SIMON & SCHUSTER MEGA CROSSWORD PUZZLE BOOK

Series 4

300 never-before-published crosswords

Edited by John M. Samson

T0046047

G

GALLERY BOOKS

New York London Toronto Sydney New Delhi

G
Gallery Books
An Imprint of Simon & Schuster, Inc.
1230 Avenue of the Americas
New York, NY 10020

Previously published in 2009 by Touchstone, an imprint of Simon & Schuster

This Gallery Books trade paperback edition March 2020

GALLERY BOOKS and colophon are registered trademarks of Simon & Schuster, Inc.

For information about special discounts for bulk purchases, please contact Simon & Schuster Special Sales at 1-866-506-1949 or business@simonandschuster.com.

The Simon & Schuster Speakers Bureau can bring authors to your live event. For more information or to book an event, contact the Simon & Schuster Speakers Bureau at 1-866-248-3049 or visit our website at www.simonspeakers.com.

Designed by Sam Bellotto Jr.

Manufactured in the United States of America

20 19 18 17 16

ISBN 978-1-4165-8781-1

COMPLETE ANSWERS WILL BE FOUND AT THE BACK.

FOREWORD

RING THING   by Harvey Estes

(Letters in circles are an anagram of the riddle answer.)

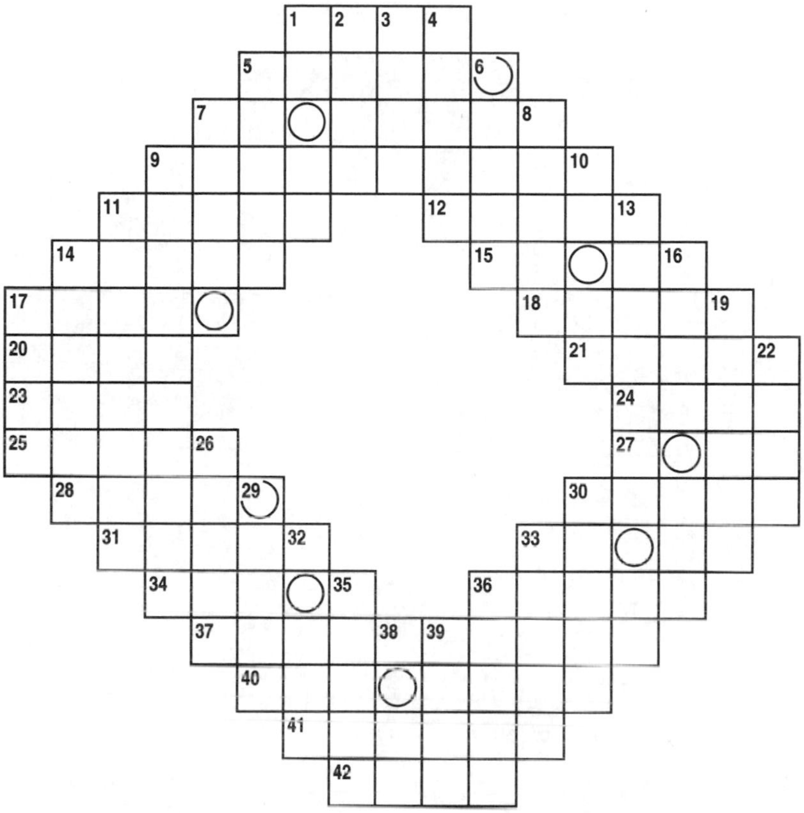

ACROSS

1 Put a worm on
5 Confidence
7 Pull-off
9 **Start of a riddle**
11 Abounds
12 Type of flare or panel
14 Small shoulders?
15 Austerity
17 Do a double take
18 Police
20 Hendrix hairdo
21 White wader
23 **More of riddle**
24 **More of riddle**
25 VCR?
27 "I before E, except after C," e.g.
28 You guys of Arabia?
30 33 Across and others
31 Family nicknames
33 Exodus memorial
34 PC support
36 Sheltered bays
37 **End of riddle**
40 Give lip service?
41 They tell you where to go
42 Change for a fin

DOWN

1 Trumps
2 Play opening
3 Levin with a nest egg?
4 Contract conditions
5 Clothes lines
6 "Coffee, ___ Me?"
7 Butler on screen
8 Ignore the cue cards
9 Friends cross it
10 Top scout
11 Eagerly unwrap
13 Duffer on a golf cart?
14 Cover some of the cost of
16 Sends another way
17 Whole slew
19 Bear
22 Els pegs
26 Get Mad again
29 Mexican munchy
30 Variety show
32 "___ Lady" (Tom Jones song)
33 Covers with carbon
35 Holy beginning
36 Lobster features
38 Go round the bend
39 Sea peril

The Margaret Award winner is RARE WORDS I & II by Arthur S. Verdesca

JOHN M. SAMSON

1 WALK AROUND THE BLOCK by Elizabeth C. Gorski

A pleasant stroll that starts at 1 Across and ends at 1 Down.

ACROSS

1 Cookie cutter?
6 Water carrier
10 "Quantum of Solace" hero
14 Father of the Dionne quintuplets
15 Violist's clef
16 "Gem City" of Pennsylvania
17 Osteopath's concern
18 Clean freak's nightmare
19 "P.S. I Love You" actress Gershon
20 Titanic letters
21 Alternate TITLE (with 57-A)
23 Matured
24 Thai cash
26 "Don't give up!"
27 Tribe of Delaware
29 "Musicophilia" author Sachs
31 Have shingles
32 Chinese dialect
33 The Karnali flows there
34 Like some divorces
36 NYC subway line
37 THEME (with "Side")
39 B. Obama, for one
42 Contaminate
43 Gloria Stivic's mom
48 Pay ending
49 Correlatives
50 Iterate
51 Ain't, in the past?
53 God, in Roma
55 Boyfriend
56 Washington nine
57 See 21 Across
60 Capp and Pacino
61 "What's ___ for me?"
62 Solves kakuro puzzles
63 Henpeck
65 Fate who spins the thread of life
66 Swarm
67 Vernel Bagneris musical "___ Time"
68 Eats
69 Effortless
70 It holds water

DOWN

1 Mint julep ingredient
2 Like "The Full Monty" strippers
3 Close connection
4 "Fields of Gold" singer Cassidy
5 Creek at the Masters
6 Conductor Kurt
7 Quell
8 "Like ___ not!"
9 Al Gore, for one
10 Got cracking
11 Paper tiger?
12 Spare part?
13 Like a job with no future
22 District: Abbr.
25 Federal energy org.
28 Paris palace
30 Ex-Yankee catcher Howard
31 Joseph Conrad's "___ of Six"
34 Dr.'s orders
35 Bard's nightfall
38 Antioxidant in foods
39 Pitcher who gave up Aaron's 715th home run
40 Roosevelt in the White House
41 "Czech Rhapsody" composer Bohuslav
44 Belle of the ball
45 Cool stretches
46 Symmetric brain parts
47 NASA city
50 Shad delicacy
52 Shop sign shorthand
53 Ones into ranch dressing?
54 Bon Jovi's "___ Life"
58 Theaters of ancient Greece
59 Prig
64 Santa ___ winds

2 "ALL YOU NEED IS . . ." by Pete Muller

The answer to 55 Across would make a good alternate title.

ACROSS

1 Film fish
6 Flambé fixer
10 Free feline?
14 Ishmael's half-brother
15 OR need
16 Some Scottish votes
17 Helena Bonham Carter movie
20 They're not needed for acoustic shows
21 Went up
22 Blue
23 Wheatback, for one
24 Shoot out
25 Famous Louvre marble
29 CEO's degree
32 Shows approval
33 It can be added to pay
34 Not mod.
35 Half in front?
36 With extreme passion
38 It might glow
39 Tea type
40 Exist
41 "Catscratch ___" (Ted Nugent album)
42 A safety gets you two
43 Baroque instrument
46 Pirate hanged in 1701
47 Irritate
48 Sue, usually, but not in a Johnny Cash song
51 Extra: Abbr.
52 Bit
55 Thompson Twins album
58 Swann who could catch a pigskin
59 Home of Interpol
60 "Definitely Maybe" is their debut album
61 Young girl
62 Last year, on Jan. 1
63 Martini's partner

DOWN

1 Feeble fellow
2 It's worth seven extra armies in "Risk"
3 Annoying ones
4 Morse bit
5 Nonplayer in the Old Globe Theater
6 Virtuous, to some
7 Build up
8 NT book
9 Boston song
10 Provide a chair for
11 Marseilles milk
12 Contact org.
13 "Gimme ___"
18 O'er in the distance
19 Cookie seen in "Rounders"
23 A famous reindeer
24 Planter place
25 At-home TV monitor
26 Put in place
27 When repeated, squeals
28 She might be super
29 "Great job!"
30 Haying machine
31 Worship
34 Leitmotif
36 Ladylike
37 MLB 2007 AL MVP
41 Be attracted to
43 Extremely yucky
44 Passionate
45 She had a hit with "White Flag"
46 Hot-dog name
48 Sate
49 "Caribbean Blue" singer
50 Olympus et al.: Abbr.
51 "Cornflake Girl" singer Tori
52 Go for a ringer
53 They hope you don't remember Alamo
54 American Indian
56 Yup
57 Thai neighbor

3 LOTS IN TRANSLATION by Bonnie L. Gentry

12 Down has been called the "Greatest Spectacle in Racing."

ACROSS

1 Raptors, e.g.
5 It may part the waves
9 Check the mailbox for
14 Turin neighbor
15 Ending with buck or stink
16 "Games People Play" author
17 Garfield's birthday extravaganza?
20 Woman of questionable values
21 Hormuz, e.g.: Abbr.
22 Clark and Orbison
23 Multiple choice, say
26 Heckle sibilantly
28 Leave a mess on the stove?
34 Completely lose patience
35 One in Orléans
36 Band together
38 Slangy smoke
39 Vigilant
42 Vote from an anti
43 Swedish sedans
45 It merged with GE in 1986
46 Maneater of myth
47 Near a VFW post?
51 Olympic swimmer's assignment
52 Part of an archipelago
53 Plotter in a play
56 Rocky Mountains Indian
58 Muchachas: Abbr.
62 Dixieland breakfast for factory workers?
66 Ice-cold
67 1492 trio member
68 "Zip-___-doo-dah . . ."
69 Certain locks
70 Shipped off
71 Can't forgo

DOWN

1 It shows RPMs
2 Biblical barterer
3 "The Practice" roles: Abbr.
4 Slip-up
5 Potent java, slangily
6 Table scrap
7 Scale in which topaz is 8
8 Clare who married Henry Luce
9 Washboard muscles
10 Passes slowly, as a day
11 The Ponte Vecchio spans it
12 500-mile race
13 Julia's role in "Ocean's Twelve"
18 Open hearing, in law
19 "The Angry Hills" novelist
24 Use a Taser on
25 Chinese secret society
27 Carb source, informally
28 Bronze mil. medals
29 Room-sized computer
30 Katey of "8 Simple Rules . . ."
31 Transmitter starter
32 Hint of hue
33 Jump involuntarily
37 Peer group?
39 Mythical mount
40 When Mercutio delivers the Queen Mab speech
41 Team encouragement
44 Isaac Asimov's neckwear
46 Hire too many
48 Ample, in dialect
49 View from Jackson Hole
50 If follower, in computer programs
53 Rock singer ___ Pop
54 51, for one
55 Organ in tadpoles but not frogs
57 Put-in-Bay's lake
59 It gets high every day
60 Toward one side of a ship
61 Husky's load
63 Old radical org.
64 Former NASCAR airer
65 It may be hard on a construction worker

4 THE YOKE'S ON THEM by Sam Bellotto Jr.

"Bones" is the nickname of 38 Across.

ACROSS

1 Festoon
5 Ice-cream mold
10 Pack tight
14 Stratosphere High Roller sound
15 Parliament closer
16 Piazza di Venezia locale
17 Dominant religion of Greece
20 "Walls of Jericho" group
21 Routing word
22 Suds
23 Journal offerings
26 Rumford–Bangor dir.
27 Manhattan breakfast order
32 Snake venom, e.g.
35 Teensy amount
36 First full spring mo.
37 Current law
38 Kirk's doctor friend
40 Square mileage stat
41 Uma's role in "Pulp Fiction"
42 Chinese export
43 Rock legend Holly
44 2004 World Series winners
48 A touch
49 Upgrade, in a manner of speaking
53 Emotional shocks
57 Constrictive neckwear?
58 Juan's vee
59 Goldfinger's "Goldfinger" goal
62 Homophone of I'll
63 Make up for
64 City SE of New Delhi
65 1962 NL homer leader
66 Basketry twig
67 Mattel products

DOWN

1 Asseverate
2 Atlantic City high roller
3 "The Fox and the Grapes" author
4 Tennis retrieval
5 Revealing
6 Showy
7 "Winterset" hero
8 Sharp comment
9 Heartfelt appeal
10 Gloated
11 Gander Mountain gear
12 One way to run
13 Long, for short
18 Mineral water
19 Egyptian dye
24 Stats for Derek Jeter
25 Mackintosh
28 Locks in Sault Ste. Marie
29 Fat in the can?
30 Opinion page
31 Peek inside
32 Lara Croft target
33 Kentucky neighbor
34 Yule
38 Second largest of the Philippines
39 Bathroom cleaner brand
40 One of the Horae
42 "Me too!"
43 Sacha Baron Cohen film
45 Some surgical implants
46 Prep a salmon steak
47 Warehouse worker
50 Fielding-practice bat
51 Tusk substance
52 Lubbock's state
53 Bookbinding step
54 John Jasper's pupil
55 With proficiency
56 Vince Carter et al.
60 Faith, at Lourdes
61 "Love Story" singer McPhee

5 PUZZLE PUN by Ed Early

The "Golden Prosperity" tower at 4 Down is located in Shanghai.

ACROSS

1 The Boston ___
5 Disorderly in appearance
11 Nutrition abbr.
14 Exam for budding attorneys
15 Madrid locale
16 Pres. monogram of 1881
17 **Start of pun about a puzzle**
20 At a bargain price
21 Clown's leg, at times
22 May of Hollywood
23 Atlantic City mecca (with "The")
26 "I cannot tell ___"
27 **Part 2 of pun**
30 Endings for sultan
31 "I was ___ come, so here I am"
32 Parisian pronoun
33 Half the North Pole exports?
35 Fox-trot maneuver
38 Sunday talk
39 Gyro bread
40 **Part 3 of pun**
45 Hawaiian goose
46 Tolkien creature
47 Shrubs of the heath family
48 Have distaste for
50 City on San Francisco Bay
51 **End of pun**
55 Norwich loc.
56 Walking
57 Nerve network
58 "Die Another ___" (2002)
59 Legislators
60 Sugar suffixes

DOWN

1 Catcher on a table
2 Kiss
3 Has some
4 The Jin Mao Tower has 88
5 Practice a dance movement
6 "Let us leave ___ came"
7 Mailman's org.
8 Feather's partner
9 Linking word
10 Legs, to oglers
11 Montreal university
12 Rayed flower
13 Squealed
18 Capital of Yemen
19 "Give ___": Try
23 Introduce
24 "___ as You Love Me": Backstreet Boys
25 Singer Watley
28 Word root
29 PM times
33 Casino action
34 "What's Hecuba to him ___ to Hecuba": Shak.
35 Bishoprics
36 "See you then!"
37 Manège maneuvers
38 Three-time PGA champ
39 Ancestor of poker
40 "We thought they'd never ___ sing and dance . . ."
41 "Romeo and Juliet" setting
42 It may be chemical or kinetic
43 Serfs
44 ___-raspberry juice
49 Brit. medals
50 Ages and ages
52 Before PQR
53 Buffalo Bills' old org.
54 "Rock and Roll, Hoochie ___": Derringer

6 NO FOUR-LETTER WORDS by Harvey Estes

All answers in this low-word count challenger are five letters or longer.

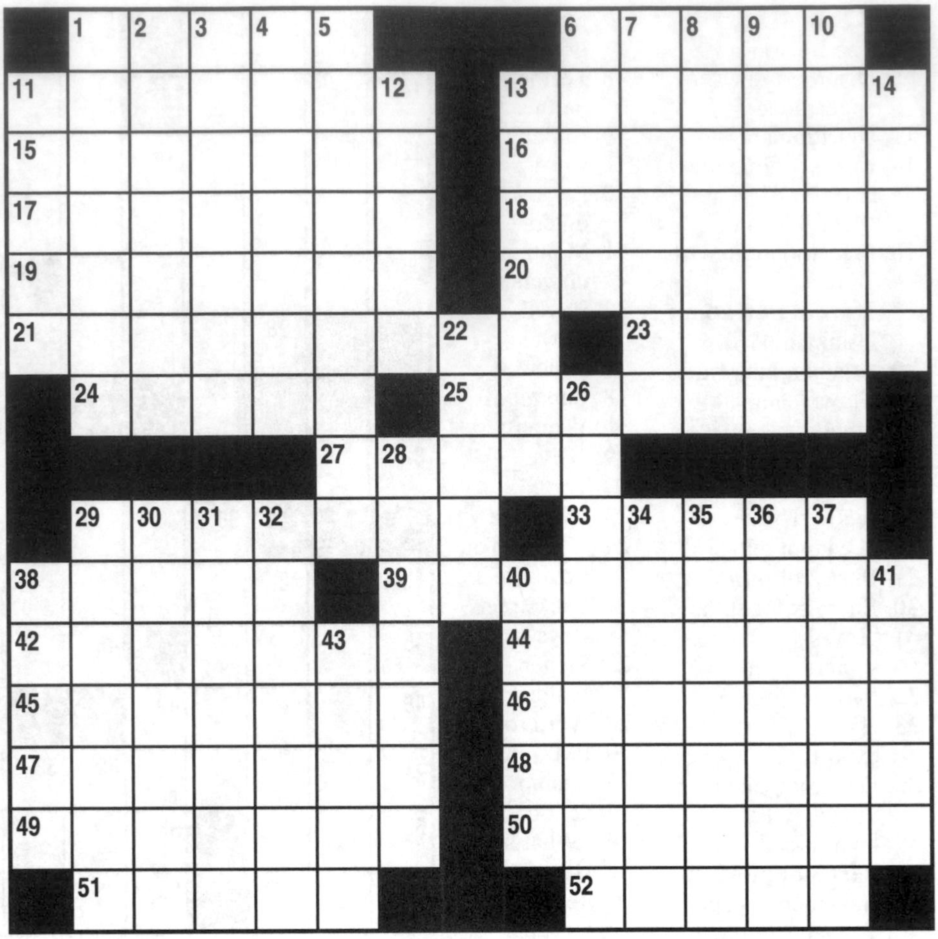

ACROSS

1 Some protests
6 Gathers together
11 Produce milk
13 Daily allowance
15 Belongs
16 Cold brew
17 Small bit
18 They're often smart
19 Yap
20 Red light of the night
21 Janis Ian song (with "At")
23 Take off
24 Feeling, Italian-style
25 Tasty bits
27 Possession question
29 "Buck up!"
33 Submersible tube
38 Swinton in "Michael Clayton"
39 Of a region
42 Two-base game
44 Ford part
45 Drones come out of it
46 Short operatic piece
47 Click beetles
48 Came to a boil
49 Starting points
50 Links challenge
51 Leaves in
52 Burning balls of gas

DOWN

1 Cheeky pairs?
2 Make
3 First Christian martyr
4 Large-scaled game fish
5 Bethlehem, for example
6 Sandy type
7 Self-made orphan of the Greeks
8 In all likelihood
9 Exact
10 Cassandra, e.g.
11 Speech therapy targets
12 First name in cosmetics
13 Works by Nicola or Giovanni
14 Difficult shot
22 Gush
26 Stops on the interstate
28 Party person
29 Grand ones, perhaps
30 White-tie, say
31 Stuart Little, for one
32 Most like streaking?
34 Least
35 Stone name
36 Seconds
37 Reasoner partner, once
38 "Ain't Too Proud ___": Temptations hit
40 Gorge
41 Very much
43 Ski start

7 ELECTRICAL ENGINEERING by Jim Leeds

29 Down is a good example of a misleading clue.

ACROSS

1 Give up the football
5 Rotisserie part
9 Kentucky college
14 Open up ___ of worms
15 Pas ___ (ballet step)
16 "___ Care": Tanguay
17 Shut out
19 Dogpatch rows
20 The savvy electrician ___?
22 Japanese volcano
23 Hush-hush maritime org.
24 "Aqua Teen" character
25 Gunny's rnk.
28 Electric Kathleen Winsor romance?
32 Skateboard pad
33 Uncommon, to Horace
34 Épée cousin
37 "___ drunk walks into a bar . . ."
39 Polo teams
40 Kind of dance
41 Take root
43 Electric state song of Kansas?
48 Rousing shout
49 Driver's complete turnaround
50 Nancy's friend
51 NBA center Ming
54 Con Edison's balance sheet listings?
58 They're often blue
60 Wall eyesores
61 Inspiring fear
62 What to stick it in the water
63 Filmmaker Riefenstahl
64 Hypnotized
65 Lincoln and Johnson: Abbr.
66 Detached portico

DOWN

1 Jeremy Irons movie
2 Graphic symbols
3 "Take Good ___ My Baby" (1961 hit)
4 Had the answer
5 IV solutions
6 Like the "b" in "bull" and the "p" in "parcel"
7 Ingrid's 1942 role
8 A step up from a tween
9 Centaur or mermaid, e.g.
10 Genesis locale
11 "The Social Contract" author
12 Cut short
13 Sobriety org.
18 Relating to a Greek ensemble
21 "Star Trek" producer Behr
26 Boxer's warning
27 Social receptions
29 Where Stephen King went to college
30 Jagged-edged
31 Antler part
34 Suffix for smack
35 Satirist Mort
36 It's punched at work
38 Water purification method
39 Polish off
42 Durango dishes
44 Bottle for baby
45 Thrice: Comb. form
46 Laughing predators
47 Grommet
52 "Lisa Bonet ___ basil (palindrome)
53 Easier to play, musically
55 Combined, in Calais
56 Andrea's boyfriend in "The Devil Wears Prada"
57 Coins of Peru
58 ___ d'esprit (witticism)
59 Fabric suffix

8 TALKING BIG by Ray Hamel

. . . with big words.

ACROSS

1 Went back out
6 Toothbrush maker
11 Tar
14 "Thunderball" villain
15 Not a social butterfly
16 Bride's response
17 Empty boasting
19 Bronx attraction
20 Highly regarded
21 Chain selling Martha Stewart products
23 Foal's mother
24 Heed
26 "Racer's Edge" sloganeer
29 Pretentious boasting
35 The out crowd
37 Got a perfect score on
38 Loaf end
39 Terminal man?
40 Noah in "Sergeant York"
41 "And that's all there ___ it!"
42 Dog biter
43 Bit of elementary Latin
44 Journalist's hope
45 Vain boasting
48 "The Masque of the Red Death" author
49 Some special agts.
50 Third baseman's asset
52 Runner Kip Keino's homeland
55 Like some cafe dining
60 Logical beginning?
61 False boasting
64 Pulver's rnk. in "Mister Roberts"
65 Egg-shaped
66 Baseball manager Francona
67 Ex follower
68 Landlord payments
69 Consort of Elizabeth I

DOWN

1 North Sea tributary
2 Jail window obstructions
3 Little snip
4 Incited (with "on")
5 Folded corners
6 Quaint adjective
7 Large cross
8 Mandela's polit. party
9 Waikiki welcome
10 Shattered
11 City near the Great Pyramids
12 Glade's enemy
13 Diamond flaw?
18 Target practice need
22 Kind of proportions
24 Underworld code of silence
25 Trunk
26 Up to ___ (acceptable)
27 Magnetic unit
28 Smooth one's feathers
30 Subordinate deity
31 Vast expanse
32 Slave who told tales
33 Droid's last name?
34 Skip a big wedding
36 Having open windows, maybe
40 Unadorned
44 Saw-toothed
46 Key of Beethoven's 7th
47 A little batty
51 Apportions (out)
52 More than suspected
53 One of a few "choice" parts?
54 Small victory margin
55 Buckling down
56 Slangy hats
57 Letter opener
58 Reactor section
59 Banded mineral
62 Abbr. on a Monopoly board
63 One in the cooler

9 INNER TUBES by Barry C. Silk

The theme reveals itself at 61 Down.

ACROSS

1 Tubular pasta
5 Sailor's "stop!"
10 Poet Lazarus
14 Yemen port
15 Stomach
16 Visualized
17 H.S. junior's test
18 Tabernacle locale
19 Like window dummies
20 Sweet potato, for one
23 "Affirmative"
25 Society page word
26 "No bid," in bridge
27 Cylinder-head part
32 Oboe and bassoon
33 The Buckeye State
34 White House monogram (1881–85)
37 Propagated
38 Machinist's tool
40 Shades from the sun
41 Long-distance inits.
42 Salary
43 One of the original Beach Boys
44 "The Man From U.N.C.L.E." star
47 "Peer Gynt" playwright
50 Fix illegally
51 Moe Berg's org.
52 Bay of Naples landmark
57 Taking action
58 JFK Library designer
59 Jigger of whiskey
62 Celebrate
63 Regional flora and fauna
64 ICBM type
65 MacMurray of "My Three Sons"
66 John who sang "Rocket Man"
67 PC "brains"

DOWN

1 Nuke
2 Driver's licenses, e.g.
3 Page with a perforated edge
4 Mad about
5 Reduces
6 Luxurious fabric
7 Essen elder
8 Foundry refuse
9 Item in a boot
10 Prison break, e.g.
11 Peach ___ (dessert)
12 Military messes
13 Peruvian peaks
21 Burden sometimes "on you"
22 VCR successor
23 San Francisco's ___ Buena Island
24 Bring to bear
28 Sum up
29 Primary participant
30 "Say ___"
31 Top-Flite position
34 Merchant vessel
35 Egyptian crosses
36 Orgs.
38 Research room
39 Census-form question
40 Symbol for torque
42 Refuses to
43 Trio in Bethlehem
44 Leased
45 Closely following
46 Vance of "I Love Lucy"
47 Departing words
48 Embarrassing mistake
49 Honeymoon quarters
53 Unspecific feeling
54 Jannings in "The Blue Angel"
55 Primer dog
56 Camp Lejeune letters
60 Sch. named for a televangelist
61 Tubes

10 MONEY CACHE* by Alan Olschwang

Asterisked clues relate to the title.

ACROSS

1 Medics
5 Dalmatian feature
9 Defense's focal point
14 Infante of baseball
15 Nautical greeting
16 Where Celtics deplane
17 Publish successively*
19 Scrat's "Ice Age" quest
20 Psyche
21 Ashen
22 "Ouch, that ___!"
23 Bushido practitioner
25 Office group
26 Visual arthropod organs*
31 Family cars
34 Algonquian language
35 Caduceus org.
36 Hebrew month
37 Suffix for alien
38 ___ Kross (rock group)
39 Netman Henman
40 Avian mimic
42 Superdome team
44 2005 Lisa Kudrow film*
47 Letters from Patrai
48 Loudly
52 Some brass
55 Organic compound
56 Forest denizen
57 Watchful
58 Radar's favorite drink*
60 Actress Braga
61 Italian noble name
62 Pub potions
63 Traction aid
64 Instrument of title
65 Attention getter

DOWN

1 Apothecary measures
2 Resistance symbol
3 Billiards stroke
4 ___ Lanka
5 Respectful bows
6 Writer Roth
7 Seep
8 Abilene suburb
9 Dessert option
10 Area
11 "Young Franken-stein" hunchback
12 A Maverick
13 Taverns
18 Chef's cover
22 Unit of loudness
24 The Golden Bears, shortly
25 Unadulter-ated
27 Two quartets
28 Tale
29 Give off
30 Fresh language
31 Bullock of "Deadwood"
32 Charles Lamb
33 Empty a certain truck
37 Miller and Martin
38 Buss
40 "It's on me!"
41 Some voters
42 Pried
43 Like shortstops
45 Illinois city
46 Genetic
49 Super stars
50 Silver streaks
51 Matzo's lack
52 Latin noun gen.
53 MP's pursuit
54 "Fascination" singer Morgan
55 Scottish Gaelic
58 Dropout's deg.
59 Easy mark

11 THE NAME GAME by Doug Peterson

37 Across is also baseball's all-time leader in runs scored.

ACROSS

1 Passel
5 Tiara sparklers
9 Note above C
14 Spell checker's find
15 Declare bluntly
16 Durance of "Smallville"
17 Stench
18 Slot machine alternative
20 1979 Best New Artist Grammy winner
22 "Big" Hawaiian
23 ABA member
24 Rabbit's foot
25 Crime-fighting org.
27 Spring bloom
31 Sounds of hesitation
34 Lanai
36 Their ads often feature cavemen
37 Baseball's all-time stolen-base leader
40 Research money
41 Dismay
42 High school subj.
43 Rebuke to Brutus
44 Succor
45 Three-sided sail
47 Felix, for one
49 Glossy paint
53 Kipling's brave mongoose
58 Quit until tomorrow
59 Bearing
60 One with bad looks?
61 Have emotions
62 Klein of fashion
63 Iraqi seaport
64 Like the Sears Tower
65 Badminton barriers

DOWN

1 Fabled baby deliverer
2 Kingdom of Croesus
3 Period of time
4 Prepare
5 Made a gift of
6 Old Nick's knack
7 Current fashion
8 ___' Pea (Popeye's adoptee)
9 Warehouse
10 Unsettled region
11 Take a shine to
12 High cards
13 La Brea gunk
19 Town east of Santa Barbara
21 Sulking
25 Playing surface
26 ___ fide
28 Get out of bed
29 Clickable image
30 iPod selection
31 Egg on
32 Trumpeter Al
33 "Beat it!"
35 Hailing from Bangkok
36 Zodiacal twins
38 Tim Wakefield pitch
39 1941 Spencer Tracy role
44 Plugging away
46 Dynamic Duo member
48 "Ran" Director Kurosawa
50 Portland's state
51 The Oscars, e.g.
52 Queues
53 Hindu melody
54 Misfortunes
55 Electee of 1908
56 "What's the big ___?"
57 Film critic Pauline
58 Corn core

12 MOVING RIGHT ALONG by Sam Bellotto Jr.

16 Across played God in the 1968 movie "Skidoo."

ACROSS

1 Reduced
5 Starfleet Academy student
10 Simba's supper
13 Biker's route
14 Nikko attraction
15 Fowl piece
16 "You Bet Your Life" host
18 Editor's conclusion?
19 Cochise's tribe
20 Word form for white stuff
21 Court fig.
22 Sea palm, for one
24 Assign
26 **Start of a quotation by 16 Across**
32 Cabinet dept.
33 Subj. for U.S. newcomers
34 Sign of late summer
35 Cpl.'s boss
36 One learning the ropes
39 Bourg is its capital
40 Be responsible for
42 Mrs. lobster
43 French ETO battleground
44 **More of quotation**
48 Male
49 Montana national forest
50 Hudson River fish
52 Steve Case's former org.
54 Field of greens
58 Finger-lickin' luau food
59 **End of quotation**
61 Further
62 Long-armed apes
63 Snakeless isle
64 Short answer
65 As like ___ (probably)
66 FedExed

DOWN

1 Lorena Ochoa's org.
2 Old West's Wyatt
3 Greek colonnade
4 Oyster-bar job
5 Comedienne Margaret
6 SALT component
7 Ross, Rigg, and Dors
8 Sign up with the registrar
9 Lone Star handle
10 They may attend galas
11 Skillfully done
12 Rough on the eyes
14 Pea-picking job
17 Emeril or Wolfgang
21 First Japanese ambassador to the U.S.
23 City on the Arno
25 Not on tape
26 "The Gondoliers" mezzo
27 Stevens in "The Farmer's Daughter"
28 Parking monitors
29 Statesman Root
30 Hardly awkward
31 Social blunders
36 Hamlet
37 Goldman on "Family Guy"
38 Lays to rest
41 Friend of Rat and Mole
43 Actress Lindsay, and kin
45 Natural aptitudes
46 Japanese inn
47 Doghouse denizen?
50 Fix a feline
51 Make perfect
53 Late-night icon
55 Beard
56 "Come ___, the water's fine!"
57 Have too little
59 World's most massive mountain
60 CAA or CIA employee

13 "PLEASE DROP IN!" by Ernest Lampert

44 Across has been called "Pavlova of the Ice."

ACROSS

1 Ike's out
6 Puccini's Floria
11 Advanced degree
14 Run to
15 Davenport occupant
16 Bill partner
17 Dabs of medium?
19 Gepetto's tool
20 Senior diplomats
21 Torpid
23 Do boring work
25 "7 Faces of Dr. ___"(1964 movie)
26 Epiphany
29 Cardinals +7, e.g.?
35 Elm extentions
37 Sq. bisector
38 Deuterium discoverer
39 You, amongst Friends
40 Wonderlands
41 Alouette, in English
42 Ponderosa guy
43 Spin-off of a sort
44 1920s–30s Winter Olympics star
45 The puck stops here?
48 Pot opener
49 Childcare writer LeShan
50 Khartoum's river
52 Hivelike
57 Astaire-Rogers musical
61 "___ Loser": Beatles hit
62 Taxis looking for a fare?
64 McGraw of baseball
65 Tomato blight
66 Musical pair
67 NYSE debut
68 Oozy
69 "Return of the Jedi" locale

DOWN

1 Minimally
2 Bats
3 "Lord knows ___!"
4 Company that coined the word "aspirin"
5 Malady
6 Idiosyncrasy
7 Cry over spilled milk
8 Babe Ruth's sultanate
9 Product books
10 Patron Saint of Scandinavia
11 Sweet Sixteen org.
12 Hamlet's cousin
13 Partner of Rinehart and Winston
18 "Peace ___ hand"
22 Little lump
24 "Rose ___": Stephen King
26 Even if, for short
27 Greeting to a spouse
28 "It's ___ Unusual Day"
30 Reunion attendee
31 Card game also called sevens
32 "Destry Rides Again" author
33 Out of this world
34 Moppets
36 Orchard measure
40 Cadillac SUV
44 Abelard's beloved
46 Brings out
47 In ___ (undisturbed)
51 Canon rival
52 NYC-based bank
53 Shoot-___ (western)
54 Como is one
55 "A flash of dew, ___ or two . . .": Dickinson
56 D. Do-Right's outfit
58 Ziegfeld's first wife
59 1968 self-titled folk album
60 Boris or Basil
63 Skate in water

14 REBUS PUZZLE by Nancy Salomon & Michael Langwald

Thematic rebus answers in the style of the game show "Concentration."

ACROSS

1 Wall St. wheeling-dealings
5 Recipe meas.
9 Cockney chap
14 Verdi opera set in Egypt
15 Overhead light?
16 Ward off
17 Neatnik's opposite
18 Not too much
19 Hot spots
20 **"Is everything okay?**
23 Help for the irregular
24 Splits
25 Half a couple
28 Talk trash to
29 Letters of credit
31 Prufrock's creator
33 Sports figures
35 Non-pro?
36 **"Something troubling you?"**
42 Miscellaneous mixture
43 Form a union
44 Heightens
48 Needle-nosed fish
49 Stock figure
52 Enron's former NYSE symbol
53 Scandalous company
55 Clued in
57 **"Are those tears I see?"**
60 Stage
62 Spreadsheet figures
63 Take the booby prize
64 Squad car sound
65 Heroic saga
66 Whole lot
67 Plains shelter
68 Not up to snuff
69 Silver skates pursuer Brinker

DOWN

1 Scolded
2 Neil Simon play locale
3 A non-alcoholic beer
4 Native Israeli
5 Warm up
6 The Sultan of Swat
7 Water-park attraction
8 Packing a punch
9 Look through books
10 Dolly of "Hello, Dolly!"
11 Willingness to hear new ideas
12 Starr in the news
13 Some commuter trains
21 Goes off
22 Dict. entries
26 Unthinking repetition
27 Hooha
30 Feedbag morsel
32 Kenny Rogers hit
33 "That's enough!"
34 Do the math
36 Had on
37 Defender Dershowitz
38 Sc-fi plot device
39 Attractive, in a way
40 Support, of a sort
41 Lineup
45 Unflappable
46 A, in Arles
47 Goody-goodies
49 Deejay's bribe
50 Up and at 'em
51 Makes arrangements for more of "Us"
54 Relative of a giraffe
56 Cardiff residents
58 "Got it"
59 Pool tool
60 L.A. hours
61 Get a move on, quaintly

15 HAPPY FEET by Billie Truitt

"Sorry, no dancing penguins here!"

ACROSS

1 Walk laboriously
5 "Look what I did!"
9 Letter-shaped steel girder
14 Move, in realtor's lingo
15 Will beneficiary
16 ___ Carta
17 Pernicious
18 Formerly, formerly
19 One who went to market?
20 Family-size apartments
23 Licorice substitute
24 Author of the "Earth's Children" series
25 Word on a towel, perhaps
28 Actress Arthur
29 Indolent idlers
33 Grape plants
34 Greenspan or Arkin
35 Painter's tool
38 Spots at the doctor's office?
41 Mysteries in the skies
42 Talk big
43 Respond to a crisis, figuratively
47 Chemical suffix
50 "___ you all right?"
51 Follow orders
52 Desert pit stop
54 Plunger targets
58 Teach one-on-one
60 Bay bobber
61 Ingrid's "Casablanca" role
62 Click "send"
63 Old Ford models
64 Down Under greeting
65 Six a.m., for most
66 In ___ (actually)
67 Brings home

DOWN

1 Like a modular home
2 Met maestro James
3 Joan Fontaine's sister
4 Distributes
5 One of TV's Huxtables
6 Space or sol prefix
7 Causes perturbation
8 Scheming
9 Graceful antelope
10 Can of worms?
11 Off-white shade
12 Film director Lee
13 Merry month
21 Ignited once more
22 Sky lion
26 "Dies ___"
27 ID thief's targets
30 Hill dweller
31 Capital of Zimbabwe?
32 Allegro
33 One piece of a three-piece suit
35 Cougar
36 At a distance
37 San Antonio beer
38 Pop's partner
39 "The Raven" poet, initially
40 Part of PTA
42 They may be leveraged
44 Like some wages
45 Recede
46 Small, rounded stone
47 Tristan's love
48 Scratches excessively
49 English class assignments
53 Adjust precisely
55 Hard work
56 Fishing poles
57 The Big Board, briefly
58 Summer shirt
59 Thurman of "Pulp Fiction"

16 NUMERICAL ALPHABET by Pancho Harrison

A tricky theme from this Denver puzzler.

ACROSS

1 Like Heidi
6 In the center of
10 Broad-topped hill
14 Call ___ to (stop)
15 Sitar selection
16 Woes
17 Root of all evil
18 Grab (with "onto")
19 Java neighbor
20 1927 Gershwin song used in 1957's "Funny Face"
22 Natural in craps
24 Tennis great Sampras
25 Golda of Israel
26 Some insurance frauds
29 Kind of jump shot
33 Last words of "The Purple Cow"
34 1962 Ray Charles country hit
35 Canine comment
36 Neighbor of Turkey
37 AOL alternative
38 1930 Gershwin song from "Girl Crazy"
41 Levi Dockers feature, often
43 Parsley family herb
44 Erin Moran TV role
45 Cotton bundle
46 Residential area, for short
47 "Ta-ta"
50 1971 Carole King song from "Tapestry"
54 Rice-A-___
55 Fork feature
57 Love poetry muse
58 Freudian topics
59 "Animal House" party attire
60 Jacket worn by Sammy Davis Jr.
61 Laundry load
62 City near Provo
63 Have confidence in

DOWN

1 ___ Club (Costco rival)
2 "How'd the game end?"
3 ". . . ___ my Annabel Lee": Poe
4 Consider overnight
5 Synthetic rubber component
6 Debate
7 Teen hangout
8 "May ___ now?"
9 Barry Humphries alter ego
10 Left-winger
11 Norway's patron saint
12 Marseilles miss: Abbr.
13 Speller's clarifying phrase
21 Knox and Dix: Abbr.
23 Not be truthful with
25 One of the Osmonds
26 Addis ___, Ethiopia
27 Summer TV fare
28 The first or fifth letter of George, e.g.
29 Pro ___ (perfunctorily)
30 Voters since 1920
31 Very, in music
32 "Fiddler on the Roof" matchmaker
34 One way to take an enemy outpost
36 Short dagger
39 Woody Allen stereotype
40 Oil of ___
41 Omen
42 Working stiff
44 Roast beef au ___
46 Second stringers
47 Cold one
48 Exercise discipline with asanas
49 Slaughter of baseball
50 "Picnic" playwright
51 Pearl Harbor's site
52 Alphabet components: Abbr.
53 Went to Wendy's, say
56 Suffix with super

17 OUT OF THIS WORLD by Alan Olschwang

18 Down is often depicted holding an ankh.

ACROSS

1 Gave a flip
6 Gym dance
9 Guy
14 Primitive calculators
15 "Xanadu" band
16 Actor Delon
17 Delicate fern
19 1969 role for Dustin
20 Peyton Manning's brother
21 Corrida competitor
22 Enclosed by
23 Some Louvre hangings
25 Charged particle
26 Governments of the wealthy
32 Kushner's "___ in America"
35 Ruby or Sandra
36 Fit for the task
37 Ways to get out
38 Tie the knot
39 Absinthe flavoring
40 Kind of rug
41 Crony
42 Slurs over
43 Post-WW2 economic aid program
46 Try truffles
47 Driver's need
51 Cannon of a sort
55 Expression of feigned amusement
56 "The Black Cat" auth.
57 Eschew
58 Melancholy
60 Slow in music
61 "Roses ___ red . . ."
62 Oncle's wife
63 Prepare for a match
64 Some enlistees
65 Assuages

DOWN

1 Speleologist
2 White poplar
3 Collared
4 Old French coin
5 Makes gin
6 San Simeon builder
7 Olla podrida
8 ___ favor
9 Cooked cereal
10 Israeli seaport
11 Thin wood strip
12 Virna in "Arabella"
13 Soon
18 Falcon-headed Egyptian god
22 Had on
24 Massenet works
25 On the rocks
27 Digger of old-time radio
28 Eyetooth
29 Footnote abbr.
30 Otherwise
31 Understands
32 First grandfather
33 "Key Largo" heroine
34 Attendee
38 "Van Wilder" director Becker
39 Dining option
41 Early forerunner of Leno
42 Root from New York
44 Confrontational
45 Franklin Mint products
48 Hamburg refusals
49 End of a French toast
50 Wired blades
51 Scotch, for one
52 Concluded
53 Anagram name of 33 Down
54 Tail-twining monkey
55 Last name in spydom
58 Reagan's first presidency
59 Pilots' org.

18 DENNIS RODMAN'S 2004 WIN by Brad Wilber

. . . and he received $222,000 for that win at 17 Down.

ACROSS

1 1969 Joyce Carol Oates novel
5 Sucker punch, e.g.
14 ___ avis
15 Violin bow material
16 Saint canonized in 993
18 Mitochondrion or vacuole, e.g.
19 Heavenly altar
20 Novel which inspired "Clueless"
22 San Francisco mayor Newsom
23 Like bath mats
25 Put through the blender
26 Rip to pieces
27 Wellsian fruit eaters
29 Under an alcohol ban
30 Second-string player
31 Cloud of negativity?
33 Green car
37 Cricket batsman position
38 Covers with black grime
40 Alarm settings, for short
43 Meadow Soprano's dad
44 Attire
45 Coolers
47 Hot air
48 Father of Hector
49 Mythical goat-man
50 Kennel exclamation
51 Saran Wrap targets
54 Took a chance
56 Rakes with gunfire
57 "Ta-ta!"
58 Grand-piano pedal
59 Ian in "Lord of the Rings"

DOWN

1 Certain cutters
2 "Our Gang" producer
3 Quixote's specialty
4 Month during le printemps
5 Emulate Pac-Man
6 Bar mitzvah dance
7 0.1 microjoule
8 Simile center
9 Anatole France satire
10 Wool-gather?
11 Split 50-50
12 More sycophantic
13 In
17 Dennis Rodman's 2004 win
21 Successor to Salyut 7
24 Multiplex mementos
25 Milne protagonist
27 Diplomatic agent
28 Creditor's claim
31 Mideast's Gulf of ___
32 Hotfoot it
34 Altar exchange
35 Casanova
36 Like Glinda the Good Witch
39 Bottom rung, in the Middle Ages
40 Waldorf salad ingredients
41 Rita in "Carnal Knowledge"
42 Solo racing boats
44 Actor Gulager
46 "Weird Al" Jackson song parody
47 Sarastro in "The Magic Flute," e.g.
49 Wring one's hands
52 Grace ___ Owen ("L.A. Law" role)
53 End of many e-mail addresses
55 Oh, in Cologne

19 THREE MEN IN A TUB by Jim Leeds

And who do you think they be?

ACROSS

1 E-mail from Hormel?
5 Mountain spike
10 Swing
14 Pakistani language
15 Florist's draw
16 Arrow poison
17 Lampblack
18 Macanudo product
19 Thom the loafer?
20 The butcher admits ___
23 Pray
24 Japanese-American
25 "Arms and the Man" playwright
26 "Gladiator" director
30 Veggie served with 1 Down
31 Kind of wagon
33 Roy Orbison hit
34 Livingston in "Office Space"
35 The baker is ___
39 Early sixth-century date
40 Muslim republic
41 Kyushu volcano
42 Word in Montana's motto
43 Precincts
45 "Ibis" poet
48 Good for something
50 PETA prefers them faux
53 The candlestick maker ___
57 ". . . ___ may never meet again" (Johnny Mathis lyric)
58 A wolf raised him
59 Former "Wheel of Fortune" host
60 Reach a maximum
61 CORE leader Roy
62 Savvy about
63 Former Russ. states
64 Michael in "The Quiet American"
65 Deprivation

DOWN

1 Raw fish dish
2 Prefaces
3 Brewer Coors
4 Mangle
5 Certain horse in a race
6 Van Gogh masterpiece
7 Roman coverup
8 It abuts Yemen
9 Fragrant ointment
10 Big wheels for big wheels
11 Chin cleft
12 Got tough with
13 Stress
21 Adds diacritical marks to Hebrew letters
22 Svelte
27 Carbon copy
28 "___ the fields we go . . ."
29 "Bye!"
32 Big do
35 American rates
36 Custer's Last Stand conflict
37 Raw sienna
38 Leaving
39 Comical Canadian singing duo
44 Spangle
46 Cantillate
47 PC key
49 Pursues
51 Ballet ___ de Monte Carlo
52 Bishopric group
54 Mabius of "Ugly Betty"
55 Siberian river
56 Prefix for bus

20 AN INCONVENIENT TRUTH by Larry Shearer

Be sure and watch Al Gore's documentary before solving this one.

ACROSS

1 Inexplicit
6 Shut tight
10 Fall birthstone
14 Mistreat
15 Declaration in court
16 Disaster relief org.
17 Congressional investigation?
19 Skedaddled
20 ___ empty stomach
21 Free
22 Arousing
23 Jamaican music
25 Unnatural
27 On the other hand
29 Five Nations tribe
33 Publicist's anathema
38 Dodge truck
39 Peter in "The Maltese Falcon"
40 Fool
42 Demolish
43 It merged with Chevron in 2005
45 Many St. Augustine residents
47 Rests
49 Carried the day
50 It's worth one point in Scrabble
52 Skewer morsels
57 Veteran sailor
60 De Gaulle's birthplace
62 Composer Stravinsky
63 AAA mem.
64 What a sentry might say?
66 Okefenokee possum
67 Singer Young
68 Contest spot
69 Vodka brand
70 "This ___ sudden!"
71 Fools

DOWN

1 It's in the air
2 Have ____ to pick
3 Solzhenitsyn's prison
4 Taking advantage of
5 Donne's dusk
6 Whirled
7 Crack
8 Mountaintop abodes
9 Like wedding cakes
10 One desperate for a bug spray?
11 Soccer legend
12 VISA alternative, briefly
13 ___ Day (Billie Holiday nickname)
18 Sight often seen at a theatre
24 Side by side
26 Straight
28 Disapproving sound
30 Shoreline shelter
31 Fit to ___
32 Maglie and Mineo
33 Make obscure
34 Crack
35 Discontinue
36 Hype restraint?
37 Polite address
41 Lawn coating
44 "Sweet ___" ("Wakiki Wedding" song)
46 Keepsake
48 Playground features
51 "Love Me Tender" singer
53 Coffin holders
54 Very destructive 1972 hurricane
55 Wilderness Road trailblazer
56 Sp. misses
57 Fools
58 Running ____
59 Building block
61 Composer Schifrin
65 21st President's monogram

21 JOBS OF SILICON VALLEY by Matt Ginsberg

Techies should be familiar with 40 Across.

ACROSS

1 Pocket food
5 Basque stream
9 French sight-seer
13 One seeing a lot of red
14 Calligrapher's fine points
15 Chris craft
16 Librarian's credo
19 "Annie" couple
20 Crew's control
21 Yakov Smirnoff's birthplace
22 Poly-sci finals
23 Child guidance
24 Poor judgment
27 Talked over and over
31 Like an unwatched pot
32 End notes
33 Motor attachment
34 Attractive ironwork
38 British byes
39 Four front
40 Jobs of Silicon Valley
41 Regular guys
44 Selling points
45 Fiction material
46 Advanced degrees
47 Birthday gift
50 "Cheers" stoolie
51 Beginning of a hickey
54 Householder
57 Zodiac sign
58 Razor handle
59 Broadway opening
60 Left at sea
61 Make a stink
62 Crowd noise

DOWN

1 Example of model behavior
2 High-handed remark
3 Rolodex nos.
4 Art, nowadays
5 Put down stakes
6 Last stands
7 Mel Ott's 1,860
8 Watch this
9 Crude ships
10 Do these justify the means
11 Urban ends
12 Turner in "Peyton Place"
15 Speaking points
17 Register ring
18 Robin's home
22 Colored part of a ball
23 Pesach feast
24 Thai cabbage
25 One trying to avoid charges
26 Code maker with a dotty history
27 Digs like pigs
28 One working on the cutting edge
29 École attendee
30 Saturday night specials
32 What the little birdie told Scrooge
35 Circus boosters
36 Intake problem
37 Mustang racers, once
42 Son of Kong
43 Buggy places
44 Barely move
46 Dame intro
47 Driving hazard
48 Dynamic beginning
49 Locale for a den mother
50 Parker in "The Great Debaters"
51 Art follower
52 Logical introduction
53 Mayberry drunk
55 Camel hazard
56 Talker's gift

22 HOUR OF DECISION by Edna Greenberg

A fine example of lateral symmetry and Marxist philosophy.

ACROSS

1 Adjective for cell or pile
8 "I Love ___"
15 Emphatic denial
16 Article lower in a hierarchy
17 **Start of a quip by Groucho**
19 "Just a ___ at . . ."
20 Prepare the sails for another cruise
21 Train line for Nassau County, NY
22 Remains on the lee side
25 Computer keyboard key
28 **Part 2 of quip**
29 Screw thread cutter
32 Hutton in "American Gigolo"
34 Mark Twain's burial place
36 Engine at a red light
37 "None ___ the lonely heart . . ."
40 Legal scholar Guinier and others
41 Brother of Groucho
42 Chicago–Detroit dir.
43 In need of ___ of paint
44 **Part 3 of quip**
47 List ender
50 Brewery supply
51 Shin preceder
55 **End of quip**
58 Mother in "Ah, Wilderness!"
59 Crag
60 Subway rider's convenience
61 Pass a rope through a hole
62 Eon segment
63 Annoy
64 Private talk duo?
65 Deli choice
66 65 Across, for one

DOWN

1 Burgundy and Bordeaux
2 Melville novel
3 Ames or Errol
4 Sharp flavors
5 Germ or prof finish
6 Fix in the mind
7 Australian cries
8 Birthplace of St. Francis
9 Darts, for one
10 Fortas or Burrows
11 Springfield or Enfield
12 French possessive
13 Writer Earl ___ Biggers
14 Retired, as a prof.
18 Before, before
23 Oscar winner Charlize
24 Egyptian laborer
25 Shakespeare's Age: Abbr.
26 "Your Love Is King" singer
27 Cosby's "I Spy" costar
29 Martinez of baseball
30 Operatic solo
31 Tense input?
33 Loathsome
35 Solvent which decomposes food
37 Bird that likes wasps
38 Distasteful
39 Mosaic chips
45 Caustic stuff
46 Linotype feeders: Abbr.
47 "Movie Home Companion" author
48 "We're off ___ the wizard . . ."
49 No liability
52 Dropped the ball
53 Dred Scott, for one
54 Highly agitated
56 Trevino and Strasberg
57 Nickname of Hockey's Phil

23 THREE SHORT STACKS by Bonnie L. Gentry

Breakfast just isn't the same anymore.

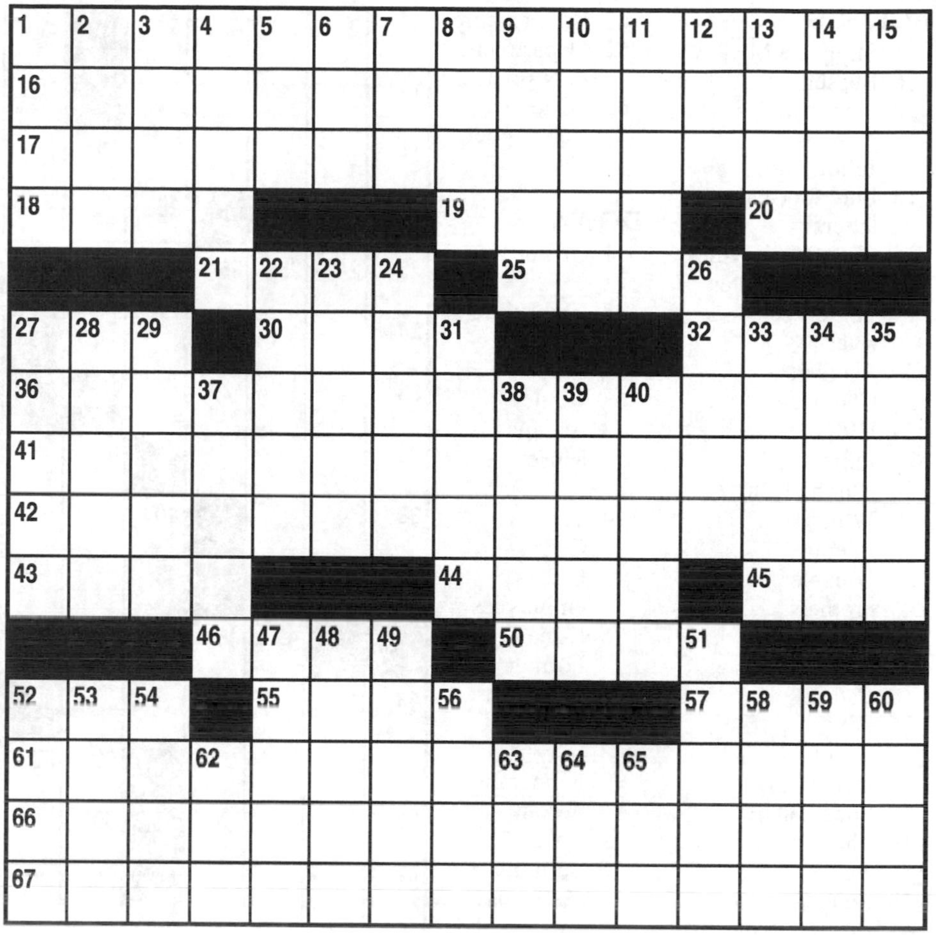

ACROSS

1 Bone breakers
16 Choice in academia
17 Cause trouble
18 Social or septic starter
19 CPR deliverers
20 Spawning fish
21 Alternatives to PCs
25 Mark with a branding iron
27 Immature newt
30 "The Purple People Eater" singer Wooley
32 They'll never get off the ground
36 Hard to wrinkle
41 Isn't pleasant to remember
42 Order sought by an accused before trial
43 Handyman's gadget
44 Author of "I Kid You Not"
45 Land in l'eau
46 "She's a Lady" songwriter
50 Many moons
52 Badly
55 Burned, to a nerd
57 Russian leader until 1917
61 Covered-dish supper favorite
66 Radar jamming and decoy flares, e.g.
67 When procrastinators get going

DOWN

1 Gp. advocating adoption
2 Go to the dark side
3 "My eye!"
4 Staked thing
5 Young fox
6 Just past five o'clock?
7 "Now I've got it!"
8 What the last piggy got
9 Solicits, with "up"
10 Deliberately annoy
11 "The Gondoliers" flower girl
12 Man-mouse link
13 Short iron, for Tiger
14 Action-denoting suffix
15 Cartoonist Silverstein
22 Nincompoops
23 Capablanca's game
24 Asian inn for caravans
26 Adjust a document setting
27 Striking success
28 Middle Corleone brother
29 "I love you," to Luis
31 Fast-tempoed jazz
33 Pastoral people of Kenya
34 Up to the point that
35 Memorial marker
37 Province of central Spain
38 Yemeni city
39 Conventioneer's badge
40 Outlet, e.g.
47 Nick of "North Dallas Forty"
48 Show obeisance
49 Capital of Ghana
51 Act the troubadour
52 Manco Capac's people
53 Pilfered goods
54 Ill-mannered oaf
56 Current blockers
58 Tender
59 Architect William Van ___
60 Conclude one's case
62 Gov. J. Shaheen's political ID
63 Shooting location
64 Houston of the Republic of Texas
65 Placido's "that"

24 GIRL IN A BLUE HOUSE by Bernice Gordon

The "Blue House" is where 17 Across lived and is now a museum.

ACROSS

1 Slipped a Mickey
6 Russell ___ College
10 Pair of mules
14 Nobelist Joliot-Curie
15 Pitchfork-shaped letters
16 Sharpen a scythe
17 "Roots" painter
19 Ponte Vecchio's river
20 Pie fruit
21 Clan wear
23 URL
27 Inhibit
28 Blubberheads?
29 Whirlybird
30 Intent
33 Oscar-winning brothers
34 Adage
35 Daughter of Cadmus
36 Frozen-waffle brand
37 Dialectics
38 Sphere start
39 The Indigo Girls, e.g.
40 Rajah's consort
41 Like the fishing cat
42 Suffix for rocket
43 Sugar bowl team?
44 "Valse ___": Sibelius
45 Ammonia compound
47 "Confounded!"
48 Witchy groups
50 "I don't give ___!"
51 Aid in a felony
52 Dolores Olmedo Patiño Museum display
58 Rail
59 "The Night of the Hunter" screenwriter
60 City on the Songka river
61 Effect a cure
62 Department in N France
63 "Ode to a Baby" poet Nash

DOWN

1 "What's the ___?"
2 Eight-time Norris Trophy winner
3 Indiana U. Museum designer
4 Terminal
5 Circus Circus employees
6 E-mails junk
7 Former Davis Cup coach
8 Indy 500 winner de Ferran
9 Recondite
10 Split up
11 17 Across was a "self" one
12 Soprano Moffo
13 Bright light
18 Rodin sculpture (with "The")
22 Smidgen
23 Give in
24 Re-entry parachute
25 Husband of 17 Across
26 Casino city
27 Land of Cotton
29 Security deposits
31 Pokey person
32 Acted cheeky?
34 ___ Carlo
37 Lubber
38 "___ stands now . . ."
40 Somerset Maugham story
41 Plains Indian
44 Gillette's ___ II razor
46 Noted conductor
47 Sun-___ tomatoes
48 Mazuma
49 "Bolero" instrument
50 Feller
53 Teamwork deterrent
54 Quarter horse not worth a nickel
55 Connective word
56 Sevruga delicacy
57 Its symbol is Sn

25 SOUPS DU JOUR by Alan Olschwang

Chowderheads have a definite solving edge here.

ACROSS

1 Dog star
5 Nemeses
10 Commandment word
14 Gaudy
15 Make ends meet
16 Troubles
17 Where to find a good Irish stew in the Buckeye State?
19 Wait at the light
20 Actor Delon
21 Signal after the danger has passed
23 Flowers' places
26 Bread cover
27 Sticker stat
30 Where to find a good minestrone in the Peach State?
35 Vacuum's lack
36 Stadium section
37 Suit material
38 Speaker's platform
40 Social sufferers
43 Famed surrealist
44 Nullify
46 QED part
48 Low sound?
49 Where to find a good borscht in the Gem State?
52 Old French coin
53 Attired
54 Spill the beans
56 Came into view
60 Debonair
64 Lemming cousin
65 Where to find a good bouillabaisse in the Lone Star State?
68 Mild expletive
69 Musical study
70 Headland
71 They're opposed
72 Balance-sheet item
73 Safer

DOWN

1 Captain Pierce portrayer
2 Kind of music
3 Sousaphone
4 Off-the-cuff remark
5 Prohibit
6 Bother
7 Okinawa port
8 Novel ending
9 1966 U.S. Open winner
10 Personalized
11 Trapper's quest
12 Stew pot
13 Patron
18 Languid
22 Bus. leaders
24 Exhaust
25 Hook's mate
27 Palindromic address
28 Keyboard instrument
29 Beams
31 Transgressed
32 Fats units
33 Abode for Ice Cube?
34 Kindergarten quintet
39 Makes it
41 Dull
42 Funnyman Mort
45 Mr. Applegate's accomplice
47 Skoal or prosit
50 Bent out of shape
51 Conceive
55 Park of California
56 With: French
57 Cartoon possum
58 Think out
59 Clobber
61 Skater's jump
62 Roses' place
63 Latin infinitive
66 Amin of Uganda
67 Ready to run

26 MEMBERS OF THE CLAN* by John Underwood

Asterisked clues are all members of the clan.

ACROSS

1 Philosopher David (1711–1776)*
5 Noble Italian family
9 Arafat's successor
14 "Law & Order: SVU" star
15 Tiptop
16 "The Sound of Music" family
17 Disraeli's rival*
19 Certain Web surfer
20 One-horse carriages
21 "Goldfinger" star*
23 Bose rival
25 Get under one's skin
26 "Sweet Afton" poet*
30 "What's going ___ there?"
32 ___-El (Superman)
35 Langston Hughes poem
36 "A Study in Scarlet" author*
39 Lacking legal force
40 According to schedule
41 Negri in "Madame Bovary"
42 THEME
44 Prep for Kings College
45 Switch positions
46 In ___ (shortly)
47 "Rob Roy" author*
48 Maui music maker
49 Monterrey munchie
52 Subject of a Shakespeare tragedy*
56 Bay of Whales locale
61 Crazy Spanish numbers?
62 Two-time UK prime minister (1886–1937)*
64 Pay for lunch
65 Workplace protection org.
66 Shortest bk. in the Bible
67 Instructional book genre
68 "The ___ the limit!"
69 Audiometer inventor*

DOWN

1 Like falsetto
2 The Bruins' school
3 Tight-fisted
4 JFK stats
5 Cake message for Alice
6 Brindisi bride
7 X
8 Major suit?
9 Kaput
10 Yankee Stadium location
11 Christian in "Batman Begins"
12 Takeoff artist
13 Sprightly
18 Pub crawlers
22 Shropshire and Wiltshire
24 Make up
26 Parlor pastime
27 Complete reversal
28 Players play them
29 Big Easy acronym
31 Astro ending
32 Former capital of Japan
33 Shell out
34 Listed
36 Mollycoddle
37 Whenever
38 Crude group
43 Likes right off
47 Comme ci, comme ça
48 Wolfgang Lüth's vessel
50 Literary cockroach
51 Score endings
52 One not afraid of the limelight?
53 Kind of phobia
54 Masticate
55 Membership care gps.
57 High muck-a-muck
58 "¿Quien ___?" ("Who knows?")
59 Carrier to Ben-Gurion
60 Over and above: Abbr.
63 Grill

27 MIXED NUTS by Kevin George

Four theme entries relate to the title.

ACROSS

1 Stripe
6 Balkan native
10 It's a long story
14 In town
15 Banned orchard spray
16 Shrinking Asian sea
17 Bowl
18 Homer Simpson's mom
19 Rock's Jethro ___
20 Trendy
21 Action-movie stand-in
24 Gallic girlfriend
25 "Wheel of Fortune" category
26 Some like to rub it in
31 "See ya" in Sonora
32 Shakespearean verb
33 Snatch
36 Drift
37 New Orleans footballer
39 Pet plant
40 Helpful connections
41 Hwys.
42 October stones
43 "Marie Antoinette" star
46 Theater opening
49 Rogers and Clark
50 Biennial statistics
53 Poor service?
56 Inflamed ending
57 Color quality
58 Vice President before Gerald
60 Diving position
61 Whitney and Manning
62 Miniscule
63 Late Orly birds
64 "Round and Round" rock group
65 "Holy cow!"

DOWN

1 Bridge contract
2 Mower maker
3 Passed with flying colors
4 See 22 Down
5 Television varieties
6 Jackson of "Pulp Fiction"
7 North Carolina university
8 Tirade
9 "Troy" star
10 General Motors division
11 Caribbean island
12 Exasperates
13 Formal avenue
22 "Wizard of Oz" character (with 4-D)
23 "We're in trouble!"
24 Basic unit
26 It's a wrap
27 Japanese noodle
28 Vardalos and Peeples
29 Lyric poet
30 Stone weight
33 Poker expert Johnny
34 Art supplies
35 Former
37 Less forgiving
38 He lost twice to DDE
39 PC "brains"
41 Cambodian cash
42 Spacecraft orbiting Mars
43 Gifts
44 Jim Varney character
45 Commandment word
46 Jimmy of "NYPD Blue"
47 Whale constellation
48 It's handed down
51 "Return of the Jedi" dancing girl
52 Troop group
53 String together
54 Highlands dialect
55 Woody and Buzz Lightyear
59 Mile High Center architect

28 BEAT THE CLOCK 9:22 by Ernest Lampert

Consider yourself a whiz if you can solve this one in 9:22 or better.

ACROSS

1 Meat tenderizer
7 Most blue
15 Relationship involving love and jealousy
17 Retreating army's defensive maneuver
18 Prudential rival
19 Moved carefully
20 "The Pittsburgh Kid" of the ring
23 "Breakfast in Bed" artist
26 Sgt.'s address
27 Windy City team
28 Nicholas II was the last one
32 Ecological community
34 Note
36 Tchaikovsky's "___ Cantabile"
39 Tiger Woods' real first name
40 Skimmers
42 Cottonwood relative
43 Gray ___
44 Antiaircraft fire
47 Shogun's capital
48 Scale model
50 Cy Young winner Saberhagen
51 ___ the hole
54 Myanmar, in the past
56 Walks down Madison Ave.?
62 Simultaneously
63 Craving ones
64 Cinch

DOWN

1 Pricing word
2 Took the cake, say
3 Shell-game item
4 Firth of Clyde island
5 "Splendor in the Grass" screenwriter
6 Sinuous dance of the East
7 Bonn boulevard
8 Suffix for cow or can
9 ___ Fail (Irish coronation stone)
10 Be silent, in music
11 Shredded
12 Support
13 Wild plum
14 Keep an eye on
16 Maui neighbor
20 Secret doctrine
21 He speaks his mind
22 Pest
24 To a degree
25 Botanist's angle
27 Recent: Comb. form
29 SWAT team member
30 Submit
31 Make a better hitch
33 Hindu religious sage
35 Site of Theo. Roosevelt National Park
37 Drainpipe part
38 It's inside: Abbr.
41 Slopes habitués
45 Less than right?
46 Piranha
49 Key word
50 Bêtes noires
51 Mordant
52 Feature of Beldar from Remulak
53 Tolkien tree creatures
55 "September ___": Diamond
57 Honshu bay
58 Bluejacket
59 Track-and-field org.
60 Paper size: Abbr.
61 Harry Connick, Jr. album

29 CAUSTIC CRITIQUE by Ed Early

The author of the searing review below can be found at 37 Down.

ACROSS

1 Radio type
5 Irritate
10 ___ Raton
14 Stage direction
15 "The Philosophy of Right" author
16 Coup d'___
17 Trick ending
18 Persian Gulf export
20 **Start of a sardonic literary review**
22 Sp. equivalent of Frau
23 Arrive at a judgment
24 Vestiges
26 Neighborhoods
27 U.S. Public Health agcy.
30 "___ of those who . . ."
31 Orientation instruments
33 **Part 2 of review**
36 Whirling Sicilian dance
38 Gramophone inventor Berliner
39 "Treasure Island" monogram
40 Acela, for one
45 Basketball pros
47 **See 37 Down**
48 Aiport near Disney World
49 **End of review**
53 Constant busy signal, e.g.
55 Parting words
56 Guitar chord
57 Century 21 listings
58 Peter Fonda title role
59 Collision souvenir
60 ___ al-Arab (Iraqi river)
61 Foxx of Comedy

DOWN

1 Prosecutor's aide: Abbr.
2 Nurture
3 Swindle
4 Oldest of the Brady girls
5 Garlic relative
6 This spot
7 Lab gel
8 Bogs
9 Ex-governor Spitzer
10 Turpin of slapstick
11 ENT instrument
12 Egyptian capitalist?
13 Encyclopedia sections
19 Namaqualand locale
21 Binges, briefly
25 Eros
27 Prefix for space
28 Amusing, in an odd way
29 Lets the A/C run
31 Clock std.
32 Music to shuffle by
33 Shakedown cruise, for one
34 Hearty partner
35 Xenon, argon, et al.
36 Made for a mortise
37 **Author of review (with 47-A)**
40 Padre's sister
41 Serve more coffee
42 Fit for cultivation
43 1954 Patti Page hit
44 Took home
46 Certain undergrads
47 Brittany seaport
50 Cry of delight
51 Home-loan agcy.
52 "___ of wit well play'd": Shak.
54 1/3 a wine

30 STEWART'S GRAND CRU? by Matt Ginsberg

The answer to that question can be found at 38 Across.

ACROSS

1 Baby swallows
5 Fake handle
10 Herb for the judicious
14 Code beginning
15 Car opener
16 City on the Oka River
17 Song tribute to Marilyn Monroe
20 Bud holder
21 "None missing"
22 Little suckers
25 Strong light
26 A many-splendored thing in Italy
30 Rice concoction
33 Brown bread
34 Buck back
35 Grande opening
38 Stewart's grand cru?
42 Switch "ups"
43 Ruler with a line
44 Head lights
45 Gas range
47 Gets across
48 Make a hash of
51 Cause of a class struggle
53 Disbelief
56 Battery components
60 Hard up
64 Spotted
65 Tax extension
66 Commedia dell'___
67 Azurite and tinstone
68 "Picnic" beauty queen
69 Stage mom in "Gypsy"

DOWN

1 Doctor's bag?
2 Brief investments
3 House opening?
4 Marquis name
5 House of games
6 A blooming necklace
7 Board seller
8 "A Bug's Life" princess
9 Satirist Mort
10 Careless catchphrase
11 First sign
12 Art class
13 Hostel opening
18 Exists from a long time ago
19 Cinder ending
23 First-rate
24 Factotum
26 Air head
27 Climactic sound
28 Crew's control
29 They stand before U
31 Evening out
32 Brick measure
35 Avis adjective
36 Coward's confession
37 Epinicia
39 J. D. holder
40 A time to dye
41 Western agreement
45 Where the buoys are
46 A bettor item
48 "Attila" operatic title role
49 Wolverine's kin
50 A one and a two
52 Plum pit
54 E-mail attack
55 Intro to physics
57 VA neighbor
58 Tropical tuber
59 They flew for nearly 35 years
61 "The butler ___ it!"
62 Bank contents
63 Half a snicker

31 ISLAND FEATURE by Pete Muller

A tropical topic from this native New Yorker.

ACROSS

1 Half a dolphinfish
5 From the barrel, to Capp
10 Bridge
14 Regents, for example
15 Ukelele has one
16 Big Brown hair
17 **A collection of letters**
20 Island near Maui
21 Type of wonder
22 Some layers
25 Brass, for example
26 A Kennedy
30 Pliocene and Pleistocene
33 German beer saint
34 Pop
35 Japanese sash
38 **What's special about the collection: Part 1**
42 English Beat genre
43 Informative android?
44 Waste producer
45 One keeping track
47 Wahine's welcome
48 Where two become one
51 Pair
53 Ahi steak, e.g.
56 First name in strikeouts
60 **What's special about the collection: Part 2**
64 Last name in couture
65 Foreigner
66 They're seen at SFO
67 It's in Paris but not in New York?
68 Spay
69 When doubled, quickly

DOWN

1 Joe Cocker's "Cry ___ River"
2 It could be a double
3 LOL
4 Committing words
5 North of Virginia
6 Marcel, say
7 Spike TV, formerly
8 Staring
9 Type of platter
10 Some blouses
11 Inquiring group
12 "___ it goes . . ."
13 Informative
18 "The Prophet" poet Gibran
19 Solitude can be found here
23 Olympian drink
24 Saw
26 "Beowulf," for one
27 Go down
28 Certain skirt
29 Bridge whiz Culbertson
31 Chicago Fire scapegoat
32 Tesla namesake
35 ___ buco
36 Matt Helm's wife
37 It could be bad or good
39 Tokyo, once
40 It's shortest at noon
41 "Rhapsody in Blue" carrier: Abbr.
45 "Surfin' ___": Beach Boys
46 "Strong Enough" singer Sheryl
48 "Like me"
49 Marx brother?
50 Porsche SUV
52 Attach
54 Turtle Bay locale
55 Fossey or Parkinson
57 MGM studios cofounder
58 Intro painting class
59 Mont. neighbor
61 Perfect marks
62 Newcastle or Sierra Nevada
63 Fed. stipend

32 EMINEM by Barry C. Silk

37 Across was a 2008 Microsoft acquisition target.

ACROSS

1 Highland hats
5 Measured (with "up")
10 Karaoke need
14 Month in Israel
15 "We hold ___ truths . . ."
16 Voiced
17 Chatterbox
19 Made the putt
20 Historic beginning?
21 Butterfinger's comment
22 Ready for
24 Hungry person's query
26 MD's diagnostic tools
27 French friend
28 "P" or "D" on a coin, e.g.
32 Sine language?
35 "CSI" interruption
37 Google competitor
38 Mata ___
39 Piquant
41 Page (through)
42 DVD player button
44 Egyptian queen, for short
45 Dodge model until 1990
46 Jim Cramer show
48 Tonic's partner
50 Summer quaffs
51 Targeted
55 Mortgage payment add-on
58 Island of Napoleon's exile
59 Suffix with social
60 Alcove
61 Hollywood heavyweight
64 Surfer's sobriquet
65 Sports complex
66 Very knowledgeable
67 Practice boxing
68 Frisco footballer
69 Sam and Dave's label

DOWN

1 Devil Rays' home
2 Gussy up
3 Pirate's pal
4 Full-house letters
5 Swiss winter resort
6 Optimist's phrase
7 Supreme Greek deity
8 NYC hrs.
9 Remove a rack
10 NBA 1978–79 MVP
11 "If ___ the Zoo": Dr. Seuss
12 German philosopher
13 Nevada county
18 Space
23 Feel sorry for
25 Writing utensil for Copperfield?
26 Gnatlike insect
28 Virile
29 "Uh, excuse me?"
30 Horse of a different color?
31 UN leader Annan
32 Van Morrison's former group
33 Indian prince
34 Outraged
36 Bad habits
40 Jellystone Park denizen
43 Heading on a list of errands
47 "Seinfeld" character
49 Muslim leader
51 Dress style
52 Finger or toe
53 Pasadena neighbor
54 Fax precursor
55 Terminates
56 Mulligatawny, for one
57 Musical wrap-up
58 Roulette bet
62 ". . . ___ quit!"
63 Cries of pain

33 CHIVALRY LIVES by Sarah Keller

The real title can be found at 54 Across.

ACROSS

1 Break fasts
4 Pinnacle
8 Movie trailer
14 Tell falsehoods
15 Well-heeled?
16 To a great degree
17 Like emergency lights
19 "It was my best effort"
20 Loose coins
22 Moving about
25 Ho's instrument
26 Neighbor of Isr.
27 Monitor option
31 Pres. Jefferson
32 Med. report
33 "___ Ben Jonson!": Young
38 Charge card term
42 Native of Yemen's capital
43 Big Band follower?
44 Clinton cabinet member Federico
45 Attendee at a pre-nuptial party
49 "Stupid me!"
52 Craggy height
53 Edward James in "Selena"
54 Chivalrous act/PUZZLE TITLE
59 Valentine message
60 Educational milieu
64 Fetches
65 "Comin' ___ the Rye"
66 Swiss peak
67 Most reasonable
68 Pt. of AAA
69 Encouragement at the bullring

DOWN

1 Pole worker
2 Feel sick
3 Surrey spot?
4 On land
5 A la mode
6 Jazzman Thelonious
7 It may be cutting
8 Alan of "Growing Pains"
9 Choice offering
10 Taj Mahal site
11 Kick targets
12 Mournful song
13 Winona in "Mr. Deeds"
18 Imitates a peeping Tom
21 S–W filler
22 Ad ___ per aspera
23 Bus station handout, for short
24 Hidden treasure
28 Reno's st.
29 Enjoy the slopes
30 Vice President Spiro
34 Turn off
35 Revoke, to a lawyer
36 Classic laundry detergent
37 Les ___-Unis
39 "TV Guide" entries
40 Test for collegiate srs.
41 Saturn or Mercury
46 "No kidding"
47 Web site address ending
48 NASCAR racer Jeff
49 "Catch-22" lieutenant
50 Horse or soap follower
51 Confine
55 Three times three
56 Computer input
57 "Talking Vietnam" singer
58 Rows
61 Long March leader
62 Under the weather
63 Troglodyte

34 TWO CENTS' WORTH by Ed Early

Dan Blocker played the character at 22 Across.

ACROSS

1 Zoo attractions
5 Be a partner in crime
9 Windy isle off Venezuela
14 Percussion instrument
15 "Shark Tale" dragon fish
16 Kind of module
17 **Start of a popular adage**
20 More at liberty
21 Finish finish?
22 "Bonanza" character
23 Even chance
25 Brontë governess
27 Ivan or Peter
29 "Waiting to ___" (1995)
34 Clark's "Mogambo" costar
37 Well partner
40 Preserved, in a way
41 **Middle of adage**
44 Best of the lot
45 Amusing in an odd way
46 Black-maned horse
47 Most of Libya
49 Polio vaccine developer
51 Relatively few
54 Cognitive
58 Active European volcano
62 Tip off
64 Static
65 **End of adage**
68 Shine up the car again
69 Roanoke's Virginia
70 Much more than a walk
71 Applicant's aim
72 Word in a New Year's carol
73 Idiophones

DOWN

1 Astern
2 Guerrero of baseball
3 Leprechauns
4 Most cunning
5 Growler contents
6 Cookbook instruction
7 Borden bovine
8 Light brown to brownish orange
9 Styled after
10 Gordon in "Boardwalk"
11 "Once more ___ the breach . . .": Shak.
12 Expressions of contempt
13 Wonder Woman's adversary
18 Saladin's enemies
19 Not there
24 ___ Alto
26 Top-flight
28 Orange cover
30 Paul Newman title role
31 What a Persian is not
32 Capp's hyena
33 Whirling current
34 Impressed
35 Evil anagram
36 Sign in an antique shop
38 TV-show recorder
39 His teammates called him "Country"
42 Nice hot time
43 Jack in "The Rare Breed"
48 Cowardly Lion's fellow traveler
50 ___ Berry Farms
52 Pinochle declarations
53 Bronco Hall-of-Famer
55 Royal headwear
56 To one side
57 Onion relatives
58 To be, to Deneuve
59 That time
60 Eye source in "Macbeth"
61 Way away
63 Forsaken
66 Prefix for moron
67 French-born?

35 ELUSIVE CONNECTION by Larry Shearer

. . . and that connection can be found at 63 Across.

ACROSS

1 Some GI's
5 Dense ice cream
11 Duffer's delight
14 Indian tourist site
15 Danny Kaye was an ambassador for this org.
16 Patterned after
17 Handlers of stolen bonds?*
19 Racket
20 Rather
21 In a natural state
23 Peters out
26 Tear asunder
27 Kettle and Bell
30 Personal authority
33 D sharp's equivalent
35 Top-of-the-line criminal restraints?*
39 "Man-o-war on the port bow!"
41 "What's the rush?"
42 Calligraphy character?*
46 ___-Wreck
47 Dishwasher cycle
49 Outdo
50 Exclamation accompanying goose bumps
53 Strip
55 Updates machines
58 Suitable places
62 Show
63 Elusive connection in clue* answers
66 Mamie's hubby
67 Unruffled
68 Po tributary
69 Corporate component: Abbr.
70 Vacation spot
71 Dry run

DOWN

1 Boodle
2 E–J filler
3 ___-raspberry juice
4 Lebanese seaport
5 Laugh heartily
6 Cleveland–Toronto dir.
7 Vietnam Memorial designer Maya
8 Charge of wrongdoing
9 Harry Potter, for one
10 Spirit ___ Louis
11 Princess Leia's mother
12 Unfamiliar
13 Corp. division
18 "It's my pleasure!"
22 Jolt
24 "Star Trek" sequel, to fans
25 Paul Anka's "___ Beso"
27 Large city close to Phoenix
28 Daniel Mason's "___ Country"
29 Skirt feature
31 NFL stat.
32 Achieve a sensational success
34 Outstanding, in a way
36 Source
37 Album insert, informally
38 Album insert, informally
40 Taxonomic suffix
43 Ties up
44 Article in "Der Spiegel"
45 Standby maritime force, in the UK
48 Shakespearean work
50 Hair feature
51 Method of spiritual healing
52 Clergyperson's title: Abbr.
54 Fanfare
56 Gen. Bradley
57 Dieter's watchword
59 Camouflage
60 They might be tight
61 Game with 32 cards
64 ___ Paulo
65 Leb. neighbor

36 "WHERE, OH WHERE?" by John Lampkin

40 Across is an interesting clue.

ACROSS

1 Tore
6 Hot stuff
10 Knack
14 "Beetle Bailey" character
15 Amazes
16 On ___ (equipotent)
17 Indy 500 sound
18 Where the Three Little Pigs live?
20 Letter abbr.
21 Strangely
23 It can follow someone
24 SONY rival
26 Merganser features
27 Where to cry after a gutter ball?
31 Beethoven symphony "undedicated" to Napoleon
32 Bloom's buddies
33 Inc., abroad
36 Tucker
37 Sharks girl, on Broadway
39 Tend
40 Down, but with nothing to do with 3 Down
41 Flexible mineral
42 Tidy up
44 Where to kiss Big Bird?
46 Guru's quarters
49 Exchange positions
50 Bar
51 Arch preceder
53 Tee for Zorba
56 Where the Beatles made bad jokes?
58 Roof issues
60 "___ Three Lives"
61 "Vissi d'___"
62 Like "The X-Files"
63 Actor Grant
64 Adjudge
65 Chopper blade

DOWN

1 Heart song
2 Pensioner's org.
3 Grid work
4 Freudian concern
5 Devilish
6 Yes man
7 MP's quarry
8 Actual
9 "Don't ___!"
10 Ancient ship
11 "No bid"
12 Aspect
13 Lock
19 1994 Peace Nobelist
22 "Forceful" theory
25 "I cannot tell ___"
26 Comet, e.g.
27 "All ___ are off!"
28 "Mi chiamano Mimi," e.g.
29 The "A" in James A. Garfield
30 Welcome wreath
33 Poor excuse for tardiness
34 Every family has one
35 Bumper ding
38 Here, in Chihuahua
39 Links rental
41 Not fine
43 On-line seller
44 Calvados, e.g.
45 Favor
46 Jellied garnish
47 Winning 1974 Super Bowl coach
48 Sharpener
51 Lunar depression
52 A chip, maybe
54 Sony cofounder Morita
55 ___-friendly
57 Boy
59 Classified ad abbr.

37 BEATLES GIRLS by Holden Baker

The girl asked "to play" at 27 Across is Mia Farrow's sister.

ACROSS

1 Gator's cousin
5 "Barbershop" star
9 Fawns' papas
14 Scotch mixer
15 Agnew's plea, for short
16 "To ___ Mockingbird" (1962)
17 Bruin penalty killer
18 London apartment
19 Bonehead
20 **"Wearing the face that she keeps in a jar . . ."**
23 Win over
26 Deportment
27 **"Won't you come out to play?"**
31 Spanish 1 verb
32 Confine, as farm animals
33 Rob of "The Evidence"
37 Ben & Jerry's rival
39 Carpentry grooves
41 Grime fighter
42 Steven Bochco series
44 Went white
46 "Every child. One voice." org.
47 **"Hold your head up you silly girl . . ."**
50 Weapons cache
53 Card game for two
54 **"A girl with kaleidoscope eyes . . ."**
58 Figure at a roast
59 Splinter group
60 English subway
64 Crucifixes
65 Peel
66 Sharif or Bradley
67 Rendezvous
68 Boot attachment
69 Visitor of "Deep Space Nine"

DOWN

1 CBS drama set in Las Vegas
2 Fabled bird that never lands
3 Praiseful poem
4 Life's work
5 Deduced
6 Rum mixer
7 Panache
8 Dorothy's dog
9 Giant slalom, e.g.
10 Neatness
11 Get straight
12 Geographic teaching aid
13 Nymph's pursuer
21 Reindeer herdsman
22 Pres. from Yorba Linda
23 Collectible Ford flop
24 "I ___ Lover": Mellencamp
25 Actress Hannah
28 Inappropriate
29 "Well, lah-___"
30 Paul Prudhomme's sister
34 Sot
35 "___ Joe's"
36 Trunk item
38 White, long-haired Russian dogs
40 College period
43 Most suspicious
45 Painter Anthony Van ___
48 Rembrandt van ___
49 National Aviation Hall of Fame site
50 Not foggy-headed
51 Scuttlebutt
52 "Star Trek" doctor
55 Recipe amts.
56 Jalopy
57 Off-white shade
61 Thurman in "Kill Bill"
62 Declare illegal
63 Cooperstown stat

38 PUN AND GAMES by Matt Ginsberg

Richard Davalos played 17 Across in 1955.

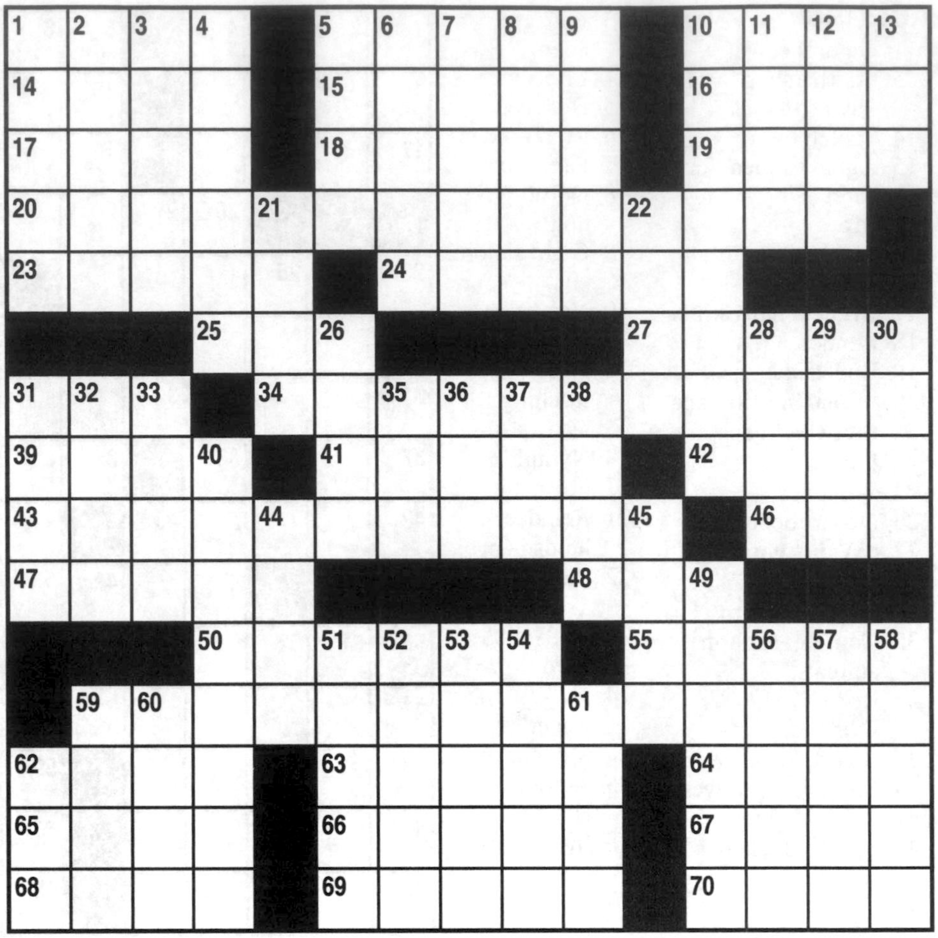

ACROSS

1 Come crawling back
5 Checked for the last time
10 Lucky number in Monte Carlo?
14 Ritzy cracker
15 Santa follower
16 Dodge City lawman
17 Cal Trask's twin
18 Clip joint
19 Man of war
20 Lose focus?
23 Be constructive
24 Car bombs
25 Key contraction
27 Blood line
31 Alter egos
34 Piscine operator?
39 Odile's black skirt
41 Syrian political party
42 Head for a bar
43 Madrid water conduit?
46 A crowd, for Florence
47 Himalayan hazards
48 Fireworks sound
50 Where to find directors?
55 Big dipper's condiment
59 A matter of principal?
62 It brings people closer
63 Art supporter
64 Colored part of a ball
65 Change furniture
66 Do a make-up job
67 Go easy
68 NRA mem.
69 Checks for letters
70 Mona's surname

DOWN

1 Oak product
2 Worker who makes connections
3 Wishful thinking
4 Enclave of SE France
5 Spanker
6 "What's in ___?"
7 Having square footage
8 Collars for preppies
9 Silvio of "The Sopranos"
10 Quarantines
11 Peer group member
12 Game in the woods
13 Decorates with Charmin, briefly
21 Short highways
22 Rickman in "Sweeney Todd"
26 Massages
28 Cut-up
29 Ruler with a line
30 Mourning line
31 Half small
32 Short copy
33 Ballpark figure
35 Bit of cheer
36 Cheesecake ingredient
37 Frequent flyers stat
38 Columbus' home
40 Local personality
44 "___ She Great" (2000)
45 In business
49 Luke Skywalker's portrayer
51 Fleece
52 Bring up
53 Chicken company
54 Lost one's balance
56 The king of Champagne
57 Takes it from the top
58 Confused between ports
59 Bossy comments
60 Punch lines
61 Bath suds
62 Eva's half sister

39 OPPOSITES ATTRACT by Frances Burton

Our test solvers gave the clue at 38 Across an A+.

ACROSS

1 Juan's room
5 Pipe part
9 Eighty-six
14 Larger-than-life
15 By way of
16 Abdul of music
17 ___-do-well
18 Thought twice
20 Exams requiring no explanations
22 Scant
23 Nancy's "Rhoda" role
24 Gown's partner
27 Butch Cassidy, by birth
30 Smeller
34 Above it all
36 Unit of work
37 Bank of facts
38 Pointless college studies
42 Fail to mention
43 Follows Oct.
44 "The Age of Reason" author
45 Musical unit
46 Partygoers
49 Sun
50 Nothing
52 Troubles
54 Queries requiring no explanations
61 Baja and Sinai
62 Sword
63 Macaroni salad option
64 Poker stake
65 Hollow
66 Church officer
67 Fortnight's fourteen
68 Building wings

DOWN

1 Broadcast
2 Copycat
3 Stead
4 Realty units
5 Difficult situation
6 Louise's partner
7 Geologic divisions
8 Chew over
9 Do 50 in a 30
10 Greek prophetess
11 Old car coat
12 Pub pints
13 Launching site
19 Andy Capp's heady brew
21 Louse up
24 Chicken
25 Where Col. Travis died
26 Put forward
28 Axe handle
29 Parabola
31 Damascus, e.g.
32 Pool member
33 Artist's stand
35 Pretended
39 Americans, south of the border
40 Marker
41 Bowl over
47 Perspiring
48 Mixes a salad
51 Privileged
53 Screen out
54 Shout out
55 City in Oklahoma
56 Campus area
57 Forearm bone
58 Milky gem
59 Dudley Do-Right's love
60 Comes across
61 Edgar Award eponym

40 SHAPELY by Alan Olschwang

The Boston terrier at 26 Across was first seen in 1902.

ACROSS

1 Noose
6 Highlanders
11 Atlas page
14 McCann Erickson employees
15 Come to terms
16 Under the weather
17 Arlington landmark
19 Besides
20 Romance novelist Victoria
21 ". . . ___ I will be married to a sponge": Shak.
22 Like some interests
24 Cream puff
26 Buster Brown's dog
27 "The Graduate" plot device
33 Grad's pursuit
36 Where Hercules fought a lion
37 Sri Lankan primate
38 Province
40 Scorch
42 Kind of roast
43 Intends
45 Monte Carlo roulette bets
47 ___ vivant
48 Stock item of kitchens
51 German coal basin
52 Gasped
56 Agitate
59 Breadbasket
61 Producer De Laurentiis
62 Troy, NY, campus
63 Where it's okay to drop the ball
66 Sushi bar offering
67 Harden
68 Solecism
69 HST's successor
70 Like some stadiums
71 Makes trades

DOWN

1 Tool with a headstock
2 Impromptu
3 Olfactory offense
4 Of an atrial partition
5 Billfold filler
6 Turnstile proceeds
7 Culture medium
8 A bit of a joule
9 His papacy began in 936
10 Mali neighbor
11 Campanella had a hand in it
12 Vera's leader?
13 Trudge
18 Butterflies
23 Mexicali mister
25 Charged particle
26 Like "Macbeth"
28 Key with one sharp
29 Mortise mate
30 Chow
31 Prom transport
32 Sport's channel
33 Door part
34 Vowel-rich cookie
35 Bridges in "Norma Rae"
39 Pizzelle flavoring
41 Vents like Vesuvius
44 Inclined
46 Start-up loan org.
49 Hispanic
50 Last
53 Miss USA's wear
54 Sign up
55 They walk the walk
56 Mr. Mertz
57 Kind of column
58 Go the extra ___
59 Richard in "Nights in Rodanthe"
60 Like Goodwill goods
64 Reticent
65 Proof abbr.

41 LITERALLY SPEAKING by Jim Leeds

A more devilish clue for 22 Across would be "Lucifer's grandson."

ACROSS

1 Kansas motto word
7 Critical pan from an ovine member?
10 Future reading material?
14 "Absolutely certain!"
15 In progress
17 Children's nursery rhyme
19 Formed a connection
20 Montana tribe
21 Ketch kin
22 Pappy Yokum's grandson
25 Indian lentil dish
26 Mini-albums, for short
29 Chopper
31 Freshwater duck
34 Carpe diem
38 Gutter site
39 La-la lead-in
40 Photographers
42 Sticky substance
43 During
45 Oft-repeated phrase from "The Wiz"
47 Spike the punch
48 After due
49 Miss-handled
50 Spawn
52 Soviet auto
54 Former Cremona coin
58 Common site in Ft. Lauderdale
61 Reveres
64 1978 Faye Dunaway film
67 Wooden dowel used in shipbuilding
68 One of a kind
69 In ___ (actual existence)
70 Factory agent
71 Marne mornings

DOWN

1 Sufficiently
2 Tone for Stieglitz
3 Tropical fruit
4 Stores on a farm
5 Rents
6 Stub ___ (stumble)
7 Sticker
8 Folk rocker DiFranco
9 Uses an abacus
10 Church dignitary
11 Back then
12 Myanmar neighbor
13 "Damon and Pythias," for one
16 "Yipes!"
18 Dietary info
23 Maxwell Anderson play (with "The")
24 Semester testers
27 Jim and Tammy's old club
28 Basic Halloween costume
30 "I've got my ___ you!"
32 Swear
33 Economist Keyserling
34 Newcastle abundance
35 Milkseed tuft
36 Coffee additives
37 First mes of the año
41 Melbourne to Canberra dir.
44 Will beneficiary
46 Fix boundaries
51 Soon
53 Nonpro org.
55 Kuwaiti's neighbor
56 It's been seen before
57 Buffoons
58 Little bit, to L'il Abner
59 Hoity-toity put-ons
60 Yonder
62 Thing to beat
63 Endo of tennis
65 Whitewash the truth
66 Bavarian peak

42 "... AND NOT A DROP TO DRINK" by Bonnie L. Gentry

Ben Affleck played 33 Down on the silver screen in 2003.

ACROSS

1 Brief words?
5 Stays for another hitch
10 Bangkok money
14 Worsted fabric
15 Wedding reception party?
16 Pigmented peeper part
17 De Gaulle alternative
18 One thrown at a rodeo
19 Be a little hoarse
20 Less than diddly
21 Enought to put you to sleep
23 "Hee Haw" humor
25 Needing to cool down, maybe
26 1973 news topic
31 Northwest's 2008 merger partner
32 "Coming to America" prince
33 "What ___ care?"
36 Capital south of Lillehammer
37 Chatty flappers
38 It's no. 1 on the Mohs scale
39 Sporty cars
40 Embroidery loop
41 City in a Porter song title
42 Slice an onion, say
44 Fundraising dinner unit
46 Wilbur's pal
47 Excellent excuse
51 Freud focus
54 Vehicle seen at a roadside diner
55 "The Audacity of Hope" author
56 Admit frankly
57 McDonald's founder Ray
58 Jordanian cash
59 Fretted fiddle
60 They move in a charged atmosphere
61 They're in control of their faculties
62 Range in "The Sound of Music"

DOWN

1 Bingo hall cry
2 "Me neither!"
3 Attendance takings
4 The Kingsmen drummer
5 A lot of summer TV
6 Long-distance runner Zátopek
7 West Coast school
8 "Fur is dead" org.
9 Shores
10 A matter of grave importance?
11 Popeye's "stop!"
12 Anyone's pronoun
13 Aquafina alternative
21 "The Sopranos" actress de Matteo
22 Apothecaries' weight
24 Mort Walker pooch
26 Mudpuppy
27 Daring exploit
28 American psychic Edgar
29 In ___ (constricted)
30 Hardly o'er
33 Matt Murdock's alter ego
34 Hispanic huzzahs
35 Zero-calorie drink
37 Liz Taylor's third husband
38 Diggs in "Rent"
40 Trodden trail
41 "Frasier" actress Gilpin
42 Earvin Johnson and namesakes
43 Imprisons
44 Prefix meaning "wing"
45 7-Up flavor
47 Glide behind a motorboat
48 Irish Rose's guy
49 "Sweater Girl" Turner
50 Supermodel David Bowie married
52 Sticky matter
53 They take night flights
56 Gardner in "Mogambo"

43 HOLLYWOOD LEGEND by Doug Peterson

. . . and that legend can be found at 61 Across.

ACROSS

1 35th prez
4 Dolls up
10 "May I speak?"
14 Tram cargo
15 British pop star Williams
16 Danny DeVito sitcom
17 1956 epic featuring 61-A (with "The")
20 Was a straphanger
21 Signal on stage
22 Rap's Dr. ___
23 1931 crime film starring 61-A
28 Fail to see eye to eye
31 "Toddlin' Town" trains
32 "Grody!"
33 Mystique
34 Sink stopper
38 1944 film noir costarring 61-A
43 Mex. miss
44 Teensy bit
45 Novelist Kesey
46 Question starter
49 Most uncool
51 1973 sci-fi movie starring 61-Across
55 Gaza Strip gp.
56 Portuguese king
57 Goes barnstorming
61 Actor awarded an honorary Oscar in 1973
66 Minnelli of "Cabaret"
67 Kind of cracker
68 Swift bird
69 Actress Remini
70 "The Tigger Movie" character
71 Receiving line figure

DOWN

1 Writes quickly
2 Banjo ridge
3 Number-picking casino game
4 Wastefully extravagant
5 CD-___
6 Apple competitor
7 Advanced deg.
8 ___-nez
9 Inveigle
10 Chowed down
11 Ranch crew
12 Not included
13 Tightwad
18 Rum mixer
19 Repast
24 Test choice
25 Garr or Hatcher
26 Like a famous Italian tower
27 "NBA Fastbreak" channel
28 July 4th disappointments
29 Inventor Sikorsky
30 Not ajar
35 Take a shine to
36 Colorado natives
37 "Peer ___"
39 Turn on the waterworks
40 Industrious sort
41 Raison d'___
42 Traveled fast
47 Munich mister
48 Jumpy
50 A part of
51 Bit of witchcraft
52 Enduring hit
53 "Yikes!"
54 Big cat, in Córdoba
58 Played for a sap
59 "Quo Vadis" setting
60 Deliberate slight
62 Sound of contentment
63 Flat-bodied fish
64 "Just as I suspected!"
65 Limbo prop

44 "SURPRISE!" by Ed Early

Canadians will know the answer to 20 Across.

ACROSS

1 Intoxicating Polynesian drink
5 Refurbishes
10 Unpleasant amount
14 With, to Jacques
15 Notched
16 Crew concurrence
17 **Start of a quip**
20 Dollars in a "toonie"
21 Often a subject
22 Blunder
23 Topmost point
24 "Walk Like ___": The 4 Seasons
25 Tec
28 British counterpart of 4 Down
29 Playful activity
32 Barbecue morsel
33 Came home, in a way
34 Flower holder
35 **Quip: Part 2**
38 Nary a one
39 Musical wind emitter
40 Squeezed, in a way
41 Tease
42 Once again
43 Hardships
44 Dump closure
45 Hannity of FOX News
46 End of the line?
49 Jemima or Millie
50 Towel inscription
53 **End of quip**
56 ___ Blanc
57 Off-stage remark
58 Life of Riley
59 Devious maneuver
60 Destined
61 Word with fox or turkey

DOWN

1 "Critique of Judgment" author
2 Frankly admit
3 Presidential power
4 Austrian "alas!"
5 Poisons
6 Have words
7 Lawns after being cut
8 Pressure unit
9 Like some millionaires
10 Apply lightly
11 Court cry
12 "Kiss From a Rose" singer
13 Latin infinitive
18 Nightmares
19 Truckful, e.g.
23 "Get ___ on!"
24 Mentally alert
25 Neckless lizard
26 Southeast Asian capital
27 "Guten ___" ("Good evening!")
28 Macaroni shape
29 Round figure
30 Person found on the aisle
31 Require-ments
33 Oft-rattled sword
34 Churchill's trademark
36 Not ready for the concert stage
37 Take off
42 On the surface of
43 Caused distress
44 LX, in Torino
45 Jacket material
46 Motorist's convenience
47 Organic compound
48 Jean in "The Da Vinci Code"
49 Working
50 Listen attentively
51 "___ many words"
52 Let it stay
54 Stars and Bars org.
55 11/11 VIP

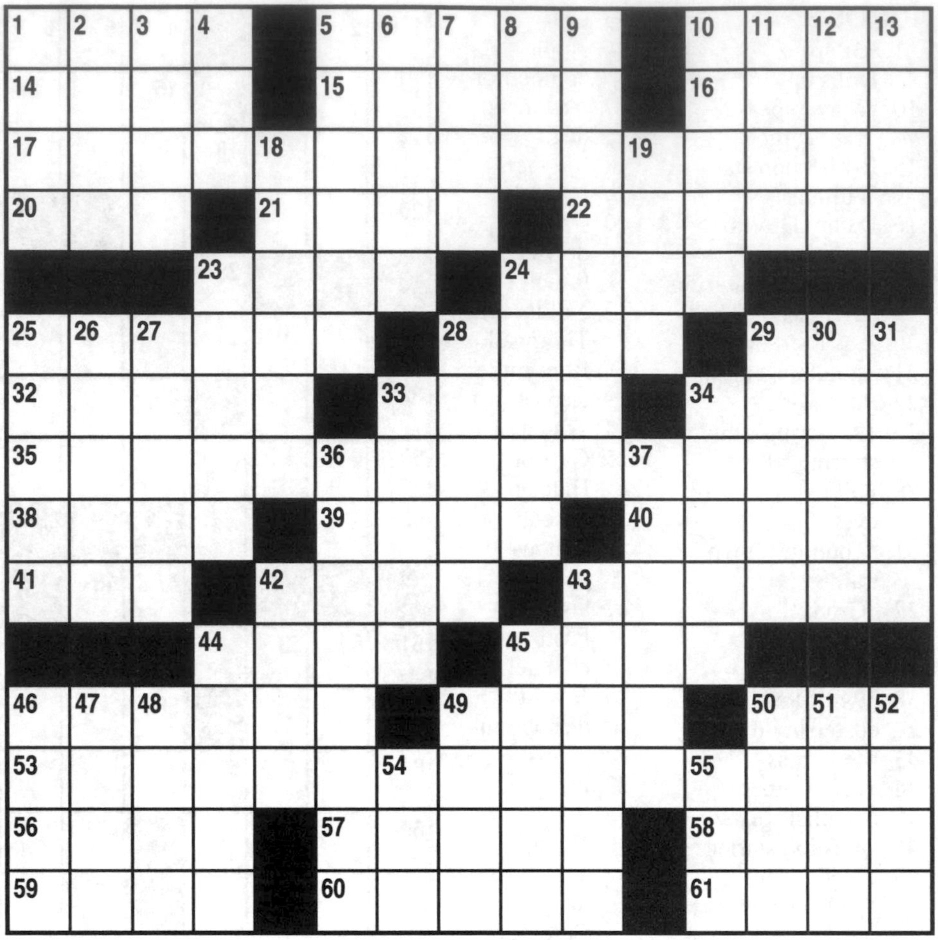

45 EYELETS by Billie Truitt

A no-nonsense homophonic challenge.

ACROSS

1 "Get out!"
6 Deli choice
10 Cyberclutter
14 "There's ___ in the bucket"
15 Honey factory
16 Create
17 Outdoor hotel employee
18 Cools down
19 Paperless exam
20 Former Caribbean piracy center
23 Nebraska native
24 Miners dig it
25 Bribe
26 Maple drip
29 City on Lake Tahoe
31 Major suffix
33 Material for a homemade valentine
35 Bit of style
37 One who's up
38 1972 Staple Singers hit
42 Wicker willows
43 Buying binge
44 "All I ___ Do": Sheryl Crow
45 Road or young suffix
46 Take a break
50 Gobbled up
51 It lies in front of the door
53 This instant
55 Sgt. or cpl.
56 Airline seating choice
60 Opposite of riches?
62 Friend of Big Bird
63 Choppers
64 Divisible by two
65 Kind of bargain
66 Orange box
67 Part of a three-piece suit
68 Round of applause
69 Derby competitor

DOWN

1 One who delivers
2 Virtuous
3 Deodorant type
4 Out of the wind, at sea
5 "Ditto!"
6 Ultra-formal
7 Puerto ___
8 Reluctant
9 Basil sauce
10 Unhealthful air
11 Moocher
12 Rap sheet letters
13 Blanc who voiced Bugs
21 Loses it
22 News bulletin
27 Angel or Devil Ray
28 Combustible heap
30 Many a time
32 Romantic rendezvous
34 None of the above
36 1951 NFL champions
37 Mole's hole
38 Site of the earliest presidential caucus
39 Aspiring atty's exam
40 Genealogy topics
41 Drivers hear it calling
45 "A Streetcar Named Desire" character
47 Make beloved
48 Big name in lawn care
49 Long-tailed finch
52 First Hebrew letter
54 Margaret Hamilton role
57 "Money ___ everything"
58 Sign for the superstitious
59 Emperor during Rome's Great Fire
60 Lean on the accelerator
61 Forum greeting

46 ELEMENTARY by Barry C. Silk

17 Across was inducted into the Rock and Roll Hall of Fame in 2001.

ACROSS

1 Movie studio with a lion mascot
4 Happening place
9 Bone marrow lymphocyte
14 Yeoman's "Yes!"
15 Hamburger with fries, e.g.
16 Maybelline rival
17 "Bohemian Rhapsody" vocalist
19 Keep treating a black eye, maybe
20 Greek vowel
21 Prefix with state
22 Entraps
23 Take for granted
25 Palindromic time
26 1964 Presidential candidate
32 Hodges of the Dodgers
35 Traffic jam
36 The Scales, astrologically
37 "Let us know," on an invitation
39 Org.
41 Wet forecast
42 "Hello" from Hilo
44 String quartet member
46 Blushing
47 Magician of note
50 Traditional knowledge
51 Kind of photograph
55 Carve
58 Gold ingot
60 Not pro
61 Assume as fact
62 1984 Tony Award winner for "The Real Thing"
64 Napoleon's force
65 Admission of defeat
66 Dubious "gift"
67 Josh
68 Tropical ray
69 ACLU concerns

DOWN

1 Mario Puzo subject
2 Spinning toys
3 Swim competitions
4 Outfield surface
5 Standards
6 German river
7 Classic soft drink
8 Unit of work
9 Long-winged creature
10 Ionic Breeze boast
11 Arab chieftain
12 Scarf material
13 Soapmaking substances
18 Paint amateurishly
22 Old French coin
24 Bathroom rug
25 Italia seaport
27 Bail out
28 Pulitzer poet Komunyakaa
29 Uphill lift
30 Toledo's lake
31 Money in South Africa
32 Mortarboard tosser
33 Ibiza, e.g., to Spaniards
34 Ukrainian city near the Polish border
38 Steve Carlton's former team
40 Least obscure
43 One taken in
45 Bullring cheer
48 TV component
49 Strong cart
52 Reason out
53 Bikini blast, in brief
54 Thpeakth like thith
55 Cross words
56 Apple throwaway
57 West Point letters
58 Lugosi in "Ninotchka"
59 Johnny Bravo's city
62 Huck Finn's raftmate
63 NYC subway overseer

47 COMIC BOOK HERO TO MOVIE STAR by Ray Hamel

24 Across was the world's first space satellite.

ACROSS

1 Sudden muscle contraction
6 Art ___
10 Take forcefully
14 British tar
15 George McGovern's birthplace
16 Symphony venue
17 Oak fruit
18 Hilarious character
19 Garfield's foil
20 Movie heroine of 1968
22 Japanese noodles
23 Paul Newman film
24 1957 launch
26 Weeps loudly
30 Title for A. Sharpton
32 Place for a plug
33 Be wise to
34 Robin's class
36 Side-to-side measurement
40 Peel of "The Avengers"
41 "Peanuts" lad
43 Desperately urgent
44 Online health information source
46 Leisurely pace
47 At any time
48 "___ favor, amigo"
50 Ryan in "Kate & Leopold"
51 Scoundrel
52 Homburg
56 Feel bad for
58 Great Basin state
59 Movie hero of 1995
65 Feng ___ (art of placement)
66 Pierre's yours
67 Anthony of "General Hospital"
68 Bring home
69 Frau's husband
70 Come to be
71 Hose problem
72 Singer Heidi Klum married
73 Slangy legs

DOWN

1 Ribs order
2 Printing measure
3 Pablo's passion
4 Certain Balkan
5 Chatty bird
6 Movie hero of 2003
7 What the good guys battle
8 Loses heat
9 How some books are available
10 Movie hero of 2007
11 Home-buyer's concern
12 Story of a sort
13 Hardly promising
21 Out in the country
25 Detroit-based labor org.
26 Distort
27 "Lean ___" (1989 movie)
28 Box office failure
29 Movie hero of 1982
31 Spider-Man villain
35 Movie heroine of 1984
37 Powerful female performer
38 Voyage with Captain Kirk
39 "Take this"
42 Proceed without a pause
45 Homer Simpson exclamation
49 Indian monarchs
52 They may be blown
53 Hawke of "Dead Poets Society"
54 First Lady after Hillary
55 Special student
57 Borders
60 Mrs. David Copperfield
61 Let
62 Reduce
63 Jazz combo rhythm keeper
64 Changes color

48 GENERAL KNOWLEDGE by Harvey Estes

Another clue for 16 Across could be "Met fan."

ACROSS

1 "Godmother of Punk" Smith
6 "Catch my drift?"
15 Solidarity
16 Lorgnette user
17 Numbers
18 Eases aches
19 Saucy one
20 It's on the map
21 Make (out)
22 Uptown, in NYC
24 NASA vehicle
25 Lewdness
28 Tyrant
33 Orchard stones
34 Exigency
36 Bag
37 Half of an old radio duo
38 From the keg
40 Domingo delivery
41 Garment worker
43 Game-stopping call
44 Part of Ripley's phrase
45 Tightens up
47 Lab warning
49 End of the yr.
51 Stat for Santana
52 Pres. Davis headed it
53 Like Robocop
58 Paints poorly
60 Michigan athlete
61 Man and Wight
62 Some T-men
63 Like old chips
64 Student loan assessment
65 Does desire?

DOWN

1 Gets by rudely
2 "La Dolce Vita" actress
3 Walk of Fame locale, informally
4 Threads
5 Consonant
6 Qualified
7 Autobahn auto
8 Olympian goal
9 Put a tag on
10 Flower clusters
11 Alaska's first governor
12 Part of n.b.
13 Judge
14 Highlands tongue
23 "The Godfather" composer Rota
26 Buffoons
27 Tibetan legends
29 Periwinkle
30 Exceptionally selective
31 Mintaka locale
32 Makes a crowd cry
35 Utmost
39 Nectar source
42 Old name for a Cincy team
46 Hush-hush
48 Bit in a salad bar
50 "Crazy" singer
53 Do laps
54 Went lickety-split
55 Lanchester of "Bride of Frankenstein"
56 Hoosier Bayh
57 Hill builders
59 Film canine

49 WITTY-BITTY by Jim Leeds

Perhaps the clue at 42 Down should be "Roll for Dustin?"

ACROSS

1 Fruity quaffs
5 Toronto team, for short
9 Family-sized auto
14 Japanned ware
15 Shawm offspring
16 Drudge
17 Question for a designing woman?
20 Rubinstein and Webern
21 Large open vessel
22 Palindromic turkey
23 Elg in "Les Girls"
24 Harris Rabbit
26 Create cryptograms
27 CBS series of 1980–81
28 Three, in Milan
29 Heated
31 Rembrandt van ___
32 Aiming aid
33 Med. plan
34 Hawaiian hamburger?
39 Apple Day mo.
40 Architect ___ Ming Pei
41 Til now
43 Hawaiian singer, to the uninitiated?
46 Pile
47 Tow job
48 Chemical endings
49 Working in a mess?
51 Shaky dish
52 "Miss Peach" lad
53 Tucker ___-Cat
54 Fraudulence
55 Lithographer Nathaniel plus harem?
59 Cornerstone abbr.
60 Keds rival
61 Persian sprite
62 Lateen-rigged boats
63 Set of beliefs
64 In addition

DOWN

1 "Boogie Man" subject Lee
2 "Symphonic Minutes" composer
3 High spirits
4 "Dragonwyck" author, and family
5 See 3 Down
6 Certain type group
7 Second person
8 Do time
9 Expectorated
10 Eet's Kellogg's pal
11 Canine world
12 Refer (to)
13 Requisite
18 Some Scottish precipitation
19 Sound heard at Little Bighorn
24 One of the Magnificent Seven
25 Bolshevik's flirtatious gesture?
26 Cut short
28 Long odds or 12:50
30 Both: Prefix
32 "Sheep May Safely Graze" composer
35 Daily weather statistic
36 Tidy sum
37 Like some grills
38 Those who answer
42 Role for Dustin
43 Prepared for winter driving
44 Spate
45 Close by
47 Fannie Farmer specialty
50 Santa tracker
51 Dreidel spinner, often
53 Bros
54 June 6, 1944
56 Inflamed
57 Macao coin
58 Veto

50 9:15 by Bonnie L. Gentry

42 Across was also a 1961 film that starred Ruby Dee and Sidney Poitier.

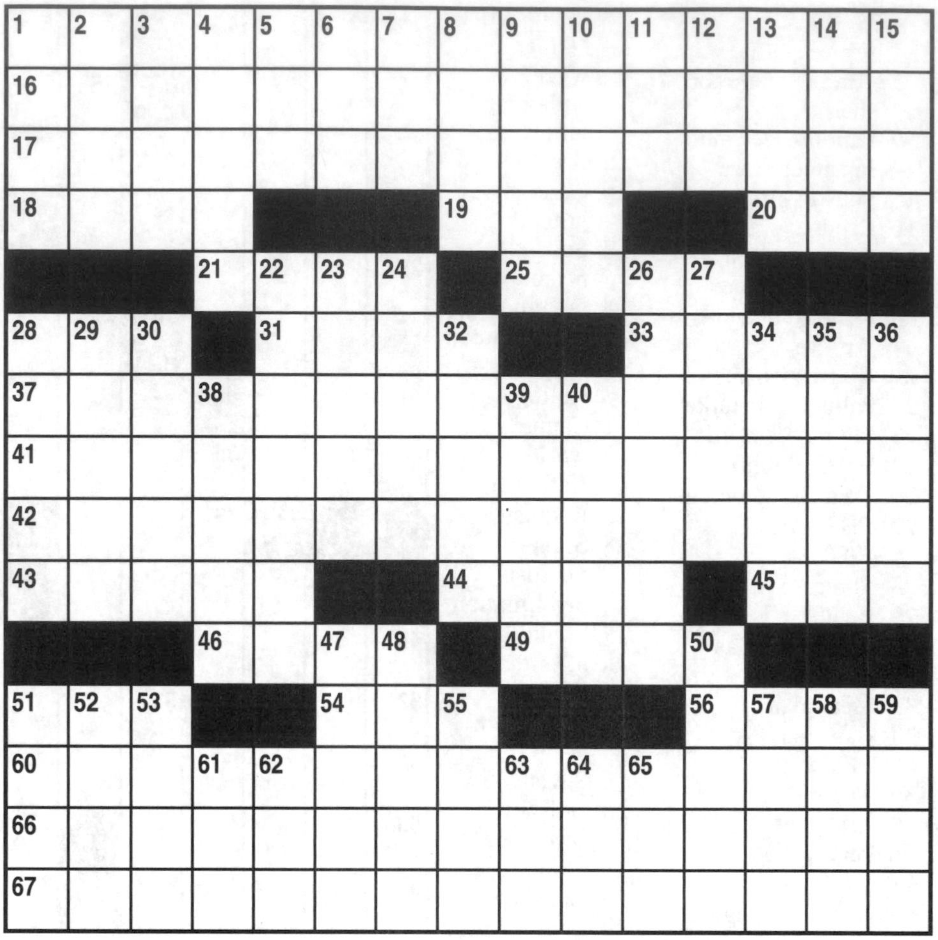

ACROSS

1 Range exercises
16 Grieved bitterly
17 It ended with Oklahoma's statehood
18 Minnesota quarter bird
19 Major ISP
20 Schmear accompanier
21 General picture
25 "Volsunga ___"
28 Other name indicator
31 Film ___
33 Cause to be red-faced
37 Edward Albee play (with "A")
41 Dr. Seuss had a celebrated one
42 Lorraine Hansberry Broadway play
43 Indian dignitary
44 Will be, in a Doris Day song
45 The Eisenhower years, e.g.
46 "Saving Private Ryan" event
49 Koppel and Kennedy
51 Dixie letters of 1861
54 "Bad Behavior" star Stephen
56 Capital founded by Pizarro
60 Michelangelo's tools of the trade
66 It may have a virus
67 America's Dairyland export

DOWN

1 Box kite's lack
2 95 for Am or 100 for Fm: Abbr.
3 Give a makeover to
4 Auctioneer's word
5 Former queen of Spain
6 End of a KO count
7 What most Laker games are played on?
8 County setting of the Scopes Trial
9 Gordie Howe's defunct team
10 2008 First Lady of France
11 Plane or cycle prefix
12 Gomez Addams' cousin
13 In the 40s, say
14 Coin that debuted on 1/1/02
15 Netherworld river
22 Cut marks on
23 Copycat's comment
24 Saturn satellite
26 Holy Grail pursuer
27 Taper off
28 Negative campaign feature
29 Knightley of "Pride & Prejudice"
30 Haggard hero Quatermain
32 Kathie Lee's ex-partner
34 Absinthe flavor
35 Clean, but good
36 Salon dye
38 "When ___ last . . .": Donne
39 IQ-test creator
40 Cavern, in poetry
47 Firth of Clyde island
48 1923 Literature Nobelist
50 Cover with ectoplasm
51 Work on a wad of gum
52 ___-Am (Dr. Seuss character)
53 Second in a Latin series
55 Naysayer
57 "Makes sense to me"
58 Sears department
59 Der ___ (Adenauer moniker)
61 Emcee's device
62 Chess rating
63 Blues Brother Aykroyd
64 Roosevelt's "Tree Army," for short
65 LBJ's veep

51 "CHARGE!" by Matt Ginsberg

It's unusual to find the same clue 17 times in one puzzle.

ACROSS

1 Charge
5 What Edna wouldn't give Mr. Incredible
9 Charge
13 Draftworthy
14 Boneheads
15 Charge
16 Charge
18 Graces the stage
19 Put on the feed bag
20 Bone head?
21 Dull
23 Weasel words
25 Sweeper or skip
27 Mirrored
29 Like some tires
32 Charge
35 Exert a calming influence
37 Bird from a green egg
38 Folding words
40 ___ & Perrins
41 Charge
43 Charge
44 Grosses out
47 LLD rcpt.
48 Charge
50 Without
52 Stashes away
54 Don't give this up
58 "Citizen Kane" model
60 Hurricanes' mascot
62 Kalashnikov alternative
63 Once mo'
64 Charge
67 Space (out)
68 Charge
69 High school breakout?
70 Tavern sign abbr.
71 A Dixieland quartet, perhaps
72 Redness exemplar

DOWN

1 Shoddy
2 Succeed
3 LBJ and GHWB
4 Chihuahua sound
5 Charge
6 Nahuatl speaker
7 Luau fare
8 Civic rivals
9 Went by sea
10 Charge
11 Gentle rebukes
12 Tarheel State motto word
14 Buttered up?
17 ___-garou (werewolf)
22 Dyed a robin's-egg color
24 Garry Kasparov's birthplace
26 Regular drink orders
28 Center of the Greek universe
30 Discharge
31 Charge
32 Soprano Te Kanawa
33 Moslem ruler
34 Charge
36 Charge
39 The scales of justice have two
42 Child's play
45 MDMA, familiarly
46 Man's inhumanity to man
49 Pulled down
51 JPL org.
53 Starr's 1964 stand-in
55 Charge
56 Celebrated hole
57 IQ test inventor
58 It can be purple
59 Easily bruised items
61 Wood knot
65 El operator
66 Charge

52 THIS AND THAT by Barry C. Silk

42 Down was a good example of a 17 Across.

ACROSS

1 Locale of many u-turns
8 Multivehicle collision
15 Chip away at
16 Glucose-creating enzyme
17 Team superstar
19 Tangles
20 Air France destination
21 Reading and others: Abbr.
22 Etching fluids
23 Clio, Erato or Urania
24 Laptop surfer's connection
25 Inarticulate pauses
26 In support of
27 Confronts
28 Total
31 Waste of taxpayer's money, usually
32 Greek for "wooden sound"
34 Habit
37 Where pawns move
41 Hard thing to swallow
42 Pain in the neck
43 Hydrocarbon ending
44 Innocent, e.g.
45 Baseball no-no
46 Used a telescope
48 Sci-fi staples
49 Legislative grp.
50 Square of Manhattan
51 Edmund Randolph was the first one
54 Cross-reference words
55 Daughter of King Minos
56 Proof goof
57 Bedroom fixture

DOWN

1 Cheat
2 Otalgia
3 Reversion
4 Took some courses
5 Ltr. accompaniment
6 Highest degrees
7 "And how!"
8 007 foe
9 Box elder, for one
10 Comrade in arms
11 Dot on a subway map: Abbr.
12 Stack found on a farm
13 Turnpike toll, e.g.
14 Keep going
18 Cheesesteak mecca
23 Japanese soup
24 Decreases in strength
26 Hanky-panky
27 Depression
29 Heavy water, for one
30 Greek singer accompaniment
31 Bookworm's counterpart
33 Signal to a road hog
34 Play the peacemaker
35 Horse for Cat Manzi
36 Informant
38 Active volcanos and earthquakes
39 Narrow, as bridges go
40 Street vendor
42 NBA great Abdul-Jabbar
45 Language group that includes Zulu
46 Spirit that's willing?
47 Figures in geometry
49 Bapt. or Meth.
50 Munich address
52 ___ hunch
53 Gallivant

53 INITIAL OBSERVATION by Michael Langwald

Michael thought up this quip while watching a popular CBS show.

ACROSS

1 Plays a part
5 Something to follow
9 OK, in a way
14 Ancient mariner
15 Language of Pakistan
16 Absurd
17 **Beginning of a quip**
20 Zen enlightenment
21 Warbled
22 Take home
23 "No One" singer Alicia
25 All tucked in
27 Joseph of ice-cream fame
30 Fill
32 Pellet pistol
36 Farm sounds
38 Narc's find, perhaps
40 Audacity
41 **Middle of quip**
44 Omit a syllable or two
45 Edible shell
46 Persuaded
47 Take offense at
49 Rear
51 Word of possibility
52 Not "fer"
54 Snorkeling site
56 Smooth talkers have this gift
59 Handbag
61 More watchful
65 **End of quip**
68 "Goodbye, Pierre"
69 Knock off
70 Eastern European
71 Katmandu's land
72 Looks at
73 Beatles album

DOWN

1 Tropical cuckoos
2 Conclusion
3 Boor's lack
4 Trembled
5 Japanese dish cooked tableside
6 Psychic Geller
7 Bad day for Caesar
8 Big brasses
9 "Ratatouille" hero
10 Football lineman
11 Acquire
12 Stud fee?
13 Just in case
18 Loads from lodes
19 "The King and I" role
24 Tour of duty
26 TV's "___ Anatomy"
27 Uncool coal
28 Inspector Lestrade's creator
29 They're often reflective
31 "Enigma Variations" composer
33 Prepare
34 Throat dangler
35 Square
37 Cassette half
39 Arise
42 Like Hamlet
43 In unspecified manners
48 Jackson of singing siblings
50 ___ moss
53 Care for
55 Mouthing off
56 FBI operative
57 Glorified gofer
58 Radar image
60 One way to stand by
62 Vacation destination
63 And others, for short
64 Common request
66 Mauna ___
67 Scot's refusal

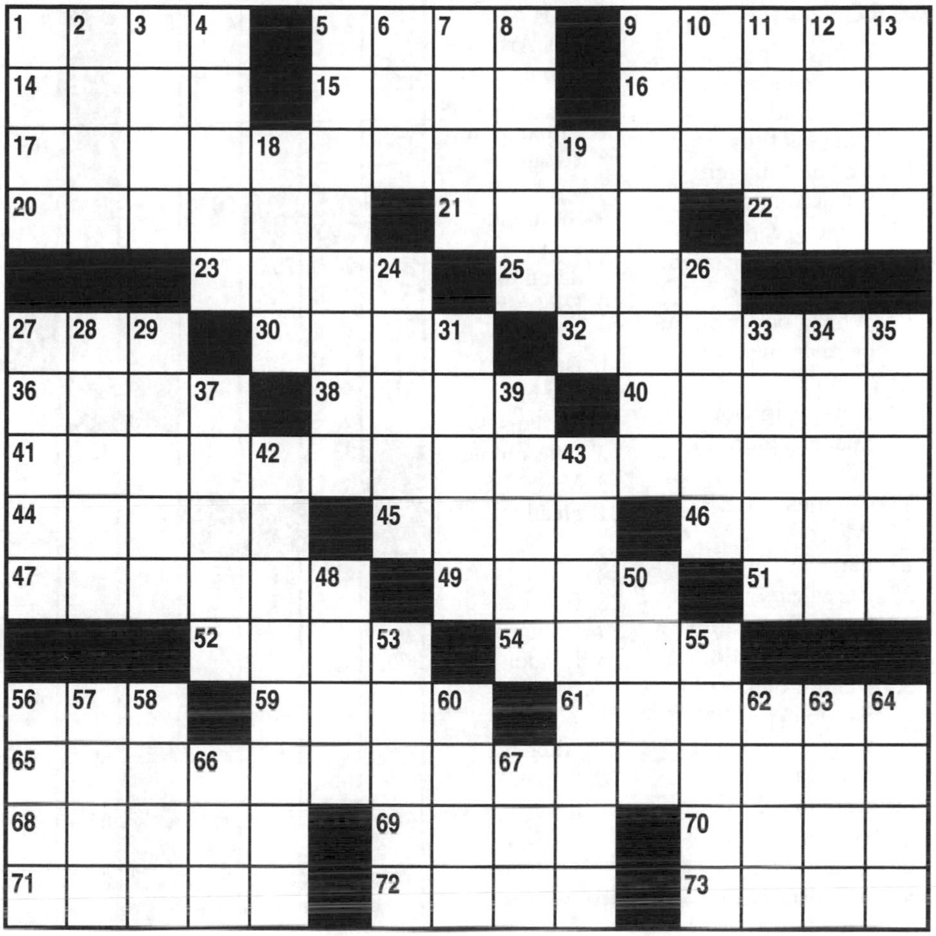

54 CAR TALK by Larry Shearer

. . . with apologies to Click and Clack.

ACROSS

1 Longstocking of children's books
6 1978 Michael Douglas film
10 Recipe smidgen
14 Substitute for
15 Yemen seaport
16 What a boxer might eat
17 What a boxer might be restrained by
18 Connect
19 Tenn. neighbor
20 Space exploration treaty?
23 Campus letter
26 Water barrier
27 Faint
28 Prowl cars
31 Cockney greeting
32 Stone memorial
33 Central theme of a Sandburg biography?
39 Degrade
40 Certain Johns
42 Wasted
46 Tropical fruits
48 An absence of musical discernment
49 Simon, Twain, and Nelson
50 Zoo emergency?
54 Vingt-___ (blackjack)
55 Setting for Ferber's "Cimarron": Abbr.
56 Author Loos
60 Pet that only needs water
61 Financial aid criterion
62 Musical staff sign
63 Sawbucks
64 Stirs in
65 "Ole Buttermilk Sky" bandleader

DOWN

1 Bud
2 Diamonds, slangily
3 Kind of meeting
4 Last words of a chain letter, perhaps
5 Start of a MacArthur quote
6 Spicy cuisine
7 Emanation
8 "Count ___!"
9 Sigmund Freud's daughter
10 High school events
11 Breakfast place, perhaps
12 Less ample
13 Mobs
21 Head's opposite
22 Static ___
23 Compass dir.
24 Influence
25 Lender-offered safeguard: Abbr.
28 "Thou ___ not say I did it": Shak.
29 Provoke
30 Actress Mary
32 Family group
34 "Lost Horizon" director
35 Honorary U.K. title
36 Della Femina started one
37 Sheltered area
38 Accounting period
41 Griddle sound
42 Introduce
43 Abhor
44 Sci-fi author Ursula
45 Spa attractions
46 Supermodel Carangi
47 Empty
49 Loads
51 Writer Jaffe
52 Barely accomplished (with "out")
53 Iditarod entry
57 French pronoun
58 Casual attire
59 Hottest cont.

55 CHALLENGER by Brad Wilber

One can only wonder how 1 Down interprets the prestissimo passages.

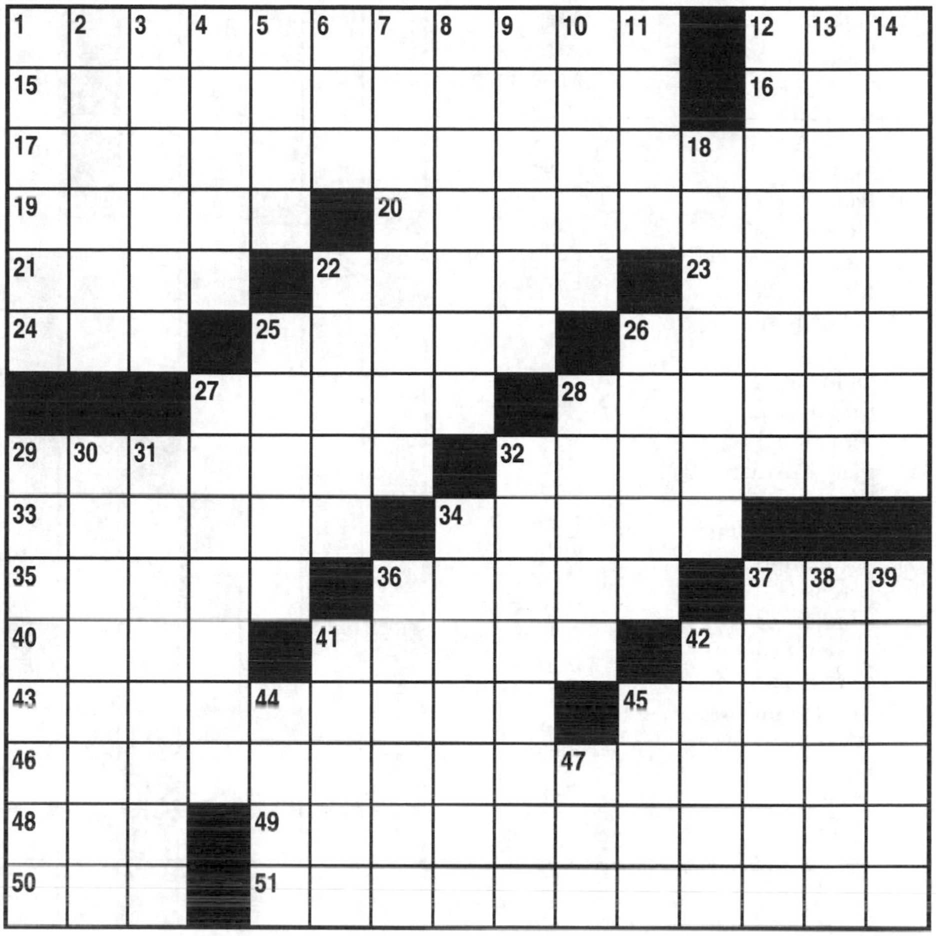

ACROSS

1 Fresh ones
12 "American Experience" airer
15 Spanish-titled ABBA song
16 It can be blonde or dark
17 "The Water Horse" creature
19 "Double Stuf" cookies
20 In stealth mode
21 Grand Portage Natl. Monument site
22 Jason's faithful dog
23 Relinquish
24 Direction from Berlin to Frankfurt
25 Dali's "___ Reflecting Elephants"
26 Medieval merchant guild
27 2002 U.S. Open winner
28 Revue for which Bob Fosse won a 1978 Tony
29 19th-century Seminole leader
32 Tarot reader's topic
33 Short holidays?
34 Sirens
35 Not at all ruddy
36 Chicago Board of Trade building statue
37 "Somebody Get ___ Doctor": Van Halen
40 Tasso patron
41 They're left to deckhands
42 Skating venue
43 Cabaret singer
45 "___ in Tempore Belli": Haydn
46 1990 Schwarzenegger vehicle
48 Ethyl follower
49 Onetime "American Idol" signoff
50 RUF ___ (German sports car)
51 Spirit messengers in Cherokee lore

DOWN

1 Violinist Mintz
2 Native New Zealanders
3 Sherpa's concern
4 Address for the PM of Canada
5 Khaki palette
6 ___ Zion Church
7 Fellini film starring Anthony Quinn
8 Starfleet Academy grads
9 Vanderbilt grounds
10 Macrame, essentially
11 Painter ___ di Pietro
12 Cato's "greatest of all virtues"
13 Goes unnoticed, perhaps
14 Drill handler
18 Trigonometric ratios
22 MP collars
25 Summons to the trough
26 Celestial instruments
27 London theatre district
28 Ceilings at planetaria
29 Herd-trailing African flier
30 Stupendous
31 Flamenco percussion
32 Rear seating section
34 Red-carpet tux source
36 Sporty Mercury
37 "The First Circle" setting
38 Grant spiritual awareness
39 Changes with the times
41 Georges who wrote "Life: A User's Manual"
42 Mottled horse
44 1980 Best Picture nominee
45 Screen door material
47 Gumshoe

56 NMI by Harvey Estes

43 Across also starred in the 2003 film "Calendar Girls."

ACROSS

1 "___ that pass in the night . . .": Longfellow
6 From A to B, musically
10 Pac-10 team
14 "Roger that"
15 La., once
16 Mouth part
17 Letter-perfect steak?
18 Ohio native
19 Certain something
20 Star of "Adam-12"
23 Put away
25 Pt. of 57 Down
26 "Moonlight Serenade" bandleader
30 Trio of fashion characters
33 Thespian focus
34 Julianne of "The Hours"
35 "The Bourne Supremacy" org.
36 Start of a rhyme about a tiger
37 Skyline feature
38 Dorm dweller
39 Start of a Faulkner title
40 Invite info
41 Measure precisely
42 High pts.
43 "The Queen" Oscar winner
45 Take off
47 Overlooks
48 Attorney general under Richard Nixon
53 They're often stroked
54 Manicurist's tool
55 Sorbonne student
59 Head for the hills
60 Smoke conveyor
61 "The Christmas Song" cowriter
62 Slug follower
63 Utilize gravity
64 Mail type

DOWN

1 Army NCO
2 Mischievous sprite
3 Simpson judge
4 Cash from an ATM?
5 Part of TSE
6 Editor's notation
7 Polo on the screen
8 St. Patrick's land
9 Red-carpet event
10 Eurasian chain
11 Where you don't make a federal case of it
12 Anecdotes
13 Way out
21 Sleep acronym
22 As to
23 Most foxy
24 Score in a basketball game?
26 Bit of hope
27 Push forward
28 Tours locale
29 "Two Women" star
31 Protracted tactics
32 Weighed down
37 Badge wearers
38 Set of ringers
40 "Freedom" rock duo
41 Gin-and-lime drinks
44 Springfield bartender
46 Dawn
48 Racer Gordon
49 Eye rakishly
50 Register
51 Fingerprint, perhaps
52 Take seriously
56 Mound stat
57 "West Point of the South"
58 Conger

57 SOUNDS LIKE by Sarah Keller

20 Across was also the site of the 1988 Summer Olympics.

ACROSS

1 Yonkers race
5 Mirror sliver
10 Some marine mammals
14 Not against
15 Free-for-all
16 "Where Eagles ___" (1968)
17 Choir member
18 Big ape
19 Garden of "delight"
20 Hyundai headquarters
22 Fabrications
23 Velvet finish?
24 Different from
26 "A Study in Scarlet" hero
30 Salami hangout?
32 Police poster pseudonym
33 Fa followers
38 It may be stacked
39 "Yes ___!"
40 Parka part
41 Motown Sound
43 Parsonage
44 Pupil's surrounder
45 Poker bluffs, at times
46 Hair goo
50 Pocketbook
51 Resident of 19 Across
52 Seafood entrée
59 Puerto ___
60 Pumping organ
61 Opening to space
62 One-third a hit by The Byrds
63 Jacques Tati role
64 Auntie of Patrick Dennis
65 Hazardous driving condition
66 Tipped at the casino
67 Small fastener

DOWN

1 "___ the night before . . ."
2 Upset
3 NFL legend Graham
4 Gee
5 Cigs
6 Long-legged bird
7 Questionable orchard spray
8 Russo in "Get Shorty"
9 1st Fifth Republic president
10 Digger of "The Life of Riley"
11 Spokes, e.g.
12 Runnel
13 Have a feeling
21 Cask sediment
25 Entertainer Peeples
26 Derisive taunts
27 Spread in a tub
28 Stead
29 Spot for a spree?
30 Day at the movies
31 TVA output
33 "Spanish Eyes" ayes
34 Bangkok native
35 Charged particles
36 Two pills, perhaps
37 Famous Horace work
39 Deadeye
42 Central
43 Epiphany kings
45 Conquered the rapids
46 They're found at the junkyard
47 Hatred
48 Close-up lens
49 Surrounded by
50 Milton on "Texaco Star Theater"
53 Wine prefix
54 Fall short of
55 Souvlaki ingredient
56 King in a Shakespeare tragedy
57 Humorist Bombeck
58 Open-___ shoes

58 MISLEADING CLUES by Matt Ginsberg

. . . and all question marks have been removed after these clues.

ACROSS

1 Office communiqué
5 RCMP's "SWAT" unit
8 China setting
12 Aweather antonym
13 Cut corners
15 "Shall we?" response
16 Slow-paced
18 Boulle citizenry
19 That fellow
20 Lacking support
22 Sidereal altar
23 Doing some knitting
25 Camel's resting place
27 Zorro's title
28 Charged swimmer
30 Emulate Demosthenes
31 Service song
33 Sign of a big hit
34 Suffix for Michael
37 Refusenik refusals
39 "Mad" people, for short
40 Hitching posts
43 Eau de Cologne
46 Like Halloween
47 Hydroxide solution
48 Book review
52 The Shirelles hit
54 Red Bull competition
56 Brick measure
57 Handle differently
59 Just scratch the surface
60 They're taken out and beaten
62 Sixty
64 Douay Bible book
65 Circulation director
66 The heavens, to Atlas
67 GE Building muralist
68 East end
69 Tableland

DOWN

1 "Chances Are" singer
2 Lily maid of Astolat
3 Ethel in "Gypsy"
4 Brit. lexicon
5 Roster ending
6 Start a new game
7 Hair piece
8 It's put before the carte
9 Become Reno-vated
10 Came again
11 Ones doing rush work
13 Bus. drivers
14 In heat
17 Support group
21 Toots of crosswords
24 Steal, ironically
26 Sung syllable
29 Finger board
32 Brief reply
33 Lab series
34 Score keepers
35 No place for a draft dodger
36 Unacquaintance
38 Play ground
41 'ard rain
42 Caboose
44 Blowholes
45 Where It.'s at
47 Work up the Dial
49 Martino replaced him in "The Godfather"
50 Wax-winged flier
51 Wright in "Track of the Cat"
53 Forgetful river
55 "___ My Mind Wander": Willie Nelson
58 Yellow line
61 Sound stage
63 Amazon end

59 FLYING STARTS by Alan Olschwang

17 Across was "Glamour's" first redheaded covergirl.

ACROSS

1 Fences the loot
6 Cowardly Lion player
10 Stoma
14 Curve in a shoreline
15 Next to putt, in golf
16 Egg
17 Actress Everhart
18 Popular seafood entrée
20 Sewing stitch
22 Former Houston pro
23 Poisonous snake
26 Peggy or Pinky
27 Speaker's skill
29 "Old Folks at Home" subject
32 Unfounded rumor
33 Corporate chief
34 QB option
38 Awry
39 Centum start?
40 Musical speeds
41 Type of type
42 Taro dish
43 Risk takers
44 Sister series of "Merrie Melodies"
46 Spa treatment
50 Sort of serve
51 "Shanghai Noon" director
52 Pot-roast ingredient
53 Indulged in vanity
56 Excludes
58 Ladder levels
62 Play a child's game
63 Skye in "Gas Food Lodging"
64 Supplementing the hard way
65 Ripened
66 Females of the species
67 Opening

DOWN

1 S&L's org.
2 Coal holder
3 Incite
4 Not that
5 Some base runners
6 One way up
7 MP's pursuit
8 Entertain, home-style
9 Pumpernickel source
10 Set forth
11 Rounded convex molding
12 Monarch
13 A corundum
19 Elsa's reply
21 Instrument of conveyance
23 Songwriters' org.
24 Mystic
25 Terror
28 Old Olds
30 Project Galileo org.
31 Put a freeze on travel?
34 Lima's land
35 Polish the prose
36 Binge
37 Wimp
39 Belittle Winnie?
40 Dilapidated
42 Kitty
43 Added color
44 Come down
45 They're privileged
46 Great java
47 Remove a ship's supporting system
48 Device to restrict current
49 Acknowledged applause
54 Ancient alphabet character
55 Coach K's U.
57 "___ for Silence": Grafton
59 Pen point
60 New homonym
61 NCO

60 STRAIGHTFORWARD by Ed Early

A themeless construction devoid of misleading clues.

ACROSS

1 "A ___ of robins . . ."
5 Very desirous of
13 Volcano encircling Mount Vesuvius
14 Any
16 Oust
17 Kangaroo or wombat
18 Pontiac SUV
19 Borden bovine
20 Northern ___ apple
21 "___ Mir Bist Du Schön": Andrews Sisters
22 High schooler
23 Takes a taste
24 "Let ___ Cake" (Gershwin musical)
27 Remote batteries
28 Commemorative tablet
29 Toward Des Moines, from Cheyenne
31 Evening party
32 Like many pads
33 Elevator for earls
34 Benedict XVI's office
37 Indifferent
41 Dishonor
42 Garden tool
43 Sliding screen in Japanese homes
44 Monthly expense
45 Sound of disapproval
46 Schroeder of tennis
47 "___ be my pleasure"
48 Singer Shore
49 Peru city with Inca ruins
51 Like city driving
53 Show feelings
54 Tirade deliverer
55 Nemeses
56 Generous spirit
57 Sign on a car lot

DOWN

1 Shaving-cream brand
2 Spills out the contents
3 "Peter Pan" pirate
4 Baby soother
5 Like Shoemaker–Levi's discovery
6 Checking out a tip, to detectives
7 Lines on greeting cards
8 Rose-colored dye
9 Test choice
10 Little devil
11 Causing more of a din
12 Seize and hold in a firm grip
13 "South Pacific" extra
15 French president's palace
23 Fasten, in a way
25 "Finally!"
26 Once and again
28 Waiting-room furniture
30 "___ Wednesday" (1966)
31 Command to Fido
33 Where breakers break
34 Religious community
35 Encouragement for a wrongdoer
36 Infamous box opener
37 Prescription data
38 Richard Preston bestseller (with "The")
39 Thrown out
40 Mischievous pranks
42 Vishnu worshipers
45 Door support
48 "Rats!"
49 Philippine island
50 Fringefoots
52 Course standard

61 OLD TECHNOLOGY by Pete Muller

An interesting character study by this Manhattan musician.

ACROSS

1 Select
4 Some files
9 Pay-upon-receipt items
13 Former capital of San Marino
15 Home to some cats
16 To play it you need a thin reed
17 Zambezi dweller
18 Long
19 Word with salt or land
20 They get paid
22 Child's cry
24 Drives away
26 R, 38 Across
27 Corrodes
28 New Jersey county
30 Drag queens, usually
31 Hertz rival
32 Uh-uhs
34 "Moondance" key
38 **TITLE: Part 3**
41 The ___ Ducks
42 Howard Hanson symphony
43 Greystoke's foster parents
44 "Get me outta here," on a PC
45 Talk to
47 Thou-shalt-not
50 D, 38 Across
52 Ahead
53 Fancy dress
55 Style
56 Undress with the eyes
57 East, south of the border
59 Lofgren who played with Neil and Bruce
62 Magellan's org.
63 Global warming creations
64 Little brat
65 2008 DNC chairman
66 Forearm bones
67 Bloke

DOWN

1 "Ain't 2 Proud 2 Beg" group
2 Make known
3 Asking for a hand?
4 Charles and Robinson
5 Fat Tire, for one
6 Hasty
7 August birthstone
8 N follower
9 **TITLE: Part 1**
10 Legitimate awards
11 Cruller
12 Penetrates (with in)
14 **TITLE: Part 2**
21 Costa Rican peninsula
23 Krispy ___
24 It's not usually voluntary
25 "___ got a girl for you!"
26 Amazon, for one
29 Where Wall St. is
30 Kenyan tribesman
33 Distress call, 38 Across
35 Street sign
36 "Golden Boy" playwright
37 Bowling alley button
39 "Don't worry"
40 Laser output
46 Exec. most likely to cook the books
47 You hold it for a while for interest
48 Bane of swimming pools
49 Wing wood
50 First name in mystery
51 Pampers, say
54 It's white and comes in bricks
55 It could be more
58 It can be white, black, or green
60 Infielder Merloni
61 Porky's place

62 ONE OF SEVEN* by Kevin George

Opening answers to clues* relate to the title.

ACROSS

1 Poor marks
4 Balkan cars of yore
9 Place for winners
14 Casual Friday nonessential
15 Chicago film critic
16 Muse with a lyre
17 Some gametes
18 She wears bulletproof bracelets*
20 Guitar part
22 Get up
23 Frozen floater
24 Accelerate
26 Dolphin Hall-of-Famer
28 Farsi speaker
30 Expect
32 Closet type
33 Hurled
34 Dated
37 Droop
38 Corp. bigwig
40 RR stop
41 Elephant tail?
42 Draft choice
43 Cuzco natives
45 Goes without, in a way
47 "Flowers in the ___" (1987)
48 Spider's legs, e.g.
49 Joan of Arc, for one
52 First course, to Europeans
55 1998 Sarah McLachlan hit
56 Rock or Stone
58 No-win situation
61 Pluto, e.g.*
64 Bird-related prefix
65 Student/teacher, for one
66 Do penance
67 Bamboozle
68 Rub out
69 Basil-based sauce
70 Couplet

DOWN

1 Waist-length jacket
2 Lincoln's bill
3 Profound transformation*
4 Longbow wood
5 WW2 menace
6 Mystery or horror
7 9 Across, for example
8 Holy Fr. women
9 Hardly any
10 Isaac Asimov novel
11 Japanese noodle dish
12 Like some contrasts
13 Kingdom near Fiji
19 Backpedal
21 Batman's creator
25 Nickname for Las Vegas*
27 Verify a FedEx delivery
28 "Casablanca" role
29 Yemeni money
31 Weakling
33 Centers of attention
34 Whoopi Goldberg comedy*
35 Kitty food
36 "She Done Him Wrong" star
39 Trick into wrongdoing
44 Overlay material
46 Holed out from the tee
47 Pioneering game systems
49 Mom, in Mazatlan
50 Negative campaign waging
51 Calf catcher
53 Pulling the cat's tail et al.
54 Dilfer in Super Bowl XXXV
57 How to turn on a light, perhaps
59 Proclaim
60 Brown bagger
62 Adversary
63 Auto racer Fabi

63 WHERE TO FIND SOME SUPER JOBS by Ernest Lampert

Those super jobs can be found at 17 Across.

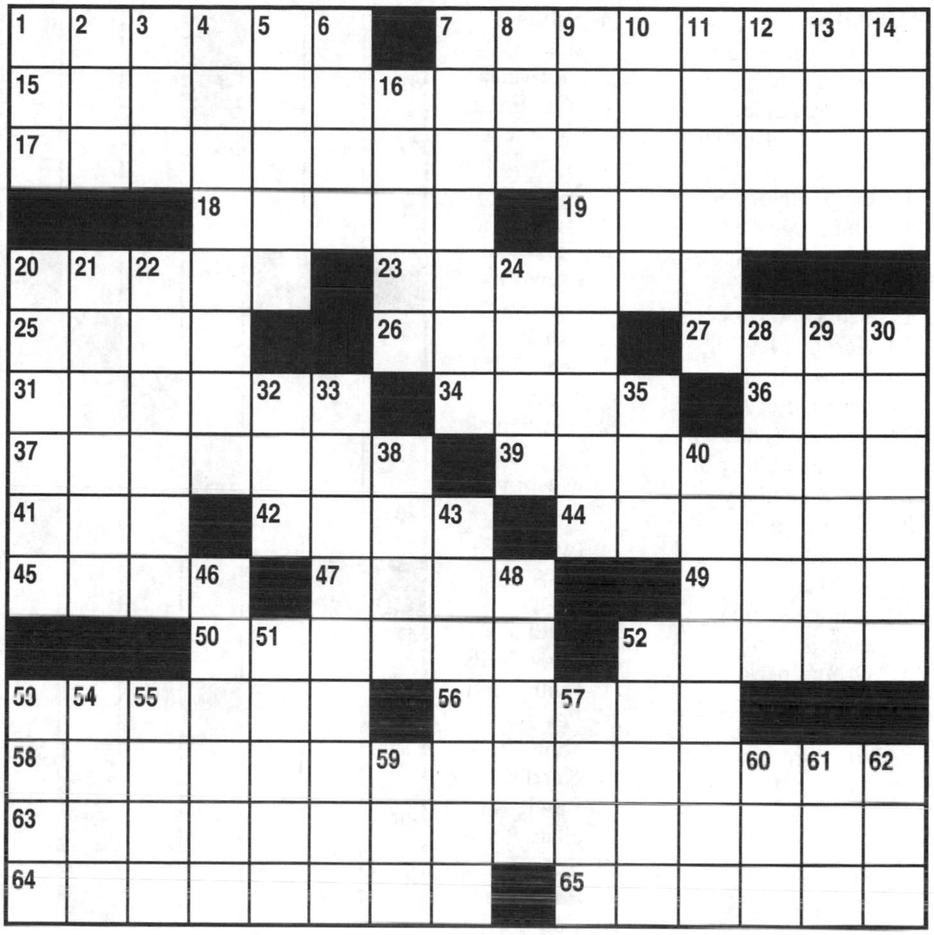

ACROSS

1 Took a powder
7 Social worker's backlog
15 Contract term
17 Where to find some super jobs
18 Heavy-faced type
19 Most opportune
20 French poodle, e.g.?
23 Testify under oath
25 Ty Treadway, for one
26 Hibernia
27 X-ray units
31 Russian city on the Don
34 Brouhaha
36 Two-finger sign
37 Rand Corporation employee
39 Fabric fit for a king
41 Tre + tre
42 Inverness native
44 Firmly set
45 Gds.
47 Dollar rival
49 Parker in "The Great Debaters"
50 Harvard president (1933–1953)
52 Landed
53 Unmitigated
56 Melee
58 The way up a lighthouse
63 Heartfelt harangue
64 One speaking out
65 Tabloids monster

DOWN

1 Untilled tract
2 Annie's protector (with "The")
3 B.B. King's label
4 Naughty operetta heroine
5 Ken Kesey's middle name
6 "Tarnation!"
7 Vainglory
8 Public hanging?
9 "Peanuts" pianist
10 Remove, in law: Var.
11 "True Colors" singer
12 Yorkshire river
13 "___ Death": Grieg
14 Airport sign abbr.
16 Tenerife volcano
20 Sacramental oil
21 Like a cobra
22 1940s internees
24 Underpin
28 1975 Belmont Stakes winner
29 PC key
30 Placed in the Open
32 Mantra sounds
33 Weedy parcel, often
35 Guido's gold
38 Smoked salmon
40 Cooks up
43 Oater badge
46 Game similar to euchre
48 Lift
51 Broadcasting
52 "Based on ___ story"
53 In the Red
54 Tach readings
55 Blue Jay star Alex
57 Noun suffix
59 Hostess ___ Balls
60 Coolers, briefly
61 Asian honorific
62 Cyclops feature

64 SOLDIER ON by Paula & Barry Silk

Joe Isuzu would get a kick out of solving this one.

ACROSS

1 1952 campaign name
4 Stingy person
9 "Bei Mir Bist Du ___"
14 Opposite of SSW
15 Flabbergast
16 "Common Sense" pamphleteer
17 See 37 Across
19 Nervous feeling
20 Turns on
21 Safari site: Abbr.
23 Irritated (with "up")
24 Disney collectible
25 Earth's galaxy
27 Big name in spreadsheet software
30 Konica's 2003 merger partner
31 Orbital period
32 Seeming eternity
33 Colors over
36 Blowup: Abbr.
37 Isuzu SUV
39 PC monitor
40 ___-faire
42 Decompose
43 Computer key
44 Like Iron Man
46 Land of the Rising Sun
47 Shared a boundary with
49 Minister, slangily
50 Brown, for example
51 Half a Gabor?
52 Princess topper
56 Stallone hero
58 See 37 Across
60 Bathtub feature
61 Astaire with a skirt
62 B'way notice
63 "The Playboy of the Western World" author
64 Informative
65 Sock ___ (informal dance)

DOWN

1 "Picnic" dramatist
2 James ___ Polk
3 Fed. job-discrimination watchdog
4 Subdued shade
5 Motivate
6 "Get Smart" spy agency
7 Book before Neh.
8 Hold
9 Handheld firework
10 Optimist's word
11 See 37 Across
12 Southend-___, England
13 Meshlike
18 Veggie preparer
22 Broccoli piece
25 Studied secondarily (with "in")
26 Pay stub abbr.
27 Needle holes
28 Lawless character
29 See 37 Across
30 Cattle call?
32 Goofs
34 Columnist Bombeck
35 British gun
37 Pacific, for one
38 Okra bit
41 Former California fort
43 Mayhem
45 Washington airport
46 Largest of the Channel Islands
47 Ornithophobiac's fear
48 Reproductive gland
49 Fancy wheels, informally
52 Ship's complement
53 Snack
54 Money since 2002
55 Sporty car feature
57 1988 Hanks film
59 Suffix with chlor-

65 36 ACROSS by Jim Leeds

60 Across is a classic example of spot-on wordplay.

ACROSS

1 Rime
5 Mason's investments partner
9 Sweetened the pot
14 Cinder's remnant?
15 Suffix for oxygen
16 Mildred Ratched, for one
17 Gulf port
18 An irate Ms. Evert?
20 Ipse ___
22 Dairy case item
23 Habitude
24 TWA rival, once
26 Capek play
27 Anoint
30 Give me the tab, Mr. Donahue?
33 Menagerie
34 Fan site
35 "Oh, dear!"
36 TITLE
42 Dismantle, in Devon
43 Holocaust rescuer Sendler
44 Arrow's path
45 Greet Mr. Lauer?
51 "Sure!"
52 Volga tributary
53 "Apollo 13" vehicle
54 Like tartare
55 Hostile behavior
58 Edible agave
60 Storm troopers?
63 "The Chronicles of Clovis" author
64 Go for
65 "Hello, ___!" (Marty Allen greeting)
66 Sarah Brightman album
67 Wed
68 Meth.
69 Rose rose to fame with them

DOWN

1 Lead
2 Getting up there
3 Son of Tsar Nicholas II
4 Eastern honorific
5 Ballet's "Le ___ des Cygnes"
6 Antifreeze alcohol
7 "Madama Butterfly" matchmaker
8 Voodoo amulet
9 Fix the phone cord
10 Make like Morris
11 Amoebas, e.g.
12 Curvaceous character
13 "Jersey Boys" director McAnuff
19 Semitic house of prayer
21 Neon fish
25 "Excuse me . . ."
28 2200 hrs.
29 Fall back
31 "The Naughty Lady of Shady ___"
32 Plain-Jane
35 Early Irish alphabet
36 "Old Dog ___": Foster
37 Aesopian animal
38 Béarnaise ingredient
39 Hook, line, and sinker fishermen
40 Blood pigment
41 Them
45 Made like Rover
46 Popular bakeware brand
47 Scottish landowners
48 Pinball palace
49 Turned aweather
50 Mark and Shania
56 Dry
57 Deucy beginning
59 Narc's mark
60 Sei school
61 Boise's county
62 Rigid

66 SHERLOCKIAN SKILL by Bonnie L. Gentry

The title can be found again at 51 Across.

ACROSS

1 Bose of Bose Corp.
5 Tourney hotshot
9 Singer Stefani et al.
14 Computer file list
16 Yet to come
17 Quasimodo's love
18 Late conductor Georg
19 "Fly Away Home" bird
21 Polo crossed it
22 Short spout
23 Recreational kind of fishing
31 Steamed up
32 One voting for
33 Feeder of the Fulda
34 Check for accuracy
35 Wall paper?
39 Pastureland
40 "ER" areas
42 Theater-funding gp.
43 Old Russian oppressors
45 Pledge on the stump
49 Directional ending
50 "___ poor, wayfaring . . ."
51 SHERLOCKIAN SKILL
57 Cozy corners
58 Best Actress of 1997
60 Jezebel player of 1938
61 Preludes to operas
62 Latin for "for this"
63 Teachers' favorites
64 Get set for a shot

DOWN

1 Summertime cooler
2 Catchall abbr.
3 "Aeneid" starter
4 Simulate a historic event
5 Ballparks
6 Like wind-formed caves
7 Mother of the Valkyries
8 Cannon in "Deathtrap"
9 Commodities futures listing
10 "Yay!"
11 Some coral reef predators
12 NBA Hall-of-Famer Thurmond
13 Reagan Era prog.
15 Entered without an invitation
20 Something in your eye
23 Palindromic Honda
24 Betel palm
25 Jazz pianist Art
26 "Knockin' On Heaven's Door" singer
27 Old wheels
28 Ike's two-time opponent
29 Future viewers
30 Expunge
36 Permanent way to write
37 Takedown unit?
38 Cartoon insect superhero
41 Chat with
44 Freeway closer
46 Trig. measurement
47 Tiny squealer
48 Go-carts
51 Open to all
52 Longtime Delaware Senator
53 Breakfast restaurant chain
54 Campbell of "Relative Strangers"
55 Cologne coin
56 Sega competitor in the 16-bit market
57 Wizards and Magic org.
59 Twice, a nasty fly

67 "ZOUNDS!" by Doug Peterson

1 Across authored 86 novels and 14 short-story collections.

ACROSS

1 Western writer L'Amour
6 Bar mixer
10 Open a crack
14 "One way" indicator
15 Sign of sadness
16 Chucklehead
17 General at Gettysburg
18 Green Gables orphan
19 Black & Decker rival
20 Secure position
23 Slender swimmer
24 Foam football maker
25 Influential German school of design
27 Conduit
30 Leprechaun's land
32 Craggy peak
33 2007 BCS Championship winners
34 "Just ___ suspected!"
35 Reverberated
38 Dog bred for hunting
42 "Attention!" opposite
43 Sass
44 Actress Vardalos
45 Up to, informally
46 Spot for a nosh
47 Sea swirl
48 Err in calculating the age of
51 Study all night
53 Hubbub
54 Like the Hulk
59 Bellow in a bookstore
61 Texan's tie
62 Bright courtyards
63 "This is a disaster!"
64 Toiling away
65 67 Across's grade
66 Dozes off
67 Former frosh
68 Ford flop

DOWN

1 Heads for the hills
2 Creme-filled treat
3 Russian mountain range
4 Element found in seaweed
5 Stockholm citizen
6 Five-legged ocean dweller
7 Wine prefix
8 Waltz river
9 Bout site
10 TV interruptions
11 Engage in waggery
12 French farewell
13 Moves on casters
21 Garage lubricant
22 Ronald Reagan's nickname
26 Santa syllables
27 "Guilty," for one
28 "___ it obvious?"
29 Washington inlet
31 It has a kick to it
35 Run out
36 City near Tulsa
37 WW2 turning point
39 Placed
40 Moor's faith
41 Waterproof fabric
46 Conquistador Hernando
47 Got melodramatic
48 Wall builder
49 Neighbor of Oregon
50 Hefty horns
52 Taper off
55 Movie snippet
56 Java servers
57 Evening, casually
58 Wonka's creator
60 ___ Alamitos, CA

68 SELF-CENTERED SINGER by Harvey Estes

Some people should sing solo . . . so low that no one can hear.

ACROSS

1 Forgers
7 Turns to mush
11 Que. neighbor
14 Triumph
15 Saint Paul's sphere of influence, e.g.
17 Loves
18 Press release packets
19 Retired speedster
20 Verse weather
22 Breaks in relations
23 ___ generis
24 Protective headgear
27 Major African artery
28 Seesaw sitter of verse
30 Archenemy
32 Animator's unit
33 Ballroom dance
35 Hearty pastries
37 People who say 7 Down, seemingly
40 Dutch Guiana, today
42 Two-masters
46 Toy boy
47 Tease mercilessly
50 Stimulate
51 Snug retreat
53 Record blemish
55 Earlier
56 Sleek swimmer
58 Gettysburg general
59 Howe'er
60 Pebble Beach group
63 Out of it
65 Teflon, for example
66 Pooh pal
67 "Uh-huh"
68 Gift-getter's question
69 Howard on the back of a boat?

DOWN

1 Reuben cheeses
2 Rachel Smith's 2007 title
3 Sign off on
4 Simple ending
5 Pen
6 Ripped off
7 Sound of a self-centered singer warming up?
8 Inc., in England
9 Athlete lead-in
10 Rise dramatically
11 Pore, for one
12 Really irritates
13 Decorative dangle
16 Similar
21 Notre Dame is on one
25 Bygone leader
26 Where it's at
29 Cold War superpower
31 Light on one's feet
34 Arguing
36 "The First Time Ever ___ Your Face"
38 A wink and ___
39 Moon sight
40 Transparent, informally
41 Loosen, in a car seat
43 Sharp reprimand
44 Foghorn of cartoons
45 Moe and more
46 Hard to saw
48 FDR program
49 Cleans (up)
52 Prepared to drive
54 Palindromic principle
57 Water hazard
61 Winter product prefix
62 Crew implement
64 Favorable vote

69 GROUCHO SPEAKS by Ed Early

"Before I speak, I have something important to say." — Groucho Marx

ACROSS

1 Start of Paul V's papacy
5 Shirt ruffle
10 Jr. high subj.
14 "Chill Factor" hero
15 "Christ Stopped at ___": Levi
16 Abbrs. on vitamin bottles
17 Phnom Penh currency
18 **Part 1 of a Groucho Marx quip**
19 Reggae's ___-Mouse
20 Primate of Madagascar
22 Slangy assent
23 Be in store for
24 **Part 2 of quip**
27 Brazil NBA star
28 Styptic pencil ingredient
29 MLB playoff series
31 **Part 3 of quip**
35 Pre-toddler
38 Bambi, for one
39 Hit hard on the head
41 It's past due
42 Bahamas island
44 Old Mideast org.
45 Places to work out
47 **Part 4 of quip**
50 Old movie marquee name
51 Taina in "Les Girls"
52 Benzene prefix
55 Affirmation of a turndown
59 One ___ time
62 **End of quip**
65 "___ Love Her": Beatles
66 Toothbrush brand
67 Ashtabula's lake
68 Baseball's "Walking Man" Eddie
69 "___ Thy Bride": G&S
70 "From Russia With Love" killer

DOWN

1 "A League of Their Own" infielder
2 Coiffeuse's tool
3 French premier during World War 1
4 "Your silence speaks ___"
5 Nozzle
6 Detest
7 "North and South," trilogy-wise
8 "Daily Planet" photographer
9 Formal requirement
10 Server of homemade ale
11 What Harmony.com attempts to provide
12 Jack in "Call of the Wild"
13 Exams for budding attorneys
21 Rembrandt van ___
23 Feel ill
25 Fleshy fruit
26 Train car
29 "___ Without Rain" Enya
30 Canis lupis
32 Rel. to shipping
33 First deodorant soap
34 Cross inscription
36 Edinburgh hillside
37 Polite Ozark assent
39 "Love and War," trilogy-wise
40 Production batch of raw yarn
43 Nav. rank
46 Homeowner's monthly exp.
48 Absent one
49 Obi-Wan of "Star Wars"
52 On the road
53 Greek philosopher
54 Dynamic 88, for one
56 Swiss river to the Rhine
57 Norwegian speed skater Ballangrud
58 Opposite of stet
59 Microsoft Vista interface
60 Speaker of baseball
61 Befuddled
63 Stewed
64 Boating pronoun

70 MEMBER OF THE WEDDING by Barry C. Silk

26 Across was the mother of a U.S. president and lived to be 104.

ACROSS

1 Vishnu worshiper
6 LV x XL
10 Piece of glass
14 The bounding main
15 Prefix with bank or dollar
16 NYSE rival
17 "A Different World" actress
19 Prego competitor
20 Minn. neighbor
21 Tent furniture
22 Falsified a check
23 Math class subj.
24 Eliciting feeling
26 Political family matriarch
30 "___ the Roof" (1963 hit)
31 Old Testament book
32 Hosp. scan
35 "Spin City" actress
40 Grade-school trio
41 "___ Woman" (ELO hit)
42 The "I" of "The King and I"
43 Employee of Boss Hogg
47 7-Eleven drink
50 "Need You Tonight" band
51 Moorage spots
52 Upper hand
53 School dance
56 Sauce thickener
57 Member of the wedding/TITLE
60 Seaplane stop
61 New Rochelle college
62 City on the Arkansas River
63 Thunder sound
64 Having many irons in the fire
65 Bacon flavor

DOWN

1 Orange-roofed hotel, for short
2 Self-confident words
3 Brooder's place
4 Beaver's handiwork
5 Audrey Hepburn was its ambassador
6 Tryster's message
7 Hot chocolate containers
8 French vineyard
9 Playfully noncommittal
10 Equality
11 High-end violin
12 Beersheba locale
13 Radiate
18 Secluded spot
22 Canon competitor
23 Bloke
24 Carmaker Ferrari
25 Ford product, briefly
26 Essen's valley
27 Letters above 0
28 Get high?
29 "Country Grammar" rapper
32 Diner handout
33 Private, e.g.
34 "Dies ___" (Latin hymn)
36 Oodles
37 "Howards End" character
38 Shine's partner
39 Pubmates
43 Philadelphia university
44 Battle of ___ (June 1942)
45 Halo wearer, in France
46 Applies, as pressure
47 Currency substitute
48 At large
49 Throat doctor's concern
52 Many millennia
53 Panaewa Rainforest Zoo site
54 Ural River city
55 Huddle call
57 Bit of baloney
58 R&B singer Rawls
59 Bazooka, e.g.

71 ON THE LIGHTER SIDE by Matt Ginsberg

Scab or greasy spot would be an example of 36 Across.

ACROSS

1 Hook, line, and sinker
5 Flip comment
10 A crack investigator
14 Amount to be raised
15 Tiny farmer
16 Christ's following
17 Breakout
18 Stock holder
19 "Space Cowboys" org.
20 Money maker?
23 Muscateer
24 Copyholders
28 Brooks in the country
32 Pen-based
33 Short stop
36 Citrus malady?
39 Code beginning
41 Eye drops
42 Casual evening
43 Not touched up
46 Jailhouse singer
47 Lodge opening
48 Short partner
50 Fixes a clog
53 Sob sister
57 Really lie
61 Teatime for Nero
64 Spoke more than once
65 Butler's place
66 "Cheers" stoolie
67 Collars for preppies
68 Buried treasures
69 Baby bouncer
70 People with safe jobs
71 Bachelor's end

DOWN

1 Silent screen star
2 Accouter
3 Confused between ports
4 Work on moving pictures
5 Office unit
6 "What ___ mind reader?"
7 Apple for the teacher
8 Forgetful river
9 Fancy-free
10 Clubhouse "hole" number
11 Remote battery
12 IV league
13 Org. that whistled "Dixie"
21 Face of time
22 Spin backward
25 How the euphoric walk
26 One with dreads
27 Cold drops
29 Rio's follower
30 Counterfeit cops
31 Flip comment
33 Creator of cords
34 Remains barely noticeable
35 Peter and the Wolfe
37 Shout heard at the O.K. Corral
38 One of a British group
40 When people like to pay taxes?
44 English Channel swimmer
45 Chinny chatter
49 Be sneaky
51 The king of Spain
52 School board
54 Eye-catching works
55 Top of the art world
56 Abridge too far
58 Lad
59 Flight controller
60 Blow off steam
61 Invisible follower
62 Abstract ending
63 Aggravated one's condition

72 ISOLATIONISM by Pete Muller

Circular reasoning may be needed to solve this challenger.

ACROSS

1 NASCAR sponsor
4 Covering of sorts
8 Sandwich server
14 Starbucks order
15 Luau dance
16 Exotic asian fruit
17 Frosted
18 See 6 down
19 180 manuevers
20 What's inside the circles (with 38-A and 56-A)
23 Drug quantity
24 Ont. ensemble
25 Wilma Flintstone's home
28 Calling conferences?
31 Tell on
34 Put on
35 Kirk sometimes gave it to Spock
36 Name from a Beatles' song
37 Be shy
38 See 20 Across
42 Vex
43 Chandler on "Friends"
44 ___ Lonely Boys (rock group)
45 Family car
46 1974 kidnappers
47 Says yes
51 Get mad
53 Ticket buyers
55 Starbucks order
56 See 20 Across
61 Largest S.A. country
63 Not pro
64 Tax
65 Overhauled
66 Some subdivisions
67 Before
68 Repay
69 ERA, say
70 NY puckster

DOWN

1 Boondocks
2 One who does bits?
3 It's still prevalent in the music biz
4 SeaWorld whale
5 Bears or lions
6 Red, orange, and 18 Across
7 Shows or tells all
8 Photoshop option
9 Bit
10 Hard-to-field NFL kick
11 Excited
12 Looked for a seat
13 Extra periods
21 Veg-O-Matic company
22 Gathering place
26 Political columnist Maureen
27 South Bend coaching legend
29 Searches
30 Contact, in a way
32 Nobelist Windaus
33 Fifty after
36 It may be up
38 Type of brother
39 Outlaw
40 Mixup
41 Japanese shoe company
42 Drips
47 Start of a famous quote of 1/20/61
48 The Ocean State
49 Muck
50 Fingerspeller
52 River in 61 Across
54 Records
57 Call up
58 Run away
59 Singer James
60 Tilt
61 Supporter
62 Title for A. Sharpton

73 ATTACHMENTS by Alan Olschwang

The author at 34 Across will live forever in crosswords.

ACROSS

1 He played Ugarte in "Casablanca"
6 Served sushi
9 Enjoys a sumptuous repast
14 City near Camp Pendleton
16 Bartlett of pear fame
17 Baseball crowd pleaser
19 First or last of a series?
20 Deposit-slip entry: Abbr.
21 Proportions
22 Really bad character
24 Enterprise helmsman
25 Apply oneself
29 Online journal
33 Pioneering game systems
34 "Rock On" author
36 Bruin legend
37 Giant
38 Sort of serve
39 Lenya of "Threepenny Opera"
41 Corrida cry
42 Betazoid Deanna
44 Attire
45 Costner character
47 Acquitted
49 First Earl of Chatham
51 They make galleys go
52 White man
55 Coll. course
56 Begley and Begley
59 Complete surprise
63 Stage direction
64 Duration of one orbit
65 "The Gondoliers" girl
66 ___ of Reason
67 Aussie tennis star Fraser

DOWN

1 Finish third
2 "Draft Dodger Rag" singer
3 Classic cars
4 ___ Dawn Chong
5 Nanny's triplets
6 Tightened
7 Polish prose
8 Start of a mark?
9 Steamer-trunk sticker
10 Bathing
11 Words of denial
12 Danish shoe company
13 Librarians' interjections
15 Takes a long, long look
18 Infantryman
22 Stew ingredient
23 Eye emanation
24 Loretta in "Whoops Apocalypse"
25 ___ Rouge
26 Functional
27 Phoebe in "Princess Caraboo"
28 "___ by land . . ."
30 Game of chance
31 Weed-B-Gon company
32 Frat member
35 Laurey's Aunt Murphy
38 Golf club feature
40 Expressions of wonderment
43 Gyroscope part
44 Ballroom dance
46 Treats with malice
48 Play the flute
50 Footnote word
52 Fence the loot
53 Going solo
54 Deli offerings
55 Urban blight
56 Parmenides' home
57 Twofold
58 Withered
60 Explorer Johnson
61 Sea eagle
62 "Sayonara!"

74 "SURPRISE!" by Ed Early

There are times when 35 Across may be more "startling" than "welcome."

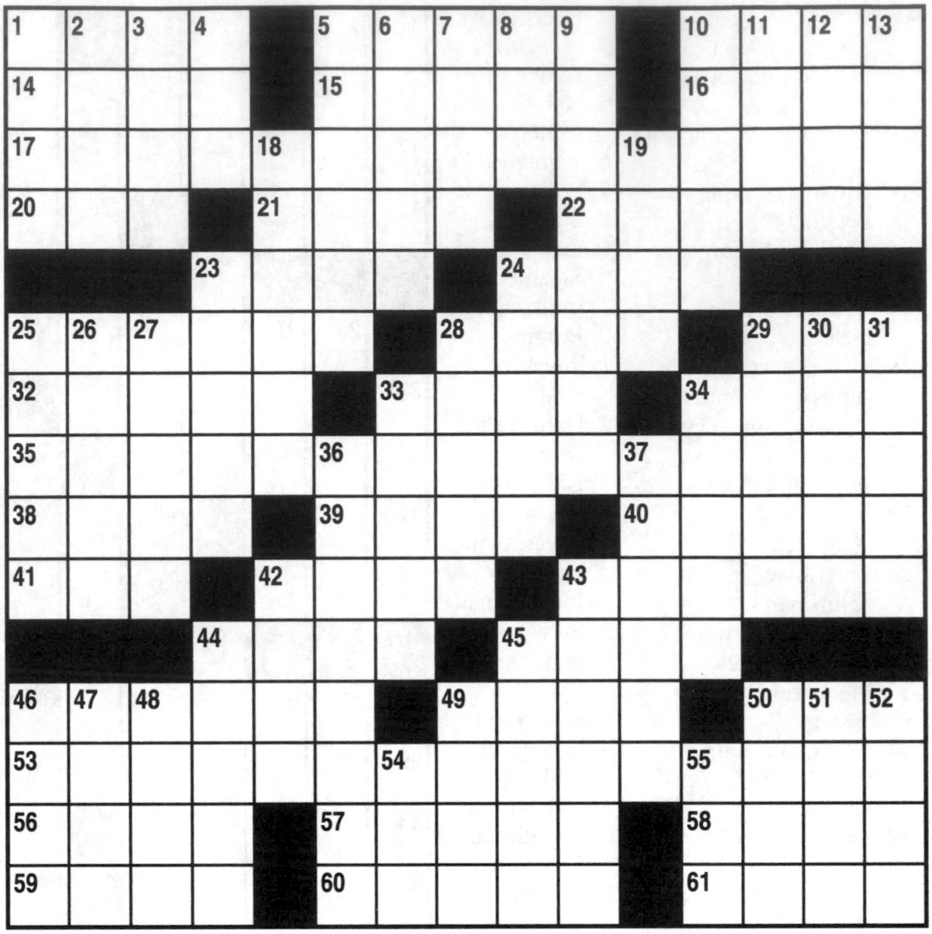

ACROSS

1 It's under one's thumb
5 In hog heaven?
10 Major in astronomy?
14 Inter ___
15 Periodically repeated event
16 Pod member
17 Springs an unwelcome surprise
20 Pitching stat
21 Ever's partner
22 Sultan's edicts
23 FBI agents
24 British can
25 Heiss and Kane
28 Heartache
29 Toning targets
32 Informed
33 The D in CD-ROM
34 Blackthorn fruit
35 Springs a welcome surprise
38 1930s migrant
39 And higher, in cost
40 Mail carriers have one
41 Sparks or Beatty
42 Ballet movement
43 Bar orders
44 Strait-laced
45 Princess Margaret, to Prince Charles
46 Silence ___ (Ben Franklin pen name)
49 Magazine James Agee wrote for
50 When doubled, a Gabor
53 Springs a startling surprise
56 ___ vera
57 Hatfield or McCoy
58 Oklahoma city
59 Money in Osaka
60 Neutral one in WW2
61 Pitcher Hideo

DOWN

1 It may be stepped up
2 Having wings
3 Chaplin's second wife
4 Brit's raincoat
5 Parts of an act
6 Youngest heavyweight champ
7 Desktop image
8 Mischievous sprite
9 Fort built by Anthony Wayne in 1794
10 Standard
11 Interpret
12 Parched
13 Contributes to
18 "To be or not to be . . ." speaker
19 Pirate's potable
23 Spiny shrub
24 Fill the tank
25 Banquet entrée
26 Came to
27 The R in IRT
28 Feeling of wounded pride
29 Time traveler, perhaps
30 Showed displeasure
31 Transmits
33 Jean material
34 Imitate a peacock
36 Billie and the Fourth of July?
37 They go with Earl Grey
42 Those for
43 "West Side Story" dustup
44 Residents of Castel Gandolfo
45 Looked through the crosshairs
46 Memorable date in 1944
47 Coat-of-arms border
48 Strikebreaker
49 Tip the dealer
50 Philosopher of Elea
51 Modelesque
52 Gucci or Ray
54 "It" girl Clara
55 Multiple layer

75 OLD WEST ANESTHETIC by Matt Ginsberg

The anesthetic can be found at 9 Down.

ACROSS

1 Big shot at a bar
5 Minn. minutes
8 Grand events
13 Eerie homonym
14 Green-headed pet
15 Woody's "Sleeper" role
16 Peer group member
17 Capital of Cambodia
18 Declaration of independence
19 "Car and Driver" features?
22 Giggly trio
23 Graphic intro
24 More to the point
27 Sale preceder
29 Rapids transit
33 Small-intestinal
34 Tearing up, perhaps
36 A new start
37 "War in the Garden of Eden" author
40 Duct opening
41 Bed material
42 Depressed area
43 Welfare state
45 TV exec Moonves
46 Fall guys
47 Bolivian bear
49 Needing some kneading
50 Five-leaved ivy
58 Trolley talk
59 In a sack
60 Commotion requiring action
61 Hurried over
62 Silly pair
63 Carries a heavy caseload
64 Dance set
65 Bisected fly
66 When people take tours in Tours

DOWN

1 Honey bunch
2 Was at the forum
3 Former capital of Italy
4 Ancestor of a text message
5 Double features
6 Axis victory
7 Baby shower
8 "Cheesy" look
9 Old West anesthetic
10 Hunter gatherer
11 Chow chaser
12 Sonic boomers of yore
14 Town's man
20 Crank up the tunas
21 Bad actors
24 Camera name
25 Ecole-ite
26 Branch headquarters
27 April ___ Day
28 Pizarro's favorite colors
30 Something to lend
31 Good chap
32 Bags it
34 Imported French wheel
35 Found under the elms
38 Clutch performer
39 Bug on the road
44 Grab some chow
46 Houseful in Britain
48 Lets the fingers do the talking
49 Piece of fish
50 Tapers
51 "___ a Song Go . . ."
52 In the pink
53 "Cool" rap artist
54 Start of a Shakespearean title
55 Keep a stiff lower lip
56 Exciting seat part
57 Flagwoman

76 SOME REAL CHALLENGES by Victor Fleming

. . . and that real challenge can be found at 74 Down.

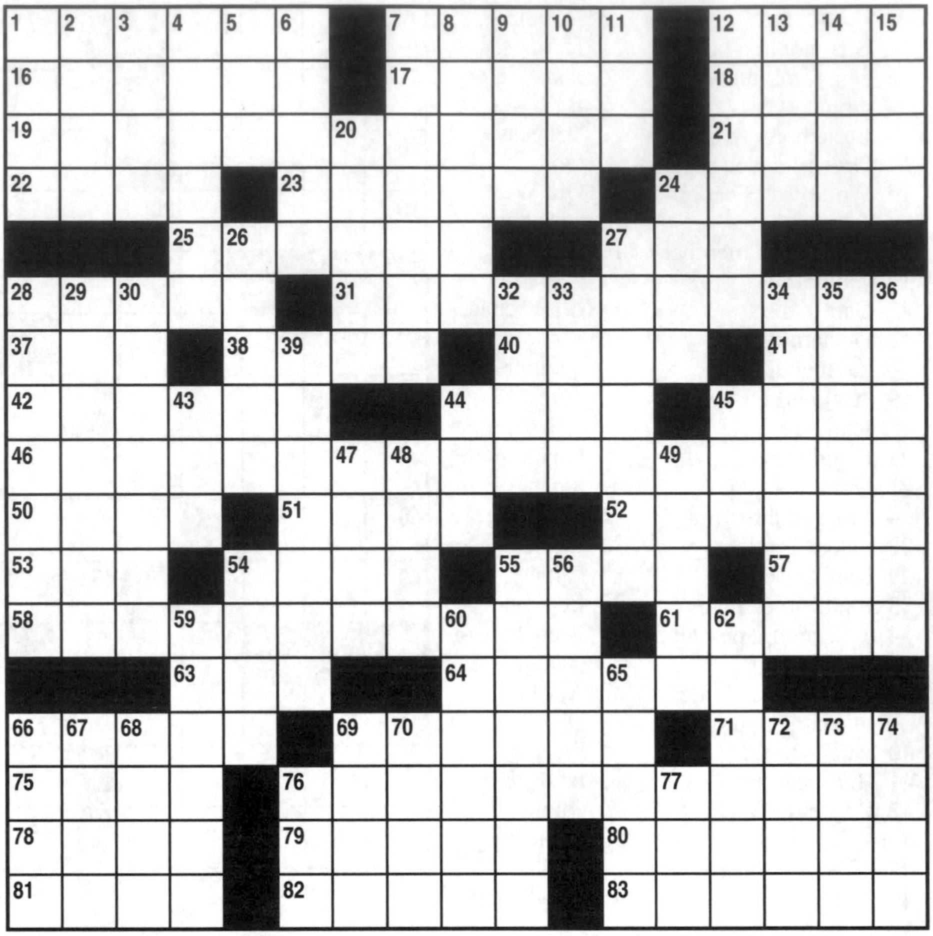

ACROSS

1 Gene in "Young Frankenstein"
7 Word before Mesa or Brava
12 Web auction site
16 Silent star Renée
17 Pueblo pots
18 Start of something huge
19 Birthday query*
21 Roll maker?
22 Load
23 Islands of Portugal
24 Familiar mothers
25 New Hampshire senator
27 Kind of range
28 EMT summoner
31 Signals that reflect back to antennae*
37 Be off
38 City on the Skunk
40 When the tardy arrive
41 Educ. site
42 Spanish jambalaya
44 Isle near Scotland
45 Have a yen
46 Beatitudes platitude*
50 Vino region
51 Blows away
52 Place for therapeutic magnets
53 Originally named
54 Dynamic opening?
55 ___ morgana
57 Online chuckle
58 Tanzanian capital*
61 Extended families
63 Landed
64 "Stat!"
66 Winter protection
69 ___-tung
71 Reminded
75 West Wing helper
76 Slum, e.g.*
78 Little shavers
79 "Justine" star
80 Comic Phyllis
81 Chuck
82 Cheeseparer
83 Really here

DOWN

1 Comic cries
2 Matinee hero
3 Brat Pack alum
4 Fade, in a way
5 One with electric organs
6 V-shaped fortification
7 Round at a Mexican bar, maybe
8 1993 A.L. batting champ
9 Roy Rogers' birth name
10 O'Keeffe home
11 Jonesboro campus
12 Clause separator
13 Earthwork
14 Mexican water
15 Subterranean edibles
20 Common color in heraldry
24 Mugger repellent
26 Range that divides Eurasia
27 Bleachers' shout to a batter
28 Halftime players
29 It's less than half its 1960 size
30 Wal-Mart worker
32 Burn balm
33 Carry on
34 Onetime Seminole chief
35 Corporate grade
36 Mideast money
39 "Sextette" was her last film
43 ___ Logic Corp.
44 Return letters
45 Mornings, briefly
47 "David Copperfield" wife
48 Off base?
49 Make official
54 Up until
55 To a greater extent
56 "It's ___ Unusual Day"
59 Way out
60 Highest point
62 Quarter
65 "___ say more?"
66 No-no for some dieters
67 "Ta-ta!"
68 Tacks on
69 Mid 11th-century date
70 Purposes
72 Modern addresses
73 Extra-wide shoes
74 Challenge that appears in clues*
76 "Batman" sound
77 Hullabaloo

77 GROCERY LIST by Robert A. Doll

What grocery does Bob shop at?

ACROSS

1 Melchior et al.
5 Luau dances
10 Lend an ear
16 Nobelist Pavlov
17 Japanese cartoon art
18 Records
19 Adjusts a clock
20 Passover month
21 Vinegary
22 The finest
25 Diane Renay hit "___ Blue"
26 One married to the mob
30 Kind of kick
33 Oenophile's concern
35 Guesstimate words
36 Fatso
38 Shade provider
40 Thumbs-up
41 Chi Omega mascot
42 Like a starched shirt
43 Always, in verse
44 Cold-shoulder
46 Thwart
47 "___ a Long Way to Tipperary"
50 Harper Lee character
52 Former California fort
53 Kind of artist
54 Horrified
56 "Photoplay" photos
59 Maui mementos
60 A deadly sin
61 Matlin in "Walker"
62 ABC's of a successful pangram?
65 Medical breakthrough
66 Charles Henry Phillips product
72 Go back
75 Affair
76 "Cheers" regular
77 Eats up
78 Important exam
79 "The Time Machine" people
80 Vespas
81 Steps over a fence
82 Cub Scout groups

DOWN

1 Catchall abbr.
2 Allege as fact
3 Ticket info
4 Madness
5 Home of Dartmouth
6 Amalgamate
7 Tilt, at sea
8 Nanking nanny
9 Dakar is there
10 Live's partner
11 Disguised, briefly
12 Blended family members
13 Asian holiday
14 "___ tu" ("A Masked Ball" aria)
15 White House advisory grp.
23 Earned
24 Lightning McQueen, e.g.
27 Like orchids
28 Clairvoyance
29 Hobbs of "The Natural"
30 Instrument in a wind quintet
31 Microwave, slangily
32 NCC-1701 is one
33 Sign of boredom
34 Building addition
37 Fight card unit
38 Dernier ___ (the latest thing)
39 Be indisposed
42 ___ of Hammurabi
44 "Mayday!"
45 QB's cry
46 Stew
48 Bit of filming
49 "Peter Pan" pirate
51 Sweater material
52 Quaker Oats cereal
53 Checked baggage
54 Cookbook phrase
55 Do goo
56 Some jeans
57 What rumrunners do
58 Bring home
60 Albanian currency
63 Helped
64 Give a benediction
65 Root ___
67 Dart about
68 "Austin Powers" character ___-Me
69 Matchless
70 Niblick, for one
71 "Lucky Jim" author
72 Dodge truck
73 Tokyo, once
74 Lift

78 LOATH OATHS by Patrick Jordan

58 Across was created by Pulitzer Prize–winning cartoonist Jeff MacNelly.

ACROSS

1 Grocery shelf lineup
5 Urban areas, slangily
10 Most leafless
16 Magnetizable metal
17 First symptom
18 Kind of bet at Belmont
19 Venus de ___
20 Landlord's document
21 Whitney's "The Preacher's Wife" costar
22 **Start of a quip**
25 "I'll take the offer, Howie!"
26 Pres. of the USA
27 Rod hidden by hubcaps
28 Conceded putt
29 Adjective for a slum
33 Rooster's weapon
35 Firth of Clyde port
36 Filling station fixture
37 Helpful hints
40 The Venture in "King Kong," e.g.
42 Wimbledon shot
43 **More of quip**
48 Airy courtyards
50 Ginger or pale follower
51 Deerstalker projection
52 **More of quip**
57 Wield diligently
58 Purple martin of the funnies
59 Nitwit
60 Loud laughter or thunder
61 OutKast's genre
64 "Disappear" band
66 Ruthless rule
68 Blow away
70 Jack in "The Comancheros"
73 Lyndon's female beagle
74 Beguiling trick
75 **End of quip**
80 Authorize
83 "Hollywood" author Gore
84 "I, Claudius" outfit
85 Disposed (of)
86 Alpine ridge
87 Tear's partner
88 Hall of fame candidates
89 "A thing of beauty . . ." poet
90 18-Across payout factor

DOWN

1 Hendrix at Woodstock
2 Operatic number
3 Dicer's turn
4 Alp topper
5 Ise or Mecca, e.g.
6 Singles
7 Expo '70 site
8 Spay or neuter
9 Fills with resolve
10 Spot to sack out
11 Hewing tool
12 Brooks in "Cop"
13 Itchy skin problem
14 Like a romance novel
15 Superior in stature
23 Feel poorly
24 Soda aisle brand
28 Express sorrow
29 Paintball field sound
30 "___ the raven . . ."
31 Shadow's middle
32 Tango move
34 Hesitant syllables
38 Recite the Hail Mary
39 Hardly hollow
41 Chi-omega link
43 Driving club
44 Meeting reminder, perhaps
45 "Quaking" tree
46 1992 Rangers retiree Ryan
47 With a straight face
49 "___ been real!"
53 Outpaced every opponent
54 Sinister spells
55 Nimble-minded
56 Apertures for some voyeurs
60 Sequel's subtitle, often
61 Cake mix additive
62 Tchaikovsky's "Piano Trio in ___"
63 Wine taster's asset
65 Language akin to Czech
67 TD signaler
69 Serengeti grazer
71 Engulfed in flames
72 Princess in the Golden Fleece myth
76 Horsepower fraction
77 Went after weeds
78 Quaint "Yikes!"
79 Its moons are Phobos and Deimos
81 Squiffed
82 MSS markers

79 UNDERCOVER FORCE by Chase McFarland

Can you uncover this undercover force below?

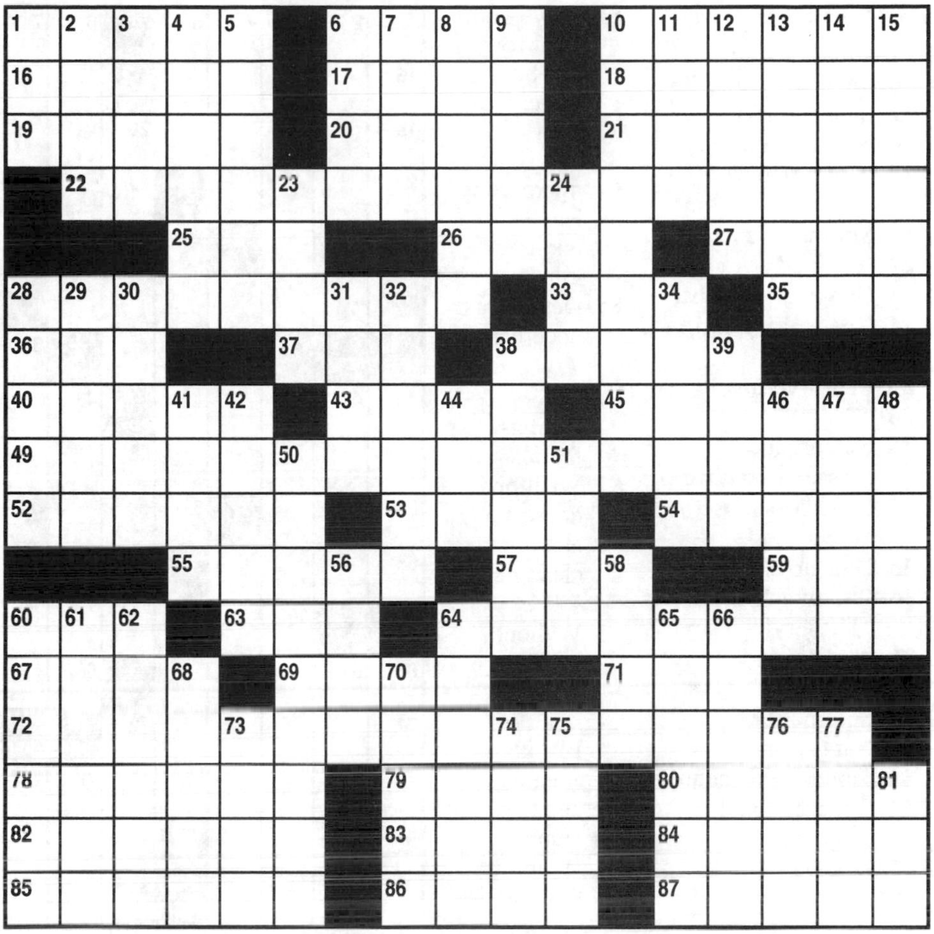

ACROSS

1 Extend an invitation for
6 "Poor me!"
10 Deep-dish dish
16 Sports show ending
17 Popular techno musician
18 Bearing red tags, maybe
19 Point a finger at
20 It won't let you be objective
21 Initial
22 Lima founder
25 Auto of old
26 ___ the crack of dawn
27 High-school subj.
28 Exes with joint custody
33 Crunch targets
35 "Just ___ am, without . . ."
36 Constellation near Norma
37 ___ es Salaam
38 Savage
40 Deep-red apples
43 On the agenda
45 Goes for the passer
49 Gallup product
52 Salon worker
53 Reagan cabinet member
54 "Pagliacci" role
55 Keach or Lattislaw
57 Cruise or Mix
59 Party member, briefly
60 Soft shoe
63 "Baudolino" author
64 Swimming pool game
67 Small batteries
69 Child support?
71 Flight board abbr.
72 They ended with the Peace of Callias
78 13th-century Italian sculptor
79 Breakfast acronym
80 "___ the Tiger" ("Rocky III" song)
82 Pouting
83 Etta of old comics
84 Mil. rank
85 It gives you an out
86 Huxtable and Lovelace
87 "Whole ___ Shakin' Goin' On"

DOWN

1 Wall St. maven
2 Philosophical concept
3 Reliant or Aries
4 2004 Emmy nominee Braun
5 Can tail?
6 Both up front?
7 Trixie Flagston's mom
8 Item with beads
9 Computer bulletin board administrator
10 Red board?
11 "Il Trovatore" role
12 Tavern sign abbr.
13 Pro ___ (for one's country)
14 Oldmobile models of 2000
15 Essence of orange blossom
23 Like Davidson College
24 Steve Allen successor
28 Quibbles
29 "Are you in ___?"
30 Namby-___ (silly)
31 Brussels-based alliance
32 The Heisman, for one
34 Kind of double
38 "La Isla ___": Madonna
39 Hockey's Phil, familiarly
41 Some pipe joints
42 Spanish dice roll
44 Noche follower
46 John Havlicek's nickname
47 Eero's father
48 Camera technique
50 Whimsical eccentrics
51 Sikorsky or Stravinsky
56 Scoop site
58 Thom of footwear
60 Chatterbox
61 Crew action
62 Salad type
64 Worked as a combination
65 "Animal Farm" author
66 Invoke
68 Land's end?
70 Eleniak of "Baywatch"
73 Till compartment
74 Kappa preceder
75 Studios, maybe: Abbr.
76 Four-sided fig.
77 Hearth buildup
81 Boca's st.

80 JUDGE DREAD by Bonnie L. Gentry

"You know you've had a bad 'Idol' performance when . . ."

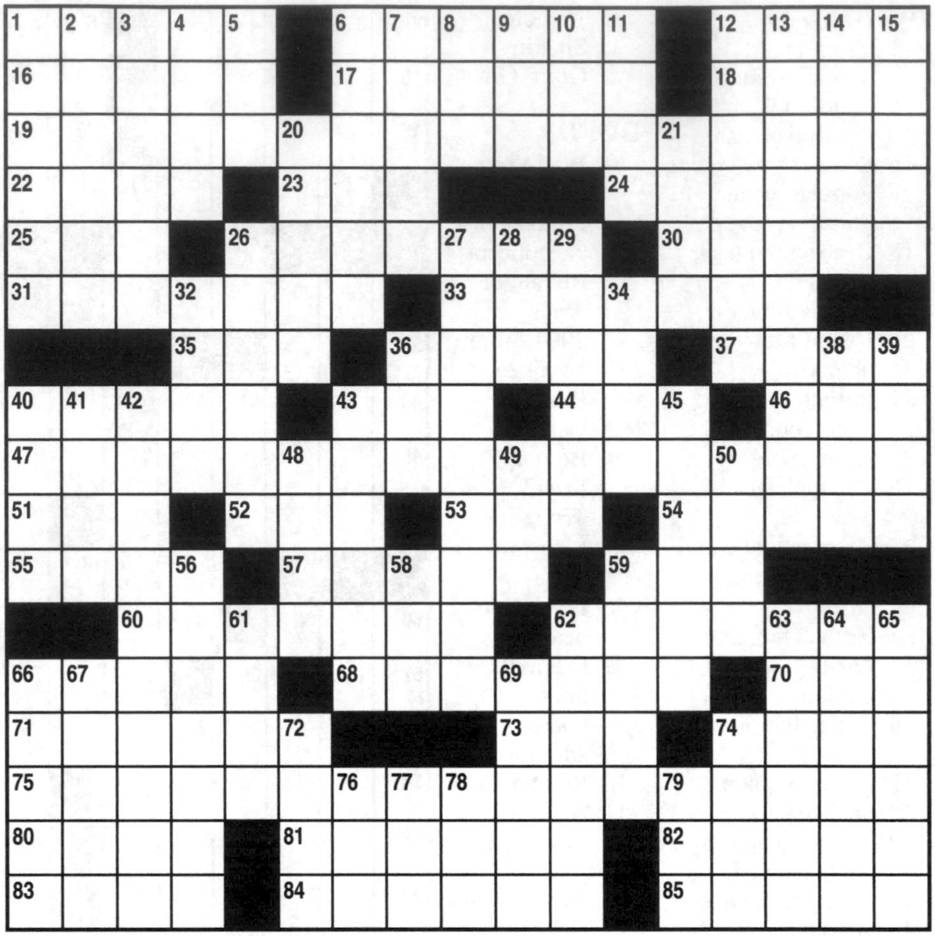

ACROSS

1 Out on a limb
6 "Are you game?"
12 Suspicious of
16 Bob's partner
17 Is nuts about
18 Cut with a scythe
19 **Simon says . . .**
22 Reclined
23 Unagi, at sushi bars
24 One making shrill barks
25 Like wee-uns
26 "Got it!" concordance
30 Massey of old films
31 Pioneer in close-up magic
33 Gun stock
35 Whitaker's costar in "The Crying Game"
36 Athletic shoe feature
37 Solomonlike
40 Gangly one
43 Tibetan milk source
44 Congressional creation
46 JetBlue competitor
47 **Randy says . . .**
51 Catch, as a perp
52 It can be seen during el día
53 Part of UNLV
54 Opie player
55 Exile site for Napoleon
57 Half-speed, e.g.
59 Sighing sound
60 Affront to neighbors
62 Governing bodies
66 Prospectors' discoveries
68 Justifiable
70 Two halves
71 Go into banks, perhaps
73 "Yoo-___!"
74 Parks of civil-rights history
75 **Paula says . . .**
80 1986 Peace Nobelist Wiesel
81 Move to the front row, maybe
82 Solicitious phrase
83 Part of a microscope
84 Have a one-track mind
85 Destroy, as documents

DOWN

1 Riding-wear fabrics
2 What one doesn't pay at a clearance sale
3 Without breaking a sweat
4 "The Blackboard Jungle" author Hunter
5 Wilming-ton's st.
6 Greet silently
7 Writer St. Johns
8 ". . . ___ a lender be"
9 Give 100%, say
10 Word in William Shatner titles
11 First words to stand for
12 Tribal precepts, by and large
13 Palo Alto–based IT network
14 Already spoken for
15 Phantom's milieu
20 Hotelier Helmsley
21 Hold back Cupid
26 Encirclements, of sorts
27 1995 Batman portrayer
28 Middle of a famous palindrome
29 "Magic Hour" novelist Susan
32 Select at random
34 Design with acid
36 Mushroom topper
38 Pieced together
39 Nervously irritable
40 "Same Old Lang ___": Fogelberg
41 Santa's revenge
42 Said "nyah, nyah, nyah"
43 Coward's color
45 Bossy boss
48 Katharine in "Shenandoah"
49 Confucian "way"
50 Capital east of Riyadh
56 Responses to bridge bids?
58 Element below plata in the periodic table
59 "Facetious" fivesome
61 This, to Cervantes
62 Piglets
63 Out-of-bounds, so to speak
64 Nutrition shake brand
65 Tamper-resistant
66 RCA or EMI
67 Seed structure
69 '89 World Series winners
72 Overseas union unit
74 In clover
76 Civil War soldier
77 Pluralizer, often
78 Sacramento newspaper
79 Frank McCourt novel

81 BROKEN PROMISES by Patrick Jordan

The five-letter answer to 5 Across is not TENOR.

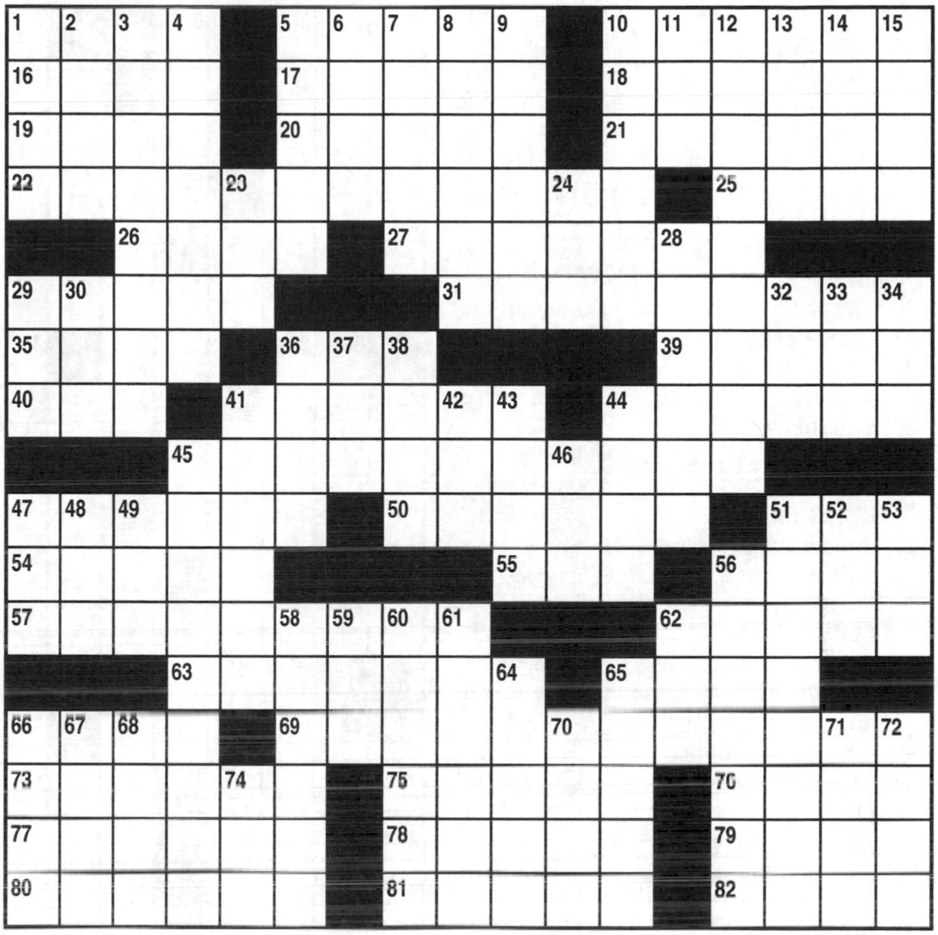

ACROSS

1 Scout's badge holder
5 Barbershop quartet member?
10 Seal of approval
16 Quarterback's cry
17 Bother greatly
18 Talk over again
19 Novel notion
20 Asian palm
21 1804 Beethoven symphony
22 Plush bed or sofa item*
25 Did in
26 Oceanarium wrigglers
27 Ingenue's quality
29 Like an epigram
31 Stern lecture tool?*
35 Buck or sock add-on
36 British leaders, briefly
39 Submit taxes online
40 Meditative sect
41 Crop-menacing insect
44 Concerns for fashionistas
45 Ed Sullivan's "Toast of the Town," e.g.*
47 Receive willingly
50 Closed (in on)
51 **Promise broken in clue* answers**
54 Base manned by I Don't Know
55 Make the last payment on
56 "Heartburn" author Ephron
57 "The Blackboard Jungle" actor*
62 Quick kisses
63 "My bad!"
65 Beyond, at first?
66 Provide a cure for
69 Lava stream*
73 Thrill
75 Brother of Moses
76 "___ Rose" ("Music Man" tune)
77 Written reminiscence
78 Had a go at
79 Polo Ralph Lauren rival
80 Script segments
81 Weensy preceder
82 Gen-___ (boomers' offspring)

DOWN

1 Gangster's knife
2 Errand runner
3 Anatomy class display
4 Dismissal, slangily
5 Auditorium array
6 47-stringed instrument
7 Finished some leftovers
8 Former Czech president Havel
9 Plus others, in Pliny's day
10 Twisted woolen yarn
11 ___ Lingus
12 Elite group
13 Car-denting stones
14 Verb suffix
15 Spring phenomenon
23 1960s TV action star Ron
24 Lacto-___ vegetarian
28 Steering arm attachment
29 Candy in collectible dispensers
30 Ticked-off feeling
32 Storage crib
33 GOP member?
34 Bullets legend Unseld
36 Freighter's destination
37 Long-distance inits.
38 Canal opened in 1869
41 What a Newfoundland isn't
42 Sault ___ Marie
43 Veteran's counterpart
44 At which point
45 Brilliant red
46 Piglet parent
47 Off-road vehicle
48 X, to Xenophon
49 Title for JFK or LBJ
51 Compete on "American Idol," say
52 Sitcom planet
53 "What ___ I thinking?"
56 Blockbuster rival
58 Nomadic types
59 One of Pooh's pals
60 Recently
61 Message in a corporate image ad
62 Chest muscle, for short
64 "Beyond the Sea" subject Bobby
65 She honeymooned on 52 Down
66 Some alteration targets
67 Major suit?
68 Gadget company of cartoondom
70 Refusals
71 Gas leak evidence
72 Gum globs
74 Casting vote's cause

82 AFTER ALL* by Sam Bellotto Jr.

22 Across is now a national park on the Bristol Channel coast of England.

ACROSS

1 He's a good feller
6 Porks off
11 Redd of "The Royal Family"
15 Crystal-lined rock
16 Dotty
17 "Enquirer" blurb
18 Stevie Wonder hit of 1973*
20 Lady of Seville
21 E-mail chuckle
22 "Lorna Doone" setting
23 YouTube offerings
25 "Storms in Africa" singer
27 Rocky pinnacle
28 Sooner than
29 Police band broadcast*
36 Star on Sirius
38 Pelouze product
39 "There will ___ laughter": Orwell
40 Centennial number
41 "The Cyclops" has just one
43 NPR's Glass
44 Comic from Copenhagen
45 Shakespeare play that opens in Rousillon*
49 Make a new bow
50 Pet
51 Son of Gad
52 Match, in a way
53 LAX guesstimates
54 Nonsense
56 Perceptions
58 1989 Don Bluth animated film*
61 Sale word
62 Road-map abbr.
63 Dial abbr.
67 The Mishnah is part of it
70 Sawhorse, basically
73 Prefix for biology
74 Arthur of "Hoop Dreams"
75 Like many a winning vacation package*
78 Esfahan coin
79 Duo, plus five
80 Actress Sokoloff
81 Conservative Party predecessor
82 "Things We Said ___": Beatles
83 Terry or Drew

DOWN

1 Mentally acute
2 Element 54
3 Shannon or Parker
4 Fanfare
5 Glacial snowfield
6 Snowbirds' meccas
7 Dope
8 Polygraph flunker
9 New Haven student
10 Truckling
11 Cheese-knife type
12 Sioux speaker
13 One of the phobias
14 Present day?
16 "American Idol" judge
19 Like the thylacine
24 "___ be darned!"
26 Bonobo
28 Where Gingrich got his PhD
30 Alb covering
31 GPS units, iPods, PDAs, etc.
32 Without a stitch
33 Rosie O'Donnell's middle name
34 Fireplaces
35 Popular British TV actress Gordon
36 Orlando Pirates home
37 Digital ID?
40 "And the wine ___": Psalms 75:8
42 Reporter's end
44 "Penny Lane" was on this
46 Not at all clumsily
47 Buck's tail
48 "You ___ crazy!"
54 Most near absolute zero
55 Bully on "The Simpsons"
57 Roxy Music's Brian
59 Wildebeest
60 Nautical call
64 Janis Joplin album
65 Relegate
66 Winged Godzilla foe
67 Open pie
68 Financial allowance
69 "All in the Family" producer
70 Given the O.K.
71 Spanakopita cheese
72 Farmer Hoggett's wife in "Babe"
76 Banh ___ (Vietnamese crepe)
77 NTSC alternative

83 ENCORE PRESENTATION by Victor Fleming

50 Across may be a good place to start solving.

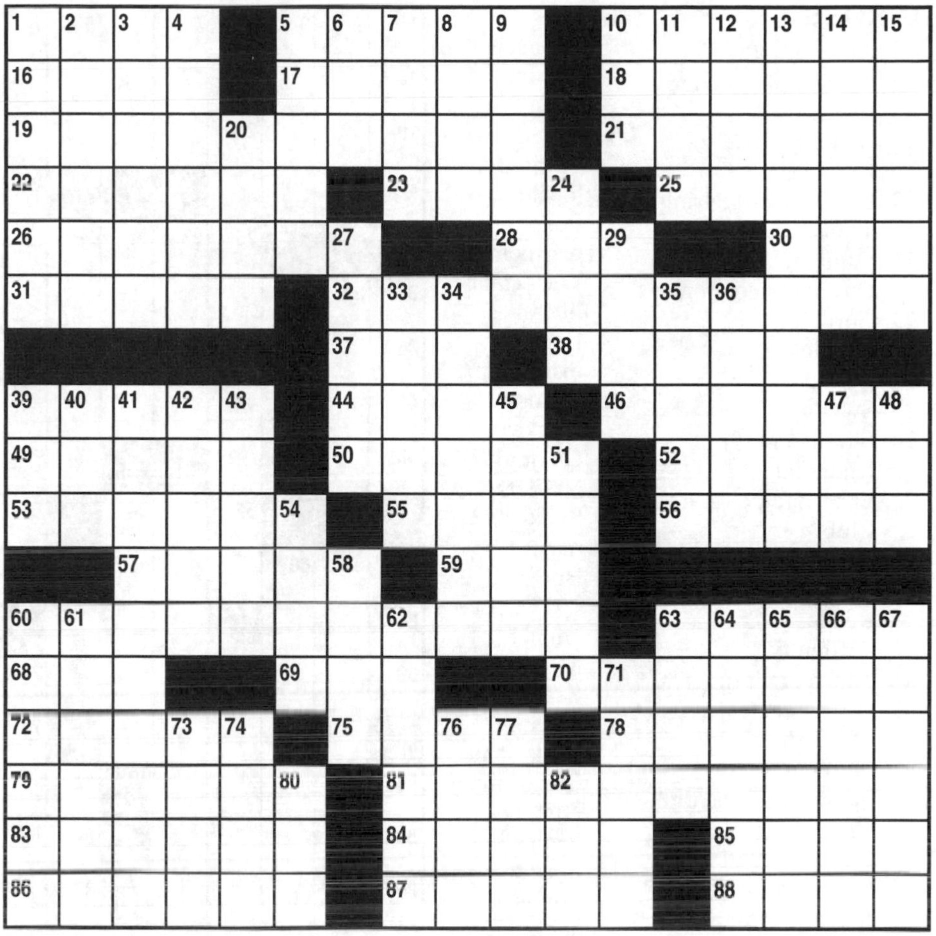

ACROSS

1 Suburban additions?
5 Frond growers
10 Memory-filled spans
16 Go squishy
17 Village ___
18 Source of Tiger's frustration
19 Not in balance*
21 Like some hot desserts
22 Basket twigs
23 Hop and jump partner
25 Fudd of toons
26 Some stanzas
28 Langley initials
30 Embitterment
31 Forestry units
32 Paid expenses*
37 Writer Tarbell
38 Goes it alone
39 Tended
44 Places for patches
46 Chinese hard-liner
49 Find repugnant
50 TITLE, WHEN ENCORED*
52 Inclination
53 Beyond acceptable limits
55 Ventimiglia of "Heroes"
56 Company with a blue globe logo
57 Renaissance instruments
59 "Hinky Dinky Parlay ___"
60 In uncomfortable surroundings*
63 Is adjacent to
68 ___ cit. (footnote abbr.)
69 "___ Night Like This": Dylan
70 One who's out early
72 Atoll
75 Globule
78 Showed shortness of breath
79 Formal fiddle
81 Hardly competitive*
83 On or before deadline
84 Kind of roll
85 Sculptor Nadelman
86 Mortified
87 Good feature
88 U.S. hwys., e.g.

DOWN

1 Duty
2 In fewer words
3 Ava's role in "Mogambo"
4 Fla. beach spot
5 Leading the pack
6 Early autumn setting in Cambridge
7 "How the Other Half Lives" author
8 Dinette spot
9 Yule visitor, briefly
10 9 Down helper
11 Profusion
12 Iridescent stone
13 Not available*
14 Golfer Green
15 Cordwood measures
20 Miner's quest
24 Some charts
27 Prefix for gyra
29 Quark's place
33 Disrepute and then some
34 Like some audiences
35 Seize
36 Alley Oop's love interest
39 Made use of a sedan
40 Blood-typing letters
41 Fictitious*
42 Silken and firm, e.g.
43 Pontificate
45 Wise old head
47 Recovery place
48 Pro ___
51 Civil War authority Shelby
54 Move, realtor-style
58 Mail off
60 "Twelfth Night" countess
61 ___ around (prying)
62 First first lady
63 "Do you have Prince Albert in ___?"
64 Headline
65 Adjust, as the level of a projector
66 ___ Beanie Babies
67 Swamp grasses
71 Rush
73 Oscar-winner Kazan
74 Rice and Robbins
76 Cries of discovery
77 Writes
80 Divided court feature
82 Tommy who sang "Jam Up Jelly Tight"

84 JAVA DEVELOPMENT by Kevin George

Matt Ryan was a 68 Across in 2008.

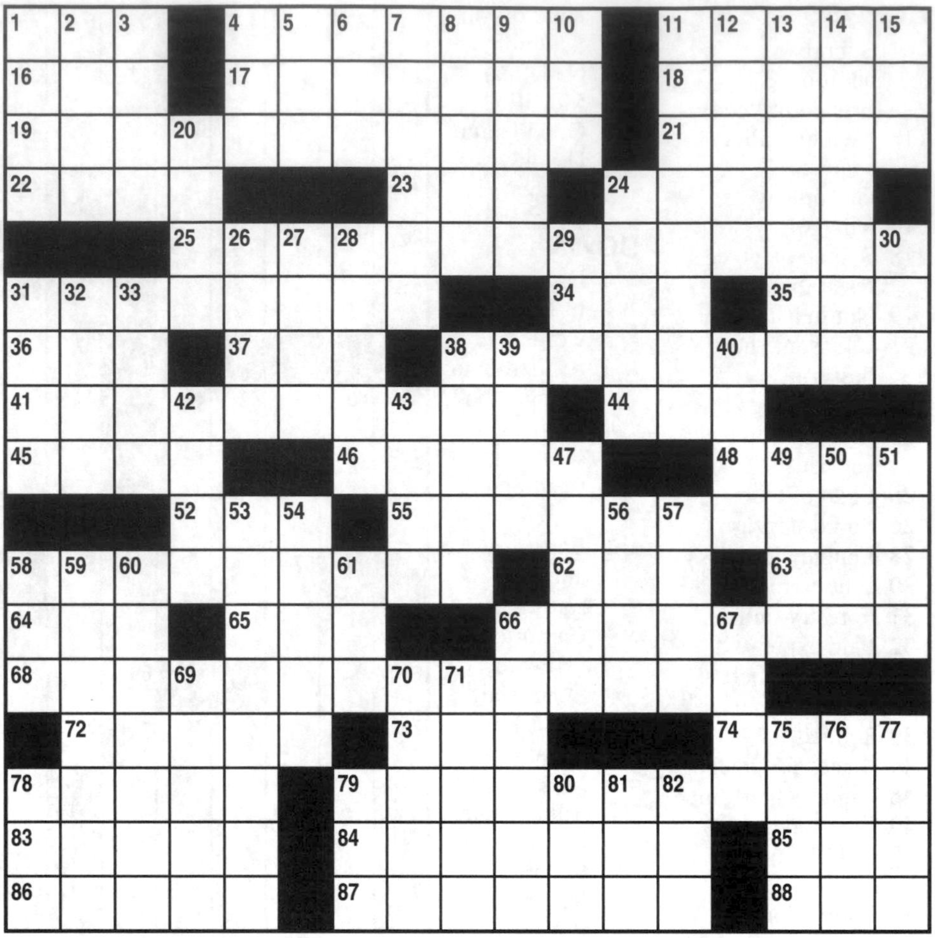

ACROSS

1 Glass of NPR
4 Sudden hirings and firings
11 Gushing flattery
16 Crew need
17 Phrase heard during a police raid
18 Stun gun
19 Coven concoction
21 Curly hair or freckles
22 Further
23 Swell
24 Simon and Diamond
25 Entrée at the Friars' Club?
31 Exercise form
34 "___ Mine": Beatles
35 Difficulty
36 Top-secret grp.
37 ___-Lucia Cortez of "Lost"
38 Mementos
41 Same old, same old
44 Omelet ingredient
45 Chinese: Prefix
46 Legal claim
48 Just one of those things?
52 Jersey cager
55 Behave appropriately
58 Change place?
62 "Mazel ___!"
63 French way
64 Instructional material?
65 German 101 article
66 Descendant of both Madrid and Mongolia?
68 Elite draftee
72 Transported
73 Mai ___
74 Mid-month time
78 Petrol unit
79 Badly bludgeon
83 Al Yankovic hit that went gold
84 ___ Field Airport, nka O'Hare
85 ER pronouncement
86 Hebrew leader?
87 Number one
88 "___ for Silence": Grafton

DOWN

1 Spirit Lake locale
2 Poker table perimeter
3 They can be liberal
4 Educ. institution
5 Ground breaker
6 Colorado NHLers
7 Stick-y meals?
8 Bug
9 1957 Oscar winner Miyoshi
10 Seat of worship
11 Ávila saint
12 Star of many Nintendo games
13 For fun
14 Publish anew
15 Clubber Lang portrayer
20 Chanel of fashion
24 Echo, for one
26 Silicon Valley auctioneer
27 Suffix with duck or seed
28 Online greeting
29 Push
30 Superstation letters
31 Added stipulations
32 Morales of "Vanished"
33 Drought relief
38 Criticize
39 Menu choice?
40 Qtys.
42 NFL Hall-of-Famer Howie
43 Neighbor of Pakistan
47 Tally
49 Mata ___
50 Fuego fighter
51 Prom attendee
53 White canines
54 Retro Ford of 2002
56 "Me neither!"
57 Emergency order, briefly
58 Adobe Reader file
59 Primary
60 Strangler's weapon
61 It has 12 meses
66 Piaf and Wharton
67 Pass over
69 Type of mall or steak
70 In ___ (unborn)
71 Springarn Medal org.
75 Threads
76 Morlock victims
77 Resting places
78 Open field
79 Droid
80 Select
81 Spanish Main cargo
82 Home security company

85 " 'S WONDERFUL!" by Jay Sullivan

19 Across is a Scary clue!

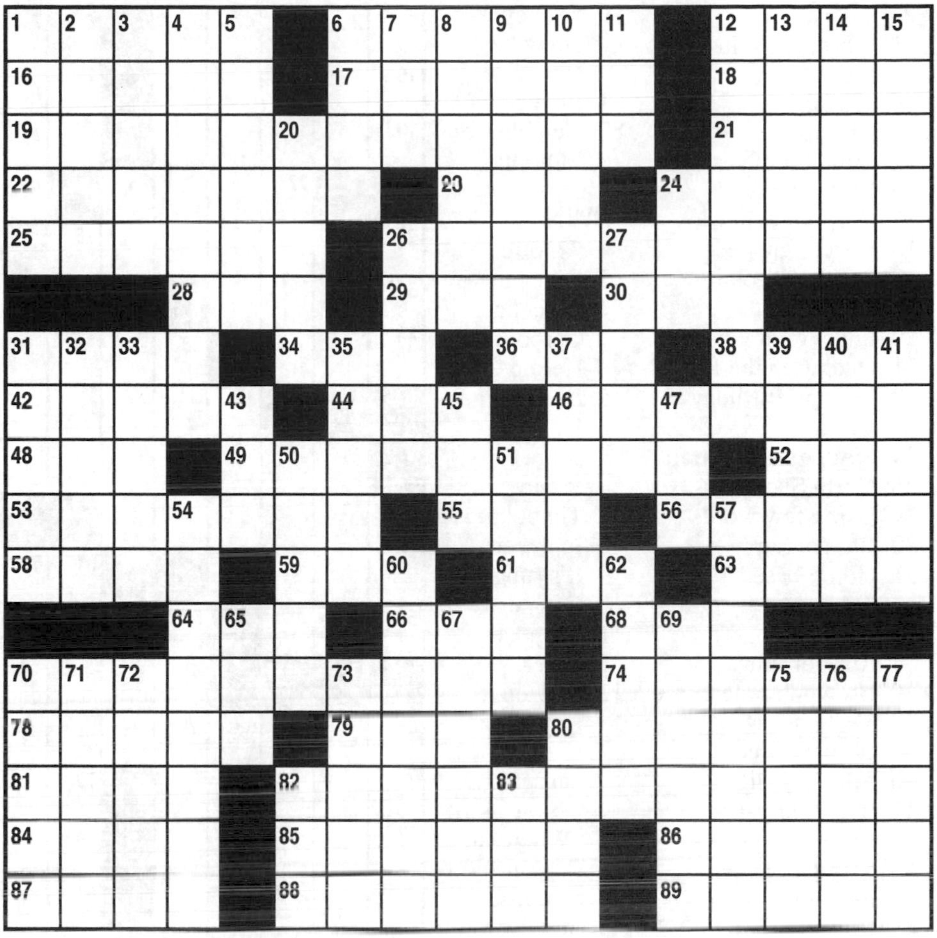

ACROSS

1 Unwanted growth
6 Caped Crusader's domain
12 They have teeth in them
16 Some fellers
17 Wing it
18 "I was afraid of that!"
19 Where "Wannabe" gets a lot of air time?
21 Remote possibility
22 Melisande's lover
23 Kind of will?
24 Spring part
25 Sordid
26 Mast?
28 Wavy area
29 Overnight letter
30 Yellowfin tuna
31 Newton's ___ of motion
34 Overhead item
36 Serengeti sight
38 They have pull
42 Milo of the movies
44 The price you pay
46 Nonstop
48 Words of praise
49 Batting .200?
52 Just deserts
53 View from Maui
55 An Ivy Leaguer
56 Serviceable
58 Punjab separatist
59 Yolk container
61 Treebeard's doc?
63 One whose business is taking off
64 It could be toast
66 Swiss sight
68 Sancho Panza's mount
70 Candy store?
74 Hire all new actors
78 Like some AA batteries
79 NATO mbr.
80 Eroded
81 Fox fave, familiarly
82 Crew's cruise?
84 Went downhill
85 It's more than a promise
86 After lunch, perhaps
87 "The Eagles" cofounder
88 Familiar with
89 Less loco

DOWN

1 Social insects
2 Boot out
3 Nellie's "South Pacific" lover
4 Formerly chic
5 Blessed event?
6 Some heaters
7 Fertilization sites
8 "Assumption of the Virgin" painter
9 Coming down hard
10 Coral construction
11 Chess group
12 Spunk
13 Enterprise officer
14 Recurring theme
15 Book store
20 Physician's request
24 Butt end
26 Long-necked lute
27 Hot spot
31 Impends
32 Likewise
33 Large gastropod
35 Places in the heart
37 On order
39 Go figure
40 Stir up
41 Display disdain
43 Stock quote
45 Luck of the draw
47 From ___ Z
50 Where to pick up dates
51 Took time out
54 "Is that so?"
57 Il Duce follower
60 Take prisoner
62 Paris pie
65 Since Jan. 1
67 Dilly-dallied
69 Regards
70 Catch wind of
71 Dentist's request
72 School of Paris
73 Andy in "The Devil Wears Prada"
75 It's not free of charge
76 Old age
77 It's in development
80 Regards
82 Apt name for a cook
83 GPS measurement

86 BLUE MATERIAL by Richard Silvestri

Words spoken by Ariel in "The Tempest" inspired the composition at 15 Down.

ACROSS

1 Wore a hole in the rug
6 Whirlpool alternative
11 Little bit of scat
16 Wide open
17 Corporate division
18 Sovereign
19 Put the check in the mail
20 Snow removers
21 Quaker in the forest
22 "Happy Birthday" writer
24 **Start of a question**
26 North Star
29 Using few words
30 Bass organ
31 Home-based hardware
33 Somewhat
34 Run for fun
37 Brewpub order
38 Vectors' counterparts
40 Mountain lion
41 In memory
42 Column type
44 **Middle of the question**
48 Bud
49 Camden Yards player
50 Level
51 Auto annoyances
53 Feathery accessory
56 Homer Simpson's father
57 Tenant organization
59 Blazed a trail
60 "Bang a Gong" group
61 Like 37 Across
63 Call for
65 **End of the question**
70 Run a rag around
71 Subside
72 "Silas Marner" author
74 The Jetsons' dog
77 Moon vehicle
78 Right-hand page
79 Coast condition?
80 "Nancy Drew" author
81 Imbue
82 Neighbor of Ethiopia

DOWN

1 72, often
2 Get better in the cellar
3 Garbo role
4 Heroic
5 Discourage
6 Egyptian cobra
7 Where Timbuktu is
8 In the air
9 It's rung in
10 Categorizes
11 Found a caller
12 Step on it
13 Brand that goes to the dogs
14 Onion's kin
15 "Where the Bee Sucks" composer
23 Skydiver's line
25 Ryder Cup team
26 Major golf tourney
27 Upton Sinclair novel
28 Muffler
32 Passel
34 2007 Ellen Page film
35 Persian poet
36 Sal, in the song
38 Bowl over
39 Kind of committee
40 Accumulation
41 Hook's helper
42 Took to task
43 Office seekers
44 Kaffiyeh wearer
45 Tailor's concern
46 Sea east of the Caspian
47 Floor worker
48 Monastery address
51 Cads
52 Shoulder piece
53 "Billy Budd" composer
54 Poetic preposition
55 Bunyan cutter
57 Stick together
58 Area code preceder
60 Melee
62 Supermarket marking
64 Canvasback comment
65 Gloomy
66 Orchestral reed
67 Roof feature
68 Tommy's gun
69 Make an entry
73 Do better than
75 Bit of sunshine
76 Feast-famine filler

87 HIDDEN RIFT by Billie Truitt

A puzzle that's a bit cracked.

ACROSS

1 U-bend under a sink
5 Clothing
11 Award of Valor org.
15 Circle dances
17 Like clothes in a hamper
18 Bring in
19 Low-tech calculators
20 Dream up
21 Bach's "Mass in ___"
22 Phrase seen on a vending machine
24 Excessive
26 Hold contents
27 German industrial region
29 Trojan War epic
32 Signs of relief
33 Store door
36 Day-___ paint
37 Doo-wop syllable
38 U.S. Open tennis stadium
39 Take a taste
40 Mary-Kate or Ashley
42 Pre-1917 monarch
45 Stairwell sounds
47 Cheer heard at a Nittany Lions game
50 Spicy Southern stew
53 ___-bitty
54 Horseshoe-shaped letter
58 Unrefined find
59 Ceremonial splendor
61 Just average
63 Ticked off
64 "May it never be!"
68 Installments, briefly
69 Kind of pointer or tag
70 Jekyll's alter ego
71 Queen of daytime TV
73 Totally lost
75 Create a rift/PUZZLE TITLE
78 Sugar lump
80 One-dimensional
82 Mark the end of ___
83 "___ do you good!"
84 S.O.S. alternative
85 Exorbitant
86 Kiter's holding
87 Welcomes warmly
88 Merrie ___ England

DOWN

1 Compared to
2 Telemarketer's tactic
3 Plains native
4 Indiana cagers
5 Fungal spore sacs
6 Bull-fighter
7 Jams
8 Dockers' gp.
9 Election-night data
10 First lady's garden?
11 Interstellar cloud
12 Inherited
13 Jackie's second
14 Raggedy doll
16 Croon or warble
23 Have a snack
25 MGM lion?
28 "Citizen Kane" model
30 It can be a lot
31 Onetime Tunisian rulers
32 In the past
34 Abominate
35 "Take ___ Train"
37 Busybodies
41 Bird of the future
43 Short-tempered
44 Hill dweller
46 Clothing line
48 Pal of Christopher Robin
49 Proofreader's find
50 Seethe
51 Major in astronomy?
52 Not throw-away
55 John Steed's partner
56 Collected
57 Pop-ups, e.g.
60 Angora sweaters
62 Yours, to Yvette
65 Go over again
66 Ford flops
67 Sherpa, perhaps
68 Right away
72 School support gps.
74 Isle of exile
76 Scientology's Hubbard
77 Collar location
78 Geometric fig.
79 4 x 4, for short
81 An end to peace?

88 BLANK EXPRESSIONS by Jill Winslow

That's not a misspelling in the answer at 19 Across.

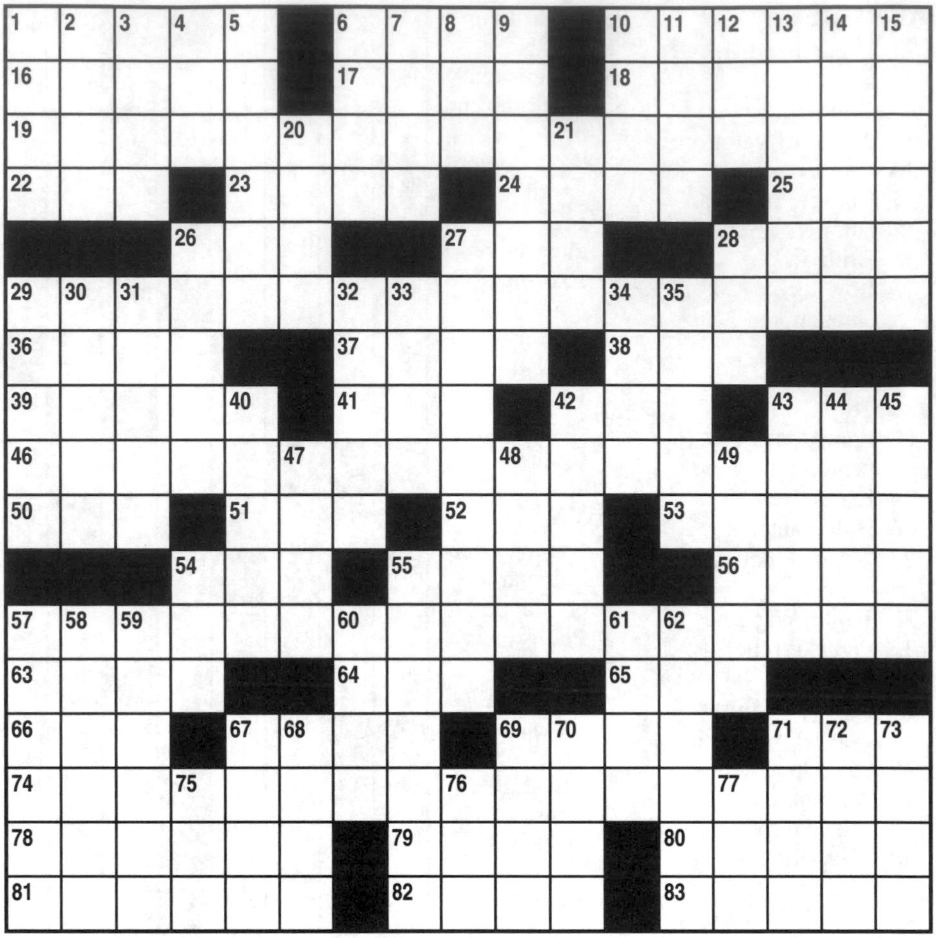

ACROSS

1 Concert piano
6 Scratch target
10 Aftershock
16 CSA general
17 Vicinity
18 Halcyon
19 **With her marriage she got ___**
22 Kwanzaa mo.
23 Long-legged wader
24 Airplane, for short
25 Mr. Jinks, for one
26 Verb suffix
27 Form W-9 info
28 Former Cosmo great
29 **Stiff the exorcist and ___**
36 French department
37 Lena in "Romeo Is Bleeding"
38 D-Day craft
39 Laughter units
41 Flagstick
42 It can hold its liquor
43 007's "GoldenEye" car
46 **What's the definition of a will? (___)**
50 Go follows it
51 "You got it!"
52 Fishing essential
53 Get in the net
54 Org. with a motto
55 Not belonging to others
56 Flying pest
57 **Shotgun wedding: A ___**
63 Come close
64 R. Shapiro, notably
65 Wriggly swimmer
66 Spring runner
67 In good health
69 Show satisfaction
71 "What guy?"
74 **A chicken crossing the road ___**
78 Must
79 First name in architecture
80 Crown
81 Most peculiar
82 Dog food brand
83 Book of Mormon book

DOWN

1 Alum
2 Descartes
3 Baldwin in "Pearl Harbor"
4 Not a rerun
5 Bond girl Richards
6 Branches
7 God struck by a spear in "The Iliad"
8 Great white hunter milieu?
9 Stays in there
10 Bygone ruler
11 Fix up
12 Commit a no-no
13 "I hate those ___ to pieces!": Mr. Jinks
14 Discounted
15 Finished the defense
20 Help out
21 Unpleasant sounds
26 S-curves
27 Ocean spray
28 Calif. hrs.
29 Mystical people
30 Take the podium
31 In the dark
32 Ring boundaries
33 Charles Lamb
34 Eastern European
35 Rob in "Nostradamus"
40 Definitive word
42 India.Arie hit
43 "___ Devil" (first 3-D film)
44 Friend of Robespierre
45 "Christina's World" painter
47 Like Marlee Matlin
48 Out of the picture
49 Helpful one
54 Put money down
55 Raised to a bishop
57 Place to 54 Down
58 Lowered in prestige
59 Put away a dish at night
60 "Wild Hogs" director Becker
61 Enlarge
62 Take down a peg
67 Beach shelters
68 Heaps
69 Hoopoe, e.g.
70 Son of Seth
71 Accompanied by
72 You can dig it
73 It doesn't happen again
75 "Tapestry" label
76 Verbal vote
77 ___ for tat

89 SHOP TALK by Patrick Jordan

11 Down was a song on their 1975 album "Wish You Were Here."

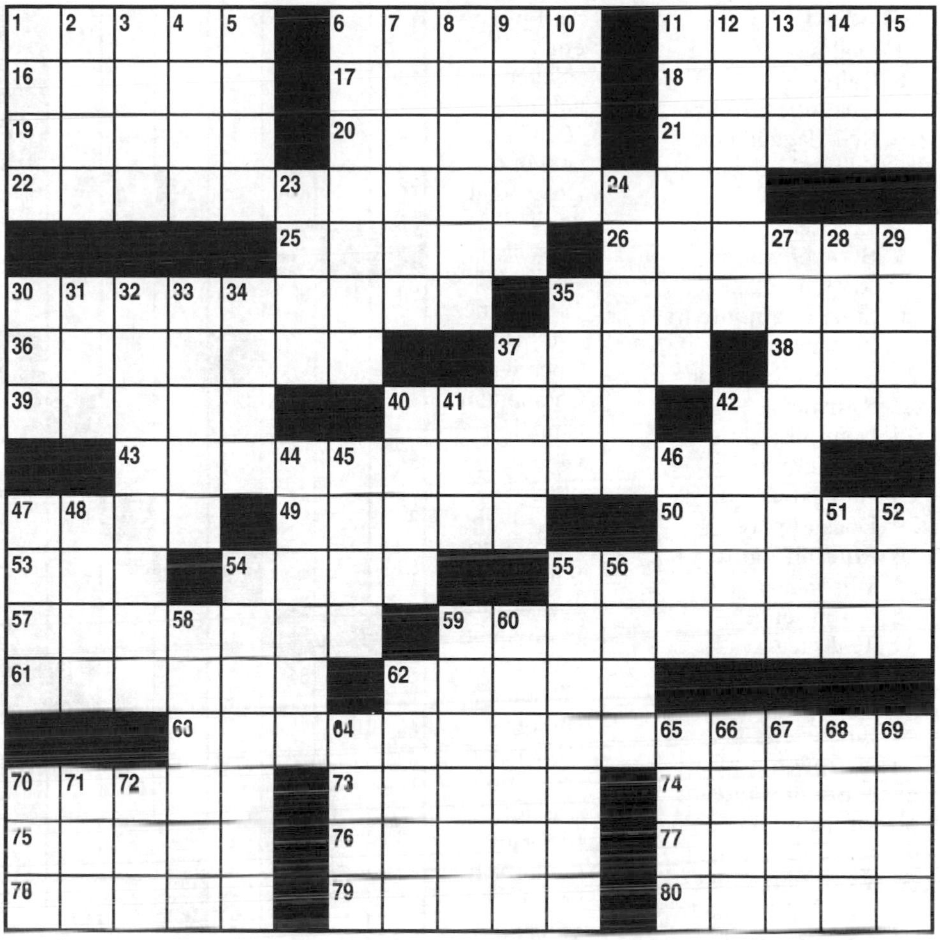

ACROSS

1 Walks in the waiting room
6 Abundant amount
11 Subzero temperature sign
16 Take flight to unite
17 Book before Joel
18 Parsley family herb
19 Less experienced
20 Sorrowful statement
21 Filibuster broadcaster
22 **Quip: Part 1**
25 Terrific time
26 The Blue Angels, e.g.
30 **Quip: Part 2**
35 Coin creation process
36 Fixed-payment plan
37 Brood
38 Gun, in gangster flicks
39 "Guideposts" editor Norman Vincent
40 Inherently
42 Shuts down
43 **Quip: Part 3**
47 Ready, briefly
49 Going hungry
50 Takes way too much of
53 Dinny's master Alley
54 Excessive quantity
55 Portuguese wine
57 Emulates Elvis
59 **Quip: Part 4**
61 Inheritance tax target
62 Publisher Nast
63 **Quip: Part 5**
70 Shirtless basketball team
73 Present at birth
74 Sign off on
75 Successful job applicant
76 Leaning
77 City where Galileo taught
78 Put forward
79 Reacts to a haymaker
80 Hits a housefly

DOWN

1 Durable do
2 Jai ___
3 Part of Batman's disguise
4 Pentathlon event
5 Middle Ages menial
6 Portrayer of Irma and Tess
7 Marks in a list
8 Fielding percentage element
9 Handed out hands
10 Marquis de ___
11 Pink Floyd's "Welcome to the ___"
12 Sunday paper piece
13 Autumn chill
14 Chant at the Olympics
15 Rep.'s colleague
23 Demise notice
24 Chiang Kai-shek's capital
27 Antacid ingredient
28 "Zounds!" alternative
29 Ping-Pong partitions
30 Blasting or thinking follower
31 1969 Three Dog Night hit
32 Chaotic place
33 Cup-shaped flower
34 Security interest
35 Engage in slam-dancing, say
37 TV's eloquent equine
40 Fizzling-out sound
41 Grandmother of Enos
42 Tribal bigwig
44 Keir of "Bunny Lake is Missing"
45 It's hard to bear
46 Cryptogram's key
47 Be a model student?
48 Bingo card quintet
51 Post-meal morsel
52 Highlander's "Hardly!"
54 Makes arrangements for
55 "Tin Lizzies"
56 Impressionist
58 Not as humble
59 Kim's "The Facts of Life" role
60 Summonable by phone
62 Box from an orchard
64 Watchdog's warning
65 Mouths, in slang
66 Raptor's ripper
67 Alan in "Paper Lion"
68 Force to flee
69 "Jabberwocky" starter
70 "Steady as ___ goes!"
71 "Kid-tested, mother-approved" cereal
72 High dudgeon

90 BAD GROWING CONDITIONS by Barry C. Silk

52 Across was also a pen name of Jonathan Swift.

ACROSS

1 Otalgia
8 Balmy
12 Quantities: Abbr.
16 Red-flagged item
17 Sikkim's global area
18 City near Sparks
19 Body of water south of Orsk
20 **Start of a quote by 83 Across**
22 Rod McKuen song
23 Sadistic
25 Gene Vincent's "___ Lovin' "
26 Hams it up
29 Doesn't play
30 **More of quote**
35 Was in charge of
36 For instance
37 Texas tea
38 ___ Kan dog food
41 Trying experience
43 Fibula, e.g.
45 Narrow furrow
47 **More of quote**
50 Of the hipbone
51 "Tosca" highlight
52 Word said with a wave of the hand
53 Chicago hrs.
54 Concorde
55 Early second-century year
56 Chinese menu name
57 **More of quote**
62 Flood
65 PC key
66 Make ___ (phone)
67 Geo model
69 Va. neighbor
73 **End of quote**
75 Pizza topping
78 Away from the wind
79 Some time ago
80 Department stores
81 Pocket protector user
82 Lacking width and depth
83 **Source of quote**

DOWN

1 Mus. key with four sharps
2 Rhine tributary
3 Anti-piracy org.
4 "Never sold before!"
5 "CSI" network
6 Do ground work?
7 "Just as it should be!"
8 1960s dance
9 1968 U.S. Open winner
10 Cambodian capital
11 Ginnie ___
12 Songlike
13 Thaws
14 Fed. security
15 Some convertibles
21 Eponymous source of "Dracula"
24 Buttons in "Sayonara"
27 Byzantine wall art
28 Electric toothbrush brand
29 Sidekick
30 Line around the globe
31 Ex-British PM Macmillan
32 Breaks up
33 "Crime and Punishment" heroine
34 Appearance
38 Yamaguchi on skates
39 "Say it ___, Joe!"
40 Bora Bora enclosure
42 That, in Toledo
43 Tournament spot
44 Geisha's sash
45 Inflexible
46 Word ignored in indexes
48 Survive
49 Offer a viewpoint
54 ___ Thérèse, Quebec
55 Optimum snorkeling conditions
57 Projected
58 Tangelo trademark
59 Exchanged words?
60 "___ who?"
61 Stretching muscle
62 Six-Day War general
63 Nice school
64 Longtime "Today" host
67 Ivy in Philly
68 Kind of pudding
70 Irene of "Fame" fame
71 Opposin'
72 Did "Time"
74 "Hinky Dinky Parlay ___"
76 Ray of the Indigo Girls
77 "America's Next Top Model" network

91 SPEECH THERAPY by Victor Fleming

Elijah rode 2 Down on the highway to heaven.

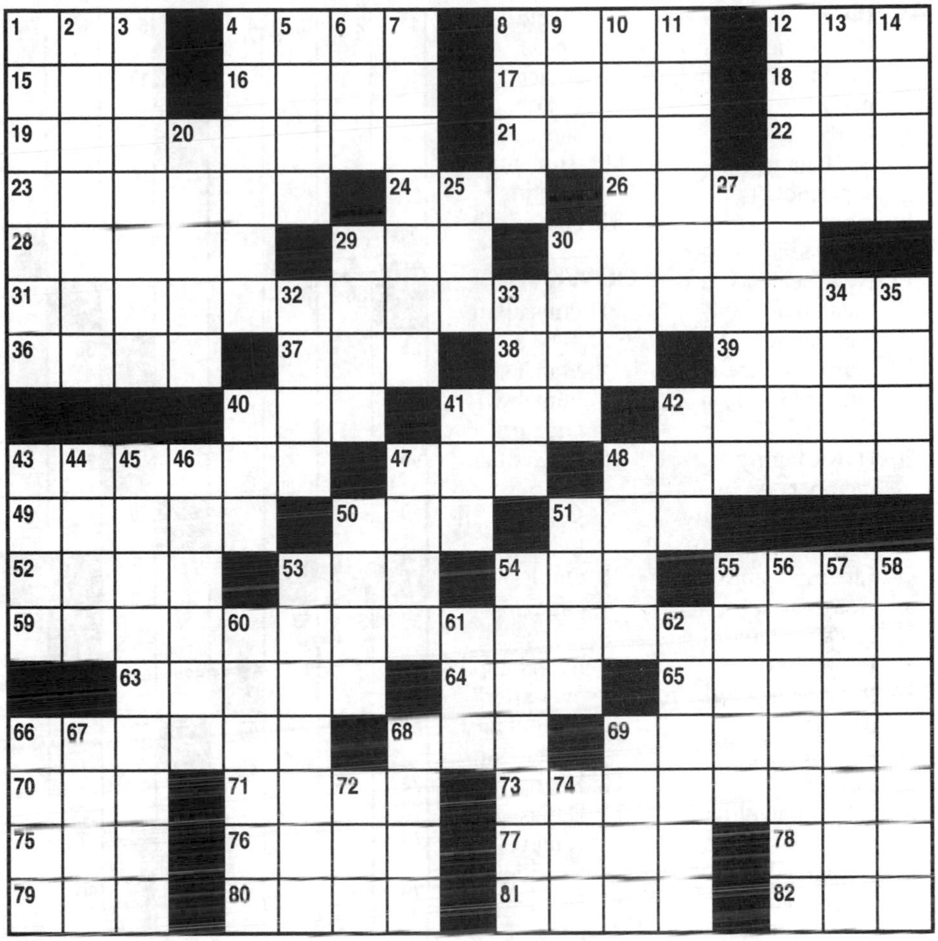

ACROSS

1 UML sublanguage
4 Early TV host
8 Peak in les Alpes
12 Zap
15 Sorority letter
16 Yokel
17 Bluff in Banff
18 Brazilian port
19 **Source of quotation (with 73-A)**
21 Envelope abbreviation
22 Pose a poser
23 Prior
24 Diddley and Derek
26 Not similar
28 Kinswoman
29 Favoring
30 Was meddlesome
31 **Start of a quotation**
36 Camp Swampy pooch
37 Rip-roaring time
38 Long fish
39 "Go on!"
40 Iams eater
41 Scarf for Mae West
42 Have a hankering
43 Sea spots
47 **Middle of quotation**
48 African menace
49 Freshmen, usually
50 "How wonderful!"
51 One of the gang
52 Ticket info
53 Mini-albums
54 Not tough at all
55 Yarn spinner
59 **End of quotation**
63 Hardly domestic
64 HMO concern
65 Protection
66 Chase scene din
68 ___ Plaines
69 House of games
70 Make advances on
71 Errand runner
73 **See 19 Across**
75 "The Wedding Banquet" director Lee
76 Drove like mad
77 Part of a pot
78 Inc. kin
79 More, in Cancún
80 Figure of Arthurian legend
81 Impoverished
82 Meth.

DOWN

1 Magic city
2 Elijah's transport
3 What Rittenhouse Square apartments aren't
4 Radio button
5 Kinswoman
6 "Alias" network
7 Pump shoes
8 New corp. hires
9 Food morsel
10 Au ___
11 Play with matches?
12 Playground "coward"
13 Exposure
14 Coupling
20 Right-hand page, in printing
25 Sch. in Tulsa
27 Apartment occupant
29 Apartment
30 "Not guilty," e.g.
32 Gets on, so to speak
33 Marquee sign
34 Boaters pull them
35 "The ___ Reader"
40 Barnum and 109
41 "Poppycock!"
42 Fashion inits.
43 "Me!"
44 Appear to be
45 Jumps over
46 Salmon, at times
47 Go for
48 El alternative
50 German automaker
51 Go by
53 Dodger's forte
54 Photographer's cover
55 Hanger-on
56 Laura ___ Wilder
57 Grapefruit juice property
58 Transmits twice
60 Like baroque architecture
61 Skater of cinema
62 Not as small
66 Did the butterfly
67 New Rochelle college
68 Owner's proof
69 Pilot leader?
72 Red Baron's Fokker ___
74 "Mrs. Lennon" singer

92 JOINT EFFORT by Norma Steinberg

56 Across can be seen in New York's Museum of Modern Art.

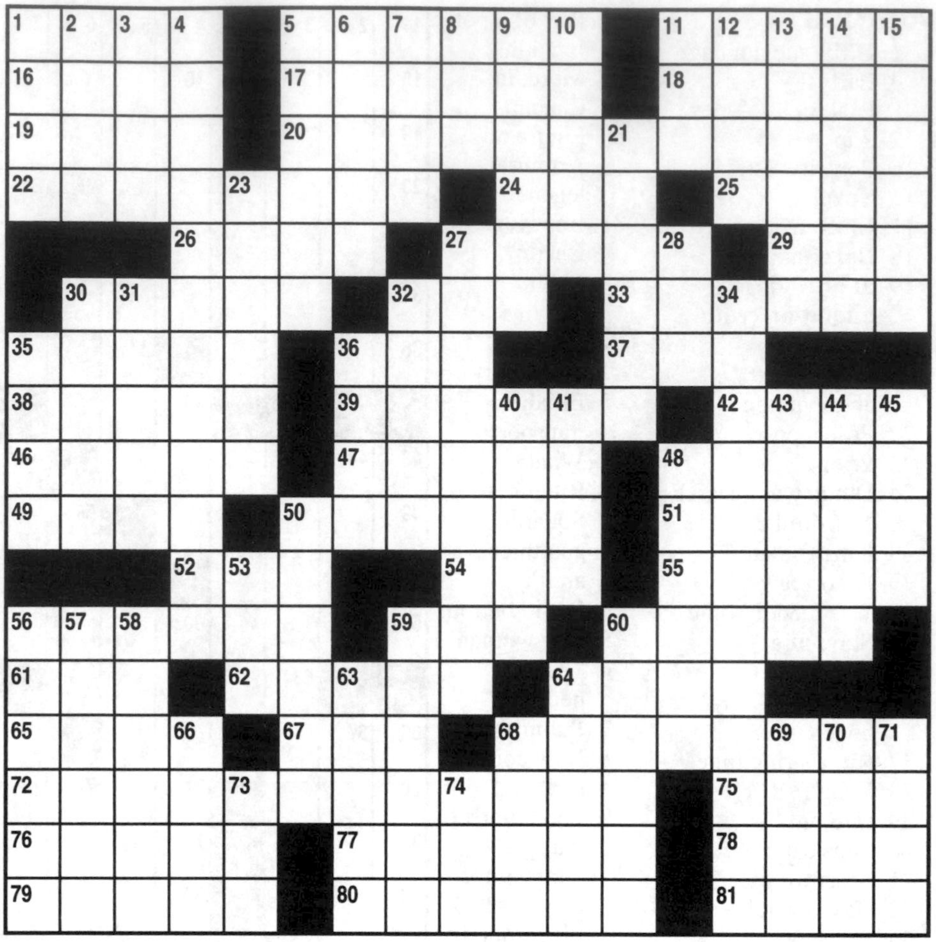

ACROSS

1 Put on the line
5 "With boughs of holly ___ . . ."
11 Harbor sights
16 Somalian supermodel
17 Aphrodite's beloved
18 New Zealand native
19 Incan homeland
20 Deliberately ignore
22 Gummed labels
24 Hur or Gurion
25 Exist
26 Hawk family member
27 Defeated, slangily
29 Diarist Anais
30 Electrical units
32 Actor Diesel
33 Heeds the alarm
35 Put at 000
36 Rand McNally product
37 Author Rand
38 Follow
39 Like some alliances
42 Diner sign
46 He played Zorba
47 Sleep soundly?
48 Zellweger in "Leatherheads"
49 Progeny
50 Basic pantry item
51 Ruhr Valley city
52 Mouse-sighting cry
54 "¡___ favor, amigo!"
55 Coffee package info
56 Van Gogh's "The ___ Night"
59 Farm layer
60 Embers
61 Rocky outcropping
62 "Ragged Dick" author
64 Postprandial sound
65 Iranian coin
67 To, to Hans
68 Expressway
72 "Cheers" patrons, e.g.
75 Add and delete
76 Parisian waterway
77 Placid
78 Lease subject
79 Put on, as a show
80 Romantic meetings
81 Heroic tale

DOWN

1 Pulls apart
2 "___ a Man": Ciardi
3 Punjab wrap
4 Give in
5 Sides of an issue
6 Really, really like
7 Online chuckles
8 ". . . ___ lived happily ever after"
9 Capital city on the Tajo
10 Hearth heap
11 Dallas campus
12 Corridor
13 Element called I
14 Knighted conductor André
15 Sea nymphs
21 Street sign
23 Tabby's baby
27 Rapper
28 Hudson's frequent costar
30 Locale
31 Davis in "Harry and Son"
32 Pat's cohost
34 Funny jokes
35 Demands: Abbr.
36 Has to
40 Synthetic fabric
41 Contemptuous expression
43 Adams who wrote "Born Free and Equal"
44 Adolescents
45 Gmail command
48 Converted, in a way
50 NASA success
53 Pitching stat
56 Cause of burnout
57 Latrine
58 Mecca locale
59 Playboy Mansion resident
60 "___! Foiled again!"
63 Sheraton patron
64 Charred
66 Yearn
68 Polo shirts
69 "Why, the very ___!"
70 Chess VIP
71 Blues guitarist Baker
73 Tiny
74 Help with the dishes

93 COMICAL CLUES by Matt Ginsberg

Joe Cocker covered 59 Across in 1970.

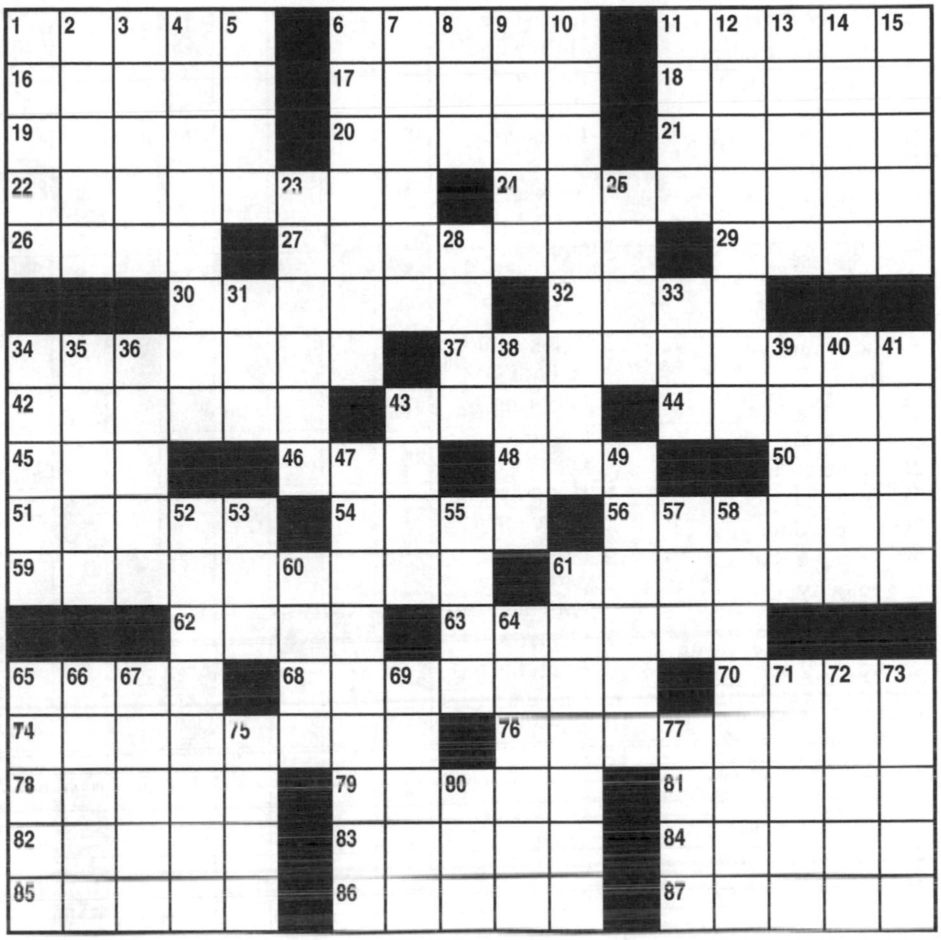

ACROSS

1 Pest-removal word
6 Trickle-down effect
11 ___ deux
16 Flip comment
17 Head lights
18 The end of many attorneys
19 Shake in bed
20 Study aid
21 A little night music
22 Gets a handle on
24 One who's always right
26 Add ends
27 Tried to lose
29 Have a fling
30 Lord of the ring
32 Beginning of a cure
34 Calling up trouble
37 Adam or Eve?
42 What the clueless have
43 Sicilian volcano
44 Sting
45 Violin string
46 British ram
48 Abbr. for Roget
50 Mouth opening
51 Backbreaker for a camel
54 Nair rival
56 Twisted
59 1967 Box Tops hit
61 Gets back to business
62 Route LXVI, e.g.
63 Coin
65 Start to kick
68 Tennis player who often raised a racket
70 Fork setting
74 Spinning out of control
76 Gilda "SNL" character
78 "Mission possible" group
79 Like a not-so-fine whine
81 Letter opener
82 Check some stock
83 Replace with dots
84 Mexican cigar
85 A lot of assassins
86 Orders to go
87 Guys who use come-on lines

DOWN

1 Bred winners
2 Carbon copy
3 A way with numbers
4 Helped
5 Heated competition
6 Brew that will make you wise?
7 Person in charge of liner notes?
8 Russell Crowe's middle name
9 Knight stick
10 "Oremus"
11 Kind of tense
12 When people like to pay taxes?
13 Technique for viewing some slides
14 ___ Salaam
15 Still-life subjects
23 Roundup rope
25 Compass points
28 Artist's pad
31 Sweet ending
33 Withdrawal problem
34 Fear of Frankfurters
35 River's end
36 Saltpetre
38 Part of RIT
39 Do a make-up job
40 Italian shroud city
41 Big pictures
43 Blade for Aramis
47 Like military boots?
49 Reunion attendees
52 Turn into an extraterrestrial?
53 Believer in spirits
55 Formerly, formerly
57 Louis XVI, e.g.
58 Made the cut
60 Work behind bars
61 Fixes a clog
64 High-stepping occasion
65 Union member
66 Whits
67 Slip cover
69 Gamut
71 First ding in the morning
72 "What's in ___?"
73 Exorcist's concern
75 "The Secret Storm" family
77 "¿Cómo ___?"
80 Start of a pleasing expression

94 "SHAPE UP!" by Arlan and Linda Bushman

Orodruin is another name for Mount Doom (see 39 Across).

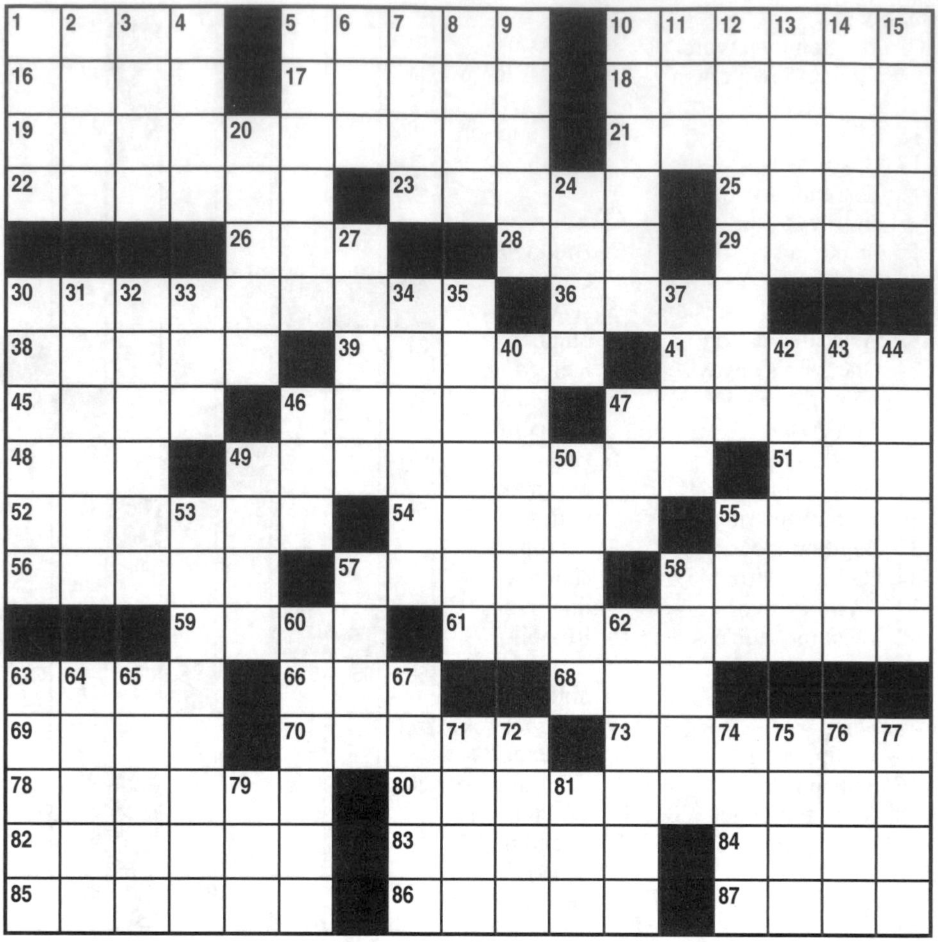

ACROSS

1 Marine prowlers
5 Hitchcock gem?
10 Fissures
16 Three Rivers river
17 Speculate
18 Superficial
19 Ready-made response
21 On the go
22 Ultimatum
23 Like much testimony
25 "Casablanca" croupier
26 Tread softly
28 Give way
29 Lively dance
30 Voyager's FTL velocity
36 Strike out
38 "Swan Lake" swan
39 Traveler to Mount Doom
41 Lab cultures
45 Utter a harsh cry
46 Waive
47 Hooded jacket
48 Puppeteer Baird
49 Penicillin source
51 "The Bourne Identity" org.
52 Throw
54 Sully
55 Kind of iron
56 Mariner's friend in "Waterworld"
57 "Rooster Cogburn" star
58 Beatles vamp
59 River of Aragon
61 Home of the Fighting Irish
63 Zenith
66 Man from Moo
68 Old hand
69 Drawn
70 Black suit
73 Musketeer of fiction
78 On the line
80 Martini adornment
82 Dorm cohort
83 Impassive
84 Hollywood's Raines
85 Bug
86 Links coup
87 Some browsers

DOWN

1 Not in condition
2 "This could be bad!"
3 Whirring sound
4 Handful
5 Hoofer's move
6 Not participate, with "out"
7 Quarries
8 From the top
9 Ciphers
10 Morph
11 Ad ___
12 Hyde, to Jekyll
13 Muck
14 "Seven" or "10"
15 Peachy
20 Blunder
24 Swiss watch name
27 "Robinson Crusoe" author
30 Rock
31 Brody in "The Pianist"
32 Venetian bridge
33 Layer
34 Corrections list
35 Summer doldrums
37 Set down
40 Piece with pips
42 Roofed passageway
43 Wrinkled morsel
44 Glided along
46 Small ___
47 PC keyboard tag
49 Spill the beans
50 A point ahead
53 Employee scheduling perk
55 Semi section
57 Moth's temptation
58 Abbreviated
60 Rise rapidly
62 Stupor
63 Video game pioneer
64 "Cry, the Beloved Country" author
65 Guilder replacements
67 Throb
71 Gamma preceder
72 Skyline obscurer
74 Thunderstruck
75 Eight furlongs
76 Vacation spot
77 Sheriff's badge
79 Oft-bracketed word
81 Shale extract

95 BOOB TUBE by Lisa Damiano

The title is appropriate for the quip below.

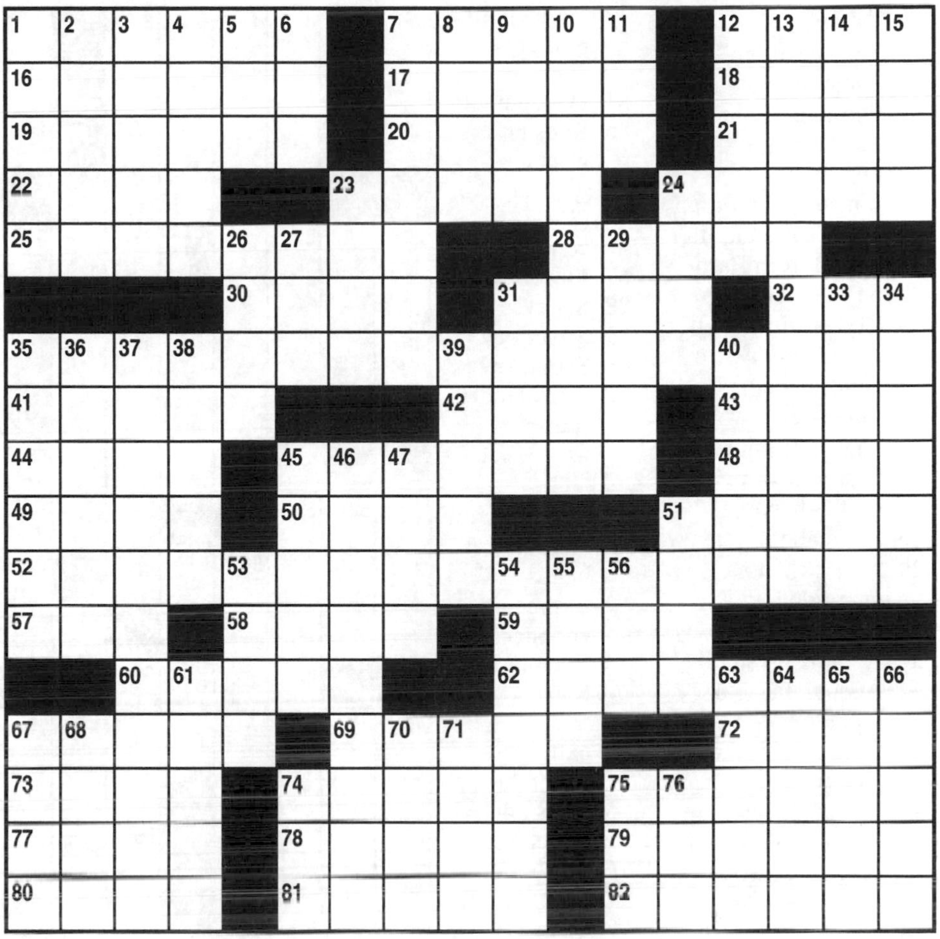

ACROSS

1 Andy Warhol's genre
7 Gogol's "___ Bulba"
12 Afrikaner
16 Put topsoil on
17 As a friend, to Michele
18 Women's magazine
19 One-cellers
20 Spring sound
21 Bank guarantor: Abbr.
22 ___ facto
23 "Biography" network
24 "The Prince of ___" (1991)
25 **Start of a quip**
28 Darkness prefix
30 TV horse
31 Subatomic particle
32 Members of AMA
35 **Part 2 of quip**
41 "Don Carlos" princess
42 Prefix meaning 100
43 "River has ___; Mississippi has four"
44 "Hallelujah, I'm ___" (folk song)
45 **Part 3 of quip**
48 Resolution
49 The scarlet letter
50 Cockney's distinction
51 Start of a Neapolitan song
52 **Part 4 of quip**
57 Cookbook abbr.
58 Chevy pickup
59 No, in Hilo
60 Relief giver
62 **End of quip**
67 Mandalay Bay VIP
69 Bootlicker
72 Eternally
73 Devon in "2 Fast 2 Furious"
74 "Divina Commedia" author
75 Get rid of potholes
77 Slow migration
78 Pass in the Sinai
79 Amatory
80 Container weight
81 Blacksmith's block
82 Purpose

DOWN

1 Braid
2 What Marilyn Monroe had
3 Bel ___ cheese
4 New Jersey's Perth or South
5 Blakey of CNN
6 Dolphin stats
7 Diva Renata
8 At another time
9 Police action
10 Jason Bourne et al.
11 Composer Romberg
12 Be appropriate to
13 Virginia's nickname
14 Nobelist Wiesel
15 45s and 78s: Abbr.
23 Pub offerings
24 Musical sound
26 CCCII x III
27 Paul's role in "Exodus"
29 French nobleman
31 Michelin tire
33 Mano a mano code
34 Pot winner, e.g.
35 "___ Up" (Queen song)
36 Brooklyn Dodgers field
37 Stereo system component
38 Mischa the violinist
39 Midwest hub
40 Use a divining rod
45 Cabaret
46 Throw a party
47 McCarthy aide Roy
51 City on the Oka
53 Start of North Carolina's motto
54 Short end of the stick
55 Like caviar
56 Whole shebang
61 Two peas in a pod
63 Greyhound station
64 Egg-shaped
65 "Mighty Lak' a Rose" composer
66 Straight up and down
67 Power unit
68 Dance at a bar mitzvah
70 Where "Lost" is found
71 "Volsunga Saga" king
74 Conductor's deg.
75 Potuguese king
76 Shore bird

96 BEDROOM SCENES by Patrick Jordan

. . . and these scenes are all rated G!

ACROSS

1 Pursuer of the Penguin
7 Pop in on
12 ___ regia (gold dissolver)
16 Finish a respiration
17 Fable's moral, often
18 Sound from Barney on "The Simpsons"
19 Crystal-lined stones
20 Arcade coin
21 Wildly popular fad
22 Punta del ___
24 Fairy tale with a bedroom scene (with 40-A)
26 Avila abode
29 "Attack!," to a guard dog
31 "Rumor has it . . ."
32 Appetizing smell
34 Acquaintance of Estragon
37 Comment to the playgoers
40 See 24 Across
42 Puts on the record
43 Linus's constant companion
44 Oman money
46 They used to spin LPs
47 Fairy tale with a bedroom scene (with 72-A)
51 Join a quilting bee
54 Vice squad concern
55 Metrical unit
59 Oft-coiffed dog
62 Fairy tale with a bedroom scene
64 Hawk's home
65 Contentious matter
66 Mall or mine follower
67 Absorb academically
69 0° longitude hrs.
71 Budgetary reductions
72 See 47 Across
76 "Uh-huh"
78 1/6 inch, to a printer
79 Takes in
81 Disreputable
85 Rooster's weapon
86 ___-Lay (35-D company)
87 More frilly
88 Set eyes on
89 Silver or Scout, say
90 Joints under spats

DOWN

1 Request with clasped hands
2 Fireman's chopper
3 Even if, to a bard
4 Was extremely profitable
5 Pints poured in pubs
6 Pest-control targets
7 Tannery vessel
8 Role model
9 "The Interlopers" author
10 "No need to explain the punchline"
11 Virginia, in statehood rank
12 Shoulder-to-shoulder
13 Dug out, as marble
14 Light a fire under
15 Did a spoof of
23 When prime time starts in NYC
25 Be recumbent
26 Fuel injector's predecessor, briefly
27 Seed covering
28 Spritzer ingredient
30 Romantic murmur
33 Hieroglyphic cross
35 Corn-chip brand
36 God whose throne is named Hlidskjalf
38 Four-time NBA MVP
39 Sidewinder's shape
41 They're a-laying in song
42 1985 John Malkovich film
45 Private high school
48 Tawdry toupees
49 "Do the Right Thing" pizzeria
50 Random sampling
51 Hydropathic treatment site
52 Help-wanted ad abbr.
53 Soccer event since 1930
56 Creamy color
57 Burlesque bit
58 Recipe amts.
60 Regimen-related
61 Judah's mother
63 Clumsy fellow
65 Not entirely
68 Navigation hazards
70 Electricity pioneer Nikola
72 Cathedral area
73 Jack Frost's assaults
74 Canal opened in 1825
75 Pre-deal payment
77 Country crooner Jackson
80 Lawn patch
82 Have an affliction
83 Suez terminus?
84 Soph and sr., e.g.

97 WIDE-OPEN SPACES by Frank Longo

An 80-word themeless challenger.

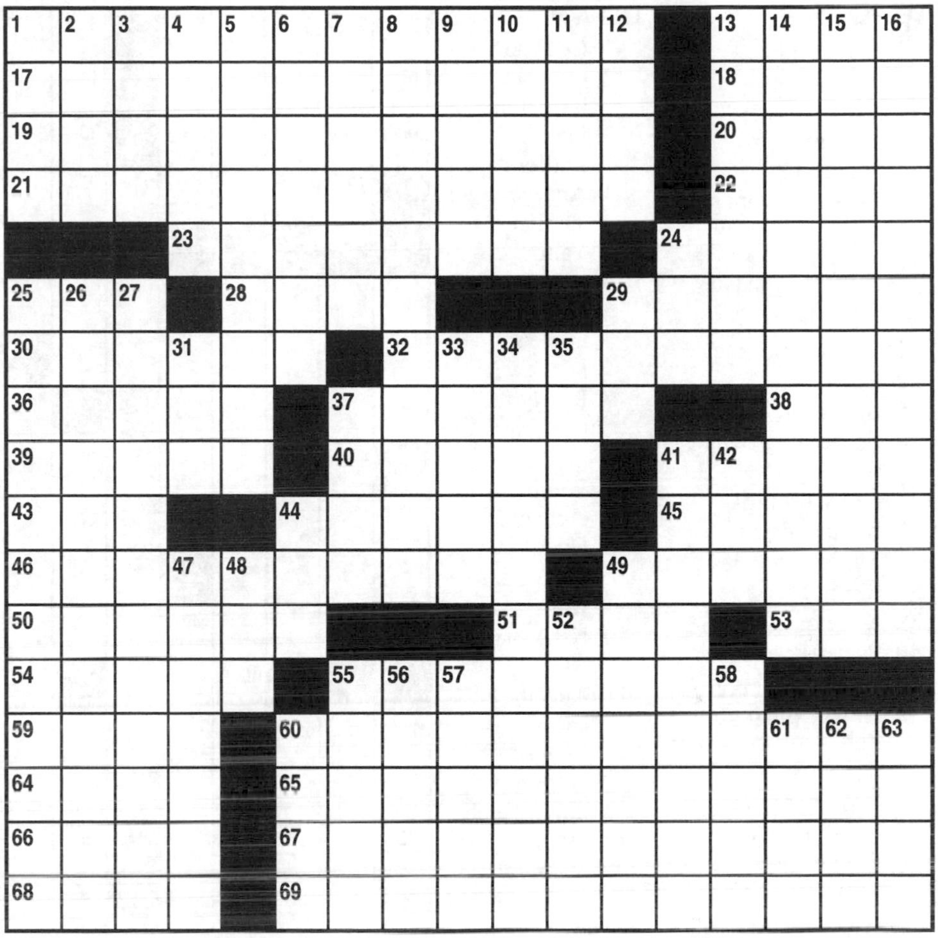

ACROSS

1 A user may burn one
13 Wonka portrayer
17 String quartet instruments
18 Profess
19 Mutual influences
20 Coquettish trick
21 Words of concurrence
22 Je ne ___ quoi
23 Stuff in a pencil
24 Puerto Rico's chief port
25 Garmin's navigation
28 Cole ___ (fashion label)
29 Scribe
30 Mandrake the Magician's sidekick
32 Home to Central Michigan U.
36 Take ___ (go sightseeing)
37 "Bye-bye!"
38 It used to streak in the sky
39 Dept. concerned with cleaning up
40 Tree knots
41 Napoli night
43 Apt to artifice
44 Wait longer than
45 ". . . has ___ and hungry look": Shak.
46 Deejay of top 40 countdowns
49 Cranks up
50 Editorializes
51 Timewalker of Valiant Comics
53 Bishop's bailiwick
54 Car parker
55 "My Big Fat Greek Wedding" star
59 I, O or U, but not A or E: Abbr.
60 Forestry
64 She ranks in Raipur
65 Opposite of patriotic
66 "Behold!," at the Forum
67 Connector of many calls
68 Wedded trio?
69 Warbling women

DOWN

1 Year in Trajan's reign
2 Vietnam's Ngo ___ Diem
3 Ecclesiastical court of appeal in Rome
4 Professeur's charge
5 "Never Surrender" singer
6 Rampaging
7 Maker of Nehi
8 Holdups
9 Put right
10 Old comic actor Eric
11 Company eschewer
12 "Sum" is a form of it
13 TV's "___ Creek"
14 Annual LPGA Tour event in France
15 Land of Opportunity neighbor
16 Some action words are in it
24 Potpie bit
25 Like hotbeds
26 Chief residence of the Dalai Lama until 1959
27 Expressionless, hushed state, as from being stunned
29 Little, in Limoges
31 Chinese emperor ___ Tsung
33 Razz
34 Cytosine, thymine, and uracil
35 Going down the wrong road, perhaps
37 Gull-like bird
41 Needle stone
42 Boff ending
44 Lets go through
47 Bond and No, e.g.
48 In the time left
49 Base greeter?
52 Like some lots and stares
55 ___ verde (Portuguese wine)
56 St. Louis suburb
57 Camper's activity, informally
58 Puts securely away
60 Cheeseheads
61 Spanish indefinite article
62 Few and far between
63 Club with lodges

98 UTTER NONSENSE by Jay Sullivan

Hustlers should know the answer to 43 Across.

ACROSS

1 Sweet thing
6 The end of ___
11 Downs town
16 "Norma" or "Martha"
17 Peace proponents
18 Figure of speech
19 "Beyond the Sea" subject (2004)
20 Nullifies
21 Biblical prophet
22 Yodel?
25 Substitute for
26 Something Sajak sells
27 Not working
32 In custody
37 Typically
38 Ski boost
39 King or queen
40 Rapid Ryan
41 Playground retort
43 Blue-striped pool ball
44 Cuss?
48 Casting choice
49 Small praise
50 Becker of "L.A. Law"
52 Sacred Egyptian bull
54 Welcome sights
55 More voluble
57 Dated
59 Symbol of witchcraft
60 Racer blade
61 Ladies' men
63 "Oops!"?
71 Roulette bet
72 They're related
73 Southfork family
75 One who takes potshots
76 Act badly
77 "It's true"
78 Backboard, familiarly
79 Intuit
80 Join forces

DOWN

1 Coal porter
2 October birthstone
3 Famed fiddler
4 Apt name for a colleen
5 Yahoo honcho
6 Dutch uncle's nephew?
7 Ready for hanging
8 Lloyd Webber title character
9 Over-exposed, in a way
10 NRA or NCAA
11 Anesthetic gas
12 Way of getting things done
13 1998 National League MVP
14 Autobahn auto
15 It's what's for dinner
23 Unable to cut it
24 Dip stick?
27 Dapper fellow
28 Atomic alternative
29 Crusaders' foe
30 Shrinking sea
31 Scam
33 Test group
34 1998 Oscar winner
35 Biblical prophet
36 Home room
38 Sets straight
41 Even so
42 Prayerful figure
45 Think well of
46 Sound of music
47 Mother of the Valkyries
48 Rarer than rare
51 Afore of yore
53 Larry, Curly, and Moe
55 "Time will tell"
56 MIT or VMI
58 Is undecided
59 Forensic evidence
62 Green border
63 Rugged rock
64 Make a stir
65 Colorado town
66 Deli inventory
67 What's cooking
68 Lottery exclamation
69 Taylor of "Six Feet Under"
70 Put in stitches
74 "I'm impressed"

99 RENOWN PHRASE by Patrick Jordan

The original name of 21 Across was Truman Streckfus Persons.

ACROSS

1 Galileo Galilei Airport site
5 Denver boot, for one
10 In force
15 Tweak text
16 Mansion's counterpart
17 At peace
18 Simeon's mother
19 Ancient Athens marketplace
20 "M*A*S*H" procedure
21 **Truman Capote quip: Part 1**
24 They're filled with bills
25 Tango maneuver
26 Canonized mlle.
27 With intervening space
30 "Gets down" at a disco
34 Rorschach or road follower
35 **Quip: Part 2**
40 Alts.
41 Mashes a mosquito
42 Celebrated shortstop Pee Wee
43 English Lit assignments
45 Science of motion forces
48 Hunter on high
49 Snobbish sort
50 Vaudeville legend Eddie
51 **Quip: Part 3**
55 "What ___ you thinking?"
56 Costing a dime
57 Supermarket fleet
58 Hearth particle
61 Store receipt word
62 Quatrain composer
64 **End of quip**
72 Kind of couplet
73 Mountain bike options
74 Skin cream additive
75 Fixes upright
76 Water or rust, chemically
77 Made a present of
78 Office array
79 Parachute fabric
80 Set one's sights on

DOWN

1 Money, in slang
2 Skull session result
3 "The King and I" backdrop
4 In essence
5 Yawning pit
6 Corporate symbols
7 Anthony Eden's earldom
8 European blackbird
9 Modeling material for kids
10 ___ Beach, FL
11 Desert description
12 Reads (through)
13 Foundry bar
14 Plow innovator John
17 Visit briefly
22 Unintelligible Addams
23 1958's Best Picture
27 For each
28 Czar known as "the Great"
29 Tear into
30 "All ___ are off!" ("No guarantees!")
31 Game extensions, briefly
32 Long-necked frog eater
33 "Ignore the dele"
35 Fall heir to
36 Imitate a shrew
37 Dairy youngster
38 Chaperone, e.g.
39 Enthusiastic agreement
41 As of
44 Simpleton
45 Sailing speed unit
46 Short notice?
47 Fish-fowl connector
49 "Together" prefix
52 Monkeyshines
53 Decode a bar code
54 Shape in a honeycomb
55 Light bulb number
57 Animation studio sheet
58 Throbbed
59 ___ Khan (Kipling tiger)
60 Start of Ed's late-night intro
62 Veteran TV announcer Don
63 Gridiron retiree Merlin
65 Prepare to fire
66 Hobbyists' buys
67 Cheesecake adjective?
68 Pony Express delivery
69 Oil of ___
70 Crafted burlap
71 Cry out for

100 TURNING POINTS by Elizabeth C. Gorski

The embedded title can be found at 43 Across.

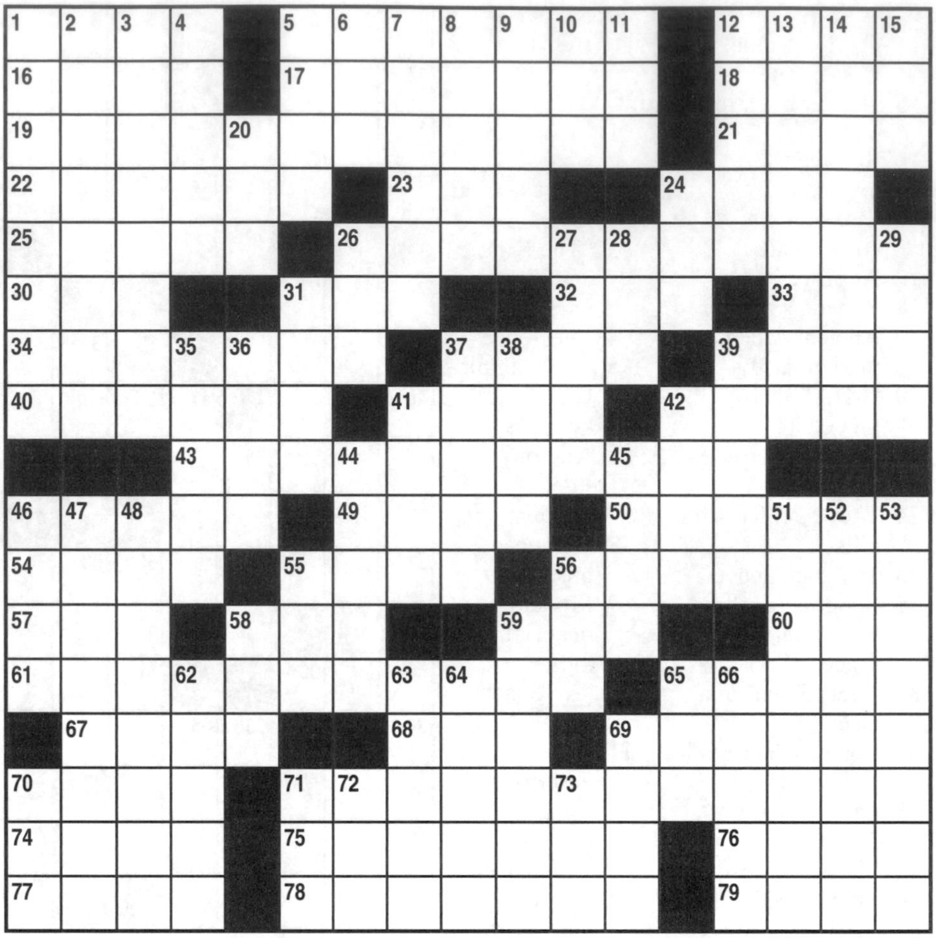

ACROSS

1 Neat as ___
5 Athlete who's very goal-oriented?
12 Cut from the same cloth
16 An ex of Burt
17 Fleece producers
18 Marco's "well"
19 Patient wear*
21 QED middle
22 Hitching posts?
23 Hemingway's "In ___ Time"
24 They're developed by Mr. Universe
25 Future docs' exams
26 1960s pop song by the Winstons*
30 Veggie burger's base
31 Agcy. once led by Leon Panetta
32 CPR experts
33 Queen of Thebes, in mythology
34 Pull back
37 Ltr. holders
39 "___ Rebel": Crystals
40 Per se
41 Surveyor's measure
42 Thin cookie
43 TITLE
46 "Rush, Rush" singer
49 Reverse
50 "Law & Order" actor Farina
54 Places with going rates?
55 Foil's cousin
56 Bridge expert
57 Compass user's suffix
58 Comedienne Charlotte
59 Dart game locale
60 Stanley, for one
61 Bit of nasty gossip*
65 Caterpillar's rival
67 Assn. of lodges
68 Singer DiFranco
69 "Brady Bunch," e.g.
70 Claude of champagne fame
71 One-time ABC police drama*
74 ". . . ___ take this charm from off her sight": Shak.
75 Got by
76 Barbra's "Funny Girl" costar
77 Stop dreaming?
78 Legendary king of Athens
79 Eye piece

DOWN

1 Granada landmark
2 Sticks in a game room
3 Split seconds
4 Try to bite, as one's heels
5 Yoga class needs
6 Dock workers' gp.
7 Composure
8 Home of Queen Beatrix (with "The")
9 Tough nut to crack
10 Gaping mouth
11 ISP choice
12 Red as ___ (embarrassed)
13 Babushka
14 Sort of
15 Common URL ending
20 Agcy. with many agents
24 Opp. of negative
26 Small quantity?
27 Original ELO member
28 Hosp. units
29 Loud laugh
31 Koko Head island
35 "Tell Me Something Good" band
36 Earth Hour subj.
37 Slowly destroy
38 Grammy winner Peter
39 Blue Rodeo's "___ Hit Me Yet"
41 Prom-night nightmare?
42 House bird
44 Indian coin
45 River of Germany
46 Guinness of "Star Wars"
47 Island of French Polynesia
48 Warning on a Christmas present
51 Happy hour?
52 "You bet!"
53 Vatican City basilica
55 Shucker's spike
56 Pierre, S. ___
58 It may be toast
59 Way out of Manhattan
62 Funny Fields
63 The Pine Tree State
64 Karenina and namesakes
65 Tony winner McAnuff
66 Praise
69 Foam
70 Small gull
71 NYC subway line
72 "Well, ___-di-dah"
73 ___ d'esprit (witty comment)

101 "HUMOR ME!" by Robert A. Doll

22 Across has a champagne, cigar, and tank named after him.

ACROSS

1 Hardens
7 Any day now
11 Comment to the audience
16 Be a buttinsky
17 Miler's concern
18 Puts on cargo
19 Melodious
20 Emulate Chagall
21 "Three Billy Goats Gruff" baddie
22 Speaker of quote
25 ___ Anne de Beaupré
26 Purple shade
27 Parts of a min.
31 Ethnic cuisine
34 Nextel Cup org.
39 Quote: Part 1
43 Like Silver's rider
44 In ___ res
45 Flat-topped rise
46 Predispositions
47 Bleep out
49 More than twice
51 Time on the job
52 Move like molasses
56 Beaver State city
58 Blue-ribbon
59 Quote: Part 2
61 Kind of union
63 Long, long time
64 Just for men
65 Slammer unit
67 Literary monogram
70 Win at "Last Comic Standing"?
79 Antilles native
80 "Triple" ice jump
81 Snarl
82 Endangered perissodactyl
83 Untouched?
84 Branch of the deer family?
85 Forefinger
86 See 2 Down
87 Pine products

DOWN

1 "Heartbreak House" playwright
2 "Real Men" singer (with 86-A)
3 "___ go bragh!"
4 1961 space chimp
5 Leans, at sea
6 High-hatter
7 Design detail
8 Four-letter word
9 Takes up space
10 Jawaharlal
11 Tennis great Gibson
12 Madras dress
13 Hollywood favorite
14 Apple rival
15 Immigrant's class: Abbr.
23 New Jersey cagers
24 Manhattan sch.
27 Drucker of "Green Acres"
28 Jet seat
29 Tylenol #3 ingredient
30 Fair-___ beauty
32 Limelight lover
33 Forum greeting
35 Horse-drawn vehicles
36 Amour-propre
37 Rabbit ears
38 Court matter
40 "Big" Syracuse conference
41 Equal: Comb. form
42 Dirty dog
46 Fabergé cologne
48 Beluga yield
50 "For ___ a jolly . . ."
51 Cul-de-___
53 Graduate school challenge
54 Sharp turn
55 Help-wanted abbr.
57 Curate's
59 Editor's mark
60 Brings into play
62 Early refrigerator
66 Himalayan capital
68 Rose oil
69 Spruce Goose, e.g.
70 Chemistry Nobelist Otto
71 Like the Kalahari
72 Tarzan's transport
73 Late-night name
74 Pub potables
75 Pangolin's meal
76 Wrinkly fruit
77 Secluded valley
78 Half a matched set
79 Dernier ___ (the latest thing)

102 DROPPING ACID by Richard Silvestri

Listen to "Lucy in the Sky With Diamonds" while solving this one.

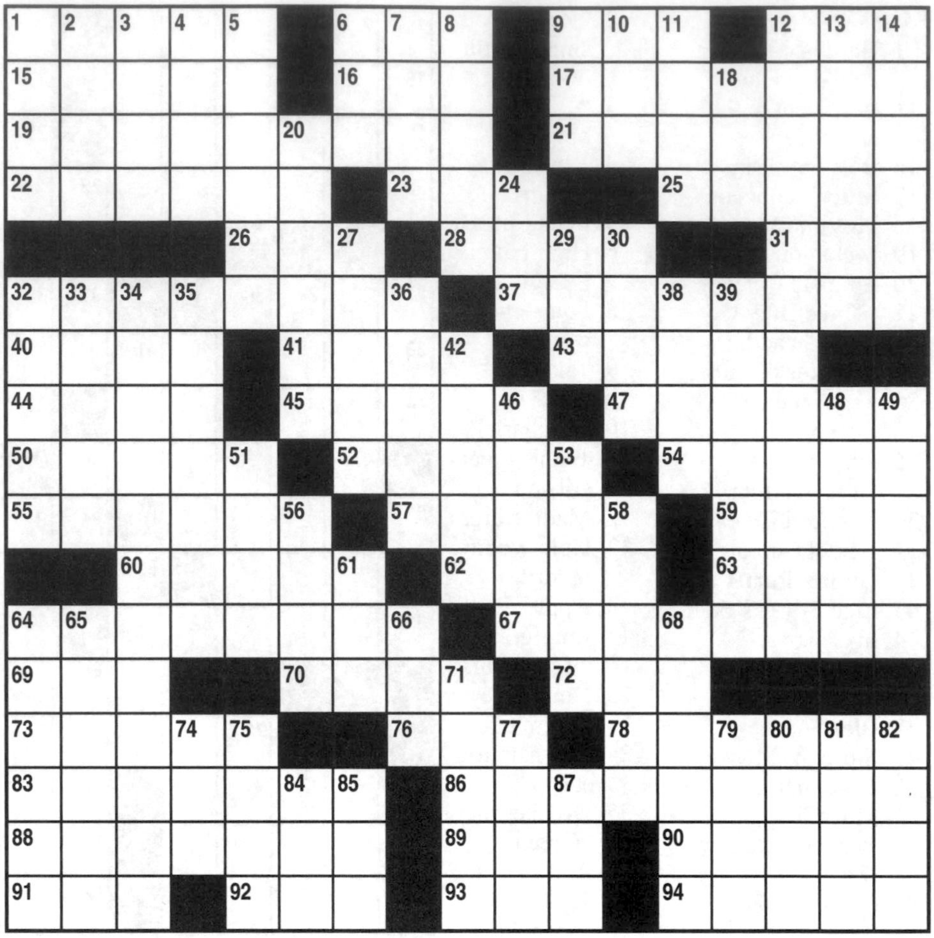

ACROSS

1 Tracking device
6 Do Little work
9 Red-white-and-blue monogram
12 "___ Didn't Care"
15 In solitary
16 Snitch
17 Cuban capitalist?
19 Close observation of commotion?
21 Moved like a dragonfly
22 Musically jarring
23 Asian holiday
25 Big name in farm equipment
26 Offshore structure
28 Abadan coin
31 Speak with forked tongue
32 Traffic snarler
37 Like the surface of the moon
40 Shark's offer
41 Mrs. Helmer
43 Candidate's concern
44 Troubles
45 Sweater size
47 Established as fact
50 Tour de France vehicles
52 Glyceride
54 On ___ (carousing)
55 Genetic
57 Port in a storm
59 "Bus Stop" playwright
60 Muscat inhabitant
62 Heat, e.g.
63 Begins litigation
64 Couric's workplace
67 Some chickens
69 Every last bit
70 Social rebuff
72 AEC successor
73 Good, in Guatemala
76 Prospector's aid
78 Rope for a trail boss
83 Kook
86 Infantile Dickens novel?
88 Crew competition
89 Blow away
90 Grace
91 Compass dir.
92 Radical '60s gp.
93 The acid dropped in this puzzle
94 Bartok and Fleck

DOWN

1 ___-tat-tat
2 Piles
3 Didus ineptus
4 Ere long
5 Word on a wanted poster
6 It may be abstract
7 War ender
8 Old number?
9 TV band
10 Mule of song
11 Gung-ho
12 Chip money?
13 "The ___ Queene": Spenser
14 By all means
18 Had a bite
20 UFO crew
24 Initial X, perhaps
27 Folklore dwarf
29 Uris hero
30 Aladdin's discovery
32 Legal out
33 General Powell
34 Result of a Berkeley degree?
35 Trouser junctures
36 Compactor input
38 The O'Hara place
39 Vanity case?
42 Sacrifice spot
46 Burton of "Star Trek: TNG"
48 Champing at the bit
49 Go formal
51 Top player
53 Scouting work
56 Sonny Shroyer role
58 Not quite
61 Chemists get a charge out of it
64 Pyle player
65 Gives the slip to
66 The word, at times
68 Deified beetle
71 Elephant of kiddie lit
74 Tony Parker's org.
75 Feedbag filler
77 Lowly member of the board?
79 Insulting
80 Fan's favorite
81 Taj Mahal site
82 Till section
84 Old Ford model
85 Vegas opening
87 Emmy winner Arthur

103 NINE-PIN REALITY by Victor Fleming

"The Peter Principle" author on everyday existence.

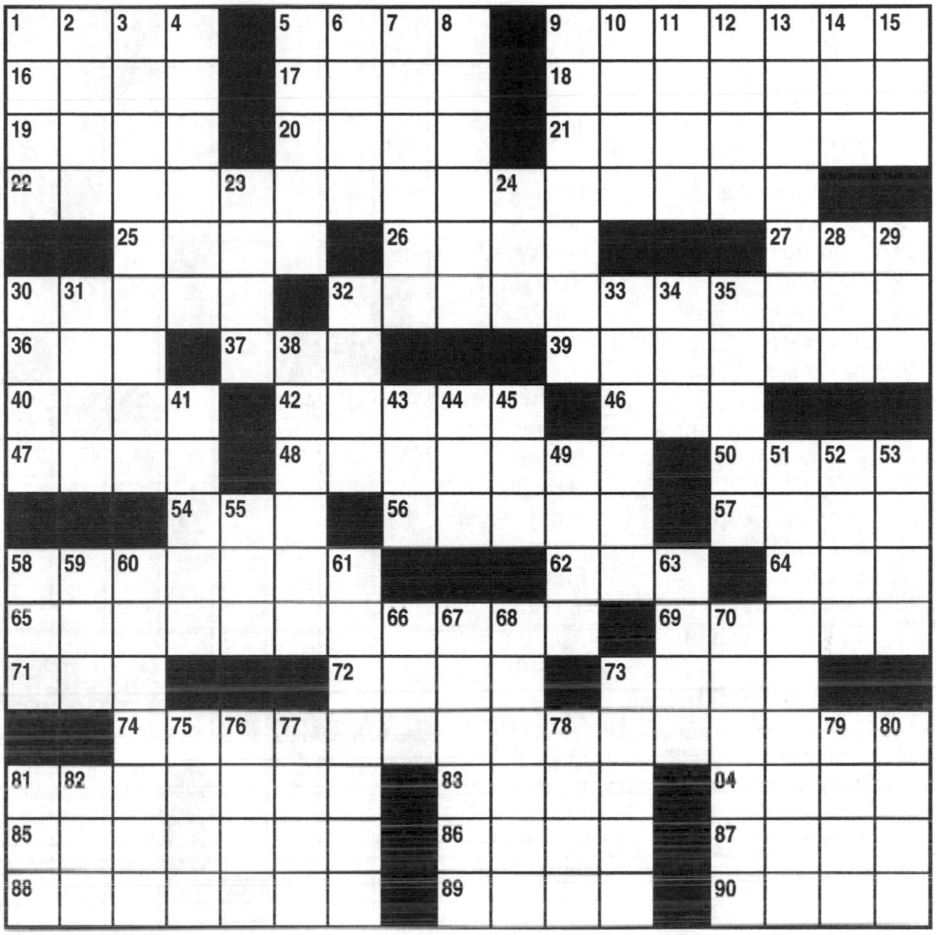

ACROSS

1 Key letter
5 Mr. Woodley of "Blondie"
9 Allan Sherman camp
16 Came to rest
17 Skin-care brand
18 Put in a crate
19 NFL Hall-of-Famer Ronnie
20 "The Plot Against America" author
21 Ariel, for one
22 **Laurence Peter quotation: Part I**
25 Some time ago
26 Not with
27 Shoshonean
30 African cape name
32 **Quotation: Part II**
36 Boss's Day mo.
37 Slow start
39 "Apostolados" artist
40 Tikrit's land
42 Sevilla now
46 Get prone
47 1984 Peace Nobelist
48 **Quotation: Part III**
50 Fill to the gills
54 When Dijon gets hot
56 Bergen-born, say
57 Bygone pol. units
58 Firm
62 Sushi bar order
64 Fields persona
65 **Quotation: Part IV**
69 Like some pain
71 Prefix for center
72 Presently
73 Operation memento
74 **Quotation: Part V**
81 Sidelong pass
83 1962 Ursula Andress film
84 Winter forecast
85 Piram or Eschol
86 Toaster brand
87 Result of overexercise
88 Badenov and Godunov
89 Godunov's no
90 Marsh growth

DOWN

1 Bouncer?
2 Morlocks' victims
3 Payment in kind
4 Come to
5 Flicka or Silver
6 North Carolina university
7 Wicker material
8 Manually
9 Resembling an emerald, say
10 Sen. Chuck Hagel follower?
11 Plot element?
12 Specify
13 Generally
14 "Agnus ___"
15 Subjoin
23 Frozen beverage brand
24 Capt.'s underlings
28 Private eye
29 That, to Juan
30 Sports equipment manufacturer
31 Stockings shade
32 #1 tennis player of 1975
33 "Let me think about it"
34 ___ Friday's
35 Head lock
38 Mariners' ___ Field
41 Leeds line
43 Have control of
44 Kanga's kid
45 Land south of the Medit.
49 Like many eBay items
51 Word
52 Home-run gait
53 Town in the Euganean Hills
55 Rubble-maker
58 Filly, but not a billy
59 Something to draw from
60 Earhart, e.g.
61 Gives 100%
63 Delicate, as fabric
66 Barracks bed
67 Caulfield of fiction
68 Oomph
70 Rubicon crosser
73 Schnozz
75 Pak of the LPGA
76 Kristofferson in "Millennium"
77 "I can't believe ___ the whole . . ."
78 Pulitzer playwright
79 Architect Mies van der ___
80 Scand. tongue
81 Area of experimentation
82 Te-___ cigars

104 ADAPTION SEQUEL by Bonnie L. Gentry
"Hooray for Hollywood!"

ACROSS

1 Assigned jobs
6 Flockhart role
12 Pullman, for one
15 Slippery as ___
16 Unsound
17 Dance for a luau
18 **Part I of a quip**
20 Opposite of nope
21 Intend on
22 Scholarship allowance
24 "___ make a long story short . . ."
25 Castle's protection
27 Tests without pencils
31 **Part II of quip**
36 Dark times, in literature
37 What children shouldn't touch in the kitchen
38 Sex researcher Hite
41 Frere's sister
43 She played Carmela
44 Dallas hoopster
45 **Part III of quip**
49 Monument's age: Abbr.
50 Captain in "Moby Dick"
52 Cézanne contemporary
53 Does a laundry chore
55 Extremists
57 Roseanne's first last name
59 **Part IV of quip**
64 Ranee's wrap
65 "Othello" heavy
66 Small business course?
68 Music shop fixtures
72 Cognitive
74 Do some tub-thumping
77 **Part V of quip**
79 Thumbs-up voters
80 Ecological systems
81 Tastiness
82 More than miffed
83 Bull Run general Jeb
84 Fake handle

DOWN

1 Forces down
2 Having hands, clockwise
3 Ratifying body
4 One with an address
5 Shutter part
6 Degree from Parsons, perhaps
7 Implying an origin
8 Fit up against
9 Appropriate for kids K–12
10 Mounted on
11 U-shaped musical instrument
12 Signal to enter
13 Menu attribution words
14 Pep rally word
17 Moisturize
19 "Time and tide wait for ___"
23 Negative links
26 Photo ___ (PR occasions)
28 Like one end of a battery terminal
29 Assessed, as a tax
30 Dieter's bane
32 Caught sight of
33 Thomas Crown caper
34 Deck suit complement
35 Other, in Oaxaca
38 "Street" intelligence
39 "Oh, yeah, that's funny"
40 Escapee, at times
41 Hearing or sight, e.g.
42 Tijuana yell
46 He played Yuri in "Doctor Zhivago"
47 Lowland, poetically
48 Factory owners: Abbr.
51 Cuts evenly
54 Monopoly avenue
56 Kept in the loop, briefly
57 Seek financial aid?
58 Subject for a wine connoisseur
60 Jack's Soviet counterpart
61 Poughkeepsie college
62 Army creatures?
63 Gauguin's Tahitian autobiography
67 Cards and Bucs
69 Does a bank job
70 Pitch ___ (react angrily)
71 ___ En-lai
73 She, in Venice
74 33 or 45, e.g.
75 Parseghian of Notre Dame
76 Shoemate of Wynken and Blynken
78 "Saving Private Ryan" craft, for short

105 BY ANY OTHER NAME by Billie Truitt

Would they sound as sweet?

ACROSS

1 Harry Potter's rival
6 Dance studio support
11 Stage name of Tracy Marrow
15 Lindsay Lohan hit
17 Natural soothers
18 It was lost for want of a nail
19 Australian penguin
20 Number for nine?
21 Judge's seat
22 Christina Claire Ciminella
24 Snack from a kosher deli
25 Barrel rider's venue
26 German article
28 Indy 500 entrant
31 Reginald Dwight
36 "Cuchi-Cuchi" girl
37 Spec attachment
39 Shortly
40 Deadly viper
41 Nellie for whom a toast was named
43 Appear to be
44 Declan Patrick McManus
48 Board haphazardly
50 Weaker alternative to a pen?
51 Some upperclassmen: Abbr.
54 Tiny points of land
55 "See ___ care"
56 Gordon Sumner
58 Yvette Marie Stevens
61 Watches closely
63 City on the Rhone
64 "Love & Pride" singer Davis
65 Reference book
69 Geraldine Halliwell
74 Agitate
75 Hindu principle
76 Highest
77 Big fusses
78 Actress-director Keaton
79 Boxer's sequence
80 Paul Hewson
81 Apollo's birthplace
82 Yucky

DOWN

1 Attract
2 Giuliani of politics
3 "You got that right!"
4 Hair stylist, at times
5 Venezuelan river
6 Bluegrass instrument
7 MLB family name
8 14-line verse
9 Alter again
10 Fig. from a mechanic
11 Novel ID
12 Milky spiced tea
13 Ages and ages
14 One kind of support
16 ___ message
23 Mountaintop homes
24 Doghouse
27 ___ about (gossiped)
28 Color TV pioneer
29 Sighs of relief
30 Alpha star in Auriga
31 Intrude
32 Hebrew heroine who dispatched Sisera
33 Assimilation process
34 Rams and bulls, e.g.
35 53-D, for one
38 Group of Oct. ballgames
41 "The Turing Option" coauthor
42 Dating from
45 Symbol of Wales
46 Essential organs
47 Three-bagger
48 Photo, for short
49 "Sort of" suffix
52 Single-helix molecule
53 Cpl.'s superior
56 Picking up
57 Frontier trading post figure
59 Immobilize
60 "The Muppet Show" drummer
62 ___ the ground
64 "The Eve of St. ___": Keats
65 Yemeni or Saudi
66 Heading on an errand list
67 Pride member
68 In addition
70 Tiny prefix
71 "Leave ___ Beaver"
72 Milk dispensers
73 Heroic verse
75 Build on

106 FUNNY MEN by Ray Hamel

68 Across is the only month that can start and end on the same day.

ACROSS

1 Serves perfectly
5 Puffed-up dessert
12 Cowgirl's footwear
16 Tennis score
17 Dress
18 Problem to face?
19 Form of therapy
21 Visible
22 Like Wikipedia
23 Crossword sign
24 Voice above a tenor
25 Contractor's fig.
26 Everly Brothers hit
30 Tailor's line
32 Ship to Colchis
33 Chemist Hahn, et al.
34 Computer insert
40 Pep rally intangible
41 Not at home
42 Gremlins and Pacers
46 Like some angels
49 Runoff source
51 K–4
52 Thom in shoes
54 "But will it play in ___?"
55 May Day disaster of 1886
58 Hurriedly
62 Word after paper or razor
63 "The Wasteland" monogram
64 Showing concern
68 Short mo.
70 Richie Rich's collar
71 Court grp.
72 Live wire, so to speak
75 Make ___ (get along)
76 "Sisters" star
80 Hold, as an opinion
81 Pop singer Gloria
82 They're found under layers
83 Sleuthing canine
84 Space shuttle manuever
85 Kind of job

DOWN

1 Pet food brand
2 Ethanol source
3 Russia, to Reagan
4 Round following the quarters
5 Inventory-reduction effort
6 Special ___
7 Lines at the checkout scanner?
8 Quite a ways
9 Just caught
10 Denis of "Rescue Me"
11 "___ World" ("Sesame Street" segment)
12 Extrusive volcanic rock
13 Spotted cat
14 Ring combination
15 Joins, as with a mortise
20 Ergate
26 ___ de coeur
27 Back then
28 Secret society
29 Atlantic food fish
30 "The Glass Bead Game" author Hermann
31 Drive out by force
32 Breathing woe
35 Composer Khachaturian
36 Flask hit
37 Base VIP's
38 Dancer Miller
39 Get back into business
42 Pablo's passion
43 Scout's honor
44 Madison Avenue awards
45 Announce
47 In need of salt
48 Rotating disk
50 Saturate
53 Partnership for Peace org.
55 Coop resident
56 Letter that follows pi
57 Caboodle's partner
58 Underlying plan
59 Has compassion for
60 Cousin of the snipe
61 Field of stars?
65 Nintendo enthusiast
66 Belittle
67 1877 Twain collaborator
68 "Read this"
69 Ceased to be
72 Fashionable initials
73 RAM units
74 Ural River city
77 DDE's rank
78 More than now and then
79 Bluejacket

107 POTPOURRI by Barry C. Silk

47 Across was also known as Connie Mack Stadium for many years.

ACROSS

1 ___-faire
8 How many walk along the beach
16 Sweated
18 Amendment construing judicial powers
19 Eggs are a rich source for it
20 Skipper's opposite
21 Jennifer Lopez film
22 Noted exile
23 Chicago sights
24 Massage
25 Charlemagne's domain: Abbr.
26 First year of Cornelius' papacy
27 Photographer's diaphragm
30 Catch, run, and throw
32 Mackerel sharks
33 Ailurophobe's dread
34 Multichannel system
36 Madison's st.
37 Costco alternative
38 Is in the past?
39 Constantinople's empire
43 Concern
46 Fused together
47 Phillies' old home
49 Ringside shout
50 Apple core?
51 "Welcome" sights
52 Erupt
54 Varnish base
55 Draft picks
57 Einstein Bros. product
58 1958 World Cup phenom
59 Trying people: Abbr.
60 Partner of games
61 Breezily informative
64 Eastern principle
65 Org. searching for signals from space
66 More aloof
70 San Francisco Bay lighthouse
72 Feeding tubes
73 Gone with the wind
74 Tyrannical
75 Skeptical type
76 Reserve

DOWN

1 Soap containing pumice
2 Opposed to, in oaters
3 Trace amount
4 Bites
5 "American Idol" judge Cowell
6 Site reading?
7 Zoroastrian scriptures
8 "Wouldn't It Be Nice" group
9 Sacrificial settings
10 Tighten, maybe
11 Square
12 Waterlogged lowland
13 Where a weighted bat is swung
14 1887 La Scala premiere
15 Master piece?
17 Less stimulating
26 Beehive division
27 SALT subjects
28 Indian chief
29 1959 hit for Paul Anka
31 Definitely no Yankee fan
32 Had a problem with
34 Pinata filling
35 Diamond covers
36 When repeated, a Western city
40 Some are "telephoto"
41 Katmandu locale
42 Bring out
44 They give people lifts
45 Day planner, e.g.
48 It keeps your powder dry
53 Got tight
55 Historic 1942 surrender site
56 Catchall abbr.
57 Zippo fuel
58 Dragon killed by Apollo at Delphi
60 Washington State conveyance
62 Rushing sound: Var.
63 Mawkish
65 Greek portico
67 "Must have been something ___"
68 Protection
69 Flair and Ocasek
71 Exercise target

108 FLIPPING THE THREE-TOED SLOTH by Victor Fleming

This one wins the most original title award!

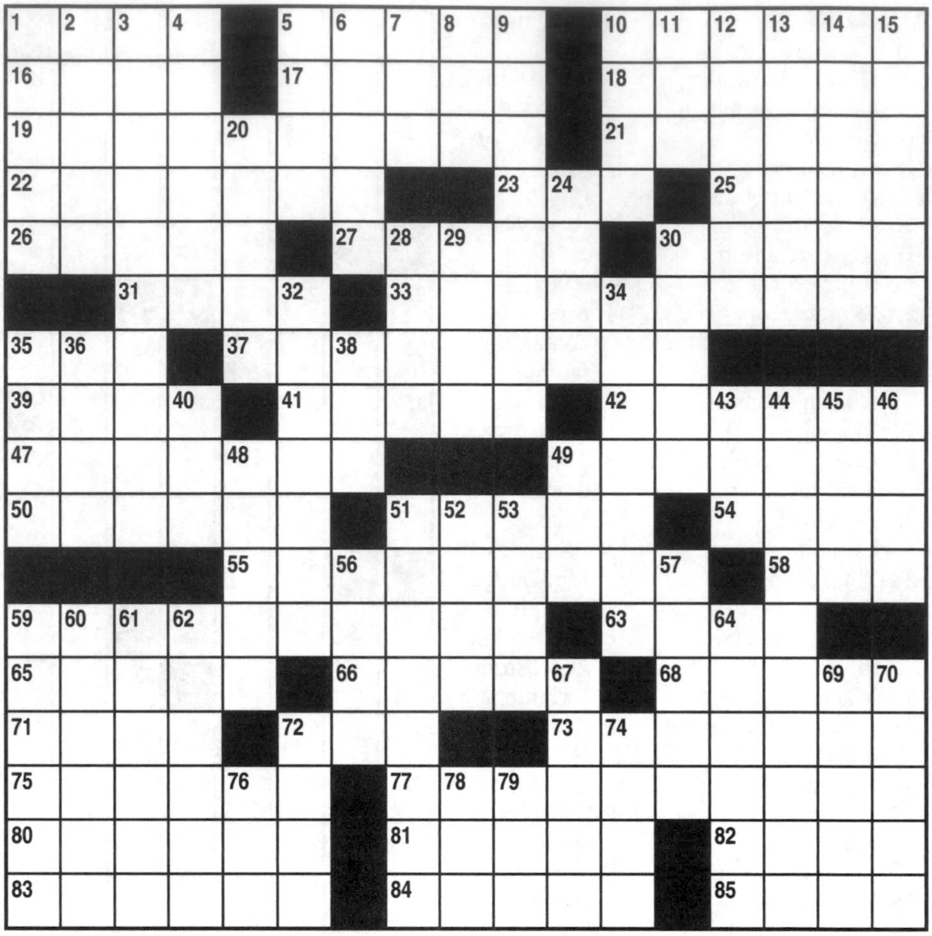

ACROSS

1 Clerical apparel
5 Sunbow producers
10 Monopoly maker
16 Tipper, for one
17 "Go ahead with your question"
18 Toyota model
19 Hansen, if married to Frankie?
21 Taste
22 Red Sea Republic
23 Country rtes.
25 They may be black or red
26 Drift
27 Après-ski drink
30 Civic club president, often
31 Rare blood type
33 Corrupt pitcher Luis?
35 Battle of ___ (1st Allied victory of WW1)
37 Helen Reddy hit
39 Queen Noor's predecessor
41 Roger Rabbit and Porky Pig
42 "Okay by me"
47 Wall images
49 Quiet
50 Filmdom's Nastassja
51 Hopping arcade character
54 Stop following?
55 Credit card charge
58 Myrna in "The Thin Man"
59 Journal of milking activity?
63 Butts
65 Feminine ends
66 Shampoo directive
68 Ankles
71 Paving block
72 Ricky, to Harriet
73 Primes
75 Clarifier's words
77 Pathway used as a test?
80 Word after yes or no
81 Keep an ___ the ground
82 Chase of "Now, Voyager"
83 Two-seater
84 Patrol mission
85 RAF awards

DOWN

1 Shoelace end
2 Noted wine valley
3 Bonk De Palma on the head?
4 Relayed
5 Guy
6 Father of famous twins
7 Go downhill fast?
8 Badge material
9 Baseball no-nos
10 Accidents
11 Marchetta in "Material Girls"
12 A hero may have it
13 "Una Paloma ___" (1975 hit song)
14 Bad
15 Quick round of tennis
20 Went astray
24 Andrews or Carvey
28 One of the Ringling brothers
29 "Misery" star
30 Old lab heaters
32 Hear about (with "of")
34 Classic party game
35 Wine holder
36 For grades 1 to 12
38 Cuban article
40 Rag's source of income
43 Fat mouse in "Cinderella"
44 Persian train fares?
45 Kellogg's waffle
46 Kids' rhyme starter
48 Signs off on
49 Boxer's sound
51 More old-fashioned
52 Stock holder
53 Tarzan portrayer's family
56 Robert de ___
57 Trouble constantly
59 Stop
60 Swamp fever symptom
61 Trainee or detainee
62 Impede
64 Birthplace of Penélope Cruz
67 Sister of Terpsichore
69 Watch word
70 Mallorca y Tenerife
72 Blossom support
74 Tar Heel State campus
76 Mamie Eisenhower, ___ Doud
78 "Diff'rent Strokes" actress
79 U.S. tax law book

109 EXTINCT ANIMALS by Robert A. Doll

The extinct insect at 79-A has been spotted recently in 2007 and 2008.

ACROSS

1 GI garb, for short
5 Blood-typing letters
8 ___ Blue (Danish cheese)
12 Painter Lippo Lippi
15 Oversight
17 2003 Johnny Cash hit
18 "The One I Love" group
19 Extinct cat?
21 Wood sorrel
22 Pigtail, e.g.
23 Pants part
24 Doofus
26 Take a powder
28 Extinct horse?
30 Health
35 Hidden cost, at times
36 Lachrymosity result
37 Length × width = ___
38 Pooh-poohs
40 Divine
41 Crossworder's crutch: Abbr.
42 Not very friendly
43 Princess tormentor
45 Extinct antelope?
51 Paranormal ability
52 Rock of Cashel locale
53 Harvard's Pennypacker Hall, e.g.
55 Mill fodder
59 Dell dude?
61 Creative spark
62 City near Sparks
63 Clean bass
64 Anxiety
66 Extinct fish?
69 Guinness suffix
70 Ravel classic
71 Babe in the woods
74 Minimum
78 "Don't tase me, ___!"
79 Extinct insect?
82 Total jerk
83 Palio course
84 Transfuses
85 "Holy cow!"
86 Artist Magritte
87 Emulate Bode Miller
88 Patty ___

DOWN

1 Search thoroughly
2 From the U.S.
3 Red giant in Cetus
4 Be undecided
5 Go public with
6 "Where the ___ Are" (1960)
7 Grimm beginning
8 Secluded
9 Doggie Daddy's son, familiarly
10 Starbucks option
11 Hoisted, nautically
12 Expressed displeasure
13 Pianist's time to shine
14 Passionate
16 Red Sea republic
20 Stumblebum
25 Former Yugoslav leader
27 Letter abbr.
29 Breathed
30 Roll of bills
31 Mystery writer Ambler
32 Poland's Walesa
33 Ice-cream portion
34 Music genre
39 Less restricted
40 Cumberland ___
44 Come forth
46 Chihuahua checker
47 Part of Einstein's theory
48 For the time being
49 Rich supply
50 Aphrodite's lover
54 Bell and Barker
55 Assortment
56 Moral anguish
57 Nearby
58 Just a little
60 All excited
63 "How Stella Got Her ___ Back" (1998)
65 Speck in the ocean
67 Great passion
68 Dundee denial
72 Cow-headed goddess
73 Depression
75 Au fait
76 Put on eBay
77 Put your big toe in the water
80 One of Alcott's "Little Men"
81 Chi follower

110 PATCHWORK QUILT by Brad Wilber

1 Down was first seen as host of the Food Network's "$40 a Day."

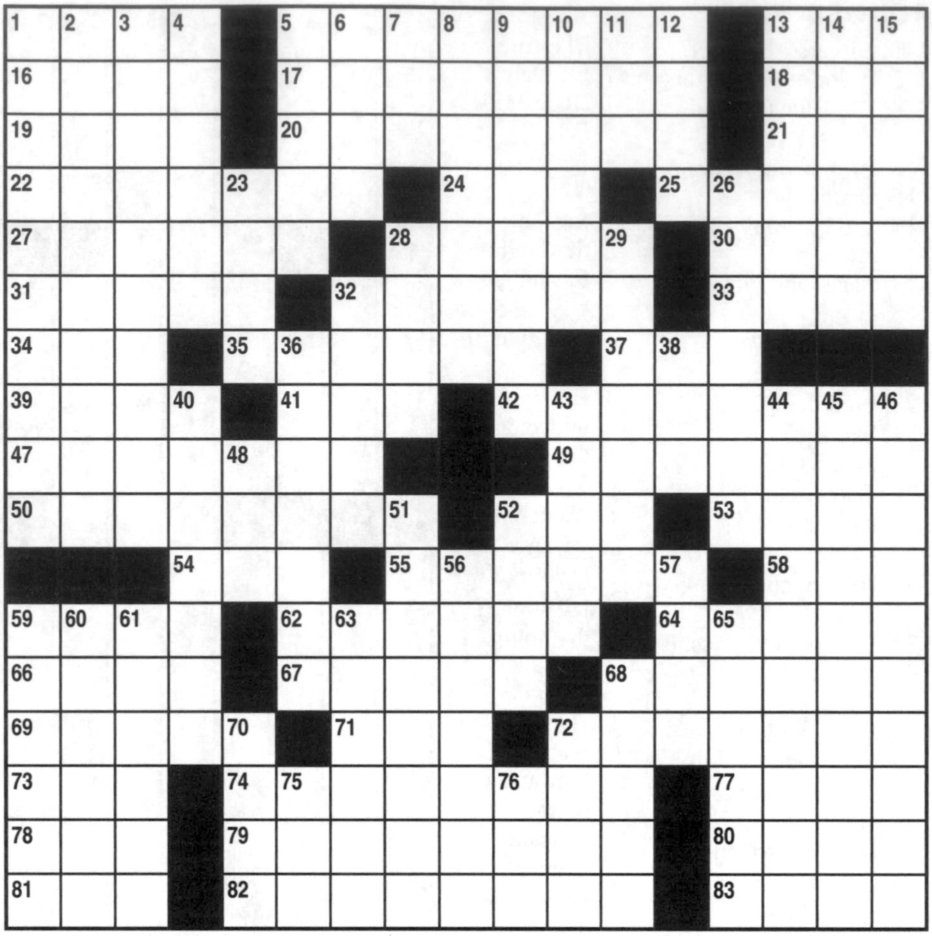

ACROSS

1 Hindu avatar
5 Aesop's hare, e.g.
13 They interrupt surfing
16 Impulse transmitter
17 Concha locale
18 Start of three John Wayne movie titles
19 Twinkletoes opposite
20 Come out of hiding
21 Long-jawed fish
22 Paul in "Now, Voyager"
24 "Not ___ million years!"
25 Camp David Accords participant
27 Shoelace tips
28 Unwelcome summer cloud
30 Stick in the fridge
31 Pension law acronym
32 Winless thoroughbred
33 Feudal worker
34 Triangle part
35 African pest caught in cloth traps
37 Some AOL missives
39 Fan sounds
41 Metric wts.
42 West End musical group
47 Bunkers' Queens neighborhood
49 Netherlands queen
50 Noncommittal reply
52 Burlesque prop
53 Russert and Robbins
54 E, on golf leaderboards
55 Come up with
58 Spot fixer?
59 Lebanese designer Elie
62 Duck portrayer in "Peter and the Wolf"
64 Intimate nightclub
66 Karen Carpenter, for one
67 George of "Cheers"
68 Capital of Zimbabwe
69 Pope in 1605
71 As well as
72 Mauritania neighbor
73 Deep Purple frontman Gillan
74 "To Althea, From Prison" poet
77 Yielded
78 White House advisory gp.
79 Not fleshed out
80 Lag b'___ (Jewish holiday)
81 Nice time of year?
82 Certain peerages
83 "I Remember Mama" son

DOWN

1 Dunkin' Donuts pitchwoman
2 Lube from a gun
3 Does double duty, in a way
4 Guitarist Segovia
5 Bullwinkle adversary
6 Had second thoughts about
7 Downed
8 Drew Carey and Mike Myers, e.g.
9 Paintball accessories
10 Make fizzy
11 Scandal sheet
12 Sierra Club logo, essentially
13 Sock pattern
14 It's always relegated to the bottom
15 Noncommittal reply
23 "L'___ c'est moi"
26 Best Supporting Actor of 1982
28 Hoods' pieces
29 Abuse verbally
32 Emmy winner Mullally
36 "Ironweed" setting
38 Kingston Trio hit of 1959
40 Derby of Akron
43 WW2 torpedo vessel
44 "The Weakest Link," for one
45 Marty McFly's specialty
46 Mean Joe Greene, Mel Blount et al.
48 Retrovirus component
51 "Amapola" singer Helen
52 Outdo
56 Rife
57 Israel's first UN delegate
59 Like the Aral Sea
60 Orioles' div.
61 Pronto
63 State animal of 65 Down
65 "Alis volat propriis" state
68 Jimmy Choo trademark
70 Female role in "Spring Awakening"
72 Take for a ride
75 River to the Volga
76 From ___ Z

111 SPLITTING THE . . . by Victor Fleming

We'll let you figure out the rest of the title.

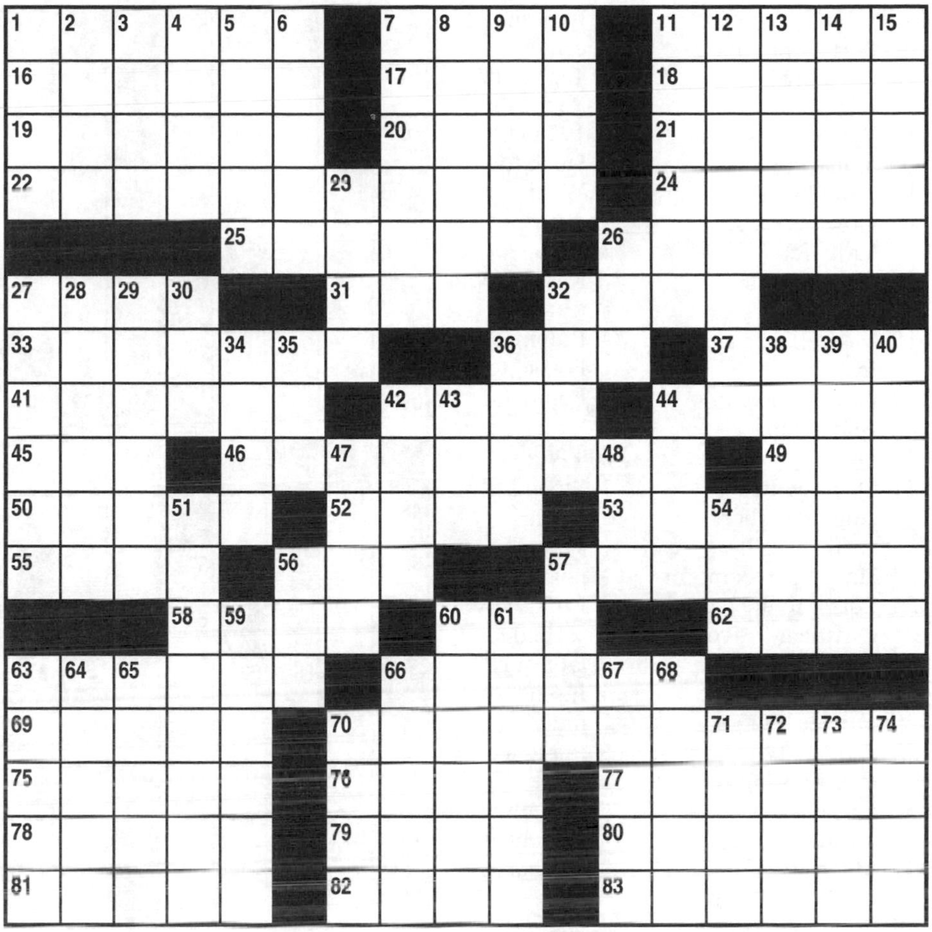

ACROSS

1 Alley denizen
7 Layered haircut
11 Wood that glides in models
16 Creed in "Rocky"
17 Not stay fresh
18 Phillips of "Star Trek: Voyager"
19 Hire, as counsel
20 Designer Gucci
21 Corruption partner
22 Ague, e.g.
24 Water's components, e.g.
25 Fitting worker
26 Caged warbler
27 Kind of guy
31 Spiritual path
32 Rip end
33 Spaced out
36 Short of
37 Ancient Persian poet
41 Key West rental
42 Largest of seven
44 Campfire treat
45 "Got it!"
46 Lack of a key
49 Keydets' sch
50 Roberto Duran's "I quit!"
52 Drudge of the Web
53 Chinese noodle dish
55 No condensation
56 In need of changing
57 Minoxidil brand name
58 House
60 Spanish sight seer?
62 Tech sch. grad
63 Dress option
66 Bed toppers
69 "___ my case!"
70 Down deep
75 Butler from Charleston
76 Diane Sawyer's birth name
77 Fabled cow owner
78 Vacation rental
79 "Post" page
80 Sartre classic
81 FIVE ARE SPLIT IN THIS PUZZLE
82 Some attendance figs.
83 Minus sign twin

DOWN

1 Maeve Binchy's "___ Road"
2 Vienna-based cartel
3 Caterpillar successor?
4 Potter's supply
5 Elite
6 Tony winner Pinkins
7 Basic food item
8 Big name in hotels
9 Strong devotion
10 Euclidean subj.
11 Cupholder
12 Haphazardly
13 Tibetan capital
14 Less dicey
15 Jittery
23 Slugger Johnny
26 Coquettish
27 1997 Demi Moore title role
28 What a liner may get caught on
29 Japanese floor covering
30 Takes too much of, with "on"
32 Spiced Indian tea
34 Aliases
35 Oxy-5 target
36 Riverbed deposit
38 Occupy
39 Giving guns to
40 "Misery" director
42 Sculpture student's subj.
43 Stood no more
44 Clean Air Act target
47 Broken mirror, say
48 Driver's caution
51 Familiarize
54 Daisy ___ Yokum
56 Retail storefront?
57 Actor's meat
59 Seattle's Best offerings
60 Juice source
61 Internal Islamic battles
63 About
64 Nirvana attainer
65 "___ evil"
66 Unilever brand
67 Butcher shop choice
68 Early Athenian democrat
70 African lily
71 Angry
72 Biological groups
73 ". . . ___ it Memorex?"
74 Jackalope, for one

112 TONSORIAL TUTORIAL by Patrick Jordan

Floyd is the name of the tonsor on 71 Across.

ACROSS

1 Portal uprights
6 Hash browns veggie
10 Word with screen or second
15 Stupid sort
16 Governor's bailiwick
17 Capital in the Andes
18 Mowgli's bear friend
19 Fateful force in Buddhism
20 Drove
21 Opera with a singing barber (with "The")
24 Have the receipt for
25 Puts into the record
26 City near Provo
27 Cause nose-wrinkling
29 Tomato's tinge
30 Agreeably sharp-tasting
32 Bipedal ranch creature
35 Made an effort
37 Dispatches anew
39 Shorthand pro
40 Inventorying aid, briefly
43 Medical suffix
44 Musical with a demonic barber
48 Moslem ruler
51 Tined tools
52 "Frasier" episode, e.g.
56 Some bank collections
58 Vinyl benzene
60 "Mazel ___!"
61 Purposes
63 Pan Am rival, once
64 Appease completely
65 Cutting side
67 Skilled combat pilot
70 Pioneer's house material
71 Sitcom with a folksy barber (with "The")
75 Arledge of "ABC News" fame
76 Certainty
77 Peninsula bordering Israel
79 Near the center
80 Tapped out
81 Shriver's 1978 U.S. Open foe
82 Wind-deposited silt
83 Nolan Ryan's debut team
84 Ralph and Potsie, to the Fonz

DOWN

1 Sloop sail
2 Bruce Wayne portrayer
3 From Italy's second-largest city
4 Insensitive individual
5 Put in a crib, say
6 Brought to Broadway
7 Culinary gadget
8 Highest degree
9 Loath to listen
10 Water pistol discharges
11 Wholesale removal
12 Bone-to-bone connector
13 Road, in old Rome
14 Kerfuffle
16 Did some ice dancing
22 With respect to
23 Precede
24 Metal-bearing minerals
28 Leavenworth locale
31 "I smell ___!"
33 1,501, at the Forum
34 Battleship inits.
36 "That really hurts!"
38 Downy ducks
40 Fingerprinting liquid
41 Wallace in "Cujo"
42 England and Hardin
45 Graphite remover
46 Fluency
47 No longer yielding milk
48 More than capable
49 Day-___ paint
50 Finish (with)
53 Former CBS anchor Harry
54 Contrary to propriety
55 Deprivation
57 Ambushing robbers
58 Bind with a bandage
59 Dash dial
62 "On Language" columnist William
63 Illusionist's repertoire
66 Force units
68 "Otherwise . . ."
69 German industrial hub
71 Seed appendage
72 Preschooler's prohibition
73 SALT concern
74 Place that's buzzing with activity
78 "___ Your Thing": Isley Brothers

113 PRETTY WELL OILED by Ray Hamel

"Pump Action" was Ray's alternate title.

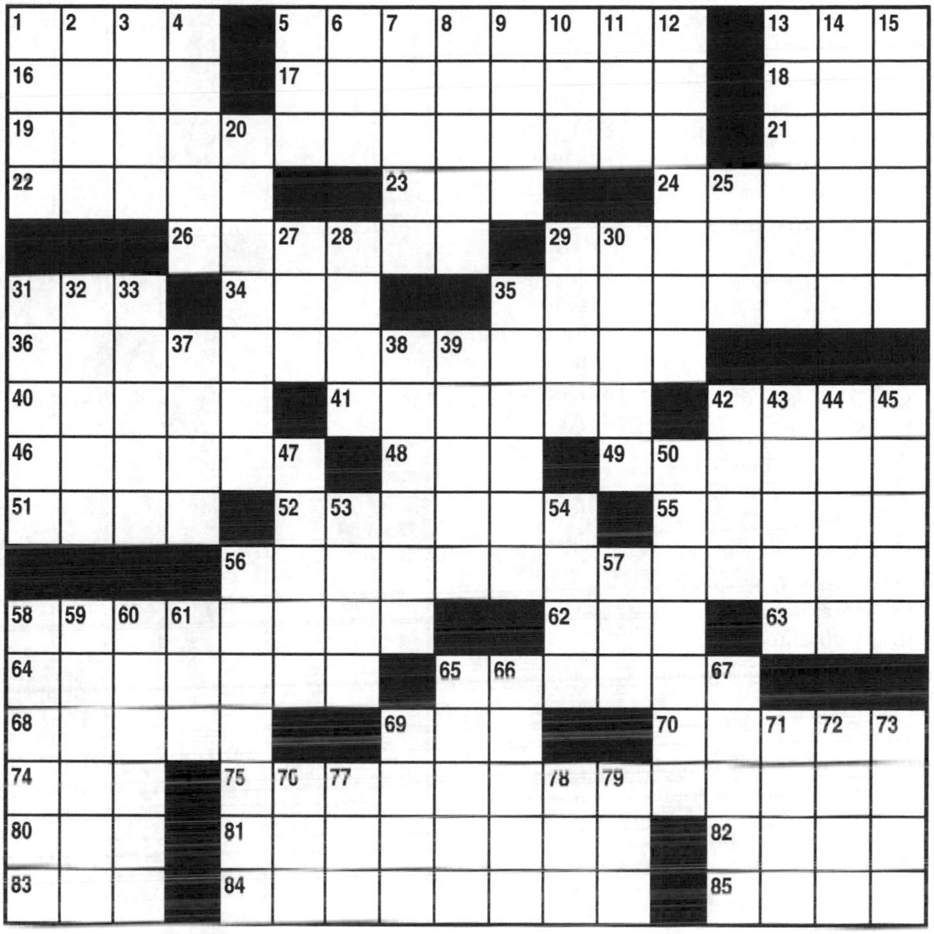

ACROSS

1 Float easily
5 Give up
13 Bookie alternative
16 First Amendment advocacy grp.
17 Kind of court
18 WWW address
19 Statistical variation
21 Kind of cross
22 Dixie's animated partner
23 French article
24 Use a loom
26 Purplish red
29 Indian River exports
31 Meditation syllables
34 Prefix with state
35 With reluctance
36 Baltic Sea arm
40 Washer's neighbor
41 Prima ballerina
42 Principe, for one
46 Up until today
48 "The View" network
49 Conductor Damrosch
51 Stereotypical gamer
52 Make a gradual transition
55 Birthplace of Gene Autry
56 "Ann Vickers" novelist
58 Jain Temple city
62 Andalusian aunt
63 Jeanne or Bernadette
64 Remember with a poem
65 Bricklayers
68 Watch for
69 Golfer's number
70 Femur spot
74 Dispirited
75 Pasta well-suited for clam sauce?
80 Contact's place
81 One of the Prairie Provinces
82 Bibliography abbr.
83 ID with two hyphens
84 Won over
85 Reagan's Secretary of the Interior

DOWN

1 Mud-daubing insect
2 Curtain opener
3 Linen source
4 Toga alternative
5 Jamaican music
6 "Wag the Dog" ploy
7 Provide
8 William Morris employee
9 Tenuous
10 1967 NHL Rookie of the Year
11 Rock's ___ Fighters
12 Wisconsin's motto
13 Power failure
14 Take a bus
15 Like B.B. King's music
20 "Blade II" director
25 USN rank
27 Dog sound
28 Teeming
29 Track figure
30 Extend a contract
31 Utah city
32 Diving bird
33 More mischievous
35 Singer Keys
37 Chase (off)
38 Source of the Mississippi
39 Big prize in medicine
42 Rival of Jimmy and Bjorn
43 Loads
44 Lawful
45 Wipe away
47 Bruce of "Hill Street Blues"
50 Coca-Cola's home
53 Get a pot going
54 Trivial complaints
56 "I can live with that"
57 Samba city
58 Puts a halt to
59 Without exception
60 Weighted down
61 Modern F/X field
65 Home of the Knights Hospitalers
66 Culet and cuirass
67 Nag
69 Ballet maneuver
71 Crumb
72 Camping nuisance
73 Sword handle
76 Leia's love
77 It may be living or dead
78 Fortas or Burrows
79 Scoundrel

114 SWELLING RANKS by Harvey Estes

13 Down can be found in the novel and film "A Clockwork Orange."

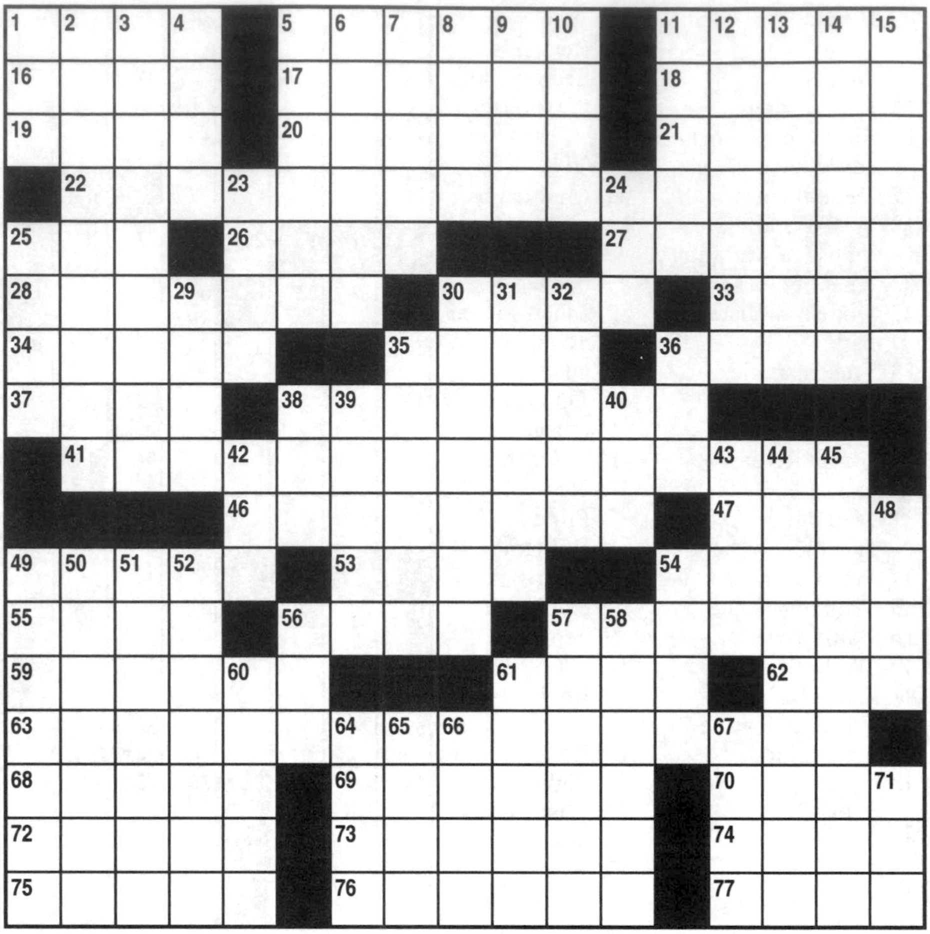

ACROSS

1 Circle segments
5 Punishes corporally
11 Get a bead on
16 "___ interesting!"
17 Mysterious
18 Piquancy
19 Eve's first home
20 Mel or Jose
21 Drawing room
22 Be candidly selfless?
25 PIN taker
26 Plenty angry
27 "So long"
28 In more of a hurry
30 "Let's see now, where ___?"
33 Part of a spy name
34 Molecule members
35 Mural site
36 More unusual
37 Eliot protagonist
38 Begin
41 Irritated rock band?
46 Unsightly sights
47 Carbon compound
49 Prom transports
53 "Sister Act" extras
54 Desert bloomers
55 What you can take from me
56 Public relations output
57 Funhouse fixtures
59 Brewer of song
61 Words before camera or rock
62 Pt. of AARP
63 Prize for grouchy kids?
68 Vietnamese capital
69 Not recognized
70 Jump up
72 Eventually become
73 Apartment dweller
74 Very top
75 RBI and ERA
76 Wetland birds
77 Crockpot contents

DOWN

1 Blvd.
2 Republican, by location
3 Vanilla beverage
4 Milli Vanilli's lip action
5 "Thinking of You" singer
6 Like better
7 Very bitter
8 Antidrug agent
9 Patella site
10 Manor worker
11 Analyze for gold
12 Famed Rio beach
13 Korova ___
14 Altar server
15 Kind of reunion
23 Reformer Jacob
24 Baseball card stat
25 Arab of song
29 Fed. agents
30 Combat area
31 Takes in, say
32 Hillside
35 Crumples into a ball
36 USPS beat
38 Crazy like a fox
39 Lilliputian
40 Pkg. purveyor
42 Jennifer Lien's "Voyager" role
43 Goneril's dad
44 Wrong
45 Hunchback's home
48 Mailing to Santa
49 Gate closers
50 Repetitive
51 Daniel Hillard's ex
52 Flare, as nostrils
54 Sticking point
56 Stable staple
57 Fridge stick-on
58 Some computer files
60 Cuts class
61 Rest room sign phrase
64 Holiday period
65 A hundred sawbucks
66 Country in a Beatle song
67 Wistful word
71 Basilica bench

115 JA-PUN-ESE FOOD by Richard Silvestri

Cry "Yatta!" ("I did it!") after solving this one.

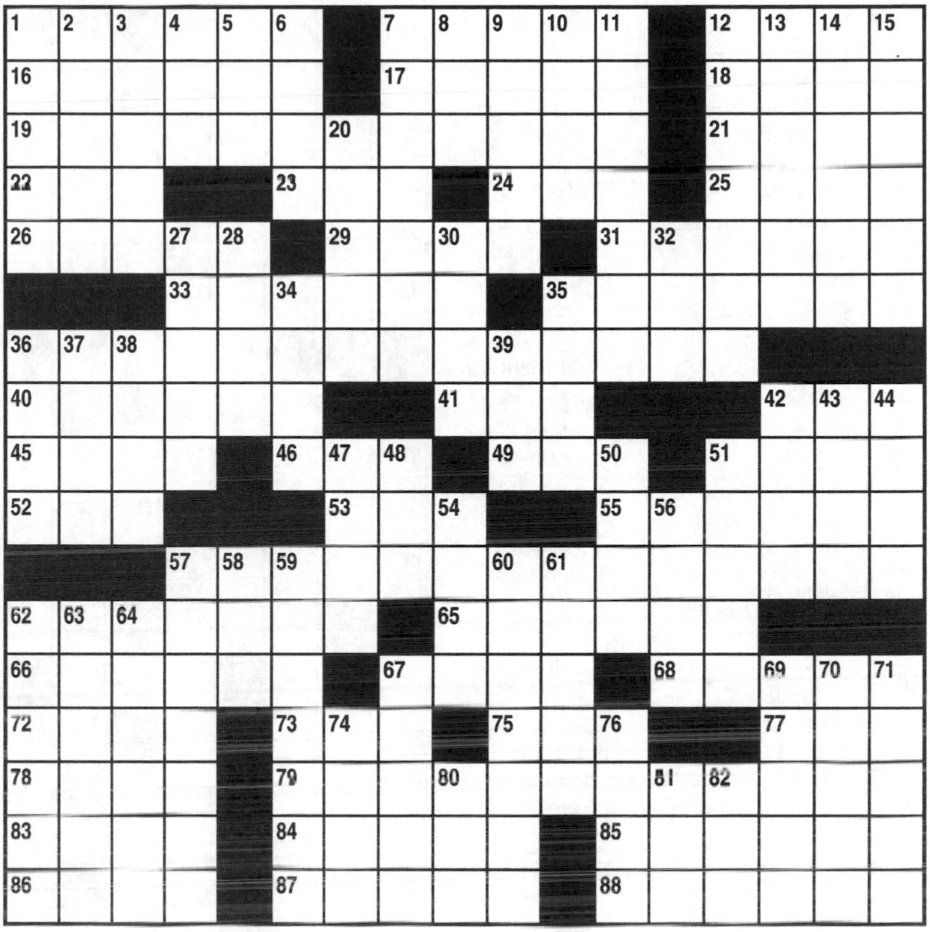

ACROSS

1 String along
7 Surf
12 Bellicose Olympian
16 Walking on air
17 Say "nothin' "
18 Become engaged
19 Gag order at the Japanese restaurant?
21 Sleuthing duo's dog
22 Dedicated lines
23 Crackers or bananas
24 So far
25 "All in the Family" producer
26 Michener epic
29 Place for a dip
31 Pope's emissary
33 Clog
35 Put under
36 Hissy fit at the Japanese restaurant?
40 Use a compass
41 Jersey hangout
42 MPG raters
45 Turku resident
46 Took a load off
49 "Which came first?" thing
51 Political coalition
52 Guitar's little brother
53 Minorca's capital
55 Ear specialist
57 Japanese restaurant song?
62 More clever
65 V-2, for one
66 Battery terminals
67 Someone I remember
68 "Bolero" star
72 Basilica center
73 River of Russia
75 Suffix for self
77 Old greeting
78 Judd's "Taxi" role
79 Spectacle at the Japanese restaurant?
83 Ready to eat
84 Highborn
85 Columbus Day event
86 Ottoman rulers
87 Siouan language
88 Let off the hook

DOWN

1 Stop on a line
2 Slip away from
3 Chicle source
4 Stage actress Hagen
5 Plaines preceder
6 Dutch export
7 Winnow
8 Rumble in the Jungle winner
9 Record material
10 Carmela on "The Sopranos"
11 Colonist
12 Combination
13 Change place cards
14 It's left behind
15 Was generous
20 Key letter
27 Quaker in the woods
28 Phaser setting
30 Milky gem
32 E-mail address ending
34 Scraps for Scrappy-Do
35 Daddy deer
36 Vegan's protein source
37 Composer Satie
38 Hog's word
39 Social-page word
42 "Boola Boola" singers
43 Swanky
44 Broadway opening
47 Child god
48 Greek cross
50 Stare stupidly
51 Savage
54 Gumbo veggie
56 Ready for recycling
57 Quick-reference aids
58 Medieval malediction
59 "Make up your mind!"
60 Name on a slate
61 Internet payment method
62 Dudley Do-Right's home
63 Handy watch?
64 Nine-day devotion
67 Deadly snake
69 Aircraft equipment
70 Get out of
71 In A, e.g.
74 Smart foes
76 Brewery need
80 Taina in "The 39 Steps"
81 Peke's perch
82 Soc. Security supplement

116 MEAN TIME by Patrick Jordan

"The First Lady of the Theater" can be found at 19 Across.

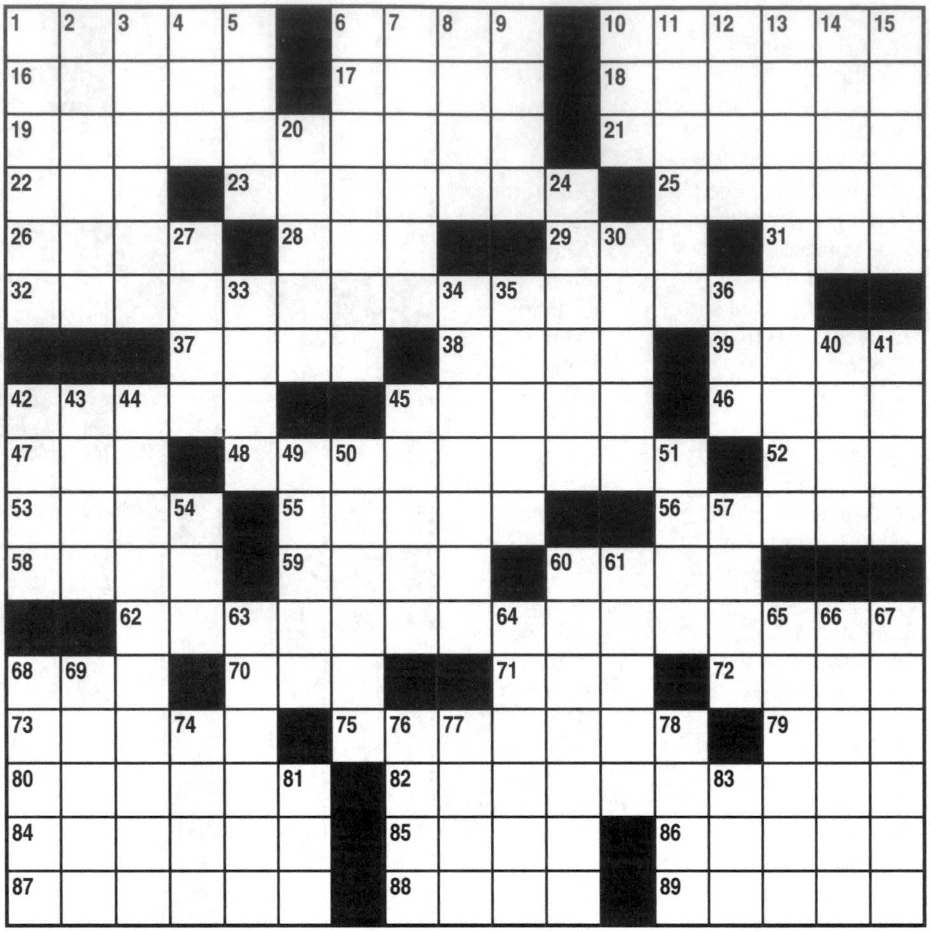

ACROSS

1 Donkeys' ancestors
6 Corp. chiefs
10 Parts of putters
16 Far from firm
17 "Six" prefix
18 Thick stew
19 **Speaker of quip**
21 Execute excessively
22 Chum
23 Sovereign's topper
25 Mary in "The Maltese Falcon"
26 "How sweet ___!"
28 Word with canal or candy
29 Fess (up)
31 Choleric emotion
32 **Quip: Part 1**
37 In ___ (at heart)
38 Mythical bowman
39 Some hooded snakes
42 Brown-coated ermine
45 Prepare French toast
46 Denver's elevation, famously
47 Sphere at a coronation
48 **Quip: Part 2**
52 Apply blades to blades?
53 "Crossroads of the South Pacific"
55 Verbal fanfares
56 Certain sport shirts
58 Tomahawks and such
59 One who watches
60 Calcutta cover-up
62 **Quip: Part 3**
68 AOL exchanges
70 Innermost pt.
71 Sampan propeller
72 Rosalind of "M*A*S*H"
73 Heart
75 Small herding dog
79 Superlative syllable
80 Graduated
82 **Quip: Part 4**
84 Make the scene
85 Tofu source
86 "Three Tall Women" playwright
87 Kind of line to sign
88 Zoning director's map
89 Elegantly attired

DOWN

1 Barbecue receptacle
2 Close-fitting dress
3 ___ Mae (student loan agency)
4 Make last (with "out")
5 Coordinate, colloquially
6 Pretense
7 Pooh's gloomy chum
8 Yoked team
9 Freelancer's encl.
10 Initials that delight angels
11 Castro's capital
12 Grows gray-haired
13 Loudly, to Liszt
14 Elizabeth I's dynasty
15 Keep in a crib, say
20 Gardeners, on occasion
24 Camry company
27 Where Namath played
30 Bremen's river
33 ___ spumante
34 Shore dinner, e.g.
35 Squares up
36 Edward Jones Dome athlete
40 Trudge
41 Plies a needle
42 Davenport or settee
43 Fruity Pebbles rival
44 Decorative collectibles
45 Audiocassette marking
49 1945 Alamogordo event, briefly
50 Parfait features
51 Gaelic speaker's homeland
54 Suffix for shrew
57 Multivitamin metal
60 Tries to smack
61 Condor's quarters
63 Eight-note interval
64 "See? I wasn't lyin'!"
65 "Inside ___" (TNT postgame show)
66 Holy Saturday follower
67 "Wait a bit longer"
68 Blue line
69 Brewery or biology prefix
74 Buttonhole, for one
76 Fastening gadget
77 Organic compound
78 Perón and Marie Saint
81 Mars's hue
83 Stately shader

117 ON THE TABLE by Arlan and Linda Bushman

60 Across are the sources of many bumper snickers.

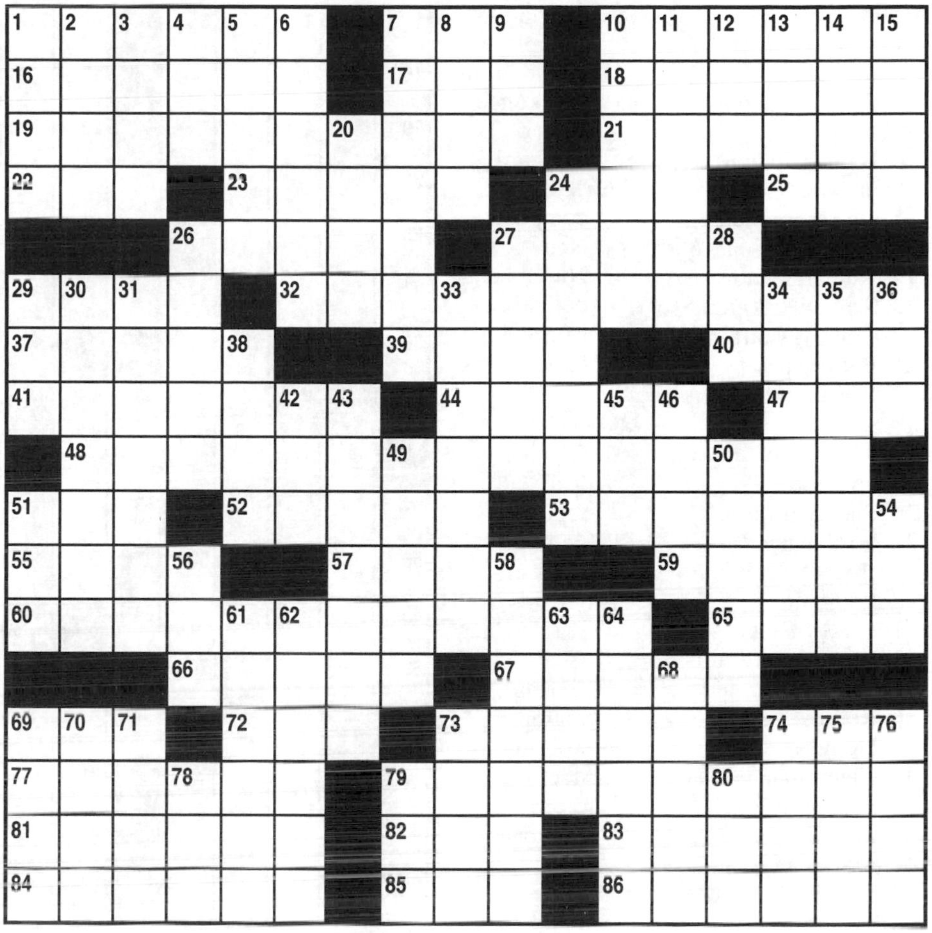

ACROSS

1 Impassive
7 Flinch
10 Small firecrackers
16 IVP dye
17 Cobbler
18 Overseas travel option
19 North Dakota's "Sunflake City"
21 Comb obstruction
22 "Yo!"
23 Chilling
24 Off-road ride, for short
25 Antediluvian
26 On the nose
27 1943 penny material
29 EPA concern
32 Giant upset of 2008
37 Serbian President Tadic
39 Uniform
40 Cookie fresh-baked in 1912
41 Tabletop griller
44 Kind of shark
47 Aussie swimmer Thorpe
48 Ace of clubs
51 Weeks per annum
52 Flavor
53 Taciturn
55 Religious image
57 Eastern ties
59 Set down
60 Conceits of car owners
65 ___ buco
66 "American Pie" locale
67 Rite site
69 Spree
72 Game pieces
73 Sound of displeasure
74 Char's tote
77 Brusque
79 Wimbledon trophies
81 Krypton, for one
82 Word of support
83 Official count
84 Milne moper
85 Tread softly
86 Frank's comic-strip pal

DOWN

1 Exhale audibly
2 Sped
3 Jazz singer Anita
4 Memorial designer Maya
5 Book section
6 Checkmate
7 Brownies
8 Boost
9 Thumbs-up
10 Parlor piece
11 Tremble
12 Pedestal topper
13 Emilia's treacherous mate
14 Visor
15 Husky haul
20 Its players know the score: Abbr.
24 In danger
26 To her, some things are "loverly"
27 Describe concisely
28 Wall St. deal
29 Decline
30 Napoleon's birthplace
31 Address
33 Wine concoction
34 Lines up
35 Fatigues
36 First name in horror films
38 Salutation word
42 Greek vowel
43 Unwrap hurriedly
45 Waiting rm. locale
46 Behold, to Livy
49 Chivalrous
50 Deck with laurels
51 Tyler in "Lord of the Rings"
54 ___-Magnon
56 Goose egg
58 Ravenous
61 Strengthen metal
62 Mimieux of movies
63 62 Down's "Time Machine" role
64 Posture
68 Incense
69 Wisecrack
70 Competent
71 Overcast
73 Featured Prado artist
74 Dwell on
75 Comics penguin
76 Attention getter
78 Kids' card game
79 Once around
80 TV info source

118 "GIVE ME SOME 79 DOWN!" by Victor Fleming

A breathtaking experience!

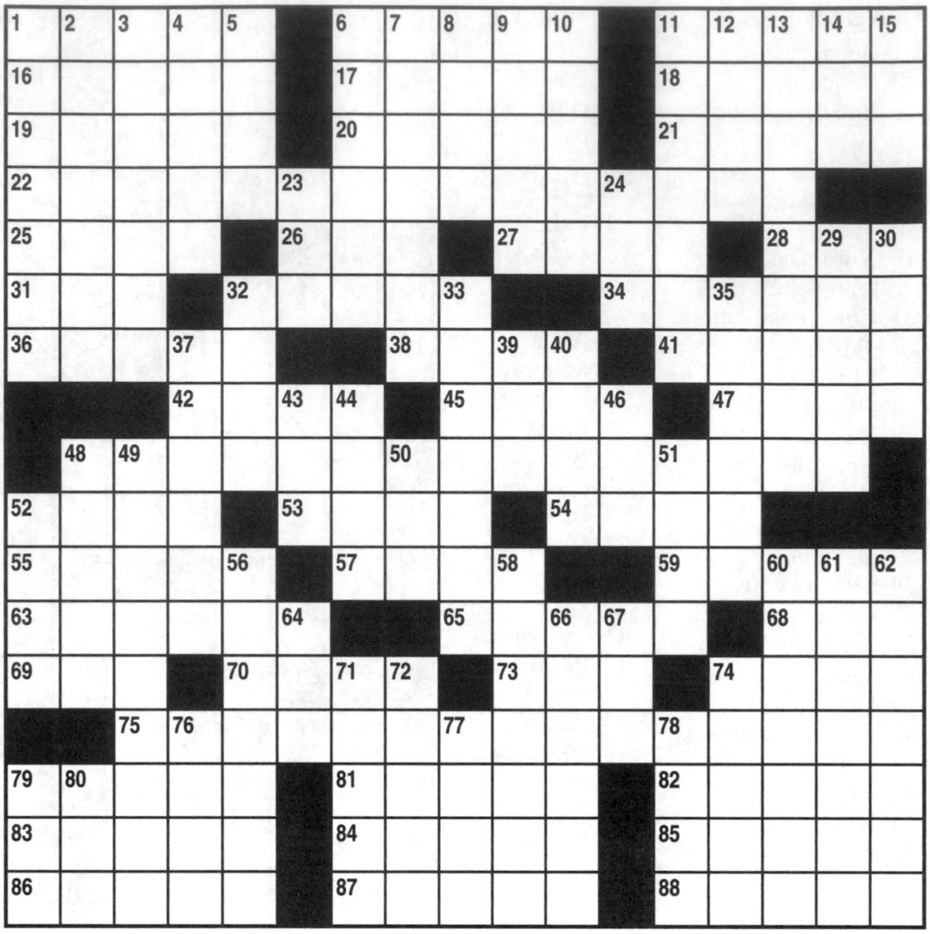

ACROSS

1 Hitter of 61 in '61
6 Influences
11 One who shoots hoops
16 Former Italian queen
17 Golfer Baddeley
18 Half a '60s dance
19 Numeric leader?
20 Seat of Siskiyou County, California
21 Battery part
22 Where to find tom yum
25 "A vote for ___ a vote for . . ."
26 Slangy refusal
27 Ford make, for short
28 Polite title
31 Part of ETA
32 Literally, "for this"
34 Ricardo, to Mertz
36 Robins' homes
38 Delight
41 Cleo of jazz
42 Brinker in books
45 Folk forename
47 Makes angry
48 "Barney's Version" author
52 Gander or bull
53 ___ City, Baghdad
54 End of a fitting phrase
55 "Fleas" poet Nash
57 Garage item
59 Words of clarification
63 Brandy Norwood role
65 Cutting light
68 Inflation meas.
69 Spanish guitarist (1778–1839)
70 Composition of some beds
73 Spring resort
74 "I cannot tell ___"
75 NOW president (1991–2001)
79 Briskly
81 Words after get or grab
82 Charley Weaver's hometown
83 Figure skater Slutskaya
84 De Gaulle's birthplace
85 "Okie From Muskogee" singer Haggard
86 "Bertha" composer Ned
87 Nuremberg defendant
88 Musical upbeats

DOWN

1 Butcher
2 Roll call report, perhaps
3 Fixings
4 "It's ___ Kiss": Cher
5 Coal-rich German region
6 Follows the doctor's order
7 Pumbaa in "The Lion King"
8 Field
9 Pansy of Dogpatch
10 Deadfall
11 Pulpit's locale
12 Uncle's partner
13 French word list
14 Days of yore
15 Ham holder
23 Quash
24 Former "Jeopardy" host Fleming
29 Central
30 I-40 and I-30
32 "It's ___ state of affairs!"
33 Kaleidocolors maker
35 Executed perfectly
37 Triplets
39 Do something human
40 Chicago Cubs manager (1982–83)
43 Big inits. in video games
44 Improvise vocally
46 World Series mo.
48 Cartoon "Mr."
49 First glasses, e.g., comparatively
50 Busyness
51 Will beneficiary
52 May day honorees
56 Blue Jackets, e.g.
58 Louisiana namer
60 Filled pastries
61 Turning point
62 Tinted tees
64 Alpine river
66 "Eek!" producer
67 Wax producer
71 Perfume bottles
72 ___ off the old block
74 Russian republic
76 Teen concern
77 One loved by Hercules
78 Spice Girls member
79 WORD FOUND IN 8 ANSWERS
80 In favor of

119 WORD SALAD by Doug Peterson

3 Down was the second American to fly in space.

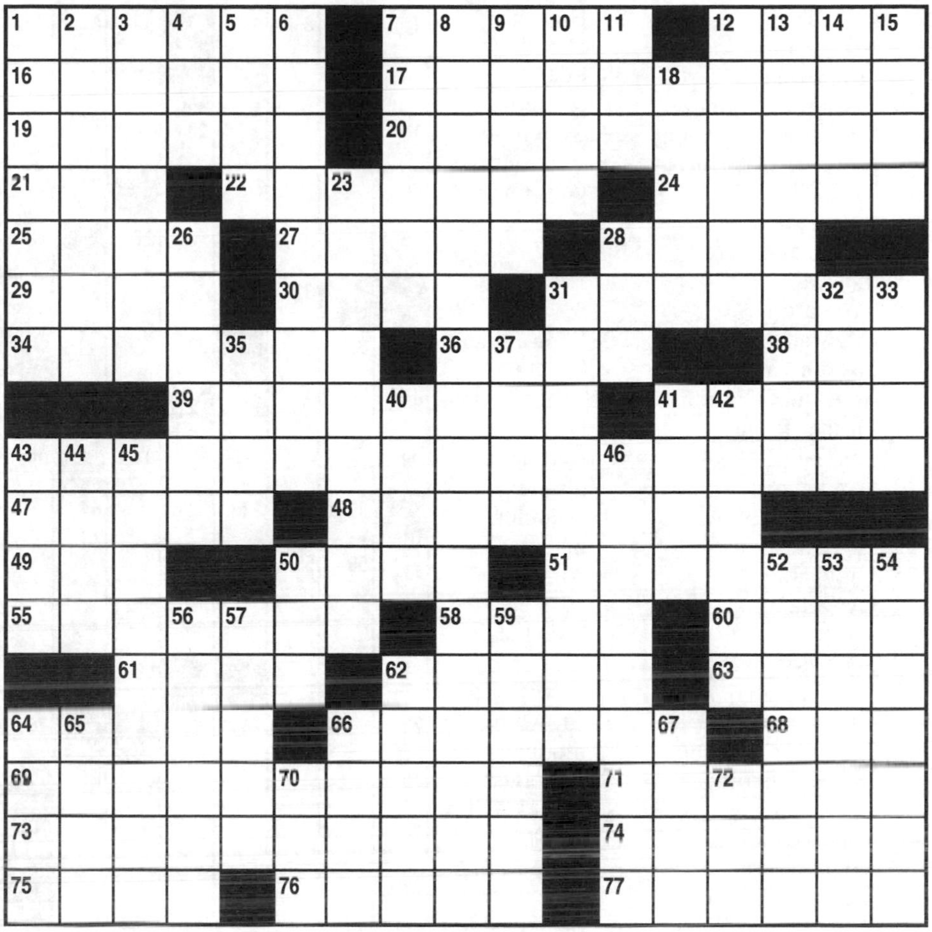

ACROSS

1 Convertible, colloquially
7 Mount in Exodus
12 Qualified
16 Moon of Jupiter
17 Stiff jacket feature
19 Body-shop application
20 Unbelievable
21 ___Tafari
22 Lincoln, in a Whitman poem
24 Drops in a mailbox
25 Otherwise
27 Ivy League member
28 Gnu group
29 Disheveled one
30 Wine lover's prefix
31 1945 conference site
34 Stock-ticker sights
36 Natasha's negative
38 Grp. with a noted journal
39 Divided into installments
41 "See ya!"
43 Where Reno was once located
47 Developed
48 Court, in a way
49 Pops
50 Bakery purchase
51 "SNL" alum Joe
55 Jubilance
58 ___ arms (outraged)
60 One of Donald's nephews
61 Saturates
62 Howlin' Wolf's music
63 LAX listings
64 Bradley and Epps
66 Beckons
68 Merlot holder
69 Superman's home
71 Camden Yards player
73 Place-setting piece
74 Hammock user
75 "Ol' Man River" composer
76 They may be spliced
77 Urban two-wheelers

DOWN

1 Quash
2 How music is sensed
3 Project Mercury astronaut
4 Alley prowler
5 Crude acronym?
6 Like some mirrors
7 "Miracle on 34th Street" director George
8 Capra classic set in Bedford Falls, NY
9 Away from home
10 Before too long
11 Post-op stop
12 Thicket trees
13 Risky social arrangement
14 Finish a flight
15 Work units
18 First signs
23 Keeps trying
26 Walt Alston's 1955 home
28 On a roll
31 Dixie desserts
32 "You said it!"
33 Trade center
35 Taylor tyke of reruns
37 Pained cry
40 Halls of music
41 Old Ford models
42 Oscar winner in "Cocoon"
43 Shade of green
44 Orenburg's river
45 Seltzer-bottle liquid
46 Gullywasher
50 ___ Gatos, CA
52 Defeat at the polls
53 Propelled a Schwinn
54 Pearl harborers
56 Earthling, in sci-fi novels
57 "There, there"
59 Signs of life
62 Ina in films
64 Siberian metropolis
65 Apportion
66 Volcano top
67 Milkshake flavor
70 USPS parcel
72 DSL co.

120 COAUTHOR by Buddy Richard

Joseph Conrad's "Heart of Darkness" was the basis for "Apocalypse Now."

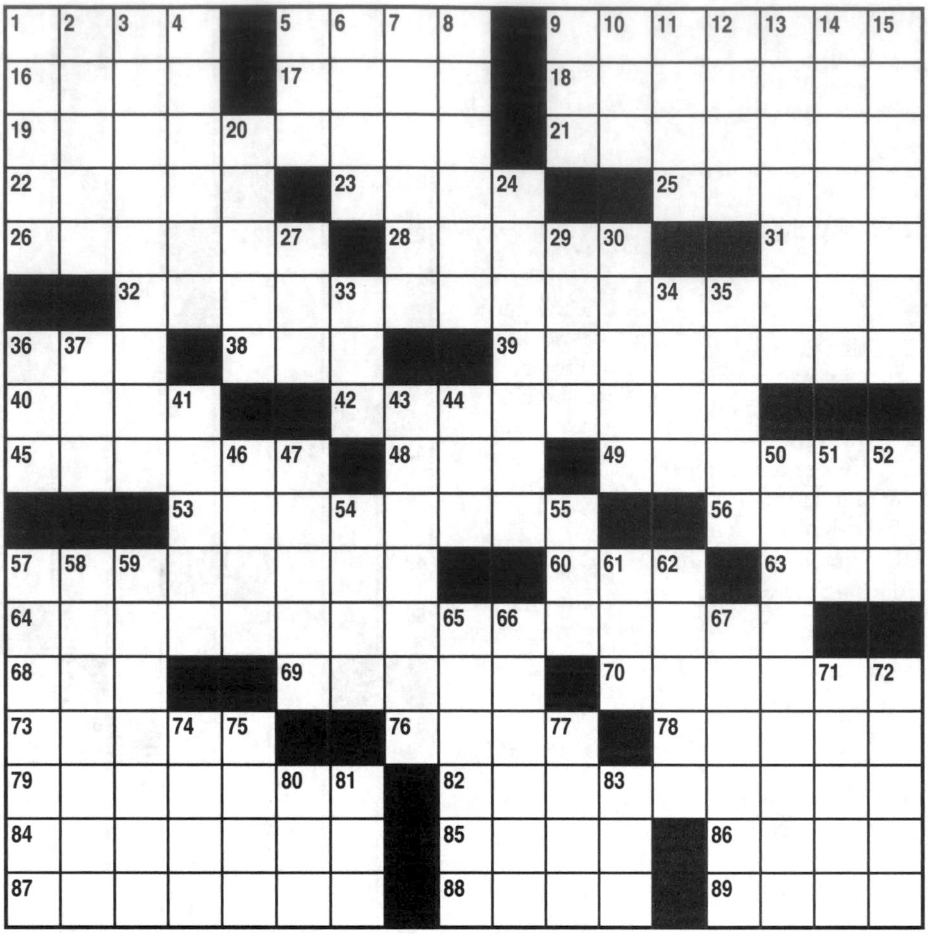

ACROSS

1 Now companion
5 "Immediately!"
9 They're obvious
16 "Houston, ___ got a problem!"
17 "The Night They Invented Champagne" musical
18 "You are ___, sir" (McMahon line)
19 **Joseph Conrad quotation: Part I**
21 Further from rational
22 Caravel of Columbus
23 ___'acte
25 Laughable
26 "Angela's Ashes," e.g.
28 Spenserian verb
31 La-la intro
32 **Quotation: Part II**
36 "Favorite" relation
38 Bishop's bailiwick
39 Ugly sights
40 Relative of a Salchow
42 Seattle's Best brew
45 Birthplace of Saint Ignatius
48 **Quotation: Part III**
49 Rumor unit, perhaps
53 Ranked a tourney differently
56 Convenience for an ed.
57 Illustrative story
60 ER figures
63 "Care for a spot of ___?"
64 **Quotation: Part IV**
68 USN petty officer
69 "Cats" poet
70 Try again
73 Torch's work
76 Long ago, long ago
78 Give to
79 1997 Hawke movie
82 **Quotation: Part V**
84 Rome description
85 Choice
86 Zaire's Mobutu ___ Seko
87 Have an effect
88 FCC concerns
89 System that can improve your image?

DOWN

1 Afternoon hr.
2 Figure skater known as "The Golden Girl"
3 Betting phrase
4 Calculus inventor
5 Amt. on a 1040
6 Web locale
7 Conference need
8 Browning product
9 It merged with AT&T in 1999
10 Howard or Turcotte
11 Bearish start
12 Where rials are spent
13 Dole or Pryor
14 Three-time Wimbledon champ
15 They may be winning or losing
20 Train company stocks
24 Ring leader?
27 Bar choice
29 Lid annoyance
30 "If ___ walls could talk . . ."
33 Start of a laugh
34 She, in Salerno
35 Embarrassing guests
36 "Old pal" of song
37 Kitchen utensils maker
41 TV producer Michaels
43 Metallic marble
44 Third degree?
46 Groucho's grimace
47 TV's "___ World Turns"
50 Chumpish
51 Apply
52 Pastureland
54 Series ender
55 Orthodontist's deg.
57 Neptune's photographer
58 Repeat
59 Wrote for another
61 JEC successor
62 Warfare tactic
65 Former justice Abe
66 Sweater's remark
67 Beat
71 "For every Bird ___": Dickinson
72 Episc. title
74 Other, to Ochoa
75 Half of Mork's greeting
77 Ride herd on
80 Curbside container
81 City council rep.
83 ___ publica

121 "DON'T ASK ME Y" by Billie Truitt

59 Across is the subject of many New Year's resolutions!

ACROSS

1 Post-injury program
6 Lover of Daphnis
11 British sitcom, for short
16 Cookbook author Prudhomme
17 Common letter sign-off
18 Worth
19 Where a browbeater goes shopping?
21 More than annoyed
22 Palindromic "before"
23 Gingerbread house nibbler
24 Trust
25 Helen of Troy's mother
27 Even score
28 Pretentious
29 Prepare a treatise on a card game?
33 Copier problem
36 Make certain
38 "Lord, ___?": Matt. 26:22
39 Exist as a group
40 Tampa neighbor, briefly
41 Piece of land
42 Hobbyist's knife brand
44 Have ___ with (know somebody)
45 Beat decisively
48 Distort
49 "The Count of ___ Cristo"
51 Plains native
52 Edmondton team
54 Man of the future
55 Shiny balloon material
57 Kind of bond
58 Moreover
59 Part of a rotund silhouette?
61 "No restrictions ___ kind!"
63 Geisha's sash
64 Go by
68 Sporty scarves
70 Dutch beer brand
73 Whirlpool tub
74 Occupy, as a table
75 Very dirty field hand?
77 Bikini, notably
78 "The Tortoise and the Hare" author
79 Make better
80 Prize money
81 So last year
82 Movie producer Carlo

DOWN

1 Revolting one?
2 Toughen
3 Sank, as a putt
4 The whole enchilada
5 Birch or Evan of Indiana
6 Popular poison in whodunnits
7 Rocking toy, to a tot
8 Gospel writer
9 Hurler Hershiser
10 Ballpark fig.
11 Amelia Earhart, for one
12 Old dance sites
13 Parka worn by a dandruff sufferer?
14 Mobile beginning
15 "___ there, done that!"
20 Ripens
24 Cherokee Sal's creator Harte
26 Go-ahead
28 Japanese watchdog
30 Boy king of ancient Egypt
31 Expose to public scorn
32 "___ Mio"
34 Main line
35 Cat chorus
36 When two hands meet
37 Porcupine with a medical degree?
40 Brazilian dance
41 Bit of potpourri
43 Out
46 Yuletide greenery
47 Messenger
50 Prepare for war
53 Robbins of Baskin-Robbins
56 Longings
57 Group within a group
60 The whole enchilada
62 Stable infants
65 Skier's vacation spot
66 Used up
67 Famed New York restaurateur
68 On the double
69 Part of LASIK
70 Bailiwick
71 America or Manners
72 Type of year
75 Mountain pass
76 Latin lover's verb

122 F+ by Arlan and Linda Bushman

The title is not reflective of the grade our test solvers gave this one.

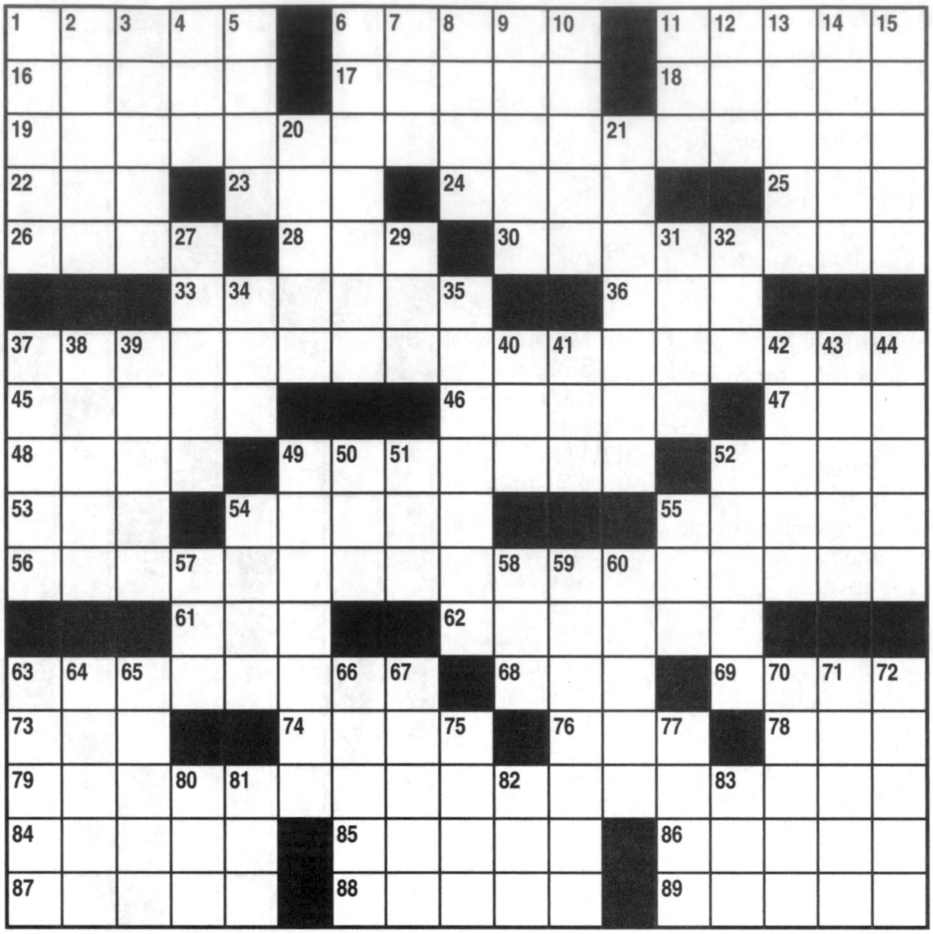

ACROSS

1 Hands-on noshes
6 Blockbuster
11 Arugula dish
16 Stand by
17 Frayed
18 Hirsch of "Into the Wild"
19 Sinbad, for one?
22 Monk title
23 Inexperienced one
24 Pastry concoction
25 ASCAP rival
26 Give a cheer
28 Ditto
30 Sorting station
33 Crafty
36 Deck number
37 What Boris Karlof made?
45 Deceive
46 Zest source
47 Berberian of opera
48 Symphony member
49 Noted translation software
52 Surveyor's map
53 Key preposition
54 Increase
55 Sicily neighbor
56 Getting bonked on the head by an apple?
61 Galoot
62 Cabinet find
63 Food on sticks
68 NFLer Manning
69 Olden days
73 Words of praise
74 City on the Oka
76 DDE's opponent
78 Caesar of comedy
79 Sheep and geese mixed together?
84 Betelgeuse home
85 Place
86 Rouse
87 ___ Martin Lagonda Ltd.
88 Bar serving amounts
89 Gathering storm

DOWN

1 Boardwalk treat
2 Mindful
3 Ring of plotters
4 Flax derivative
5 Rung
6 Visit briefly
7 "Spy vs. Spy" magazine
8 Working hard
9 Vapor
10 Many-headed monster
11 Bishop's domain
12 Doc bloc
13 Pole dance
14 Historic mission
15 Coarse cloth
20 Flat-topped hill
21 English blue cheese
27 Cafe order
29 Couple's possessive
31 Describe in detail
32 Sugarloaf setting
34 Pi follower
35 Frog hangout
37 Emotionally reserved
38 Journalist's worry
39 Arrowsmith's wife
40 Firm up
41 Ins. option
42 "My Eyes Adored You" singer
43 Versifier's muse
44 "Paradise Lost" figure
49 Jester
50 Director Lee
51 Prickly husk
52 Easy mark
54 Course
55 Astronaut Jemison
57 Prevailed
58 Compete
59 Keys
60 Fence's supplier
63 Warming quaff
64 Spray target
65 Send payment
66 Mastery
67 Donnybrook
70 Levant of levity
71 ___-Tikki-Tavi
72 Car with a "horsecollar" grille
75 Stead
77 Sharp rebuke
80 Casper's comment
81 Wayfarer's spot
82 Galley need
83 In arrears

123 MONOGRAM MEMBERS by John Underwood

. . . and all these monograms have two things in common.

ACROSS

1 HCH member
6 JEC member
10 JQA member
16 Lash of old westerns
17 Allies' adversary
18 Sci-fi author Le Guin
19 Man from Muscat
20 Satirized (with "up")
21 Bread maker?
22 WGH member
24 FDR member
25 Degrees for attys.
26 Perfume the air
27 Fishy bunch
31 Gov. Landon et al
32 Polygraph flunker
36 "___ a Symphony": Supremes
37 Road on a Beatles album
39 Objets d'art
40 "Beetle Bailey" creator Walker
41 Verdi's "___ Miller"
42 Like the Riddler
43 Vet
44 WJC member
46 Saint in Brazil
47 Left port
49 1300 hours
50 Sampling of opinions
51 Jimmy of the "Daily Planet"
52 Capital of Ghana
53 Swab the deck again
54 "Little" kid of comics
55 Wings
56 Nephew of King Arthur
57 Sherpa's home
59 The sun as deity
61 LBJ member
63 RBH member
68 Two-person bike
69 Neutron's locale
71 Frat pledge persecutor
72 "Truth ___?" (party game)
73 Storm
74 Lose ground
75 RWR member
76 JKP member
77 DDE member

DOWN

1 Wooden shoe
2 One-L priest
3 Composer Khachaturian
4 ___ fever
5 Lake Wobegon creator
6 Gently maneuvered (into)
7 Jumps for Mao Asada
8 ___ Tin Tin
9 D-day amphibian
10 Shea Stadium locale
11 Russian range
12 El Al passengers
13 Former Georgia senator
14 Advertising award
15 "Babi ___": Yevtushenko
23 Indisposed
24 Hang tough
26 More sharply defined
27 USG member
28 Bach work
29 Act of derring-do
30 Granola bar bit
31 Truancy
33 Exasperating
34 Pigged out
35 GRF member
37 "___ Wiedersehen!"
38 Like some glasses
39 Horse transport
41 Called the shots
42 Tattoo honoree
44 Aniston, familiarly
45 Watering place
48 Spartan king killed at Thermopylae
50 By means of
52 "'Tis a pity!"
53 Worked on the Southfork
55 Prehistoric primates
56 "Blimey!"
58 Calendario leaf
59 From the beginning
60 American watch company
61 Italian Adriatic port
62 S ___ (thrift)
64 ___-kiri
65 World's shallowest sea
66 ___-Mix Concrete
67 Harriet Beecher Stowe book
68 Sugarbush lift
69 Ham's refuge
70 "The Bonesetter's Daughter" author

124 QUESTIONABLE CLUES by Bonnie L. Gentry

Clues with question marks signify puns . . . as you'll soon discover.

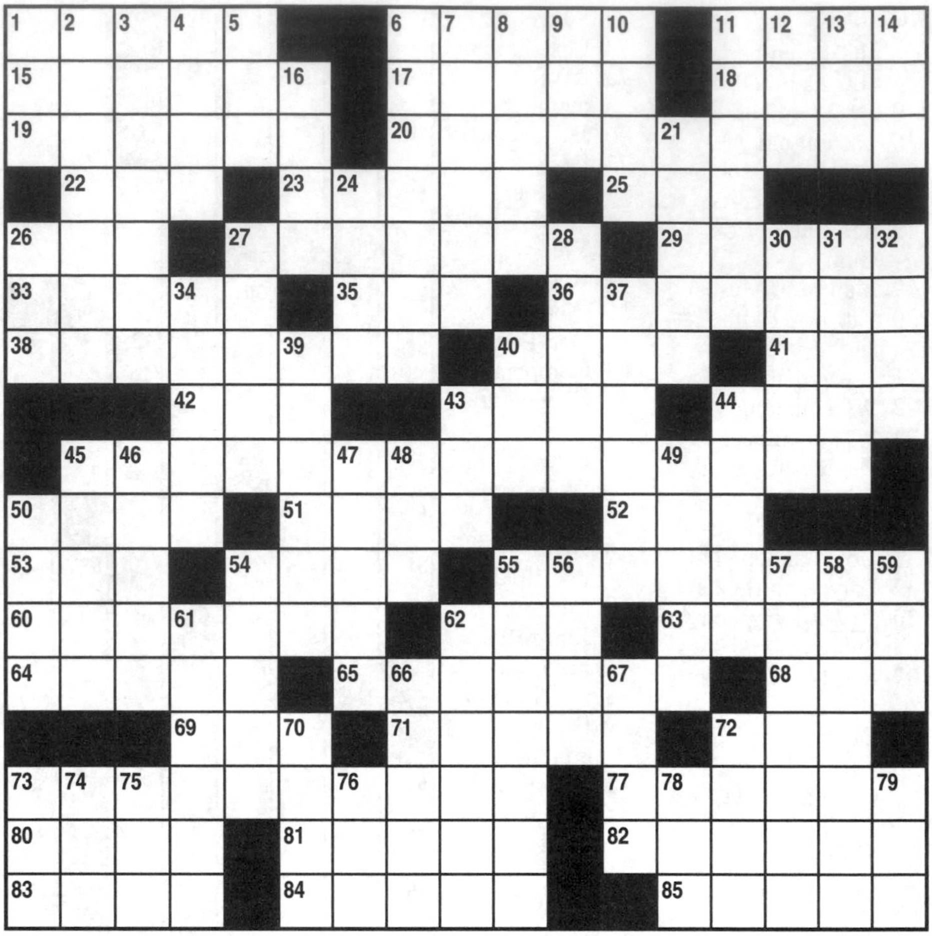

ACROSS

1 Addition sign?
6 Acid head?
11 Horsepower source?
15 Iron product?
17 Separatist?
18 Ltr. of approval?
19 Fixed one's eyes?
20 John Hancock site?
22 Part of a return address?
23 Castle with a lot of steps?
25 Spade for digging up dirt?
26 Sweet ending?
27 Those who shouldn't live in glass houses?
29 Do a hair-raising job?
33 Steps along the Seine?
35 India Inc.?
36 Digital window?
38 Check mate?
40 Movie trailer?
41 Quick draw?
42 Took the cake?
43 Taken in by a doctor?
44 Is on the bottom?
45 Red plot?
50 Match ends?
51 Middle sax?
52 Is for two people?
53 The dark side?
54 Gets better?
55 The high cost of leaving?
60 One who's always off?
62 Non-ewe?
63 Make-up name?
64 Dig deeply?
65 Meter maid?
68 Self starter?
69 The same partner?
71 Eau de Cologne?
72 Better this than dead?
73 High jink?
77 Key rings?
80 Knight time?
81 Supreme leader?
82 Bus stations?
83 Welfare state?
84 Passes notes?
85 All-night bar?

DOWN

1 Emergency measures?
2 Exhibitionist?
3 Go bumper to bumper with?
4 Canal zones?
5 Follower of Mao?
6 Like some firm elbows?
7 Brought up the rear?
8 Lay low?
9 Mariners' catcher?
10 Lucky strikes?
11 Well-invested group?
12 The start of it all?
13 Soldier material?
14 Church lady?: Abbr.
16 Text massage?
21 Social activist?
24 Part of a stage?
26 Poetic ego-booster?
27 Mattress handle?
28 Cry before dinner?
30 Tall story?
31 Deep place?
32 Thought patterns?
34 Acts hawkish?
37 Foreign correspondent?
39 Bad-smelling flower?
40 A Bonn vivant?: Abbr.
43 Smash letters?
44 Flower holders?
45 Had a peak experience?
46 Scout master?
47 Remove the dirt from?
48 They're out of this world?
49 Butter up?
50 Banks with style?
54 Magic place?
55 Old green coats?
56 Closing on Sunday?
57 Moor jealous?
58 Shot putters?
59 Law closing?
61 Attended to pressing needs?
62 Work on moving pictures?
66 Church keys?
67 Parking place?
70 Tight positions?
72 Mechanical starter?
73 Thesis intro?
74 Do ground work?
75 Shortly before?
76 Crowd in old Rome?
78 Main man?
79 Flightless bird?

125 THE GOOD, THE BAD, AND THE UGLY by Martha C. Patty

21 Down wasn't that bad. It climbed to #1 in the UK charts in 1963.

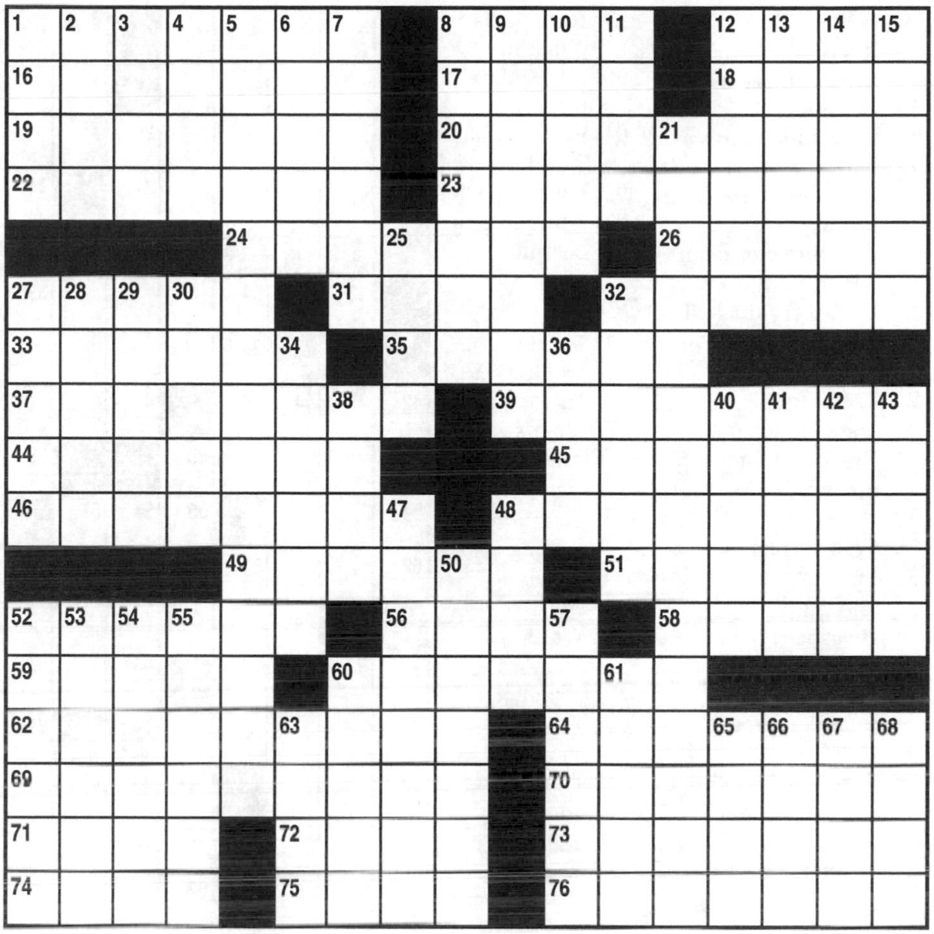

ACROSS

1 Ishmael's father
8 "No ___"
12 Moses in a 1971 Jerry Reed song
16 "Il Trovatore" heroine
17 Mythical Hun king
18 Shetland's tail?
19 Amazing
20 Told lies about
22 Bivouac item
23 Tribunal of old Israel
24 December 31
26 Sheer fabric
27 Go ___ for
31 Toe woe
32 Before deadline
33 1950 Isaac Asimov work
35 Kind of council
37 Sensation of mistrust
39 Drool
44 Start of a backwoods opinion
45 Like many classical aphorisms
46 One after another
48 UGLY feud
49 Zero
51 Popular mint
52 Like some traffic
56 Threat extremes?
58 Hybrid garment
59 Reduce to a pulp
60 Like a hungry lion
62 Singer Humperdinck
64 Mrs. John Quincy Adams et al.
69 Determined to have
70 Ape
71 Reader of crosswords?
72 "___ Marlene" (1944 song)
73 Places where hits are taken
74 Model
75 Acid-resistant wood
76 DNA component

DOWN

1 College grad
2 Nota ___
3 Phoenix kin
4 Anthologies
5 GOOD 1993 Parton/Lynn/Wynette album
6 Golfer Palmer, informally
7 Rival acquired by Whirlpool
8 Rubber
9 Stephen King's "Hearts in ___"
10 "... ___ flowing with milk and honey": Ex. 3:8
11 Ho Chi ___
12 Tarzan's realm
13 "Tuesdays With ___": Album
14 "Strange Interlude" playwright
15 Gateway to Australia
21 BAD Elvis Presley song
25 "The Godfather" composer
27 Conical homes
28 "___ Ben Jonson!": Young
29 Termite, say
30 Old adders
32 Skill
34 Tastelessly affected
36 Kind of coat
38 Monogram ltr.
40 Former White Sox owner Bill
41 A hard ___ follow
42 13th-century invader
43 Opposite of kill
47 RAZR company
48 Angle
50 Slob's opposite
52 Accelerated
53 Locate on the dial
54 They may be vital
55 South Carolina river
57 Flint is a form of it
60 Even the score again
61 One for whom all roads lead to roam
63 It goes to waist
65 "Put ___ writing!"
66 ___-Flush
67 Heaps
68 Zaire's Mobutu ___ Seko

126 COOLIDGE BREAKS HIS SILENCE by Patrick Jordan

Talk about a presidential leader!

ACROSS

1 Interior
6 Increases the kitty
13 Least bit
16 Like a loud crowd
17 Do voice-over work
18 Luau instrument, briefly
19 Barrel maker in an Alberta city?
21 Discovery docked with it in 1997
22 Intertwine
23 Trunk topper
24 Dark brown hue
26 Branco or Bravo preceder
27 Called one's own
29 Web surfer's stop
32 Further
33 Gave a pitch
36 Bearing protuberances
38 Empire with a sedative effect?
42 Entr'___
45 Servitude symbol
46 "Spring forward" abbr.
47 "It just came to me!"
48 Caroler's leapers
50 Make a miscue
52 Exxon ship
54 Priest in I Samuel
55 Superman's nemesis Luthor
58 Passport verification
61 E-mail command
62 Fortress built from Italian turnovers?
66 Mexican-American man
67 Stupid sort
70 Ear cleaner brand
72 Apply crudely
74 ___ Na Na (Woodstock group)
75 Daily grind
77 Acknowledged the bride's entrance
79 Breathtaking serpent?
81 Graphite eradicator
83 "Glass Bell" novelist Anaïs
84 Amateur criminal's mug shot?
88 Pixel
89 Removed by plucking
90 Dressed to the ___
91 Baseball bat wood
92 Unity
93 Antiquing chemicals

DOWN

1 Mugger repeller, perhaps
2 Shah's subjects, once
3 Sour cream serving
4 Icelandic epic
5 Windpipe
6 "___ way you slice it"
7 Table salt, chemically
8 Three, in Toulouse
9 Crumbling away
10 Tree tapper's collection
11 Salt Lake City athlete
12 Cuzco's country
13 Fund-raising event
14 Steinbeck's Joad family, e.g.
15 ___ Haute, Indiana
20 "Cross my heart!"
25 Butte's larger kin
28 Garage band's sample
30 Barbarous barber Sweeney
31 Haagen Dazs rival
34 Cooled with cubes
35 Irrigation barrier
37 Aware of
39 Moxie
40 At that point
41 Gridiron division
42 1964 Tony winner Guinness
43 Pop machine option
44 Infinitesimal fraction
49 Parking meter feature
51 Witty comment
53 Realization remark
56 Town on the Chisholm Trail
57 Lucy Lawless role
59 Briny bodies
60 Pollen producer
63 Microwaves
64 Tunnel center?
65 "My ___" (1979 hit for The Knack)
68 Garlicky poison gas
69 Swordsman with a second
70 Press conf. segment
71 The Supremes et al.
73 "Hooch"
76 Lengthy lock
78 Morph or plasm prefix
80 Inspires wonder
82 "I don't give ___!" ("Who cares?")
85 Oat bristle
86 "School Daze" director Spike
87 HQs for some sgts.

127 "I'M IN!" by Richard Silvestri

This is one title to take literally.

ACROSS

1 Explorer, for one
4 "The ___ Girls" (2001 Sorvino film)
9 Disharmony
15 Sixteen-wheeler
16 Beat, in a way
17 String along
18 Minuet movement
19 First name in makeup
20 Shake down
21 Actual approximation?
24 City on the Humboldt
25 Print-shop worker
26 At an angle
28 Rustic
32 Daniel Boone's brother
33 Grounded flyer
36 Bank depositor's facial expression?
40 Part of a foot
44 Lehigh and Lafayette, e.g.
45 Wouk work
46 Biblical dancer
48 Anticipatory time
49 ___ too many (gets drunk)
50 Spud spot
51 Brace
53 "Jurassic Park" beast
54 Question asked of a charades player?
57 Annapolis grad.
58 Part of R&R
59 "Damn Yankees" team
64 Undivided
67 Crow home
68 Pamplona runner
71 Dentistry as a hobby?
75 Military command
77 Shout from the stands
78 Takeover action
79 Guru
80 Gold standard
81 Mem. of the bar
82 Size up
83 Twisting
84 ___ Moines

DOWN

1 Sister of Venus
2 Kayak cousins
3 End of the rainbow?
4 Top four
5 Rigging attachment
6 Hostile to
7 Abounds
8 Noted toy company
9 Woody Allen film
10 Animator Avery
11 Put on a scale?
12 Cult figure
13 Bifurcate
14 Opposite of veto
15 Bacon bit
22 Little lust boy?
23 Iceman's aid
27 Minneapolis suburb
29 Pink in the middle
30 Bird, in combinations
31 As-it's-happening broadcast
33 Delight in
34 It's part of the act
35 Fax forerunner
37 ". . . ruler of the Queen's ___" G&S
38 Flashes of light
39 75%, perhaps
40 Private lines
41 Troublesome gas
42 Argil and kaolin
43 Sounds of merriment
47 Beat one's breast
49 Song of praise
51 Path starter
52 Cast object
55 Athletic awards
56 Grub
60 Foursome
61 Narcotic sedative
62 Slackens
63 Like a dive
64 Fill with joy
65 Part of a drink order
66 One of the Allens
68 The Crimson Tide
69 Western tribe
70 Glasses glass
72 Consort of Zeus
73 It's all downhill from here
74 Affectedly aesthetic
76 Lusitania's call

128 GROUCHO THE CRITIC by Ed Early

14-D will always be remembered for the catch he made in the 1954 World Series.

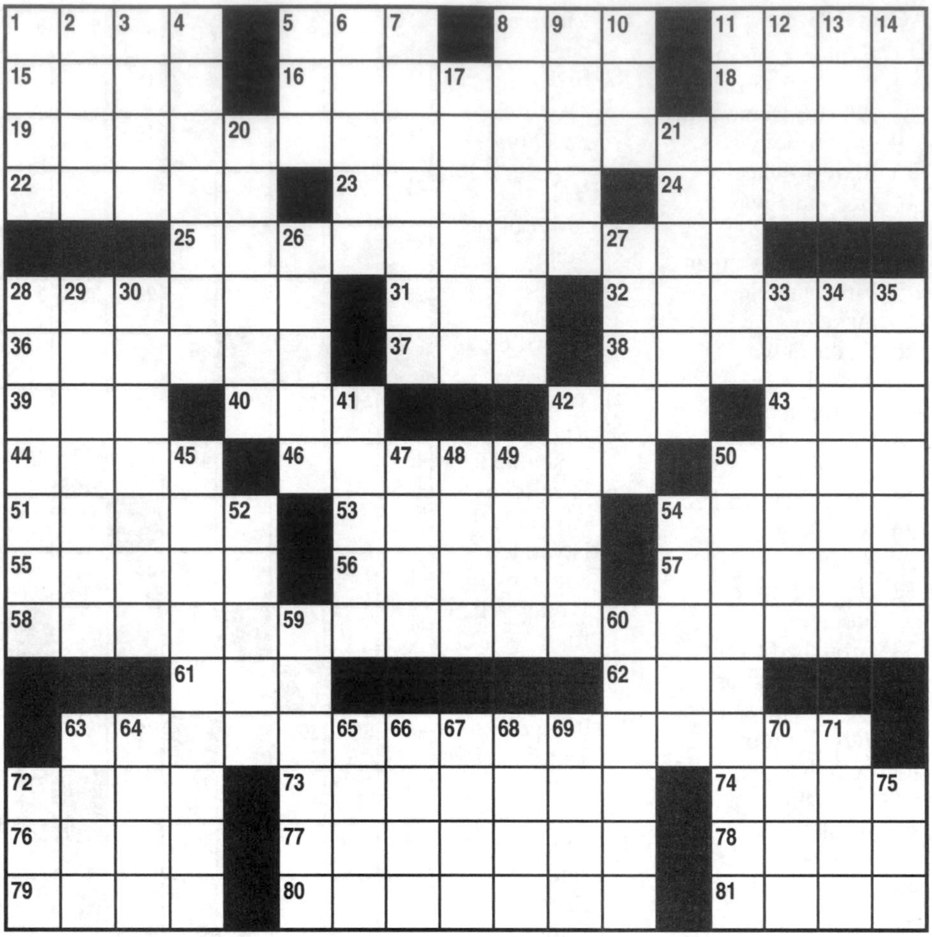

ACROSS

1 Salutary clubs
5 Car sticker stat
8 DDE
11 High-end cheese
15 "Felicity" star Russell
16 Ends up in a padded cell
18 Home of Wyeth's "Christina's World"
19 **Start of a Groucho review**
22 Free-for-all
23 Piston great Thomas
24 Electrical units
25 **Part 2 of review**
28 Sedative
31 Jeremy's "Entourage" role
32 1975 Isabelle Adjani title role
36 Stove burner?
37 Heathrow arrival of yore
38 Wright in "The Steel Trap"
39 ___ in Charles
40 Four Monopoly sqs.
42 Dancer Lili Saint-___
43 Hydroplane support
44 Miss Brockovich
46 **Part 3 of review**
50 Strong ___ ox
51 Edward James in "Stand and Deliver"
53 "Let me repeat . . ."
54 "Palookaville" actor Adam
55 Western director Sergio
56 "Long time ___"
57 Klemperer and Preminger
58 **Part 4 of review**
61 Waxman in "Hollywood Ending"
62 Observe
63 **End of review**
72 Charlie of early whodunits
73 Desperate
74 Green cup
76 Injured
77 Monkey's uncle?
78 ___ lot (very little)
79 March time
80 Trying one?
81 Telephone service

DOWN

1 No-fat milk
2 Ending for milli-
3 Nutmeg skin
4 Court huddle
5 Exec. level
6 Kind of sci.
7 Japanese entertainers
8 "This is no joke!"
9 Blues singer McDonald
10 Icelandic letter
11 Authorize
12 Barbie or Ken
13 Amo, amas, ___
14 "Say Hey Kid" of baseball
17 They enjoy the slope
20 Spay
21 Tax scofflaw
26 "Three's Company" nurse
27 Part man, part goat
28 Seminole chief
29 Dove for gems
30 "I, Robot" author's memoir
33 Rent
34 Boomer of football
35 Kind of raceway
41 "Goosebumps" author
42 Relinquished
45 Much ado about nothing
47 Lake Placid org.
48 Part of Ovid's name
49 ___ Bien Phu, Vietnam
50 "Begin the Beguine" clarinetist
52 Glacial pinnacle
54 "When I take my Sugar ___"
59 Mire
60 "As God is my judge!"
63 It's usually dull
64 Hounds' prey
65 Aussie animals
66 Ivan who produced "Gog"
67 Sutherland solo
68 Without purpose
69 Khartoum river
70 Tucson college, briefly
71 Developer's layout
72 Sorority letter
75 UFO passengers

129 IT'S IN THE SOUP . . . by Harvey Estes
. . . but hard to chew. (See 37 Across)

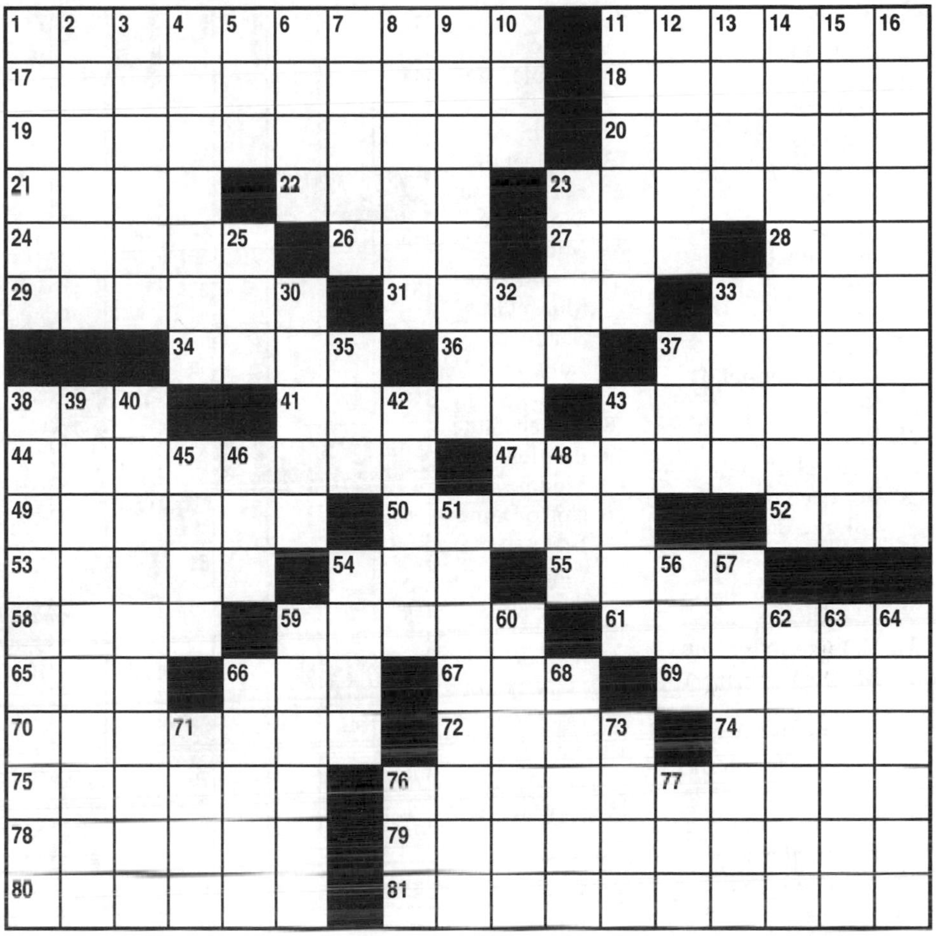

ACROSS

1 Gathering of politicians, informally
11 Printing goof
17 Comment on a tedious trip
18 Dugout items
19 Some models
20 Ring source
21 Pt. of AARP
22 "Ah me!"
23 Asmara's land
24 June portrayer
26 Elev.
27 Indian export
28 Give it a go
29 Next to bat
31 Items sent to record companies
33 Checked item
34 Plug away
36 McKellen in "The Da Vinci Code"
37 It's in the soup but hard to chew
38 Light wood
41 Vieira's show
43 Seasonal numbers
44 Classic children's song
47 Tired writer?
49 Just
50 Tart
52 Object in a courtroom
53 Best example
54 Cold response
55 West Wing worker
58 Straight up
59 Was lost in thought
61 "Pretty nice!"
65 Gallery objects
66 Syr. and Eg., once
67 Sharer's word
69 One of the Marxes
70 Earns
72 Small detail?
74 Where to spend a kip
75 Sorrowful cry
76 Pig out, e.g.
78 Rent collector
79 Eclectic magazine
80 Will's subject
81 Private talks

DOWN

1 Sporty Chevy
2 Up
3 Prepared for a blow
4 Matching pair
5 Lush locale
6 Place of fiction
7 Longtime Dolphins coach
8 Official messenger
9 Aeschylus trilogy
10 Horror director Craven
11 Cuts ridges into
12 Craze
13 Body of soldiers
14 One way to sell
15 Winner at Bull Run
16 Examination prose
23 College on the Thames
25 "The Name of the Rose" writer
30 Pool
32 Waffler's answer
33 Complain constantly
35 Fortune
37 Back muscle
38 Letter clarification
39 Old calculators
40 Weary traveler's cry
42 Sweetie pies
43 Room on board
45 Words before arms
46 Conduit bend
48 Cooperstown stat
51 Chimney deposit
54 Make, as CDs
56 "How dumb of me!"
57 Latin list shortener
59 D preceder
60 Circle in Washington
62 Former German chancellor Willy
63 High point
64 Medicine givers
66 ". . . lead ___ into temptation . . ."
68 Big name in "Chicago"
71 Bart Simpson sister
73 Fame's Irene
76 Kind of instinct
77 Rouge or noir

130 A SHORT WEEK by Edgar Fontaine

A clever challenger from this native New Englander.

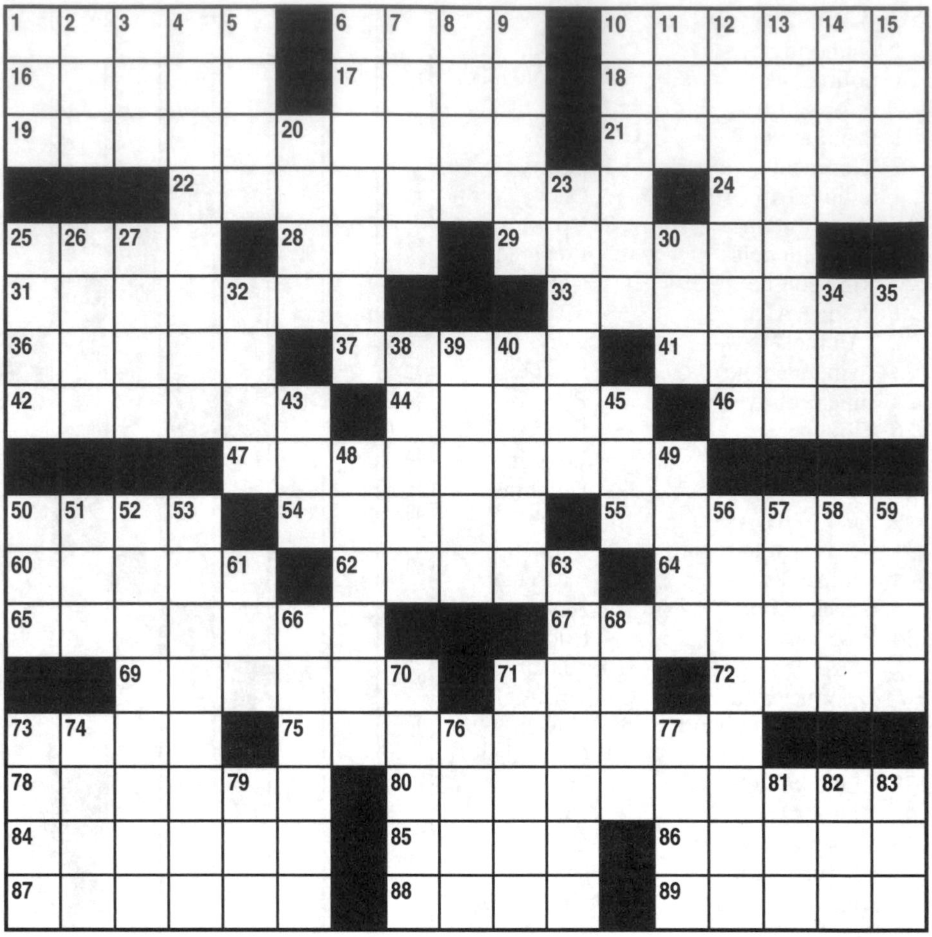

ACROSS

1 Post sans postage
6 Actress Freeman
10 Volcanic rock
16 Bicyclist Armstrong
17 Leave out
18 Muse of astronomy
19 Interminable on d 6?
21 Rag
22 Most stick-in-the-mud
24 Strain
25 Pawn
28 Genteel affair
29 For each one
31 Glutton on d 5?
33 Overlooked
36 Cultivated land
37 Blaspheme
41 Hang in loose folds
42 Moonshine's Irish kin
44 Ration
46 "Irish" Meusel of baseball
47 Milano Mr. on d 2?
50 Pain in the neck
54 "__ Davis Eyes"
55 Pulpits
60 Misbehave
62 Advisers of old
64 Invisible emanations
65 Make right
67 Secure on d 4?
69 Luanda's land
71 Part of USSR
72 Caustic substances
73 Negligible amount
75 Bones of the spinal column
78 Attach anew
80 Hot on d 1?
84 Safe and sound
85 Clarinet's cousin
86 Noted Barton
87 Ramada chain, e.g.
88 School misfit
89 Matches, as tracks

DOWN

1 Ernie Keebler, e.g.
2 Spoil the finish
3 "Wheel of Fortune" buy
4 Move like Midori
5 Period after Mardi Gras
6 Shapers
7 Longines rival
8 Not absolute
9 Perplexed
10 Meddle
11 Notre Dame first name
12 Make out on d 7?
13 Civil War battle site
14 Norseman Ericsson
15 Not at all sweet
20 Overdo the TLC
23 Goad
25 Web address start
26 Miami or Lima location
27 Beantown center?
30 Hail Mary target
32 Those people
34 Starting center?
35 Second smallest st.
38 Pine away
39 Type type
40 Notorious Hiss
43 Head, slangily
45 Rocky crag
48 Cuddle
49 Kind of hog
50 Moccasin
51 "Foucault's Pendulum" author
52 Unbent
53 Sad ER employee on d 3?
56 In a dour manner
57 Where Helen lived
58 Field event
59 Inquires
61 Mumblety-___ (jackknife game)
63 Mopped the deck
66 Envies
68 Pantyhose shade
70 Incendiarism
71 Man of Castilla
73 Imitate Gene Krupa
74 Biggest Little City
76 Soho subway
77 What rainbows are
79 Dot-com's address
81 Golf's Baker-Finch
82 Nils Diaz's org.
83 Neon or Neon-need

131 DIAMOND DEED by Pancho Harrison

The subtitle can be found at 43 Across.

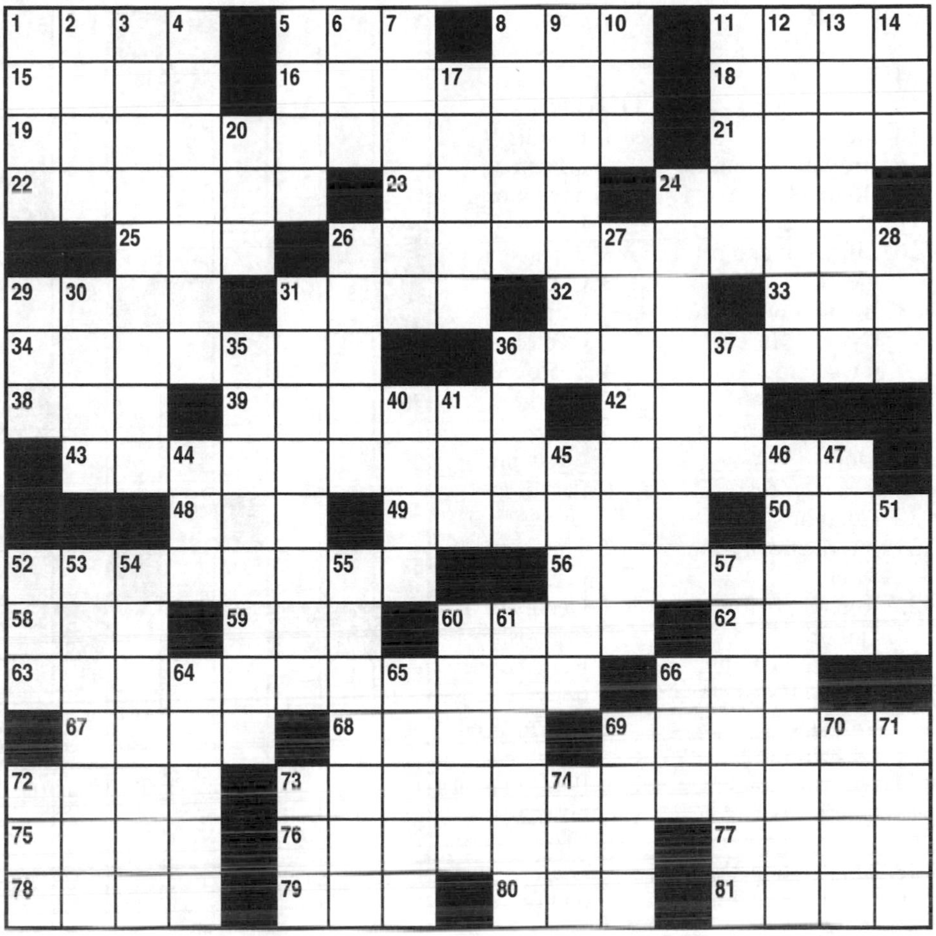

ACROSS

1 Poetic foot
5 Treasury Dept. division
8 Crater edge
11 Mock words of understanding
15 Lady of the haus
16 José who wrote "Juiced"
18 Like morning meadows
19 Unaided
21 Creek at the Masters
22 Poppy derivative
23 Late 19th-century hairdo
24 Macadamize
25 Letterman's network
26 Aldrich Ames, for one
29 1847 Melville novel
31 Heloise offering
32 Text scanner: Abbr.
33 Haw's partner
34 Old film developer
36 Bellagio porters
38 Telecom giant
39 Corrida charger
42 ___ de toilette
43 SUBTITLE
48 Ballpark fig.
49 Scold
50 Meaningful nos. for Mensa
52 Vitamin C sources
56 Wear down
58 Trophy, sometimes
59 French friend
60 Bank regulating org.
62 Impertinent one
63 Count Fleet's feat
66 Nail, in a way
67 Freshwater duck
68 RC or Coke
69 Noxious effluvia
72 D.C. figures
73 Springfield simpleton
75 She sheep
76 Kittenish
77 They may be electric
78 Memo heading
79 Arlo, to Woody
80 Date
81 Where el sol rises

DOWN

1 "That being the case . . ."
2 "What ___-off!"
3 Stuffed-pasta dish
4 Bête noire
5 Arctic Blast maker
6 Cheery sound?
7 Big name in tools
8 Record voice-overs again
9 Arctic Ocean sight
10 Rocker's foe, in '60s London
11 "Kind of ___": Buckinghams
12 Rope puller's cry
13 Tonsor Todd
14 Frustrated utterances
17 Hog's honker
20 USMA grads
24 Bettor, at times
26 "That goes for me, too"
27 Syncretic
28 Logos, e.g.: Abbr.
29 "Birds ___ feather . . ."
30 Clothing consumer
31 Super Bowl intermission
35 Setting for many M*A*S*H scenes
36 Physics Nobelist Niels
37 Tampa Bay player, to fans
40 Eyes
41 Rural address abbr.
44 Golfer's need
45 Have a TV dinner, say
46 Elsa and Nala
47 Prefix with distant
51 Longtime Richard Petty sponsor
52 Sales slip: Abbr.
53 Thornton Wilder play
54 Circus pitchman
55 Mini-flute
57 One on the lam
60 Nashville legend Red
61 Animated miners
64 Obsolete
65 Director Polanski
66 Point
69 Thirty-two laps in the pool, say
70 Shed skin
71 "As I Lay Dying" father
72 Shar-___ (dog breed)
73 Some PCs
74 "A Boy Named ___"

132 NFL INSIDERS by Bonnie L. Gentry

The Pinto's rear fuel tank was another example of a 60 Across.

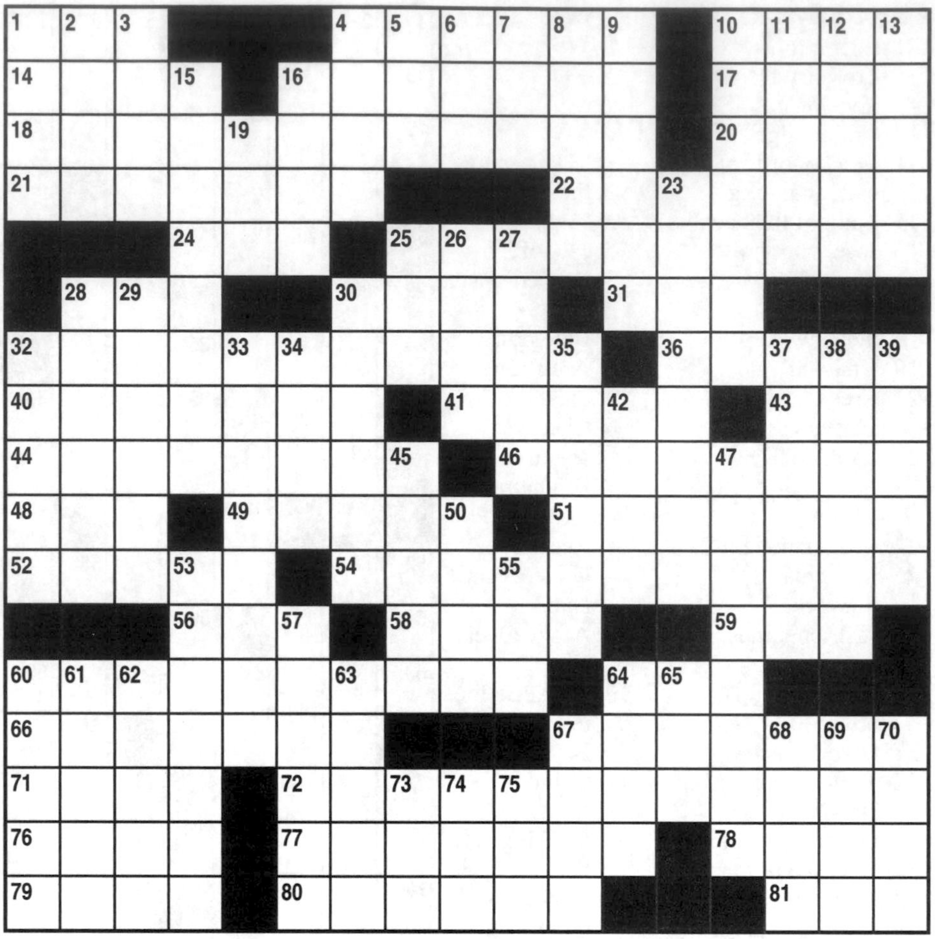

ACROSS

1 Limited number
4 "C'mon!"
10 Green-light
14 Inca fortunes
16 Brownish oranges
17 Bogotá boy
18 Fail spectacularly
20 Lift a hot dog off the grill
21 Break down
22 Cyprus Museum locale
24 Picnic discard
25 Healthy breakfast food
28 Reagan proj.
30 Hussein's queen
31 Interjections from Rocky
32 Referee, before a kickoff
36 Puts in the hold
40 Like half a cyclical romance
41 Related maternally
43 ___ vous plaît
44 Overturns
46 Form a hypothesis
48 Emulated the Sprats
49 "Taxi" mechanic
51 Court arbiter
52 Former NYC restaurateur
54 1966 James Bond spoof
56 Upper-left button on a phone
58 One of Jacob's wives
59 Jennet
60 Cause of a bridge collapse, perhaps
64 Cadence count
66 Chopstick, e.g.
67 Rower
71 Helgenberger of "CSI"
72 Jason's quest
76 Prefix with business and chemical
77 Dispense, as justice
78 "The Witches" author
79 Lennon's "Beautiful Boy" subject
80 Size up
81 Part of AT&T

DOWN

1 Fictional circum-navigator
2 End of the old switch
3 Captain Queeg's creator
4 SoHo studio
5 Goethe's "The ___-King"
6 Part of a chorus line?
7 Theology inst.
8 Occupant of Friendship 7
9 Become bony
10 Down, at a diner
11 Place to post notices
12 "The Nanny Diaries" nanny
13 Exercise systems
15 Arrangement methods
16 Social rebuff
19 Wall St. deal
23 Make unavailable to the public
25 Dizzy Gillespie's genre
26 Lifeline, maybe
27 Fail to be
28 Beethoven's "Appassionata," e.g.
29 Something not to change in midstream?
30 51 past
32 Andean shrubs
33 Weaknesses
34 "Pygmalion" heroine
35 Overly enthusiastic
37 Father of Anubis
38 Mummifies
39 Cause of some skids
42 New driver, typically
45 Haunted house dangler
47 Recidivated
50 2-D measure
53 Rubbing out
55 Animal's gullet
57 Puzzlement
60 "Twenty Years After" author
61 French story
62 "Apostle of California"
63 Ice sheets
64 Knife handle
65 Web site
67 Load to bear
68 Packinghouse product
69 Aleve target
70 Liam Neeson film
73 ROTC grads
74 "Gidget" star
75 Goddess in a chariot

133 "ER" CANCELLED by Billie Truitt

Don't stick an "N" in the name at 37 Down.

ACROSS

1 Action-movie scene
6 Collar location
10 Freak out
15 Women's group?
16 Amtrak's bullet train
18 Red, green, yellow, or white veggie
19 Late party at the neighbors' house?
21 He ran against Clinton and Bush
22 Bye-bye
23 "This is ___ for Superman!"
25 Purina competitor
26 Pumpernickel ingredient
27 Shortly, briefly
29 School of thought
30 She was Dear to many
33 Phony story?
36 Eastern way
37 Burst of laughter
38 Govt. securities
39 Chatty bird
41 Basketball commentator Elmore
43 Spin
44 Memoir of a lepidopterist?
49 Major League family name
50 Larry King's channel
51 Kitchen magnet?
53 Intermediary
56 Chocolate tidbit
58 Campfire seat
59 Laboratory funding?
63 "Anything ___?"
64 Young pond dweller
65 Very much
66 Common site of knee injuries
68 Had on
70 Baylor's home
71 Vacation souvenirs
75 Starr witness Linda
77 How to cook maize evenly?
79 Show opener
80 Key material
81 Half a record
82 Ghostly pale
83 Jump in the rink
84 Precipitous

DOWN

1 Small talk
2 Holy circle?
3 Alice's Restaurant customer
4 Lookout
5 Post of manners
6 Slangy refusals
7 Make a scene?
8 Academic showoff
9 Wood who played Frodo
10 Elephant gp.
11 Most draftable
12 Helicopter rescue, at times
13 Sweetie pie
14 Lays to rest
17 Win by ___
20 V-formation fliers
24 No longer ill
27 Cove
28 Multiplexes
30 Twenties dispenser
31 Indiana political name
32 U2 frontman
34 New Haven inst.
35 Use crayons
37 Jules Verne's Fogg
40 Come to
42 Big Apple initials
43 Confrontation
45 Anne ___ Lindbergh
46 Not sour
47 Kind of booth
48 Med. plans
52 Candle count
53 Dunk some Darjeeling
54 Improvements, of a kind
55 World's fastest biped
57 Secret supply
60 Orange box
61 Priam's wife
62 Bleach brand
63 Draw forth
67 Quest for a mate?
69 Fencing implement
71 E-mail sign-off
72 Took the subway
73 Nest site
74 Lose it
76 Slammer
78 U-turn from SSW

134 "HELLO, I MUST BE GOING" by Patrick Jordan

Alternate clue for 82 Across: Cinderella's horses, subsequently.

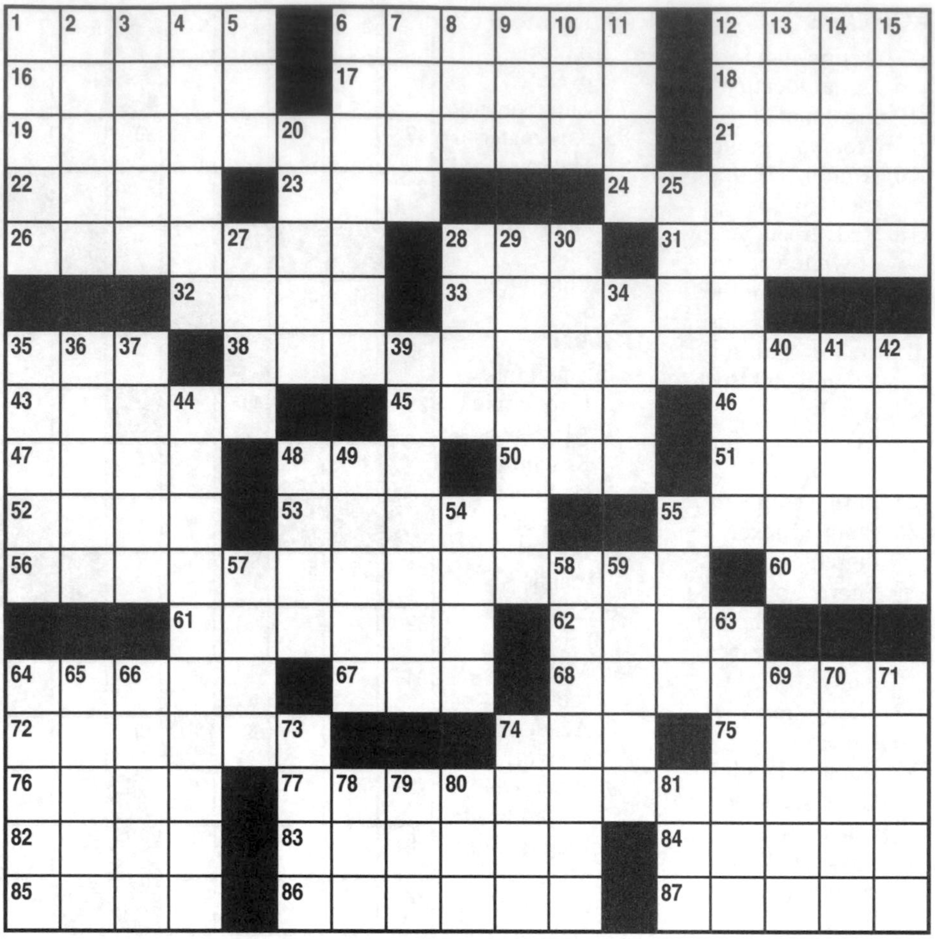

ACROSS

1 Zestfulness
6 Park pigeon's perch
12 Kid around with
16 Those who oppose
17 Riding on
18 "Render ___ Caesar . . ."
19 Greeting to a seismologist?
21 Rabin's predecessor
22 Dee who duetted with Elton
23 Asphalt ingredient
24 Branch out, as a business
26 Boom box feature
28 UPS delivery
31 Donnybrook
32 Ship captained by Vicente Pinzon
33 Earned an honorarium, perhaps
35 Fannie or Ginnie follower
38 Greeting to the Invisible Man?
43 Not suitable
45 Put into circulation
46 Laboratory vessel
47 In ___ (unmoved)
48 Certain stock buyer, briefly
50 Elevs.
51 15th New Testament book
52 Poker player's assertion
53 La Scala's location
55 Packers powerhouse Favre
56 Farewell to an escaped convict?
60 Pronoun for every second hurricane
61 Checked the flavor of
62 "In your dreams!"
64 1988 Summer Games site
67 Pension-paying govt. org.
68 Quarantine
72 Shares the value of
74 Porter or stout
75 "I see ___ moon rising . . .": CCR
76 Petunia, to Harry Potter
77 Farewell to a farmer?
82 Cinderella's horses, formerly
83 "Rambo" genre
84 Plymouth cofounder John
85 Barreled along
86 Bowling or boxing, but not hockey
87 Batik practitioners

DOWN

1 Stares stupidly
2 Like a square
3 Vampire vanquisher
4 Brownish orange hue
5 WWII spying org.
6 Reminiscent of a desert
7 Ski lift type
8 NASA affirmative
9 ___ chi (exercise program)
10 Cremains container
11 Cutting side
12 Cleared with a bound
13 Bryant's former teammate
14 Horror author R. L.
15 Teeming throng
20 Shorthand pro
25 Wolverine's squad
27 It's worn with a sporran
28 Some crockery
29 Flute-playing Hindu god
30 Entire range
34 Souvenir shirts
35 iPod output
36 Psychological inner self
37 "Weird" Al Yankovic parody
39 1960 Elvis musical
40 Analyzes, with "up"
41 "War of the Worlds" world
42 Inspire ecstasy in
44 Emphasized
48 Irving and Tan
49 Thigh-slapping jokes
54 Costar of Farr and Farrell
55 Vivacity, to Verdi
57 Corridor
58 Final part, redundantly
59 County bordering Suffolk
63 How the tone-deaf sing
64 Coal beds
65 Furnish gear for
66 Krugerrand's weight
69 Bear patiently
70 Whip wielder at a circus
71 Blissful spots
73 Fawn's father
74 Briefly, to a bard
78 Defrosting target
79 Env. enclosure
80 Lucy in "Shanghai Noon"
81 Diminutive degree

135 WHAT THE DOCTOR OUGHT TO ORDER by Lucile Sloan

October 4, 1957 is the official date of 33 Across.

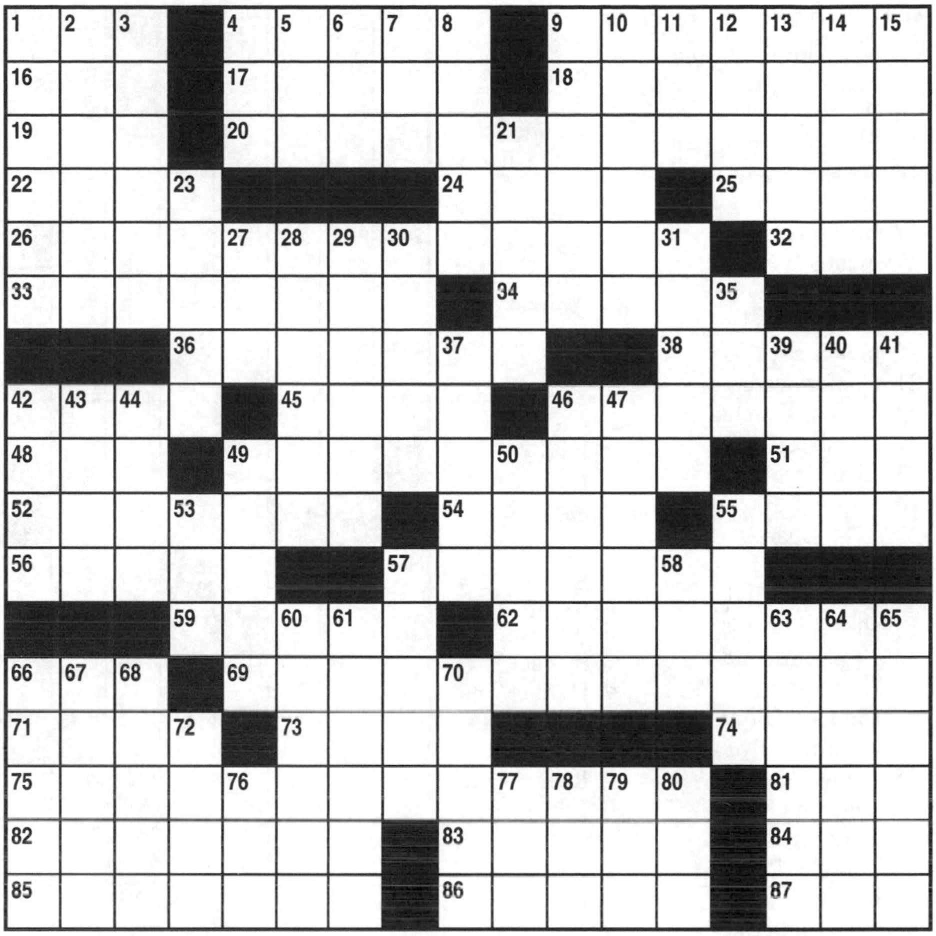

ACROSS

1 NASCAR sponsor
4 Make a law of
9 Has a long step
16 Hardly paleo
17 Alvin of Broadway
18 Charge for using
19 "Take Me as ___": Faith Hill
20 **Josh Billings quote: Part I**
22 Fall ___ grace
24 Orr teammate, familiarly
25 Cave effect
26 **Quote: Part II**
32 Take sustenance
33 It started with Sputnik
34 Bridge phrase
36 Went wild
38 About to receive
42 WW2 Axis leader
45 Parker in "Old Yeller"
46 Seat of Webster County, Ia.
48 Fla. neighbor
49 **Quote: Part III**
51 Dudgeon
52 Some bundles of joy
54 Phys. activity
55 Knocked off
56 "Woman Eating Oysters" artist
57 Mediterranean vessels
59 VW preceders
62 Taking a powder on the mound
66 "Freaks" director Browning
69 **Quote: Part IV**
71 "Bring ___" (2000 cheerleading movie)
73 Dobbin's restraint
74 Tropical starchy root
75 **Quote: Part V**
81 Part of a wd.
82 Tee transfers
83 Ex-New York governor
84 Games org.
85 Not mind
86 Work until smooth
87 Suffix with propyl or butyl

DOWN

1 Emulates a police dog
2 Begin to cry
3 Home of Cal Poly
4 Creepy crawler
5 "Forget it!"
6 Is for more than one?
7 Train section
8 Gershwin's "Of ___ Sing"
9 Gain admission quietly
10 "Receiving poorly," in CB talk
11 Untrustworth y one
12 "Woe ___!"
13 Low card
14 ___-Sketch
15 Not ___ (far from optimal)
21 "My Fair Lady" setting
23 Smaller than small
27 Granting grp.
28 Virile
29 White-tailed herons
30 Franklin, religiously
31 Bagnold and Blyton
35 Noted Tokyo-born singer
37 Milo of "Ulysses"
39 Bank-window initials
40 "The Lord of the Rings" creature
41 Walter ___ Hospital
42 Bandage in a way
43 Portrait studio ___ Mills
44 Jolts
46 Sans
47 Soprano Stratas
49 Quotable Yogi
50 Version's start
53 ___ au vin
55 "Ours ___ to reason why . . .": Tennyon
57 Desi's daughter
58 0, in soccer
60 Pilgrim's goal
61 Smaller than small
63 Rome's home, in France
64 "The Honeymooners" character
65 Aerospace measure
66 Marshmallowy
67 Comic actress Cheri
68 "Ice Age" birds
70 New York hoopster
72 Spanish kid
76 Corn throwaway
77 Cloister sister
78 Other side
79 Mia in "Pulp Fiction"
80 Signal at Sotheby's

136 IT'S ELEMENTARY by Robert A. Doll

60 Across was Secretary of Transportation from 1993 to 1997.

ACROSS

1 Museum Folkwang locale
6 Put to the test
11 Place for a pumpkin
16 Gene Tierney classic film
17 More "compos mentis"
18 Plains tribe
19 Heavy-metal pioneers
21 Copier need
22 Weight Watchers member
23 Like Dracula
24 Shows
27 "The Dean Martin Show" dancers
30 Showered and shaved, say
32 ___ Marquette
33 Linda ___ (Supergirl)
34 Alternatively
35 All worked up
37 Big name in furniture rental
38 Dorothy Parker quality
39 Like Catherine Zeta-Jones
42 Apiece
44 Tennessee Williams classic
49 ___ the finish
50 Dapper
51 "Platoon" setting
53 Cathedral recess
56 Scrooge
58 Eight furlongs
59 ___ generis (unique)
60 Clinton cabinet member Federico
61 Speck
65 Party staple
68 Most warmed-up
69 Lexington's Rupp et al.
70 Brunch fare
72 Japanese cooking wine
73 Sure thing
78 "Silas Marner" author
79 Nighttime kitchen invader
80 Stevie Wonder's "My Cherie ___"
81 College bigwigs
82 Cruel sorts
83 Animal hides

DOWN

1 "The Lord of the Rings" figure
2 Freelancer's enc.
3 ___ rosa
4 Learned
5 Compatriot
6 African menace
7 Hard to find
8 Prefix with red
9 Reef dweller
10 Like some wine
11 Soup, in a French restaurant
12 In a crowd of
13 Grapefruit cousin
14 Fan, at times
15 Can't be swayed, in jargon
20 "Aqua ___ Hunger Force"
23 Stinging colonist
24 All over again
25 Dig find
26 Haile Selassie disciple
28 Kick ___ storm
29 More than dislike
31 He ran away with the spoon
36 French wine region
37 Comedian Margaret
39 Hit the jackpot
40 Some paints
41 Barrio resident
43 Boo-hoo
45 Backgammon impossibility
46 Diamond cover
47 In reserve
48 Horseshoe ___
52 Track event
53 Red-faced
54 Childish
55 Sight of the Tunguska blast
57 ___ Paulo
58 Buy before a sale, e.g.
60 Double agents
62 Hebrew letters
63 Thespian's quest
64 Work boot feature
66 Negatively charged particle
67 Like some stock
71 Cheese nibblers
73 Ora ___ nobis
74 Cranberry area
75 Cambodia's Lon ___
76 Director's cry
77 Store posting: Abbr.

137 SHIFTY SLOGANS by Doug Peterson

19 Across won the Daytona 500 in 1991.

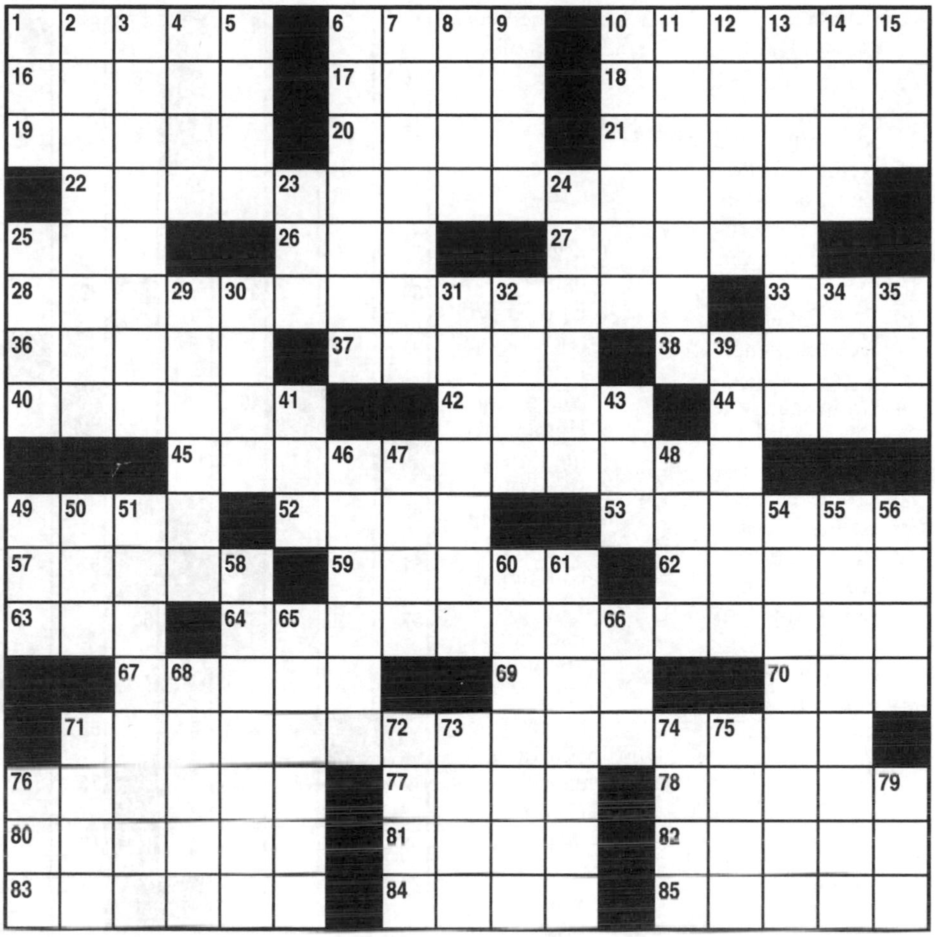

ACROSS

1 Goes for a dip
6 Some laptops
10 Togo, e.g.
16 River craft
17 Father of Ham
18 Meeting handout
19 Legendary NASCAR driver Ernie
20 "The River Sings" singer
21 Makes fine food?
22 Bisquick slogan?
25 Magnate Onassis
26 Calendar-watch abbr.
27 Beehive State resident
28 Bausch & Lomb slogan?
33 Glum
36 Associate of Freud
37 Right-hand page
38 Opposing force
40 Bellyached
42 Hardly a squeaker
44 Emmy winner Falco
45 AAA slogan?
49 Cocktail garnish
52 "Skedaddle!"
53 Prankster's cry
57 Madrid museum
59 Make fun of
62 Not at all
63 Droop
64 Formula 409 slogan?
67 Boca ___
69 Watch attachment
70 '50s political inits.
71 Speedo slogan?
76 Lemonlike fruit
77 Kind of vaccine
78 Sacred stand
80 Alternative to macaroni
81 Wile E. Coyote supplier
82 Unpleasant residue
83 End of a threat
84 Racing circuits
85 Elizabethan earl

DOWN

1 Chem. or phys.
2 Result of a hitch in the service?
3 Sweet-talk
4 Zoo barrier
5 In the mail
6 Mistakenly
7 Pep rally sight
8 BLT spread
9 ___-Pei dog
10 Hero of Super Bowl III
11 Work up
12 Sophomore's grade
13 Furious
14 German border river
15 Mil. landing site
23 Dee follower
24 Head for the hills
25 Steed with speed
29 Tested by lifting
30 BlackBerry rival
31 Cratchit's employer
32 "Believe ___ Not!"
34 Brest buddy
35 Turn blue
39 Trojan War counselor
41 Two-out plays: Abbr.
43 Dress (up)
46 Hallowed site
47 Lather
48 "The World of Suzie ___" (1960)
49 Vinyl spinners
50 401(k) cousin
51 "The Treachery of Images" painter
54 Italian table wines
55 Event with a friendly crowd
56 Leaves speechless
58 Auto extras
60 Freeway feature
61 Noggins
65 '80s White House nickname
66 Stat for a Mariner
68 Pop singer Lavigne
71 "New Look" designer
72 Stable newborn
73 Predator of the deep
74 Ming thing
75 Maladies
76 ___-Magnon
79 Stout of whodunits

138 BUSH THE LEADER by Billie Truitt

A puzzler's tribute to the 43rd president . . . or is it?

ACROSS

1 Costco competitor
5 Darrow defended him
11 Journalist Drudge
15 Neutral shade
16 Piano adjusters
17 Jiggly dessert
18 Range unit
19 One on the stump
20 Erie Canal city
21 Keep the ship's log?
24 Brain scan letters
25 "Not guilty," for one
26 Promotes
30 Centric starter
32 Body slam consequence?
36 Sniffs out
38 Fellow
39 Gluttony or pride
40 One of the five W's
41 Supermarket division
43 Rollercoaster segments
44 This life's struggles?
48 Root ___
49 Spread out
50 Juanita's year
51 Word to a family doctor
52 "Dig in!"
53 Winter sculpture
57 Sound of rustling gift paper?
62 Almanac tidbit
63 "Hogan's Heroes" character
64 Drying oven
66 Genealogy word
67 Prepare used clothes to drip dry?
72 Babble on
75 Dad's sister, affectionately
76 MP's quarry
77 Reno or Jackson
78 "Can't wait!" in Canterbury
79 On one's rocker?
80 Telescope sight
81 Canned heat
82 Units of work

DOWN

1 Kelp
2 Grow together
3 Man to marry
4 Bird feeder fat
5 Kitchen island seat
6 Homecoming times?
7 Even (with)
8 Anti-fur gp.
9 Cupid's counterpart
10 Ukr. and Est., once
11 Shooting star
12 Will Smith title role
13 Convalescent's need
14 Grind ___ halt
17 "A ___ Wine, a Loaf . . .": Khayyám
22 Ages
23 Blood-typing letters
27 Rug fiber
28 "Fun, Fun, Fun" car
29 Payroll IDs
31 More up-to-date
33 Shake up
34 Like an easy job
35 MacLachlan of "Desperate Housewives"
37 Little ones
41 Company with a spokesduck
42 McGregor in "Stormbreaker"
43 Three, perhaps
44 "___ the Champions": Queen
45 Post-injury program
46 Diner sign
47 Sworn in
48 Cry like a baby
53 Grand Central, for one
54 Fabled racehorse
55 Everlasting
56 1956 Kentucky Derby winner
58 Tankard metal
59 Editor's mark
60 Yes, to Yvette
61 Computer network device
65 Shorthand expert
68 Constant carpers
69 Mex. neighbor
70 Treater's phrase
71 Alleviate
72 Sleepover attire, briefly
73 2008 Chinese calendar icon
74 Santa in California

139 SOPHISTICATED LADY by Norman S. Wizer

A felicitous title and the name of a classic Rosemary Clooney recording.

ACROSS

1 Repository
6 Liturgical vestments
10 Sinbad's land
16 Ice house
17 12/26 event
18 They're made at bars
19 Rosemary sang with his band
21 Quartet + trio
22 Memorabilia
23 Went through channels?
25 Fontaine offering
26 Marvin and Merriweather
28 Cinerary vessel
29 It's found on the streets
33 1951 Rosemary Clooney hit
37 ___ corpus
40 Mushroom
41 Deal maker
42 The footlights
43 Source of suds
46 1954 Rosemary Clooney hit
49 1952 Rosemary Clooney hit
52 Clio winners
53 Poke
55 Kind of symmetry
56 Puts down
58 Idle
59 1954 Rosemary Clooney film
64 Put another way
65 New Zealand bird
66 Beat down
70 Trip of sorts
71 Tickle
75 Thailand language
76 Rain cloud
80 1954 Rosemary Clooney film
82 It's between the pages
83 Pundit
84 Spine-tingling
85 Set
86 Got with difficulty
87 Break in

DOWN

1 Life-giving
2 Time past, time past
3 Radii companions
4 She played Mrs. Charles
5 Blue-ribbon
6 Free from doubt
7 Ricky Martin's music
8 Political group
9 Withered
10 Jenny may be one
11 Charlotte of "Diff'rent Strokes"
12 Gran Paradiso, e.g.
13 Bayou boat
14 Prototypes
15 Perceptive
20 Reuners
24 Scratch up
27 Hound's clue
30 Seductive singer: Var.
31 21st Greek letter
32 In ___ signo vinces
34 Inauguration Day vow
35 Washington slugger
36 Banded quartz
37 Silly fence?
38 Kept in the cellar, perhaps
39 Turkish governors
42 Meal with matzoh
43 Destiny's Child, e.g.
44 Word of consolation
45 Gomer of Mayberry
47 Put on the books
48 Hied
50 Computer input
51 Have being
54 E-commerce giant
56 NFL passing stat
57 "Golden Girl" Arthur
58 Normandy beach
59 Monkey ___
60 Flight to freedom
61 Chemical "twin"
62 Just a little bit
63 Dressed
67 On the qui vive
68 Victor ___ Hugo
69 Puzzling problem
72 Enya's language
73 News source, at times
74 Home of Keebler elves
77 Like Peck's boy
78 Put into practice
79 Change on the Ginza
81 Yellow Monopoly bill

140 IT MARCHES ON by Jinx Davidson

40 Across ranks behind Great Britain and Iceland in size.

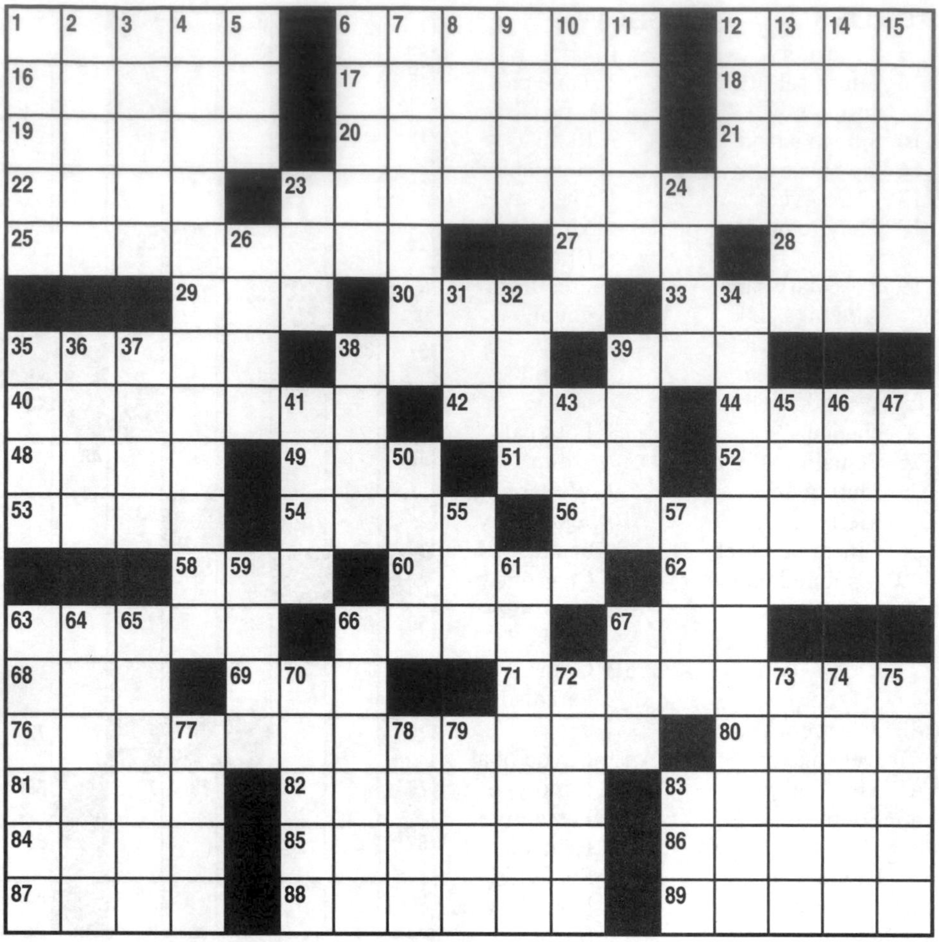

ACROSS

1 Backslide
6 Single-minded theorizer
12 Glen Gray's Casa ___ Orchestra
16 Lands in the ocean
17 Kansas city suburb
18 "About" preceders in charges
19 Bellyaches
20 Infection result, perhaps
21 Cold pack
22 Stall
23 "In other words . . ."
25 More elliptical, in a way
27 Shucker's unit
28 Bracket type
29 Old can material
30 Check number
33 Sajak or Trebek
35 Willy of "Death of a Salesman"
38 Morales in movies
39 LDS-related campus
40 Europe's 3rd-largest island
42 Swing site
44 Girl from 40 Across
48 Toy ball brand
49 Goad, with "on"
51 Was idle
52 Jean-Claude Van Damme film
53 De follower?
54 Flying formations
56 Herring delicacy
58 Poetic tribute
60 Subsequently
62 Evil one
63 Greeting
66 Laceration
67 Brother's title
68 Court winner
69 Env. content
71 Ration out
76 "It's been a pleasure"
80 Slip ___ (blunder)
81 Stare open-mouthed
82 Philippine province
83 Hard wear?
84 Bank claim
85 "Mad" man
86 Fred's familial partner
87 Muffs
88 Manages
89 Loan security

DOWN

1 Trunk attachments
2 "Modern Man in Search of ___": Jung
3 Costa del Sol feature
4 Overly nostalgic sort
5 Snaky shape
6 Israeli leader Dayan
7 Mrs. ___ cow
8 "I'm taking a siesta!"
9 "___ small world!"
10 Eye shadow?
11 Seed coat
12 Gray wolf
13 "Hold on!"
14 Spirit
15 Diamond-shaped pattern
23 Take the cake
24 Junior's son
26 "Dennis the Menace" girl
31 Grab a bite
32 Goes on TV
34 Storage units
35 Swimmer Jeremy
36 Three-layer treat
37 Raconteur Griffin
38 Cusp
39 Eliza follower?
41 Torino Olympic mascot of 2006
43 Toward the rising sun
45 Zoning unit
46 By and by
47 Zoomed
50 Kind of therapy
55 Neptune's realm
57 Bushy do
59 Blockhead
61 Roentgenologist's place
63 Quibble
64 Patisserie product
65 Good rebounder, usually
66 "The Rose of ___"
67 Winter health concern
70 Self-contained entity
72 Hardly rational
73 Zeniths
74 "A Confederacy of Dunces" author
75 "Snowy" bird
77 Retreats
78 "Stop the clock"
79 Rice and Robbins
83 Miami Heat home

141 PROMPT JUDGMENT by Patrick Jordan

Lon Chaney, Jr., and Benicio del Toro have both played 24 Across.

ACROSS

1 Passages between peninsulas
7 Pick up vibes about
12 Cello's range
16 Lebanese University site
17 Fusion weapon, for short
18 Diva's rendition
19 **Quip by E.V. Lucas: Part 1**
21 Adept at deception
22 Hydropathic facility
23 Asparagus shoot
24 Hairy howler of horror
26 Having a screw loose
28 Texas Revolution fort
29 Pas' partners
32 Nebr. neighbor
33 Throw off one's trail
36 **Quip: Part 2**
39 Mme., in Mazatlán
42 Performs adequately
43 Grinner's emotion
44 "Get Smart" enemy org.
45 Welcome
46 "Seventh heaven"
48 Signs of bad shock absorbers
49 Bridge builder James
50 Strategist's concoction
51 Gesture to a general
52 "Reach for the ___!" ("Stick 'em up!")
53 **Quip: Part 3**
56 Frugal shopper's concern
57 UAE member?
58 Pegs, briefly
59 Echo-testing shout, often
62 Stropped item
64 Globe girder
67 Bombastic outbursts
69 Big bankroll
72 Patty or Selma, to Bart
73 **Quip: Part 4**
76 Popular fashion
77 Without letup
78 Tick away
79 "Mush!" yeller's vehicle
80 "Clash by Night" playwright
81 IOU writer

DOWN

1 Curve-billed wader
2 Twice-monthly tide
3 Succotash bean
4 Memorable span
5 Soaking spots
6 Retreat a little
7 Massage technique
8 "The Great Movies" author Roger
9 Guy Fawkes Day mo.
10 Small fishing duck
11 Spain's most voluminous river
12 Throw for a loop
13 Coffee shop lure
14 Early riser's hr.
15 Refuse
20 Wasn't quite perpendicular
25 ___-in-waiting
27 Cheerleader's repertoire
29 Tiny buzzers
30 Greenland wear
31 Bullet train adjective
32 Gordian or granny, e.g.
34 Contends (for)
35 Absorbed the cost of
37 Applications
38 Not getting any younger
39 Slender hunting dog
40 Broke down
41 Size up
44 Pop-flavoring nut
46 International alliance
47 "Today" talker Matt
48 Door frame upright
50 Upsilon follower
51 Gave quite a turn to
53 Sulky puller's pace
54 Duffer's obstacles
55 "The Gift of the Magi" device
56 Like an armadillo
59 Gets wind of
60 Sharing a value
61 Fencing move
63 "You ___ serious?" ("Is this a joke?")
65 Melville book set in Tahiti
66 Rip apart
68 Brogue's bottom
69 Reacted to a tearjerker
70 "Not to mention . . ."
71 One who tints togs
74 Skein formation
75 Slap the cuffs on

142 TRIPLE THREAT* by Elizabeth C. Gorski

18 Across was first staged in 1901 and is actively produced today.

ACROSS

1 Nae sayer
5 Sprints toward
11 Blondie drummer Burke
15 Name on an IRA
16 Like some bonds
17 University of Hawaii locale
18 Title by 78 Across/SUBTITLE
20 Words heard by mice
21 Bless with oil
22 "Excuse me . . ."
23 Gift for Rapunzel
24 Checkbook record
26 It's abuzz with activity
28 Level
31 Double-wide pram*
36 Knock, slangily
37 Pricey
38 Bonn article
39 Ketel ___ vodka
40 Shake hands on
42 Monster's loch
45 Italian soprano Renata
47 30, at times*
50 World Cup chant
51 "Right!"
52 Defeat Federer in the first round
54 Sun god
55 Constellation near Scorpius
57 "Mama" Elliot
59 Mozart's gift
60 Marathon ender*
64 Queue after Q
65 Its capital is Pristina
66 Mariposa lily variety
68 Low point
71 Bullfrog genus
73 Throat soother
77 Plath's "Tale of ___"
78 Russian physician/playwright
80 A word from Mork
81 Foster's brown-haired girl
82 "___ Rock": Simon & Garfunkel
83 Tulip supporter
84 Skillful
85 Richie Rich's collar

DOWN

1 Mex. miss
2 Joe McCarthy's counsel Roy
3 Other, in Cancun
4 Belief in God
5 Bollywood star Aishwarya
6 Nocturnal bear
7 Detroit on Broadway
8 Leaves Earl Grey in hot water
9 It'll eat you out of house and home
10 Takes too much
11 Classic supermodel Tiegs
12 Stead
13 Antlered critters
14 Slam dance
16 Knowing
19 Med. specialty
23 Tracheal branch
25 Swahili honorific
27 Come into being
28 Christian denom.
29 Poker variety
30 Haifa native
32 "Your honor, ___ my case . . ."
33 Egyptian water lilies
34 Request
35 ___ Speedwagon
37 Economics measure
41 Mik Kaminski's group
43 Boston Pops sect.
44 Took a bit of needling
46 Alley in the comics
48 Parisian papas
49 Gets better
50 East of Germany
53 Capote, to friends
56 Decorated
58 Boil over with anger
61 Downwardly mobile sort
62 Incarnation
63 Words of protest
64 Yankee Stadium newbie
67 Upper-level coll. entry test
68 Bobbsey and Robertson
69 Rat-___
70 Novel set in the year 10,991
72 Years in old Rome
74 Palaver
75 Jacob Epstein's "Ecce ___"
76 "Mrs. Bridge" author Connell
78 Classic Steely Dan album
79 Op. ___

143 WEATHER OR NOT by Arlan and Linda Bushman

Santa's throwing the party at 19 Across.

ACROSS

1 Ridiculous
7 Brace (oneself)
11 Recklessness
16 Oil-rich sultanate
17 Son of Seth
18 Steer clear of
19 North Pole party?
21 Patches
22 Headstrong
23 Dance partner
24 Record label letters
26 Journey of 2009?
27 Kind of shot
28 Playwright Shepard
31 Time span
34 Flat cause
37 Jungle hacker
39 Solon consideration
40 Snaps
41 Prison in 1971 headlines
42 ___ around
44 Ways
45 Finding time to relax, e.g.?
48 Drive (out)
51 Meal makings
52 Beguile
56 Broadway musical
57 Antediluvian
58 Nitty-gritty
59 Fickle demeanor?
63 Andean honchos
64 Stake
65 Miniature
66 Winter Palace occupant
68 Minn. neighbor
69 Souter attire
71 Superficial
74 Excellent
76 Frosty's concern?
79 Stand-up's delivery
80 On the house
81 Singly
82 Hound's clue
83 Popular sneakers
84 Packed compactly together

DOWN

1 Mideast garment
2 Cold call?
3 To the point
4 Golden Rule word
5 This pulls a bit
6 Pronouncements
7 Italian treat
8 Lined up
9 Like some cheeks
10 Mar. event
11 Celebrated
12 Baker
13 Best personal asset
14 Maximum
15 Draper's meas.
20 Scorched, in Montreal
23 Oodles
24 Austen classic
25 Defensive feature
27 Swiss capital
29 Keystone's place
30 Snafu
32 Copse
33 "Men in Trees" star
35 Court responses
36 Austere
38 ___ chi
42 Wesley Snipes vampire flick
43 Newt, once
44 Sophia Loren hubby Carlo
46 Sucker, informally
47 Peg
48 Rebuff
49 Colliery
50 Picketing
53 Carom
54 Philosopher Watts
55 "Hey!"
57 Orchestral tuner
58 No laughing matter
60 Most favorably
61 Paid the penalty
62 Matters for discussion
67 Put on again
70 Auspice
71 Close attention
72 Model
73 "How sweet ___!"
74 REM-time wear
75 "Arabian Nights" flier
76 RMN rival
77 Sharapova coup
78 Combine

144 DIJON VU by Richard Silvestri

The definition below is not according to Webster's.

ACROSS

1 New Zealand aborigine
6 Toll area
11 Hacienda brick
16 Out of this world?
17 Big name in morning TV
18 Steakhouse order
19 Worked on pumps
20 Pizza places
21 Minimum
22 **Start of a definition of "Dijon vu"**
25 Blue
26 Towhead
27 Satisfied the munchies
28 Chevy Colorado predecessor
29 Fermi's study
32 Scoutmasters, mostly
36 Small swallow
38 The time of your life
40 WWW addresses
42 Flight formation
43 Driver's target
45 Leather-___ (very loud)
47 Nut-brown quaff
48 **Middle of definition**
52 Jackie's 1968 husband
53 Disclaimer
54 "The Eve of St. Agnes" writer
55 The big house
56 Put in one's two cents?
57 Camel dropping
60 Is, for two
61 Competitive plus
63 Cub Scout groups
65 Point to the left?
67 Simile words
69 "Magic Man" group
71 Batter's success
74 **End of definition**
80 Dreadlocked dude
81 Hopping mad
82 Heathen
83 Phenol compound
84 In a spin
85 Emulate Cicero
86 In need of cash
87 Intrinsically
88 Triple trio

DOWN

1 Brig twosome
2 Hilo hello
3 Drunk as a skunk
4 Boating hazard
5 Owing
6 Stretch out
7 "The Stepford Wives" author
8 It may be hidden
9 Energy
10 Kind of mgr.
11 Equivalent of G sharp
12 Reduced the fare
13 Oil of crosswords
14 "You'd ___ Nice to Come Home To"
15 Rebuke from Caesar
23 Where Zeno taught
24 Best Picture of 1948
28 Noted Graf
30 Arctic plain
31 Bacchanalia
33 Incarnation in human form
34 Strike out
35 Crop starters
36 Fearful
37 "The Legend of Sleepy Hollow" author
39 "Pipers piping" number
41 Mt. Rushmore loc.
43 Condition
44 Role for Radner
46 Persian Gulf fed.
49 Lugosi portrayer
50 Bar mitzvah, e.g.
51 Parliament prize
58 Wrap with bandages
59 Basil, for one
62 Egg-roll time
64 Lad
66 Treat badly
68 Nobody's fool
70 Empire State Indians
71 "Crocodile Dundee" star
72 Hopping mad
73 Article of faith
74 Uno + dos
75 Diner specialty
76 :, in analogies
77 Cuff
78 Pirelli product
79 Las Vegas game

145 SIX THAT SOUND THE SAME by Regimen L. Evers

34 Across enrolled at Stanford in the fall of 2007.

ACROSS

1 Goombah
4 Act inconspicuously
10 Tell to sit a spell
15 "Don't have ___, man!"
17 White fur
18 Nebraska Indian
19 Ride rider's shout
21 Hidden mikes
22 Clinton's 1993 inauguration started one
23 City southwest of Padua
25 Take without asking
26 Ohio college
29 Where Wales is
31 Center in central Florida
34 Honolulu-born golfer
38 Movie cowboy Lash
39 Cornrow
40 German industrial center
41 Free-swinging Ruben
43 Figure of speech
45 "___ Tu" (1974 hit)
46 Developing
49 Habit
53 Two twelfths
54 Coming from both sides
56 Word before box
60 Bolt to get hitched
63 Horoscope writer Sydney
64 Xbox 360 rival
66 Hiding hiker of kiddie lit
67 Old convertible name
68 Over
70 "___ take arms against . . .": Shak.
71 Blurt out
75 Picks via polls
79 Herald's locale
81 Yes to a Frenchman
84 Spaniard's "these"
85 Soda jerks hand them out
86 Camping equipment
87 Pad user
88 Walk like a baby
89 Wave carrier

DOWN

1 One of 16 in chess
2 Workout consequence, maybe
3 Movie mogul Marcus
4 "The Merry Widow" composer
5 George's lyrical brother
6 CPR user, sometimes
7 It's insurable
8 It's carried on the shoulders
9 Shoved off
10 Actress Clara
11 Ellis Island visitors
12 Gets smaller
13 Inferior product
14 Fading star
16 Two and three a.m., say
20 Word processor user
24 Sniggler's catch
27 Roadie's burden
28 Measure of thickness
30 Peter Fonda's favorite role
31 Threat ender
32 Eyes or ears
33 Tribe of Canada
35 Purina product
36 Put in a position?
37 Captain Hook's alma mater
42 Singer DiFranco
44 Quart divs.
47 Cut from the payroll
48 Normandy battleground of '44
49 Arrivers' comment
50 Dental school exam?
51 No jock
52 Ring rampager
53 Dump closure?
55 "His" and "Hers" items
56 Workers make them
57 Pepys, for one
58 Tuition classification
59 Footstool
61 Dessert wedge
62 Nietzsche article
65 San Francisco hill
69 Clueless
72 Clueless
73 One with a painted body
74 Oriole or cardinal
76 2.0 grades
77 Something to whistle
78 Madrid Mlle.
80 Equi- relative
82 "Cracked" competitor
83 Mouse catcher

146 THERE'S MONEY IN IT by Jay Sullivan

60 Across is a popular dance in Lafayette, Louisiana.

ACROSS

1 Jeanne d'Arc, par exemple
7 S&L offering
11 Pleased as punch
15 NAFTA component
16 Made the cut
17 A Golden Girl
18 What banks pay in Romania?
20 Think piece
21 Cut down to size
22 Sun star
23 Inexpensive Delhi footwear?
29 Big tops
30 PC program extension
31 Helping that doesn't help the waist
36 Dredge up
38 Soliloquize
39 Snake alarm
40 The eyes have it
44 Sought a second term
45 Net earnings, in Nogales?
49 Volunteer's response
51 Gave the slip
52 Zsa Zsa's sister
55 In stereo
57 First-class sailor
60 Cajun jig
61 Disney picture
64 Monk's music
65 Polish gambler's preference?
68 Shylock's trade
72 Geronimo, for one
73 "Don't think so!"
74 Saudi currency venture?
80 Course elective
81 Capital of central Asia
82 Indelicate
83 Care for
84 Chicano bears
85 At first, perhaps

DOWN

1 Mineo of the movies
2 Leader of the pack
3 Post-op stop
4 Discouraging words
5 Least original
6 Ferber and Everage
7 One of the Pleiades
8 Pipsqueak
9 Some TV's
10 Summer Mass. hours
11 Put on a happy face
12 Pocket full of gold
13 Gone fishing, perhaps
14 Howie Mandel offering
16 Coil
19 Floor decor
22 Annual awards event
23 Household cleaners
24 Sci-fi craft
25 Undefiled
26 It's quite a stretch
27 Beat the heat?
28 No longer in the U.S. Army
32 Bread spread
33 Old salt
34 Small inheritance
35 AARP member
37 Sugar suffix
38 Not worth ___ cent
41 Bargain-basement
42 Veg out
43 It'll never fly
46 Unfortunately
47 Accident-prone
48 Mad men, briefly
49 Resident of the former Biafra
50 Patriots' victory
53 Wind instrument
54 Mound builders
56 Mom or pop
58 Tier
59 Yellowfin tuna
61 "Othello" setting
62 Net receipts
63 Like doilies
66 Karate-like exercise program
67 New Mexico canyon
68 Military outfit
69 In need of liniment
70 Well-versed in
71 Tear up
74 WBC result
75 Suffers from
76 Small serving
77 Thing of the past
78 Dolt
79 Rebel leader

147 CLUES TO AMUSE by Matt Ginsberg

The answer to 8 Down is not SHOE SOLE.

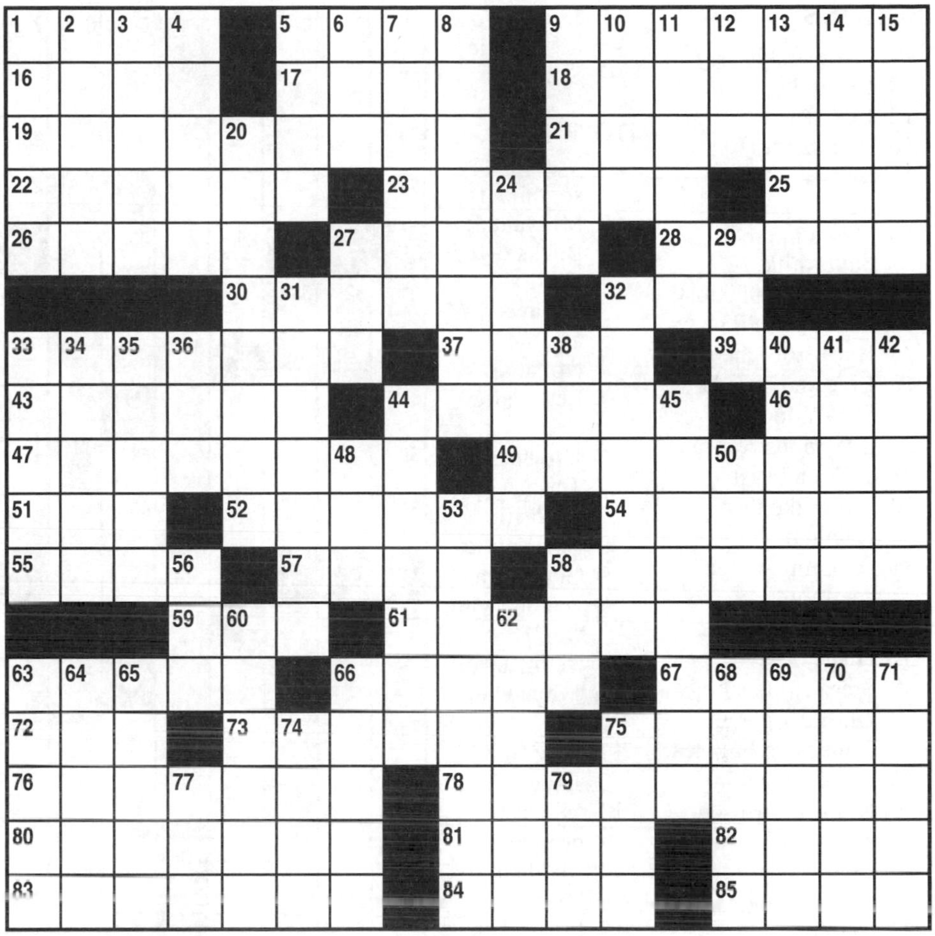

ACROSS

1 High points of a Swiss vacation
5 Bean head
9 Fare trade
16 Limited support
17 Actress Spelling
18 Medium settings
19 Some say it's bliss
21 Payers of flat fees
22 Trend follower
23 What this is
25 Modern "art"
26 Abridge too far?
27 Major 2001 bankruptcy
28 Page in "Juno"
30 "Night at the ___" (2006)
32 "XXX" org.
33 Gets back to business
37 Maegashira's sport
39 A bit of chemistry
43 Mohair
44 Words after "we meet"
46 Private address?
47 Where "stop" is a period
49 Pointless
51 Cockney's main Web page
52 Make an outstanding design
54 Alarmist
55 Exchange letters
57 Extra-wide width
58 Not right at all?
59 Singing the blues
61 "Key Largo" star
63 Black item
66 Family heads
67 Blast from the past
72 Rebel with a cause
73 Lock on a key
75 Dynamic beginning
76 Acted the ham
78 Entrance fee
80 Acknowledgment of error
81 Casual evening
82 French bean?
83 Bill sponsor
84 Hellenic letters
85 Flanders river

DOWN

1 Bring up the rear
2 Head producer
3 Chris craft
4 Change channels
5 "M*A*S*H" character?
6 Alternative to smoking
7 Like federal tax laws
8 Cobbler's bottom
9 Emoticon "eyes"
10 Man of war
11 The back of the choir
12 Pops in the fridge
13 Intestinal
14 "Nothing runs like a ___"
15 Düsseldorf neighbor
20 Come again
24 Rhea Silvia's son
27 Soup starter
29 "___ note to follow sew . . ."
31 Gun shy
32 Breather
33 Sing at Sing Sing
34 Other side
35 Checks figures
36 "Ulalume" poet
38 Dog's best friend
40 Chair person
41 Basso's house
42 Shooter's target
44 Examples of low life
45 Down time?
48 Copper head
50 Peabody in "Midnight"
53 Water wings?
56 Brooklyn follower
58 Head for Vegas
60 Dined downtown
62 Redact jointly
63 Country squares
64 Lion's amount
65 Town car
66 Product of the press
68 Peevish
69 Spooky sounding tribe
70 Struck from the Bible
71 Skin bracer
74 Emperor that fiddled around
75 Binders
77 "Love ___ Simple Thing"
79 Training org.

148 TWO WRONGS MAKE A . . . by Robert A. Doll

19 Across are enshrined in the National Aviation Hall of Fame in Dayton.

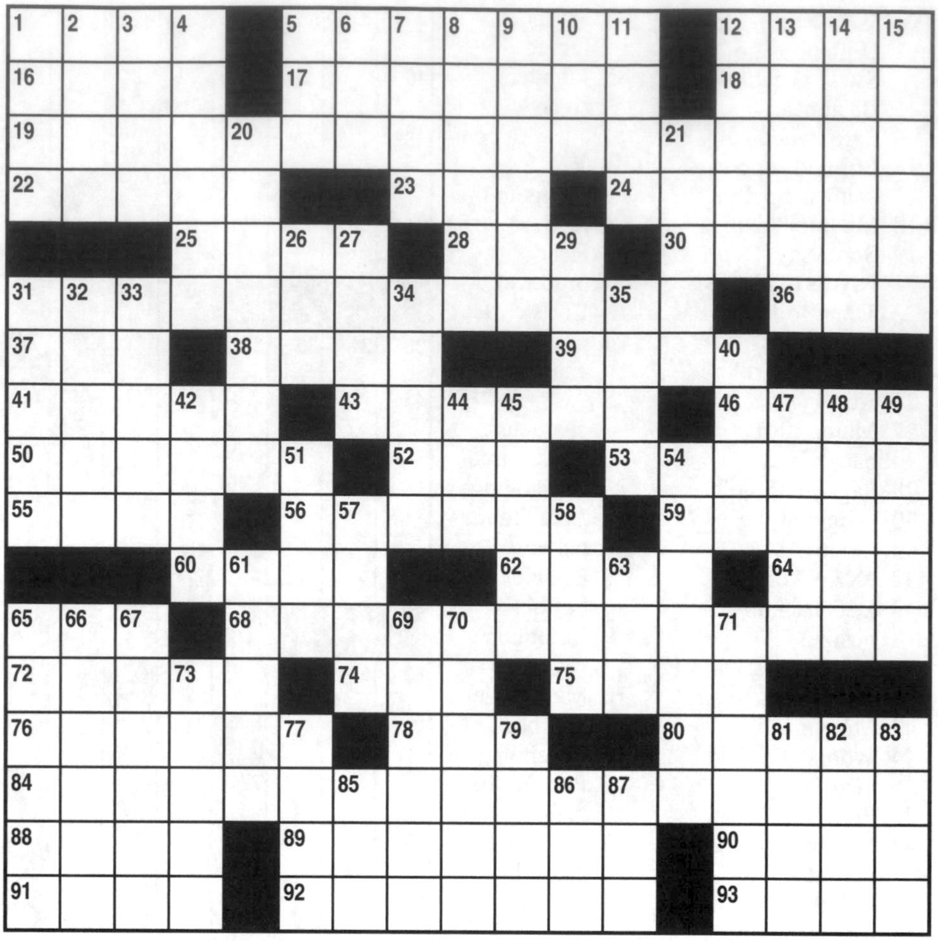

ACROSS

1 Comparable (to)
5 Exalted
12 CCCP
16 Plumb crazy
17 Verona's "Piazza dei ___"
18 "Fly's in the buttermilk, ___ . . ."
19 They made history on 12/17/1903
22 Blast from the past
23 Live and breathe
24 S, to a pilot
25 Luxurious resorts
28 Tolkien beast
30 More like the Kalahari
31 "Coming of age" ceremony
36 Hilary Duff song
37 Disney deer
38 Stern's opposite
39 Glasgow gal
41 Minnesota Fats feat
43 Block, in a way
46 Kon-Tiki Museum site
50 Messy
52 Not worth a ___
53 Buckle
55 Crystal ball user
56 Turns inside out
59 Knox and Courage
60 Fill to excess
62 Mao's successor
64 Sensitive subject, to some
65 John ___ Passos
68 Precisely punctual
72 Dispatch boat
74 Berne's river
75 "Take ___!"
76 Derelict
78 Acapulco aunt
80 Give a shave forward
84 Pen one to Penn. Ave
88 Groundless
89 Howard Hughes owned one
90 Joie de vivre
91 Refusals
92 Moves closer to the aisle
93 Stiff hair

DOWN

1 Voice below soprano
2 Milwaukee Bucks owner Herb
3 Put away, as a game
4 Not at all
5 Letter after chi
6 18-wheeler
7 Turkish honorific
8 Emcee lines
9 Gets on the wagon (with "up")
10 Be mistaken
11 "Vaya Con ___"
12 "My Boo" singer
13 Mideast prince
14 Reddish brown
15 Prayer beads
20 In the La-Z-Boy
21 Surfers concerns
26 Back of the boat
27 Design detail
29 Rodeo ropee
31 Romulus slew him
32 Cockamamie
33 Small sample
34 Make smile
35 Whaler's spear
40 Ho-hum
42 Churchill and McCartney
44 Anderson's "High ___"
45 Best
47 Fine fiddle
48 Send packing
49 Beginning
51 Himalayan bigfoot
54 Hamid Karzai, for one
57 Lyra's brightest star
58 Dispatched
61 Cropped up
63 Ultimate degree
65 "Origin of Species" author
66 Exaggerate
67 Neat as a pin, for one
69 Sour sorts
70 Diamond feat
71 Chopin pieces
73 Positions
77 One doesn't rate well
79 Met solo
81 Remove from a manuscript
82 No-see-um
83 Peak near Taormina
85 Shake a leg
86 Med. specialty
87 Parisian possessive

149 ADDING INSULT TO . . . by O. C. Hayes

This puzzle may suffer from a lack of respect.

ACROSS

1 Light type
7 American Samoa, e.g.: Abbr.
11 Nav. officers
16 Part of a pizza ad, often
17 Hirsute biblical twin
18 Endangered gazelle
19 NASCAR family
20 Whitey Ford's pitching coach
21 Use an atomizer
22 Lowering the price of ewes?
25 Adult pup
26 Kibbutz grandpa
27 Egyptian deity
31 Movers' inventory
34 ELO album
38 Showcase next to a book of regulations?
42 Clever
43 Day-___ paint
44 Domesticated
45 Foreman KO'er
46 Divided into segments
51 Braz. neighbor
52 Bowflex features
54 Home-financing org.
55 Jot in a log
57 Eras in which we didn't get what we wanted?
62 Recreational vehicle
63 Leo component
64 Scrimmage wear
65 Perceived
67 Deuces
70 Cause the loss of safely shipped parcels?
78 Scouting group
79 Switch tail?
80 Eats into
81 Render nugatory
82 12 Down is one
83 "Tear down this wall" speaker
84 Illegal take
85 Brit. gallantry awards
86 Convictions

DOWN

1 Gulf war missile
2 Novelist Morrison
3 Filmmaker Meyer
4 Cartel founded in 1960
5 1963 U.S. Open winner
6 Follow
7 Research site
8 Mr. Morales
9 Precipitate
10 Ladder features
11 Where imbibing guests pay
12 Planters pitchman
13 Serious
14 "___ the Wild Wind" (DeMille movie)
15 Designing
23 Dark shade
24 Pre-Windsor name
27 Items checked at the door
28 Kind of steak
29 Mom's argument ender
30 Coppertone no.
32 Frank Gifford was one
33 Capital of Manche
35 Where Helen Keller grew up
36 Took down a notch
37 Unavailing
39 Mil. titles
40 Popeye's "Positively!"
41 "Angel"
47 Exec who deals with money
48 None of that?
49 Tackle's teammate
50 Initial follower
53 Turns in
56 Pointer
58 Dazzling display
59 Feather: Prefix
60 Body art
61 Port city or the lake it's on
66 Exercise
68 Make, as an effort
69 Jag
70 Fleming villain
71 Prefix for sphere
72 Piccadilly statue
73 Unworkable
74 Certain horse
75 Barely better
76 Musical chairs goal
77 Payroll IDs
78 Hunter of film and song

150 ABBEY ROAD REUNION by Barry C. Silk

A reunion held within the circles in the squares.

ACROSS

1 Loosened (up)
7 Classify
13 Lisa Simpson, to Bart
16 Words after "because"
17 Taser, e.g.
18 It's used at Gallaudet U.
19 Colorful testudinate
21 Second Amendment advocacy gp.
22 "Show Boat" author Ferber
23 Ranked player
24 August 15, 1945
26 Timid type
31 Toward the stern
33 Justice Dept. worker
34 USN clerk: Abbr.
35 Tie with a clasp
36 Salvation Army founder
38 Injured party
41 Its symbol is Sn
42 Beige
43 Barbara of "Mission: Impossible"
45 Pod opening?
47 Viper on the Gadsden flag
53 State confidently
54 Bundles of dough
55 Took advantage of
56 11th-century date
59 "Panther in the Basement" novelist
61 Worked at a nabe
62 Zwei halved
64 Cyclone center
65 Litigator's org.
67 Globetrotter Nellie
68 Ottawa official
73 Billy Joel's "The Downeaster ___"
74 Smashnova of tennis
75 Lays down the lawn
78 Cigarette substance
79 Krispy Kreme offering
84 Mil. academy
85 Like farmland
86 Attached, in a way
87 Once named
88 Mooring rope
89 Emphasize

DOWN

1 Paper towel, e.g.
2 "It's ___ state of affairs!"
3 Cause for a delay in play
4 Avian chatterbox
5 Ballpark fig.
6 Accomplishes the task
7 Pontiac SUV
8 Jordanian's neighbor
9 Apr. season
10 Settle on
11 Divinity school subject: Abbr.
12 Rome's Fontana di ___
13 1993 baseball film (with "The")
14 Sabra
15 Mercury astronaut Deke
20 Door ding
25 Responsibility
27 Root word?
28 First U.S. capital
29 Age
30 Articulates
31 Prep a perp
32 Central points
37 Horn of plenty?
38 Itinerary word
39 Divided
40 Steele and Hood: Abbr.
43 City on the Weser
44 Dry gulch
46 Daunting burden
48 "The Loco-Motion" singer Little ___
49 Looney Tunes devil, for short
50 Fair-haired lass
51 Ship stabilizer
52 Watery swirl
56 Payload measure
57 Encroach on
58 4, to 1/4
60 Sun. address
61 Bygone Mideast fed.
63 Mae West play
65 Part of A.D.
66 Humdingers
69 Indian prince
70 Crystal of country music
71 Rear-___
72 Peter of Peter and Gordon
76 Pairs
77 CSX stops: Abbr.
80 Steve Carlton's was 3.22
81 Murphy's is well-known
82 Abbr. on a barbell
83 "Vamoose!"

151 PRETTY MUCH SET by Steven E. Atwood

"Brantford, Ontario tribesman" would be another clue for 57 Across.

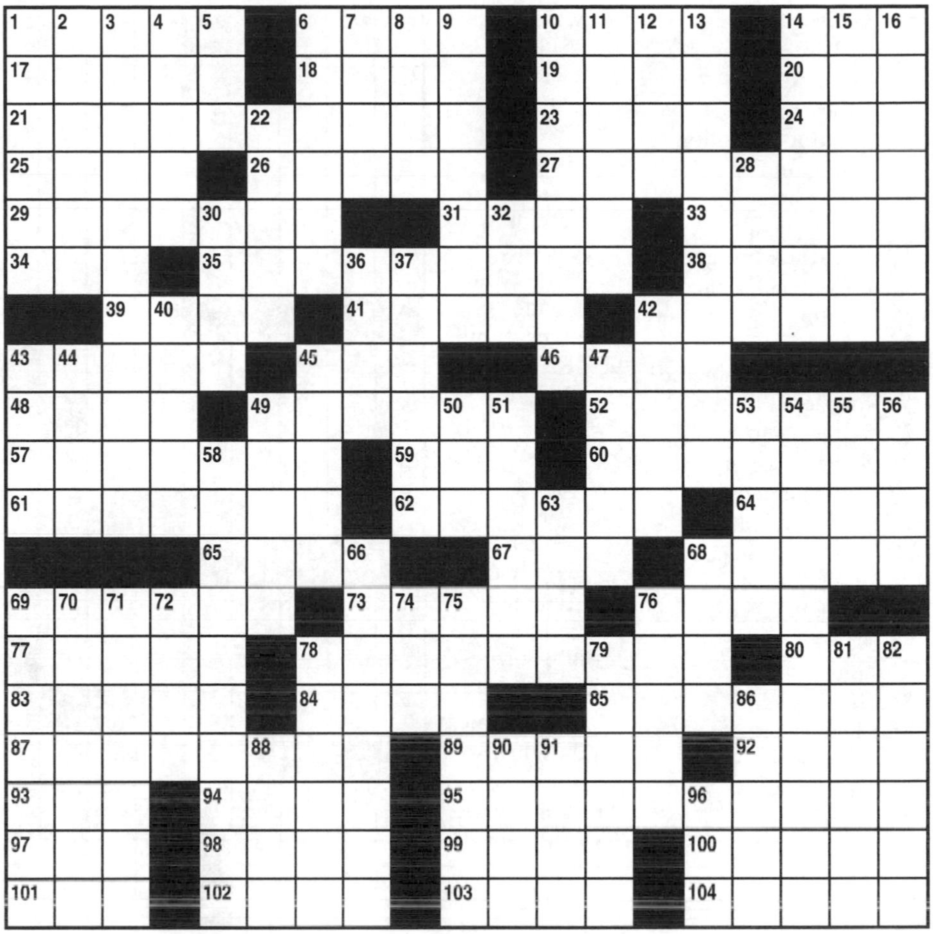

ACROSS

1 Nose or numeral type
6 Environmentalist Leopold
10 Eagles coach Andy
14 Corneille drama (with "Le")
17 Build up
18 Cervine creature
19 "All ___": Sinatra
20 Hwy.
21 SET
23 ". . . to buy ___ pig"
24 Deadly snake
25 Unique person
26 Play
27 SET
29 Church superstructure
31 College, e.g.
33 Basel river
34 Ages
35 SET
38 Polite addresses
39 Evil Disney lion
41 Canadian peninsula
42 Shoppers' cartways
43 Cause to converge
45 NFL linemen
46 Richard Pryor's daughter
48 Over, to Otto
49 Declarations
52 "Destry Rides Again" heroine
57 Member of a New York tribe
59 Time period
60 Boring
61 Junk yard, to some
62 Black sheep
64 Mammoth
65 Leopold's codefendant
67 Through-the-teeth utterance
68 Petty
69 Clown McDonald
73 Comparable to a beet
76 Peyton Manning, for one
77 Académie
78 SET
80 N.T. book
83 Glacial pinnacle
84 TV radio station
85 To ___ (somewhat)
87 SET
89 Yucca relative
92 Mountain in Thessaly
93 Purina brand
94 1963 role for Shirley
95 SET
97 To hear: Span.
98 Medical suffix
99 Speaker in the field
100 "Doctor Zhivago" producer
101 Make lace
102 The "N" of Rock's CSNY
103 Clockmaker Thomas
104 Mork, by birth

DOWN

1 Rest
2 Tooth: Comb. form
3 SET
4 Lit
5 Gotham paper, initially
6 Flips over
7 She played Glinda in "The Wiz"
8 Regard
9 Decrees
10 Tesla model
11 Devitalized
12 Muslim leader
13 SET
14 Skull-related
15 "My treat!"
16 Bring down
22 Goof-off
28 Words of discovery
30 Electronic organizers
32 Pile
36 "Taxi" driver's nickname
37 Wind-sprint
40 Preserves
42 Buenos ___
43 A hothead has a short one
44 Take orders from
45 Indian royal
47 Out to get
49 Stringed instrument of India
50 Treasure from the Atocha shipwreck
51 Like paint applied too thickly
53 Nothing: Lat.
54 SET
55 Hurricane of 1989
56 River of France and Belgium
58 SET
63 Pakistan's official language
66 Strong adverse reaction
68 Style
69 Do another take of
70 South Pacific island group
71 Mathematician Wiener
72 Kyrgyzstan range
74 NYSE unit
75 Meals
76 Gave up
78 Hindu mystics
79 Extravagant
81 Former Spanish currency
82 Turn toward the port
86 Dig
88 Latin for "bear"
90 Environmentalist Al
91 Landed
96 NYSE event

152 "NOBODY'S PERFECT . . ." by Elizabeth C. Gorski
". . . except me!"

ACROSS

1 Robert of "The Sopranos"
5 "Too bad . . ."
9 Lacking hydration
13 Windjammer
17 Fate who spins the thread of life
18 Bordeaux bridge
19 Formula One racer Takuma ___
20 Aust. state
21 In 2007 he homered for the 600th time
23 Winter ammo
25 **Start of a quip**
27 Units named for physicist Nikola
28 Author LeShan and others
29 Plays bass?
33 Carnegie Hall figure
34 Small apts.
35 Head cases?
37 "Toy Story" pig
38 Virility
39 Knack
44 Type of colony Australia was
45 Personality profile info
46 Kane's "Rosebud"
47 Lawmaker of Athens
52 **More of quip**
56 Sights from a cruise ship
57 Pack animals?
58 Tortilla chip topper
59 Emulate Fred Astaire
61 They've got a lot of pull
62 Lack of competence
67 "___ Be In Love": G. Brooks
68 Immature
69 Reveals, in verse
70 "Kyle XY" actress Apanowicz
75 President Sarkozy's predecessor
76 Green stroke
77 Hutton in "American Gigolo"
78 **End of quip**
82 Piece for Yo-Yo Ma
85 Camel in a pack
86 Garfield's pal
87 David Bowie's model wife
88 Joseph Conrad's "___ of Six"
89 Condo owner's bill
90 Roy Orbison's "___ Dooby"
91 Part of ASCII
92 Brit. companies
93 Family tree figures

DOWN

1 Unmoved
2 Bakery sales
3 Tangle, as in a net
4 Promenade
5 Cathedral recesses
6 Kook
7 "I'm waiting for a response . . ."
8 Budding actor's dream
9 Small groups?
10 Called
11 Langston Hughes poem
12 Ruin
13 Skips the night on the town
14 Prince of Broadway
15 Wight or Man: Abbr.
16 J. Major et al.
22 Anniversary unit
24 Russian pancakes
26 Gp. formed in 1948
30 Color shade
31 German border river
32 Steam heat sound
34 Nasser's successor
35 D. Parton's music genre
36 Biology text subj.
37 People of Rwanda
38 Swim team events
39 Madonna's "Take ___"
40 "If you like ___ coladas . . ."
41 Tick's counterpart
42 Bardot's brainstorm
43 File extensions
44 Ford ID
46 Fly-by-night
47 Clean the deck
48 "This can't be!"
49 Mythical mother of twins
50 "Put a lid ___!"
51 Schnapps shots
53 Country singer Travis
54 Neighbors
55 Mariposa lily variety
59 Relating to sugar
60 Dogpatch adjective
61 Chubby Checker song
62 CEO's employer
63 Japanese musical drama
64 Singer DiFranco
65 Fashion designer Luella
66 Coeur d'Alene locale
67 Type of illusion
69 Rank beginner?
70 Bryn ___ College
71 Money of ancient Rome
72 Hawaiian cave
73 Tooth bone
74 Heavenly bodies?
76 Talking point?
77 Juristic exams
79 Man of Pisa
80 Pleased as punch
81 Like fine wine
82 Bill's partner
83 Shogun's capital
84 Ad add-on

153 JAYWALKING by Fred Piscop

4 Down is an example of a riddle clue.

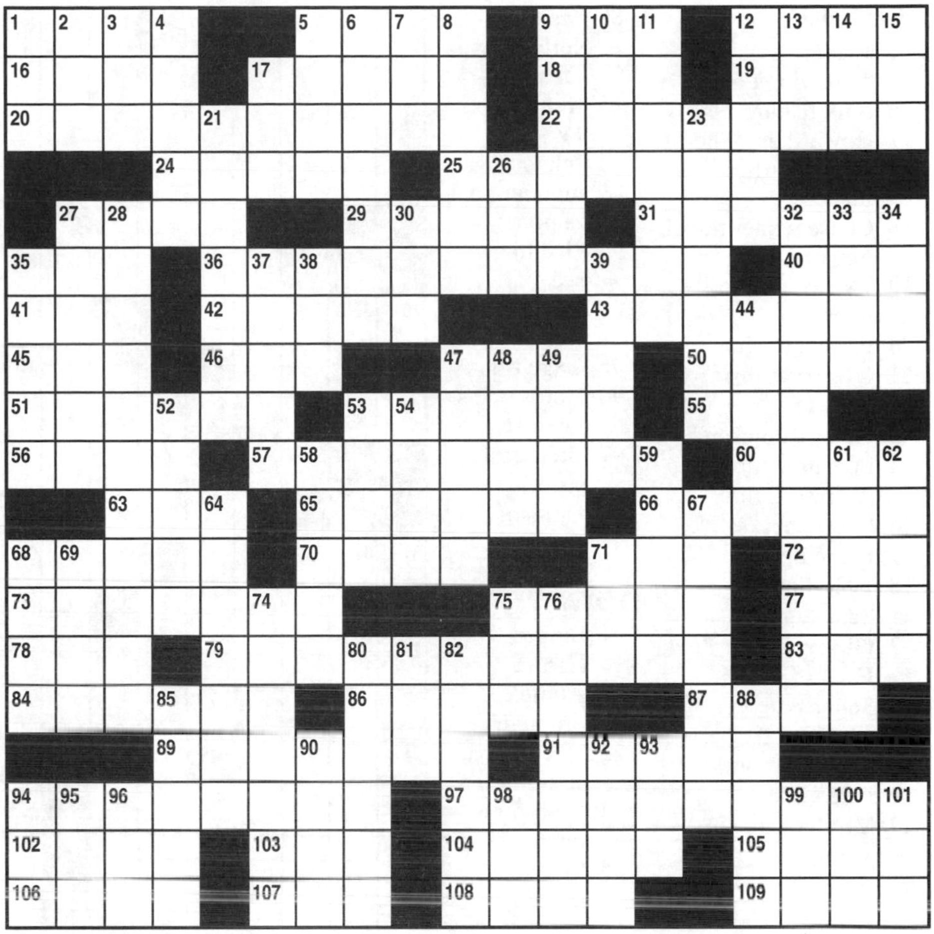

ACROSS

1 They're blind, to bleacher bums
5 Turnstile feature
9 Dickensian epithet
12 Graph line
16 USB connection
17 Popular aerobic program
18 Menu term
19 Catch a Greyhound
20 Canine martial arts expert?
22 "Cabaret" director
24 Played over
25 WW2 meal
27 "I haven't got it ___!"
29 Disney mermaid
31 Surveyor's aid
35 ___ Friday's (restaurant)
36 Astrological sign of some Oslo natives?
40 LL Cool J's "All I Have" partner
41 Place to turn in
42 River through Hesse
43 Deejay's wear
45 Houlihan's rank: Abbr.
46 Do Chisanbop
47 Eastern wrap
50 Janet in "Psycho"
51 Game similar to euchre
53 Dallas bowl
55 Unagi, at the sushi bar
56 Ricky player
57 Waterway allowing some leakage?
60 Scissors beater
63 Suffix with social
65 Latest word
66 Craps natural
68 Charades player
70 Flapper Betty
71 Absorbed, as a loss
72 Shogun's capital
73 "Hanging chads" state
75 Male: Comb. form
77 Swerve at sea
78 "When oysters ___ season"
79 Singer that passes mustard?
83 Workplaces for RN's
84 Farmer's device
86 Cretan capital, formerly
87 Great work
89 Rio beach of song
91 Denis of "Rescue Me"
94 "Hero" singer Enrique
97 The return of Borg?
102 Medieval defense
103 Fighting Tigers' sch.
104 Slowly, on scores
105 Bamako's land
106 Boston orchestra
107 Chucklehead
108 Upper hand
109 Dixie pronoun

DOWN

1 Big Brown
2 Comfy shoe
3 Old hand
4 It has an eye but cannot see
5 Thompson of "Pollock"
6 Foe of Hearns and Hagler
7 Sentence part: Abbr.
8 Withstood hardship
9 Arnaz signature tune
10 Jillions
11 Bar regular
12 Rice-___
13 Letters after nus
14 Check-cashing needs
15 Take a tour of
17 Norse war god
21 It may be used in frying
23 Sign on a lawn
26 Stephen of "Citizen X"
27 Pianist Paderewski
28 Japanese singer with a killer voice?
30 Vitamin qty.
32 Ode to nightwear?
33 Designer to Jackie
34 "The lady ___ protest . . ."
35 Like track events
37 Realm of Herod
38 Moth-eaten
39 Lorelei's river
44 Name on an 84 Across
47 Bra part
48 Toiling away
49 Knock about
52 Choir's place
53 Mob bigwig
54 Word on a dollar
58 Confederate general Early
59 In again
61 Trees of Lebanon
62 Has down
64 Elbow straightener
67 "Il Trovatore" heroine
68 Producers: Abbr.
69 "Would ___?"
71 Modifying wd.
74 Knocks off track
75 Gator tail?
76 "Soul Food" actress
80 Gets slick
81 Skater Naomi Nari ___
82 Give power to
85 Loses on purpose?
88 Miniature
90 Von Braun's org.
92 De Tirtoff's alias
93 "It's ___-brainer!"
94 Sitter's handful
95 Icky stuff
96 Pool unit
98 Elly May's pa
99 Rte. recommenders
100 Off one's feed
101 Zip

154 HANDLE WITH CARE by Reggie Evers

11 Across was Mayberry's county clerk played by Jack Dodson for six years.

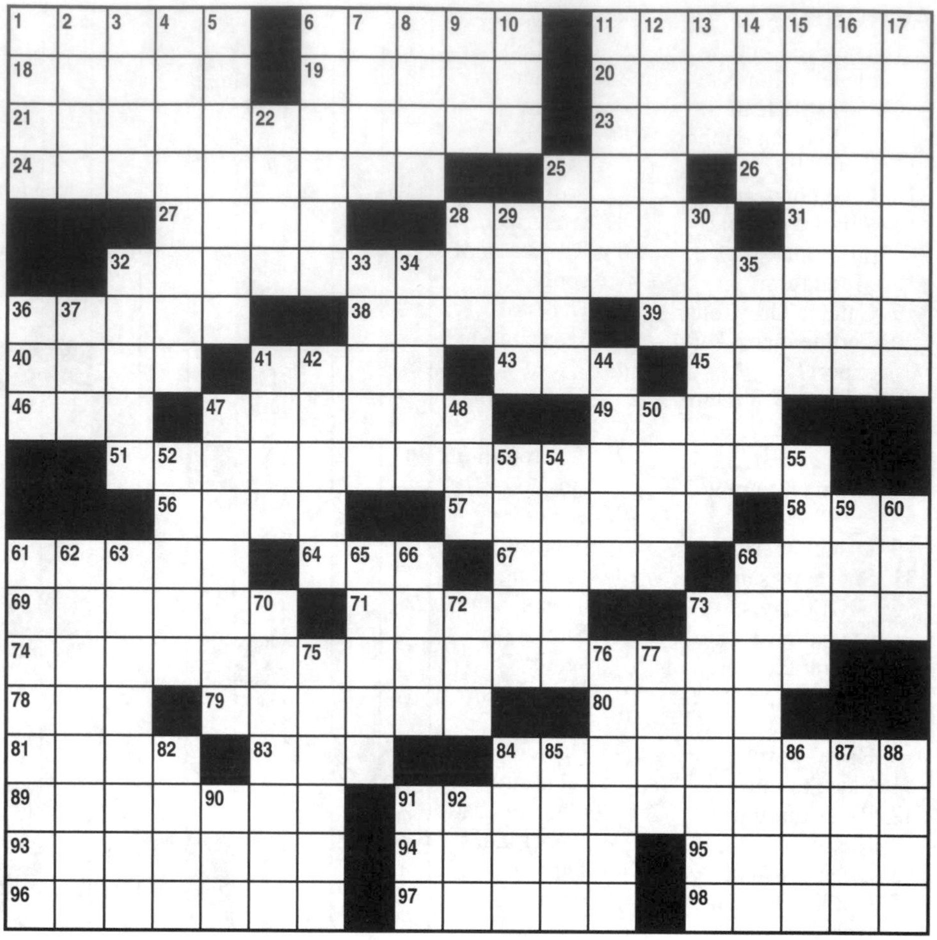

ACROSS

1 Joanna of "Growing Pains"
6 Sink feature
11 Howard on "The Andy Griffith Show"
18 Cause winter travel impairment
19 "No you're not!" retort
20 Falling (over)
21 **Observation: Part I**
23 Actor Robinson
24 Puts up with
25 Actress Aulin
26 Seine specks
27 Bjorn opponent
28 1927 Ford
31 Scat syllable
32 **Observation: Part II**
36 Schnozzle
38 "A Dog of Flanders" author
39 Pale violet
40 Middle name in Memphis
41 Go up against
43 Evasive center?
45 Did a fall chore
46 Dolt
47 Rickey of baseball
49 Bob bit?
51 **Observation: Part III**
56 Met, say
57 Token of victory
58 Frequently, to yeats
61 Ebbing and flowing
64 Word after legal or medical
67 Quintillionth: Prefix
68 PC command
69 Lake near Syracuse
71 Pub lights
73 Headliner's cue
74 **Observation: Part IV**
78 Writer Rosten
79 Vet helper
80 Nobelist Morrison
81 Reason for detention, maybe
83 Account
84 Unsuitably applied handles
89 Made of certain twigs
91 **Observation: Part IV**
93 Inhabiting mountainous regions
94 "I'd like to see ___" (diner's words)
95 Gage title
96 Holds one's interest
97 Breakfast strip
98 Units of force

DOWN

1 Singer Eartha
2 Audio problem
3 Not walk a straight line
4 Club for a pitch
5 Show hostility toward
6 Tried to lose
7 Singer-actress Martha
8 John of "Roots"
9 Pocatello sch.
10 Here–there connector
11 Barbecue stick
12 Propelled a Schwinn
13 VCR remote button
14 Literally, "merry," in Basque
15 Chick flick chat?
16 Be at the heart of
17 Dish discussed in "What's Up, Tiger Lily?"
22 Primary
25 Collections of Scandinavian myths
28 CDVI + DXCVI
29 Ye ___ Antique Shoppe
30 State of mayhem
32 Dotty
33 A dazed boxer may hear it
34 Starsky's partner
35 Khan of R&B
36 Brazil saint
37 Depression agcy.
41 R&B singer India.___
42 Iraqi seaport
44 Went out?
47 Starkville mascot
48 In a lather (with "up")
50 Galba's successor
52 Walking ___ (ecstatic)
53 Malaysian swinger
54 "I beg to differ!"
55 "Kemo sabe" utterer
59 New Deal monogram
60 Abnormally
61 Laborious
62 Like strawberries in the spring
63 Asking questions of, in a way
65 Standing to lose a bundle
66 Hollow
68 Hardly prompt
70 Chisholm Trail stop
72 Olive not meant for martinis
73 Didn't heed
75 Dwellings
76 Why many love crossword solving
77 Prohibition
82 ___ good example
84 Not much time: Abbr.
85 Pay–mind link
86 All tied
87 Cubist painter Magritte
88 Indian titles
90 Duster
91 Origin of Frankenstein's monster
92 Org. with a highly regarded journal

155 RELIGIOUS SERVICE by Dave Mackey

36 Across is nicknamed the Pineapple Island.

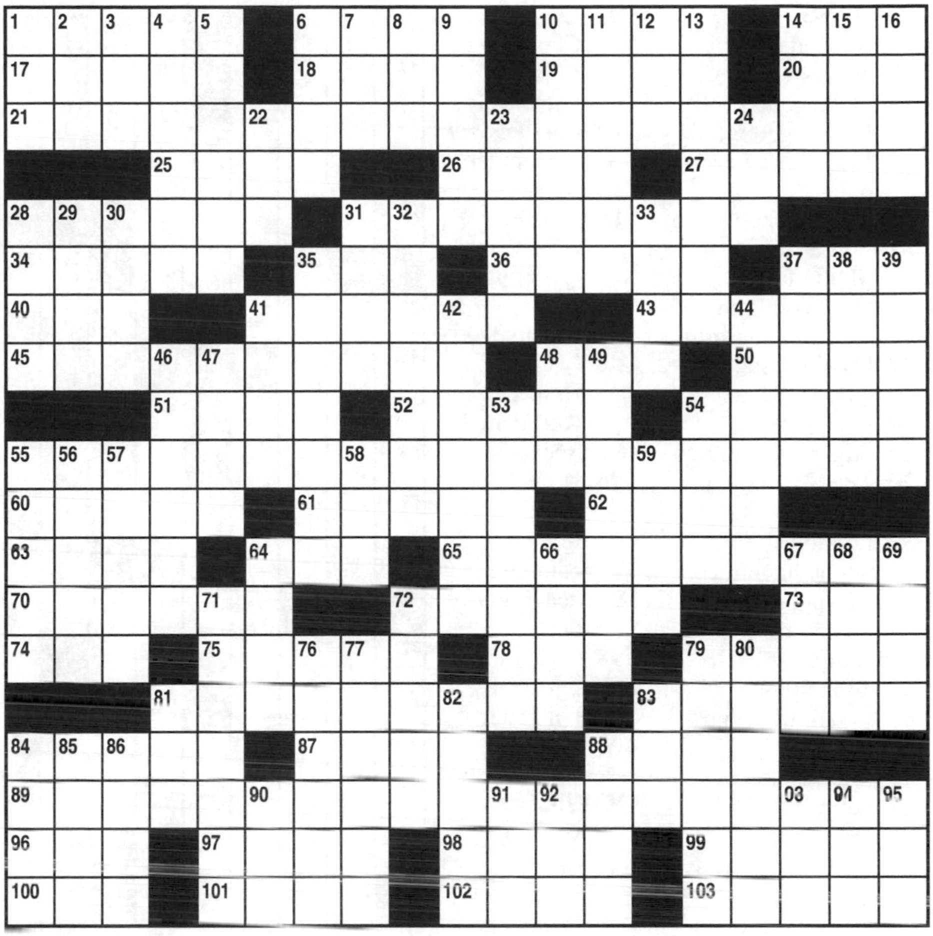

ACROSS

1 Cry of discovery
6 Some retinal receptors
10 Fastener
14 Subway car displays
17 Peter who sang "I'm Henry VIII, I Am"
18 Robt. at Antietam
19 Saarinen of Gateway Arch fame
20 ___-de-sac
21 **Part 1 of a quip**
25 "Beautiful Freak" group
26 "Take ___ I Am": Faith Hill
27 Court defense
28 ". . . owed by ___ to so few": Churchill
31 Roaring Twenties night spot
34 "Nixon in China," e.g.
35 Request a doggie treat
36 Sixth-largest Hawaiian Island
37 Fat farm
40 Peace, in Russia
41 Record again
43 Rodeo ropes
45 **Part 2 of quip**
48 Prior to, in poetry
50 It's curved, at times
51 "That's the Question" host Bob
52 "Mon ___ D'Amerique" (1978)
54 Baccarat call
55 **Part 3 of quip**
60 Location of Van Gogh's "Bedroom"
61 Courtyards
62 ___-mutuel wagering
63 Roger in "Nicholas Nickleby"
64 History
65 **Part 4 of quip**
70 Slew
72 Pro tem
73 Its HQ is the Pentagon
74 Expedited mailings: Abbr.
75 It merged with the C. of I.O.
78 Ancient way to say ancient
79 Sheikdom of song
81 Mugger
83 Certain horse race
84 Novelist Walker
87 Home of Russell Sage College
88 Bad fate
89 **End of quip**
96 Golfer Se Ri ___
97 Chocolate-syrup brand
98 Polite contraction
99 Some MoMA hangings
100 Most AARP members
101 Torrey Pines scores
102 Any time now
103 Done in

DOWN

1 "Crouching Tiger, Hidden Dragon" director Lee
2 See 3 Down
3 Half a chocolate drink
4 Evoke affection
5 MTV news reporter Altschul
6 Guns the motor
7 Spanish cheer
8 German article
9 Note from the boss
10 "Stairway To Heaven" singer
11 Ford's press secretary
12 Early Dadaist
13 Sweetums
14 Clearasil target
15 Club fees
16 Canon EOS et al.
22 Bridge authority Culbertson
23 Zora ___ Hurston
24 Kid with a trombone
28 Sleep prefix
29 Ronny Howard role
30 He invented the "Wheel"
31 Complete collections
32 FedEx Cup org.
33 Tributary of the Rhine
35 Hacky sack
37 Artery opener
38 City on the Columbia
39 ___ Martin
41 Former "Biggest Loser" host
42 Catalina maker, once
44 Lack of coordination
46 Way out
47 Campanella and Disney
48 Inventor Whitney
49 Holla back
53 Purify
54 North Atlantic hazard
55 Gets bent out of shape
56 Mountain nymph
57 Like months without oysters
58 Ear: Comb. form
59 Performed with the chorus
64 Gordon Shumway and others
66 Toni competitor
67 Pierre's loc.
68 Florida's ___ Sound
69 Baskin-Robbins rival
71 Abates
72 "Everything's clear here!"
76 More whole-grain
77 Record book entries
79 Not seeing eye to eye
80 French flutist
81 "The Hound of the Baskervilles" auth.
82 Mornings, colloquially
83 "Native ___": Wright
84 Current draw units
85 When repeated, a Jim Carrey film title
86 Finishes a comic strip
88 What Rhett didn't give
90 Makeup aisle, initially
91 NBA's "Ming The Merciless"
92 ___ Paulo
93 Repeated syllable in a Rihanna song
94 Nintendo game platform
95 IRS ID

156 PARTNERS IN RHYME by Jay Sullivan

Jay thanks Mr. Porter for the clue at 66 Across.

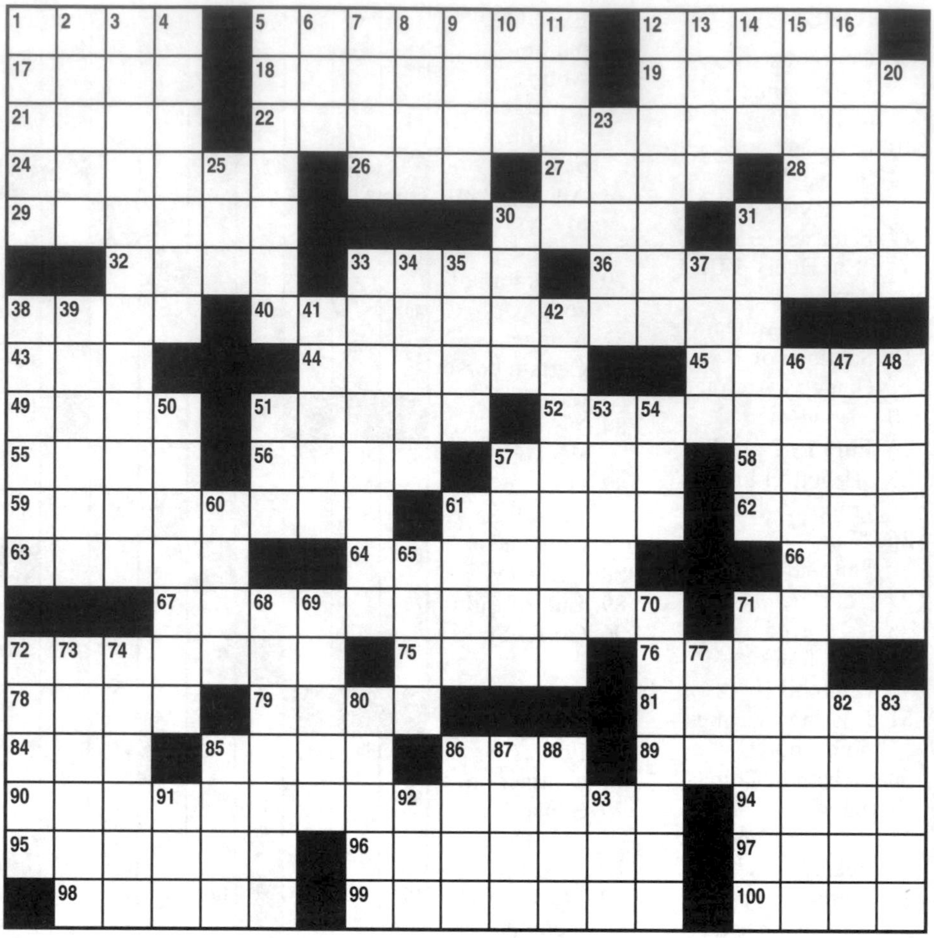

ACROSS

1 Spotted cavy
5 Makes waves
12 Did a greasy job
17 Exchanged words
18 Musical "sweet potato"
19 Did a make-up job
21 Left at sea
22 Mount up?
24 Sports column
26 Company quorum
27 Missouri state quarter back
28 It's a scream
29 Sugar substitute?
30 That's what you think
31 London site for public hangings
32 Kissing couple
33 Men behaving badly
36 Took home
38 ___ fide (in bad faith)
40 Need to nosh?
43 Latin lover's profession
44 "A Life for the Tsar" composer
45 Wired
49 Caesar's cohort
51 Name for a snow-covered peak
52 Some titleholders
55 Shrinking lake of Western Asia
56 "The Children of the Poor" author
57 What's more
58 Pair of rattlers?
59 Australian euro
61 More than capable
62 Where Greek tragedies were performed
63 Daze of our lives
64 House honcho
66 Birds do it; bees do it
67 Played without a contract?
71 Turndowns
72 Reign man
75 From scratch
76 "Believe ___ Not!"
78 Grant and Gehrig
79 Linguist Chomsky
81 Enjoys immensely
84 Loss leader?
85 Unpopular spots
86 Fleeced beast
89 ___ bundle (loses big-time)
90 It's made by Harper?
94 Kurt denial
95 Spews forth
96 "I kid you not"
97 Lowest common denomination
98 "What if," informally
99 Laid back
100 Ill at ease

DOWN

1 Whistled sharply
2 Really fancy
3 Where the horses hang out?
4 Columbia River town
5 Have
6 One of Henry V's five?
7 Make a sudden move
8 Gunslinger's dare
9 Venice attraction
10 Stopping point
11 Subway fare
12 "Madama Butterfly" debuted here
13 Four Corners state
14 Hunk's pride
15 Win over
16 Strike out
20 Gave a head fake
23 Do something constructive
25 It may be carved in stone
30 Author Dinesen
31 Become fond of
33 Steam organ
34 Folic, oxalic, and malic
35 Fashionable letters
37 Start to morph?
38 Long-tailed parrots
39 Lacking principle
41 Dame Marsh of mystery
42 Shop tool
46 Leadfoot's malady?
47 Brosnan TV role
48 "The Federalist Papers," essentially
50 Gene variations
51 Baby, it's cold outside!
53 Chilled garnish
54 Biodegrade
57 "The Gentleman Is ___" ("Allegro" number)
60 On ___ with: comparable to
61 Arkin or Alda
65 Dutch treat
68 Short and sweet
69 Capital of Denmark
70 Like a '60s T-shirt
71 Never ever
72 Student of the Sorbonne
73 Back biters
74 Stop short
77 Main man
80 Race of Norse gods
82 Playing for a sucker
83 Kind of raid
85 Newspaper section
86 Smoother
87 High in the Andes?
88 Another world
91 Friendly introduction?
92 Jeanne d'Arc, par exemple
93 Sorry state

157 FOUR EVERS AND A DAY by Harvey Estes

13 Down is a four-time Daytona 500 winner.

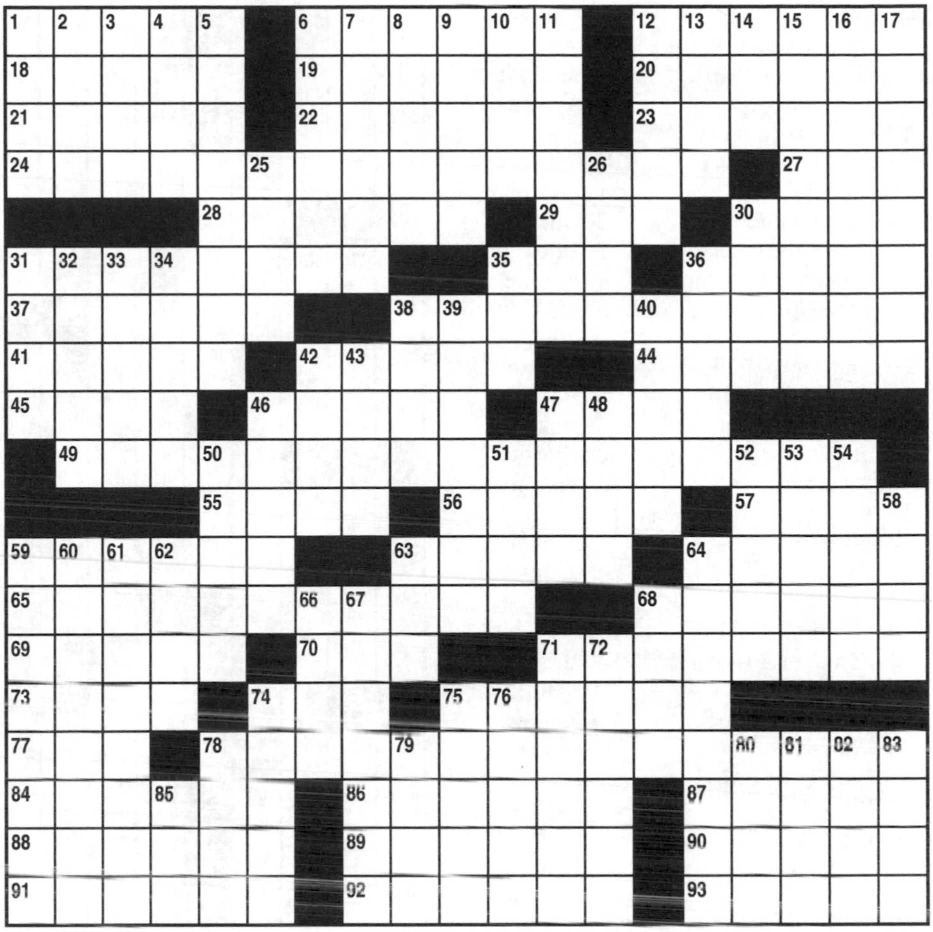

ACROSS

1 Prayer attributed to David
6 Monastery heads
12 Screenwriter's work
18 Foil maker
19 Necktie
20 Roman ruler
21 Billiards bounce
22 Until now
23 Milano of "Charmed"
24 EVER
27 JFK's branch
28 Hits the sauce
29 Snake sound
30 Very French
31 Puzo family name
35 Cattle call
36 Response to "Am not"
37 Donny or Marie, by birth
38 EVER
41 Burton of "Star Trek"
42 "Chill out!"
44 Bends over
45 DC VIP
46 How some issues are debated
47 Bamako's land
49 EVER
55 Preindication causing trepidation
56 Diarist Nin
57 Ballot bit
59 "Becker" star
63 In the thick of
64 Short-winded
65 EVER
68 Henry's Anne
69 Like cut-rate bread
70 Gun the motor
71 Free rider
73 Bluish green
74 Winter product prefix
75 Bar regular
77 Peppy piano piece
78 DAY
84 Roma's country
86 Aplenty
87 Synthetic fiber brand
88 Foundation material
89 Is gaga over
90 Soup scoop
91 Says "It's on me"
92 Least wacko
93 Bridges in "Airplane!"

DOWN

1 Walk nervously
2 Belgrade resident
3 Farm division
4 Bird in a crazy simile
5 Sow with a "too soft" bed
6 Director's cry
7 Third place medal
8 Sheriff's shield
9 Racing paths
10 London gallery
11 Oater topper
12 Confidence games
13 Racer Yarborough
14 King of Spain
15 Definitely will
16 Says no to
17 Windows over doors
25 In a minute
26 "Time ___ the essence!"
30 The Supremes, e.g.
31 Cosby's "I Spy" costar
32 Cheri of "Scary Movie"
33 Baltimore footballer
34 Tibet's capital
35 Cowboy Tom
36 Monkeyshine
38 Shakespeare title starter
39 Go out in a small boat
40 Florida keys, e.g.
42 Catch rodeo-style
43 Kind of jacket
46 Ditties for the deity
47 Corp. recruits
48 Hit the ground
50 Wild West knot
51 Dr. Jones' nickname
52 Amtrak offering
53 Tiny insectivore
54 Cushy class
58 Contradict
59 Word after school or business
60 Aardvark, for example
61 March Madness feature
62 Bear market order
63 Teen tube fave
64 Council's meeting place
66 Composer Thomas
67 Diner sign substance
68 Churlish chap
71 Mall units
72 Most faithful
74 Makes a fly die
75 Traffic cone
76 Prefix with mentioned
78 Salon offering
79 "Presto!"
80 By word of mouth
81 Menu option
82 Lean (on)
83 Downhill racer
85 Pastoral place

158 " 'TIS THE SEASON . . ." by Roger Coburn

Rod Stewart covered 14 Down in 2006.

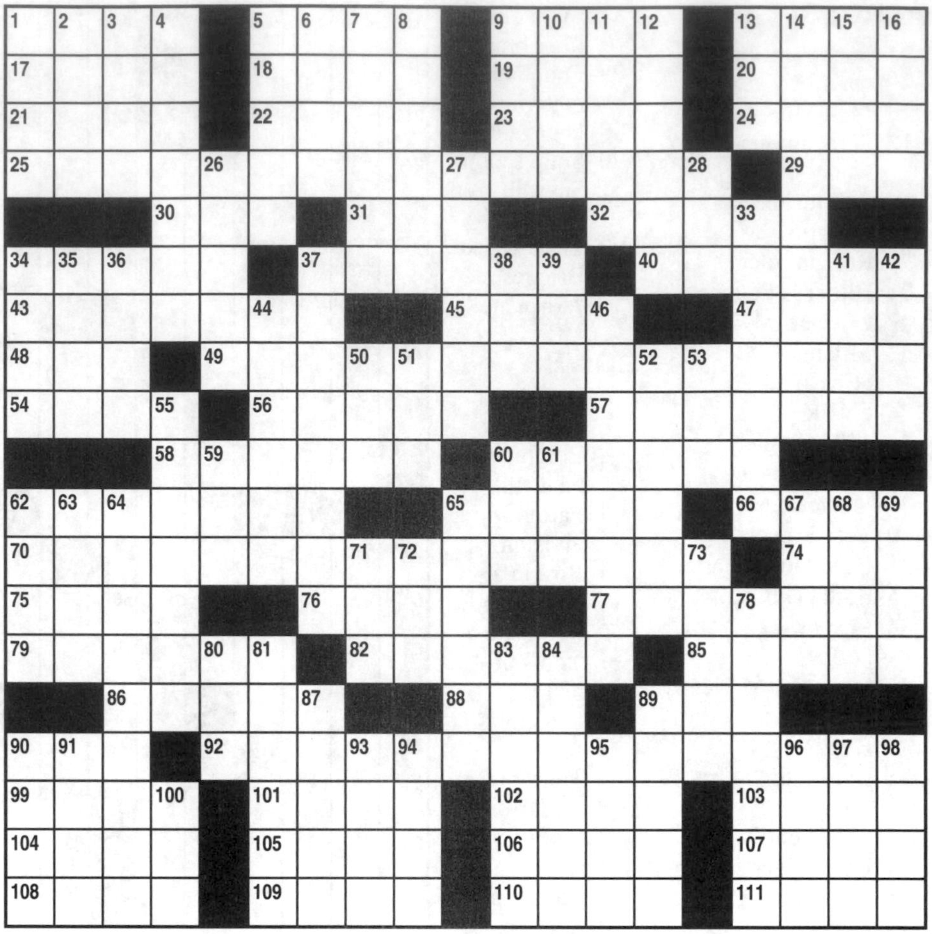

ACROSS

1 Prep veggies
5 Jessica, on film
9 Boring tools
13 Resistance units
17 Moon goddess
18 Forsaken
19 Neil Diamond hit
20 Row on a calendar
21 Spore sacs
22 Lie's pp
23 Earthen jug
24 Superboy's gal
25 **Start of a quip**
29 It's hard to get out of
30 Visionary
31 Listener
32 Fissure
34 Spoken
37 Tell
40 Something to draw
43 Snake or a worm
45 Competes
47 It follows a yodel
48 Function
49 **Part II of quip**
54 Place for chow
56 Belief
57 Tenants
58 Flexible
60 K2 guide
62 Bit of gunpowder
65 Bailiwick
66 It's ususally hourly
70 **Part III of quip**
74 Unit of light
75 Feet of ___
76 Vulnerable bone
77 Nasal twang
79 Greedy ones
82 Ranges
85 First quarter tide
86 Leaf swelling
88 Humorous one
89 Mine and yours
90 Confess to
92 **End of quip**
99 Arrest
101 Twelve ___ (Tara's neighbor)
102 Opponent
103 Redolence
104 Humorist Ferber
105 Svelt
106 Come-on
107 Arm bone
108 Presage
109 Tailors
110 Wound reminder
111 Appear

DOWN

1 Hammer part
2 Quiet
3 Tale opening
4 Aching
5 It's behind the stores
6 Fill a truck
7 He'll take a kickback
8 Yearly
9 Commotions
10 Lobo
11 Popular scent
12 Delays
13 Wise bird
14 "It's a ___": Bonnie Tyler
15 It shows choices
16 Shoo
26 Darken
27 Fertile
28 Rent out
33 It'll cut curves
34 Astringent
35 Misplace
36 Must pay
37 Emendments
38 Metal in terne metal
39 Conger
41 Cry from a ride
42 Sauces
44 Mini Cooper dashboards
46 Like wornout shoes
50 Author Deighton
51 So far
52 Varmint, for real
53 Clairvoyance
55 Spread out
59 1st Earl of Marlborough
60 Harden
61 Cry from Alf
62 Diplomacy
63 Queen of scat
64 It may be rude
65 Fame
67 Old radio alphabet word
68 Swallow
69 Sir Paul and Lady Heather, e.g.
71 Sighs
72 Gear
73 Accumulate
78 Oxide lead-in
80 Goose the engine
81 Glabrous
83 They're taken in triage
84 Indigenous
87 Knowing
89 Willow rod
90 Wallet fillers
91 African pasture
93 Take off the top
94 Beliefs
95 Lab burner
96 Unoccupied
97 Number of Bach symphonies?
98 Small amount
100 Computer link

159 GIRLIE MEN by Edgar Fontaine

Ed thanks Mr. Schwarzenegger for suggesting this title.

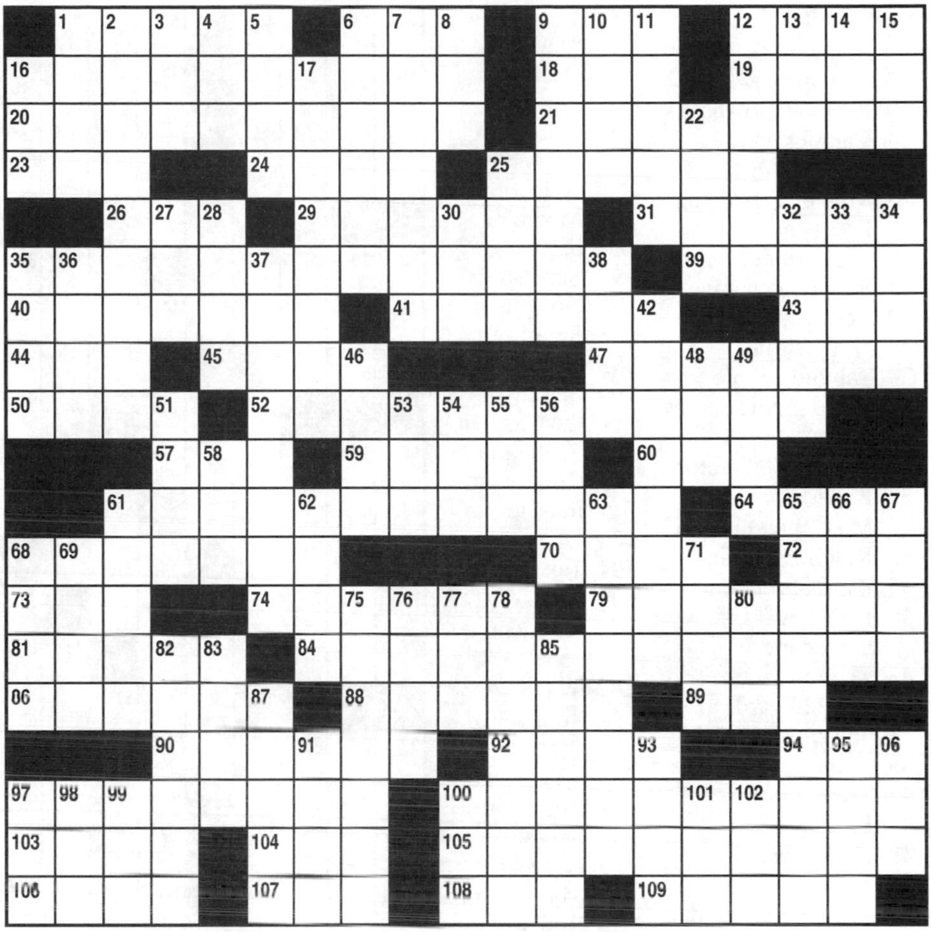

ACROSS

1 Nincompoops
6 QB protectors
9 Word said with a salute
12 Kill, in a way
16 Pirate ships' kin
18 Waste not
19 Love personified
20 Josephine in "Some Like it Hot"
21 Delight
23 Rand of "The Fountainhead"
24 "Larry Legend"
25 Diacritics
26 Left-of-center front?
29 Couple's attendant?
31 Cleared
35 Euphegenia in "Mrs. Doubtfire"
39 Three-time AL batting champ
40 Rough
41 Relax
43 Bottom line
44 Kind of wheels
45 Sushi supplies
47 Eyelash makeup
50 Slog (through)
52 Hildegard in "Bosom Buddies"
57 Here, to Henri
59 Rhone tributary
60 One fifth of CCCV
61 Edna in "Hairspray"
64 Don Rickles remark
68 Computer memory
70 Part of a Happy Meal
72 To boot
73 Black gold
74 Beveled, as a timber
79 Berle and Friedman
81 Pass-the-baton race
84 Dorothy in "Tootsie"
86 Audition
88 Medicinal shrub
89 Short trader?
90 Rights, in law
92 Millennium divs.
94 ___ pro nobis
97 Trattoria offering
100 Daphne in "Some Like It Hot"
103 Henry's number
104 Ref's decision
105 Presumptively
106 Prepares to be shot
107 Dict. listing
108 Anti-Vietnam War org.
109 Like some divorces

DOWN

1 Quarterback Aikman
2 Big name in 97 Down
3 Wrigley Field greenery
4 Middle of a game?
5 Torn ticket
6 Toward the posterior
7 Cookware
8 Deep-fryer sound
9 Mary Wilson, for one
10 Man, for one
11 Chaucer pilgrim
12 Liege subject
13 Outback runner
14 Rocky hill
15 "Get a lode of this!'
16 Bake sale org.
17 Sister Euphemia in "Nuns on the Run"
22 Saab model
25 Leaning
27 Kind of iron
28 "Splendor in the Grass" screenwriter
30 Twice the rad.
32 Red Sea peninsula
33 By any chance
34 "Star Trek: TNG" android
35 Dudley Do-Right's org.
36 Face-to-face exam
37 Fits of crying
38 Samporo sport
42 Italian architect Andrea
46 Cookbook direction
48 Mystery novelist Rohmer
49 Cheat sheet
51 Christian name
53 Spaniard's "that"
54 Part of rpm
55 Sellout indicator
56 Collectible frames
58 Half a dance?
61 Jocund
62 Oversee
63 Buffy in "Bosom Buddies"
65 Weapons of mass destruction
66 Gossipy Barrett
67 Ship's petty officer
68 Variety
69 Factor in ticket pricing
71 ___ Romeo
75 Type of bridge?
76 Proteins produced by a male gland: Abbr.
77 UFO crew
78 Chuck out
80 Reassign: Abbr.
82 Vietnamese attire
83 Mongolian tent
85 Sisters' daughters
87 Sweetie
91 Jet black
93 Urban blight
95 ___-poly
96 "Take your pick"
97 Campers, for short
98 Junior's junior
99 "Skedaddle!"
100 Magistrates: Abbr.
101 Suffix in linguistics
102 "No ___": Duran

160 CONVERSION FACTORS by Richard Silvestri

Wordplay sure to evoke a measured response (of groans).

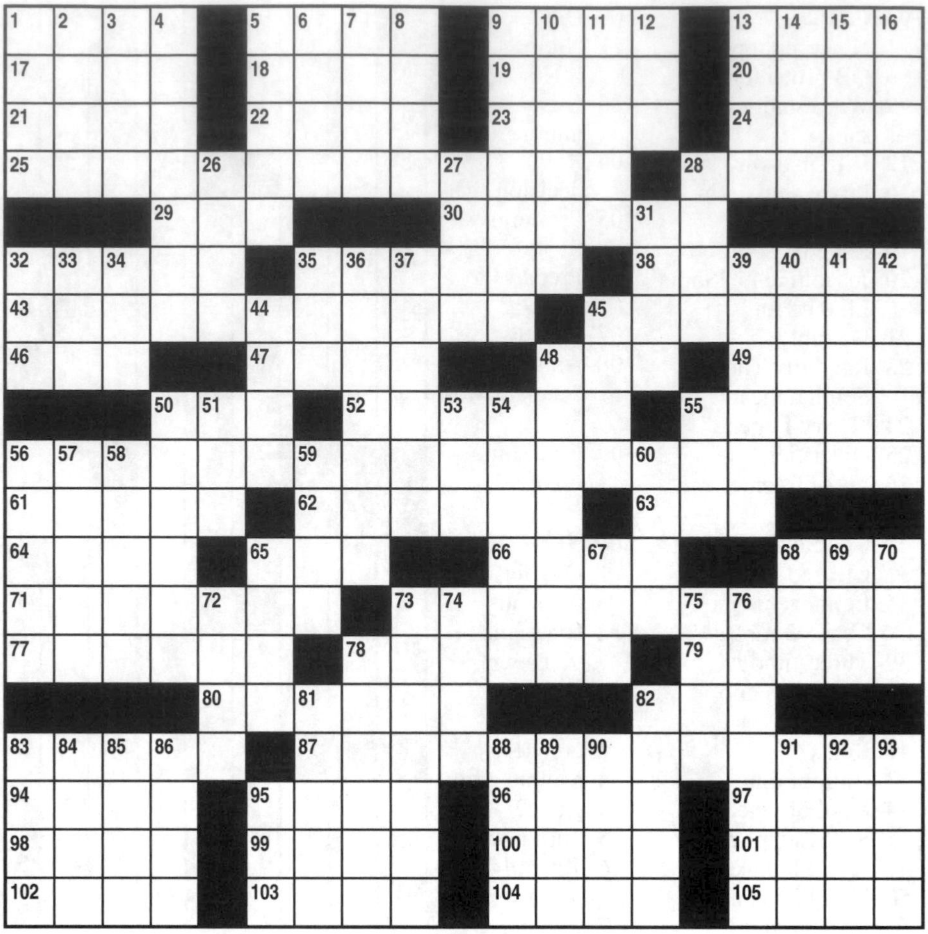

ACROSS

1 Element #30
5 Mental power
9 Roll-call no-show
13 Campus area
17 1813 battle site
18 Making a crossing
19 Four-star review
20 Pull strings?
21 Salt, to a chemist
22 Louver piece
23 Holly shrub
24 Tabloid couple
25 1,000 grams of wet socks?
28 "Platoon" director
29 Expert ending
30 Mass-market book?
32 Role for Dustin
35 Kind of republic
38 Do a new horoscope
43 The time it takes to sail 220 yards at one nautical mph?
45 Raphael subject
46 Tribute in verse
47 Exactly
48 Pocket-watch adjunct
49 Painter Jan van der ___
50 Center of Louisville
52 Carpentry tool
55 Red card
56 2,000 members of the family Mimidae?
61 Swift
62 Soup ingredient
63 Free electon, e.g.
64 Bickering
65 Place to plant
66 Signaled, on the stage
68 Cry of insight
71 Threatens
73 Basic unit of laryngitis?
77 Car-radio feature
78 Force
79 Bring to bear
80 Thin plate
82 Rocky weapon
83 Windshield adornment
87 16.5 feet in "The Twilight Zone"?
94 Cricket field
95 Videophile's collection
96 Medicine ball?
97 Supreme Norse god
98 Small flute
99 Try to lose
100 Sea east of the Caspian
101 Paella pot
102 Contract a muscle
103 Unearthly
104 Tax
105 Bug repellent

DOWN

1 Founder of Stoicism
2 "If ___ the Zoo": Dr. Seuss
3 Agreeable
4 Ma, for one
5 Refuse
6 Seaplane stop
7 One of the jet set
8 Latticework strip
9 Leaving the depths
10 1983 Peace Prize recipient
11 Hot spots
12 Superman nemesis Luthor
13 Go cold turkey
14 Biblical preposition
15 Port of Yemen
16 Capitol feature
26 "Time ___ the essence"
27 Gulf state
28 Husky burden
31 League member
32 "Room Service" studio
33 As well as
34 Wing-tip tip
35 Good buddy
36 Panicky
37 Vague idea
39 Arrive
40 Lend ___ (listen)
41 Bergen dummy
42 Bakery display
44 Tel. or elec.
45 Cut, as grass
48 Washout
50 Japanese woofers?
51 Something to flip
53 W–L stat.
54 Slalom wear
55 Cable letters
56 Walk heavily
57 Balloon filler, perhaps
58 Editorialize
59 Corrida cheers
60 "The Counterfeiters" novelist
65 ___ carotene
67 Subj. for aliens
68 Blow away
69 Part of HRH
70 Public hangings?
72 Monastic chamber
73 Billy Joel song
74 Persian poet
75 Alligator ___ (avocado)
76 Deep red
78 Block material
81 The reel thing?
82 Smucker's product
83 Tip one's hat
84 Harmful effects
85 Bistro
86 Football great Karras
88 October birthstone
89 Desperately urgent
90 Macedonian or Montenegrin
91 Lay off
92 Lifeline of Egypt
93 Biting bug
95 ETO chief

161 HOPPIN' MAD by Robert A. Doll

Trekkies should know the answer to 1 Down.

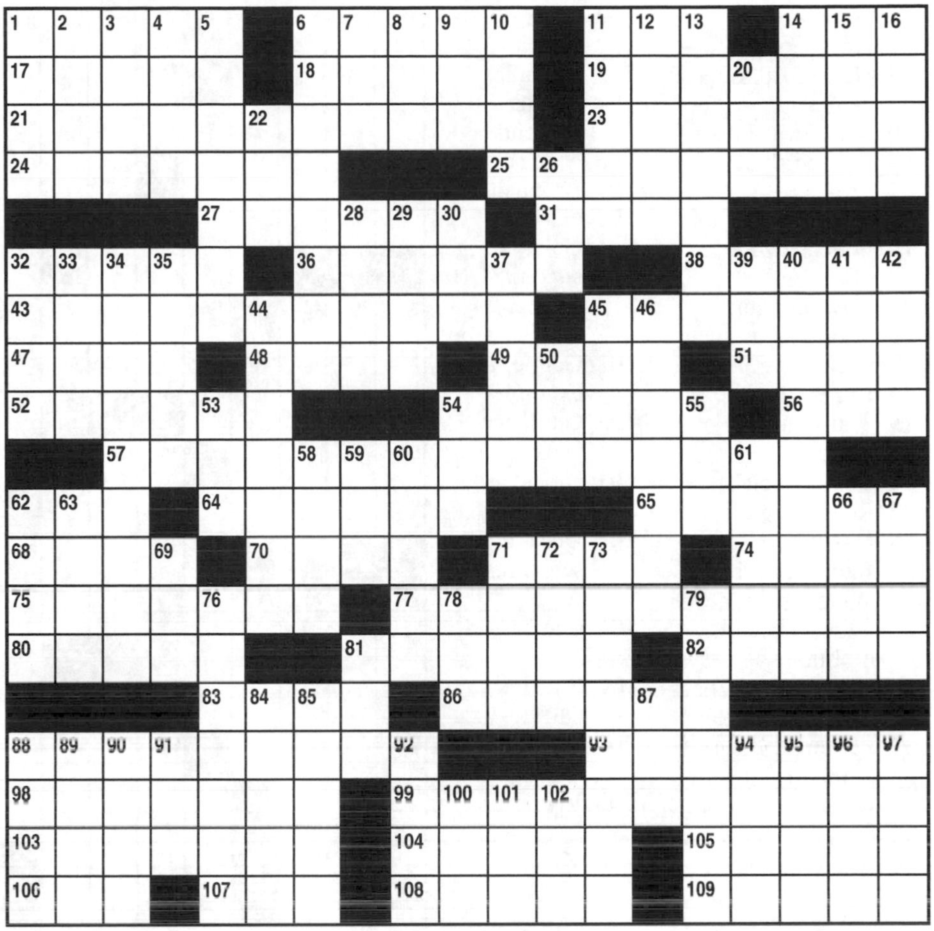

ACROSS

1 Fable finale
6 Mouton ___ (Bordeaux wine)
11 Bank letters
14 JFK watchdog
17 Give the slip
18 Like some angles
19 Sources
21 Carry on
23 Idahos' kin
24 Severe
25 Carry on
27 Sort of
31 Veronica in "The Blue Dahlia"
32 ___-ski
36 What pupils do at times
38 Broadcast
43 Carry on
45 Tree farm
47 J.D. Hogg, familiarly
48 Ancient theaters
49 Realtor's map
51 "I'd walk a ___ for a Camel"
52 Back at sea
54 Gave up
56 Mack of early TV
57 Carry on
62 ___ Claire
64 Place to find Lawrence?
65 Rubbernecks
68 Sign of apprehension, perhaps
70 Hibernia
71 Popular cuisine
74 Glazier's item
75 Epcot location
77 Carry on
80 Final authority
81 Periodic Table items
82 Must-haves
83 Spanish appetizer
86 Scout groups
88 Carry on
93 Ruled
98 Ernst & Young worker
99 Carry on
103 Authors
104 Wet behind the ears
105 Down the hatch
106 Novelist Deighton
107 "Didn't I tell you?"
108 Harbingers
109 Hagar's dog

DOWN

1 Vulcan mind-___
2 Done with
3 Pro ___
4 Hoo-has
5 Hugo Chavez supporter
6 Gushed, in a way
7 Be a thespian
8 Fitting
9 Greek H
10 Office fill-in
11 Major artery
12 Tacoma, for one
13 Get the wrong message, perhaps
14 Feudal estate
15 Not pro
16 Like some D.A.'s
20 Fed. property manager
22 Half a sawbuck
26 Martinique, par exemple
28 "Better half"
29 Inter ___
30 Soviet rocket base Kapustin ___
32 "Dancing Queen" group
33 Major-leaguers
34 In a relaxed manner
35 Prop for Picasso
37 Home for Hiawatha
39 Any doctrine
40 Stress
41 Agatha contemporary
42 Not the original color
44 Like some guests
45 Astronaut's insignia
46 Part of a place setting
50 "Well, ___-di-dah!"
53 Scandinavian rug
54 Half a dance
55 "Silent Spring" subject
58 Gambling game
59 John Doggett's org.
60 Hint
61 Expire, as an insurance policy
62 Swelled-heads
63 Certain something
66 Arthurian lady
67 Jiffs
69 ___ de deux
71 Alpine transport
72 Saint topper
73 Losers
76 Jots down
78 Giant Giant
79 Guts
81 More, in Madrid
84 Prior to, old-style
85 Stakes race money
87 Confident solver's tool
88 Cry like a baby
89 Angler's need
90 Asgard denizen
91 Margaret Edson play
92 Start of a conclusion
94 The G in GTO
95 Archibald of the N.B.A.
96 Anon's partner
97 Groundbreaking golfer Jim
100 Escort's offering
101 Born
102 Nadia's feat

162 GET IN THE SWIM by Billie Truitt

The subtitle can be found at 98 Across.

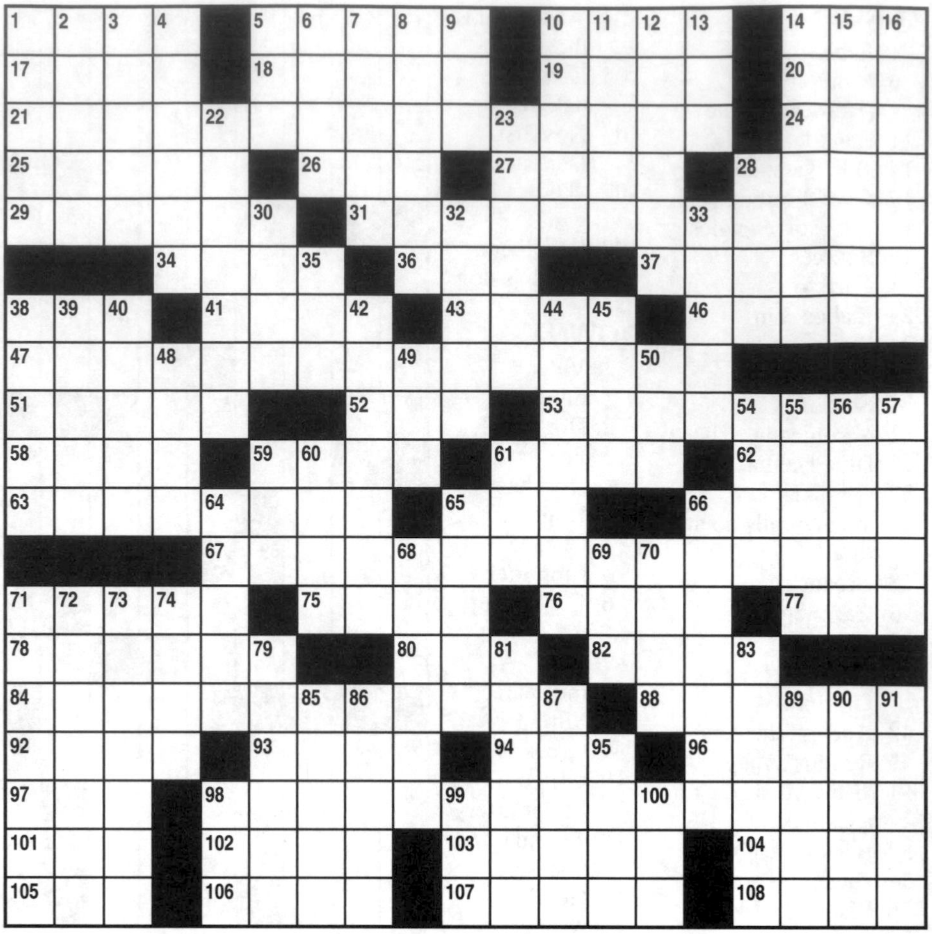

ACROSS

1 No-win situation
5 Half of Ethiopia's capital
10 Wall St. debuts
14 Retired flyer
17 Pro-___
18 Helen's abductor
19 Scheherazade offering
20 Hawaiian tuna
21 "Looking at the positives . . ."
24 Little beauty
25 Translator's obstacle
26 Young socialite
27 Rear or deer
28 Unsullied
29 Babe Ruth rival
31 What a baby needs to do to become mobile
34 Like some chances
36 Sgt. or cpl.
37 Feminist Steinem
38 Santa in California
41 Biblical kingdom
43 Golden Rule word
46 In the midst of
47 Opera that inspired "Miss Saigon"
51 Rumor sources?
52 Poor grade
53 Is forced to make a retraction
58 Running shoes brand
59 Library ID
61 McNally's partner
62 Don Juan type
63 Cornhuskers' state
65 Young pond dweller
66 Knight in "Jurassic Park"
67 Nostalgic phrase
71 How some stocks are sold
75 "Now hear ___!"
76 Colorless
77 Guitar pioneer Paul
78 Sweet-faced child
80 Big Apple sch.
82 Lund in "Casablanca"
84 Deli sandwich choice
88 One who works with acid
92 Colleges, to Aussies
93 Han's love
94 La mer contents
96 Nice school?
97 Brouhaha
98 Gary Coleman sitcom/SUBTITLE
101 Kind of tape
102 Condo, for example
103 Gardener's packet
104 Nevada resort city
105 Decade segments: Abbr.
106 Catches on to
107 Backpack part
108 Twosome

DOWN

1 Right, in Rouen
2 Jackson of "American Idol"
3 Top story?
4 Yells heard at a rodeo
5 Police alert, for short
6 Rhymester
7 Disney's little mermaid
8 London's Great Bell
9 Shade of blonde
10 "___ the bag"
11 Emulate Picasso
12 New tricks non-learner
13 "Didn't I tell you?"
14 Cactus with arms
15 ___-Williams
16 Interval between cause and effect
22 Insignia
23 Seat of power
28 Senior moment?
30 Stay a while
32 Far from obtuse
33 Some heavy soils
35 Dangerous crowd
38 Jordan's capital
39 Easily duped
40 Ignore the script
42 Spa option
44 Picked up the check
45 The end ___ era
48 Wing-shaped
49 Gymnast's goal
50 Inc., in Britain
54 Word to follow king or snow
55 Like some pains
56 Prevention measure?
57 Fortnight pair
59 Suffix meaning "or so"
60 Card game for three
61 D.C. stadium
64 "Based on ___ story"
65 Gut course
66 Man of many words?
68 Bad singer's problem
69 Indian honorific
70 Y chromosome carrier
71 AIG number-cruncher
72 Rumble from the sky
73 Geological divisions
74 Synagogue cabinets
79 Reporter's credit
81 Online newsgroup system
83 Agreement
85 Suit
86 Breaks in relations
87 Home-fries ingredient
89 Cornball
90 Verdugo in "Moon and Sixpence"
91 Fix the fairway
95 Meat stamp letters
98 Broke ground
99 First of September?
100 Recipe abbr.

163 CAN YOU FIND IT? by Buddy Richard

Hint: It's in the box.

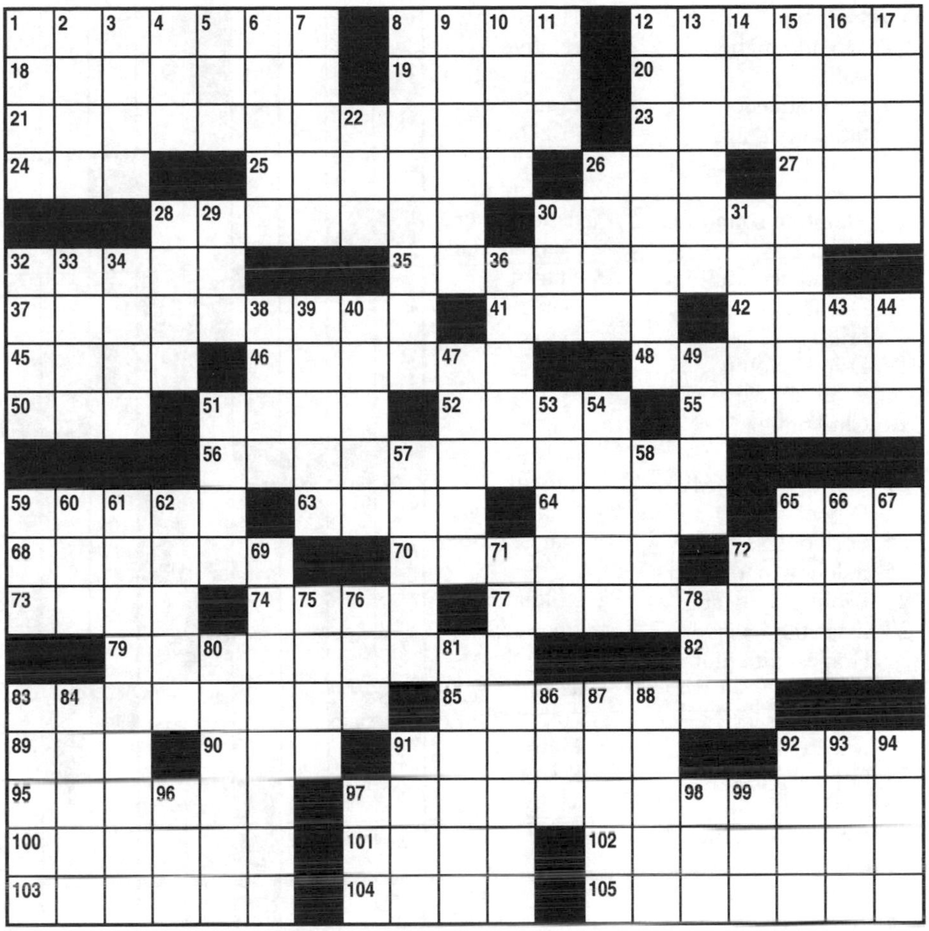

ACROSS

1 Grayish-red hue
8 "Jabberwocky" opener
12 Cease go-with
18 Brown shades
19 Millions of years
20 Astronomy Muse
21 Caveat about change (with 30-A)
23 Landlord
24 Dump
25 Opt
26 Capital letters in UTAH?
27 Tent leader?
28 Fish hawks
30 See 21 Across
32 Fall faller
35 Words to an admiral
37 Recant
41 Latin 101 verb
42 Clears
45 Short-story awards
46 Wasting time
48 Certain reception
50 "___ calls?"
51 Spheric beginning?
52 French eye
55 Liability's opposite
56 Kind of kit
59 McCartney hit of 1984
63 IRS data
64 Chits
65 Welby and Kildare
68 Green enactment
70 Gain again
72 "Later!"
73 Get from ___ (progress)
74 "Piece of cake!"
77 Advice to the stunned
79 Allen Ginsberg et al.
82 Gossip
83 One third of a 1945 Cahn-Styne song
85 Came from behind
89 Charismatic Christian sch.
90 Male sheep, in Shropshire
91 Doctor's order
92 Radio settings
95 One who inappropriately appropriates
97 Burger King slogan
100 Plant swellings
101 In excess of
102 Beatles' manager Brian
103 It bought Carnation in 1985
104 Firms
105 Cashes in

DOWN

1 Narc trailer?
2 Exalted feeling
3 Prayer recipient
4 Cytoplasmic acid
5 Clandestine maritime org.
6 Wall Street index, for short
7 Ethyl acetate, e.g.
8 Popular marinade
9 Like pine scent, say
10 Huber of tennis
11 Pilot's heading
12 It makes one uninteresting
13 Puts up
14 Swedish flier
15 Muses
16 Red Cloud, for one
17 La Brea attraction
22 Dating abbr.
26 Kind of bean
28 Metal rock group
29 Foul mood
30 Flood control
31 Conclusion
32 Razor choice
33 City near Le Havre
34 "Fine by me!"
36 More than ready
38 ___-Honey
39 Fesses up
40 Overwhelms with sweetness
43 Driving point
44 Congeal
47 "It's ___!"
49 Clods
51 "___ pinch of salt"
53 Piston great Thomas
54 "Arrowsmith" wife
57 Way to eat pastrami
58 Blockhead
59 Azov or Caspian
60 When the NLCS and ALCS are played
61 TVs, slangily
62 Even if
65 "Titanic" soundtrack singer
66 "Cast Away" vessel
67 Living room item
69 Treat as though helpless
71 Ones who try
72 Alluded to
75 Individually
76 Mother bear
78 Look at
80 ". . . quite the bargain!"
81 Globetrot
83 "Two Women" Oscar winner
84 Take support from
86 Café go-with
87 Coating
88 "God willing!"
91 Word processing command
92 ___ bit (slightly)
93 Hurt severely
94 Assn. and org., e.g.
96 Subway sandwich
97 Razorback
98 Currency shop abbr.
99 AAA recommendation

164 "NAME THAT TOON!" by Patrick Jordan

58 Across is also the name of a mixed drink.

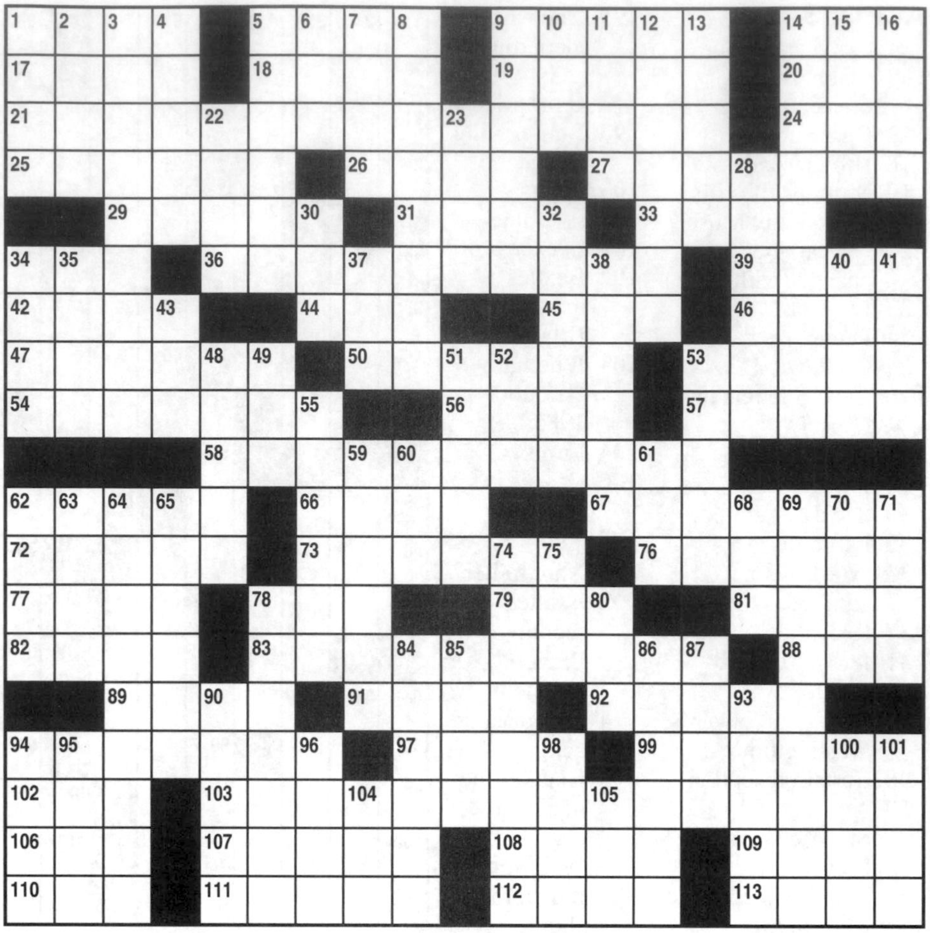

ACROSS

1 Melodramatic lament
5 Dermabrasion target, perhaps
9 Brazilian ballroom dance
14 Shootout sound effect
17 Diet successfully
18 Dashboard device, briefly
19 Ezio's "South Pacific" role
20 Christian or Cenozoic
21 Star of "Blow Me Down" (1933)
24 Fork out
25 Salchow performer
26 Bibliography abbr.
27 Does the Twist
29 Horses with muted coats
31 "The Mikado" wardrobe items
33 Offer from Monty or Howie
34 Kept tabs on the kids
36 Star of "Going! Going! Gosh!" (1952)
39 Animation fan's collection
42 Prof's handout
44 Luau serving
45 Cambridgeshire town
46 For each
47 Not quite
50 Put points on the board
53 Buscemi of "Billy Bathgate"
54 Playground fixtures
56 Indulge in idleness
57 Took a hatchet to
58 Stars of "Salt Water Tabby" (1947)
62 "Occupant" author Edward
66 Jai ___
67 They dangle in delis
72 Heading (for)
73 Some Winter Olympics entrants
76 Keyboard expert
77 The Cowboys' home, familiarly
78 Hackberry relative
79 Organ with a drum
81 "Enchanted" girl of film
82 Gas brand named after Standard Oil
83 Star of "Crazy Over Daisy" (1950)
88 Spider's snare
89 Nautical lockup
91 ". . . pretty maids all in ___"
92 Mikhail's first lady
94 Thought of as comparable
97 Metros and Prizms
99 Malty mugfuls
102 Rev
103 Star of "The Coo-Coo Bird" (1947)
106 Tom Collins component
107 Hearing-related
108 Buggy obstacle
109 Casino offering
110 Moviedom's Helm or Flint
111 Place for 113 Across
112 Rigging supporter
113 Broadway backdrops

DOWN

1 Brenner Pass range
2 "Behold!"
3 Saccharine alternative
4 Handle
5 Caterer's heat source
6 93 Down, for one
7 Throbbing sensation
8 Orator's art
9 Trap hermetically
10 "___ glad you came along!"
11 Inch fractions
12 Post-shampoo option
13 Eaglet's nursery
14 Star of "Odor-able Kitty" (1945)
15 Adjective for some vaccines
16 Means partner
22 Leap or light follower
23 "The Thief of Baghdad" actor
28 Obey an eviction notice
30 Gullible sort
32 "Bless you" prompter
34 Briny expanses
35 Wheelbase boundary
37 Coifs, for short
38 Tribal dignitaries
40 Valentine sentiment
41 Went full tilt
43 Calendar pgs.
48 Wholly gratified
49 Only even prime number
51 "American Graffiti" soundtrack song
52 British rule in India
53 As a wallflower would
55 Jack-o'-lantern feature?
59 She has a degree
60 Long shot at a derby
61 "Flushed Away" character
62 French clergyman
63 Hi's honey, in the funnies
64 Star of "Falling Hare" (1943)
65 1960s TV role for Agnes
68 Darwinian forebear
69 "Laverne & Shirley" setting
70 Lake Superior's ___ Royale
71 Wield a bayonet
74 Towering trees
75 Like Emmett Kelly's clown face
78 Barely beat
80 Karel Capek work
84 Design with diamonds
85 Theater mogul Marcus
86 Gregarious ghost
87 Toy for breezy days
90 "___ the best of times . . ."
93 1990s White House pet
94 Incubator inhabitants
95 Cryptogram solution, often
96 Explorer with a talking backpack
98 It's slurped by rude diners
100 Jamboree shelter
101 Popular plays, briefly
104 Trygve's U.N. successor
105 Genetic trigram

165 LOST LOVE by E.G. Harris

50 Down is also a translation of the Bible.

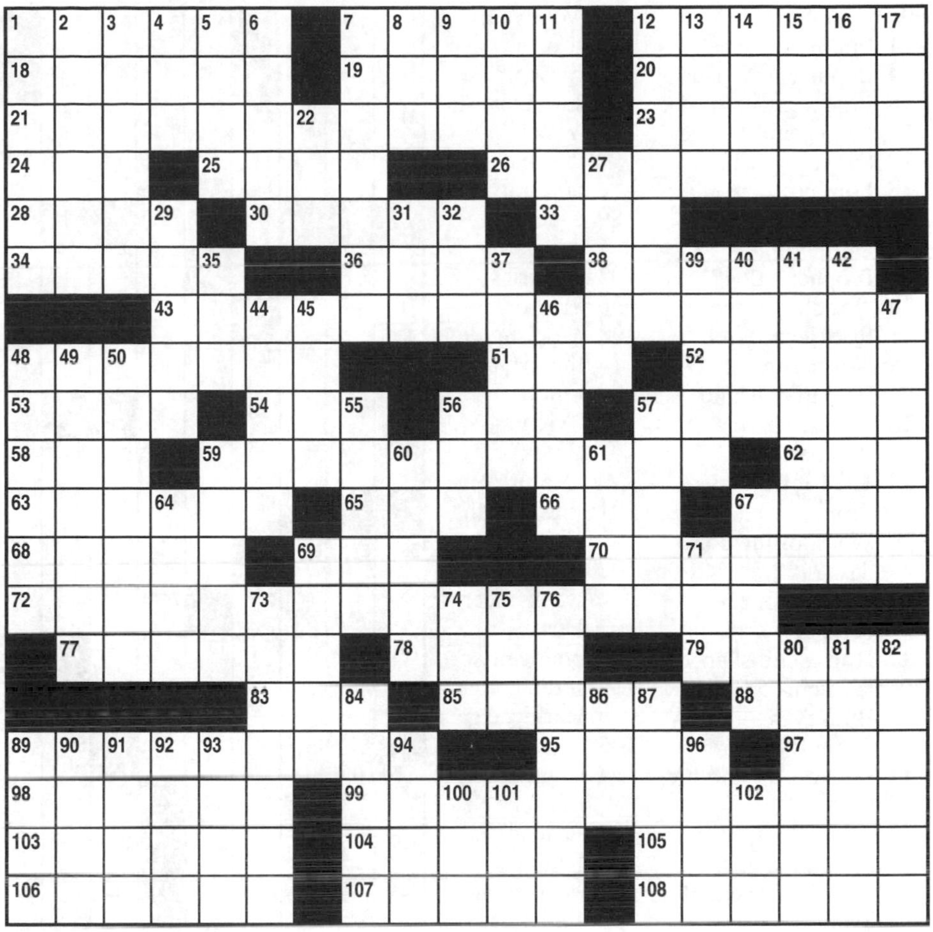

ACROSS

1 Goes off course
7 Ariz. neighbor
12 Weather-changing current
18 Ratted out
19 Part of CSI
20 Riot participant, maybe
21 Hires apartment?
23 Mason of "The Goodbye Girl"
24 Across the st. from
25 18 wheeler
26 Beatnik postal carrier?
28 Naval Academy freshman
30 "The Thinker" sculptor
33 Architect Maya ___
34 Begin's peace partner
36 Red rind contents
38 Makes off with
43 Disarm meek folks? (with 59-A)
48 Greenhorns
51 Mauna ___
52 Puccini heroine
53 Numbered piece
54 Folkie DiFranco
56 1 of 100 in DC
57 Embark, as on a journey
58 Voice of Bugs
59 See 43 Across
62 Pod beginning
63 Riles up
65 Wide size
66 Mere taste
67 Huxtable son
68 Ease off
69 Harsh review
70 Gun barrel cleaners
72 Where knights wipe their feet?
77 Take back to the lab
78 Steer clear of
79 Karate acquisitions
83 Make funny faces
85 Tours ta ta
88 Daytime TV drama
89 Baseball players?
95 Get better
97 "Evita" narrator
98 Coral islands
99 Oreo with the main course?
103 "It's crazy but true!"
104 Dixie talk
105 Into the breeze
106 Wept wildly, maybe
107 Two sides in a battle
108 Game in which love means 0

DOWN

1 Barbershop sharpeners
2 Big song and dance
3 Fled and wed
4 Buffalo's summer hrs.
5 39 Down and others
6 Contemptuous smile
7 1957 Chuck Willis hit
8 Light bark
9 Dogpatch diminutive
10 PC competitor
11 Postembryonic
12 City near Los Angeles
13 Shaped meat dish
14 "Cheers" regular
15 "___ wrap!"
16 Classic soft drink
17 By word of mouth
22 Comedian Philips
27 Campbell of "Martin"
29 Grounds
31 "If I knew you were coming ___ baked a cake!"
32 King Cole
35 Gumshoe, for short
37 Free-for-all
39 "Melrose Place" name
40 "There'll be ___ time . . ."
41 South African monarchy
42 Tied down
44 Bosc and anjou
45 "It comes ___ surprise"
46 Ice grabbers
47 Bug zapper sites
48 Polite turndown
49 Where drinks are on the host
50 Common speech
55 "Let me try again . . ."
56 That girl
57 March honoree, for short
59 Soeur's counterpart
60 Sees to
61 Runs on TV
64 State on the Seine
67 Grove components
69 Build
71 "Boys of summer" org.
73 Seeped through
74 "Got it!"
75 Chew for Bossy
76 Eric Burdon's old group
80 Commit unalterably
81 Sesame seed paste
82 Cyclist's choices
84 Showy bloomers, briefly
86 Slippery one
87 Not edited for TV
89 Cause of misery
90 Wee particle
91 Japanese WW2 general
92 Parcel of land
93 Sommer of the screen
94 To be, in Bordeaux
96 Inside scoop
100 Hit the limit, with "out"
101 Fleecy female
102 Have the deed to

166 WOOF! by Pancho Harrison

Volleyballers should get the clue at 83 Across.

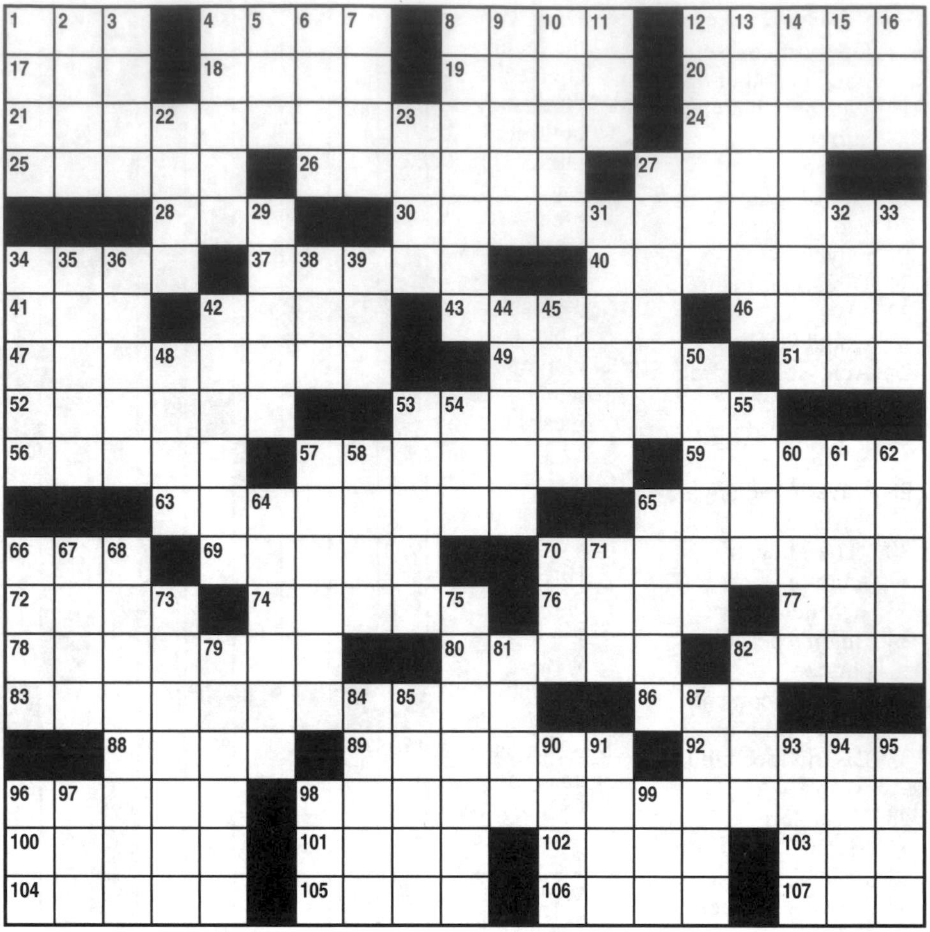

ACROSS

1 Put money on
4 Popular A/V jacks
8 Pipe part
12 Falana and Montez
17 Santa ___ winds
18 Ford crossover
19 Indian spiced tea
20 Unmoving
21 Prophetic dog?
24 "Fiddler on the Roof" patriarch
25 Northernmost Hawaiian island
26 Zoo denizen
27 Plot part
28 1974 John Wayne film
30 Wear for the dog days?
34 "Born From Jets" company
37 Horseshoe-shaped lab item
40 Buckeyes
41 B'nai B'rith org.
42 Sign on for another hitch
43 No-fat Jack
46 Executive gps.
47 Obedience school exams?
49 Laura Petrie's cry
51 Half of a figure eight
52 Skimpy suit
53 Planters pitchman
56 Dined at a diner, say
57 Dog for Devo?
59 Daytime dramas
63 Kuala Lumpur's land
65 Bleach
66 ___ Moines
69 Prepares, in a way
70 Ancestry of a curly-tailed dog?
72 Wax-coated cheese
74 At right angles to the keel
76 Mystique
77 Photocell
78 Footboard-headboard connector
80 Composes
82 ___ Helens, WA
83 Volleyball team mascot?
86 La-la lead-in
88 WW1 German admiral
89 Mackerel cousin
92 Sty cries
96 Taxi ticker
98 Working dog that pays rent?
100 "Men in Black" creature
101 Prefix with China
102 End-of-the-week cheer
103 Dusk, poetically
104 Indian or Harley, e.g.
105 ___ majesty (high treason)
106 Peacock tail features
107 Winnebagos, for short

DOWN

1 Catch some rays
2 One-named New Age singer
3 "The Forbidden Fragrance"
4 Dig discovery
5 LP successors
6 Turkish title
7 Spotted
8 Chumps
9 Walking papers, slangily
10 Steve of country music
11 Between pre- and post-
12 Chinese nut
13 Like many old-time schoolhouses
14 Influence
15 Legend ender?
16 Sault ___ Marie
22 Poet's foot
23 Dr Pepper rival
27 Kutcher in "What Happens in Vegas . . ."
29 Cheese, in Chihuahua
31 Bust a gut over
32 Demolition needs
33 Sound of a leak
34 Latin dance
35 Rewrite for the screen
36 "The Sandbox" playwright
38 Boy king of ancient Egypt
39 Increases
42 Sale item label
44 Dad
45 First South Korean president
48 Washington Huskies, e.g.
50 Baloney
53 Beethoven's "___ Solemnis"
54 Tech sch. in Troy, NY
55 Slave away
57 Sing like a bird
58 Stevenson title character
60 Slanting
61 Remains unresolved
62 Hägar the Horrible's dog
64 Be a go-between
65 Most awful
66 Mazar in "GoodFellas"
67 River of Hesse, Germany
68 Cruel, and liking it
70 "Iron Man" Ripken
71 "Rattle and ___" (U2 album)
73 Diana Rigg role
75 "You can't be serious!" tennis champ
79 "Juarez" Oscar nominee
81 Like the Gobi
82 Postal delivery
84 Chophouse choice
85 Horned croakers
87 Mouth parts
90 Chapeau site
91 Bacchanalian bash
93 Pirate or Padre, for short
94 Chicken ___
95 D.C. bigwigs
96 Brit's raincoat
97 Ron who played Tarzan
98 "The Family Circus" cartoonist Keane
99 French co.

167 "AW, SHUCKS" by Richard Silvestri

94 Across was also the MVP of that exciting game.

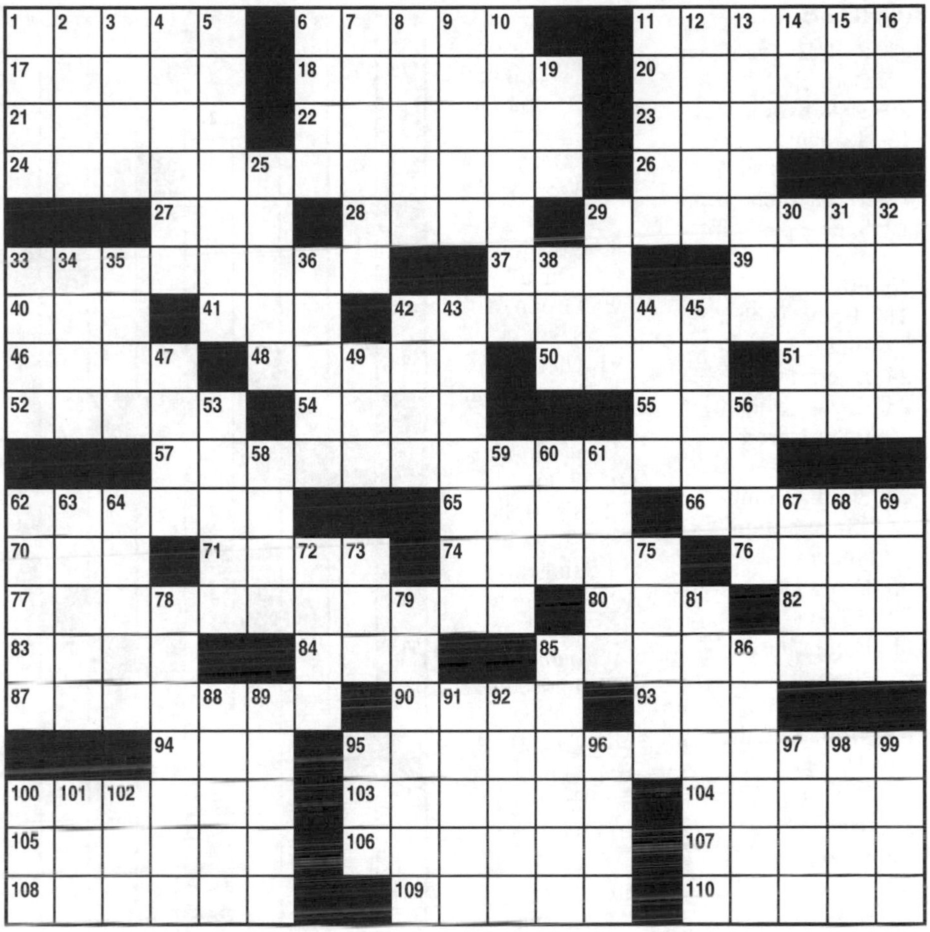

ACROSS

1 Bonobo's kin
6 Of the foot
11 Skier's delight
17 Bookstore section
18 Weak
20 Emulate Earhart
21 Old World lizard
22 Sends the money
23 Hit the roof
24 Made by a British soldier?
26 Seaside soarer
27 Occupational ending
28 Former polliwog
29 Sister of Apollo
33 Diminish
37 Sapporo sash
39 Put first things first
40 Tell's home
41 Long-time NBC show, for short
42 Flyfishing bear, e.g.?
46 Source of a twist
48 Raspberries' "___ the Way"
50 Work in Vegas
51 "Bambi" character
52 Charlatan
54 First-floor apartment
55 Took inventory?
57 Burlesque theater?
62 Snitch
65 Pouting grimace
66 Pot
70 Psyche part
71 No contest, perhaps
74 Lisa Marie's father
76 Satanic stuff
77 Misbehaving tree?
80 Thesaurus wd.
82 Verb-forming suffix
83 Where it's at
84 "Losing My Religion" group
85 Left high and dry
87 Catch
90 Arnold or Wilbur
93 Salt Lake City athlete
94 Manning in Super Bowl XLII
95 Thoreau work in hock?
100 System starter
103 Salad ingredient
104 Cheap smoke
105 Get in
106 Trawling equipment
107 Navajo dwelling
108 Bullet with a visible path
109 Inclines
110 Battery terminal

DOWN

1 Shoot the breeze
2 Quasimodo's creator
3 Leader at a mosque
4 "___ Dearest" (1981)
5 Missal contents
6 Henry VIII's last
7 Singular
8 Take exception
9 Pal
10 "3rd Rock from the Sun" star
11 Message machine
12 Impossible to miss
13 One who says "I do"
14 TVA project
15 Fraternity letter
16 Flushed
19 Chi. clock setting
25 Off the beam
29 Staff member
30 Sacred song
31 Goddess of peace
32 Fancy fiddle
33 Gang's territory
34 "Turandot" tune
35 Slip shade?
36 Overflow
38 Breakfast partner
42 One of the common people
43 Egg white
44 Colombian city
45 On the border of
47 Obligation
49 To some extent
53 Ed Norton's neighbor
56 Folklore monster
58 Caning memento
59 Hercules' captive
60 Chevy truck of yore
61 Washington or Jefferson
62 On edge
63 Over
64 Track figures
67 All fired up
68 Volume
69 Musher's vehicle
72 Brontë heroine
73 Mimic
75 Vermont product
78 No-frills
79 Form a jury
81 Boris' partner in crime
85 Comedy's Mr. Wright
86 "Principia" author
88 Still kicking
89 Kitchen gadget
91 Song from the 60's
92 Twin Cities suburb
95 NBA Hall-of-Famer Unseld
96 Scotch water?
97 Canceled, to NASA
98 Old oath
99 Unit of force
100 Prepare for framing
101 Mess up
102 Part of a chorus line?

168 SOUL SEARCHING by Jim Page

Of the group below, 84 Across was the only one not to sign with 57 Across.

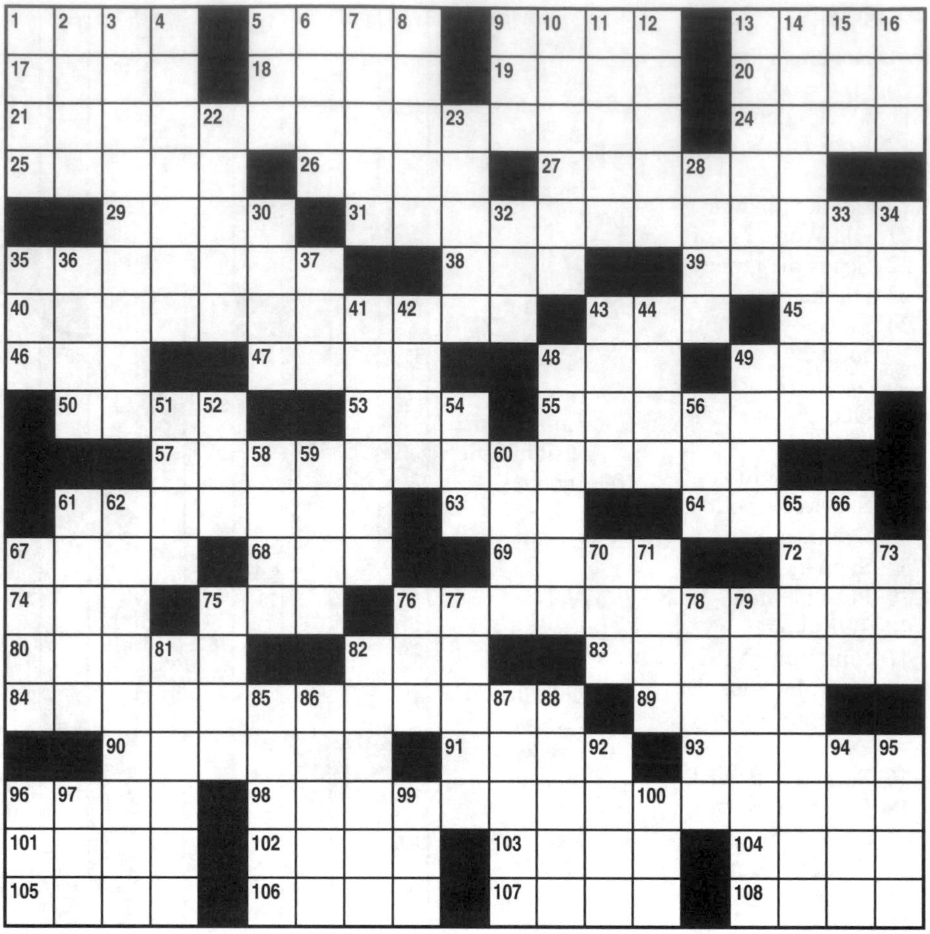

ACROSS

1 Rick Blaine's love
5 Bark cloth
9 Shadowbox
13 Sea hail
17 Chemical salt?
18 Yerba buena, e.g.
19 Senate page, for one
20 Fill a hold
21 "Being With You" singer
24 Blimp front
25 Kazan resident
26 Bakery aroma
27 Fearful
29 Football foul
31 "Superstition" singer
35 Disconnect a trailer
38 Bubkes
39 Haggard of Nashville
40 "Baby Love" group
43 Workout unit
45 "___ Been Thinking About You"
46 Foot-pound relative
47 "Kalifornia" director
48 Focus of a sleep lab
49 "Amores" poet
50 Balanchine ballet
53 Go over to the other side
55 Uplifts
57 Berry Gordy founded it in 1957
61 Anastasia, e.g.
63 Flying Cloud of yore
64 Kind of equity offering
67 Sally ___ bread
68 Pound puppy
69 ". . . ___ you ain't my baby?"
72 180° turn
74 New Hampshire river
75 Talking-___ (scoldings)
76 "I Want You Back" singers
80 Paint solvent
82 GameCube successor
83 "Death in the Afternoon" figure
84 "Baby Workout" singer
89 Pooch from China
90 Group of seven
91 Margot in "Superman"
93 Antique photo tone
96 Palm smartphone
98 "My Girl" singers
101 Where to find Lima beings
102 First-rate
103 Some are cream
104 U.S. Army medals
105 Dramatis personae
106 Nothing special
107 Start of a URL
108 Rushing yds., e.g.

DOWN

1 "Meet me ___ Louis . . ."
2 Prayer wheel user
3 It's hard-boiled and deep-fried
4 Acid neutralizers
5 Your of yore
6 Inflatable mattress
7 Cowpoke pokers
8 Monk's superior
9 ___ Quentin Prison
10 Flower part
11 Really fancy
12 Keep getting "Mad"
13 Like Super G
14 Western Digital product
15 "Deep Space Nine" security chief
16 Flexible wood
22 Verdi aria
23 Dancing Castle
28 Circumstance partner
30 Family mds.
32 Strength
33 Sonny Crockett's alligator
34 Swamp thing
35 Sun-dance tribe
36 Drag-racing org.
37 Charlemagne's reign: Abbr.
41 Tom Clancy Xbox 360 game
42 Paramount
43 Write a second draft
44 Near East nabob
48 Cap a wine bottle anew
49 Picardy river
51 OPEC member
52 Fish–fowl connection
54 Misreckon
56 Wartime pres.
58 "Dora the Explorer" squirrel
59 Load to bear
60 Affirmative Action org.
61 Home of the Golden Hurricane
62 "Invasion of the Body ___" (1956)
65 Roadside sign
66 "Whip It" band
67 Cobb in "Twelve Angry Men"
70 Suffix for sex
71 Dove, e.g.
73 "___ darn tootin'!"
75 Outing
76 Fashion designer Sander
77 Supermaket area
78 Military experiment, briefly
79 How some get admitted to the bar?
81 Barely make ends meet
82 Improves a road
85 James and Kett
86 Rebel yell
87 Sex appeal
88 ___ in the bud
92 Undo a dele
94 Western pyramid builder
95 Coadjutant: Abbr.
96 Richest PGA tournament
97 Stephen in "Breakfast on Pluto"
99 Saxophonist Macero
100 Nile biter

169 DQ MENU by Arlan and Linda Bushman

A recent visit to Dairy Queen inspired this theme.

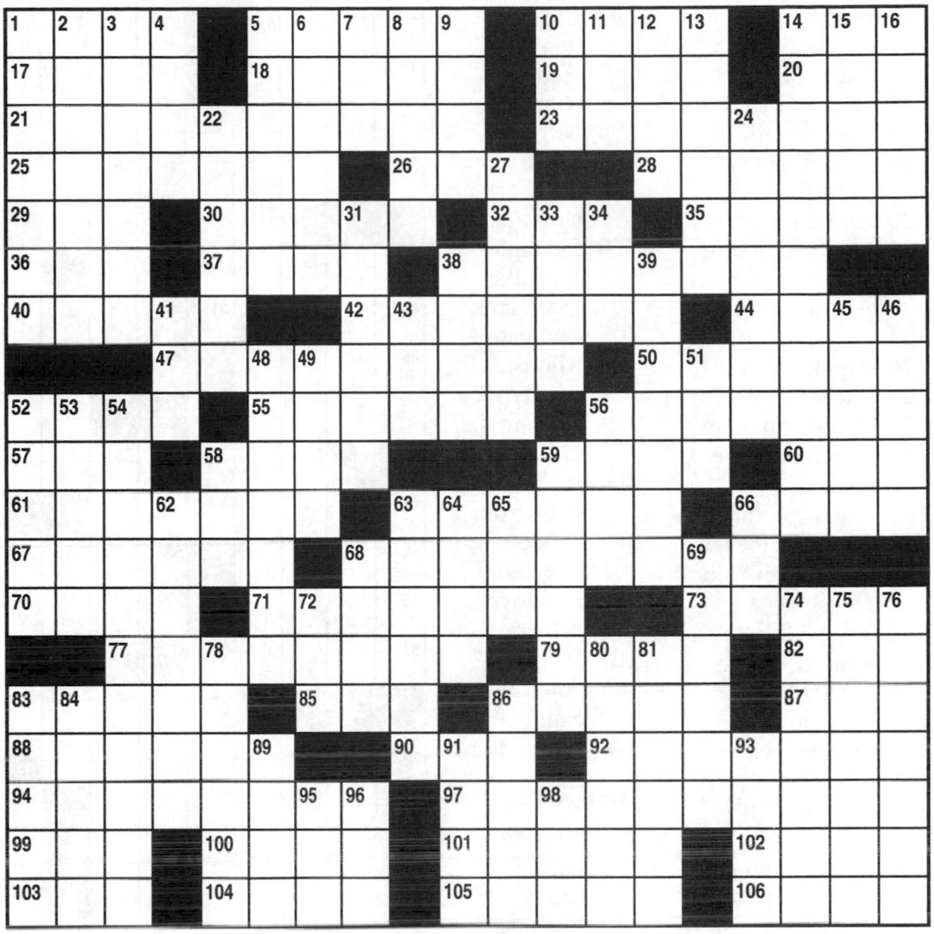

ACROSS

1 Repartee
5 Moxie
10 Tiddlywink, for one
14 Mar. event
17 Not fooled by
18 Big Bird cohort
19 Spread
20 Flock member
21 One given to over-the-top reactions
23 Daily splashes, perhaps
25 Dinger
26 Pen mate
28 Stable anti-pest protection
29 Inexperienced one
30 Reagan attorney general
32 Fall behind
35 Copies, briefly
36 Arapaho neighbor
37 "The West Wing" actor
38 "Star Trek" warrior race
40 Fixed up
42 Results in
44 ___ vitae
47 Hoosier statesman who wrote "Standing Firm"
50 Not celebrated
52 Some vegetable containers
55 Cary's "Charade" costar
56 Roman province
57 Dijon honey
58 Verve
59 Cloverleaf segment
60 Urban add-on
61 Garage alternative
63 1971 Beatty title role
66 Fruity quaffs
67 What Dinah Shore wanted people to see in their Chevrolets
68 Persian Gulf capital
70 Pouches
71 Walden guy
73 Payola
77 Shake a fist at
79 Kett of old comics
82 Ante relative
83 Umbrage
85 Command to dobbin
86 It's upriver from Tours
87 Stew morsel
88 Bursts forth
90 Morpheus protege
92 Falls back on
94 Farm males
97 Dulcinea's champion
99 QB's boo-boo
100 Hershiser of baseball
101 Assembly
102 At any time
103 Wood ash derivative
104 Fleet
105 Politician Kefauver
106 Buntline and Beatty

DOWN

1 Riding breeches namesake city
2 On the way
3 Put your foot down hard
4 Volume
5 Hollywood staple
6 Thinned out
7 French article
8 Jenna, to Jeb
9 Numbers game
10 Dopey confederate
11 UN-based workers grp.
12 Psyche
13 "C U When U Get There" rapper
14 1994 Doc Holliday portrayer
15 Honeyed
16 Analyzes
22 Marine force
24 78 Down, notably
27 Fearlessly
31 "Buenos dias," for instance
33 Knowing
34 Fangorn Forest dweller
38 Danny known for tongue-twisting songs
39 Epicure
41 Freudian constructs
43 Ring bearer
45 Link up
46 Dancer de Mille
48 Recount
49 Step down
51 Wee dram
52 Treaties
53 College World Series city
54 Not a paraphrase
56 Rum-soaked cake
58 Diddley and Jackson
59 Welch of filmdom
62 Exercise regimen
63 Heavy ribbed fabric
64 CBS morning anchor Julie
65 Ontario motorist's org.
66 Schedule abbr.
68 Fuss over
69 2001 Australian Open winner
72 Crone
74 Say yes
75 Lost sleep (over)
76 Promos
78 Mary Lou on a Wheaties box
80 Twisting force
81 Highway headaches
83 Jeopardy
84 O. Henry forte
86 Loudmouths
89 Toxin fighters
91 Brink
93 Field workers
95 Gun
96 Underhanded
98 "Ready or ___ . . ."

170 OFF-ROAD VEHICLE by Clare Hansbrough

33 Down was visited by Ann Curry of "The Today Show" in 2007.

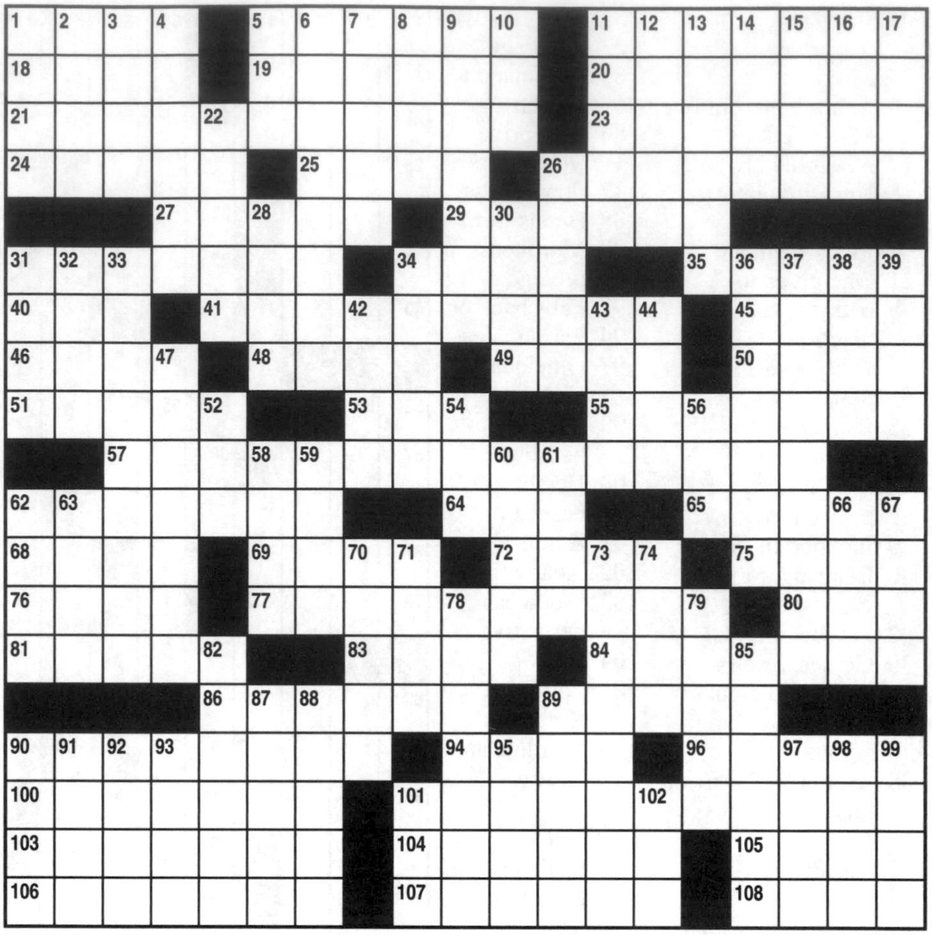

ACROSS

1 Has title to
5 Gung-ho
11 "Puh-leeze!"
18 London lad
19 Julia's role on "Seinfeld"
20 Castle feature
21 Macho attitude?
23 Nature worshiper
24 Arrow shaft
25 "___ fan tutte"
26 Alpine tea?
27 Succotash beans
29 Strike obliquely
31 Grappler in the sticks
34 Circus performer
35 Ab strengthener
40 Game with "Skip" cards
41 Cry of "Look, Alfred!"?
45 NASDAQ counterpart
46 Slap on
48 Film fish
49 "For heaven's ___!"
50 Do a spit take
51 Movie crowd member
53 Put in a pet
55 High beams
57 Alternative to laughing gas?
62 Number on a letter
64 Brazilian map word
65 Land units
68 Reassuring response
69 Not taken in by
72 Soybean dish
75 Commercial suffix with Star and Sun
76 Chaucer piece
77 Minnelli singing in clubs?
80 Mai ___ cocktail
81 First words in "Ozymandius"
83 Badminton projectile
84 Strictly required (with "de")
86 Revolutionary Brando role?
89 High flat areas
90 Competitions in feathery wraps?
94 Nay and uh-uh
96 Early caucus participant
100 Examples of beefcake
101 "Star Trek" character who isn't the elite type?
103 Sparing the rod
104 High standards
105 Shade makers
106 Hangover helpers
107 More fanciful
108 Nair competitor

DOWN

1 "Bound for Glory" singer Phil
2 Put an edge on
3 Be specific about
4 Takes part in a bee
5 Pt. of AARP
6 One way to order
7 Angelic auras
8 Social reformer Jacob
9 Flu fighter
10 "Hold it!"
11 Give rise to
12 Type of button
13 Comes to mind
14 Butts into
15 "Gandhi," for one
16 Fit together
17 Sundance's gal
22 Sam of "Jurassic Park"
26 Tex-Mex topping
28 "You're putting ___!"
30 Produces eggs
31 Ill-bred
32 Some have it to grind
33 Bottom spot
34 Laugh derisively
36 On hand for sale
37 Compose on a keyboard
38 Keyboardist, of a sort
39 Sunday seats
42 Runner Zatopek
43 Stew veggie
44 "Hud" Oscar winner Patricia
47 Word that one tacks onto tax
52 Mil. drop site
54 WBA stats
56 Where St. Pete is
58 Heartthrob
59 NBC stalwart
60 Beyond full
61 Meal for a moth
62 Tubular pasta
63 Mosque leader
66 Jacob's hairy brother
67 Ruin a martini, to 007
70 Brass section
71 Tending to business
73 Clearance event
74 Israeli weapons
78 Moorish kingdom
79 Another time
82 Flowering shrub
85 Arthur Ashe Stadium event
87 In the thick of
88 Royal pains
89 Rock genre
90 Java neighbor
91 Crude letters
92 Top drawer
93 Oily
95 European auto
97 Beguiling trick
98 Very top
99 Anti-Greeley cartoonist
101 Op. ___
102 Bib. setting

171 "AMEN, TO THAT!" by Elizabeth C. Gorski

The answer to 38 Across is obviously not Jon Arbuckle.

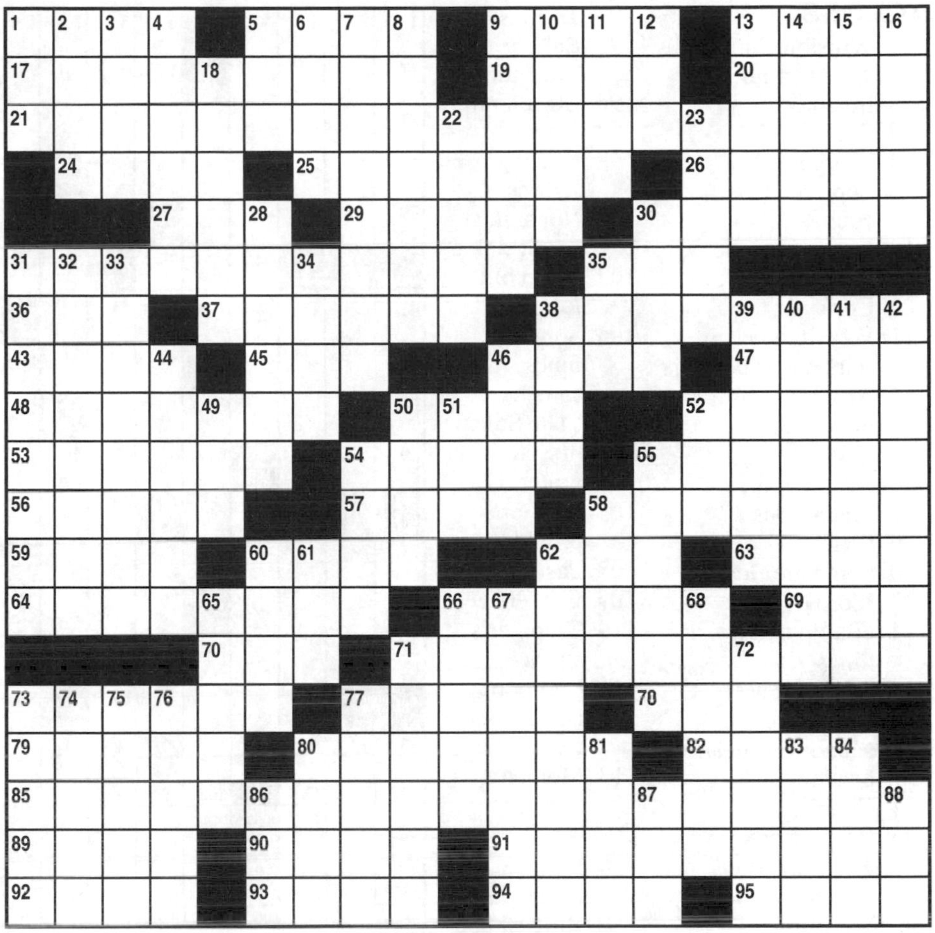

ACROSS

1 Kane's "Rosebud"
5 Cyclotron bits
9 Soothing lip ointment
13 Supplements
17 Proof of purchase
19 "Now ___ it!" ("Understood!")
20 Bananarama, e.g.
21 **Start of a thought**
24 Motorola phone
25 Hired gun
26 Hamilton in "The Terminator"
27 Brain scan
29 How prima ballerinas dance
30 Moving chair
31 **More of thought**
35 Character on "The Simpsons"
36 Queen of Thebes, in mythology
37 Uses finger paints
38 Odie's owner
43 Sitarist Shankar
45 ___-relief
46 Classic ref. works
47 Kitchen floor, for short
48 Kick in a swimming pool
50 Enya's homeland
52 Leaf division
53 Opera singer's concern
54 Unintended reaction to a sermon
55 Revolt
56 "The Water Horse" hero
57 Crunchy cookie
58 Ma and Pa of '50s films
59 Not working
60 Where Zeno of Citium taught
62 Dorm overseers, for short
63 Dispatched
64 Get lost in one's thoughts
66 Diva Franklin
69 Boise's county
70 Cash dispenser
71 **More of thought**
73 Feuding (with)
77 Legislate
78 PBS program
79 ___ New Guinea
80 Hold
82 Rogers and Scheider
85 **End of thought**
89 Wisdom of the ages
90 Eyelid woe
91 "Stay for a while . . ."
92 Pro team?
93 DC fundraisers
94 "And Morning ___ with haste her lids . . .": Emerson
95 Ladies of Andalusia: Abbr.

DOWN

1 Maine–Texas dir.
2 Big cat player in "The Wizard of Oz"
3 Zeno of ___
4 Washington in "Philadelphia"
5 "Sort of" suffix
6 Cheers for El Toro
7 Patron saint of children
8 Oxford word-jumbler (1844–1930)
9 Circus tent
10 See eye to eye
11 Icky look
12 Homeowner's doc.
13 Room at the top
14 Have a Cosmo
15 The "D" in LED
16 Detecting device
18 Kind of fracture
22 Hemidemisemiquavers, e.g.
23 Audibly
28 Frolic
30 45 and 78
31 Emergency care
32 Really big snake
33 With fondness
34 Scorch
35 Support
38 "Gosh . . ."
39 First invitees
40 Wrapper of Greek cuisine
41 Slur
42 Susan Lucci, for one
44 Released
46 Soup pasta
49 One of the family
50 Poet Pound
51 Computer attachment?
52 Service area at Daytona
54 Tabloid photographer's attachment
55 FedEx anew
58 "Greatest American Hero" portrayer
60 Broadway show displays
61 Skye cap
62 Where truckers recharge their batteries
65 Early-warning device
66 Beginning of a Dickens title
67 "I Love Lucy" family
68 Having no principles
71 Foot divisions
72 Paints a picture
73 With competence
74 Sierra Nevada lake
75 Beethoven wrote only one
76 Befools
77 Britannica set: Abbr.
80 "I could ___ horse!"
81 Southern side?
83 Orbital period
84 Fiji's capital
86 Medium ability
87 Workout equip.
88 Financial-page ratios

172 GETTING IN GEAR by Robert A. Doll

21 Across is what you'd call big-screen entertainment.

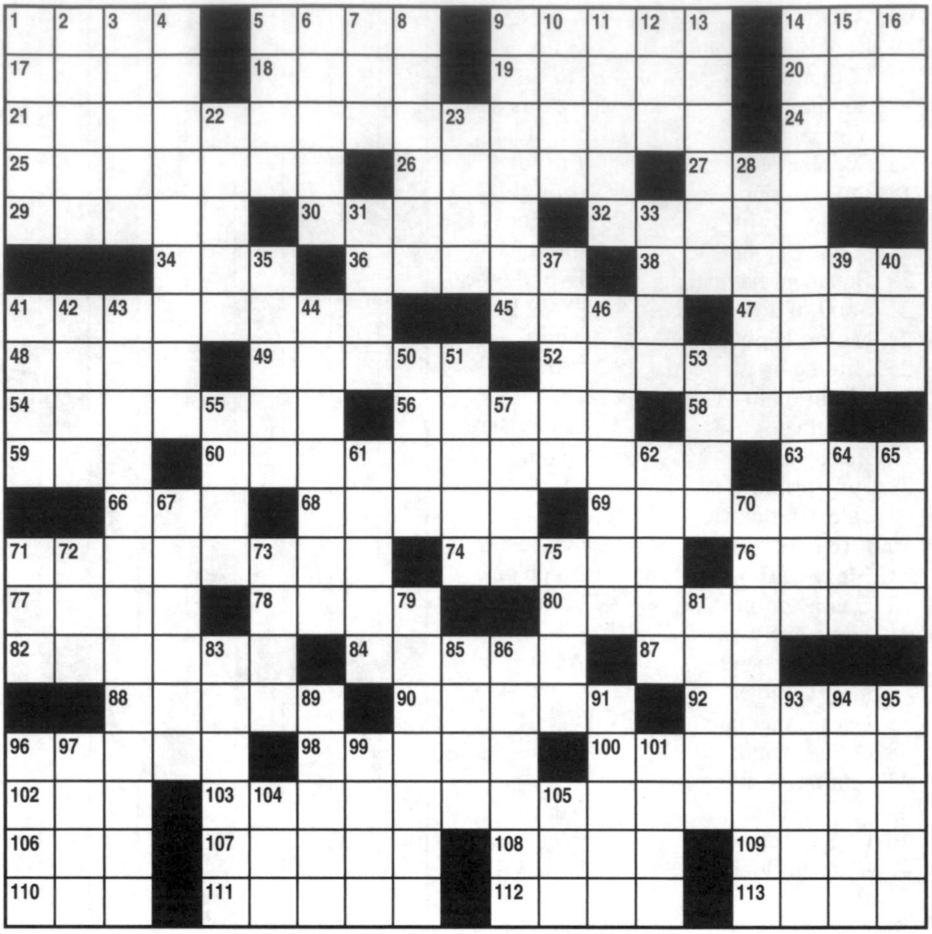

ACROSS

1 Winston Churchill's "___ Country"
5 Inventory
9 Saw
14 "Forget it!"
17 Supreme Court count
18 Looped handle
19 Four-star reviews
20 Corn serving
21 Where to watch stars under the stars
24 Arthur Godfrey's instrument
25 Gist
26 Do-nothing
27 Pretentious
29 Lieu
30 Some are floating
32 More devious
34 eBay purchase, at times
36 "Haven't we met before?" et al.
38 Mount Carmel locale
41 Cunning
45 Basilica area
47 The E in BPOE
48 Screen symbol
49 Wingtips
52 Ashamed
54 Notorious London prison
56 Kind of letter
58 Buzzing about
59 Grand Prix feature
60 Jellystone fuzz
63 Genetic letters
66 "To Autumn," e.g.
68 ". . . tall buildings in a single ___"
69 Fashionable jeans
71 Tiger Woods, to Buick
74 Fort Knox unit
76 Staying power
77 Racetrack fence
78 Greek H's
80 Subatomic particle
82 Lucky charm
84 Old Chevys
87 H. Rider Haggard novel
88 Michelle Phillips and Cass Elliot
90 Trumps
92 Bakery emanation
96 Close-knit group
98 Fencing swords
100 Not animal or vegetable
102 52, in old Rome
103 Source of funds, for some
106 "The Sultan of Sulu" writer
107 Foie Gras providers
108 Paste
109 Ear-related
110 Grappler's surface
111 Boo-boo
112 Nordstrom rival
113 Moments

DOWN

1 Peruvian peaks
2 Blue-ribbon position
3 Pernod flavoring
4 Like some blouses
5 Nonclerical
6 Word with ear or peace
7 Mach 1 breaker
8 Gauguin's paradise
9 Amu Darya's outlet
10 Palm fruit
11 Maintains
12 Neth. neighbor
13 Lamb pieces
14 Ring position, after a knockdown
15 They used to be acorns
16 Rare trick-taker
22 Finish with
23 ___ Prairie, MN
28 Enjoy a book for a second time
31 As well
33 More than stretched the truth
35 Seed coat
37 Parsley piece
39 Scratch (out)
40 Dr. Leary's drug
41 Dine's partner
42 Sews up
43 It's not to be taken with a grain of salt?
44 Palate cleanser
46 Mauritania neighbor
50 Light brown
51 Duffer's stroke
53 Like Eddie Felson
55 Copycat
57 Wing ___ prayer
61 Sacred text
62 Passage and spring
64 NASA scrub
65 NAACP part
67 "A diller, a ___ . . ."
70 Dark sides, at times
71 Hurler's stat
72 "China Beach" setting
73 Stiff hair
75 Musical mark
79 More likely to pass a breathalyzer
81 Gregorian ___
83 Come forth
85 Flying formations
86 Take stock of
89 Cut off
91 Butcher's coat
93 Emulate Cicero
94 David Blaine forte
95 Guinness and Baldwin
96 Secretive sort
97 Verdi heroine
99 Baja bread
101 Rubs the wrong way
104 Always, to a bard
105 Extinct New Zealand bird

173 BEING THERE by O.C. Hayes

A 1979 Peter Sellers film inspired this title.

ACROSS

1 Dives in
8 "Yeah, right!"
14 End table item
18 1984 PGA champ
19 Bad vibrations
20 Evening, in Paris
21 Shines coming through the door
24 Some mkt. deals
25 "___ is human . . ."
26 Automat, e.g.
27 Make ___ for it
28 Silk producer
32 LAX announcement (with 49-A)
37 Art supporter
42 Marching together
43 Protective embankment
45 Certain bond
46 Popular camera
47 Bibliophilic suffix
49 See 32 Across
51 Genesis plot
52 Explorer ___ Anders Hedin
53 Red Cross procedure
54 Actor Beatty
55 Small merganser
56 Mtn. stats
57 "Star Wars" syst.
60 Glasgow landowners
62 Lighten up?
63 Bufo marinus
64 "Took me by surprise!" (with 75-A)
67 Do sums
68 Word with eye or pie
69 "New Look" designer
70 Repressed
72 Ferrous sulfate target
73 Have a funny feeling
75 See 64 Across
78 Vault features
80 Supports for specs
81 Unwelcome one
85 Paper for a pad
87 Musical symbol
91 How credits may be listed
96 "Sula" author Morrison
97 Cause to sparkle
98 Ex-president Obote, for one
99 Graph line
100 Parlor piece
101 Nags at

DOWN

1 WWW code
2 Saudi, for one
3 Zaire's Mobuto Sese ___
4 Mad. and Lex.
5 "Angela's Ashes" sequel
6 About to use one's sand wedge
7 Dress up
8 "Soy of Cooking" author
9 Randolph and Patty
10 Model
11 Wear and tear
12 Loser to JFK
13 First name in mascara
14 Professional school hurdle
15 Super!
16 Prefix meaning little
17 Zebras, to lions
22 Director Clair
23 Seldom seen
27 "Right on!"
29 Decorative loop
30 "This is spooking me!"
31 Got off track
32 German article
33 Mean-spirited
34 Reprimanded gently
35 Take ___ the chin
36 Campus official
38 Friend of Françoise
39 Seven-seater
40 Bambi relative
41 Count Basie's "___ Darlin'"
44 ___ & Whitney (aircraft engine manufacturer)
47 Not in favor of
48 Indian leader's residence
50 They line up next to ctrs.
52 Forge worker
55 Fernando's leader?
57 "Me, too!"
58 "Splish Splash" singer
59 Luggage attachment
60 CEOs, e.g.
61 Coupe's cousin
62 Paul in "Little Miss Sunshine"
63 Not us
64 Fingers, as in a lineup
65 Go kaput
66 Ca++ is one
68 Top naval brass
71 1959 Ricky Nelson hit
72 Ranch land
74 Major Hoople's holler
76 Tide variety
77 Go light (on)
79 Flightless birds
81 Stuffed food
82 Strong as ___
83 Rice-A-___
84 Showy flower
86 Foil's cousin
87 Hyperbolize at high volume
88 "The NeverEnding Story" writer
89 Injury's aftermath
90 100 make 1,000
92 "Riddle-me-___"
93 Scrap for Rover
94 Lucrative
95 Dorm VIPs

174 INVISIBLE ALIENS by Jay Sullivan

These UFOs will never be uncloaked.

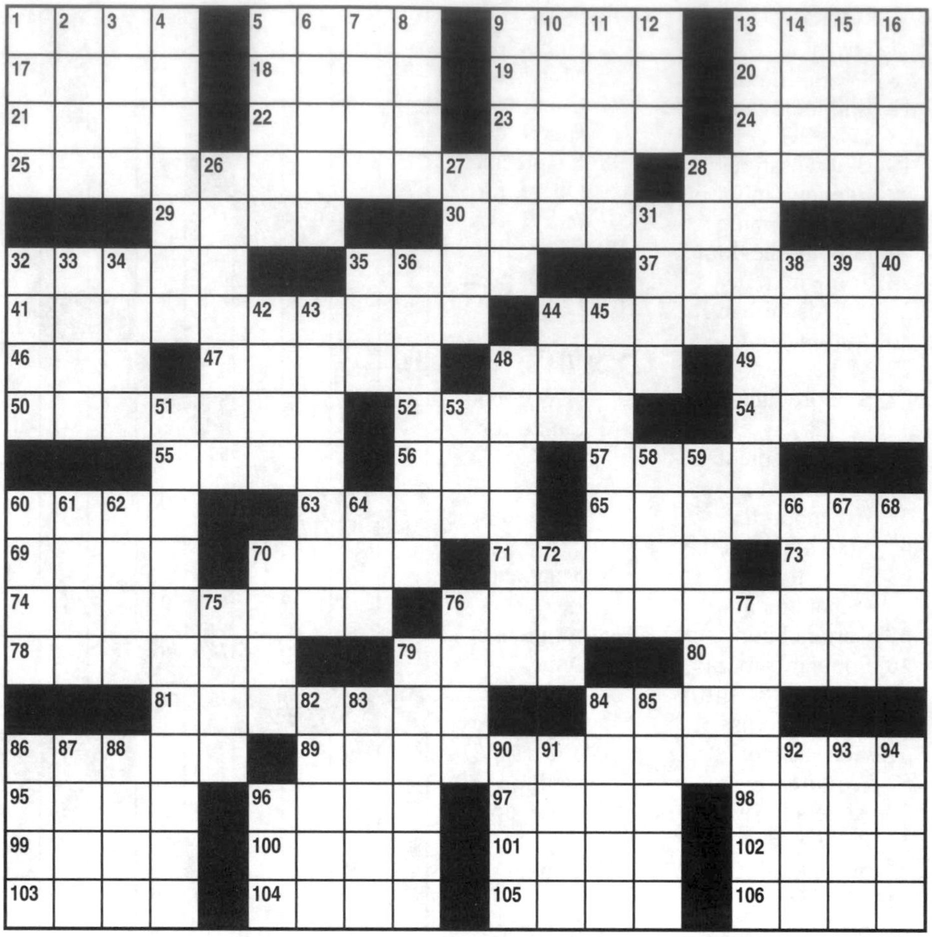

ACROSS

1 Tanganyika or Chad
5 Pro's con
9 Walk all over
13 God of Jezebel
17 Avenged
18 Hangs a right
19 Genesis grandson
20 Sea World cetacean
21 Proceed
22 Lighten up
23 Purges
24 Chops meat
25 Foreign exchange concern?
28 Sea spots
29 Excited about
30 Dig up
32 ___-garde
35 Puts on
37 Wind deity
41 Low barkers?
44 Hogwarts witch
46 Manning man
47 No dice!
48 Idiomatic stopping point
49 Matted cotton
50 Erudite
52 Sahara shortage
54 Commotions
55 No Mr. Nice Guy
56 Bottom line
57 Cabbage batch
60 Soft rock
63 Wind section
65 Where the Shannon flows
69 Hunt for
70 Not fair
71 Vex
73 Overly
74 ___ Islands of the Bering Sea
76 Fish out of water?
78 Already?
79 Be lost in thought
80 Your father's favorite
81 Running wild
84 Stop order
86 Test group
89 Toreador's wear?
95 Stop order
96 Mower maker
97 Bean town?
98 In a bad way
99 Border line
100 In good time
101 Technical support caller
102 One who makes do
103 Anxiety
104 Dept. store inventory
105 Order to go
106 Used cars, perhaps

DOWN

1 Indecent
2 Say so
3 Numbers game
4 Cello supports
5 One who acts for actors
6 "Super!"
7 New Age pianist
8 Catch phrase
9 Shows over
10 Place for a cold one
11 Gin kin
12 Scout leader?
13 Russian dance party?
14 Shrinking sea
15 Wile E. Coyote's supplier
16 Short retrievers
26 It's trendy
27 Hamburger holders
28 News note
31 Red state
32 Explorer Tasman
33 A river runs through it
34 World piece
35 Small inheritance
36 Epic journey
38 Truckful
39 "Once more ___ the breach . . .": Shak.
40 Match makers
42 Show-jumping obstacle
43 Experience
44 Lay low
45 They're in retirement
48 Distressed ones?
51 Amplifier?
53 Paul Newman title role
58 Setting for Camus' "The Plague"
59 Release
60 Recipe shortening?
61 Start to bat?
62 "Fantasy Island" props
64 One who wears little clothing
66 Somewhat
67 Me neither
68 Scoop or poop
70 It's out on a limb
72 Bridge response
75 They're all charged up
76 Roll up
77 Keyboard instrument, of old
79 "Mailman" of the NBA
82 Gov't. obligation
83 Continental capital
84 Some people
85 Fail to share
86 Cordon Bleu graduate
87 Haul aboard
88 Low life
90 It's a sign
91 Greet the judge
92 Nevada town or county
93 Go downhill fast
94 Rolls roller
96 Flat hat

175 OLIO by Arlan and Linda Bushman

Samuel Gerard is the name of 1 Across.

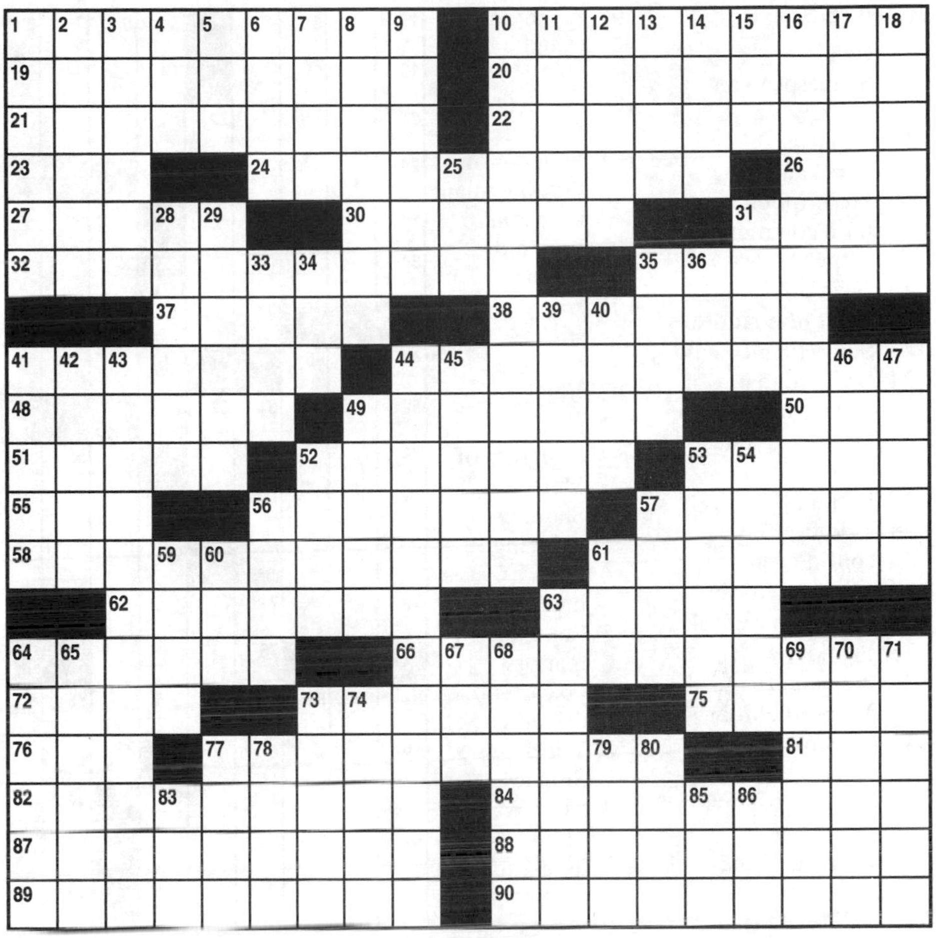

ACROSS

1 Tommy Lee Jones "Fugitive" role
10 TV and radio, for example
19 Bowling-ball feature
20 Shy groom's suggestion
21 Bad luck
22 A clamdigger can dig here
23 Meditation chants
24 She wrote "Consuelo"
26 Outrage
27 Blue cartoon figure
30 Psychic aids
31 UK awards
32 Do secretarial work
35 Watch on fixedly
37 Assigned places
38 Do a slow burn
41 Tex-Mex cuisine favorites
44 Ernest Borgnine TV series
48 Circumvented
49 "My Name Is Aram" author
50 ___ kwon do
51 Freud colleague
52 Turned tail
53 General under Jackson and Lee
55 Six, in Parma
56 Kane's appellation
57 Wall off
58 Bouncing one
61 "Now that I think about it, you're right"
62 First European to cross Lake Michigan
63 Boutonniere spot
64 Fill in with sediment
66 Last lap
72 PBS flagship station
73 Winter hazard for river traffic
75 Ancient Roman women's wear
76 Philip of "Kung Fu"
77 Formal events
81 Gardens of London
82 Like Achilles and Hector's fight
84 Camping gear
87 Rams
88 NASA goal
89 Feeling
90 Gym regular

DOWN

1 Maximum
2 Dance "like my sister Kate"
3 Tousle
4 "Mad Men" airer
5 President between USG and JAG
6 Haircut style
7 Improve on
8 Amos and Louisa May
9 Give the eye to
10 Celestial spectacle
11 Elite invitees
12 Vending stock
13 Overarch
14 Pinochle display
15 Voltage letters
16 On purpose
17 As measured by square units
18 Bear witness
25 Coll. senior's test
28 Occupy
29 Miss a step
31 Tournament type
33 Cargo
34 Tours connections
35 Dingle
36 Pitches
39 "Apocalypto" dialogue language
40 Oil of ___
41 Sumptuous spread
42 Catkin-bearing tree
43 "Hey Jude" was written for him
44 1991 Reese Witherspoon film (with "The")
45 Derange
46 Esteem
47 Barks
49 "Le Fils des étoiles" composer
52 Brook
53 Sniggling sorts
54 Singles' place
56 Confined space
57 Clan division
59 George Romney's son
60 Film comedy of 1994
61 Occurred
63 Super Mario of hockey
64 Overwhelms
65 Take a whiff
67 Spanish eye
68 1962 MLB MVP
69 Stein companion
70 "Monty Python" alum John
71 Mooring rope
73 Qom dweller
74 Literary anthology
77 Oaxaca abode
78 Give off
79 Feminine suffix
80 Headliner
83 Punch lines?
85 UN Security Council mem.
86 Sasebo sash

176 LONE STAR STATE by Frank Longo

An original riddle by a cosmic cruciverbalist.

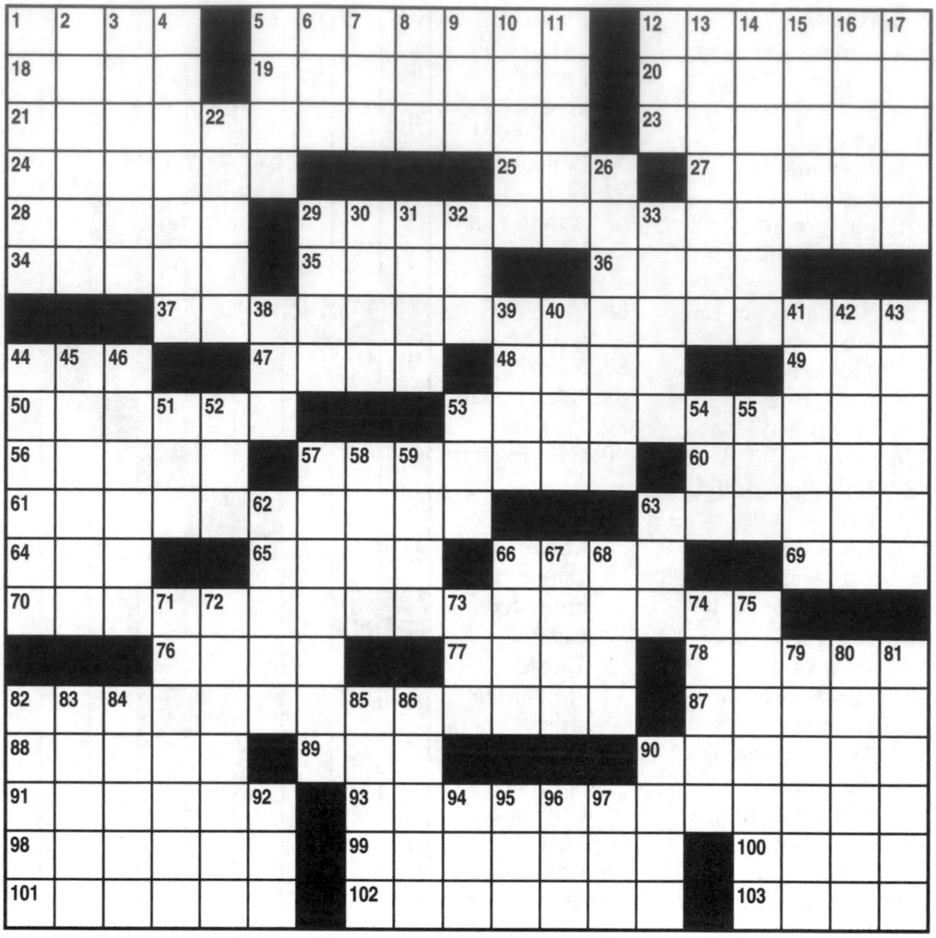

ACROSS

1 Can
5 Shakespearean usurer
12 Bananas
18 Arras auxiliary
19 Prescription drug for a common viral ailment
20 "Can do!"
21 **Start of a riddle**
23 Some financial aid
24 Deemed to be
25 Leader of the rap group Wu-Tang Clan
27 Bichon ___
28 Free from confinement
29 **More of riddle**
34 Words on a check
35 It's not good
36 2.2 pounds
37 **More of riddle**
44 "Sleepless in Seattle" hero
47 From a past era, in a past era
48 Home to some workers
49 Salute in verse
50 WW2 threats
53 **More of riddle**
56 It's a dyeing art
57 Subject for Quincy
60 Family figure
61 **More of riddle**
63 Professor's prize
64 Family figure: Abbr.
65 Botanical coat
66 Fix firmly
69 89-A floor
70 **More of riddle**
76 Zoning board calculation
77 Protected, nautically
78 Places to pick dates
82 **End of riddle**
87 Sing in a full voice
88 "I'll take that as ___"
89 Java, e.g.
90 Gallimaufry
91 It may be preconceived
93 **Riddle answer**
98 Carom
99 ___ oxide (laughing gas)
100 Gospels follower
101 Founder of the Akkadian kingdom
102 Like old Russia
103 Home in the sticks?

DOWN

1 Ices
2 Daughter of Metis
3 Shudder-inducing
4 Mars of movies
5 Some Fr. martyrs
6 Oxcart driver's cry
7 Wide-ranged Sumac
8 "The Wave Field" landscape sculptor
9 Time after time, in verse
10 French educator of the deaf
11 Serious weed in the South
12 Having one sharp, musically
13 Neighbor of Newport News
14 "Pirates of the Caribbean" captain
15 1970–72 CBS sitcom
16 Refuter's response
17 Portrayer of a Clampett
22 Mot Cot Pagoda setting
26 Invite to one's place
29 Be a canary
30 "Heroides" penner
31 Piccolo relative
32 Faena shout
33 Entangled
38 Help-wanted notice?
39 Thug's knife
40 Mass-consumed stuff?
41 Home of many jets
42 Be faithful (to)
43 Rained cats and dogs
44 Tribeca maker
45 Lowers
46 Mark with differently colored spots
51 What a flat lacks
52 Bout terminator
53 Actress ___ Park Lincoln
54 Mineral suffix
55 Get into, in a way
57 Rounds up
58 Versailles valentine
59 Walter ___ Mare
62 1976 Olympic swimming star John
63 Prefix with athlete
66 Beast on a borax box
67 Ready to receive a pass
68 Due
71 Stock boy's task, at times
72 Ciudad Bolívar is on it
73 "The Karate Kid" dojo Cobra ___
74 Takes along
75 Solid foundation
79 Say "There, there" to
80 Provides a seat for
81 Superlatively slippery
82 Isn't resolved
83 Capri or Sicilia
84 Bollywood soundtrack instrument
85 False show
86 Royals in saris
90 Riven was its sequel
92 Robb of baseball
94 Volos vowel
95 Go wrong
96 "___ ever!"
97 Like some scores: Abbr.

177 WITH WITH by Harvey Estes

45 Down is also a neighborhood of Chicago.

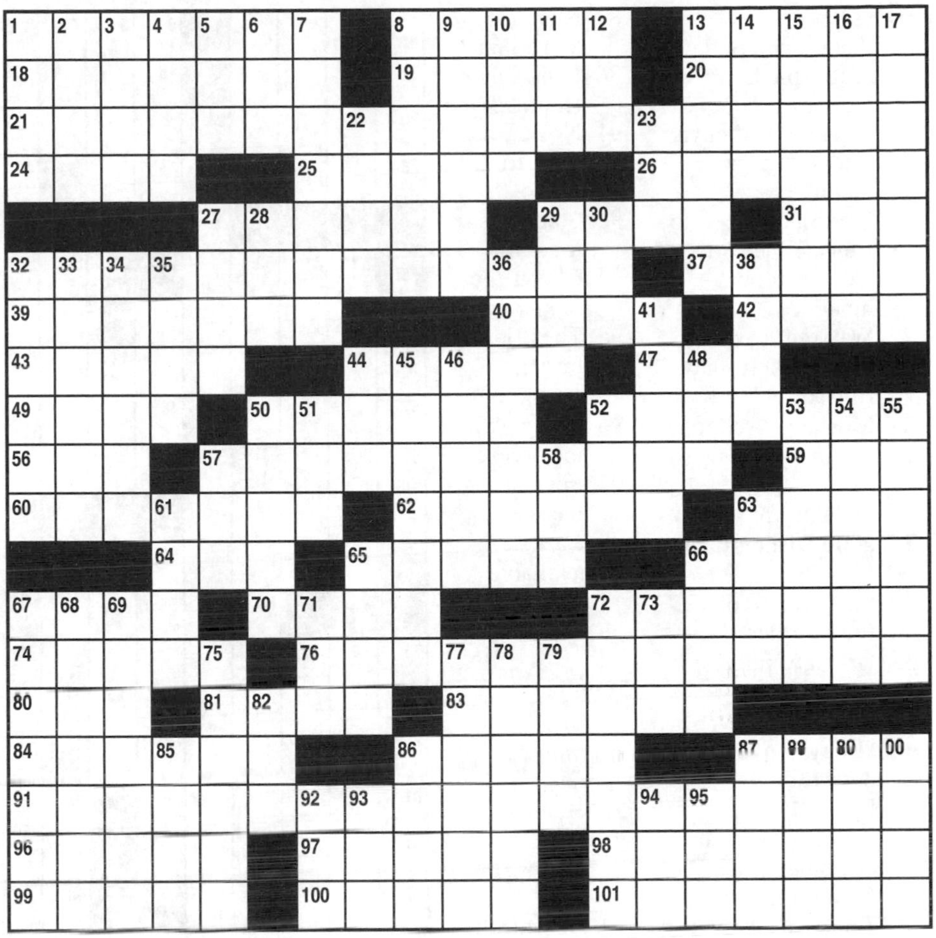

ACROSS

1 Prepared, as a memo
8 Adjust to fit
13 Scenic view
18 Shake up
19 Kind of eclipse
20 Autumn color
21 In seventh heaven (with "with")
24 Highlander's tongue
25 Danish physicist Bohr
26 Em or Mame
27 "Couldn't tell ya"
29 Six years for a senator
31 Charged item
32 Barely punctual (with "with")
37 Cause of yawning
39 Soapbox speakers
40 Mother of "Brothers & Sisters"
42 Canadian pump name
43 Ford pardonee
44 Quick raid
47 Feathery stole
49 Bit of change
50 Opening words
52 Get back (to)
56 José's huzzah
57 In anticipation (with "with")
59 Pal of Pooh
60 Sets of numbers
62 Come-ons
63 Eliot's Adam
64 "Dig in!"
65 Kramer of "Seinfeld"
66 ". . . and ___ well"
67 Greek salad cheese
70 Penthouse feature
72 Sauce with a bite
74 Escapades
76 Not seriously (with "with")
80 Significant period
81 Medical care orgs.
83 Grassy plains
84 Witt of "Law & Order"
86 Brake components
87 Brake component
91 Realistically (with "with")
96 Close to
97 Role for 57 Down
98 "Walk on the Wild Side" singer
99 Listerine targets
100 Fructose or glucose
101 "Rumor has it . . ."

DOWN

1 Diggs of "Private Practice"
2 "Son of Frankenstein" shepherd
3 Papal name
4 "To be" to Henri
5 Long in Morse
6 Versatile vehicle, for short
7 Lucy's gang
8 ET and Alf
9 Michelin competitor
10 Hill builders
11 "Fiddlesticks!"
12 Three, in Italy
13 Remote button
14 Religious image
15 Recluses
16 Long and tiresome
17 Hall in "Martial Law"
22 Flintstones' pet
23 Hertz offering
27 "___ a roll!"
28 Aachen article
29 "Iliad" setting
30 Racket extension
32 Corporal or sergeant
33 Baltimore ballplayer
34 Prepared for takeoff
35 "Put ___ my bill"
36 Ample ex, for example
38 Tide variety
41 Helps with a holdup
44 Venom, to Spider-Man
45 Place for a hot time tonight?
46 Choir attire
48 ___ Kosh B'Gosh
50 Satellite service
51 ACLU concerns
52 "The Facts of Life" actress
53 Ultimatum ender
54 "Forget it!"
55 Performs adequately
57 Arthur in sitcoms
58 Juan's that
61 Faucet malfunction
63 Not so exciting
65 Corporate VIPs
66 Basic principles
67 Cheap quarters
68 Stud site
69 Double-crosser
71 Simpson case judge
72 Adds sparkle to a tree
73 Year in Yucatán
75 Changes gears
77 "The Wizard of Oz" witch
78 Heavy overcoat
79 Per person
82 Investors' Fannie
85 Good buddy
86 Animated show on Nickelodeon
87 Like some losers
88 Rainbow bands
89 Draft-eligible
90 Swirling water
92 Printers' measures
93 Athenian T
94 Bit of baby talk
95 Pirates' drink

178 TREE HUGGERS by Russell G. Brown

The size at 60 Across is not officially recognized by the AKC.

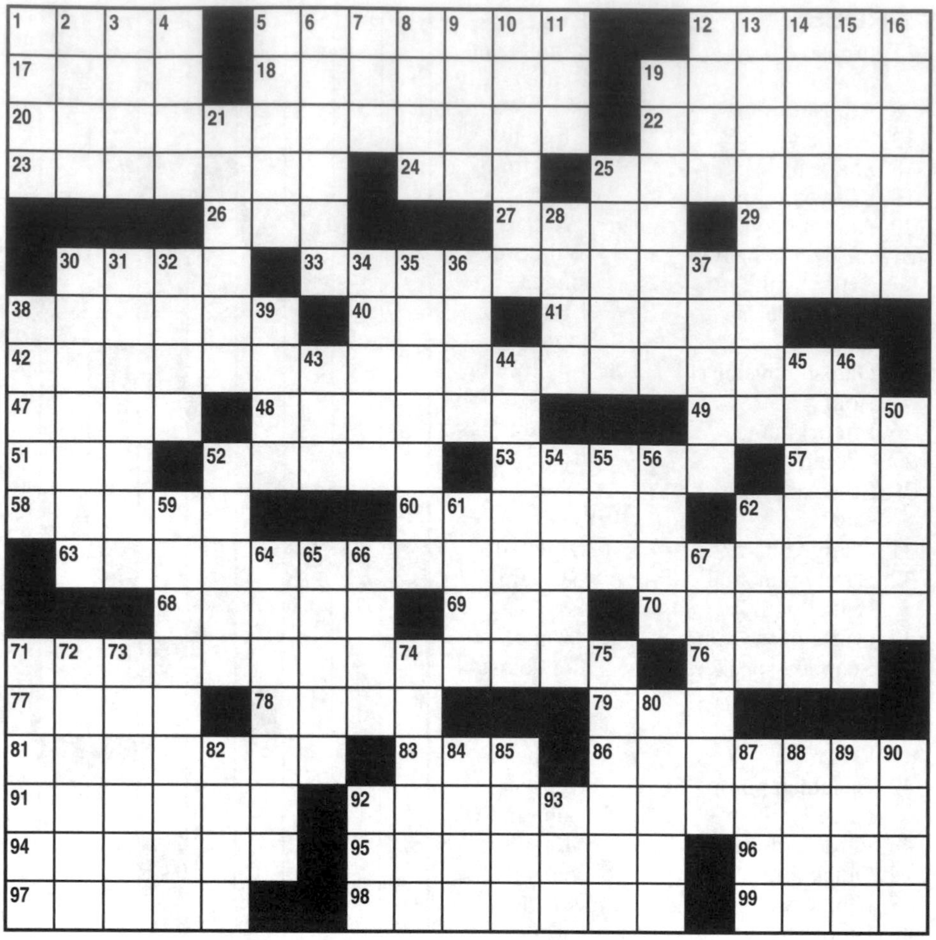

ACROSS

1 Abbott and Selig
5 Angel pitcher Kelvim
12 Operatic bad guys, frequently
17 Upon
18 Maximally acerbic
19 Renaissance artist
20 Golden-brown lunatic?
22 Way out
23 1977 Robert Shaw film
24 Mustangs' school
25 Put in a good word for
26 Tallahassee school
27 2006 Disney/Pixar film
29 Like silv. or plat.
30 Put in order
33 Graph of interest to Mrs. Smith?
38 Mexican beer
40 "Baby, it's cold outside!"
41 Eyes
42 Andrew Jackson campaign pitch?
47 Kauai, for one
48 Tater Tots company
49 For a particular purpose
51 Australian ratite
52 Some petty officers
53 Wore
57 That, en español
58 Philippine president Ramos
60 Poodle size
62 E.B. White's trumpeter
63 Mothproof furniture boast?
68 Daisuke of karaoke fame
69 Mlle. after marrying
70 "Gossip Girl" girl
71 Wooden "SNL" characters?
76 Banks on TV
77 First-floor apartment
78 Lose brilliance
79 Pal of Nancy
81 Long items of winter apparel
83 Necessary keg adjunct
86 Lens-shaped legumes
91 Nearer, my God, to thee?
92 Stuckey's journal?
94 Chews the scenery
95 Theatrical trailer, for example
96 Move with the breeze
97 Lends for a fee
98 Cars available only in black
99 Cartoon unit

DOWN

1 Thai monetary unit
2 Home of Zion National Park
3 Nap fitfully
4 Tore
5 Anglo-Saxon drudges
6 Make a hot rod hotter
7 Dele
8 Middle Earth nasties
9 It might be light or steel
10 Per se
11 66, e.g.
12 Texas metropolis, familiarly
13 Wasted away
14 Sprite rival ___ Mist
15 2004 Internet worm
16 Hexapod
19 Lose one's cool, in a way
21 Bequeathed
25 Pet names of John Cleese, in a sketch
28 Individually
30 Like some faults
31 Stand in the doorway
32 Cad
34 Tin Man before Haley
35 Wannabe in a beret
36 Gunk
37 Antiseptic
38 Cutpurse
39 Suffix for buck
43 Soph., Jr., and Sr.
44 Title for a Hindu sage
45 Tougher
46 Cry of adoration
50 Party line?
52 Voice of Fudd
54 Took the stage
55 "Am I that dumb?"
56 Lola Granola's love
59 A desperate housewife
61 Farmer's wife in "Babe"
62 Not bad, for an old man?
64 High-level asphaltists
65 People of Panama
66 Hear and obey
67 Alloting
71 Ritzier
72 It's gross at times
73 Kevin of "Weeds"
74 Straight one
75 Light medieval helmet
80 Responds cattily
82 Skeins
84 Nailed a final
85 Lay macadam
87 Baker's unit, for short
88 State University in Ames
89 Lend for a fee
90 Scottish isle
92 EPA unit, frequently
93 Zero

179 FIRST-NAME BASIS* by Patrick Jordan
The theme is explained at 98 Across.

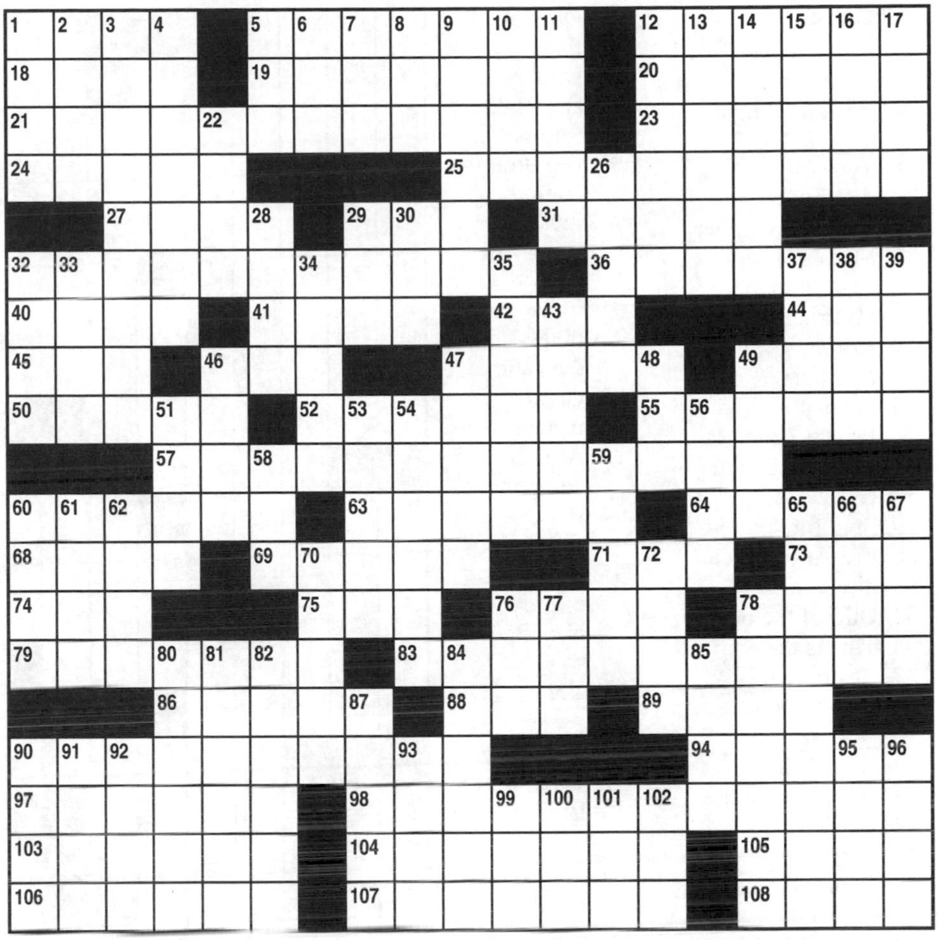

ACROSS

1 Pie target, in slapstick
5 Some rabbits and goats
12 Had a jones for
18 Israeli diplomat Abba
19 Least distant
20 Prayer beads
21 Annoyance in traffic*
23 Mont Blanc adjective
24 "Cheers" prop
25 TV's Pacific Princess, e.g.*
27 Straitlaced
29 Saddler's tool
31 Taking precedence
32 Early radio receivers*
36 Causing hardship
40 Ear or brain feature
41 Keen enjoyment
42 Quid-quo connection
44 Go ___ (lose it)
45 Malty draft
46 Elevenses quaff
47 Bit of drudgery
49 Profess bluntly
50 News sources
52 Won over
55 Paul Bunyan tale, e.g.
57 S'mores ingredient*
60 Miss Kitty ran one
63 Lead ore
64 Sings the praises of
68 Knock off
69 Treat with 46 Across
71 Aves. and blvds.
73 Item in a gladiator's arsenal
74 Back the other way
75 Aardvark victim
76 Heckler's comment
78 Canadian gas brand
79 In a snarl
83 Fan club's purpose*
86 Crowned head
88 "___ the economy, stupid"
89 Townshend of The Who
90 Attar source*
94 Guy, slangily
97 Enticingly unfamiliar
98 **What clue* answers start with**
103 Presentable
104 Pelt procurer
105 It ends with Holy Week
106 Joints covered by spats
107 Briny expanse
108 "Saratoga Trunk" author Ferber

DOWN

1 Admit, with "up"
2 Share a boundary
3 Covered boudoir furnishing
4 Prepare to cash
5 One, some, or all
6 Maude's widower on "The Simpsons"
7 Fierce freshwater fish
8 "Give me a raise, ___ resign!"
9 Uprising
10 "Wait ___" ("Be right there")
11 Throat infection, for short
12 Skull sections
13 Deodorant option
14 Aim (to)
15 Fruitless
16 Coastal eagle
17 Batik practitioner
22 Dismounted
26 Viny shelter
28 Puzzle with dead ends
29 Braying equine
30 Word with suit or blanket
32 Chowder tidbit
33 93 Down, for Angelina
34 Dog walker's restraint
35 Elliptical geometry solid
37 Best-loved, slangily
38 First preposition in "The Raven"
39 Lecherous
43 1956 Japanese sci-fi flick
46 Starchy tropical plant
47 Dishwasher process
48 White-rumped grazer
49 India tourism center
51 "___ You Babe" (1965 hit)
53 Hayride conveyance
54 Kia model
56 Elongated swimmers
58 Ques. counterpart
59 1985 baseball retiree Rod
60 Carpet dealer's meas.
61 Force field phenomenon
62 Veldt predator
65 Like circus peanuts
66 Sitcom pioneer Arnaz
67 Block off
70 Coast Guard newbie
72 Cut from the roster
76 Note quickly
77 Golf great Ernie
78 "Golden Girl" Getty
80 Gingerbread house visitor
81 Wolflike
82 Picks at the polls
84 Gloomy
85 Second mortgage, briefly
87 Canyoneering crafts
90 "The Scarlet Letter" stigma
91 Beefy beasts of burden
92 Hard blow
93 "Tomb Raider" heroine Croft
95 Football Hall of Famer Swann
96 Whodunit terrier
99 Decide
100 DHL rival
101 Date regularly
102 Underwired undergarment

180 HEDGE FUN by Jay Sullivan

79 Across is also the home of Southern Oregon University.

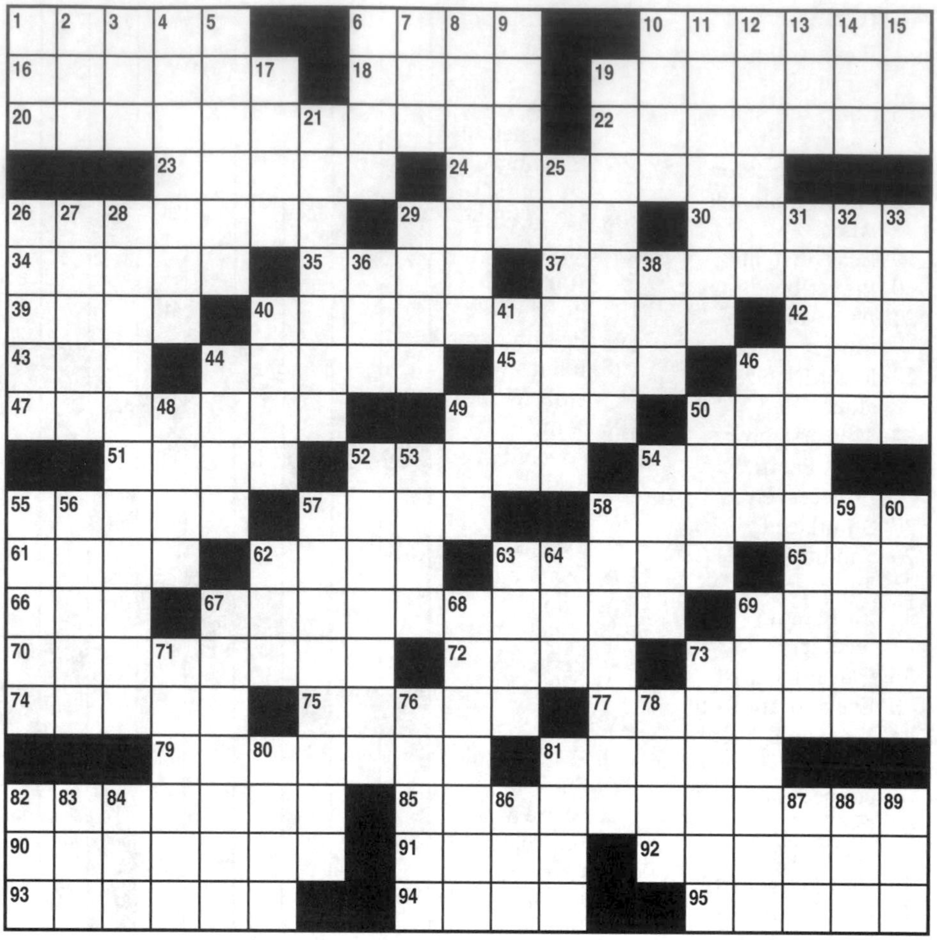

ACROSS

1 Lake Louise neighbor
6 Rash treatment
10 "___ Fables"
16 Type of rhododendron
18 Stowed away, say
19 Mom's sisters
20 Market maker in electric utilities?
22 Konrad Adenauer, familiarly
23 Tears up
24 Private timberland
26 Gray general at Gettysburg
29 Stag film?
30 "12 Angry Men" director
34 Bird of the bayou
35 This is the end
37 Restrained
39 Way to go
40 %%%?
42 Big 12 inits.
43 HMO personnel
44 Stave off
45 Regarding
46 Country dance
47 Like a horseshoe
49 Bruce Lee TV role
50 Idaho city
51 Sod crackers
52 Tot's cots
54 Type type
55 Lose one's balance?
57 It has many feet
58 Joyce title character
61 Fraternity party
62 Sweat spot
63 Ferber and Best
65 That's a laugh!
66 Ready for war
67 In cash?
69 "Variety" pic
70 Bare-bones
72 Noble
73 Lawrence's partner
74 Hardly a fancier
75 Pointless
77 Inside out
79 Oregon Shakespeare festival site
81 Does a fishing chore
82 Dudley Do-Right, for one
85 Big drop in commodities?
90 They will carry on
91 It can carry a tune, and then some
92 Go no further than
93 Amplifier component
94 Recipe shortening?
95 Valley east of the Sierra Nevada

DOWN

1 Protestant denom.
2 Type of dye
3 Backwoods turndown
4 Spotted
5 Plains predator
6 New Mexico tourist town
7 Say what?
8 Sheltered
9 Bank job?
10 "Clan of the Cave Bear" author
11 Signs up
12 It may be carved in stone
13 "There Will Be Blood" subject
14 Treat like a dog
15 Short course
17 Slightly
19 Complementing
21 Gave it another go
25 They're blowing in the winds
26 Hidden
27 Stravinsky and Sikorsky
28 Bear wear?
29 Lithuanian or Latvian
31 Bear's order?
32 A lot of sissies?
33 World's end, in ancient times
36 More than oft
38 Four seasons of Seville
40 Jacques-___ Cousteau
41 Volvo rival
44 Did a Little bit
46 Brown and Silver
48 Primo
49 Cattrall of "Sex and the City"
50 Girl scouts?
52 Flower part
53 Water hazard
54 Hostile reaction
55 Hard ticket, most likely
56 Winter weather wear
57 Inn stock
58 Hazy
59 Advice to Alice
60 Did a farrier's job
62 Bear's option
63 Coup target
64 June beetle
67 Magnetic unit
68 Parodies
69 Merely ostentatious
71 Rough house
73 Rankles
76 Out of shape
78 Is in the running
80 Bring on board
81 "This ___ for you!"
82 "The A-Team" star
83 Crew's control
84 Start to lateral?
86 Selling point, ideally
87 Cockney's aspiration
88 Boot
89 Diamond wgt.

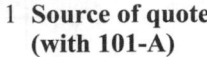

181 EYE CONTACT by Victor Fleming

The quote below is from "Gap Creek," a 2000 Oprah Book Club selection.

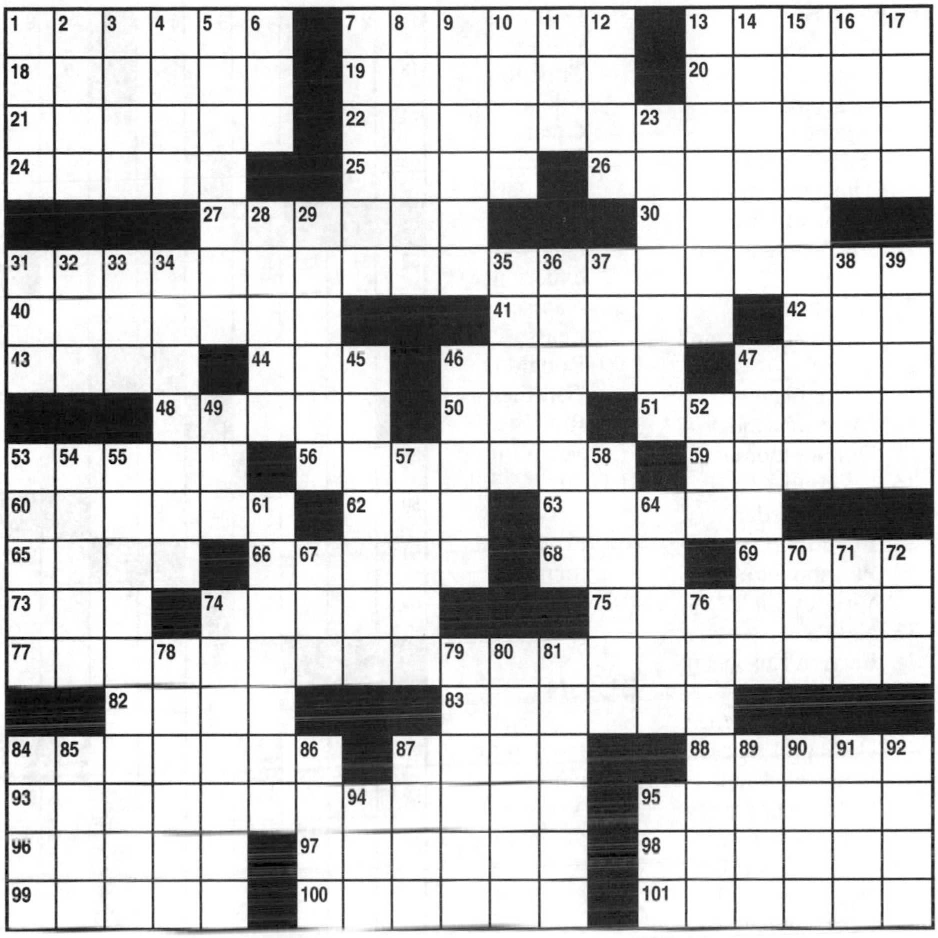

ACROSS

1 **Source of quote (with 101-A)**
7 Goaded
13 Wish starter
18 He gets a lot of interest
19 Kind of tutoring
20 Sheer fabric
21 Again and again?
22 **Quote: Part I**
24 Not assent
25 Irving title character
26 Spuds from Boise
27 Most pathetic, as an argument
30 Israeli conductor Daniel
31 **Quote: Part II**
40 Wall-to-wall alternative
41 Jots
42 Santana's "___ Como Va"
43 Danny in "The Secret Life of Walter Mitty"
44 Half a Teletubby's name
46 Zhou ___
47 Old knife
48 Rock layer
50 Maui memento
51 Smiths
53 ___-Bismol
56 **Quote: Part III**
59 Italian marble center
60 Hardy's pal
62 Dada pioneer
63 "Turn the ___" (A/C request)
65 Singer Guthrie
66 Hoffman the radical
68 "___ haw!" (cry of delight)
69 Zoroastrian spirit
73 1970s Cambodian leader
74 Make ___ (vend something)
75 Offspring of Japanese immigrants
77 **Quote: Part IV**
82 Sedaka or Simon
83 NY Mets' division
84 Fuel gases
87 Picnic side
88 Tower supports
93 **Quote: Part V**
95 Bother incessantly
96 Pulitzer winner Carl Van ___
97 "Songs in ___": Keys album
98 Free from care
99 Handbag material
100 They make connections
101 **See 1 Across**

DOWN

1 Causes of some spinning wheels
2 Govt. workplace watchdog
3 Put under?
4 Shamrock land
5 Change the hue of
6 Due follower
7 Swiss psychologist
8 Loosen the ropes
9 "M*A*S*H" member
10 LeBron's target
11 Mass. political initials
12 Mal's prefix
13 Guts
14 Yon partner
15 Binary 7s
16 Spar, e.g.
17 Photog. blowups
23 Shelley poem
28 Normally (with "as")
29 Maniacal leader?
31 Tibetan beast
32 60 minuti
33 Slangy spin
34 Bernstein or Toscanini
35 Frisco pro
36 It may be religious
37 Acting expert Hagen
38 Batik artists
39 ___ doctor (gets treatment)
45 Friendly
46 Split to unite
47 What's his face
49 Clod chopper
52 Med. plan option
53 "Here's a ___ drew up"
54 ___ corn
55 Direction to a driver
57 More deviously misdirected
58 Rest of the afternoon
61 Fourth part of a relay
64 Old peso fractions
67 "Rubbish!"
70 Scared shout
71 Routing word
72 Nova Scotia hrs.
74 "Simply stupid!"
76 Lacking enthusiasm for
78 ___ up (got weepy)
79 One way to stand
80 Enchantment
81 Ax wielders
84 Itinerary guesses
85 Big chunk of moola
86 "Jaws" actor Robert
87 Con's place
89 Pugilist Max
90 Like an excited dog's tail
91 Tabula ___
92 Uzi kin
94 "I did not want to know that!"
95 Looker's leg

182 "PLAY BALL!" by Robert A. Doll

Solve this one with a hot dog and a beer.

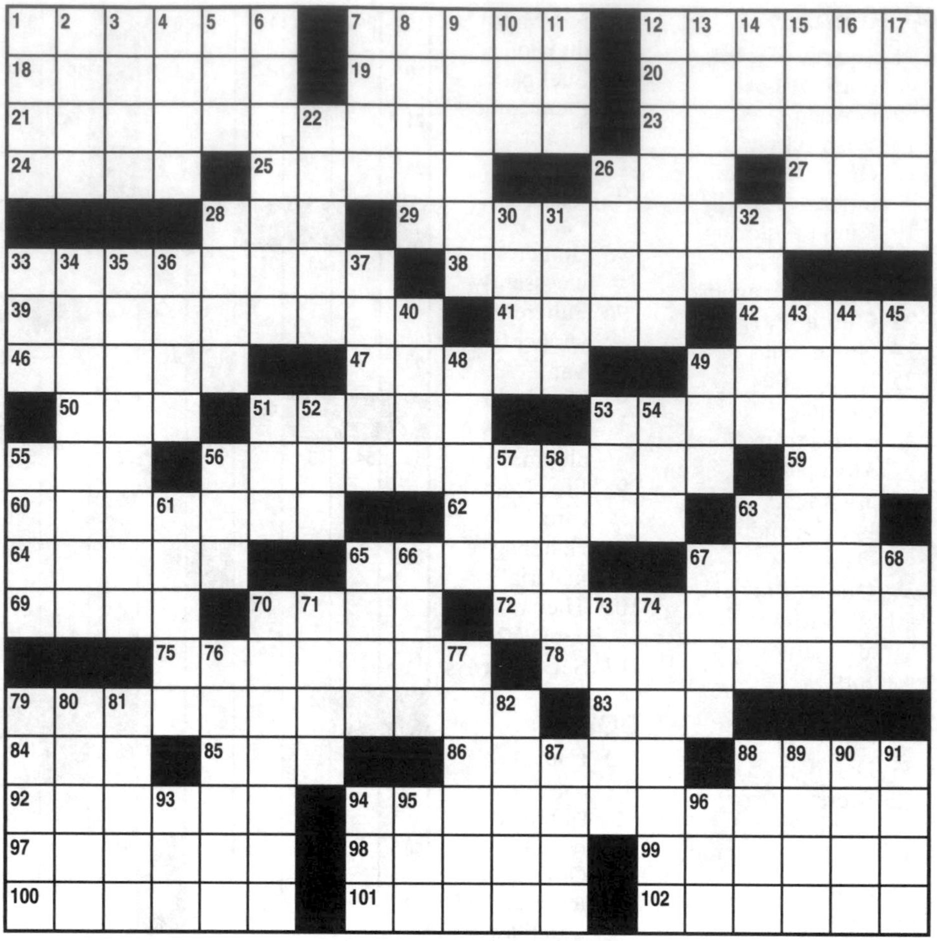

ACROSS

1 Astronomical distance
7 Hasty Pudding bigwig
12 Wears away
18 Theater district
19 Tropical vine
20 Just between you and me
21 Hot time at Progressive Field?
23 Marie ___ magazine
24 Burst of wind
25 Dutch bloomer
26 ___-Ban
27 Fo proceeder
28 Luau loop
29 Pressboxer at Wrigley Field?
33 Names
38 Eastern European
39 Turner Field accomplishment?
41 Cathedral recess
42 Umpire's shout
46 Witches powwow
47 Sonnets and such
49 Nigerian port city
50 Half a sawbuck
51 Queen's land
53 Grows gracefully
55 Roman sun god
56 Winding path at AT&T Park?
59 General ___ (Bo Duke's car)
60 Kind of election
62 Kind of wave
63 Make a lap
64 Stevie Wonder's "My Cheri ___"
65 Jazz singer Diana
67 Broken
69 Deliver a tirade
70 Muse of history
72 Comerica Park bloom?
75 Uniform adornment
78 Denigrate
79 Error at Busch Stadium?
83 Pro ___
84 Forum greeting
85 Safari sight
86 Hammerstein creation
88 Young socialites
92 Golf ball feature
94 Time to celebrate at Great American Ball Park?
97 Hair-___ (scary experience)
98 Nabisco treats
99 Ronald in "Brother Rat"
100 Sci-fi thing
101 "It ___ All Velvet" (Tormé memoir)
102 Sweater pattern

DOWN

1 Victorian
2 Hokkaido native
3 X-ray units
4 Open, in a way
5 Greek H
6 Be competitive
7 End of the Jewish calendar
8 Guillermo del Toro horror film
9 Place for a bell tower
10 Louisville to Cincinnati dir.
11 Cup handle
12 Coop flier
13 Trust
14 Wood sorrel
15 Vagabond
16 Spine-tingling
17 Have the helm
22 CSN's "___: Judy Blue Eyes"
26 Guns the engine
28 Chattel mortgage
30 "Gil ___"
31 You can skip it
32 Further shorten, maybe
33 Agatha Christie's "The ___ Murders"
34 Some financial statements
35 Place to party
36 Baker's need
37 Magnificent number?
40 Balance sheet minus
43 Kid's meal discount condition
44 Divine
45 Actual being
48 Haile Selassie disciple
49 Herbert of Pink Panther films
51 Triple Crown winner ___ Barton
52 "That ain't ___!"
53 Neighbor of Ga.
54 Chat room chuckle
55 Bandy words
56 Needlefish
57 Cheerful tune
58 Improvise
61 Quiet
63 NaCl
65 Volleyball winner
66 Eurasian deer
67 Barbershop request
68 Salon supply
70 Steinbeck's row
71 Waikiki wingding
73 See
74 Euripides drama
76 "Winnie the Pooh" character
77 Marks in Spanish class
79 Close-knit group
80 Deadly flu strain
81 Invoice word
82 Hose material
87 Musical symbol
88 Party pooper
89 On pins and needles
90 Jezebel's idol
91 "Auld Lang ___"
93 Telekinesis, e.g.
94 Brouhaha
95 Swing ___
96 Always, to a poet

183 SEND IN THE CLONES by Elizabeth C. Gorski

51 Across finished his career with 938 stolen bases.

ACROSS

1 Ivans IV and V
6 Topnotch
12 New York City mayor (1974–77)
17 Accumulate (debt)
18 Certain hand-holding events
19 Grasso and Fitzgerald
20 **Part I of advice**
22 Heaps in a laundromat
23 Crummy joint?
24 "Spider-Man" director Sam
26 "A League Of Their Own" outfielder
27 "For Your Eyes Only" villain
28 Squire
32 Window above a door
34 For fear that
36 Travel allowance
38 Tower's makeup
39 **Part II of advice**
45 Seldom seen
46 Mane area
47 "ER" sets
48 Small pickle
51 "The Base Burglar" Lou
53 Boorish
54 Domestic science class
55 "In India's sunny ___ . . .": Kipling
56 Agressive poker player
58 John of "Good Times"
59 Point one's finger at
60 Card cheaters
61 Trammel
62 "My Getaway" singer Watkins
63 Feels fluish
64 **Part III of advice**
71 Hold up
72 Bird of passage
73 River of Flanders
76 Famed Ottawa chief
79 "Ave Maria" composer Charles
81 Menlo Park monogram
82 "___-La-La": Shirelles
83 Party gift
85 Marks
87 ___-miss
89 **Part IV of advice**
93 Coeur d'___ Lake
94 Nicole Kidman's top feature?
95 Dark
96 Retrogressing
97 Girl Scout units
98 Shapes with a hammer

DOWN

1 Like a council on "Survivor"
2 Surgeon's stitch
3 He believes the universe has a soul
4 JFK's Secretary of State
5 Backbone
6 Corp. jet user
7 White-handed gibbon
8 Ogden Nash poem (with "The")
9 "The Lion King" villain
10 Hill competition?
11 Showing activity
12 "Mad About You" singer Carlisle
13 Bev Bevan was its drummer
14 Besieged site in 1836
15 Sir's counterpart
16 Being, to Caligula
18 Sample for the lab
21 Spellbinding
25 Papier-___
29 Cheer for El Toro
30 "Losing My Religion" band
31 Bill at Trader Vic's
33 Grounded jet in 2000
35 Liz of "Gilmore Girls"
37 Biologist's study
40 Gardening tool
41 Toll rd.
42 Brooklynese pronoun
43 Call for food
44 Techie's clientele
48 Kofi Annan's country
49 Batter's dream
50 Ham it up as Hamlet
51 Prep school jacket
52 Salty Margarita glass area
53 Composer ___-Korsakov
55 Overcast factor
56 System with a track record?
57 "___ Wanna Do Is Have Some Fun"
59 Cookout, for short
60 USPTO, for one
62 Leg bone
65 Large coffee container
66 For a price
67 Lively dance
68 "Coast to Coast AM" topic
69 Disco guy on "The Simpsons"
70 George Costanza's mom
74 Brings home a pizza
75 Pushes one's buttons?
76 Van Dine detective Vance
77 Sagebrusher
78 Head off
80 Wither away
82 "Pygmalion" playwright
84 Make over
86 "Mecca" singer Pitney
88 Up positions
90 Letter after Pi
91 Dog show sound
92 "___ for Burglar": Grafton

184 ALL IN THE FAMILY by Robert A. Doll

The clue at 58 Across is not a question.

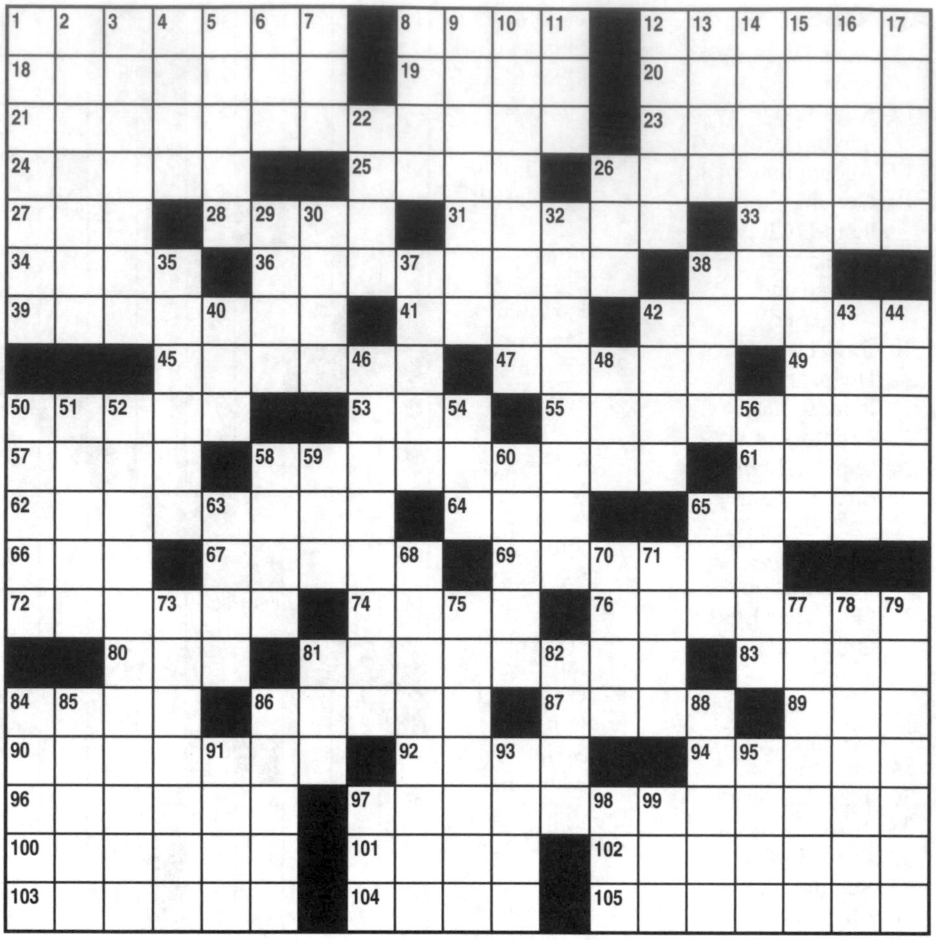

ACROSS

1 Skycap's bailiwick
8 St. Louis landmark
12 Fish out of water
18 Worn down
19 "Encore!"
20 Loosen, in a way
21 "Sugaring Off" painter
23 Land of Robert Burns
24 Door part
25 Luau strings
26 Restraints for Fido
27 "Silent Spring" subject
28 Floor model
31 Earthy pigment
33 Epitaph starter
34 Many moons
36 Dorothy Gale lived with her
38 Debussy's "La ___"
39 Most profound
41 Humerus neighbor
42 Nighttime critter
45 Scuttlebutt
47 Start of a refrain
49 Genetic info carrier
50 Fess up
53 Virgo mo.
55 Fanlights
57 Lowly laborer
58 What parent
61 First word of "Jabberwocky"
62 Mingle
64 Quadruple ___ loop
65 Four farthings
66 Louisville Slugger wood
67 Payed to play
69 Pick-me-up
72 "You ___ worry"
74 Rod's partner
76 Gumble on "The Simpsons"
80 Embarrassed
81 He's been at dinner tables since 1943
83 ___-Foot Sue (Pecos Bill's gal)
84 Get smart
86 Inscribed pillar
87 Bit of gossip
89 Genetic stuff
90 Frat boy type
92 Lab gel
94 Attach a codicil
96 Utter
97 "Hee Haw" banjoist
100 In a New York minute
101 E-mail
102 One who spread the Word
103 Looked after
104 "The Thin Man" pooch
105 Most cheeky

DOWN

1 Capital on the Tigris
2 Condense
3 Aid recipient
4 Chain ___
5 Threw in
6 Special person
7 Author LeShan
8 Wild and wooly
9 Damask extract
10 Waxing moon
11 "For ___ a jolly . . ."
12 Contemplative sort
13 Ancient Peruvian
14 Pie-eyed
15 G.K. Chesterton detective
16 Less friendly
17 Coquette
22 Elementary particle
26 Moonscape traverser
29 Bridge position
30 ___ swan
32 More rib-sticking
35 Thin strip of wood
37 "Swan Lake" wear
38 Bell-curve figure
40 Grab a bite
42 Sheep's cry
43 Emasculate
44 Like a windbag
46 Dessert wine
48 Met display
50 Like Barry B. Benson
51 Not too swift
52 Sisters of Charity of St. Joseph's founder
54 Skedaddle, in Dogpatch
56 Stems opposites
58 Pessimist's word
59 Opal's mo.
60 Lofty
63 Big name in mapmaking
65 ___ stirpes
68 Makes known
70 Support, in a way
71 Chaplin prop
73 Lose heart
75 Polished
77 Italian for "to the tooth"
78 Small streams
79 Fixed
81 Colorado Indian
82 "A ___ in the hand . . ."
84 Comics sound
85 Mountain ridge
86 In place
88 Foremost
91 Purple shade
93 Lick ___ promise
95 Lion's share
97 Fed. property overseer
98 Drivel
99 Make like

185 PENCIL PLEASER by Doug Peterson

Tom Selleck was considered for the lead role in 56 Across.

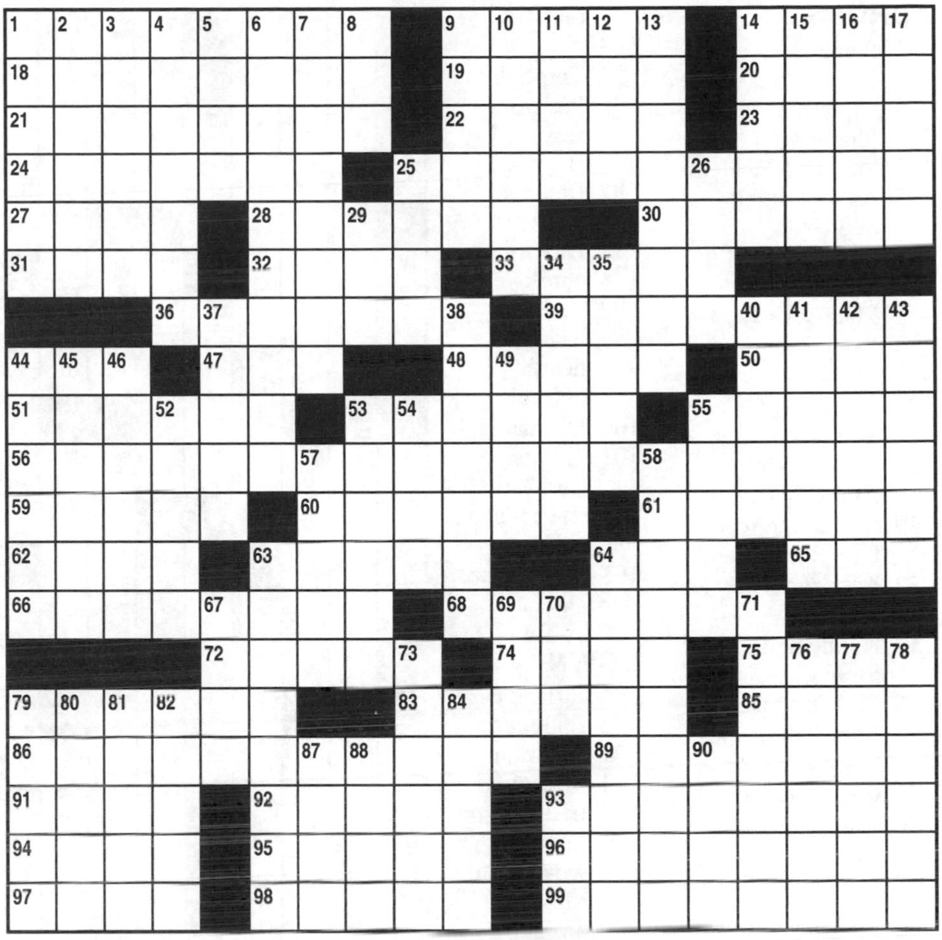

ACROSS

1 Conjectures
9 Play for time
14 Calla lily's family
18 Language of Zagreb
19 "Pagliacci" role
20 Make commercial, in a way
21 Keep
22 Illinois city
23 Start of Mongolia's capital
24 Suffixes
25 Lashless whips
27 Bank holding
28 Horse stable
30 Baja break
31 Film composer Schifrin
32 "Idylls of the King" lady
33 Pianist Rubinstein
36 Mexican munchie
39 "Hulk" star
44 RR stop
47 Blood-typing system
48 Like a 4-F
50 Keep ___ profile
51 Three-horse sleigh
53 Type of oil
55 Minute Maid Park player
56 Highest grossing film of 1981
59 Build a wing, say
60 Quaint cooler
61 Dieppe darling
62 Nancy Drew, for one
63 Vermont ski town
64 Hole starter
65 Hyphenated ID
66 Haydn's "The Creation," e.g.
68 She vanished in 1937
72 Lacking in resonance
74 Song from "Hair"
75 Sources of nickel
79 Doing time
83 Coveted statuettes
85 About to be served
86 Wastes time
89 Raven rival
91 Yuletide
92 Library taboo
93 Entry in a spaceship log
94 Cold capital
95 Ralph in Cooperstown
96 Bibb and iceberg
97 Audition
98 Part of FAQ
99 Wall-climbing flora

DOWN

1 Oscar winner Maximilian
2 Sister of Erato
3 Short poem
4 French line of defense
5 Lay ___ thick
6 Unattached establishment?
7 Corrodes
8 ___-Caps candy
9 Escalator part
10 "See, I was right!"
11 Pro foe
12 Sphinx, in part
13 Forte
14 Sky-blue
15 Caramel-and-chocolate candies
16 Not fitting
17 Bright bunch
25 Funny Foxx
26 Mag. publisher's concern
29 By way of
34 Automatic response
35 Court activity
37 Like Cutty Sark casks
38 Mayberry matron
40 Juice the goose
41 Tabernacle tables
42 "Lone Wolf McQuade" star
43 Roused
44 Sphere starter
45 Worker on the Street
46 "Search me!"
49 Manhattan neighborhood
52 Unexpected wedding response
53 Caterpillar's quarters
54 Not many
55 "My Name Is ___ Lev": Potok
57 Nonviolent protest
58 Rhode Island
63 Land once called Serendip
64 One with a craving
67 Mayberry tippler
69 Children's song start
70 New Deal agcy.
71 Got in shape
73 "Here's the thing . . ."
76 Tie the knot again?
77 Devonshire city
78 Italicize, perhaps
79 Otherwise
80 Lariat loop
81 Silver and Grey
82 Parcel out
84 Bucktoothed Mortimer
87 French kings
88 Rooter's sound
90 Art deco notable
93 Utah airport

186 ONE SIZE FITS ALL by Ed Early

Uncover the quip and you'll realize how fitting this title is.

ACROSS

1 Place
5 Robin Cook novel
9 Aquarium fish
13 Shampoo
17 Supermodel Heidi
18 A single-malt Scotch
19 Tricycle
20 Frijoles pot
21 Mass servers
23 PayPal founder Musk
24 Unbelievable one
25 **Start of a quip**
28 Lizard fish
29 Atahualpa subject
30 ___ bad to worse
31 OPEC member
32 Between RMN and JEC
34 Kaline and Simmons
36 Frost's Muse
39 **Part 2 of quip**
44 Pollywogs
45 Cager Danilovic
46 Bind
47 RR stop
48 "Le Monde" article
49 Strip of equipment
52 No-goodnik
53 **Part 3 of quip**
60 Couple
61 Davis in "Speechless"
62 Roxy Music founder
63 Spider-Man foe Doc ___
64 Fifth-century Pope
66 Food wrap
69 Reagan prog.
72 **Part 4 of quip**
77 Angling hang-ups
78 Kyushu volcano
79 Make known
80 Porgy's love
81 Appease completely
83 Friend of Hi and Lois
85 Actor Morales
86 **End of quip**
93 Calais cop
94 Old Tokyo
95 "___ Through the Park One Day"
96 Big dope
97 Rabin's predecessor
98 Day-to-day employee
99 "That's ___ haven't heard before!"
100 Discharge
101 "L'Arc en Ciel" artist
102 Cheers at a ballgame
103 Cle. Indian chiefs

DOWN

1 Jutland cape
2 Bad mood
3 Guardian
4 Flowing out
5 Irish seaport
6 Plaintive woodwind
7 Mexican holiday date
8 Williams of "Happy Days"
9 General
10 Lucre
11 Standoffish
12 Testimonial speakers
13 1941 Lon Chaney role
14 Others, to Ovid
15 Pole or Czech
16 Fabled race loser
22 AAA map abbr.
26 Berkeley school
27 Temple scroll
31 Erroneous
32 Crunch
33 Legal object
35 Ninth MLB commissioner
37 "Bobby Shaftoe's gone ___ . . ."
38 A lot
40 Buyer
41 ___ Cologne
42 Sicilian stew
43 The Phantom's creator
48 Monitor type
50 "Children of the Albatross" author
51 Pancreatic enzyme
52 "12 Miles of Bad Road" network
53 Just ___ on the map
54 German fox
55 Occupied
56 Prayer start
57 Don Juan saved her
58 Greenland explorer
59 Mrs. Shakespeare
64 ___ tender
65 Resort on Long Island Sound
67 Twinings product
68 Elvis Presley's label
69 Fingerpainting technique
70 Dior, for one
71 Checkpoint demands
73 Goes ballistic
74 Seville saint
75 Sushi seaweed
76 Beloved son of David
82 Prince among men, in Dubai
84 Frowzy
85 Wing not for flying
86 B-2 homes
87 Trough fare
88 "Big Cat" of baseball
89 Correct copy
90 Infantry
91 Outstrips
92 Patronage

187 TAKE 10 by Steven E. Atwood

Exactly ten.

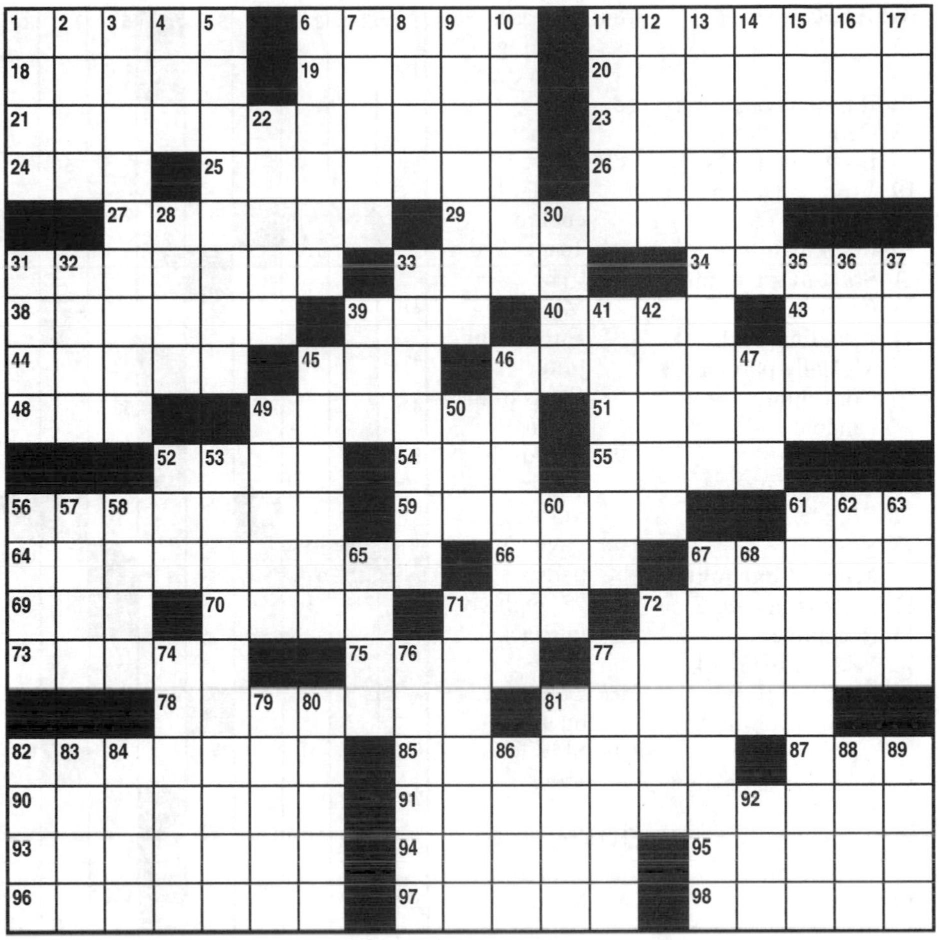

ACROSS

1 Make an impression on
6 TV monitor, of sorts
11 Piles up
18 Narrow
19 Greek goddess of peace
20 Ritzy, to the max
21 TAKE
23 "Never Be You" singer Cash
24 Russian for "peace"
25 Nail-pulling tool
26 Son of Agamemnon
27 Bring into parity
29 Most acute
31 Gym rat
33 Delaminate
34 Fry lightly
38 Steps
39 Step, on the floor
40 Clothes line
43 Rare color?
44 Fixes
45 Snoop
46 TAKE
48 Latin conjunction
49 Keanu's costar in "Speed"
51 ___ International
52 Mickey's creator
54 Plasma ingredient
55 Short routines
56 One to bounce things off
59 Effect
61 Fortnight couple: Abbr.
64 TAKE
66 Flagon filler
67 Selassie of Ethiopia
69 Soft shoe
70 Fisher in "Wedding Crashers"
71 Mo. you can eat oysters
72 Ancient Mexican
73 Downs town
75 Brand of an automotive degreaser
77 "Sounds of Silence" graffitist
78 Full of energy
81 Leads
82 Bonnie in "Die Hard"
85 Fordable
87 Soft-shoe
90 Winter coats
91 TAKE
93 RSVPer
94 Match
95 Grandmas
96 Wobbles
97 "___ by a Little Girl": Conkling
98 Buddy

DOWN

1 Opposite of stern
2 Move on the runway
3 TAKE
4 La Méditerranée, e.g.
5 TAKE
6 It can hurt you, they say
7 Brittle
8 Large quantity
9 They're covered by air filters on cars
10 Squirt
11 Cook wear
12 "Sicko" director
13 TAKE
14 California mount
15 En route
16 Serf
17 Fr. holy women
22 Word with "fancy" or "smarty"
28 ___ the Impaler
30 Other
31 Cirrus machines
32 Locust, for one
33 Mother lode
35 "A God in Ruins" author
36 Bedouin abode
37 Pushing the envelope
39 As needed: Rx
41 Pave the way for
42 Word on a ticket
45 Cover a beat
46 Plunder
47 Scale notes
49 Pours over
50 Anonymous party in a lawsuit
52 Woo successfully
53 TAKE
56 "Then You Look ___": Celine Dion
57 Eliminate
58 Carpet cleaners
60 Last: Abbr.
61 TAKE
62 "The Mocker Mocked" painter
63 Religious subdivision
65 Sitar music
67 TAKE
68 Mont Blanc, par exemple
71 Busily active
72 Some combos
74 No longer sick
76 Open with a pop
77 Beats
79 Hog rider
80 Demolishes: Brit.
81 Crest competitor
82 Entice
83 Feminine ending
84 Magician's bird
86 Land parcel
88 Not much
89 Cantina coin
92 Clavell's "___-Pan"

188 BAR JOKE by Ernest Lampert

Jan sings about 59 Across in the movie "Grease."

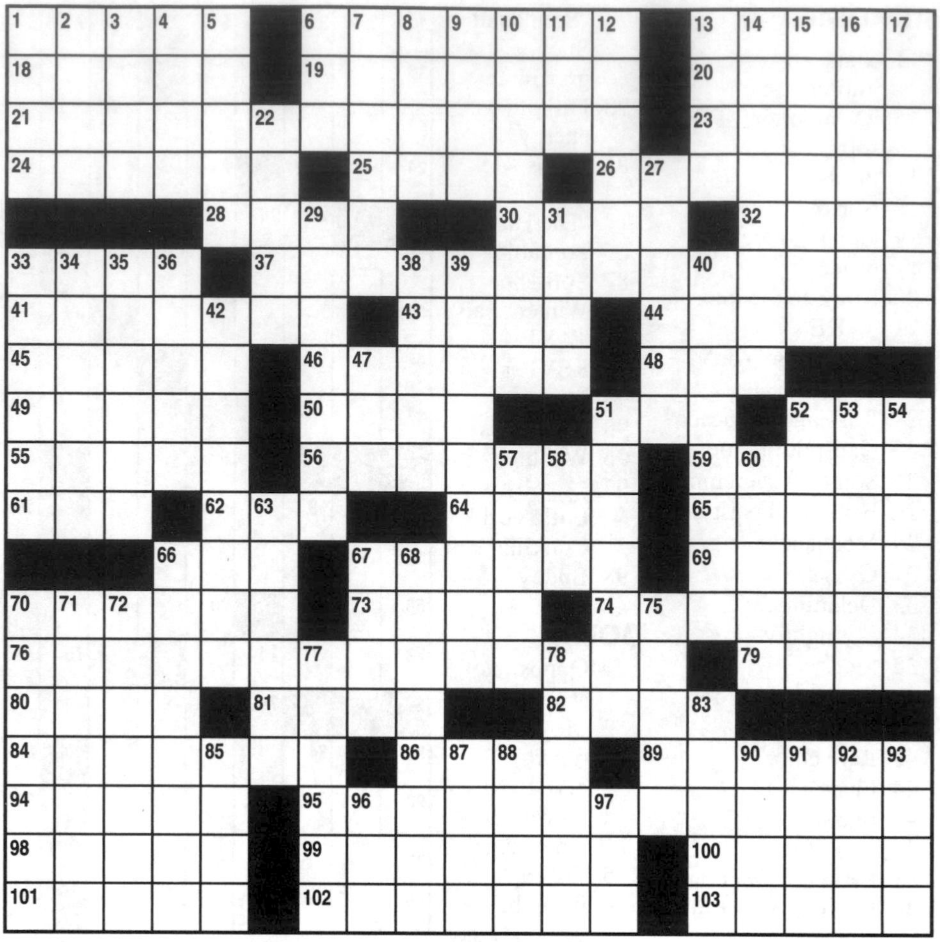

ACROSS

1 ___ Janeiro
6 Circular
13 It has movable frets
18 Cedric of "Little Lord Fauntleroy"
19 Virginia Dare's colony
20 Franklin bill
21 **Start of a bar joke**
23 Clueless
24 Aquafina rival
25 McNally partner
26 Convention handout
28 13 for Al
30 Geologic periods
32 Boarding site
33 Rubs out
37 **More of bar joke**
41 Attacks in a rage
43 Receptive
44 Wide of the mark
45 "The Devil and Daniel Webster" writer
46 Negative campaign features
48 ___ in Eddie
49 Tomato blight
50 "Star Trek" navigator
51 Get off the fence
52 Neth.
55 Crane cousin
56 **More of bar joke**
59 Bucky Beaver's toothpaste
61 Whimsical
62 Conductor ___-Pekka Salonen
64 Robert ___ (gin drink)
65 Abalone
66 Small counsel
67 Potsdam Conference attendee
69 Legal pleas, for short
70 Chorus from the flock
73 Uffizi display
74 Bleeth of "Titans"
76 **More of bar joke**
79 That's "Conolly" spelled with ___
80 Aussie greeting
81 Sami
82 Sports figure
84 "Grease" dressing-room items
86 Life's partner
89 Game similar to euchre
94 Tsar called "The Moneybag"
95 **End of bar joke**
98 Coins of the realm
99 One of the Oxford Martyrs
100 Taylor's party
101 "Symphony in Black" et al.
102 Condenses on a surface
103 Slow, on a score

DOWN

1 24th Senate Majority Leader
2 Soaps creator Phillips
3 Leavings
4 Qatar's capital
5 "Uncle Vanya" woman
6 Tahiti war/peace god
7 Lament
8 Tennis star Mandlikova
9 What the connected may have
10 Weigher, without a scale
11 Ticker-tape letters?
12 Troi of "Star Trek: TNG"
13 Hoodwink
14 1 and 2, e.g.
15 Taqueria offering
16 Pigged out
17 Active chemical
22 "___ Pass": Uris
27 Word after fast or sound
29 Boris Badenov's friend
31 Defeats regularly, in sports lingo
33 Words after baron or side
34 Feather an arrow
35 Regalia
36 Summons from the boss
38 Caterwauls
39 Place for an eagle
40 MRE forerunners
42 Gasoline-price factor
47 MADD concern
51 Like the jack of spades
52 Lincoln's first vice president
53 Early Ping-Pong score
54 Well-known London captain
57 Kind of wrench
58 Lilliputian
60 Free sample, perhaps
63 Paperclip alternative
66 Adjournment
67 Powerful DC lobby
68 They may be identical or fraternal
70 Doodlesack
71 George Bush's prep school
72 Inflexible
75 Viper
77 Calif. barrio city
78 Spider snare
83 Lower
85 Runs out of steam
87 Prefix with -syncratic
88 "They Call ___ Tibbs"(1970)
90 Long (for)
91 Scout leader?
92 USAF noncom.
93 Station on Route 66
96 Conned
97 Corp. news announcements

189 BIG PROBLEMS by Robert A. Doll

73 Across was founded in 2006.

ACROSS

1 Green activity
5 "La ___ Aux Folles"
9 "Little Latin ___ Lu": Kingsmen
13 Looking down from
17 Chemistry class
19 Romance lang.
20 Egg on
21 Big problem
23 Mah-jongg piece
24 Dazed and confused
25 Canine shelters?
26 Plumber's snake
27 Marlon's 1972 role
30 Corot painting style
32 Thane of Glamis
36 Big problem
40 Burn balm
41 Erratum
43 Roll-call vote
44 "I told you so!"
45 Arctic gulls
47 Meal
51 Photo finish
53 Tyler's predecessor
55 2002 Olympics venue
58 M, to Einstein
59 Big problem
62 One-spots
64 Lofty standard
65 French flag
68 Sashimi kin
70 Timber trouble
72 Old and feeble
73 San Diego Wildcats' org.
74 Hightailed it
77 Give off
79 Cruise stopover
80 Big problem
85 Lancelot's son
87 Instigated
88 Walt Kelly critter
89 Prison weapons
92 More hopeful
94 Rostropovich's instrument
99 Went like the dickens
100 Big problem
103 Arab chieftain
104 In the sack
105 Be suspicious
106 Military meal
107 Wait
108 Hops kiln
109 Carson's successor

DOWN

1 Hummus holder
2 Newton, for one
3 Garb
4 Sloth's home
5 Swing master Calloway
6 Whichever
7 Controversial prison, for short
8 She loved Narcissus
9 Kind of bug
10 Jazz fan, most likely
11 Country crooner Brad
12 Building addition
13 One of a Vivaldi foursome
14 H.S. math
15 Eye rakishly
16 Ibsen's "___ Gynt"
18 Critical
22 Continental coin
26 State in NE India
28 "The Addams Family" cousin
29 Butterfly-shaped gland
31 Resident's suffix
32 Moonshine mix
33 ___-Seltzer
34 Nell Gwyn, for one
35 Pessimistic, to brokers
36 Lindy's dance
37 Institute
38 Match parts
39 Driver's devices
42 Composed
46 ___ semper tyrannis
48 In a fitting way
49 Asian honorific
50 "___, the piper's son . . ."
52 Little Bo-Peep product, once
54 Do wedelns
56 Hitchcock thriller
57 Sapporo sash
60 Needlefish
61 Andean tuber
62 "Pronto!"
63 Rough Riders' battlefield
66 Earthen pot
67 Cattail, e.g.
69 "Reversal of Fortune" star
71 Crossword blogger Parker
75 Hyperbola part
76 Capital of Kenya
78 Children's game
81 Frogmen
82 Put away
83 Next to
84 Valhalla V.I.P.
86 In the neighborhood
88 Trumpeter Louis
89 Goblet feature
90 Main Web page
91 Rainbow goddess
93 "Tiger-in-your-tank" gas
95 Catchall abbr.
96 Old Italian money
97 Fannie Mae transaction
98 Able to see right through
100 Catch in the act
101 Your, to Yves
102 Final: Abbr.

190 GOING SOLAR by Arlan and Linda Bushman

101 Across is located near Luxor.

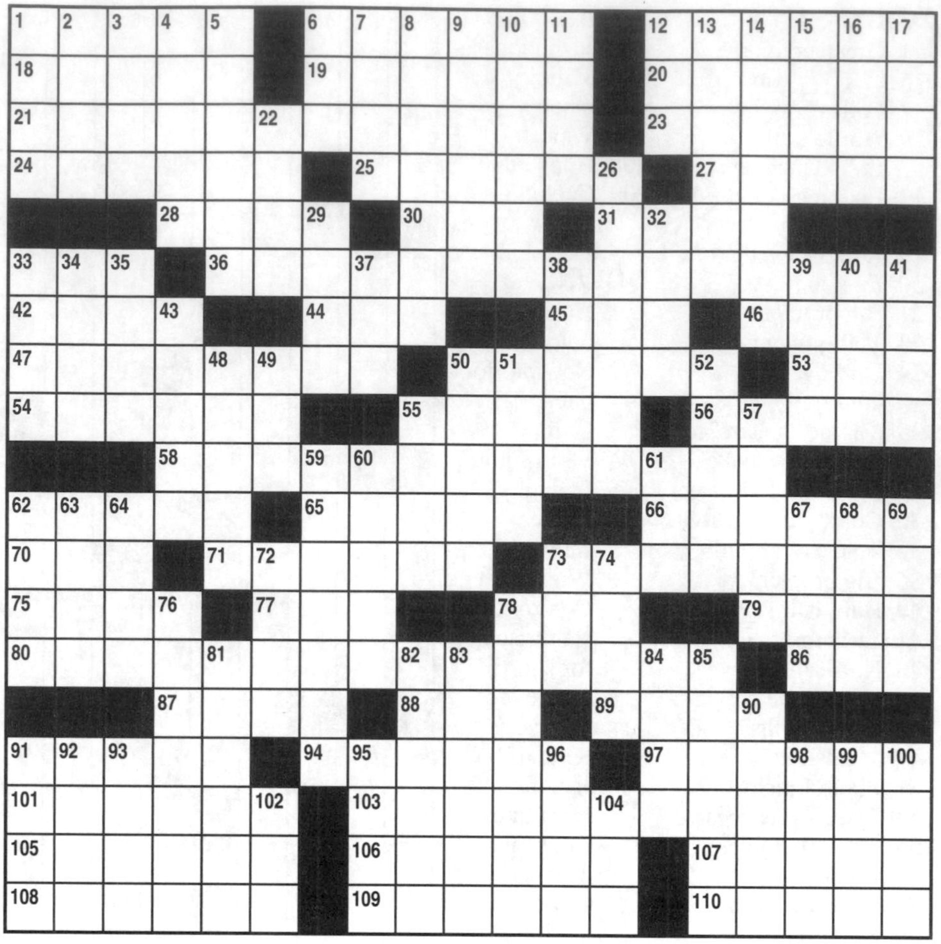

ACROSS

1 Yarn
6 Volcanic materials
12 Provide
18 Another time
19 ER screening
20 Minutiae
21 Company's solar products arm?
23 Empty pride
24 Sounds of admonishment
25 Pull the wool over
27 Turns over
28 Petitions
30 Authorize
31 Holiday shorthand
33 Part of TGIF
36 Symposium on solar technology?
42 Southwestern art mecca
44 Guitar kin, briefly
45 Wrong (with "all")
46 Consequently
47 Swap
50 Quaking
53 Hard feelings
54 Title for Japanese emperor
55 Tread heavily
56 Stand
58 Public debate on solar's role?
62 Win all games of a series
65 Pleasure trip
66 Illegal enterprises
70 Website visit
71 With-it
73 Kind of key
75 Social group
77 Duke's org.
78 Feel bad about
79 Hideo of baseball
80 Promotional claim about solar's popularity?
86 Just out
87 Initial stake
88 PBS benefactor
89 Good earth
91 Many-eyed giant
94 Time span
97 2004 Will Smith film
101 Major Egyptian ruins site
103 Solar researchers?
105 Winter hanging
106 Low tie score
107 Backs, in a way
108 Dewey, to Donald
109 Hillary's Everest partner
110 Fill (out)

DOWN

1 Almanac tidbit
2 Develops
3 Be unwilling
4 Happy tunes
5 Arrives (at)
6 "The Hills" airer
7 Lacking interest
8 French tragic ballet
9 Posted
10 Tropical rodent
11 Call (for)
12 Off-road ride, for short
13 Dust-up
14 Subtlety
15 "Metamorphoses" poet
16 Observance
17 Goodly stretch
22 Home furnishings chain
26 Passage
29 Close-fitting
32 Tone down
33 Detail
34 Prepare for takeoff
35 Punch
37 Squeeze (out)
38 Hindu mystic
39 Pupil setting
40 Ruffian
41 Coward of the theater
43 Contour
48 Take up
49 Present
50 Hard-hearted
51 Paddock denizen
52 Model decoration
55 Russet, slangily
57 Poplar variety
59 Thrown out
60 Dressing option
61 Clinch
62 Persian monarch
63 Bacchus province
64 Sundance's gal
67 Harrow rival
68 Apple choice
69 Hoodwink
72 Large number
73 Aggregate
74 Centerboard
76 True-blue
78 Inconsiderate driver
81 Marked down
82 Brendan Fraser comedy "___ Man"
83 In short supply
84 Film genre
85 Free-trade barrier
90 Big wheel
91 Analogous
92 Meet event
93 Valise
95 Son of Zabulon
96 Sight from Messina
98 Undoing
99 They're uneven
100 New Age musician John
102 London's ___ Gardens
104 Ottoman governor

191 L DORADO by Brad Wilber

All kidding aside, 50 Across is one of Joni's biggest hits.

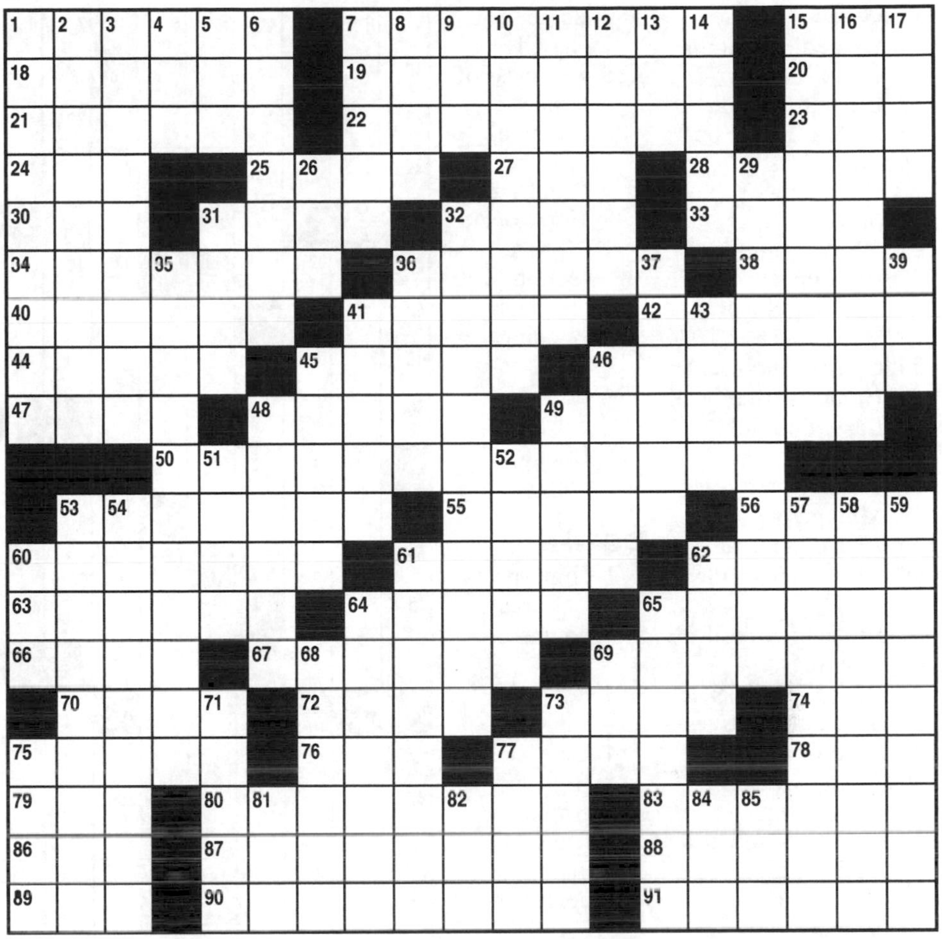

ACROSS

1 Victor in "My Darling Clementine"
7 Heebie-jeebies
15 Bout-promoting org.
18 It's been known to wipe out
19 Billie Holiday's birth name
20 "There Will Be Blood" subject
21 Opportunities to swing
22 Architectural space above an arch
23 Colorado Indian
24 Atomic energy agcy. since 1974
25 "Get Smart" bad guys
27 Carried out
28 Electric battery inventor
30 Seek favor with
31 Superlative eBay adjective
32 "Litany for the Whale" composer
33 Like some shoppes
34 Manhattan tunnel
36 California birthplace of Jessica Alba
38 Grave
40 Exhibiting decorum
41 Waves made sound at the salon
42 Punch bowl adjuncts
44 Split
45 Throng
46 Tap
47 Thornfield Hall governess
48 Jack in "The Little Dictator"
49 Connived
50 Joni Mitchell hack work?
53 Lost momentum
55 Parties with poi
56 Capone nemesis
60 "Chicago Tribune" et al.
61 Jane Goodall subject
62 Ski run
63 Game "point"?
64 Riyadh native
65 Subject to catcalls
66 Socialite Sedgwick
67 ___ Artois beer
69 Captain of industry
70 Tudor widow Catherine
72 Storm cloud product
73 One of the Jackson Five
74 Accept, as an excuse
75 Hawaiian island once owned by James Dole
76 Coddling recipient
77 "Mr. Mom" actress
78 Trevino of golf
79 Boston Marathon mo.
80 Einsteins
83 Lets in
86 Neckline shape
87 Miss, in a way
88 Monte ___ sandwich
89 Dull finish?
90 1980s hair fads
91 German baked treat

DOWN

1 Concurrently
2 Steelers' founding owner
3 It lacks buttonholes
4 "Nashville Star" cable network
5 Pt. of AARP
6 "Tobacco Road" writer Caldwell
7 Stupefy with infatuation
8 Yodeler's range
9 Cartel-busting gp.
10 "Muscles from Brussels" actor
11 Dark blues
12 Company with a spokescow
13 "Maid of Athens, ___ we part . . .": Byron
14 Battleship blast
15 Con man's rhetorical question
16 When a diehard dies hard
17 "Alexandria Quartet" finale
26 "What's more . . ."
29 Virginia
31 Unicorn feature
32 "The Father of the United Nations"
35 MLB's post-1920 period
36 Scylla or Charybdis
37 Socially dominant types
39 Id follower
41 Reproved a snorer
43 Zenith
45 "Shaft" scorer Isaac
46 Malfunction
48 Fans of cheesecake?
49 Turban-clad mystic
51 Bjorn's 1976 Wimbledon opponent
52 "A Dog of Flanders" author
53 Metaphor for a cat's tongue
54 Nancy Drew's hair color
57 Found
58 Tony, for one
59 Saw
60 "Lost" actor Daniel ___ Kim
61 Camus play set in ancient Rome
62 Churchy La Femme's pal
64 Like an island
65 Place for a bowler
68 1995 Sandra Bullock film
69 Russian launch of 1986
71 Strictness
73 To-do list entries
75 Black soap
77 Seismologist's field: Abbr.
81 "Die Meistersinger" heroine
82 ___-disant
84 Joanne in "All the King's Men"
85 Karaoke need, for short

192 ITALIAN METROPOLITAN by Anna Carson

36 Across is also a '60s band.

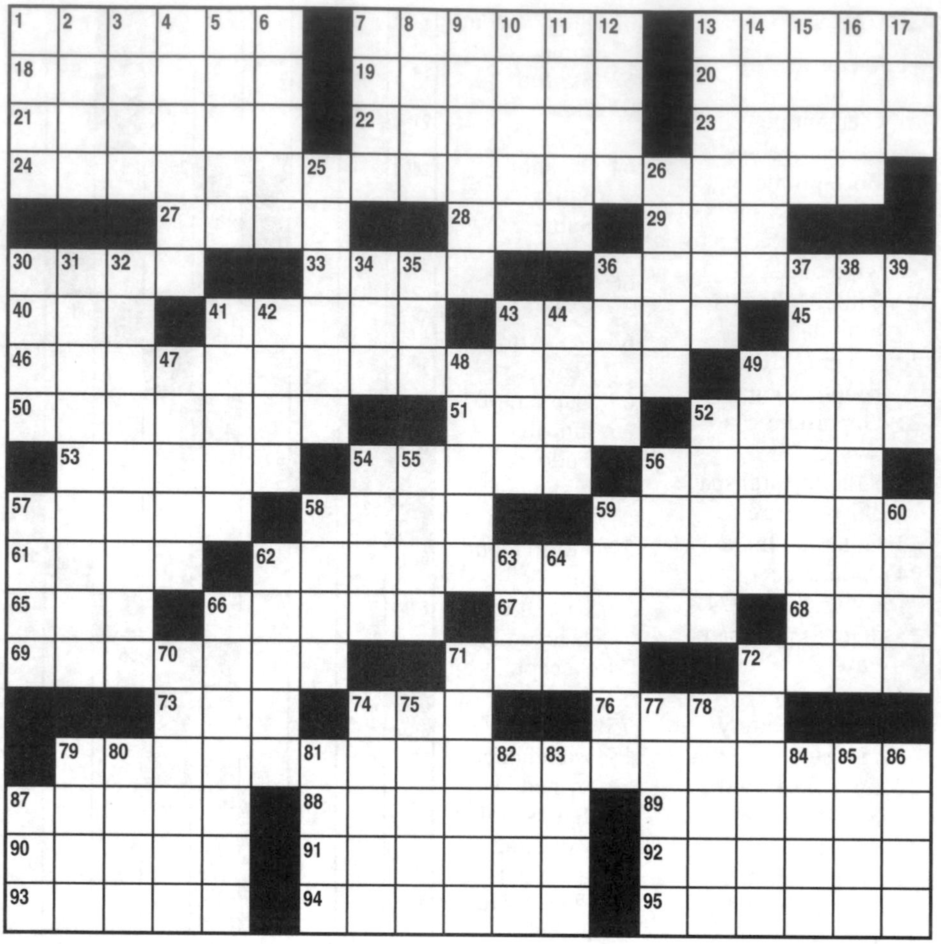

ACROSS

1 Uncredited authors
7 Curt refusal
13 Come to a point
18 Attack like a lion
19 For voices
20 Beginning of a prayer
21 Alaska native
22 Riles up
23 Winning Super Bowl coach in 1974
24 Constantine's realm
27 Humorist Bombeck
28 Last of a drink
29 Rhine feeder
30 Catches on to
33 Min. parts
36 Chocolate treats
40 Ab ___ (from day one)
41 Big name in foil
43 Cunning
45 Vote of confidence
46 Shade alternatives
49 Seat for a tot
50 Angler with a moving line
51 Garfield's sidekick
52 Zeal
53 Light lunch, perhaps
54 Hall's singing partner
56 Bracelet attachment
57 Feline nonet
58 On top of that
59 Small potatoes
61 Words before instant
62 Brunch dish with spinach
65 Long distance inits.
66 Beach Boy Wilson
67 Destroy gradually
68 "Runaway" rocker Shannon
69 Waffle type
71 Penetrate slowly
72 Norm's wife on "Cheers"
73 Giant Mel
74 Name divider
76 Former rival of Jimmy and Bjorn
79 Layered dessert
87 Somewhat, slangily
88 Keenness of mind
89 Danny of "Do the Right Thing"
90 Horse opera
91 MoMA section
92 One hunting
93 Bedding item
94 Some coffees
95 Literary Papa

DOWN

1 High spirits
2 "___ real nowhere man"
3 Squirrel haunts
4 Gets back at
5 Big-top employee
6 Big blow
7 Tenn. neighbor
8 "Well, hell!"
9 Doctrines
10 One response to "How do you know?"
11 Madrid meat
12 Choice word
13 Extra
14 Touted trumpeter
15 Rain buckets
16 First name in whodunits
17 Food package info
25 Jeff Gordon's org.
26 Wedge drivers
30 Poly sci subj.
31 From that point on
32 In vain
34 Awfully long time
35 Car at a stand
36 Sweeping force
37 One-sided win
38 Morning coffee, for one
39 Clairvoyant
41 Ayn Rand's shrugger
42 Told tales
43 French novelist André
44 United, to Ionesco
47 Talk show host Degeneres
48 "What a ___ hooey!"
49 Big cheese processor
52 Roomy dress
54 Gymnast Korbut
55 Pt. of AARP
56 Acceptance on the street, slangily
57 Elm extension
58 Feudin' with
59 Globe circler
60 Ward of "Sisters"
62 Millay's Muse
63 Appomattox figure
64 Blast furnace input
66 Cameo
70 Chin beard
71 Gobs
72 Ben of "Roots"
74 Williamson in "The Seven-Per-Cent Solution"
75 Piano exercise
77 Let out
78 Containing more cubes
79 Genesis boatwright
80 Art deco illustrator
81 Mary's pet
82 Uncool sort
83 Wayside havens
84 Sommer in "A Shot in the Dark"
85 Pub brews
86 Humorist Sahl
87 Palindromic plea

193 CLOSING UP SHOP by John Greenman

An unusual theme idea . . . but will it play in 71 Across?

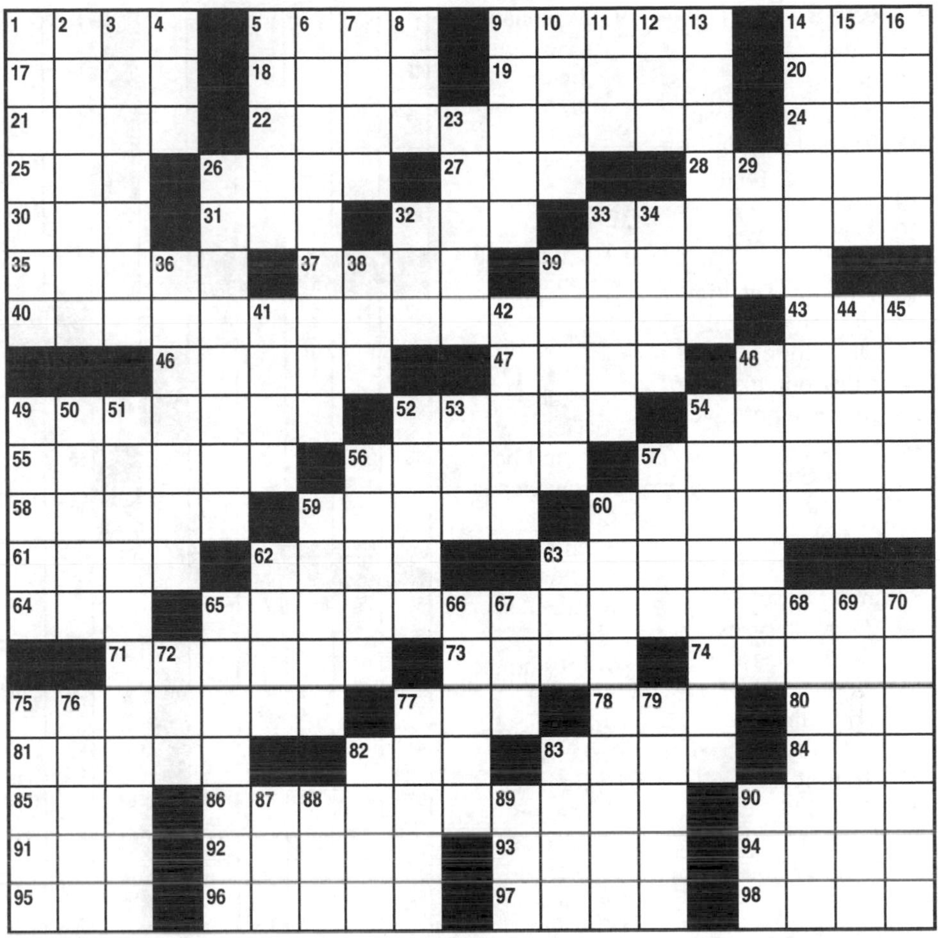

ACROSS

1 Robust
5 Gossip: sl.
9 Hip-related
14 Saperstein of basketball
17 Pedro's years
18 Opposed to
19 Papal administration
20 Hecht or Hogan
21 Wields oars
22 Fold a meat-packing business?
24 Poetry or painting
25 Burrowed
26 Burmese hill-dweller
27 Originally called
28 Landholder
30 Shake a leg
31 Actor Linden
32 "Ben-___" (1959)
33 At a time to come
35 Texas landmark
37 College sci. course
39 Regained consciousness
40 Fold a laundry business?
43 "Heroes" network
46 Anchorage
47 Wee songbird
48 Home to over half of humankind
49 Garbs
52 Bizarre
54 Group's character
55 Orcas
56 Less tainted
57 Punctual
58 Got one's goat
59 Howled like a lamb
60 Siesta shawls
61 Dregs
62 Operatic voice
63 Visionary?
64 Pasture
65 Fold a snack-food business?
71 City in Illinois
73 Of poems
74 Macho one
75 Skill
77 Ampersand
78 Application
80 Larter of "Heroes"
81 Less cooked
82 Newcastle Brown, e.g.
83 "How sad!"
84 Flit
85 Append
86 Fold a 24-hour business?
90 Tug-of-war team
91 Do macramé
92 Buoy one's spirits
93 Thugs' guns
94 Tropical cuckoos
95 High, rocky hill
96 Friend of Pythias
97 Filled cookie
98 Contained

DOWN

1 Miner's helmet
2 "Becket" playwright
3 It might be used on hills
4 Double curve
5 Russian country house
6 Asthma remedies
7 Shock
8 Embarrassing sound, often
9 More gelid
10 Mandolin's kin
11 Lyricist Gershwin
12 Be on the sick list
13 Electrode-cell powder
14 Fold a cruise line?
15 City in Kentucky
16 Contest mail-in
23 Football's Rockne
26 Didn't bathe?
29 Covered with dew
32 Cry of contempt
33 Lumberjack, at times
34 Portent
36 Baby toys
38 Imprecise ordinal
39 Kitchen utensil
41 Fills with fury
42 Rough wool fabric
44 Ecological life zone
45 Boxes
48 Kind of case
49 "Where there's ___, there's . . ."
50 Magi, e.g.
51 Fold a compact business?
52 Seemingly
53 Yorkshire river
54 Fortifies
56 Turkish bigwig of yore
57 Feedbag contents
59 Fundamental principle
60 Conjecture
62 Captain's insignia
63 Naval CIA
65 Curb legally
66 Trio of trios
67 Even's opposite
68 Envision
69 "Have Gun Will Travel" hero
70 Most sarcastic
72 She-sheep
75 Institute in Brooklyn
76 Click and Clack's medium
77 Outlander
79 Authority
82 Chorister
83 Hebrew month
87 Wing
88 On the ___ (fleeing)
89 At an earlier period
90 Aphid's lunch

194 PLUS FOURS by Harvey Estes

You won't find any four-letter words below.

ACROSS

1 Solid
7 Smiths' places
13 Intentionally lose
18 Product of a dull lecture, perhaps
19 Apply oil to
20 Kent portrayer of film
21 Without exception
22 Digs on the trail
23 Stand for a portrait
24 Alley-oop toss, e.g.
25 Hartman portrayer
26 Duck
27 "Capiche?"
29 Meaning
30 Carries on
31 Gymnast's helper
33 In any case
38 Victorian types
40 Literate boast?
41 Hardly top-of-the-line
45 Misinform
46 Drafting aids
47 "Uh-uh!"
53 Stick out
55 Haunted house noises
56 Easily bent
57 Drive off
58 Hides, like a dog
60 Property paper
61 With the fewest bubbles
63 Frank option
64 Chip rakers
69 Influences
71 Letting out
72 Husband of Pocahontas
75 Advantage
76 To some extent
84 Cooler rooms
85 Accept eagerly
86 Japanese religion
87 Designer Calvin
88 Ascribe
89 Sawbuck
90 Tape over
91 Doth knock for a loop
92 Drive-thru requests
93 Winona in "Beetlejuice"
94 Least significant
95 Monster's nickname

DOWN

1 Label with a handle
2 Slipknot loop
3 Brown in the kitchen
4 Ticket word
5 Don't belong together
6 Camping enthusiasts
7 Queue up
8 Like a short play
9 Lies on the beach
10 Japanese knife
11 Register
12 Stashes
13 Serious betrayal
14 Tar stop
15 Takes umbrage at
16 Direct workers
17 Tosses, as the sea
28 Devonshire dad
32 Unskilled labor
33 Wasn't well
34 Singer Lopez
35 Yorkshire city
36 Really enjoy
37 Like loads
38 "Candle in the Wind" lyricist Taupin
39 Some Scots
42 Kind of vertebra
43 Heavy blows
44 Person's pump
48 Lacking
49 Coward's lack
50 Orb-related
51 Put aside
52 Pounding parts
54 Like a cartoon cookie-maker
59 A natural location?
62 Strict adherence to rules
64 Salty snack
65 Carousing
66 Tethered
67 Put to work, in Winchester
68 Light lager
70 Experience with delight
72 Standing
73 Spouts
74 Gossip (with "the")
77 ___ fatale
78 Jaguar's prey
79 Author Hite
80 Female deer
81 Laura of "ER"
82 SNL's Cheri
83 Like Leif

195 RAILWAYS by Richard Silvestri

Take a ride on the Short Line.

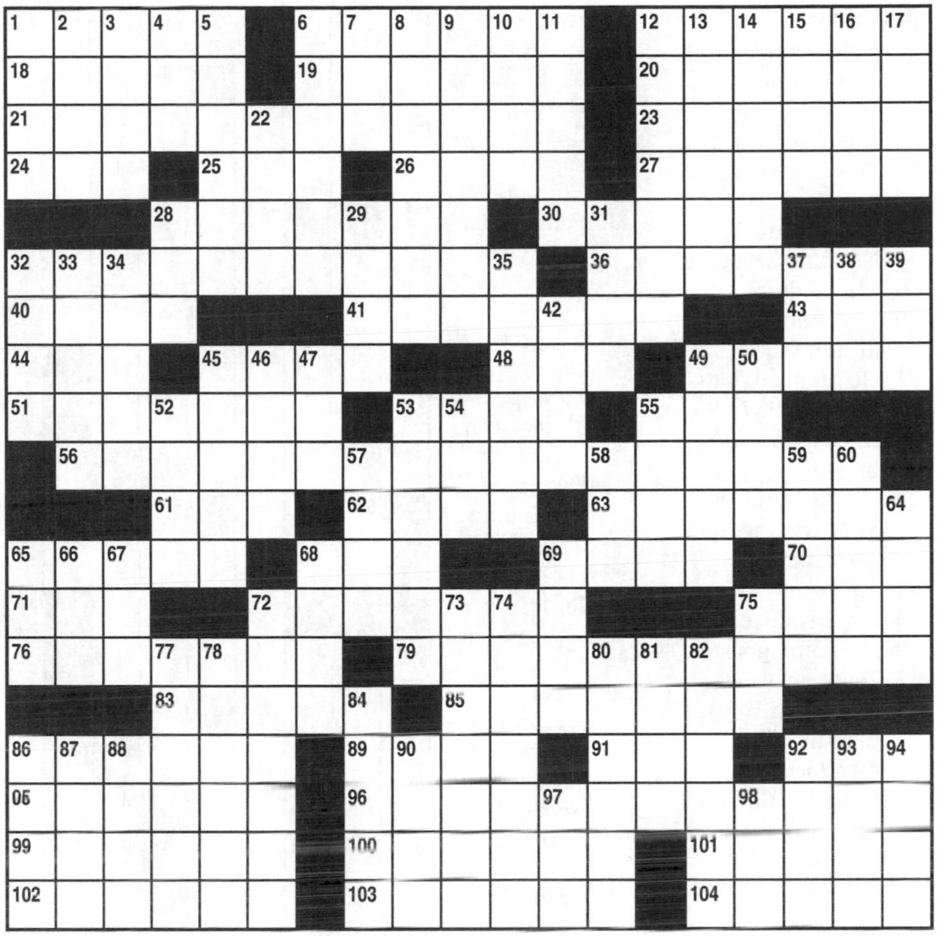

ACROSS

1 Dreadlocks wearer
6 Tutu, e.g.
12 Attack
18 Beat
19 City on Lake Ontario
20 Go to extremes
21 Ironworks income?
23 Gets tight
24 Big jerk
25 Gift for a malihini
26 Fairy-tale villain
27 Makes like a peacock
28 Small animal
30 Raggedy-edged
32 Patrick's mom?
36 Do repeatedly
40 Module
41 Categorizes
43 Bouvier des Flandres, for one
44 Penn., in NYC
45 Chowder morsel
48 Charlottesville sch.
49 Mouth, slangily
51 "Pequod" weapon
53 Like some pen points
55 Bit in a horse's mouth
56 Forward-looking baker?
61 Put away
62 Microscope part
63 Beginning to develop
65 Volkswagen model
68 Sorrow
69 Ice in the ring
70 P.O. delivery
71 In the style of
72 Sardou play that inspired Puccini
75 Flash of inspiration
76 Hood
79 Nation in need of ZPG?
83 Incensed
85 "Friends" actor
86 Boil
89 "Cheerio!"
91 Part of the Treasury Dept.
92 "___ Jane run . . ."
95 Pull in
96 St. Peter?
99 Two-___ (short film)
100 One of the Gallos
101 Slacken
102 Hayseeds
103 Friars events
104 Put a strain on

DOWN

1 Huge amount
2 Baseball family name
3 Garden pest
4 Canterbury can
5 Washington ___ U.
6 Like a lad
7 School of thought
8 Certain winners
9 They're in the closet
10 One in the hole
11 Name on a check
12 Meat-and-vegetable stew
13 Loath
14 Facing
15 Limerick languauge
16 Arabian Sea gulf
17 Pitch
22 Bring up
28 Food additive
29 Husky group?
31 "Lovely" Beatles woman
32 Drivel
33 Tavern sign
34 Queen topper
35 Lester and Loretta
37 Wood-shaping tool
38 Overly
39 Freud subject
42 Camper driver
45 Terra ___
46 Folk tales
47 Whichever
49 Low man at La Scala
50 Problem ending
52 H.S. exam
53 Not bound by
54 Chemists get a charge out of it
55 Anthem opening
57 It may thicken
58 Bambi's aunt
59 African grassland
60 Step inside
64 Salver
65 Problem on the expressway
66 "Evil Woman" band
67 Bar bill
68 Skin blemish
69 "Meet the Press" host Marvin
72 Front men?
73 Yellow raisin
74 Splits
75 Corporate abbr.
77 "Like a" phrase
78 See the world
80 Black and Walker
81 Things in tholes
82 Oust the incumbent
84 Old number?
86 Player of golf
87 Treat with milk
88 Long haul
90 Dynamic beginning
92 Sam and Dave's label
93 Painter of an Art Deco alphabet
94 Looked at
97 Suffix for winning or losing
98 Timberwolves' org.

196 WESTERN LEGEND by Ray Hamel

Hugh O'Brian was the first actor to play Wyatt Earp on TV.

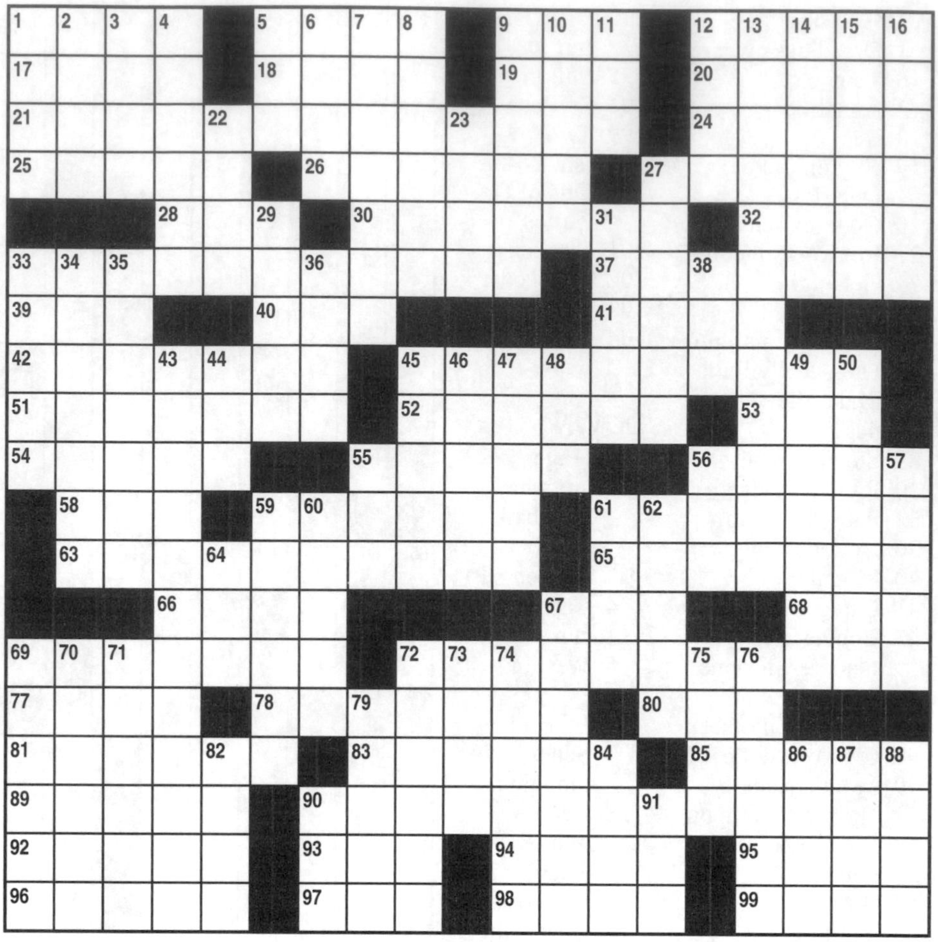

ACROSS

1 "Have You Heard" singer James
5 Crips, for one
9 Checkers, e.g.
12 French clergy
17 Lendl of tennis
18 ___ Woods National Monument
19 Mil. address
20 Line outside the theater
21 He played Wyatt Earp in 1957
24 Lexicographer's interest
25 Guy with the mike
26 This evening, on a marquee
27 Told (on)
28 Seize suddenly
30 Do-nothing's state
32 Teutonic article
33 He played Wyatt Earp in 1993
37 Informed
39 Reno-to-Elko dir.
40 Singer-songwriter Corinne Bailey __
41 Outside categorization (abbr.)
42 A way to serve chicken
45 He played Wyatt Earp in 1955
51 Singing and dancing, e.g.
52 Mercedes-Benz model category
53 Faulkner's "___ Lay Dying"
54 Norwegian church type
55 Bluesman "Sleepy John"
56 Sporty Ford
58 Nero's 151
59 Cry over
61 "Arabian Nights" hero
63 He played Wyatt Earp in 1946
65 Takes in astonishedly
66 Vocalist Vikki
67 For this or that
68 Sweet ending?
69 Amanda of "L.A. Law"
72 He played Wyatt Earp in 1967/1988
77 Hazzard County deputy
78 Current units
80 Female in a wool coat
81 Outperformed
83 "___ the Chief"
85 Ties up
89 Major oven maker
90 He played Wyatt Earp in 1939
92 Fabricated stories
93 Mil. svc. unit
94 Across the street, perhaps
95 One point of cuisine?
96 Access
97 Spelling contest
98 Aruba, for one
99 Deli side

DOWN

1 See eye to eye
2 Egg
3 Deal breaker?
4 It may be criminal
5 D. Sawyer show
6 Mom's sister
7 Salade ___
8 Starbucks order
9 Fisher-Price acquirer in 1993
10 Alternatives to foils
11 And not either
12 Color similar to teal
13 He played Wyatt Earp in 1958
14 "Take a hike!"
15 University of Oregon site
16 Like bye recipients
22 Dramatic king
23 Flower pot site
27 Archaeological booty
29 Done to blackness
31 Emma in "Delirious"
33 "Endymion" writer
34 Debar?
35 Cask-fermented beer
36 Succumbs to gravity
38 Top-left key
43 He played Wyatt Earp in 1994
44 Plastic ending?
45 George on "Seinfeld"
46 Square-dance group
47 Last queen of Italy
48 Vegas head
49 Boomer of football
50 Site of some bombers
55 Rock genre out of Washington, D.C.
56 Waiter's reward
57 Match.com clinic
59 Scenic route
60 Zimbalist of "The F.B.I."
61 Periods in history
62 Roomy
64 School shout
67 Pounding tools
69 Discuss the pros and cons of
70 Kind of show
71 Like some diets
72 "State Fair" actress Crain
73 Lacking imaginativeness
74 "Law & Order: SVU" star Christopher
75 Saddle working tools
76 Does a double-take, say
79 Aspect
82 Not knotty
84 Lustrous gem
86 Slinky, basically
87 Largest volcano in Europe
88 Ratatouille, e.g.
90 Obstacle, to Shakespeare
91 Charlemagne's domain: Abbr.

197 SAME IN THE END by Robert A. Doll

We all have our 15 minutes of fame, although 104-A had a few minutes more.

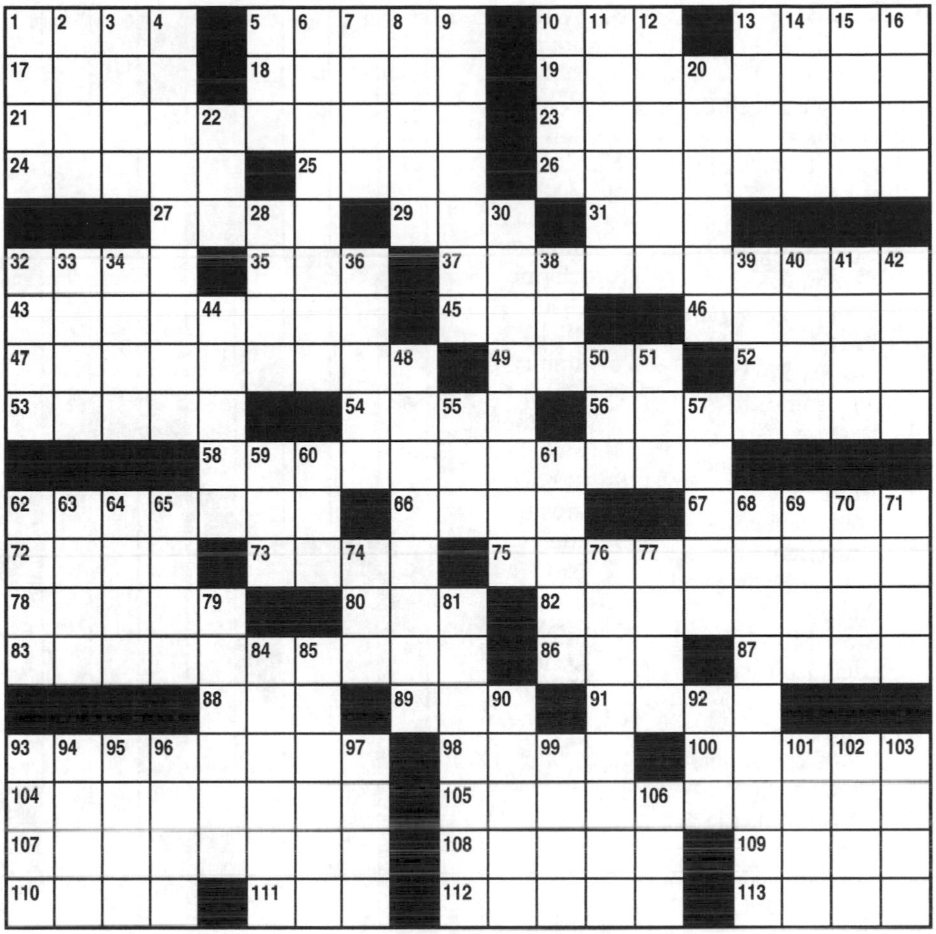

ACROSS

1 Final notice
5 Obey Darwin's theory
10 Honshu honorific
13 Balmoral cousins
17 ___ Martin (cognac)
18 Hem again
19 Handel work
21 Starbucks choice
23 Hard Italian cheese
24 Beasts of burden
25 JFK postings
26 Intruded
27 Garden buttinsky
29 The ___ Lady ("Twin Peaks" character)
31 Luau souvenir
32 Culture medium
35 "My Name Is Asher ___": Potok
37 Cherry choice
43 Trigger, for one
45 Bard's "before"
46 Passover meal
47 Sports enthusiast's tidbit
49 Letter opener
52 Head for the hills
53 City on the Ruhr
54 Chip's cartoon chum
56 Athletic awards
58 Fresco master Brumidi
62 Cruise times
66 Allege as fact
67 Fisherman's ___
72 Future J.D.'s hurdle
73 Spinnaker, e.g.
75 Recovery
78 Allegro ___ (music direction)
80 Morse click
82 Elementary particle
83 Fancy Ford of yore
86 Acme order from Wile E. Coyote
87 Drop-off spot?
88 Half a bray
89 Agatha Christie's "The ___ Murders"
91 Mother of Helios
93 Compact items
98 Clandestine 51 is one
100 Big dos
104 "88 Minutes" star
105 Tartini clarinet piece
107 Allies invasion area
108 Chills
109 Nights before
110 Eye problem
111 Mason Williams' "Classical ___"
112 Get-go
113 Tabula ___

DOWN

1 Marine menace
2 Lillie and Arthur
3 Little devils
4 Used an Olivetti
5 Hyperbola part
6 Heir's benefactor
7 "___ were . . ."
8 Prison-related
9 Golf group
10 Frosh, next year
11 Pupil surrounder
12 Button materials
13 Went like the dickens
14 Dry as a bone
15 Subcompact
16 Any day now
20 Invigorating drinks
22 Application
28 "Boola Boola" singers
30 Le Carré's "The Constant ___"
32 Basilica area
33 Goons guns
34 Word for Yorick
36 Annuls
38 Riddle-me-___
39 Bulk
40 Just lying around
41 At no time, poetically
42 Mine finds
44 Recipe direction
48 California island
50 The Louisville Lip
51 Cartoon Chihuahua
55 John
57 Namely
59 Tiebreakers, briefly
60 Eavesdropping org.
61 1545 council site
62 Smelting waste
63 CCCP, American-style
64 Astronaut's insignia
65 Hockey's Mikita
68 The other side, in a sense
69 Fired up
70 "You ___?": Lurch
71 Arctic sight
74 Despot Amin
76 Octopus feature
77 The Great Bambino
79 Cornell's home
81 The T in ATF
84 Crew member's task
85 Uganda neighbor
90 Sing like Bing
92 Cup handle
93 Staffs
94 All the time
95 Nimble
96 Showed up
97 Some beans
99 1961 chimp in space
101 1972 Kentucky Derby winner ___ Ridge
102 Addition column
103 McGwire's 1999 rival
106 NYC time

198 CALL YOUR REPRESENTATIVE by Bruce Venzke

The Rockefeller in the clue at 1 Across was John D., Sr.

ACROSS

1 Rockefeller handouts
6 Hefty competitor
10 Amphora
13 H.S. junior's exam
17 Rice-___
18 Saab concept car
19 Commando weapon
20 Verdant
21 **Will Rogers quote Part 1**
23 **Quote: Part 2**
25 90° from ESE
26 Beaut
27 Desert of southern Israel
29 Some Japanese-Americans
30 Ward of "Once and Again"
32 Site of Kublai Khan's pleasure dome
34 Whirlpools
35 East German secret police once
37 Houston squad member
40 Combo vaccination
41 **Quote: Part 3**
47 Year in Rio
48 "You're going ___?"
49 Joe Buck's pal
50 Big "Big" star
52 Washroom, briefly
53 "For Your Eyes Only" villain
54 Ming relic
58 Glue factory candidates
61 **Quote: Part 4**
63 Slasher film sounds
65 "The Time Machine" people
66 Forenoons, in brief
68 Belfast inits.
70 Perfume ingredient
71 Boneless cut
73 Bunco artist
76 Pioneer cell phone co.
77 **Quote: Part 5**
80 Source of royal insomnia?
82 Wrigley gum brand since 1984
83 E. Spitzer, e.g.
84 Discrete unit
86 Loch monster's moniker
89 Marine shade
93 "SNL" alumna Oteri
94 Old Oldsmobile model
96 "I have a dream" source: Init.
98 News agcy. formed in 1958
99 **Quote: Part 6**
101 **Quote: Part 7**
104 Québec's ___ de la Madeleine
105 Bart's grandfather
106 Adjudge
107 Presentation aid
108 Bag of pretzels, perhaps
109 Opposite of masc.
110 There are 10 million in a joule
111 Flashy Chevy

DOWN

1 Occurs to (with "on")
2 Sherlock's love
3 Bel Air or Biscayne
4 Roxy Music founder
5 Be a stool pigeon
6 SWAT team gear
7 Sister of Jackie Onassis
8 "Gladiator" setting
9 Like many ballparks
10 Rope fiber
11 Sea of ___ (Black Sea arm)
12 Eve's origin
13 Kilt pattern
14 Public grant to private enterprise
15 Napping
16 True believer
22 Uncle Miltie's sponsor
24 Permanently funds
28 Its capital is Hagatña
31 Batty wood?
33 Williamson in "Excalibur"
34 Sexually provocative
36 "The Gondoliers" flower girl
38 "Que" follower, in song
39 Pre-1917 dictators
41 It was a Blazer until 1995
42 Firing ___ cylinders
43 Apt. alternative
44 Multicolored horse
45 Bill
46 Copters do this
51 Beaver cleaver?
55 Gutteral cry of frustration
56 Do in, Biblically
57 Ruhr River city
59 Ford that debuted in 1995
60 Silvery fish
62 Enterprise counselor Deanna
64 Sonata section
67 The slammer, slangily
69 Poker pot starters
72 Joke response
74 Caps
75 Theatrical backers
77 Some paints
78 Billy in "Titanic"
79 New Deal program: Abbr.
80 Jelly ingredient
81 Surround, in a way
85 From Killarney
87 Eat away at
88 Stahl and Kroft colleague
90 Search
91 In a dither
92 Bride's path
94 Rubik creation
95 Romantic duo in tabloids
97 Capital of Ukraine
100 Big ox
102 ___ the question
103 Not, to a Scot

199 INNER SOL by Lucille Sloan

The clue at 54 Across is right on the money.

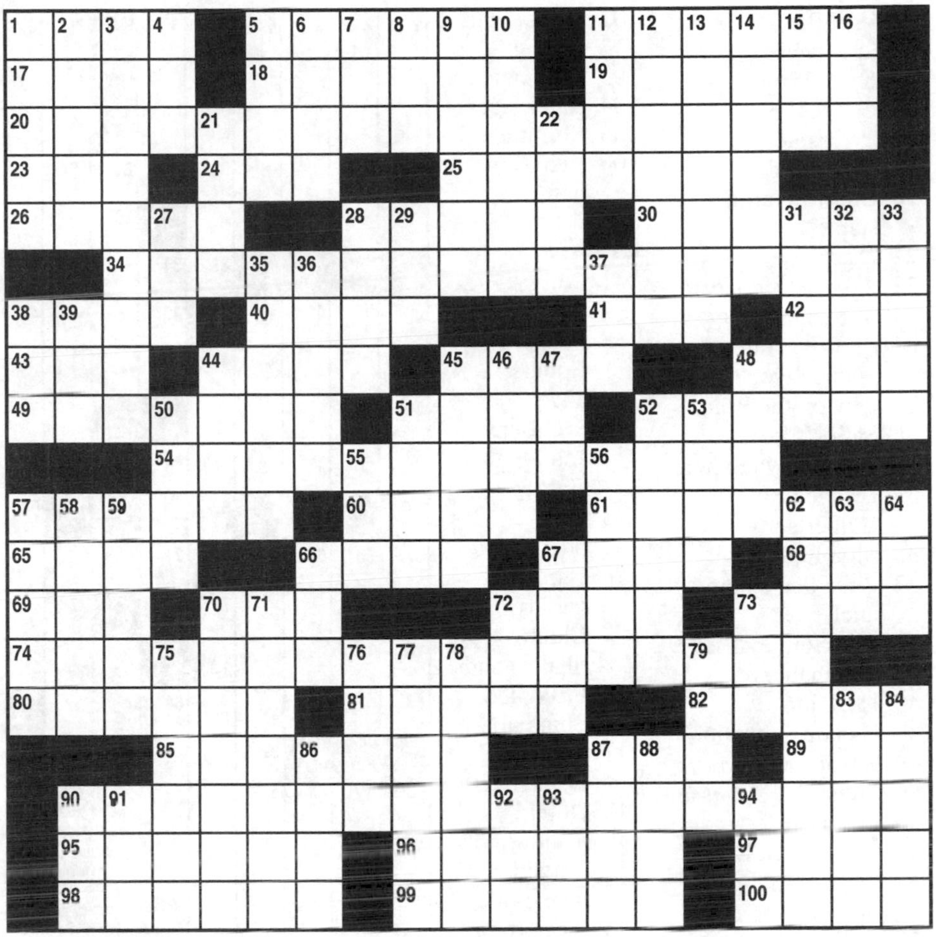

ACROSS

1 Land leader?
5 Cleans the floor
11 "Enduring Love" novelist Ian
17 "Are you out ___?"
18 End's uniform part
19 Baroque
20 Dictionary phrase
23 P.D.Q. mem.
24 Absorb, as costs
25 Person receiving a deed
26 Slangy assents
28 One who's learning
30 Weissmuller role
34 Big East's Scarlet Knights
38 It may be flipped
40 Home of the Phoenix
41 LSAT takers
42 Grier of "Jackie Brown"
43 Marilu on "Evening Shade"
44 Peevish state
45 Ghana neighbor
48 Apple discard
49 Was part of the pack
51 Not bats
52 "That's being taken care of by me!"
54 Coined phrase?
57 Music box?
60 Well intro
61 Opts for
65 Kind of view
66 Stub ___
67 ___ majesty
68 Piniella of baseball
69 Place below Eur.
70 Logical conclusion
72 Superciliousness
73 Nut
74 Indicators of sleeplessness
80 Impassive
81 Ducts
82 Highly skilled
85 Menu heading
87 Lock sight
89 Nest egg letters
90 "Law and Order" series
95 1957 Presley hit
96 Crude petroleum component
97 Vocal pitch
98 Candy brand
99 Mariners
100 ___'acte

DOWN

1 Modest and then some
2 Rocky prominence
3 Marian's "The Music Man" role
4 Opposite of ques.
5 1986 World Series site
6 "Who ___ and art and . . ." (hymn lyric)
7 The PGA's "Big Easy"
8 Bird on Australia's coat of arms
9 City in eastern China
10 Head the cast of
11 Dawn, to Donne
12 Informal animal
13 Makes lovable
14 Stakes money
15 Dug, with "up"
16 Verne harpooner
21 Cranmer's concern
22 Island east of Java
27 Barbarian
28 Meth., e.g.
29 Swabber's org.
31 Like some jacket hoods
32 Electronic game pioneer
33 K. Hernandez was one
35 Not likely to bite
36 Root of Yale
37 Abbr. on a brandy label
38 Ride provider
39 Reproductive cells
44 Drinks slowly
45 Spreadsheet section
46 Weight
47 Some appliances
48 "Follow me"
50 Tax
51 Minuteman's place
52 Actually
53 Asinine shoe?
55 Mob pariah
56 Sponges, so to speak
57 Grouches
58 Skim, as soup
59 Stevedore's concern
62 Approach
63 Immoderately
64 STAR
66 Insert
67 Is untrustworthy
70 Fruit that resemble pears
71 Oft-prophesied about era
72 Certain colonist
73 Paved the way
75 Place for an arm
76 Big name in daredeviltry
77 Medieval stewards
78 Like some maintenance
79 Edible roots
83 Fine stuff
84 ___ Tots
86 John and Charlotte
87 Feast (on)
88 Pious agreement
90 35mm camera
91 "The Raven" poet
92 Single dance move?
93 Topper for a lass
94 Beehive State athlete

200 DROPS FROM THE START by Robert A. Doll

The clue at 45 Across can be interpreted two ways.

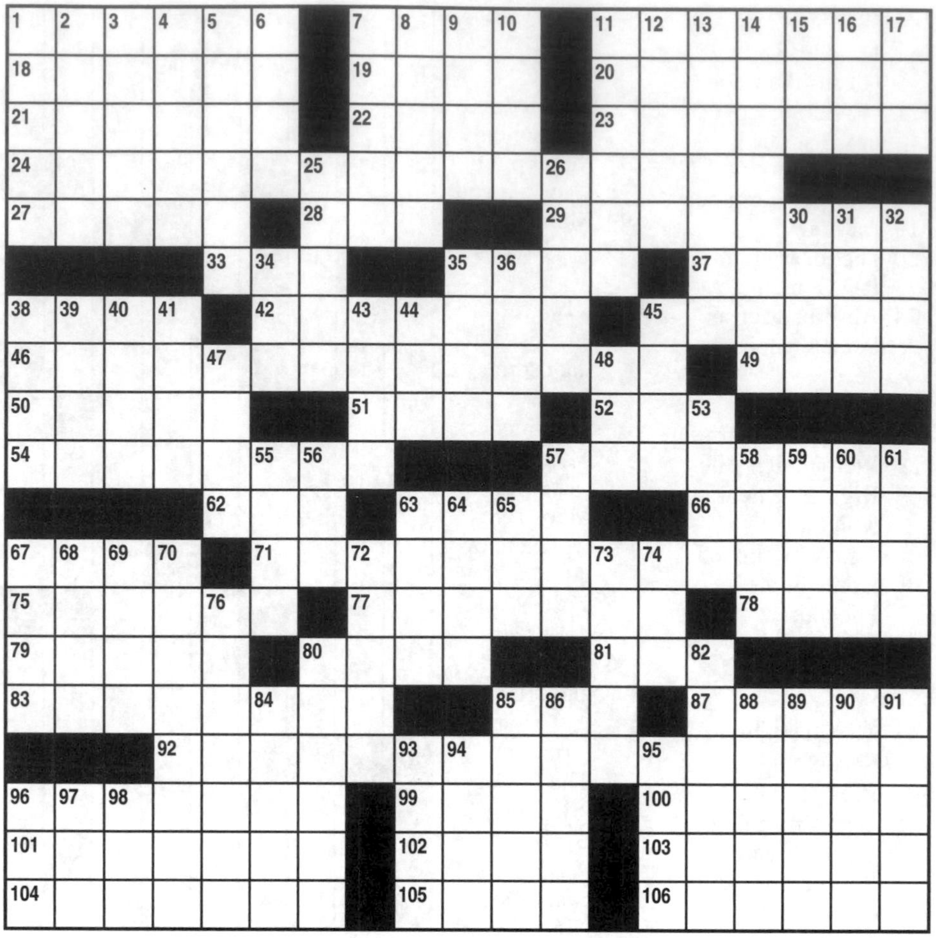

ACROSS

1 Spectacles
7 Kind of rat
11 Concoct
18 ___ aspic
19 Chills and fever
20 Chef Boyardee staple
21 Dress styles
22 Arborist's concern
23 Stress, in a way
24 La Brea couple who pitched woo?
27 City on the Ruhr
28 Sailor's assent
29 Chemistry lab item
33 Bridge guru Culbertson
35 Mountains
37 Pinballer Tommy's uncle
38 Port Stanley's lake
42 Laughable
45 Desk job
46 Bad bug situation?
49 Response to Marco
50 Fugard's "A Lesson From ___"
51 Giant great Kyle
52 Get-up-and-go
54 Sound
57 Self-important
62 ___ Paulo
63 Bring on
66 Cree craft
67 Chooses (with "for")
71 Packers' field?
75 Beat to death
77 Surpassed
78 Not so much
79 Lexington's Rupp is one
80 Crossword humor
81 Go on to say
83 Rotary Club meeting, often
85 More, in Madrid
87 Inedible orange
92 Space Shuttle's ET?
96 Taira no Kiyomori, for one
99 Corn bread
100 Huxley's last novel
101 Spark
102 Gloria Patri ending
103 Complete
104 Light lager
105 Multitude
106 Like some hair

DOWN

1 Polity
2 Tabs
3 Mideast leaders
4 Vice President John ___ Garner
5 Forever, poetically
6 Garden-variety
7 Chump
8 Shake hands
9 Prompted
10 Ship part
11 Sunday excursions
12 Hotel posting
13 Turned inside-out
14 Place for a crop duster, often
15 Bygone bird
16 Final: Abbr.
17 Cap-a-___ (head to foot)
25 Authority
26 Playful aquatic animal
30 "For ___ us a child is born . . ."
31 High school subj.
32 Architect Saarinen
34 PC linkup
35 Emily's ___
36 Fairy-tale opener
38 Greek H's
39 Tick off
40 Computer image
41 Barely gets by (with "out")
43 About, on a memo
44 Conservative leader
45 Decorative pitcher
47 Egyptian fertility goddess
48 Aries mo.
53 Somewhat, to Salieri
55 Huge loss, in jargon
56 Mauna ___
57 Jason's ship
58 France, under Caesar
59 Infant photographer Geddes
60 Auction actions
61 Miss Durbeyfield
63 Pirouetted
64 Stones
65 South Bend college
67 Kind of agreement
68 Cuzco's country
69 In that case
70 Inner ___ (secret places)
72 Hood or Rushmore
73 Grind the teeth
74 "Galloping Ghost" Grange
76 Hot and dry
80 More laggard
82 Fails to
84 Related on the mother's side
85 Word with land or strip
86 Player's rep
88 ___ dog cocktail
89 Be of use to
90 Film noir, e.g.
91 Wrapped up
93 Sushi fish
94 ___ erectus
95 Goes quickly
96 Weaken
97 "Wheel of Fortune" purchase
98 Wire number

201 FAB HITS by Harvey Estes

79 Across is a place in a novel by 111 Across.

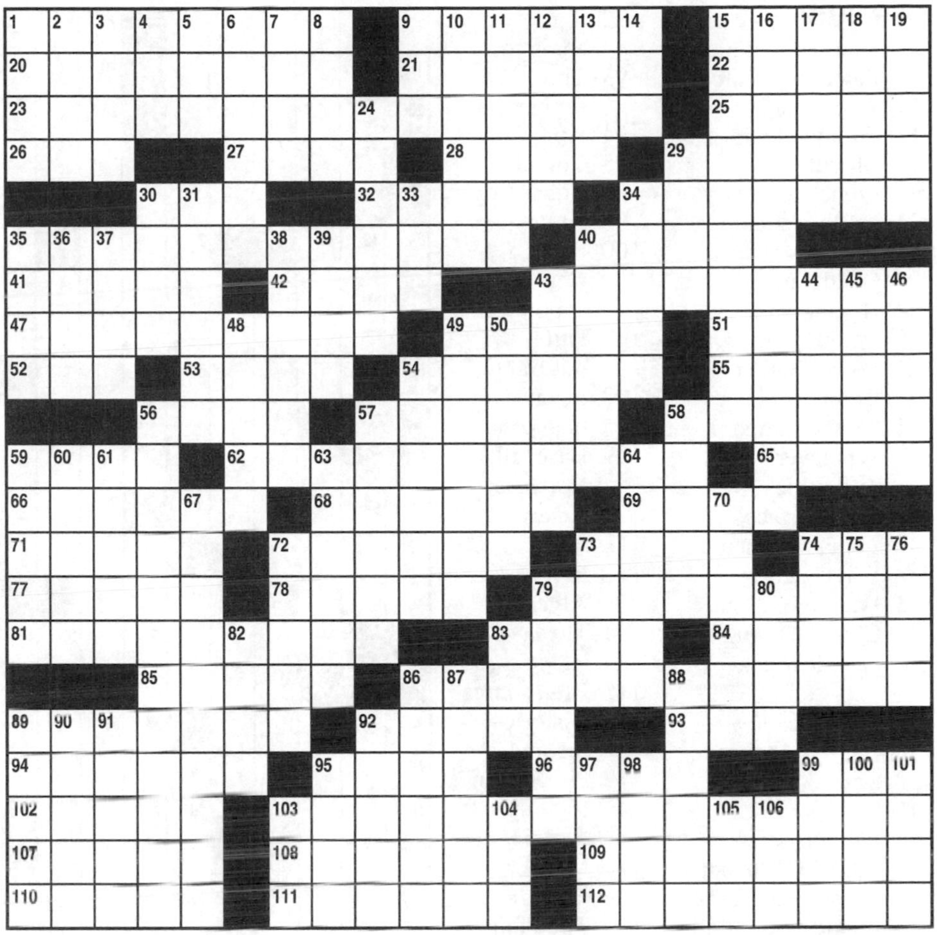

ACROSS

1 Took the beltway around
9 Free from care
15 Trait bearers
20 All told
21 Big bullies
22 Avoid capture
23 1966 Beatles #1 hit
25 Of few words
26 Many mins.
27 Can't stomach
28 Like a case from long ago
29 Showing prejudice
30 Pay ender
32 Highly skilled
34 Tornado parts
35 1965 Beatles #1 hit
40 Upper body
41 Kind of supervision
42 "I thought we ___ deal!"
43 Stork stat
47 Worth of a business
49 Cook in butter
51 Specter of the U.S. Senate
52 Regular or high-test
53 Toothpaste types
54 Litterbug's leavings
55 Formed a stack
56 Ian of "Alien"
57 Mexican state bordering Arizona
58 Saskatchewan's capital
59 Novel ending
62 1968 Beatles #1 hit
65 Type of seller
66 Court figures
68 Links up
69 "An apple ___ . . ."
71 Bird's sound
72 Some computers
73 Bard's home
74 Funny guy
77 Swashbuckling Flynn
78 Some German autos
79 Utopia
81 Stars on the wane
83 "Looks like trouble!"
84 Slangy farewell
85 Talk show tycoon
86 1969 Beatles #1 hit
89 Oily disinfectant
92 Burton of "Star Trek"
93 Train cos.
94 Hang in there
95 Auntie of Broadway
96 Part of UTEP
99 Site for three men in a tub
102 "I was elsewhere" excuse
103 1966 Beatles #1 hit
107 Pretty Boy of crime
108 Meeting schedule
109 Get snockered
110 Elaborate parties
111 "Lost Horizon" author
112 Barbeau of "Maude"

DOWN

1 Birch of Indiana
2 Belgian border river
3 Good buddies
4 Leather worker's tool
5 HBO rival
6 "Big deal"
7 Lanchester of "Bride of Frankenstein"
8 Bk. of the Pentateuch
9 SDI weapon
10 Followed the trail of
11 The Continent
12 At an angle
13 Cell-phone button
14 Language ending
15 Fit the mold?
16 1966 Beatles #1 hit
17 Tend with tenderness
18 Ford flub
19 Lawn starters
24 Chin covers
29 Songwriter Bacharach
30 Ark. neighbor
31 "C'mon!"
33 Domingo, for example
34 Links cries
35 Zesty flavor
36 Brainstorming product
37 Loin and shank, e.g.
38 Louise's film cohort
39 Rolled items
40 "Venus of Urbino" painter
43 Pack animals
44 Kate's sitcom companion
45 Adolescents
46 Stop with
48 Puts on eBay, e.g.
49 Legislative houses
50 Places to call home
54 Part of A.D.
56 1967 Beatles #1 hit
57 Church councils
58 Household hazard
59 Register
60 2008 Dodgers coach
61 Sporty Ford, for short
63 City on Lake Superior
64 Arizona tribe
67 Round solids
70 Bait buyer
72 Martian marking
73 "Cat on ___ Tin Roof"
74 On the side of
75 Helm location
76 Teri of "Mr. Mom"
79 Everest guide, often
80 Hamelin menace
82 Memphis middle name
83 Thurman in "Bee Movie"
86 Make firm
87 Take too far
88 Farmer
89 Grain husks
90 Esther of "Good Times"
91 "The Hollow Men" poet
92 Jacket flap
95 Traveling trio
97 Court records
98 Fail to grip the road
99 British carbine
100 Working stiff
101 Composer Thomas
103 "Fiddlesticks!"
104 Prohibition
105 Lyon king
106 Having four sharps

202 PUTTING IT POLITELY by Tucker Smith

The "King of Country Music" can be found at 95 Across.

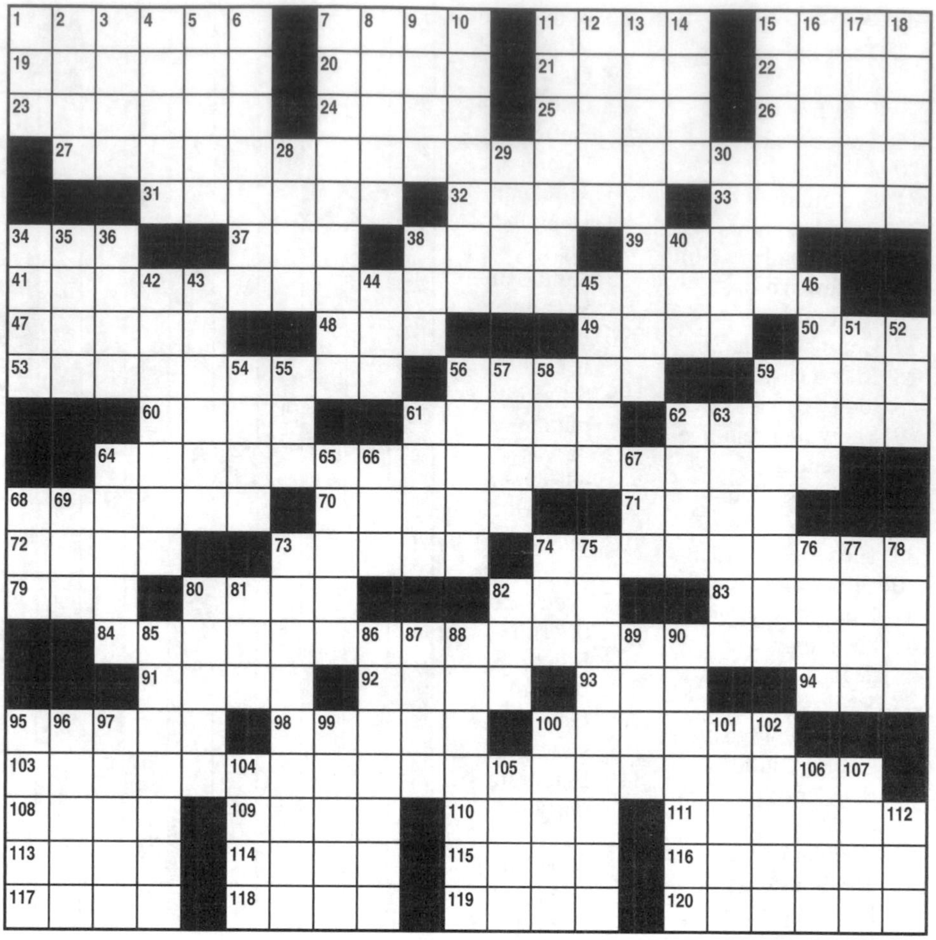

ACROSS

1 Atami entertainer
7 Pay attention to
11 Two-master
15 Torah holders
19 Ill will
20 French auxiliary
21 Buffalo's lake
22 Pride member
23 Off the mark
24 Hood's blade
25 Thomson in "Other Voices, Other Rooms"
26 "Fame" singer Irene
27 Whatever difficulties
31 Gem surfaces
32 "What Women Want" actress
33 Walton of "The Compleat Angler"
34 Decide to leave, with "out"
37 Lush meadow
38 C&W's McEntire
39 Barrie pooch
41 Macho mantra
47 Eskimo digs
48 "Bambi" character
49 Dessert cart items
50 La mer, essentially
53 "Wait a minute!"
56 French Revolution figure
59 Ming artifact
60 Israeli diplomat Abba
61 Belt clip-on
62 Burnout consequence
64 Show remorse
68 Trick
70 Filed items
71 Crucifix letters
72 Course finale
73 Suit fabric
74 Home entertainment medium
79 Jerry Stiller's son
80 Nincompoop
82 Links statistic
83 Graceful
84 Words before "full speed ahead"
91 Taurus tankful
92 Stack acronym
93 Three R's supporter
94 King Cole
95 Country singer Roy
98 Union part
100 Reagan Court appointee
103 Fail miserably
108 Science magazine
109 Baseball's Hershiser
110 Ad award
111 Rum drink
113 Port of Algeria
114 Theda of the silents
115 Bran source
116 Historical records
117 Phoenician trading center
118 Mayberry jailbird
119 They follow exes
120 Get plenty of sleep

DOWN

1 Hurdle for srs.
2 Wyatt of the West
3 Memo opener
4 Complement to earmuffs
5 Civic maker
6 Constitution component
7 Thinks twice, perhaps
8 Guiding beliefs
9 Moran of "Happy Days"
10 Fan
11 Cat's assent
12 PGA "army" leader
13 Playing by ear
14 Levi's mother
15 Moorish castle
16 Steer stopper
17 "M*A*S*H" locale
18 Carroll creature
28 Souvenir buys
29 Holds up
30 Some brown-baggers
34 "Door's open, come ___"
35 Walt Kelly strip
36 Cheat at pinball
38 Genetic info carrier
40 Malt drink
42 Biting midge
43 "What a shame"
44 Bank acct. entry
45 Illusory paintings
46 "Sailing to Byzantium" poet
51 Fire residue
52 One-eighty
54 What will be
55 To some extent
56 Sweet sap source
57 Processes wine or cheese
58 Room opener
59 Check-cashing requirement
61 Fuddy-duddy
62 "Rule, Britannia" composer
63 Early release
64 Fudd's voice
65 Lunch time, for some
66 Former Mideast org.
67 Suffix with human or fact
68 Cotillion honoree
69 Program file extension
73 Sniff out trouble
74 Dye container
75 German military decoration
76 Lay-thick connector
77 Queens ballpark
78 That's French
80 Smokeless tobacco
81 Chemical ending
82 Get-up-and-go
85 Disconnected
86 Cage of films
87 Comparison connector
88 "Unbelievable!"
89 Peer at a page
90 California observatory Mount
95 Going on
96 Toyota sedan
97 Of an armbone
99 Cheri of "Scary Movie"
100 Hotel upgrade
101 Totally ridiculous
102 Actor Claude
104 Gray wolf
105 Oil of ___
106 Maine, to Monet
107 Yellow Sea feeder
112 AOL or EarthLink

203 OLLA PODRIDA by Harvey Estes

46 Down is also the name of a college in Amherst, Massachusetts.

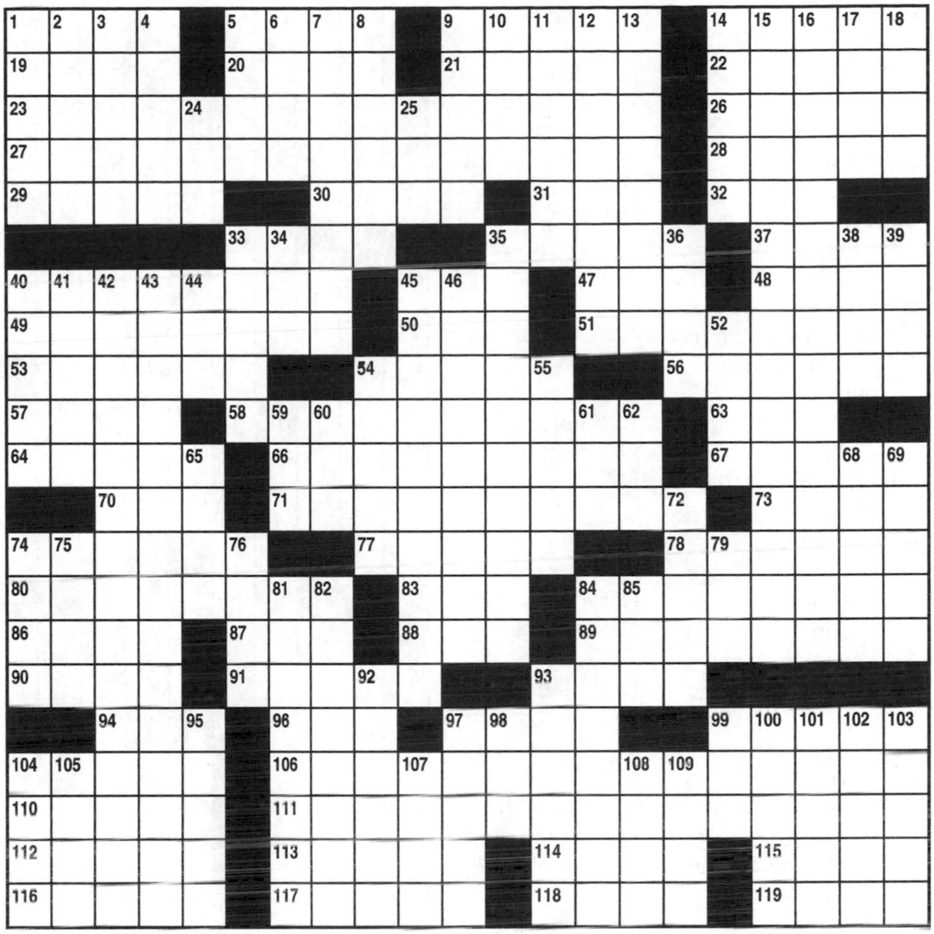

ACROSS

1 Oliver's partner
5 "Sorry . . ."
9 See-through sealer
14 Avid golfer's wife
19 Switch add-on
20 Vein contents
21 It could be a grand
22 Cheri of "Scary Movie"
23 Executive's climb
26 Playful aquatic critter
27 Passing the bar?
28 Jumping the gun
29 Fifth wheel
30 Exploits
31 D.C. summer hrs.
32 MGM rival, once
33 Dijon dad
35 They chase flies
37 Cork's country
40 Remove minimally
45 Sailing pronoun
47 Broadway bio
48 British arm
49 Sound quality
50 Back tap
51 Caught
53 Draws a bead on
54 Bar stock
56 Shantytown composition
57 Solidify
58 Ray trap
63 Disencumber
64 Beat Ken
66 Obstinate
67 E'er
70 6-pointers
71 Make wedding plans
73 Dietary, in ads
74 Like R versus PG-13
77 Matched furniture
78 "Thank U" singer Morissette
80 Artery without blockage?
83 Art, today
84 Stray
86 Ernie's roommate
87 Sch. subj.
88 Guitar master Paul
89 Advance trials
90 Italian noble family
91 Apple supports
93 Piped up
94 "Exodus" character
96 Olympics chant word
97 Big bucks and small
99 "Same here!"
104 Practiced, as a trade
106 Thinks out loud
110 Just know
111 Dumbo, notably
112 Crew on a ship
113 ___ Cologne
114 Lod lander
115 And so
116 Private meeting
117 Pfeiffer in "Brothers in Arms"
118 Unit of force
119 Talk like Popeye

DOWN

1 Shakers and Quakers
2 Hike
3 Main trunk
4 Kind of stock
5 Mrs. Dithers of "Blondie"
6 Mubarak, for one
7 Goes site-seeing?
8 Fly in the tropics
9 Crosses
10 West Wing worker
11 Baba Wawa portrayer
12 Personal account
13 Not for recycling
14 Beau
15 Hillary Clinton book
16 Motown players
17 First name in pitching
18 Lean
24 Hurrah for Jose
25 Stay flat
33 Pound and others
34 Georgia O'Keeffe's pair
35 Chats
36 Fanny
38 Projector load
39 Pair in a line
40 Crude site
41 ___ Selassic
42 Chances are
43 Personal stakes
44 Aunt in "Bambi"
45 "Go Down, Moses" and others
46 Black and white pig
52 Mother of "Brothers & Sisters"
54 Stands the test of time
55 Like a snicker
59 Places for MDs
60 Appomattox figure
61 Spacewalk, at NASA
62 Do-over
65 Belgian border river
68 Listing
69 Green lights
72 Like cornstalks
74 Ceremonial garb
75 Henchmen
76 "Mahogany" star
79 Not long.
81 Put into motion
82 Hymn about the Day of Judgment
84 How deserts are populated
85 Corn starter
92 Plunder and pillage
93 Placed in the Open
95 Latin clarifier
97 Gifted person
98 Heading abbr.
99 Chip accessory
100 "Devil ___ Heart": Beatles
101 Papal crown
102 Ice grabbers
103 Sitting pretty
104 "Hey!"
105 Cordelia's father
107 Beef unit
108 Pearl Buck heroine
109 Soccer great

204 HAT TRICK by Alyssa Brooke

1 Across is also a sci-fi series with Hayden Panettiere.

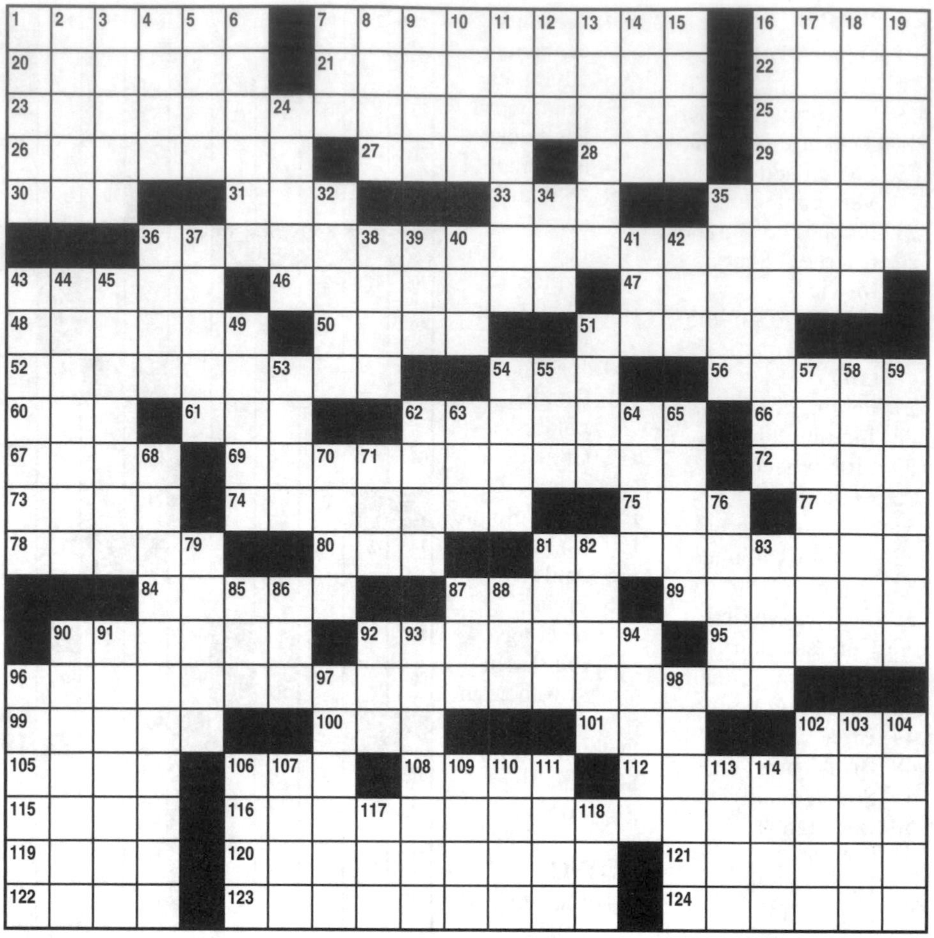

ACROSS

1 They save the day
7 Going back to an earlier time
16 Serious sign
20 Ax to grind
21 Fleeting
22 Glowing review
23 Comedy about Gandhi?
25 Captain Hook's ally
26 Money coming in
27 Vincent Lopez theme song
28 Brown from the sun
29 Galley propellers
30 Canonized Mlle.
31 Printer's measures
33 Sign of a hit
35 We–please bridge
36 Try to penetrate a lineup?
43 Panoramic view
46 Made noise in the stable
47 College officer
48 Buries
50 Picnic infestation
51 Airport transports
52 Cool Sean Combs?
54 Coffee, in slang
56 Artless ones
60 Dawber of "Mork & Mindy"
61 "Star-Spangled Banner" preposition
62 Egyptian symbols
66 Monogram pt.
67 To some degree
69 Nutritionist's talk?
72 Andrews in "Laura"
73 Trig ratio
74 Serial segment
75 Chairman of note
77 Lunch holder
78 Walk stiffly
80 Place for a price
81 Divination book about eggs?
84 Roundup rope
87 Its HQ is in Brussels
89 Hitting position
90 Woman's shoe feature
92 "My Own Private Idaho" director Gus
95 Old-timer
96 Cry of "Big deal! Indiscretions!"?
99 Canary call
100 Thus far
101 PIN requester
102 Indy 500 sponsor
105 "Yeah, sure"
106 DVR attachments
108 Foreboding
112 Sedatives
115 The N in N.B.
116 Source of a blood feud?
119 Irk big-time
120 With all sincerity
121 Like some fingerprints
122 Eye problem
123 Woos musically
124 Diplomatic agents

DOWN

1 Wig components
2 Plumed wader
3 "The Canterbury Tales" pilgrim
4 Round-buyer's words
5 Forbidden fruit site
6 Gunmaker Colt
7 Letters in some church names
8 Having a hard time choosing
9 Bullets and shells
10 Kind of cutlet
11 Lickety-split
12 RR terminal
13 Name in a heart, perhaps
14 La Douce of film
15 Greenish blue
16 As people claim
17 "Oh, my!"
18 Muscle that rotates a part outward
19 Liam in "Breakfast on Pluto"
24 Porto Novo's land
32 Place
34 Mayberry mail service
35 Hammerin' Hank
36 Let be, editorially
37 "SNL" announcer Don
38 Itsy-bitsy
39 Elev.
40 Massage reactions
41 Baseball card stat
42 Tight-lipped
43 Concert comp
44 Occupy
45 Staying power
49 Holey utensil
51 Levi's mother
53 Leaky faucet sound
54 Eyre of fiction
55 Killer whale
57 Needing help
58 Put up the cash for
59 Walk in a crooked line
62 Urban air problem
63 Spanish hero, with "El"
64 The Crimson Tide, to fans
65 Census output
68 Be a raconteur
70 Brother of Jermaine
71 Former Congressman Hutchinson
76 Four pairs
79 Gold weight
81 Neighbor of Aust.
82 Civic-minded company?
83 Dutch painter Frans
85 Posed for pics
86 Maxwell Smart, for one
87 U-turn from SSE
88 "Just ___ suspected!"
90 Harbor vessel
91 In a pleasing manner
92 Saturn SUV
93 Johnny Carson character
94 From bottom ___
96 Wasp woes
97 Maryland mollusk
98 Medical vial
102 Fifth-century Pope
103 Lilliputian
104 Attention-getting sounds
106 Not that
107 Weather indicator
109 Ferber or Best
110 Scored 100 on
111 Blush libation
113 "No man ___ island . . ."
114 Play's end, perhaps
117 Comic actress Charlotte
118 ACLU concerns

205 "AHOY, MATEY!" by Arlan and Linda Bushman

In 2007 Mr. Symington went public about the 1 Across he claimed to have seen.

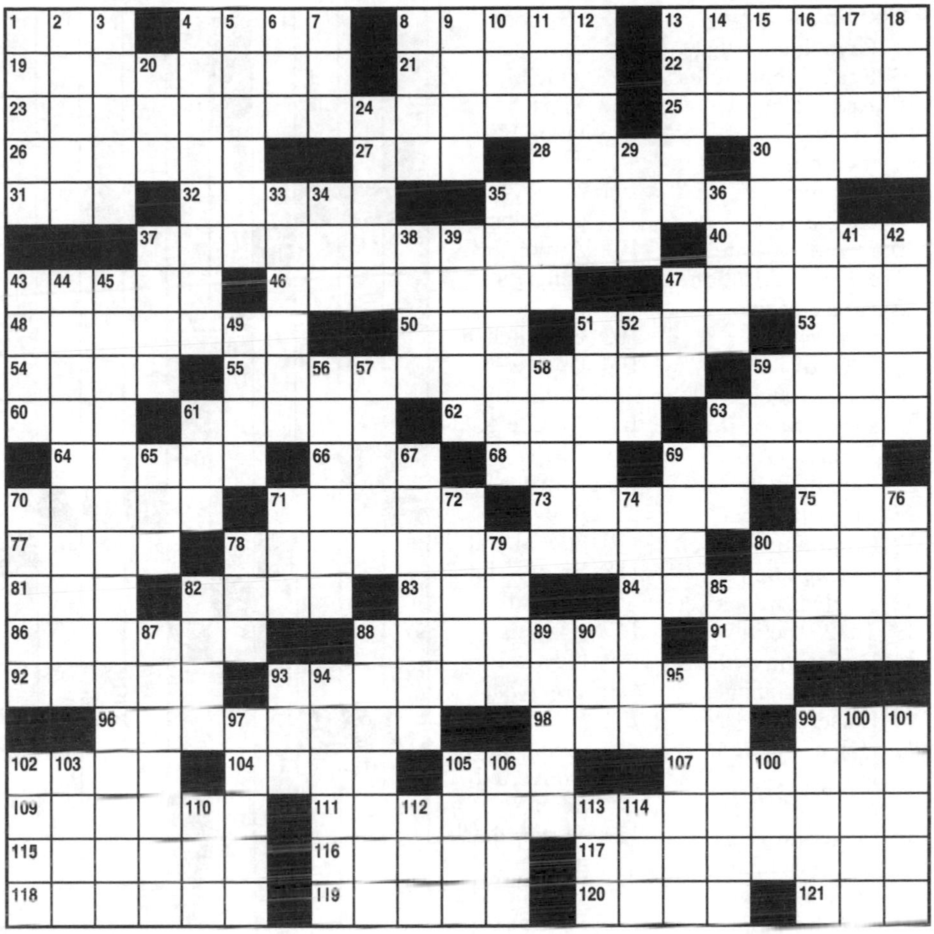

ACROSS

1 What Gov. Symington saw on 3/13/97
4 Time to beware
8 Blows hard
13 Dismay
19 On the stout side
21 "Middlemarch" author
22 Actress North
23 Name on a ballerina's boat?
25 Con game victim
26 Group with shared culture
27 Took in
28 Super Bowl XXXVI year
30 Barley bristles
31 Lunar New Year
32 Dolphins home
35 Porter tote
37 Name on a songwriter's boat?
40 ___ the test
43 Travel documents
46 South Seas islands, collectively
47 Worked together
48 Old-time desk slot
50 Concession
51 Wilbur's friend
53 Result
54 Goddess of discord
55 Name on a chef's boat?
59 "Judith" composer
60 Mos of "Be Kind Rewind"
61 Have for sale
62 Lyric poem
63 His and her
64 Retro hairdos
66 Dismiss
68 What to do at 77 Across
69 Appeals
70 Obscure
71 Venus offspring
73 First name in cosmetics
75 Pharaonic symbol
77 Kitzbühel peaks
78 Name on Intel's boat?
80 Twinge
81 Dangerous current
82 Heaps
83 Hawaiian acacia
84 Thoughtless criticism
86 Words of regret
88 Peso division
91 Observances
92 Attack from all sides
93 Name on Sunoco's boat?
96 They're kept in the freezer section
98 Just for laughs
99 Old saying
102 Hand, informally
104 Vega's constellation
105 Brace
107 Book of prophecies
109 Richards of "Jurassic Park"
111 Name on Ernestine's boat?
115 Campfire treats
116 Strong point
117 Golfer's concerns
118 "Dust in the Wind" band
119 Profoundness
120 Impertinence
121 Flap

DOWN

1 Discomfit
2 Champagne glass
3 Not quite must
4 Vower's declaration
5 Uses a ladle
6 Night class subj.
7 Moo ___ pork
8 Lift up
9 Beekeeper of film
10 Cone producer
11 Chemist's derivation
12 Frustrate
13 Savory jelly
14 21st Greek letter
15 Magic steed of myth
16 Name on impatient kid's boat?
17 Pugilist Spinks
18 Optical device
20 Valet
24 Acadia National Park site
29 Vital addition
33 Famed Harlem theater
34 Slicker
35 Boo-boos
36 Parodied
37 Shooting marbles
38 Surprised reaction
39 Battery part
41 Gym bag find
42 More fishy
43 Contended
44 Outside the realm of daydreams
45 Name on an enemy's boat?
47 Sea, to Henri
49 D-Day boats
51 Fashionable
52 Deplore
56 Supernatural
57 Giraffe cousin
58 Comic bits
59 "I knew it!"
61 Turf
63 ___ Cool (Green Day drummer)
65 Lat. neighbor
67 Some change
69 Pumpkin, for example
70 West Indies native
71 Union letters
72 John Ridd's wife
74 Give a warning
76 Guinea pigs, often
78 Furtive
79 Brussels group
80 Seller's admonition
82 Old, in Bonn
85 Crossings
87 Honey raw materials
88 Disinfect
89 Charged atom
90 Max ___ Sydow
93 Bloke
94 On a world tour
95 Escorts
97 Stylish manner
99 18th Greek letter
100 Let out a sigh
101 "___ glum?"
102 Halloween piece
103 Rombauer of cookery
105 Waste allowance of old
106 Accompanying
108 Tropical bird
110 PBS funder
112 Special insight
113 Porsche 904 ___
114 Pro's vote

206 BREAKING OTT IS HARD TO DO by Harvey Estes

Alternate clue for 28 Down: Dubya's father, to Yale.

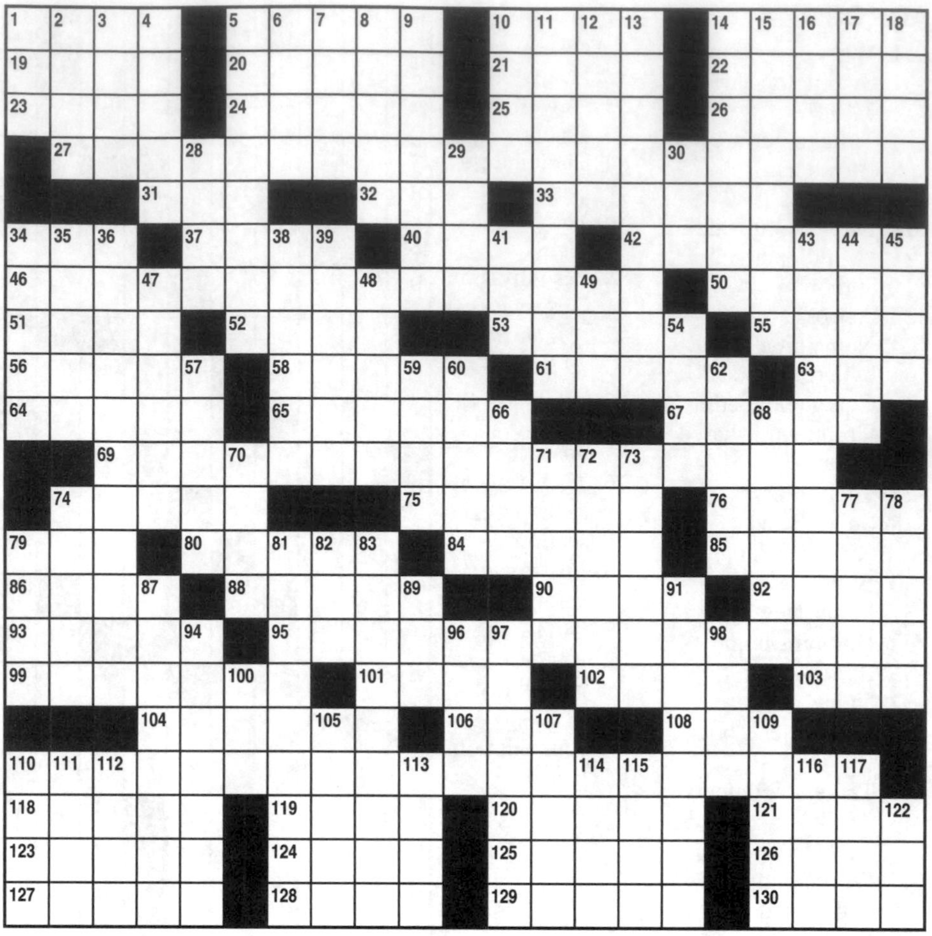

ACROSS

1 Give this for that
5 Bea's sitcom role
10 Arizona city
14 "You ___ mouthful!"
19 Hemingway nickname
20 Knot-tying site
21 Picnic infestation
22 House of two Henrys
23 "Son of Frankenstein" shepherd
24 Roundup rope
25 Standing on
26 Rep with a cut
27 Communicate well
31 Chicago trains
32 Fizzled firecracker
33 Tube repetitions
34 Beginning with law
37 Diamond judges
40 Raise Cain
42 Helper in crime
46 Ultimatum about a pet
50 Jacket material
51 One mo' time
52 Pianist Peter
53 Disadvantage
55 Scissor sound
56 Classmate of Dobie
58 Come up
61 Just beat, with "out"
63 USMC barracks boss
64 Firebug's crime
65 Tick of the clock
67 The sky, for some
69 Best loan conditions
74 Mazda model
75 Mexican ma'am
76 Chin dimple
79 Patriotic soc.
80 Per ___ (yearly)
84 Michelangelo masterpiece
85 Nametag word
86 Reformer Jacob
88 Frightfully strange
90 Live ___ (be in the closet, e.g.)
92 Auction web site
93 Prior to
95 "Nobody runs the table"
99 Most favorably situated
101 Money-object bridge
102 Armchair athlete's channel
103 Got hitched
104 Gym wear, familiarly
106 AOL, e.g.
108 Peri's "Frasier" role
110 "Let's do it!"
118 Ex of "The Donald"
119 Hyena's hideaway
120 Trims back
121 Bit of moonshine
123 Converted pounds
124 Misses the mark
125 Leg shackles
126 Pink, in a steakhouse
127 Shangri-las
128 Cager Thurmond
129 Universal donor
130 Asian sea name

DOWN

1 Undercover agent
2 Droll folks
3 Price phrase
4 Cole Porter title city
5 Good shooters
6 Hit the ground
7 Orrin Hatch's state
8 Saw socially
9 Sign of a goof
10 Polite address
11 Joined, redundantly
12 Got to second base, perhaps
13 Veggie with spears
14 She's often depicted holding a lamb
15 Caesar's successor
16 Creative spark
17 Syllable preceding "The witch is dead!"
18 Comedian Johnson
28 Dubya, to Yale
29 "The Wedding Singer" star Sandler
30 Heart of the matter
34 Town square
35 Pilot's OK
36 Unholy ghosts?
38 "May I?"
39 Reddish-brown horse
41 Nautilus locale
43 Repetitive motion problem
44 Royal decree
45 Debtor's car, maybe
47 "Bewitched" mother
48 Say-so
49 Lennon's mate
54 "Once and Again" actress Ward
57 Old juice booster Bryant
59 Blue-bootie babies
60 Came to a halt
62 Get rid of
66 Meyer of "Saw"
68 Free-for-alls
70 Neck hair
71 Exploding suns
72 Bug catcher on the road
73 Two-way devices
74 Battleship to remember
77 Moth drawer
78 Played (with)
79 Defeat decisively
81 Like fresh snow
82 Swiss canton
83 Mod wear
87 Audits, as a class
89 Curve shape
91 Strong joe
94 Service that isn't sung
96 Tending to the problem
97 Dangerous place to dance
98 Chimp in space
100 Bank charge
105 Papal crown
107 Like an Anjou?
109 Referee, slangily
110 Company with a swoosh
111 "Metamorphoses" poet
112 Chaucer piece
113 Celtic tongue
114 Stage item
115 Russo of "Tin Cup"
116 In the vicinity
117 Movie plantation
122 Ott "broken" in 5 answers in this puzzle

207 CHALLENGER by Harvey Estes

57 Across was named for the wife of George III.

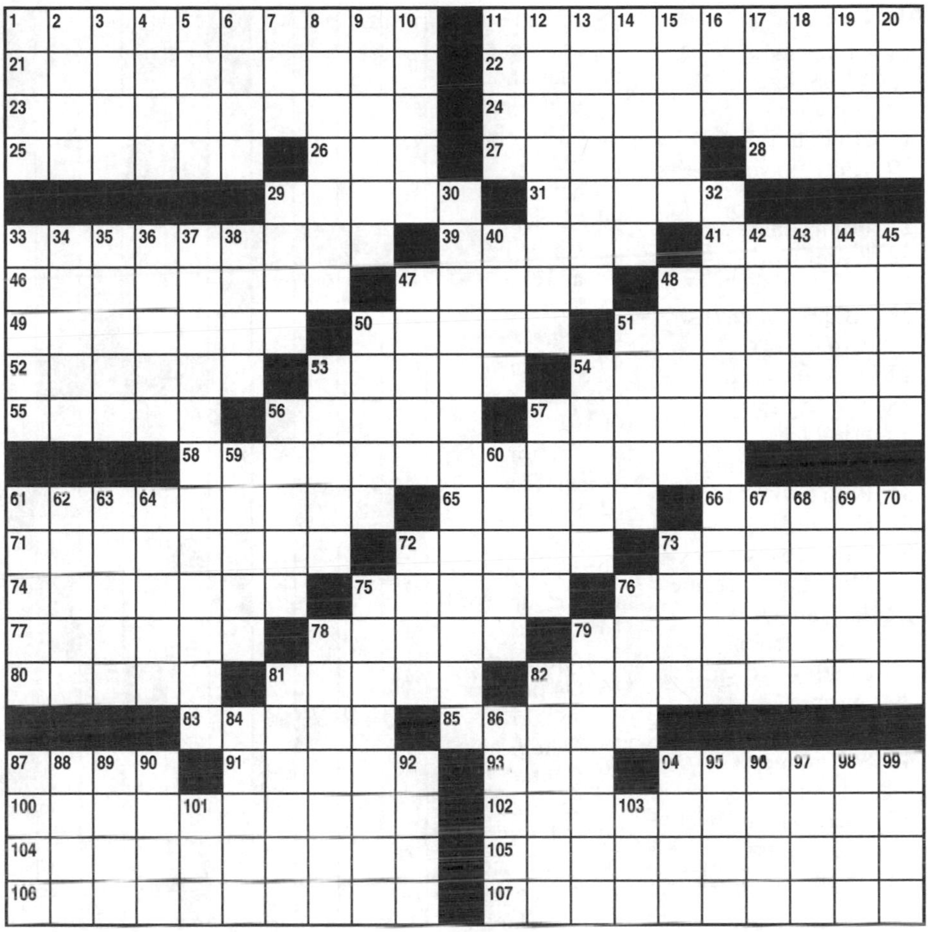

ACROSS

1 It can be a pane
11 Patti Page song of 1957
21 Dry amendment
22 It's served warm and cold
23 Unmistakable
24 Really physical
25 Many a bridesmaid
26 Canadian map abbr.
27 Stuff in a closet
28 Diggs of "Private Practice"
29 Industrious group
31 Paris parents
33 Fond attachment
39 Levels
41 Wear pink and orange
46 Protester's prop
47 Hardly sophisticated
48 Help in climbing
49 Cut off
50 Understood
51 Rock hurlers
52 Fancy
53 Office buys
54 Tries to hit
55 Ford folly
56 Florentine exile
57 City of 87 Across
58 Billy Joel hit
61 Whirlybird
65 Sheds tears
66 Duke of Hollywood
71 Marshy ground
72 Top dog
73 Code word for "S"
74 More impudent
75 Slight variation
76 Be relevant (to)
77 Folks with mikes
78 Stand out
79 "A Season in Purgatory" author Dunne
80 June portrayer
81 Confidence game
82 Reflects
83 Our, in South Bend
85 Big pictures
87 CSA member
91 Polish sites
93 Wall St. group
94 Hot hunk
100 Way across the ocean
102 Right now
104 Seemingly endless
105 Be vaguely aware
106 Ambience
107 4-minute milers, e.g.

DOWN

1 Bodybuilder's pride
2 Leslie Caron title role
3 Processes wine or cheese
4 Pointer's word
5 "To be" to Henri
6 It's got teeth
7 Guitar master Paul
8 "Yadda, yadda, yadda"
9 Big Apple isle
10 Skittish horse
11 Silicon dioxide stone
12 Application for aches
13 Educational office
14 Provides provender
15 Out on a limb
16 Dawber of "Mork and Mindy"
17 Send out
18 Caesar's sidekick
19 Singer Anita
20 Mark of omission
29 Like some straits
30 "What's up?" . . . "Not much," e.g.?
32 Ghost of a final exam victim?
33 Tolerate
34 Stuck together
35 Clean between the teeth
36 Ewing matriarch, on "Dallas"
37 A son of Ramón Estévez
38 Starter for bag or board
40 Eye part
42 Tempo marking
43 What you can give it
44 Jack of nursery rhymes
45 Undue speed
47 Social group
48 Mall constituent
50 Gist
51 Pillow covers
53 Sees people
54 Docile followers
56 Lavish lover
57 Breaking and entering, e.g.
59 Krypton and others
60 Make a swap
61 Smoldering fragment
62 "Blame It on the Bossa Nova" singer
63 Adorn
64 First, second, and third
67 Prudential rival
68 Legacy from mom or dad
69 Brief moment
70 "Over There" soldiers
72 Say a few words
73 Interstate roller
75 Ozone layer, e.g.
76 Humpback herds
78 Furrowed
79 Gull
81 Carb contributor
82 Small disaster
84 From the keg
86 Hikers' routes
87 Big wine valley
88 Rudely abrupt
89 Bit to split
90 Photo process
92 Pop singer from Nigeria
94 Tyler Perry's "Diary of ___ Black Woman"
95 Big rackets
96 Tending to business
97 In one's birthday suit
98 Body passageway
99 Salty septet
101 Jrs. superiors
103 Match a poker bet

208 FILM NOIR by Fred Piscop

The call-in joke at 76-Across started in 1907 and is still going, unfortunately.

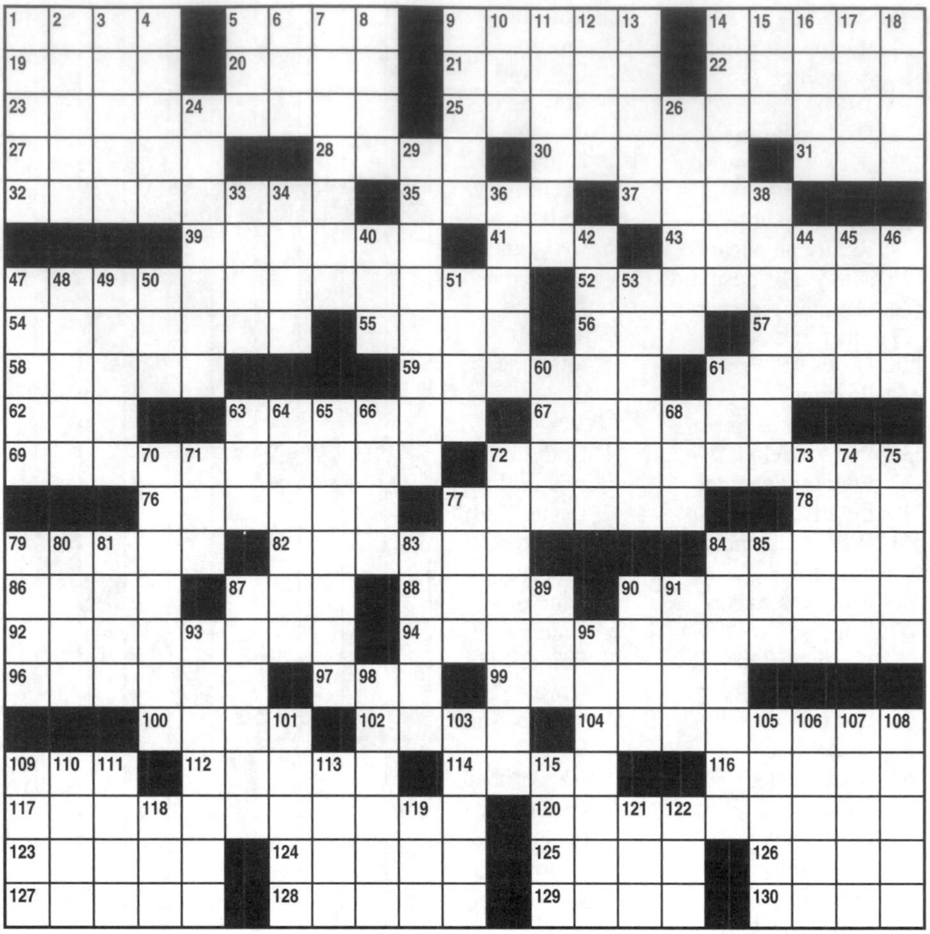

ACROSS

1 Chip's pal
5 ___-Seltzer
9 "Ora pro ___"
14 Hit bottom?
19 "Put ___ writing!"
20 Cold one
21 From square one
22 Relief work?
23 "Pitch Black" actor
25 "Black Narcissus" actress
27 Priscilla's John
28 The Big Easy, briefly
30 Brunch offering
31 Prefix with profit
32 Captain's log entry
35 "Brokeback Mountain" heroine
37 ___ blocks (construction puzzle)
39 "Sacred" birds
41 ___ standstill
43 Subsidiary theorems
47 "Bad Day at Black Rock" actor
52 "Meet Joe Black" actor
54 Item with a thumb hole
55 Farming prefix
56 Sun. delivery
57 "Fashion Emergency" host
58 Old Dodge
59 "Sorry, all full!"
61 In other words
62 Original "King Kong" studio
63 Undergrad path
67 1951 movie alien
69 "Little Black Book" actress
72 "Black Sheep" actor
76 "Do you have Prince Albert __?" (prank line)
77 Senior members
78 Figs.
79 Starbucks order
82 Outfielder's cry
84 Isn't straight
86 Genesis victim
87 ___ Dee River
88 Prized, to a philatelist
90 Marathon-er's need
92 "The Black Stallion" actress
94 "Black Christmas" actress
96 Electric eye, e.g.
97 N.Y. hrs.
99 Track gait
100 Refs' calls
102 Author Dinesen
104 Produce, in a way
109 Torah holder
112 Parting word
114 "Ain't!" rejoinder
116 On the up and up
117 "The Black Dahlia" actress
120 "Men in Black" actor
123 Turn aside
124 ___ Haute
125 Slaughter in baseball
126 King of comedy
127 Sugar source
128 Promo creator
129 "Zounds!"
130 Foreign: Comb. form

DOWN

1 Met performers
2 Not straight
3 Yorba ___
4 Rear-___ (auto mishap)
5 Justice Fortas
6 "___ Miz"
7 Most clever
8 Alice's chronicler
9 Tennis star Rafael
10 U.K. bestowal
11 Short-tailed feline
12 Novello of old films
13 Tender spots
14 Acted the jezebel
15 Marketing unit, in ads
16 Call from the flock
17 "Quo Vadis?" role
18 "Hee Haw" radio station
24 Files charges against
26 Having no axis extremities
29 Pasta dishes
33 Look out for?
34 Get pooped
36 Giuliani was one
38 Excited, slangily
40 Timeline chunk
42 Get off the hook
44 Silent type?
45 24-hr. conveniences
46 Blue-pencil notation
47 Touch off
48 Skier's wear
49 Prufrock's creator
50 Bio word
51 Toot one's horn
53 Hang in
60 Passable
61 TGIF part
63 Keglers' org.
64 More risqué
65 Tchotchke holder
66 Monologist of note
68 Plugs
70 Targeted ones
71 Hydrocarbon suffix
72 Seek treats
73 Diarist Nin
74 "Holy Sonnets" poet
75 Blue-book filler
77 "Pulse" phone feature
79 Long. crossers
80 Busy as ___
81 Gull kin
83 Track paces
84 Symbols of victory
85 Ambulance inits.
87 Mad magazine content
89 NASA "walk"
90 Fill beyond full
91 Bygone era
93 Speedy one-seaters
95 Headed for the entrance
98 Render harmless
101 Rapper's sibling
103 "Great Circle" novelist
105 Big name in real estate
106 Unlike a klutz
107 Business bigwig
108 Prefix with centric
109 Ill-fated whaler
110 Tear apart
111 "Red Balloon" painter
113 Was in the hole
115 ___'Pea
118 Oils and such
119 New Deal agcy.
121 Mauna ___
122 Trip producer

209 LIVING UP TO ONE'S NAME by Elizabeth C. Gorski

We hope 101 Across has a sense of humor.

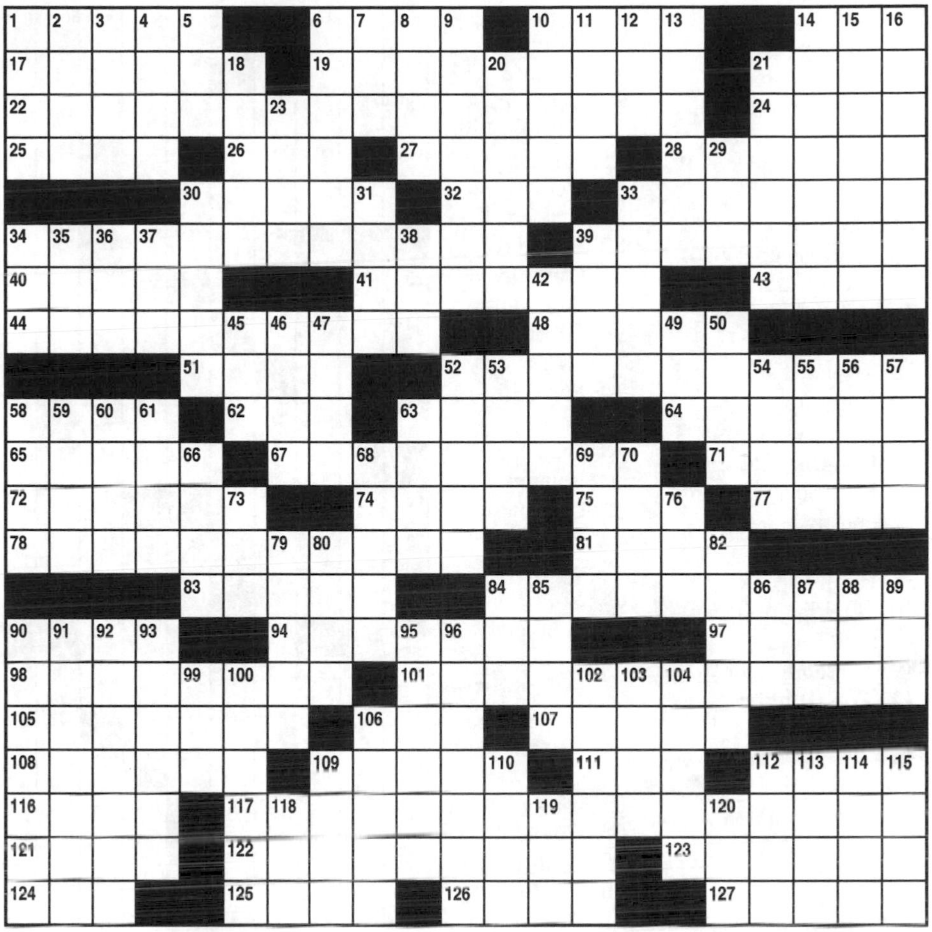

ACROSS

1 Native-born Israeli
6 Goad
10 Magazine item
14 Nourished
17 Herbivorous lizard
19 Type of deli salad
21 Uffizi collection
22 "Wishin' and Hopin' " singer who took a powder?
24 Carson's predecessor
25 "I could ___ horse!"
26 Queen's servant
27 Patient person?
28 African river
30 Takes on
32 Ben Franklin's deg.
33 Equipped
34 Fibrous folk singer?
39 Long Island's gateway to Fire Island
40 Muppet pal of Bert
41 One with collections
43 Former Israeli president Weizman
44 Plumbing problems
48 Kind of acid
51 Comments from a pro?
52 Elegant crime family boss?
58 Opera orch. sections
62 Cry from Homer Simpson
63 "And ___ goes . . ."
64 Type of equality
65 Big cheese
67 Cheerful "Honor Thy Father" author?
71 Vampire
72 Sports venues
74 Leftists, for short
75 Dock workers' gp.
77 Part of SASE
78 Begrimed "Father of Chicago Blues"?
81 Trial balloon
83 Punk's smile
84 1961 Elvis film
90 Rack collection
94 Allow in again
97 Led Zeppelin's "Whole ___ Love"
98 Does Mickey Mouse work?
101 Lustful "American Idol" judge?
105 File covers
106 Japanese musical drama
107 Chars
108 Hair salon professional
109 Siouans
111 Wall Street whiz
112 Down Under: Abbr.
116 Carry-on, maybe
117 Humble "Night On Bald Mountain" composer?
121 Yalies
122 2007 Keira Knightley film
123 Library-sponsored activity
124 "Losing My Religion" band
125 Word with heart or shoulder
126 Blows away
127 Vineyard pick

DOWN

1 Fries or coleslaw, e.g.
2 Oaxaca water
3 Head and shoulders, in sculpture
4 Pro ___
5 Whatever
6 Fleet, e.g.
7 Key letter
8 Containers of coffee
9 Clothes fit for a king
10 In ___ (hard-pressed)
11 Track event
12 Bad beginning?
13 Not off
14 Blunt "What About Bob?" director?
15 Place for stuff
16 Mocking sort
18 The same size
20 Gmail attachments
21 Helicopter model
23 Lima's land
29 Yak genus
30 Laughing critter
31 Thick carpet
33 Wardrobe for Mrs. Gandhi
34 Tie the knot
35 Canadian-born hockey great
36 Words with roll or bagel
37 502, in an inscription
38 Apt. compartments
39 Valentine openers?
42 Henri's health
45 Gene's dance partner in "Singin' in the Rain"
46 Carroll of "Topper"
47 Workplace safety org.
49 Oslo's land: Abbr.
50 Autumnal birthstone
52 They make amphibious landings
53 Renoir's output
54 Some MP3 players
55 "Darling, Je Vous ___ Beaucoup"
56 Polished surface
57 Minnesota's Saint ___ College
58 Did the butterfly
59 Highway sign word
60 Piccolo, for one
61 Transport
63 Main attraction
66 Produces eggs
68 City in the Shasta Valley
69 In ___ (unmoved)
70 Robert ___ cocktail
73 Personal ad shorthand
76 Fireplace heap
79 Buenos ___
80 Very, in Vichy
82 Locker room applications
84 Storage area
85 Brit. companies
86 Yan's pan
87 Instinet, for one: Abbr.
88 Midori, the Olympic skater
89 Fleming who created Goldfinger
90 Cute rodent
91 French chef in "Right, Ho Jeeves"
92 Minuscule singer with a falsetto?
93 Happy face features
95 Fitful sleep
96 Spiritual guru
99 Bass behind the bar
100 Airport area
102 Pastry kitchen staples
103 Rattles
104 Shady resting place
106 Without letup
109 Pop hero
110 Diving duck
112 Thickening agent
113 Food stamp org.
114 Do without
115 Amy's costar on "Judging Amy"
118 Prefix meaning "ear"
119 Half of deux
120 Rule, briefly

210 MY FAIR BRADY by Harvey Estes

The title has nothing to do with 25 Down . . . or quarterback Tom.

ACROSS

1 Show opener
5 Shady retreat
10 Bygone monarch
14 Truth stretchers
19 Manor head
20 Nada
21 Earthenware jar
22 Mork's supervisor
23 Clean floors, e.g.?
26 Fritter away
27 Coming up
28 Try hard
29 Light up
30 Heir's concern
31 Chaplin spouse
32 Hydrocarbon ending
33 "___ who?"
34 Barely speak
36 "Field and Stream" rival?
39 Thread holder
42 Appealingly shocking
44 Cheri of "Scary Movie"
45 California cop gp.
46 Costume for "I, Claudius"
47 Aspirin targets
49 "WKRP" actress Anderson
53 Nasdaq cousin
54 Anouk of "La Dolce Vita"
55 Like a roving knight
56 Castillo of baseball
57 Flower cluster
59 Scott of legal fiction
60 Fairy-tale baddie
61 Failed as a mason?
66 High-strung
67 Drink for Dracula
68 Afflicting
70 Swenson of "Benson"
71 Fine fabrics
73 Evita portrayer LuPone
75 Hoedown honey
76 Laid-back
77 Jane Fonda film
78 Powder holders
79 Sigh words
80 Afternoon TV fare
82 Venetian voyager Polo
83 Private pupil
84 Ocean surface?
89 Sound off
91 Outrage
92 Salt source
93 Glorified gofer
94 Parrot perches
98 Licorice liqueur
100 Chronicles
102 Random criticism
103 More cunning
104 Golfer's cry over a lost wood?
106 Archipelago component
107 Bête noire
108 Hot spot
109 Draft status
110 Fits together
111 Decked out
112 Deuce toppers
113 Author Simone

DOWN

1 Title role for Jude Law
2 Woes of toes
3 Have faith in
4 Musher's race
5 Atlantic island group
6 Rampant
7 Deli order
8 Phil of folk
9 Art of speaking
10 City in "Italia"
11 Language closely related to Czech
12 Skin moisturizer
13 St. Louis NFLer
14 It's good for climbing hills
15 Present-day Persia
16 Town of St. Francis
17 Way past ripe
18 React to snuff
24 The bottom line
25 The Brady kids, e.g.
29 Send to the tummy
32 Consumed
35 With a feather
36 Pungent cheese
37 Punk hairstyle
38 Huge number
39 High-five sound
40 Rose Bowl site
41 Job vacancies
43 A, in Arles
46 Cheat at pinball
47 Roll-on brand
48 Swamp critter
50 Total
51 Slim or Fats, e.g.
52 "Sort of" suffix
54 Teen tribulation
55 Continental cash
58 "Looks like it"
59 Steakhouse offering
60 D-Day was its turning point
62 Thickheaded
63 Hit the ground
64 Decide on
65 "Blueberry Hill" singer Domino
66 Reason for extra innings
69 Tickled-pink feeling
71 Did figure eights, say
72 Kind of male
73 Like the driven snow
74 Pro Bowl side
78 Member of a discussion group
79 Where to see attractive models
81 In a way
82 Muffler maker
83 Gov't. security
84 Gets two by the backboard
85 Vague warning
86 Pauline's problems
87 It has a peel for physical comedy
88 Washed the soap off
90 Inviting smells
95 Stood out in the crowd
96 Oscar winner Marisa
97 Great bargain
99 Nair rival
100 Asian sea name
101 Burn a bit
102 Polo animal
104 Telly initials
105 Give a line to

211 INFERIORITY COMPLEX by Victor Fleming
Talk about being made to feel small!

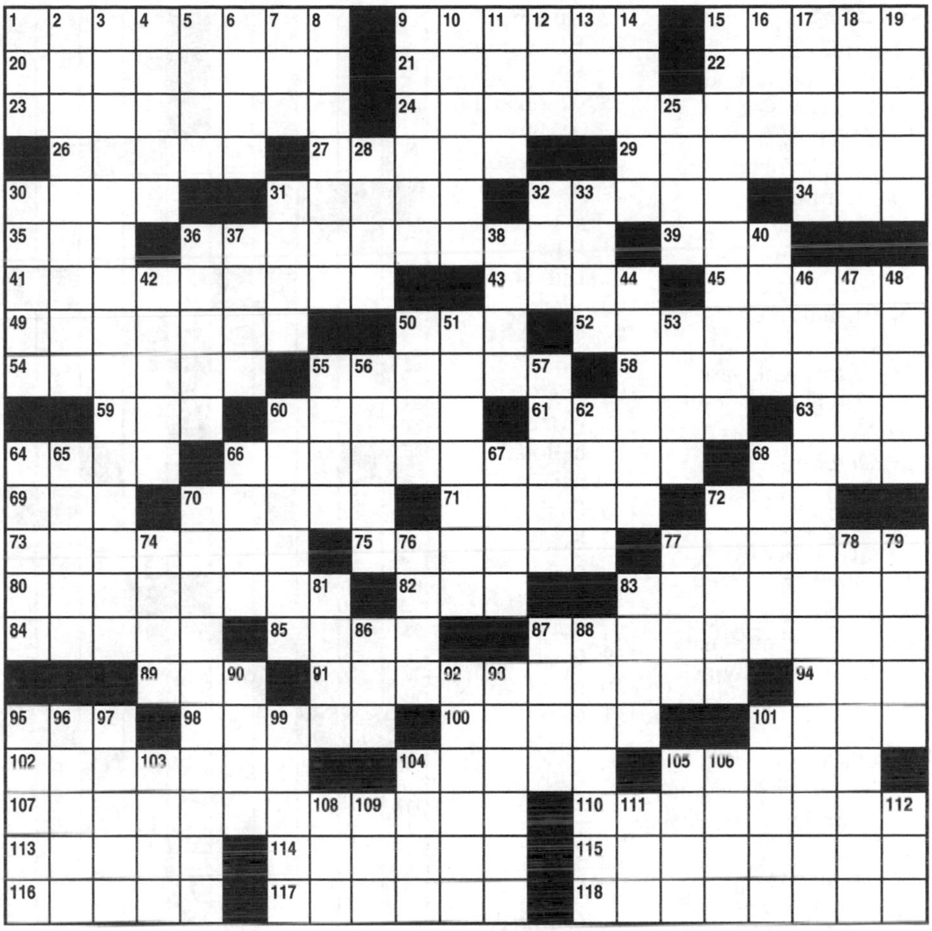

ACROSS
1 "Unfinished Symphony" composer
9 Tejano singing star
15 Jennifer in "Flashdance"
20 Lose it
21 Was not caught by
22 Berg of atonal music
23 "Farewell, ___" (1965 Baez album)
24 Package-store purchase for 80-A?
26 Canon's subj.
27 Projected part
29 Mediterranean evergreen
30 They may be performing
31 Adds strength, with "up"
32 Prescribed food selections
34 Bowl stats
35 Stomach
36 Card game for 80-A?
39 Cry of discovery
41 Orcas' features
43 Puts on paper
45 "___ Mio"
49 Like stuff bought at amazon.com
50 Type letters?
52 What 80-A scatters things to (with "the")?
54 Sonata components
55 Hasta follower
58 Range of vision
59 Unknown John
60 Deceptive gridiron moves
61 One putting on cargo
63 Debut on the mkt.
64 "There oughta be ___!"
66 Interstate rig for 80-A?
68 PDQ
69 ___-di-dah
70 Spade player, familiarly
71 Pets, informally
72 In times past
73 Crowds may get their addresses
75 Working cat
77 Queen toppers
80 What he was after being cut down to size?
82 Nth, for short
83 Budget problem
84 Equally out yonder
85 Takes the plunge
87 Make proportionally smaller
89 Mormons: Abbr.
91 Hotel chain for 81-A?
94 Looie's subordinate
95 Andrea Bargnani's org.
98 Covered transport
100 Pale purple shrub
101 Without bounce
102 Kazakhstan city
104 Brothers' superior
105 Lowly laborers
107 Baseball event for 80-A?
110 Plant feeders
113 Actress Aimée
114 Kansas motto word
115 Electioneering data source
116 Low-cal drinks
117 Condo contract condition, perhaps
118 One giving a make-up, perhaps

DOWN
1 Fed. loan agency
2 She who's low in the loft
3 Triumphant gesture for 80-A?
4 "Gold" of the silver screen?
5 Machete kin
6 Sermon topic
7 O-___ Ishii ("Kill Bill" character)
8 Aerialist's swing
9 Cause to lose it
10 "Despite that . . ."
11 "Auld–Syne" connection
12 Miami summer hrs.
13 Book before Esth.
14 Sun-dried brick
15 Where Huggies may be gifts
16 USPS mail-sorting product
17 Scrub a launch
18 Bummed around
19 Crossword blades
25 ___ Morgana (mirage)
28 Curious George's creators
30 Honey-colored
31 Shiny on top?
32 Hip-hop Dr.
33 Has no life
36 Lover of Daphnis
37 Some deer
38 Versed in
40 Terse disclaimer
42 Word with golf or grass
44 Bergman and Borg, e.g.
46 How 80-A stands independently?
47 Parkinsonism treatment
48 Bar at the bar
50 Over
51 Given to blushing
53 Hearing in open court
55 Certain bond, slangily
56 "Coming to America" prince
57 Motrin competitor
60 Kind of puzzle
62 Oriole, e.g.
64 Western airline
65 Maurice Jarre's "___ Theme"
66 "Cheers" cheer
67 Toward Tennessee, from Arkansas
68 Put in ___ word for
70 Promenades at shores
72 Napoleonic forces
74 Big name in nonstick cookware
76 Unseat
77 King of rhyme
78 Tyne Bridge locale
79 Bishops' council
81 Lost movie fish
83 Traffic cop?
86 Mafia leader
87 WW2 battle site
88 Talk a blue streak
90 Fill beyond full
92 Hubbard who wrote "A Message to Garcia"
93 Fall folk?
95 Twangy
96 Traditional Shrovetide dish
97 Comeback to "Are so!"
99 Wilson in "The New Yorker"
101 Doesn't hold
103 Scary symptom
104 Chick's tail?
105 Rain, but just barely
106 One-named costume designer
108 That, to Juan
109 Computer program, for short
111 Chopper's implement
112 Short camera type

212 ALL-AROUND NUISANCE by Arlan and Linda Bushman

. . . and that nuisance is lurking at 111 Down.

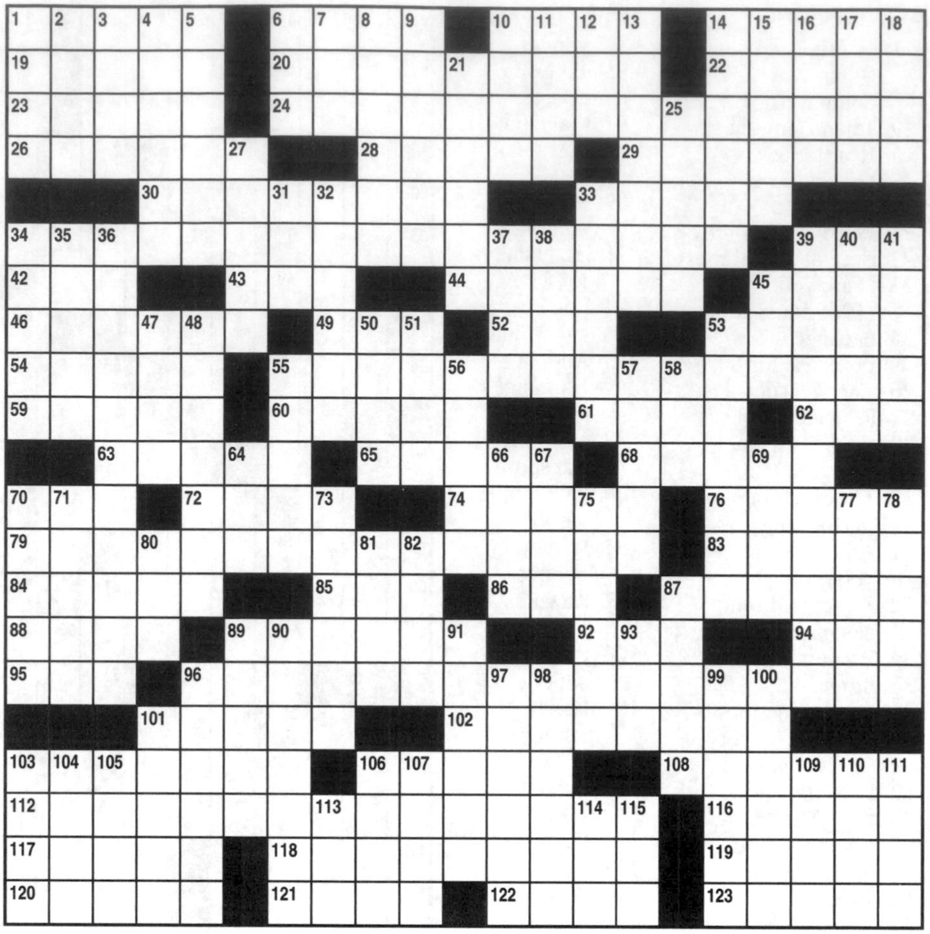

ACROSS

1 Fritter away
6 Stare open-mouthed
10 Lincoln in-law
14 Mocking
19 Lucy's friend
20 Gesture of deference
22 Trail figure
23 Clay pigeon sport
24 Sit-in, for one*
26 Societal no-nos
28 Works with yarn
29 Movie blooper bit
30 No constraints
33 Determine value
34 Yoko Ono résumé entry*
39 Cry of discovery
42 Chopper
43 Jazz style
44 Italian diva Renata
45 Courter of rhyme
46 Engrosses
49 Mathematical constants
52 Battery designation
53 Spanish missionary Junipero
54 Exonerate
55 Joey Dee & the Starliters hit*
59 Villechaize of "Fantasy Island"
60 Voiced
61 Chihuahua child
62 Flight formation
63 Brute
65 Meaning
68 "Harry Potter" banker
70 Rose letters
72 Harmony
74 Last empress of Iran
76 Alan and Cheryl
79 NEO PI-R or Rorschach inkblot*
83 Not active
84 Another time
85 Impress mightily
86 Cartoon scream
87 Kind of bond
88 "Phooey!"
89 Predicted the future
92 Opponent
94 Fort Collins sch.
95 Command to dobbin
96 Wearer of rose-colored glasses*
101 Rate
102 Little cupid
103 Worry about
106 Tom Mix film
108 Peewee
112 Arizona national park*
116 High abode
117 Really bother
118 Dessert cart item
119 Quahogs
120 Rickety ride
121 German mining region
122 Panache
123 Plus

DOWN

1 Cardinal point
2 Aleutian component
3 Wooley of "High Noon"
4 Use a driver
5 Corrida charger
6 Huckabee grp.
7 Homer's dad
8 Undermine
9 Outing, of a sort
10 Wilson preceder
11 Hardship
12 LXV x X
13 Down payment
14 Have a ___ (chance)
15 Gritty prelude?
16 Home furnishings chain
17 Secretary
18 Noted art deco designer
21 Fishing nets
25 Actress Rene
27 Some Balkans
31 Comic Philips
32 Mountaineer's descent
33 Secure
34 Make thirsty
35 Outcast
36 Echo repeatedly
37 Rent-___
38 Gallivant
39 Parting word from 44 Across
40 Mount
41 Small print
45 Handful
47 Overhang
48 Arnold's offense
50 Popular tote
51 Provoke
53 Informer
55 City on the Ganges
56 Instruct
57 Dusk to dawn
58 Spike TV, formerly
64 Dict. listing
66 Outcome
67 House locale
69 Spiritual power
70 Precisely
71 Smooth transition
73 Bordeaux offering
75 Solicit
77 Sack or shift
78 Parade
80 Start of an old cheer
81 Tape breaker's shout
82 "Tiger Beat" reader
87 Country rock guitarist Dickey
89 Letter flourish
90 Nitpickers
91 Minute alga
93 Unseal, a la Shakespeare
96 Small and trim
97 Fine arbitrarily
98 Clairol rival
99 Home of Odysseus
100 Gourmet mushrooms
101 French revolutionary
103 Blueprint detail
104 Sport
105 Vocalist James
106 Concert halls
107 Yonder
109 Some stashes
110 Play charades
111 Nuisance surrounding clue* answers
113 Generation
114 Jamaican music
115 Half a score

213 MOVIE REWRITES by Clare Hansbrough

. . . and all these rewrites are close to their original films.

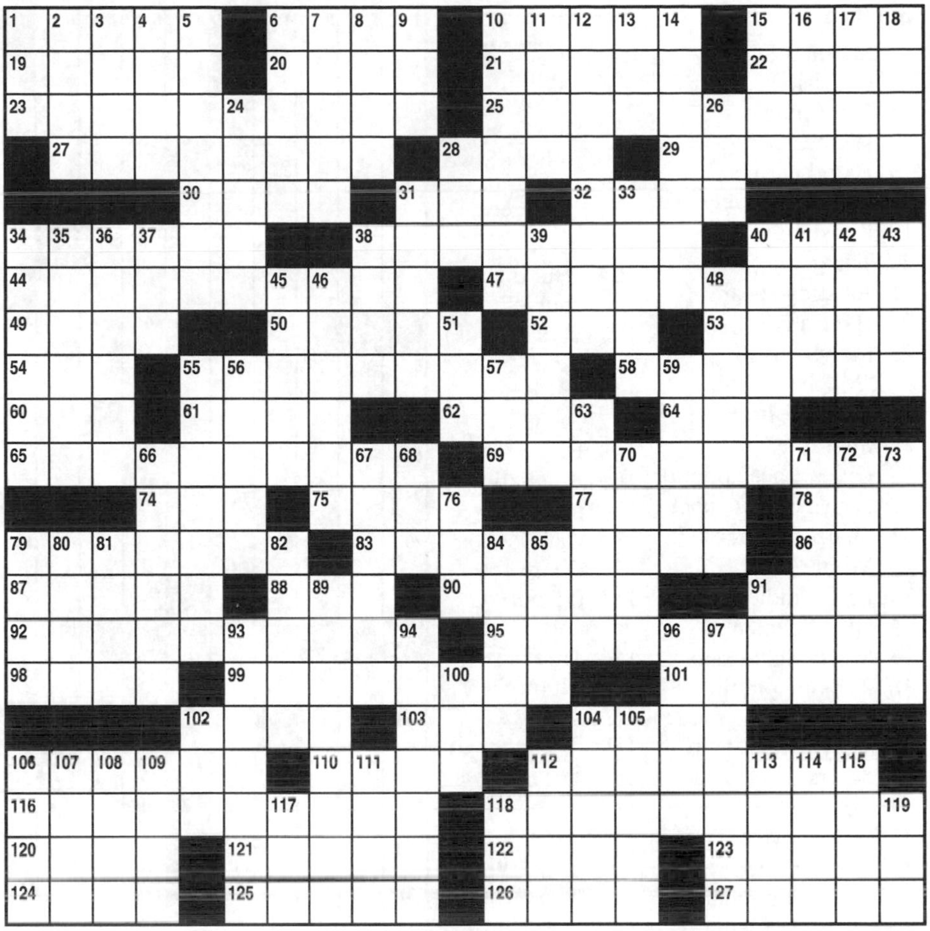

ACROSS

1 Make changes to
6 "Hey, bud!"
10 Special talents
15 Hock
19 Slapstick comedy
20 Confident words
21 Aimee of "La Dolce Vita"
22 Big name in oil
23 1971 James Caan film
25 Prude dressed like a bum?
27 One Patriot to another
28 The majority
29 Kiddy baseball league
30 "___ I a stinker?": Bugs Bunny
31 Statehouse VIP
32 Noose material
34 Pigeonhole
38 Arrive fashionably
40 Hits the slopes
44 2000 animated Mel Gibson film
47 More attractive portion?
49 Lower digits
50 Prudential rival
52 Bard's above
53 Painter Matisse
54 Cries of pain
55 Low-rate period
58 Head scratcher's words
60 Wagon track
61 Nick's time
62 Gardeners' tools
64 Myrna of "The Thin Man"
65 1987 Mel Brooks film
69 Finds homes for dogs?
74 Wear and tear
75 King of tragedy
77 Word after sotto or viva
78 ___-mo replay
79 Evening meals
83 Footnote indicators
86 Rocky peak
87 Tax month
88 Antonym (abbr.)
90 Bloodhound's guide
91 Composer Thomas
92 1990 De Niro film
95 Stuff safe to eat?
98 Wraps up
99 Nitwit
101 Ready to go
102 Anjou alternative
103 Gallery objects
104 "WKRP" actress Anderson
106 Outré or exit
110 "Don't throw bouquets ___ . . ."
112 Saturday night specials, e.g.
116 1941 Bogart film
118 Crown prince in gaudy robes?
120 Resolve, with "out"
121 Nash of funny verses
122 And so
123 Rich dessert
124 Pita sandwich
125 Carrots, to snowmen
126 Get the ball rolling
127 Did a blacksmith's job

DOWN

1 SAC site
2 Shopping area
3 Buffalo's lake
4 "March Madness" org.
5 Jutland's country
6 Galileo, for one
7 "Ivanhoe" writer
8 Right in the head
9 "Star Trek: ___"
10 Flame-based cooker
11 Wayside retreats
12 Dash or marathon
13 Place for three men
14 Pilot
15 Tiny opening
16 "There ought to be ___!"
17 Carry on
18 NASDAQ alternative
24 Strike down
26 Name divider
28 Tat word, often
31 Fixin' to
33 Cheri of "Scary Movie"
34 Troupe group
35 Make an appearance
36 Sonora snooze
37 Mil. training site
38 Like kittens and puppies
39 Toy train maker
40 Songbird Crow
41 ___ fu
42 As to
43 Comedy sketch
45 1994 trade pact
46 Vend again
48 Opts for
51 Light wood
55 Alone (with "by")
56 Bran plus
57 Caveman of comics
59 Patch of color
63 Being thrifty
66 ___-dart (blue succory)
67 Accept eagerly
68 Swedish flier
70 ___ del Sol
71 Houston nine
72 Jean Harlow was one
73 Hurting to the max
76 NFL linemen
79 Wise guy
80 Atop of
81 Egg on
82 Loafer bottoms
84 Big splash
85 Clarinet part
89 Demonstration sights, perhaps
91 One path to the WWW
93 Sentiment
94 Tribal healers
96 Finishes a flight
97 O'Hare departures
100 Old preposition
102 Mass transit vehicle
104 Like a sumo wrestler
105 Tear producer
106 Tory rival
107 Light and delicate
108 "Son of Frankenstein" shepherd
109 Cry of frustration
111 Family diagram
112 Plucked instrument
113 "I'm in trouble now!"
114 Pianist Peter
115 Something to build on
117 Kind of trip
118 GM make
119 Badly chafed

214 "I'M BEING OBJECTIVE" by Theresa Yves

A good one for the me-first generation.

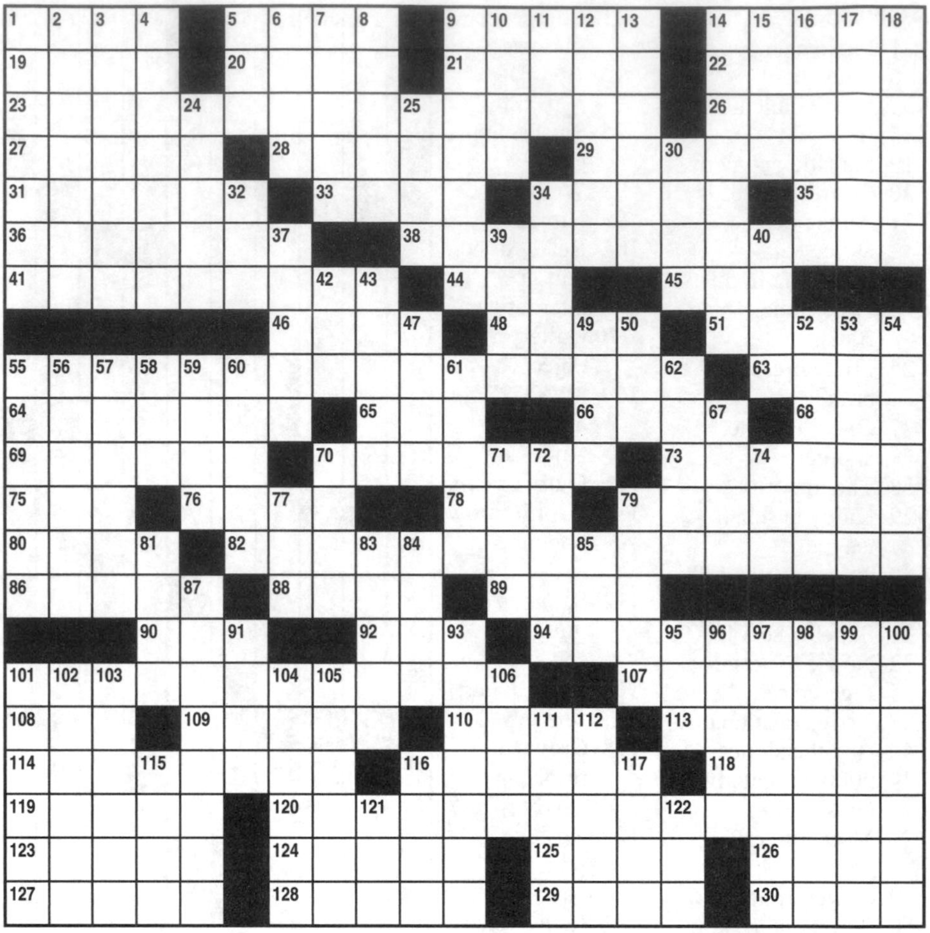

ACROSS

1 Spelling of television
5 Electronic synthesizer
9 Blood partner
14 Lower, as prices
19 Roasting place
20 The goods
21 Jousting spear
22 Have a cow
23 Marsh gas in "Macbeth"?
26 Lay to rest
27 Sing like Crosby
28 Gives a heads-up to
29 "Love Songs" poet
31 Sharp as a tack
33 Military color
34 Early fiddles
35 NFL linemen
36 Make big, as hair
38 Zoologist in the middle of the road?
41 They love to take orders
44 Court VIPs
45 Genesis vessel
46 Is left with
48 In a willing manner
51 "The Lion King" king
55 Impromptu anthropology group?
63 "Rats!"
64 Completely finished
65 "Seinfeld" uncle
66 Fabled archer
68 "At Seventeen" singer
69 "Jurassic Park" menace
70 With 82 Across, invite from a UFO?
73 Detest passionately
75 "My Big Fat Greek Wedding" actress Vardalos
76 Hit the keys
78 Antidiscrimination letters
79 Realistic display
80 Suffix with refer
82 See 70 Across
86 Fail to keep a poker face
88 Author Bellow
89 Uppity sort
90 Either of two NT books
92 Mexican month
94 "But of course!"
101 Scrappy auto exec?
107 Eastern event
108 Have life
109 Emphatic turndown
110 Daredevil's desire
113 Pitch to the noggin
114 Theatrical
116 Bit on the cob
118 Puts through a food press
119 Hub-to-rim lines
120 Vengeful dirty look?
123 Reef ring
124 Heavenly hunter
125 Verdi opus
126 Passionate love
127 Smoothes wood
128 Battery units
129 Picked straws
130 Bk. of the Pentateuch

DOWN

1 Males that meow
2 Across the ocean
3 Check the bill
4 Using one's own staff
5 Lots of secs
6 Draft eligible
7 From way back
8 Summer intern, maybe
9 Open truck
10 Criminals break them
11 Put a halt to
12 Nova follower
13 Right after this
14 Barbershop essential
15 Hit the runway
16 Wedding sites
17 Gracefully slender
18 Religious dissent
24 Primes the poker pot
25 Study in a panic
30 Sports car, briefly
32 Old World cont.
34 Drop by
37 English coppers
39 Spanish surrealist
40 Fail to grip the road
42 Chest muscle
43 Furry wrap
47 Hook's ally
49 Suffix with major
50 Finder's take
52 Rum cocktail
53 Rodeo bull
54 Temper
55 Eliot's miser
56 Runaway bride in "The Graduate"
57 Fleecy fabric
58 Banned bug killer
59 Least bit of concern
60 Way to serve ham
61 Church composition
62 Immigration island
67 Ill-gotten gains
70 Prefix with physics
71 Golf pegs
72 Taxi tooters
74 JFK info
77 Mil. stores
79 Charger's woes
81 Behold, to Brutus
83 Unfounded story
84 Guinness of "Star Wars"
85 Pal of Pooh
87 Polish targets, perhaps
91 Run amok
93 Previews, as movies
95 Where spokes meet
96 End of ___
97 Taught the ropes
98 Without ulterior motive
99 Words to a tot
100 Least wordy
101 Bay of Bengal port
102 Publication goofs
103 String along
104 "I, Robot" author
105 Chicago suburb
106 Light as a feather
111 Links legend Sam
112 Drink made of fermented milk
115 Not spicy
116 Sailor's speed measure
117 Valuable vein
121 Be laid up
122 Wet behind the ears

215 DYNAMIC TRIOS by Frances Burton

Three diamonds are usually set on 27 Across.

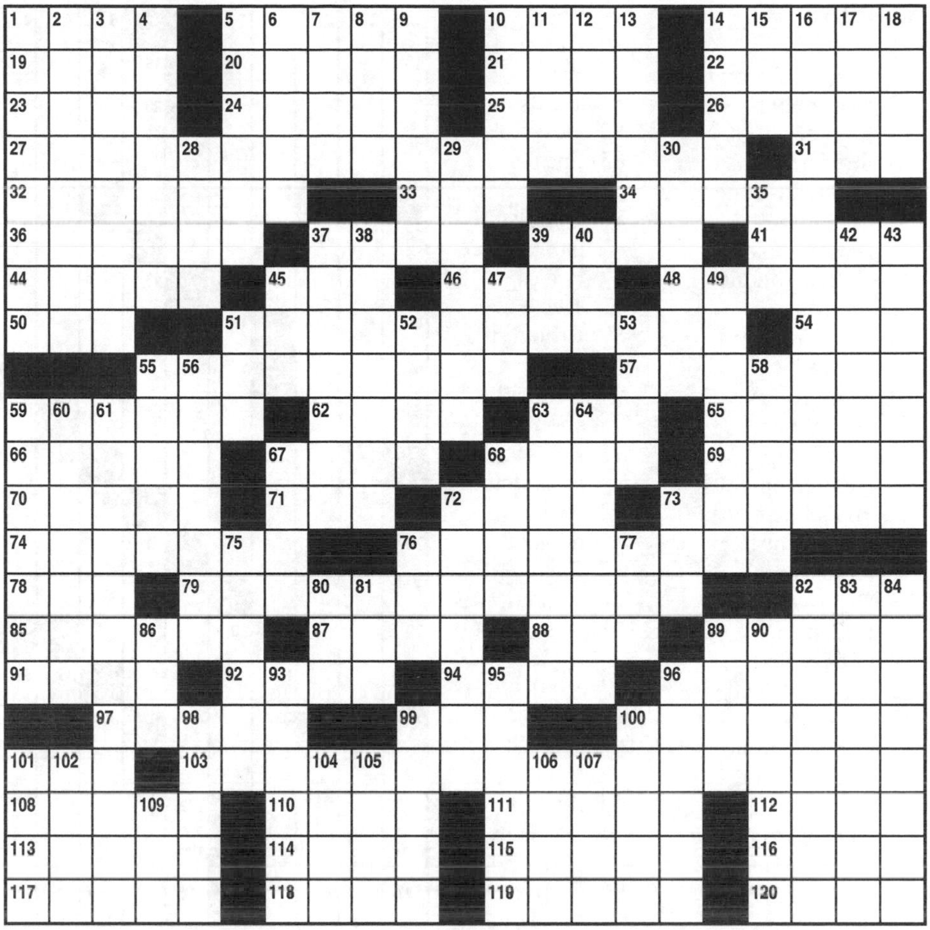

ACROSS

1 Like "King Lear": Abbr.
5 Hair ornament
10 Anthropologist Margaret
14 Bwana's Indian cousin
19 Go down
20 Welsh dog
21 Emerald, e.g.
22 It goes before the fall
23 God of thunder
24 Freshwater mammal
25 Go belly up
26 Railroad
27 A ring for all seasons
31 Ten-gallon
32 Tipperary locale
33 Singer O'Connor
34 City in India
36 Muslim princes
37 Ornamental cord
39 Ukraine's capital
41 Singles out
44 Framework
45 Thicken
46 Quirk
48 Stay clear of
50 Naval off.
51 Skirmish-line command
54 Proustite, e.g.
55 Large labor union
57 Large shell
59 Ruler
62 Mahjong piece
63 Good place to get money
65 Golden measure
66 Cowgirl Dale
67 Limping
68 Swellhead
69 Marble
70 Lawrence's mount
71 Marvin or Majors
72 Food thickener
73 Buffy, for one
74 Synthetic fabric
76 Important sign
78 Greek letters
79 Caesar's boast
82 Shell game prop
85 Seesaw
87 Latvian port
88 QB misfire: Abbr.
89 Graceful birds
91 Adam's third boy
92 In addition
94 Mental pain
96 Pirate storage places
97 Out of sorts
99 Guy Fawkes Day mo.
100 Wrap
101 Gershwin or Levin
103 Two-person hand game
108 Was foolishly fond
110 Big pile
111 Brazilian city
112 Love god
113 Moolah
114 Great lake
115 Twist
116 Well-defined track
117 Anesthetic
118 Kisses off
119 Squeezes by
120 Arctic transport

DOWN

1 Beach attire
2 Control tower figure
3 Cookie seasonings
4 Softer
5 Pooh-poohs
6 Well-known
7 Food scraps
8 S-shaped molding
9 Oktoberfest skirt
10 Annoys
11 Isaac's son
12 Came to rest
13 Four-flush
14 Sales pitch
15 Biceps locale
16 Resounding cheer
17 Dilbert's light bulb
18 Three stars in Orion
28 Cut back
29 Cups, caddies, draining trays, etc.
30 Echo
35 Ad ___ committee
37 Rap's ___ Boys
38 "Give me that ___ religion . . ."
39 Stanley in "The Right Stuff"
40 "Mission: Impossible" org.
42 Like a cloverleaf
43 More angelic
45 Precious stone
47 Belonging to hubby
49 ___ beet (Swiss chard)
51 Wharf pest
52 High-pitched cry
53 Metrical unit
55 Dogma
56 Subjugate
58 Sea wreckage
59 Forswears
60 One in a temporary shelter
61 "Finito!" at Wimbleon
63 Anjou native
64 London suburb
67 Secluded valley
68 Rani's garment
72 Vending-machine drink
73 Enjoy Aspen
75 Shipworm
76 Mediterranean tree
77 World Series mo.
80 Treasury Dept. division
81 Compete
82 Idyllic
83 Provide with power
84 Appraised
86 Despite the fact that
89 "___ a Lady": Tom Jones
90 Equivocators
93 Chinese fruit
95 Get even for
96 Cools down
98 Send off for
99 Bandannas protect them from sunburn
100 Close shave
101 Run in neutral
102 Overwhelming defeat
104 "Ol' Man River" composer
105 Anted up
106 Writer Ayn
107 Male party
109 Before

216 ER by Fran & Lou Sabin

The Stage Deli at 47 Across can be found on 7th Avenue in New York City.

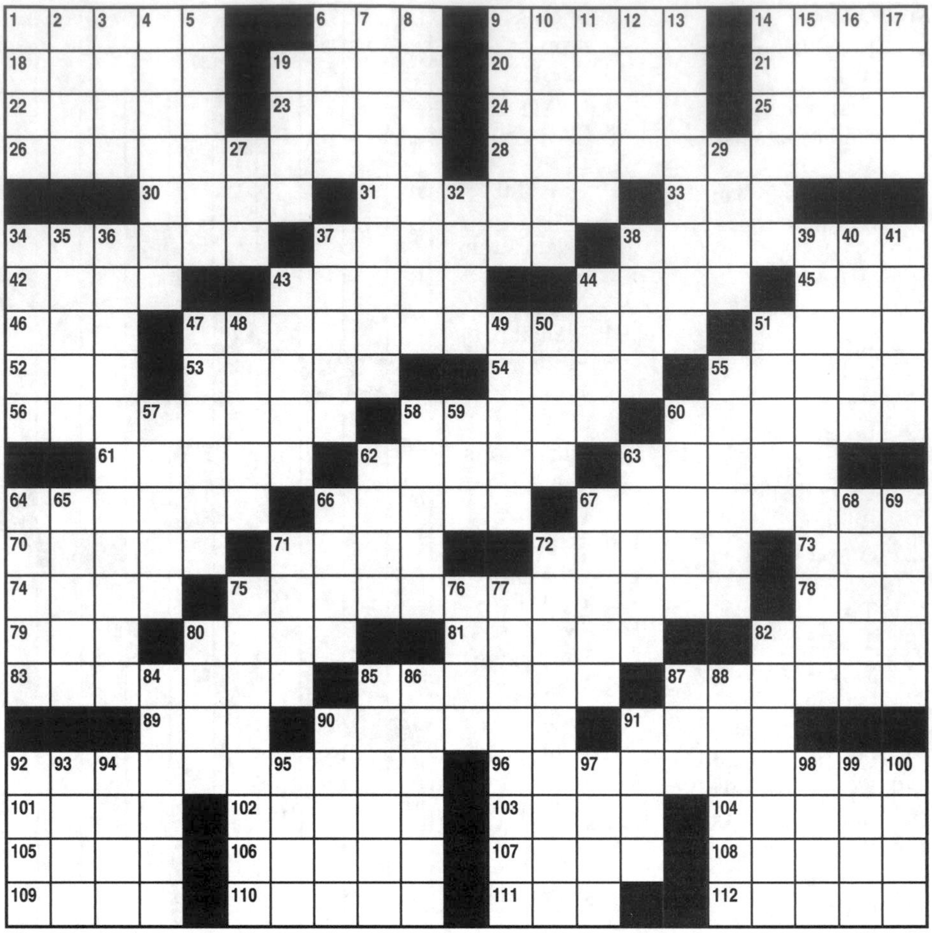

ACROSS

1 Spa
6 Diamond crown?
9 Sommelier's study
14 Logger's tool
18 Suddenly
19 It may be done in full
20 Battery post
21 College biggie
22 M. Zola
23 Cuba in "Chill Factor"
24 More reserved
25 Disagreeing
26 "Surf's up!" announcement?
28 Ted's blazer?
30 Baobab or banyan
31 Aplenty
33 "You kidding?!"
34 Indian snack
37 Glossy duds
38 Indy 500 leader
42 Hoofbeat
43 "Them" author
44 Fries or slaw, e.g.
45 "The Wire" carrier
46 Big Board listing
47 Comedienne's Stage Deli namesake?
51 Candidate's goal
52 ___ -jongg
53 Kashmir's river
54 Clobber
55 Manuscript page
56 Conference handout
58 Speak hastily
60 Door-to-door salesman
61 Fleming at the Met
62 Take out
63 Birthday girl, usually
64 Practiced cartography
66 Building block
67 Procrastinator's promise
70 Exhibition
71 Ligurian Sea feeder
72 Letter's final line?
73 ___ Victor
74 "No prob!"
75 Light-fingered one at the gym?
78 Table type
79 "Just ___!"
80 Kett in a strip
81 Treats meat
82 Dover export
83 Speaks uncertainly
85 Upholstered parlor piece
87 Foe of Two-Face
89 Brooklyn's finish
90 Feel sad about
91 First name in architecture
92 Newborn's nook?
96 Source of goat cheese?
101 Aesir's leader
102 1960's dress style
103 Juillet follower
104 Stand for 100 Down
105 "Lovely!"
106 Dead duck
107 Wise one
108 Embarrassing moment
109 Stem-to-stern structure
110 Watchful ones
111 Interrogate
112 "___ Foolish Things"

DOWN

1 Max of ring and film fame
2 Spitballs, BBs, etc.
3 Working gumshoe
4 Ski-lift stop
5 Villainous expressions
6 ___ avis
7 Melinda's money man
8 Rabid fan
9 Tend to
10 Acquires (debts)
11 Bete ___
12 Opening scene?
13 Wooer's tune
14 Cochise, memorably
15 Bond's screen debut
16 Greek's sixth letter
17 Stage direction
19 Walk around
27 Eng. rocker Chris
29 One's heart may do it
32 Victorian affectation
34 Mischief-maker
35 Basilica site
36 Birth certificate, e.g.?
37 "Here's to you!"
38 Small dose
39 Place for a board meeting?
40 Drop down
41 Eggbeater's blade
43 Like 80 Across
44 Smith & Dale routine
47 Steamboat Willie's creator
48 Signed, sorta
49 Put to work
50 Package handler?
51 "The Third Man" escape route
55 Eloped
57 Calyx leaf
58 Freshwater waterway
59 Hyde's hideout
60 Nabe guy
62 "The Country Girls" author O'Brien
63 Heiress Duke
64 Brilliant bird
65 Foodie lure
66 Kind of code
67 Cutesy laugh
68 Town 35 miles from Gainesville
69 See the light?
71 Leaf-cutters
72 Physically demanding
75 Cheap crossing
76 Plasm preceder
77 Turnip's kin
80 "And what ___?"
82 Inner man
84 Food enhancer
85 Certain fishing boat
86 Glowing coals
87 Endangered insect
88 Collar
90 Corned-beef solution
91 Caesarean delivery?
92 Bop
93 Jim Davis's pooch
94 Worldwide staple
95 Overfeed
97 Adana citizen
98 "That's it!"
99 Camera part
100 "Fish Magic" painter

217 GOING WILD by Pancho Harrison

An example of 97 Across can be found in Warren County.

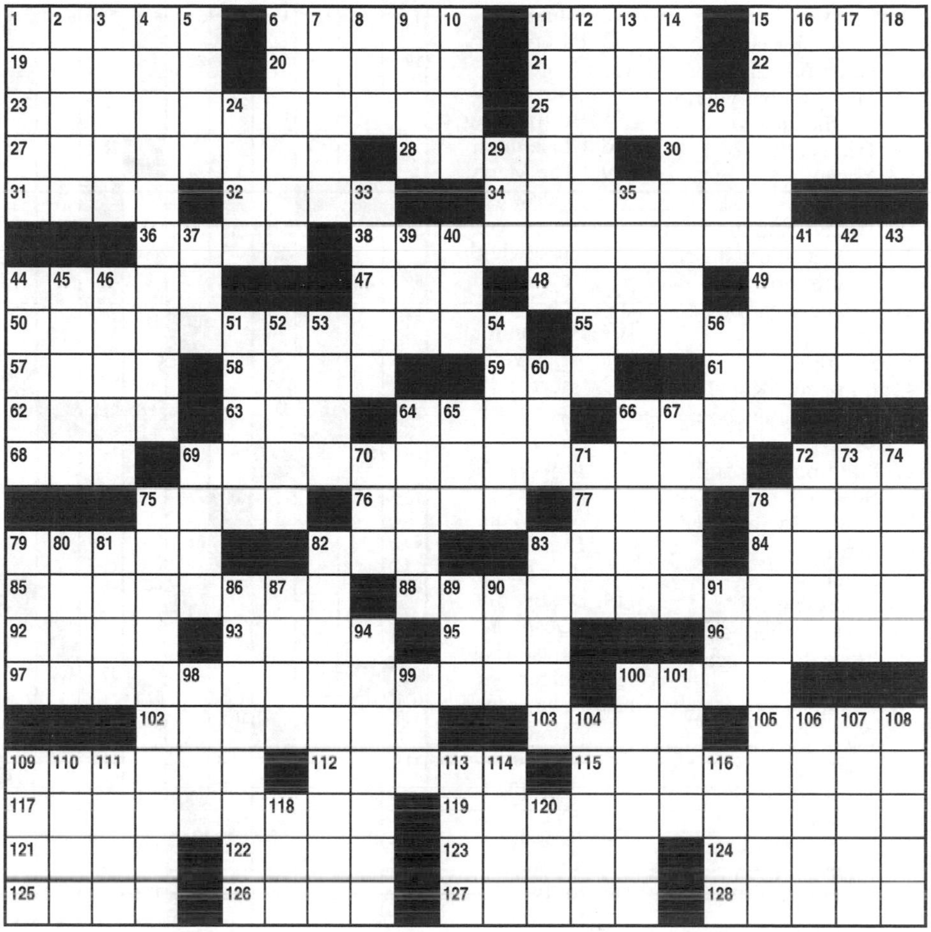

ACROSS

1 Schleps
6 It may be sold in bolts
11 Explorer of Nickelodeon
15 Spot's master
19 González in the 2000 news
20 French actress Anouk
21 Privy to
22 Taj Mahal site
23 Runaway cat?
25 Spa feature, often
27 Hairdo that requires a scrunchy
28 Luke's father in "Star Wars"
30 Browbeat
31 Cornerstone abbr.
32 Tournament ranking
34 Feature of a sloth support system?
36 Typhoon that devasted Guam
38 Silly play by the river bank?
44 Pricey
47 Luau instrument
48 Spilled the beans
49 Brewery equipment
50 Road hog spinning out of control?
55 Vacation spots
57 Dodge Super Bee engine
58 Seagoing: Abbr.
59 Sailor's affirmative
61 Blue ___ special
62 Run into
63 Cigarette box: Abbr.
64 "Your Love Is King" singer
66 Hi's partner in the comics
68 CIA precursor
69 Carved pumpkin with a canine face?
72 Droop
75 Australian wild
76 Ice-dancing team
77 Huntington loc.
78 "American Gigolo" star
79 Buzzing
82 Vixen's lair
83 Dance with Virginia?
84 Lie low
85 Rocker Lewis, known as "The Killer"
88 They're puffed on in Minnesota?
92 Rain-starved
93 Tombstone lawman
95 "The Tell-Tale Heart" author
96 In unison
97 Short-hop transportation?
100 "Doggone it!"
102 Trail-mix ingredients
103 Trillion: Comb. form
105 Fancy
109 Put on a hook again, as a worm
112 Red-waxed cheeses
115 "The Guns of ___" (1961)
117 "G.I. Jane" star
119 Three, for the Goldilocks play?
121 Interminable time
122 ___-friendly
123 Reynolds Wrap maker
124 "In ___": Nirvana album
125 Parts of mins.
126 Throw out
127 Composer Saint-___
128 Gull relatives

DOWN

1 Phoenix neighbor
2 Mixed bags
3 Old-fashioned denial
4 "Calm down!"
5 Hissy fit
6 More crafty
7 City NNE of Paris
8 "Peg ___ Heart" (1913 song)
9 Be inclined
10 Prefix with -gon
11 Misrepresent
12 Exactly
13 Shad delicacy
14 Brazil boa
15 Fearless Tasmanian team?
16 "The Firebird Suite" composer Stravinsky
17 Gator's kin
18 Drumlin's relative
24 "The Right Stuff" org
26 Gram molecules
29 Paperboy's beat: Abbr.
33 Skepticism
35 ___ up (hide)
37 Speedometer meas.
39 End of many a match
40 Tetley product
41 It means nothing in Nogales
42 Proofer's mark
43 To be: Lat.
44 Bonehead
45 Larch and Linden
46 Kind of chair
51 Machu Picchu people
52 "You betcha!"
53 Greasy glop
54 Corporal O'Reilly
56 "Wheel of Fortune" turn
60 Longing
64 Word on the street?
65 Bonavena's 1970 opponent
66 Seesaw, for one
67 Some exams
69 Peer group
70 One way to go
71 Ever-so-quaint, to a Brit
72 Timex competitor
73 Cosmetician Elizabeth
74 Skein gang
75 Dodos
78 Pen for another
79 Not completely closed
80 Repeated word in a Doris Day hit
81 Lou Grant's paper
82 Backsides
83 Butler in an epic
86 Psychiatrist's urging
87 Vittles
89 Photo-___ (press events)
90 Luau chow
91 Barnyard bleat
94 Caters basely (to)
98 "___ to please!"
99 Top-secret org.
100 Daytime soaps
101 Sitar master Shankar
104 Bankrupt energy giant
106 "Odyssey" author
107 Bury
108 Office correspondence
109 Dietary data, briefly
110 Clown shoe width
111 Univ. hotshot
113 CEO degrees
114 Emmy winner Ward
116 "Are you some kind of ___?"
118 Bear, in Barcelona
120 Top fighter pilot

218 SILLY SIBILANCY by Jay Sullivan

The propeller-capped friend of 59 Down was aptly named Beany.

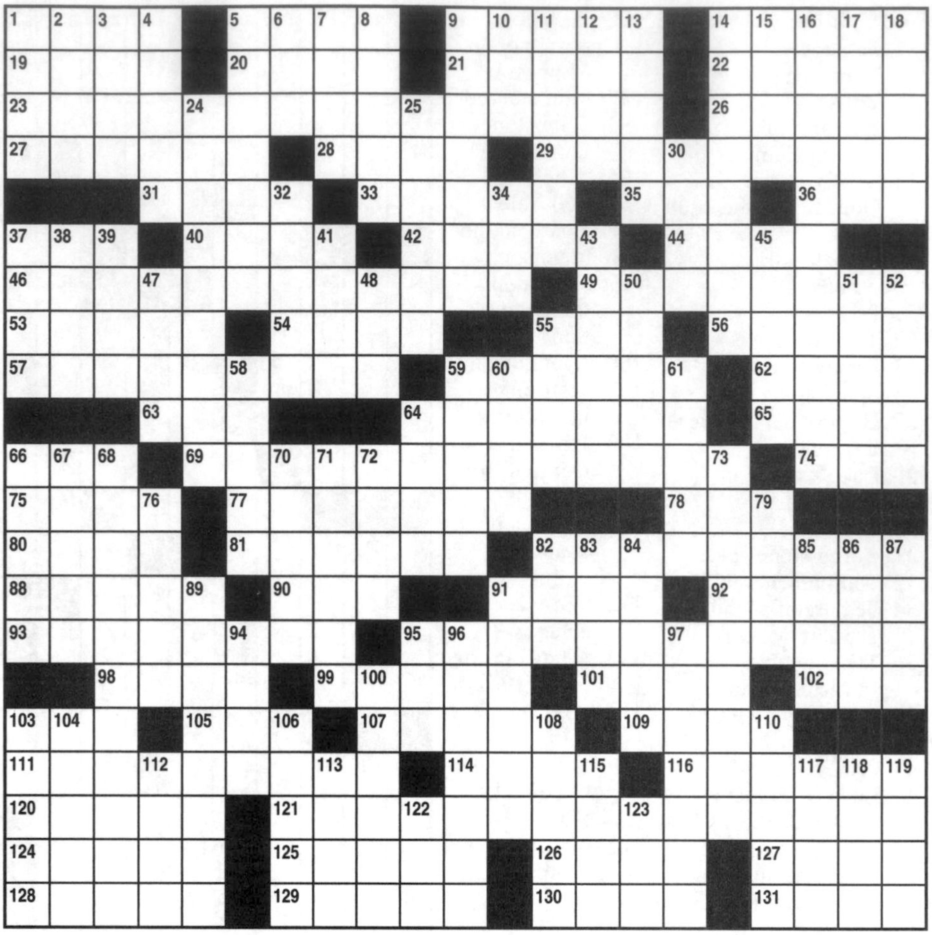

ACROSS

1 No longer under construction
5 They can put you in a tight squeeze
9 Tribe native to Yosemite
14 Hung on to
19 Treats a sprain
20 ". . . ___ dust shalt thou return"
21 Japanese cartoon style
22 Scold
23 Immanuel Kant?
26 Computer encoding sys.
27 Saint born in Avila
28 Slapstick props
29 "Three's Company" actor
31 Pinches
33 Texas leaguer?
35 On the other hand
36 Piece de resistance?
37 Bat wood
40 Architect Mies van der ___
42 Chaplin persona
44 MTA commuter system
46 Detectives' dinner, at times?
49 On the payroll
53 Pueblo pots
54 Make advances
55 English cathedral town
56 Arafat
57 Acid rain, for example
59 Mustard plant oil
62 1963 role for Liz
63 Quarterback Manning
64 Calm
65 Hard rain
66 Transport for Sinbad
69 Failure to yield the right-of-way?
74 Party crowd mbr.
75 Earth sci.
77 Per ___: for example (Italian)
78 Connecticut quarter arbor
80 Verne voyager
81 Conductor Barenboim
82 Like "sic" often
88 They're entitled
90 Stop on the way home
91 Apply lightly
92 Filing aid
93 Part of a winter foursome
95 Bullfighting?
98 Close in on
99 "The Merry Widow" composer
101 Get a wiggle on
102 Rebel leader
103 Pack animal
105 ___ kwon do
107 Short and sweet
109 Word processor settings
111 "The Wild Bunch" director
114 Delany of "Desperate Housewives"
116 Vulgar
120 Renaissance painter Veronese
121 Bargeman's song?
124 "Oprah" alternative
125 Early Schwarzenegger title role
126 Long, long time
127 Contemporary auctioneer
128 News-story openers
129 Biases
130 Does doilies
131 Running things

DOWN

1 Paul Lo Duca's glove
2 Distress signal
3 Popular game
4 Ruhr Valley steel town
5 Fly in the ointment
6 Half and half
7 Looking down on
8 Director Coppola
9 One who knows the score
10 ___ New York minute
11 Solomon's specialty
12 Melville's tale of the South Pacific
13 ___ G: smooth-jazz saxophonist
14 How an exotic dancer might be clad
15 "Now I get it"
16 High five?
17 "All in the Family" character
18 Belief in a supreme being
24 Consequently
25 Virginia city
30 Some seaweed
32 Former Dolphin Don
34 Trade center?
37 All wet
38 ETO battleground (07/44)
39 "Clue" room
41 Kind of scholar or collar
43 Head of the House
45 "Our Gang" producer
47 Cabbage cousin
48 Overdue for take-off?
50 "You've got to be pulling ___"
51 Refrain from farming?
52 Whimsical
55 Hydroxylated hydrocarbon
58 Like a bike
59 Seasick sea-serpent toon
60 Lhasa ___
61 Impromptu
64 Ready to eat
66 Tears up
67 Three-time Clooney role
68 "Wait till your father gets home"?
70 Light ___ (feathery)
71 Culinary herb
72 Mus. chord
73 Acknowledges applause
76 "Camelot" composer
79 HUD secretary (1989–92)
82 Tippling point
83 Heavy hitter
84 In the vicinity
85 Dabbling duck
86 Superior's inferior
87 Small force
89 ___ of the Cross
91 Like a shark's fin
94 Persian Gulf country
95 Pastoral parent
96 Ends a sentence
97 Perfume bottles
100 Natural gas component
103 Fencing feint
104 Black Panthers cofounder
106 They have lots of extras
108 Finish up by
110 Sub-Saharan region
112 "Twittering Machine" artist
113 Rampaging
115 On naval maneuvers, say
117 "Sticks and Bones" playwright
118 Glitch or hitch
119 Ice cream brand
122 Uh-uh
123 Nap sack

219 BRAIN BUSTER by Harvey Estes

Cryptic clue for 72 Down: Litigants in uncomplicated spats.

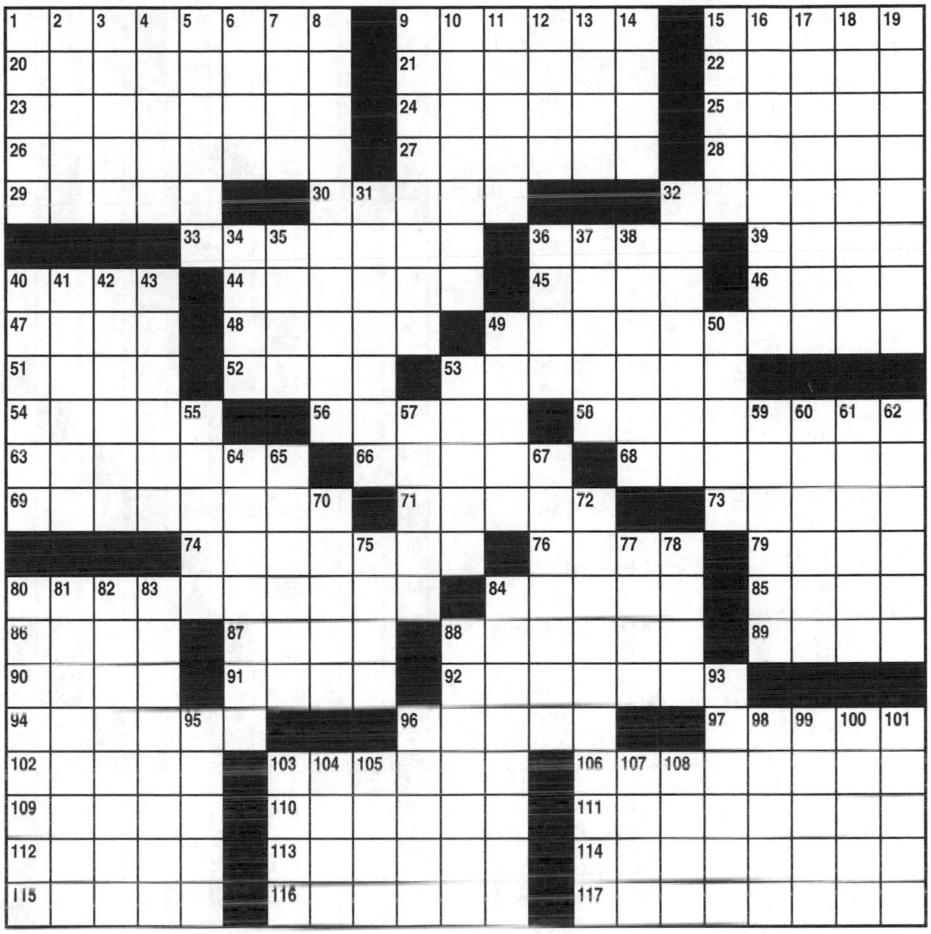

ACROSS

1 50 Cent and more
9 7-10 and others
15 Dash
20 Roman carrier
21 Friday companion
22 Deck out
23 Sandlot sport
24 Like the Trojan horse
25 Grenoble ground
26 "Ready to go!"
27 Some young predators
28 Dostoevsky novel, with "The"
29 Heart recipient, e.g.
30 Pumps and such
32 Bush follower
33 Drawing tools
36 Didst take a chair
39 Soviet news agency
40 Salsa rating
44 Throws with effort
45 Big name in Dixieland
46 Coup target
47 Actress Falco
48 Question source
49 Imitate them
51 University of North Carolina
52 No layabout
53 Settle the score
54 All thumbs
56 Pine product
58 Like an oft-visited page
63 Votes out
66 Put off
68 Song and dance
69 Sweet sandwiches
71 Thoroughly enjoyed
73 Sign supporters
74 Acid users
76 Card, for one
79 Agrippina's son
80 Leads
84 Papal crown
85 Extreme right of Dixie?
86 Gyro component
87 Best of the theater
88 Rationality
89 Hockey nickname
90 Burns up
91 Do boring work
92 Type of protection
94 Apple tools
96 Ace, maybe
97 Church areas
102 Pointless
103 Making a bundle
106 Cold storage
109 "Cape Fear" actor
110 John's "Grease" costar
111 Emulate Ben Franklin
112 ___ over (assisted)
113 Tops
114 Drove (out)
115 Wet spots
116 Bring relief to
117 Mudslingers

DOWN

1 Like many a fan
2 Memorable mission
3 Galileo, for one
4 Inscribed column
5 Pool furniture
6 "Ah me!"
7 Get to
8 When it rains it pours?
9 Big glass
10 Great facility
11 Quiet times
12 Dot in the ocean
13 Bender
14 Hems, for example
15 "Socrate" composer
16 Came before
17 Water
18 Bacchanalian activity
19 Letters get smaller on them
31 Hung around
32 "Get your paws off!"
34 "If ___ my way . . ."
35 Sonora simoleon
36 Fired off
37 Caught a bug
38 "Sons and Lovers" actor Howard
40 Person with a message
41 "Couldn't tell ya"
42 This way
43 Excavate further
49 Woman told to walk away
50 Ahead of the game
53 Shower sights
55 VCR, e.g.
57 Store at many a mall
59 This minute
60 Choirs may stand on them
61 Bag
62 Early explorer of Florida
64 Rare contributors
65 Leave the country
67 Meet by chance
70 Pundit Alexander
72 Suit bringers
75 Dutch export
77 Art deco illustrator
78 Beach catch
80 Don
81 Irrational distrust
82 Deep greens
83 Someone you miss
84 Follow too closely
88 Like a pig
93 Arid expanse
95 Marsh growth
96 Turning point
98 Bluffer's game
99 Hotel upgrade
100 Banana oil, e.g.
101 Lawn starters
103 They're down around the neck
104 Kind of sax
105 It may be a stretch
107 Skelton's Kadiddlehopper
108 Brontë woman

220 RUDOLPH'S TEAMMATES by John Greenman

Original clues with a holiday theme.

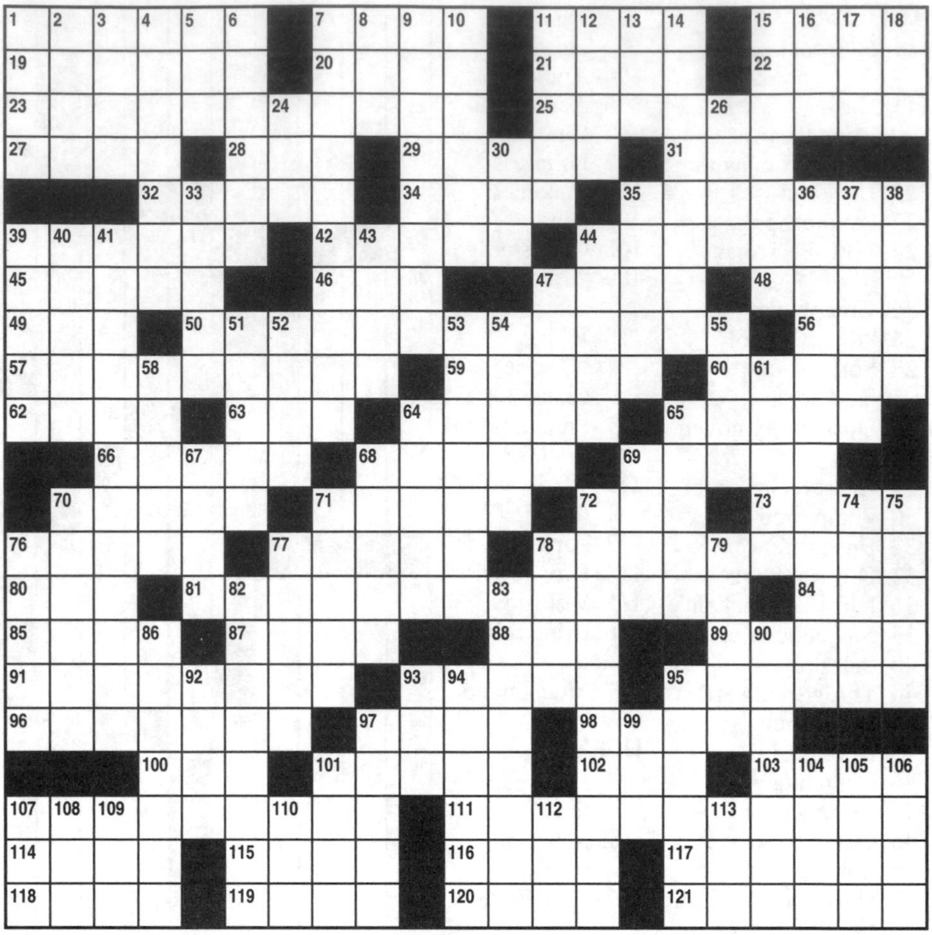

ACROSS

1 Party or banquet
7 Zulu warrior band
11 Cornmeal mush
15 Wrestling surfaces
19 Delphic seer
20 Currish
21 Vera preceder
22 R&B singer India.___
23 DONNER
25 DANCER
27 Observant one
28 ___-de-la-Cité
29 Shreds
31 Vex
32 Ina in "The Black Orchid"
34 ___ avis
35 Cause of affliction
39 Sloping rise
42 Mosque figures
44 Recipe measure
45 Bridget Fonda, to Jane
46 Jaunty cap
47 Julie of "Big Brother"
48 Annoyingly self-satisfied
49 Plaint akin to "baa"
50 PRANCER
56 Ripen
57 Imagines
59 Ph.D. exams
60 Jury, for one
62 Having digits
63 2005 Prince hit
64 Breadth
65 Orbit
66 Hollow
68 Shakespeare's Andronicus
69 Nightspot
70 Lei Day greeting
71 Locker picture
72 Dawn riser
73 Arden and Plumb
76 Jasmine Guy hit single
77 Crimean people
78 Most impassive
80 Ambassador's res.
81 BLITZEN
84 Federal Acquisition Service org.
85 NC university
87 To be, to Brutus
88 Stout relative
89 Reuben James sinker
91 Reflect
93 Country snger Haggard
95 Do a batik-like craft
96 Synthetic plastic
97 South of France
98 Saw parts
100 Moving vehicle
101 Spurious
102 Scam
103 "The Last King of Scotland" subject
107 VIXEN
111 DASHER
114 Shortly
115 Begum's garb
116 Otherwise
117 Plant maladies
118 Toodle-oo
119 "Auld Lang ___"
120 Pair
121 Ambers, e.g.

DOWN

1 Top-drawer
2 Donnybrook
3 Notoriety
4 Sharp, as wit
5 Peru port
6 Top off a drink
7 Without regret
8 "Give ___ break!"
9 Deli meat
10 Pantleg part
11 Native-born Israeli
12 Alack's partner
13 Gretchen of films
14 Fish-gathering birds
15 Price increases
16 Jackie's second
17 Metal alloy
18 Yellow, black or red
24 "When We Were Kings" figure
26 Son of Aphrodite
30 Start of MGM's motto
33 Baldwin and Guinness
35 Clairvoyants
36 CUPID
37 Dug into wood
38 NBC newsman Richard
39 Not reached, as quotas
40 Alicia de Larrocha's instrument
41 COMET
43 Injures
44 Oarlock
47 Rodeo wear
51 Muhammad's favorite wife
52 Model
53 Matins division
54 Bevy
55 Heroic poem
58 Figure of speech
61 Bowed
64 Egyptiian peninsula
65 Novelist Cather
67 Rachael Ray, e.g.
68 Give alms regularly
69 Condemn
70 Small sea strait
71 Outdated
72 Respect, in the hood
74 Prose piece
75 Condition
76 Bustles
77 Sample
78 Use eBay
79 Eskimo
82 Bacon asset
83 With ostentation
86 "Smells Like Teen Spirit" group
90 Comports oneself
92 Ducky color?
93 Jet fighter plane
94 Elicited
95 Sore
97 Pluck
99 Geologic span
101 Née
104 "Rent" heroine
105 Hit single by Nas
106 "Untouchables" crimefighter
107 Full-figured
108 Last Spanish queen
109 Bon ___
110 Wray in "King Kong"
112 2002 Winter Olympics host
113 Netherlands city

221 LAST STOP by Fred Piscop

Ironically 6 Down is not related to his idol "Bird."

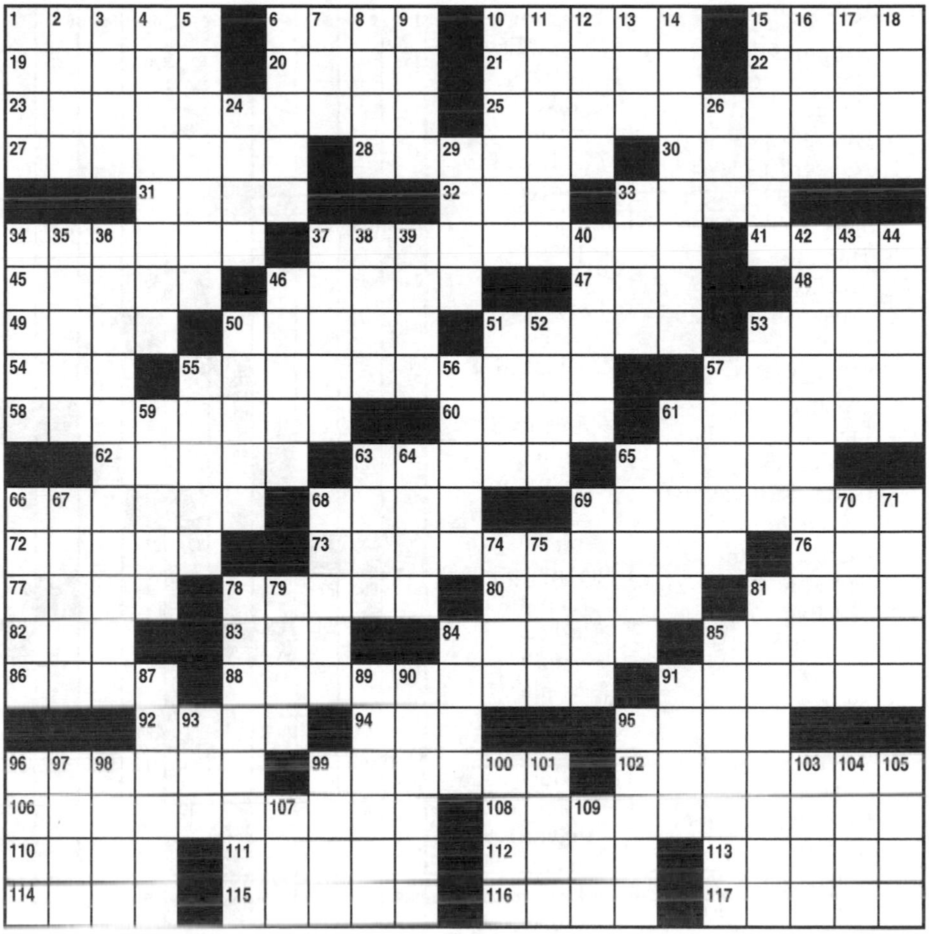

ACROSS

1 Dieter of rhyme
6 Voodoo charm
10 They may be vaulted
15 "Beetle Bailey" dog
19 Admiral Byrd book
20 Case for the MPs
21 Black Monday event
22 Set to drive
23 Stoop
25 Grasp
27 Cause to jump
28 The Keys, e.g.
30 Calendar listings
31 Kent State's state
32 "The College Widow" author
33 Wroclaw's river
34 Spoon-fed, say
37 Recovering
41 Pack away
45 They carry tunes
46 Like chiffon
47 "La ___ en Rose"
48 2001 Smith biopic
49 News agency established in 1925
50 Pet store buys
51 Something tasty
53 X, Y or Z
54 Green prefix
55 Auto magazine since 1949
57 You can dig it
58 Hung back
60 Scout's venture
61 Duped, in a way
62 Was visibly angry
63 Secluded spots
65 Steinway item
66 Norton player
68 Jillions
69 O. Henry et al.
72 Drops out
73 The "4" of "7 – 4 = 3"
76 Weasel word?
77 Shovels it
78 One of the Four Hundred
80 Cliff dweller's abode
81 Filmmaker Riefenstahl
82 Reinking on Broadway
83 PBS benefactor
84 Like a tumbler
85 Irish tenor Tynan
86 Patches, in a way
88 Envelope directive
91 Noggin
92 Greasy spoon sign
94 Prefix with soak or sort
95 Ad mustache makeup
96 Richard of Rambo films
99 Result in
102 Big Brother's state
106 Starbucks brew
108 Stretch too thinly
110 Concession add-on
111 It'll hold water
112 It may be hitched
113 Touch up
114 Go slowly
115 Eastern VIPs
116 Taylor Hicks, e.g.
117 "Foxfire" author

DOWN

1 Some bunts, for short
2 Whodunit kernel
3 Gossipy Barrett
4 Some sci-fi villains
5 Uses a ring, maybe
6 Jazz saxophonist Parker
7 See red?
8 "Woodstock" songwriter Mitchell
9 Bygone GM make
10 Give in
11 For now
12 ___ Club (merchandising chain)
13 Eerie ability
14 Rendered unreadable
15 Rightmost column, perhaps
16 Eagle Scout, say
17 Revival spot
18 Churchill Downs info
24 Dropped in value
26 Time to revel
29 Costar of Bolger and Haley
33 "Come ___!"
34 Dog to beware
35 At full gallop
36 Close chum
37 1977 Burns film
38 Not e'en once
39 It makes the grade
40 Duck
42 Like Liberals, some say
43 "Thimble Theatre" name
44 ___ up (got hip)
46 Packed to the gills
50 Brooklyn island
51 Blue cheese line
52 Tat artist's stock
53 Rice-___
55 Performers in whiteface
56 Role for Clark
57 Liver, for one
59 Bee and Em
61 Hideous one
63 Pack to the gills
64 Piercing site
65 Loon-like bird
66 RC and others
67 PABA part
68 Like the flying lizard
69 "___ in my hand the final envelope"
70 Having a key
71 Craven's lack
74 Go bananas
75 Court score
78 Lamp locale
79 Some July births
81 Hot-dogger's cry
84 Sacked out
85 Some Times Square knockoffs
87 Picked up
89 Game one
90 Plays the market
91 "Good one!"
93 Suffix with pent
95 Tasty fungus
96 Winter woe
97 Churn up
98 Trevi toss-in, maybe
99 First name in denim
100 Doughnut shapes
101 "Ars Amatoria" poet
103 Depilatory brand
104 ___ way, shape, or form
105 Annex: Abbr.
107 NFL Hall-of-Famer Barney
109 Shogun's capital

222 GOOD ADVICE by Matt Ginsberg

Looks like the advice offered at 27 Across was taken.

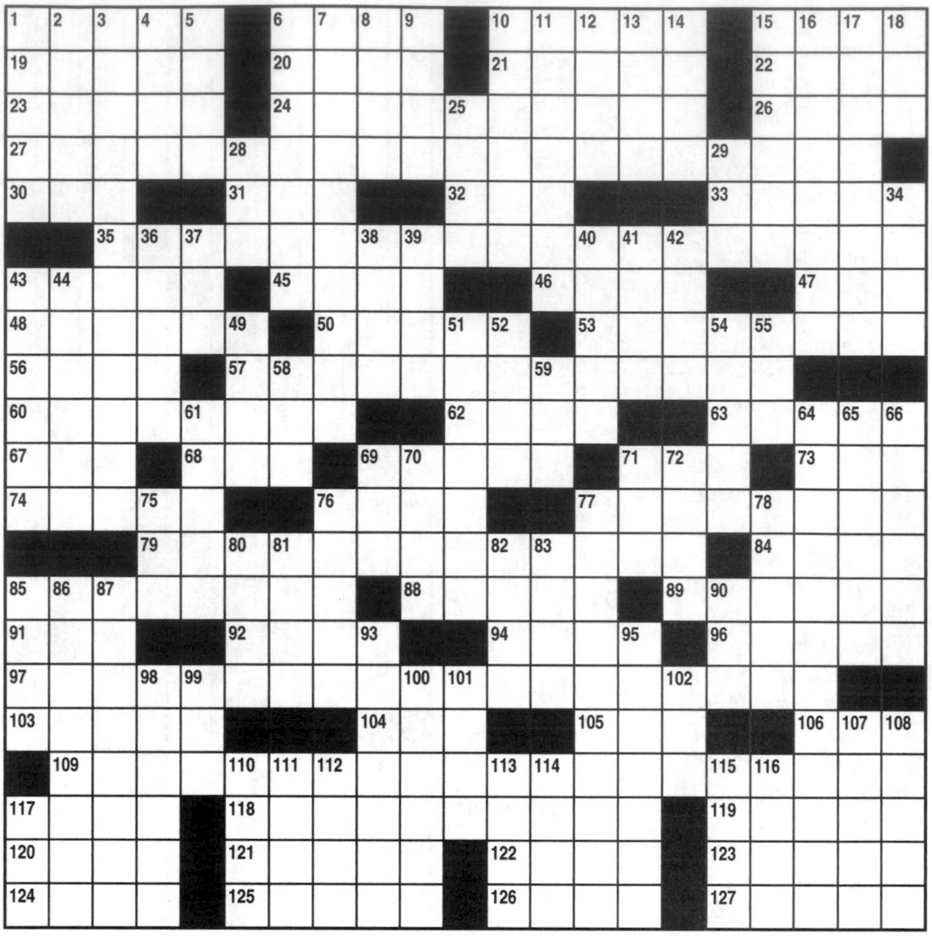

ACROSS

1 Generous donation
6 Hairy Genesis character
10 Uncouth
15 Not certifiable?
19 "Donkey Kong" hero
20 Turn
21 Mucho
22 What there oughtta be
23 "Chinatown" producer
24 Incomprehensible, facetiously
26 Goddess of victory
27 Advice for Daimler? (2007)
30 Draft pick?
31 The Eagle, briefly
32 J.A. Prufrock's creator
33 Su Lin or Zhen Zhen
35 Advice for Wile E. Coyote?
43 Cousteau invention
45 Schlep
46 Silicon Alley loc.
47 Silicon Alley loc.
48 Good to go
50 Lovers' lane?
53 Roots (through)
56 Dwyane of the NBA
57 Advice for Mary, Queen of Scots?
60 Like Cruella de Vil
62 Superblack
63 "Fuhgeddaboudit!"
67 Playwright Levin
68 The provide TLC in the ICU
69 Horses have it
71 Apt. elts.
73 Is for you?
74 Lovable bear
76 Circumnavigator Phileas
77 French delicacy
79 Advice for Lot's wife?
84 Dextrous opening
85 Separate
88 Hook-sinker connector
89 "Chico and the Man" setting
91 Treebeard, e.g.
92 Part of n.b.
94 Brett Favre activity
96 Take up again?
97 Advice for Paris?
103 Life-preserver stuffing
104 Drowned valley
105 Chickadee cousin
106 Intended kidnap victim in a 2001 Pixar hit
109 Advice for Capt. Edward J. Smith?
117 Mini-marathon, briefly
118 Widely circulated advertisement
119 Divine comedian?
120 Railroad missing from a Monopoly board
121 Dig deeply
122 "Ben-Hur" costume designer
123 Nook or cranny
124 Sagan's subj.
125 Bo and Daisy
126 Talc-to-diamond scale
127 1998 role for Malkovich

DOWN

1 End-all
2 Tangle, and disentangle
3 "Touch of Grey" band
4 Isn't right?
5 Snack
6 Revert to the state
7 Vow
8 Ayla creator
9 Kazakh mountain
10 Rider
11 Play lists?
12 Spherical starter
13 Double ___ Oreos
14 Anti-DWI grp.
15 Birkenstock, e.g.
16 Making true
17 Unassisted observer
18 Dolly, for one
25 "The Great American Novel" author
28 Antiquity
29 Vs.
34 Electrical extravaganza
36 "Father of Modern Drama"
37 "Fuhgeddaboudit," in Glasgow
38 Narc chaser?
39 "Concetta" pianist
40 Pachisi-like board game
41 "Fuhgeddaboudit"
42 Quince, e.g.
43 Felt like it
44 Charlie's "Stardust" costar
49 Minnesotan
51 Using as a bed
52 Endless periods
54 Parson's place
55 Bother
58 Kiang or onager
59 Beach banjo
61 Dehumidifier
64 Backup activity
65 Agri-useful
66 Playground rebuttal
69 Great ball of fire?
70 Mind's I's?
71 Sinbad's avian adversary
72 Gumshoe Hammer
75 2008 Pepsi Center event: Abbr.
76 Guitarists' concerns?
77 They come out at night
78 Krypton and argon
80 "I came"
81 College founded by King Henry VI
82 Hung on to
83 Jaded feeling
85 Flatten
86 Asthmatics' aids
87 "Go!"
90 JFK info.
93 United charge
95 Muslim minority
98 Kitchen appliance
99 ___-Katy
100 Electronic flow controllers
101 Seed locations
102 Not Rx
107 Weed-B-Gon company
108 Curved moldings
110 Amos' succ.
111 Karachi language
112 Laid off, in baseball
113 Van Morrison's first band
114 1992 title role for Dustin Hoffman
115 She wouldn't give the Incredibles capes
116 Fly, for one
117 Chinese export

223 "GIDDYUP!" by Billie Truitt

A ride down the bridle path.

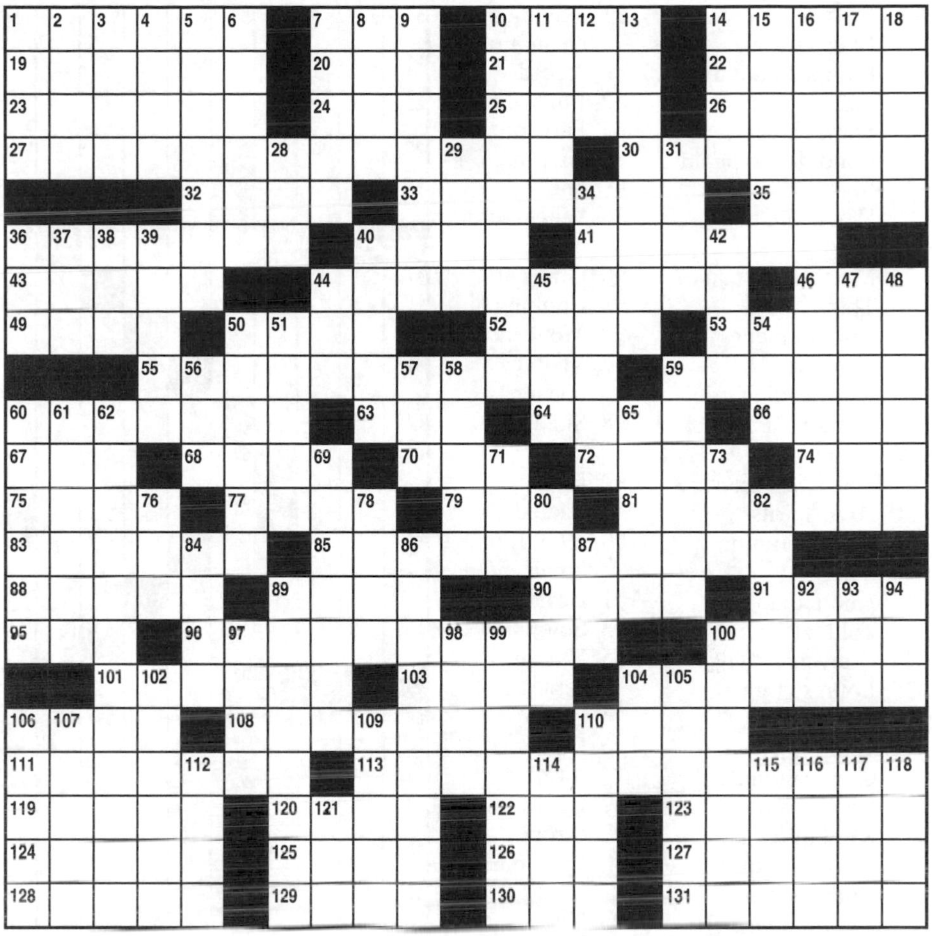

ACROSS

1 Stratagem
7 On vacation
10 "Be that ___ may"
14 Used a stopwatch
19 Four-faced god
20 Mary in "Look Back in Anger"
21 A bit off-color
22 Shake off
23 Catches some Zs
24 Pentagon fig.
25 Fort in Arlington
26 Borden mascot
27 Settle a debt
30 Methuselah, for one
32 Pucker-producing
33 Authorize
35 The good life
36 Hood's forte
40 Yarn producer?
41 Paradise
43 ___ Major
44 Spotty soup legumes
46 4, on the phone
49 One of the Redgraves
50 Fundamental particle
52 It's a real gas
53 "The Wild Duck" playwright
55 One who avoids conscription
59 Low-tech hauler
60 Come by
63 Expert
64 Birds' beaks
66 River through Hamburg
67 Thanksgiving, for one: Abbr.
68 "Rose Is Rose" boy
70 Not firmed up yet, on a schedule
72 Military meal
74 Memorial architect Maya
75 Pedro's aunts
77 Amber brews
79 Stars and Stripes land
81 Colored a shirt at camp, perhaps
83 Wild
85 Sorceress of Arthurian legend
88 Response to "Who broke this?"
89 Res ___ loquitur
90 Smooth-talking
91 Lounge around
95 Suffix for legal
96 Discovery site of ancient gnostic texts in Egypt
100 ___ Hawkins Day
101 Corkscrew pasta
103 Stash of cash
104 Made corrections
106 Whistle blowers?
108 Eyelash enhancer
110 Frost lines?
111 Folk religion adherent, perhaps
113 Scheherazade's stories
119 Trend
120 "What's ___ for me?"
122 Tummy muscles
123 Asparagus units
124 Nut case
125 "Reader" of crosswords?
126 "What, me worry?" magazine
127 Meteor impact site
128 No ___ barred
129 Cast off
130 Roses–red connector
131 **They lead off eight answers**

DOWN

1 Cook's meas.
2 Alice's restaurant patron
3 Normandy city
4 Those folks
5 Ascribes
6 Weinberger who served Reagan
7 Word of obligation
8 Set loose
9 Pen up
10 Moon's first visitor
11 Greet
12 Cool down
13 One from Innsbruck
14 Prepared to drive (with "up")
15 "Let me get back to you on that"
16 1966 Wilson Pickett hit
17 Falco and Adams
18 Mower maker
28 Make an attempt
29 Advanced biol. course
31 Skinny
34 Something to prove
36 It's sometimes repaired by knee surgery
37 Line of light
38 Larry King's channel
39 Yoga practitioner
40 Park of "Star Trek: Enterprise"
42 Powerful auto engine
44 It's at home on the range
45 "___ there, done that"
47 VW Beetle in the movies
48 Mean
50 Exploit successfully
51 "___ the same about you"
54 Pre-AD
56 Ocasek of the Cars
57 Columbus Day mo.
58 Fix, as software
59 Change into bone
60 Bring into harmony
61 Dockers product
62 March Madness game
65 Tropical nut
69 Beale Street's city
71 Jehoshaphat's father
73 It makes waves
76 Bottom line
78 Slugger Sammy
80 Battery terminal
82 "Blowin' in the Wind" composer
84 Season for hot-cross buns
86 Fortified with bulwarks
87 Year in Nero's reign
89 Founder of the Jesuits
92 Like a sock with no mate
93 Stretch out
94 Took by the hand
97 Objectives
98 Red giant in Cetus
99 "To Kill a Mockingbird" state
100 Part-time player
102 Donny or Marie
104 Long, long time
105 Decent sort
106 Toothed wheel
107 Año nuevo month
109 Queeg's command
110 ___ deux (dance)
112 Annoys
114 Letter-shaped girder
115 Drive or reverse
116 Milliner's stock
117 Picnicker's shade
118 Ukr. and Est., once
121 Ultimate degree

224 DIAMOND DESIGN by Harvey Estes

37 Down won seven Olympic gold medals that year.

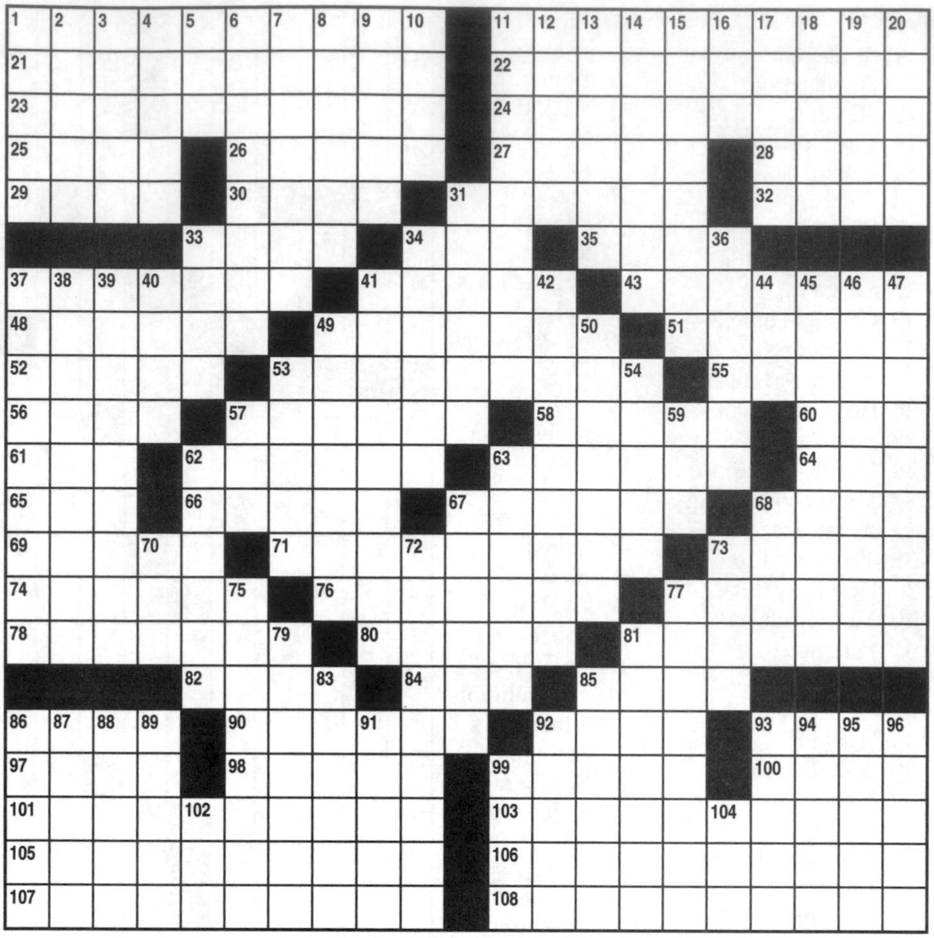

ACROSS

1 Et cetera
11 European relative of Tyra?
21 Stark choice
22 Candidate type, in film
23 Harsh and then some
24 Marie's last name?
25 Think
26 Commitment symbols
27 One needing prier restraint?
28 Slammer
29 North Sea feeder
30 High spirits
31 Demonstration noise
32 Knotted up
33 Told tales
34 Convenient enc.
35 Long swimmers
37 Strolled, in "The Ten Commandments"?
41 Really rains
43 Kind of radar
48 Squirrel's stash
49 Coerce
51 Hall-of-Fame QB Bob
52 Edit for radio, maybe
53 Look here
55 Quite quickly
56 Rosebud owner
57 Long-eared pet
58 In a straight-faced way
60 Ryder rental
61 Winter product prefix
62 Hit on the head
63 Prolonged attacks
64 Wren's wing
65 Homeboy
66 Israeli seaport
67 Draft orders
68 Eastern cuisine
69 Ryan of "Pippin"
71 Inelegant language
73 Sends packing
74 Musical ineptitude
76 Places
77 Biker's protection
78 Czech runner
80 Appointed
81 Having a clean moral record
82 Lofty lines
84 Paris potable
85 Nirvana, for one
86 What there oughta be
90 Grabs at
92 Cooking aid
93 Move slowly
97 Vision opener
98 Shade of black
99 Prison-related
100 1939 film home
101 Bearing
103 Screwball
105 Without serious injury
106 Dakar dweller
107 Downtown
108 Strong emotions

DOWN

1 Hookup spot
2 Long story
3 Uncool sort
4 The Velvet Fog
5 Many mins.
6 Efforts
7 Bad-mouthed
8 Smoothed out
9 Suit material
10 Dos follower
11 Blockbuster
12 "Care to?"
13 Chant
14 Hightailed it
15 Vessel documentation
16 Patty's place
17 What to give it
18 Capone cohort
19 "Born to Be Wild" gorilla
20 Bergen sidekick
31 Came down with
33 Minnesota's WNBA team
34 Lathered
36 Uses a hose
37 1972 Olympic swimming star
38 Salty exhibitions?
39 Sleepy
40 Historic canal
41 Sports training time
42 Persevered, with "on"
44 Deck spot
45 Go off to college
46 Snowballs
47 Does another hitch
49 Complete supply of office things
50 Sea nymphs of myth
53 Lose it
54 Yield and more
57 Down around the neck
59 Article at the Louvre
62 Bottom-of-the-line
63 Like booty
67 Hindu teachers
68 Motorist's payout
70 Prefix with con
72 Junkman, e.g.
73 Give in
75 Cabernet, for example
77 Quadruped pair
79 Protein in hair and nails
81 Crusader's foe
83 Red, once
85 Bunch member
86 Storage spot
87 Téa in "Spanglish"
88 Carve up
89 Wuss
91 Pound parts
92 Persona non grata
93 Nationality prefix
94 2000 presidential candidate
95 Wave feature
96 Can't stand
99 Furtive summons
102 Room opener
104 Part of a graduate's ensemble

225 TOWN TUNES by Lou Kirkley

"I Wanna Go Home" is the alternative title for 28 Across.

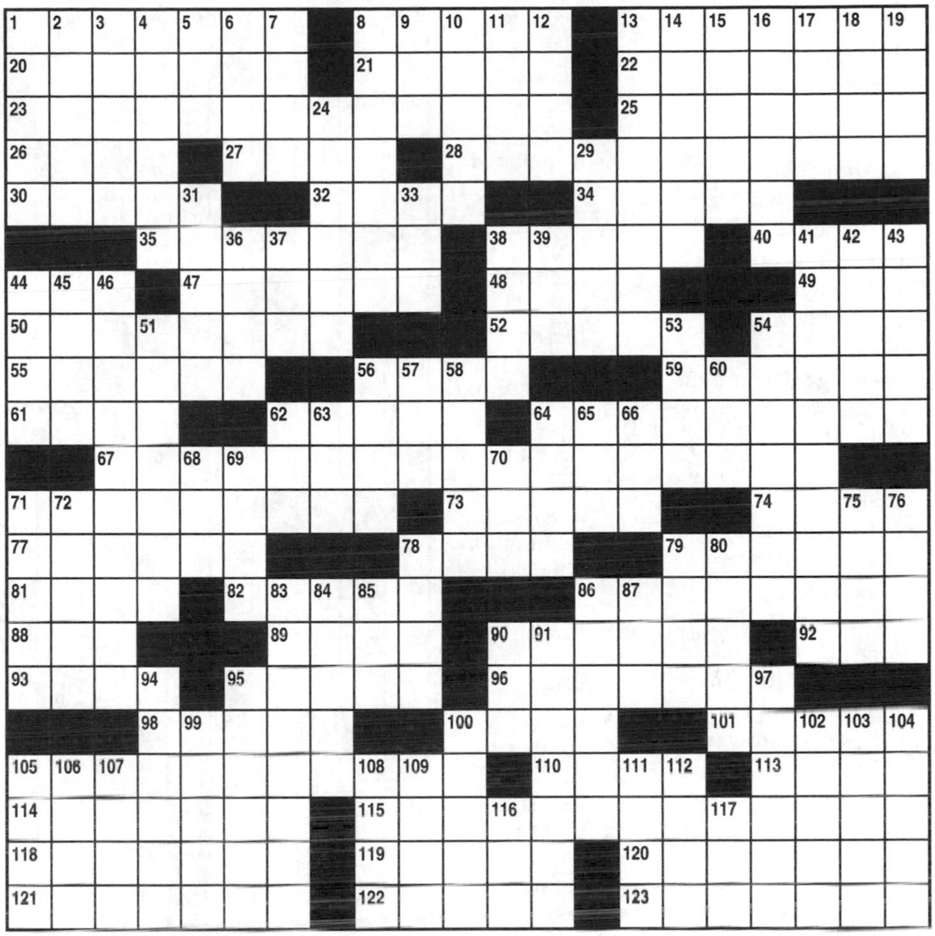

ACROSS

1 Runs toward
8 Egypt's Nasser
13 To the point
20 Working together
21 Poet's muse
22 Woke up
23 Glen Campbell song (with 64-A)
25 Had faith in
26 Existed
27 Store in a hold
28 Bobby Bare song
30 "Let ___!"
32 Carla portrayer on "Cheers"
34 Textile trademark
35 Kind of counter
38 Collar attachment
40 List finish
44 Words of assent: Var.
47 Treat, as table salt
48 Pine for
49 Sumac of Peru
50 Head honchos
52 Jacobi of "I, Claudius"
54 Ending for auto
55 AARP concern
56 Dithers, to Bumstead
59 Cause to sparkle
61 Salt on a chemist's table
62 Bend over
64 See 23 Across
67 Tony Bennett song (with 71-A)
71 See 67 Across
73 Type size
74 Jermaine Jackson's brother
77 Use for support
78 Fur stole
79 Elbow-bender
81 Skin moisturizer
82 Mall binge
86 Aspen and Vail
88 Big, fat mouth
89 Painter Magritte
90 Profits
92 Roadside warning sign
93 Part of CBS
95 Spoke (up)
96 Bart Starr's number at Green Bay
98 Wipe away
100 Lanchester of "Bride of Frankenstein"
101 Holy, to Jose
105 19th-century minstrel song
110 Ray Stevens' "Ahab the ___"
113 Harness the wind
114 Fellini, for one
115 Lovin' Spoonful song
118 The artist formerly known as Knowles
119 "Of ___ Sing"
120 Swimmer's malady
121 "The Faerie Queene" poet
122 Sea birds
123 Use a whetstone on

DOWN

1 Synagogue official
2 To date
3 Furnish food
4 Cultural, as cuisine
5 "Got it?"
6 Skin designs, briefly
7 Skip past
8 "Wow!"
9 Onassis, to friends
10 Sister of Eva and Zsa Zsa
11 Done to ___
12 Trent of Mississippi
13 Liquid dumped on winning coaches
14 Going astray
15 66, for one
16 Clout
17 Italian wine city
18 Nair rival
19 Jacuzzi effect
24 Finicky cat
29 PG assigner
31 Skating event
33 Wide size
36 Farm layer
37 "___ bodkins!"
38 They're neither Rep. nor Dem.
39 Wallace of "E.T."
41 Cruelly oppresses
42 Prized violin
43 Surgical glove material
44 Words before end or impasse
45 Eastern discipline
46 Covert govt. force
51 TV's "Science Guy"
53 "It Had to Be You" lyricist
54 Architect
56 Laddie
57 "Oh wow!"
58 Broccoli bit
60 Canon camera name
62 Rd. crossers
63 HBO competitor
64 Golf peril
65 Giant Mel
66 Pizzeria output
68 "The Name of the Rose" author
69 Fish propellers
70 Eastern title
71 Wears at the edges
72 Pass along
75 Dark greenish blue
76 Roughly
78 Lawn invader
79 Ill humor
80 Desert havens
83 One who doesn't look good in stripes
84 Fasten anew
85 Chemical suffix
86 African adventure
87 Scout Carson
90 CIO partner
91 In relation to
94 Nonstick surface
95 Royal home
97 Jeff Gordon's org.
99 Showers
100 Ruhr valley city
102 Equal rights org.
103 Tenth part
104 "Full House" twins
105 Spatter guards
106 Lone Star sch.
107 Dunaway of "Network"
108 Pay your share (with "up")
109 Bert in "Ship Ahoy"
111 Pub brews
112 Dull as dishwater
116 Half a bray
117 Historic period

226 NINE/TENTHS OF THE LAW by Pancho Harrison

The cookie in the clue at 107 Across is usually found as an answer.

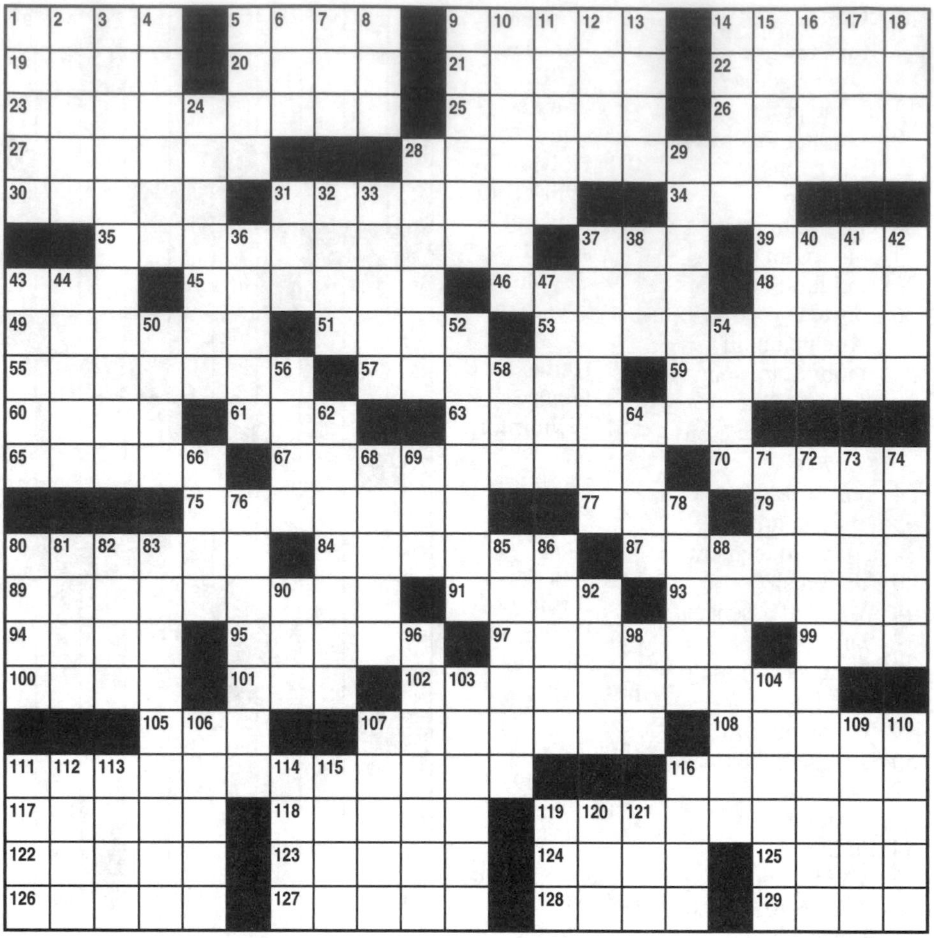

ACROSS

1 Mr. Perot
5 Online periodical, briefly
9 In flames
14 Mrs. Schumann
19 "Manhattan Mary III" artist
20 Frigid follower
21 Johnnycakes
22 Felt poorly
23 James' territory?
25 Bridge declaration
26 Microphone holder
27 Petal perfumes
28 Johnny's political stance?
30 1984 Vardon Trophy winner Calvin
31 Ask for
34 A Stooge
35 Sean's cutlery?
37 Tackle moguls
39 Some microwaves
43 Prefix with metric
45 The get-go
46 Overact (with "up")
48 "Chicago" Tony winner Neuwirth
49 Spilled the beans
51 Certain Slav
53 Brad's rodeo critters?
55 Big bash
57 Penitent one
59 Some scouts
60 Flaky mineral
61 Small batteries
63 Comes to
65 Siskel's onetime partner
67 Ringo's arduous journey?
70 1992 Nicholson title role
75 Strove for (with "to")
77 The Pistons, on scoreboards
79 ___ circles (field phenomena)
80 Libyan language
84 Argues back
87 Z's
89 Richard's work hours?
91 12-point type
93 More senseless
94 Pizazz
95 Peddler's merchandise
97 Mascara targets
99 Weep
100 Campus mil. program
101 "Am ___ brother's keeper?"
102 Oscar's literary circle?
105 Flying Solo
107 Oreo maker
108 Lent a hand
111 Jack's sand irons?
116 Commotion
117 Tinseltown trophy
118 Scent
119 What Rob's Pebble Beach numbers?
122 Get underway
123 Koran's religion
124 PayPal's parent company
125 Cafeteria dispensers
126 Decaf brand since 1903
127 Tilts
128 Broadcasts
129 Sound of a leak

DOWN

1 Summarize
2 Make a delivery?
3 Real troopers?
4 Upper house
5 All ___ (paying attention)
6 Farrow in "Rosemary's Baby"
7 Lob's path
8 Grok
9 Each
10 Like a dandy
11 Unsuitable
12 Defendant in court: Abbr.
13 Petrol brand
14 Electronic keyboard maker
15 One who pitches out?
16 Jai ___
17 Clinton's attorney general
18 Annex: Abbr.
24 Took a particular direction
28 Sidetrack
29 Lovestruck
31 Wild blue yonder
32 Lennon's in-laws
33 Initial entry on a form, perhaps
36 "Birthday Girl" heroine
37 Smiled smugly
38 Pioneer Carson
40 Block part?
41 Competent
42 Appt. with a shrink
43 "Who's there?" response
44 Old Indian title
47 ". . . partridge in ___ tree"
50 Bump on a log
52 Nail wood over windows, say
54 Criticize harshly
56 Struggle for air
58 Region above Sask.
62 Cook in a wok
64 Just makes it
66 Mai ___ (rum cocktails)
68 Rocky ridge
69 NBA stat
71 Eight: Comb. form
72 Glass-paneled entryways
73 Vestibule
74 Mimicking behavior
76 Big name in bikes
78 South Vietnam's last president
80 "Happy Feet" composer
81 Move, in Realtor-speak
82 "I smell ___!"
83 Standard of excellence
85 Mel of country music
86 Oodles
88 Opens certain fasteners
90 "___ Legend" (2007)
92 "Hold on ___!"
96 "Waltzing Matilda" vagabond
98 "The Sopranos" airer
103 Construction girders
104 Big top
106 Main artery
107 City of Zambia
109 Brings in
110 Jumper
111 Profit's opposite
112 This, in Tijuana
113 Shoe seller Thom
114 Banshee's cry
115 Celtic language
116 180-degree turns, slangily
119 Meadow
120 ___-Wan Kenobi ("Star Wars" character)
121 Armed conflict

227 CELEBRITY DINNER by Robert A. Doll

Looks like Bob's supplying the entertainment to the dinner below.

ACROSS

1 Geoducks
6 Normandy battle site
10 Elevated
14 Nicktoon's "___ Mikey"
19 Macho sort
20 Egg on
21 Hodgepodge
22 Paragon
23 Writing desk
25 Give a second thought
27 Hollywood Canteen bread?
29 Famed Ferrara family
30 Pantry pest
31 Master Melvin of baseball
32 Sites for rites
36 Bloodhound's cue
39 Magazine contents
41 "Mayday!"
44 World's lowest lake
46 Hollywood Canteen potage?
49 Around the bend
50 Camel cousin
52 Bit for Mr. Ed
53 The S in OSU
54 Bumbling
56 Wee hour
57 Tighter
60 Gumbo ingredient
61 Hollywood Canteen Moselle?
64 Dixon Ticonderoga end
66 Actress Zadora
67 Took action
68 Menlo Park monogram
69 Become more mysterious
73 Hollywood Canteen course?
81 Ready to eat
82 Ice cream treat
84 Clandestine Feds.
85 Princess topper
86 "Belling the Cat" author
88 ___ Paulo
89 Thespian
91 Gordian, for one
92 Hollywood Canteen dessert?
96 Let off the hook
98 The piper's son
99 Film classic "Driving ___ Daisy"
100 Florida State athletes, for short
102 Turned down
103 Make a selection
104 Chowed down
105 "Drillbit Taylor" actor Wilson
107 Hollywood Canteen béchamel?
117 Octoberfest attire
118 French Riviera resort
119 Licorice plant
120 Delta deposit
121 Assist
122 Laser gas
123 Peel's partner
124 Words of understanding
125 New Jersey cagers
126 Steals a glance

DOWN

1 Emeril, for one
2 ___ majesty
3 Gremlins and Hornets
4 Snickers' parent
5 Sneaky shooters
6 Gracious loser
7 Three-wheelers
8 Handed down history
9 Baltic Sea feeder
10 Argonauts' home
11 Native Alaskan
12 Prevarications
13 Tennis score
14 Bomb measures
15 Grownup
16 Ring
17 Butter units
18 Schooner filler
24 Mortarboard attachment
26 Bakery emanation
28 Brinker of Haarlem
32 Wing-it
33 Sierra ___
34 Be quiet, musically
35 Take in, as a stray
37 Mercury model of the '60s
38 Stat for Phil Hughes
39 Let up
40 Allot, with "out"
41 Rips off
42 Like "The Twilight Zone"
43 Pickle unit
45 Hilo hello
47 Content word
48 Greek portico
51 "Wheel of Fortune" purchase
55 Use an old Olivetti
57 ___-baked potato
58 Verdi opera
59 Bring up baby
62 Takes home the trophy
63 Icelandic saga
65 Musical notation
68 Fifer's drum
69 Beer choice
70 "Old MacDonald" letters
71 English racecourse
72 Drudge
73 Spicy cookies
74 Hollyhood hunk
75 Hasty Pudding bigwig
76 Make a lap
77 "American Idol" star Clay
78 Oahu porch
79 Greeted the day
80 Out of style
83 "Snail mail" org.
87 Mollycoddled
89 Be under the weather
90 Night flight
93 Gee follower
94 ___ cordiale
95 Concrete or tone follower
97 Camera accessory
101 Petrarchan poem
103 More than pleasingly plump
104 Edward Rochester's daughter
106 Rolling Stones drummer
107 Jonathan Larson musical
108 Mrs. Lou Grant
109 Mozart's "___ fan tutte"
110 Sale condition
111 Muscat is there
112 Spa attire
113 Bern's river
114 Itch
115 Clydesdale noise
116 Ages and ages
117 Carol syllables

228 MIDDLE STICKS by Harvey Estes

Lonesome Polecat and Hairless Joe were the brewers of 56 Down.

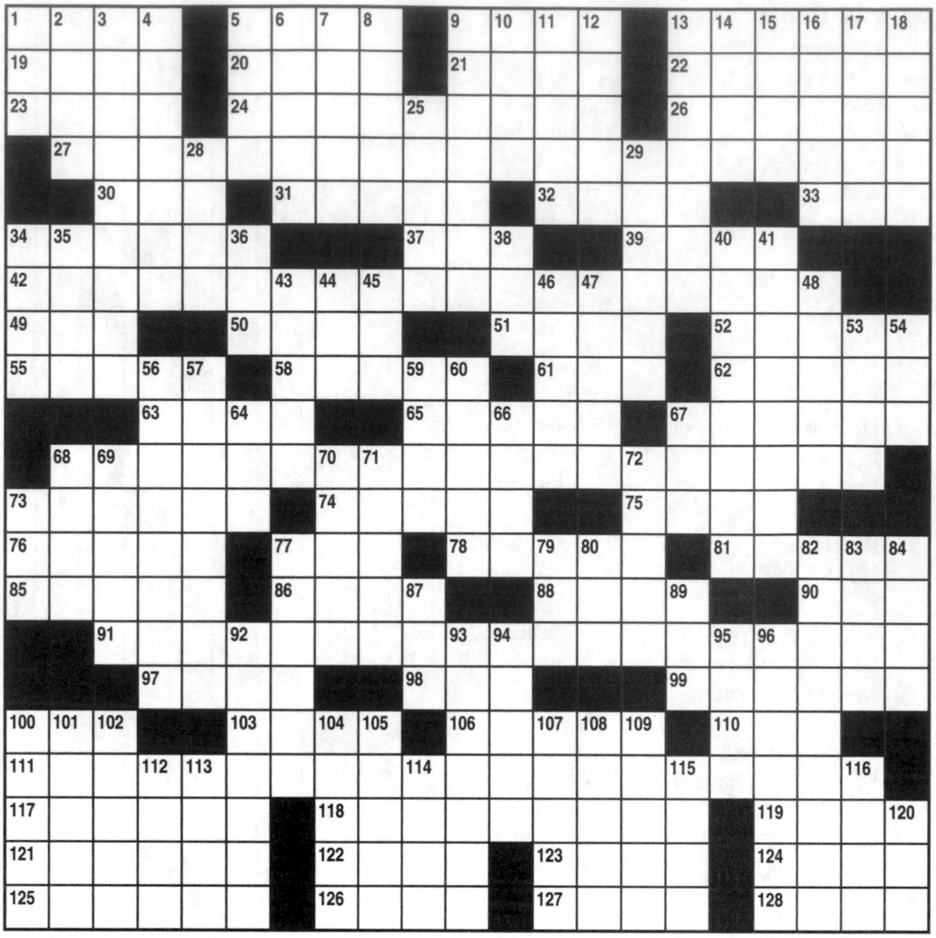

ACROSS

1 "Dancing Queen" group
5 Melville sea tale
9 Bottleneck blocker
13 Yanks' org.
19 Bacon portion
20 Throw out
21 "You said a mouthful!"
22 Trail shelter
23 Groan causers
24 Conductor Arturo
26 Designer Pierre
27 Photojournalist mag employees?
30 Opposite of ESE
31 Twill fabric
32 Jacob's first wife
33 Gees come after these
34 Phone interference
37 "The Name of the Rose" author
39 Alcatraz (with "the")
42 Really fast sci-fi guy?
49 Command for DDE
50 Mar. Madness source
51 Wrestling style
52 Shirts and skins, in gym class
55 Dahl's Willy
58 "C'est moi" to Arthur
61 Gaping chasm
62 Some used cars
63 "___ never fly!"
65 Opponent for Ike
67 Painter Peter Paul
68 Beverage for kids?
73 Became understood
74 Klingon or Vulcan
75 Nothing, in Nantes
76 Peruvian ancient
77 Prefix for early man
78 Christine of "Chicago Hope"
81 Tailor's joints
85 Extends one's enlistment
86 Old Italian coin
88 Impetuous ardor
90 Beer source
91 Forestry workplace?
97 ___ about
98 Fifth scale note
99 Shed, as feathers
100 Docs' bloc
103 Spinoff group
106 Ennui, with "the"
110 Burnt ___ crisp
111 Southern town, from a music perspective?
117 Prime Minister Gandhi
118 Mythical moola source
119 Haggard horses
121 For skin
122 Naturalist John
123 Therapist's response
124 "See you later"
125 "The Tatler" essayist
126 ABA member
127 Publisher and punster Bennett
128 Farthest reaches

DOWN

1 Nile reptile
2 Down in the dumps
3 Something to jump on
4 Bitter liqueur (var.)
5 "Beatle Bailey" dog
6 Invaders of Spain
7 Davis of "Do the Right Thing"
8 Movie trophy
9 Baseballer Jose
10 Forget
11 Of the kidneys
12 Cutler's product
13 Still stuff
14 Table extension
15 Jason Lee's "My Name Is ___"
16 MacDowell of "Groundhog Day"
17 Leave without paying
18 Shades
25 "Ragged Dick" author Horatio
28 Foolish fellow
29 Mia of "Rosemary's Baby"
34 Great deal
35 Puente or Jackson
36 Turner ntwk.
38 "___ bodkins!"
40 Vitamin C sources
41 Connector of song
43 How to respond to an insult
44 Rebellion leader Turner
45 Pump product
46 Sometime poisonous plant
47 Net letters
48 Watched wide-eyed
53 First name in the Louvre
54 Snake sound
56 Joy Juice of Dogpatch
57 Rowan in "Bean"
59 Lanai neighbor
60 Henry Ford's son
64 Sportscaster Berman
66 Glinda portrayer in "The Wiz"
67 Baseball card stat
68 Nape growth
69 Rack up
70 Comic Cheech
71 Mild oath
72 Heep of fiction
73 McCartney title
77 Red table wine
79 Farm female
80 Special attention, for short
82 Getting into more trouble
83 Tear gas spray
84 Risked a citation
87 Tummy muscles
89 Marseilles moniker
92 Like accurate plats
93 Word after highway
94 Put to rest
95 Snapshot, commercially
96 Walk ostentatiously
100 Etching materials
101 "Water Lilies" artist
102 Tennis great Agassi
104 List divider
105 Rainbow fish
107 Top floor
108 Simple basketball game
109 Snide expression
112 Thin coin
113 River to the Caspian
114 Mad mood
115 Coral habitat
116 "Omigosh!"
120 "___ yer ol' man!"

229 THE WB NETWORK by Ray Hamel

"Demi" is another term for 32 Across.

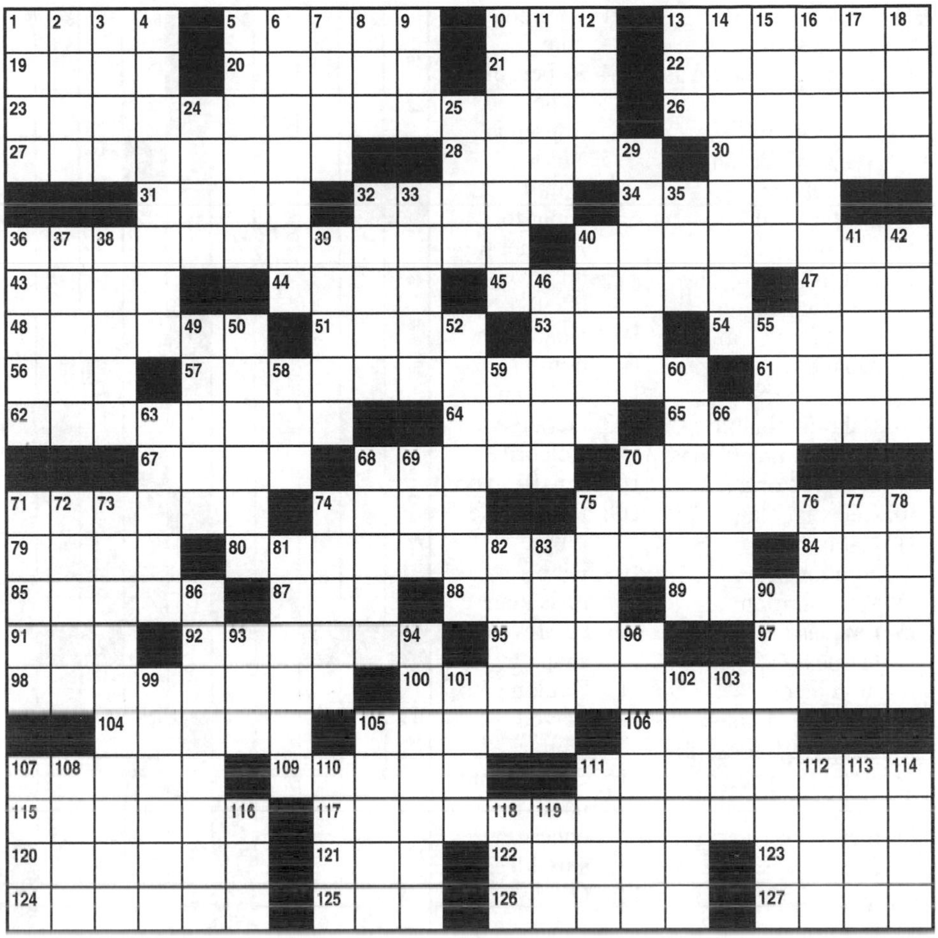

ACROSS

1 Dark and atmospheric
5 The ultimate troublemaker
10 Demographic balance: Abbr.
13 Melted
19 Author Bombeck
20 Fury
21 Fury
22 Nothing more than
23 IFO, at times
26 Drive members
27 Mexican treats
28 Al or Al Jr.
30 River through Rome
31 ". . . ___ saw Elba"
32 Small Champagne bottle
34 Atelier prop
36 Old gang breakers, of song
40 What Eliza Doolittle did not do
43 Food item sold in bars
44 Part of Mork's greeting
45 Casserole holder
47 Neither mate
48 "___ Down a Dream": Tom Petty
51 Immobile Stratego piece
53 Italian artist ___ Bartolommeo
54 Friend of Fran
56 Reagan proj. nicknamed "Star Wars"
57 Carabao
61 Course starts
62 Time-related
64 Sounds from Sussex sleepers?
65 Prince Siegfried's love, in ballet
67 Crucifix letters
68 Miata maker
70 "Jekyll & Hyde" actress Linda
71 Part of Johannesburg
74 Toxin fighters
75 Kind of vigil
79 Real, in Germany
80 Hamper, perhaps
84 French head
85 Small bottle
87 Start of a tile game
88 Pull into a slip
89 Pull out
91 Lunar New Year
92 Three Muscateers?
95 Lousy eggs
97 Take the testimony of
98 Carpet store purchases
100 Peeping Tom protection
104 "The Break-through" singer Mary J.
105 Puts on cargo
106 Right on the map
107 Movie ogre
109 Give a shout out to
111 Bouts of otalgia
115 Looked sharply
117 Dayton flyers
120 Wooden boxes
121 Count Basie's "___ Darlin' "
122 Metropolitan
123 Caesar's "he loves"
124 Augments
125 Lab subj.
126 Delicious
127 Tater ___

DOWN

1 Wee salamander
2 Cookie often twisted apart
3 "___ helpless as a kitten up a tree . . ."
4 Fingered a crime boss
5 Gotland's country
6 Call up on charges
7 Folder features
8 "One Day ___ Time"
9 Rangers' org.
10 Chaim Weizmann, for one
11 "To your health!"
12 DNA carrier
13 HBO rival
14 Thermal energy dissipator
15 More pretentious
16 Party pooper
17 Model Macpherson
18 Hair colorer
24 Mata of spydom
25 Ceasefire
29 Put the cap back on
32 Ventriloquist ___ Wences
33 Investigate
35 Close relative of humans
36 Deserving of a Razzie
37 Shake
38 Jeans material
39 Biblical ziggurat
40 Wall hanging
41 Apartment sign
42 Record over
46 Norwegian interjection
49 Toddler's obstinate reply
50 Like a one-lane bridge
52 Carrion seeker
55 Embryos' homes
58 Clavell's "___-Pan"
59 Gave supper to
60 A lot
63 Michelangelo masterpiece
66 Al ___ (pasta preference)
68 Phifer of "ER"
69 It may follow you
70 Bugler in the wild
71 Dividing walls
72 Landscapist's color
73 Rather ordinary
74 Works at a checkout counter
75 "I didn't ___ be here"
76 Verdant
77 Amateur on the surf
78 Stadium levels
81 Mental pictures
82 "___ nuit!"
83 Folic and formic
86 Small cousin of the parrot
90 Small talk
93 Play to the camera
94 Language that gave us "Kwanzaa"
96 Call bad names
99 Warnings
101 Hippie's "Gotcha!"
102 Noble's estate
103 Exam for a future J.D.
105 Karaoke words
107 Pound gp.
108 Range rover
110 Leatherworking tools
111 Recedes
112 Blood prefix
113 "He was" in Caesar's time
114 Atlantic crossers, once
116 Brit. medal
118 Word repeated before a hike
119 Refrain syllable

230 CHEF'S SPECIAL by Arlan and Linda Bushman

The CIA at 58 Across is the Culinary Institute of America.

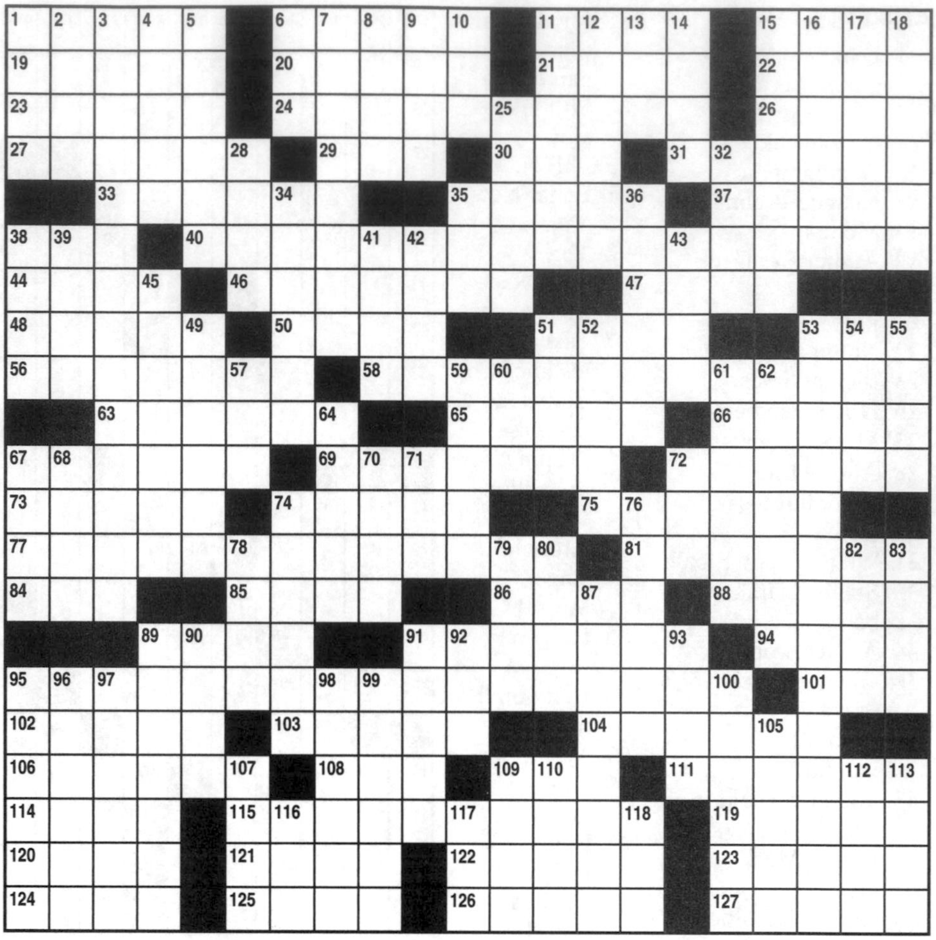

ACROSS

1 Trumps up
6 Clint Eastwood was one
11 Bar material
15 Very, in Verdun
19 Go-between
20 Dollar rival
21 Not more than
22 Zorba's quaff
23 More winsome
24 Hard Rock Cafe's Japanese counterpart?
26 Bahrain notable
27 Aquarium denizens
29 Ensign's org.
30 Celestial altar
31 Natural gas component
33 Waiting room
35 Laziness
37 Harnesses (together)
38 Bishop's domain
40 Loopy gift ideas for a cook's special day?
44 Figure on Irish euro coins
46 Dermal designs
47 Even
48 Everyday
50 Ger. neighbor
51 Rotter
53 Forthwith
56 Financial cushion
58 Must-have for a CIA student?
63 Dissertations
65 Daytime favorite
66 Mooed
67 Crazy Horse tribe
69 Boxes
72 Three-stripers
73 Dress style
74 The Velvet Fog
75 Paycheck recipient
77 Smoothie machine for tailgate parties?
81 Sort of chilly
84 Pt. of a line
85 "Star Wars" mentor
86 Go for
88 City W of Montgomery
89 Overarch
91 Unpredictable
94 Robert of "The Sopranos"
95 Mario Batali's shout to Rachael Ray on "Iron Chef"?
101 Roadside bomb
102 Demean
103 Derisive
104 Celebrity
106 Small cavern
108 Portuguese king
109 Bit of resistance
111 Freshwater snapper
114 Kaplan who played Kotter
115 Catchy brand name for a cheese shredder?
119 Overly sentimental
120 Dutch export
121 Mezzanine section
122 Have words
123 In conflict
124 Young socialites
125 Sized up
126 Irksome
127 Wound up

DOWN

1 Almanac tidbit
2 Shivers
3 Crime more serious than stealing recipes?
4 First on Juan's calendar
5 "Ghost Story" author Peter
6 Gaping mouth
7 Famous French roundelay
8 Shoots the breeze
9 Gulf sultanate
10 Cubs great Santo
11 Parting, to Shakespeare
12 Formally sworn
13 Entirely
14 WW2 journalist Ernie
15 Climber's purchase
16 Japanese appetizer
17 Online publications
18 Most vexed
25 Tyne and Tim
28 Foul mood
32 Youngster
34 Farmers group
35 ___ Paulo
36 Relating to advanced devices
38 Have no truck with
39 Uncomplicate
41 URL starter
42 Qatar capital
43 Fodder place
45 Poker holding likely to win as is
49 Actress Sobieski
51 Little Boy Blue tote
52 Remove
53 Recent bar partner arrival?
54 Pointed arch
55 Combines
57 Brownies org.
59 Eminent
60 Part of a mil. address
61 Grassy plains
62 Rhine siren
64 Upbraid
67 Lummoxes
68 Merriment
70 Province
71 JFK debater
72 B'way posting
74 Chophouse orders
76 On the go
78 Tom Clancy hero
79 Neutral tone
80 Hearty laugh
82 One of Hook's men
83 Candy or cider type
87 Leave in a huff
89 Networks
90 Artist Mondrian
91 Vocalist Gorme
92 Shad delicacy
93 Euro division
95 Worked the checkout line
96 Wear away
97 Broad-trunked tree
98 Push too far
99 Tried to lose
100 Candy filling
105 Kept in touch
107 Rubberneck
109 Grimm creature
110 Monopolizes
112 Merino hangouts
113 Fictional Jane
116 Acuff of music
117 Criticism
118 Tripoli ruler

231 FLUSHED WITH SUCCESS by Bonnie L. Gentry

. . . and making out royally too!

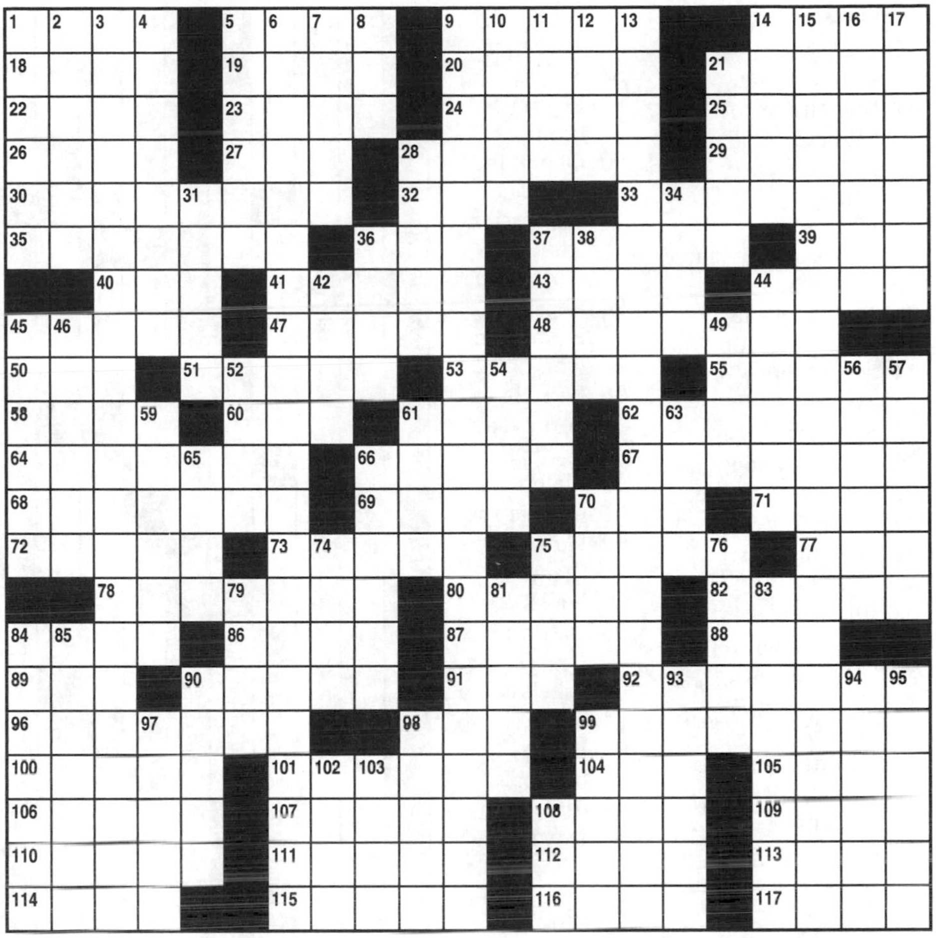

ACROSS

1 Meter man?
5 Norwegian hero
9 Cabinet department
14 Big name in cosmetics
18 School founded by Henry VI
19 Russo in "Get Shorty"
20 Stradivari's mentor Nicolo
21 1983 Indy 500 winner Tom
22 Where not to throw bouquets?
23 Give off, as fumes
24 O-shaped
25 Former UN leader Kofi
26 Window frost
27 Chat room "I think"
28 Line at the track
29 Starbucks order
30 Used to advantage
32 Run after D
33 "King Kong" attire
35 Native New Yorker
36 "Bambi" aunt
37 Zimbalist of "The F.B.I."
39 Turn into compost
40 St. with only three counties
41 Smidgen
43 Mining strike
44 Porch chair material
45 Home of the NHL's Lightning
47 Relevant, in legalese
48 Can help?
50 It began in A.D. 800
51 Brit's boob tube
53 Midwestern hub
55 Racetracks, often
58 Start of a counting rhyme
60 Not professional
61 Salt Lake City collegians
62 Willa Cather heroine
64 Begin, as an adventure
66 Jerky sort
67 Satisfied customer's request
68 New Jersey city
69 Spots in la mer
70 Billy's cry
71 Astronaut's beverage
72 Comparably healthy
73 Bergen who spoke for Mortimer
75 Deborah and Graham
77 One-tenth of a percent of a cool mil
78 Black Sea resident
80 Experienced, quaintly
82 Stage combat props
84 "___ nome" ("Rigoletto" aria)
86 French twist, e.g.
87 Corkers?
88 Letters on Boot Hill
89 Part of a PC-resetting combo
90 It keeps a cook tied up
91 Grafton's "___ for Corpse"
92 Hoist
96 Oakland, Berkeley, etc.
98 Shipping unit: Abbr.
99 Notoriously
100 Beyond what's needed
101 They're unmentionable
104 "Serendipities" author
105 Slush Puppie parent
106 Bizet opera priestess
107 Wilder's "Silver Streak" costar
108 "No ___" ("Sure!")
109 Author/illustrator Silverstein
110 Billionaire Khashoggi
111 "Saturday Night Live" alum Cheri
112 Stops squeaking
113 What a chapeau covers
114 French door component
115 "The Gondoliers" flower girl
116 Place to see dashes
117 While beginning?

DOWN

1 Red suit
2 Deck out
3 TENS
4 Seriously involved
5 Subsidiary of Heinz
6 JACKS
7 It's negative
8 Honoree from a past war
9 QUEENS
10 In the company of
11 Italian province in the Puglia region
12 Mayberry elbow-bender
13 KINGS
14 Kournikova and Pavlova
15 ACES
16 It may be standing
17 Girl of a 1925 Broadway hit
21 Venue of 1692 trials
28 Swag man
31 Fanfare
34 Orange covering
36 "Just you wait, ___ 'iggins . . .": Doolittle
37 West Texas town of song
38 Lou Gehrig's number
42 Without expending much energy
44 Make merry
45 It has an emission mission: Abbr.
46 Punta ___, Chile
49 Emerald City visitor
52 Race in The Time Machine
54 Does an alteration
56 Subject of a property claim
57 Military nicknames
59 "Do you love me?" response?
61 John Wooden Center locale
63 Close in on
65 Matter of interest
66 Begin the broadcasting day
70 Boot camp fare
74 Part below a cornice
75 Munroe of "Charlie's Angels"
76 Noted missionary Junípero
79 Apartment worker, familiarly
81 Brockovich et al.
83 Ivories tickler of Paris
84 Esoteric doctrines
85 Shady promenade
90 Early invader of India
93 "Survivor" host Jeff
94 Makes roads slippery, in a way
95 Shoelace holder
97 Aga Khan's god
98 Aspen Edge producer
99 Home with a view
102 Output of Tintoretto
103 Tournament exemptions
108 Little barker, briefly

232 PROGRESS by Fred Piscop

Getting from point A to point B can be difficult at times.

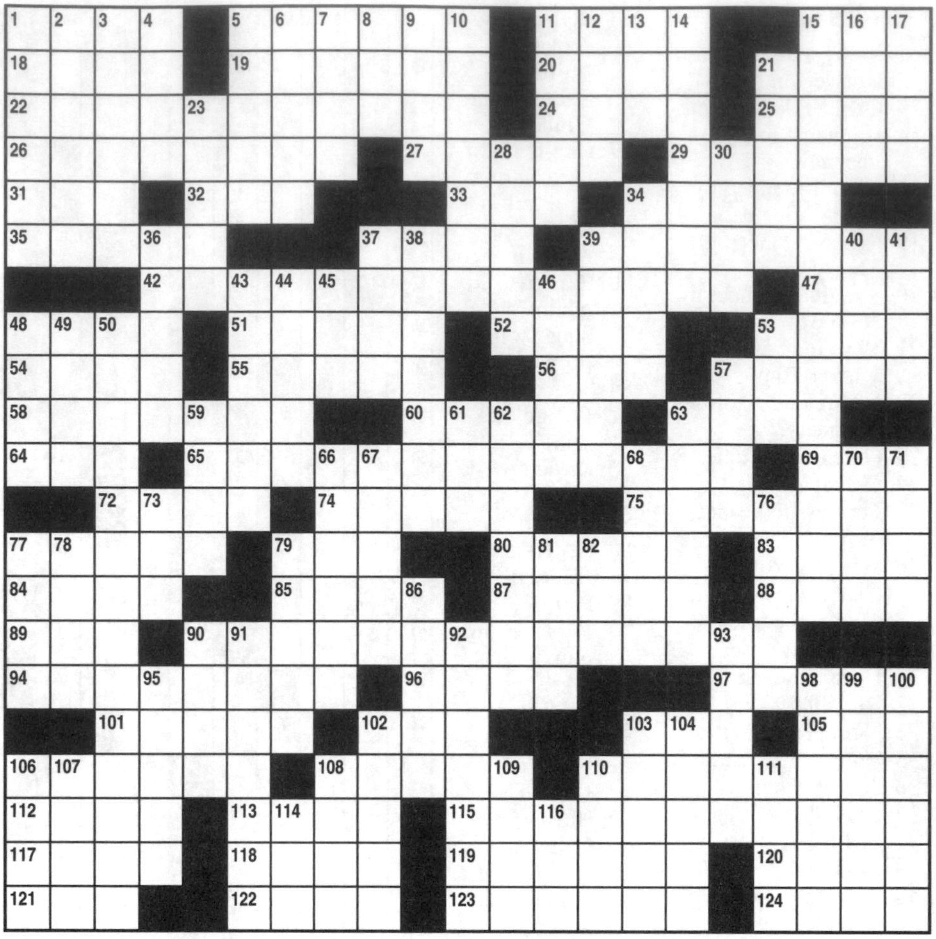

ACROSS

1 Easy win
5 Foot-care Dr.
11 Signature spot
15 "Where ___?"
18 Baseball exec Minaya
19 Classic bug-assembly game
20 It may be gray
21 Mmes. of Malaga
22 Fumigation option
24 "Casablanca" café owner
25 Sundance's gal
26 Don, as a negligee
27 Treeless expanse
29 Makes out
31 Downing Street address
32 Illiterates' marks
33 Old Serbian capital
34 Cal. sequence
35 Cooper's part
37 Nae sayer
39 Obama, by birth
42 Risking firing, perhaps
47 Grand __ (wine words)
48 Author Turgenev
51 Ruhr Valley city
52 Mideast capital
53 Composer ___ Carlo Menotti
54 Whole bunch
55 Showy bloom
56 Monopoly quartet: Abbr.
57 Pinto and others
58 Resort spot
60 Sour-tasting
63 Suck in
64 Some ER cases
65 The "have" in "I have arrived," e.g.
69 Omaha Beach craft
72 Dole's running mate
74 ___ Yello (soft drink)
75 More like a wimp
77 Home of the Ashanti
79 Place with an EIK
80 Largish combo
83 BB's and such
84 Sherman ___, Calif.
85 Like a tuned string
87 Circus supporter
88 Slightly
89 Peyton's brother
90 One of the Abstract Expressionists (1903–74)
94 Short Beethoven work
96 Ferrell portrayed her on "SNL"
97 Slalom paths
101 Orange spot
102 How-___ (handy books)
103 California's Big ___
105 Jukebox input
106 Home brewer's directions
108 Royal king?
110 Apse locale
112 Spread unit
113 Cold caller's success
115 1962 Ray Stevens hit
117 Part of a hat trick
118 Desktop item
119 Gerald Ford, nee __ King Jr.
120 Hand-waver's cry
121 Tirana is its cap.
122 House Speaker before Dennis
123 Movie preview
124 Toon Le Pew

DOWN

1 Tributes, of sorts
2 Folded fare
3 Place with slips
4 Stage item
5 Tea go-with
6 Team with a horseshoe logo
7 Freddie the Freeloader, e.g.
8 Ear-related prefix
9 Like a wet noodle
10 Hezbollah's land
11 Bellyaches
12 Bocelli showstopper
13 Wine bottle word
14 Second try, in a studio
15 A prosthesis
16 Board game ending
17 "Stupid ___ stupid does"
21 Seven: Prefix
23 Boxcars pair
28 Kitchen protectors
30 Gun cleaner
34 Goya subjects
36 Directional devices
37 Graf ___
38 Transportation giant until 1999
39 Monarch of 1387–1422
40 County Galway's ___ Islands
41 Order members
43 ___ to (precede)
44 Vintage auto
45 Guinness suffix
46 "Here's another nice mess . . ." speaker
48 ___ facto
49 Went head to head
50 Expensive seafood menu item
53 Prefix with political
57 Short 'dos
59 "___ Camera"
61 "Silent" prez
62 Affixes, in a way
63 Tutti-___
66 Classic Chevy
67 Back off
68 "The Seven Year Itch" actor
70 Circular opening?
71 Sulky puller's pace
73 USNA grad
76 Cars "Born From Jets"
77 Gets a move on
78 Symbol of virtue
79 Observe Yom Kippur
81 "Beetle Bailey" pooch
82 Annual b-ball event
86 Painful pang
90 Riding on
91 Goes head-first
92 Unified whole, in psychology
93 Causing goose bumps
95 Disney mermaid
98 Late bash
99 Pitch one's tent
100 Naval builder
102 Council city
103 "Socrate" composer
104 Ballpark worker
106 Shankar selection
107 Green's sci.
108 Word after Joe or low
109 Quaker address
110 OPEC amts.
111 Miner's hat attachment
114 Star of the rotation
116 Simile center

233 PARTS AND CRAFTS by Clare Hansbrough

The clue at 29 Down appears backwards.

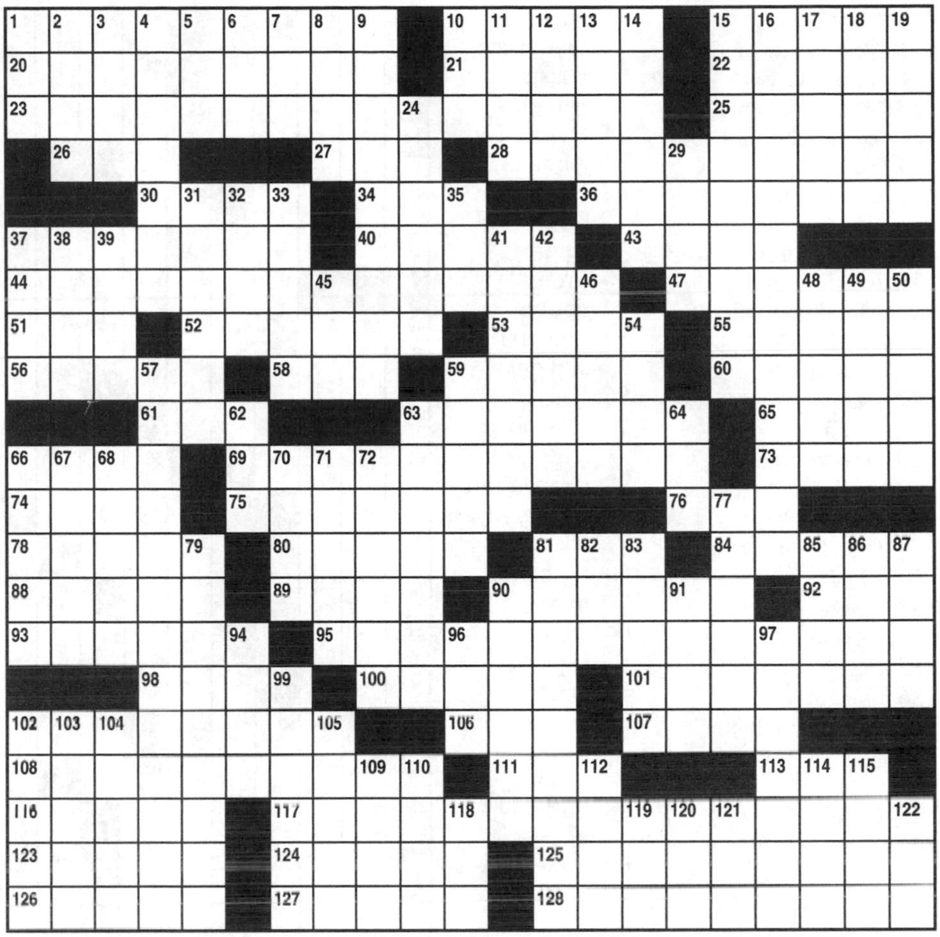

ACROSS

1 Proposals put before the people
10 Read the riot act to
15 Heaps
20 1942 Allied victory site
21 Just not done
22 Debussy title that means "the sea"
23 Hands reaching out to the needy?
25 The bounding main
26 Rebellion leader Turner
27 Overtime creator
28 Calms
30 Trust, with "on"
34 Student stat
36 Crispy snacks
37 Shooting marble
40 Burn with water
43 Boxer Spinks
44 Water carrier's aide?
47 Longhorns, e.g.
51 Math subj.
52 Former cager Bob
53 Oversupply
55 E-mail remark in caps
56 Rifle attachment
58 Retired speedster
59 Farm machine
60 Two-masted vessel
61 Tigers of the NCAA
63 Molded one's muscles
65 Jupiter's wife
66 Goya subject
69 Push, then stagger?
73 Soothsayer's clue
74 Out of town
75 Caviar carriers
76 Fashion monogram
78 "Simple" pie eater of rhyme
80 Bowler's tough spare
81 Airline to Oslo
84 Millennia upon millennia
88 Bowie's weapon
89 Sport with mallets
90 Halloween figure
92 Pot pie spheroid
93 Quick drawing
95 Representa-tive accord?
98 Bucket of bolts
100 Paragon of virtue
101 Inventors' safeguards
102 Under pressure
106 Neighbor of Wyo.
107 "Dukes of Hazzard" deputy
108 Rough weather
111 Magneto portrayer McKellen
113 Alternatives to Macs
116 China's Zhou ___
117 Sulk near a diamond?
123 Go-between
124 Bottle size
125 More than tempted
126 McDowall of "Planet of the Apes"
127 Utopia and Shangri-la
128 Oscar, for example

DOWN

1 Bodybuilder's unit
2 Impressive style
3 FDR's pooch
4 Stately shade-giver
5 Dorm VIPs
6 Singers of "Unbelievable"
7 Keanu in "The Matrix"
8 Malicious gossip
9 Pilot's protection, briefly
10 Mary or Agnes: abbr.
11 Upper limits
12 Penetrating reed
13 Plunders
14 On the back
15 Possible imposition
16 Walk like a harried debtor?
17 "In other words . . ."
18 Let out
19 Sea birds
24 Swinger of old
29 Stout Guinness
31 Bolts with a beau
32 Biographical focus
33 "Byzantium" poet
35 Rhine feeder
37 Pool sites
38 Baby's dusting
39 Breakfast brand
41 Molecules that bind to receptors
42 More like dishwater
45 Parts of gals.
46 Napped leather
48 Generational symbol
49 Filthy follower
50 Hawke of "Hamlet"
54 Partner of tried
57 Stage version of "The Good Earth"?
59 Lisa of "The Cosby Show"
62 Merchandise ID
63 Pudding ingredient
64 Practice, as a trade
66 Face protectors
67 Quick as ___
68 "Ray" star Foxx
70 Grating sound
71 Dr. Seuss' "Hop ___"
72 "Who shot J.R.?" show
77 Serenaded
79 It's needed
81 Easy-to-answer questions
82 2 on a phone dial
83 Skiers' venue
85 Kind of tournament
86 Snug retreat
87 Talk trash
90 Entered
91 ___ uproar (tumultuous)
94 Doth own
96 Metal container
97 Break
99 "Us" rival
102 Shave sheep
103 Ballroom dance
104 Het up
105 Sci-fi extra
109 Trumpet muffler
110 British carbine
112 Nair rival
114 Pt. of CD
115 Venetian blind strip
118 Taxing org.
119 Govt. medicine watchdog
120 Make a doily
121 ACC school
122 Change color

234 BOUNCES AROUND by Norm Guggenbiller

The Chrysler Building in New York was designed by a team lead by 29 Across.

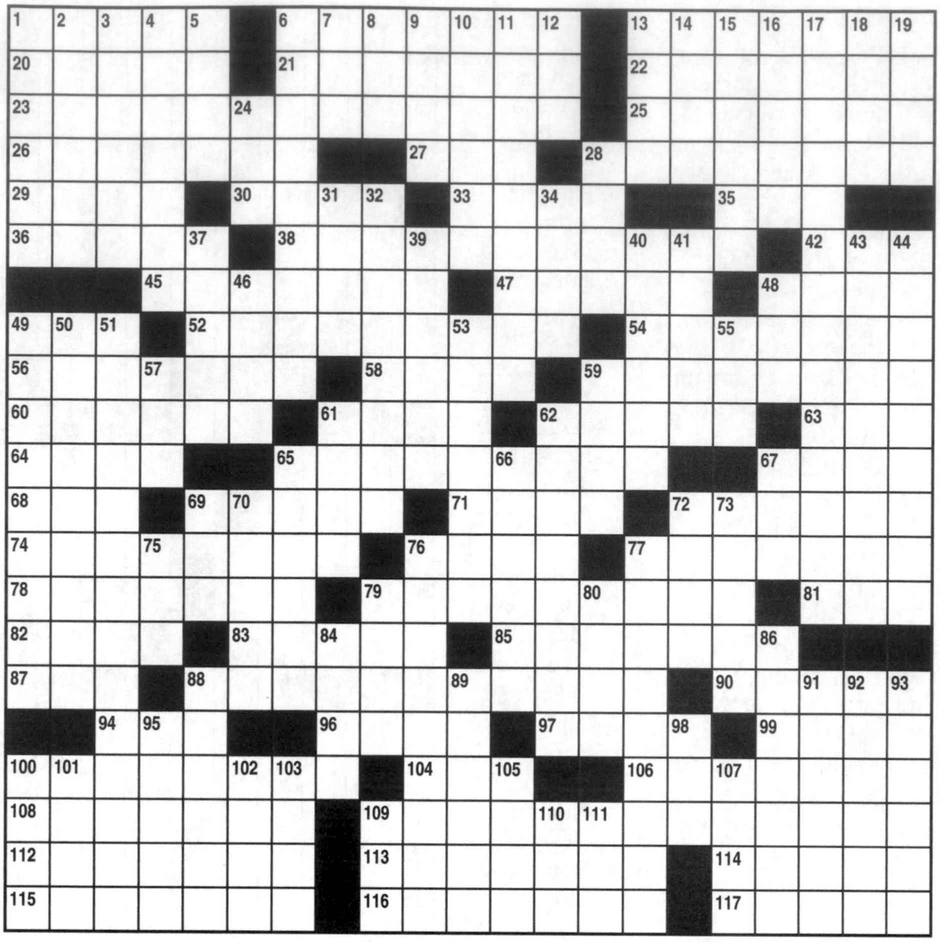

ACROSS

1 Had the means
6 Turnpike exit
13 Accumulates
20 Discombobulated
21 Shrewd
22 1984 Emilio Estevez flick
23 What Foreman was to Ali
25 Metal container?
26 Remington competitor
27 Canyon producer, briefly
28 "Good going!"
29 Architect William van ___ (1883–1954)
30 "Just ___!"
33 Seeger of the Weavers
35 Permit
36 Obscured
38 Gem State baker
42 Old TV control abbr.
45 Omelet folder
47 Promulgate
48 Place to moor
49 Hockey's Tikkanen
52 Rules out beforehand
54 Stir-fry tidbit
56 Lugs
58 Santa ___ (hot winds)
59 Track officials
60 Former offenses
61 Does something
62 Pares pounds
63 NFL linemen: Abbr.
64 Capital of Latvia
65 Empty a piggy bank, in a way
67 Waikiki locale
68 Book before Phil.
69 Take ___ at (guess)
71 Song holder
72 Winery position
74 "You can quit now!"
76 Aware of
77 Do a museum job
78 More pliant
79 Designs
81 Thing in court
82 Not a dup.
83 Lunar valley
85 New toothpaste boast, perhaps
87 One of 100: Abbr.
88 Don Quixote's squire
90 From ___ bottom
94 Something to slip on
96 Eat
97 ___ alone (solo)
99 Orange-red variety of chalcedony
100 Lutheran hymns
104 Delivery experts, briefly
106 Dangerous Rhine maiden
108 Puff's land, in song
109 Infielder's bane/ PUZZLE TITLE
112 Squaring things
113 Passer of information
114 Draw a bead on
115 Protects
116 Trypanosomiasis carriers
117 Extends across

DOWN

1 Short rest
2 Lord Jim portrayer
3 Loan shark
4 Folk tales
5 "James and the Giant Peach" author
6 Up and down
7 Dandy
8 Showman Ziegfeld
9 Chime
10 "Return to speed," in music
11 British holiday pastries
12 Rep's take
13 Singer India ___
14 Jazzman Saunders
15 Former NASA program
16 Exploration probe
17 Sade song
18 Net
19 Old knife
24 South American tuber
28 Moistens
31 Cabinet dept.
32 Late worker's option, possibly
34 Chuck
37 Word before deck or hand
39 Stomping grounds
40 "Live Music Capital of the World" city
41 Time for brunch
43 "Where I'm pointing"
44 Calms
46 Some Guggenheim works
48 Portion of a ton: Abbr.
49 Strong brews
50 Sacred writing
51 Esteem
53 Debonair
55 Surgery sites
57 Mauna ___
59 Flexible Flyer, for one
61 Latin lesson word
62 Canoodling, in granny's day
65 Have the lead
66 Kia model
67 Stuttgart sunrise direction
69 National League city: Abbr.
70 He-Man's sister
72 Polo of "Meet the Fockers"
73 Desirable trait
75 Court stat.
76 Some private meetings
77 Merchants
79 Like some textbook publishers
80 Auto executive Ferrari
84 Some TV screens
86 Source of Vitamin C
88 Enclose securely
89 Small stone
91 Fashion designer Picasso
92 Hole-cutting tool
93 Lyrical poets
95 "The Red Badge of Courage" author
98 Piggy
100 Punch-card leftover
101 Table d'___
102 Afford
103 Hosp. procedures
105 Usher in
107 Nucleotide chains
109 NYC's first subway line
110 Detmer and Cobb of sports
111 Minute

235 ALL IN THE GAME by Harvey Estes

. . . and the game is played at 107 Across.

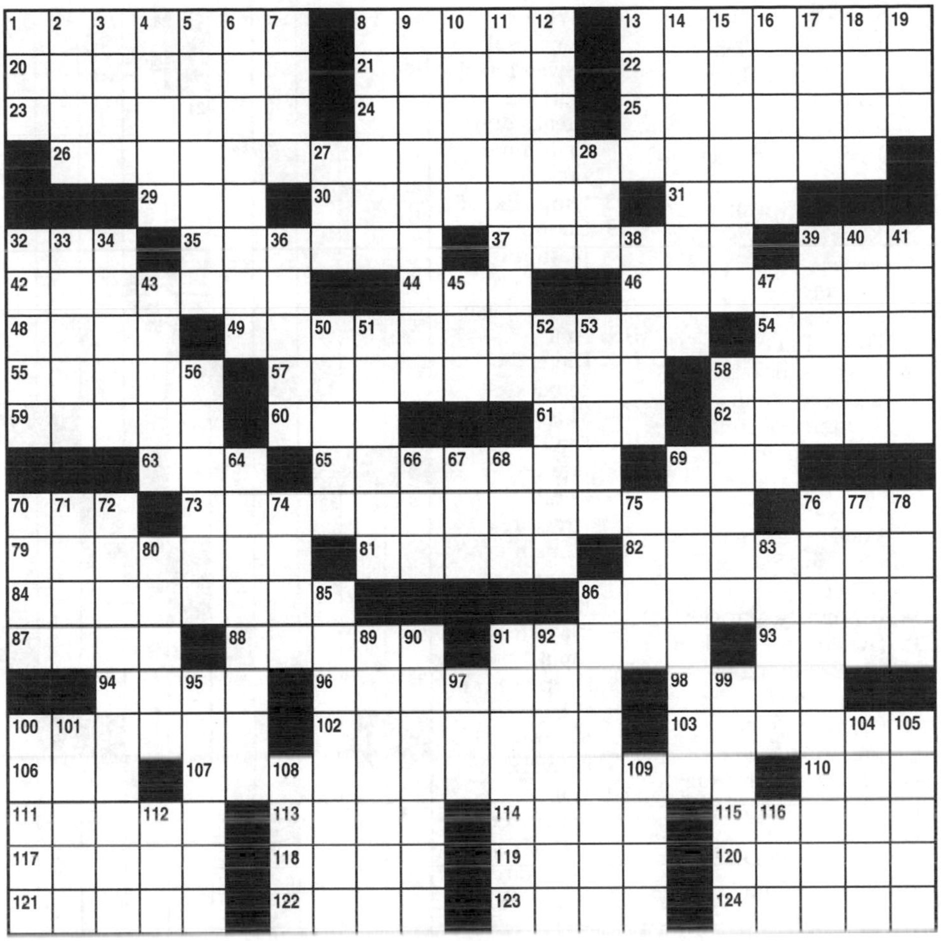

ACROSS

1 Pawn
8 Splinter groups
13 Riot-squad gear
20 Tom, Dick, or Harry
21 "___ man for himself!"
22 Diplomat's aide
23 Soft drink choices
24 Well-grounded
25 Tank type
26 Tells a keyboardist to scram?
29 Not neg.
30 Corny joke
31 Cotton gin inventor Whitney
32 AOL or Earthlink, e.g.
35 Good condition
37 Move like Elvis
39 Pt. of TGIF
42 Gonzaga University city
44 CIO partner
46 Kind of carpet or cat
48 Water-skiing locale
49 Suffers jeering?
54 Lima's nation
55 Amtrak offering
57 They let things go
58 Offers drinks to
59 Ethel or Fred
60 Singer Sumac
61 Dye container
62 Conductor Previn
63 Lay turf
65 Drop like a rock
69 Hurrah for Jose
70 Place to enter a PIN
73 Aussie hoppers gone bad?
76 Buddhism branch
79 Gets back in business
81 Pokes fun at
82 1968 hit by the Turtles
84 Wake-up calls
86 Strongholds
87 Schindler's roster
88 The whole shebang
91 Sell very high, perhaps
93 "Over here . . ."
94 Simple partner
96 Like some officials
98 Gershwin with a nest egg?
100 "Cut that out!"
102 Mud holes
103 Lulls
106 Windy City, briefly
107 WHERE TO PLAY THE GAME?
110 Eur. nation
111 Textile trademark
113 Butt of jokes
114 Debussy subject
115 Newscaster Couric
117 Shirker's phrase
118 Grease monkey's job
119 Museo holdings
120 Make changes to
121 Dry runs
122 JFK predictions
123 Meg of "In the Cut"
124 Needing cleaning

DOWN

1 ER practice
2 Fly-ball paths
3 Kind of support offered by Dell
4 Prying person
5 Ham Fisher's boxer
6 Piling up
7 Left on a map
8 Draconian
9 Vanish
10 Salsa singer Cruz
11 Love complications
12 Greenstreet in "Casablanca"
13 Fight for breath
14 Wheaties stars
15 Shoplifter
16 "Bloody" Tudor sovereign
17 Very top
18 ___-Pei (wrinkly dog)
19 He's a doll
27 Elev.
28 Benjamin of The Cars
32 Muslim faith
33 Wild blue yonder
34 Hearth tool
36 On one's guard
38 Make ___ (blog)
39 Mr. Hyde, e.g.
40 Harder to find
41 Lavatory sign
43 Ancient Brits: Var.
45 Govt. loan source
47 Book part
50 Office subs
51 Skier's course
52 Cuts at an angle
53 Take the soapbox
56 Islands off Portugal
58 Pickpocket's prize
64 Fund a charity
66 Radar anomaly
67 Singer Davis
68 New York blvd.
69 Exxon Valdez disaster
70 Asian inland sea
71 Hatcher of "Desperate Housewives"
72 Makes assertions like Elsie?
74 Northern capital
75 Kind of cutlet
76 Provider of menagerie uniforms?
77 Seaside soarers
78 Snug retreat
80 Lodge
83 Try to bite, like a pup
85 Leaves for a moment
86 2003 Billy Bob Thornton movie
89 "Open sesame!" sayer
90 Papal representatives
91 Dazzling
92 Period in history
95 Shoulder firearms
97 Pfc.'s superior
99 Caused a stink
100 Very little
101 Violent spasm
104 Word-processor command
105 In sorry shape
108 Lascivious look
109 ___ there, done that
112 911 respondent
116 "___ my brother's keeper?"

236 PARDON SHOT by Patrick Jordan

55 Down was an advisor to JFK during the Cuban Missile Crisis.

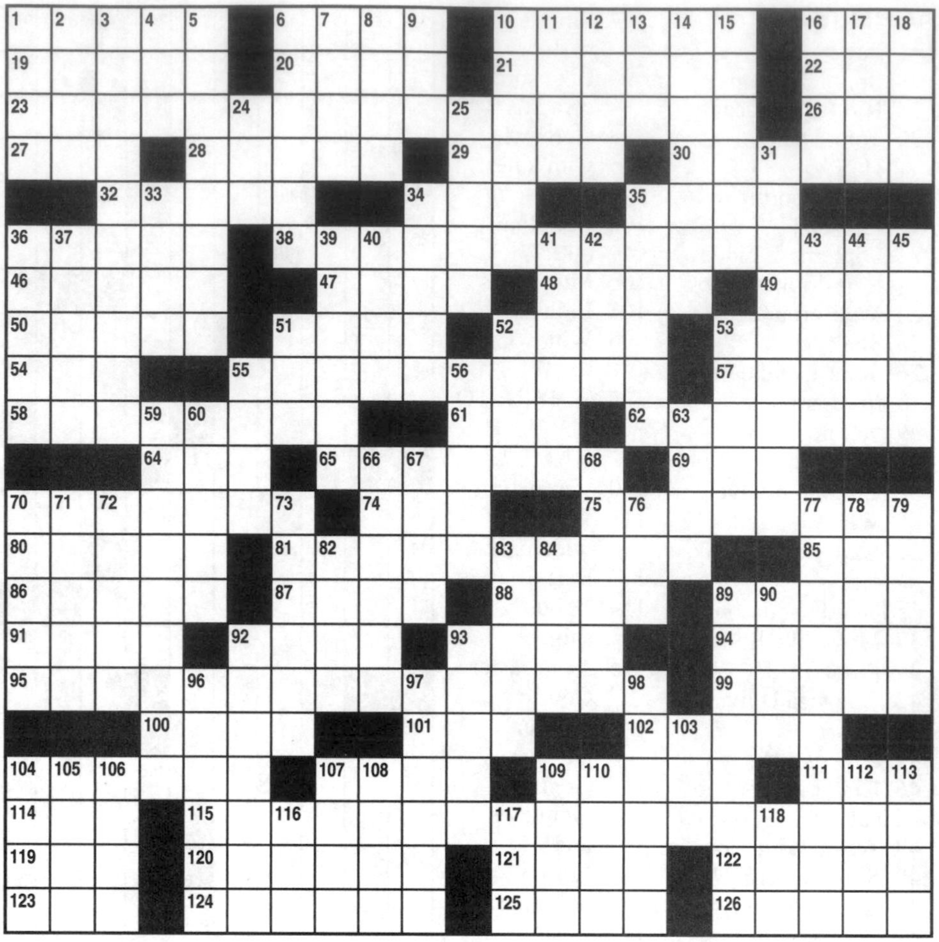

ACROSS

1 Explorer da Gama
6 ___ II (razor brand)
10 Nibble on indifferently
16 Rock concert stage effect
19 Splashdown site
20 Kaneohe Bay's locale
21 Lewdness
22 Sorehead's emotion
23 **Quip: Part 1**
26 Copier blockage
27 Cub Scout unit
28 Sentimental sort
29 Caviar sources
30 Contacts via computer
32 Frankie who sang the "Blazing Saddles" theme
34 It's mostly nitrogen
35 General ___ chicken
36 Modify formally
38 **Quip: Part 2**
46 Carlo or Cristo preceder
47 Charlotte's creations
48 Reddish-brown horse
49 Priceless?
50 Made a fillet of
51 Plumlike fruit
52 Actress Ryan of "Boston Public"
53 La Scala solos
54 "Strange Magic" band, to fans
55 **Quip: Part 3**
57 Car wash step
58 Most lanky
61 From ___ Z
62 Some Mapquest lines
64 Mrs. Juan Peron
65 Sect led by Ann Lee
69 422-year dynasty
70 Facing the pitcher
74 Preceding, poetically
75 Matthew's "Friends" role
80 Comment from the conquered
81 **Quip: Part 4**
85 Nuptial affirmation
86 Castle-ringing trenches
87 "Beetle Bailey" barker
88 Installed, as carpeting
89 Classify
91 "What nonsense!"
92 "Swan Lake" skirt
93 Breaks down
94 Eight fluid drams
95 **Quip: Part 5**
99 Choir platform
100 Oldest pro baseball team
101 Amt.
102 Dieters' setbacks
104 Muscular
107 Rio Bravo liquido
109 Coral structure
111 ". . . ain't heavy, ___ my brother"
114 Blast furnace input
115 **Quip author**
119 "The Simpsons" network
120 Tour conductors
121 Pub selection
122 Courtyards
123 Aardvark's victim
124 Keyboard symbol above the hyphen
125 Be abuzz (with)
126 Flophouse adjective

DOWN

1 Render ineffective
2 Dull pain
3 Musical son of Yoko Ono
4 Cleveland cager, briefly
5 Unilateral
6 Not numerous enough
7 The Kon-Tiki, for one
8 "Hello, sailor!"
9 Unlikely dog show entrant
10 A ___ (deductive)
11 Roof overhang
12 Pool hall poles
13 Chess piece, briefly
14 See 55 Down
15 Tony Soprano's organization
16 Vijay Singh's homeland
17 Thumb-sucking stage
18 Treasure chest baubles
24 32,000 94-Acrosses
25 Crossword diagrams
31 With amicable intent
33 Pre-deal payment
34 Harry's veep
35 Prepares for pugilism
36 "Jurassic Park" DNA preserver
37 "Cabbage" or "lettuce"
39 Big-eyed nestlings
40 Flying Cloud and Royale 8
41 Claire in "Key Largo"
42 Hole on SpongeBob
43 Pickling solution
44 LCD component?
45 Assents
51 "Mayday!" relative
52 Ballet jump
53 Firth of Clyde island
55 1970 Pulitzer winner (with 14-D)
56 Sulu portrayer George
59 Arrives
60 Trellis climbers
63 Spring event
66 Grow more intense
67 Folk guitarist Guthrie
68 Rift between factions
70 Trampy type
71 Emotionally distant
72 Clink glasses
73 Emulates a tiler
76 Mortar trough
77 Leo's cut?
78 Draw out
79 Dogie snarer
82 Start of Caesar's last query
83 Coin in Krakow
84 Chows down on
89 Dian Fossey's subjects
90 Render unusable
92 It's hardly chicken feed
93 Mark for a sale
96 Yanni's genre
97 Wet sneaker's sound
98 Vanity case?
103 Without exception
104 End table adjoiner
105 Anemiac's need
106 Call to a queue
107 He's Vinick on "The West Wing"
108 Giggling foursome?
109 Up to the task
110 Obstacle for George of the Jungle
112 Seat of Garfield County, OK
113 Stick around
116 Put out of sight
117 Doffable item
118 Mineralogy suffix

237 RIVERS RUN THROUGH IT by Fran & Lou Sabin
Subtitle: WHERE HAVE ALL THE FLOWERS GONE?

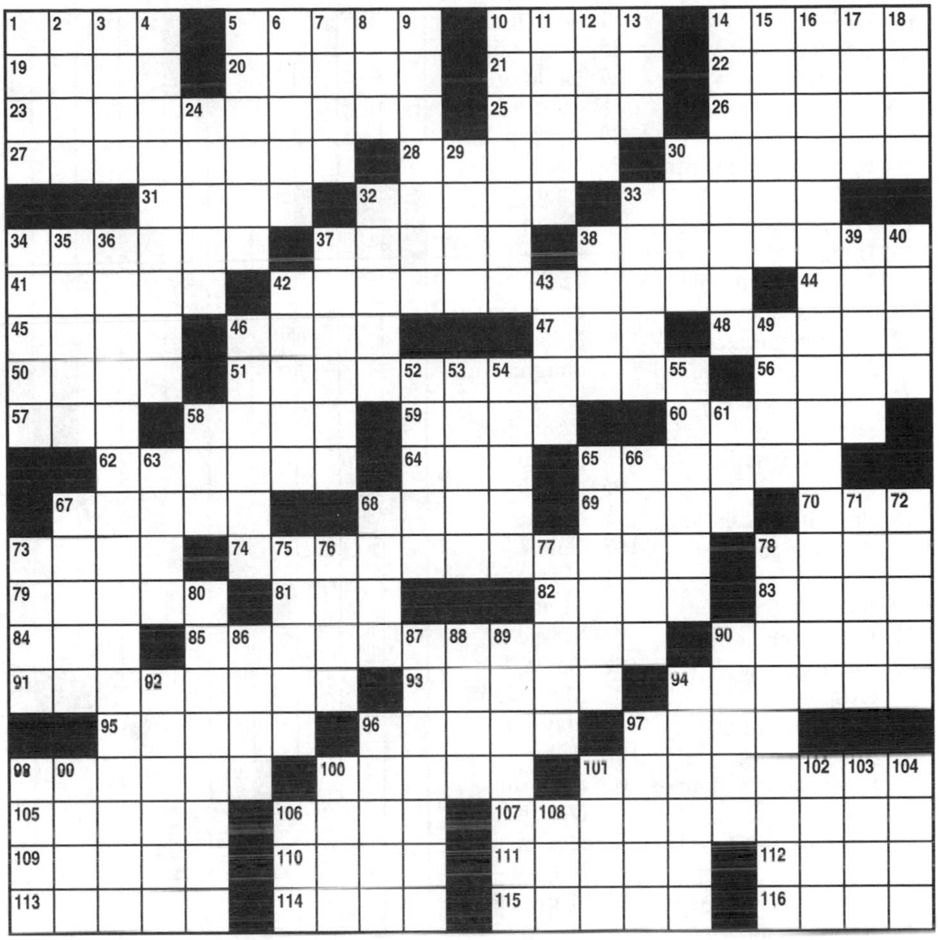

ACROSS

1 Gentle one
5 Lowlife
10 Baylor U.'s city
14 Side with 10 Down, perhaps
19 "A Death in the Family" playwright
20 Alps or Apennines, say
21 Israel's Abba
22 Delhi royal
23 Lettered mystery writer?
25 A few
26 Pillow stuffing
27 Buy-out
28 BYOB provision
30 Applicant's offering
31 Squaw Valley lift
32 Affix firmly
33 Glass insets
34 Six-line stanza
37 Fin
38 Subaru model
41 Despises
42 Chaplin classic
44 Writer Santha Rama ___
45 Selfish sort
46 "Bee Season" star
47 Fearsome movie street
48 Majorettes do it
50 Cross characters
51 NBA Rookie of the Year (2003–04)
56 Alma mater of 85 Across
57 Building annex
58 "Boston Legal" suit
59 King's entertainer
60 Score
62 Rings out
64 "What a good boy ___!"
65 Like totem poles
67 "A Room with a View" reverend
68 Layout
69 Much put-upon pup
70 Stretcher carrier
73 Gardner or Kenton
74 Taj Mahal builder
78 Studio head
79 Ex-Bear coach Mike
81 Building site
82 Ridicules, in a way
83 Bring aboard
84 Chemical suffix
85 Buster Crabbe movie persona
90 Ovine Muppet
91 Give new meaning
93 At warp speed
94 Jake of "The Sun Also Rises"
95 Put to the test
96 Sister of Calliope
97 Set right
98 Vietnamese, e.g.
100 Mythical bottle resident
101 Math curve
105 Persian dialect
106 "Tuna Fishing" painter
107 New Year's party handout
109 Cheep
110 Longoria and Peron
111 Dinner invitee
112 Submission enc.
113 Like Eloise
114 Soapy soak
115 "Both ___ Now": Joni Mitchell
116 "___ right!"

DOWN

1 Hang tough
2 Havana water
3 Like 1 Across
4 Fathers
5 Haberdashery item
6 Decathlete Johnson
7 ___'acte
8 Fraudian focus
9 Wool-gathering
10 Omelet order
11 Dealing with
12 Political group
13 Customer's allotment, often
14 Most eco-friendly
15 Ups the ante
16 Wind tunnel's sphere
17 Pour down
18 Suffering drought
24 Bench garb
29 From here to eternity
30 Black-and-blue, in a seafood restaurant
32 Bill addition
33 ___ de terre (potato)
34 "On the Beach" author
35 Atelier sight
36 Michelin Primacy MXV4s, e.g.
37 Business magazine
38 Photo supply
39 3 A.M., for many
40 Make a decision
42 75th U.S. attorney general
43 Greenish-blue
46 Displayed anger
49 Noah of "E.R."
52 Phrase after best or last
53 Wanderer
54 Juncture
55 Comic reading
58 "Hi-De-Ho Man" Calloway
61 Greeting from Galba
63 Onion's kin
65 Contest-entry form
66 Space sellers
67 Pickler's purchase
68 Way to go
71 Harry Potter's fat aunt
72 Long Celtic baskets
73 River to Kassel
75 Warner who played Charlie Chan
76 Smoke detector
77 Rollye James medium
78 "Hot corner" at AT&T Park
80 Natural liking for
86 Impostures
87 Aspic or parsley, e.g.
88 Yemen neighbor
89 Sweeps subject
90 China Clipper airline
92 Takes away
94 Tams, French-style
96 Gulf of Aqaba seaport
97 Pool player's ploy
98 Small units?
99 "I never ___ purple . . ."
100 Cuppa joe
101 Multicolored
102 "I'll take it!"
103 Suffix for Congo
104 His temple was in Athens
106 Ball girl
108 Arles assent

238 OBEDIENCE SCHOOL 101 by Harvey Estes

AKA members should easily dog-trot right through this one.

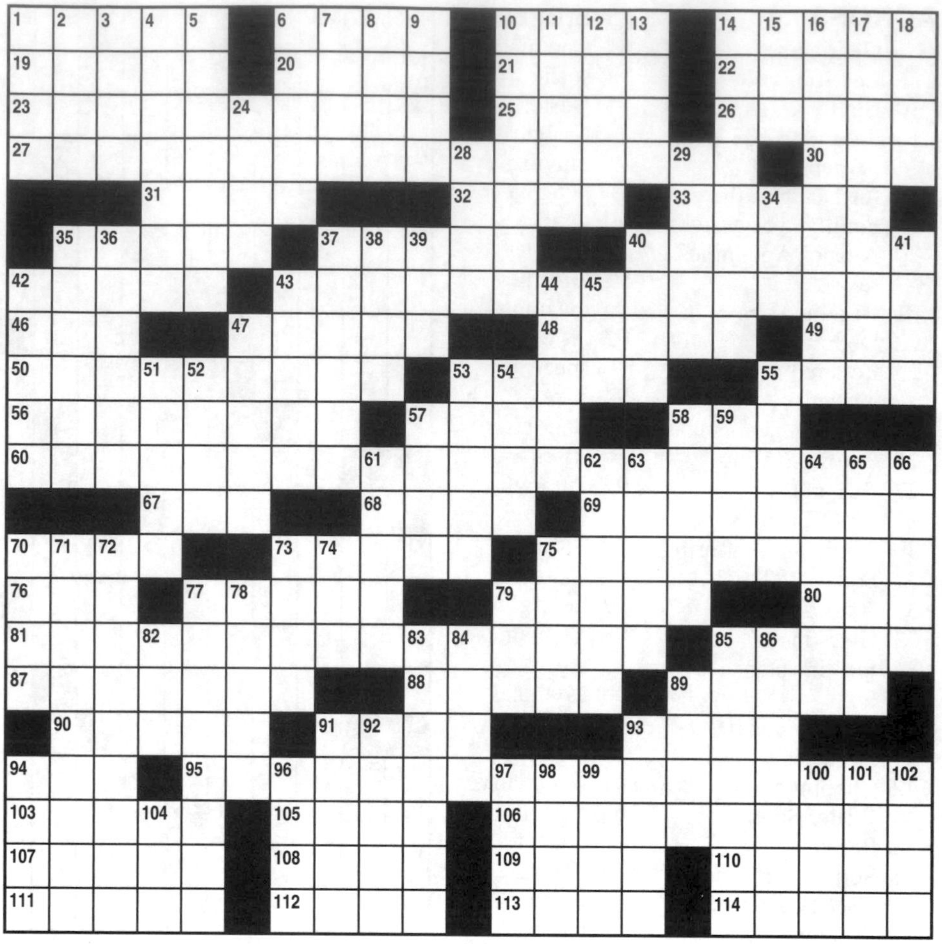

ACROSS

1 Legal analyst Van Susteren
6 "Star Trek" counselor
10 Robin Williams title role
14 Distinctive time
19 Boca ___
20 Capetown currency
21 Track shape
22 His pen name was Saki
23 Portly guy at a port?
25 Wife of Charlie Chaplin
26 Pass the threshold
27 Emulate Jack and Jill
30 Solo of "Star Wars"
31 Hoity-toity attitude
32 The majority
33 Drop in
35 Refs' decisions
37 Send-up
40 Shakespeare's Fairy Queen
42 "Bolero" composer
43 Reprieve
46 Summer in Savoy
47 Reef buildup
48 Karate acquisitions
49 MSNBC competitor
50 "Easter Parade" star
53 Electron tube
55 Prefix meaning "middle"
56 Number, at the print shop
57 Cartoonist Peter
58 Site for three men in a tub
60 Tell lies
67 Work for eds.
68 Irish tongue
69 Quality of beef that obviates beefs?
70 Fifth-century Pope
73 Angelic auras
75 Proceeds in a lawsuit
76 Son of Prince Valiant
77 Shutterbug's request
79 Mustard choice
80 Arles article
81 Take it easy
85 Turn edible
87 Build up
88 Terra firma
89 Art capable
90 "The Evil That ___" (Bronson film)
91 Jed's daughter
93 Naomi's daughter-in-law
94 Comedian DeLuise
95 Chuck Berry classic
103 Cara of "Fame"
105 Mine, on the Marne
106 Oater
107 Mrs. Mertz player
108 Ruhr refusal
109 Send out
110 Dustin Hoffman biopic
111 "I'm at the ___ my rope!"
112 Dharma's guy
113 Early lessons
114 Rob of "Melrose Place"

DOWN

1 1996 Wimbledon winner
2 Teen party
3 Maine, to Monet
4 Like accurate plats
5 Formicary
6 Spyglass Hill bunkers
7 Pro follower
8 "Tell me ___ haven't heard!"
9 Old-fashioned poem
10 Laze around
11 Declares
12 Charged
13 Land map
14 Retiree's status
15 "Let us spray," e.g.
16 Precariously situated
17 Artistic works
18 Warning device
24 Warring world in "War of the Worlds"
28 Melville novel
29 Boot out
34 Day after saying "TGIF!"
35 Take a break
36 Get back at
37 Mason's secretary
38 Talk-show pioneer
39 Animated Olive
40 Prefix with photo
41 Part of A.D.
42 Brings in
43 Conductor Georg
44 Online lit
45 Crossed out
47 Feline features
51 Where Dolphins play
52 Squid squirts
53 Smeltery waste
54 Memo opener
55 Unexpected help
57 Hendrix hairdo
58 Gravy spot
59 Early video game
61 Trojan beauty
62 Wood of Hollywood
63 Dry out
64 Outfits
65 Group of discussion groups
66 Ruhr industrial center
70 Zap
71 "Happy Days" actress
72 Getting better
73 Follow a trail
74 In such a way
75 Rhythmic swing
77 Keel bumper
78 "Wedding Bell Blues" singer Marilyn
79 Austrian article
82 Arrid rival
83 Going deeply (into)
84 Zany Martha
85 Dirty digs
86 Wishful (that)
89 Baby-faced
91 Befuddled Fudd
92 Sarge's superior
93 Takes a breather
94 Take the plunge
96 Singer k.d.
97 Carla portrayer of "Cheers"
98 Big flop
99 Google CEO Schmidt
100 Let off steam
101 Flying fisher
102 Discouraging words
104 Sgt. or corp.

239 CAMPAIGN STAFFERS WANTED by Yakov BenDavid

It's hell-bent-for-election time below.

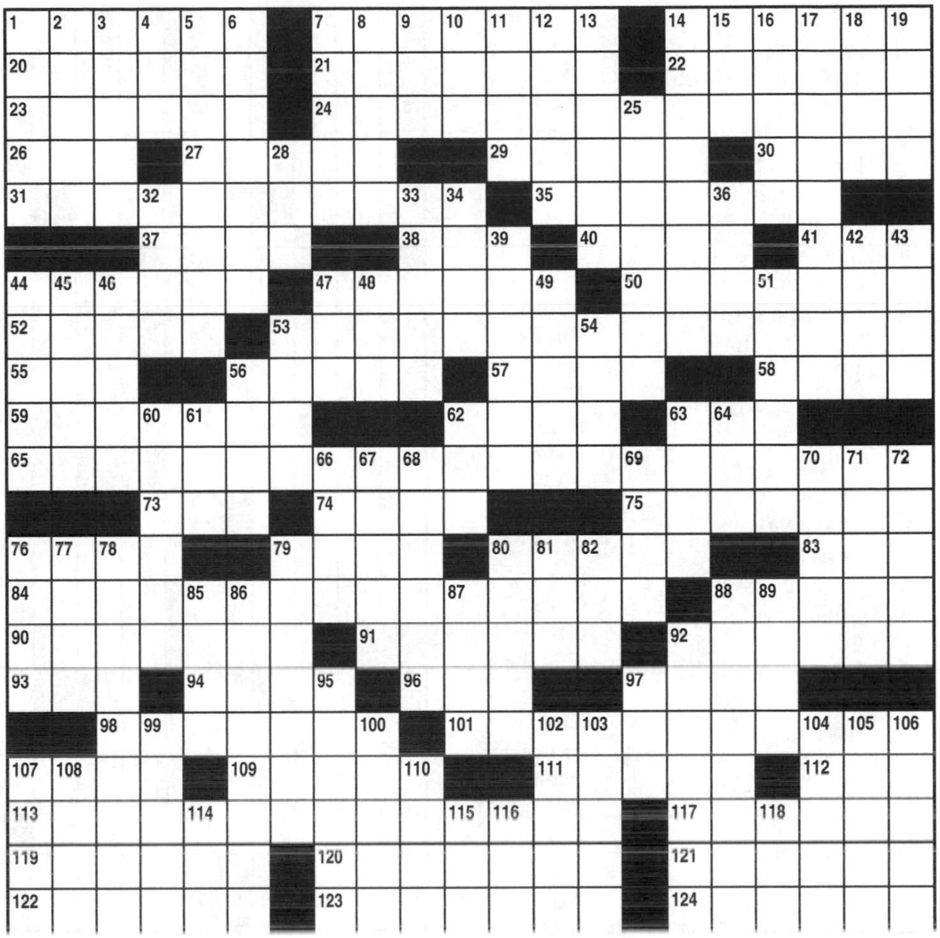

ACROSS

1 Jawaharlal's daughter
7 Narnia's creator
14 Where to go cold turkey?
20 Flew
21 Like VMI before 1997
22 Openings
23 Like instructions, often
24 Upholsterers wanted, because they can . . .
26 Sharp turn
27 Fishing spot
29 Henri's health
30 Govt. watchdog
31 Dry cleaners wanted, because they can . . .
35 Waist pinchers
37 Parks who stood up by sitting down
38 Yes, in Yokohama
40 Linguist Chomsky
41 Writer LeShan
44 Mississippi marshes
47 Ultimatum words
50 Gratifies
52 Scarlett's love
53 Lumberjacks wanted, because they can . . .
55 Bloom attachment?
56 "I thought I'd ___ shame!"
57 Stable call
58 Naval noncoms
59 Luxury digs
62 Mekong River land
63 McCullough's "John Adams," e.g.
65 Stove repairmen wanted, because they can . . .
73 Simile center
74 Neeson in "Schindler's List"
75 1st Russian Federation President
76 Shell rival
79 Faction
80 Seven-time Emmy winner Ed
83 Pub brew
84 Equestrians wanted, because they can . . .
88 Horrible Viking
90 Rooter at Citi Field
91 The G-7, for example
92 Singer-songwriter Lyle
93 Number of weeks per annum
94 Stringed instrument
96 ___ volente (God willing)
97 Soccer star nicknamed "O Rei"
98 Rotary engine cylinder type
101 Figure skaters wanted, because they can . . .
107 Reebok rival
109 Louvre pyramid architect
111 Maine college town
112 Enero to enero
113 Geologists wanted, because they can . . .
117 Must pay
119 Jeremiah preceder
120 Native New Yorkers
121 Blush or flush
122 Most unflushed
123 Recipients of NEA funding
124 Hang on

DOWN

1 Rodeo and Trooper maker
2 Grannies
3 Doleful ditty
4 Project conclusion?
5 Assist (to)
6 Speech
7 Stunt
8 Satisfy
9 Lawyer's deg.
10 911 responder
11 Nursery cries
12 Intestinal
13 Appliqued
14 Bargain opportunity
15 GOP fund-raising grp.
16 "Some Like ___"
17 Plays a child's game, perhaps
18 "Oh, wow!"
19 Mrs. Bugsy Siegel
25 Waste away
28 Govt. watchdog
32 Jog
33 Bundle
34 Polio vaccine developer
36 Scottish uncles
39 Meteorologist's line
42 Sample
43 Deadly biters
44 Fedora features
45 Loads
46 Lawyer questions, often
47 Expose, poetically
48 Classic car
49 Company in 2002 scandal
51 Foregoing profit
53 ___-Japanese War
54 "Don't ___ me, bro!"
56 Nick Jr. explorer
60 Equilibrium
61 Conditions
62 Abner's radio partner
63 Stand at a funeral?
64 Archipelago unit: Abbr.
66 Brewer, for short
67 Lyme disease carriers
68 Enjoyed a soak
69 They may be seeded
70 Lexicographer's concern
71 Southernmost city of Israel
72 Pet of 88 Across
76 Web programming language
77 "Able was I ___ saw Elba"
78 Like "The Colbert Report"
79 Italian Riviera resort
80 Sci-fi droid
81 Chicago–Miami dir.
82 Clear
85 Can. province
86 Part of DST
87 Crude group?
88 Like many October pumpkins (with "out")
89 Dodo's class
92 "La forza del destino" heroine
95 Wife to José
97 Favoring
99 Jack in "The Great Dictator"
100 Dinner commemorating the Exodus
102 ___ home (out)
103 Head lock
104 ___ Calais (Strait of Dover)
105 Lay to rest
106 Everybody's opposite
107 "You're ___!": Archie Bunker
108 Traveler's need
110 Fails to be
114 Some batteries
115 Muumuu go-with
116 Coolers, for short
118 Old English letter

240 FAMILIAR FACES by Sarah Keller

For many years 118 Across was clued erroneously as "Alley Oop's wife."

ACROSS

1 Nev. neighbor
6 Manhattan Project creation
11 Fragrant flower
15 Hombre's home
19 Muscat native
20 Way to be in love
21 Horse course
22 Dead-end jobs
23 **Start of a quote by Ogden Nash**
25 Makes retroactive
27 Oscar Night VIP
28 Bake eggs
30 Accustom
31 Draft letters
32 Slave away
33 **Quote: Part 2**
35 Morning hrs.
36 In that case
37 Old White House nickname
38 Turndowns
39 Basra native
42 "Ta-ta!"
44 Fish cleaners, at times
48 Excavated more
49 Big name in kitchen foil
51 "___ was saying . . ."
52 On the wagon
56 **Quote: Part 3**
60 Coke or Pepsi
61 Pouts
62 Hybrid elm variety
63 Paint layer
64 Dollar coin, familiarly
67 **Quote: Part 4**
69 Brian in "Titanic" (1953)
71 ___-TASS news agency
72 Loss of muscle coordination
75 Knight wear
77 Calf-length skirt
78 **Quote: Part 5**
84 Makes preparations
86 Classic opener
87 Battier of the NBA
88 Like a chimney sweep
89 Heartfelt
92 Baseball stats
93 Lazarus and Goldman
94 "Vanish, ___ shall give thee . . .": Shak.
97 Sundial number
98 "Ah, me!"
100 ___ Vegas
101 **Quote: Part 6**
105 Arouse
107 Bill's partner in love
110 Have ___ of tea
111 Religious splinter groups
112 Cornet relative
114 "It's a done deal!"
116 **End of quote**
118 "Return of the Jedi" dancer
119 Handed-down history
120 "I Hated, Hated, Hated This Movie" author
121 Many a blacksmith
122 Rallye rds.
123 Insulting tip
124 Feel
125 Some pre-state areas: Abbr.

DOWN

1 Casino freebies
2 Bigwigs in the Middle East
3 Puts on cargo
4 They're not party people: Abbr.
5 Choice steakhouse choice
6 Valuable violin
7 It goes with lox and cream cheese
8 Frankfurt's river
9 1051 in old Rome
10 Percy ___ Shelley
11 Batman's sidekick
12 Egg producer
13 Joint that often causes pain
14 Caribou kin
15 Construction site sight
16 Fall
17 2-channel sound
18 Stocks and bonds
24 "The Dukes of Hazzard" lawman
26 They jackknife
29 Plymouth Rock layers
33 Holler's partner
34 Island strings
35 Greenish-blue gem
36 Crunchy munchie
39 R.E.M. record label
40 Antique auto
41 High nav. rank
42 Superhero accessory
43 Martinique et Tahiti
45 Mean
46 "Hard Road to Glory" author
47 Some striker parents
50 Very attentive
53 Crude dude
54 Distinctive flair
55 Have status
57 Coffee brand
58 Where It. is
59 "I love you," in Spanish
64 Ninny
65 Gas or elec.
66 Emmy-winning Thompson
67 Former Montreal team
68 Compete
70 Alternate to incarceration
73 Sneaker
74 Bide-___
75 "The King and I" role
76 Deli breads
79 Bundle
80 Crew members
81 E-mail closer
82 Aristotle's H
83 Cobb and Treadway
85 Big Easy team
90 Dispose (of)
91 Stretched tightly
94 Henry Clay, notably
95 Filmed over
96 Pierce with a skewer
99 Setbacks
100 Pride member
102 Scintillas
103 Long
104 Largish combo
105 Clairvoyants
106 Gov. security
107 Use crayons
108 Champion skater Brian
109 Humdingers
112 ATF employees
113 Laugh line?
115 Pampering
117 U.K. award

241 PURR-FECT CLUES by Arlan and Linda Bushman

85 Across was the debut single for Cat Stevens.

ACROSS

1 Machine parts
5 Cat impressions
11 Unmatched
14 Pace, to Cat Manzi
18 Home state of the Bengals
19 Triumph
20 Pain in the neck
22 "Dora Maar With Cat" artist
24 "The Incredible Hulk" star
25 Where to find a stranded cat, perhaps
26 Step face
28 In reality, in Tours
29 Prepare to run
30 Hold off
32 Sharp turn
35 Creator of a grinning cat
39 Fishing net
42 Muskeg
45 ___ show (spectacle)
46 Troy prince
48 Spoils
49 Sets
51 Pot contents
52 Tropical food fish
53 Choice morsel
55 Unbending
57 "Cat Ballou" star
60 Celestial altar
61 Destiny
62 Attached, in a way
64 One with an E-3 pay grade
66 Overturn
67 Catty remark?
68 Links shot
70 Robert and Alan
73 Bark person
75 Paddock sights
76 Cat's canines
77 Showman Ziegfeld
79 He starred with a cat in "Bringing Up Baby"
82 Unruly child
83 Beatle who loved cats
85 "I ___ My Dog"
86 Dhabi preceder
88 Like housecats
89 "Diana" vocalist
90 Sensei's skill
93 Cat copy, possibly
95 Mariner's hdg.
96 Pretentious sort
98 "The Cat and the Mouse" composer
101 Say again
103 Brewery object
104 Kind of job
107 Flexible wood strip
109 Heroic tales
112 Herd members
115 Creator of Maggie "the Cat"
118 "Cat's Cradle" author
120 Unplugged, musically
121 Lights into
122 Vintners' valley
123 Olympus Mons site
124 Larter of "Heroes"
125 Defer
126 "___! The Cat" (1965 Broadway musical)

DOWN

1 Egyptian Christian
2 Midwest hub
3 Heckled
4 Cirque du ___
5 Snare activator
6 Room to relax?
7 Money-grubbing
8 Small crude dwelling
9 "Catman" Criss played for this group
10 Plumlike fruit
11 Undivided
12 Failure
13 Kuwait cash
14 Lasagna-loving cat
15 He voiced a cat in "Shrek the Third"
16 Emblem
17 Look after
19 Health ins. choice
21 Bisques
23 ___ cat (jaguarundi)
27 Beach Boys title girl
31 Not in port
33 Tankard filler
34 Dockworker's org.
36 Unit of power
37 Went full tilt
38 20 quires
40 Film ___
41 James of blues
42 Luxuriates (in)
43 Coming up
44 "Cat, You Better Come Home" author
47 Hubbub
50 Summer capital of British India
52 Takes in
54 Cell occupant
56 Particolored cat
57 DJ spins
58 Cats and dogs event
59 A-list ones
62 Loki associate
63 Well-ventilated
65 Watchful
68 Scoop holder
69 Cat accessory of rhyme
71 Bohr's study
72 Mouselike mammal
74 Slender
75 Bird of ill omen
77 Envelope part
78 Optical device
80 Fierce looks
81 Newspaper section
82 Treat for kitty
84 First atomic-powered sub
86 Obstacle for Hannibal
87 Means of escape
91 Battery designation
92 Cat quarry
93 Seaside
94 Come to
97 Leary of comedy
99 Rough
100 Justify
102 "Giant" ranch
105 "Popeye" cartoonist
106 Big band drummer Gene
107 Did the crawl
108 Typewriter type size
110 Aliases, briefly
111 Spew forth
113 Funny pair?
114 Sports figure
116 Thickness measure
117 Ecol., for one
119 "Tom and ___" (1994 film)

242 LIFE PARTNERS by Clare Hansbrough

93 Across is mentioned in "The Ballad of Jed Clampett."

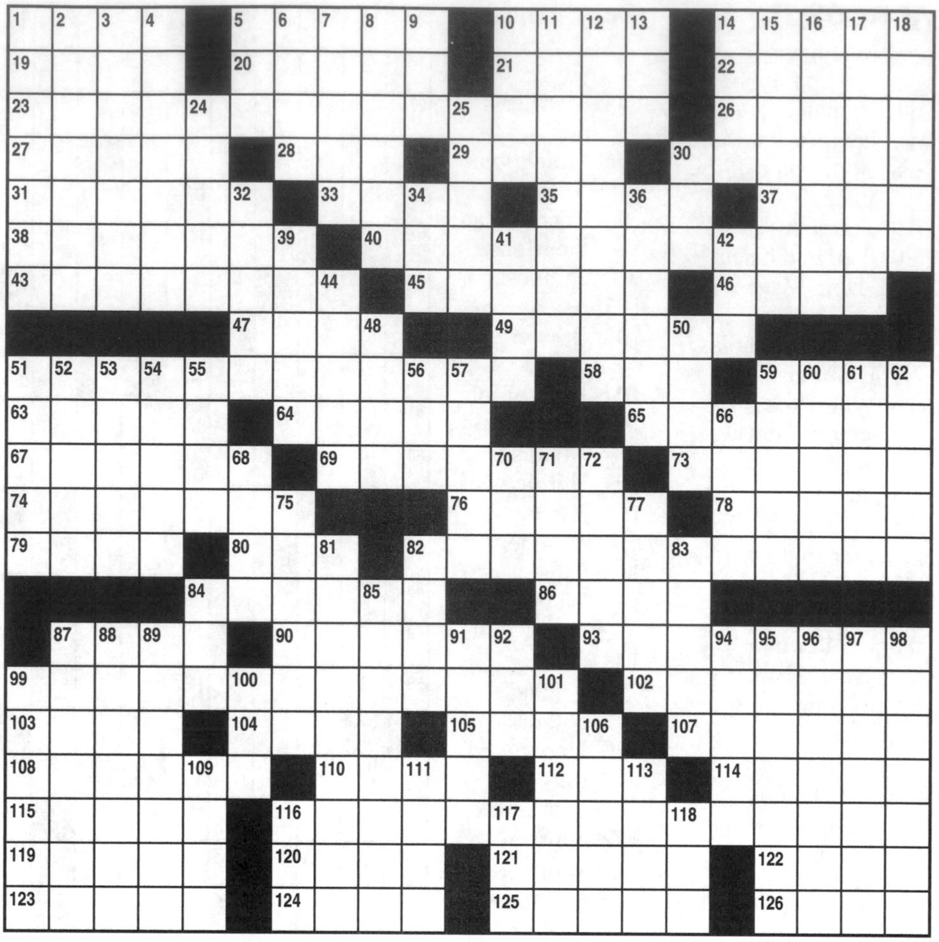

ACROSS

1 Nickelodeon explorer
5 "The ___ Were": Streisand
10 Fit to be tied
14 Capital of Ghana
19 Big brutes
20 Polynesian greeting
21 Autobahn auto
22 Units of laughter
23 Be financially independent
26 Start of a legal conclusion
27 Tuckered out
28 "Verrrry . . ."
29 Scottish isle
30 Disgruntled fan's cry
31 Closed in on
33 Like cotton candy
35 Allies' enemy
37 Jason's craft
38 Stirs up
40 Extra scores, in baseball
43 Note-taker's tablet
45 Tennis star Williams
46 Weightlifting units
47 Garfield's sidekick
49 Fitzgerald figure
51 Dress code, sometimes
58 Poseidon's province
59 Pub missile
63 Roll-on brand
64 Palindromic principle
65 Judges establish it
67 Added support to
69 Fair ones in distress
73 Hyundai model
74 Present adornment
76 Wherewithal
78 "American Idol" judge
79 Leather stickers
80 Fall mo.
82 Emulate Ethel Merman
84 Disco pulser
86 Comical Bombeck
87 Catch sight of
90 Dinnerware items
93 Black gold
99 Prompt you to act
102 Give the letters for again
103 "Song of the South" syllables
104 Hugging limbs
105 Jungle warning
107 Type of column
108 Available to rent
110 Series ender
112 Boxing stat
114 Lint collector
115 Put in two cents worth
116 Novel need
119 "The Manchurian Candidate" heroine
120 "Star Wars" creature
121 Storage spot
122 Wanton look
123 Asparagus piece
124 D.C. bigwigs
125 Can't avoid
126 Canadian gas brand

DOWN

1 Aquafina rivals
2 Ever so lavish
3 Put back
4 Heart protector
5 Tedious card game
6 Mtn. stats
7 Toys on strings
8 Goldberg in "The Color Purple"
9 Perrier, to Pierre
10 Fair-to-middling
11 Kite-flying place
12 Medicines for muscle strain
13 Polar worker
14 One mo' time
15 Transportation cost
16 Resolve
17 Gives notice
18 Houston team
24 "I'm not ___ complain, but . . ."
25 Get the suds off
30 Trojans' sch.
32 Bus station
34 Us, in Ulm
36 "Be right with you!"
39 Egyptian Peace Nobelist
41 Try to persuade
42 Suffix with station
44 Ate elegantly
48 "Giant" author Ferber
50 Sheep calls
51 Obese "Star Wars" character
52 Turn indicator
53 Swim stroke
54 Breaks, as a habit
55 Shangri-La
56 Word after pro
57 "C'est moi" to Arthur
59 "The Ref" star Leary
60 San Antonio siege site
61 Boca ___
62 Guitar sound
66 Slugger Sammy
68 "Stop that!"
70 Long swimmer
71 After curfew
72 Quick drink
75 Inertia
77 Ancient region of Mesopotamia
81 Trilogy's center
82 Aleph follower
83 Takes money from citizens
84 Sault ___ Marie
85 Seat at Cheers
87 Bubbly beverage
88 Just so
89 Pacific group
91 Ahead of time
92 Winter product prefix
94 Les of Clinton's cabinet
95 Turntable axis
96 Sneakers, for short
97 Famed New York eatery
98 Fast for fiddlers
99 Party handouts
100 China's Sun ___-sen
101 Fanning in "I Am Sam"
106 Alex Haley miniseries
109 At no time, in verse
111 Torah holders
113 Comedy sketch
116 IRA type
117 Cry of contempt
118 "The Name of the Rose" author

243 BEAT THE CLOCK: 14:52 by Alyssa Brooke

An easy-to-medium Sunday-sized challenge.

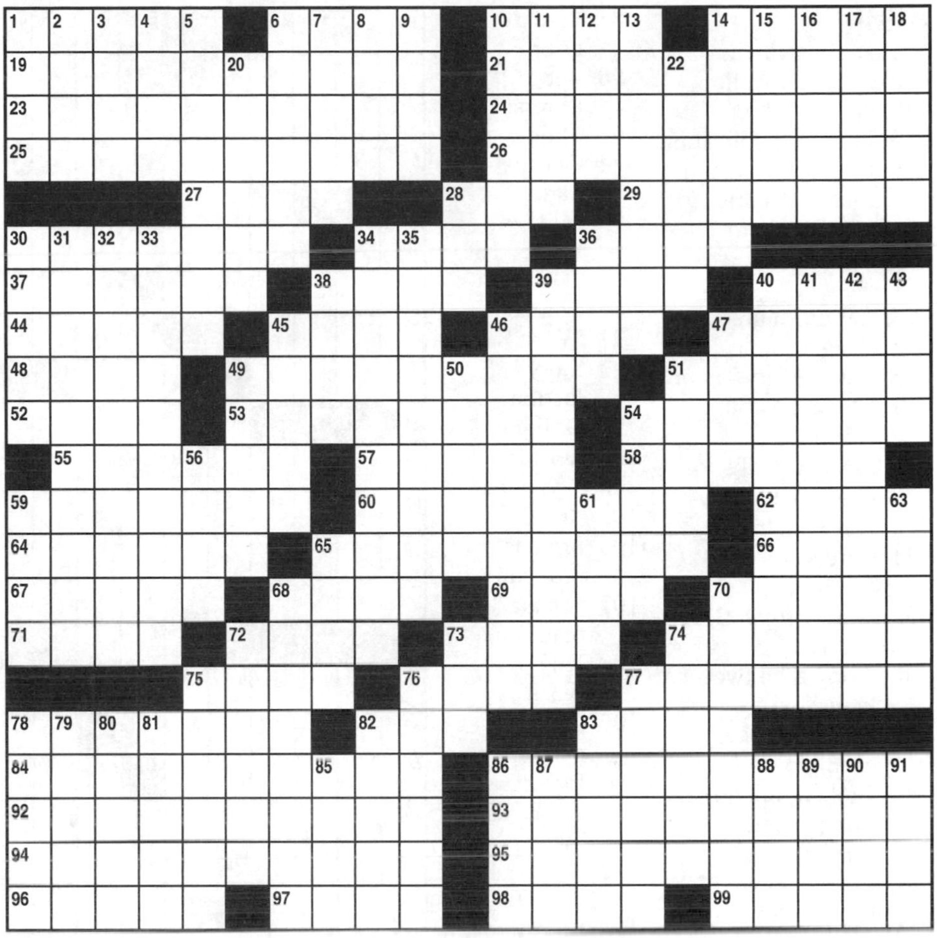

ACROSS

1 Shucks
6 Choice of juice?
10 Legal cover-up?
14 Turns over
19 Crisp
21 "Get in line!"
23 Jim Carrey's detective role
24 Directly confront
25 Golf groups
26 Signs, as an agreement
27 Scores 72 on, perhaps
28 Reel holder
29 Make further modifications to
30 Mellow tones
34 POTUS part
36 Yarn source
37 Without a sour note
38 Bikini feature
39 College figure
40 Tip
44 Shifts direction
45 Balkan dweller
46 Puppy bites
47 Tea choice
48 Mideast land
49 From abroad
51 Feeds a crowd
52 Some gobblers
53 Citizenry
54 Elizabeth ___ Browning
55 Singer Ronnie
57 Jolie's "Girl, Interrupted" costar
58 Deliver a message
59 Establish a better foothold
60 Vine support
62 Sci. course
64 "Becket" actor
65 Selectively block
66 Bride-___
67 Like a thicket
68 Frontier nickname
69 Contact piece
70 Lonesome George of comedy
71 Highlands tongue
72 N. Car. neighbor
73 Soprano role in "Lohengrin"
74 Most immaculate
75 Lech's look
76 1974 CIA-spoof movie
77 Western endings
78 Ductless organs
82 Food preservative
83 Tears
84 "Mad About You" star
86 Crushing underfoot
92 Completely destroy, perhaps
93 "Blame It on the Bossa Nova" singer
94 Said again
95 Endurance sports events
96 Church officer
97 Snaky swimmers
98 It seems like forever
99 Namely

DOWN

1 Scrap
2 Former NYC mayor
3 Road that led to Rome
4 Church section
5 Gets harder to climb
6 SAG members
7 Cronies
8 Not looking good
9 Workers in columns
10 Ladies' men
11 Running
12 Sucrose source
13 Hash houses
14 Unpopular senate figure
15 Online sales
16 Failed to
17 Overdramatize
18 Casa dweller
20 Closeout tag
22 Screw feature
28 Flag thrower, at times
30 Turning point
31 Wind instrument
32 Laundry items
33 Unleashes
34 Like a tough nut to crack
35 Battle reenactor's cry, perhaps
36 Take bounding steps
38 Sow's opposite
39 Delicious masher
40 No fans
41 Florida lake
42 To an ultimate advantage
43 Follower of gab or slug
45 Cuts off
46 Goody-goody
47 Skin
49 Sudden burst
50 Anwar of Egypt
51 Wedge-shaped mark
54 Good grade
56 Shoe bottom
59 Teased mercilessly
61 Geraldine Chaplin's mom
63 Gets all mushy
65 Klinger portrayer
68 Requiem Mass hymn
70 It's over a barrel
72 Finish
73 Capable, facetiously
74 Punch, for example
75 "My Fair Lady" lyricist
76 Reduces to confetti
77 Like King Kong
78 Skyline feature
79 Wall covering
80 Completely clear
81 Choice
82 "South Pacific" nut
83 Ham medium
85 Fill completely
86 Stiff bristle
87 Brit's wheel
88 Legal plea, for short
89 Wax
90 Science magazine
91 Snug retreat

244 -TERS by Harvey Estes

Try to figure out the title before you solve 105 Across.

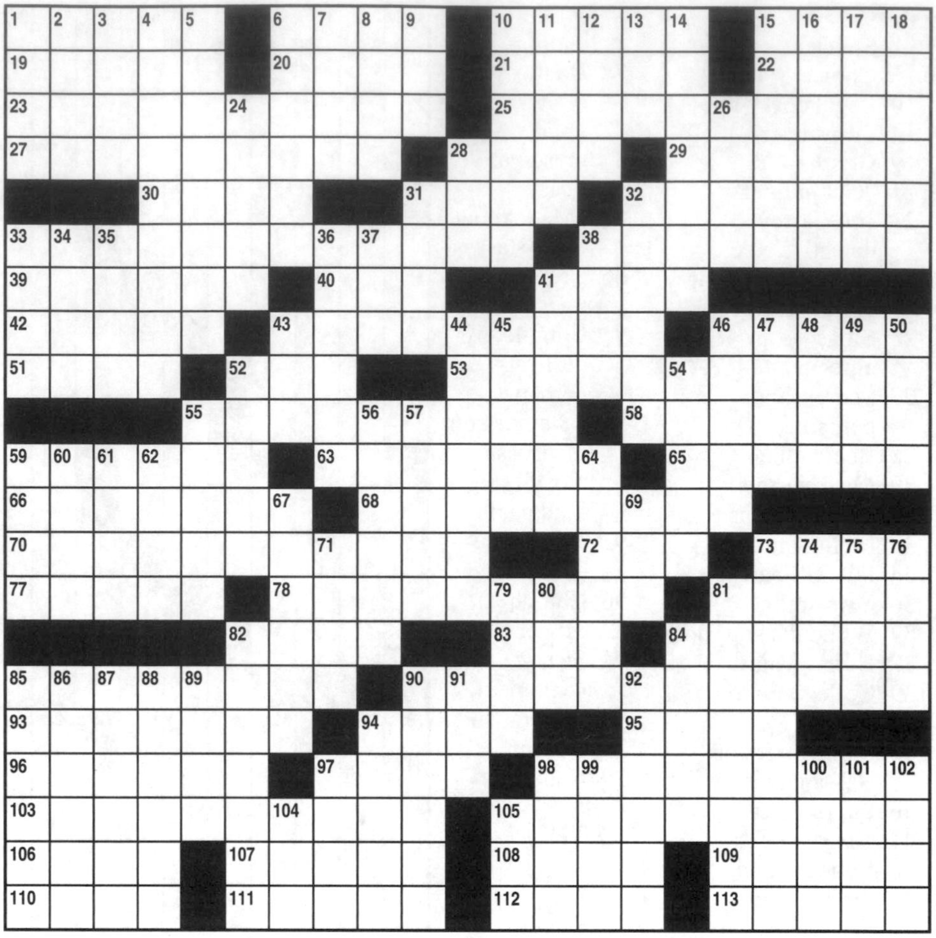

ACROSS

1 Highway exits
6 Impala, to a lion
10 Dijon darling
15 Prep for publication
19 Prufrock's creator
20 Metallic fabric
21 Christmas story villain
22 Ho Chi ___ City
23 -ter of Maureen Reagan
25 -ter of Mary Tudor
27 "Give me your word!"
28 Stare stupidly
29 Orion, with "the"
30 Royal address
31 Card spots
32 Big birds
33 -ter of Elijah Blue Allman
38 Array with two kings
39 Bicycle spoke, for example
40 Quibell, in Quebec
41 Long-jawed fish species
42 Really enjoyed
43 Universally loved sitcom star
46 Out in front
51 Be abundant
52 Sticky seed case
53 -ter of Lorna Luft
55 "Whip" of facetious punishment
58 Way of Springsteen's band
59 Bootlegger's cornfield measure
63 Divides
65 Bread units
66 Result of iron deficiency (var.)
68 Unwraps in a hurry
70 -ter of King Arthur
72 Turner of an uprising
73 Computer clickers
77 Extra charge
78 Downward plunges
81 Kind of bear
82 Kind of tense
83 Greeting to Maria
84 Dextrose and fructose
85 Like a grinning cat
90 -ter of Loretta Lynn
93 Major babes
94 Queens' ___ Park
95 Midnight fridge visit
96 "Do it again!"
97 "West Side Story" faction
98 Obliging
103 -ter of Wynonna
105 -ter
106 Friends' pronoun
107 "Dallas" matriarch
108 Ice house (var.)
109 Market purchase
110 Beer, slangily
111 Serve
112 Sound of a bell-raiser
113 Like a confusing explanation

DOWN

1 Workout tallies
2 What there oughta be
3 Wee bit
4 Banana benefit
5 1973 Johnny Nash tune written by Bob Marley
6 Krypton, in science fiction
7 Shankar of sitar
8 Give out
9 Twenty Questions answer
10 Bargain-basement
11 Chips in
12 Pennsylvania city
13 Peri's "Frasier" role
14 Some taters
15 Corrects, as text
16 Says "I agree"
17 "Is it hot ___ or is it just me?"
18 Need a drink
24 Rock's "Pillow Talk" partner
26 Burger rolls
28 Card table cry
31 Do the honors at tea
32 Shiny car trim
33 Suffix with Dixie
34 Can't stomach
35 "Zip-___-Doo-Dah"
36 Has a hankering
37 Howl in the moonlight
38 Biblical wedding site
41 Star watchers
43 Same old grind
44 Bygone times
45 Middle distance runner
46 Writer Chekhov
47 Greek queen of heaven
48 Mt. sign
49 Sheltered on the sea
50 Morse clicks
52 Neighbor of Nigeria
54 Spot in the water
55 John Lennon song
56 Clothing ensemble
57 Ryan of "Love Story"
59 Vasco da ___
60 It's given in agreement
61 Fat in the can
62 Toy block brand
64 Shakespearean specialty
67 Sites of rites
69 "Swan Lake" step
71 Peace of mind
73 Seaport of Somalia
74 "As ___ Dying"
75 Poet Sandburg
76 Highlands tongue
79 Ponies up
80 ER hook-ups
81 Field of boxers
82 Under the table
84 Insult responses, perhaps
85 Deals from the bottom, say
86 Fuji's island
87 Deeply embedded
88 Furry wraps
89 Sign up
90 Kind of block
91 Fix, as a fight
92 Carrier's load
94 Ham medium
97 Big gap
98 Batting area
99 Earthenware jar
100 Minimally
101 Propeller head
102 Small club
104 "The Wedding Planner" actress, familiarly
105 With it

245 ARBOR DAZE by Pancho Harrison
"I think that I shall never see . . ."

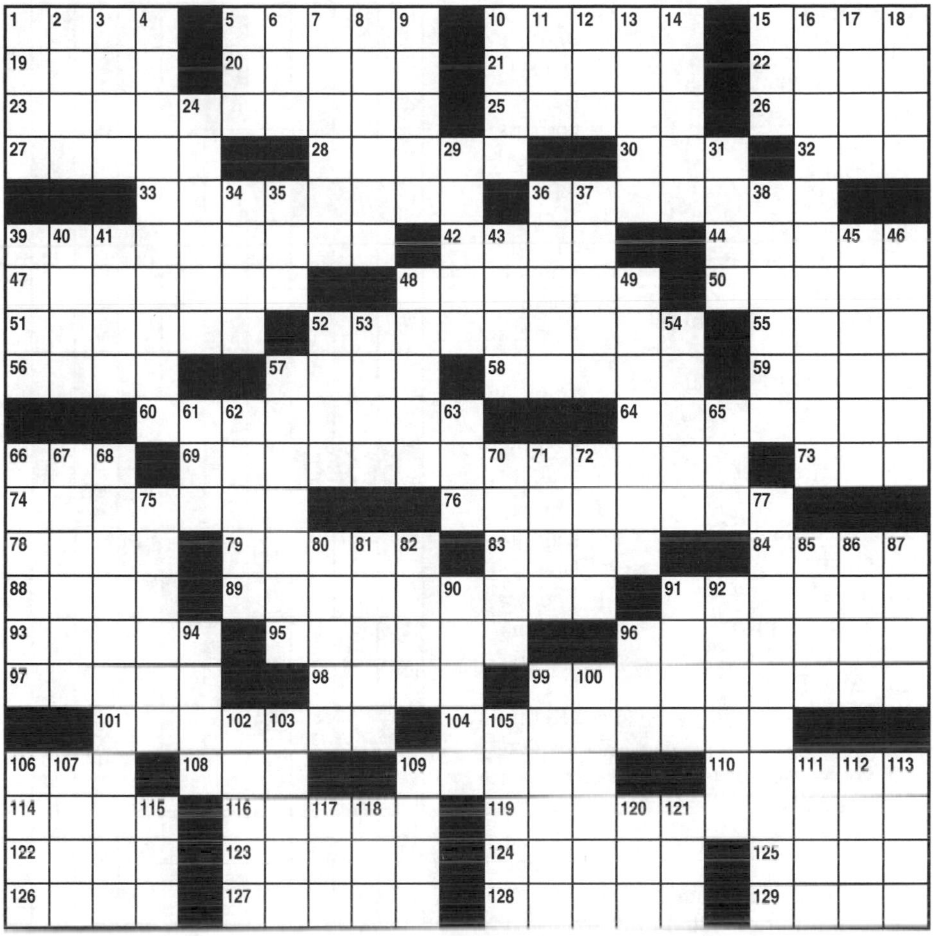

ACROSS

1 "Bonanza" brother
5 Land of the rising sun
10 Oodles
15 Chairlift alternative
19 Madame in "The Balcony"
20 Words before and after "for"
21 Eva of Argentina
22 Fictional detective Wolfe
23 Lost conifer?
25 Violet starter?
26 Show's partner
27 Dalmation features
28 Blender brand
30 Edwards or Andrews: Abbr.
32 Flirtatiously shy
33 Mount St. Helen action
36 Acute distress
39 Gangsta eucalyptus?
42 Remove from text
44 Italian lawn-bowling game
47 All fouled up
48 Glib speech
50 Witch craft?
51 In a meddling way
52 Evergreen dealer?
55 Napoleon and Nero: Abbr.
56 Org.
57 Corn bread
58 "Fear of Flying" author Jong
59 "___ Ben Adhem"
60 Insane
64 Nonprofessional
66 Storage container
69 "Great Society" lime?
73 MapQuest request: Abbr.
74 Fit to be tied
76 Worries, slangily
78 Give ___ to (prompt)
79 Tummy trouble
83 Ticks off
84 Leprechaun's land
88 "No skateboarding," e.g.
89 Monogamous ties, according to Bartletts?
91 Feudal lords
93 Hawke in "Training Day"
95 At the table
96 Busts a gut over
97 Brief fight
98 Not yet final, in law
99 Banyan seen on "Barney Miller?"
101 Game played with five dice
104 Agrippina's brother
106 Davis or Stanley, e.g.
108 It's found in veins
109 Beginning, slangily
110 First name in cosmetics
114 Alkali neutralizer
116 In unison
119 Alamo tune?
122 Fit to be tried
123 14 pounds, in London
124 Disney mermaid
125 Therefore
126 Didst kill
127 High-strung
128 Summarize
129 Elton, Paul, and Mick, e.g.

DOWN

1 Goals
2 Loser, in '50s high school slang
3 "Are not!" rejoinder
4 Criminal genius
5 Painter Vermeer
6 "Brokeback Mountain" director Lee
7 Hallucinogenic cactus
8 Swabbie's affirmative
9 Unfamiliar with
10 Egg on
11 Cartoon frame
12 Carney in "Harry and Tonto"
13 Hip-hop head wear
14 Major mix-up
15 "We know drama" cable channel
16 One in search of a specific driftwood?
17 "Alice's Restaurant" singer
18 ___-poly
24 Tel Aviv's land
29 Be over by
31 Lettuce variety
34 ___-daisy
35 Second afterthought: Abbr.
36 Site for rites
37 "___ say more?"
38 Irritated with
39 Queen Latifah in "Beauty Shop"
40 Some, in San Juan
41 Part of WMD
43 To be, to Henri
45 Poor excuse
46 "There's no doubt in my mind!"
48 Primp
49 Hires new actors
52 Enamored (of)
53 "Picnic" playwright
54 Aquino's successor in the Philippines
57 Like some jury rooms?
61 She, in Sao Paulo
62 Put together
63 CD players?
65 Singer DiFranco
66 Prejudices
67 Provoke
68 Hardly a good Christmas tree?
70 In debt
71 Bovine bunch
72 Scottish refusals
75 Soprano Scotto
77 Quells rioters
80 "Sleuth" star Michael
81 Bert's muppet pal
82 Slugger's stats
85 ___ many words
86 Size up, in a way
87 This, in Tijuana
90 Chilling
91 Vegan staple
92 Taxi flagger
94 Greenwich Village neighbor
96 Gas pump abbr.
99 "Earth in the Balance" author
100 "Ali" or "Ray," say
102 Totally wreck
103 Piquant
105 Even, at Shinnecock
106 Pop music's "Mama"
107 Berkeley school
109 Will of "Jeremiah Johnson"
111 Singer Amos
112 MIT grad: Abbr.
113 They can be inflated
115 "Do the ___!" (soft drink slogan)
117 End of an Alley?
118 Denver–Minneapolis dir.
120 Where grass roots
121 Eiger, for one

246 STARTING TEAM by Fran & Lou Sabin

Answers to clues* are members of the starting team.

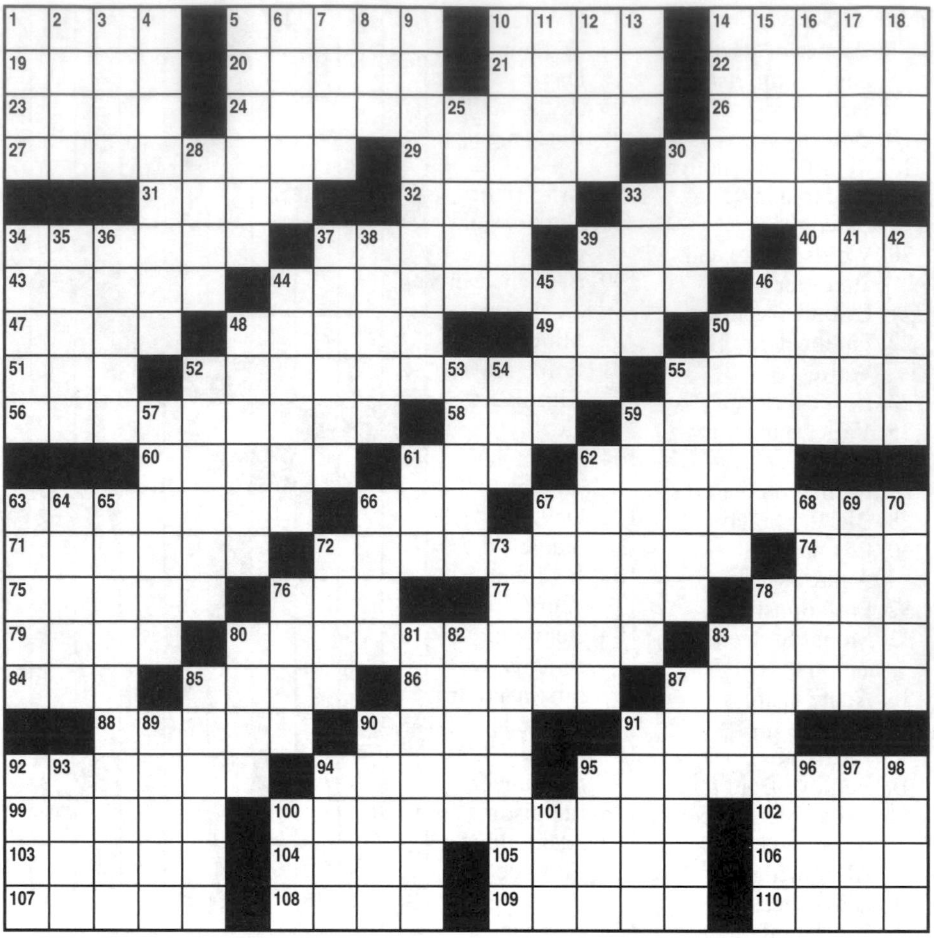

ACROSS

1 Licorice candy
5 Class-change alert
10 Tricky move
14 Film featuring "Baby Mine"
19 Smell ___
20 Budget ___ Car
21 Kind of agreement
22 "Don't enter!" alert
23 "It's ___ vu all over again!"
24 Home turf of 100 Across
26 Crabwalk
27 George Eliot classic*
29 Three-time PGA champ
30 ER signs
31 Knee-slappers
32 Number crunching
33 Road Runner box
34 Upward mobility?
37 Chanel product
39 Grass measure
40 "Travels in Hyperreality" author
43 Wind-driven clouds
44 Stage actress noted for her Peter Pan*
46 High school highlight
47 Fill fully
48 Motherly prefix
49 Oaxaca whoopie
50 Native Polynesian
51 Name that means "greatest"
52 Pave, in a way*
55 Hound dog
56 Ancient Chinese aristocrats
58 Hoosier fabulist
59 Cannons
60 Tic-tac-toe act
61 Sugar Loaf site
62 Stray's affliction
63 Running out
66 Mummer's topper
67 Achilles's warriors
71 Many a ski lodge
72 Big surprise*
74 Drink like Figaro
75 Luges
76 Panama
77 "___ Andy Warhol" (1996)
78 Beans, perhaps
79 Roofer's repair spot
80 "Once is enough!"*
83 Municipal
84 Jeanne d'Arc, for ex.
85 Tender to the touch
86 Moralist's principles
87 Gerents
88 Riata loop
90 Head line
91 Theater clearer?
92 Passover fare
94 "Return To Sender" is one
95 Stretch innings
99 Pleaides pursuer
100 STARTNG TEAM*
102 Shivery
103 Hollow pasta
104 Focal points
105 Compelling sort
106 Jane Austen heroine
107 Champing at the bit
108 Guitar ridge
109 Still-life objects
110 Way down

DOWN

1 Zip
2 Set to explode
3 Lower California
4 "City Slickers" scene
5 Silvery
6 Yorkshire city
7 Henry VIII's 4th
8 Atlas abbr.
9 TV, radio, newspapers et al.
10 Language-code stone
11 Heep of "Bleak House"
12 Pronounced
13 Cantab's rival
14 Square-dance figure
15 Tie up
16 Oscar-winning Simone Signoret film*
17 Meal ender?
18 Tram fillers
25 Employed
28 Dog holders?
30 Tennessee jocks
33 Silent entertainment
34 Shillong's state
35 Gia in "The Angry Hills"
36 Film insert
37 Thai coin
38 Cheese food
39 Moolah
41 Kitchen tool
42 Puts aside
44 Club activity
45 Catch some Z's
46 Gave the old one-two to
48 Gyrene
50 Page's border
52 Wise words
53 Pale yellow
54 It turns singles into doubles
55 Clever remark
57 Malicious marquis
59 Francis "the Swamp Fox"
61 Give 'er the gun
62 Like Arthur and Guinevere
63 Improves eyesight, in a way
64 Singer's key
65 Prohibiting*
66 Celebrate
67 Kenyan native
68 Castor Oyl's sister
69 Low point
70 Building plans
72 Critic's response
73 "Don't be so serious!"
76 Attendee's answer
78 Shut up
80 Quick bite
81 Allow back in
82 Roman courtyards
83 Make jerky
85 Ado Annie, for one
87 "Midnight Special" singer
89 Oxygen with an odor
90 Noun category
91 Peggy Lee hit
92 Gloomy Gus, notably
93 Surface section
94 Lysol target
95 Arcade name
96 "It Matters ___": Faith Hill
97 Dwelling
98 Buffet
100 Sitcom alien
101 Dr. of the rap world

247 BEASTLY by Edgar Fontaine

27 Across is Sparky Lyle's too.

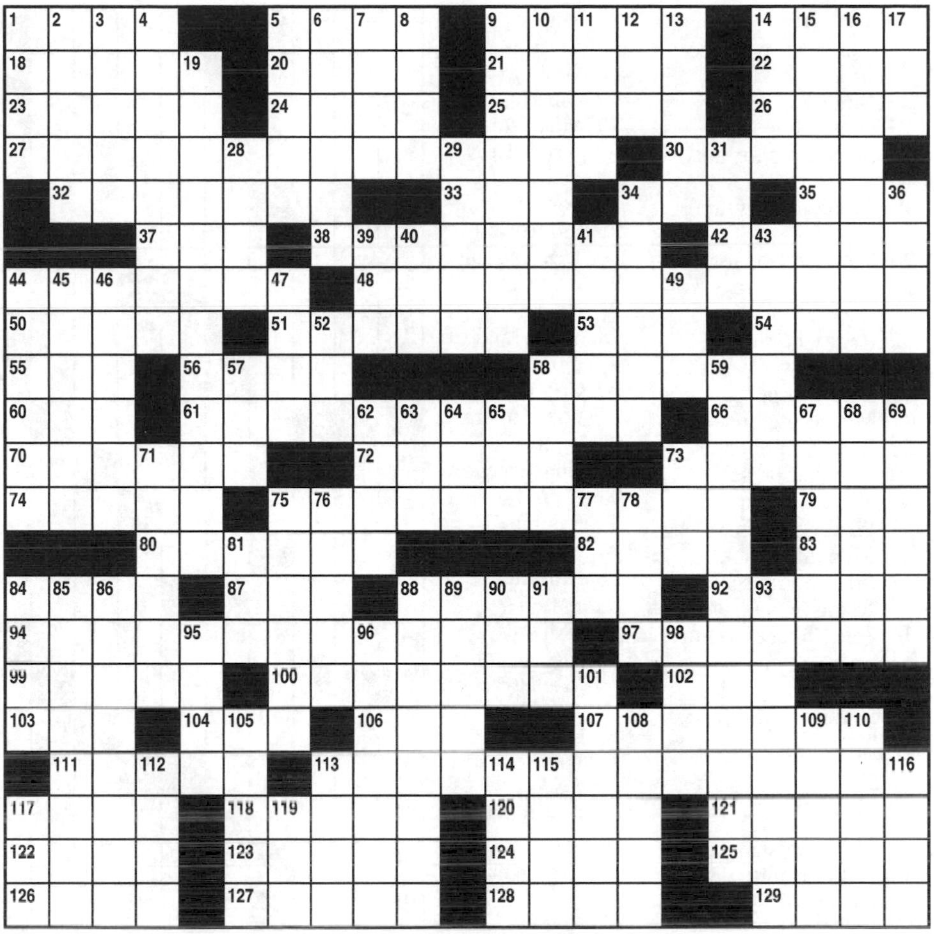

ACROSS

1 Support group?
5 Gives in the middle
9 Milk source
14 Humorist Bombeck
18 Talks wildly
20 Mitch Miller's instrument
21 Gaucho's accessory
22 Luminous sign
23 Paperback alternative
24 Very short time: Abbr.
25 British __
26 Platte River tribe
27 Craig Stadler's trademark
30 Anklebone
32 Even smaller
33 Fish with a long snout
34 Queen of the fairies
35 Part of A.A.R.P.
37 10 gm
38 Tact
42 Earl Scruggs' instrument
44 On the left, on the Left Bank
48 Avocado
50 Minute translucent marine life
51 Called
53 "Put a lid on it!"
54 Church benches
55 Sect leader?
56 Scottish hillside
58 Peter of 59 Down
60 USNA grad
61 Double basses
66 Prefix with red
70 Fix, as leftovers
72 Yemeni's neighbor
73 Dieter's concern
74 Comic actor Arnold
75 John Hurt character in 1980
79 Austin–Dallas dir.
80 Confutes
82 Himalayan legend
83 Roadhouse
84 Samoan port
87 Eyebrow's shape
88 Belonging to them
92 Famous
94 Judicature
97 Diane and Tom
99 Computer key
100 Jenny McCarthy in October 1993
102 Dogfaces
103 Shogun capital
104 Don't waste
106 Stat for "Big Papi"
107 Fazed
111 True inner self
113 False sorrow
117 Large number
118 Pope of 1049–54
120 "Galveston" songwriter
121 Plant problem
122 Top of the head
123 Be of one mind
124 Doozy
125 "The Canterbury Tales" pilgrim
126 Side squared, for a square
127 Active sorts
128 Goblet feature
129 J. D. of baseball

DOWN

1 Suds
2 Morocco's capital
3 American chameleon
4 Accumulated
5 English Channel feeder
6 Laughable
7 Takes off
8 Breakaway group
9 Gout cause
10 Sink add-on?
11 Chip's cartoon chum
12 Hiver's opposite
13 Bob Marley fan
14 Organic compound
15 Prodigal son, later on
16 City west of Regina
17 T or F, e.g.
19 Swamp plant
28 Sound of dismay
29 Nimble
31 Short term?
34 Ideology
36 Rocky peaks
39 Ring bearer, maybe
40 Legal deg.
41 Social stratum
43 Add
44 Fall flowers
45 January birthstone
46 "You Wanna Be A Star" singer
47 Catchall abbr.
49 "Just as I suspected!"
52 Slithery swimmer
57 Same old, same old
58 Lena of "Chocolat"
59 1968 film (with "The")
62 Rivals
63 Enfant terrible
64 Code word
65 Courtroom evidence
67 Limited
68 On-base one
69 Makes right
71 Infuriate
73 Posed
75 The Continent
76 Maj.'s superior
77 Norse war god
78 Base meal
81 Legal profession
84 Jamaican fruit
85 London police cruiser
86 Recite as a chant
88 Children's chests
89 Like fertile soil
90 Piece of history
91 Morticia's cousin
93 Dug mollusks for Rockefeller?
95 Jack-in-the-pulpit
96 Flattop
98 Chills and fever
101 Like some mushrooms
105 Pre-entree course
108 Vinyl collectible
109 Gung-ho
110 Got off the tee
112 It comes to mind
113 Part of a nuclear reactor
114 Mail carriers in Harry Potter novels
115 O.T. book
116 Mulligan, for one
117 Place to be pampered
119 Id's kin

248 ROLL CALL NAMES by Victor Fleming

An amusing subtitle can be found below.

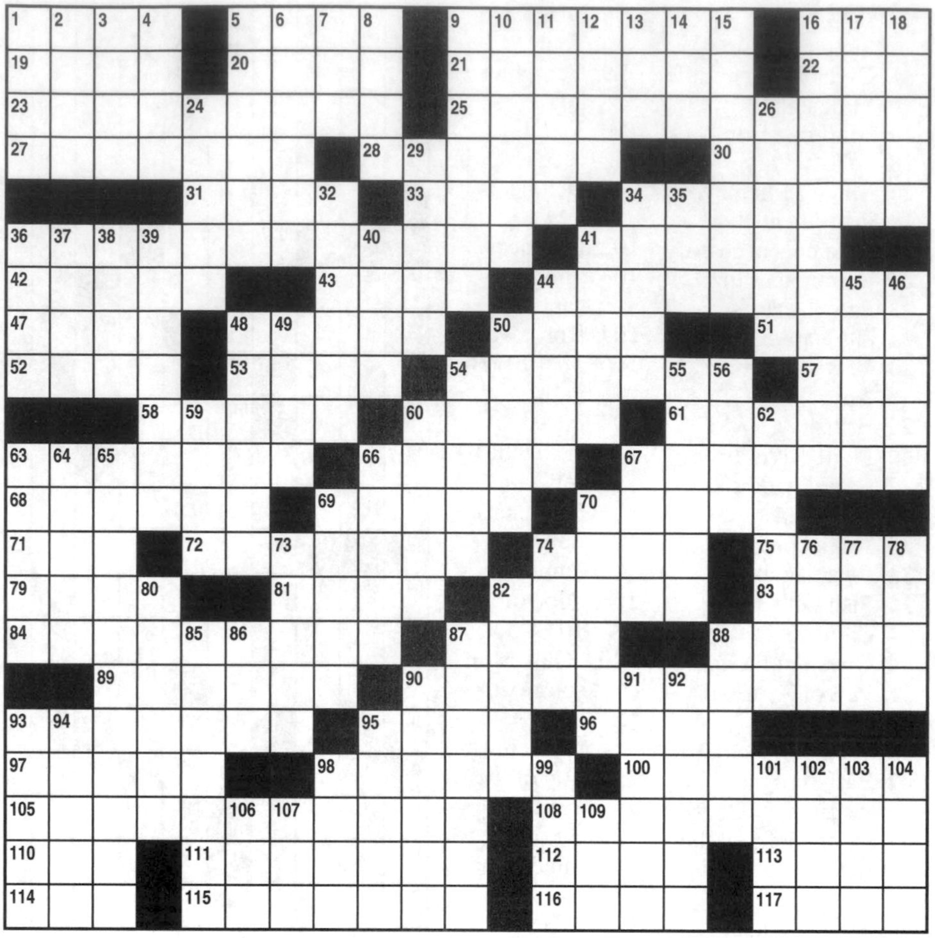

ACROSS

1 Oppenheimer who produced "Get Smart"
5 Clothed
9 Selects, as for duty
16 Sauna locale
19 Amazing Rhythm ___
20 Whence venison
21 Xerxes or Ataxerxes, e.g.
22 It may be run
23 Give Elwes a wish?
25 Kiss a Pope?
27 Muscovite, for one
28 Reno neighbor
30 And and or, say
31 Not esa or otra
33 Works of Henry Mancini: Abbr.
34 Like the Jays against Ryan on 5/1/1991
36 Tell Chaucer to hurry up?
41 Hindu dignitaries
42 Hades, for Pluto, e.g.
43 "Louis___" (Somers opera)
44 Former Florida governor
47 Manning stats
48 Bulletin follower?
50 Reject
51 "The Aba-Honeymoon" link
52 Häagen-___
53 Aussie colleges
54 **Puzzle subtitle: Part I**
57 Elephant eater of myth
58 Gave off coherent light
60 Nation that's long, tall and narrow
61 E-mail software named for a writer
63 Canadian province
66 **Subtitle: Part II**
67 Merged with
68 Of the Middle Ages
69 Evil one
70 Roadside inn
71 Bruins Hall of Famer
72 **Subtitle: Part III**
74 Armyworm, eventually
75 Nightclub routines
79 Helvetica, for one
81 "La Fille Perdue" playwright
82 Indian craft
83 Those folks
84 Only child of the King
87 Maverick or Starr
88 Soak up
89 Clearings
90 Make sci-fi writer Brown drill?
93 Pool wear
95 Pioneering U.S. feminist
96 Bug fighters
97 Hag
98 Some kind of a nut
100 Connors contemporary
105 Injure Shakespeare?
108 Look for Thomas?
110 Coll. major
111 Adriatic nation
112 "Ah so!"
113 Morales of "Resurrection Blvd."
114 River near Balmoral Castle
115 Hero worship
116 Mix
117 Gone, maybe

DOWN

1 Jaromir of the NHL
2 Brown shade
3 Bodies that get sailed
4 IRS data
5 Where liner notes may be found
6 Wilderness shelter
7 ___ Lingus
8 Prohibitionist groups
9 Wear
10 Amoroso or oloroso
11 Gives the ax
12 Is vexing to
13 Leader of law and order?
14 Scand. land
15 Tax reducer
16 Throw rocks at Ozzy's wife?
17 What homers are hit out of
18 Bottomless pit
24 Supermodel Cheryl
26 "Balm in ___" (Lanford Wilson play)
29 Lessened, with "down"
32 Fearful
34 Spanish 101 word
35 Swinger's middle?
36 Foray
37 Wrist-elbow connector
38 Kind of bath
39 Made life hard for
40 Needle bearers
41 Esther of "Good Times"
44 Union general at Shiloh
45 Stop, at Cape Canaveral
46 Former Portuguese colony
48 Stir
49 Fit to serve
50 Kid
54 Burmese diplomat U ___
55 Breathe fire and fury
56 'Hood arrogance
59 Emirate denizen
60 It may be pounded
62 Acted like a pupil
63 Gompers grp.
64 Poet Jones
65 Cheats Carlin?
66 No-Bob connection
67 Short pic
69 "Done!"
70 Quite a while
73 Travelocity.com info
74 Rival of Julius
76 Burn on the grill
77 Actress Polo
78 Match, informally
80 Knack
82 Marseille menu
85 Hardly sought peace
86 Hoo-ha
87 Tile protector, of a sort
88 Boxer's restraint
90 Byzantine dome art
91 Aromatic seed
92 Violent, perhaps
93 Short timetable
94 Juice type
95 Appalachian Trail's northern terminus
98 Fan sound
99 Vagary
101 Augusta National has 18
102 Further
103 "Fly Like an Eagle" singer
104 Markey of Tarzan films
106 Seine scene
107 Dumbbell abbr.
109 Service

249 "AM I BLUE?" by Bonnie L. Gentry

You might say these are members of the Blue Man Group.

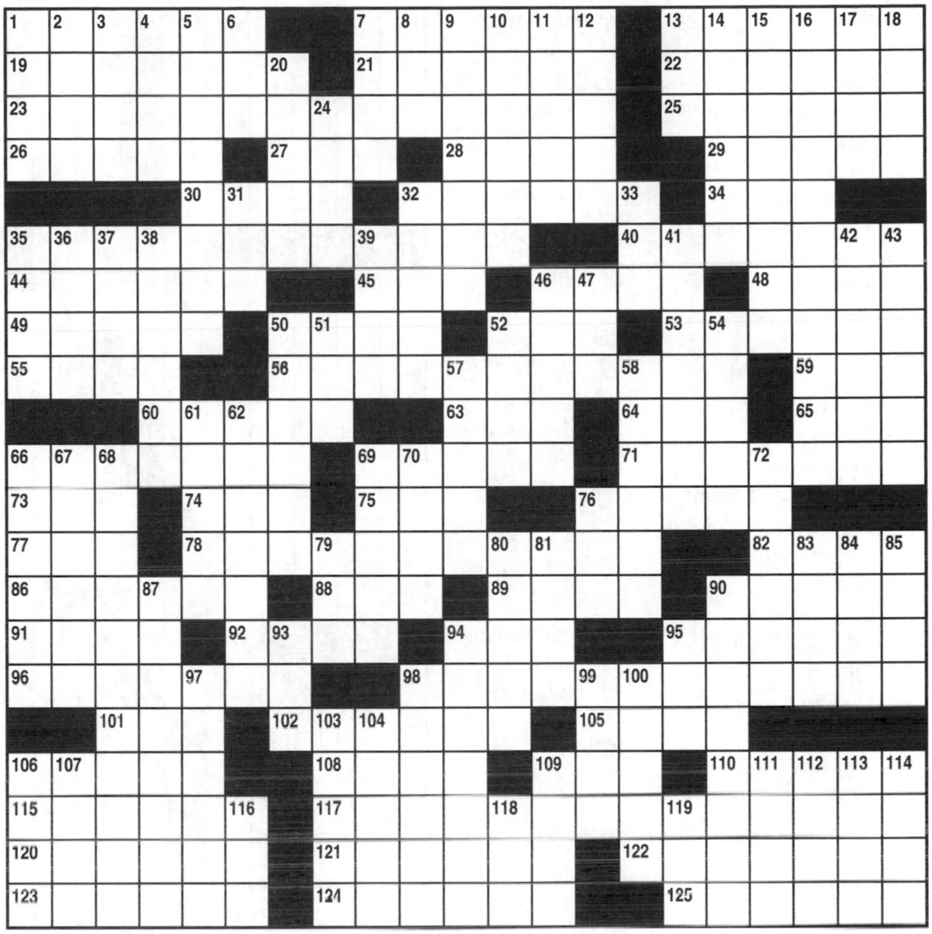

ACROSS

1 Chock-full
7 Japan, to the Japanese
13 Daredevil's retort
19 Up against
21 Place for elvers
22 How uncut grass goes
23 "Blue Streak" actor
25 Act the Pied Piper
26 NHL great Hull
27 Go one way or the other
28 Med. school course
29 Shocks to the system
30 Notes from shy folks?
32 "Battleship Potemkin" city
34 Old fort near Monterey
35 "Blue Hawaii" actor
40 Warren denizens
44 Pinpoint
45 Like some jobs
46 Prop in a Chuck Barris show
48 River of Bern
49 Wrongs
50 ChapStick Moisturizer ingredient
52 Junior Olympic Games org.
53 Rowers
55 Sch. of technology
56 "NYPD Blue" star
59 Delivery drs.
60 Several Norwegian kings
63 Coppertone bottle abbr.
64 Lucy in "Kill Bill"
65 NY Mets' division
66 Be of good cheer?
69 Licorice-scented herb
71 Disrespects
73 2009, por ejemplo
74 Drop a pop-up
75 Play the slots
76 Plague
77 Wishy-washy suffix
78 "Blue Velvet" singer
82 "Little Girl Blue" lyricist
86 Sawyer's "GMA" predecessor
88 Put to the test
89 Turnarounds
90 Engraving tool
91 Wall St. whizzes
92 Thanksgiving side dish
94 Less than med.
95 Tool in a Communist emblem
96 When you can start to drive
98 Artist who had a Blue Period
101 Carry with difficulty
102 Martian features
105 It's grown for the sake of Japan?
106 Give the slip to
108 Fridge posting
109 Be gluttonous, say
110 Cry of innocence
115 Aware of, slangily
117 "Rhapsody in Blue" composer
120 Like the Amish, e.g.
121 Kazan in "Gigli"
122 Appearing to be
123 Singers John and Bonnie
124 Welles and Bean
125 Rouse

DOWN

1 Portal post
2 At some distance
3 "But wait, there's ___!"
4 Pup without papers
5 Entitlement claimants
6 Cheadle in "Reign Over Me"
7 Speaker between Tom and Dennis
8 -y and then some
9 Besought
10 J.C. of malls
11 Ocean threats
12 Tomsk turndowns
13 Meteor tail
14 Road-gang work, e.g.?
15 Where Mimmsie Starr got pinched
16 "Song Sung Blue" singer
17 Little faith?
18 Poetic tributes
20 Miller product
24 Basilica area
31 What flowers do, in poetry
32 Of yore
33 Prince Valiant's son
35 Grades 1–12
36 It might be unsecured
37 Some were Betamax
38 "You are not!" comeback
39 In two shakes
41 Trials and tribulations
42 Amplifier setting
43 They can be dulled
46 Faux pas
47 Lord's Prayer start
50 Grammatically, grammatically
51 Clinton cabineteer Aspin
52 Hooded killers
54 Heraldic hue
57 Disciples' query
58 Pilgrims John and Priscilla
61 Ich ___ dich
62 NASCAR, e.g.
66 Inveigh against
67 Check again
68 He was Jake Blues
69 Chasm
70 "Scream" star Campbell
72 Cornell University city
76 Gainsborough's blue subject
79 Mooch
80 Desensitizes
81 Legendary archer
83 NASDAQ quotes
84 Fam. members
85 Palm smartphone
87 One not on the Dean's List
90 Permit holder
93 NRC predecessor
94 Port of southern Italy
95 [Not my mistake]
97 "Ha ha, very funny"
98 Dialect
99 Not a rehash: Abbr.
100 Needle bearers
103 ___-Saxon
104 Absence of musical skill
106 Washstand jug
107 Grammy-winning Ford
109 Catches a glimpse of
111 Electrical impedance units
112 Noodlehead
113 Smaller than compact
114 Caltech grad
116 It turns out looies: Abbr.
118 Pink lady ingredient
119 Fighter at Vicksburg

250 FOUR AND OVER by Harvey Estes

A masterful construction devoid of three-letter words.

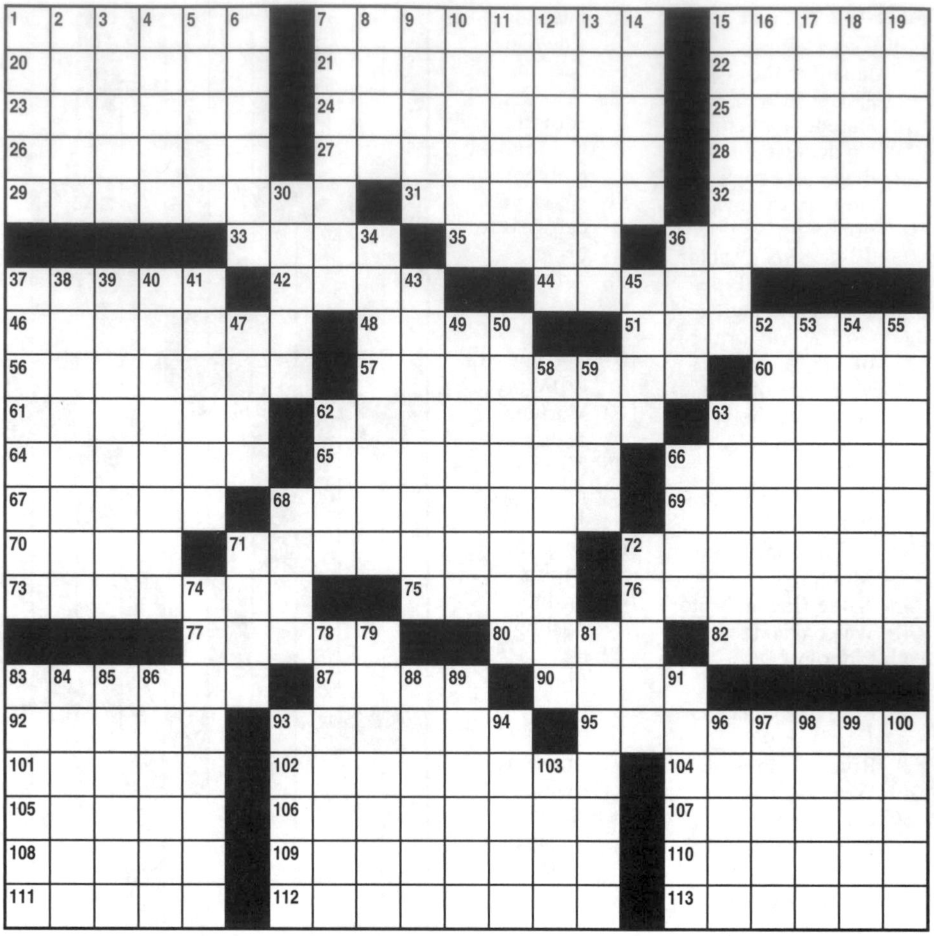

ACROSS

1 Moneybags
7 Campaign promises, often
15 Milan's La ___
20 Slip collection
21 Island activity
22 Guilty and more
23 Less frivolous
24 Cast a spell on
25 Knitting need
26 Vote out
27 They know the score
28 Paper mark
29 Deli order
31 Go through again
32 Allow to be known
33 Tammany skewerer
35 Sour fruit
36 Plain as day
37 Bleach target
42 Brand
44 Palace figures
46 From the heart
48 Expressed, as farewell
51 Mold over
56 Goes at it
57 Nonunion workplace
60 Historic stretches
61 Work up
62 Middle of a square, maybe
63 Stayed awake
64 Michelin rival
65 Frame parts
66 Fifth-century scourge
67 Flu variety
68 Devotees' reads
69 Whole bunch
70 Battery component
71 Digressions
72 Jewelry designer Elsa
73 "The Breakfast Club" actor
75 Playboy's gaze
76 Fertility deity
77 You may find it in Java
80 Common carrier
82 Not so naïve
83 B neighbor
87 Waiter's place
90 Seeks wet gold
92 Butler of film
93 Hard times
95 Old-fashioned water conduit
101 Steer stopper
102 One in a balloon
104 Gazed dreamily
105 Ultimately become
106 Sort of
107 Lacking credit
108 Sling ammo
109 Couldn't stand
110 Hold out a carrot to
111 Steps on a scale
112 React to a blow
113 Held out

DOWN

1 Ready to walk
2 NBA venue
3 Lock
4 French king Hugh
5 One may shed this
6 Kilt pattern
7 Teddy part
8 Moth variety
9 Take in, perhaps
10 Analyzes grammatically
11 "___ be the day!"
12 Act without restraint
13 Room recesses
14 Word on a cheese wrapper
15 Small scope
16 Bordeaux output
17 Make bubbly
18 "Highway to Heaven" star
19 Give thumbs up
30 Rigging supporters
34 Forbidding
36 Type of school
37 Decide when to become one
38 Some April births
39 Match misuser
40 Set apart
41 Trafalgar Square honoree
43 Top of a "golden stair"
45 Schoenberg's "Moses und ___"
47 Trickle through the cracks
49 Most of a canine
50 Diplomatic arrangements
52 Protect from the air, in a way
53 Craftsmanship
54 Goddard of "Modern Times"
55 Trellis for branches
58 Part of a force
59 Fuse sound
62 Spanish dessert
63 Moves suddenly
66 Heston's jailors, in a sci-fi film
68 Disconcert
71 Maryland athlete, for short
72 Pamphleteer Thomas
74 What the kind rewind
78 Property recipient, legally
79 Change places
81 Shake alternatives
83 Bust
84 Eastern religion
85 One way to meet
86 Bring into harmony
88 Oater neckties
89 Famous Papa
91 Patriot Adams
93 Bootleggers' worries
94 Present presenter
96 Reed in "It's a Wonderful Life"
97 Sign supporters
98 Alaskan language
99 English coppers
100 Beat barely
103 Exploitative type

251 DAYS ARE SHORT by Holden Baker

The title is also the name of an Arlo Guthrie song.

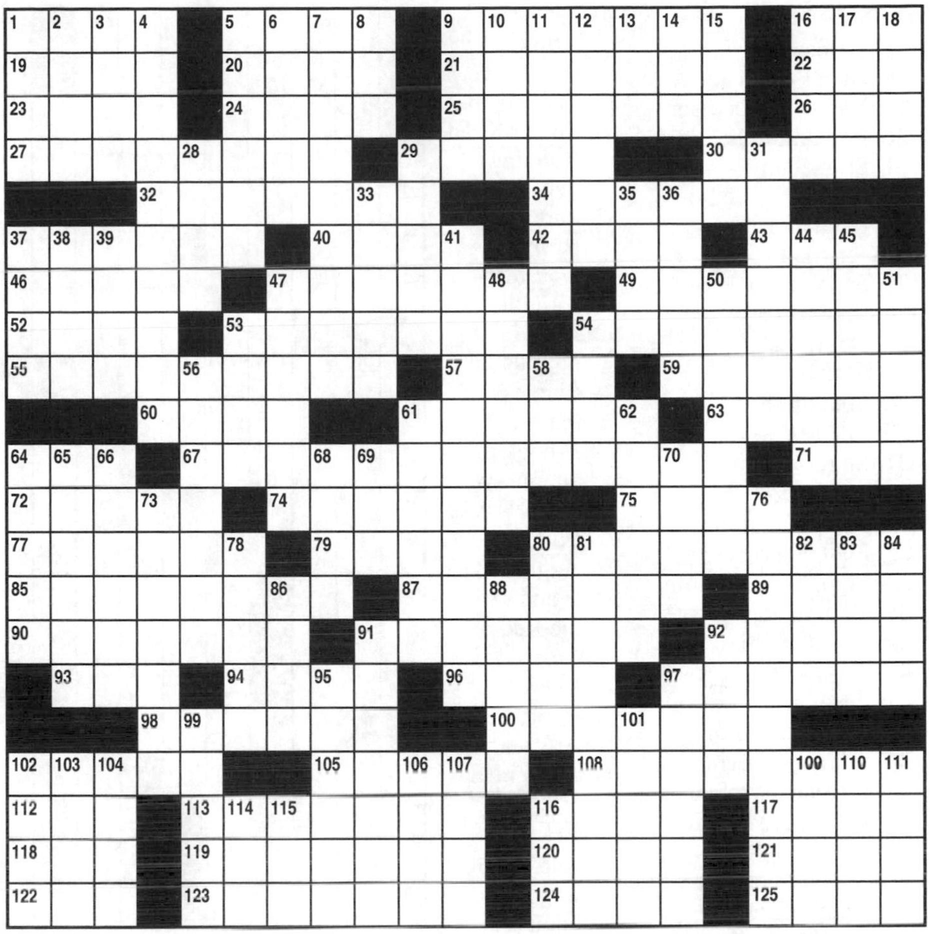

ACROSS

1 Maid of the ___ (Niagara Falls tour boat)
5 Knocks over
9 David's foe
16 It may be circular
19 Genesis twin
20 Jai ___
21 Synthetic fat
22 "Muskrat Ramble" composer Kid
23 The Blue Devils
24 Union election overseer
25 Japanese mats
26 Hilary ___ Swank
27 Occurring sporadically
29 Towering
30 "Is this seat ___?"
32 Reveries
34 National paper
37 Stinger ingredient
40 Broccoli ___
42 Musical ending
43 Bearded sheep
46 ___ lazuli
47 "That's a lie!"
49 Fuse metal parts together
52 All worked up
53 Tackles way too late
54 Early Beatles hit
55 Proof that silence is golden?
57 Others, to Ovid
59 "No Exit" playwright
60 Marketing prefix
61 Antarctic penguin
63 "SNL" numbers
64 H. Rider Haggard novel
67 Joseph Smith's followers
71 Biblical jawbone source
72 "Gloria ___, et Filio . . ."
74 Alpine echoes
75 Former NYC paper
77 Small task
79 1936 Oscar winner as Pasteur
80 Softest looking, as clouds
85 "Arabian Nights" hero and namesakes
87 Yes men
89 Justice Bader Ginsburg
90 Glow
91 Souvenir clothes
92 Roman courtyards
93 Keanu in "The Matrix"
94 Spiced tea beverage
96 Legal wrong
97 Encourage
98 Job time for most
100 Early TV cop
102 Western capital
105 Caterpillar, for one
108 Restore to confidence
112 Tolkien monster
113 Easter Island
116 "Lucky Jim" author
117 Manipulates
118 Apprehend
119 Hot-tub disinfectant
120 "The Naughty Lady of Shady ___"
121 Scholar of Islamic law
122 Nightmarish street?
123 Picks out
124 101 course: Abbr.
125 Wife of Bath's offering

DOWN

1 "One man's ___ is another man's Persian": Kaufman
2 Goes to bat
3 H.H. Munro
4 "___ Music Club" (Sheryl Crow album)
5 Became empty, as a well
6 Kukla's pal
7 Venetian boat song
8 Close relative
9 ___ guy (clutch player)
10 Norway's patron saint
11 Wet burrito garnish
12 "Why? Because ___!"
13 Well Fargo convenience
14 Angle opening
15 Must
16 Laze in the tub
17 "The Temple of Dullness" composer
18 Casino developer Steve
28 Bookie's numbers
29 Exams for future D.A.'s
31 Eight hours, for most
33 Pirate pal
35 Economist Smith
36 Gogol's "___ Bulba"
37 Dull and boring
38 Prego competitor
39 Military mail drops
41 When some daring robberies take place
44 Hearth goddess
45 All-points bulletins, e.g.
47 Fourscore and ten
48 Except if
50 Literary work of ancient Greece, e.g.
51 Kind of rehearsal
53 Silents star Negri
54 Sundial numeral
56 Mrs. Bill Gates
58 Stevedores' org.
61 Playoff sites
62 Walks onstage
64 Fishgig
65 "Bleeding" Kentucky county
66 On-line business
68 Male turkeys
69 Relative of .com
70 Cancún crowd?
73 1987 Woody Allen film
76 Threadbare threads?
78 Sunk fence
80 Magnetic beginning
81 Paul Shaffer's boss
82 Money across the pond
83 Commotion
84 One of those things
86 "M*A*S*H" soft drink
88 Spanish red wine
91 Ill-fated ship of 1912
92 Rotational line
95 Burning
97 Pencil part
99 Belgrade residents
101 Deke
102 Ulna or radius
103 Like a valedictory
104 SALT subject
106 Smallest of the litter
107 Competes
109 DDE's alma mater
110 Genuine
111 J.D. Salinger heroine
114 "___ you kidding?"
115 D.C. insider
116 HBO's "Da ___ G Show"

252 LIGHT MOTIF by E.G. Harris

Another clue for 94 Across would be "hard copy."

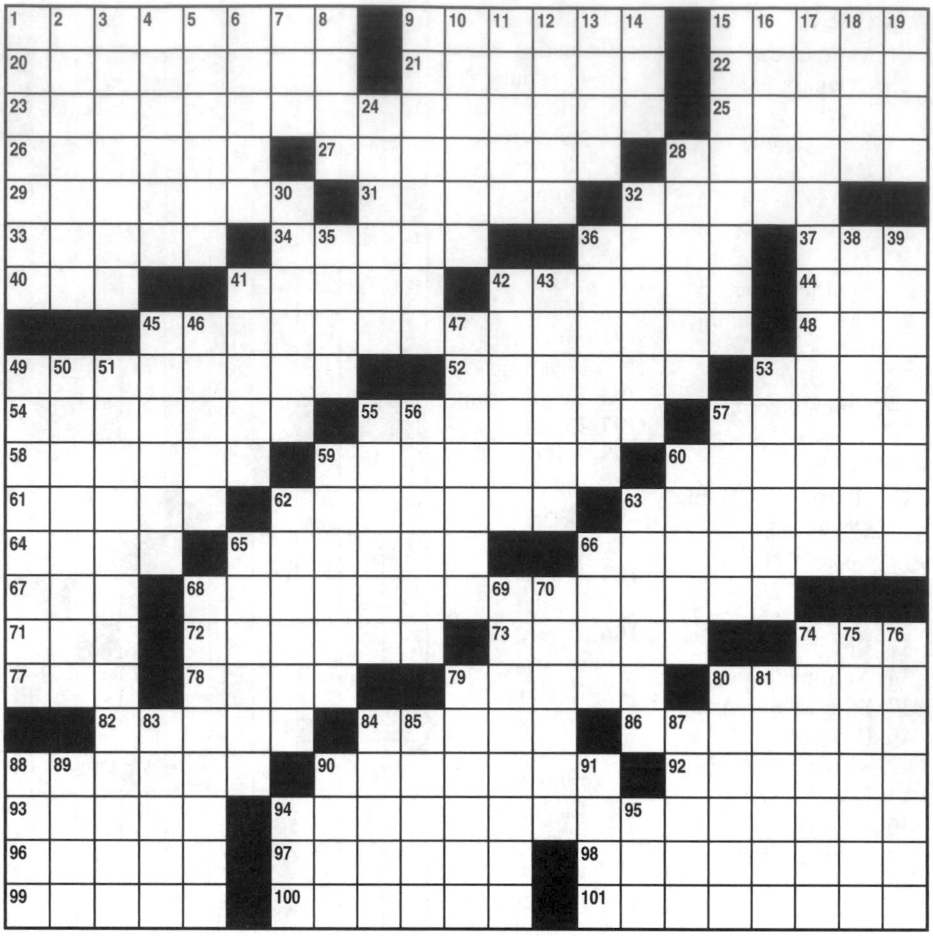

ACROSS

1 Cascades peak
9 Attack from above
15 Nasser's successor
20 Relating to heraldry
21 Showy bird's mate
22 Luncheonette lure
23 Osculatorily certified?
25 Scout's job
26 Like tears
27 Delirium ___ (d.t.'s)
28 Small prayer?
29 In any case
31 Start of a legal conclusion
32 Tempo marking
33 First and reverse
34 Preparing to bloom
36 Harry Potter prop
37 Cereal box no.
40 Jay's announcer
41 Early heat
42 Eastern religion
44 Sturgeon steerer
45 It connects to a calf
48 Part of a whiz kid's report card?
49 Southern taste treat
52 Mitty of fiction
53 Word by a door handle
54 Letting out
55 Charged
57 Short-fused
58 Chowing down
59 Less loquacious
60 "Live and learn" and others
61 Fred's sis
62 Bubba Blue's friend
63 Mint
64 Butler's quarters?
65 Most sneaky
66 Joint recesses
67 Rocks
68 Where Merry Men made merry
71 Sounds of surprise
72 Churches may adopt them
73 Leaves at the altar
74 Make moos
77 Take home after taxes
78 Sexologist Shere
79 Bamboo eater
80 New York strip alternative
82 Fish organs
84 Singer Khan
86 Running mate of 1972
88 Part's partner
90 Gourmet sprinkle
92 Debs in politics
93 Single-master
94 E-book alternative
96 Batter's woe
97 Vote out
98 Augments
99 B and O at the Red Cross
100 Black Sea locale
101 Arts and crafts item

DOWN

1 Rub the right way
2 Took out, in a way
3 Classified
4 More pious
5 Places for fans
6 What opponents take
7 Espied, to Tweety
8 Set down
9 Small ball
10 Joined together
11 Casino gear
12 Drop it or take it
13 Own (up)
14 Print measures
15 Susan in "The Banger Sisters"
16 No longer exist
17 Soulless sole
18 Mine, to Marcel
19 Darkens in the light
24 Concerning Mohawks, e.g.
28 Wise teacher
30 Burdensome
32 Kind of gentry
35 Rock musician Lofgren
36 Biting time
38 Receiver sound
39 Lab reports
41 "I haven't a ___ to wear!"
42 Fires up
43 Biker's protection
45 Hun head
46 "I Fall to Pieces" singer
47 Vouched for
49 Genesis 1 topic
50 Aspirin target
51 Money markets and the like?
53 Former cager Bob
55 Crafty
56 Some sculptures
57 Wrongful acts
59 Late bash
60 Customs
62 Loads of ships
63 Justice Abe
65 Like a rebel yell
66 Bread bane
68 Lugs
69 Capital city once called Batavia
70 Last movement
74 Some hippie gatherings
75 Without variety
76 "___ Gonna Take It"
79 Zita and linguini
80 It's self-evident
81 Site of three rings
83 Melodramatic words on arriving
84 Break off
85 One hell of a destination
87 Ibsen's Gabler
88 "Hey, over here!"
89 Formal friend
90 Put in the mail
91 Light afternoon meals
94 Sonny & Cher, e.g.
95 Buffalo's summer hrs.

253 128 CLUES by Harvey Estes

103 Across declined a Nobel Peace Prize.

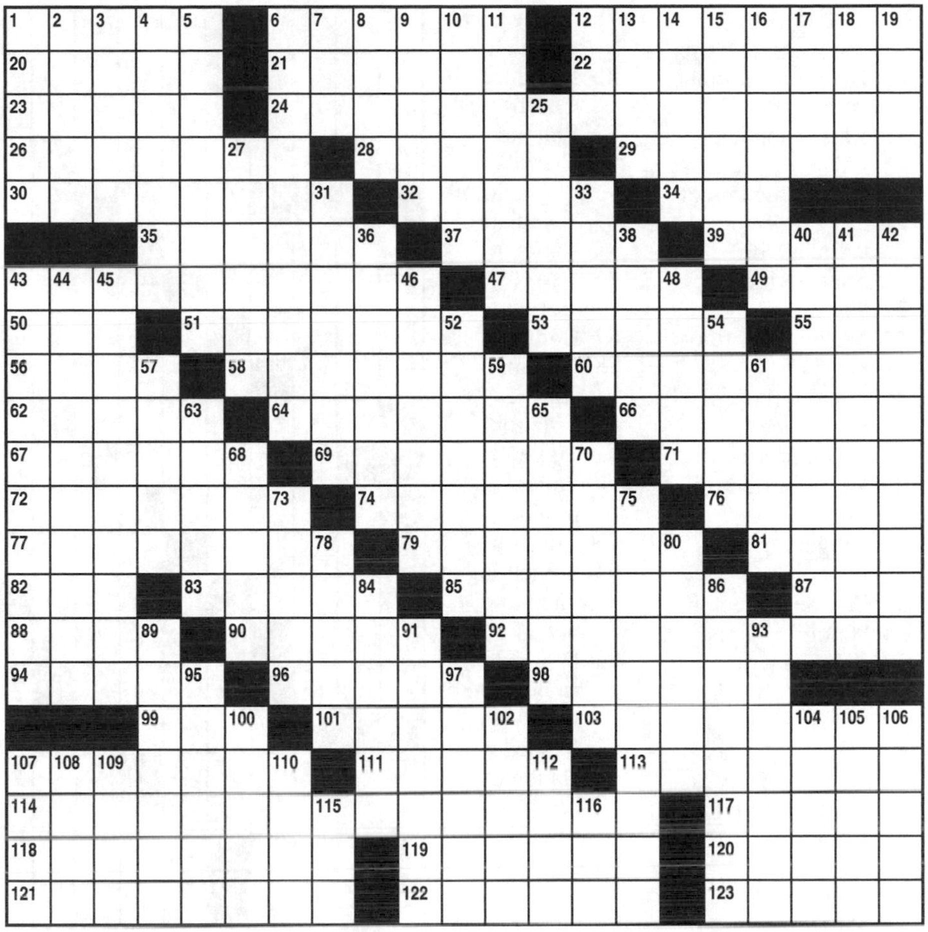

ACROSS

1 Woody woe
6 Turns edible
12 Fountain
20 ___-nez
21 Cracker type
22 Stroke
23 Three wood
24 Clothing worn to be removed
26 Diet
28 Old school item
29 Off-Broadway's "The Beauty Queen of ___"
30 More like a romance novel
32 "I Love Lucy" role
34 Long-faced
35 Summer resident, perhaps
37 Macho dude
39 Hook up again
43 Nothing-fancy breakfast item?
47 Bank takebacks
49 Gambling city
50 Slippery one
51 Meter site
53 "The Count of Monte Cristo" author
55 Minor player
56 Dotted-line command
58 Reduced in rank
60 Trigger, e.g.
62 Moaned and groaned
64 More demanding
66 Stripped bare
67 Alfalfa, for one
69 One who creates a trust of property
71 Tomei of "Alfie"
72 One of the Titans
74 River near Rutgers
76 Shade of black
77 "Casino" costar
79 Pygmalion creation
81 "The Mod Squad" character
82 Heart exam
83 Put one's foot down
85 Is important
87 U-turn from NNW
88 Sent a dup
90 Stout vessel
92 Private school honcho
94 Mystic deck
96 Blue hue
98 Widen
99 Eminem's mentor, briefly
101 Totally befuddled
103 Vietnamese official
107 Charlotte, and others
111 Author Calvino
113 Type of crow
114 Stupid scheme
117 College figures
118 Operation headed up by Eisenhower
119 Bottled spirits
120 Words in a Kilmer simile
121 Mosaic pieces
122 Plato's place
123 Bakery need

DOWN

1 Choir terminators
2 Try to bite
3 Thou
4 Peter of "Newhart"
5 Project, perhaps
6 Get more for Uncle Sam
7 Rest stop
8 Stones in some food
9 "South Pacific" hero
10 Broadway Joe
11 Lay on thick
12 Oil can letters
13 Silicon dioxide stone
14 Knuckleheads
15 Show up
16 Put down
17 Queen of the Heavens
18 Farm team
19 Nabors role
25 Was rife
27 Ungrammatical theological statement?
31 Ruling groups
33 Drink greedily
36 Bounce back
38 Rover
40 Chronic lapser
41 From a certain perspective
42 Booted disco figure
43 Federal housing for animals?
44 Chrysler handle, once
45 "I Have a Rendezvous with Death" poet
46 Cause for a "safe" call
48 Oregon's capital
52 "All's Well That Ends Well" count
54 Titanic seeker's tool
57 Give halftime stats
59 Biblical femme fatale
61 Bit of street art
63 Claire of "Romeo and Juliet"
65 Turned
68 Craves, with "for"
70 Kind of comb
73 Macbeth and Duncan, e.g.
75 Creweler's container
78 First words in "Ozymandias"
80 Big naval group
84 Cobbler container
86 Rest time
89 Walks unsteadily
91 Savings
93 Give off
95 Clef designation
97 Front runner
100 Wrong move
102 Dress shape
104 Papal crown
105 Puts an edge on
106 Advent
107 Totally gone
108 Do road work
109 Angers
110 Gilbert of television
112 Garfield's sidekick
115 Suffix with ox
116 U.S. trading partner

254 E FOR EFFORT by Fred Piscop

3 Down was heard singing "Indian Love Call" in the movie "Mars Attacks!"

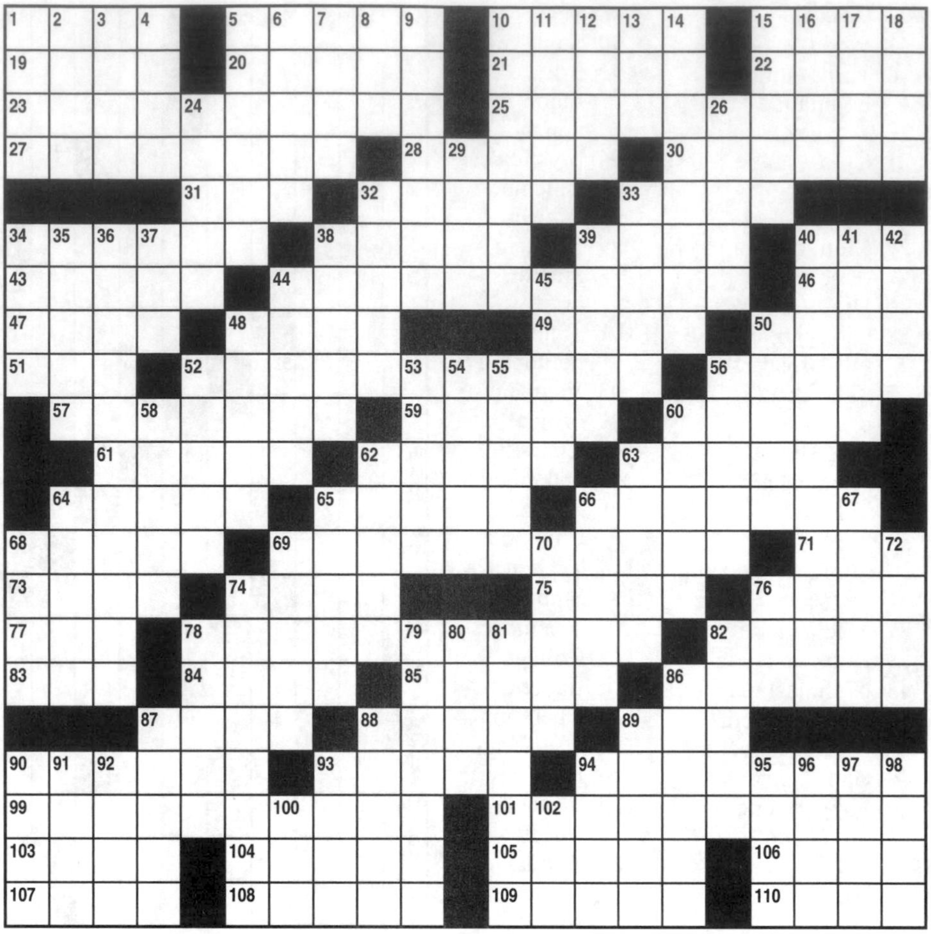

ACROSS

1 Moonshiner's mix
5 Handled without care
10 Rats' hangout
15 CD-___
19 First name in scat
20 ___ Hirsch of "Alpha Dog"
21 State a view
22 "Yeah, sure"
23 Malicious sort's hairdo?
25 Penalty for cowardice?
27 Headquarters
28 War reporter, e.g.
30 Provoke
31 Tangent of 45°
32 First sign
33 Shuttle protector
34 "Gimme" putts
38 Russian writer Bonner
39 Peel off
40 Day-___ paints
43 Edgar or Tony
44 Product for lazy oenophiles?
46 "___ vu" (apartment ad phrase)
47 Scout group
48 ___ time flat
49 "Today 4 U" musical
50 ___ Valley, Calif.
51 Verdi's "___ tu"
52 Zebra meat?
56 Broke, in a way
57 Oozes forth
59 Word on a jar top
60 Buggy places?
61 Homeric epic
62 Leveling devices
63 When maror is eaten
64 In short supply
65 Classic 1953 oater
66 Really enjoyed
68 Bit of garnish
69 Chiropractor?
71 Chair part
73 Animal house?
74 "New Look" creator
75 Full of oneself
76 Transcript figs.
77 24-hr. convenience
78 Nonsensical riposte?
82 Designer Geoffrey
83 Pint-size
84 Ciardi's "___ a Man"
85 "Gladiator" setting
86 Barrel cleaner
87 Bothers
88 Quarter feature
89 Title for Jagger
90 Pollen producer
93 Bone up
94 Something to do in the nude
99 Dog that smells like air freshener?
101 Haunted house sound?
103 Server's edge
104 With a haircut, it's two bits
105 Get around
106 Super review
107 Draw pints, say
108 They're tender
109 Force units
110 Spy Aldrich

DOWN

1 Stocking pattern
2 Boxer's bowlful
3 Yodeler Whitman
4 Can't take
5 Praline nuts
6 Tickle
7 Informant's wear
8 Bend shape
9 Proposed Mormon state
10 Versatile legume
11 They're pointless
12 Like a joker, maybe
13 Blowup: Abbr.
14 Turn to a new setting
15 Springfield, e.g.
16 Village Voice bestowal
17 Pull-down item
18 Aerobics prop
24 Treasury offering, once
26 Dorian Gray's creator
29 Winona's "Dracula" role
32 "Matter of Fact" columnist
33 Use the old bean
34 Surveillance evidence
35 With it, in a sense
36 Wintry conditions in Hawaii?
37 Tee off
38 Heath's "Brokeback Mountain" role
39 Fret over
40 Worker on a dirt farm?
41 Bar stock
42 "Amores" poet
44 How losses appear
45 Snake, to Medusa
48 Where ___ (hot spot)
50 Not so dotty
52 Going after, in a way
53 One of the Coens
54 Pen group
55 Like track events
56 Henry VIII's house
58 Natural talent
60 Cattle breed
62 Bake, as eggs
63 "Socrate" composer
64 Sudden rush
65 Speak pompously
66 ___ Flow (Scottish channel)
67 Clog clearer
68 Beanery side
69 Googlers' destinations
70 Like Bo Peep's flock
72 Teacher's deg.
74 Witchy woman
76 Rare find
78 Gets on
79 Dispositions
80 Like much folk mus.
81 Entered again
82 Ribs et al., for short
86 Salon jobs
87 Make better
88 Carlton in the Hall
89 Chukka boot material
90 Hit the cuspidor
91 Clammer's concern
92 Has ___ (is connected)
93 Wildcard symbol
94 It connects banks
95 Subtle glow
96 There's no I in it
97 Monied one
98 ___ out (just makes)
100 E'en if
102 Wrigley Field flora

255 DOUBLE DUTY by Jay Sullivan

109 Across is an example of an oxymoronic clue.

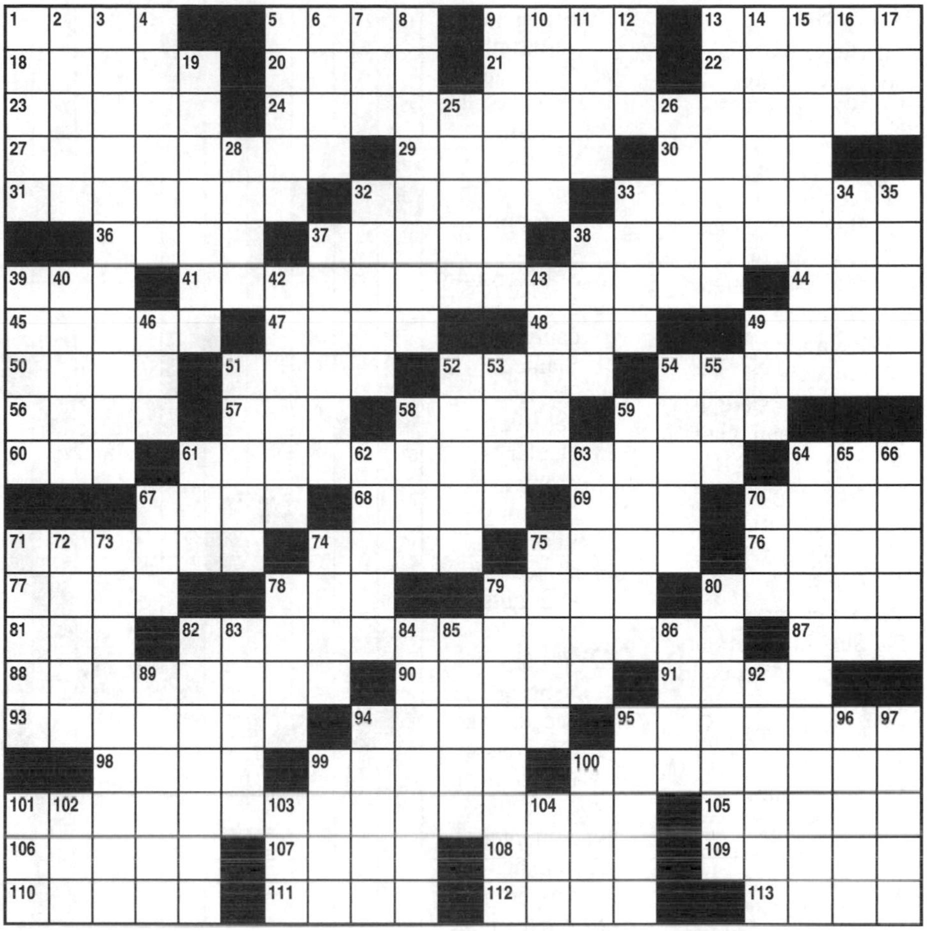

ACROSS

1 Country name
5 "Wanted" poster option
9 Not fooled by
13 Out, of sorts
18 City along the Mohawk
20 Little girl of "David Copperfield"
21 Sans lettuce
22 Wicker worker
23 Place for a pin
24 Cost-saving company vehicle?
27 Ones who think for themselves
29 Cardinals, Orioles, and Blue Jays
30 Remus relation?
31 "Coppelia" composer
32 ___ on (incited)
33 Forward thinker
36 Nervous as ___
37 Allude (to)
38 "We're done here"
39 Way off
41 Two-tone decor?
44 Sushi sauce
45 It's a sign
47 Customer support caller
48 Masked
49 Whimper
50 Gone fishing, perhaps
51 Set in motion
52 Third person
54 Sylvan
56 It may be made in spades
57 Cross product
58 Fed up
59 Willing
60 This miss
61 Quarterback option?
64 "Don't think so!"
67 Sound companion?
68 Gutless one
69 Transcribed letters
70 It's what's for dinner
71 "Twelfth Night" duke
74 'Bama team
75 Refuses to
76 It's on the agenda
77 Hack it
78 Front end?
79 Wood-splitting tool
80 It's in a pickle
81 Blow away
82 Oyster poacher?
87 Big mover
88 Tearful
90 Virtue ___ own reward
91 Easy stride
93 Reason for sneezin'
94 "I dunno"
95 Superior substructure
98 Low life
99 ___ Olay
100 One day
101 The "Wright Flyer" on taking off?
105 Band stand
106 Fracas
107 It may be attached to the house
108 Plot line
109 X-Men woman
110 They engage in fancy footwork
111 Davy Crockett portrayer Parker
112 1969 "Miracle" team
113 Celtic New-Age singer

DOWN

1 Passed judgment
2 Story of Paris
3 Manic-depressive Arctic resident?
4 Vinegary
5 They're outstanding
6 They'll never fly
7 Gore and more
8 In great need of
9 Warm-up acts
10 Barely beat (with "out")
11 Fail to recycle
12 Round figure
13 Build up
14 Clutch performers
15 Ran up
16 Loudness unit
17 Red state?
19 "Arabian Nights" character
25 Chad neighbor
26 It plays a supporting role
28 Alien-life research prog.
32 Conger catcher
33 Drop down, say
34 Decelerates
35 In secret
37 "The Barber of Seville" soprano
38 Water down
39 Glitz
40 It could lead to marriage
42 In a charming fashion
43 "Be cool"
46 Fleeced beast
49 One of the Pep Boys
51 South Carolina motto word
52 Bad spell
53 "I'm afraid so"
54 Attended
55 Mantra chants
58 Family matter
59 Flying fish eater
61 Whopper topper
62 Come full circle
63 Does a correctional worker's job
64 American buffalo?
65 Ring site
66 Macho types
67 "For shame!"
70 Holiday purchase
71 Gainesville neighbor
72 "Laugh-In" name
73 Sight for sore eyes
74 Sitting duck
75 Realize a novel idea
78 "The Brothers Karamazov" brother
79 Con
80 They'll take your order
82 Major factors
83 In other words
84 They come with strings attached
85 Thwart in court
86 Jack in "The Comancheros"
89 Small stream
92 Tiny
94 Heckling
95 Dust Bowl product
96 It's abrasive
97 Skin suffix
99 Comics canine
100 Pique experience
101 Child hood
102 One way to start a phyte?
103 Seasonal worker?
104 Wood whacker

256 "TAKE DIS TO HEART" by Anna Carson

53 Down is a tuition-free school where students work on-campus.

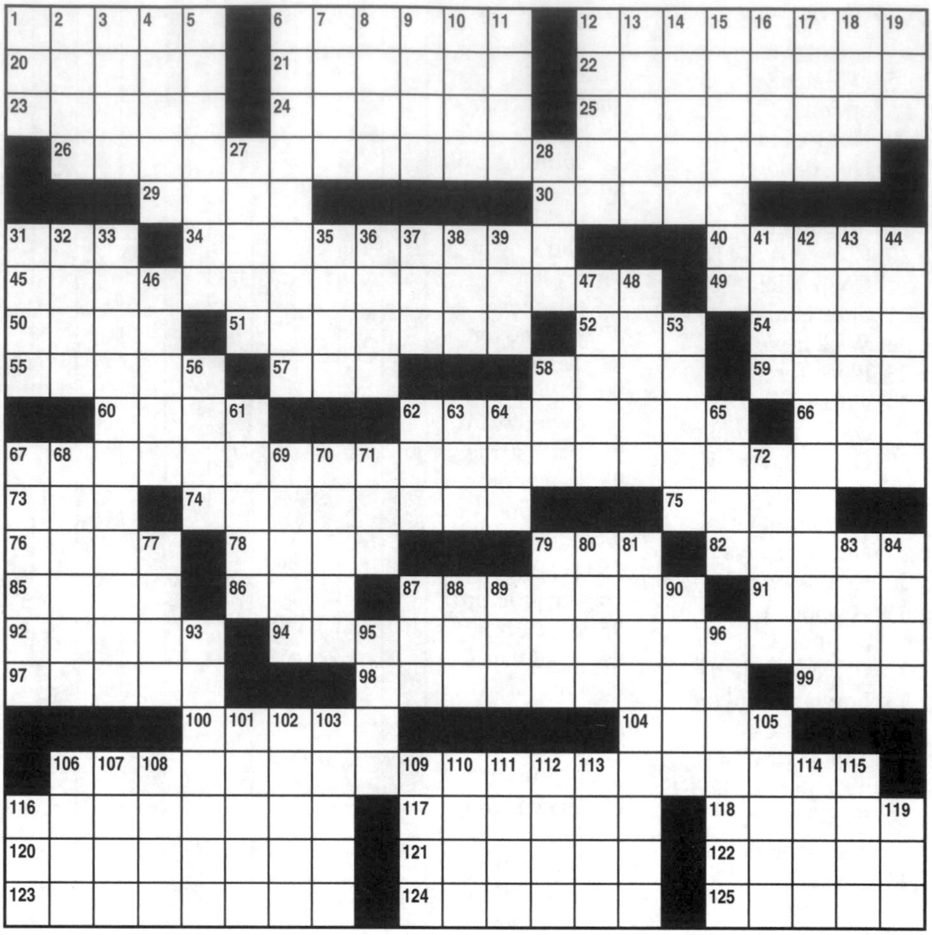

ACROSS

1 Brake parts
6 Move away
12 Where to find a hack
20 Inside story
21 Conjured up
22 Hawaiian dance
23 Hopkins of "Gimme a Break"
24 No more than
25 Pagan, perhaps
26 One whose customers are users
29 Cosmonaut Gagarin
30 Make ___ (blog)
31 Nest egg
34 Pay attention
40 "Holy cow!"
45 Boring
49 Art gallery
50 She, in Cherbourg
51 Places of worship
52 Rip off
54 Colada fruit
55 Attach, as a button
57 Scale tones
58 Raise Cain
59 Capone feature
60 Some binary digits
62 Vatican City sight
66 Sorbonne summer
67 Saw about advance notice
73 "Eeew!"
74 Darwin's hypothesis, and more
75 No longer in port
76 Grant basis
78 "___ Walked Into My Life" ("Mame")
79 Air rifle ammo
82 Tiny leftover
85 Alan in "What Women Want"
86 Life story
87 Basking places
91 Up to speed
92 Oafs
94 Basilica of St. John Lateran statues
97 Mar. honoree
98 Sleeper units
99 Novelist Umberto
100 Big name in vermouth
104 Goofs up
106 Travolta film of 2001
116 "Just because"
117 Acropolis figure
118 Solid ground
120 More captivating?
121 Slanted
122 Try to deceive
123 Ocular problem
124 Most angry
125 Like someone with guts?

DOWN

1 "Spring ahead" syst.
2 Cold desserts
3 By yourself
4 Cozy and contented
5 Flapjack flipper
6 What's left
7 Even once
8 Apple leftover
9 Just managed, with "out"
10 Pastrami palace
11 Ice cream case name
12 Cricket sound
13 Kind of feedback
14 Jell-O servings
15 Puts hand to head
16 "Imagine ___!"
17 Station wagon, for one
18 N.Y. Met, e.g.
19 Patriotic soc.
27 Take by force
28 Like them apples?
31 Mid-month date
32 Preside over
33 In a tizzy
35 Thin coin
36 Nile biters
37 Islanders' org.
38 Fleecy female
39 Some batteries
41 Empty spaces
42 4-time Wimbledon singles champ
43 Visit a bloodmobile, e.g.
44 Took in
46 "Fistful of Dollars" director Sergio
47 Poet's muse
48 OK, on a walkie-talkie
53 Kentucky college
56 Pond denizen
58 Striped shirt wearer
61 Indian honorific
62 Cold war abbr.
63 Overtime cause
64 Ends of letters
65 Get smart with
67 Big exams
68 Spotted cat
69 Equip anew
70 Not in any way
71 Before, old-style
72 Brief summary
77 "Star Trek" android
79 Expressed, as farewell
80 Dover denizen
81 Whoopi Goldberg comedy
83 Obi-Wan player
84 Cancún coin
87 School zone caution
88 Ab ___ (from the start)
89 NASA vehicle
90 Like a sourball
93 Runs in the altogether
95 Rocker Clapton
96 Tel Aviv native
101 Davis of "Do the Right Thing"
102 Hardhearted
103 Barely burn
105 Kind of mail
106 Industrious one
107 "___ put it another way . . ."
108 Ft. or yd., e.g.
109 Emcee's platform
110 "Suffice ___ say . . ."
111 ___-Pei (wrinkly dog)
112 Distant prefix
113 Colleges, to Aussies
114 Algonquian language
115 Kett of the comics
116 Atomic energy org.
119 Hic, haec, ___

257 CLOSE ASTERN by Elizabeth C. Gorski

The real title can be found at 109 Across.

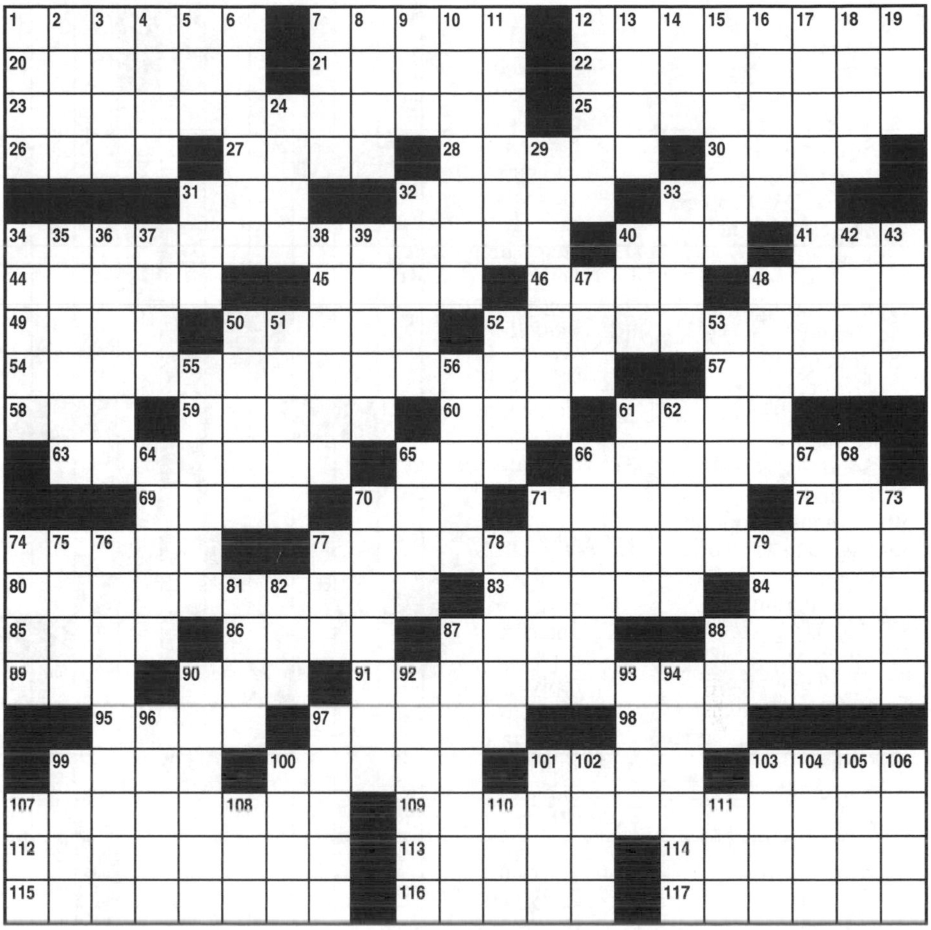

ACROSS

1 Little fish in a big pond?
7 State bordering Bangladesh
12 "Much appreciated!"
20 Biblical son of Amoz
21 Backs, anatomically
22 Spots on Rush Limbaugh's show
23 Layered lunch order*
25 They're swiped at banks
26 Bowlers and the like
27 Flip a coin
28 "Gosford Park" maid
30 Former GM line
31 Compete
32 Former center of Los Angeles
33 Big pie slice
34 It's done on Monday*
40 "The Black Cat" writer
41 Aegean island for tourism
44 Middle East leaders
45 Pale drinks
46 "___ have thunk it?"
48 Sp. girl
49 Legal start
50 It's developed by Mr. America
52 Mario Puzo novel
54 Jerry McGuire's signature cry*
57 Captain's cry
58 Bottled French import
59 Moorehead of "Bewitched"
60 Sister
61 Langlaufer's lift
63 Tackle
65 ABA member
66 Exam done on sight
69 Sweet'___ (sugar sub)
70 Early morning TV show
71 Knowledgeable about
72 "___ I Kissed You": Everly Brothers
74 Allegro ___ (very fast)
77 The Impressions hit*
80 In joint custody?
83 "Being There" director
84 Whitaker's 2006 Oscar role
85 Corp. jet users
86 Workout count
87 Head-turner
88 "Feast of Saint Nicholas" artist
89 Eminem collaborator
90 "Fantasia" frame
91 Home bodies?*
95 Fast partner?
97 Rich kid of "Nancy"
98 Aromatherapy setting
99 Sluggish
100 Tennis legend Ivan
101 "Oh, now it's clear . . ."
103 Mr. Everest stat
107 Czech or Serb, e.g.
109 TITLE
112 Customized cell sound
113 Green-skinned pear
114 Renaissance man Girolamo
115 Whenever
116 Iron-fisted rulers
117 Hastings locale

DOWN

1 Wolverine St.
2 Madonna's "La ___ Bonita"
3 Maritime: Abbr.
4 Bird beaks
5 NATO counterpart
6 "Supposing . . ."
7 Supplements
8 Seeds
9 Hindu address
10 Has one's head in the clouds?
11 "Das Lied von der Erde" composer
12 Hiker's path
13 Not fancy?
14 Decatur food conglomerate
15 Virginia in "The Hours"
16 Furry-eared cutie
17 "Heart Full of Soul" group*
18 Likelihood
19 Enterprise letters
24 Winter air
29 Novel by Elizabeth Berg
31 Columnist Marilyn ___ Savant
32 Lunch hour
33 Pop in the fridge
34 Backslide
35 Siouan people
36 Put it on the line?
37 Backspin
38 German cathedral city
39 "___ Gold" (1997)
40 D.C. player
42 Platte Valley tribe
43 Yemen capital
47 "You, over there!"
48 Selling point?
50 "I ___ differ"
51 Old TV's "See ___"
52 Wide-headed fastener
53 Motor coil
55 Long-jawed fish
56 Available now
61 Laid-back sort
62 Miss Boop
64 "Nearer The Moon" author Nin
65 "Famous" chip manufacturer
66 Half a fourth or fourth a half
67 Botanist's study
68 Neatened (up)
70 "Showgirls" actress Gina
71 "Steppenwolf" author
73 Redgrave and Swann
74 American Indian
75 Futurist
76 Crams in
77 Baby food
78 Cowboy show prop
79 "Do I dare to ___ peach?": Eliot
81 Scott in the 1857 news
82 Ann Patchett's "___ Canto"
87 Sweatpants, e.g.
88 Org. for a start-up, maybe
90 Prefix meaning "hidden"
92 Hag or Joe Jackson's "Black Betsy"
93 Friendly opener?
94 Pickle jar items
96 Gong used in Yoruba music
97 Descartes and Magritte
99 Mexican singer Miguel
100 Smallville girl
101 "Take ___ leave . . ."
102 Erwin and Ungar
103 "Shady Lane" trees
104 Grazing places
105 Osprey's cousin
106 Type of auto engine
107 Stat for Joba Chamberlain
108 Geologic time division
110 Classic Steely Dan album
111 Letters of credit

258 BY THE NUMBERS* by Ray Hamel

Donald Klopfer was the other cofounder and the year was 1925.

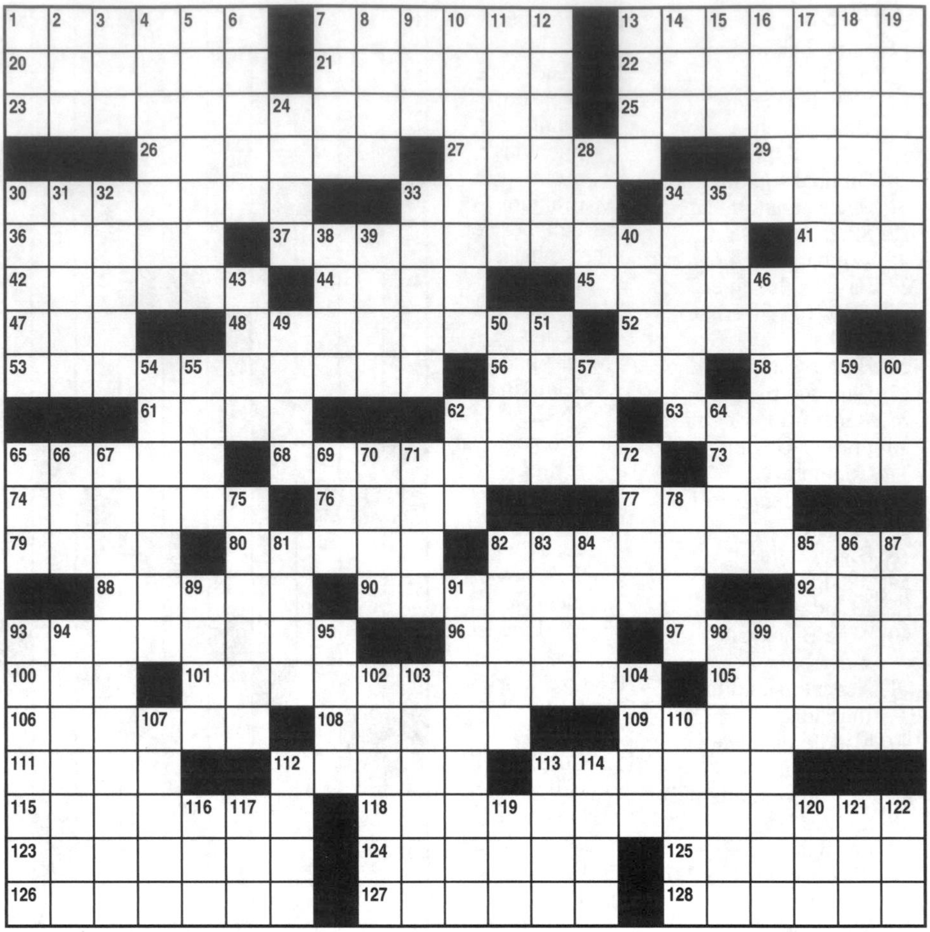

ACROSS

1 Longstocking's creator Lindgren
7 Do sum thing wrong?
13 Source of Internet revenue
20 Illegal DVD copier
21 "Twelfth Night" countess
22 Payload measure
23 Line through Greenwich*
25 Timothy in "Rollercoaster"
26 "Hägar the Horrible" cartoonist
27 Sonora sendoff
29 Pianist Gilels
30 Carpooler's option
33 Big bang source?
34 Continent with the most nations
36 Red as ___
37 Publisher cofounded by Bennett Cerf*
41 Cleveland cager
42 One paying a flat fee
44 Ogle
45 Surround
47 Approx.
48 Enjoys immensely
52 Key-related
53 Property*
56 ___ disturb
58 Clark's workmate
61 Folies Bergère designer
62 Gun-barrel diameter
63 Bits of dust
65 Prickly plants
68 1994 Kathleen Turner film*
73 One with a rucksack
74 Prepares tapes for reuse
76 Secure, in a way
77 NASA acceleration unit
79 Finnish architect Saarinen
80 Greet the day
82 Bread choice*
88 "Got me!"
90 Pregame gathering
92 YMCA instruction
93 Formal dress code
96 ___ avis
97 Fight
100 Long stretch
101 Phone-service option*
105 Theater parts
106 Pretzels and peanuts
108 Inclement
109 Eternally young
111 Work the land
112 "We ___ please!"
113 Largemouth bass feature
115 Effortless beyond compare
118 Make the scapegoat of*
123 Sharpening device
124 Log-on name
125 Wood for Woods
126 Rap genre
127 Holders over shoulders
128 Latino singer Jon

DOWN

1 "Killer" program
2 End of a private's reply
3 Prefix with angle or pod
4 Talks aimlessly
5 Utter repeatedly
6 ___ rum
7 Early part of the day
8 Foe of Bjorn
9 A Caesar
10 American employees
11 Royal headwear
12 Flaky pastry
13 UN reps.
14 "In excelsis ___"
15 Mil. rank
16 What Commodus called Marcus Aurelius
17 Precise timepiece*
18 Burlesque
19 Make a servant of
24 Washstand accessory
28 Siouan people
30 More sound
31 Unpleasantly plump
32 Roman hearth goddess
33 Fred Astaire's sister
34 Fancy neckwear
35 Sinn ___ (Irish organization)
38 Thomas Edison's middle name
39 Hair No More alternative
40 "Do ___ others . . ."
43 While beginning
46 North Carolina's capital
49 Summers on the Riviera
50 Movie star
51 Comparison figure
54 Releases from the poky
55 Buffalo's county
57 Start to con?
59 Nickname in a 1950s political slogan
60 Soviet place-name letters
62 Scrooge's expression
64 "That was close!"
65 Bee chaser?
66 "___ you decent?"
67 Capital vice*
69 Lilly of pharmaceuticals
70 Coarse speech
71 "Interesting"
72 Hood's honey
75 Seasonal mall employees
78 "Because of You" singer
81 Exasperate
82 Strong indignation
83 Mata ___
84 Woman in "The Good Earth"
85 Nice school?
86 Chevets
87 Head lock?
89 Crick site
91 Pen occupant
93 Setting for "The Great Gatsby"
94 Capital of the Solomon Islands
95 K–12, scholastically speaking
98 Make ready
99 Political tract
102 Cat of Tennessee folklore
103 Talented one
104 Clothes
107 Hang on
110 Adorns unnecessarily
112 Razor introduced in 1977
113 Send by UPS
114 Williams and Kennedy
116 Mag. big shots
117 Hardened
119 Part of a chorus line?
120 Mendes in "Hitch"
121 Major ref. work
122 Charlton Heston's org.

259 G-RATED by Jay Sullivan

49 Across is a gimme for Harry Potter fans.

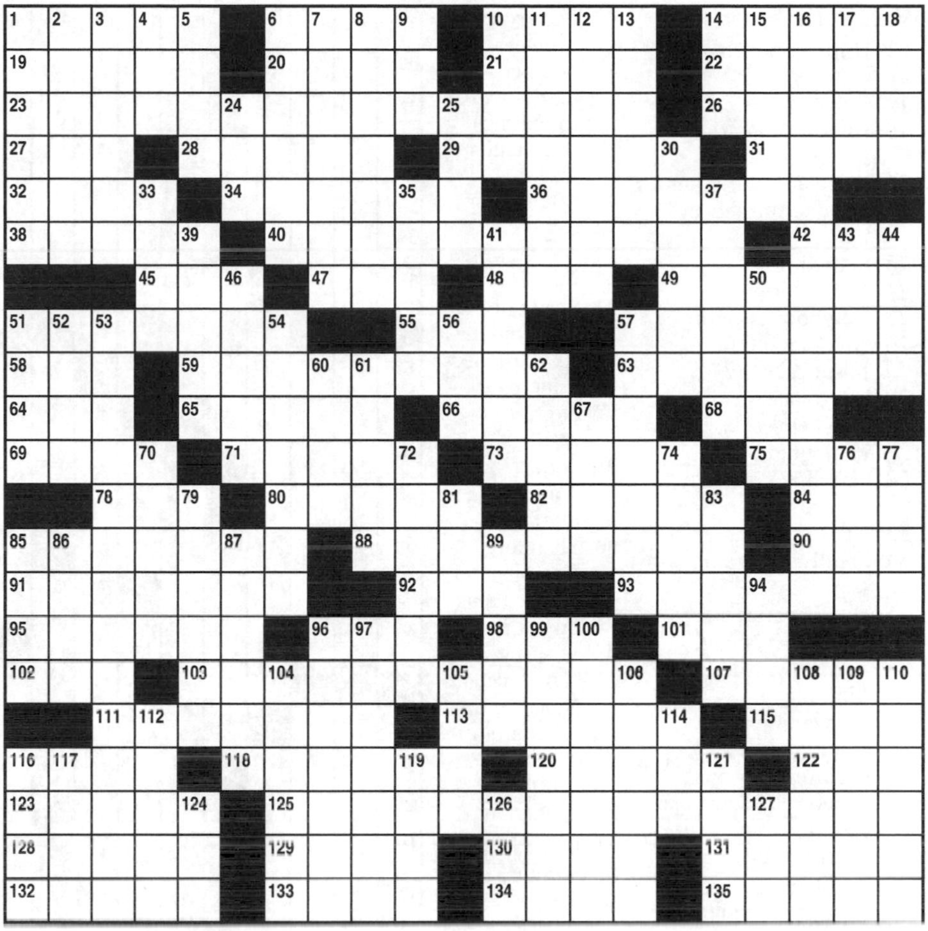

ACROSS

1 Toothbrush handle
6 Jrs. exam
10 Greasy kid stuff
14 "Ghosts" writer
19 Small part for a big actor
20 Bold type
21 Regarding
22 Mother Judd
23 El cereal?
26 Diogenes, for one
27 C section
28 Comic Radner
29 Most liable
31 Be all leers
32 They're tapped out
34 Mickey Mouse org.
36 Back-breaking
38 Former acting President
40 Engine-noise detector?
42 Make up your mind
45 Child's play
47 Pinch
48 UFO crew
49 Draco of Slytherin
51 Japanese film actor Mifune
55 One of dose things?
57 One who focuses on the bottom line
58 Silk tie
59 Settle a score?
63 Recluse
64 "When Harry Met Sally" costar
65 Go bad
66 Pun postlude, perhaps
68 Smidgen
69 Get it together
71 Bad company
73 Go with the flow
75 Country girl
78 Buried treasure
80 To reiterate . . .
82 Packed like sardines
84 Like Ike
85 "The Three-Cornered Hat" composer
88 "I'm really really sorry?"
90 The Eastern "Way"
91 Tough competitor
92 GI destination in the 60's
93 Split
95 "Your wish is my command."
96 He's cool
98 TV show-stoppers
101 Miss-named
102 Bionic Woman's org.
103 Palatial mansion?
107 Capital of Morocco
111 Non-moving motor parts
113 The lower limits
115 Former Italian capital
116 You can take it to the bank
118 Spheroidal
120 Gator kin
122 Main man
123 Out of this world
125 "Is dinner on the table?" answer
128 Western necktie
129 Pelvis parts
130 Motley rock group?
131 Poker play
132 Palindromic principle
133 It's pretty much out of gas
134 Cobra kin
135 Barely beat

DOWN

1 Eight is enough for these
2 Sporting chants
3 "Cocoon" Oscar-winner
4 Fowl piece
5 5-time Wimbledon winner
6 Prince of England
7 Orders to score
8 Commentator Huffington
9 No small matter
10 Role for Reagan
11 Carousing
12 Breaks in
13 Desk accessory
14 Business letters
15 Cajun country
16 The National Anthem et al.?
17 Pianist Gilels
18 Pleasant
24 That's a relief
25 States
30 Whole lotta shakin'
33 Clockmaker Thomas
35 Musical mnemonic
37 Stated one's address
39 Babes in the woods
41 Hoisted by one's own ___
43 One who engages in fancy footwork?
44 Sidon's sister city
46 Beef
50 Truman's birthplace
51 Jones and Joad
52 Marriage vow
53 Caret?
54 Bill Clinton, as a Rhodes scholar
56 Math class
57 By an order of magnitude
60 Snooty affectation
61 Twilight, of old
62 Doughnut-shaped
67 Japanese aboriginal
70 Stick one's neck out
72 It's nothing in Napoli
74 Easy basket
76 Gentleman caller
77 Each
79 Burial place of Samuel Clemens
81 Filmmaker's union: Abbr.
83 Tennis player known as "The Rocket"
85 Rat Pack nickname
86 Those were the days
87 Having missed the start of
89 Fine fiddle fabricator
94 Beef dish
96 Historian of the French Revolution
97 French border region
99 Chorus girls
100 Agitates
104 Provide the price of freedom
105 Main villain
106 Plays to the gallery
108 Rest stop sight
109 Get excited
110 Designated
112 What we have here
114 "Mein Gott!"
116 Is unable to
117 Burn balm
119 Bandleader Jones of jazz
121 Saharan
124 The puck stops here
126 DVD manufacturer
127 Walk all over

260 128 ANSWERS by Brad Wilber

. . . and exactly 128 clues.

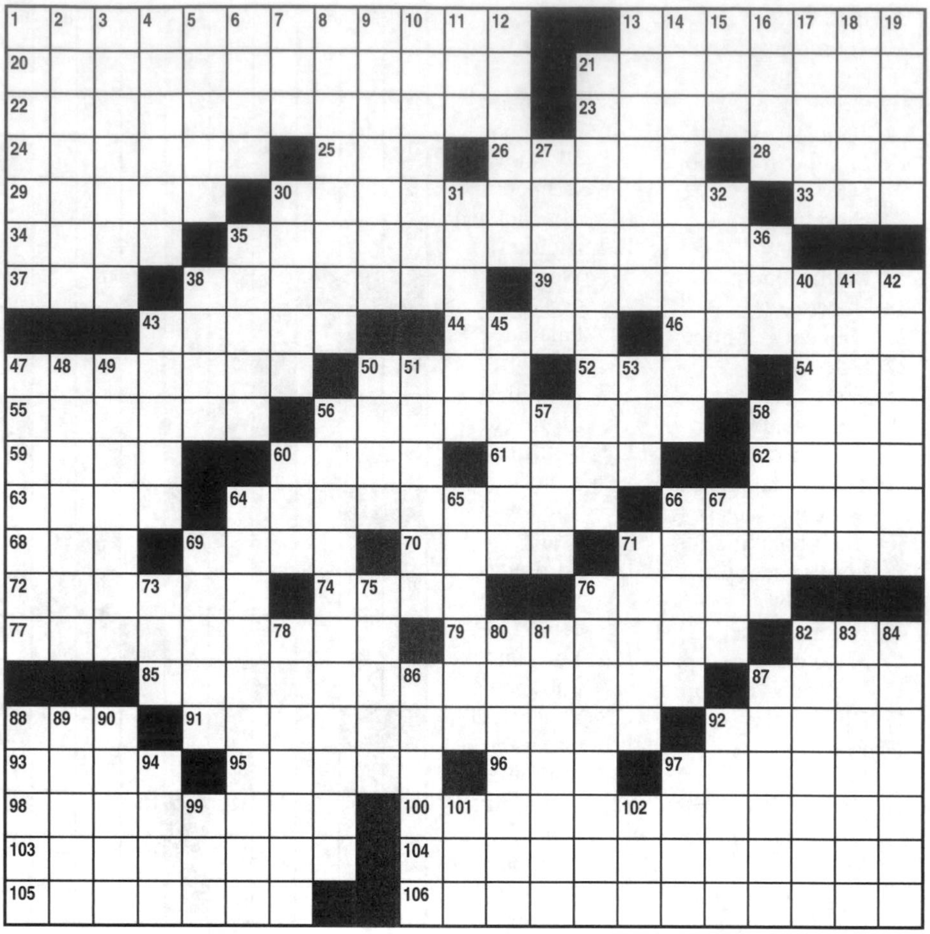

ACROSS

1 Hollywood Bowl, e.g.
13 Con
20 Attack on Pearl Harbor film
21 Maryland menu item
22 "Undue Influence" author
23 Settled
24 Tribal carvings
25 Neighbor of Serb.
26 "In Search Of . . ." host (1976–82)
28 Life-or-death
29 Geometry class computations
30 Coach K's strategy, perhaps
33 ABA member
34 Smallville's famous son
35 Numismatics study
37 Bill Cosby's deg.
38 Achieve through diplomacy
39 It's waiting to be filled
43 Performs abysmally
44 "Ditat ___" (Arizona motto)
46 Undisturbed, as artifacts
47 "Touche!" elicitors
50 Milieu for a Power Seller
52 Spandau Prison's last resident
54 Airline to Oslo
55 Canyon tones
56 Caught the pitcher napping, maybe
58 René of salons
59 Haggis ingredient
60 Periodic table "ID"
61 Collected wisdom
62 Hercules's concubine
63 Pithy truths
64 Most like a matinee idol
66 "Yeah, right!"
68 Rhoda's mother
69 City on Kyushu
70 Fangorn Forest race
71 Place to get staples?
72 Orange Broadband Prize winners
74 Sable automaker, slangily
76 Kevin's "Bull Durham" role
77 "D.C. Cab" theme song singer
79 "Charlotte's Web" author
82 Tee options, briefly
85 Ticker-tape event
87 ___'Pea (cartoon foundling)
88 One stands to lose it
91 WKRP, e.g.
92 If-___ (programmer routines)
93 Shade of bleu
95 Y-chromosome carriers
96 Principle
97 Zagreb residents
98 Some Annapurna climbers
100 Theodore Dreiser work
103 Where teens take turns
104 Meeting place
105 "Of Mice and Men" setting
106 "Canterbury Tales" stops

DOWN

1 Risked
2 Went by Vespa
3 Ersatz
4 Accost
5 Tabloid twosomes
6 Snyder and Lehrer
7 Mr., in Helskinki
8 Anvils, e.g.
9 Tweaks in search of harmony
10 "Necessaries," in old lingo
11 Eet's cereal box pal
12 ___ Maria Rilke
13 Battle venue for Sergeant York
14 Oscar-nominated "Forrest Gump" actor
15 Face on a fin
16 Like some lattes
17 "American Pie" exchange student
18 Hybrid tennis garment
19 Precept
21 Placed, say
27 "___ See Him" (Reba album)
30 "Let's Make a Deal" letdowns
31 Intricate
32 Preppy collars
35 Restaurant freebies
36 Yearbook gp.
38 Going rate?
40 Slip into one's birthday suit
41 Dell Inc., notably
42 Like Hayworth's hair
43 Civil wrongs
45 Oxford finisher?
47 "Il Barbiere di Siviglia" composer
48 OPEC dropout of 1993
49 Bleacher bums pastime
50 Sight from Taormina
51 Male kangaroo
53 Ending for morph or graph
56 Ran roughshod over
57 One of the Cartwrights
58 Crib
60 "Of all lies, ___ is the least untrue": Flaubert
64 Obsolete Kodak product
65 Consume
66 Hot
67 Shake, as a tail
69 Soapmaking acid
71 Radar screen features
73 P.O. item
75 Combs of Murderers' Row
76 Smoothies
78 Oversize reference books
80 Fidel Castro's predecessor
81 Usurped
82 Administer an oath to
83 Something often honorable
84 Abates
86 Boot camp affirmative
87 Characteristic of him, not you
88 Touches down
89 High-end Hyundai
90 Adele, to Jane Eyre
92 Hint
94 Beatles' sitar teacher
97 Included on a memo
99 Cariou of Broadway
101 Aunt and rearer of Dionysus
102 Singapore shortwave sta.

261 MUSICAL MEDLEY by Arlan and Linda Bushman

"Pakistan pass" would be another clue for 5 Down.

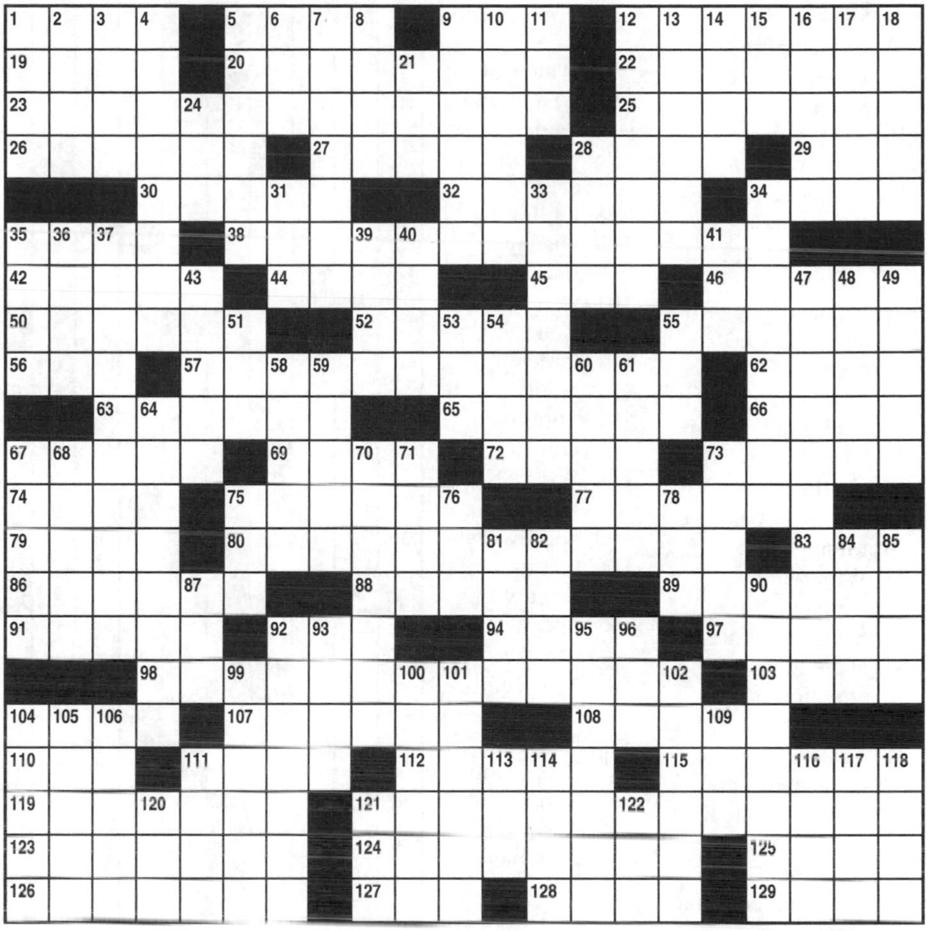

ACROSS

1 Part of a big plot
5 Bauhaus artist Paul
9 Some attire, briefly
12 Characteristics
19 Silas Marner device
20 Feature of many a tool
22 Retail complex habitué
23 Analysis of mainstream music?
25 Field of study that encompasses Area 51
26 First U.S. space station
27 Surrounded by
28 Deli order
29 Cambodia's Lon ___
30 Ketch milieu
32 Sway
34 Holiday song title word
35 Resist openly
38 "Hard" musical arrangement?
42 Skin balms
44 Vintage soda
45 Small ammo
46 Party people
50 Cleaning challenge
52 Shed ___
55 Conference
56 It's a scream
57 Expert on Tejano music?
62 Dam consort
63 Serve
65 Merriment
66 Donald Duck, to Huey
67 Flashy jewelry, slangily
69 Convenes
72 Cry from a sheep
73 Stingy
74 Unwind
75 Categories
77 Personal attendants
79 Deputy
80 Accepting blame for gangsta music?
83 Short flight
86 Chews out
88 "Jetsons" pooch
89 Writer's comparison
91 Apia's place
92 Comics prince
94 Vaulted recess
97 Put off
98 Dear Led Zeppelin music?
103 Sporty car feature
104 Nigerian-born vocalist
107 "Rambo" actor Richard
108 Erie Canal city
110 Sense of self
111 Chinese dynasty
112 Aware, with "in"
115 Walk softly
119 Seaplane component
121 Exploring Motown music?
123 Streetcar
124 Small quantity
125 Marine hunter
126 Biting wit
127 Tap flow
128 Navajo neighbors
129 Swamp thing

DOWN

1 Skiing mecca
2 Dish preparer
3 Cordlike
4 Put to work
5 Pink Floyd's "Up the ___"
6 Resinous substance
7 Improve upon
8 Land south of Moab
9 On the double
10 Liquor measure
11 Operative
12 Lucky charms
13 Overland trek
14 Furrow maker
15 Wing
16 Friend
17 Append
18 Flair
21 Shine, in ad speak
24 Pouchlike appendage
28 Wild guess
31 Insurance giant
33 Involve in conflict
34 Winter outfit
35 Lady's title
36 Nobelist Wiesel
37 Insight into Woody Guthrie music?
39 "Star Trek" villain
40 Suits
41 Cry of surprise
43 Baseball commissioner Bud
47 Change from big bands to combos?
48 Portable light
49 Fret about
51 Angkor ___
53 Med. test
54 Starbuck's captain
55 Use a crowbar
58 Where a gob goes
59 How to sign a contract
60 Furlough
61 Flower yield
64 Chamois is one
67 Yellowish alloy
68 Expensive camera
70 Versailles' Grand ___ Palace
71 DC group
73 Not so hot
75 Sporty autos
76 Friday's rank
78 Vegas opener
81 Mine runner
82 Ambition
84 Tub contents
85 Criminal, in police lingo
87 ___ es Salaam
90 Cousin of 89 Across
92 Radar, for one
93 Waltz revivalist Andre
95 Attentive observer
96 Polish off
99 Seconds
100 Straighten out
101 Homage
102 Petrol units
104 Clan divisions
105 Marketplace of yore
106 Generous one
109 Pres. title
111 Dreyfus Affair figure
113 Final: abbr.
114 Genesis twin
116 Enervate
117 Previously
118 Old-style exclamation
120 Special attention
121 Resort amenity
122 Crackerjack

262 MORK OF DISTINCTION by Theresa Yves

24 Down is also the 1996 Oscar winner for Best Picture.

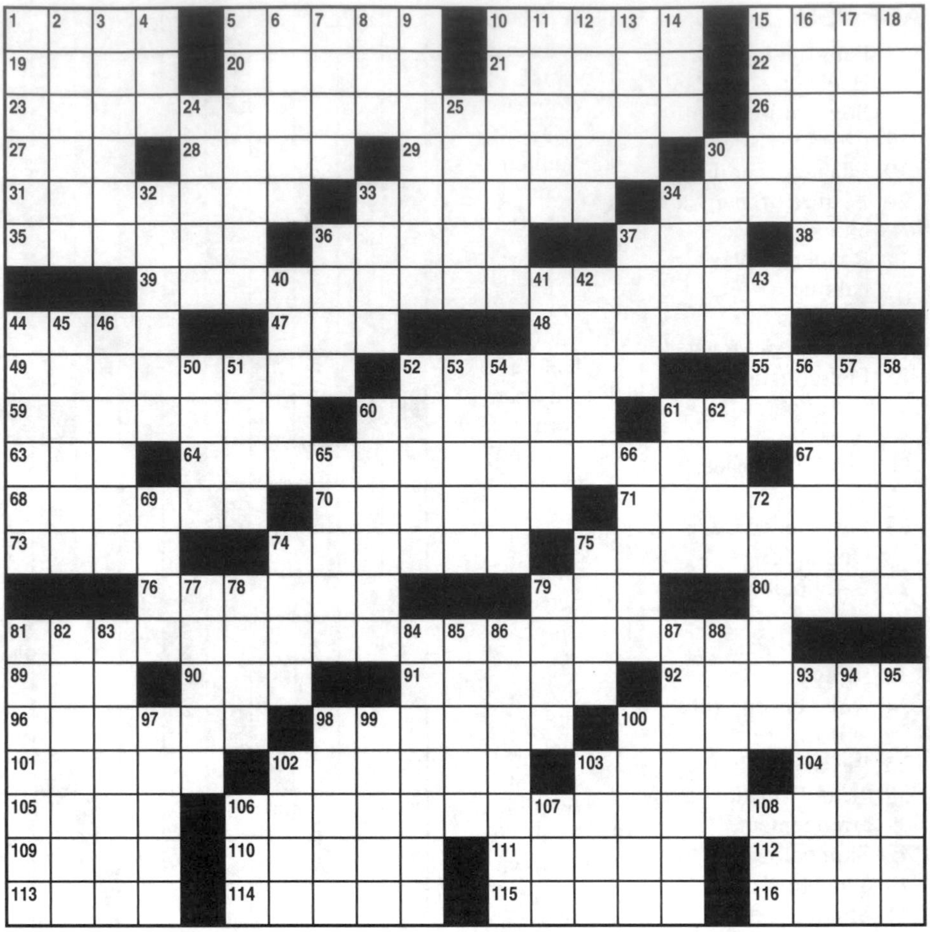

ACROSS

1 Sighed phrase
5 Legendary soul seller
10 Busy hub airport
15 Like, with "to"
19 Be abundant
20 Reel person
21 Strip locale
22 Jay of TV
23 Indiana Jones film set on Orson's planet?
26 Neeson of "Schindler's List"
27 "The Matrix" role
28 On the apex of
29 Intensely passionate
30 Indian state
31 With vigor
33 Vinny, in a movie
34 Sri Lanka, formerly
35 Have the attention of
36 Booze
37 Mai ___
38 Bullring bravo
39 Attack erroneously through the media?
44 "___ the Arab" (Ray Stevens song)
47 Card came
48 Blind spot's location
49 Shogun, and others
52 Sawbones
55 Chinese dynasty
59 "Bobby" director Emilio
60 Lech of Solidarity
61 In the rear
63 Book ending
64 Entertaining ham?
67 NFL defensive positions
68 With no joy
70 Proclamations
71 "Nice!"
73 Jupiter's wife
74 Sires
75 Grab hold of
76 Deli staple
79 Poet's before
80 Harsh sound
81 Unlikely nerd in the running?
89 Suffix for concert
90 Forever and a day
91 Watch for
92 Disreputable lenders
96 Argentine area
98 Until now
100 Disney's Lady, for one
101 "___ to Be You"
102 Greeley's advice
103 Tommy's gun
104 Where St. Pete is
105 Hardly drab
106 Get in a food fight with plastic utensils?
109 Meek and mild
110 Major happening
111 Zoo sounds
112 Type of club
113 First name in pitching
114 Present, for one
115 Shopaholic's binge
116 HI, once

DOWN

1 Immediately
2 Right after this
3 Major Vietnam river delta
4 Modern music genre
5 More like marbled, as meat
6 Blessing prompter
7 Lone Star coll.
8 Org. or grp.
9 Bring forward
10 Quarterback
11 Artist Toulouse-Lautrec
12 "Encore!"
13 "The Fountainhead" author
14 NY hrs.
15 Film noir setting
16 "Lake Wobegon Days" writer
17 Having debts
18 One who'll run
24 Wells' partner
25 Certify, with "for"
30 Stoop
32 Talk nonsense
33 Guitar neck attachment
34 Permission request
36 Soaks up rays
37 Dorothy's best friend
40 Spreading plant
41 Places for watches
42 Give halftime stats
43 White lie, sometimes
44 Like some anchors
45 Pain in the butt
46 Camelot's king
50 Race track shape
51 "Ratatouille" hero
52 '50s First Lady
53 Put in office
54 Fender flaws
56 Capital of Montana
57 Trips around the sun
58 Clear, as a drain
60 Woman's shoe
61 Alice's Restaurant patron
62 Go once over lightly
65 Appears to be
66 Tended to a squeak
69 Camouflage
72 Seoul man
74 Hoedown setting
75 Spunk
77 Coming up
78 London privies
79 Falco of "The Sopranos"
81 Take a bit from, as savings
82 Rampaging
83 Stress hard
84 Brownie, a few years later
85 Swimming (in)
86 Talks a blue streak
87 Sling mud
88 Do an Oscar winner's job
93 Thumb through, as pages
94 Raines' "New York Times" successor
95 Buffy is one
97 Comic strip section
98 Subway coin
99 Buck of "Hee Haw"
100 Mall constituent
102 Was philanthropic
103 Box without a ref
106 Ran into
107 Absorb, with up
108 Army NCO

263 GRAMMY SONG OF THE YEAR SINGERS by Harvey Estes

Anagram the circled letters to get the Grammy Song of the Year for 1962.

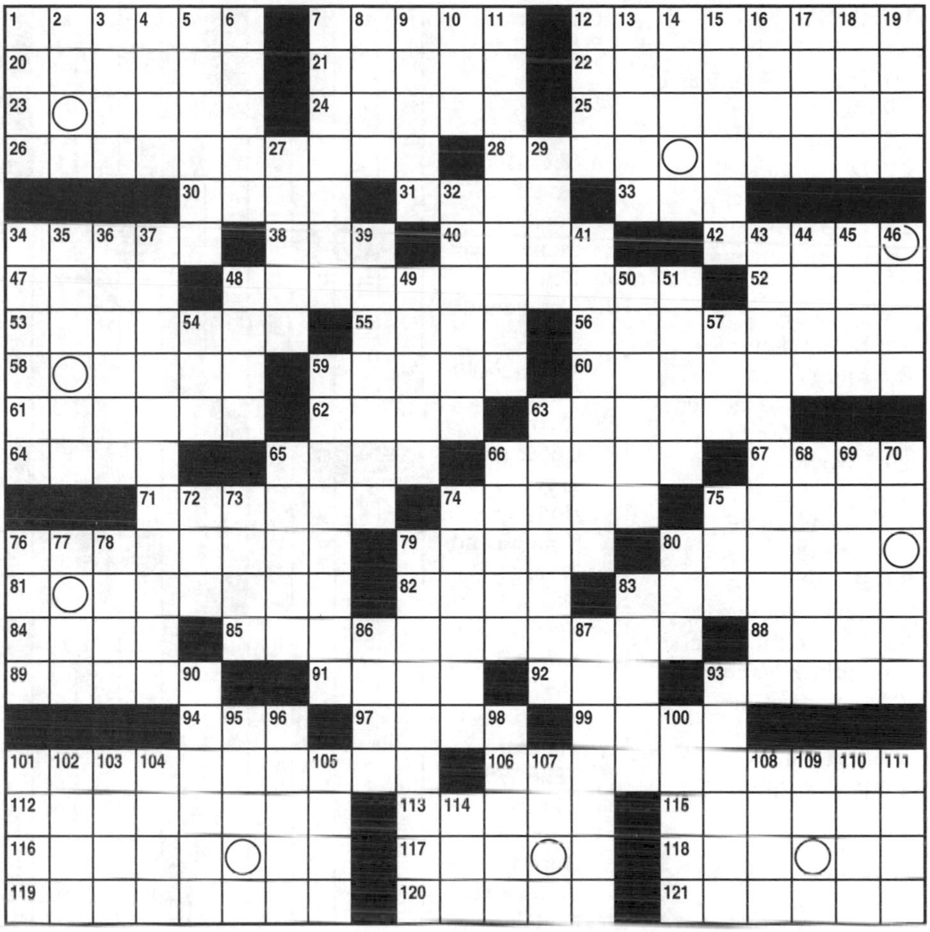

ACROSS

1 Seafood restaurant option
7 One that gives up
12 Richard Burton, for one
20 "Arsonist" cow owner
21 Whodunit start
22 Draft locale
23 Rung
24 Sunday dinner fare
25 They're not quite octaves
26 "My Heart Will Go On" singer (1999)
28 "Fallin'" singer (2002)
30 Dry as a bone
31 Diva's offering
33 Cable trademark
34 The Pyramids, e.g.
38 Potpie tidbit
40 Yale grads
42 Cut off from escape
47 Buffalo's lake
48 "Streets of Philadelphia" singer Bruce (1995)
52 Get out of bed
53 Is of value, slangily
55 Latvian port
56 Texas town
58 Ways to go
59 Dress fold
60 San Francisco columnist
61 Makes fit
62 Get under one's skin
63 Alpine alternative
64 Be abundant
65 Seemingly forever
66 Bette's "All About Eve" role
67 Croquet site
71 Cell dweller
74 Cursor controller
75 ___ Picchu, Peru
76 Uncompromising person
79 Keep the duck moist
80 Chopper, briefly
81 Santana hit
82 Precollege
83 Mame and others
84 City on the Tiber
85 "Unforgettable" singer (1992)
88 Seep slowly
89 Washstand accessories
91 Kind of appeal
92 Mandela org.
93 Laura of "ER"
94 Second afterthought abbr.
97 Unwelcome obligation
99 Blessing
101 "You've Got a Friend" singer (1972)
106 "Don't Know Why" singer (2003)
112 Does a surgeon's job
113 Totally ridiculous
115 Lighter fuel
116 Clothing supporter
117 Desmond of "Sunset Boulevard"
118 Set straight
119 Directly across from
120 Frat man
121 Affirmatives

DOWN

1 Campus mil. grp.
2 Skin moisturizer
3 Place for a wish
4 South Pacific island
5 Gladiators' places
6 Winona of "Girl, Interrupted"
7 Chuck Willis hit
8 Switch suffix
9 Beloved princess
10 Printers' measures
11 Costs
12 "Let's see now, where ___?"
13 To-be, in politics
14 "Rosemary's Baby" author Ira
15 Sword case
16 Goose sound
17 Trumpet muffler
18 White as a ghost
19 Costner character
27 Totally uncool
29 Café au ___
32 Bob Marley's music
34 Try to rip
35 Baltimore athlete
36 Teeny-tiny
37 "From a Distance" singer (1991)
39 Diving suit hose
41 Aquarium creature
43 "Tears in Heaven" singer (1993)
44 Pfefferberg in "Schindler's List"
45 Man or Wight
46 Sign gas
48 Get smart with
49 Nobel physicist Bohr
50 Pop up
51 "Taxi" character Elaine
54 The other woman
57 Baseball card stat
59 Campus sit-ins, e.g.
63 L.L. Bean competitor
65 Cushy class
66 Dayan of Israel
68 Film director's cry
69 Breathe noisily
70 "General Hospital" extras
72 U-turn from SSE
73 Sound stressed
74 California beach site
75 Jamaican "mister"
76 In this case
77 Say it's so
78 Winter coating
79 Sense of ___ (feeling at home)
80 Give a line to
83 Foil maker
86 Soon, to Shakespeare
87 Having coffee, say
90 Pie fight soundtrack
93 Cause harm to
95 Kind of dish
96 Trapshooting
98 Catch in a trap
100 "Hot dog!"
101 Comedic actor James
102 For one
103 Gather from the fields
104 "___ put it another way . . ."
105 "Now it's clear"
107 Round-buyer's words
108 Singer Redding
109 Scottish refusals
110 Non-PC suffix
111 Studio stages
114 Neither companion

264 "WOW!" by Roger Coburn

The clue at 20 Across usually leads to Corona.

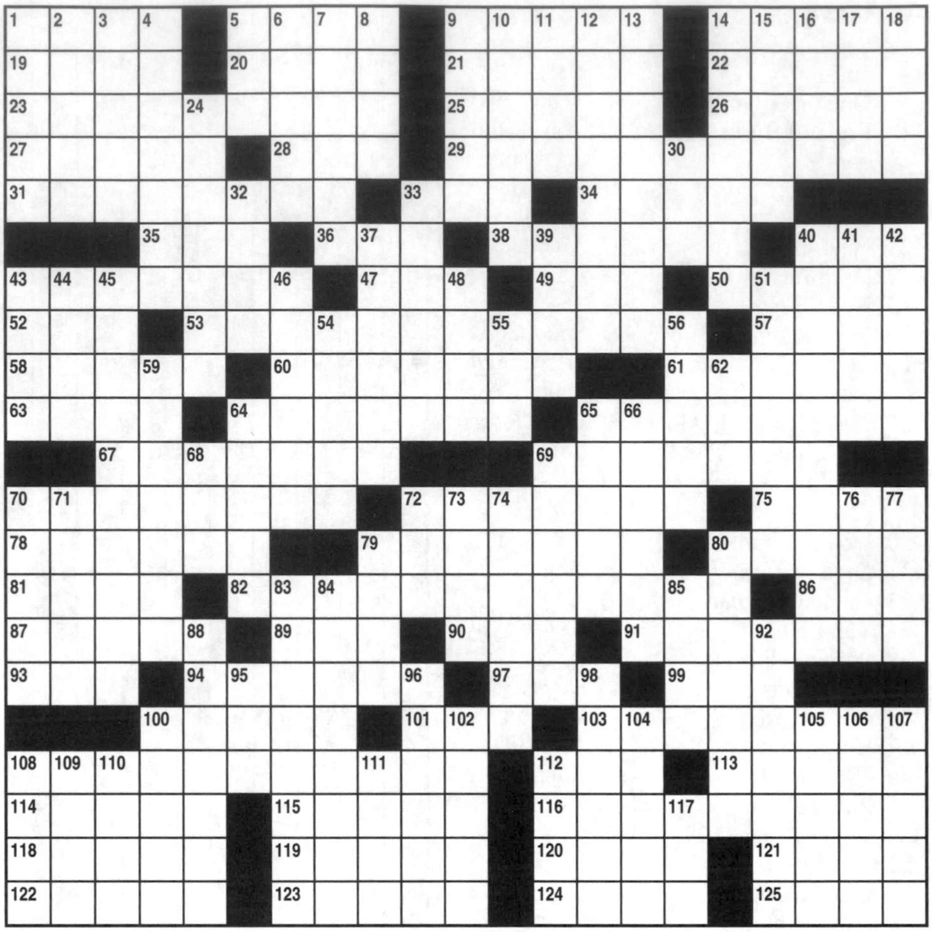

ACROSS

1 A job for Perry
5 Highlands language
9 Burning
14 Award
19 Dumbfounded
20 Mexican beer
21 Like some communities
22 Insect stage
23 "Wow!"
25 Labor camp
26 More recent
27 Related to mother
28 Long-nosed fish
29 "Wow!"
31 "___ Evil" (horror-game series)
33 Harden
34 Tenement level
35 Respectful address
36 Turkish leader
38 Larry, for one
40 Mel, on the diamond
43 Puget capital
47 In toto
49 Biker buddy
50 More consistent
52 Low sound
53 "Wow!"
57 To be, to Deneuve
58 Rests against
60 Moocher
61 Go ahead, taste it
63 Swelling
64 Most inner
65 Pampered
67 Live-forevers
69 Lines of a sort
70 It's in the bag
72 Like an empty tank
75 Fight venue
78 Emoting, perhaps
79 Cotton workers
80 10th-century king of England
81 Tabula ___
82 "Wow!"
86 Provocative network
87 Serengetti grazer
89 Thanksgiving staple
90 Christmas staple
91 Finds
93 It breaks early
94 Go overboard
97 Sheriff's asst.
99 Pocket money?
100 Lets out
101 Compound curve
103 City in South Dakota
108 "Wow!"
112 Cover the gray
113 Body
114 Condescend
115 Passage
116 "Wow!"
118 Florida room
119 Key, of a sort
120 Der ___ (Adenauer)
121 Pedecaris in "The Wind and the Lion"
122 Become accustomed
123 Winter woes
124 Country girl
125 Dweeb

DOWN

1 Chair man
2 Long past, in the past
3 Living room pieces
4 Swelled head
5 Annex
6 Rule
7 Beethoven piece
8 MIT grad
9 Texas A&M student
10 Fissures
11 "___ be a cold day in . . ."
12 Sop up again
13 Chisel, for one
14 Turkish tower
15 Smoothing cloth
16 "It's beginning to ___ on me!"
17 1958 fiction Pulitzer Prize awardee
18 British peer
24 Sphinx slayer
30 Follow closely
32 Gray actress
33 Like Sevier Lake
37 Lively dances
39 It'll give you a lift on the slopes
40 "Wow!"
41 Coating alloy
42 Cornered
43 Arab League sultanate
44 Timber wolf
45 "Wow!"
46 Part of AWOL
48 Mobster Diamond
51 Fabled fox
54 Dueling blades
55 Longtimer
56 Preppy jackets
59 Of the third
62 "Night Court" bailiff
64 Down Under dog
65 German magazine
66 A whole bunch
68 Bar mitzvah gift
69 Kind of hammer
70 Felt for
71 Central Florida city
72 Singing job
73 Ever and ___
74 Hair nets
76 Hood, in other words
77 ___ Ventre Indians
79 Places for Nautilus equipment
80 Squires
83 Basket case
84 Stately, in music
85 Achy or angry
88 Highlands schoolmaster
92 Gut area
95 Storage place
96 Please be ___
98 Kickback
100 Samantha in "The Collector"
102 Marks in blue pencil
104 Slaps around
105 Wear away
106 Gravel ridge
107 "Is there ___ to this madness?"
108 Unoccupied
109 Spirited opening
110 Hokkaido indigene
111 Keel locale
112 Pigeon pea
117 "Amen to that!"

265 GROUP MEMBERS by Norman S. Wizer

Here's a good Monday, Monday puzzle.

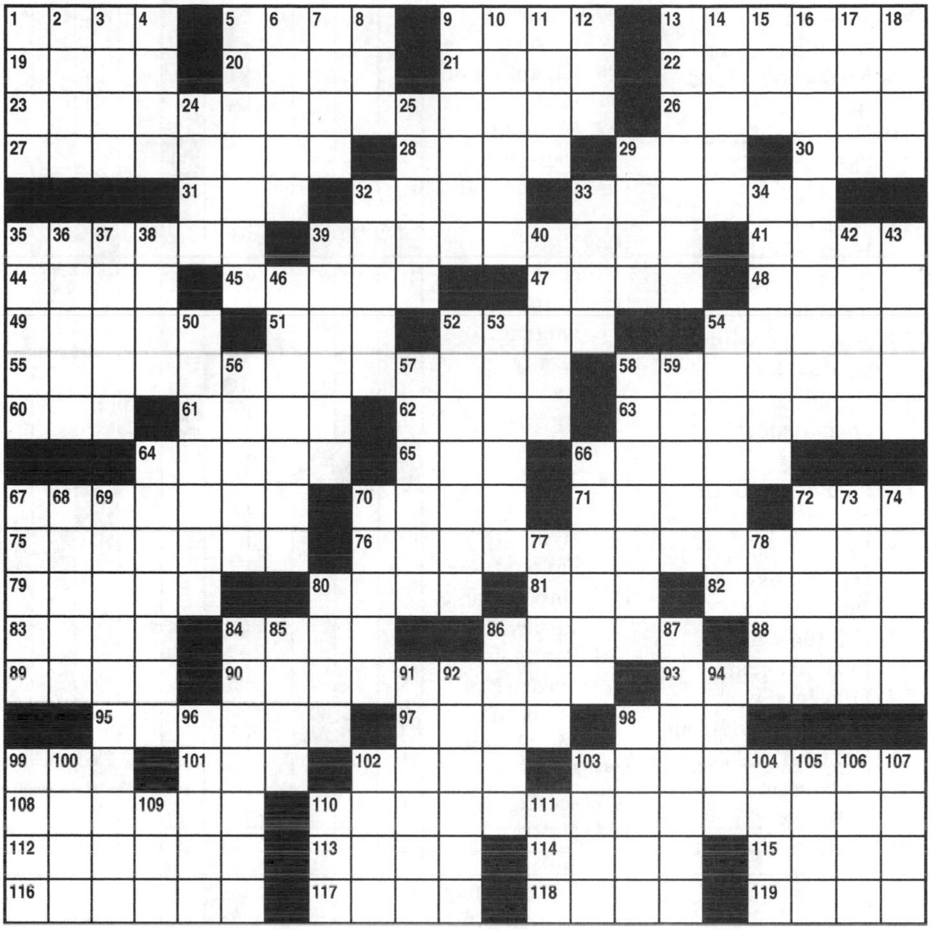

ACROSS

1 Distillery tanks
5 SeaWorld performer
9 Midmorning
13 Peeping Tom's eyeful
19 Colorful fish
20 Royal Crown brand
21 Cousins of the eland
22 Beat in a heat
23 Title holders?
26 Japanese-Americans
27 Popular sandwich
28 Far East weight
29 Roadside bomb
30 NYC–Boston dir.
31 Kenyan runner Keino
32 Lollobrigida in "Beat the Devil"
33 Online broker
35 Once in a blue moon
39 Some shooting stars?
41 Monumental
44 Feller
45 Earthen embankments
47 Partner of wheel
48 Lowland
49 Amassed (debt)
51 Brooklyn pronoun
52 Pierre loc.
54 Wishful one
55 Big Al, the elephant
58 Flagrant
60 Shaker ___, OH
61 Melissa Etheridge's "___ Am"
62 Moderate
63 Egyptian dynast
64 River into the Seine
65 Pippa Passes, KY campus
66 Blackjack table request
67 Cut out for
70 Woody's offspring
71 "The Night of the Hunter" screenwriter
72 Very, in Valencia
75 Compressed
76 Ingmar Bergman's "Scenes ___"
79 Future butterflies
80 Corner sign
81 Topper
82 Juno's robe
83 Basque for "merry"
84 "Hard Hearted Hannah" composer
86 Whined
88 2001 Judi Dench film
89 The skinny
90 Formal document from Benedict XVI
93 Persevere
95 Brewer, of sorts
97 "Fatha" Hines
98 Pou ___ (vantage point)
99 Alt. spelling
101 Cartoon collectible
102 Start of a fall mo.
103 He was born on the fourth of July
108 Discharged matter
110 Reddish-brown furniture wood
112 Woebegone
113 Sister of Cronus
114 Scoundrel
115 Swan genus
116 "___ Fables"
117 Barbecue badly
118 "I Love Lucy" landlord
119 Visitor of "Deep Space Nine"

DOWN

1 Sotto ___ (in an undertone)
2 Squeal like ___
3 Piquancy
4 Some dams
5 Shirley MacLaine book (with "Out")
6 Make a new plan
7 Lake in Nigeria
8 Ditty
9 Tennessee lizard
10 In ___ and out the other
11 "The Clan of the Cave Bear" author
12 Workload for eds.
13 King Lear's eldest daughter
14 "Under Two Flags" novelist
15 Wino's woes
16 "Zorba the Greek" star
17 Full of oneself
18 Cash Bundren's father
24 Powerful shark
25 Swabs not meant for decks
29 Chichén ___ (Mayan ruins)
32 "Brave New World" caste
33 OT book
34 Follower
35 Douglas in "Superman II"
36 Praise profusely
37 Horne and Headey
38 Wallop
39 Early arrival
40 "It's ___!" ("You're on!")
42 Graff of "Mr. Belvedere"
43 Popular breath mint
46 "The Mary Tyler Moore Show" star
50 Due
52 Shell Oil shell
53 URL suffix
54 Hits the nail on the head
56 Oberon in "Wuthering Heights"
57 Italian pizza chain
58 Military unit
59 "See ya"
64 Sense of unease
66 Her "camel" is famous
67 Senate-hearing station
68 40 acres and ___
69 Ozark bananas
70 TV/radio union
72 New Zealand native
73 Sweet tangelos
74 Homebrewer's need
77 ___ in the conversation
78 "The Way ___": Bruce Hornsby
80 Seven, in Paris
84 Kind of court
85 London lockup
86 Jewish feast day
87 Junked a junker
91 Womanizer
92 Luzon peninsula
94 ___ contendere
96 Make a scene
98 Bandy-bandy, e.g.
99 Whoopi's "Rat Race" role
100 Flu symptom
102 Mount Kaala locale
103 Foe of Doctor Strange
104 Ghostbuster Spengler
105 Hacienda room
106 Soon enough
107 "Deathtrap" heroine
109 Bay Area airport
110 "Leaving for a minute," in chat slang
111 "Woof!"

266 SERIES OF DESPAIR by Harvey Estes

93 Down is also a deodorant dispenser.

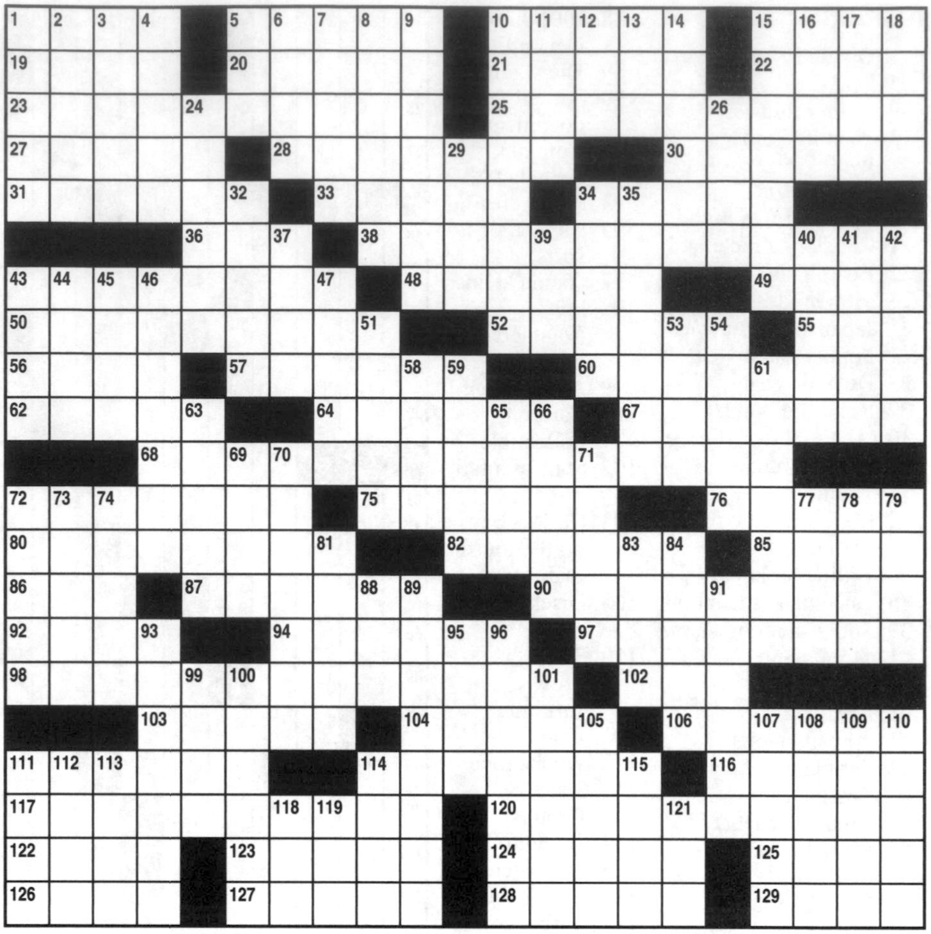

ACROSS

1 Missile housing
5 Mushroom cloud maker
10 Brazilian dance
15 "M*A*S*H" vehicle
19 "Dukes of Hazzard" deputy
20 TV, radio, etc.
21 Hold forth
22 Black and white sandwich
23 Agonies of checkmate?*
25 Pillsbury Doughboy, e.g.?*
27 Namely
28 Meet by chance
30 "Gunsmoke" star James
31 Has the wheel
33 Double agents
34 Did stage work
36 Across the st. from
38 Political debate?*
43 Telephone timesaver
48 Band equipment handler
49 Continental coin
50 Complainer's society?*
52 Least tan
55 When doubled, a chocolate
56 Debussy's "Clair de ___"
57 Slip away
60 Stepping
62 "Go ahead, ask"
64 Necktie
67 Pipe openings
68 What answers to clues* are
72 Snide retort
75 Mexican ma'am
76 Köln's river
80 Artillery wagons
82 Tiny bits
85 La Douce of film
86 Absorbed, as a loss
87 "Will & Grace" or "Ellen"
90 Psychologist's performance art?*
92 Races the engine
94 Automaker's woe
97 Featured players
98 Dreaming of id?*
102 Metered transport
103 Get the suds off
104 Yearly account
106 European language family
111 As a surprising fact
114 Tykes' clothing chain
116 Favored few
117 Unbelievable stories?*
120 Parental burden?*
122 "Mamma Mia!" band
123 Wed in secret
124 Native Alaskan
125 Fashion mag
126 Pt. of NCAA
127 Bell-bottoms, e.g.
128 Hornets' homes
129 Discouraging words

DOWN

1 Religious groups
2 Words before water
3 "Camelot" composer Frederick
4 Davis of "Do the Right Thing"
5 Sound booster
6 Den denizen
7 Disgrace
8 Bit of bait
9 Type of artery
10 Cajole
11 Alice's Restaurant patron
12 Former Red head
13 Air conditioner meas.
14 Cause to sparkle
15 No-name name
16 Buffalo's lake
17 Slippery swimmers
18 Snow pea holders
24 Went boldly
26 Boat people
29 Pianist Peter
32 Rack item
34 Cocked, as a hat
35 "Ta-ta!"
37 Buddies
39 Govt. medicine watchdog
40 Puzzle cube inventor
41 Pilotless plane
42 "Yesterday" and "Tomorrow"
43 Belt maker's tools
44 "No dice!"
45 Baseballer Martinez
46 Regular Joe
47 Susan of "All My Children"
51 Uncovers
53 Put in the mail
54 Home run, or home fries source
58 Remove the skin from
59 Makes level
61 African pullover
63 Lock of hair
65 Per person
66 Pair on a bike
69 Mine, to Mimi
70 Nissan sedans
71 Goldman's partner
72 Gobble (down)
73 Western film
74 Spaghetti strainer
77 Goofs up
78 "While ___ it . . ."
79 Catches forty winks
81 Public spectacle
83 Big Mac man
84 Marner the miser
88 It turns out lts.
89 Lethargic feelings
91 More high-minded
93 "Yeah, I'm up to it!"
95 Allow to use
96 Photographer
99 Frisbee, for example
100 Marching together
101 Early release
105 Pear-shaped instruments
107 "Zelig" director Woody
108 String section member
109 Milan's land
110 Signs over
111 Mar. Madness source
112 Planets or peepers
113 Tosses gently
114 Continued, with "on"
115 Closed
118 Menu phrase
119 Horror star Chaney
121 Alf and others

267 ALL-AMERICAN MOVIES by Holden Baker

49 Across received an Oscar nomination for Best Actress in that film.

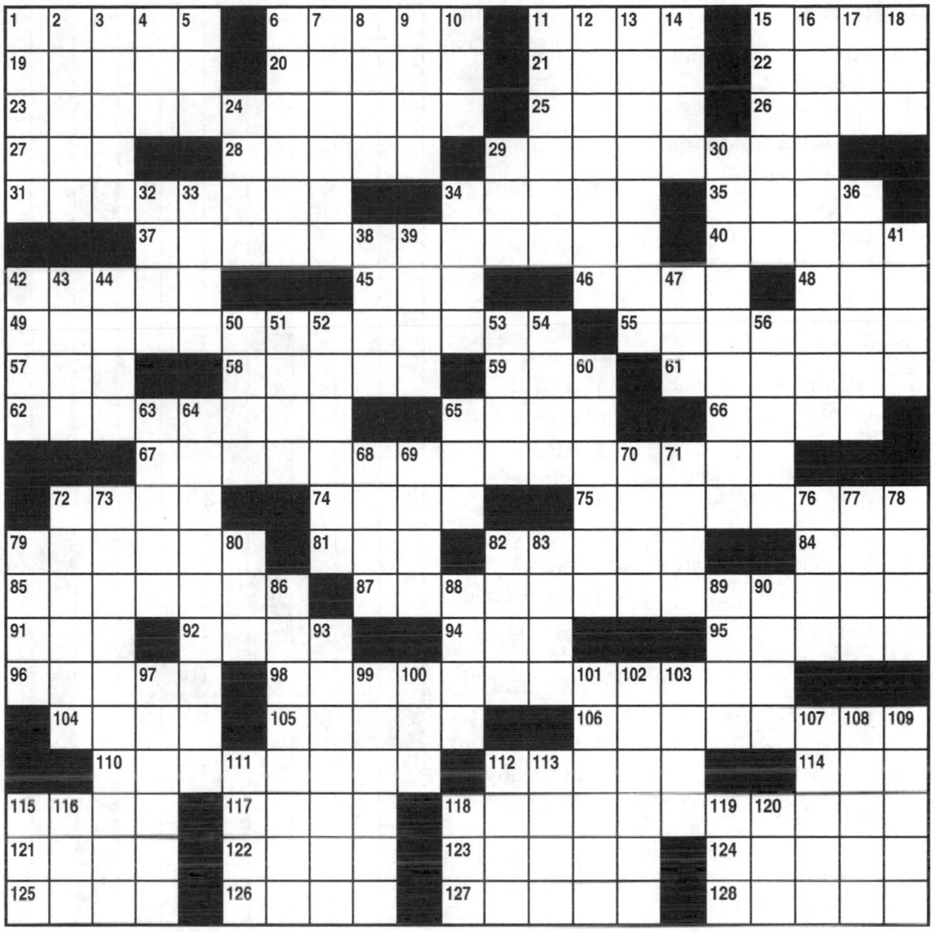

ACROSS

1 Offshoot of Toyota
6 V.P. John ___ Garner
11 Key of Bruckner's Symphony No. 7
15 Special talent
19 Voyageur's transport
20 Situation after a leadoff single
21 Whatever she wants, she gets
22 Concept
23 "American Gigolo" star
25 Watered down
26 Necessity
27 Former Irish coach Parseghian
28 Wilson's thrush
29 Highway warning
31 Home of Les Canadiens
34 Stalin's police chief
35 New Jersey five
37 "American Graffiti" actor
40 Baloney
42 City of the Ruhr
45 "Paris Sky Chief" carrier
46 Zaire's Mobutu ___ Seko
48 Mediterranean fruit
49 "American Beauty" star
55 Laundry job
57 ___ room (game area)
58 O.K. Corral brothers
59 Grazing locale
61 Binges
62 Jewelry item
65 Sherilyn in "The Dukes of Hazzard" (2007)
66 Remove from office
67 "American Graffiti" star
72 McClure of "The Virginian"
74 Dullea in "2001: A Space Odyssey"
75 To a higher degree
79 Classical lyric poet
81 Part of many Québec names
82 Many Apples
84 Fiesta-taurina cheer
85 Still on the plate
87 "American Buffalo" star
91 Diarist Anais
92 "Have it ___ way!"
94 Immigrant's course: Abbr.
95 "Maid of Athens, ___ part": Byron
96 Legionnaire Beau
98 "American Splendor" star
104 Star Wars princess
105 Leg part
106 American daily
110 Used a sieve
112 Short pants
114 ". . . ___ quit!"
115 Imperial Iranian, once
117 Might's partner
118 "American Psycho" star
121 Iditarod terminus
122 Argued, as a case
123 TV studio sign
124 Funafuti, e.g.
125 "Balderdash!"
126 Georgia and Uzbekistan, formerly: Abbr.
127 Fate
128 Series opener?

DOWN

1 "Get outta here!"
2 City in Egypt or Illinois
3 Early Peruvian
4 "That feels good!"
5 School org.
6 Spouse's denial
7 Pier in "Somebody Up There Likes Me"
8 At no time, to the poet
9 E.A. Robinson's Richard
10 Pilot's heading
11 Matador's foe
12 Certain sweaters
13 Surveying instruments
14 Painters Vermeer and Steen
15 Fred's dancing partner
16 Recognizes
17 Fixed charge
18 Young 'un
24 KOA camper
29 Gridiron official, for short
30 Place between
32 "How do I love ___?"
33 Rave's companion
34 ___ B'rith
36 Small piano
38 Self-help program part
39 Possesses
41 They're poached legally
42 Work for
43 Old-time dagger
44 1960s civil-rights org.
47 Brillo rival
50 Big name in tape decks
51 Apiece
52 Strokes of luck
53 Cardinal or Diamondback, e.g.
54 Autry or 63 Down
56 Have faith in
60 "Thou canst not then be false to ___." Polonius
63 Benny Goodman's drummer
64 Interstellar distance measure
65 Depression prez
68 No longer working: Abbr.
69 "Mon ___!"
70 Nina in "An American in Paris"
71 Violinist Camilla
72 Radcliffe or Craig
73 Treasure cave door opener
76 Where the heart is
77 What there oughtta be
78 Hawaiian goose
79 Performed, as arias
80 War on Poverty org.
82 Grammarian's answer to "Who's there?"
83 Pfefferberg in "Schindler's List"
86 Marriage
88 Dreamcast maker
89 Boba ___ ("Star Wars" character)
90 Cold, in Cancun
93 Grace Kelly's prince
97 Contributes to the church
99 Plumbing pipes
100 Pot top
101 Shiite or Sunni
102 Kansas motto ender
103 Hobart is its cap.
107 Serve
108 Good thing to be on
109 A common 29 Across
111 Roadies' burdens
112 Lollobrigida in "Woman of Rome"
113 Banned orchard spray
115 Showcase for Belushi, Curtin et al.
116 ___ polloi
118 Stir-fry pan
119 "Seesaw, Margery ___"
120 From ___ Z

268 MINGLE-MANGLE by Arlan and Linda Bushman

"Kartoffelpuffer" would be another clue for 23 Across.

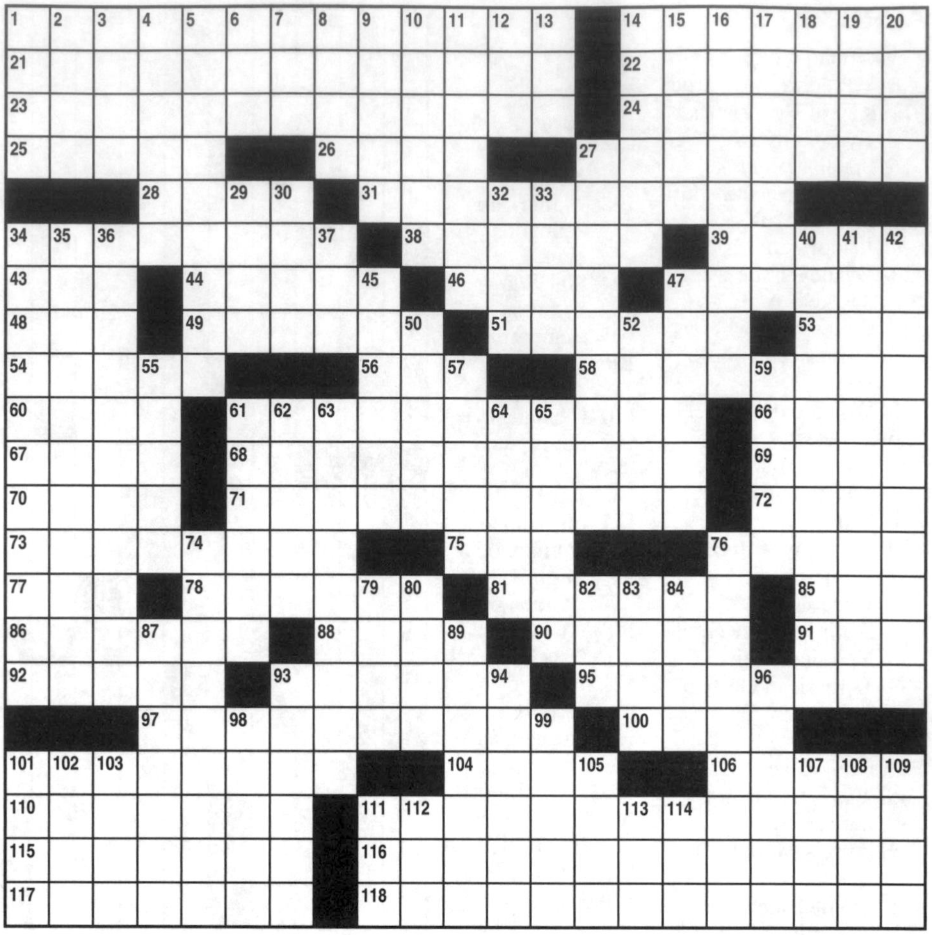

ACROSS

1 Feature of a quaint village
14 Networks
21 50-dollar gold coin
22 Artist's board
23 Latke
24 Personal data reluctantly shared?
25 Hypothesize
26 Veer away, with "off"
27 Accomplished in a tactful way
28 Oppose
31 Sampled reduced-calorie beer
34 Military dining area
38 Underscore
39 Like Oscar Wilde
43 Tribute, of a sort
44 Phony
46 Coup d'___
47 Spirited meeting
48 Never, in Berlin
49 Yukon neighbor
51 Puts up
53 Dance piece?
54 Police front man
56 Former RR regulator
58 "The Hound of the Baskervilles" setting
60 Stylish
61 Treasure locale in a Bogart film
66 "There'll be ___ time . . ."
67 Joule fractions
68 Snoopy
69 Divulge
70 Narrow inlets
71 Securely in the Land of Nod
72 View from Toledo
73 Hindu noblewoman
75 Doo-wop syllable
76 Shift
77 It may be pint-sized
78 Dementieva and Vesnina
81 Remove all doubt
85 Integers, e.g.
86 Lower-lying sections in a tract of land
88 Mother bears, in Malaga
90 Resound monotonously
91 ___-de-sac
92 "I have no idea how ___ it"
93 Brings to bear
95 Kit and caboodle
97 Majors
100 Fill to excess
101 Docility
104 Super Bowl highlight, often
106 Minstrel Allan-___
110 Sitter's prop
111 Somehow or other
115 "Blue period" artist
116 Somerset Maugham title
117 Convinces of
118 Cuts fat from the budget

DOWN

1 Joe Btfsplk's creator
2 Tale of the South Seas
3 Risks
4 Ponytail alternative
5 Accessory for keeping a car tidy
6 "Baudolino" novelist
7 Skip, as on water
8 Piece of cake
9 Basic belief
10 Greyhounds, often
11 One of a trio in a famous French motto
12 Bugling creature
13 Peg
14 Victor's claim
15 Popular New Age musician
16 Most slushily icy
17 Mosaic piece
18 Hellenic vowels
19 Homeowner's pmt.
20 Furrow insert
27 Felson in "The Hustler"
29 Jester
30 Exercise system
32 Art deco designer
33 Costly
34 Halloween song
35 Columnist's pronoun
36 Looking to the future
37 Lambda followers
40 What a babbling person is evincing
41 Student's happy cry
42 In an uncaring manner
45 Aspen feature
47 "The Devil Wears Prada" actress
50 Pungent
52 Whittle
55 St. Gregory's bishopric
57 Spanish dwellings
59 Caesar's mom
61 Rope fibers
62 Words after "hole" or "all"
63 Semiannual events
64 Baryshnikov, to friends
65 "It's about time!"
74 Oboe's sound quality
76 Small cup
79 Between ports
80 Famed puppeteer Tony
82 Dam, for one
83 Large servers
84 Lee of "Stump the Stars"
87 Generous
89 Speech flaw
93 1963 AL MVP Howard
94 Austere
96 "Little" storybook fowl
98 Painting surface
99 Paretsky and Teasdale
101 Spigots
102 Two-time Indy winner Luyendyk
103 Midpoint of the next century
105 Perplex
107 Lends a hand
108 Theater box
109 Chemical suffixes
111 Org. for Roddick
112 Govt. loan insurer
113 Bushy-tailed mammal
114 Dada pioneer Jean

269 A MAN AND HIS MOVIES by Fran & Lou Sabin

Frank Sinatra's most enduring role was not Maggio, it was humanitarian.

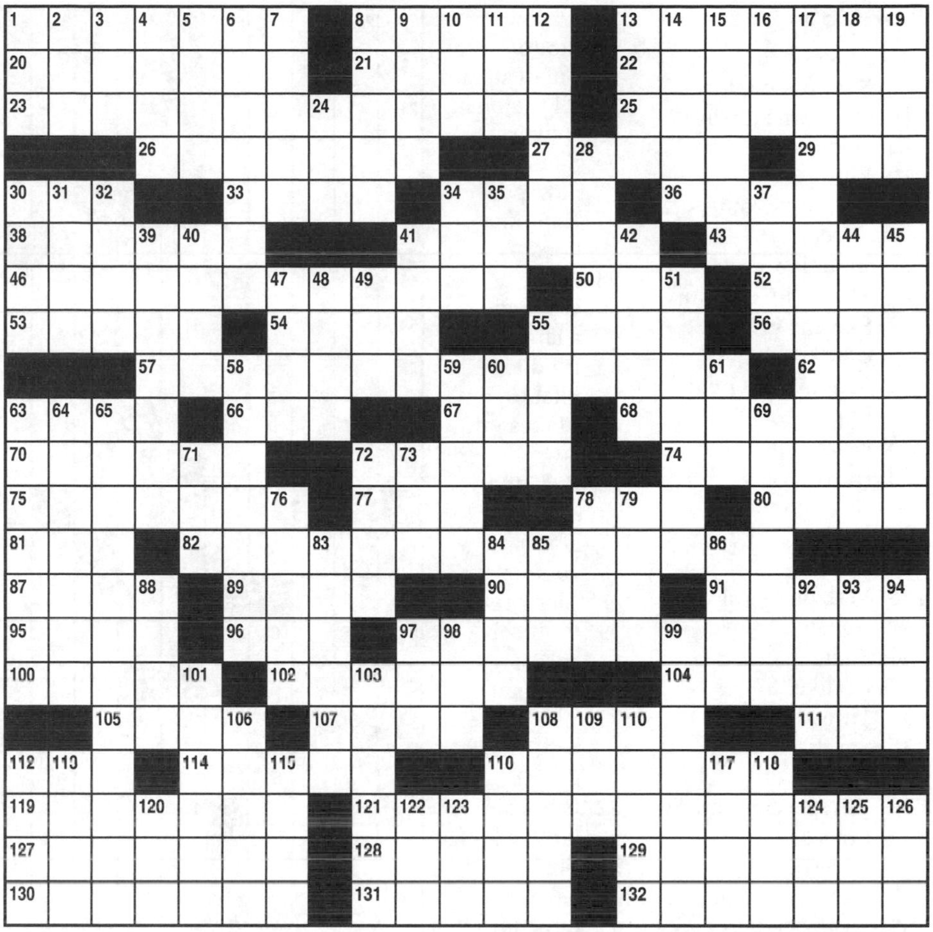

ACROSS

1 Brian of "Brian's Song"
8 Showed shock
13 Model of excellence
20 Cotopaxi locale
21 Ready for action?
22 Generally speaking
23 Where Sinatra was Charlie Reader (1955)
25 Gold rush necessity
26 Barely restrained
27 "That's ___!"
29 Garden supply
30 Core muscles
33 Low, strong cart
34 Roseanne, at times
36 Really big
38 Card game for four
41 Cocoa alternative
43 Claire in "Shopgirl"
46 Where Sinatra was Tony Rome (1968)
50 Fracas
52 Keflavik bedtime story?
53 They're perfect!
54 Give one's word
55 Cookbook direction
56 One-up, courtwise
57 Where Sinatra was Tony Manetta (1959)
62 Grammarian's case: Abbr.
63 "___ who!"
66 Cacophany
67 Oedipus, titularly
68 Montmartre artist, Maurice (1883–1955)
70 Fate a.k.a. the Spinner
72 Sweet-singing thrush
74 Basket-weaver's supply
75 Foul-mouthed folks
77 Green climber
78 Wimple wearer
80 Being, to Nero
81 Strip pup
82 Where Sinatra was Alfred Boone (1955)
87 Desert areas
89 Major up above
90 Arizona Indian
91 "Do" a wedding
95 D-Day beach
96 Fall guy
97 Where Sinatra was Joe Leland (1968)
100 "Cry, the Beloved Country" author
102 Sucker
104 Lacking
105 Funny guy
107 Gave a buzz
108 Road hazard
111 Slalom route
112 Shad spawn
114 River through Rome
116 Biting comeback
119 Helen Keller's birth state
121 Where Sinatra was Clarence Doolittle (1945)
127 DVD copiers, e.g.
128 Expert on 38 Across
129 Censor, essentially
130 Looks about to fall
131 Chopin work
132 Willing?

DOWN

1 Treat warmly
2 Fish affliction
3 Hustler's tool
4 Blanchett in "Little Fish"
5 Music halls of yore
6 Count Fleet's jockey
7 "Ten-hut!" is one
8 Low-rated mag
9 La-di-da
10 Links goal
11 House letter?
12 "Go home!"
13 Early late-night name
14 Its capital is Shillong
15 Spoke harshly
16 Altar in the sky
17 Where Sinatra was Nathan Detroit (1955)
18 Kitchen staple
19 Campus outcast
24 Santana stat
28 Yule symbol
30 Famed palindrome opener
31 Deep-headed nail
32 Order addition
34 Voyage beginning
35 One-time LSAT taker
37 Mother of the Titans
39 Heredity rulers
40 Annabeth in "Mystic Pizza"
41 Downed by Paul Bunyan
42 Parting shot?
44 Menu listing
45 City in a Bacharach song
47 Colombian city since 1536
48 Knotted
49 "Excusez-___!"
51 Filibuster tactic
55 Like Roger Rabbit's wife
58 Skunky
59 Low pair
60 "Away from ___" (Julie Christie film)
61 Mabuse, No et al.
63 Manage to find
64 Province above Montana
65 Where Sinatra was Barney Sloan (1954)
69 Repeat oneself
71 Barnyard squawker
72 MasterCard rival
73 Mendes in "Hitch"
76 Subway support
78 Tonsorial target
79 Kind of pricing
83 Reach for the stars
84 At that time
85 "Scarface" prop
86 Behold!, in the Forum
88 "Git!"
92 Time's partner
93 Poetic times
94 Junkie's "downers"
97 X, in a way
98 Road animal?
99 It leads to a mate
101 Score music
103 Service center?
106 Kitchen aid
108 "Total Recall" star
109 Champagne apéritif
110 Cartographer's addition
112 Totally involved
113 Some of this, some of that
115 Trio member, often
116 Dust off
117 Woolly ones
118 "La Boheme" in rock
120 Swing it!
122 "___ a chance!"
123 Bordeaux vineyard
124 Mrs. Eddie Cantor
125 Solve
126 It folded in 1806: Abbr.

270 "NICE CATCH PHRASE!" by Pancho Harrison

Clara Peller became famous for saying 4 Down.

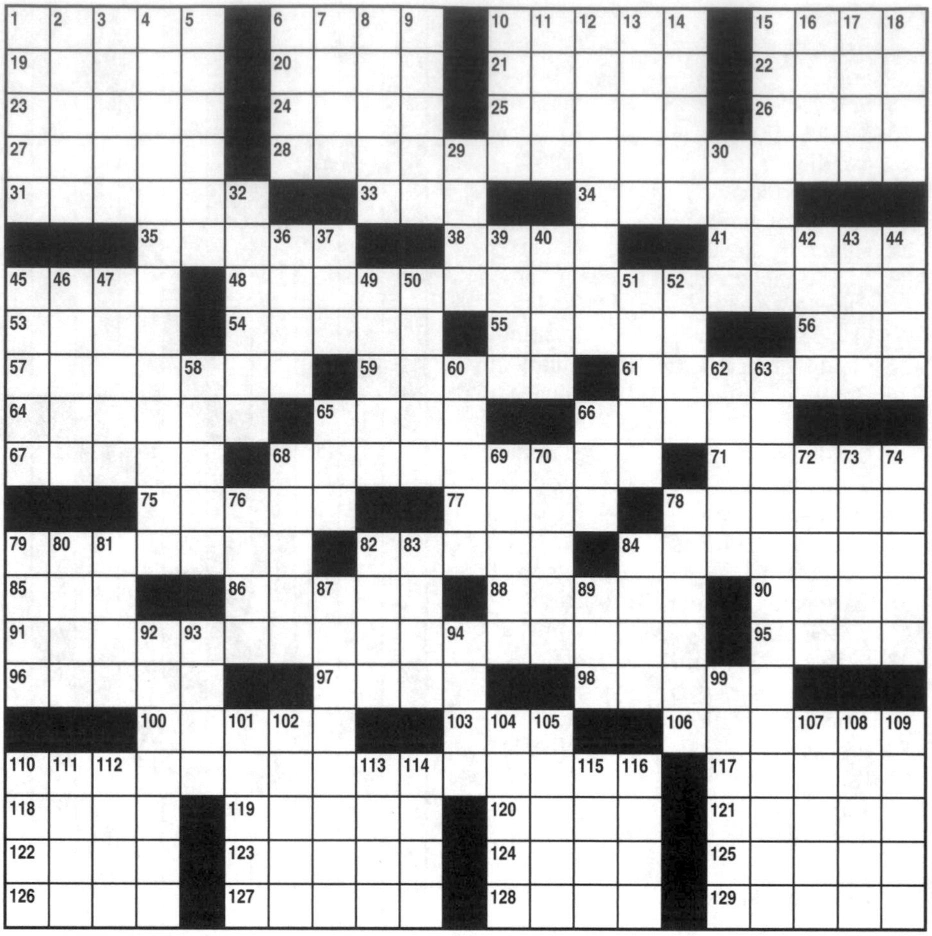

ACROSS

1 Makes beer
6 Summer coolers
10 ___ home (away)
15 Cutup
19 Fitting
20 Rob of "Brothers & Sisters"
21 Imitative
22 State with certainty
23 Stevens in "Five Card Stud"
24 Shallowest Great Lake
25 Drug cop
26 Holly in "Moonlight Mile"
27 Stick out like ___ thumb
28 Verizon Wireless slogan
31 Plant again
33 Gallivant
34 Thread holder
35 South Carolina motto word
38 Nevada city on I-80
41 Emcees
45 Aerosol output
48 L'Oreal slogan
53 Seating sect.
54 What Rhett didn't give
55 Warn
56 Ron who played Tarzan
57 Makes a scene?
59 In ___ (not yet born)
61 Show time
64 Make possible
65 Battery fluid
66 Transpire
67 Tony-winner Patrick
68 Chevy trucks slogan
71 Range rover
75 Studio stand
77 Comedian Sahl
78 Idolize
79 Orange spice
82 Term of address in "Roots"
84 Word with water or deposit
85 "Chances ___"
86 Contribute to the mix
88 Money motto starter
90 Small stream
91 KFC slogan
95 Bawls
96 San Diego newspaper
97 Rallying cries
98 Radiant
100 Kindled again
103 Product pitches
106 Makes into law
110 Red Bull slogan
117 Drum kit component
118 Think (over)
119 Protuberances
120 Suit part
121 "___ the bag!" (sure thing)
122 Biblical brother
123 Stag
124 "Frisco Lil" director Kenton
125 They're troubled, often
126 Miracle site in John 2:1
127 Malayan palms
128 Regard
129 "Frasier" terrier

DOWN

1 Patch in an Uncle Remus tale
2 Washer cycle
3 Some frozen waffles
4 Wendy's slogan
5 "Sophie's Choice" Oscar winner
6 A Baldwin
7 Nickelodeon's little explorer
8 J.R. of "Dallas"
9 "Ciao!"
10 Said twice, an Orkan farewell
11 Brilliantly colored fish
12 Yawn-inducing
13 Tunesmith's org.
14 Detailed, informally
15 King Arthur's realm
16 The Bard's river
17 Nevada gambling mecca
18 Challenge in many an oater
29 Poetic tributes
30 "Jerry Maguire" actor Jay
32 Campaign event
36 Merlot and Chianti
37 Mozart's "L'___ del Cairo"
39 King of tragedy
40 DEA weight unit
42 Ballpark near La Guardia
43 Pisa tower feature
44 Eyelid problem
45 Surfer's need?
46 Skater Slutskaya
47 Beanpole
49 Frenzied way to run
50 Prepare for a takeoff?
51 Ruin partner
52 Ex follower?
58 Limpid
60 Wax-coated cheeses
62 Blades in "Assassination Tango"
63 Volkswagen slogan
65 Feel poorly
66 World Series mo.
68 Tennis great Ivan
69 Violin bow application
70 Sumatran simian, for short
72 Comical opening?
73 Pulsar toothbrush maker
74 Actresses Gwyn and Carter
76 Fly like an eagle
78 Enigma
79 Out of danger
80 Seed covering
81 Wet lowlands
82 Flaky mineral
83 Egyptian cross
84 Synthesizer pioneer
87 Scoundrel
89 ___ few rounds (spar)
92 Vegetarian ape
93 Altitude: Abbr.
94 "___ Her Standing There": Beatles
99 Like some inspections
101 Wertmuller and Horne
102 Capri, for one
104 Cut into cubes
105 Bug a bedmate
107 Checked out before a heist
108 "Lemon Tree" singer Lopez
109 Smell or taste
110 G3 or G4 computer
111 Polka player?
112 Secluded valley
113 Wine prefix
114 Purposes
115 Mighty wind
116 Wineglass part

271 CLASSICAL PIECE by Ed Early

76 Across is Richard Edwards' only surviving play.

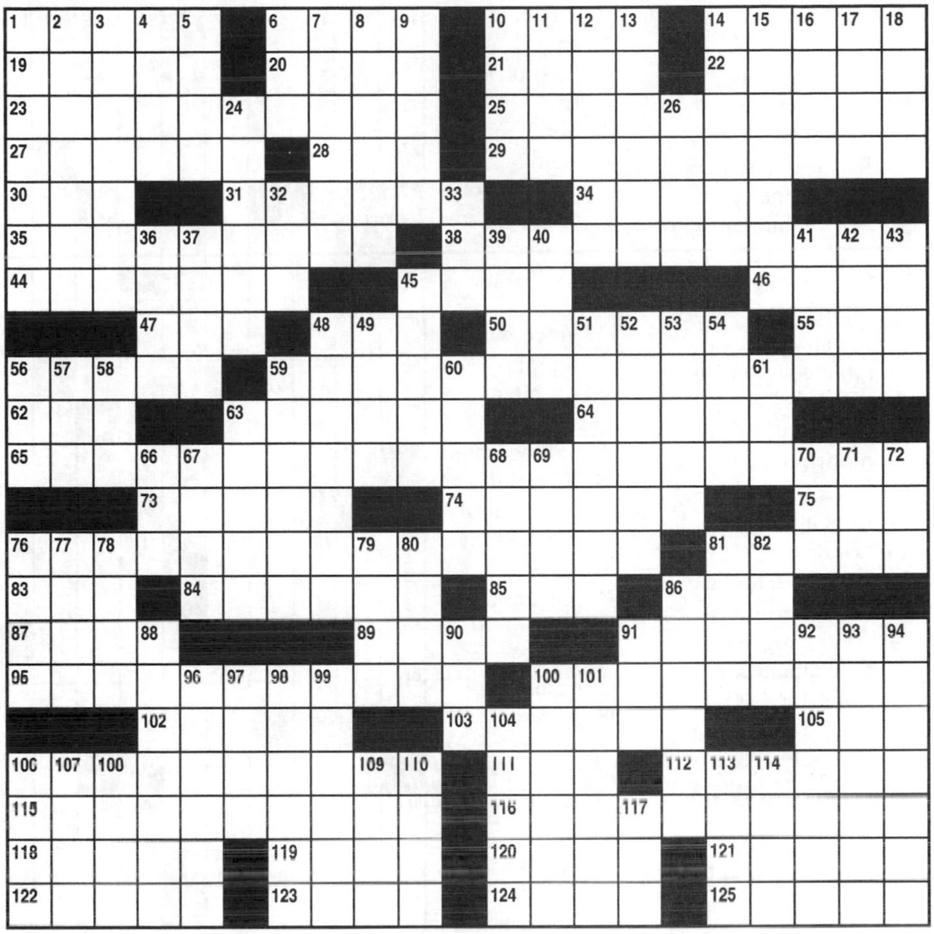

ACROSS

1 Roman holiday
6 Pesky biter
10 Pear-shaped fruits
14 Horseshoe-shaped lab item
19 ___ a limb
20 Opera set on the Nile
21 Aruba, for one
22 Innovative
23 Borodin opera
25 "The Carnival of the Animals" composer
27 Breaks up a sentence for analysis
28 Kennel warning
29 Vapor from a liquid
30 Neighbor of Leb.
31 Two Chicago mayors
34 "Goodbye, Mr. Chips" star
35 Wagnerian opera
38 Tolstoy classic
44 Trajan's successor
45 Sanctuary
46 Ancient Mideast kingdom
47 Stipulations
48 Grafton's "___ for Corpse"
50 Trembling
55 WW2 price-fixing agcy.
56 Singer Nixon
59 "The Ring Cycle" opera
62 Spheroid
63 Dark brown Indian deer
64 "A Million ___" (Kiss song)
65 Shakespeare comedy
73 Comic prefix
74 Stickball venue
75 Mendacity
76 Richard Edwards play
81 "Mack the Knife" composer
83 "The Crying Game" star
84 "Spectator" essayist
85 Strange
86 Mercator creation
87 "Bel piacere" is one
89 "___ Her Go": Frankie Laine
91 In any case
95 Rossini opera
100 Verdi opera
102 Beauty parlor name
103 Pilotless aircraft
105 Hardy follower
106 Holes 11–13 at Augusta
111 Ninny
112 Baltimore suburb
115 "La Gioconda" composer
116 "The Woman Who Strayed" opera
118 Holy Roman emperor crowned 962
119 Gentleman's give-up
120 Mice, to cats
121 Went astray
122 Dnieper tributary
123 Daly of "Judging Amy"
124 Play up
125 Kind of fit

DOWN

1 Like a fashion plate
2 "1984" superstate
3 Unlike 007's martini
4 Loads
5 Avoid ending
6 Moo goo ___ pan
7 Carp
8 Worshipped
9 Sojourn
10 Royal treasury
11 Aoki of the PGA
12 Helpful "Wizard of Oz" witch
13 Forward
14 Open a jacket, perhaps
15 The "you" of "Here's to you!"
16 Iris surrounding layer
17 Tendency
18 "What ___ can go wrong?"
24 Apocrypha book
26 Minister to
32 Bourg's department
33 Nor. neighbor
36 Smile
37 Poodle name
39 "The Kite Runner" boy
40 "The Fountainhead" author
41 1966 Batting champ
42 ___ Crunch cereal
43 Online periodical
45 Rigel, for one
48 Water closet
49 "Let ___ Me": Everly Brothers
51 Jerk
52 Hams it up
53 "It's ___ Unusual Day"
54 Cleave
56 Extinct ratite
57 Mtge. type
58 MLB stat
59 Female street urchin
60 Dada founder
61 Paris rapid transit org.
63 City north of Bombay
66 Br. military award
67 D.C. 100
68 "Some Like ___" (1959)
69 Puzzle pattern
70 Skull & Bones member
71 Feel ill
72 Cowboy great Renfro
76 Stalemate
77 Flying prefix
78 Camelot coat
79 Ballet bend
80 Shriek
81 Vietnam Memorial
82 Dueling sword
86 Greek peak
88 French lace city
90 Bygone old
91 What we all do
92 Sinatra's "Young ___"
93 Race official
94 Supercell spin-off
96 Gulf of Naples resort
97 French possessive
98 Slightest
99 Figure skater Albright
100 First Communion gift
101 Foot arch
104 Fiennes in "The English Patient"
106 Eel, for one
107 Speck
108 Tolkien creatures
109 Distinctive flair
110 Bat mitzvah, e.g.
113 Anon partner
114 Normandy river and town
117 It's kept behind bars

272 HEADLINE ABOUT . . . by Harvey Estes

"Good Morning Baltimore" is the opening number of 47 Across.

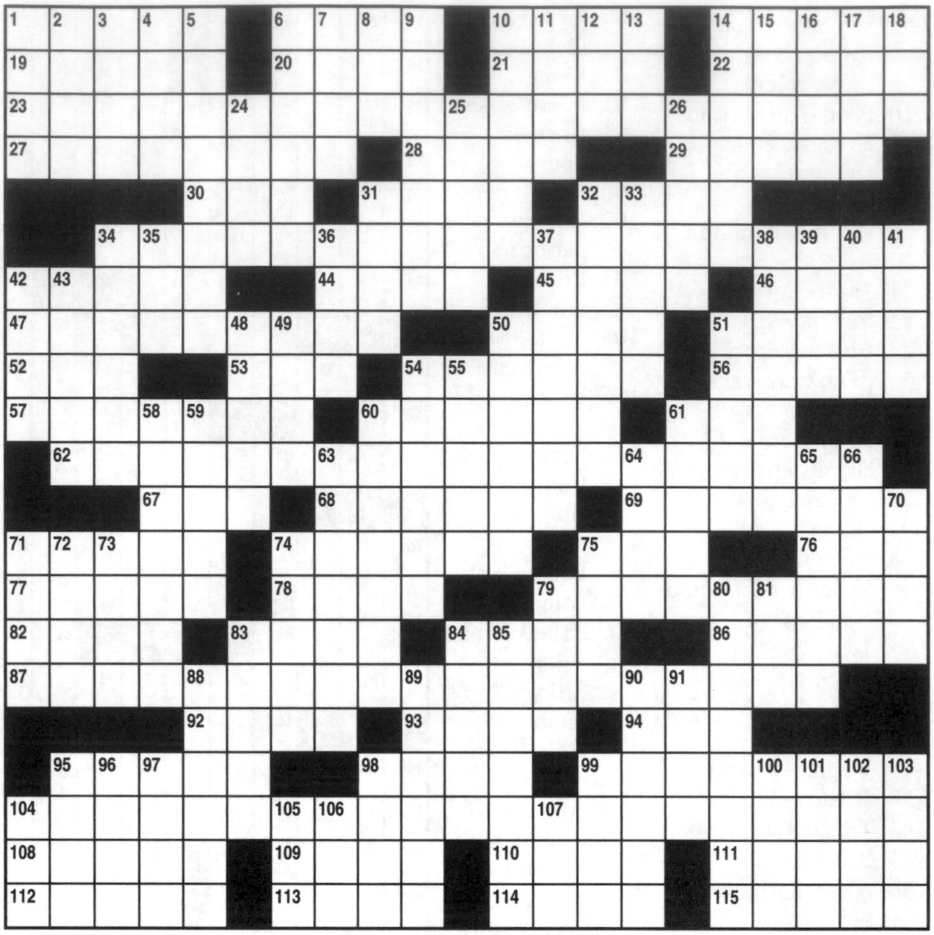

ACROSS

1 Koran focus
6 Hunting target
10 Give out
14 Cease-fire
19 Royal headpiece
20 Add to the staff
21 "___ inhumanity to . . ."
22 Summer program, often
23 . . . an Arkansas athlete supporting officials?
27 Constitution modifiers, e.g.
28 Dressy garments
29 Lent a hand to
30 "Bali ___"
31 Pseudo-esthetic
32 Hippies' homes
34 . . . a gangster's comeupance?
42 Look for
44 Flightless bird of Uruguay
45 Fathers' brothers, for short
46 Nape growth
47 Musical named for an aerosol
50 ___-à-porter
51 Church areas
52 Make sense, with "up"
53 Soft toss
54 Gardener's charges
56 Hungarian composer Franz
57 1956 Marilyn Monroe flick
60 Try to rip
61 Spring mo.
62 . . . a toon becoming a baseball scout?
67 ___ gratia artis
68 Francis or Dahl
69 Campus community
71 Ideal spots
74 "Tijuana Taxi" trumpeter
75 Pull a boner
76 By way of
77 Undeliverable letter
78 Have-not's condition
79 Taxpayer's ordeals
82 Les Etats-___
83 Toy boat spot
84 First 007 flick
86 Sheriff's band
87 . . . an idiot being put in charge?
92 Goes out with
93 Voice below soprano
94 Architect Maya ___
95 Saltine brand
98 Home of some bubbly
99 Arp and his ilk
104 . . . a rancher offering a defiant gesture?
108 Alaskan tongue
109 Baseball number
110 Greek sandwich
111 Brunei native
112 Fritter away
113 Chopped down
114 Lightly burn
115 Mall constituent

DOWN

1 Razor brand
2 "Schindler's List" star Neeson
3 Lounge (around)
4 "Star Trek" actor Eisenberg
5 Construction workers
6 Zhivago portrayer
7 Nervous twitches
8 Genesis vessel
9 Escape
10 Beginning stage
11 Nannies' cries
12 Corporation abbr.
13 Chiding sound
14 Statement of the obvious
15 Foxx of "Sanford and Son"
16 Dangle a carrot before
17 Fed a line
18 Nav. officer
24 Boo-Boo or Pooh
25 "I'm ___ here!"
26 Green sculptures
31 In need of a pain reliever
32 Clinton Chief of Staff Leon
33 S&L units
34 Proclaimed to be true
35 Geometric fig.
36 Middle East denizen
37 Basement fixture
38 Served as a game official
39 Talk trash
40 Don Juan's mother
41 "___ la vie!"
42 Melville captain
43 Roll tightly
48 Stratagems
49 Catch rodeo-style
50 Babysitter's employer
51 First in a series
54 Removed the rind from
55 Arrange in tiers
58 Unamplified, to guitarists
59 Short-winded
60 Undersea weapon
61 Capital of Ghana
63 Natural gifts
64 Popeye and Bluto
65 Bring up to date
66 Santos portrayer on "The West Wing"
70 Move carefully
71 "Y'all cut it out!"
72 Merrill in "Butterfield 8"
73 Sign over a door
74 Battery part
75 Switch ending
79 Prefix with China
80 Like an angry mob
81 Hudson in "Cars"
83 Song of praise
84 Mississippi plain
85 G and X, to movies
88 What the heirs split
89 Discussed, with "over"
90 Characteristic quality
91 Bona ___
95 French novelist Émile
96 Meadow moms
97 Isolated, with "off"
98 Top-flight
99 Explorer of Nickelodeon
100 "___ first you don't succeed . . ."
101 Missile holder
102 Former Russian ruler
103 Eye problem
104 Cornfield sound
105 Evidence type
106 Movie passes, informally
107 Coiffure color

273 ECLECTIC CHALLENGE by Clare Hansbrough

25 Down ironically appeared in the 1989 movie "High Stakes."

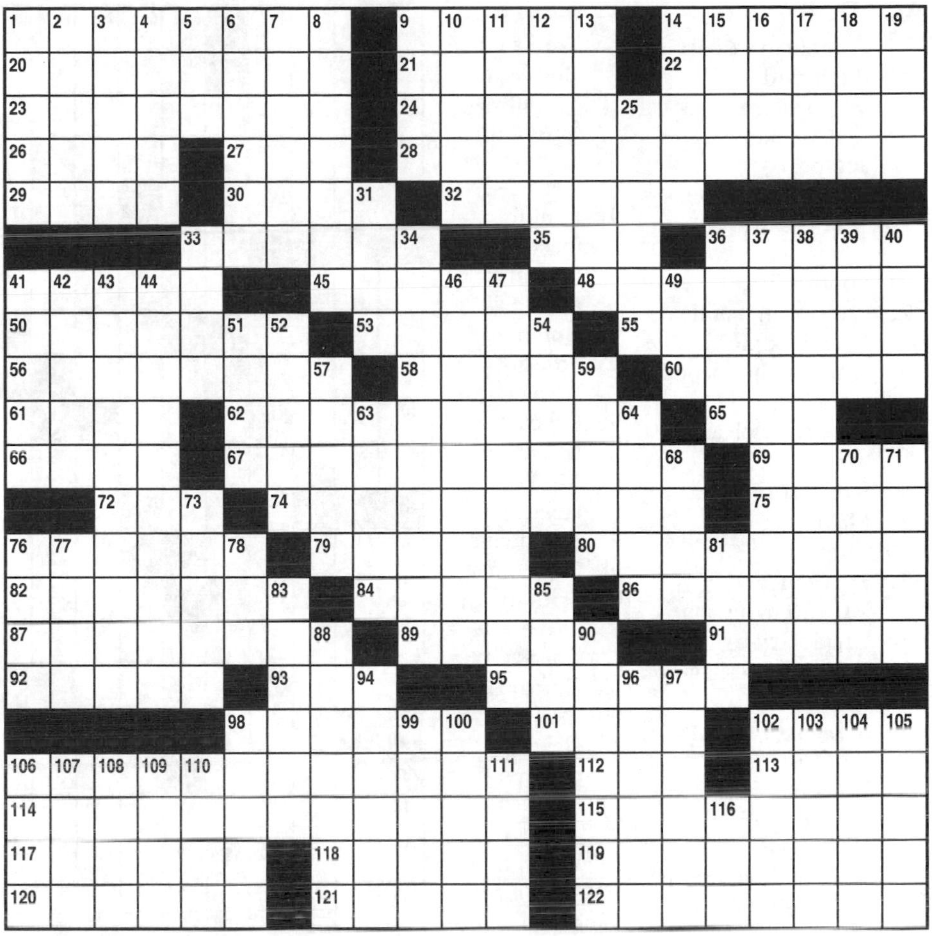

ACROSS

1 Hearts, for example
9 Around
14 Supreme Court aides
20 Ogled
21 Words before a time
22 Words to the flock
23 Give lip service to?
24 Rights
26 Linguist Chomsky
27 Pound sound
28 Home of Bert and Ernie
29 Omar in "The Mod Squad"
30 Hebrides island
32 Contaminate
33 Daffy companion
35 Night class subj.
36 "See ya!"
41 Jonah's three-day home
45 Hanger-on
48 Kahn in "Blazing Saddles"
50 Fixes spines
53 Conger catcher
55 Theater districts
56 Court crowd-pleaser
58 Loses luster
60 Oil producer
61 Made a case
62 Return requirements
65 Flyers org.
66 Fair
67 KFC fried-chicken recipe, e.g.
69 Bush and Clinton
72 Go off
74 Titanic and more
75 Pop singer from Nigeria
76 Stage offerings
79 Coming up
80 Paul in "Cinderella Man"
82 Love story
84 Place atop
86 Mesopotamia dweller
87 Comedian who inspired Billy Crystal
89 Blue material
91 Ball lofter
92 Fellas
93 Canal beast of burden
95 Simple chords
98 Split
101 Not tricked by
102 Serious sign
106 Welcome sight in an emergency
112 Social finish
113 Christmas musical prop
114 T.S. Eliot poem
115 Greyhound charges
117 "The Tatler" founder
118 Another time
119 "Interview With the Vampire" author
120 "Cheers!" and more
121 Linz cake
122 Safe havens

DOWN

1 "Star Wars" flick attacker
2 Man of morals
3 Rundown
4 Oil containers
5 Come together
6 Slow piece
7 Female prison guard
8 Going on and on
9 The heat
10 Crimson-clad
11 June portrayer
12 Port vessel
13 Particle theory
14 Take after
15 Trent of Mississippi
16 Islamic leader
17 French bank
18 Surrealist Paul
19 Pt. of DOS
25 Sarah Michelle of Buffy fame
31 On the safe side
33 Withhold
34 Thoroughly ingrained
36 Find out
37 Nevertheless
38 Turned on
39 Chimp in space
40 Staff symbol
41 Finishes filming
42 "You there?"
43 Mariner
44 Be inactive
46 School chum
47 Dardanelles' former name
49 Line across a cir.
51 Verb with thou
52 Rockets
54 German empire
57 "Beetle Bailey" character
59 Shoot
63 Ideal locations
64 Retro photo
68 Bygone leader
70 Lapel label
71 Rouen's river
73 Assigns a number
76 Bore
77 Kind of model
78 Bio., e.g.
81 Gullets
83 Naval standard
85 Actor Robert De ___
88 Forced hot-air
90 Hotel amenity for Verne Troyer?
94 Releases
96 Bring into harmony
97 Abstains, in brief
98 Bears
99 Chest opening?
100 Character part
102 Prairie State hub
103 "Sound of Music" character
104 Give a seat to
105 Rhinoplasty targets
106 Fleet
107 Words in a ratio
108 Emmy winner Perlman
109 Flock members
110 Intuited
111 Word in a New Year's song
116 Not agin

274 LETTERHEADS by Fred Piscop

. . . and they're all in alphabetic order!

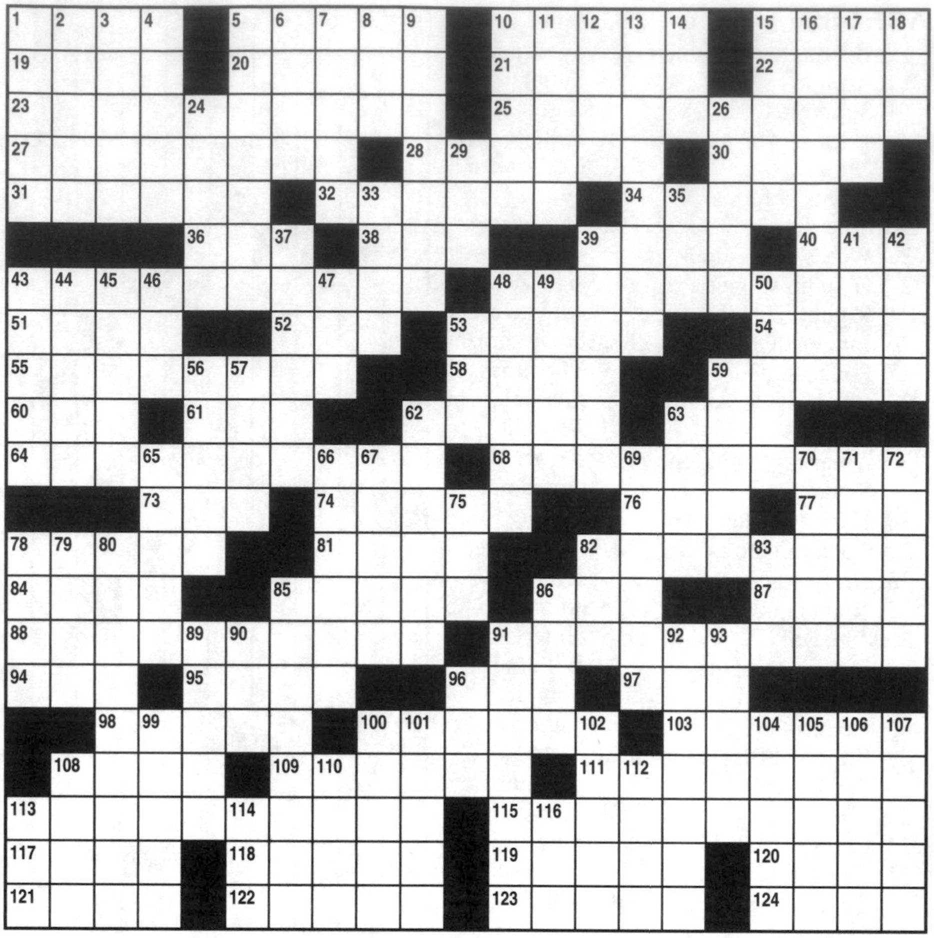

ACROSS

1 Prelude to a duel
5 Pitch card
10 Volvo alternatives
15 "Major Barbara" author
19 It's chopped liver
20 "Fra Diavolo" composer
21 Foolish folks
22 Prefix with nautical
23 Yearbook pic omitting the second string?
25 Relatively obscure song?
27 Summer time?
28 Mayo, e.g.
30 Chow
31 Types in
32 Valve-moving part
34 Greek New Ager
36 Don the feed bag
38 Made one
39 Saragossa's river
40 Warriors' org.
43 What hundreds are printed on?
48 Dealer in Normandy invasion memorabilia?
51 Home of Interstate H1
52 DHL rival
53 Traffic tieup cause
54 ___ cava
55 High-end Volkswagens
58 Suffix with myth
59 Screen bit
60 California's Big ___
61 Ltd., stateside
62 Babble away
63 Canal mule
64 Where to dump spam?
68 Close eye on a camera setting?
73 Caplet, e.g.
74 Diamond sides
76 ___ mater (brain cover)
77 It's impure
78 Pub order
81 Whales the tar out of
82 Film with dancing hippos
84 It's a crock
85 Works on a stud farm
86 ___ au vin
87 Sewed up
88 One-day-a-week fed?
91 Item for toasting the beginning of an attack?
94 Bummed
95 Full of streaks
96 Oil can letters
97 Mr. Potato Head appendage
98 Online mag
100 Tries to win
103 Driveway stones
108 Harrow rival
109 In need of clearing, perhaps
111 Piece of percussion
113 Worth of a certain Mac?
115 Maintenance man on a ski lift?
117 Awful-smelling
118 It's what's happening
119 Port of old Rome
120 Celestial spectacle
121 Looks over
122 Tales of derring-do
123 More despicable
124 From square one

DOWN

1 "The Maltese Falcon" sleuth
2 Pig language?
3 Treaty topic
4 Treaty topic
5 Mends, for a time
6 Valley of Essen
7 Wolf pack member
8 Subway Series player
9 Do well
10 Buffalo skater
11 Gold, e.g.
12 Atlas section
13 Lights out, to junior
14 Vane dir.
15 Leftovers holder
16 Relative humidity affects it
17 Current jumps
18 "Iron Chef" prop
24 Code name
26 Bocelli, for one
29 Mail order abbr.
33 Blows away
35 Some hangings
37 Joe Six-Pack's overhang
39 Aerie babe
41 Nota ___
42 Shrinking sea
43 Thicket of trees
44 Book after Micah
45 Butler's lady
46 Wimpy's payback time: Abbr.
47 Second ltr. addendum
48 Some joes
49 Mild maledictions
50 Walled city in Spain
53 Fallen orbiter
56 Mosaic worker
57 Like a backup file, maybe
59 Handle clumsily
62 Retailer J.C. ___
63 Board game turn
65 Backpedaler's words
66 Like a pigpen
67 Pageant wear
69 Clear as mud
70 Puccini classic
71 Gets blubbery
72 They may roll
75 Pothook shape
78 Mill input
79 Soprano Gluck
80 Four-time British prime minister
82 Egg ___ yung
83 Have the blahs
85 Oscilloscope curve
86 Guitarist Atkins
89 Beef cut
90 Mus. slowing
91 Bear, so to speak
92 VIP MC
93 Fireplace item
96 Ambulance chaser's advice
99 Model's asset
100 It follows a knockdown
101 "Golden Boy" playwright
102 Beats it
104 Noted phrase-turner
105 ___ a sour note
106 Chaucer traveler
107 Backbreaker?
108 Where to do your bidding
110 Soccer stadium cheers
112 Indy's Luyendyk
113 High dudgeon
114 ___ out (loaf)
116 Pack org.

275 "IT'S ACADEMIC!" by John Greenman

22 Across is in Milwaukee; 103 Across is in New Orleans.

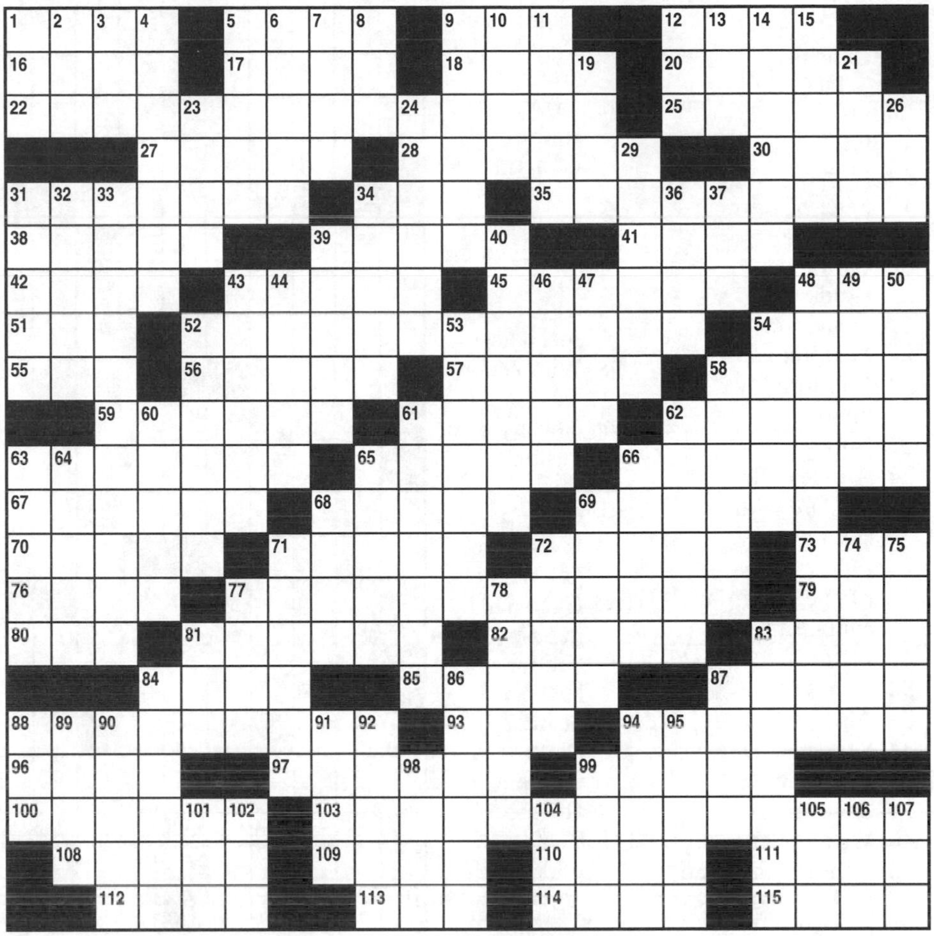

ACROSS

1 At any time
5 Alum
9 Way off
12 Lakelet
16 Italian cash
17 Put through a sieve
18 Roman war god
20 Of an eye part
22 Sensenbrenner Hall, for one?
25 Hyades locale
27 Coaxes
28 Apse structures
30 Divorce mecca
31 Visions
34 Upper-level coll. entry test
35 NYC campus cutups?
38 Zeniths
39 Common contraction
41 Cart
42 Grab (onto)
43 São ___, Brazil
45 Change for the better
48 Morticia, to Wednesday
51 Cochlea site
52 Student orientation, Greenville-style?
54 Washed-out
55 Sow's domain
56 Nom de plume, e.g.
57 Record of one year
58 Crowds
59 Kind of burner
61 Old European coin
62 Iran, once
63 Cleaning supplies
65 Leonine features
66 Verandas
67 Gilded, e.g.
68 Assigns roles
69 Buddhist doctrine
70 Bitter to the taste
71 Panfry
72 Arrange in rows
73 Cargo amts.
76 Surly
77 News scoops for "The Crimson"?
79 Pasture
80 Double curve
81 Tin alloy
82 Nobles
83 Building wings
84 Recherché
85 Conscript
87 No-see-ums
88 Raised at a Providence school?
93 NY horal system
94 Progress
96 Great Plains state
97 Gaucho's blanket: var.
99 Trunk
100 Amalgamates
103 St. Charles and South Claiborne Avenues?
108 Biblical witch's home
109 Joins a jury
110 Only fair
111 Malice
112 Multigenerational tale
113 Ellipsis element
114 Golf stroke
115 Say it isn't so

DOWN

1 Samara producer
2 By way of
3 Be off the mark
4 Dirgelike song
5 Shorthand system name
6 Baptisms, e.g.
7 Biblical book
8 Marginal grade
9 Conquered
10 "I smell ___!"
11 Summarize
12 Situate
13 Spawn
14 Of nerves
15 Venturesome one
19 Antitoxins
21 City in Sweden
23 Samovars
24 Clinton's gift to Rich
26 Poseidon's call
29 Eton or Harrow
31 Gurus
32 Virtuosity
33 Atlanta school's entrance exams?
34 Whoop-de-dos
36 Make a bundle
37 Magna ___ laude
39 What "to err" is
40 States of altered consciousness
43 Throbbed
44 Sign of the Ram
46 Lab equipment
47 Dictum
48 Huntington school ordinance?
49 Dated pop tune
50 Arizona flattops
52 Like vampires
53 Heckler
54 Fringe benefits
58 God of commerce
60 Gapple with a knot
61 Scoundrel
62 Mortgage fees
63 Alarm
64 Hocus-___
65 Purplish hue
66 Small bottle
68 Jinrikisha
69 Wide-awake
71 Lumberjacks, often
72 Toward the stern
74 Popular frat letter
75 Rakish
77 Rosemary, for one
78 Numb
81 Dutch oven
83 Supported
84 Landlocked African nation
86 Meal
87 Slash
88 Baby's dropcloth
89 Othello, to Olivier
90 "Buckeye Bullet" of track
91 Beanery sign
92 Celtic soothsayer
94 Boost
95 Grain disease
98 Chorister
99 Friends' pronoun
101 Weimaraner, e.g.
102 Murcia Mrs.
104 Clairvoyance
105 Prayer
106 Yang's companion
107 Foxy

276 SPORTS CENTER I by Harvey Estes

Clever cuts and double dribbles—NBA style.

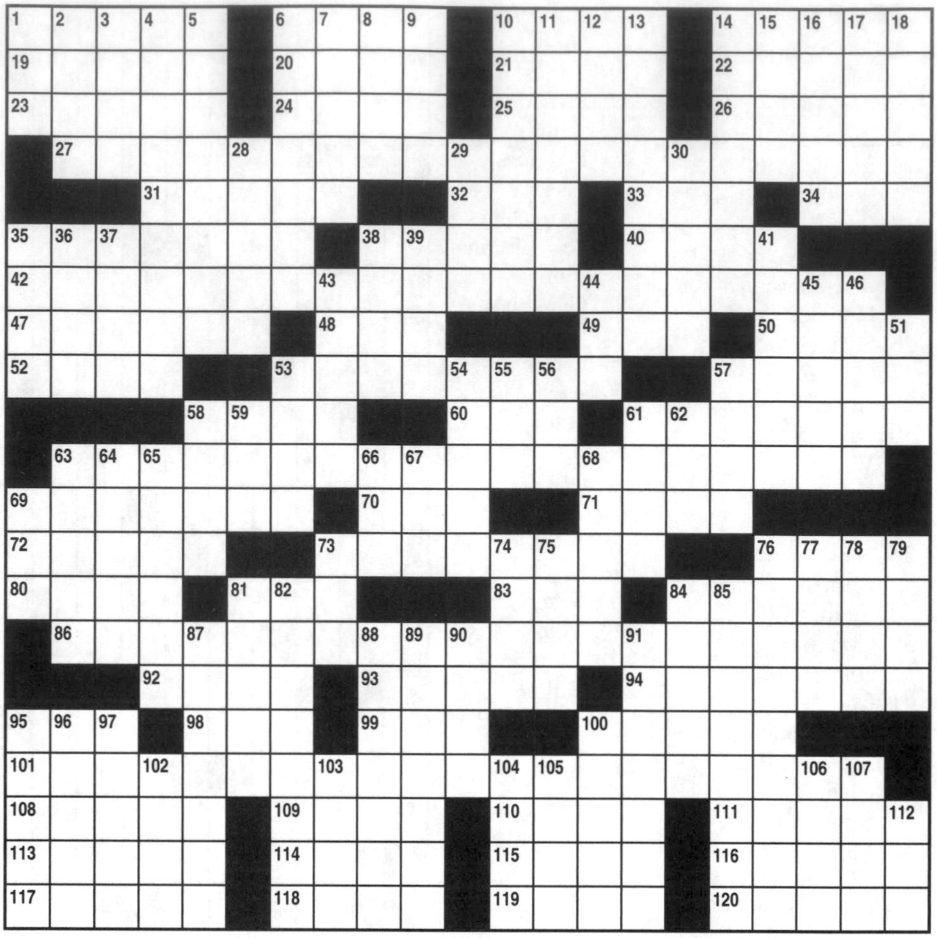

ACROSS

1 Dana of "MacGyver"
6 Lozenge
10 Pool exercise
14 Line of gab
19 Peter of Herman's Hermits
20 Cartoonist Goldberg
21 Tennis star Mandlikova
22 Comfortably inviting
23 Cul-___
24 Aussie colleges
25 Declare with certainty
26 Future oak
27 Magic cager pitted against a King?
31 Patton's vehicles
32 Hero ending
33 Alt. spelling
34 Service charge
35 On the loose
38 Shoestrings
40 Wedding exchange
42 Genius game plan in the Toyota Center?
47 Sign up
48 Net destination
49 Howe'er
50 Cry of frustration
52 Pfefferberg in "Schindler's List"
53 Unyielding
57 Film about Mexican painter Kahlo
58 Former Atlanta arena
60 Sci-fi contemporary of Ani
61 Pool wear
63 Cager finding an open man?
69 Bud and Colin
70 Hustle and bustle
71 Alpo alternative
72 Barbeque accessories
73 Sweepers' utensils
76 Guitarist Clapton
80 Tempest in a teapot
81 Infamous Amin
83 Pub offering
84 Woke up
86 Cager who went for the bronze?
92 NBA Hall-of-Famer Archibald
93 Come up
94 Damaged in battle
95 CPR specialist
98 Wimbledon unit
99 Ghostly pale
100 Pastor's flock
101 Cager's take-home pay?
108 Guadalajara good-bye
109 "Tell me ___ haven't heard!"
110 Class reunion attendee
111 Beef and pork
113 A-list notable
114 Explorer of Nickelodeon
115 Old Italian money
116 Banana oil, e.g.
117 Running total
118 Pt. of AAA
119 Pencil filler
120 Court employee

DOWN

1 Purpose
2 Big name in theaters
3 ___ Nostra
4 Daughter of Nicholas
5 Reworks, as a course of action
6 Tipsy
7 Ladder steps
8 Memorial announcer
9 Cuban coin
10 Algonquian tribe member
11 Most like a perm
12 Don Juan's mom
13 "Pistol Pete" of basketball
14 Caviar variety
15 Somewhat, in music
16 "See ya!"
17 Like Stephen King stories
18 Paul of "Hollywood Squares"
28 Iron bar
29 Shaving mishap
30 Ham's medium
35 Throat clearer
36 Collette of "In Her Shoes"
37 Rest in a conversation
38 Manor head
39 Human rights org.
41 Naps noisily
43 Cube creator
44 Sault ___ Marie
45 Scold mildly
46 Biblical witch's home
51 West. alliance
53 Difficult obligation
54 Bomb squad machine
55 Aladdin's monkey
56 Nervous twitch
57 Own (up to)
58 Big-eyed birds
59 Adjusted prefix
61 Sauna bath sites
62 Dawber of "Mork and Mindy"
63 Take care of a spill
64 "If only!"
65 Reveals true feelings
66 Mer contents
67 Mag. execs
68 Longtime Mets announcer Ralph
69 Pressure meas.
73 Social reformer Dorothea
74 Handles roughly
75 Burn alleviator
76 Type of syndrome
77 Debtor's car, maybe
78 Body passageway
79 Toe woe
81 ICBM part
82 Pepsi One, for one
84 IHOP, for one
85 Broadcast news
87 Passes with care
88 Cutting-edge jobs
89 Like Titania and Oberon
90 Mudville team
91 Was overrun
95 Put into law
96 Jason's wife
97 Trouser material
100 Dern of "Jurassic Park"
102 Rocker Billy
103 "Dukes of Hazzard" deputy
104 Hard to believe
105 "Night" writer Wiesel
106 Scandal suffix
107 British carbine
112 Sellout initials

277 SPORTS CENTER II by Harvey Estes

Snappy slapshots and deft dekes—NHL style.

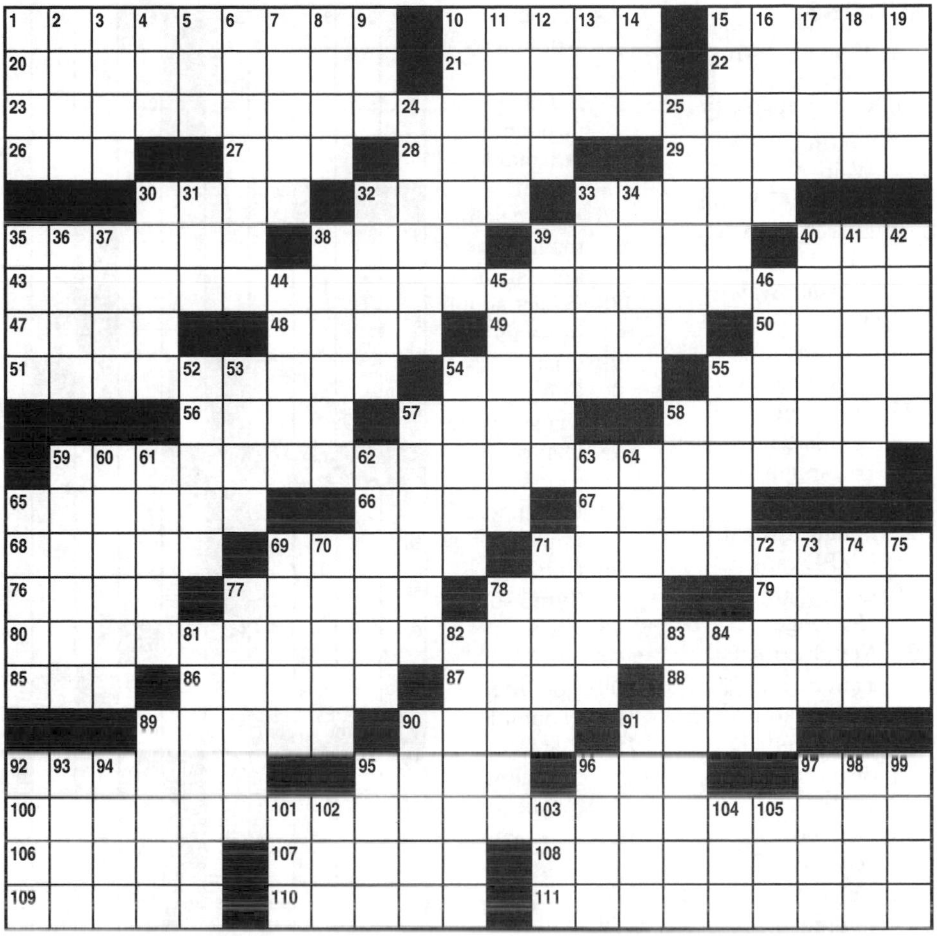

ACROSS

1 Rafah locale
10 "The Republic" writer
15 Classic toothpaste
20 Glaciers
21 Sci-fi maid, maybe
22 Also-ran
23 Texas puckster playing in the West Bank?
26 Pic blow-up
27 Auto racer Fabi
28 Anthem opening
29 Water rompers
30 ". . . gyre and gimble in the ___": Carroll
32 Hit flies
33 Woodwind instruments
35 Richards of "Jurassic Park"
38 R.E.M.'s "The ___ Love"
39 Wolf's warning
40 Dollar divs.
43 Progress by a D.C. puckster?
47 Pump name in Canada
48 C&W's McEntire
49 Thin soup
50 Round buyer's words
51 Cough medicine amounts
54 Highly-polished
55 Quintain rhyme scheme
56 Hurler Hershiser
57 Kind of point
58 Oozed out
59 Militant New York puckster?
65 Informal truce talk
66 Very French
67 "You betcha!"
68 Come after
69 "A League of ___ Own"
71 Rob Reiner's mock rock band
76 Cause a jaw to drop
77 Grove components
78 Barbers' challenges
79 "Not that!"
80 Impervious to an Alberta offense?
85 "___ changed man!"
86 Hot-blooded
87 Baltic Sea tributary
88 Daring exploits
89 Readies for release
90 Yale grads
91 "___ match?"
92 Straw-colored
95 Voting unit
96 Year in Madrid
97 Carrier to Swed.
100 Western puckster who excels at golf?
106 Put in office
107 West Side Story heroine
108 Nonviolent shooter
109 Tickle pink
110 "By the ___ Get to Phoenix"
111 IOU holders

DOWN

1 "The Immoralist" novelist
2 Open ___ of worms
3 Georgia statesman Miller
4 Manual communication syst.
5 Refrain syllable
6 Treaty subject
7 Watch again
8 Words after stick
9 Pro bono TV ad
10 Run-of-the-mill
11 Yogurt choice
12 Columnist Van Buren
13 It tests the water
14 Giant Mel
15 Sibling's threat
16 Pound and Poe
17 New York tennis stadium
18 At no time, poetically
19 Octopus abundance
24 Ivanhoe's lady love
25 "Yay, team!"
30 Cowboy's cry
31 Darth, as a boy
32 Uppity folks
33 Burger topper
34 Bonkers
35 Knocks for a loop
36 Harsh sound
37 Playground comeback
38 Verdi opera
39 Mischievous imp
40 Party offering
41 Tree fall call
42 Golf great Sam
44 Watery porridge
45 Can't stomach
46 Comedian George
52 Like some checking accounts
53 Become threadbare
54 On the wagon
55 State Farm rival
57 Tomei of "What Women Want"
58 Uzi relative
59 Little chicken
60 Sci-fi author Le Guin
61 Thrown with force
62 Hard as nails
63 Nas, e.g.
64 Off the mark
65 "GoodFellas" star Joe
69 Lovers' lane event
70 Tests the weight of
71 Bumps and bruises
72 Mucho
73 Just one of those things
74 Beheaded Boleyn
75 Poker prizes
77 Making level
78 Italian family of art patrons
81 Spaghetti spec
82 Hawaiian island
83 "Oops!"
84 Wimbledon unit
89 Dead-on
90 Borden bovine
91 Grimm guardian
92 Hightail it
93 Lounge around
94 On a cruise, say
95 Wall of earth
96 Thickening agent
97 Kind of wrestling
98 "This guy walks into ___ . . ."
99 Payroll IDs
101 911 respondent
102 "A Man and a Woman" composer
103 Letters on the Enterprise
104 Dernier ___ (last word)
105 Back muscle, for short

278 SUPERMAN by Reggie Evers

Reggie's grid design inspired this title.

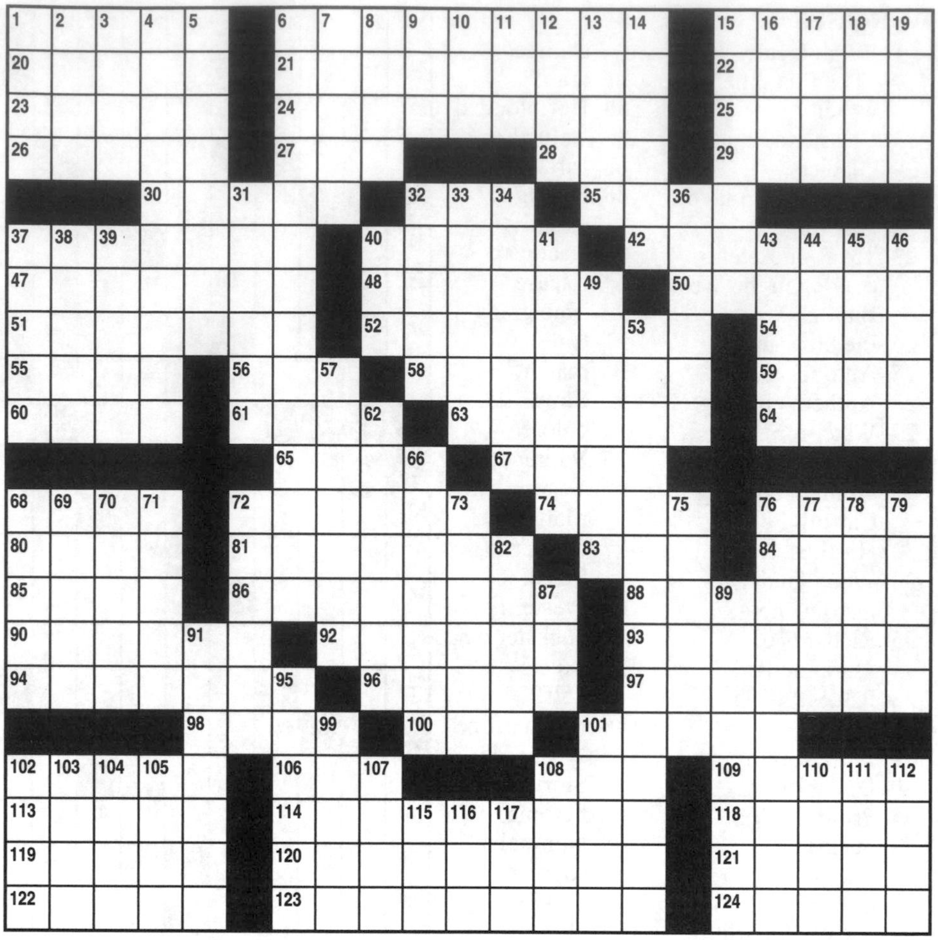

ACROSS

1 "Sound of Music" surname
6 WHAT THIS IS
15 Getting on
20 Weird
21 Old English coin
22 Drive in Beverly Hills?
23 Pleasant way to walk
24 Where some diplomats work
25 Free from confusion
26 Late-night host's family
27 Fanciful story
28 NYPD rank
29 On ___ (by challenge)
30 Metallic man
32 Jean or Jacques
35 Bank stamp abbr.
37 Advanced discussion-group course
40 Gauchos' accessories
42 Carrier who comes round daily
47 Skintight outfit
48 Sound setup
50 Like some bonds
51 Painting people
52 PSI measurer
54 Looking down
55 "___ and Day" (1988 hit)
56 Suitable
58 Running back's malady
59 Arch type
60 Prizms and Metros
61 Cy Young Award winner Saberhagen
63 Taj Mahal employee
64 11/11 honorees
65 Singing brothers
67 Spanish crowd?
68 British maid
72 Blood designation
74 Head set?
76 Intestinal parts
80 Commanded
81 Cotton's bane
83 Corker
84 ". . . that would have ___ a member": Groucho
85 Adaptable aircraft
86 Where some magazines are issued
88 Forget about, in a way
90 Cast
92 Falling-shapes game
93 Clairol product
94 Dutch post-impressionist
96 Crashed
97 Syrup source
98 Techie's client
100 Rod divs.
101 Is durable
102 Flame throwing, maybe
106 A.A. Milne character
108 ___-jongg
109 Hall-of-Fame Brave
113 Fight division
114 Different
118 Fancy flapjack
119 Present time
120 View from Calabria
121 '50s Pirates slugger
122 Trimmed the lawn
123 WHAT THIS IS
124 In good shape

DOWN

1 Jimmy or jack
2 Old Scandinavian letter
3 ___ angle (tilted)
4 They might not be in order
5 Images
6 Pater Noster
7 ___ up (overact)
8 River to the North Sea
9 Curator's deg.
10 Graphics file format
11 Paul or Brown
12 Earl's wife in "Neighbors"
13 Look of loathing
14 Gambler's claim to winning
15 Santa Anita race track site
16 Winner's medal
17 Brain trust offering
18 Dear's partner
19 Cause for an R-rating
31 A screwdriver may be on it
32 Untagged, in tag
33 1993 AL batting champ John
34 Ann-___ ("Bye Bye Birdie" actress)
36 Profession
37 Faddish language
38 Otherworldly
39 Rhode Island's is "Hope"
40 Explorer's org.
41 Lobsters, e.g.
43 D. Paterson's title in 2007
44 Combine companies
45 On ___ (cutting down)
46 April and June
49 Defeat in the long jump, say
53 Takes one's turn without hesitation
57 Hoo-ha or brouhaha
62 Soap boxes?
66 Too good to be true
68 "Dr. Phil" venue
69 Yoga leader
70 Prettify
71 Enter over
72 Bluegrass sounds
73 Trumpeted
75 Valkyries' props
76 Social director, of a sort
77 Heads up
78 Cushy course
79 "It's ___ in the right direction"
82 Goes wrong
87 Old streaker
89 Haberdashers' items
91 ___ Knee (Dee Brown topic)
95 Kind of couplet
99 Revolving part
101 Kind of printer
102 1948 Chemistry Nobelist Tiselius
103 Crucifix
104 Communicated using notes
105 In bygone times
107 "Horrors!"
108 Soy-based Japanese soup
110 Brand of contact lens solution
111 Golf or tennis championship
112 Campus misfit
115 Dusseldorf dessert
116 Coll. mentors
117 Vane dir.

279 OPTIONS EXPIRATIONS by Bonnie L. Gentry

Where have all the bears and bulls gone?

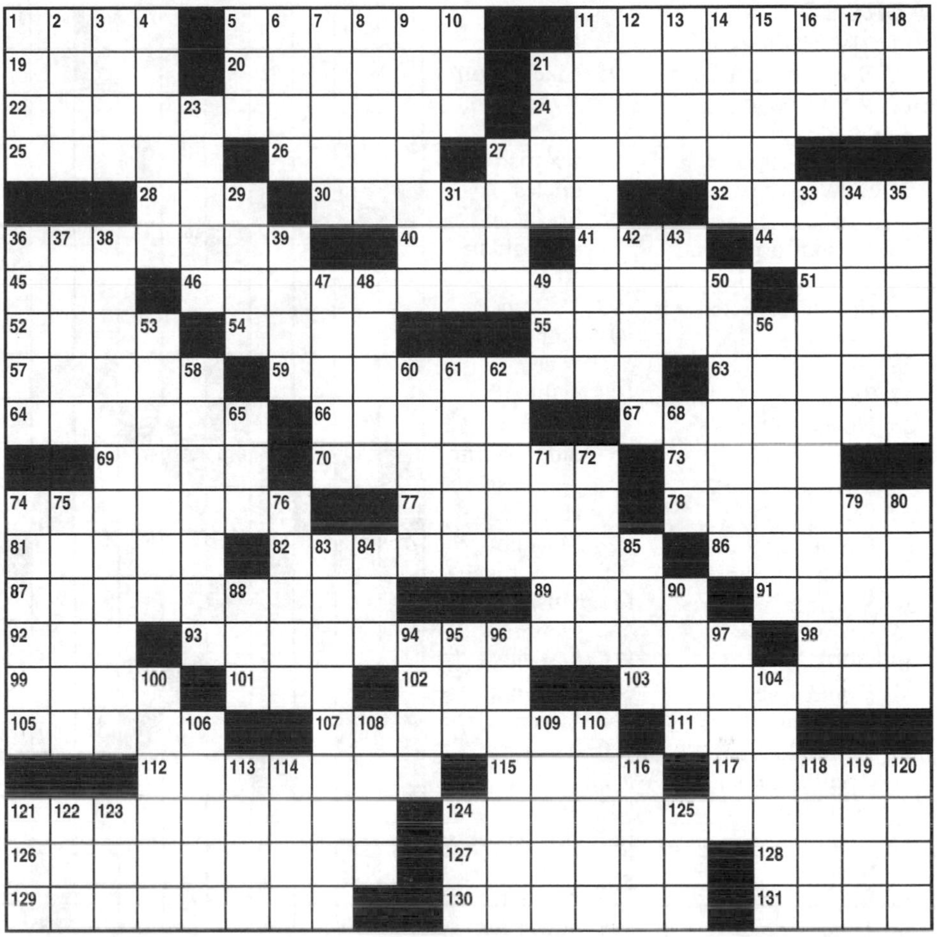

ACROSS

1 Seashore scavenger
5 Oil industry leaders
11 Acrobatic feat
19 Kofi Annan's middle name
20 Key without sharps or flats
21 Drummed out
22 Ristorante entrée
24 Inclined to be bold
25 Walk laterally
26 Bausch & Lomb brand
27 Powerful combos
28 Part of VSOP
30 Firefighter, at times
32 Miles and Wang
36 Printer's layout
40 Summer setting at the NYSE
41 "Calling all cars" letters
44 Quotable Yankee
45 Org. for court figures
46 What a snake oil salesman might have
51 Mined-over matter?
52 Rose passed him
54 Gin flavor
55 Inveigher
57 Some brass
59 Whitsunday
63 Conclude from the evidence
64 Stop, as a flow
66 Inscribed monument
67 Common cleanser
69 O'Hara estate
70 Capable of being stretched
73 Half of oct-
74 Renowned
77 Onetime NFLer
78 Wall Street type
81 Town ordinance
82 Assimilates anew
86 Part of a subway entrance
87 Taking for granted
89 Move merchandise
91 Suffix with opal or fluor
92 Airline that filed for bankruptcy in Oct. 2004
93 Sachems
98 Maria of the Met
99 Word command
101 Neighbor of Libya: Abbr.
102 Ding-a-ling
103 Truck stop sign
105 They may get a licking after dinner
107 Spoke wrongly
111 Diminutive
112 "The Cup of Tea" painter
115 FBI guy
117 VAT part
121 Dynast
124 Barney Fife, for one
126 For the time being
127 Part of E. I. du Pont
128 Pony's gait
129 Momentarily dazzling
130 Perform major surgery
131 Gas company with toy trucks

DOWN

1 Gund Arena hoopsters
2 East Coast hwy.
3 Tiny amount
4 It may be stuffed in a box
5 Bogart's "Key Largo" costar
6 Mythical matchmaker
7 More mature
8 Cat-___-tails
9 Abstainer
10 Mr., in Madras
11 Union negotiation topics
12 Mgr.'s aide
13 Work on a wad of gum
14 Bolshoi rival
15 Fashion designer Johnson
16 Verdi aria "___ tu"
17 Where Harry Reid is a Sen.
18 50's political monogram
21 Prop for Dr. House
23 Monica of tennis
27 Production
29 Forehead-slapper cries
31 What leads to an F
33 What a debatable point leaves
34 "No argument here"
35 ___ Mist (7 Up rival)
36 Munich and Warsaw
37 ~, mathematically
38 Professor's time out, say
39 Touch
42 Early Brits
43 Arg. neighbor
47 Verb for thou
48 Busybody
49 Tempest in a teapot
50 Carpenters, at times
53 1971 Woody Allen film
56 Tuition classification
58 Bungle
60 Potato sack wt., maybe
61 Adamson's "Forever Free: ___ Pride"
62 Home of the Ramses Hilton
65 Flying Solo
68 Justice Dept. staffer
71 Cocoon creator
72 Set firmly
74 Site of the Sun Bowl
75 Pestle's partner
76 Fife flourish
79 Dana in "The Nude Bomb"
80 Joaquin's "Walk the Line" costar
83 Hard to figure out
84 CIA operative
85 Old dagger
88 Bygone relative of the kiwi
90 20-20, e.g.
94 MIT part: Abbr.
95 Pedicurist's target
96 Stand with shelves
97 Forbes of Forbes
100 Tertiary Period segment
104 Family life, figuratively
106 ___ Domingo
108 Agenda detail
109 Ascribes
110 Pop singer Taylor
113 End for hip or hoop
114 Calcutta attire
116 Tiny time unit: Abbr.
118 Old Milano moola
119 ET airmada
120 Small salamanders
121 Kitchen spray
122 Laudatory lines
123 Chickadee relative
124 Corp. board member
125 Irritated (with "up")

280 BLOC-HEADS by Ed Early

Hopefully the sector below is disenfranchised.

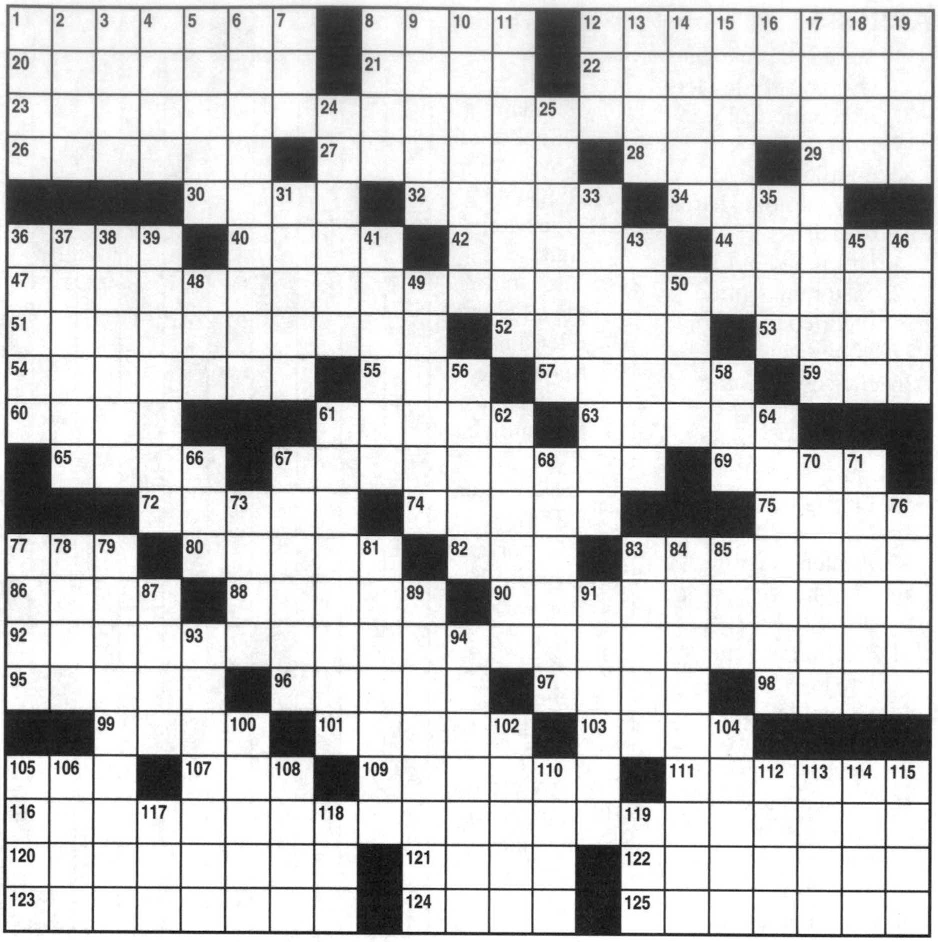

ACROSS

1 "1984" country
8 Scandinavian saint
12 Wrote verse
20 Shades of yellow-pink
21 Suave skunk Le Pew
22 Person-to-person
23 **Wry remark about the electorate: Part 1**
26 Iron deficiency
27 Ta-tas
28 Never, to Hans
29 "Star Trek: Voyager" role
30 "No ___!" ("Nothing to it!")
32 Hobbyist's knife
34 Salinger title girl
36 Seized item
40 2,051
42 Diving duck
44 Flip over
47 **Remark: Part 2**
51 Apply subtlety to gain an edge
52 One of the Seven Sages
53 Ethereal prefix
54 Tunes
55 Russian car
57 Dost observe
59 Music genre
60 Oscar Robertson's nickname
61 Sausage
63 Draw ___ on (aim at)
65 Like some misses
67 **Remark: Part 3**
69 Barcelona structure
72 ___ dozen (cheap)
74 Daybreaks
75 Russell in "Captain Ron"
77 ". . . we gotta go, ___ my-o"
80 Hoodlums
82 Butter-and-sugar unit
83 TV's "One Day ___"
86 Big name in pet food
88 Waits at the light
90 Needlework pro?
92 **Remark: Part 4**
95 Like a foon
96 Word form of "nine"
97 Scottish uncles
98 Socks on sale, often: Abbr.
99 1/8 ounce
101 Faints (with "over")
103 "Dilbert" character
105 Santos saint
107 ___ Vashem Holocaust Museum
109 More musty
111 Music store section
116 **Source of remark: Taken ___**
120 American dugouts
121 Statute
122 How snorers sleep
123 Plunders
124 Suffix for young
125 Tempers steel

DOWN

1 Employee-safety org.
2 "Freebie and the Bean" star
3 Dakota Fanning's sister
4 Radio letters
5 Stiff penalty?
6 As one
7 Suffix for malt
8 Thomas Friedman's page
9 Pope Victor II's predecessor
10 Mollify
11 Egyptian fishing boats
12 School of whales
13 ". . . ___ you noblest English!": Shak.
14 Start of a kid's counting rhyme
15 Does the math
16 Itemized bill: abbr.
17 Safari park guide
18 Berlin duck
19 GPA spoilers
24 Casals and Picasso
25 ___ Unidos
31 Stage direction for "all"
33 Springs further
35 Film-rating org.
36 Compass point
37 Enter gradually
38 Solemn promise
39 Empty a hold
41 "How's the fire?" answer?
43 "Friends" character
45 Tiber tributary
46 Social outcast
48 Depart
49 Mirror graffiti in "The Shining"
50 Bay State motto word
56 Part of YWCA
58 Pencil-game word
61 Chain breaker
62 Prospered
64 Marshall Thompson TV series
66 Slugger's swing
67 Borrower
68 Holding the bag
70 Swain
71 Big name in meat
73 American naturalist (1838–1914)
76 U. of Maryland athletes
77 Miss Kitty's friend
78 PTA milieu
79 Symbols of welcome
81 "Keystone Kops" creator Mack
83 Summits
84 Gets drunk
85 "The Ice Storm" director Lee
87 Open-court hearing
89 Conn men
91 Mustang competitor
93 In the recent past
94 Largest flatfish
100 Ornamental evergreen
102 Sundial pointer
104 Kline in "Dave"
105 Dirty Harry's org.
106 Luyendyk of racing fame
108 Use an épée
110 Bavarian river
112 Omniscient
113 Sarah McLachlan hit
114 Vex
115 TV Tarzan's kin
117 Pail partner
118 Forerunner of the CIA
119 Genetic stuff

281 SALTBOXES by Alan Olschwang

Examples of New England colonial houses will not be seen below.

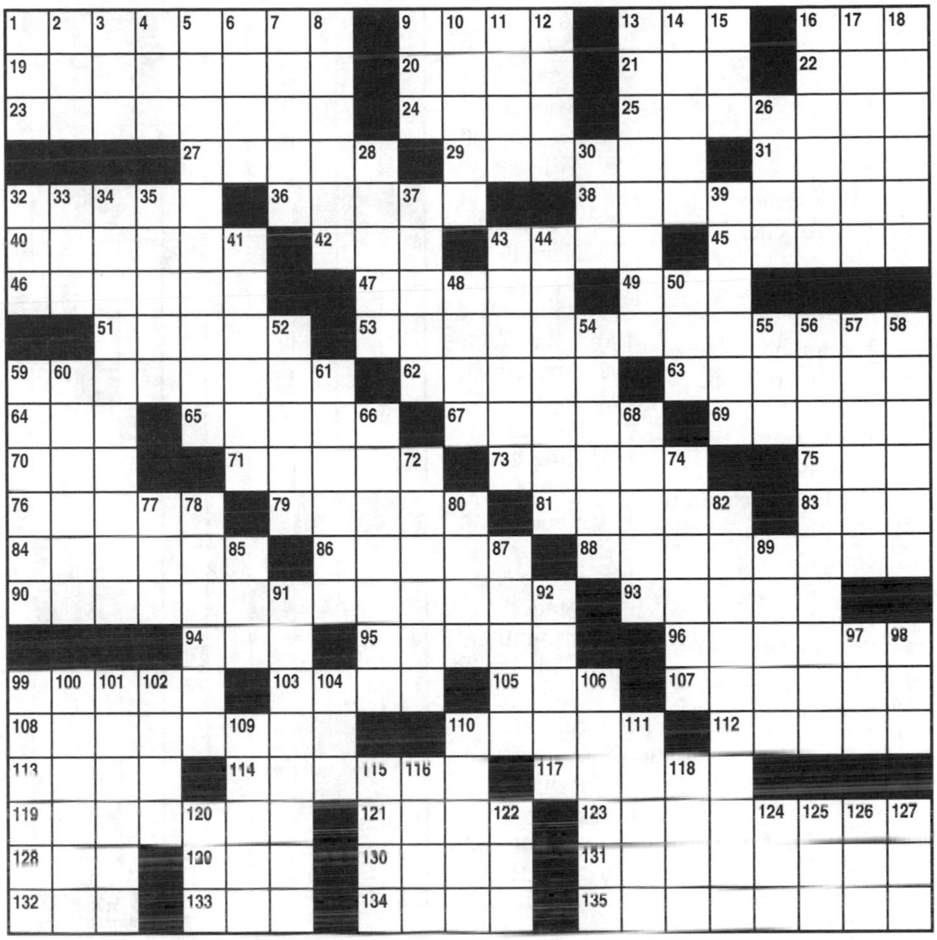

ACROSS

1 Treadwheel runners
9 Memory unit
13 Mounty
16 CST, MST, ___
19 Tree-dwelling
20 Get dirty
21 Formerly
22 Letter from Patrai
23 Like flotsam
24 Atmosphere
25 Deli devices
27 Gets one's attention, in a way
29 Kind of control
31 New Haven seniors
32 Shiraz native
36 Arrests
38 Adirondacks resort
40 Parental admonition
42 Reagan Era acronym
43 Red Sea vessel
45 More modern
46 Bacchante
47 "___ jolly swagman . . ."
49 Bonavena's 1970 opponent
51 Shackles
53 Unique
59 Conclusions
62 Growing outward
63 Ukraine peninsula
64 Shem's brother
65 Doldrums
67 "Paint Your Wagon" song girl
69 Accumulate
70 Bread buy
71 French states
73 Adolescents
75 C. Rice's former org.
76 Cordage fiber
79 Indian lute
81 Made a new hole
83 Average grade
84 Great deals
86 Star-crossed lover
88 "The Way We Were" opener
90 Historic building in Salt Lake City
93 Holy water holder
94 Poet kicked in "I Am the Walrus"
95 Swashbuckler Flynn
96 Bacon products
99 Enchantress of Greek mythology
103 Costner or Stack role
105 City on the Danube
107 Took ten
108 2005 Peter Mullan film
110 Adams and Brickell
112 Harvard ___
113 Provides a crew
114 "Oedipus" composer
117 Tina in "Waterworld"
119 Mosque tower
121 Mail
123 Fissure
128 "Exodus" hero Ben Canaan ___
129 CBS reporter Bob
130 Opera solo
131 No place for a bull
132 Congress mem.
133 Former governor of Algiers
134 Dollars for quarters
135 Piths

DOWN

1 Possesses
2 "Chances ___": Mathis
3 Executive's deg.
4 Sort of story
5 Havana cabaret
6 Architect of crosswords
7 Break ___ (defect)
8 Winter woes
9 Order of the Arrow org.
10 Part of a letter closer
11 Swing ring
12 It overthrew Babylonia
13 Mary Ann Summers, for one
14 He leers
15 Taro dish
16 Undergrad major
17 Thornbird
18 Quarterback, often
26 Last Supper room
28 Words of agreement
30 Bilbao bear
32 Big Blue
33 Short-story award
34 Wind gauge
35 Hirschfeld hidings
37 High point
39 "Peer Gynt" dancer
41 Channel swimmer Gertrude
43 Ready water for drinking
44 More speedy
48 Sugar source
50 DMV doc.
52 Acts as usher
54 Be suitable for, old style
55 Alastair in "School for Scoundrels"
56 Free from slavery
57 Renter
58 Roman symbol of power
59 Sacramental oil
60 Stops, as a ship
61 "The Killer Angels" author
66 Disco lights
68 El Misti's range
72 "Three's Company" actress
74 Fort of Charleston Harbor
77 Escape
78 Romeo or Juliet
80 Author Earl ___ Biggers
82 Clingy crustacean
85 Hostess ___ Balls
87 In high spirits
89 Charlotte's dessert?
91 57 Down et al.
92 "Dallas" matriarch
97 Still
98 Weathermen forerunner: Abbr.
99 Two in 1,000,000?
100 "Ninotchka" actress
101 Enzyme used in making cheese
102 Sala holder
104 Hurricane component
106 Threaten
109 Green tractor
110 Microscopy dye
111 Some underclassmen
115 Work with Rocky
116 Pippin part
118 Island wreaths
120 Reel partner
122 Psych exam
124 Heavy weight
125 M. Leinart's alma mater
126 Riddle-me-___
127 Romulans, to Kirk

282 24/7 by Billie Truitt

4 Down was first cultivated by the Incas.

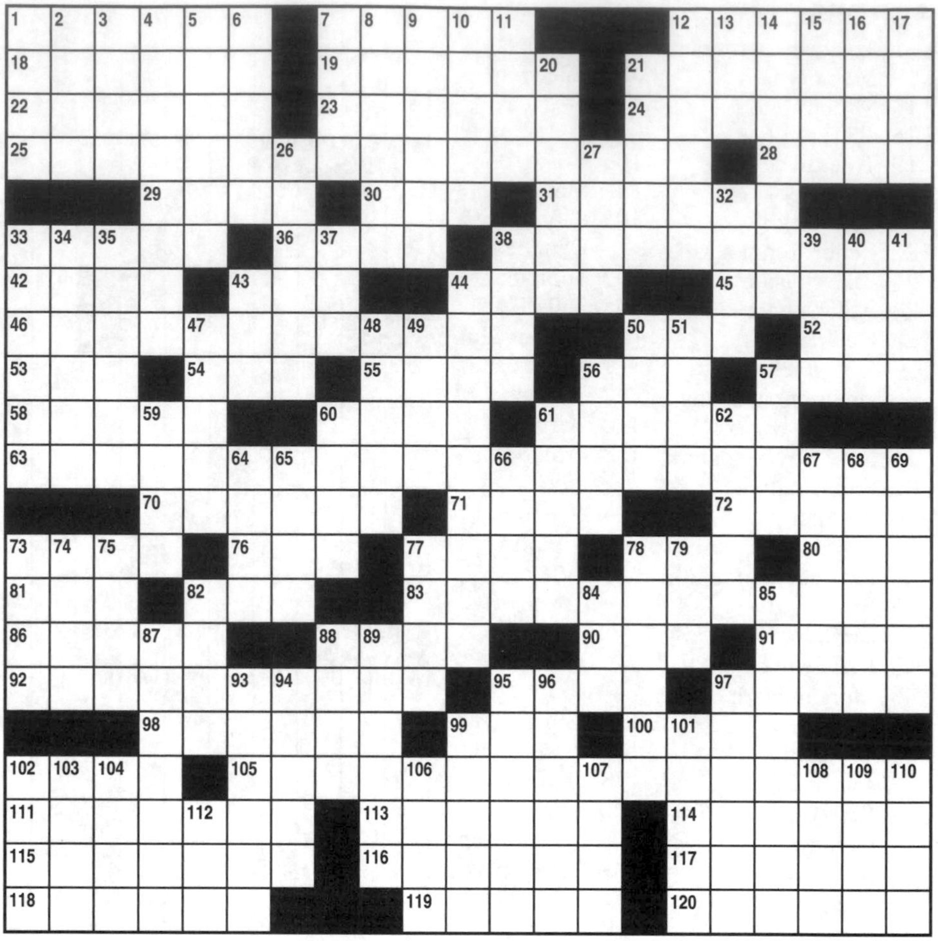

ACROSS

1 Make airtight
7 Dixie side dish
12 Lying face up
18 Surfing, in a way
19 Nutcase
21 More speedy
22 Lack of energy
23 Graceful antelope
24 Mythical beast
25 24
28 Natural healer
29 "___ there, done that"
30 Letter from Greece
31 Worthy goals
33 Wickerwork willow
36 Bubble bath contents
38 7
42 Grandma
43 Spy org.
44 Yours and mine
45 Original
46 7
50 Jazz reed
52 Altar in the Southern sky
53 Student's email letters
54 Stout relative
55 Inborn talent
56 First of three X's
57 500-mile race
58 Rock of comedy
60 Apple products
61 Mediterranean arm
63 24
70 Object of Jason's quest
71 Batting stats
72 Foul spirit
73 Frozen dessert chain
76 Mary Kay of cosmetics
77 Far from shore
78 Scary word?
80 "Either you do it, ___ will"
81 Corn unit
82 Vinyl collection
83 7
86 Quickly
88 Diner sign
90 Sound of contentment
91 Village Voice award
92 7
95 British actress Nell
97 Military bigwigs
98 "A Streetcar Named Desire" role
99 Battery size
100 Cain's father
102 Amateurish
105 24
111 Pie vegetable
113 How some games end
114 Vietnamese port
115 "Love Me Tender" inspiration
116 "This I gotta hear!"
117 Stir up
118 Au naturel (with "in")
119 Emerald, essentially
120 "Old Rough and Ready"

DOWN

1 Take to the cleaners
2 Sicilian resort town
3 Yankee or Mariner, briefly
4 Succotash ingredient
5 Peacemaker
6 "___ Porridge Hot"
7 Key with two flats, briefly
8 Accelerated, with "up"
9 Enters
10 Miss America's headwear
11 Garage event
12 Summer shoe
13 Wire service initials
14 "Blue Period" painter
15 Adored one
16 Fictional Wolfe
17 Sea eagle
20 Comparatively crafty
21 Like a legal pad
26 Not outdoors
27 Harem rooms
32 Short-tailed wildcat
33 Batting next
34 Greeted
35 Protect, in a way
37 Motor City org.
38 Check for fingerprints
39 They say he was Terrible
40 Unlikely party animal
41 Dispatch, as a dragon
43 Pt. of a V-8
44 Less-busy time
47 Flip-chart stand
48 Playing marble
49 In clover
50 Communicate manually
51 Passed with flying colors
56 Herbal array
57 Memo opening
59 A bit doubtful
60 "How ___?"
61 Like pond scum
62 Optional accessory
64 Harvest
65 Short meeting?
66 Winnebago owner
67 Slide subject
68 English folk dance
69 Licorice-like seeds
73 Eye drop
74 Guitarist's accessory
75 Stoker who wrote "Dracula"
77 Blows away
78 Swahili sirs
79 Sound of wonder
82 Hot cross bun season
84 Bad hair ___
85 Quiet period before the eruption
87 Hotel reception feature
88 Pueblo pot
89 Undisturbed
93 Talmud language
94 "Can you believe that!"
95 Ankle protector
96 With great caution
97 Split ingredient
99 Let up
101 ". . . I ___ my way"
102 Babysitter's challenge
103 Nope
104 "You bet!"
106 Radio dial
107 Secluded valley
108 Sandbox toy
109 Taken with
110 Bavarian river
112 Like

283 WORKING STIFFS by Fran & Lou Sabin

If you think the world is your oyster, take a job as a 25 Across.

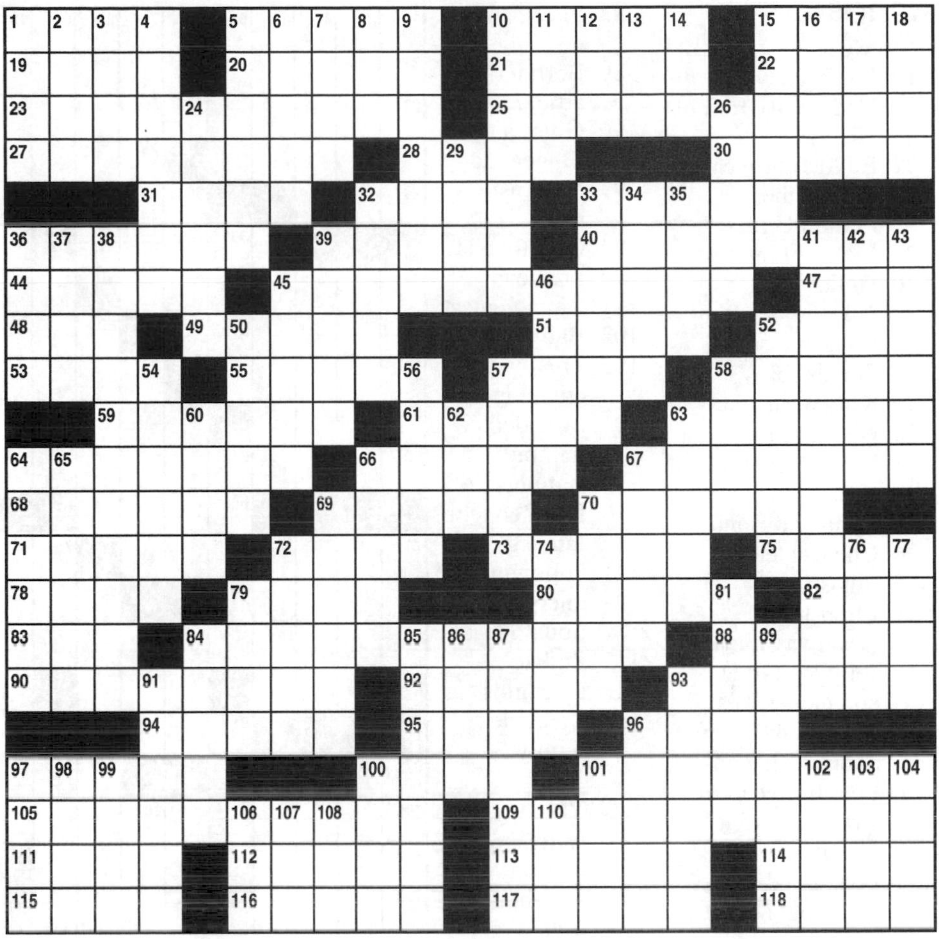

ACROSS

1 Big name in jeans
5 They may be oreganato
10 Cop-out
15 Reunion group
19 Like 100
20 Goes after
21 Piano part
22 Holiday destination, perhaps
23 Office worker
25 Dishwasher
27 Editorial paste-ups
28 Deep Throat's contribution
30 Remediate
31 Old French coins
32 Deceptive chap
33 Photo texture
36 Neruda and Casals
39 Knock off
40 Deeply involved
44 Ice Palace leaps
45 Diner server
47 Full-throated cry
48 Many an ode opening
49 Scrub off
51 Noble air, say
52 Cereal flakes
53 Austrian town since 1212
55 In a rut
57 Moonstone
58 Starting point
59 Hem in
61 Have a ball
63 Cool as ice
64 Rock hound's field
66 Competitor
67 Polite bus passenger
68 Folks in the same class?
69 Baneful
70 Performance enhancer
71 Weight factor
72 Trifling matter
73 Sign from the bench
75 Three-card monte, e.g.
78 Oasis nibble
79 It has rabbit ears!
80 ___ artery
82 More than enough
83 Printemps follower
84 Counterfeiter
88 U. of Maine's town
90 Makes notches in knives
92 Eastern biggies
93 Took off
94 Bikini event
95 Defensive maneuver
96 Colombian city since 1536
97 Child's play?
100 Bus rider
101 Slick
105 Executive interviewer
109 Gumshoe
111 ___-Lackawanna
112 Vocally enhanced
113 Ear or circle preceder
114 Burger order
115 Household problem
116 Story lines
117 Dressed to the nines
118 Make a move

DOWN

1 "___ and the Swan": Yeats
2 On and on and on
3 Bulletproof garb
4 Quill dipper's fount
5 Greek drama group
6 Doesn't have
7 Expresses curiosity
8 Pearl ___ Bailey
9 A la mode
10 Duds
11 Onion's cousin
12 Mount near ancient Troy
13 It may close at 3 A.M.
14 "___ Be Around"
15 "Sleigh Ride" instrument
16 "Sweetie!"
17 Final word, at times
18 Hardly a BMOC
24 Lots of laughs
26 Machine for a 23 Across
29 Greasy spoon fare
32 ___ Lemon (Crayola color)
33 Like serfs and peons
34 Broadway backer
35 Ness and staff
36 Birmingham bean
37 Neural transmitter
38 Statistician
39 Mom in the kiddie pool
41 Vet
42 Comedy writer-director May
43 Less perceptive
45 2003 Jessica Alba film
46 Drive hard
50 Gymnastic event
52 "Yankee Doodle" lyricist
54 Offer comfort
56 Clichéd
57 Round figures
58 Grumpy guy
60 Caesar or Cleopatra
62 One of the Gabors
63 Inscribed pillar
64 Rock hound's collection, perhaps
65 Treat as the same
66 Leaf collector
67 Way up or down
69 Fossa's home
70 Two-time U.S. Open queen
72 Funny things
74 Big cat, in Chihuahua
76 Elite
77 General attitude
79 Find intolerable
81 "Enough!"
84 Stop-smoking aid
85 Doral perils
86 God of love
87 Spare target, at times
89 Aggressive poker players
91 Staged a bust
93 Working stiff's reward
96 Thirst for
97 "Look over here!"
98 CD-burning software
99 Bovine flyswatter
100 Centipede's pride
101 Pub draw
102 Miami five
103 "Iris" director
104 Quite involved
106 Strike caller
107 Zip
108 Fight ender
110 Genetic factor

284 HALVE THE LAST WORD by Tucker Smith

21 Across is also the title of a James Dickey novel.

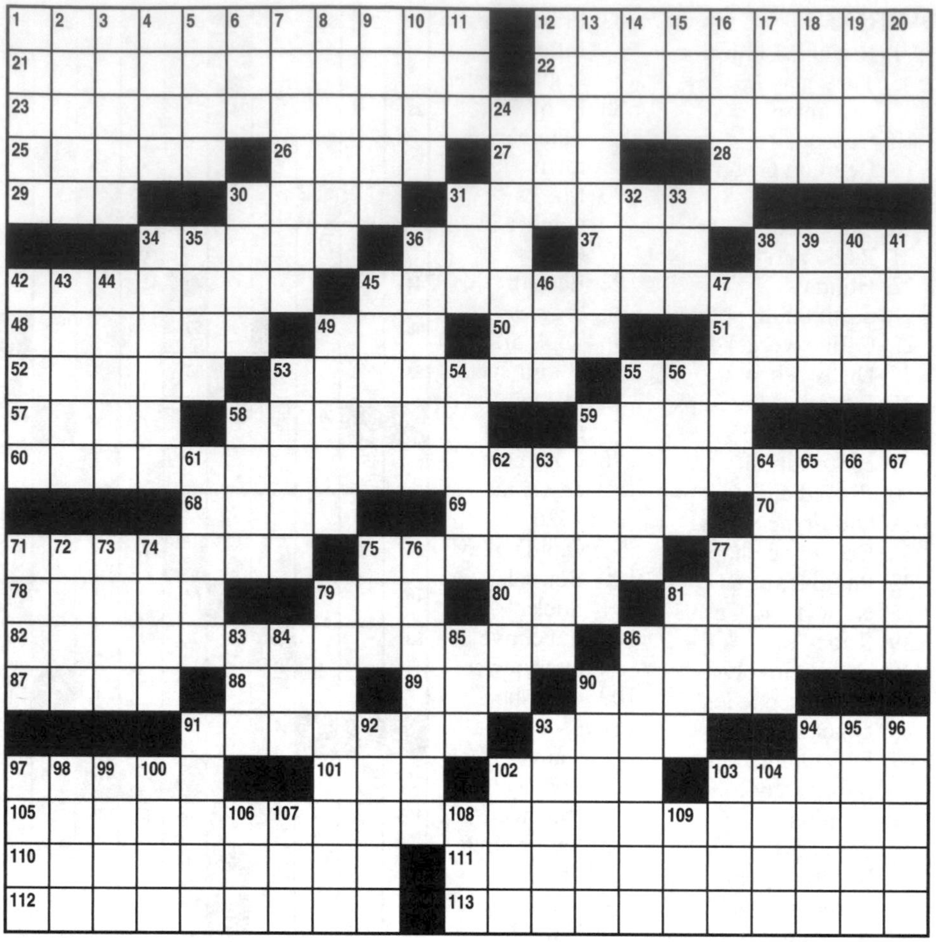

ACROSS

1 Muse
12 Put in abeyance
21 Ned Beatty film of 1972
22 Editor, at times
23 Yet another immoral cruise?
25 Fields of interest
26 Dollar bills
27 Take home after taxes
28 Stands for
29 Kind of instinct
30 NY Met, e.g.
31 Many Christmas trees
34 Emulated Bond
36 Chinese tea
37 Smash into
38 Elton John broadway musical
42 Jelly Roll of jazz and namesakes
45 "Star Wars" movie about male ghosts?
48 Free from care
49 Bray beginning
50 Slippery one
51 Pencil end
52 Halle of "Monster's Ball"
53 Devoid of moisture
55 Get more of the suds out
57 Rock's Clapton
58 Exactly this way
59 Norm's wife on "Cheers"
60 What dawns with a final ale?
68 Hill habitants
69 Air combat mission
70 Ristorante beverage
71 Monopoly Place
75 Way of Springsteen's band
77 McEnroe foe
78 Optimist's words
79 Biblical Samuel's mentor
80 Tiny amount
81 ___ franca
82 Comment about exciting parents?
86 Refreshment stand
87 Pressure on astronauts
88 Put a scuff on
89 Berliner's article
90 Gives a beep
91 Singer Judd
93 Newcastle's river
94 Org. for Els
97 Freeload
101 Kennel guest
102 Baby barkers
103 Treat with contempt
105 Stranded without stationery?
110 Led Zeppelin fan, e.g.
111 Following unconventional ideas
112 Zodiac arachnids
113 Bedrock family

DOWN

1 Luggage clip-on
2 Jawaharlal of India
3 Hard rain
4 Tuscany city
5 Currier's companion
6 MLK's title
7 Spaces between leaf veins
8 Bronzed, in a sense
9 Part of ICBM
10 Phil of folk music
11 Neighbor of Ariz.
12 Coat of paint
13 It's below B flat
14 With one sharp
15 Jane or John
16 Molecule constituents
17 Umpire's cry
18 Wonderful life beginning
19 Bump off
20 Sea divers
24 Written down
30 Mudville team
31 Sea shell seller
32 Recyclable item
33 911 respondent
34 Collar stiffener
35 Flower shop purchase
36 Slice in a Big Mac
38 Mine, on the Marne
39 Hacker's cry
40 Game rooms
41 Fork over (with "up")
42 Silents actress Normand
43 "SNL" alumna Cheri
44 Hook up again
45 First extra inning
46 "You there!"
47 Winfrey of "The Color Purple"
49 Leno and Letterman
53 Hits with horns
54 Accomplish, archaically
55 Equip anew
56 Art deco illustrator
58 "Emma" author Austen
59 Attempted to remove a chad
61 Big-top employee
62 Sitcom sewer worker
63 Sleep phenomenon
64 Major happenings
65 Subtle coloration
66 Needless
67 Fireballer Ryan
71 Tell all
72 For whom the bell tolls
73 Zeus, to Romans
74 Guitarzan's audience
75 Conduit bend
76 Every knot has one
77 Sausage unit
79 Old-world
81 Nathan of "The Producers"
83 Author Tan
84 Rather
85 Hamm of soccer
86 Keep company (with)
90 Word divider
91 Sassy kid
92 Food, clothing, and shelter
93 ___-frutti
94 Stop by
95 Somber
96 Range of South America
97 Showy flowers
98 Crude cartel
99 Palindromic male name
100 Blacken on the grill
102 Medication option
103 ERA or RBI
104 "The Elder" of Rome
106 Bears' home, briefly
107 Vintage automaker
108 Female flyer
109 Word after young

285 FEMALE COMPANIONSHIP by Harvey Estes

86 Down is also the title of a Marilyn Monroe film.

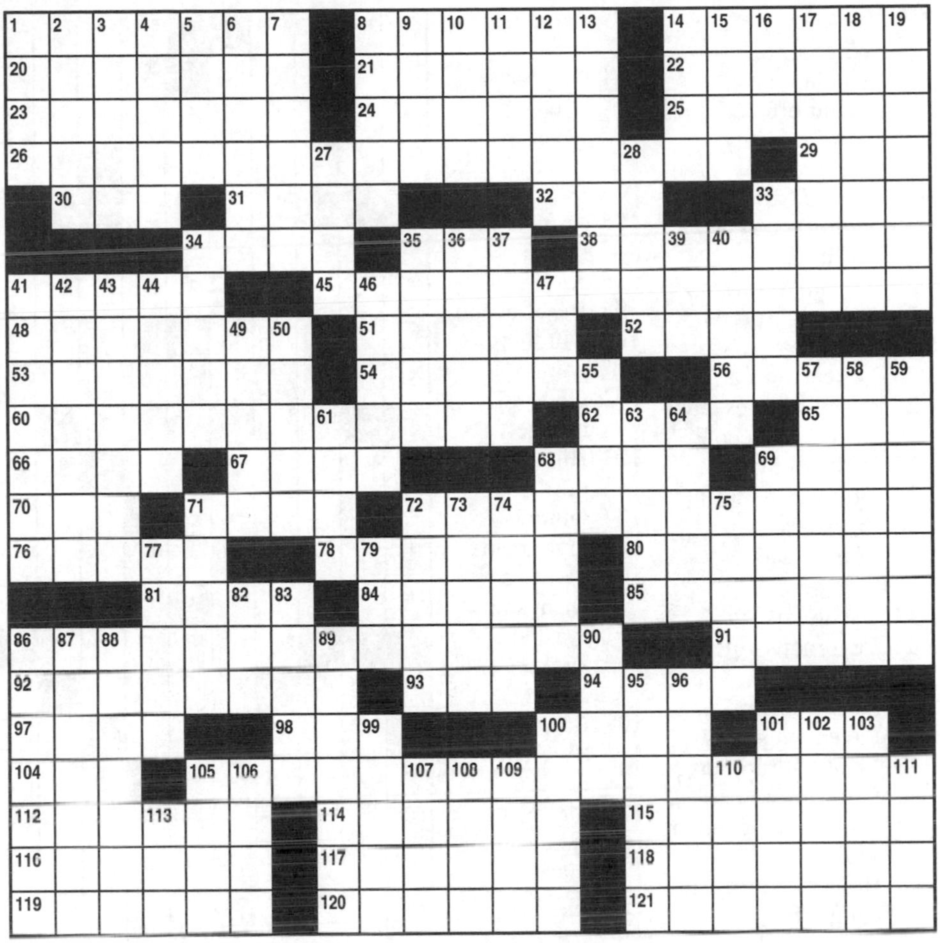

ACROSS

1 Space clouds
8 Beats
14 Big naval group
20 Some newsletter pictures
21 This second
22 Paul of "Mad About You"
23 Better than any other
24 Kind of oil
25 Tooth buildup
26 Where water splashes in a shower?
29 Gator add-on
30 Wide size
31 Sky sightings
32 Broadway bio
33 Roth offerings
34 Military lockup
35 QB feats
38 "That was no joke"
41 Knocker's reply
45 Wise-guy Carolina team?
48 Copes
51 Chicago hub
52 "___ ask you!"
53 Share fairly
54 Dubuque natives
56 They bray
60 Where to find singer Bill's chair?
62 Bull: Prefix
65 Mai ___ cocktail
66 Darth's daughter
67 Send out
68 Tampa Bay team, for short
69 Fix sox
70 Wall St. group
71 Shoe holder
72 Pungent fish dish?
76 Alley wanderer
78 Seaport of Italia
80 Some fuels
81 Thick chunk
84 Gone up
85 With the least delay
86 Low wages?
91 Acknowledge
92 Belonging naturally
93 Before, in verse
94 Prudent
97 Old pros
98 ___ de mots (pun)
100 Pub offering
101 Katie Couric's network
104 Generation separator
105 Compete in dreary journalism?
112 "I, Robot" author
114 Old-phone user
115 Brand of playing cards
116 Image receiver
117 Cover stories
118 Omitted
119 Lash out at
120 Free from worry
121 International accord

DOWN

1 Duke's st.
2 "Dallas" Miss
3 Hull section
4 ___ creek (stuck)
5 Café enhancer
6 Hot dog brand
7 Graf of tennis
8 Treaties between countries
9 Four Corners toucher
10 Type of wolf
11 Stuffed shirt
12 Brilliant success
13 Cruise
14 Comedian Johnson
15 Cabooses's spot
16 Fallen Russian station
17 Fertility deity
18 Broadcast snafu
19 Rap sheet entries
27 Heavy mists
28 One of us
33 Vonda Shepard's "It's ___ Kiss"
34 Generated, in Genesis
35 Resort lake
36 Haggard
37 Valuable violin
39 Rocker Brian
40 Engaged in hostilities
41 Antelope with an auto?
42 Most tangy
43 More wintry, in a way
44 West Side Story heroine
46 Somewhat wet
47 Kobe currency
49 Anesthetic of old
50 Brief summons
55 "Star Trek" phaser setting
57 Like colored glass
58 From the heart
59 Serenades
61 French goose egg
63 Aspirin targets
64 Be of ___ (help)
68 Sound of a spring
69 Pipe cleaner
71 Liv of "Jersey Girl"
72 Have one's say
73 Emphatic turndown
74 "Mr. Belvedere" actress Graff
75 River of Lyon
77 Hearth waste
79 JFK info
82 "Exodus" role
83 Cinema canine
86 Horseshoe Falls location
87 Covers completely
88 Worse than bad
89 Axes to grind
90 Loretta of "M*A*S*H"
95 Scarf down
96 Filmmaker Spielberg
99 Of service
100 Analyze, as a sentence
101 Orange container
102 Conductor's wand
103 Talent hunter
105 "Both Sides Now" singer Mitchell
106 Race track shape
107 "Aquarius" musical
108 North Sea feeder
109 Control, with "in"
110 Schism
111 Art deco illustrator
113 Hamm of soccer

286 R&R by Richard Silvestri

An example of 47 Across would be Evita in "Rent."

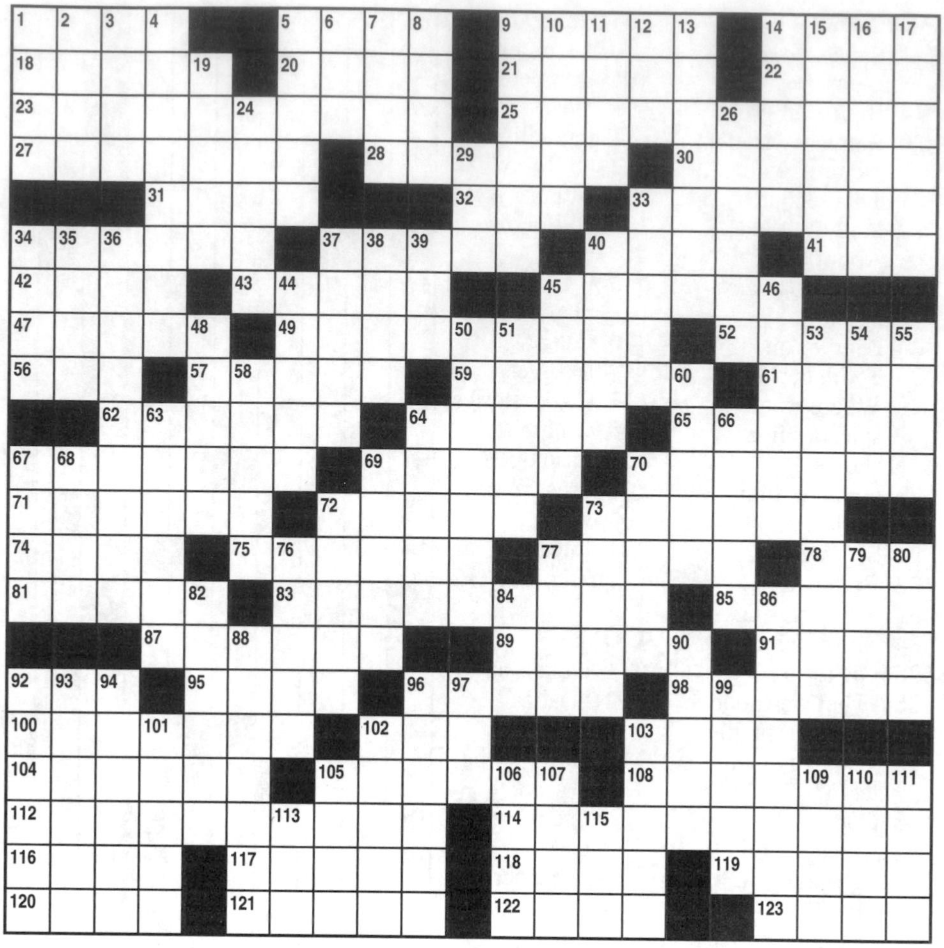

ACROSS

1 Wirehair of whodunits
5 Guitar effect
9 Word in many Christie titles
14 Fan's favorite
18 Part of a cowboy outfit
20 Trojan War hero
21 Beast of Borden
22 Soup bean
23 Policeman's anger?
25 One who goes from steeple to steeple?
27 Walk all over
28 Go over the wall
30 Sidetrack
31 Classic cars
32 Step on it
33 Babar's queen
34 Venomous vipers
37 Blotch
40 Auto pioneer Benz
41 Pavement sealer
42 Plant with fronds
43 Fall flower
45 Whalebone garment
47 Japanese dog
49 Howard putting up paintings?
52 Not spelled out
56 Race the engine
57 Positive-yardage plays
59 Shudders in shock
61 Evening, in ads
62 Used the fat end of the pencil
64 Like a hoodlum
65 The "it" girl?
67 Dire follower
69 Fill with glee
70 Tanning device
71 City on the Po
72 Gray
73 Steersman's responsibility
74 Yemeni seaport
75 Theater district
77 Gem State capital
78 Sound from the bleachers
81 Off-peak call?
83 Obvious drubbing?
85 Alley pickup
87 Humble
89 Montezuma, e.g.
91 Spumante source
92 Metric measurement syst.
95 Prepare for action
96 Kayak kin
98 Bit of bacon
100 Climbing palms
102 Go for the bronze?
103 Huff and puff
104 Ointment ingredient
105 "Wasted Days and Wasted Nights" singer
108 Back
112 Blue-collar tirade?
114 Moray's dance?
116 Maritime eagle
117 Maltreat
118 Reagan's first secretary of state
119 Flip-chart support
120 Senior member
121 Eye enhancer
122 Just
123 Old Ford models

DOWN

1 Money in the bk.
2 Toots the restaurateur
3 Cassette contents
4 Open to view
5 Raises a red flag
6 Steely Dan album
7 Carry on
8 Central lines
9 Stop
10 Take the honey and run
11 "___ forgive those who . . ."
12 Get even with
13 Shelties, at work
14 Amo, translated
15 Strip
16 Why Fat Tony won't talk?
17 Actress Ali
19 Exodus celebration
24 Apollo 14 astronaut
26 Small creek
29 X
33 Chile partner
34 At a distance
35 Fake out, on the ice
36 One (wine) for the road?
37 Roadside establishment
38 Till section
39 Neighbor of Bol.
40 Eccentric
44 Acts skittish
45 Short-billed rail
46 Lock horns
48 From the top
50 Middle Earth?
51 Stunted
53 Smoker's allergic reaction?
54 Piece of news
55 Tar Heel's rival
58 First woman in Parliament
60 Collar fasteners
63 Came down
64 End of Montana's motto
66 Llama locale
67 Obedience school command
68 Hoo-ha
69 Novelist Glasgow
70 Hotel offering
72 Leaves for lunch
73 Way to go
76 Champagne buckets
77 Dumb guy
79 Museo display
80 One with will power?
82 Papal representative
84 Kurosawa's adaptation of "King Lear"
86 Rustic
88 Inorganic substance
90 Grammer role
92 Made common caws?
93 In great quantity
94 Breastbones
96 Easy gallop
97 Word of partnership
99 Arnold's co-conspirator
101 Spoken for
102 Full of suspense
103 Lipton or Lee
105 Roman satyr
106 Sonic bounce
107 Leather color
109 Take five
110 It's for the birds
111 Corner shapes
113 Sacrifice fly stat
115 Zilch

287 QUADRUPLE-U by Fred Piscop

89 Across earned his doctorate at Johns Hopkins University.

ACROSS

1 "Misery" star
5 "Total Recall" author Paretsky
9 Medea rode on it
13 Prepared to burgle
18 Wolf's look
19 Ornery sort
20 ___ terrier
22 Let up
23 Eater of a poisoned apple
25 Broom-___
26 Untouchables, e.g.
27 Links reservations
28 Worker on a scaffold, perhaps
30 Balaam's mount
31 Bring home
32 Pal of Dobie Gillis
33 Weeder's need
34 Have a nosh
35 De ___ (from the start)
36 Part of a bray
38 Daniel of "Wise Blood"
42 Fashion inits.
45 Huxley opus
49 Kimono go-with
50 Pseudopod former
52 H.S. subject
53 Masses
55 Multi-state lottery
58 IOU's
60 Hills' opposites
61 Scattered
62 "By the way" on a memo
63 Timely event
64 Jam session highlight
65 Body art, slangily
66 Painter of Helga
70 Saddler's tool
72 Attorneys' degs.
74 Explorer Tasman
75 Harpers Ferry loc.
76 River in a 1957 movie
78 More fit
80 Hummingbirds do it
82 Sweetie
84 Act
86 '60s chess champ Mikhail
87 Pianist Claudio
88 Liberal arts major, for short
89 President with a Ph.D.
94 Eerie ability
95 Basin go-with
97 Mdse.
98 The "ten" in "hang ten"
99 "Go on . . ."
100 Unlock, to a poet
102 Orderly grouping
103 Cocks and bulls
104 Celestial altar
107 Tidal extreme
112 Players
114 Catchall column
115 Téa of "Deep Impact"
116 Shrub once used for archery ammo
117 Dictator's aide
118 Cook in a wok, maybe
119 Body shape
120 Development unit
121 Completely wreck
122 Cattle zapper
123 Newcastle-upon-___
124 Glad rags

DOWN

1 Spain's ___ Brava
2 A de Mille
3 Bitter ___ (laxative drug)
4 "Contract With America" first name
5 Glob of cream cheese, in deli-speak
6 Diva's bit
7 "Darn it all!"
8 Japanese novelist Kobo ___
9 Pull off
10 Illusory goal
11 Decorates richly
12 Word on a dollar
13 Chocolate source
14 Puts down
15 49 Across, e.g.
16 Suffix with super
17 Tick's host, maybe
21 Slangy refusal
24 Where to pop one's cork?
28 All wet
29 Have puppies
32 Solemn sound
36 Show derision
37 A dwarf planet
39 Deep serving dishes
40 Heckelphone cousin
41 Reformer born in Denmark
42 Big, fat mouths
43 Hawley-___ Tariff Act
44 Creator of Ben-Hur
46 Not yet expired
47 Prone to complaining
48 Long-gone bird
51 Rolls rival
54 Left Coast NBAer
56 Designers' degs.
57 Novelist Rand
58 Show fear
59 Serenade the moon
63 Lilith's portrayer on "Cheers"
64 ___-Pei (wrinkly dog)
67 Delirious one
68 General under Lee at Gettysburg
69 New Deal inits.
71 Theme from "Doctor Zhivago"
73 Oater challenge
77 Ham ___ (overact)
78 Abbey area
79 Totally botch
80 Oregon volcano
81 Bygone GM brand
82 Dagwood's dog
83 Work on a quilt, maybe
85 Physician-turned-wordsmith
86 Adjust a bit
90 Walpole's "The Castle of ___"
91 In a stew
92 Bone-dry
93 "Encore!"
96 Ivanhoe's love
101 Unwritten, in law
102 Illicit affair
104 BP acquisition
105 Corporate makeover, for short
106 El Misti's range
107 Utterly confused
108 Grid great Graham
109 Put an edge on
110 Urban transports
111 Haul in
112 "Betty Zane" novelist
113 Police jacket letters
116 EIK's place

288 STRAIGHTFORWARD APPROACH by Jim Purkey

91 Aross was "Time's" 2001 Person of the Year.

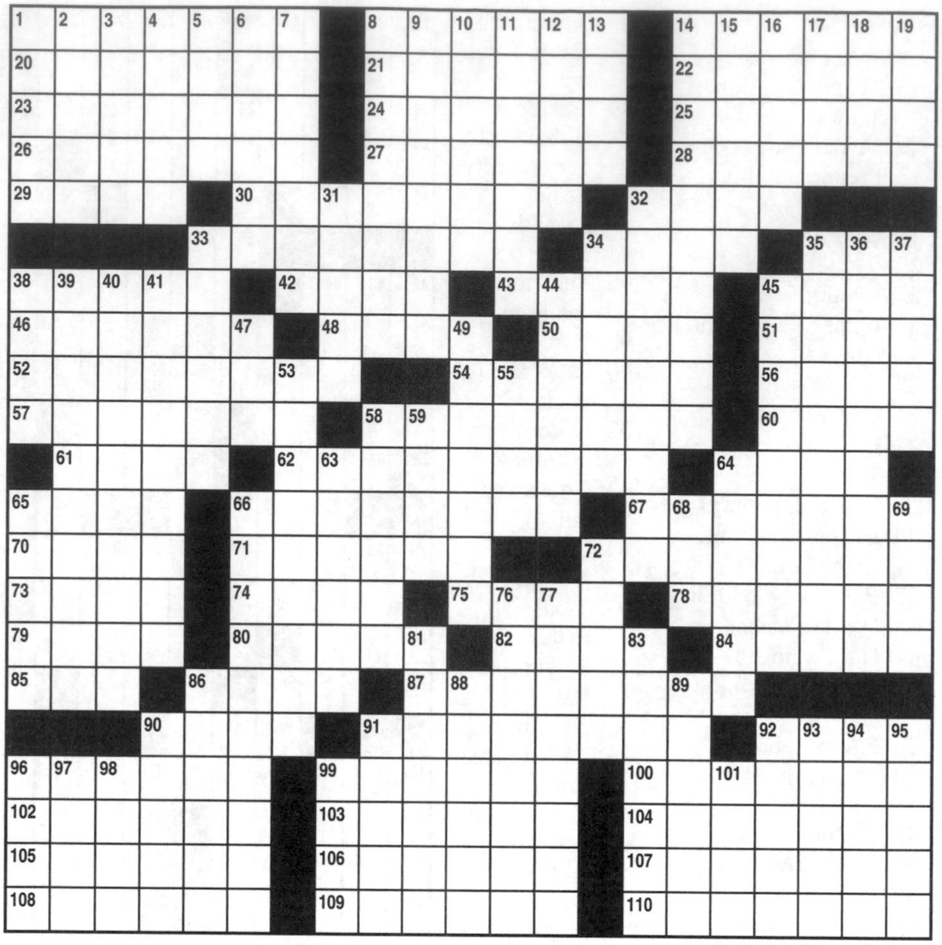

ACROSS

1 Rapper's noise
8 "Faust" author
14 Type of iron
20 1968 hit by the Turtles
21 Like hands with roamin' fingers?
22 Not digital
23 Member of a noted colony
24 Wait on
25 Nocturnal reptile of Tennessee
26 Rise above
27 Some warnings
28 Covered with canvas
29 Appealing
30 Compounds used in medicines
32 Disney lioness
33 Glacial deposits
34 Guadalajara girl
35 Monopoly buys, briefly
38 Emerson work
42 Kitty chip
43 Make right
45 Beatitude heirs (with "the")
46 Drop off the radar
48 File holder
50 Blows the minds of
51 Goofing off
52 Rubber bands and such
54 Rococo
56 "Leaving Las Vegas" costar
57 Painting copy
58 Footwear insert
60 Minority group
61 Risky business
62 Vehicle for an unpaved way
64 Put in order
65 "Exodus" author
66 Easy
67 Musical mark
70 Zip
71 Forces forward
72 Halogen-family member
73 Roman wrap
74 Get smart with
75 Watered down
78 This second
79 "While ___ it . . ."
80 Gospel
82 Taking care of business
84 Odd Couple half
85 Mass. setting
86 Bubble source
87 Elite athletes
90 Rhein port
91 Mayor Dinkins' successor
92 iBooks, e.g.
96 Police order
99 Removed air from Tupperware
100 Kind of insurance
102 In the dumps
103 Shoot for, with "to"
104 Ancient Tuscany
105 Juice source
106 Souvenir from a slugger
107 It may be under a coat
108 Words of warning
109 Church councils
110 Ties that bind

DOWN

1 Some used cars
2 Still in the game
3 Fax forerunner
4 Inflamed
5 Suit material, perhaps
6 Musical composition
7 Batter-dipped dish
8 Subway wall art
9 Contours
10 Heir's concern
11 Saint of Avila
12 Top tapper
13 Pair in a line
14 Type of attitude
15 Bassett in "Mr. 3000"
16 Zoologists' study
17 Motorist's headache
18 Without peers
19 "Holy cow!"
31 Finishes a flight
32 Good blackjack scores
33 Lili Taylor's "___ Pizza"
34 LaGuardia alternative
35 Device used in mystery writing
36 Disinclination
37 Shooting type
38 Even a single time
39 Goods locations
40 Getting testy with
41 Flier's choice
44 Miles Hawkins' alter ego
45 Lose, as an opportunity
47 Popular fruit drink
49 Most unflappable
53 Twin-hulled vessel
55 Lee's men
58 Least buggy
59 Sledding spot
63 Tears to pieces
64 Ranking
65 Set free
66 Nickname of cager Maravich
68 One-time connection
69 Groucho's smirk
72 "West Side Story" girl
76 Shouted, down south
77 Loop components?
81 Turn type
83 Most brown
86 They're often pickled
88 Ida in "High Sierra"
89 Mob member
90 Small hill
91 Overly effusive
92 Handles roughly
93 Radiant glows
94 "Crazy" singer
95 Sports figures
96 Melville novel
97 Serve drinks
98 Art deco illustrator
99 Part of a combo
101 Haus wife

289 SILVER-SCREEN QUOTES by Harvey Estes

For the record, it was Clyde who spoke 66 Across.

ACROSS

1 Uses cotton balls
5 Auto engine type
9 Pt. of VMI
13 William Tell, e.g.
19 And higher, in cost
20 "Believe ___ not!"
21 "Limp Watches" painter
22 Camry maker
23 Lascivious look
24 Chaplin spouse
25 Jelling agent
26 Classified item
27 **"Casablanca" quote**
31 Vague warning
32 Mixologist's measure
33 Attemped coups
36 L.A. hrs.
37 Ask along
40 Detonator
41 Scandal suffix
42 **"Gone with the Wind" quote (with 64 A)**
47 Bahrain biggie
50 Goneril's dad
51 Golden years org.
52 Fields of study
53 Low A
55 Hits the slopes
56 Wire-bending tool
58 Like some questions
59 Chevy SUV
62 Raptor's weapon
64 **See 42 Across**
66 **"Bonnie and Clyde" quote**
71 Hatfield, to a McCoy
72 Gold standard
73 "La Bohème," e.g.
74 Says "cheese"
77 Midnight fridge visit
79 Hindu teachers
80 Arrow shaft
81 Gold layer
82 Apéritif follower
85 ___ Hashanah
86 **"Some Like It Hot" quote**
91 Hosp. fluid feeders
92 Off the hook
93 Sherman's costar on "The Jeffersons"
94 Pig's eye opening?
97 Acts between parties
100 Change of a five
102 Smithereens
104 **"Sunset Boulevard" quote**
108 Set the dial
110 Breaks bread
111 Queens stadium name
112 Conveyance weight
113 Hanging loose
114 K through 12
115 Short pegs
116 "A Summer Place" costar
117 Klemperer of "Hogan's Heroes"
118 Juror, in theory
119 Makes mistakes
120 Slim swimmers

DOWN

1 '50s music style
2 Riles up
3 Ammo unit
4 Wizard's weapon
5 How hurricanes hit the coast
6 Put in the overhead rack
7 College in New Rochelle
8 Stellar source of a certain radiation
9 Boise's state
10 Continually find fault with
11 Pole or Czech
12 Source of inflation
13 '80s Republican strategist Lee
14 Surf sounds
15 Pessimistic person
16 Workout follower
17 Hellenic H
18 Outrageous
28 "Yeah, right!"
29 Illustrator Silverstein
30 Corleone's creator
34 Howe of sewers
35 Talk trash
38 Type of sweater neckline
39 SEP, e.g.
40 "Where Angels Fear to Tread" author
42 Don't exist
43 Water-skiing locale
44 Mai ___
45 Coalition type
46 Blast furnace input
47 Irish pop singer
48 Personal appearance
49 Words before many words
54 Poe poem
55 Sauce source
56 Criminal plan
57 Soft toss
59 Dos follower
60 Naval off.
61 Outing on a wagon
63 Astronomical altar
65 Hydrocarbon ending
66 Crumple, with "up"
67 One way to fall
68 Film fish
69 Singer Kristofferson
70 Dress decoration
72 Model makers' purchases
74 Triple Crown jockey Cauthen
75 "Alice" setting
76 Not in the pink
78 One of the Khans
79 Way to be in Seattle
80 Sink opposite
81 Tries for a Hail Mary, maybe
82 Regular at a meal
83 Nolan Ryan stat
84 Fliers mil. post
87 More frequently
88 Town near Long Beach
89 Place on piles
90 Commercial award
94 Cooling-off period
95 Brain-related
96 Some poplars
98 Conversational filler
99 Heed the alarm
100 Cock ___ walk
101 Emphatic turndown
103 Lauder of cosmetics
105 Lock manufacturer
106 Belgian border river
107 Chastity's mother
108 Shooting marble
109 Western Native American

290 "JERSEY BOYS" BOYS by Harvey Estes

The title repeats itself at 62 Across.

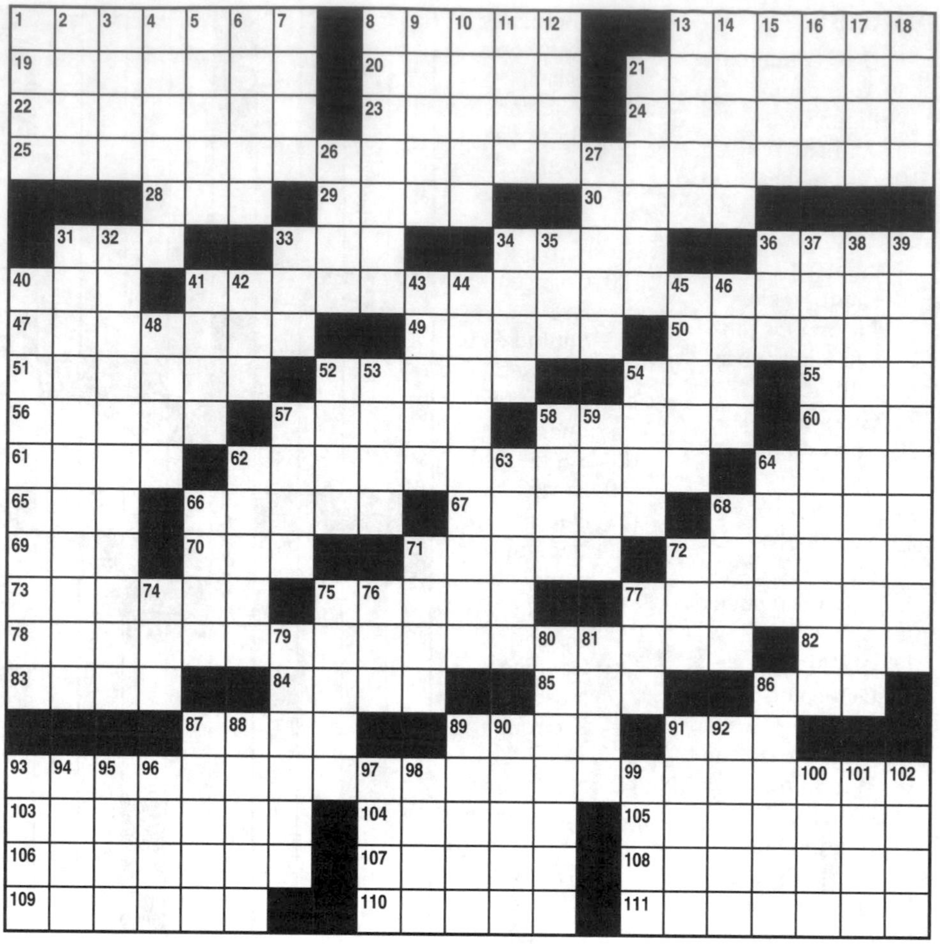

ACROSS

1 Deadlock
8 Beef and pork
13 Tune from "Sound of Music"
19 Pool sphere
20 Give consent
21 "Love Is a Battlefield" singer
22 Neighbor of Latvia
23 The color of money
24 Hyundai model
25 Roman patsies?
28 Before, in verse
29 Movie locations
30 Series ender
31 Ns, in Greek
33 Null tennis serve
34 Fork over, with "up"
36 Fly-ball paths
40 Chaney of chillers
41 Going to Fort Lauderdale?
47 Incans, e.g.
49 Out in front
50 Beads used in prayer
51 Actress Mimieux
52 Powder used in soap
54 Tank contents
55 Fleur-de-___
56 Somewhat, slangily
57 Batman foe
58 Dublin denizens
60 Trade-monitoring agcy.
61 Lanchester of flicks
62 "Jersey Boys" boys
64 Old Russian leader
65 China's Sun ___-sen
66 River triangle
67 Fargo's partner
68 Unwelcome, after "non"
69 JFK info
70 Elev.
71 Chart holder
72 Become intense
73 Serenade
75 Dish name
77 Crank up without the key
78 Senior Olympics with skiing?
82 "___ the ramparts . . ."
83 Snug retreat
84 Go ape
85 Canyon edge
86 T or F, on exams
87 Matching
89 Pound sterling, informally
91 Hosp. scan
93 Male students that flunk?
103 Place to meditate
104 Cover story
105 Not in custody
106 Venus and Mars
107 ___ Haute, Indiana
108 Promotional come-ons
109 Most unusual
110 Speak indelicately
111 Takes whatever

DOWN

1 Rapper on "Law & Order: SVU"
2 Sled imperative
3 Folk singer Seeger
4 Places to call home
5 More stable
6 Toast serving
7 Carrier to Tel Aviv
8 "X-Men" villain
9 Wading bird
10 Geometry calculations
11 Young adult
12 Put in the mail
13 Reese of "Touched by an Angel"
14 Phrase before fours
15 Gave a buzz
16 Latin accusation
17 Tudor queen
18 Roth offerings
21 Like meringue
26 Revelatory cry
27 Foul-smelling
31 Unlikely to explode
32 Gets it
33 OCS grads
34 Top spot
35 FDR program
36 MGM motto word
37 Conversion into cash
38 Unflattering portraits
39 Big-city building
40 Sees
41 Pro follower
42 Having four sharps
43 Taxi passengers
44 Freebie programming
45 Hula skirt material
46 "Fiddlesticks!"
48 Jazz singer James
52 Boxing match
53 Gumbo pod
54 Cotton seed removers
57 Shake up
58 Wight, for one
59 Throw, as dice
62 Serious offender
63 Race of Norse gods
64 Where something may stick
66 Spreadsheet entries
68 Catches on to
71 Suffix with kitchen
72 Till the field
74 Clock std.
75 Elton John's instrument
76 Part of the U.K.
77 "Very interesting . . ."
79 Watch places
80 Harder to clean
81 West Wing worker
86 All shook up
87 Many reference works
88 Lawman Earp
89 Part of a ream
90 Shaded area
91 Lauder of lipstick
92 Big splash
93 Printing goof
94 Wrestling ploy
95 "Omigosh!"
96 Bête noire
97 Domino of music
98 Didst kill
99 "Peanuts" oath
100 First name in pitching
101 Very nasty sort
102 More, to a minimalist

291 B MOVIES by Arlan and Linda Bushman

25 Across was also a Morgan Freeman film title.

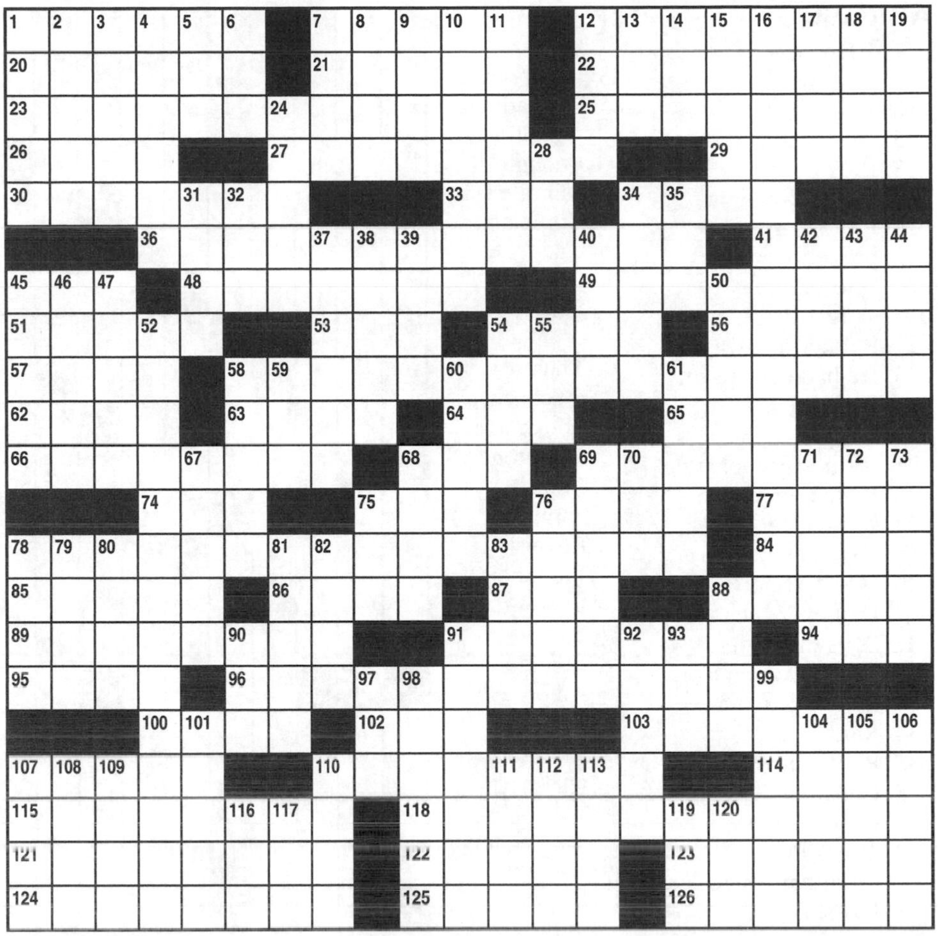

ACROSS

1 Symbol of Roman authority
7 Tel Aviv's twin city
12 Headquarters
20 City in Kansas or Ontario
21 Free as ___
22 Wrinkled
23 Film about an inmate's out?
25 Bill Withers song
26 Feminine suffix
27 Cruise liner area
29 Yarn unit
30 Marine race
33 Coach Parseghian
34 "Prince of Egypt" character
36 Rockumentary for Deadheads?
41 Revise
45 Cable choice
48 Biblical liar
49 Greek eggplant dish
51 Ashley's "GWTW" rival
53 Howl
54 Ex-Pirate Matty
56 Chasing
57 Word of honor
58 Film about a bragging bloodsucker?
62 Entangle
63 Jaipur aristocrat
64 Run smoothly
65 Pitch source
66 Deep
68 Angelico title
69 Moseys along
74 Skedaddle
75 Marie's quaff
76 Warm greeting
77 Bryce Canyon locale
78 Hapless, Hope-less road film?
84 Juncture
85 Blackjack request
86 Salinger title girl
87 Bela cohort
88 Wish whiz
89 Craftspeople
91 Go on and on
94 Concession
95 Gradually withdraw
96 Taboo film about Anastasia's stepsister?
100 Postern
102 Bump-log links
103 Restricted
107 Hogwarts item
110 Most dense
114 Presage
115 Berate
118 Film wetlands preservation?
121 Double-dealers
122 Calliope sister
123 Kevin in "A Few Good Men"
124 Packed in like ___
125 Court shot
126 Shows contempt

DOWN

1 Entrance hall
2 Conciliate
3 Fleeced
4 Warning
5 Flock member
6 Give way
7 Boosted launch acronym
8 "Fernando" group
9 Edict
10 "___ child is loving and giving . . ."
11 German typewriters
12 Shipwreck
13 Individual
14 Hamm of soccer
15 Dada artist Max
16 Documentary about a turf accountant with good numbers?
17 Novelist Rice
18 Big rig
19 Utopia
24 Clinton's 2008 rival
28 El alternative
31 "She's All ___" (1999)
32 Jack's inferior
34 Porcine feature
35 Com cousin
37 Loosen up
38 TV title town
39 Irish county
40 Mine, in Montreal
42 Input
43 Alibi ___ (excuse makers)
44 Pastry concoction
45 Defeat soundly
46 Eames creation
47 Paris transport
50 Vaccine developer
52 Film about acquiring a Las Vegas casino?
54 Water color
55 Abner's partner
58 Go one better
59 Solo in space
60 Landscaping item
61 Helpful
67 Havens
68 Outcome
69 Flare, usually
70 Hand-based comm.
71 Waist-length jackets
72 Stern's medium
73 Station denizen
75 It can be slippery
76 Small hill
78 Warm up
79 Take on
80 Vocalist James
81 Skating champ Sonja
82 Org.
83 Peter Fonda role
88 Light weight
90 Behave
91 Displaying virtuosity
92 Dogsled husky who became world famous in 1925
93 Wide sash
97 Joey's mom
98 Nail application
99 Eat in small bites
101 Cremona violin maker
104 "A Confederacy of Dunces" author
105 Winter of music
106 Classroom fixtures
107 Diner orders
108 ___ avis
109 Epps of "House"
110 Concert pianist Myra
111 "What'd ___" (Ray Charles)
112 Words to Brutus
113 Run (over)
116 Colin, to Tom
117 Half of sei
119 Gore and Cheney, e.g.
120 Long spell

292 ROUND AND ROUND by Matt Ginsberg

The subtitle can be found at 63 Across.

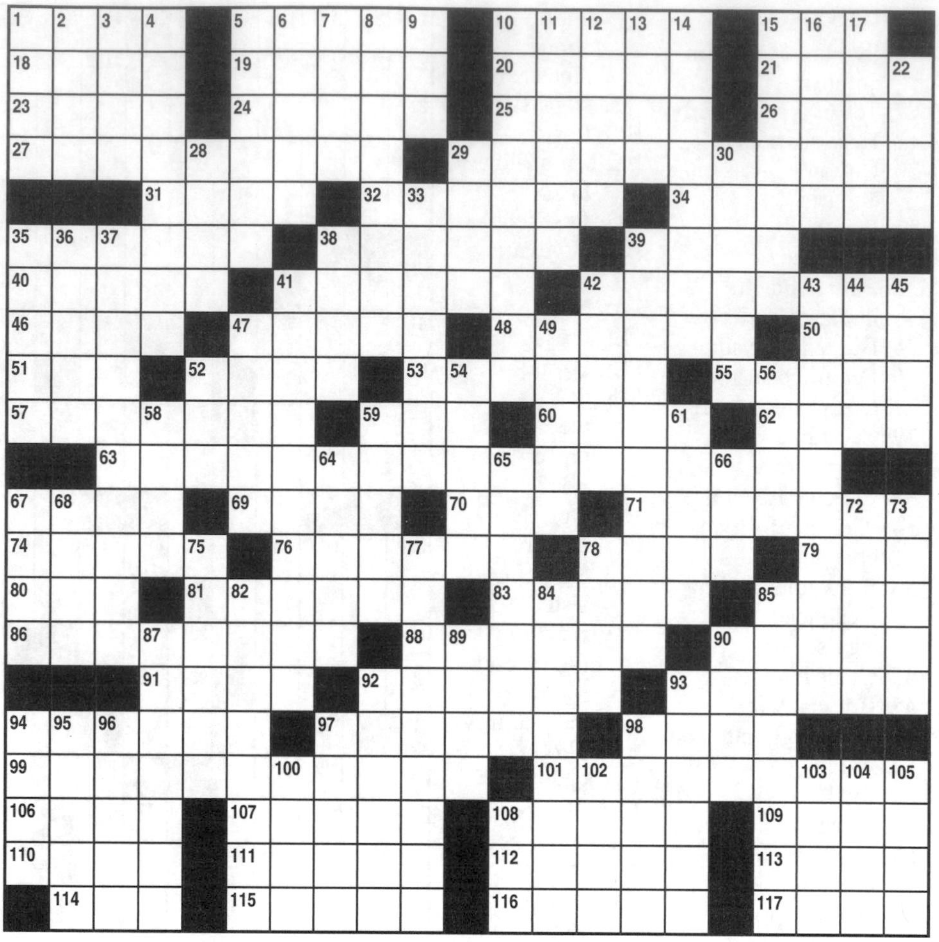

ACROSS

1 1 Down
5 1 Across
10 5 Across
15 10 Across
18 Bow accompaniment
19 Protozoan propellors
20 "Good Times" actress
21 Soldiering away
23 He had designs on Jackie
24 Deep
25 It's always negative
26 Pinta companion
27 "Dollar foolish" opposite number
29 "Coal Miner's Daughter" star
31 Senator Bayh
32 "What do you have to lose?"
34 Rant
35 Political concerns
38 Curb
39 Cowpoke
40 "Brokeback Mountain" hero
41 Lavalike
42 Going over
46 Slave loved by Radames
47 April honorees?
48 A flat
50 UAR mbr.
51 Jeanne d'Arc, e.g.
52 Courier, e.g.
53 "___, She Said" (1991)
55 Chip accompaniment
57 Pork, typically
59 A real ball of fire
60 Hindu god taking the form of a snake
62 BBC, familiarly
63 SUBTITLE
67 Pound, in Plymouth
69 Plain Jane
70 Spring for
71 Flattop crew
74 Prepare for takeoff?
76 Partial
78 Play hooky
79 "___ haw!"
80 Mineral suffix
81 America, to Borat
83 Layabout
85 O'Grady of "Eight Is Enough"
86 Rugrats
88 Bordeaux, e.g.
90 Chopin's "Minute ___"
91 Those muchachas
92 Spoke in a monotone
93 French composer Edgard
94 Fictional tiger
97 Savvy
98 Sounded sonorously
99 In advance
101 Cartoon character voiced by Tom Kenny
106 Dillydallies
107 Sur's opposite
108 Gene Vincent's "Be-Bop ___"
109 Silk wrap
110 Align
111 What Chicken Little mistook for the sky
112 Gangster Lansky
113 Narrow fissure
114 115 Across
115 116 Across
116 117 Across
117 105 Down

DOWN

1 30 Down
2 It's often left hanging
3 Hagman's TV costar
4 Milk of ___
5 "Uh" sounds
6 Connect
7 "Bummer!"
8 Diet, exercise, etc.
9 Tommy Lee Jones role
10 Apprenticeships
11 Lighter heavyweight
12 Elite roster
13 Sicken with sweetness
14 Whitewater independent counsel
15 Baseless rumors
16 Site of Woolworth's first store
17 Forklike
22 15 Across
28 Marilyn's "Let's Make Love" costar
29 Burns' "since"
30 Cheesecake
33 Broadway hope
35 67 Down
36 Country singer Cochran
37 Too small
38 Dig (up)
39 Automotive cylinder seal
41 Jungle gym
42 Perfume container
43 Michigan national park
44 "WSJ" subject
45 22 Down
47 Loud
49 Actress Duncan
52 Office machine
54 Emulate running mates?
56 Genesis fatality
58 Dress type
59 Ben Hogan rival
61 Firefighter Red
64 Actresses Moran and Gray
65 Glowing
66 Brief swim
67 94 Down
68 Till
72 Flat rates?
73 45 Down
75 Throbbed
77 Baptism, e.g.
78 Arctic transport
82 Like baseball or football
84 Marie in "Tugboat Annie"
85 Generosity
87 Corrupt
89 Oral tradition
90 Wedding gown designer Vera
92 Eldest of the Karamazov brothers
93 Joan of "Knots Landing"
94 114 Across
95 United hub
96 Going
97 Centenarian Thurmond
98 Golden Glove third baseman Scott
100 Concentrations
102 The last emperor
103 Telly Savalas, for one
104 Not a CC
105 73 Down
108 UN fig.

293 WHIRLED CHAMPIONS by Clare Hansbrough

“Whirled,” in a jumbled sense.

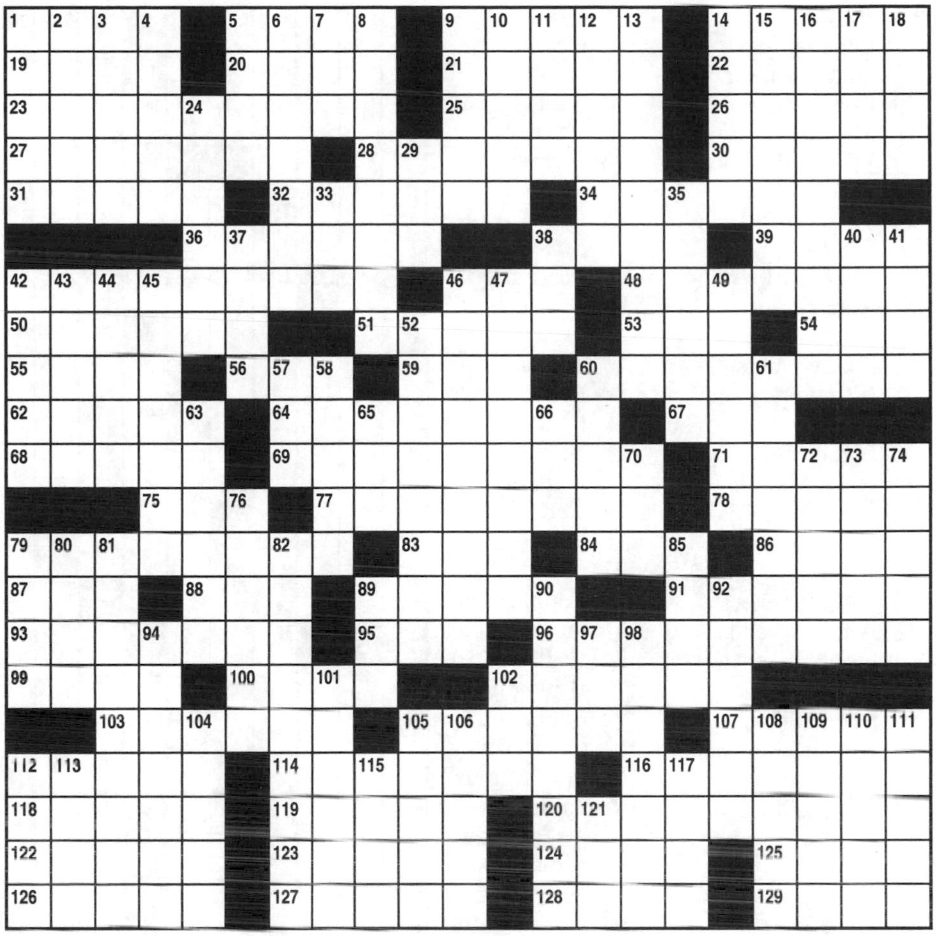

ACROSS

1 Some watch faces
5 Stunning triumph
9 Best part
14 Secret supply
19 Baldwin of “30 Rock”
20 Gumbo pod
21 Vital carrier
22 For a specific purpose
23 Manly brooches?
25 Watts in King Kong’s hand
26 New Orleans footballer
27 Sauteed
28 1951 Polo Grounds hero Bobby
30 Major blood group
31 Abraham’s spouse
32 ET and Alf
34 Laugh riot
36 Top stories
38 “Aren’t   lucky one!”
39 Asian desert
42 Korean War sitcom MP?
46 Hippie’s digs
48 The Wright brothers, e.g.
50 Angola’s capital
51 Islamic leaders
53 Mates of mas
54 Slap cuffs on
55 Mayberry cell dweller
56 Catch forty winks
59 Tar Heels’ sch.
60 Hatchet man
62 Get dressed
64 Fran of TV’s “The Nanny”
67 Cybersearch result
68 Cartoon canine
69 Groups of cleaning supply stores?
71 Playground retort
75 Go back
77 Lethargic feelings
78 Biker’s invite
79 Watering holes
83 Printing widths
84 Young chap
86 Choir perch
87 Prussian pronoun
88 Tempest in a teapot
89 Mob scenes
91 Big union letters
93 Early Christian sectarian
95 T or F, on some exams
96 Prisoner’s accident?
99 Start of a rhyme about a tiger
100 Eat up, with “down”
102 Without a sound
103 Line of clothing
105 Free-for-alls
107 Suffix with bed or home
112 Patsy Cline’s record label
114 Reno resident
116 Acupressure technique
118 Bean or Welles
119 Actress Graff
120 Tool to film “five-finger discounts”?
122 Flip out
123 Eva of Argentina
124 “Omigosh!”
125 Sound quality
126 Private Pyle
127 Has the lead
128 Right in the head
129 North Sea feeder

DOWN

1 Meek types
2 Bow or Barton
3 Room style
4 Inverted “e”
5 Handle difficulties
6 Fax machine maker
7 Coffee container
8 Hodgepodge
9 Maker of EOS cameras
10 Gads about
11 Cupid’s counterpart
12 Not more than
13 Principle karate blows?
14 Social group
15 Twenty-four hours past
16 Dale’s buddy laments?
17 Give an edge to
18 Plasm starter
24 In stock
29 “___ got the whole world . . .”
33 Fleur-de-___
35 Go back over
37 Counterfeiters’ nemesis
38 Driver’s licenses, e.g.
40 Sons of, in Hebrew
41 Copyright page abbr.
42 Coagulates
43 ___ a limb
44 Pitcher Satchel
45 John Hancock, e.g.
46 Arrest a prophet?
47 One who says, “Saith,” say
49 “For unto us a child is born” source
52 Intrude forcefully
57 USN officer
58 June balls
60 Textile trademark
61 Leisurely walks
63 JFK’s vessel
65 MPG monitors
66 Ice in Ulm
70 New Deal org.
72 Geologic time
73 Bulgarian capital
74 At the peak
76 Part of a dress
79 Buster Brown’s dog
80 Adolescent affliction
81 Sound epithet for singer Cooke?
82 Sips of coffee?
85 Epithet for Yankees
89 Like crunchy carrots
90 Biology and chemistry
92 Makes room for
94 Changing never to ne’er, e.g.
97 Hurrah for Jose
98 WKRP news director Les
101 Brunch entree
102 Hearst’s kidnappers, for short
104 Not so nutty
105 Stately home
106 Shangri-las
108 Full of flavor
109 Character of a culture
110 In unison
111 Super follower
112 Rapper Snoop ___
113 Suffix with switch
115 Norm’s wife on “Cheers”
117 Keep under wraps
121 Khan’s title

294 ROYAL TREATMENT by Harvey Estes

37 Down is the subject of a 2004 documentary titled "Bush's Brain."

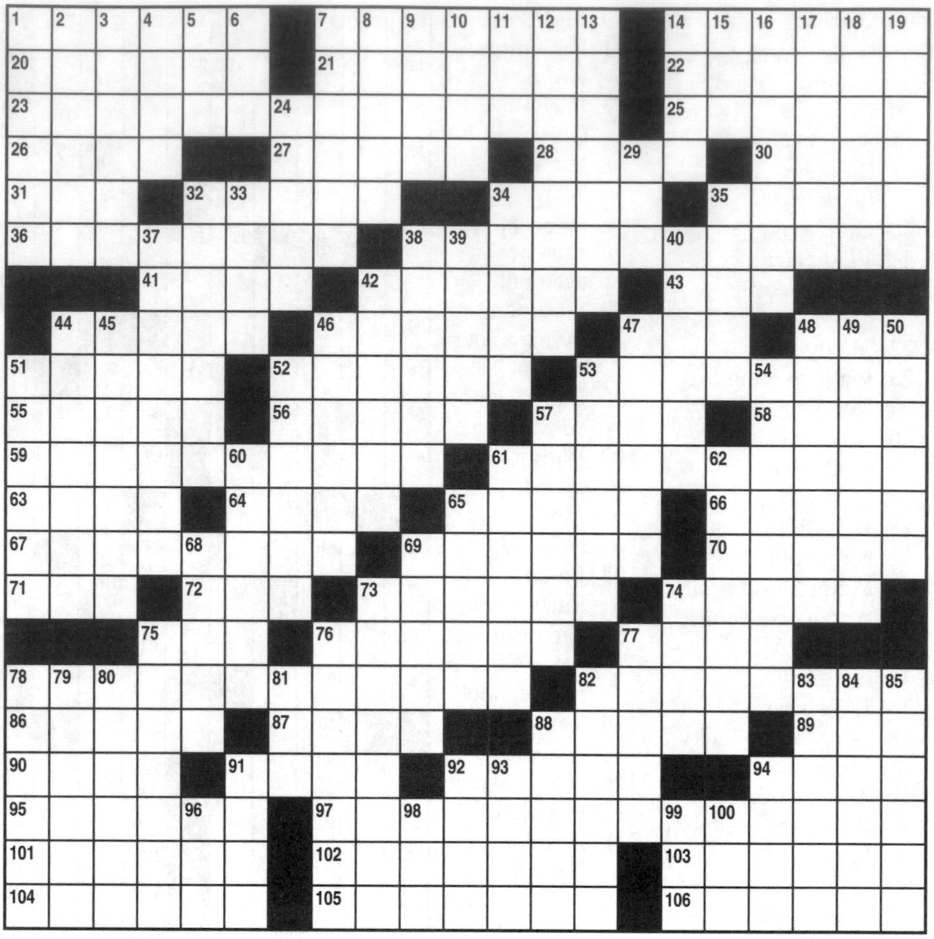

ACROSS

1 Lens settings
7 Guitarzan, for one
14 Convention pin-ons
20 Military position
21 Winnie the Pooh's creator
22 "The Murders in the Rue ___"
23 Arms profiteering?
25 Roma home
26 Hosp. workers
27 Funny incidents
28 It's pumped at a gym
30 Pod dwellers
31 Giant Manning
32 Hersey's bell town
34 Have top billing
35 Joe in "Apollo 13"
36 Gifts for execs
38 Alternative to a group discussion?
41 Face defacer
42 Sympathized with
43 Homer Simpson's neighbor
44 King of TV
46 Hour-minute dividers
47 P. Hearst's kidnappers
48 Not masc.
51 Fine fur
52 Bug zapper sites
53 Stack of fireplace logs
55 End of ___
56 Without a break
57 Fizzy drink
58 Vein contents
59 Duncan's business?
61 Better boots, e.g.?
63 Belgrade resident
64 Small coin
65 Studied, with "over"
66 Boiling mad
67 Cushy job
69 Political powwow
70 Studied, with "up on"
71 Que. neighbor
72 Thoughtful sounds
73 Even chance
74 Ease off
75 Oil can letters
76 Grain elevator features
77 Scores on a serve
78 Bearish dialogue from "Wall Street"?
82 Pub hurlers
86 Beer glass
87 Lessor amount
88 Paris parents
89 First Burmese premier
90 Gardeners' tools
91 Pencil filler
92 Capital near the pyramids
94 Ladies of Sp.
95 Bring on
97 Supply of tickets for meter maids?
101 Archeologist's prizes
102 Moved like bees
103 Like nursery rhyme blackbirds
104 Dangerous fly
105 As a group
106 Fingerprint made visible by dusting

DOWN

1 Fictitious
2 Paper fastener
3 Court activity
4 Acorn producers
5 Omega's preceder
6 DC figure
7 Glossy stuff
8 Cowboy's cry
9 Opening words of "Da Doo Ron Ron"
10 Penpoints
11 Shine, in commercial names
12 Hostile feelings
13 Change a product name
14 Hacker's cry
15 "Com" preceder
16 In a net
17 Radiant
18 South American coastal region
19 Add spice to
24 Catch basin cover
29 URL ending
32 Really funny
33 Plead innocent to
34 Shirts' opponents
35 Golfer Sam
37 George W. Bush's "architect"
38 Feeling under the weather
39 Got up
40 To be returned
42 Packing a wallop
44 Wool fat
45 Temporarily suspended
46 Poodle or pug
47 Three-dimensional objects
48 Insect with a burning sting
49 Winner of a race
50 Dovetailed
51 States as fact
52 Fire stirrers
53 Snapped out of it
54 "Yankee" dish
57 Tent show
60 Keenness of mind
61 Two halves of Congress
62 Holds up to public scorn
65 Cut's partner
68 IHOP, for one
69 Dracula's title
73 Reduce
74 Suburban plot
75 Aspen attire
76 Purify
77 Baseball's Hank
78 Souvenir shop item
79 Makes amends
80 Poke fun at
81 Hurdle for srs.
82 Pooh-pooh
83 Part of the Old World
84 Tylenol alternative
85 Minuteman's weapon
88 Studio sound equipment
91 Add-on for Congo
92 Irene of "Fame"
93 Equips for war
94 ERA or RBI
96 Office dupes, for short
98 Dawber of "Mork and Mindy"
99 Bellows of "Ally McBeal"
100 White stuff, in Dundee

295 TURNER DROPS IN by Arlan and Linda Bushman

At 15 Down, it all depends if you're pitching or hitting.

ACROSS

1 Place for seniors
7 Zoom by
11 Small craft on a large craft
20 Rostand's duelist
21 Biz honcho
22 Schedule
23 As originally positioned
24 A good price on a choice in skirts?
26 Madre's child
28 Warbler's syllable
29 Kingston coll.
30 In a huff
31 Used bombast in an election campaign?
38 Russian barley beer
40 Nobelist Wiesel
41 Aare tributary
42 Listing filler letters
43 Bray beginning
44 Seasoned
45 Some believers
48 Undercover work
53 Ancient name for Rock of Gibraltar
55 Barbarian king when pursued by enemies?
57 Uncertain
59 Recipe word
60 Hogwash
61 Southwest rival
62 Popular '50s TV series
64 Inveigle
67 Hyde Park transport
68 Much of Oceania
71 Fresh
73 Joanne of film
74 Kegler's banes
76 Island spirits
77 Lace end
79 Napoli's land
81 Draft pick
82 Relation
84 Relief lead-in
86 Thrash (about)
90 Scout jamboree training center?
95 Carved pillar
96 Trunk find
97 Become misty-eyed
99 Colossal
100 Wall St. special
101 It's a blast
103 Texas pro, slangily
104 Fuss over
105 Following behind
108 Where to find all the SROs?
112 Sully
113 Mideast garment
115 Mauna ___
116 Genesis figure
117 Took on an accountant's duty?
123 Actress Langdon
127 Spelled out exactly
128 Expanse
129 Proverbs
130 Hannibal's mount over the mounts
131 Da's opposite
132 Unruffled

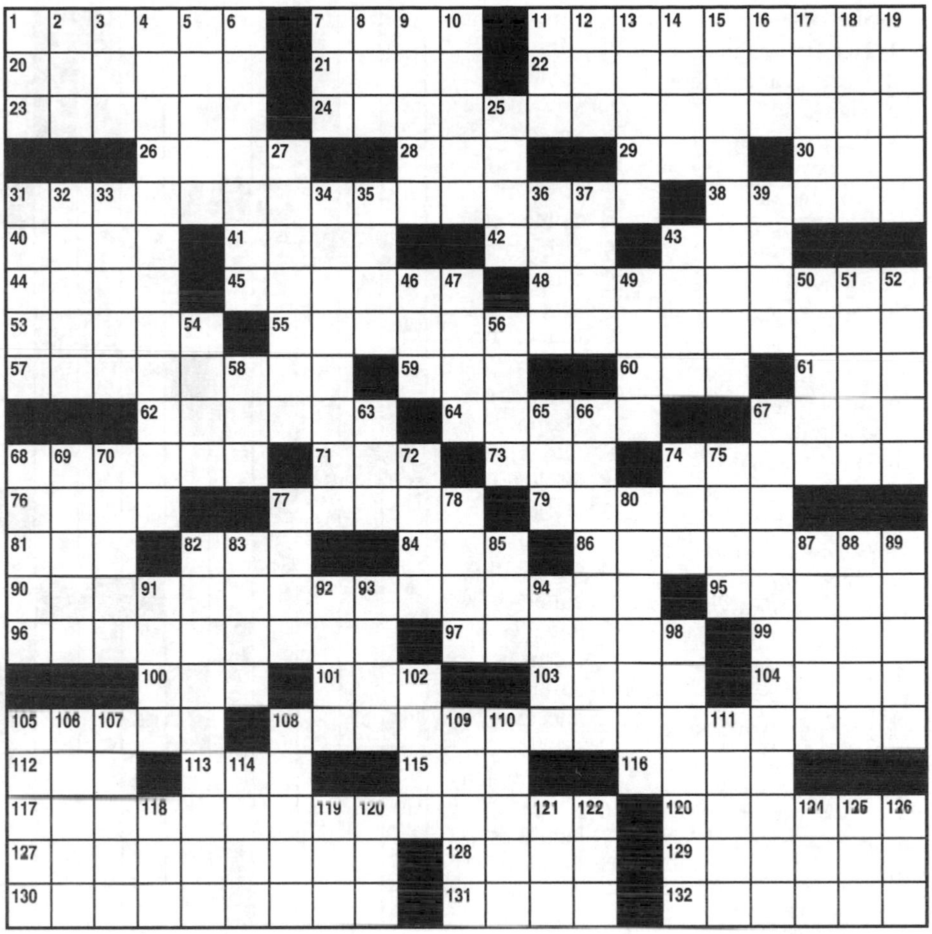

DOWN

1 A fifth of MV
2 Novelist Rand
3 Malaprop's title
4 Colorful caplets?
5 Disentangle
6 Dove, as a whale
7 Get-up-and-go
8 Rose of rock
9 Carry out
10 Muffler
11 Jeanne d'Arc, e.g.
12 Masked
13 Fill with
14 Carol tree
15 Fail or suceed, in baseball
16 Catch
17 Clinton's 2008 rival
18 Fake handle
19 Cares for
25 "Mr. Republican"
27 Person ___ (well-to-do one)
31 Attain
32 Pond buildup
33 Scientist Bohr
34 Skipping
35 Balance
36 "A likely story!"
37 It can be petty
39 Type of diagram
43 Steve Allen's "___ Steverino"
46 Faith's mate
47 Buttonhole, for instance
49 Vivacious
50 Early name in video games
51 Insinuate
52 Wax-covered cheeses
54 Bibliography notation
56 Sent packing
58 Beast of burden
63 Reef lurker
65 Hosp. procedure
66 Suggest
67 Buried tulip bulbs in the fall, e.g.
68 Most Lebanese
69 Spring harbinger
70 Rolex competitor
72 Intricate contrivances
74 ___-pitch
75 Papal name
77 Not in favor
78 Discretion
80 Enchants
82 Be on the lookout
83 Keen on
85 Any ship
87 Cache
88 Sterling
89 Went full tilt
91 Green Day, for one
92 "Ben-Hur" costume designer
93 Turn away
94 Brewery object
98 Impersonates
102 Travel expense
105 "Who's there?" reply
106 Birth related
107 Switch
108 Black Forest spa
109 Fireballer Ryan
110 Grocery section
111 Chopin piece
114 Banjo player Fleck
118 Weightlifting unit
119 Carlsbad dweller
120 Treasury div.
121 Once called
122 Hood's heater
124 Turkish honorific
125 Bottom line
126 Linguistic suffix

296 GRIME AND 115 ACROSS by Harvey Estes

The punny clue at 17 Down is not theme-related.

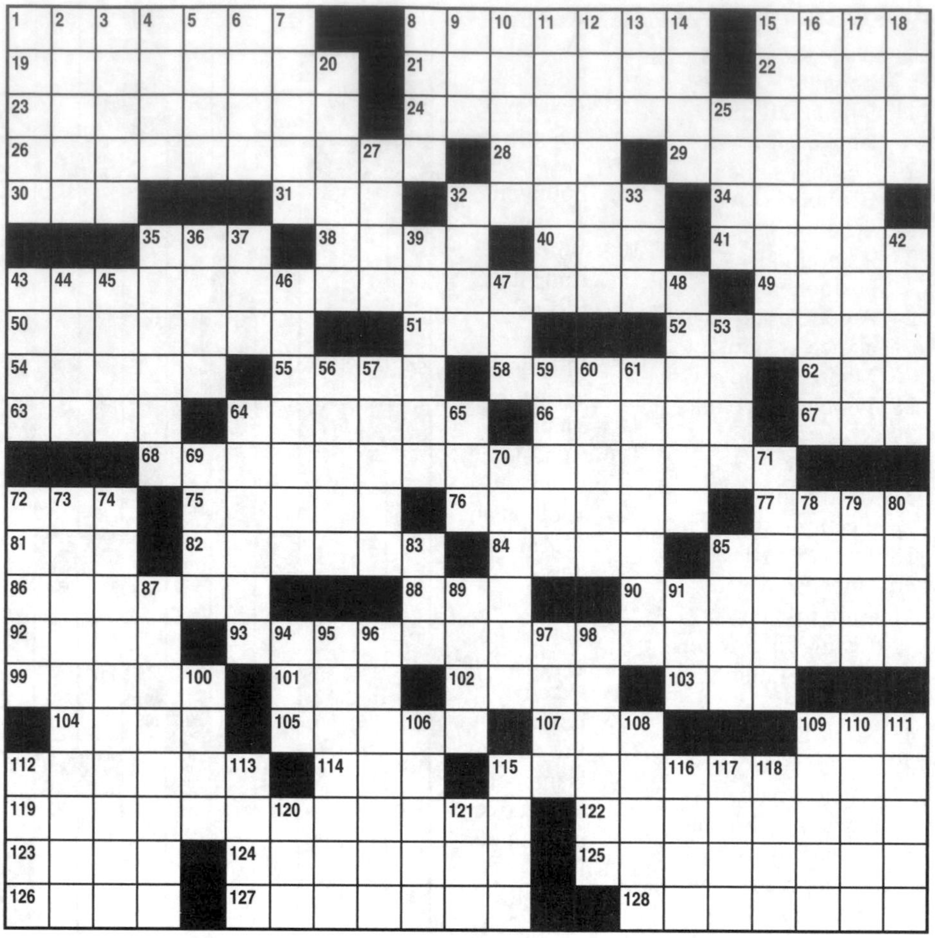

ACROSS

1 Hera or Athena
8 River near Rutgers
15 Sign over
19 How some entrées are served
21 Birmingham resource
22 Jump for Tara Lipinski
23 Call in again
24 Athenian in a teen drama?
26 Steal some computers?
28 Have the blahs
29 Hobos
30 And so forth
31 Berliner's article
32 Stop with
34 European range
35 Sense of humor
38 Laments loudly
40 JFK info
41 Mother, for Mark Antony
43 Peter and Paul's avarice?
49 Costa ___
50 Turn down
51 Letters after CD
52 Puts in the mail, maybe
54 Sure competitor
55 Thailand, once
58 Mexican cowboy
62 Volleyball gear
63 Zola's zip
64 Fashion show locale
66 Had dinner at home
67 RR terminal
68 Bad food with unjust deserts? (with 115-A)
72 "Sort of" suffix
75 Fictional Gantry
76 Laughs noisily
77 Jason Lee's "My Name Is ___"
81 Encl. to an editor
82 Cut calories
84 Femme fatale in "The Carpetbaggers"
85 Ice house
86 Apply haphazardly
88 Sturgeon stuff
90 Strong cigar
92 Munich Mister
93 Green cheese shredders?
99 First name in cosmetics
101 Some cells
102 Critic's unit
103 Sault ___ Marie
104 Marker tip material
105 Brother of Harpo
107 Old witch
109 Scale tones
112 Hyundai model
114 Originally called
115 See 68 Across
119 Author's ancestor?
122 Inherited
123 Teen malady
124 Femur neighbor
125 Poor odds
126 Asks for alms
127 Becomes blue
128 Threefold

DOWN

1 Pig out
2 Plain to see
3 Cul-___
4 Defeat decisively
5 Humorist Bombeck
6 Lamebrain
7 Rifle attachment
8 Frees (of)
9 Parseghian of football
10 "Laugh-In" cohost
11 Clique member
12 "Just missed!"
13 Prince Valiant's son
14 Hornet's home
15 Certain horn triggerer
16 Dependents, on 1040
17 Ocean mystery?
18 Civic group
20 Join the army
25 The G in EKG
27 Organic compound
32 Gas brand in Toronto
33 ___ kwon do
35 On the decline
36 Apple gizmo
37 Young'un
39 Chris of ESPN
42 Dreadlocked cultist
43 Former Russian ruler
44 Part of an espionage name
45 Fictional governess
46 Flip response to a complaint
47 Acadia automaker
48 Persian king
53 Gossip follower Barrett
56 Narrow waterway
57 Cognizant
59 Asian capital
60 To ___ (perfectly)
61 Computer command
64 Authoritative decision
65 Back gains: Abbr.
69 Go back to the drawing board
70 Troubled state
71 Soybean or sweet pea
72 "___ Really Going Out With Him"
73 Twelve drummers drumming, perhaps?
74 Encouraging
78 On top of that
79 ___-Rooter
80 Bird in a crazy simile
83 Dr. of the rap world
85 Sceptic's scoff
87 Bishops, etc.
89 Estimator's words
91 Sounds of surprise
94 "Shoe" waitress
95 Exacted satisfaction for
96 Like chopsticks
97 Surfer's paradise
98 James in "James Dean"
100 Ending for Jean or Ann
106 Hippie's catchword
108 James Dean film
109 Words before car or cop
110 Return key on a PC
111 Obdurate
112 Clean the deck
113 Torah holders
115 Letter extender
116 Hook's ally
117 Survivor, sometimes
118 St. Paul's state
120 Dundee precipitation
121 "Whew!"

297 BOOKENDS by Arlan and Linda Bushman

Famous novels are clued by their famous last words.

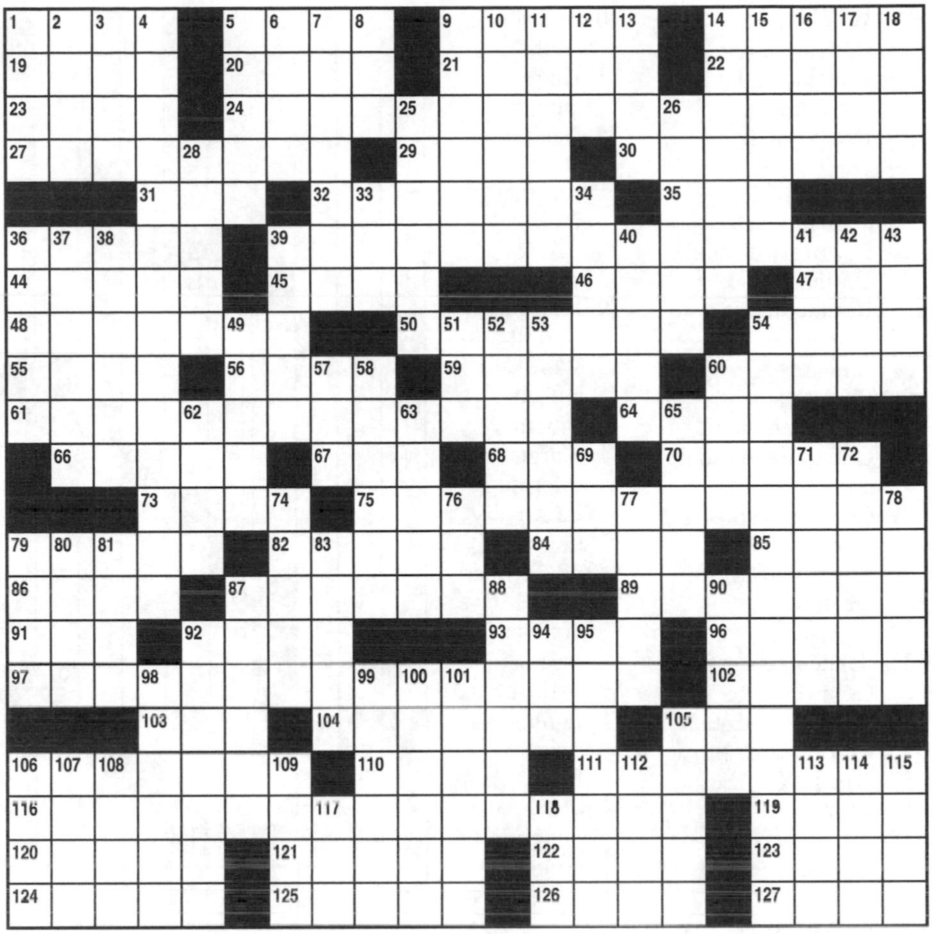

ACROSS

1 Prattle
5 Hawser
9 Impassive
14 Like some cadets
19 One and the other
20 Galatea's love
21 Potawatomi Indian of TV
22 Durance of "Smallville"
23 Pentathlon item
24 **. . . and her lips came together and smiled mysteriously."**
27 Midway game
29 River in Spain
30 Analogous
31 Tins opener?
32 Marine slowpoke
35 Break down
36 On the main
39 **". . . left the hospital and walked back to the hotel in the rain."**
44 Tonsured one
45 Swain
46 Tap brand
47 Give the once-over
48 Trumpet blast
50 Picketer's burden
54 Blue Nile lake
55 Diana in "Evil Under the Sun"
56 Grp. for amateurs
59 Cut off
60 "Jeepers!"
61 **". . . traced in space the sign of the dollar."**
64 Scruff
66 Light into
67 Buffet contraption
68 Finback school
70 Chocolate tree
73 Hebrides isle
75 **"Morning: excellent and fair."**
79 Classroom prop
82 Café addition
84 Baltic native
85 Auction units
86 Long-petaled bloom
87 Most nigh
89 Town of Arthurian legend
91 Thurman in "Gattaca"
92 "She's All ___" (1999)
93 Lena in "Casanova"
96 Seawater
97 **"After all, tomorrow is another day."**
102 Half-domes
103 Comedy world nickname
104 Calls for silence
105 Winter woe
106 Disco gear
110 90° from norte
111 Hustler's haunt
116 **". . . which is the song of the pack."**
119 Quarry
120 Bonheur and Parks
121 Agave fiber
122 Colchis-bound craft
123 Animal house
124 Bizarre
125 Knotty problem
126 Four quarters
127 Raines of film

DOWN

1 Many a trucker
2 Kachina maker
3 Ancient sun god
4 **". . . borne back ceaselessly into the past."**
5 Finger
6 Newspaperman Adolph
7 Oldtime kitchen storage piece
8 Monogram of mysteries
9 Not flighty
10 Nosebleed seating section
11 Low tie score
12 Neutral pronoun
13 Murmurs
14 Lunar phase
15 Juan's exultant cry
16 Potion holder
17 Proceedings
18 Once-tailed actor
25 Start angrily
26 Two-___ drinker
28 Headband
33 Cote remark
34 Violinist Mischa
36 TV/radio union
37 Peculiarities
38 Unattached
39 Disconcert
40 "Two Women" Oscar winner
41 Paper count
42 Gregarious avian
43 Penn name
49 Out of practice
51 Trail
52 First Hebrew letter
53 Foul-tasting panacea
54 **". . . I think this the youngest us ever felt."**
57 Tulsa campus
58 "Drat!"
60 Moonfish
62 Benefit
63 Travelocity "spokesperson"
65 Bank hldgs.
69 Jay preceder
71 Garlicky sauces
72 Pump figure
74 High repute
76 Footlike part
77 Tree bunch
78 Adlai's 1956 running mate
79 Pouring sound
80 Celeb's perk
81 Wang Lung's wife
83 Some IRAs
87 Rodin implement
88 Junco cousin
90 Game for young sluggers
92 ___ hit (double)
94 Whopper
95 Fire up
98 Prius, for one
99 Police concern
100 Scurry
101 Swimming star Williams
105 Travel guru
106 Houston pro, slangily
107 Khayyam picnic partner
108 Unwind
109 Marina spot
112 "Three Sisters" sister
113 Voiced
114 Trompe l'___ (art illusion)
115 Pianist Hess
117 Bear in Bilbao
118 Mode

298 SAVE THE CAKE FOR LAST* by Harvey Estes

8 Down was also a 1987 Supreme Court nominee of Ronald Reagan.

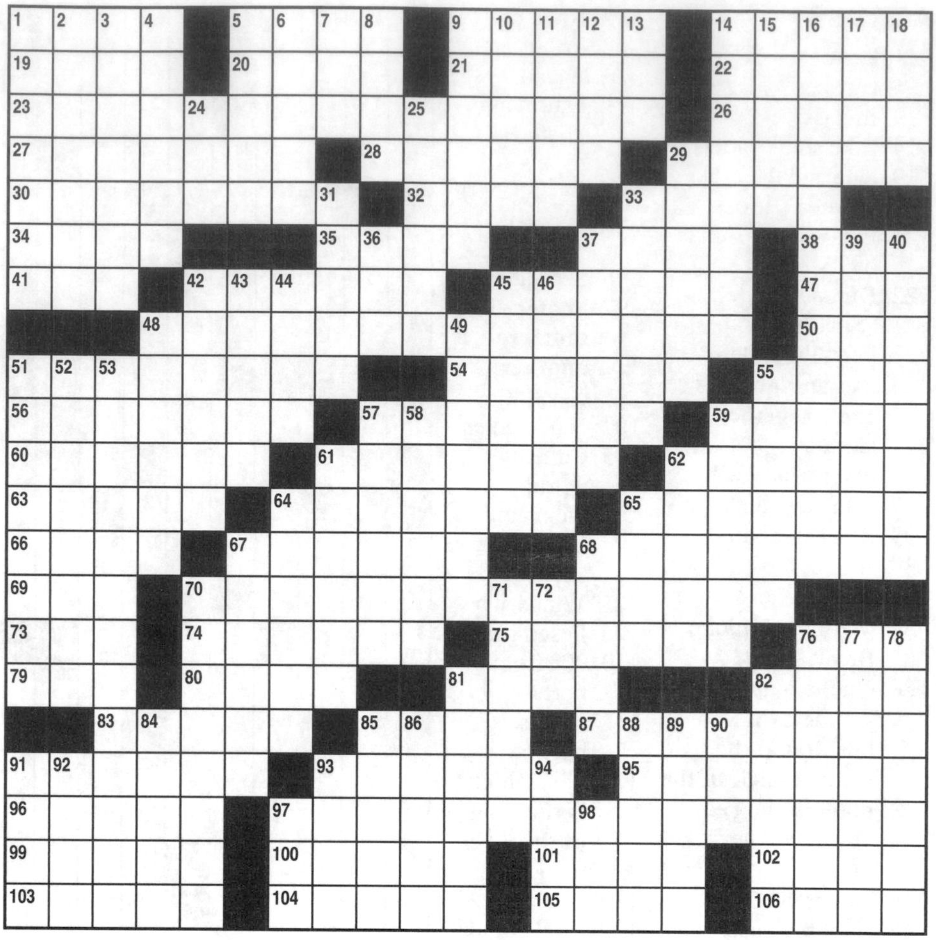

ACROSS

1 Rick's old flame
5 Chuck wagon serving
9 Puts a wave in
14 Door joint
19 At no time, poetically
20 Cry of frustration
21 Online sales
22 Bomber name
23 Man greeted by actresses*
26 Reel person
27 Get, as an idea
28 One of the martial arts
29 Campaign speech spots
30 Insectivorous creature
32 Hr. parts
33 Sanders or Goldwater
34 Senators and such
35 Kind of code or rug
37 Fox's "X-Files" partner
38 Unmannerly man
41 Hydrocarbon ending
42 Data on sales tags
45 Research papers
47 Popular vehicle, for short
48 Imbibe excessively*
50 Chest muscle
51 Military offensives
54 Purpose
55 Gangster's lady
56 England–France connector
57 Masculine and feminine
59 Underworld group
60 Fixed, but not repaired
61 Wastes away
62 Long suits
63 Milky gems
64 Firecrackers
65 Foreman's force
66 Devoid of duds
67 Singer Vic
68 Get smaller
69 Palindromist's exclamation
70 Adam's apple*
73 Huge amount
74 Beginnings
75 As a surprising fact
76 Greek consonants
79 Pink Floyd's Barrett
80 Words before "about"
81 Starbucks offering, informally
82 Overstuff
83 Audited, as a class
85 Toto's creator
87 Tight-lipped
91 Long for (with "to")
93 Bunghole's place
95 Supports a foundation
96 "Ghostbusters" goop
97 Bush cabinet member*
99 Units of distance
100 Less than
101 Revelatory cry
102 K–12, textbook-wise
103 Caring for (with "on")
104 Whistle stops
105 Grp. or org.
106 Morse clicks

DOWN

1 Physically fit
2 Made privy to
3 Niles' hometown
4 Doesn't let the issue die
5 Beckett no-show
6 Wine region of France
7 Game with "Reverse" cards
8 Swedish Chef on "The Muppet Show"
9 Noted test-marketing city
10 Vermont's Allen
11 Hurls invectives
12 Coal site
13 Kind of dog
14 Prickly problem
15 Acquire, as debt
16 No favorite of Earl Grey?*
17 Unappetizing fare
18 Hearing aids
24 Clean Air Act enforcement gp.
25 Shakespeare's king
29 Least wacko
31 Dress shop needs
33 Laundry room tubs
36 Prot. or Cath.
37 Puts off
39 Places for canvases
40 No longer chic
42 Wrinkly snacks
43 Het up
44 Pt. of IMF
45 Took care of
46 They can't stand
48 Hang loosely
49 Very similar
51 Circus performers
52 Cry from the crow's-nest
53 Little girl "ingredients"*
55 Trading center
57 Begin immediately
58 Twisty-horned animals
59 Finicky cat
61 Dues payer
62 Prepare to shoot
64 Manse dweller
65 Prefix for wolf?
67 Mr. Darko
68 Note above C
70 Part of a dentist's chair
71 Crown material
72 Armistice mo.
76 They have chambers
77 Dutch city
78 Judo teachers
81 Peers at a trial
82 Eyed impolitely
84 Woman's name meaning "loved"
85 Like "A Hard Day's Night"
86 "Our Miss Brooks" star Eve
88 Carpentry tools
89 Defraud
90 One-million link
91 Dangerous snakes
92 Picnic side
93 U2 frontman
94 Jabba the Hutt's captive
97 Cry on the set
98 Curve shape

299 RARE WORDS I by Arthur S. Verdesca

An award-winning challenger with a 23-Across theme.

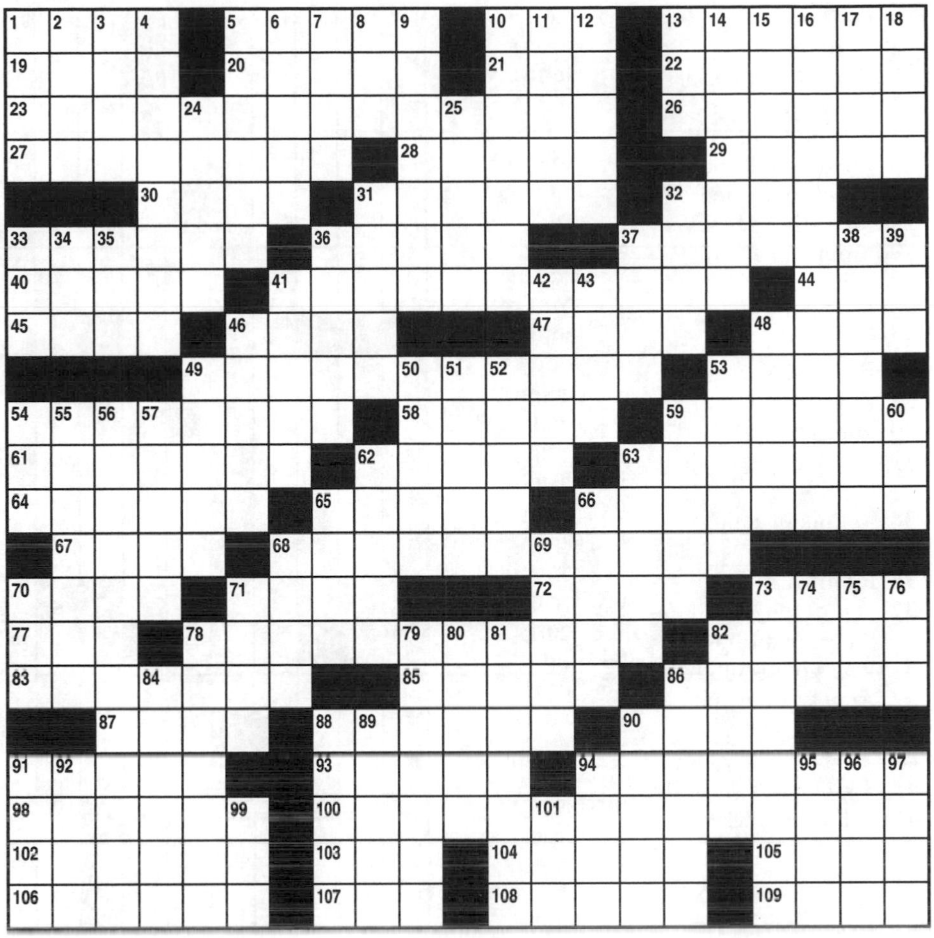

ACROSS

1 Straw grabbers
5 David Copperield's mother
10 Norm or avg.
13 1971 Beatty title role
19 Notion of Nancy
20 Automaton
21 Vet
22 Realm of Oedipus
23 Long word
26 Dances saucily
27 Added up
28 Trinidad fruit
29 Huff
30 Geo. VI's wife
31 Garth of "What I Like About You"
32 Computer list
33 Short, stocky, and muscular
36 Ignoramus
37 Turn loose
40 Proclamation
41 Counterclockwise
44 Howard Hughes once controlled it
45 One of a British group
46 Polaris bear
47 Rosalind Russell role
48 Prompting pro
49 Nail-biting
53 Breathing rattle
54 Nares
58 Skyrockets
59 Thus far
61 Lump sum alternative
62 Travis of country
63 Dropped in
64 Spheres
65 Crop up
66 Inhabitants
67 Airline since 1948
68 Elementary
70 Passageway
71 Atlas abbr.
72 Basks
73 Low
77 Green trailer
78 Hodgepodge
82 Ill-humored
83 Erase a magnetic tape
85 Plague
86 Coterie of undesirables
87 Leave out
88 Anger
90 Squealed
91 Raymond Burr role
93 Radical
94 Monument inscriptions
98 Revere
100 Hypochondriac
102 Haberdashery item
103 Morph or phon ending
104 Between, to Jean
105 Res ___ loquitur
106 Hector
107 Set-___ (fights)
108 Now alternative
109 PDQ relative

DOWN

1 Homer's daughter
2 Same as previously
3 Cantina cash
4 Succession
5 Reviewer
6 NBA twins
7 Retired
8 Wand
9 All over
10 Walleye lure
11 Bingham of "Baywatch"
12 Recipient
13 Small peaks
14 Hitching posts?
15 Singer Dion
16 Take it on the lam
17 Inamorato
18 Existence
24 Dark
25 Parrish of baseball
31 Jacob's fourth son
32 Word Daniel translated
33 Louvre Pyramid architect
34 Matt Ryan's stats: Abbr.
35 About 0.62 mi.
36 Some are compact
37 Frost-covered
38 Make a pot bigger
39 Talent for music
41 In a sardonic way
42 Sting
43 Old crones
46 Squads
48 City near Gibraltar
49 Window for plants
50 "Hamlet" courtier
51 Social grace
52 Despised
53 Bow need
54 Hound
55 Taking a sabbatical
56 Shrewd, unprincipled one
57 ___-cain (Lamech's son)
59 Brown and Turner
60 Harris and Wynn
62 "Three Coins in the Fountain" fountain
63 Like tree leaves
65 Explorer Tasman
66 "Advise and Consent" author
68 "___ Well That Ends Well"
69 With respect to
70 Concealed
71 Occasional dummy
73 Macedonia neighbor
74 Backward era?
75 Camera type, familiarly
76 Spud bud
78 Old British gold coins
79 Symbols of authority
80 Gide or Watts
81 Still on the plate
82 Reindeer driver
84 Star of a slide show?
86 Fancy dive
88 Bed covering
89 Cottonwood
90 Tapering structure
91 John Wesley's denom.
92 Himalayan setting
94 1999 Ron Howard film
95 Apple seeds
96 ___ ball (enjoys)
97 Cinch
99 Robinson or Doubtfire
101 Nice number

300 RARE WORDS II by Arthur S. Verdesca

Should the clue at 26 Across be song peddler?

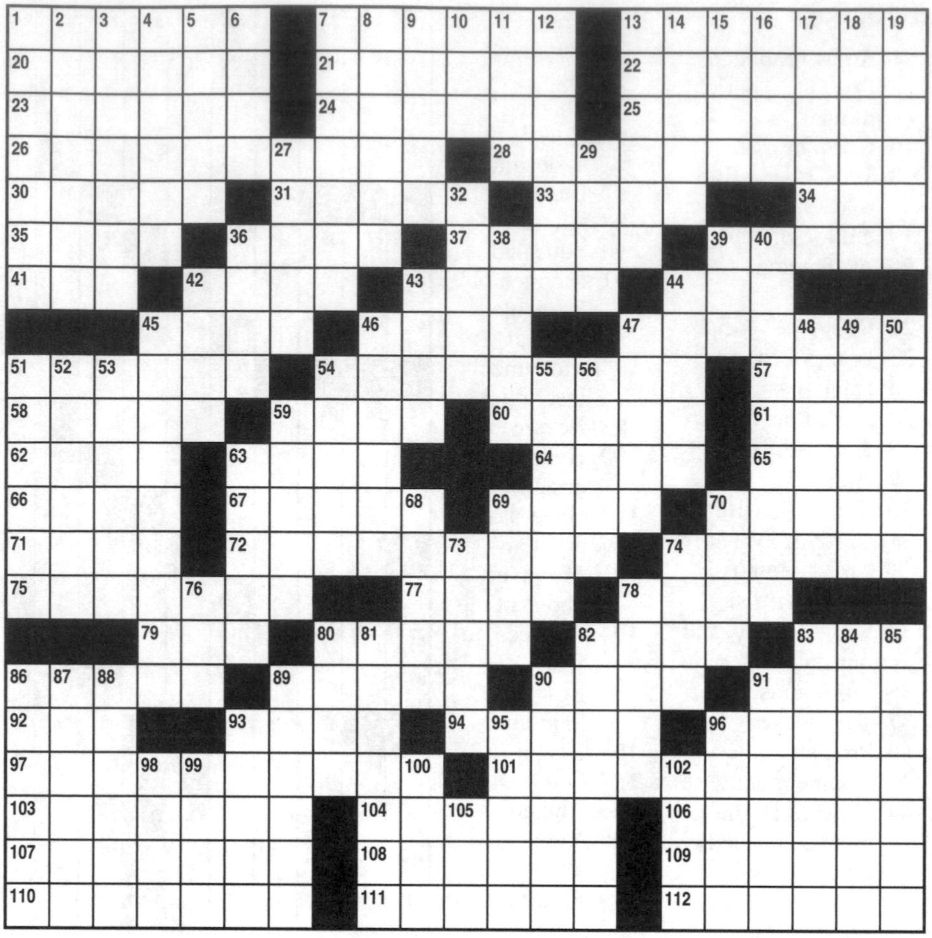

ACROSS

1 Care for
7 Envelope material
13 *Iron clamp around a champagne cork
20 French-built rocket
21 RNA component
22 More farinaceous
23 Mountain chain
24 Outgoing
25 It's full of unknowns
26 Book peddler
28 Ill temper
30 Foreign
31 Artifices
33 Nullify
34 Majors in acting
35 Split
36 Renown
37 Top of the heap
39 Sharif and Epps
41 Peer Gynt's mother
42 Attack commands
43 Brown ermine
44 Type of shot
45 Soul mate
46 Alliance est. 1949
47 Closed loudly
51 Jolly Green Giant outburst
54 War of words
57 Downsize
58 Word form for "wind"
59 Cubs' clubs
60 Derision
61 Military addresses
62 Novi Sad native
63 Pueblo resident
64 So be it
65 Skater Kulik
66 Ventura County valley
67 Olympic star in 1936
69 Leary tripped on it
70 Change a bill
71 Score after deuce
72 Baldheaded one
74 Evidence of erasure
75 Maines of the Dixie Chicks
77 Peru's "City of the Kings"
78 Wilander of tennis
79 Decennary number
80 Last of a series
82 Latin god
83 RMN's predecessor
86 Shortest river of Germany
89 Avis alternative
90 Advance
91 Food and drink
92 Vowel sequence
93 "You're lookin' at your person!"
94 Applies shingles
96 Taste
97 Sassy
101 Having very large feet
103 Treated poorly
104 Imp
106 Surface
107 Laborers
108 Subject of a will
109 Farrier's forge
110 *A person who never laughs
111 In common
112 Beliefs

DOWN

1 Lash extender
2 Baltimore nine
3 Phone link
4 Pulled some strings
5 Former Astros' Field
6 Erect
7 Docent hirers
8 Excite
9 Button material
10 Here, in Paris
11 Novelist O'Flaherty
12 Deposits along a river bed
13 Soprano Materna
14 Freezing
15 Sock or sweater material
16 Oakland A, e.g.
17 Tibia's neighbor
18 "Giant" author
19 Wipes clean
27 Flattop's foe
29 Trent of Mississippi
32 Brawl
36 Dog tag?
38 Impends
39 Schnozz add-on
40 Bigoted opponent of reform
42 Manhattan district
43 Caves in
44 "Captain Blood" actor
45 Buzz or drone
46 Jotting down
47 Fragment
48 Posted
49 Fouling up
50 Infamous Marquis
51 Former Moroccan king
52 Turning Stone Casino tribe
53 Solitudinarian
54 Carnation spot
55 Gum arabic tree
56 Droll
59 "Let's Dance" singer
63 Cabbie's invitation
68 Hawthorne's home
69 Soprano Gluck
70 Acct. nos.
73 Harshness
74 Faisal deposed him
76 Irish sea god
78 Brainy bunch
80 Mishmash
81 Ripens
82 Unclean
83 Indiana county
84 Fetched
85 Varsity wear
86 Pumpkin seed
87 Flight-recorder data
88 Air Force Academy frosh
89 In the thick of
90 Discover
91 Filming technique
93 Champagne buckets
95 Green Mupppet
96 Amiens river
98 Gather
99 Out with the buoys
100 Casement
102 Nuisance
105 RR stop

ANSWERS

FOREWORD

BAIT
SECRET
RESTAREA
WHATISMADE
TEEMS SOLAR
DELTS RIGOR
REACT BLUES
AFRO EGRET
FROM HOLE
TAPER RULE
YEMEN RITES
NANAS SEDER
TECHS COVES
WHEATFLOUR
OSCULATE
ARROWS
ONES

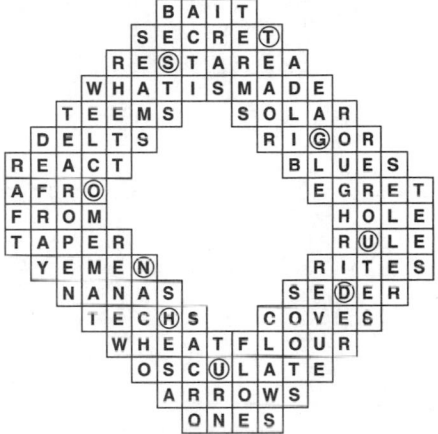

Riddle answer: DOUGHNUTS

1

B	A	K	E	R		M	A	I	N		B	O	N	D
O	L	I	V	A		A	L	T	O		E	R	I	E
U	L	N	A	E		S	L	O	B		G	I	N	A
R	M	S		S	Q	U	A	R	E		A	G	E	D
B	A	H	T		T	R	Y		L	E	N	A	P	E
O	L	I	V	E	R			A	I	L		M	I	N
N	E	P	A	L		M	E	S	S	Y		I	N	D
				S	T	R	E	E	T	S				
D	E	M		T	A	I	N	T		E	D	I	T	H
O	L	A		O	R	S			R	E	E	C	H	O
W	E	R	E	N	T		D	I	O		B	E	A	U
N	A	T	S		R	O	U	T	E	S		A	L	S
I	N	I	T		A	D	D	S		N	A	G	A	T
N	O	N	A		T	E	E	M		O	N	E	M	O
G	R	U	B		E	A	S	Y		B	A	S	I	N

2

W	A	N	D	A		C	H	E	F		E	L	S	A
I	S	A	A	C		H	Y	P	O		N	A	E	S
M	I	G	H	T	Y	A	P	H	R	O	D	I	T	E
P	A	S		R	O	S	E		E	R	O	T	I	C
			C	E	N	T		S	P	E	W			
V	E	N	U	S	D	E	M	I	L	O		B	B	A
C	L	A	P	S			O	L	A		T	R	A	D
H	E	M	I		M	A	D	L	Y		H	A	L	O
I	C	E	D		A	R	E			F	E	V	E	R
P	T	S		V	I	O	L	A	D	A	M	O	R	E
			K	I	D	D		R	I	L	E			
F	E	M	A	L	E		A	D	D	L		T	A	D
I	N	T	H	E	N	A	M	E	O	F	L	O	V	E
L	Y	N	N		L	Y	O	N		O	A	S	I	S
L	A	S	S		Y	E	S	T		R	O	S	S	I

3

T	E	A	M		C	O	M	B		A	W	A	I	T
A	S	T	I		A	R	O	O		B	E	R	N	E
C	A	T	S	O	F	T	H	O	U	S	A	N	D	S
H	U	S	S	Y			S	T	R		R	O	Y	S
			T	E	S	T		H	I	S	S			
D	E	S	E	R	T	O	N	E	S	P	O	T	S	
S	N	A	P		U	N	E			U	N	I	T	E
C	I	G		O	N	G	U	A	R	D		N	A	Y
S	A	A	B	S			R	C	A		O	G	R	E
	C	L	O	S	E	T	O	T	H	E	V	E	T	S
			L	A	N	E		I	S	L	E			
I	A	G	O		U	T	E			S	R	T	A	S
G	R	I	T	S	F	O	R	T	H	E	M	I	L	L
G	E	L	I	D		N	I	N	A		A	D	E	E
Y	A	L	E	S		S	E	N	T		N	E	E	D

4

S	W	A	G		B	O	M	B	E		C	R	A	M
W	H	E	E		A	R	I	A	N		R	O	M	A
E	A	S	T	E	R	N	O	R	T	H	O	D	O	X
A	L	O		V	I	A		B	R	E	W	S	K	I
R	E	P	R	I	N	T	S		E	N	E			
			B	A	G	E	L	S	A	N	D	L	O	X
T	O	X	I	N			I	O	T	A		A	P	R
O	H	M	S		M	C	C	O	Y		A	R	E	A
M	I	A		S	I	L	K			B	U	D	D	Y
B	O	S	T	O	N	R	E	D	S	O	X			
			T	A	D		R	E	T	R	O	F	I	T
T	R	A	U	M	A	S		B	O	A		U	V	E
R	O	B	B	I	N	G	F	O	R	T	K	N	O	X
I	S	L	E		A	T	O	N	E		A	G	R	A
M	A	Y	S		O	S	I	E	R		T	O	Y	S

5

P	O	P	S		R	A	G	T	A	G		M	D	R
L	S	A	T		E	S	P	A	N	A		C	A	A
A	C	R	O	S	S	W	O	R	D	M	I	G	H	T
C	U	T	R	A	T	E				S	T	I	L	T
E	L	A	I	N	E		T	A	J		A	L	I	E
M	A	K	E	A	P	E	R	S	O	N	G	L	A	D
A	T	E	S			T	O	L	D	T	O			
T	E	S		B	O	Y	T	O	Y	S		D	I	P
			S	E	R	M	O	N			P	I	T	A
E	V	E	N	T	H	O	U	G	H	C	R	O	S	S
N	E	N	E		E	N	T		E	R	I	C	A	S
D	R	E	A	D				A	L	A	M	E	D	A
W	O	R	D	S	M	A	K	E	O	N	E	S	A	D
E	N	G		O	N	F	O	O	T		R	E	T	E
D	A	Y		S	O	L	O	N	S		O	S	E	S

6

	F	A	S	T	S				P	O	O	L	S	
L	A	C	T	A	T	E		P	E	R	D	I	E	M
I	N	H	E	R	E	S		I	C	E	D	T	E	A
S	N	I	P	P	E	T		S	A	S	S	E	R	S
P	I	E	H	O	L	E		A	N	T	A	R	E	S
S	E	V	E	N	T	E	E	N		E	R	A	S	E
	S	E	N	S	O		M	O	R	S	E	L	S	
					W	H	O	S	E					
	F	E	A	R	N	O	T		S	T	R	A	W	
T	I	L	D	A		S	E	C	T	I	O	N	A	L
O	N	E	O	C	A	T		H	A	N	S	O	L	O
B	A	G	P	I	P	E		A	R	I	E	T	T	A
E	L	A	T	E	R	S		S	E	E	T	H	E	D
G	E	N	E	S	E	S		M	A	S	T	E	R	S
	S	T	E	T	S				S	T	A	R	S	

7

```
KICK■SPIT■BEREA
ACAN■ALLE■IDONT
FORECLOSE■FEUDS
KNEWHISANIONS■■
ASO■ONI■ERR■SGT
■■FOREVERAMPERE
■■■RISER■■■RARA
ESTOC■SOA■FOURS
RAIN■■■SETIN■■■
OHMONTHERANGE■■
OLE■UEY■AMI■YAO
■■CURRENTASSETS
JEANS■NAILHOLES
EERIE■ATOE■LENI
UNDER■SENS■STOA
```

8

```
EBBED■ORALB■GOB
LARGO■LONER■IDO
BRAGGADOCIO■ZOO
ESTEEMED■■KMART
■■■DAM■■OBEY■■■
STP■RODOMONTADE
NERDS■ACED■HEEL
USER■BEERY■ISTO
FLEA■AMAT■SCOOP
FANFARONADE■POE
■■■TMEN■■ARM■■■
KENYA■■ALFRESCO
NEO■JACTITATION
ENS■OVOID■TERRY
WYE■RENTS■ESSEX
```

9

```
ZITI■AVAST■EMMA
ADEN■BELLY■SEEN
PSAT■ALTAR■CLAD
■■ROOTVEGETABLE
YES■NEE■■■IPASS
EXHAUSTVALVE■■■
REEDS■■OHIO■CAA
BRED■LATHE■TANS
ATT■WAGE■■MARKS
■■■ROBERTVAUGHN
IBSEN■■■RIG■OSS
MOUNTVESUVIUS■■
ONIT■IMPEI■SHOT
FETE■BIOTA■MIRV
FRED■ELTON■CPUS
```

10

```
DOCS■SPOT■ALIBI
OMAR■AHOY■LOGAN
SERIALIZE■ACORN
EGO■PALE■SMARTS
SAMURAI■POOL■■■
■■■COMPOUNDEYES
SEDANS■CREE■AMA
ELUL■■ATE■■KRIS
TIM■MYNA■SAINTS
HAPPYENDINGS■■■
■■■ETAS■NOISILY
MAJORS■ENOL■DOE
AWARE■GRAPESODA
SONIA■ESTE■ALES
CLEAT■DEED■PSST
```

11

```
SLEW■GEMS■DFLAT
TYPO■AVOW■ERICA
ODOR■VIDEOPOKER
RICKIELEEJONES■
KAHUNA■■■ATT■■■
■■■PAW■FBI■IRIS
UHS■PATIO■GEICO
RICKEYHENDERSON
GRANT■ALARM■ENG
ETTU■AID■JIB■■■
■■■CAT■■■ENAMEL
■RIKKITIKKITAVI
CALLITADAY■MIEN
OGLER■FEEL■ANNE
BASRA■TALL■NETS
```

12

```
LESS■■CADET■GNU
PATH■SHRINE■LEG
GROUCHOMARX■IAL
APACHE■SNO■ATTY
■■■KELP■ALLOT■■
TIMEFLIESLIKEAN
ENER■ESL■■VIRGO
SGT■TRAINEE■AIN
SEETO■■HEN■STLO
ARROWFRUITFLIES
■■MANLY■LOLO■■■
SHAD■AOL■MEADOW
POI■LIKEABANANA
AND■ORANGS■ERIN
YES■ASNOT■■SENT
```

13

```
ALIBI■TOSCA■NTH
TOTAL■IOWAN■COO
ACRYLICPATS■AWL
DOYENS■STAGNANT
■■■REAM■■LAO■■■
AHA■STANFORDBET
LIMBS■DIAG■UREY
THOU■EDENS■LARK
HOSS■SECT■HENIE
ONTHECREASE■DES
■■■EDA■■NILE■■■
CELLULAR■TOPHAT
IMA■CABCRUISERS
TUG■EDEMA■SOLLA
IPO■SEEPY■ENDOR
```

14

```
LBOS■TBSP■BLOKE
AIDA■HALO■REPEL
SLOB■ABIT■OVENS
HOUREWEDEWWIN■■
EXLAX■RENDS■MRS
DIS■IOU■TSELIOT
■■■STATS■■■ANTI
WATTSTHUMBADDER
OLIO■■■MARRY■■■
RAMPSUP■GAR■PAR
ENE■ENRON■AWARE
■■WIREUKERYEYIN
PHASE■DATA■LOSE
SIREN■EPIC■SLEW
TEPEE■SICK■HANS
```

15

```
PLOD■TADA■IBEAM
RELO■HEIR■MAGNA
EVIL■ERST■PIGGY
FIVEROOMFLATS■■
ANISE■■AUEL■HIS
BEA■LAZYLOAFERS
■■■VINES■■■ALAN
PALETTE■MEASLES
UFOS■■■BOAST■■■
MANTHEPUMPS■IDE
ARE■OBEY■■OASIS
■■STUBBORNCLOGS
TUTOR■BUOY■ILSA
EMAIL■LTDS■GDAY
EARLY■ESSE■NETS
```

16

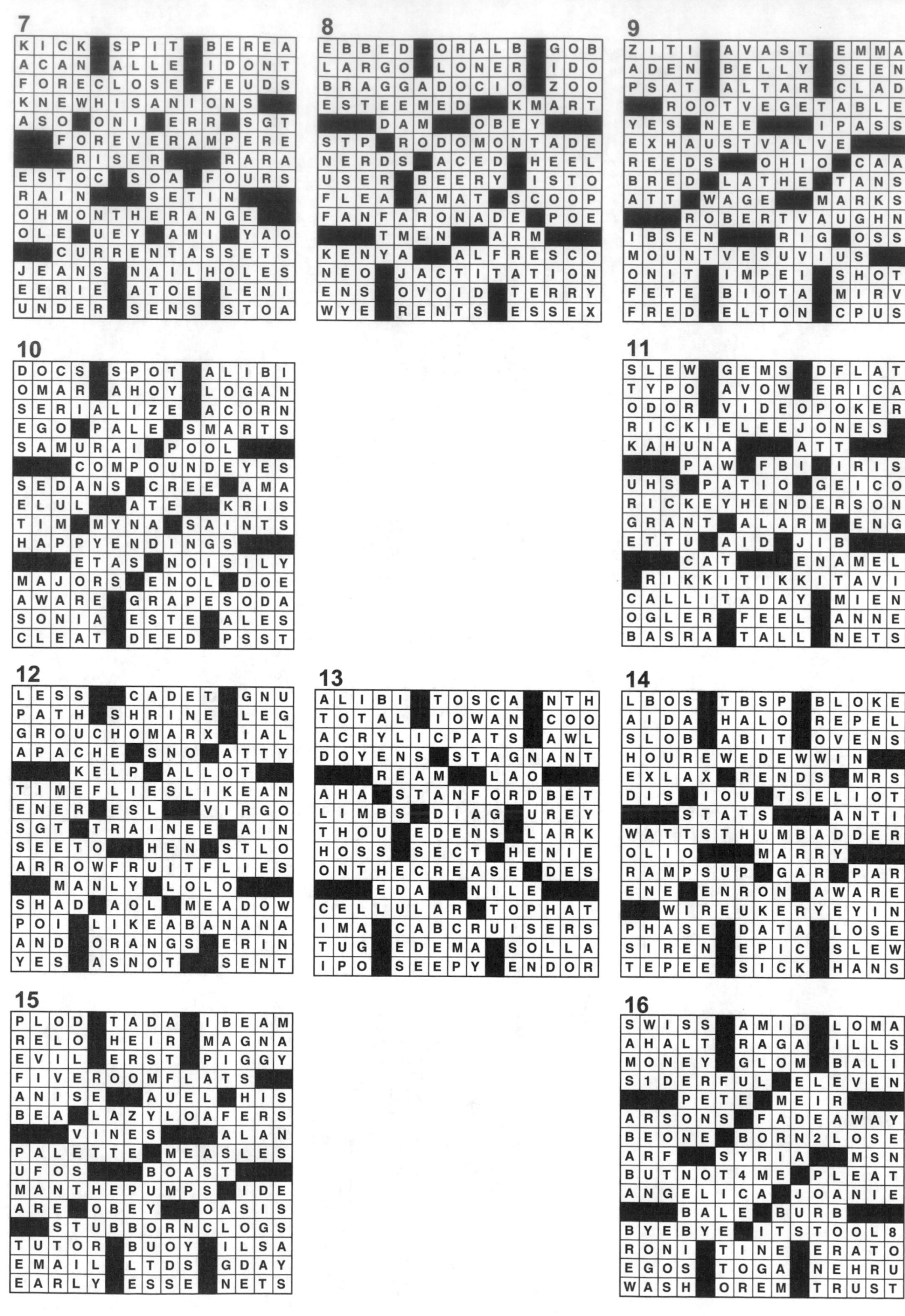

```
SWISS■AMID■LOMA
AHALT■RAGA■ILLS
MONEY■GLOM■BALI
S1DERFUL■ELEVEN
■■■PETE■MEIR■■■
ARSONS■FADEAWAY
BEONE■BORN2LOSE
ARF■■SYRIA■■MSN
BUTNOT4ME■PLEAT
ANGELICA■JOANIE
■■■BALE■BURB■■■
BYEBYE■ITSTOOL8
RONI■TINE■ERATO
EGOS■TOGA■NEHRU
WASH■OREM■TRUST
```

17

CARED HOP FELLA
ABACI ELO ALAIN
VENUSHAIR RATSO
ELI TORO WITHIN
RENOIRS ION
PLUTOCRACIES
ANGELS DEE ABLE
DOORS WED ANISE
AREA PAL ELIDES
MARSHALLPLAN
EAT LICENSE
MORTAR HAHA EAP
AVOID SATURNINE
LENTO ARE TANTE
TRAIN GIS EASES

18

THEM CHEAPSHOT
RARA HORSEHAIR
ULRIC ORGANELLE
ARA EMMA GAVIN
NONSLIP PUREED
TATTER ELOI DRY
SCRUB ANIONS
HYBRIDVEHICLE
SIDEON SOOTS
AMS TONY CLOTHE
POKEYS BLATHER
PRIAM FAUN ARF
LEFTOVERS DARED
ENFILADES CIAO
SOSTENUTO HOLM

19

SPAM PITON LILT
URDU AROMA INEE
SOOT CIGAR MCAN
HELIVESANDLOINS
IMPLORE ISSEI
SHAW SCOTT UDO
TEA LEAH RON
ASELFTORTEMAN
DII IRAN ASO
ORO ZONES OVID
OFUSE ERMINES
WAXESELOQUENTLY
ORWE REMUS GOEN
PEAK INNIS ONTO
SSRS CAINE NEED

20

VAGUE SEAL OPAL
ABUSE PLEA FEMA
POLINQUIRY FLED
ONAN UNTIE SEXY
REGGAE EERIE
BUT SENECAS
BADPRESS DAKOTA
LORRE KID LEVEL
UNOCAL RETIREES
REPOSES WON
NTILE KEBABS
SALT LILLE IGOR
AMER ADVANCENOT
POGO NEIL ARENA
SKOL ISSO ASSES

21

PITA EBRO OEIL
OWER NIBS PINTA
SILENCEISGOLDEN
ENS OARS ODESSA
ISMS STIR
BUMRAP REHASHED
ABOIL CODA OLA
HORSESHOEMAGNET
TAS TETR STEVE
STEADIES STORES
PULP NTHS
TALENT NORM DOO
REALESTATEAGENT
ARIES ATRA ACTI
PORT REEK BOOS

22

VOLTAIC APARADE
IMEANNO SUBITEM
NOONEGOESBEFORE
SONG RERIG LIRR
STAYSSAFE
ESC HISTIME TAP
LAUREN ELMIRA
IDLER BUT LANIS
ZEPPO ENE ACOAT
UNLESSTHE
ETAL YEAST RESH
BOSSLEAVESEARLY
ESSIE TOR STRAP
REEVE ERA PEEVE
TETES RYE ORDER

23

STICKSANDSTONES
PUBLISHORPERISH
CREATEANUISANCE
ANTI EMTS EEL
MACS SEAR
EFT SHEB EMUS
CREASERESISTANT
LEAVESABADTASTE
ADMISSIONTOBAIL
TOOL PAAR ILE
ANKA AGES
ILL ONCD TSAR
NOODLECASSEROLE
COUNTERMEASURES
ATTHELASTMOMENT

24

DOPED SAGE SPAN
IRENE PSIS HONE
FRIDAKAHLO ARNO
LIME TARTAN
ADDRESS DETER
CRIERS GIRO AIM
COENS MAXIM INO
EGGO LOGIC ATMO
DUO RANEE ASIAN
EER ANTS TRISTE
IMIDE DRATTED
COVENS ARAP
ABET MEXICANART
SORA AGEE HANOI
HEAL NORD OGDEN

25

ASTA BANES THOU
LOUD ADAPT AILS
DUBLINOHIO IDLE
ALAIN ALLCLEAR
BEDS OLEO
MPG ROMEGEORGIA
AIR TIER SERGE
DAIS NERDS DALI
ANNUL ERAT MOO
MOSCOWIDAHO SOU
CLAD BLAB
APPEARED SUAVE
VOLE PARISTEXAS
EGAD ETUDE NESS
CONS DEBIT ALEE

26

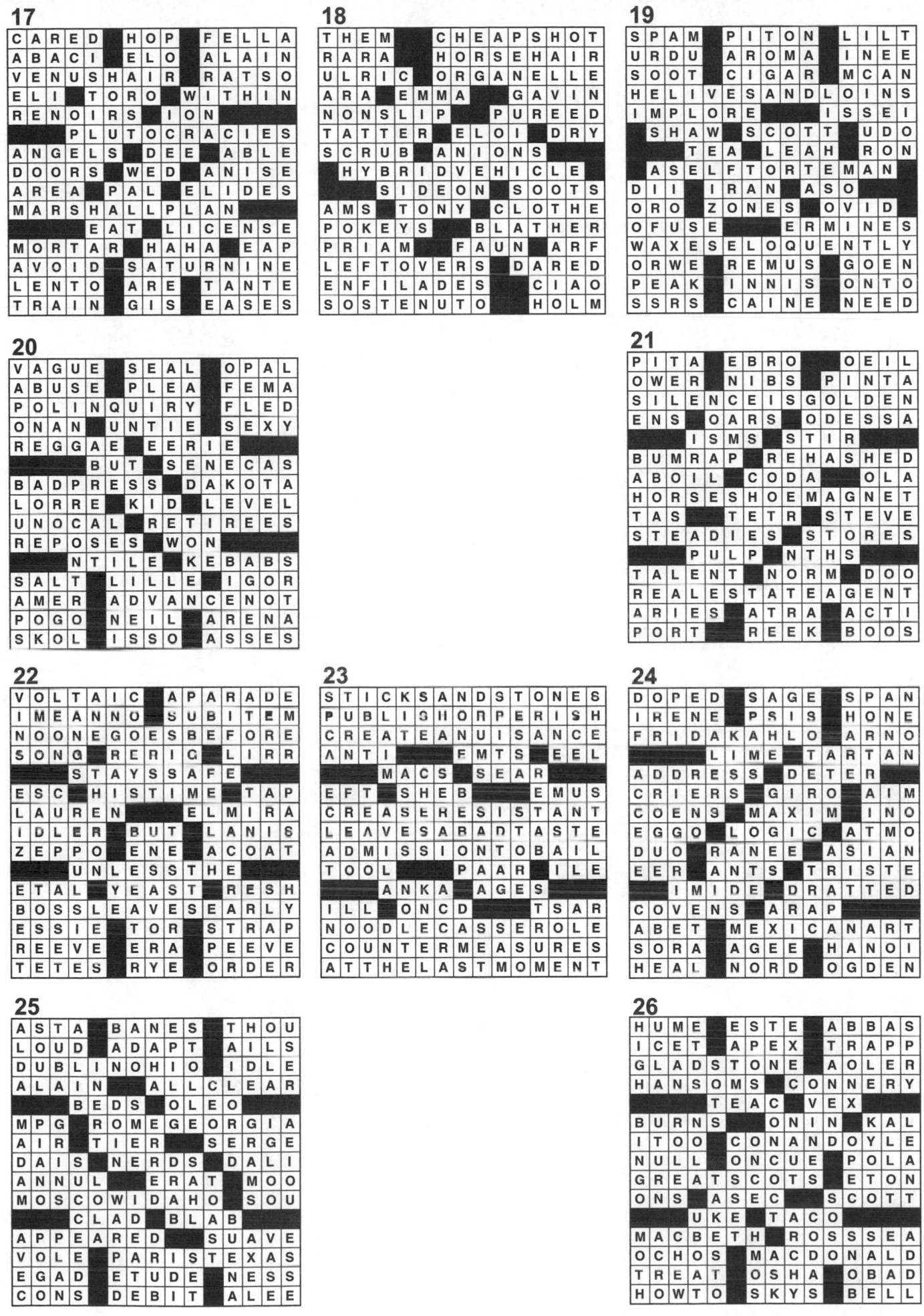

HUME ESTE ABBAS
ICET APEX TRAPP
GLADSTONE AOLER
HANSOMS CONNERY
TEAC VEX
BURNS ONIN KAL
ITOO CONANDOYLE
NULL ONCUE POLA
GREATSCOTS ETON
ONS ASEC SCOTT
UKE TACO
MACBETH ROSSSEA
OCHOS MACDONALD
TREAT OSHA OBAD
HOWTO SKYS BELL

27

S	T	A	M	P		S	E	R	B		S	A	G	A
L	O	C	A	L		A	L	A	R		A	R	A	L
A	R	E	N	A		M	O	N	A		T	U	L	L
M	O	D		S	T	U	N	T	D	O	U	B	L	E
			A	M	I	E			P	H	R	A	S	E
S	U	N	T	A	N	L	O	T	I	O	N			
A	D	I	O	S			D	O	T	H		C	O	P
R	O	A	M		S	A	I	N	T		C	H	I	A
I	N	S		R	T	E	S			O	P	A	L	S
			K	I	R	S	T	E	N	D	U	N	S	T
S	C	E	N	E	I			R	O	Y	S			
M	E	D	A	L	C	O	U	N	T	S		L	E	T
I	T	I	C		T	O	N	E		S	P	I	R	O
T	U	C	K		E	L	I	S		E	E	N	S	Y
S	S	T	S		R	A	T	T		Y	I	K	E	S

28

P	A	P	A	I	N		S	A	L	T	I	E	S	T
E	T	E	R	N	A	L	T	R	I	A	N	G	L	E
R	E	A	R	G	U	A	R	D	A	C	T	I	O	N
			A	E	T	N	A			E	A	S	E	D
C	O	N	N		C	A	S	S	A	T	T			
A	P	O		C	H	I	S	O	X		T	S	A	R
B	I	O	M	E			E	M	I	N	E	N	C	E
A	N	D	A	N	T	E		E	L	D	R	I	C	K
L	E	G	H	O	R	N	S			A	S	P	E	N
A	R	E	A		A	C	K	A	C	K		E	D	O
			R	E	P	L	I	C	A		B	R	E	T
A	C	E	I	N			B	U	R	M	A			
C	O	N	S	T	I	T	U	T	I	O	N	A	L	S
I	N	T	H	E	S	A	M	E	B	R	E	A	T	H
D	E	S	I	R	E	R	S		E	N	S	U	R	E

29

A	M	F	M		C	H	A	F	E		B	O	C	A
S	O	L	A		H	E	G	E	L		E	T	A	T
S	T	E	R		I	R	A	N	I	A	N	O	I	L
T	H	E	C	O	V	E	R	S	O	F		S	R	A
D	E	C	I	D	E				T	R	A	C	E	S
A	R	E	A	S		C	D	C		I	M	O	N	E
					G	Y	R	O	S	C	O	P	E	S
		T	H	I	S	B	O	O	K	A	R	E		
T	A	R	A	N	T	E	L	L	A					
E	M	I	L	E		R	L	S		T	R	A	I	N
N	B	A	E	R	S				B	I	E	R	C	E
O	R	L		T	O	O	F	A	R	A	P	A	R	T
N	O	R	E	S	P	O	N	S	E		O	B	I	T
E	S	U	S		H	O	M	E	S		U	L	E	E
D	E	N	T		S	H	A	T	T		R	E	D	D

30

S	I	P	S		A	L	I	A	S		S	A	G	E
A	R	E	A		R	E	N	T	A		O	R	E	L
C	A	N	D	L	E	I	N	T	H	E	W	I	N	D
	S	T	E	I	N			A	L	L	H	E	R	E
				V	A	C	S			L	A	S	E	R
A	M	O	R	E		L	E	S	T	A	T			
T	O	A	S	T		A	R	O	O			R	I	O
M	A	R	T	H	A	S	V	I	N	E	Y	A	R	D
O	N	S			T	S	A	R		A	U	R	A	E
			O	C	T	A	N	E		S	P	A	N	S
B	O	T	C	H			T	E	S	T				
A	T	H	E	I	S	M			T	E	N	T	S	
S	T	R	A	P	P	E	D	F	O	R	C	A	S	H
S	E	E	N		A	T	I	O	N		A	R	T	E
O	R	E	S		M	A	D	G	E		R	O	S	E

31

M	A	H	I		O	N	T	A	P		S	P	A	N
E	X	A	M		L	O	N	G	U		M	A	N	E
A	E	H	I	K	L	M	N	O	P	U	A	N	D	W
	L	A	N	A	I			G	U	T	L	E	S	S
				H	E	N	S			A	L	L	O	Y
E	T	H	E	L		E	P	O	C	H	S			
P	A	U	L	I		C	O	L	A			O	B	I
O	N	L	Y	L	E	T	T	E	R	S	U	S	E	D
S	K	A			D	A	T	A		H	A	S	T	E
			S	C	O	R	E	R		A	L	O	H	A
A	L	T	A	R			D	Y	A	D				
S	E	A	F	O	O	D			N	O	L	A	N	
I	N	H	A	W	A	I	I	A	N	W	O	R	D	S
D	I	O	R		H	A	O	L	E		E	T	A	S
O	N	E	I		U	N	S	E	X		W	I	K	I

32

T	A	M	S		S	I	Z	E	D		M	I	K	E
A	D	A	R		T	H	E	S	E		O	R	A	L
M	O	T	O	R	M	O	U	T	H		S	A	N	K
P	R	E		O	O	P	S		O	P	E	N	T	O
A	N	Y	M	O	R	E		M	R	I	S			
			A	M	I		M	I	N	T	M	A	R	K
T	R	I	G		T	V	A	D		Y	A	H	O	O
H	A	R	I		Z	I	N	G	Y		L	E	A	F
E	J	E	C	T		C	L	E	O		O	M	N	I
M	A	D	M	O	N	E	Y		G	I	N			
			A	D	E	S		A	I	M	E	D	A	T
E	S	C	R	O	W		E	L	B	A		I	Z	E
N	O	O	K		M	O	V	I	E	M	O	G	U	L
D	U	D	E		A	R	E	N	A		W	I	S	E
S	P	A	R		N	I	N	E	R		S	T	A	X

33

E	A	T		A	C	M	E		T	E	A	S	E	R
L	I	E		S	H	O	D		H	I	G	H	L	Y
F	L	A	S	H	I	N	G		I	T	R	I	E	D
			P	O	C	K	E	T	C	H	A	N	G	E
A	S	T	I	R				U	K	E		S	Y	R
S	C	R	E	E	N	S	A	V	E	R				
T	H	O	S		E	K	G			O	R	A	R	E
R	E	V	O	L	V	I	N	G	C	R	E	D	I	T
A	D	E	N	I			E	R	A		P	E	N	A
				S	H	O	W	E	R	G	U	E	S	T
D	O	H		T	O	R				O	L	M	O	S
O	P	E	N	I	N	G	D	O	O	R	S			
B	E	M	I	N	E		A	C	A	D	E	M	I	A
B	R	I	N	G	S		T	H	R	O		A	L	P
S	A	N	E	S	T		A	S	S	N		O	L	E

34

A	P	E	S		A	B	E	T		A	R	U	B	A
B	E	L	L		L	O	L	A		L	U	N	A	R
A	D	V	I	C	E	I	S	W	H	A	T	T	H	E
F	R	E	E	R		L	I	N	E		H	O	S	S
T	O	S	S	U	P		E	Y	R	E				
			T	S	A	R			E	X	H	A	L	E
A	V	A		A	L	I	V	E		C	U	R	E	D
W	I	S	E	D	O	N	T	N	E	E	D	A	N	D
E	L	I	T	E		D	R	O	L	L		B	A	Y
D	E	S	E	R	T			S	A	L	K			
				S	O	M	E		M	E	N	T	A	L
E	T	N	A		T	E	L	L		N	O	I	S	E
T	H	E	F	O	O	L	W	O	N	T	T	A	K	E
R	E	W	A	X		D	A	R	E		T	R	E	K
E	N	T	R	Y		S	Y	N	E		S	A	W	S

35

P	F	C	S		G	E	L	A	T	O		P	A	R
A	G	R	A		U	N	I	C	E	F		A	L	A
C	H	A	I	N	F	E	N	C	E	S		D	I	N
K	I	N	D	O	F			U	N	T	A	M	E	D
			A	B	A	T	E	S			R	E	N	D
M	A	S		O	W	N	S	A	Y	S	O			
E	F	L	A	T		G	O	L	D	C	U	F	F	S
S	A	I	L	H	O				S	O	S	O	O	N
A	R	T	L	E	T	T	E	R		R	E	N	T	A
			P	R	E	R	I	N	S	E		T	O	P
B	R	R	R			U	N	R	O	B	E			
R	E	T	O	O	L	S			N	I	C	H	E	S
A	I	R		M	I	S	S	I	N	G	L	I	N	K
I	K	E		A	T	E	A	S	E		A	D	D	A
D	I	V		R	E	S	O	R	T		T	E	S	T

36

R	A	C	E	D		L	A	V	A		G	I	F	T
S	A	R	G	E		A	W	E	S		A	P	A	R
V	R	O	O	M		P	O	R	K	P	L	A	C	E
P	P	S		O	D	D	L	Y		E	L	S	E	S
		S	A	N	Y	O			C	R	E	S	T	S
B	A	W	L	I	N	G	A	L	L	E	Y			
E	R	O	I	C	A		B	E	E	S		L	T	D
T	I	R	E		M	A	R	I	A		C	A	R	E
S	A	D		M	I	C	A		N	E	A	T	E	N
			B	E	S	A	M	E	S	T	R	E	E	T
A	S	H	R	A	M			S	E	A	T	S		
S	H	O	A	L		M	A	T	R	I		T	A	U
P	U	N	N	Y	L	A	N	E		L	E	A	K	S
I	L	E	D		A	R	T	E		E	E	R	I	E
C	A	R	Y		D	E	E	M		R	O	T	O	R

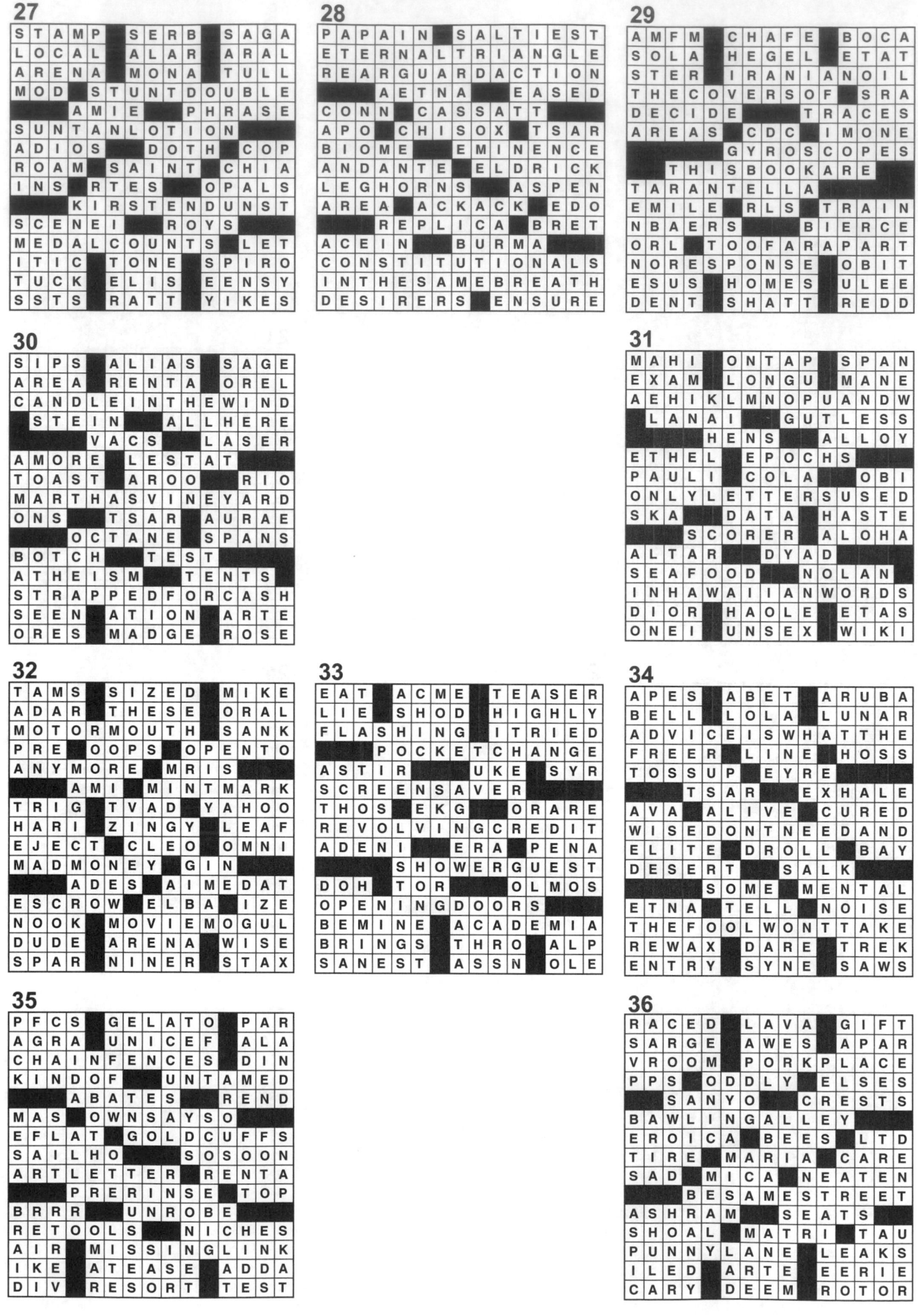

37

C	R	O	C		I	C	E	T		S	T	A	G	S
S	O	D	A		N	O	L	O		K	I	L	L	A
I	C	E	R		F	L	A	T		I	D	I	O	T
			E	L	E	A	N	O	R	R	I	G	B	Y
E	N	D	E	A	R				M	A	N	N	E	R
D	E	A	R	P	R	U	D	E	N	C	E			
S	E	R		P	E	N	I	N		E	S	T	E	S
E	D	Y	S		D	A	D	O	S		S	O	A	P
L	A	L	A	W		P	A	L	E	D		P	T	A
			M	A	R	T	H	A	M	Y	D	E	A	R
A	R	M	O	R	Y				E	C	A	R	T	E
L	U	C	Y	I	N	T	H	E	S	K	Y			
E	M	C	E	E		S	E	C	T		T	U	R	F
R	O	O	D	S		P	A	R	E		O	M	A	R
T	R	Y	S	T		S	P	U	R		N	A	N	A

38

S	W	I	M		M	A	T	E	D		S	E	P	T
H	I	H	O		A	N	I	T	A		E	A	R	P
A	R	O	N		S	A	L	O	N		A	R	E	S
D	E	P	A	R	T	M	E	N	T	A	L	L	Y	
E	R	E	C	T		E	D	S	E	L	S			
			O	E	R					A	O	R	T	A
I	D	S		S	U	R	G	E	O	N	F	I	S	H
T	U	T	U		B	A	A	T	H		F	O	A	M
S	P	A	N	I	S	H	M	A	I	N		T	R	E
Y	E	T	I	S					O	O	H			
			O	N	S	E	T	S		S	A	L	S	A
	M	O	N	T	H	L	Y	P	A	Y	M	E	N	T
Z	O	O	M		E	A	S	E	L		I	R	I	S
S	O	F	A		A	T	O	N	E		L	O	P	E
A	S	S	N		R	E	N	T	S		L	I	S	A

39

S	A	L	A		S	T	E	M		S	C	R	A	P
E	P	I	C		T	H	R	U		P	A	U	L	A
N	E	E	R		R	E	A	S	S	E	S	S	E	D
T	R	U	E	F	A	L	S	E	T	E	S	T	S	
			S	L	I	M			I	D	A			
C	A	P		U	T	A	H	A	N		N	O	S	E
A	L	O	O	F			E	R	G		D	A	T	A
P	A	S	S	F	A	I	L	C	O	U	R	S	E	S
O	M	I	T		N	O	V			P	A	I	N	E
N	O	T	E		G	U	E	S	T	S		S	O	L
			N	I	L			W	O	E	S			
	Y	E	S	N	O	Q	U	E	S	T	I	O	N	S
P	E	N	I	N	S	U	L	A	S		E	P	E	E
O	L	I	V	E		A	N	T	E		V	A	L	E
E	L	D	E	R		D	A	Y	S		E	L	L	S

40

L	A	S	S	O		G	A	E	L	S		M	A	P
A	D	M	E	N		A	G	R	E	E		I	L	L
T	H	E	P	E	N	T	A	G	O	N		T	O	O
H	O	L	T		E	E	R		V	E	S	T	E	D
E	C	L	A	I	R			T	I	G	E			
			L	O	V	E	T	R	I	A	N	G	L	E
J	O	B		N	E	M	E	A		L	O	R	I	S
A	R	E	A		S	I	N	G	E		R	U	M	P
M	E	A	N	S		N	O	I	R	S		B	O	N
B	O	U	I	L	L	O	N	C	U	B	E			
			S	A	A	R			P	A	N	T	E	D
F	O	M	E	N	T		G	U	T		D	I	N	O
R	P	I		T	I	M	E	S	S	Q	U	A	R	E
E	E	L		E	N	U	R	E		E	R	R	O	R
D	D	E		D	O	M	E	D		D	E	A	L	S

41

A	S	P	E	R	A		B	A	A		P	A	L	M
M	E	A	N	I	T		U	N	D	E	R	W	A	Y
P	P	P	S	P	O	R	R	I	D	G	E	H	O	T
L	I	A	I	S	E	D			S	A	L	I	S	H
Y	A	W	L			A	B	E		D	A	L		
			E	P	S		A	X	E		T	E	A	L
C	C	C	S	T	H	E	D	A	Y		E	A	V	E
O	O	H		L	E	N	S	M	E	N		G	O	O
A	M	I	D		E	E	E	S	O	N	D	O	W	N
L	A	C	E		T	R	E		N	E	E			
		O	V	A		O	D	A			L	I	R	A
M	A	R	I	N	A			A	D	M	I	R	E	S
I	I	I	S	O	F	L	A	U	R	A	M	A	R	S
T	R	E	E	N	A	I	L		U	N	I	Q	U	E
E	S	S	E		N	E	D		M	A	T	I	N	S

42

I	N	R	E		R	E	U	P	S		B	A	H	T
W	O	O	L		E	M	C	E	E		U	V	E	A
O	R	L	Y		R	I	A	T	A		R	A	S	P
N	I	L		D	U	L	L	A	S	D	I	S	H	*
		C	O	R	N				I	R	A	T	E	
*	G	A	T	E	S	C	A	N	D	A	L			
D	E	L	T	A		A	K	E	E	M		D	O	I
O	S	L	O		M	Y	N	A	H		T	A	L	C
G	T	S		P	I	C	O	T		P	A	R	E	E
			M	A	K	E	T	H	E	E	Y	E	S	*
	P	L	A	T	E				M	R	E	D		
*	T	I	G	H	T	A	L	I	B	I		E	G	O
S	E	M	I		O	B	A	M	A		A	V	O	W
K	R	O	C		D	I	N	A	R		V	I	O	L
I	O	N	S		D	E	A	N	S		A	L	P	S

43

J	F	K		P	R	I	M	P	S		A	H	E	M
O	R	E		R	O	B	B	I	E		T	A	X	I
T	E	N	C	O	M	M	A	N	D	M	E	N	T	S
S	T	O	O	D				C	U	E		D	R	E
			L	I	T	T	L	E	C	A	E	S	A	R
D	I	S	A	G	R	E	E		E	L	S			
U	G	H		A	U	R	A				P	L	U	G
D	O	U	B	L	E	I	N	D	E	M	N	I	T	Y
S	R	T	A				I	O	T	A		K	E	N
			W	H	O		N	E	R	D	I	E	S	T
S	O	Y	L	E	N	T	G	R	E	E	N			
P	L	O		R	E	I				T	O	U	R	S
E	D	W	A	R	D	G	R	O	B	I	N	S	O	N
L	I	Z	A		G	R	A	H	A	M		E	M	U
L	E	A	H		E	E	Y	O	R	E		D	E	B

44

K	A	V	A		V	A	M	P	S		D	O	S	E
A	V	E	C		E	R	O	S	E		A	Y	E	S
N	O	T	H	I	N	G	W	I	L	L	B	E	A	S
T	W	O		N	O	U	N		F	O	O	Z	L	E
			A	C	M	E		A	M	A	N			
S	H	A	M	U	S		E	G	A	D		F	U	N
K	A	B	O	B		S	L	I	D		V	A	S	E
I	N	E	V	I	T	A	B	L	E	A	S	T	H	E
N	O	N	E		O	B	O	E		V	I	S	E	D
K	I	D		A	N	E	W		R	I	G	O	R	S
			S	T	E	R		S	E	A	N			
P	E	R	I	O	D		A	U	N	T		H	I	S
U	N	E	X	P	E	C	T	E	D	E	V	E	N	T
M	O	N	T		A	S	I	D	E		E	A	S	E
P	L	O	Y		F	A	T	E	D		T	R	O	T

45

S	C	R	A	M		W	R	A	P		S	P	A	M
A	H	O	L	E		H	I	V	E		M	A	K	E
V	A	L	E	T		I	C	E	S		O	R	A	L
I	S	L	E	O	F	T	O	R	T	U	G	A		
O	T	O		O	R	E		S	O	P		S	A	P
R	E	N	O		E	T	T	E		D	O	I	L	Y
			F	L	A	I	R		B	A	T	T	E	R
I	L	L	T	A	K	E	Y	O	U	T	H	E	R	E
O	S	I	E	R	S		S	P	R	E	E			
W	A	N	N	A		S	T	E	R		R	E	S	T
A	T	E		M	A	T		N	O	W		N	C	O
		A	I	S	L	E	O	R	W	I	N	D	O	W
R	A	G	S		E	L	M	O		T	E	E	T	H
E	V	E	N		P	L	E	A		C	R	A	T	E
V	E	S	T		H	A	N	D		H	O	R	S	E

PUZZLE #42: * = WATER

46

M	G	M		S	C	E	N	E		B	C	E	L	L
A	Y	E		O	R	D	E	R		A	L	M	A	Y
F	R	E	D	D	I	E	H	G		R	E	I	C	E
I	O	T	A		T	R	I		S	N	A	R	E	S
A	S	S	U	M	E			N	O	O	N			
			B	A	R	R	Y	A	U	W	A	T	E	R
G	I	L		T	I	E	U	P		L	I	B	R	A
R	S	V	P		A	S	S	O	C		R	A	I	N
A	L	O	H	A		C	E	L	L	O		R	E	D
D	A	V	I	D	C	U	F	I	E	L	D			
			L	O	R	E			A	E	R	I	A	L
S	C	U	L	P	T		B	A	R		A	N	T	I
P	O	S	I	T		J	E	R	E	M	Y	F	E	S
A	R	M	E	E		I	L	O	S	T		E	S	P
T	E	A	S	E		M	A	N	T	A		R	T	S

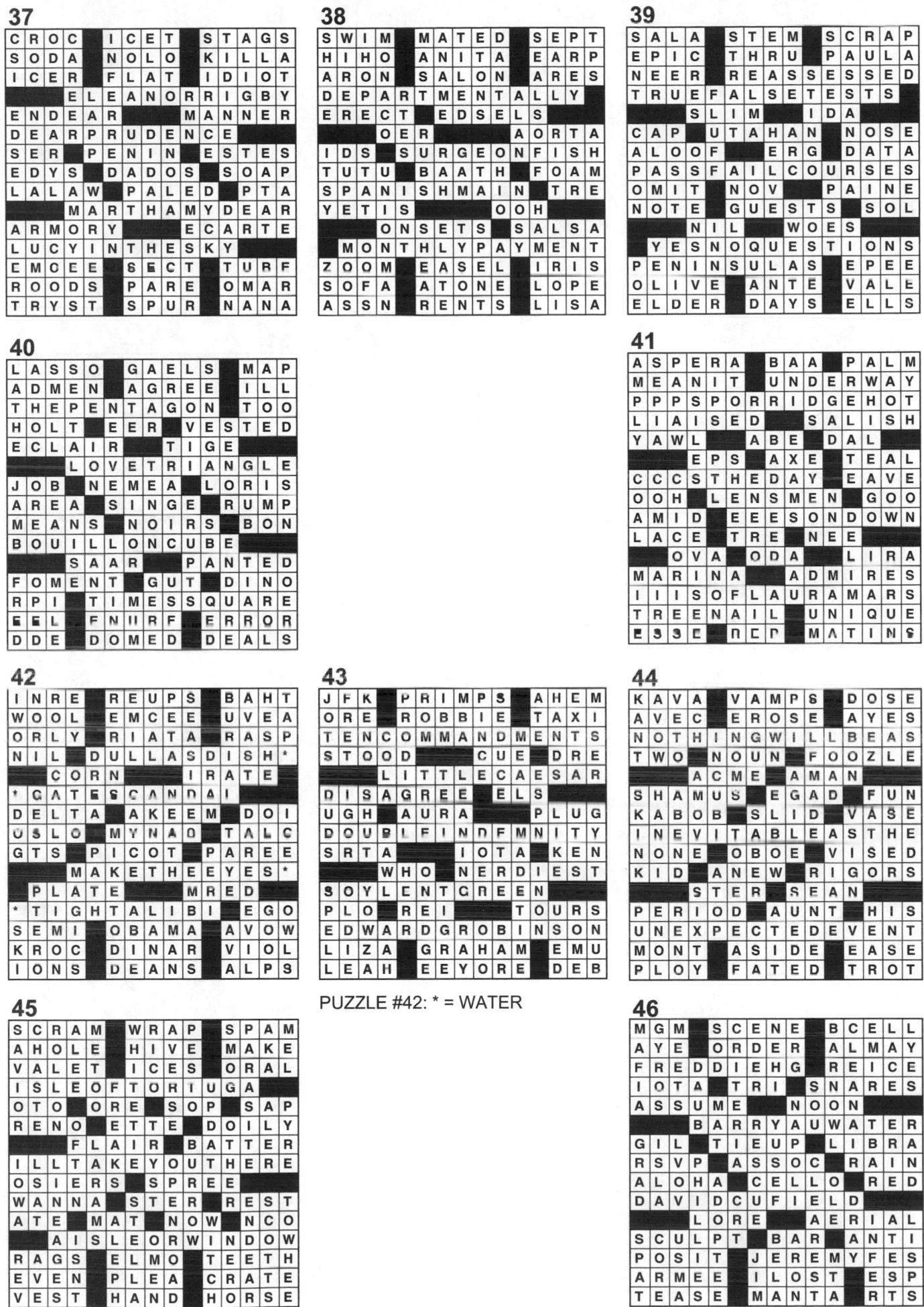

47

S	P	A	S	M	■	D	E	C	O	■	G	R	A	B
L	I	M	E	Y	■	A	V	O	N	■	H	A	L	L
A	C	O	R	N	■	R	I	O	T	■	O	D	I	E
B	A	R	B	A	R	E	L	L	A	■	S	O	B	A
■	■	■	■	H	U	D	■	S	P	U	T	N	I	K
S	O	B	S	■	R	E	V	■	E	A	R	■	■	■
K	N	O	W	■	A	V	E	S	■	W	I	D	T	H
E	M	M	A	■	L	I	N	U	S	■	D	I	R	E
W	E	B	M	D	■	L	O	P	E	■	E	V	E	R
■	■	■	P	O	R	■	M	E	G	■	R	A	K	E
F	E	L	T	H	A	T	■	R	U	E	■	■	■	■
U	T	A	H	■	J	U	D	G	E	D	R	E	D	D
S	H	U	I	■	A	T	O	I	■	G	E	A	R	Y
E	A	R	N	■	H	E	R	R	■	E	N	S	U	E
S	N	A	G	■	S	E	A	L	■	S	T	E	M	S

48

P	A	T	T	I	■	C	O	M	P	R	E	N	D	E
U	N	I	O	N	■	O	P	E	R	A	G	O	E	R
S	O	N	G	S	■	M	E	D	I	C	A	T	E	S
H	U	S	S	Y	■	P	L	A	C	E	N	A	M	E
E	K	E	■	N	N	E	■	L	E	M	■	■	■	■
S	A	L	A	C	I	T	Y	■	D	E	S	P	O	T
P	I	T	S	■	N	E	E	D	■	S	N	A	R	E
A	M	O	S	■	O	N	T	A	P	■	A	R	I	A
S	E	W	E	R	■	T	I	M	E	■	I	T	O	R
T	E	N	S	E	S	■	S	N	A	R	L	I	N	G
■	■	■	■	D	E	C	■	E	R	A	■	C	S	A
S	T	E	E	L	C	L	A	D	■	D	A	U	B	S
W	O	L	V	E	R	I	N	E	■	I	S	L	E	S
I	R	S	A	G	E	N	T	S	■	S	T	A	L	E
M	E	A	N	S	T	E	S	T	■	H	A	R	T	S

49

A	D	E	S	■	J	A	Y	S	■	S	E	D	A	N
T	O	L	E	■	O	B	O	E	■	P	R	O	L	E
W	H	A	T	S	Y	O	U	R	W	A	N	G	L	E
A	N	T	O	N	S	■	■	V	A	T	■	D	U	D
T	A	I	N	A	■	B	R	E	R	■	C	O	D	E
E	N	O	S	■	T	R	E	■	W	A	R	M	E	D
R	Y	N	■	B	E	A	D	■	H	M	O	■	■	■
■	I	S	L	A	N	D	W	H	O	P	P	E	R	■
■	■	■	O	C	T	■	I	E	O	H	■	Y	E	T
D	O	N	W	H	O	■	N	A	P	■	R	E	P	O
E	N	E	S	■	O	N	K	P	■	J	E	L	L	O
I	R	A	■	S	N	O	■	■	D	E	C	E	I	T
C	U	R	R	I	E	R	A	N	D	W	I	V	E	S
E	S	T	A	B	■	A	V	I	A	■	P	E	R	I
D	H	O	W	S	■	D	O	X	Y	■	E	L	S	E

50

T	A	R	G	E	T	P	R	A	C	T	I	C	E	S
A	T	E	O	N	E	S	H	E	A	R	T	O	U	T
I	N	D	I	A	N	T	E	R	R	I	T	O	R	Y
L	O	O	N	■	■	■	A	O	L	■	■	L	O	X
■	■	■	G	I	S	T	■	S	A	G	A	■	■	■
A	K	A	■	N	O	I	R	■	■	A	B	A	S	H
D	E	L	I	C	A	T	E	B	A	L	A	N	C	E
W	I	L	D	I	M	A	G	I	N	A	T	I	O	N
A	R	A	I	S	I	N	I	N	T	H	E	S	U	N
R	A	N	E	E	■	■	S	E	R	A	■	E	R	A
■	■	■	D	D	A	Y	■	T	E	D	S	■	■	■
C	S	A	■	■	R	E	A	■	■	■	L	I	M	A
H	A	M	M	E	R	A	N	D	C	H	I	S	E	L
E	M	A	I	L	A	T	T	A	C	H	M	E	N	T
W	I	S	C	O	N	S	I	N	C	H	E	E	S	E

51

L	E	V	Y	■	■	C	A	P	E	■	B	I	T	E
O	N	E	A	■	B	O	Z	O	S	■	O	N	U	S
U	S	E	P	L	A	S	T	I	C	■	A	C	T	S
S	U	P	■	O	S	T	E	■	O	B	T	U	S	E
Y	E	S	B	U	T	■	C	U	R	L	E	R	■	■
■	■	■	A	P	E	D	■	S	T	U	D	D	E	D
K	I	C	K	■	D	E	F	U	S	E	■	E	M	U
I	M	O	U	T	■	L	E	A	■	D	E	B	I	T
R	A	M	■	R	E	P	E	L	S	■	A	T	T	Y
I	M	P	E	A	C	H	■	S	A	N	S	■	■	■
■	■	L	A	Y	S	I	N	■	D	A	Y	J	O	B
H	E	A	R	S	T	■	I	B	I	S	■	U	Z	I
A	G	I	N	■	A	C	C	U	S	A	T	I	O	N
Z	O	N	E	■	S	T	O	R	M	■	A	C	N	E
E	S	T	D	■	Y	A	L	L	■	■	B	E	E	T

52

D	E	A	D	E	N	D	■	S	M	A	S	H	U	P
E	A	T	I	N	T	O	■	M	A	L	T	A	S	E
F	R	A	N	C	H	I	S	E	P	L	A	Y	E	R
R	A	V	E	L	S	■	O	R	L	Y	■	R	R	S
A	C	I	D	S	■	M	U	S	E	■	W	I	F	I
U	H	S	■	■	W	I	T	H	■	F	A	C	E	S
D	E	M	O	L	I	S	H	■	J	U	N	K	E	T
■	■	■	X	Y	L	O	P	H	O	N	E	■	■	■
A	T	T	I	R	E	■	H	O	C	K	S	H	O	P
P	R	I	D	E	■	K	I	N	K	■	■	A	N	E
P	O	P	E	■	B	A	L	K	■	G	A	Z	E	D
E	T	S	■	P	A	R	L	■	H	E	R	A	L	D
A	T	T	O	R	N	E	Y	G	E	N	E	R	A	L
S	E	E	N	O	T	E	■	A	R	I	A	D	N	E
E	R	R	A	T	U	M	■	D	R	E	S	S	E	R

53

A	C	T	S	■	S	U	I	T	■	L	E	G	A	L
N	O	A	H	■	U	R	D	U	■	I	N	A	N	E
I	D	C	O	O	K	I	E	B	A	N	D	I	T	S
S	A	T	O	R	I	■	S	A	N	G	■	N	E	T
■	■	■	K	E	Y	S	■	S	N	U	G	■	■	■
E	D	Y	■	S	A	T	E	■	A	I	R	G	U	N
M	O	O	S	■	K	I	L	O	■	N	E	R	V	E
B	Y	G	I	V	I	N	G	C	S	I	Y	O	U	R
E	L	I	D	E	■	T	A	C	O	■	S	O	L	D
R	E	S	E	N	T	■	R	U	M	P	■	M	A	Y
■	■	■	A	G	I	N	■	R	E	E	F	■	■	■
G	A	B	■	E	T	U	I	■	W	A	R	I	E	R
M	I	L	K	F	O	R	D	N	A	T	E	S	T	S
A	D	I	E	U	■	S	L	A	Y	■	S	L	A	V
N	E	P	A	L	■	E	Y	E	S	■	H	E	L	P

54

P	I	P	P	I	■	C	O	M	A	■	D	A	S	H
A	C	T	A	S	■	A	D	E	N	■	A	L	P	O
L	E	A	S	H	■	J	O	I	N	■	N	C	A	R
■	■	■	S	A	T	U	R	N	A	C	C	O	R	D
E	P	S	I	L	O	N	■	■	■	L	E	V	E	E
S	U	B	T	L	E	■	C	R	U	I	S	E	R	S
E	L	L	O	■	■	C	A	I	R	N	■	■	■	■
■	L	I	N	C	O	L	N	L	E	G	A	C	Y	■
■	■	■	■	A	B	A	S	E	■	■	D	O	E	S
I	L	L	S	P	E	N	T	■	G	U	A	V	A	S
N	O	E	A	R	■	■	■	S	I	N	G	E	R	S
J	A	G	U	A	R	E	S	C	A	P	E	■	■	■
E	T	U	N	■	O	K	L	A	■	A	N	I	T	A
C	H	I	A	■	N	E	E	D	■	C	C	L	E	F
T	E	N	S	■	A	D	D	S	■	K	Y	S	E	R

55

S	M	A	R	T	A	L	E	C	K	S	■	P	B	S
H	A	S	T	A	M	A	N	A	N	A	■	A	L	E
L	O	C	H	N	E	S	S	M	O	N	S	T	E	R
O	R	E	O	S	■	T	I	P	T	O	E	I	N	G
M	I	N	N	■	A	R	G	U	S	■	C	E	D	E
O	S	T	■	S	W	A	N	S	■	H	A	N	S	A
■	■	■	W	O	O	D	S	■	D	A	N	C	I	N
O	S	C	E	O	L	A	■	P	O	R	T	E	N	T
X	M	A	S	E	S	■	V	A	M	P	S	■	■	■
P	A	S	T	Y	■	C	E	R	E	S	■	M	E	A
E	S	T	E	■	P	O	R	T	S	■	P	O	N	D
C	H	A	N	T	E	U	S	E	■	M	I	S	S	A
K	I	N	D	E	R	G	A	R	T	E	N	C	O	P
E	N	E	■	S	E	A	C	R	E	S	T	O	U	T
R	G	T	■	S	C	R	E	E	C	H	O	W	L	S

56

S	H	I	P	S	■	S	T	E	P	■	U	C	L	A
G	O	T	I	T	■	T	E	R	R	■	R	O	O	F
T	B	O	N	E	■	E	R	I	E	■	A	U	R	A
■	■	■	M	A	R	T	I	N	M	I	L	N	E	R
■	S	T	O	R	E	■	■	■	I	N	S	T	■	■
G	L	E	N	N	M	I	L	L	E	R	■	Y	S	L
L	I	N	E	S	■	M	O	O	R	E	■	C	I	A
E	E	N	Y	■	S	P	I	R	E	■	C	O	E	D
A	S	I	■	W	H	E	R	E	■	G	A	U	G	E
M	T	S	■	H	E	L	E	N	M	I	R	R	E	N
■	■	S	O	A	R	■	■	■	O	M	I	T	S	■
J	O	H	N	M	I	T	C	H	E	L	L	■	■	■
E	G	O	S	■	F	I	L	E	■	E	L	E	V	E
F	L	E	E	■	F	L	U	E	■	T	O	R	M	E
F	E	S	T	■	S	L	E	D	■	S	N	A	I	L

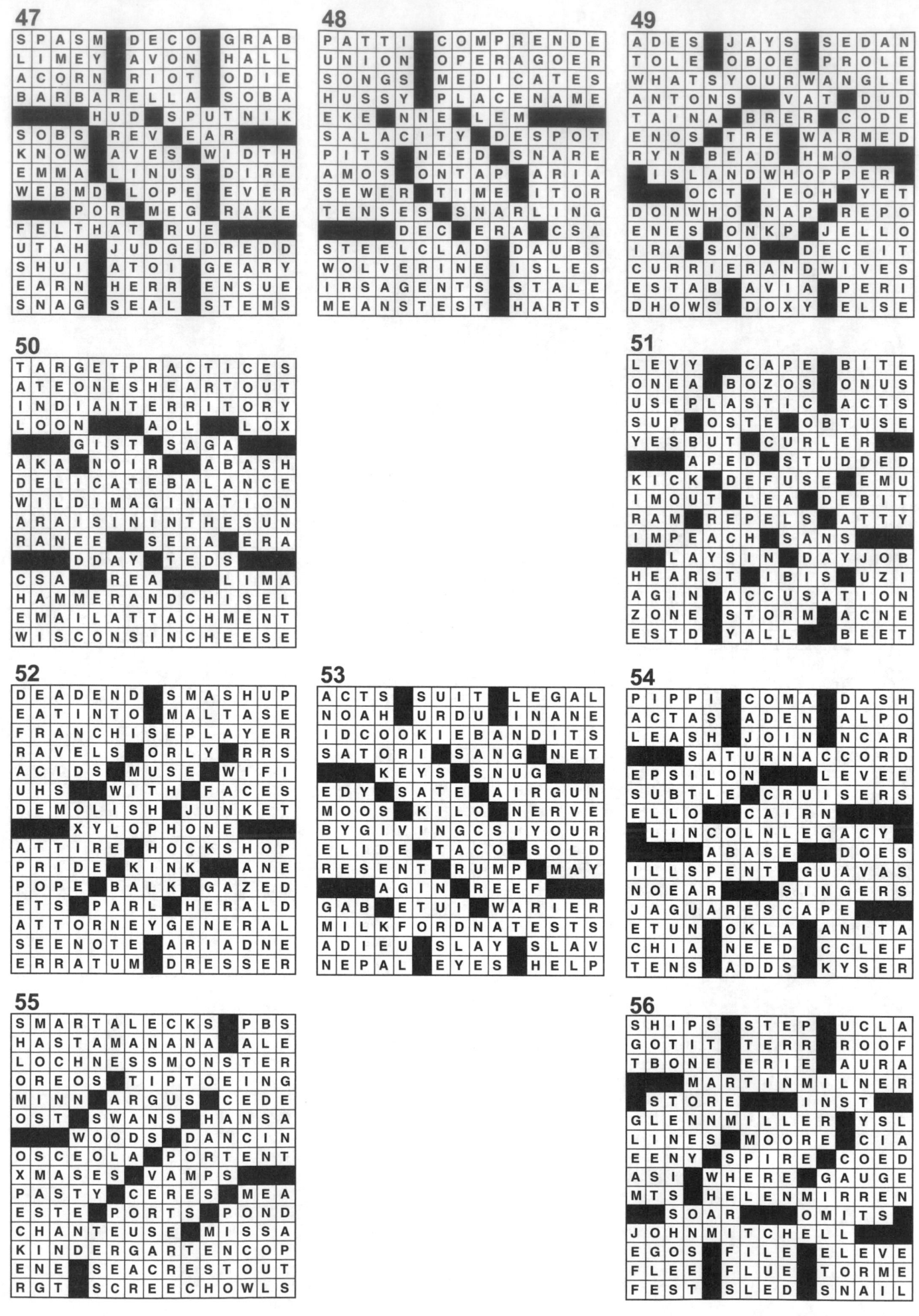

57

TROT SHARD ORCS
WITH MELEE DARE
ALTO ORANG EDEN
SEOULKOREA LIES
EEN UNLIKE
HOLMES DELI
ALIAS SOLLATIDO
HEEL SIREE HOOD
SOULMUSIC MANSE
IRIS RAISES
POMADE BAG
ADAM SOLEFILLET
RICO HEART AERO
TURN ONCLE MAME
SMOG TOKED BRAD

58

MEMO ERT ASIA
ALEE MITER LETS
TARDIGRADE APES
HIM BRALESS ARA
INACAST ASHTRAY
SENOR EEL ORATE
PSALM CRATER
MAS NYETS EDS
ALTARS RHINE
EERIE LYE AUDIT
SHALALA AIRRACE
TON RETITLE MAR
RUGS THREESCORE
OSEE HEART ONUS
SERT ERN MESA

59

ABETS LAHR PORE
BIGHT AWAY OVUM
ANGIE DOVERSOLE
SADDLE OILER
ASP LEE ORATORY
SWANEERIVER
CANARD CEO PASS
AMISS PER TEMPI
PICA POI DARERS
LOONEYTUNES
MUDBATH LET DEY
ONION PRIDED
CROWDSOUT RUNGS
HIDE IONE EKING
AGED SHES DEBUT

60

NEST COVETING
SOMMA ONEORMORE
EXPEL MARSUPIAL
AZTEC ELSIE SPY
BEI TEEN SIPS
EMEAT AAS STELE
EASTWARD SOIREE
LINY LIFT
PAPACY DETACHED
ABASE HOE SHOJI
RENT HISS TED
ITD DINAH CUZCO
STOPANDGO EMOTE
HARANGUER BANES
LARGESSE USED

61

TAP RASPS CODS
LIRA ALLEY OBOE
CROC YEARN MINE
PROS PICKMEUP
SHOOS .-. RUSTS
PASSAIC MEN
AVIS NOS AMINOR
SENTINMORSECODE
MIGHTY SEA APES
ESC DICTATE
TABOO -.. FIRST
BLACKTIE LOOK
OGLE OESTE NILS
NASA FLOES SNOT
DEAN ULNAS GUY

62

EFS YUGOS FIRST
TIE EBERT ERATO
OVA WONDERWOMAN
NECK ARISE BERG
HASTEN CSONKA
IRANI AWAIT
LINEN FLUNG SAW
SAG CEO STN INE
ALE INCAS FASTS
ATTIC OCTET
MARTYR ENTREE
ADIA ACTOR DRAW
DWARFPLANET AVI
RATIO ATONE CON
ERASE PESTO TWO

63

LAMMED CASELOAD
ESCALATORCLAUSE
APARTMENTHOUSES
IONIC RIPEST
CHIEN DEPONE
HOST EIRE RADS
ROSTOV TODO VEE
IDEAMAN PERCALE
SEI SCOT ROOTED
MDSE AVIS NATE
CONANT ACRED
ARRANT SETTO
SPIRALSTAIRCASE
EMOTIONALOUTCRY
ASSERTOR NESSIE

64

IKE PIKER SCHON
NNE AMAZE PAINE
GOODSPORT ANGST
EXCITES AFR HET
CEL MILKYWAY
EXCEL MINOLTA
YEAR EON REDYES
ENL TROOPER CRT
SAVOIR ROT HOME
ARMORED JAPAN
BORDERED REV
IVY ZSA CORONET
RAMBO GIRLSCOUT
DRAIN ADELE SRO
SYNGE NEWSY HOP

65

HOAR LEGG UPPED
ELLA ATOR NURSE
ADEN CHRISCROSS
DIXIT YOGHURT
USE EAL RUR OIL
PHILTHEBILL ZOO
ARENA OOPS
THENAMESTHEGAME
RASE IRENA
ARC WELCOMEMATT
YEH OKA LEM RAW
ASOCIAL YUCCA
GALEFORCES SAKI
ADORE DERE EDEN
MATED SYST REDS

66

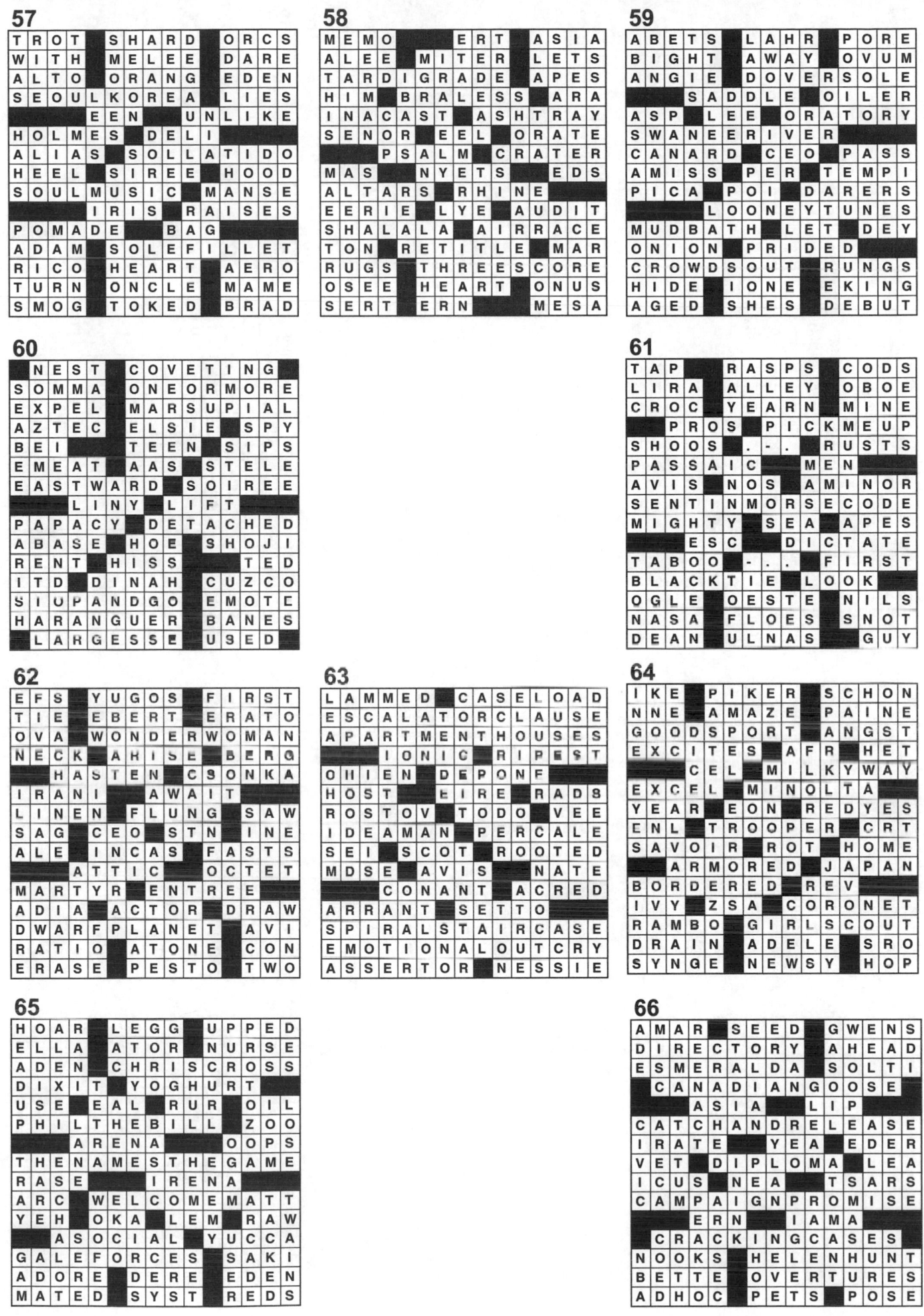

AMAR SEED GWENS
DIRECTORY AHEAD
ESMERALDA SOLTI
CANADIANGOOSE
ASIA LIP
CATCHANDRELEASE
IRATE YEA EDER
VET DIPLOMA LEA
ICUS NEA TSARS
CAMPAIGNPROMISE
ERN IAMA
CRACKINGCASES
NOOKS HELENHUNT
BETTE OVERTURES
ADHOC PETS POSE

67

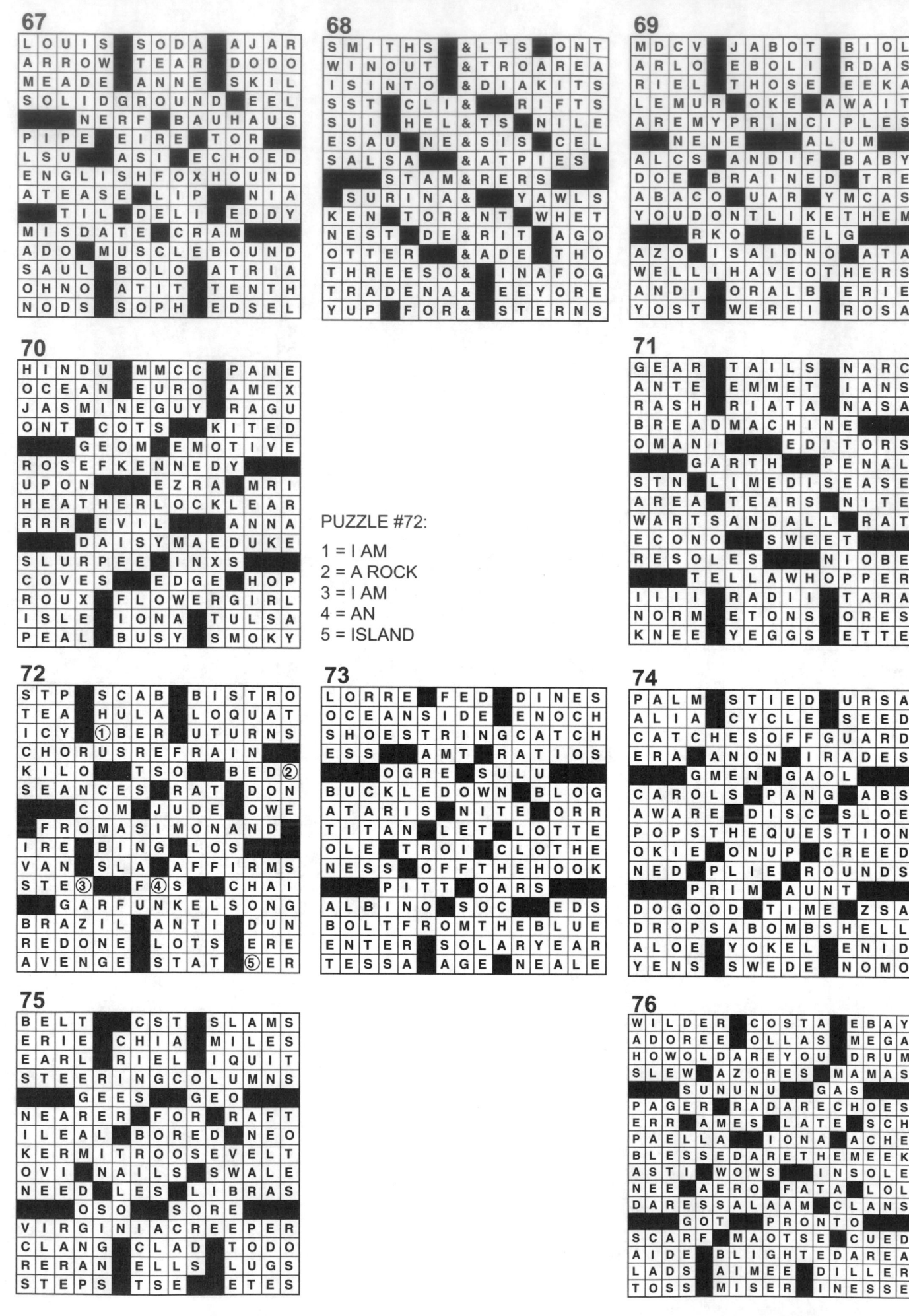

LOUIS SODA AJAR
ARROW TEAR DODO
MEADE ANNE SKIL
SOLIDGROUND EEL
NERF BAUHAUS
PIPE EIRE TOR
LSU ASI ECHOED
ENGLISHFOXHOUND
ATEASE LIP NIA
TIL DELI EDDY
MISDATE CRAM
ADO MUSCLEBOUND
SAUL BOLO ATRIA
OHNO ATIT TENTH
NODS SOPH EDSEL

68

SMITHS &LTS ONT
WINOUT &TROAREA
ISINTO &DIAKITS
SST CLI& RIFTS
SUI HEL&TS NILE
ESAU NE&SIS CEL
SALSA &ATPIES
STAM&RERS
SURINA& YAWLS
KEN TOR&NT WHET
NEST DE&RIT AGO
OTTER &ADE THO
THREESO& INAFOG
TRADENA& EEYORE
YUP FOR& STERNS

69

MDCV JABOT BIOL
ARLO EBOLI RDAS
RIEL THOSE EEKA
LEMUR OKE AWAIT
AREMYPRINCIPLES
NENE ALUM
ALCS ANDIF BABY
DOE BRAINED TRE
ABACO UAR YMCAS
YOUDONTLIKETHEM
RKO ELG
AZO ISAIDNO ATA
WELLIHAVEOTHERS
ANDI ORALB ERIE
YOST WEREI ROSA

70

HINDU MMCC PANE
OCEAN EURO AMEX
JASMINEGUY RAGU
ONT COTS KITED
GEOM EMOTIVE
ROSEFKENNEDY
UPON EZRA MRI
HEATHERLOCKLEAR
RRR EVIL ANNA
DAISYMAEDUKE
SLURPEE INXS
COVES EDGE HOP
ROUX FLOWERGIRL
ISLE IONA TULSA
PEAL BUSY SMOKY

71

GEAR TAILS NARC
ANTE EMMET IANS
RASH RIATA NASA
BREADMACHINE
OMANI EDITORS
GARTH PENAL
STN LIMEDISEASE
AREA TEARS NITE
WARTSANDALL RAT
ECONO SWEET
RESOLES NIOBE
TELLAWHOPPER
IIII RADII TARA
NORM ETONS ORES
KNEE YEGGS ETTE

PUZZLE #72:

1 = I AM
2 = A ROCK
3 = I AM
4 = AN
5 = ISLAND

72

STP SCAB BISTRO
TEA HULA LOQUAT
ICY ①BER UTURNS
CHORUSREFRAIN
KILO TSO BED②
SEANCES RAT DON
COM JUDE OWE
FROMASIMONAND
IRE BING LOS
VAN SLA AFFIRMS
STE③ F④S CHAI
GARFUNKELSONG
BRAZIL ANTI DUN
REDONE LOTS ERE
AVENGE STAT ⑤ER

73

LORRE FED DINES
OCEANSIDE ENOCH
SHOESTRINGCATCH
ESS AMT RATIOS
OGRE SULU
BUCKLEDOWN BLOG
ATARIS NITE ORR
TITAN LET LOTTE
OLE TROI CLOTHE
NESS OFFTHEHOOK
PITT OARS
ALBINO SOC EDS
BOLTFROMTHEBLUE
ENTER SOLARYEAR
TESSA AGE NEALE

74

PALM STIED URSA
ALIA CYCLE SEED
CATCHESOFFGUARD
ERA ANON IRADES
GMEN GAOL
CAROLS PANG ABS
AWARE DISC SLOE
POPSTHEQUESTION
OKIE ONUP CREED
NED PLIE ROUNDS
PRIM AUNT
DOGOOD TIME ZSA
DROPSABOMBSHELL
ALOE YOKEL ENID
YENS SWEDE NOMO

75

BELT CST SLAMS
ERIE CHIA MILES
EARL RIEL IQUIT
STEERINGCOLUMNS
GEES GEO
NEARER FOR RAFT
ILEAL BORED NEO
KERMITROOSEVELT
OVI NAILS SWALE
NEED LES LIBRAS
OSO SORE
VIRGINIACREEPER
CLANG CLAD TODO
RERAN ELLS LUGS
STEPS TSE ETES

76

WILDER COSTA EBAY
ADOREE OLLAS MEGA
HOWOLDAREYOU DRUM
SLEW AZORES MAMAS
SUNUNU GAS
PAGER RADARECHOES
ERR AMES LATE SCH
PAELLA IONA ACHE
BLESSEDARETHEMEEK
ASTI WOWS INSOLE
NEE AERO FATA LOL
DARESSALAAM CLANS
GOT PRONTO
SCARF MAOTSE CUED
AIDE BLIGHTEDAREA
LADS AIMEE DILLER
TOSS MISER INESSE

77

MAGI HULAS LISTEN
IVAN ANIME ENTERS
SETS NISAN ACETIC
CREAMOFTHECROP
NAVY GANGSTER
ONSIDE YEAR ORSO
BUTTERBALL CANOPY
OKAY OWL CRISP
EER SHUN FOIL ITS
SCOUT ORD SCAM
AGHAST CHEESECAKE
LEIS LUST MARLEE
ALPHABET CURE
MILKOFMAGNESIA
RECEDE FLING NORM
ADORES FINAL ELOI
MOPEDS STILE DENS

78

JARS HOODS BAREST
IRON ONSET EXACTA
MILO LEASE DENZEL
IALWAYSKEEP DEAL
CIC AXLE GIMME
SQUALID SPUR AYR
PUMP TIPS SHIP
LOB MYPROMISESAND
ATRIA ALE VISOR
THATSWHYIMAKE PLY
SHOE DOPE PEAL
RAP INXS TYRANNY
AMAZE ELAM HER
WILE SOFEWOFTHEM
ENABLE VIDAL TOGA
GOTRID ARETE WEAR
GREATS KEATS ODDS

79

ASKTO ALAS PIEPAN
RECAP MOBY ONSALE
BLAME BIAS LETTER
FRANCISCOPIZARRO
REO UPAT BIOL
COPARENTS ABS ASI
ARA DAR BRUTE
ROMES TODO RUSHES
PUBLICOPINIONPOLL
STYLER HAIG TONIO
STACY TOM DEM
MOC ECO MARCOPOLO
AAAS KNEE ARR
GRECOPERSIANWARS
PISANO IHOP EYEOF
INAPET KETT LTCOL
EGRESS ADAS LOTTA

80

TREED WANTTO ONTO
WEAVE ADORES REAP
ITSALLVERYKARAOKE
LAIN EEL YELPER
LIL SOHAVEI ILONA
SLYDINI ARSENAL
REA CLEAT WISE
SCRAG YAK ACT TED
YOUWEREPITCHYDAWG
NAB SOL LAS RONNY
ELBA SLOMO AAH
EYESORE SENATES
LODES WORTHIT ONE
AVIATE HOO ROSA
BUTYOUREBEAUTIFUL
ELIE RESEAT ICARE
LENS OBSESS SHRED

81

SASH SHAVE CACHET
HIKE EATAT REHASH
IDEA ARECA EROICA
VELVETPILLOW SLEW
EELS NAIVETE
PITHY VIOLINBOW
EROO PMS EFILE
ZEN LOCUST TRENDS
VARIETYSHOW
ACCEPT ZEROED VOW
THIRD OWN NORA
VICMORROW PECKS
IGOOFED META
HEAL VOLCANICFLOW
EXCITE AARON LIDA
MEMOIR TRIED IZOD
SCENES EENSY XERS

82

AXMAN RILES FOXX
GEODE SENILE ITEM
INLOVEISFAIR DONA
LOL EXMOOR VIDEOS
ENYA TOR TILL
POINTBULLETIN
STERN SCALE BENO
IOO ACT IHA BORGE
SWELLTHATENDSWELL
RETIE IRE ERI SEE
ETAS CROCK IDEAS
DOGSGOTOHEAVEN
ONLY AVE OPER
TALMUD AFRAME EXO
AGEE EXPENSESPAID
RIAL SEPTET MARLA
TORY TODAY ELLEN

83

ITES FERNS EPOCHS
MELT IDIOT LIPOUT
PROPORTION FLAMBE
OSIERS SKIP ELMER
SESTETS CIA IRE
TREES POCKETCOSTS
IDA SOLOS
SAWTO RIPS MAOIST
ABHOR OUTOF SLOPE
TOOFAR MILO PANAM
LUTES VOO
ONESELEMENT ABUTS
LOC ONA ESCAPEE
ISLET DROP PANTED
VIOLIN THERUNNING
INTIME HONOR ELIE
AGHAST ASSET RTES

84

IRA SHAKEUP SMARM
OAR COVERME TASER
WITCHESBREW TRAIT
ALSO AOK NEILS
CELEBRITYROAST
AEROBICS IME RUB
NSA ANA KEEPSAKES
DAILYGRIND HAM
SINO DROII THAT
NET ACTONESAGE
PIGGYBANK TOV RUE
DNA EIN EURASIAN
FIRSTROUNDPICK
TOTED TAI IDES
LITRE BEATTOAPULP
EATIT ORCHARD DOA
ALEPH TOPSPOT SIS

85

WEEDS GOTHAM GUMS
AXMEN AVIATE UHOH
SPICESTATION MUTE
PELLEAS ILL APRIL
SLEAZY SAILSSTAFF
SEA INN AHI
LAWS HAT GNU OARS
OSHEA TAB ONANDON
ODE SORRYSTAT DUE
MOLOKAI ELI OFUSE
SIKH SAC ENT APER
RYE ALP ASS
SWEETSSPOT RECAST
NICAD ATL ATEINTO
IDOL SCULLSESSION
FELL THREAT ATONE
FREY USEDTO SANER

86

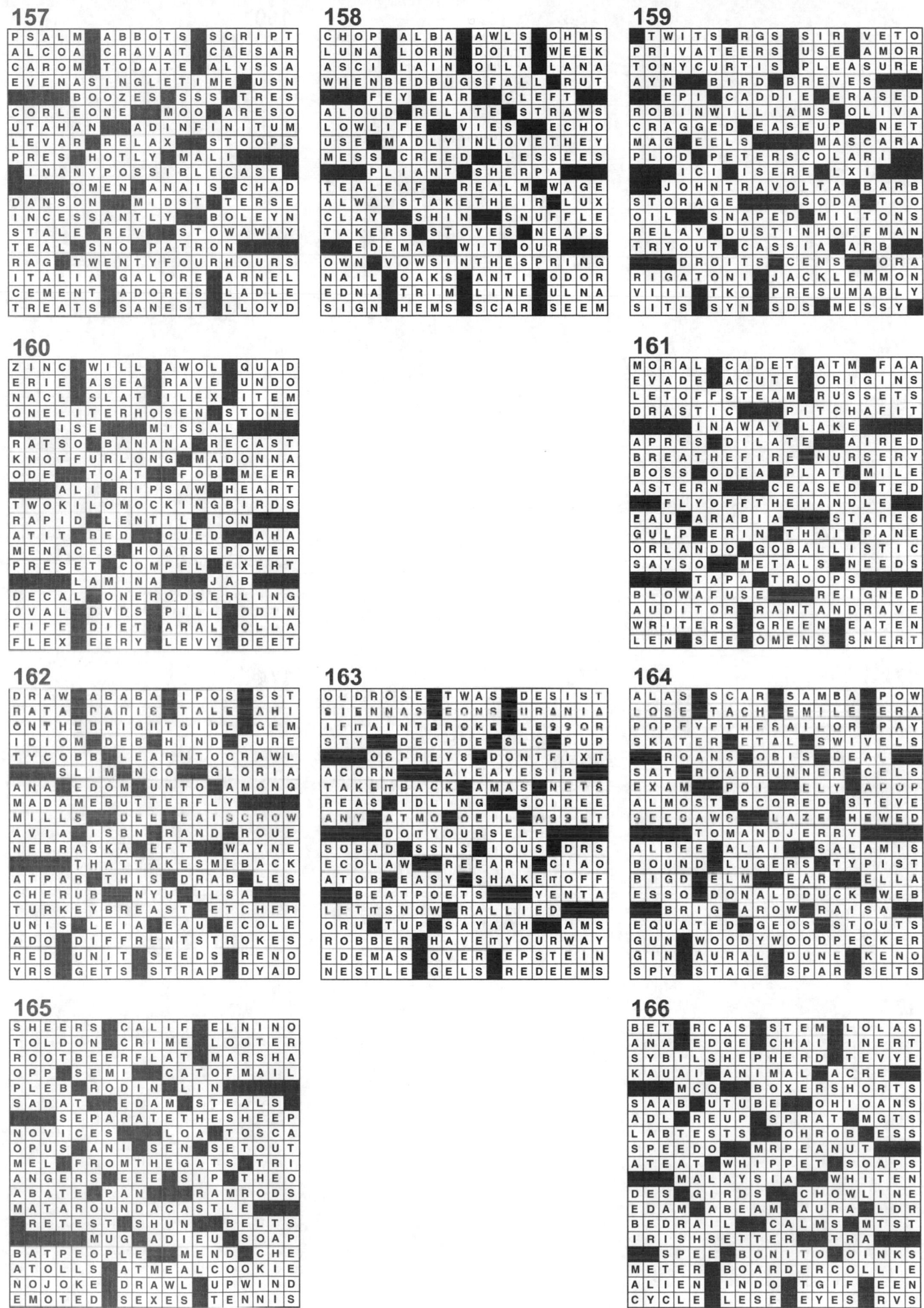

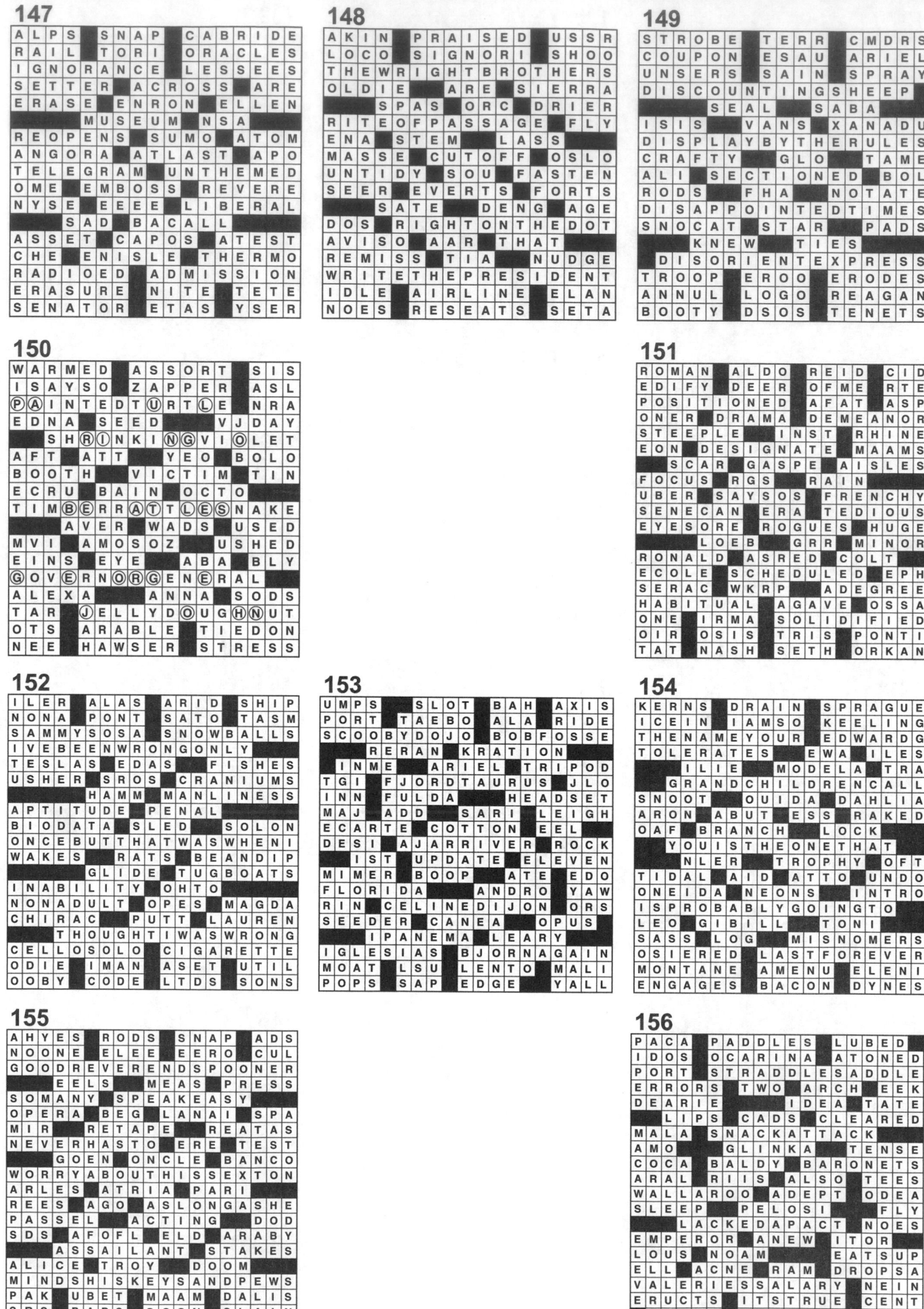

PACED AMANA TRALA
AGAPE SALES RULER
REMIT PLOWS ASPEN
ICER IFYOUCHOKE
POLARIS TERSE
GILL PCS ATAD JOG
ALE SCALARS PUMA
STORED SPINAL
ASMURFWHATCOLOR
FRIEND ORIOLE
RAZE RECALLS BOA
ABE COOP LED TREX
ONTAP REQUIRE
DOESHETURN DUST
ABATE ELIOT ASTRO
ROVER RECTO CLEAR
KEENE STEEP KENYA

87

T	R	A	P			A	T	T	I	R	E		N	C	A	A
H	O	R	A	S		S	O	I	L	E	D		E	A	R	N
A	B	A	C	I		C	R	E	A	T	E		B	M	I	N
N	O	P	E	N	N	I	E	S		U	N	D	U	E		
	C	A	R	G	O		R	U	H	R		I	L	I	A	D
A	A	H	S		S	H	O	P	E	N	T	R	A	N	C	E
G	L	O		S	H	A			A	S	H	E		T	R	Y
O	L	S	E	N		T	S	A	R		E	C	H	O	E	S
			G	O	P	E	N	N	S	T	A	T	E			
B	U	R	G	O	O		I	T	T	Y		O	M	E	G	A
O	R	E		P	O	M	P			P	A	R		M	A	D
I	S	U	R	E	H	O	P	E	N	O	T		P	M	T	S
L	A	S	E	R		H	Y	D	E		O	P	R	A	H	
		A	T	S	E	A		S	P	L	I	T	O	P	E	N
C	U	B	E		L	I	N	E	A	R		A	N	E	R	A
I	T	L	L		B	R	I	L	L	O		S	T	E	E	P
R	E	E	L		A	S	K	S	I	N			O	L	D	E

88

G	R	A	N	D		R	A	S	H		T	R	E	M	O	R
R	E	L	E	E		A	R	E	A		S	E	R	E	N	E
A	N	E	W	N	A	M	E	A	N	D	A	D	R	E	S	S
D	E	C		I	B	I	S		G	I	R	O		C	A	T
			O	S	E			S	S	N			P	E	L	E
Y	O	U	G	E	T	R	E	P	O	S	S	E	S	S	E	D
O	R	N	E			O	L	I	N		L	S	T			
G	A	L	E	S		P	I	N		V	A	T		B	M	W
I	T	I	S	A	D	E	A	D	G	I	V	E	A	W	A	Y
S	E	T		Y	E	S		R	O	D		S	N	A	R	E
			B	S	A		M	I	N	E			G	N	A	T
C	A	S	E	O	F	W	I	F	E	O	R	D	E	A	T	H
A	B	U	T			A	T	T			E	E	L			
S	A	P		H	A	L	E		B	E	A	M		W	H	O
I	S	P	O	U	L	T	R	Y	I	N	M	O	T	I	O	N
N	E	E	D	T	O		E	E	R	O		T	I	T	L	E
O	D	D	E	S	T		D	A	D	S		E	T	H	E	R

89

P	A	C	E	S		S	C	A	D	S		M	I	N	U	S
E	L	O	P	E		H	O	S	E	A		A	N	I	S	E
R	A	W	E	R		I	M	S	A	D		C	S	P	A	N
M	I	L	E	F	O	R	M	I	L	E	T	H	E			
					B	L	A	S	T		A	I	R	M	E	N
C	O	S	T	L	I	E	S	T		M	I	N	T	A	G	E
A	N	N	U	I	T	Y			M	O	P	E		G	A	T
P	E	A	L	E			P	E	R	S	E		E	N	D	S
		K	I	N	D	O	F	V	E	H	I	C	L	E		
P	R	E	P		U	N	F	E	D			O	D	S	O	N
O	O	P		G	L	U	T			M	A	D	E	I	R	A
S	W	I	V	E	L	S		T	O	O	P	E	R	A	T	E
E	S	T	A	T	E		C	O	N	D	E					
			I	S	A	G	R	O	C	E	R	Y	C	A	R	T
S	K	I	N	S		N	A	T	A	L		A	L	L	O	W
H	I	R	E	E		A	T	I	L	T		P	A	D	U	A
E	X	E	R	T		R	E	E	L	S		S	W	A	T	S

90

E	A	R	A	C	H	E		W	A	R	M		A	M	T	S
M	A	I	L	B	O	X		A	S	I	A		R	E	N	O
A	R	A	L	S	E	A		T	H	E	E	V	I	L	O	F
J	E	A	N			C	R	U	E	L		L	O	T	T	A
			E	M	O	T	E	S			P	A	S	S	E	S
T	H	E	W	O	R	L	D	I	S	M	A	D	E			
R	A	N		S	A	Y			O	I	L			K	A	L
O	R	D	E	A	L		B	O	N	E		S	T	R	I	A
P	O	S	S	I	B	L	E	B	Y	N	O	T	H	I	N	G
I	L	I	A	C		A	R	I	A		P	R	E	S	T	O
C	D	T			S	S	T			C	I	I		T	S	O
			B	U	T	T	H	E	S	A	N	C	T	I	O	N
D	E	L	U	G	E			D	E	L	E	T	E			
A	C	A	L	L		P	R	I	Z	M			N	C	A	R
Y	O	U	G	I	V	E	I	T		S	A	U	S	A	G	E
A	L	E	E		O	N	C	E		E	M	P	O	R	I	A
N	E	R	D		O	N	E	D		A	Y	N	R	A	N	D

91

O	C	L		P	A	A	R		M	O	N	T		F	R	Y
R	H	O		R	U	B	E		B	R	A	E		R	I	O
L	A	W	R	E	N	C	E		A	T	T	N		A	S	K
A	R	R	E	S	T		B	O	S		U	N	L	I	K	E
N	I	E	C	E		F	O	R		P	R	I	E	D		
D	O	N	T	T	A	L	K	U	N	L	E	S	S	Y	O	U
O	T	T	O		G	A	S		E	E	L		S	C	A	T
				P	E	T		B	O	A		Y	E	A	R	N
I	S	L	E	T	S		C	A	N		T	S	E	T	S	E
T	E	E	N	S		O	O	H		P	A	L				
S	E	A	T		E	P	S		L	A	X		L	I	A	R
I	M	P	R	O	V	E	T	H	E	S	I	L	E	N	C	E
		F	E	R	A	L		I	N	S		A	E	G	I	S
S	I	R	E	N	S		D	E	S		A	R	C	A	D	E
W	O	O		A	I	D	E		C	O	U	G	H	L	I	N
A	N	G		T	O	R	E		A	N	T	E		L	T	D
M	A	S		E	N	I	D		P	O	O	R		S	Y	S

92

R	I	S	K		F	A	L	A	L	A		S	H	I	P	S
I	M	A	N		A	D	O	N	I	S		M	A	O	R	I
P	E	R	U		C	O	L	D	S	H	O	U	L	D	E	R
S	T	I	C	K	E	R	S		B	E	N		L	I	V	E
			K	I	T	E		H	O	S	E	D		N	I	N
	V	O	L	T	S		V	I	N		W	A	K	E	N	S
R	E	S	E	T		M	A	P			A	Y	N			
E	N	S	U	E		U	N	H	O	L	Y		E	A	T	S
Q	U	I	N	N		S	N	O	R	E		R	E	N	E	E
S	E	E	D		S	T	A	P	L	E		E	S	S	E	N
			E	E	K			P	O	R		B	L	E	N	D
S	T	A	R	R	Y		H	E	N		C	O	A	L	S	
T	O	R		A	L	G	E	R		B	U	R	P			
R	I	A	L		A	U	F		T	U	R	N	P	I	K	E
E	L	B	O	W	B	E	N	D	E	R	S		E	D	I	T
S	E	I	N	E		S	E	R	E	N	E		R	E	N	T
S	T	A	G	E		T	R	Y	S	T	S		S	A	G	A

93

S	C	R	A	M		S	P	I	L	L		P	A	S	D	E
I	L	O	S	E		A	U	R	A	E		A	T	L	A	W
R	O	U	S	E		G	R	A	N	T		S	N	O	R	E
E	N	T	I	T	L	E	S		C	U	S	T	O	M	E	R
D	E	E	S		A	T	E	L	E	S	S		T	O	S	S
			T	O	R	E	R	O		P	E	D	I			
A	M	N	E	S	I	A		F	I	R	S	T	M	A	T	E
N	O	I	D	E	A		E	T	N	A		S	E	T	U	P
G	U	T			T	U	P		S	Y	N			O	R	I
S	T	R	A	W		N	E	E	T		I	R	O	N	I	C
T	H	E	L	E	T	T	E	R		R	E	O	P	E	N	S
			I	T	E	R		S	P	E	C	I	E			
S	I	D	E		N	A	S	T	A	S	E		R	O	A	D
T	O	R	N	A	D	I	C		R	O	S	E	A	N	N	E
A	T	E	A	M		N	A	S	A	L		S	T	E	A	M
T	A	S	T	E		E	L	I	D	E		T	E	A	M	O
E	S	S	E	S		D	E	L	E	S		A	D	M	E	N

94

S	U	B	S		T	O	P	A	Z		C	H	A	S	M	S
O	H	I	O		O	P	I	N	E		H	O	L	L	O	W
F	O	R	M	L	E	T	T	E	R		A	C	T	I	V	E
T	H	R	E	A	T		S	W	O	R	N		E	M	I	L
				P	A	D			S	A	G		R	E	E	L
W	A	R	P	S	P	E	E	D		D	E	L	E			
O	D	I	L	E		F	R	O	D	O		A	G	A	R	S
B	R	A	Y		F	O	R	G	O		A	N	O	R	A	K
B	I	L		B	R	E	A	D	M	O	L	D		C	I	A
L	E	T	F	L	Y		T	A	I	N	T		C	A	S	T
E	N	O	L	A		W	A	Y	N	E		S	A	D	I	E
			E	B	R	O		S	O	U	T	H	B	E	N	D
A	P	E	X		O	O	P			P	R	O				
T	A	U	T		C	L	U	B	S		A	R	A	M	I	S
A	T	R	I	S	K		L	E	M	O	N	T	W	I	S	T
R	O	O	M	I	E		S	T	O	I	C		E	L	L	A
I	N	S	E	C	T		E	A	G	L	E		D	E	E	R

95

P	O	P	A	R	T		T	A	R	A	S		B	O	E	R
L	O	A	M	E	D		E	N	A	M	I		E	L	L	E
A	M	E	B	A	S		B	O	I	N	G		F	D	I	C
I	P	S	O			A	A	N	D	E		T	I	D	E	S
T	H	E	Y	C	A	L	L			S	C	O	T	O		
				M	R	E	D		P	I	O	N		M	D	S
T	E	L	E	V	I	S	I	O	N	A	M	E	D	I	U	M
E	B	O	L	I				H	E	C	T		O	N	E	I
A	B	U	M		B	E	C	A	U	S	E		W	I	L	L
R	E	D	A		O	N	O	R				O	S	O	L	E
I	T	S	N	E	I	T	H	E	R	R	A	R	E	N	O	R
T	S	P		S	T	E	N		A	O	L	E				
		E	A	S	E	R			W	E	L	L	D	O	N	E
W	H	A	L	E		T	O	A	D	Y			E	V	E	R
A	O	K	I		D	A	N	T	E		R	E	P	A	V	E
T	R	E	K		M	I	T	L	A		E	R	O	T	I	C
T	A	R	E		A	N	V	I	L		I	N	T	E	N	T

96

B	A	T	M	A	N		V	I	S	I	T		A	Q	U	A
E	X	H	A	L	E		A	D	A	G	E		B	U	R	P
G	E	O	D	E	S		T	O	K	E	N		R	A	G	E
			E	S	T	E		L	I	T	T	L	E	R	E	D
C	A	S	A		S	I	C			I	H	E	A	R		
A	R	O	M	A		G	O	D	O	T		A	S	I	D	E
R	I	D	I	N	G	H	O	O	D		E	N	T	E	R	S
B	L	A	N	K	E	T		R	I	A	L			D	J	S
			T	H	E	P	R	I	N	C	E	S	S			
S	E	W			S	M	U	T		A	N	A	P	E	S	T
P	O	O	D	L	E		G	O	L	D	I	L	O	C	K	S
A	E	R	I	E		I	S	S	U	E		S	T	R	I	P
		L	E	A	R	N			G	M	T		C	U	T	S
A	N	D	T	H	E	P	E	A		Y	E	A	H			
P	I	C	A		E	A	R	N	S		S	L	E	A	Z	Y
S	P	U	R		F	R	I	T	O		L	A	C	I	E	R
E	S	P	Y		S	T	E	E	D		A	N	K	L	E	S

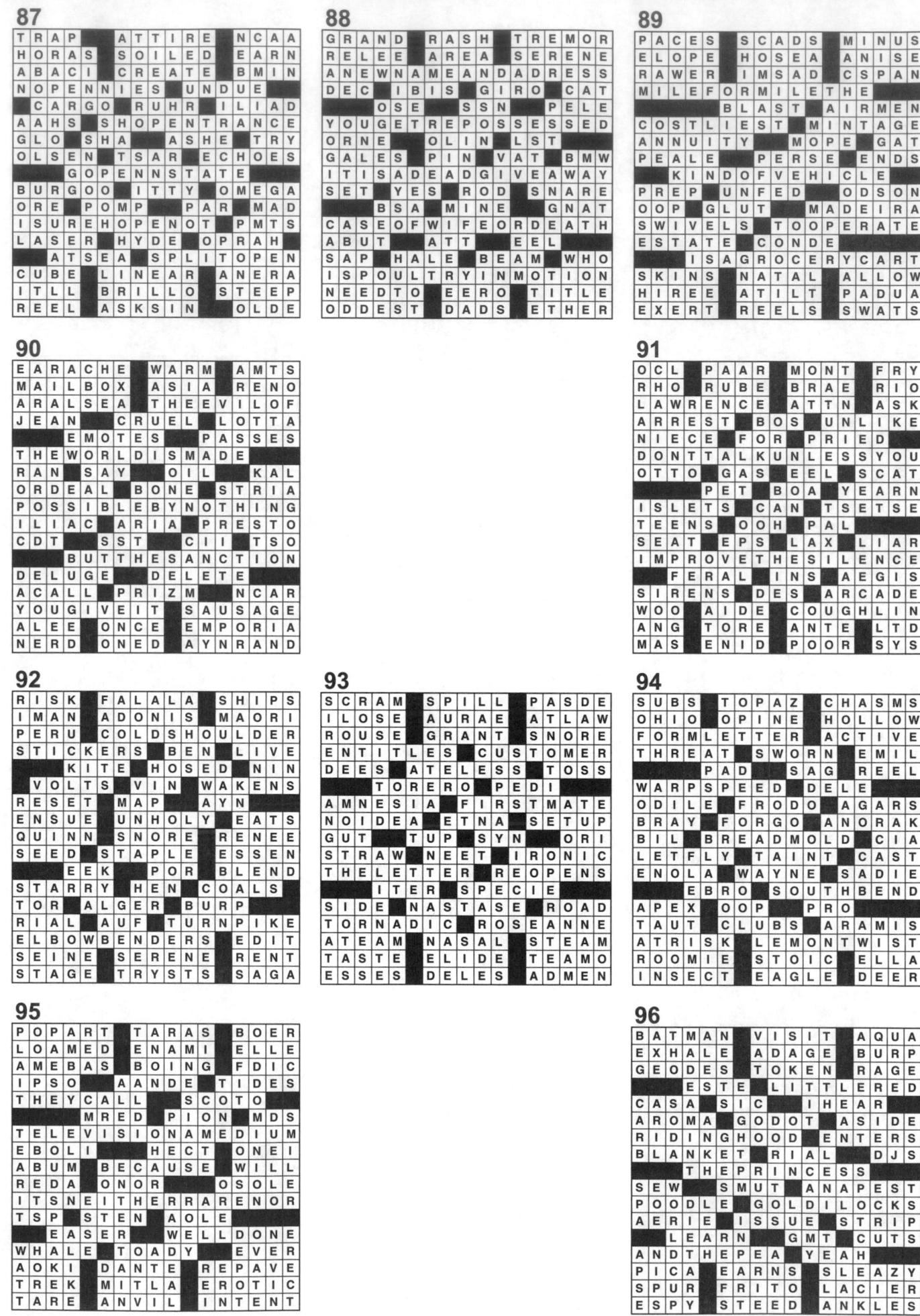

97

CDRECORDABLE DEPP
VIOLONCELLOS AVER
INTERACTIONS WILE
IHAVETOAGREE SAIS
EYELINER PONCE
GPS HAAN PENMAN
LOTHAR MTPLEASANT
ATOUR SEEYOU SST
SANIT KNARS NOTTE
SLY OUTSIT ALEAN
CASEYKASEM STARTS
OPINES IVAR SEE
VALET VARDALOS
ELEM SILVICULTURE
RANI ANTINATIONAL
ECCE PHONENETWORK
DEES SONGSTRESSES

98

HONEY ANERA EPSOM
OPERA DOVES TROPE
DARIN VOIDS HOSEA
LONGDISTANCECALL
USEAS ANE
DISABLED ARRESTED
ASARULE TBAR SIZE
NOLAN ARETOO TEN
TALKABLUESTREAK
ROD ODELET ARNIE
APIS MATS WINDIER
WENTWITH PENTACLE
OAR EARLS
CRYOVERSPILTMILK
ROUGE YARNS EWING
AIMER EMOTE NOLIE
GLASS SENSE UNITE

99

PISA CLAMP VALID
EDIT HOVEL SERENE
LEAH AGORA TRIAGE
FAMEISONLYGOODFOR
ATMS DIP STE
APART BOOGIES
TEST ONETHINGTHEY
HTS SWATS REESE
READINGS KINETICS
ORION SNOOT FOY
WILLCASHYOUR WERE
TENCENT CARTS
ASH TAX POET
CHECKINASMALLTOWN
HEROIC GEARS ALOE
ERECTS OXIDE GAVE
DESKS NYLON EYED

100

APIN MIAHAMM AKIN
LONI ALPACAS BENE
HOSPITALGOWN ERAT
ALTARS OUR PECS
MCATS AMENBROTHER
BUN OMB EMS INO
RETREAT ENVS HESA
ASSUCH AREA WAFER
FOURCORNERS
ABDUL UNDO DENNIS
LOOS EPEE DENTIST
ERN RAE BAR CUP
CATTYREMARK DEERE
BPOE ANI SEXTET
MOET BLINDJUSTICE
EHEI MANAGED OMAR
WAKE THESEUS LENS

101

STEELS SOON ASIDE
HORNIN PACE LADES
ARIOSO ETCH TROLL
WINSTONCHURCHILL
STE PUCE
SECS THAI NASCAR
AJOKEISAVERY LONE
MEDIAS MESA BENTS
CENSOR THRICE
STINT OOZE EUGENE
AONE SERIOUSTHING
CREDIT AGES STAG
CELL EAP
HAVETHELASTLAUGH
CANIB AXFL TANGLE
RHINO SANE ANTLER
INDEX AMOS RESINS

102

RADAR APE USA IFI
ALONE RAT HAVANAN
TODOWATCH FLITTED
ATONAL TET DEERE
RIG RIAL LIE
ACCIDENT CRATERED
LOAN NORA IMAGE
ILLS SMALL PROVED
BIKES ESTER ATEAR
INNATE HAVEN INGE
OMANI RACE SUEC
NEWSROOM ROASTERS
ALL SNUB NRC
BUENO MAP LARIAT
ODDBALL BABYRUDGE
REGATTA AWE ADORN
SSE SDS RNA BELAS

103

BETA HERB GRANADA
ALIT OLAY ENCASED
LOTT HOTH MERMAID
LIFEISNTALLBEER
ONCE ANTI UTE
VERDE ANDSKITTLES
OCT ESS ELGRECO
IRAQ AHORA LIF
TUTU FEWOFUS SATE
ETE NORSE SSRS
STAUNCH EEL SOT
HAVETOUCHED ACUTE
EPI SOON SCAR
ASKITTLEINYEARS
LATERAL DRNO SNOW
AMORITE EGGO ACHE
BORISES NYET REED

104

TASKS MCREAL CAR
ANEEL FAULTY HULA
MANYANAUTHOR YEAH
PLANTO STIPEND
SOTO MOAT ORALS
GETSAPLOTFORANEW
EENS HOTSTOVE
SHERE SOEUR EDIE
MAV NOVELFROM AEI
AHAB MANET FOLDS
RADICALS BARR
THESCREENVERSION
SAREE IAGO ECON
CDRACKS MENTAL
RANT OFHISLASTONE
PROS BIOTAS SAPOR
MAD STUART ALIAS

105

DRACO BARRE ICET
RUMORS ALOES SHOE
ADELIE NONET BANC
WYNONNAJUDD KNISH
RODEO EINE
RACECAR ELTONJOHN
CHARO IAL INASEC
ASP MELBA SEEMSO
ELVISCOSTELLO
PILEIN SWORD SRS
ISLETS IFI STING
CHAKAKHAN PEERSAT
LYON ALANA
ATLAS GINGERSPICE
ROIL ATMAN TIPTOP
ADOS DIANE ONETWO
BONO DELOS GROSS

106

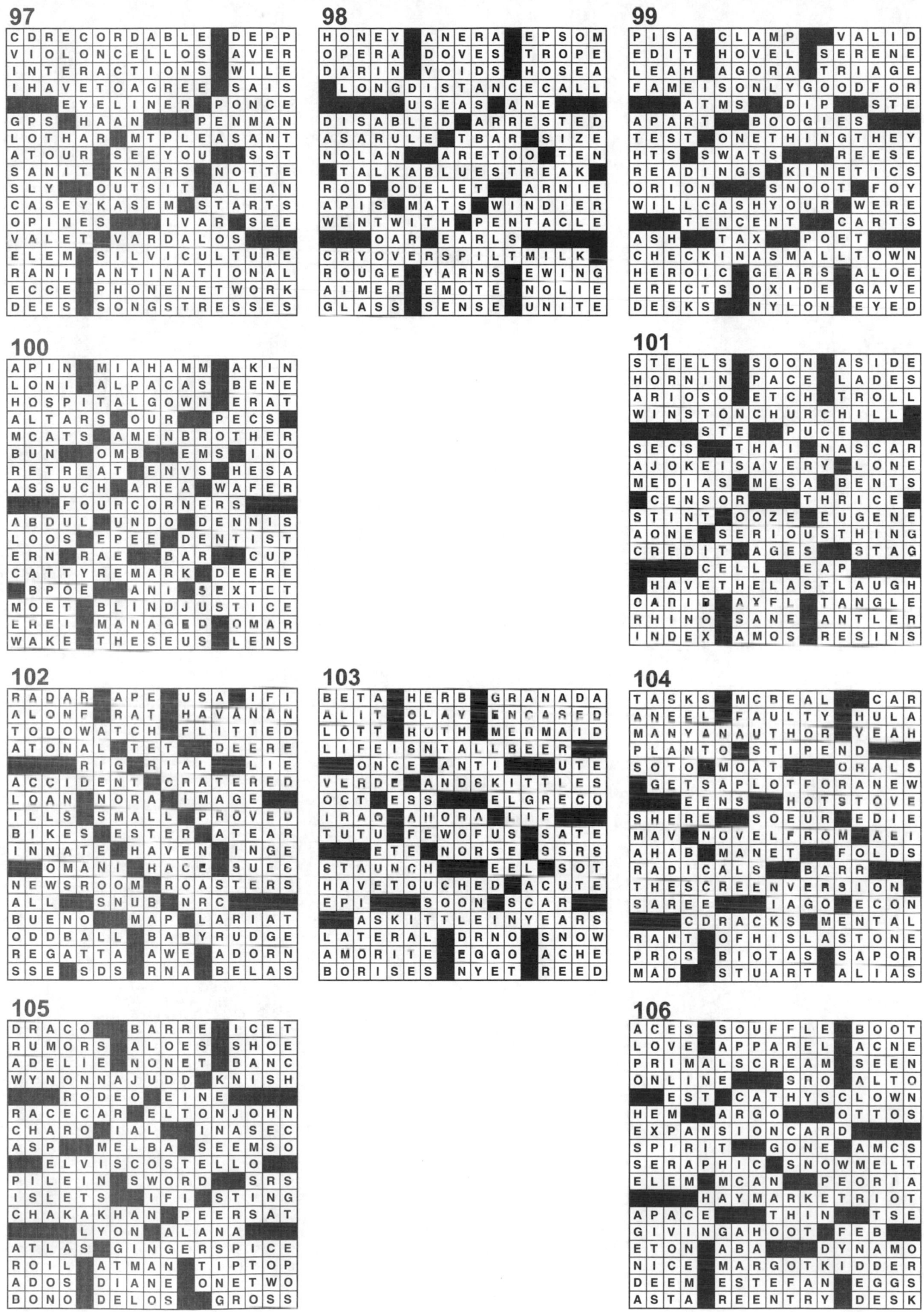

ACES SOUFFLE BOOT
LOVE APPAREL ACNE
PRIMALSCREAM SEEN
ONLINE SRO ALTO
EST CATHYSCLOWN
HEM ARGO OTTOS
EXPANSIONCARD
SPIRIT GONE AMCS
SERAPHIC SNOWMELT
ELEM MCAN PEORIA
HAYMARKETRIOT
APACE THIN TSE
GIVINGAHOOT FEB
ETON ABA DYNAMO
NICE MARGOTKIDDER
DEEM ESTEFAN EGGS
ASTA REENTRY DESK

107

LAISSEZ BAREFOOT
AGONIZED ELEVENTH
VITAMINE ATTENDEE
ANACONDA CAIN ELS
KNEAD HRE CCLI
IRIS VERBS MAKOS
CAT STEREO WISC
BJS WAS BYZANTINE
MATTERTO SOLDERED
SHIBEPARK OLE CPU
MATS GETMAD LAC
BEERS BAGEL PELE
ATTS FUN NEWSY
TAO SETI SNOOTIER
ALCATRAZ ESOPHAGI
AIRBORNE DESPOTIC
NAYSAYER SHYNESS

108

ALBS MISTS HASBRO
GORE ASKIT AVALON
LIANELAINE PALATE
ERITREA RDS ANTS
TENOR COCOA EMCEE
BNEG TAINTTIANT
CER DELTADAWN
ALIA TOONS IAGREE
SHADOWS ASSUAGE
KINSKI QBERT SIGN
ANNUALFEE LOY
DAIRYDIARY RAMS
ENNES RINSE TARSI
SETT SON READIES
IMEANT TRIALTRAIL
SIRREE EARTO ILKA
TANDEM RECON DSOS

109

CAMO ABO SAGA FRA
OMISSION HURT REM
MERCURYCOUGAR OCA
BRAID SEAT NITWIT
LAM FORDPINTO
WELLNESS FEE TEAR
AREA SCOFFS GODLY
DICT SOUR PEA
CHEVROLETIMPALA
ESP EIRE DORM
GRIST FARMER IDEA
RENO GUT EDGINESS
AMCMARLIN EST
BOLERO NAIF LEAST
BRO DODGESUPERBEE
ASS OVAL INSTILLS
GEE RENE SKI MELT

110

RAMA BRAGGART ADS
AXON OUTEREAR RIO
CLOD REEMERGE GAR
HENREID INA EGYPT
AGLETS GNATS OLEO
ERISA MAIDEN SERF
LEG TSETSE IMS
RAHS KGS SEPTETTE
ASTORIA BEATRIX
YESANDNO BOA TIMS
PAR CREATE VET
SAAB OBOIST BOITE
ALTO WENDT HARARE
LEOXI AND SENEGAL
IAN LOVELACE GAVE
NSC SKELETAL OMER
ETE EARLDOMS NELS

111

TOMCAT SHAG BALSA
APOLLO TIRE ETHAN
RETAIN ALDO GRAFT
ACHYSYMPTOM GASES
TAILOR CANARY
GOTO ZEN CORD
INADAZE SHY OMAR
JETSKI ASIA SMORE
AHA ATONALISM VMI
NOMAS MATT LOMEIN
EPIC WET ROGAINE
CLAN OJO ENGR
CASUAL QUILTS
IREST ATTHEBOTTOM
RHETT LILA OLEARY
CANOE OPED NOEXIT
ATOMS ESTS ENDASH

112

JAMBS SPUD SPLIT
IDIOT STATE QUITO
BALOO KARMA URGED
MARRIAGEOFFIGARO
OWN ENTERS OREM
REEK RED TART EMU
ESSAYED RESENDS
STENO IDTAG ITIS
SWEENEYTODD
AGHA RAKES RERUN
PLASMAS STYRENE
TOV USES TWA SATE
EDGE AIRACE SOD
ANDYGRIFFITHSHOW
ROONE CINCH SINAI
INNER BROKE EVERT
LOESS METS NERDS

113

WAFT SWEAROFF OTB
ACLU KANGAROO URL
STANDARDERROR TAU
PIXIE UNE WEAVE
CLARET ORANGES
OMS TRI AVERSELY
GULFOFFINLAND
DRYER ETOILE ISLE
ERENOW ABC WALTER
NERD EASEIN TIOGA
SINCLAIRLEWIS
CALCUTTA TIA STE
ELEGIZE MASONS
AWAIT PAR THIGH
SAD SHELLMACARONI
EYE MANITOBA ETAL
SSN ENDEARED WATT

114

ARCS SPANKS AIMAT
VERY ARCANE SPICE
EDEN FERRER SALON
SACRIFICEFRANKLY
ATM IRED BYEBYE
HASTIER WASI MATA
ATOMS WALL RARER
BEDE STARTOUT
RANKLEDZEPPELIN
EYESORES ENOL
LIMOS NUNS CACTI
ATIP HYPE MIRRORS
TERESA IAMA RET
CRANKYYOUNGAWARD
HANOI UNSUNG LEAP
ENDUP LESSEE ACME
STATS EGRETS STEW

115

DELUDE WAVES ARES
ELATED ELIDE MESH
PUTASAKEINIT ASTA
ODE MAD YET LEAR
TEXAS POOL LEGATE
STOPUP SEDATED
TEMPURATANTRUM
ORIENT LEA EPA
FINN SAT EGG BLOC
UKE MAO AURIST
IFYOUKNEWSUSHI
CANNIER ROCKET
ANODES MAMA DEREK
NAVE OKA ISH AVE
ALEX RAMENHOLIDAY
DONE NOBLE PARADE
AGAS OSAGE SPARED

116

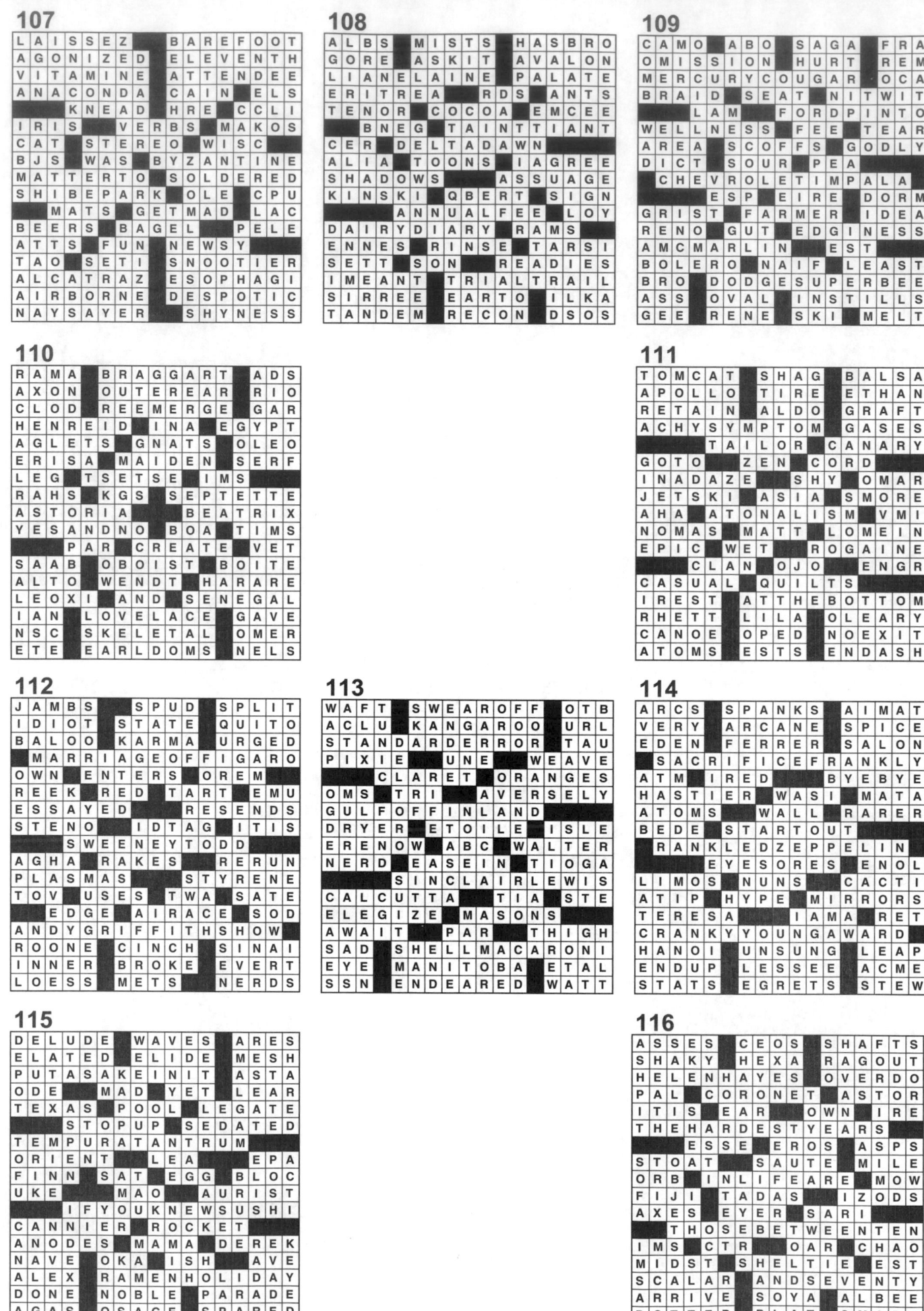

ASSES CEOS SHAFTS
SHAKY HEXA RAGOUT
HELENHAYES OVERDO
PAL CORONET ASTOR
ITIS EAR OWN IRE
THEHARDESTYEARS
ESSE EROS ASPS
STOAT SAUTE MILE
ORB INLIFEARE MOW
FIJI TADAS IZODS
AXES EYER SARI
THOSEBETWEENTEN
IMS CTR OAR CHAO
MIDST SHELTIE EST
SCALAR ANDSEVENTY
ARRIVE SOYA ALBEE
DOTTED PLAT SMART

117

STOLID SHY SQUIBS
IODINE PIE EURAIL
GRANDFORKS TANGLE
HEY EERIE ATV OLD
EXACT STEEL
ECOL THESUPERBOWL
BORIS SAME OREO
BRAZIER NURSE IAN
STARTINGPITCHER
LII SAPOR LACONIC
ICON OBIS ENTER
VANITYPLATES OSSO
LEVEE ALTAR
JAG MEN GROAN MOP
ABRUPT LOVINGCUPS
PLANET AYE CENSUS
EEYORE PAD ERNEST

118

MARIS SWAYS CAGER
ELENA AARON HULLY
ALPHA YREKA ANODE
THAIRESTAURANTS
MEIS NAH MERC SIR
ARR ADHOC TENANT
NESTS GLEE LAINE
HANS ARLO IRES
MORDECAIRICHLER
MALE SADR ATEE
OGDEN TOOL IDEST
MOESHA LASER CPI
SOR LAVA SPA ALIE
PATRICIAIRELAND
APACE AHOLD MTIDY
IRINA LILLE MERLE
ROREM SPEER ARSES

119

RAGTOP SINAI ABLE
EUROPA ETONCOLLAR
PRIMER ASTOUNDING
RAS CAPTAIN SENDS
ELSE BROWN HERD
SLOB OENO POTSDAM
SYMBOLS NYET AMA
EPISODIC LATER
JUSTICEDEPARTMENT
AROSE SERENADE
DAD LOAF PISCOPO
ELATION UPIN HUEY
WETS BLUES ETDS
OMARS CALLSTO VAT
METROPOLIS ORIOLE
STEAKKNIFE RESTER
KERN GENES MOPEDS

120

THEN ASAP TRUISMS
WEVE GIGI CORRECT
ONEWRITES INSANER
PINTA ENTR INANE
MEMOIR DOEST TRA
ONLYHALFTHEBOOK
SON SEE EYESORES
AXEL ESPRESSO
LOYOLA THE EARFUL
RESEEDED SASE
VIGNETTE DRS TEA
OTHERHALFISWITH
YEO ELIOT REHEAR
ARSON ERST GRANT
GATTACA THEREADER
ETERNAL AONE SESE
REDOUND STDS HDTV

121

REHAB CHLOE ABFAB
ENOLA YOURS VALUE
BULLYMARKET IRATE
ERE HANSEL BANKON
LEDA TIE ARTSY
STUDYPOKER JAM
ASSURE ISITI ARE
STPETE PLOT XACTO
ANIN SHELLAC SKEW
MONTE OTOE OILERS
BOY MYLAR SURETY
AND BELLYCURVE
OFANY OBI PASS
ASCOTS AMSTEL SPA
SITAT GRIMYREAPER
ATOLL AESOP AMEND
PURSE PASSE PONTI

122

TACOS SMASH SALAD
AWAIT TATTY EMILE
FABLEBODIEDSEAMAN
FRA PUP TART BMI
YELL TOO MAILROOM
ARTFUL LII
ALLTHEFRIGHTMOVES
LIETO LEMON ARA
OBOE BABYLON PLAT
OER RUNUP MALTA
FLAWOFGRAVITATION
OAF DISHES
CORNDOGS ELI YORE
ODE OREL AES SID
COMBINATIONFLOCKS
ORION STEAD AWAKE
ASTON POURS PERIL

123

CLARK EARL QUINCY
LARUE AXIS URSULA
OMANI SENT EARNER
GAMALIEL DELANO
LLDS CENSE
SCHOOL ALFS LIAR
IHEAR ABBEY VIRTU
MORT LUISA MASKED
PRO JEFFERSON SAO
SAILED ONEPM POLL
OLSEN ACCRA REMOP
NEMO ALAE GARETH
NEPAL ATON
BAINES BIRCHARD
TANDEM ATOM HAZER
ORDARE RAVE ERODE
WILSON KNOX DAVID

124

CARET AMINO OATS
CREASE LONER INIT
STARED DOTTEDLINE
IRS IRENE SAM
OSE STONERS TEASE
DANSE LTD OPENTOE
ENDORSEE GOER TUG
ATE SEEN SITS
STRAWBERRYPATCH
TKOS ALTO ARE
YIN AGES PALIMONY
RETIREE RAM ESTEE
ADORE POETESS HER
ONE RHINE RED
SHENANIGAN ATOLLS
YORE DIANA TABLES
NEED SINGS ROOST

125

ABRAHAM MAAM AMOS
LEONORA ATLI PONY
UNCANNY SLANDERED
MESSKIT SANHEDRIN
YEAREND VOILE
TOBAT GOUT TIMELY
IROBOT TRIBAL
PARANOIA SALIVATE
IRECKON SENECAN
SERIATIM VENDETTA
NOTONE TICTAC
STOPGO TEES SKORT
PUREE ROARING
ENGELBERT LOUISAS
DEADSETON IMITATE
UTNE LILI CASINOS
POSE TEAK ADENINE

126

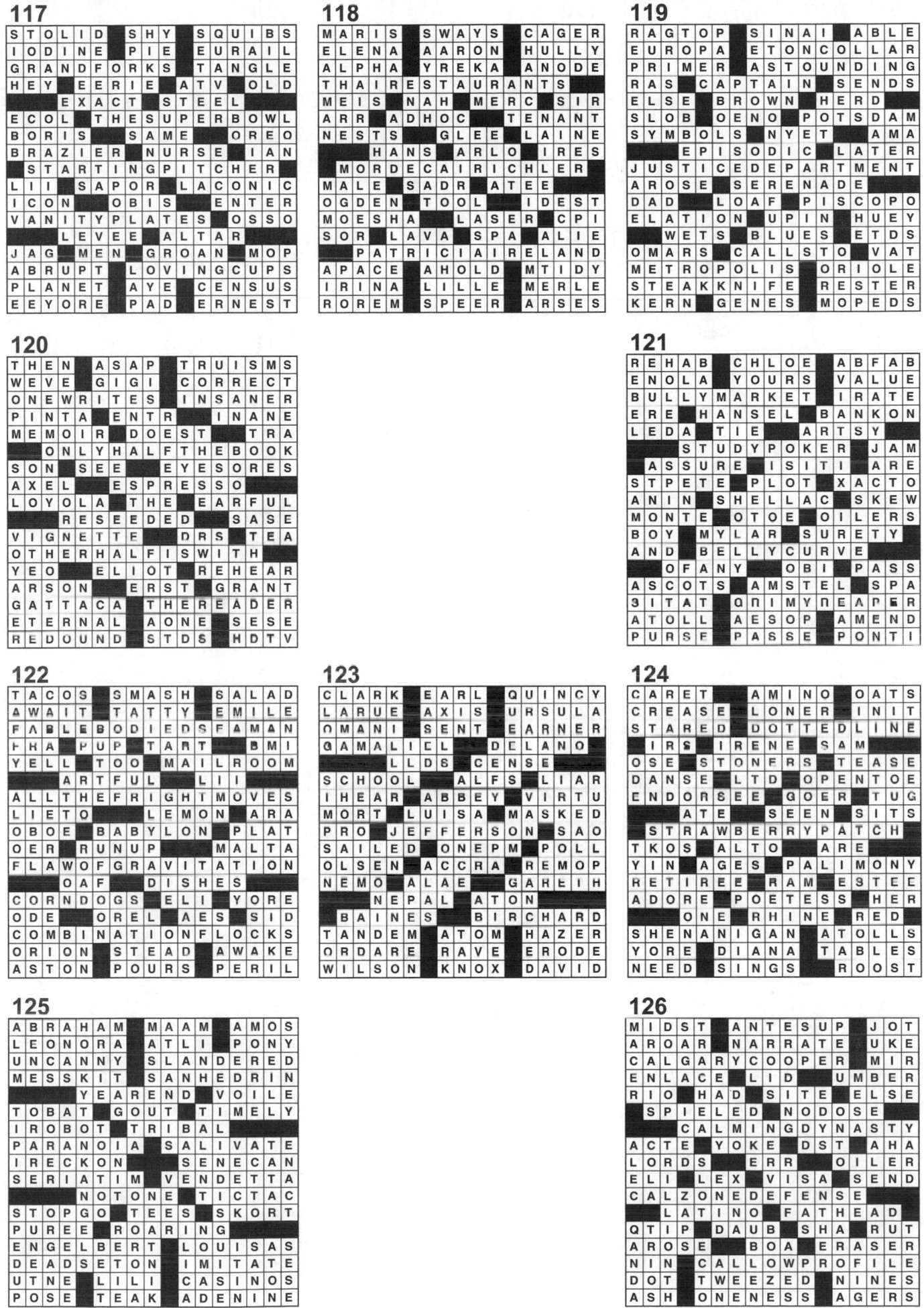

MIDST ANTESUP JOT
AROAR NARRATE UKE
CALGARYCOOPER MIR
ENLACE LID UMBER
RIO HAD SITE ELSE
SPIELED NODOSE
CALMINGDYNASTY
ACTE YOKE DST AHA
LORDS ERR OILER
ELI LEX VISA SEND
CALZONEDEFENSE
LATINO FATHEAD
QTIP DAUB SHA RUT
AROSE BOA ERASER
NIN CALLOWPROFILE
DOT TWEEZED NINES
ASH ONENESS AGERS

127

SUV AMATI STRIFE
SEMI CANED LEADON
TRIO ESTEE EXTORT
REALESTIMATE ELKO
INKER SLOPED
PASTORAL NED SST
SAVINGGRIMACE
ARCH RIVALS NOVEL
SALOME EVE HASONE
IDAHO STEADY TREX
DOYOULOVEMIME
ENS REC SENATORS
ENTIRE TEPEE
BULL TOOTHPASTIME
ATEASE CHEER RAID
MENTOR KARAT ATTY
ASSESS SNAKY DES

128

SPAS MPG IKE EDAM
KERI GOESMAD MOMA
IDIDNTLIKETHEPLAY
MELEE ISIAH VOLTS
BUTTHENISAW
OPIATE ARI ADELEH
SEARER SST TERESA
CAS RRS CYR AIR
ERIN ITUNDER ASAN
OLMOS ISAID TRESE
LEONE NOSEE OTTOS
ADVERSECONDITIONS
VAL SEE
THECURTAINWASUP
CHAN DOORDIE HOLE
HURT GORILLA AFAT
IDES ESSAYER WATS

129

CATTLESHOW SMUDGE
AREWETHERE CANOES
MINIATURES ONIONS
ASSN ALAS ERITREA
REESE ALT TEA TRY
ONDECK DEMOS COAT
TOIL IAN LADLE
ASH TODAY CAROLS
ALOUETTE BEATPOET
SIMPLY ACERB RES
IDEAL BRR AIDE
NEAT MUSED NOTBAD
ART UAR OUR HARPO
PULLSIN SPEC LAOS
PLAINT GOONABINGE
LESSOR UTNEREADER
ESTATE TETEATETES

130

EMAIL MONA BASALT
LANCE OMIT URANIA
FRIENDLESS TATTER
STODGIEST SIFT
HOCK TEA APIECE
THEATER UNNOTED
TILTH SWEAR DRAPE
POTEEN ALLOT EMIL
MONSIGNOR
PEST BETTE ROSTRA
ACTUP SEERS AURAS
CORRECT WEDLOCK
ANGOLA SOC LYES
DRIB VERTEBRAE
REGLUE SUNBURNING
UNHURT OBOE CLARA
MOTELS NERD SYNCS

131

IAMB IRS RIM AHSO
FRAU CANSECO DEWY
SINGLEHANDED RAES
OPIATE POUF PAVE
CBS DOUBLEAGENT
OMOO HINT OCR HEM
FOTOMAT BELLBOYS
ATT ELTORO EAU
HITSFORTHECYCLE
EST BERATE IQS
ROSEHIPS TIREOUT
CUP AMI FDIC SNIP
TRIPLECROWN ACE
TEAL COLA MIASMA
POLS HOMERSIMPSON
EWES PLAYFUL EELS
INRE SON SEE ESTE

132

FEW LETSGO OKAY
OROS SORRELS NINO
GOUPINFLAMES TONG
GOKAPUT NICOSIA
COB BRANFLAKES
SDI NOOR YOS
COINFLIPPER STOWS
ONAGAIN ENATE SIL
CAPSIZES THEORIZE
ATE LATKA REFEREE
SARDI OURMANFLINT
ONE LEAH ASS
DESIGNFLAW HUP
UTENSIL OARSMAN
MARG GOLDENFLEECE
AGRI METEOUT DAHL
SEAN ASSESS TEL

133

CHASE NAPE GOAPE
HAREM ACELA ONION
ALLNIGHTDIN PEROT
TOOTLES AJOB ALPO
RYE INASEC ISM
ABBY SYNTHETICFIB
TAO PEAL TNOTES
MYNAH LEN REEL
HOWIMETYOURMOTH
ALOU CNN AROMA
BROKER KISS LOG
RESEARCHCENT ELSE
EFT SORELY ACL
WORE WACO TSHIRTS
TRIPP TURNTHECORN
EMCEE EBONY SIDEA
ASHEN AXEL STEEP

134

GUSTO STATUE JOSH
ANTIS ABOARD UNTO
WHATSSHAKING MEIR
KIKI TAR EXPAND
SPEAKER PKG MELEE
NINA ORATED
MAE LONGTIMENOSEE
UNAPT ISSUE VIAL
SITU ARB HTS EZRA
IMIN MILAN BRETT
CATCHYOULATER SHE
TASTED ASIF
SEOUL SSA ISOLATE
EQUALS ALE ABAD
AUNT TILLNEXTTIME
MICE ACTION ALDEN
SPED GERUND DYERS

135

STP ENACT STRIDES
NEO FARAH LEASETO
IAM THEREAINTMUCH
FROM ESPO ECHO
FUNINMEDICINE EAT
SPACEAGE ONENO
RANRIOT INFOR
TOJO FESS FTDODGE
ALA BUTTHERES IRE
PARCELS EXER ICED
ENSOR LATEENS
QRSTU ROSINING
TOD AHECKOFALOTOF
ITON REIN TARO
MEDICINEINFUN LTR
IRONONS CUOMO IOC
DISOBEY KNEAD ENE

136

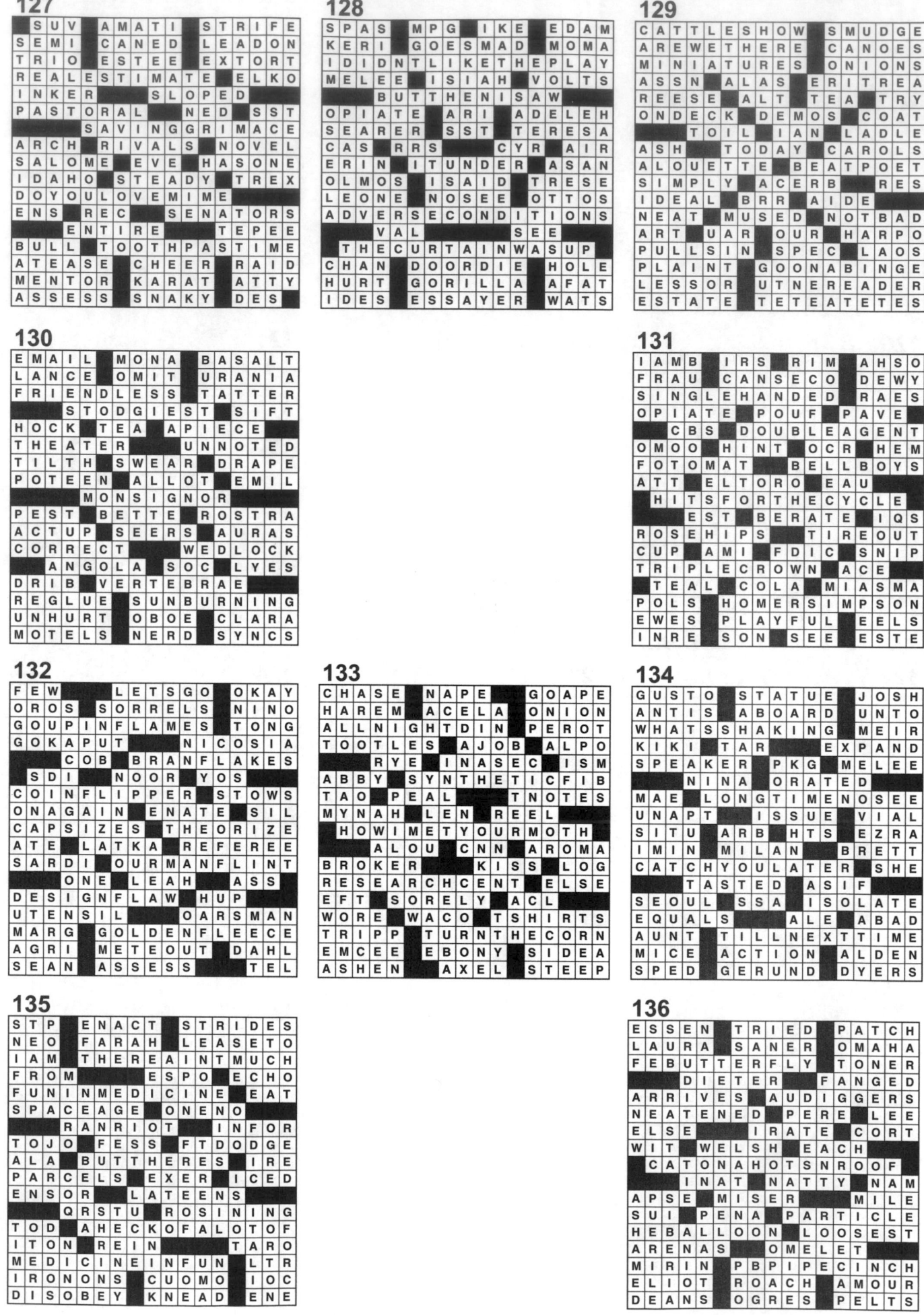

ESSEN TRIED PATCH
LAURA SANER OMAHA
FEBUTTERFLY TONER
DIETER FANGED
ARRIVES AUDIGGERS
NEATENED PERE LEE
ELSE IRATE CORT
WIT WELSH EACH
CATONAHOTSNROOF
INAT NATTY NAM
APSE MISER MILE
SUI PENA PARTICLE
HEBALLOON LOOSEST
ARENAS OMELET
MIRIN PBPIPECINCH
ELIOT ROACH AMOUR
DEANS OGRES PELTS

137

SWIMS IBMS NATION
CANOE NOAH AGENDA
IRVAN ENYA MINCES
BETTERFORBATTER
ARI FRI UTAHN
RIGHTFORSIGHT SAD
ADLER RECTO ENEMY
BEEFED ROUT EDIE
TOPSFORTOWS
LIME SHOO GOTCHA
PRADO RAGON NOHOW
SAG PRIMEFORGRIME
RATON FOB AES
DIVINEFORDIVING
CITRON ORAL ALTAR
ROTINI ACME SLIME
ORELSE LAPS ESSEX

138

SAMS SCOPES MATT
ECRU TUNERS JELLO
ACRE ORATOR UTICA
WRITEOFPASSAGE
EEG PLEA BOOSTS
ETHNO WRACKOFRIBS
DETECTS GUY SIN
WHO AISLE CARS
WRESTOFTHEWORLD
BEER SPLAY ANO
AAH EAT SNOWMAN
WRAPCONCERT ADAGE
LEBEAU OAST NEE
WRINGOUTTHEOLD
PRATE AUNTIE AWOL
JANET GAMEON SANE
STAR STERNO ERGS

139

VAULT ALBS ARABIA
IGLOO SALE SALADS
TONYPASTOR SEPTET
ANA SLUICED EAU
LEES URN ASPHALT
COMEONAMYHOUSE
HABEAS AGARIC
AGENT STAGE TAP
HEYTHERE TENDERLY
ADS NUDGE AXIAL
ABASES OTIOSE
WHITECHRISTMAS
RESTATE MOA TAMP
EGO DELIGHT LAO
NIMBUS REDGARTERS
CREASE SAGE EERIE
HARDEN EKED ENTER

140

LAPSE MONIST LOMA
ISLES OLATHE ONOR
MOANS SEPSIS BERG
BUY* WHA*ANTTOSAY
SLANGIER EAR ELL
TIN YEAR EMCEE
LOMAN ESAI BYU
IRELAND TREE LASS
NERF EGG SAT *COP
NOVO VEES SHADROE
ODE NEXT FIEND
HELLO TEAR FRA
AÇE LTR ALLOCATE
GLADTHA*TYOU ACOG
GAPE ILOILO ARMOR
LIEN NEUMAN ADELE
FRRS GETSBY ASSET

PUZZLE #140: * = TIME

141

INLETS SENSE BASS
BEIRUT HBOMB ARIA
IAMABELIEVER FOXY
SPA SPEAR WOLFMAN
BATTY ALAMO
MAS KANS EVADE
INPUNCTUALITY SRA
DOESOK GLEE KAOS
GREET BLISS JOLTS
EADS PLAN SALUTE
SKY THOUGHITMAKES
PRICE ARAB IDS
HELLO RAZOR
EQUATOR RANTS WAD
AUNT MEVERYLONELY
RAGE ONEND ELAPSE
SLED ODETS DEBTOR

142

SCOT RUNSTO CLEM
ROTH AARATED HILO
THREESISTERS EEKS
ANOINT AHEM BRUSH
STUB APIARY
SHIM TWINSTROLLER
DIS DEAR EIN ONE
AGREE NESS SCOTTO
HALFPASTTHEHOUR
OLEOLE TRUE UPSET
SOL ARA CASS EAR
TWISTEDANKLE RSTU
KOSOVO SEGO
NADIR RANA TROCHE
ATUB ANTONCHEKHOV
NANU JEANNIE IAMA
STEM ADROIT ETON

143

ABSURD GIRD FOLLY
BRUNEI ENOS AVOID
ARCTICBLAST MENDS
CONTRARY SONG
EMI AUTO FLU SAM
MONTH LOWPRESSURE
MACHETE LAW PICS
ATTICA BEEN PATHS
CHILLFACTOR
SMOKE OATS ENTRAP
NINE OLD DETAILS
UNSTABLEAIR INCAS
BET TOY TSAR ONT
ROBE COSMETIC
PRIME JANUARYTHAW
JOKES FREE APIECE
SCENT KEDS NESTED

144

MAORI PLAZA ADOBE
ALIEN REGIS FILET
SOLED OVENS LEAST
THEFEELINGTHATYOU
SAD BLOND ATE
STEN ATOM DADS
SIP AGE URLS VEE
SCREW LUNGED ALE
HAVEALREADYTASTED
ARI WAIVER KEATS
PEN ANTE ASH ARE
EDGE DENS WEST
ASA HEART HIT
THISMUSTARDBEFORE
RASTA LIVID PAGAN
ESTER AREEL ORATE
SHORT PERSE NONET

145

PAL LIELOW BENCH
ACOW ERMINE OMAHA
WHEEWHATFUN WIRES
NEWERA ESTE GRAB
HIRAM EUROPE
EPCOT MICHELLEWIE
LARUE PLAIT ESSEN
SIERRA TROPE
ERES NASCENT WONT
SIXTH STEREO
IDIOT ELOPE OMARR
NINTENDOWII WALDO
CASTRO ENDED
ORTO BLAB ELECTS
MIAMI OUIMONSIEUR
ESTAS STRAWS TENT
STENO TODDLE SEA

146

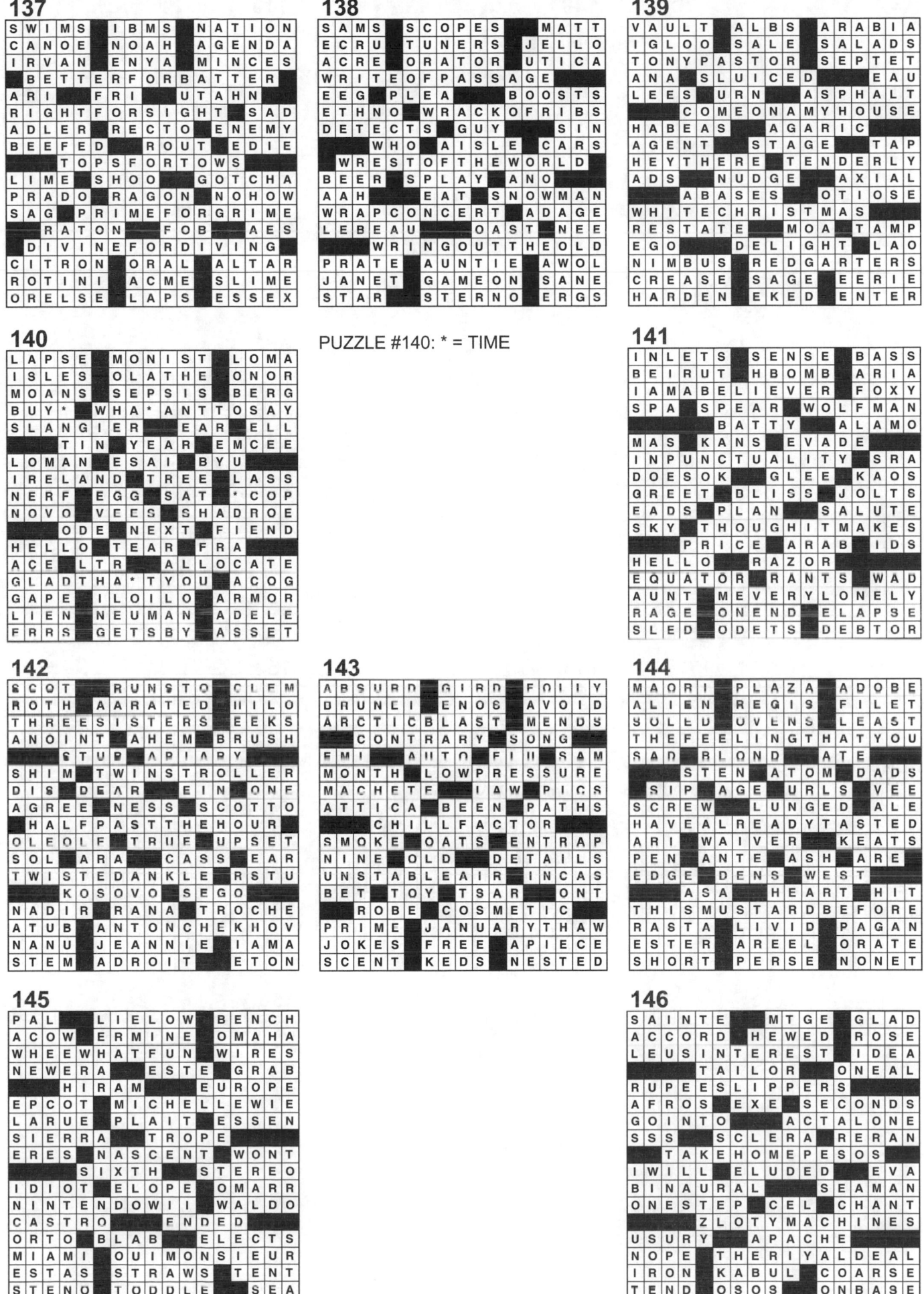

SAINTE MTGE GLAD
ACCORD HEWED ROSE
LEUSINTEREST IDEA
TAILOR ONEAL
RUPEESLIPPERS
AFROS EXE SECONDS
GOINTO ACTALONE
SSS SCLERA RERAN
TAKEHOMEPESOS
IWILL ELUDED EVA
BINAURAL SEAMAN
ONESTEP CEL CHANT
ZLOTYMACHINES
USURY APACHE
NOPE THERIYALDEAL
IRON KABUL COARSE
TEND OSOS ONBASE

147

ALPS SNAP CABRIDE
RAIL TORI ORACLES
IGNORANCE LESSEES
SETTER ACROSS ARE
ERASE ENRON ELLEN
MUSEUM NSA
REOPENS SUMO ATOM
ANGORA ATLAST APO
TELEGRAM UNTHEMED
OME EMBOSS REVERE
NYSE EEEE LIBERAL
SAD BACALL
ASSET CAPOS ATEST
CHE ENISLE THERMO
RADIOED ADMISSION
ERASURE NITE TETE
SENATOR ETAS YSER

148

AKIN PRAISED USSR
LOCO SIGNORI SHOO
THEWRIGHTBROTHERS
OLDIE ARE SIERRA
SPAS ORC DRIER
RITEOFPASSAGE FLY
ENA STEM LASS
MASSE CUTOFF OSLO
UNTIDY SOU FASTEN
SEER EVERTS FORTS
SATE DENG AGE
DOS RIGHTONTHEDOT
AVISO AAR THAT
REMISS TIA NUDGE
WRITETHEPRESIDENT
IDLE AIRLINE ELAN
NOES RESEATS SETA

149

STROBE TERR CMDRS
COUPON ESAU ARIEL
UNSERS SAIN SPRAY
DISCOUNTINGSHEEP
SEAL SABA
ISIS VANS XANADU
DISPLAYBYTHERULES
CRAFTY GLO TAME
ALI SECTIONED BOL
RODS FHA NOTATE
DISAPPOINTEDTIMES
SNOCAT STAR PADS
KNEW TIES
DISORIENTEXPRESS
TROOP EROO ERODES
ANNUL LOGO REAGAN
BOOTY DSOS TENETS

150

WARMED ASSORT SIS
ISAYSO ZAPPER ASL
PAINTEDTURTLE NRA
EDNA SEED VJDAY
SHRINKINGVIOLET
AFT ATT YEO BOLO
BOOTH VICTIM TIN
ECRU BAIN OCTO
TIMBERRATTLESNAKE
AVER WADS USED
MVI AMOSOZ USHED
EINS EYE ABA BLY
GOVERNORGENERAL
ALEXA ANNA SODS
TAR JELLYDOUGHNUT
OTS ARABLE TIEDON
NEE HAWSER STRESS

151

ROMAN ALDO REID CID
EDIFY DEER OFME RTE
POSITIONED AFAT ASP
ONER DRAMA DEMEANOR
STEEPLE INST RHINE
EON DESIGNATE MAAMS
SCAR GASPE AISLES
FOCUS RGS RAIN
UBER SAYSOS FRENCHY
SENECAN ERA TEDIOUS
EYESORE ROGUES HUGE
LOEB GRR MINOR
RONALD ASRED COLT
ECOLE SCHEDULED EPH
SERAC WKRP ADEGREE
HABITUAL AGAVE OSSA
ONE IRMA SOLIDIFIED
OIR OSIS TRIS PONTI
TAT NASH SETH ORKAN

152

ILER ALAS ARID SHIP
NONA PONT SATO TASM
SAMMYSOSA SNOWBALLS
IVEBEENWRONGONLY
TESLAS EDAS FISHES
USHER SROS CRANIUMS
HAMM MANLINESS
APTITUDE PENAL
BIODATA SLED SOLON
ONCEBUTTHATWASWHENI
WAKES RATS BEANDIP
GLIDE TUGBOATS
INABILITY OHTO
NONADULT OPES MAGDA
CHIRAC PUTT LAUREN
THOUGHTIWASWRONG
CELLOSOLO CIGARETTE
ODIE IMAN ASET UTIL
OOBY CODE LTDS SONS

153

UMPS SLOT BAH AXIS
PORT TAEBO ALA RIDE
SCOOBYDOJO BOBFOSSE
RERAN KRATION
INME ARIEL TRIPOD
TGI FJORDTAURUS JLO
INN FULDA HEADSET
MAJ ADD SARI LEIGH
ECARTE COTTON EEL
DESI AJARRIVER ROCK
IST UPDATE ELEVEN
MIMER BOOP ATE EDO
FLORIDA ANDRO YAW
RIN CELINEDIJON ORS
SEEDER CANEA OPUS
IPANEMA LEARY
IGLESIAS BJORNAGAIN
MOAT LSU LENTO MALI
POPS SAP EDGE YALL

154

KERNS DRAIN SPRAGUE
ICEIN IAMSO KEELING
THENAMEYOUR EDWARDG
TOLERATES EWA ILES
ILIE MODELA TRA
GRANDCHILDRENCALL
SNOOT OUIDA DAHLIA
ARON ABUT ESS RAKED
OAF BRANCH LOCK
YOUISTHEONETHAT
NLER TROPHY OFT
TIDAL AID ATTO UNDO
ONEIDA NEONS INTRO
ISPROBABLYGOINGTO
LEO GIBILL TONI
SASS LOG MISNOMERS
OSIERED LASTFOREVER
MONTANE AMENU ELENI
ENGAGES BACON DYNES

155

AHYES RODS SNAP ADS
NOONE ELEE EERO CUL
GOODREVERENDSPOONER
EELS MEAS PRESS
SOMANY SPEAKEASY
OPERA BEG LANAI SPA
MIR RETAPE REATAS
NEVERHASTO ERE TEST
GOEN ONCLE BANCO
WORRYABOUTHISSEXTON
ARLES ATRIA PARI
REES AGO ASLONGASHE
PASSEL ACTING DOD
SDS AFOFL ELD ARABY
ASSAILANT STAKES
ALICE TROY DOOM
MINDSHISKEYSANDPEWS
PAK UBET MAAM DALIS
SRS PARS SOON SLAIN

156

PACA PADDLES LUBED
IDOS OCARINA ATONED
PORT STRADDLESADDLE
ERRORS TWO ARCH EEK
DEARIE IDEA TATE
LIPS CADS CLEARED
MALA SNACKATTACK
AMO GLINKA TENSE
COCA BALDY BARONETS
ARAL RIIS ALSO TEES
WALLAROO ADEPT ODEA
SLEEP PELOSI FLY
LACKEDAPACT NOES
EMPEROR ANEW ITOR
LOUS NOAM EATSUP
ELL ACNE RAM DROPSA
VALERIESSALARY NEIN
ERUCTS ITSTRUE CENT
SPOSE REPOSED EDGY

157

```
PSALM#ABBOTS#SCRIPT
ALCOA#CRAVAT#CAESAR
CAROM#TODATE#ALYSSA
EVENASINGLETIME#USN
####BOOZES#SSS#TRES
CORLEONE##MOO#ARESO
UTAHAN##ADINFINITUM
LEVAR#RELAX##STOOPS
PRES#HOTLY#MALI####
#INANYPOSSIBLECASE#
####OMEN#ANAIS#CHAD
DANSON##MIDST#TERSE
INCESSANTLY##BOLEYN
STALE#REV##STOWAWAY
TEAL#SNO#PATRON####
RAG#TWENTYFOURHOURS
ITALIA#GALORE#ARNEL
CEMENT#ADORES#LADLE
TREATS#SANEST#LLOYD
```

158

```
CHOP#ALBA#AWLS#OHMS
LUNA#LORN#DOIT#WEEK
ASCI#LAIN#OLLA#LANA
WHENBEDBUGSFALL#RUT
###FEY#EAR##CLEFT##
ALOUD#RELATE#STRAWS
LOWLIFE##VIES##ECHO
USE#MADLYINLOVETHEY
MESS#CREED##LESSEES
###PLIANT#SHERPA###
TEALEAF##REALM#WAGE
ALWAYSTAKETHEIR#LUX
CLAY##SHIN##SNUFFLE
TAKERS#STOVES#NEAPS
##EDEMA##WIT#OUR###
OWN#VOWSINTHESPRING
NAIL#OAKS#ANTI#ODOR
EDNA#TRIM#LINE#ULNA
SIGN#HEMS#SCAR#SEEM
```

159

```
#TWITS#RGS#SIR#VETO
PRIVATEERS#USE#AMOR
TONYCURTIS#PLEASURE
AYN##BIRD#BREVES###
##EPI#CADDIE#ERASED
ROBINWILLIAMS#OLIVA
CRAGGED#EASEUP##NET
MAG#EELS####MASCARA
PLOD#PETERSCOLARI##
###ICI#ISERE#LXI###
##JOHNTRAVOLTA#BARB
STORAGE####SODA#TOO
OIL##SNAPED#MILTONS
RELAY#DUSTINHOFFMAN
TRYOUT#CASSIA#ARB##
###DROITS#CENS##ORA
RIGATONI#JACKLEMMON
VIII#TKO#PRESUMABLY
SITS#SYN#SDS#MESSY#
```

160

```
ZINC#WILL#AWOL#QUAD
ERIE#ASEA#RAVE#UNDO
NACL#SLAT#ILEX#ITEM
ONELITERHOSEN#STONE
###ISE###MISSAL####
RATSO#BANANA#RECAST
KNOTFURLONG#MADONNA
ODE##TOAT##FOB#MEER
###ALI#RIPSAW#HEART
TWOKILOMOCKINGBIRDS
RAPID#LENTIL#ION###
ATIT#BED##CUED##AHA
MENACES#HOARSEPOWER
PRESET#COMPEL#EXERT
####LAMINA###JAB###
DECAL#ONERODSERLING
OVAL#DVDS#PILL#ODIN
FIFE#DIET#ARAL#OLLA
FLEX#EERY#LEVY#DEET
```

161

```
MORAL#CADET#ATM#FAA
EVADE#ACUTE#ORIGINS
LETOFFSTEAM#RUSSETS
DRASTIC###PITCHAFIT
####INAWAY#LAKE####
APRES#DILATE##AIRED
BREATHEFIRE#NURSERY
BOSS#ODEA#PLAT#MILE
ASTERN###CEASED#TED
##FLYOFFTHEHANDLE##
EAU#ARABIA###STARES
GULP#ERIN#THAI#PANE
ORLANDO#GOBALLISTIC
SAYSO##METALS#NEEDS
####TAPA#TROOPS####
BLOWAFUSE###REIGNED
AUDITOR#RANTANDRAVE
WRITERS#GREEN#EATEN
LEN#SEE#OMENS#SNERT
```

162

```
DRAW#ABABA#IPOS#SST
RATA#PARIS#TALE#AHI
ONTHEBRIGHTSIDE#GEM
IDIOM#DEB#HIND#PURE
TYCOBB#LEARNTOCRAWL
###SLIM#NCO##GLORIA
ANA#EDOM#UNTO#AMONG
MADAMEBUTTERFLY####
MILLS##DEE#EATSCROW
AVIA#ISBN#RAND#ROUE
NEBRASKA#EFT##WAYNE
####THATTAKESMEBACK
ATPAR#THIS#DRAB#LES
CHERUB##NYU#ILSA###
TURKEYBREAST#ETCHER
UNIS#LEIA#EAU#ECOLE
ADO#DIFFRENTSTROKES
RED#UNIT#SEEDS#RENO
YRS#GETS#STRAP#DYAD
```

163

```
OLDROSE#TWAS#DESIST
SIENNAS#EONS#URANIA
IF(IT)AINTBROKE#LESSOR
STY##DECIDE#SLC#PUP
###OSPREYS#DONTFIX(IT)
ACORN###AYEAYESIR##
TAKE(IT)BACK#AMAS#NETS
REAS#IDLING##SOIREE
ANY#ATMO#OEIL#ASSET
####DO(IT)YOURSELF####
SOBAD#SSNS#IOUS#DRS
ECOLAW##REEARN#CIAO
ATOB#EASY#SHAKE(IT)OFF
##BEATPOETS###YENTA
LET(IT)SNOW#RALLIED###
ORU#TUP#SAYAAH##AMS
ROBBER#HAVE(IT)YOURWAY
EDEMAS#OVER#EPSTEIN
NESTLE#GELS#REDEEMS
```

164

```
ALAS#SCAR#SAMBA#POW
LOSE#TACH#EMILE#ERA
POPEYETHESAILOR#PAY
SKATER#ETAL#SWIVELS
##ROANS#ORIS#DEAL##
SAT#ROADRUNNER#CELS
EXAM##POI##ELY#APOP
ALMOST#SCORED#STEVE
SEESAWS##LAZE#HEWED
####TOMANDJERRY####
ALBEE#ALAI##SALAMIS
BOUND#LUGERS#TYPIST
BIGD#ELM##EAR##ELLA
ESSO#DONALDDUCK#WEB
##BRIG#AROW#RAISA##
EQUATED#GEOS#STOUTS
GUN#WOODYWOODPECKER
GIN#AURAL#DUNE#KENO
SPY#STAGE#SPAR#SETS
```

165

```
SHEERS#CALIF#ELNINO
TOLDON#CRIME#LOOTER
ROOTBEERFLAT#MARSHA
OPP#SEMI##CATOFMAIL
PLEB#RODIN#LIN#####
SADAT##EDAM#STEALS#
###SEPARATETHESHEEP
NOVICES###LOA#TOSCA
OPUS#ANI#SEN#SETOUT
MEL#FROMTHEGATS#TRI
ANGERS#EEE#SIP#THEO
ABATE#PAN###RAMRODS
MATAROUNDACASTLE###
#RETEST#SHUN##BELTS
#####MUG#ADIEU#SOAP
BATPEOPLE##MEND#CHE
ATOLLS#ATMEALCOOKIE
NOJOKE#DRAWL#UPWIND
EMOTED#SEXES#TENNIS
```

166

```
BET#RCAS#STEM#LOLAS
ANA#EDGE#CHAI#INERT
SYBILSHEPHERD#TEVYE
KAUAI#ANIMAL#ACRE##
###MCQ##BOXERSHORTS
SAAB#UTUBE##OHIOANS
ADL#REUP#SPRAT#MGTS
LABTESTS##OHROB#ESS
SPEEDO##MRPEANUT###
ATEAT#WHIPPET#SOAPS
###MALAYSIA##WHITEN
DES#GIRDS##CHOWLINE
EDAM#ABEAM#AURA#LDR
BEDRAIL##CALMS#MTST
IRISHSETTER##TRA###
##SPEE#BONITO#OINKS
METER#BOARDERCOLLIE
ALIEN#INDO#TGIF#EEN
CYCLE#LESE#EYES#RVS
```

167

CHIMP PODAL POWDER
HUMOR ANEMIC AVIATE
AGAMA REMITS GETMAD
TOMMYWROUGHT ERN
IER FROG ARTEMIS
TAPEROFF OBI SORT
URI SNL PAWEDCASTER
RIND GOALL DEAL ENA
FAKER ONEB LOOTED
BAWDYBUILDING
TATTLE MOUE GRASS
EGO PLEA ELVIS EVIL
NAUGHTYPINE SYN IZE
SITE REM STRANDED
ENSNARE POET UTE
ELI WALDENPAWNED
METRIC ENDIVE STOGY
ARRIVE SEINES HOGAN
TRACER LEANS ANODE

168

ILSA TAPA SPAR AHOY
NACL HERB AIDE LADE
SMOKEYROBINSON PROW
TATAR ODOR TREPID
CLIP STEVIEWONDER
UNHITCH NIL MERLE
THESUPREMES REP IVE
ERG SENA REM OVID
AGON DIE EDIFIES
MOTOWNRECORDS
TSARINA REO REGD
LUNN CUR ORIS UEY
ELA TOS JACKSONFIVE
ESTER WII MATADOR
JACKIEWILSON PEKE
HEPTAD LOIS SEPIA
TREO THETEMPTATIONS
PERU AONE PIES DSCS
CAST SOSO HTTP STAT

169

JEST SPUNK DISC DST
ONTO ERNIE OLEO EWE
DRAMAQUEEN COLOGNES
HOMERUN COB FLYNET
PUP MEESE OWE IMITS
UTE ALDA KLINGONS
REDID LEADSTO AQUA
DANQUAYLE UNSUNG
PODS AUDREY BRITAIN
AMI BRIO RAMP ITE
CARPORT MCCABE ADES
THEUSA DOHAQATAR
SACS THOREAU GRAFT
THREATEN ETTA PRE
PIQUE GEE BLOIS PEA
ERUPTS NEO RESORTS
ROOSTERS DONQUIXOTE
INT OREL GROUP EVER
LYE NAVY ESTES NEDS

170

OWNS RAHRAH SPAREME
CHAP ELAINE PARAPET
HEMENTALITY ANIMIST
STELE COSI SWISSCHA
LIMAS GLANCE
RASSLER SEAL SITUP
UNO LOTENNYSON NYSE
DAUB NEMO SAKE SPEW
EXTRA IRK RAFTERS
HAPILLTOSWALLOW
ZIPCODE SAO ACRES
IMOK ONTO TOFU KIST
TALE LOUNGELIZA TAI
IMETA BIRD RIGUEUR
ZAPATA MESAS
BOAGAMES NOES IOWAN
APOLLOS CAPTAINPICA
LENIENT IDEALS ELMS
ICEBAGS TALLER NEET

171

SLED IONS BALM ADDS
SALESSLIP IGET TRIO
WHENTHECONGREGATION
RAZR SHOOTER LINDA
EEG ONTOE ROCKER
FALLSASLEEP APU
INO SMEARS JIMDAVIS
RAVI BAS OEDS LINO
SCISSOR EIRE PINNA
TONSIL ZZZZ RISEUP
ANGUS OREO KETTLES
IDLE STOA RAS SENT
DAYDREAM ARETHA ADA
ATM ITISTIMEFOR
ATODDS ENACT POV
PAPUA ENCLASP ROYS
THEPREACHERTOWAKEUP
LORE STYE DONTLEAVE
YEAS PACS OPES SRAS

172

AFAR LIST ADAGE NOT
NINE ANSA RAVES EAR
DRIVEINTHEATERS UKE
ESSENCE IDLER ARTSY
STEAD RATES SLYER
LOT LINES ISRAEL
WILINESS APSE ELKS
ICON SHOES REDFACED
NEWGATE CHAIN ADO
ESS PARKRANGERS RNA
ODE BOUND GITANOS
ENDORSER KARAT LEGS
RAIL ETAS ELECTRON
AMULET NOVAS SHE
MAMAS BESTS AROMA
CADRE EPEES MINERAL
LII REVERSEMORTGAGE
ADE GEESE SOCK OTIC
MAT ERROR SAKS SECS

173

HASATIT OHSURE LAMP
TREVINO SEISMS SOIR
MAKESAGREATENTRANCE
LBOS TOERR EATERY
ARUN SPIDER
ESTIMATEDTIME EASEL
INSTEP ESCARP MUNI
NIKON ANA OFARRIVAL
EDEN SVEN TRIAGE
NED SMEW ALTS SDI
LAIRDS DIET TOAD
IDIDNTSEE ADD CHART
DIOR HELDIN ANEMIA
SENSE THATONECOMING
GROINS EARS
PARIAH LEASE REST
INORDEROFAPPEARANCE
TONI AERATE UGANDAN
AXIS SETTEE PESTERS

174

LAKE ANTI ROVE BAAL
EVEN GEES ENOS ORCA
WEND EASE RIDS LAMB
DROPINTHEBUCK ISLES
INTO UNEARTH
AVANT DONS AEOLUS
BASSHOUNDS HERMIONE
ELI IXNAY DIME BATT
LEARNED SHADE ADOS
OGRE SUM ROLL
TALC REEDS IRELAND
SEEK UGLY EATAT TOO
PRIBILOF FLYINGCARP
SOSOON MUSE OLDIE
ONATEAR WHOA
CLASS BULLPROOFVEST
HALT TORO LIMA ILLY
EDGE ANON USER EKER
FEAR MDSE SEND RODE

175

USMARSHAL MASSMEDIA
THUMBHOLE ELOPEMENT
MISCHANCE TIDALFLAT
OMS GEORGESAND IRE
SMURF TAROTS OBES
TYPEALETTER GAPEAT
SLOTS SMOLDER
FAJITAS MCHALESNAVY
ELUDED SAROYAN TAE
ADLER RANAWAY EWELL
SEI CITIZEN SEALUP
TRAMPOLINER WELLYES
NICOLET LAPEL
SILTUP HOMESTRETCH
WNET ICEJAM STOLA
AHN CEREMONIES KEW
MANOAMANO TENTPOLES
PLOWSINTO LUNARBASE
SENSATION EXERCISER

176

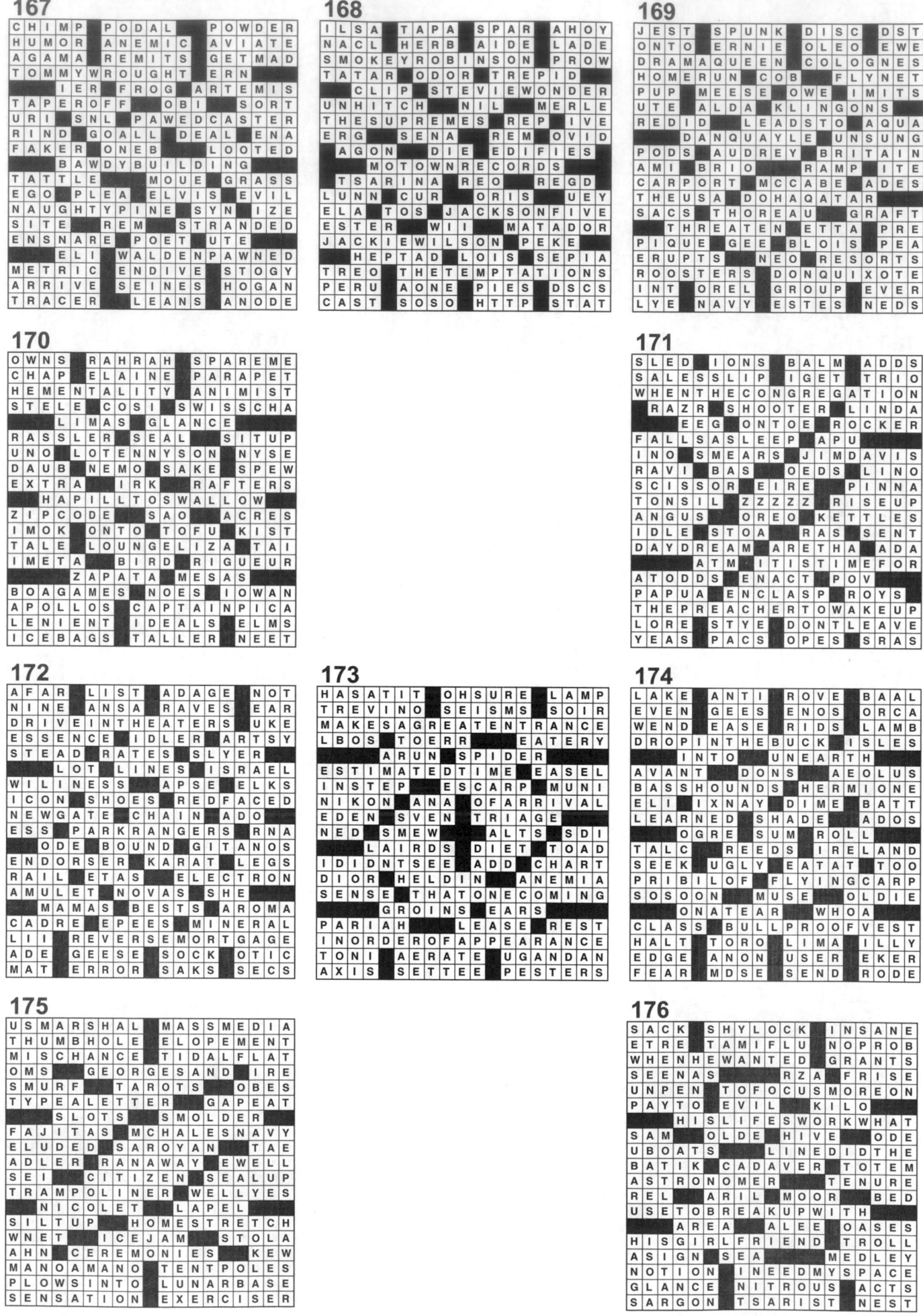

SACK SHYLOCK INSANE
ETRE TAMIFLU NOPROB
WHENHEWANTED GRANTS
SEENAS RZA FRISE
UNPEN TOFOCUSMOREON
PAYTO EVIL KILO
HISLIFESWORKWHAT
SAM OLDE HIVE ODE
UBOATS LINEDIDTHE
BATIK CADAVER TOTEM
ASTRONOMER TENURE
REL ARIL MOOR BED
USETOBREAKUPWITH
AREA ALEE OASES
HISGIRLFRIEND TROLL
ASIGN SEA MEDLEY
NOTION INEEDMYSPACE
GLANCE NITROUS ACTS
SARGON TSARIST NEST

177

TYPEDUP ADAPT VISTA
AGITATE LUNAR OCHER
YOURHEADINTHECLOUDS
ERSE NIELS AUNTIE
IDUNNO TERM ION
NOTIMETOSPARE ENNUI
ORATORS NORA ESSO
NIXON FORAY BOA
COIN PROLOG RESPOND
OLE BATEDBREATH ROO
MEDLEYS TEASES BEDE
EAT COSMO ALLIS
FETA VIEW TABASCO
LARKS TONGUEINCHEEK
ERA HMOS LLANOS
ALICIA DISCS SHOE
BOTHFEETONTHEGROUND
ABOUT MAUDE LOUREED
GERMS SUGAR SOMESAY

178

BUDS ESCOBAR BASSI
ATOP SOUREST TITIAN
HAZELNUTCASE EGRESS
THEDEEP SMU ENDORSE
FSU CARS PREC
SORT PEACHPIECHART
TECATE BRR OCULI
HICKORYSTUMPSPEECH
ISLE OREIDA ADHOC
EMU BOSNS HADON ESO
FIDEL TEACUP SWAN
CEDARCHESTTHUMPING
INOUE MME SERENA
PINECONEHEADS TYRA
ONEB FADE AMI
SCARVES TAP LENTILS
HOLIER PECANLOGBOOK
EMOTES PREVIEW SWAY
RENTS MODELTS PANE

179

FACE ANGORAS CRAVED
EBAN NEAREST ROSARY
SUNDAYDRIVER ALPINE
STOOL OCEANLINER
PRIM AWL PRIOR
CRYSTALSETS BANEFUL
LOBE ZEST PRO APE
ALE TEA CHORE AVOW
MEDIA SWAYED LEGEND
GRAHAMCRACKER
SALOON GALENA LAUDS
QUIT SCONE RDS NET
FRO ANT JEER ESSO
TANGLED IDOLWORSHIP
RULER ITS PETE
ROSEPETALS FELLA
EXOTIC FAMOUSBILLYS
DECENT TRAPPER LENT
ANKLES SALTSEA EDNA

180

BANFF TALC AESOPS
AZALEA ASEA AUNTIES
POWERBROKER DERALTE
CRIES WOODLOT
PICKETT BAMBI LUMET
EGRET REAR ONALEASH
ROAD YIELDSIGNS KSU
DRS AVERT ASTO REEL
USHAPED KATO BOISE
HOES CRIBS FONT
SPEND POEM ULYSSES
MALE PORE EDNAS HAH
ARM OUTOFSTOCK FOTO
SKELETAL EARL GORME
HATED BLUNT EVERTED
ASHLAND BAITS
MOUNTIE FUTURESHOCK
RANTERS IPOD STOPAT
TRIODE TSPS OWENS

181

ROBERT PUSHED IHOPE
USURER INHOME NINON
THRICE ALOOKCANTELL
SAYNO GARP IDAHOES
LAMEST OREN
YOUMORETHANHUNDREDS
AREARUG IOTAS OYE
KAYE LAA ENLAI SNEE
SHELF LEI SHOERS
PEPTO OFWORDS MASSA
LAUREL ARP AIRON
ARLO ABBIE YEE DEVA
NOL ASALE SANSEIS
IFITSTHERIGHTLOOKAT
NEIL NLEAST
ETHANCO CLAW IRARS
THERIGHTTIME GNAWAT
DOREN AMINOR ATEASE
SUEDE WIRERS MORGAN

182

PARSEC EMCEE ERODES
RIALTO LIANA SECRET
INDIANSUMMER CLAIRE
GUST TULIP RAY FIE
LEI CUBREPORTER
APPOINTS SLOVENE
BRAVEDEED APSE SAFE
COVEN VERSE LAGOS
FIN SHEBA FLOWERS
SOL GIANTSLALOM LEE
PRIMARY TIDAL SIT
AMOUR KRALL TAMED
RANT CLIO TIGERLILY
EPAULET BELITTLE
CARDINALSIN TEM
AVE GNU LYRIC DEBS
DIMPLE REDLETTERDAY
RAISER OREOS REAGAN
ENTITY WASNT ARGYLE

183

TSARS CLASSA BEAME
RUNUP SEANCES ELLAS
ITISIMPORTANT LOADS
BUMKNEE RAIMI MAE
ARI ESCORT TRANSOM
LEST MILEAGE CDS
TOREMEMBERTHATYOU
RARE NAPE ORS
GHERKIN BROCK RUDE
HOMEEC CLIME RAISER
AMOS BLAME PALMERS
NET TBOZ AILS
AREUNIQUEJUSTLIKE
ROB DRIFTER YSER
PONTIAC GOUNOD TAE
SHA FAVOR TARGETS
HITOR EVERYBODYELSE
ALENE REDHAIR UNLIT
WORSE TROOPS PEENS

184

BAGGAGE ARCH MISFIT
ABRADED MORE UNLACE
GRANDMAMOSES SCOTIA
HINGE UKES LEASHES
DDT DEMO OCHER HERE
AGES AUNTIEEM MER
DEEPEST ULNA BEDBUG
LATEST TRALA RNA
ADMIT AUG TRANSOMS
PEON COUSINITT TWAS
INTERACT TOE PENNY
ASH ANTED BRACER
NEEDNT REEL BARNARD
RED UNCLEBEN SLUE
SASS STELE ITEM DNA
PREPPIE AGAR AMEND
LETOUT GRANDPAJONES
ATONCE SEND APOSTLE
TENDED ASTA PERTEST

185

SURMISES STALL ARUM
CROATIAN TONIO ZONE
HANGONTO ALION ULAN
ENDINGS RIDINGCROPS
LIEN LIVERY SIESTA
LALO ENID ARTUR
TOSTADA ERICBANA
STN ABO UNFIT ALOW
TROIKA CANOLA ASTRO
RAIDERSOFTHELOSTARK
ADDON ICEBOX CHERIE
TEEN STOWE TEE SSN
ORATORIO EARHART
TINNY BEIN ORES
INJAIL OSCARS NEXT
FOOLSAROUND STEELER
NOEL NOISE STARDATE
OSLO KINER LETTUCES
TEST ASKED CREEPERS

186

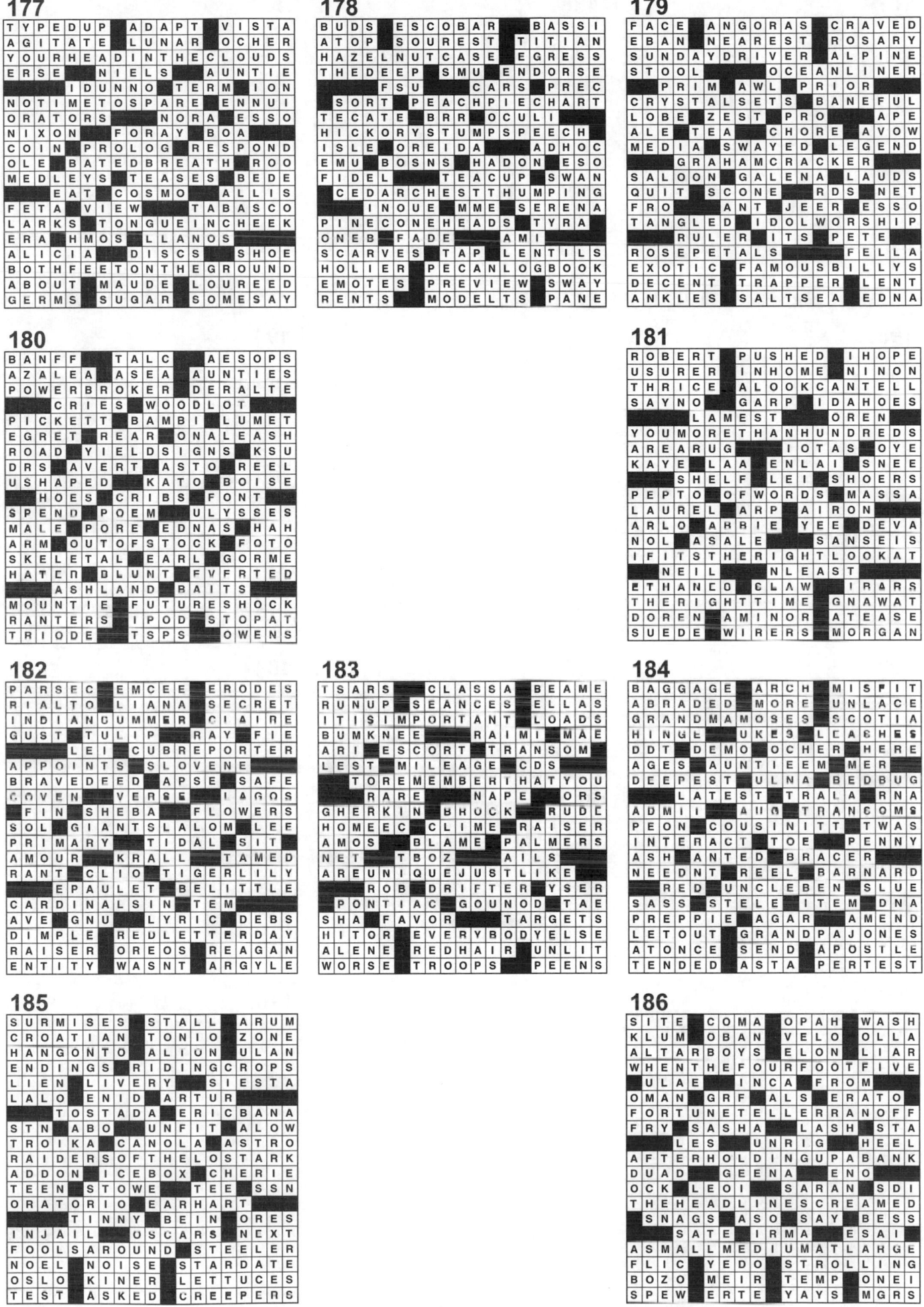

SITE COMA OPAH WASH
KLUM OBAN VELO OLLA
ALTARBOYS ELON LIAR
WHENTHEFOURFOOTFIVE
ULAE INCA FROM
OMAN GRF ALS ERATO
FORTUNETELLERRANOFF
FRY SASHA LASH STA
LES UNRIG HEEL
AFTERHOLDINGUPABANK
DUAD GEENA ENO
OCK LEOI SARAN SDI
THEHEADLINESCREAMED
SNAGS ASO SAY BESS
SATE IRMA ESAI
ASMALLMEDIUMATLARGE
FLIC YEDO STROLLING
BOZO MEIR TEMP ONEI
SPEW ERTE YAYS MGRS

187

STAMP VCHIP AMASSES
TAPER IRENE POSHEST
EXPROPRIATE ROSANNE
MIR CATSPAW ORESTES
EVENUP KEENEST
ATHLETE PEEL SAUTE
TREADS PAS SEAM RED
MENDS PRY RENDERING
SED SANDRA AMNESTY
WALT ION BITS
ADVISOR RESULT WKS
TRANSPORT ALE HAILE
MOC ISLA OCT TOLTEC
EPSOM GUNK PROPHET
VIBRANT GUIDES
BEDELIA SHALLOW TAP
ANORAKS NECESSITATE
INVITEE AGREE NANAS
TEETERS POEMS KIDDO

188

RIODE OSHAPED SITAR
ERROL ROANOKE CNOTE
INTHEMORNINGA ATSEA
DASANI RAND NAMETAG
ATNO EONS GATE
OFFS LAWYERWALKEDON
FLIESAT OPEN ERRANT
BENET ADWARS EAS
EDEMA SULU OPT HOL
EGRET HISLAWN IPANA
FEY ESA ELEE ORMER
ATT ATTLEE NOLOS
BAABAA ARTE YASMINE
ANDEXPERIENCED ONEN
GDAY LAPP ODDS
POMADES LIMB ECARTE
IVANI THEDEWPROCESS
PENCE LATIMER WHIGS
ERTES ADSORBS LENTO

189

PUTT CAGE LUPE ATOP
INORGANIC ITAL URGE
TIGERBYTHETAIL TILE
ATSEA MOUTHS AUGER
VITO REALISM
MACBETH HORNETSNEST
ALOE TYPO YEA SEE
SKUAS REPAST MATTE
HARRISON PROVO MASS
TICKINGTIMEBOMB
ACES IDEAL TRICOLOR
SUSHI DRYROT ANILE
ABA RAN EMIT ISLE
PANDORASBOX GALAHAD
INCITED POGO
SHIVS ROSIER CELLO
TORE NOWINSITUATION
EMIR ABED SMELLARAT
MESS BIDE OAST LENO

190

FABLE MAGMAS AFFORD
AGAIN TRIAGE TRIVIA
CELLDIVISION VANITY
TSKTSK DELUDE CEDES
SUES LET XMAS
ITS PANELDISCUSSION
TAOS UKE WET ERGO
EXCHANGE SCARED IRE
MIKADO STOMP EASEL
POWERPOLITICS
SWEEP JAUNT CAPERS
HIT TRENDY SKELETON
ANTS ACC RUE NOMO
HEATOFTHEMOMENT NEW
ANTE NEA LOAM
ARGUS DECADE IROBOT
KARNAK LIGHTBRIGADE
ICICLE ONEONE FUNDS
NEPHEW NORGAY FLESH

191

MATURE BADVIBES WBC
ERASER ELEANORA OIL
ATBATS SPANDREL UTE
NRC KAOS DID VOLTA
WOO MINT CAGE OLDE
HOLLAND POMONA DIRE
INLINE PERMS LADLES
LEAVE HORDE APPOINT
EYRE OAKIE SCHEMED
BIGYELLOWTAXI
STALLED LUAUS NESS
DAILIES CHIMP PISTE
ANTLER SAUDI HOOTAT
EDIE STELLA MAGNATE
PARR HAIL TITO BUY
LANAI EGG GARR LEE
APR GENIUSES ADMITS
VEE OVERLOOK CRISTO
ARD RATTAILS KUCHEN

192

GHOSTS NODICE TAPER
LEAPAT CHORAL OLORD
ESKIMO ANGERS SHULA
EASTERNROMANEMPIRE
ERMA ADE AAR
GETS SECS TURTLES
OVO ALCOA GUILE AYE
VENETIANBLINDS KNEE
TROLLER ODIE ARDOR
SALAD OATES CLASP
LIVES ALSO TRIFLES
INAN EGGSFLORENTINE
MCI BRIAN ERODE DEL
BELGIAN SEEP VERA
OTT NEE ILIE
NEAPOLITANICECREAM
SORTA ACUMEN AIELLO
OATER MODERN SEEKER
SHEET BLENDS ERNEST

193

HALE DISH ILIAC ABE
ANOS ANTI CURIA BEN
ROWS CHUCKITALL ART
DUG SHAN NEE OWNER
HIE HAL HUR SOMEDAY
ALAMO ANAT CAMETO
THROWINTHETOWEL NBC
BERTH WREN ASIA
ATTIRES QUEER ETHOS
WHALES PURER ONTIME
IRKED BAAED SARAPES
LEES BASS OPTIC
LEA CASHINONESCHIPS
PEORIA ODIC HEMAN
PROWESS AND USE ALI
RAWER ALE ALAS GAD
ADD CALLITADAY SIDE
TIE ELATE GATS ANIS
TOR DAMON OREO PENT

194

INTACT FORGES THROW
DOODLE ANOINT REEVE
TOAMAN LEANTO EASEL
ASSIST LASSER AVERT
GETTHEPICTURE SENSE
RANTS SPOTTER
ATLEAST BLUENOSES
IREAD ELCHEAPO
LIETO RULERS NOSOAP
ENDURE MOANS SUPPLE
DISPEL BURIES TITLE
FLATTEST ONION
CROUPIERS AFFECTS
RENTING ROLFE
AVAIL AFTERAFASHION
CELLS LEAPAT SHINTO
KLEIN IMPUTE TENNER
ERASE SMITES ORDERS
RYDER MEREST NESSIE

195

RASTA BISHOP HAVEAT
ALLIN OSHAWA OVERDO
FOUNDRYMONEY TENSES
TUG LEI OGRE PREENS
BEASTIE EROSE
MOTHERHENRY ITERATE
UNIT ASSORTS DOG
STA CLAM UVA BAZOO
HARPOON FINE OAT
PASTRYPROGRESSIVE
ATE LENS NASCENT
JETTA WOE KAYO LTR
ALA LATOSCA IDEA
MOBSTER FULLCOUNTRY
IRATE LEBLANC
GOTMAD TATA IRS SEE
ARRIVE HEAVENSENTRY
REELER ERNEST ABATE
YOKELS ROASTS TAXED

196

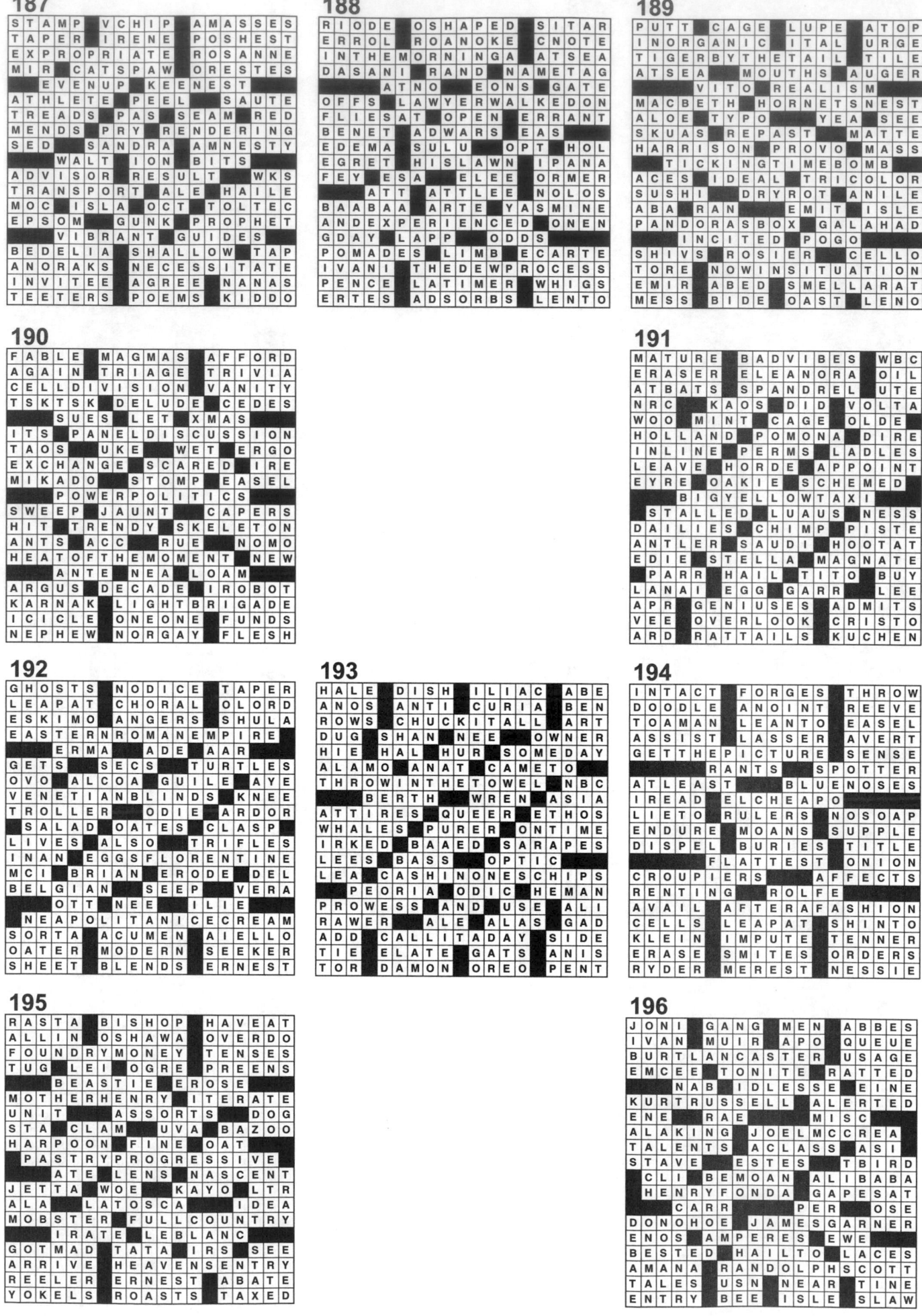

JONI GANG MEN ABBES
IVAN MUIR APO QUEUE
BURTLANCASTER USAGE
EMCEE TONITE RATTED
NAB IDLESSE EINE
KURTRUSSELL ALERTED
ENE RAE MISC
ALAKING JOELMCCREA
TALENTS ACLASS ASI
STAVE ESTES TBIRD
CLI BEMOAN ALIBABA
HENRYFONDA GAPESAT
CARR PER OSE
DONOHOE JAMESGARNER
ENOS AMPERES EWE
BESTED HAILTO LACES
AMANA RANDOLPHSCOTT
TALES USN NEAR TINE
ENTRY BEE ISLE SLAW

197

OBIT ADAPT SAN TAMS
REMY RESEW ORATORIO
CAPPUCCINO PECORINO
ASSES ETAS HORNEDIN
WEED LOG LEI
AGAR LEV MARASCHINO
PALOMINO ERE SEDER
STATISTIC DEAR FLEE
ESSEN DALE LETTERS
CONSTANTINO
SUNSETS AVER WHARF
LSAT SAIL RETRIEVAL
ASSAI DIT NEUTRINO
GRANTORINO TNT EDGE
HAW ABC THEA
MASCARAS AREA AFROS
ALPACINO CONCERTINO
NORMANDY COOLS EVES
STYE GAS ONSET RASA

198

DIMES GLAD JAR PSAT
ARONI AERO UZI LUSH
WEDONTSEEM TOBEABLE
NNE GEM NEGEV NISEI
SELA XANADU EDDIES
STASI ASTRO DPT
TOCHECKCRIMESOWHY
ANO SOSOON RATSO
HANKS LAV ARI VASE
OLDNAGS NOT SCREAMS
ELOI AMS IRA ORRIS
FILET CONMAN GTE
LEGALIZEITANDTHEN
PEA EXTRA EXGOV
ENTITY NESSIE AQUA
CHERI CIERA MLK UPI
TAXITOUT OFBUSINESS
ILES ABE DEEM EASEL
NOSH FEM ERGS VETTE

199

LALA SWEEPS MCEWAN
ORIN HELMET ORNATE
WEBSTERSUNABRIDGED
LTR EAT GRANTEE
YEAHS PUPIL TARZAN
RUTGERSUNIVERSITY
COIN ELON SRS PAM
AVA SNIT TOGO CORE
RANWITH SANE IMONIT
EPLURIBUSUNUM
CDCASE ALLS SELECTS
REAR ATOE LESE LOU
AFR QED AIRS LOON
BAGSUNDERONESEYES
STOLID VENTS ADEPT
ENTREES DAM IRA
SPECIALVICTIMSUNIT
LOVEME ETHANE TONE
REESES SEAMEN ENTR

200

SCENES PACK DREAMUP
TOMATO AGUE RAVIOLI
ALINES TREE ITERATE
TARCROSSEDLOVERS
ESSEN AYE TESTTUBE
ELY LOTS ERNIE
ERIE ASININE EDITOR
TICKINONESCRAW POLO
ALOES ROTE PEP
SENSIBLE ARROGANT
SAO SPUR CANOE
OPTS TAMPINGGROUNDS
REHASH OUTDONE LESS
ARENA PUNS ADD
LUNCHEON MAS OSAGE
TANKTOHIGHHEAVEN
SAMURAI PONE ISLAND
ANIMATE AMEN ENTIRE
PILSNER HOST STYLED

201

BYPASSED ATEASE GENES
ASAWHOLE BRUTES ELUDE
YELLOWSUBMARINE TERSE
HRS HATE COLD BIASED
OLA ADEPT FUNNELS
TICKETTORIDE TORSO
ADULT HADA BIRTHRATE
NETASSETS SAUTE ARLEN
GAS GELS DEBRIS PILED
HOLM SONORA REGINA
ETTE LADYMADONNA BEST
NOBLES UNITES ADAY
TRILL CLONES AVON WAG
ERROL AUDIS SHANGRILA
REDGIANTS UHOH LATER
OPRAH COMETOGETHER
CREOSOL LEVAR RRS
HOLDON MAME PASO SPA
ALIBI PAPERBACKWRITER
FLOYD AGENDA TIEONEON
FETES HILTON ADRIENNE

202

OFISHA HEED YAWL ARKS
RANCOR ETRE ERIE LION
ERRANT SHIV ANNA CARA
PERDITIONORHIGHWATER
FACETS TOMEI IZAAK
OPT IFA RFRA NANA
NOINTESTINESNOGLORY
IGLOO ENA PIES EAU
NOTSOFAST MARAT VASE
EBAN PAGER APATHY
BEATYOURPECTORALS
DELUDE NAILS INRI
EXAM SERGE VIDEODISC
BEN SIMP PAR LITHE
CONDEMNTHETORPEDOES
FUEL IHOP NEA NAT
ACUFF LOCAL SCALIA
FALLFLATONYOURDONKEY
OMNI OREL CLIO MAITAI
ORAN BARA OATS ANNALS
TYRE OTIS WYES RESTUP

203

STAN CANT SARAN WIDOW
EROO ORES PIANO OTERI
CORPORATELADDER OTTER
TOTALABSTINENCE EARLY
SPARE USES EDT RKO
PERE TROUT EIRE
SHAVEOFF SHE TRU STEN
HALENESS PAT ENSNARED
AIMSAT LIMES HOVELS
CLOT SOLARPANEL RID
KESEY RESISTIVE ALWAY
TDS SETTHEDATE LITE
RACIER SUITE ALANIS
OPENROAD ARE STRAGGLE
BERT SCI LES PRETESTS
ESTE STEMS SAID
ARI USA DEER DITTO
PLIED AIRSONESOPINION
SENSE TRAINEDELEPHANT
SALTS EAUDE ELAL ERGO
TRYST DEDEE DYNE RASP

204

HEROES ATAVISTIC OMEN
AGENDA MOMENTARY RAVE
IREMEMBERMAHATMA SMEE
REVENUE NOLA TAN OARS
STE ENS SRO AIMTO
SPLITTHATFORMATION
VISTA NEIGHED BURSAR
INTERS ANTS LIMOS
PHAIDIDDY JOE NAIFS
PAM OER SCARABS INIT
ABIT VITAMINCHAT DANA
SINE EPISODE MAO BAG
STALK TAG IHATCHING
LASSO NATO STANCE
TSTRAP VANSANT ELDER
SOWHATYOURWILDOATS
TWEET YET ATM STP
IBET TVS FEAR OPIATES
NOTA HATREDCORPUSCLES
GALL INEARNEST LATENT
STYE SERENADES ENVOYS

205

UFO IDES HUFFS APPALL
PLUMPISH ELIOT SHEREE
SUGARPLUMFERRY PIGEON
ETHNOS ATE MMII AWNS
TET MIAMI SUITCASE
TINPANGALLEY PUTTO
VISAS OCEANIA MESHED
INKWELL SOP MRED END
ERIS SLOOPDUJOUR ARNE
DEF STOCK EPODE THEIR
AFROS CAN SKI PRAYS
CLOUD CUPID ESTEE ASP
ALPS SILICONSHIP ACHE
RIP ALOT KOA POTSHOT
IFONLY CENTAVO RITES
BESET GALLEONOFGAS
ICECUBES INFUN SAW
MITT LYRA TWO ISAIAH
ARIANA ONERINGYDINGHY
SMORES ASSET TEETIMES
KANSAS DEPTH SASS ADO

206

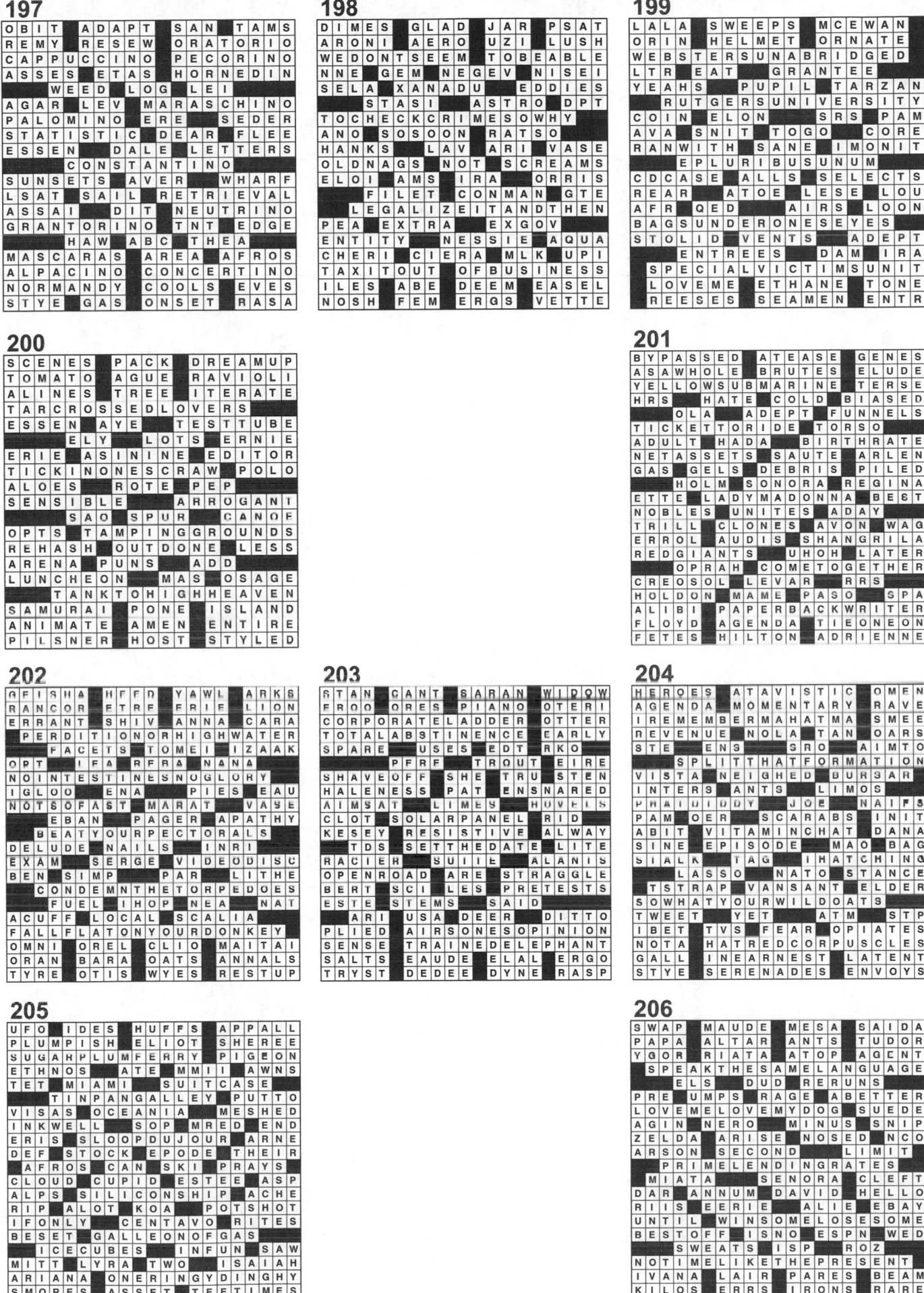

SWAP MAUDE MESA SAIDA
PAPA ALTAR ANTS TUDOR
YGOR RIATA ATOP AGENT
SPEAKTHESAMELANGUAGE
ELS DUD RERUNS
PRE UMPS RAGE ABETTER
LOVEMELOVEMYDOG SUEDE
AGIN NERO MINUS SNIP
ZELDA ARISE NOSED NCO
ARSON SECOND LIMIT
PRIMELENDINGRATES
MIATA SENORA CLEFT
DAR ANNUM DAVID HELLO
RIIS EERIE ALIE EBAY
UNTIL WINSOMELOSESOME
BESTOFF ISNO ESPN WED
SWEATS ISP ROZ
NOTIMELIKETHEPRESENT
IVANA LAIR PARES BEAM
KILOS ERRS IRONS RARE
EDENS NATE TYPEO ARAL

207

PLATEGLASS OLDCAPECOD
EIGHTEENTH PIEALAMODE
CLEARASDAY ANATOMICAL
SISTER STE LINEN TAYE
DOERS MERES
AFFECTION TIERS CLASH
BULLHORN CORNY SHERPA
ISOLATE TACIT STONERS
DESIRE DESKS SHOOTSAT
EDSEL DANTE CHARLOTTE
IGOTOEXTREMES
EGGBEATER CRIES PATTY
MORASSES CHAMP SIERRA
BRASHER SHADE PERTAIN
EMCEES SHINE DOMINICK
REESE STING MEDITATES
NOTRE EPICS
NCAR NAILS ASE ADONIS
AUTOSTRADA THISMINUTE
PROTRACTED HAVEANIDEA
ATMOSPHERE SPEEDSTERS

208

DALE ALKA NOBIS SPANK
ITIN BEER ABOVO CAMEO
VINDIESEL DEBORAHKERR
ALDEN NOLA CREPE NON
STARDATE ALMA SOMA
IBISES ATA LEMMAS
SPENCERTRACY BRADPITT
PALETTE AGRO SER EMME
ARIES NOROOM IDEST
RKO PRELAW KLAATU
KATHYBATES DAVIDSPADE
INACAN DOYENS NOS
LATTE IGOTIT LEANS
ABEL PEE RARE STAMINA
TERIGARR OLIVIAHUSSEY
SENSOR EDT CANTER
TKOS ISAK GENERATE
ARK ADIOS ISSO LEGIT
HILARYSWANK WILLSMITH
AVERT TERRE ENOS ALAN
BEETS ADMAN EGAD XENO

209

SABRA SPUR AMMO FED
IGUANA THREEBEAN ARTE
DUSTYSPRINGFIELD PAAR
EATA BEE SAINT UBANGI
HIRES LLD STOCKED
WOODYGUTHRIE BAYSHORE
ERNIE AMASSER EZER
DRAINCLOGS AMINO
AYES TONYSOPRANO
STRS DOH SOIT RACIAL
WHEEL GAYTALESE LAMIA
ARENAS RADS ILA SELF
MUDDYWATERS TEST
SMIRK BLUEHAWAII
HATS READMIT LOTTA
ANIMATES RANDYJACKSON
MANILAS NOH SEARS
STYLER IOWAS ARB AUST
TOTE MODESTMUSSORGSKY
ELIS ATONEMENT READIN
REM COLD AWES GRAPE

210

ACTI ARBOR TSAR LIARS
LORD ZILCH OLLA ORSON
FRUITOFTHEBROOM WASTE
INSTORE STRIVE IGNITE
ESTATE OONA ENE SEZ
RASP BROOKMAGAZINE
SPOOL LURID OTERI
LAPD TUNIC ACHES LONI
ASE AIMEE ERRANT LUIS
PANICLE TUROW WITCH
DIDNTDOABRICKOFWORK
TENSE BLOOD PAINING
INGA SATINS PATTI GAL
EASY KLUTE PUFFS AHME
SOAPS MARCO TUTEE
TOPOFTHEBRINE RANT
IRE SEA AIDE ROOSTS
PERNOD ANNALS POTSHOT
SLIER BRASSIECOMEHOME
ISLET BANE SAUNA ONEA
NESTS CLAD TREYS WEIL

211

SCHUBERT SELENA BEALS
BOILOVER EVADED ALBAN
ANGELINA TENTHOFBOOZE
THEOL PRONG BAYTREE
ARTS BEEFS DIETS TDS
MAW CRAZYFOURS AHA
BLOWHOLES PENS OSOLE
ETAILED ABO TWOWINDS
RONDOS MANANA EYESHOT
DOE JUKES LADER IPO
ALAW NINEWHEELER ASAP
LAH BOGIE FAVES AGO
ORATORS MOUSER CROWNS
HALFAMAN ULT NOMONEY
ASFAR WEDS SCALEDOWN
LDS MOTELTHREE NCO
NBA WAGON LILAC DEAD
ALMAATA ABBOT SERFS
SINGLEHEADER TAPROOTS
ANOUK ASPERA EXITPOLL
LITES NOPETS RETESTER

212

WASTE GAWP TODD SNIDE
ETHEL OBEISANCE HIKER
SKEET PEACEFULPROTEST
TABOOS KNITS OUTTAKE
FREEREIN ASSAY
PERFORMANCEARTIST AHA
AXE BOP SCOTTO FROG
RIVETS PIS AAA SERRA
CLEAR PEPPERMINTTWIST
HERVE ALOUD NINO VEE
BEAST DRIFT GNOME
SSE SYNC FARAH LADDS
PERSONALITYTEST INERT
AGAIN AWE EEK BEARER
NUTS SCRIED FOE CSU
GEE PERENNIALOPTIMIST
MERIT AMORETTO
SWEATIT OATER SHRIMP
PETRIFIEDFOREST AERIE
EATAT CREAMCAKE CLAMS
CRATE SAAR ELAN ASSET

213

AMEND PSST GIFTS PAWN
FARCE ICAN ANOUK OLAY
BRIANSSONG SNOBINRAGS
TEAMMATE MOST PEEWEE
AINT GOV ROPE
ASSORT COMELATE SKIS
CHICKENRUN NICERCHUNK
TOES AETNA OER HENRI
OWS OFFSEASON IFORGET
RUT NITE HOES LOY
SPACEBALLS PLACESLABS
USE LEAR VOCE SLO
SUPPERS ASTERISKS TOR
APRIL OPP SCENT ARNE
GOODFELLAS LEGALFOODS
ENDS MEATHEAD ALLSET
BOSC ART LONI
WAYOUT ATME HANDGUNS
HIGHSIERRA GARISHHEIR
IRON OGDEN ERGO TORTE
GYRO NOSES OPEN SHOED

214

TORI MOOG FLESH SLASH
OVEN INFO LANCE CALVE
METHANEOFCAWDOR INTER
CROON ALERTS TEASDALE
ASTUTE DRAB VIOLS RTS
TEASEUP MEDIANFOSSEY
SALESREPS DAS ARK
NETS LIEF SIMBA
MEADHOCCOMMITTEE DARN
ALLDONE LEO TELL IAN
RAPTOR MEETTHE LOATHE
NIA TYPE EEO DIORAMA
ENCE EXTRATERRESTRIAL
REACT SAUL SNOB
COR MES SOTHATSIT
MELEEIACOCCA SUNRISE
ARE NOSIR RISK BEANER
DRAMATIC KERNEL RICES
RADII MEANEYEFORANEYE
ATOLL ORION AIDA EROS
SANDS VOLTS DREW DEUT

215

TRAG SNOOD MEAD SAHIB
WANE CORGI ISLE PRIDE
ODIN OTTER FAIL IMPEL
PASTPRESENTFUTURE HAT
IRELAND DES DELHI
EMEERS BOLA KIEV OPTS
CADRE GEL WHIM ESCHEW
ENS READYAIMFIRE ORE
TEAMSTERS ABALONE
REGENT TILE ATM KARAT
EVANS GIMP SNOB AGATE
CAMEL LEE SAGO SLAYER
ACETATE FORETOKEN
NUS VENIVIDIVICI PEA
TEETER RIGA INT SWANS
SETH ELSE PANG CHESTS
MOODY NOV SHEATHE
IRA ROCKPAPERSCISSORS
DOTED HEAP NATAL EROS
LUCRE ERIE GNARL LANE
ETHER ENDS EDGES SLED

216

BATHS RBI WINES ADZE
AMAIN PAID ANODE PREX
EMILE ARLO ICIER ANTI
ROLLERCALL TURNERCOAT
TREE GALORE NAH
SAMOSA SATINS PACECAR
CLOP OATES SIDE HBO
ATT DILLERPICKLE SEAT
MAH INDUS NAIL RECTO
PRESSKIT BLURT HAWKER
RENEE ERASE DONEE
MAPPED ADOBE TOMORROW
ARRAY ARNO SERIF RCA
COOL SNEAKERTHIEF OAK
AMO ETTA CURES SOLE
WAFFLES SETTEE BATMAN
ESE BEMOAN EERO
CORNERCRIB BUTTERMILK
ODIN ALINE AOUT EASEL
NICE GONER GURU SCENE
KEEL EYERS ASK THESE

217

TOTES CLOTH DORA DICK
ELIAN AIMEE INON AGRA
MISSINGLYNX STEAMROOM
PONYTAIL DARTH COERCE
ESTD SEED TOEHOLD
OMAR OTTERNONSENSE
STEEP UKE TOLD VATS
CRASHINGBOAR SEASIDES
HEMI NAUT AYE PLATE
MEET CTN SADE LOIS
OSS JACKALLANTERN SAG
BUSH PAIR WVA GERE
ASTIR DEN REEL HIDE
JERRYLEE GOPHERSMOKES
ARID EARP POE ASONE
RABBITTRANSIT DRAT
RAISINS TERA WHIM
REBAIT EDAMS NAVARONE
DEMIMOORE BEARMINIMUM
AEON USER ALCOA UTERO
SECS TOSS SAENS TERNS

218

MADE BOAS MIWOK SAVED
ICES UNTO ANIME CHIDE
THESAGEOFREASON ASCII
TERESA PIES DONKNOTTS
NABS ASTRO YET OHM
ASH ROHE TRAMP LIRR
STAKEOUTFOOD EMPLOYED
OLLAS LOAN ELY YASIR
POLLUTANT CANOLA CLEO
ELI REPOSED HAIL
ROC TRAFFICSLIGHT POL
ECOL ESEMPIO OAK
NEMO DANIEL BRACKETED
DAMES INN DAUB EMERY
SNOWTIRE SPORTOFSPAIN
NEAR LEHAR HULA LEE
ASS TAE TERSE TABS
PECKINPAH DANA COARSE
PAOLO IMANOLDSCOWHAND
ELLEN CONAN AEON EBAY
LEDES SKEWS TATS LEGS

219

RAPSTARS SPLITS SPICE
ALITALIA CRUSOE ARRAY
BASEBALL HOLLOW TERRE
IMALLSET OWLETS IDIOT
DONEE SHOES LEAGUE
SIPHONS SATE TASS
MILD HEAVES HIRT ETAT
EDIE ASKER ROLEMODELS
DUKE DOER GETEVEN
INEPT RESIN DOGEARED
UNSEATS DEFER ROUTINE
MOONPIES ATEUP POSTS
ETCHERS NLER NERO
SPEARHEADS TIARA CRAT
LAMB EDNA SANITY ESPO
IRES REAM WITNESS
PARERS PILOT APSES
INANE BALING ICEHOUSE
NOLTE OLIVIA FLYAKITE
TIDED ATMOST FERRETED
OASES SOOTHE SMEARERS

220

AFFAIR IMPI SAMP MATS
ORACLE MEAN ALOE ARIE
NAMEOFAPASS BALLERINA
EYER ILE TEARS IRK
BALIN RARA SCOURGE
UPHILL IMAMS TEASPOON
NIECE TAM CHEN SMUG
MAA CAPERINGHORSE AGE
ENVISIONS ORALS PANEL
TOED SST SCOPE WORLD
NICHE TITUS DISCO
ALOHA PINUP SOL EVES
TRYME TATAR STOLIDEST
EMB FLASHINGERMAN GSA
ELON ESSE ALE UBOAT
MEDITATE MERLE TIEDYE
STYRENE MIDI TEETH
VAN BOGUS CON AMIN
FEMALEFOX CHURNDEVICE
ANON SARI ELSE EDEMAS
TATA SYNE DYAD RESINS

221

SPRAT MOJO APSES OTTO
ALONE AWOL CRASH TEED
CONDESCEND COMPREHEND
STARTLE ISLETS EVENTS
OHIO ADE ODER
BABIED ONTHEMEND STOW
IPODS SHEER VIE ALI
TASS CAGES VIAND AXIS
ECO MOTORTREND GRAVE
REMAINED HIKE CLONED
FUMED GLENS GRAND
CARNEY ALOT IRONISTS
OMITS SUBTRAHEND POP
LIES ELITE ADOBE LENI
ANN NEA AGILE RONAN
SODS DONOTBEND NOODLE
EATO PRE MILK
CRENNA LEADTO OCEANIA
HOUSEBLEND OVEREXTEND
AIRE LEVEE HIDE EMEND
PLOD EMIRS IDOL SETON

222

ORGAN ESAU GRASS SANE
MARIO SOUR LOTTA ALAW
EVANS CLEARASMUD NIKE
GETTHEHELLOUTOFDODGE
ALE LEM TSE PANDA
FINDANOTHERSUPPLIER
SCUBA TOTE SOHO NYC
ALLSET AISLE RUMMAGES
WADE WATCHYOURHEAD
FIENDISH INKY NOWAY
IRA RNS SENSE RMS ARE
TEDDY FOGG FOIEGRAS
NEVERLOOKBACK AMBI
DISCRETE SNELL EASTLA
ENT NOTA PASS REHEM
CHECKINSIDETHEHORSE
KAPOK RIA TIT BOO
LOOKOUTFORTHEICEBERG
TENK BROADSHEET DANTE
ERIE ADORE ERTE NICHE
ASTR DUKES MOHS ATHOS

223

TACTIC OFF ASIT TIMED
BRAHMA URE RACY ELUDE
SLEEPS GEN MYER ELSIE
PONYUPTHECASH OLDSTER
TART ENTITLE EASE
ARCHERY LIAR HEAVEN
CANIS PINTOBEANS GHI
LYNN PION NEON IBSEN
DRAFTDODGER OXCART
ACQUIRE ACE NEBS ELBE
THU CLEM TBA MESS LIN
TIAS ALES USA TIEDYED
UNRULY MORGANLEFAY
NOTME IPSA OILY LOLL
ESE NAGHAMMADI SADIE
ROTINI PILE EMENDED
REFS MASCARA POEM
ANIMIST ARABIANNIGHTS
TENOR INIT ABS SPEARS
CRANK UTNE MAD CRATER
HOLDS SHED ARE HORSES

224

ANDTHEREST SWISSBANKS
NOWORNEVER MANCHURIAN
OVERSEVERE ANTOINETTE
DFFM RINGS SNOOP STIR
ELBE GLEE CHANTS TIED
LIED SAE EELS
MOSEYED POURS DOPPLER
ACORNS DRAGOON GRIESE
REMIX PEEPHOLES APACE
KANE BASSET DRILY VAN
SNO CONKED SIEGES ELL
PAL HAIFA STEINS THAI
IRENE CUSSWORDS BOOTS
TINEAR LOCALES HELMET
ZATOPEK NAMED SINLESS
ODES VIN BAND
ALAW GROPES LARD INCH
TELE RAVEN PENAL TARA
TOLERATING SPACECADET
INONEPIECE SENEGALESE
CITYCENTER TRANSPORTS

225

RACESTO GAMAL GERMANE
ASATEAM ERATO AROUSED
BYTHETIMEIGET IHUSTED
BEEN STOW DETROITCITY
ITRIP RHEA ARNEL
CALORIE IDTAG ETAL
AYS IODIZE NEED YMA
TOPBRASS DEREK CRAT
AGEISM BOSS AERATE
NACL STOOP TOPHOENIX
ILEFTMYHEARTINSAN
FRANCISCO AGATE TITO
RELYON WRAP BOOZER
ALOE SPREE SKIAREAS
YAP RENE AVAILS SLO
SYST PIPED FIFTEEN
ERASE ELSA SANTO
BUFFALOGALS ARAB SAIL
ITALIAN NASHVILLECATS
BEYONCE THEEI EARACHE
SPENSER ERNES SHARPEN

226

ROSS EMAG AFIRE CLARA
ERTE AIRE PONES AILED
CAANTRACT IPASS STAND
ATTARS DEPPPOSITION
PEETE SOLICIT MOE
PENNKNIVES SKI RCAS
ISO DAYONE HAMIT BEBE
TALKED SERB PITTBULLS
SHINDIG ATONER EAGLES
MICA AAS AWAKENS
EBERT STARRTREK HOFFA
ASPIRED DET CROP
ARABIC REBUTS SHUTEYE
GERESHIFT PICA INANER
ELAN WARES LASHES CRY
ROTC IMY WILDEBUNCH
HAN NABISCO AIDED
LEMMONWEDGES UPROAR
OSCAR AROMA LOWESCORE
START ISLAM EBAY URNS
SANKA LEANS AIRS SSSS

227

CLAMS STLO TALL KAPPA
HEMAN PROD OLIO IDEAL
ESCRITOIRE REEVALUATE
FESSPARKERHOUSEROLLS
ESTE ANT OTT
ALTARS SCENT AMMO SOS
DEADSEA ORSONBEANSOUP
LOCO LLAMA OAT STATE
INEPT ONE TAUTER OKRA
BETTYWHITEWINE ERASER
PIA DID TAE
DEEPEN SIDCAESARSALAD
RIPE SUNDAE MIB TIARA
AESOP SAO ACTOR KNOT
FIONAAPPLEPIE RELEASE
TOM MISS NOLES DENIED
OPT ATE OWEN
REBECCADEMORNAYSAUCE
LEDERHOSEN MONTECARLO
ANISE SILT ABET ARGON
STEED ISEE NETS PEEPS

228

ABBA OMOO CORK ALEAST
SLAB TOSS AMEN LEANTO
PUNS TOSCANINI CARDIN
EDITORIALSTAFFOFLIFE
WNW SERGE LEAH EFS
STATIC ECO ROCK
LIGHTNINGRODSERLING
ETO NCAA SUMO TEAMS
WONKA ITSME MAW REPOS
ITLL ADLAI RUBENS
MICKEYMOUSECLUBSODA
SANKIN ALIEN RIEN
INCAN CRO LAHTI SEAMS
REUPS LIRA ELAN TAP
ROOTANDBRANCHOFFICE
ONOR SOL MOLTED
AMA SECT BLAHS TOA
CONDUCTORSBATONROUGE
INDIRA MONEYTREE NAGS
DERMAL MUIR ISEE CIAO
STEELE ATTY CERF ENDS

229

NOIR SATAN ZPG THAWED
ERMA WRATH IRE MERELY
WEATHERBALLOON CATTLE
TOSTADAS UNSER TIBER
EREI SPLIT EASEL
WEDDINGBELLS ASPIRATE
OLEO NANU TUREEN NOR
RUNNIN BOMB FRA KUKLA
SDI WATERBUFFALO TEES
TEMPORAL ZEDS ODETTE
INRI MAZDA EDER
SOWETO SERA ALLNIGHT
ECHT WICKERBASKET ROI
PHIAL MAH DOCK SECEDE
TET OMANIS NITS HEAR
AREARUGS WINDOWBLINDS
BLIGE LADES EAST
SHREK SAYHI EARACHES
PEERED WRIGHTBROTHERS
CRATES LIL URBAN AMAT
ADDSTO SCI TASTY TOTS

230

FAKES MAYOR SOAP TRES
AGENT ALAMO ONLY OUZO
CUTER WOKANDROLL EMIR
TETRAS USN ARA ETHANE
LOUNGE SLOTH YOKES
SEE BIRTHDAYWHISKLIST
HARP TATTOOS TIED
USUAL NETH HEEL NOW
NESTEGG PANFORCOLLEGE
THESES OPRAH LOWED
OGLALA CARTONS SARGES
ALINE TORME EARNER
FENDERBLENDER COOLISH
SEG YODA COST SELMA
SPAN ERRATIC ILER
BABYINEEDYOUROVEN IED
ABASE SNIDE RENOWN
GROTTO REI OHM TURTLE
GABE GRATERGOOD GOOEY
EDAM LOGE ARGUE ATWAR
DEBS EYED PESTY TENSE

231

HACK OLAV LABOR AVON
ETON RENE AMATI SNEVA
ATME EMIT TORIC ANNAN
RIME IMO FINISH LATTE
TRADEDON EFG APESUIT
SENECAN ENA EFREM ROT
DEL PINCH LODE CANE
TAMPA ADREM PULLTAB
HRE TELLY OHARE OVALS
EENY LAY UTES ANTONIA
ENTERON SCHMO REORDER
PASSAIC ILES MAA TANG
ASFIT EDGAR KERRS GEE
ODESSAN VERST EPEES
CARO UPDO IRISH RIP
ALT APRON CIS UPRAISE
BAYAREA CTN ARRANTLY
AMPLY TABOOS ECO ICEE
LEILA PRYOR PROB SHEL
ADNAN OTERI OILS TETE
SASH TESSA MEET ERST

232

ROMP SCHOLL CAST AMI
OMAR COOTIE AREA SRAS
AEROSOLBOMB RICK ETTA
SLIPINTO PAMPA ESPIES
TEN XES NIS MTWTF
STAVE SCOT HAWAIIAN
ASLEEPONTHEJOB CRU
IVAN ESSEN SANA GIAN
PILE ASTER RRS BEANS
SEASIDE ACIDY FOOL
ODS AUXILIARYVERB LST
KEMP MELLO WUSSIER
GHANA APT NONET AMMO
OAKS TAUT STILT ABIT
ELI ADOLPHGOTTLIEB
SONATINA RENO ESSES
GROVE TOS SUR ONE
RECIPE BRETT BASILICA
ACRE SALE AHABTHEARAB
GOAL ICON LESLIE MEME
ALB NEWT TEASER PEPE

233

REFERENDA SCOLD APILE
ELALAMEIN TABOO LAMER
PALMSFORTHEPOOR OCEAN
NAT TIE SETSATEASE
RELY GPA SALTINES
STEELIE SCALD LEON
PAGEOFAQUARIUS CATTLE
ALG PETTIT GLUT SHOUT
SCOPE SST BALER KETCH
LSU TONEDUP HERA
MAJA PRODANDREEL OMEN
AWAY CANAPES YSL
SIMON SPLIT SAS AEONS
KNIFE POLO GOBLIN PEA
SKETCH PACTOFCONGRESS
HEAP SAINT PATENTS
STRESSED NEB ENOS
HAILSTORMS IAN PCS
ENLAI POUTINLEFTFIELD
AGENT LITER LEDASTRAY
RODDY EDENS STATUETTE

234

COULD OFFRAMP AMASSES
ATSEA POLITIC REPOMAN
TOUGHOPPONENT IRONORE
NORELCO GMC WELLDONE
ALEN ASEC PETE LET
PERDU IDAHOPOTATO HOR
SPATULA ISSUE COVE
ESA PRECLUDES SNOWPEA
SCHLEPS ANAS STARTERS
PRIORS ACTS SLIMS RTS
RIGA SMASHOPEN OAHU
EPH ASTAB IPOD TASTER
STOPTHAT ONTO RESTORE
SUPPLER ENGINEERS RES
ORIG RILLE MINTIER
SEN SANCHOPANZA TOPTO
ICE DINE GOIT SARD
CHORALES OBS LORELEI
HONALEE INBETWEENHOPS
ATONING RELAYER AIMAT
DEFENDS TSETSES SPANS

235

CATSPAW SECTS GASMASK
PRENAME EVERY ATTACHE
RCCOLAS VALID SHERMAN
SHOOSTHEPIANOPLAYER
POS GROANER ELI
ISP KILTER GYRATE FRI
SPOKANE AFL PERSIAN
LAKE GETSTHEBOOS PERU
ACELA RELEASERS WINES
MERTZ YMA VAT ANDRE
SOD PLUMMET OLE
ATM ROOSOFALLEVIL ZEN
REOPENS MOCKS ELENORE
AROUSALS BASTIONS
LIST TOTAL SCALP PSST
PURE ELECTED IRAS
STOPIT PIGPENS LETUPS
CHI FOOSBALLTABLE IRE
ARNEL GOAT LUNE KATIE
NOTME LUBE ARTE EMEND
TESTS ETAS RYAN DIRTY

236

VASCO TRAC PECKAT FOG
OCEAN OAHU RAUNCH IRE
IHAVETOFORGIVETHE JAM
DEN SOFTY ROES EMAILS
LAINE AIR TSOS
AMEND WORLDITPROBABLY
MONTE WEBS ROAN FREE
BONED SLOE JERI ARIAS
ELO DOESNTEVEN RINSE
RANGIEST ATO STREETS
EVA SHAKERS HAN
BATTING ERE CHANDLER
ILOSE REALIZEHOW IDO
MOATS OTTO LAID GROUP
BOSH TUTU ROTS OUNCE
OFTENITUPSETSME RISER
REDS QTY GAINS
SINEWY AGUA ATOLL HES
ORE ASHLEIGHBRILLIANT
FOX GUIDES ALES ATRIA
ANT EMDASH TEEM SEEDY

237

LAMB CREEP WACO GRITS
AGEE RANGE EBAN RANEE
SUEGRAFTON SOME EIDER
TAKEOVER SETUP RESUME
TBAR RIVET PANES
SESTET FIVER FORESTER
HATES MODERNTIMES RAU
USER GERE ELM TWIRL
TEES LEBRONJAMES YALE
ELL CASE FOOL TALLY
BLARES AMI CARVED
BEEBE PLAN ODIE EMT
ERLE DONALDTRUMP TSAR
DITKA LOT APES HIRE
ENE FLASHGORDON PIGGY
REDEFINE AMAIN BARNES
TRIED ERATO MEND
ASIANS JINNI PARABOLA
PARSI DALI NOISEMAKER
TWEET EVAS GUEST SASE
SASSY BATH SIDES EYES

238

GRETA TROI GARP EPOCH
RATON RAND OVAL MUNRO
AVASTMATEY OONA ENTER
FETCHAPAILOFWATER HAN
AIRS MOST VISIT
CALLS SPOOF TITANIA
RAVEL STAYOFEXECUTION
ETE CORAL BELTS CNN
ANNMILLER DIODE MESO
PAGINATE ARNO SPA
SPEAKWITHFORKEDTONGUE
MSS ERSE LEANNESS
LEOI HALOS LITIGATES
ARN SMILE DIJON UNE
SITBACKANDRELAX RIPEN
ENHANCE EARTH CANST
MENDO ELLY RUTH
DOM ROLLOVERBEETHOVEN
IRENE AMOI HORSEOPERA
VANCE NEIN EMIT LENNY
ENDOF GREG ABCS ESTES

239

INDIRA CSLEWIS FRIDGE
SAILED ALLMALE INTROS
UNREAD PADTHEWARCHEST
ZAG CREEK SANTE OSHA
USETHEPRESS CORSETS
ROSA HAI NOAM EDA
BAYOUS ORELSE PLEASES
RHETT SPEAKONTHESTUMP
IES DIEOF BRAY CPOS
MANSION LAOS BIO
SPOTFRONTBURNERISSUES
ASA LIAM YELTSIN
HESS SECT ASNER ALE
TRAINDARKHORSES HAGAR
METSFAN SEPTET LOVETT
LII LYRE DEO PELE
RODLESS CONTROLSPIN
AVIA IMPEI ORONO ANO
PICKAGOODSLATE OWESTO
ISAIAH SENECAS REDDEN
PALEST ARTISTS ADHERE

240

CALIF ABOMB ROSE CASA
OMANI MADLY OVAL RUTS
MIDDLEAGEIS BACKDATES
PRESENTER SHIRR INURE
SSS TOIL WHENYOUVEMET
AMS THEN IKE NOS
IRAQI CIAO SCALERS
REDUG ALCOA ASI SOBER
SOMANYPEOPLETHAT COLA
MOUES LUTECE COAT
SUSANB EVERY AHERNE
ITAR ATAXIA ARMOR
MIDI NEWPERSONYOUMEET
PLANS NEO SHANE SOOTY
EARNEST ERAS EMMAS
ORI III ALAS IAS
REMINDSYOUOF STIR COO
ASPOT SECTS TENORHORN
THATSTHAT SOMEONEELSE
OOLA LORE EBERT SHOFR
RTES CENT SENSE TERRS

241

COGS TRACKS ODD GAIT
OHIO PREVAIL NUISANCE
PABLOPICASSO EDNORTON
TREETOP RISER AUFOND
EDIT WAIT HAIRPIN
LEWISCARROLL SEINE
BOG RAREE AENEAS LOOT
ANAS TEA SCAD TIDBIT
STRICT LEEMARVIN ARA
KARMA TAPED AIRMAN
SPILL HISS CHIP ALDAS
SAILOR ROANS TEETH
FLO CARYGRANT TERROR
LENNON LOVE ABU TAME
ANKA KARATE CLONE SSW
PSEUD AARONCOPLAND
ITERATE OAST DESK
SPLINE SAGAS HEIFERS
WILLIAMS KURTVONNEGUT
ACOUSTIC ASSAILS NAPA
MARS ALI SHELVE DRAT

242

DORA WAYWE SORE ACCRA
APES ALOHA OPEL GALES
SUPPORTYOURSELF IREST
ALLIN SOO IONA UNFAIR
NEARED SPUN AXIS ARGO
INCITES INSURANCERUNS
STENOPAD SERENA REPS
ODIE GATSBY
JACKETANDTIE SEA DART
ARRID TENET CASELAW
BRACED DAMSELS SONATA
BOWKNOT MEANS SIMON
AWLS NOV BELTOUTASONG
STROBE ERMA
SPOT PLATES TEXASTEA
FORCEYOURHAND RESPELL
ADEE ARMS HOAR SPINAL
VACANT ETAL KOS INNIE
OPINE STORYBOOKENDING
ROSIE EWOK ATTIC LEER
SPEAR POLS HASTO ESSO

243

SKINS ACDC ROBE CEDES
POTATOCHIP ONEATATIME
ACEVENTURA MEETHEADON
THREESOMES ENTERSINTO
PARS ROD REALTER
PASTELS PRES LIAR
INTUNE REEF COED DOFF
VEERS SERB NIPS PEKOE
OMAN STATESIDE CATERS
IOMS POPULACE BARRETT
MILSAP RYDER PREACH
RFROOTS DEANPOLE CHEM
OTOOLE FILTEROUT TOBE
DENSE DANL LENS GOBEL
ERSE VIRG ELSA PUREST
LEER SPYS SUNSETS
SPLEENS DHT RIPS
PAULREISER STAMPINGON
INCINERATE EYDIEGORME
REITERATED TRIATHLONS
ELDER EELS AEON TOWIT

244

RAMPS PREY CHERI EDIT
ELIOT LAME HEROD MINH
PATTIDAVIS ELIZABETHI
IWEARONII GAPE HUNTER
SIHE PIPS CONDORS
CHASTITYBONO CHESSSET
RADIUS EAU GARS
ATEUP RAYROMANO AHEAD
TEEM HUR LIZAMINELLI
WETNOODLE ESTREET
GALLON SUNDERO LOAVES
ANAEMIA TEARSOPEN
MORGANLEFAY NAT MICE
ADDON TAILSPINS POLAR
PAST AVE SUGARS
CHESHIRE CRYSTALGAYLE
HOTTIES RIIS RAID
ENCORE GANG COMPLIANT
ASHLEYJUDD HALFSISTER
THEE ELLIE IGLU SHARE
SUDS DOFOR PEAL MUDDY

245

ADAM JAPAN SCADS TBAR
IRMA ANEYE PERON NERO
MISSINGYEW ULTRA TELL
SPOTS OSTER AFB COY
ERUPTION ANGUISH
GUMRAPPER DELE BOCCI
INAMESS PATIER BROOM
NOSILY FIRTRADER EMPS
ASSN PONE ERICA ABOU
DERANGED AMATEUR
BIN LINDENJOHNSON RTE
INARAGE SWEATSIT
ACUE ULCER IRES EIRE
SIGN PEARBONDS THANES
ETHAN DINING ROARSAT
SETTO NISI ABEFIGODA
YAHTZEE CALIGULA
CUP ORE GETGO ESTEE
ACID ASONE POPLARSONG
SANE STONE ARIEL ERGO
SLEW HYPER RECAP SIRS

246

NIBS ALARM RUSE DUMBO
ARAT RENTA ORAL ONAIR
DEJA GENESISIII SIDLE
ADAMBEDE SNEAD VITALS
PUNS MATH MODEM
ASCENT SCENT KILO ECO
SCUDS MAUDEADAMS PROM
SATE MATRI OLE MAORI
ALI MACADAMIZE BASSET
MANDARINS ADE MORTARS
EXING RIO MANGE
LAPSING FEZ MYRMIDONS
AFRAME REVELATION LAP
SLEDS HAT ISHOT SIDE
EAVE NEVERAGAIN CIVIC
STE SORE ETHIC RULERS
NOOSE PART FIRE
MATZOH OLDIE SEVENTHS
ORION ADAMANDEVE COOL
PENNE LOCI URGER EMMA
EAGER FRET PEARS DEEP

247

```
BRAS SAGS UDDER ERMA
RANTS OBOE RIATA NEON
EBOOK MSEC ISLES OTOS
WALRUSMUSTACHE TALUS
TEENIER GAR MAB RET
DKG DELICACY BANJO
AGAUCHE ALLIGATORPEAR
SALPA TERMED SHH PEWS
TRI BRAE OTOOLE
ENS BULLFIDDLES INFRA
REHEAT OMANI SODIUM
STANG ELEPHANTMAN NNE
REBUTS YETI INN
APIA ARC THEIRS NOTED
KANGAROOCOURT SAWYERS
ENTER PLAYMATE GIS
EDO USE RBI DAUNTED
ANIMA CROCODILETEARS
SCAD LEOIX WEBB ERGOT
PATE AGREE LULU REEVE
AREA DOERS STEM DREW
```

248

```
JESS CLAD ASSIGNS SPA
ACES DEER PHARAOH TAB
GRANTCARY PECKGREGORY
RUSSIAN SPARKS LINKS
ESTA ARRS HITLESS
RUSHGEOFFREY RANEES
ALIAS RIEL BOBGRAHAM
INTS BOARD CULL DABA
DAZS UNIS THELAST ROC
LASED CHILE EUDORA
ALBERTA SHALL FEDINTO
FEUDAL FIEND MOTEL
ORR BEFIRST MOTH ACTS
FONT ANET CANOE THEY
LISAMARIE BART LEARN
GLADES MARCHFREDRIC
SPEEDOS MOTT SERA
CRONE CASHEW NASTASE
HURTWILLIAM HUNTHELEN
ENG ALBANIA ISEE ESAI
DEE RESPECT MELD SOLD
```

249

```
JAMMED NIPPON ICANSO
AFOULOF EELERY TOSEED
MARTINLAWRENCE ENTICE
BRETT OPT ANAT JOLTS
IOUS ODESSA ORD
ELVISPRESLEY RABBITS
LOCATE ODD GONG AARE
HARMS ALOE AAU OARMEN
INST DENNISFRANZ OBS
OLAVS SPF LIU NLE
REJOICE ANISE DERIDES
ANO ERR BET BESET
ISH BOBBYVINTON HART
LUNDEN USE UEYS LASER
ARBS YAMS SML SICKLE
TEETIME PABLOPICASSO
LUG CANALS RICE
ELUDE NOTE SIN NOTME
WISETO GEORGEGERSHWIN
ETHNIC LAINIE SEEMING
RAITTS ORSONS BESTIR
```

250

```
FATCAT CLAPTRAP SCALA
ERRATA HULAHULA PLEAS
DEEPER ENTRANCE YARNS
UNSEAT MAESTROS GRADE
PASTRAMI RELIVE LETON
NAST SLOE PATENT
STAIN SEAR TSARS
EARNEST BADE RESHAPE
TUSSLES OPENSHOP ERAS
AROUSE FOUNTAIN SATUP
DUNLOP LINTELS ATTILA
ASIAN FANZINES PASSEL
TEST TANGENTS PERETTI
ESTEVEZ LEER ASTARTE
CREAM SEMI SLYER
ASHARP LINE PANS
RHETT RIGORS LEADPIPE
RIATA AERONAUT MOONED
ENDUP INASENSE UNSUNG
STONE DETESTED ENTICE
TONES SEESTARS LASTED
```

PUZZLE #251: DY = DAY

251

```
MIST ROBS GOLIATH SAW
ESAU ALAI OLESTRA ORY
DUKE NLRB TATAMIS ANN
EPISODIC LOFTY TAKEN
DYDREAMS USATODY
BRANDY RAAB CODA SHA
LAPIS NOTTRUE ARCWELD
AGOG PILESON IMALOSER
HUSHMONEY ALII SARTRE
TELE ADELIE SKITS
SHE LATTERDYSAINTS ASS
PATRI YODELS TRIB
ERRAND MUNI FLEECIEST
ALADDINS AGREERS RUTH
RADIATE TSHIRTS ATRIA
NEO CHAI TORT EXHORT
DYSHIFT JOEFRIDY
BOISE LARVA REASSURE
ORC RAPANUI AMIS USES
NAB BROMINE LANE IMAM
ELM SELECTS INTR TALE
```

252

```
MTSHASTA STRAFE SADAT
ARMORIAL PEAHEN AROMA
SEALEDWITHAKISS RECON
SALINE TREMENS MANTIS
ATLEAST IREST LENTO
GEARS INBUD WAND RDA
EDD TRIAL SHINTO FIN
ACHILLESTENDON AAA
CHITLINS WALTER PULL
RENTING STORMED TESTY
EATING SHORTER MOTTOS
ADELE FORREST FORTUNE
TARA SLIEST MORTISES
ICE SHERWOODFOREST
OHS CREEDS JILTS LOW
NET HITE PANDA TBONE
GILLS CHAKA SHRIVER
PARCEL SEASALT EUGENE
SLOOP DEADTREEEDITION
SLUMP UNSEAT ADDSONTO
TYPES ODESSA STAMPSET
```

253

```
ANGST RIPENS SODASHOP
PINCE ANIMAL APOPLEXY
SPOON INTIMATEAPPAREL
EATLESS SLATE LEENANE
STEAMIER ETHEL SAD
RENTER HEMAN RERIG
PLAINBAGEL REPOS RENO
EEL TAXICAB DUMAS COG
TEAR DEMOTED PALOMINO
PINED SEVERER DENUDED
RASCAL SETTLOR MARISA
OCEANUS RARITAN RAVEN
JOEPESCI GALATEA LINC
ECG STOMP MATTERS SSE
CCED STEIN HEADMASTER
TAROT STEEL DILATE
DRE ATSEA LEDUCTHO
SPIDERS ITALO CARRION
HAREBRAINEDIDEA DEANS
OVERLORD GENIES ATREE
TESSERAE GREECE YEAST
```

254

```
MASH PAWED SEWER ROMS
ELLA EMILE OPINE IBET
SPITECURLS YELLOWFINE
HOMEBASE EMBED RILEUP
ONE ARIES TILE
TAPINS ELENA SHED GLO
AWARD INSTANTWINE RIV
PACK INNO RENT SIMI
ERI STRIPESTEAK TAMED
EFFUSES TWIST DUNES
ILIAD SHIMS SEDER
SCANT SHANE SAVORED
SPRIG SPINEDOCTOR ARM
LAIR DIOR VAIN GPAS
ATM RETURNTRIPE BEENE
WEE IMET ARENA RAMROD
ADOS STATE SIR
STAMEN STUDY SUNBATHE
PINESETTER PIPESQUEAK
ADIN SHAVE EVADE RAVE
TEND SORES DYNES AMES
```

255

```
REBA DEAD ONTO ALIBI
UTICA EMLY POOR CANER
LAPEL BUSINESSBICYCLE
EGOTISTS NINES BRER
DELIBES EGGED SEERESS
ACAT REFER THATSALL
FAR BICOLORSCHEME SOY
LIBRA USER HID MEWL
ASEA STIR CAIN WOODSY
SLAM PEN FULL GAME
HER BILATERALPASS NAH
FURY WUSS RNA FARE
ORSINO TIDE WONT ITEM
COPE IER FROE BRINE
AWE BIVALVELIFTER VAN
LACRIMAL ISITS LOPE
ANTIGEN GOTME LAKEBED
ALGA OILOF SOMETIME
INCLINEDBIPLANE RISER
MELEE LIEN AXIS STORM
POETS FESS METS ENYA
```

256

```
DISCS RECEDE CABSTAND
SCOOP EVOKED HULAHULA
TELMA MERELY IDOLATER
SOFTWAREDISTRIBUTOR
YURI APOST
IRA LENDANEAR EGADS
DULLASDISHWATER SALON
ELLE TEMPLES ROB PINA
SFWON RES RAGE SCAR
ONES STPETERS ETE
FOREWARNEDISFOREARMED
ICK THEORIES ASEA
NEED IFHE BBS SCRAP
ALDA BIO SOLARIA ABLE
LOUTS TWELVEDISCIPLES
STPAT ROOMETTES ECO
ROSSI ERRS
DOMESTICDISTURBANCE
NOREASON ATHENA EARTH
RETAKING ITALIC LIETO
CROSSEYE SOREST ILEAC
```

257

MINNOW ASSAM THANKYOU
ISAIAH DORSA RADIOADS
CLUBSANDWICH ATMCARDS
HATS TOSS ELSIE OLDS
VIE ONEAL SLAB
LOADOFLAUNDRY POE IOS
AMIRS ALES WHOD SRTA
PARA BICEP THELASTDON
SHOWMETHEMONEY TOSEA
EAU AGNES NUN TBAR
STARTON ATT EYETEST
NLOW GMA HIPTO TIL
ASSAI PEOPLEGETREADY
BEHINDBARS ASHBY AMIN
CEOS REPS PSST STEEN
DRE CEL HOUSEHUSBANDS
HARD ROLLO SPA
LOGY LENDL ISEE ELEV
EUROPEAN BOATTRAILERS
RINGTONE ANJOU ROMANI
ASSOONAS TSARS SUSSEX

258

ASTRID MISADD ADSPACE
PIRATE OLIVIA MEGATON
PRIMEMERIDIAN BOTTOMS
BROWNE ADIOS EMIL
HOVLANE ATEST AFRICA
ABEET RANDOMHOUSE CAV
LESSEE LEER ENCIRCLE
EST REVELSIN TONAL
REALESTATE DONOT LOIS
ERTE BORE SPECKS
CACTI SERIALMOM HIKER
ERASES LASH ONEG
EERO ARISE WHOLEWHEAT
DUNNO PEPRALLY CPR
WHITETIE RARA OPPOSE
EON CALLWAITING ROLES
SNACKS HARSH AGELESS
TILL AIMTO STRIPE
EASIEST PINTHEBLAMEON
GRINDER USERID DRIVER
GANGSTA STRAPS SECADA

259

ORALB PSAT GOOP IBSEN
CAMEO HERO INRE NAOMI
THEGRAININSPAIN CYNIC
ARC GILDA APTEST OGLE
DAHS DISNEY ONEROUS
SHEEN PINGSPOTTER OPT
TAG NAB ETS MALFOY
TOSHIRO DAT TOTALER
OBI FIXAGFLAT EREMITE
MEG SPOIL GROAN DAB
SYNC ENRON DRIFT REBA
ORE ISAID INOIL REP
DEFALLA MEGACULPA TAO
IRONMAN NAM DIVVYUP
NAMEIT CAT ADS NEE
OSI REGALESTATE RABAT
STATORS MINIMA LIRA
CASH OBLATE CROCS GOB
ALIEN AYTHERESTHEGRUB
NOOSE ILIA CRUE RAISE
TENET LEAD ASPS EDGED

260

AMPHITHEATER AGAINST
TORATORATORA CRABCAKE
STEVEMARTINI AGREEDON
TOTEMS BUL NIMOY DIRE
AREAS ZONEDEFENSE ATT
KENT MONETARYUNITS
EDD FINESSE OPENORDER
TANKS DEUS INSITU
RETORTS EBAY HESS SAS
OCHRES STOLEHOME FRIS
SUET ATNO LORE IOLE
SAWS DREAMIEST ILLBET
IDA OITA ENTS GROCERY
NOVELS MERC CRASH
IRENECARA EBWHITE SML
VICTORYPARADE SWEE
LAP CALLLETTERS THENS
AZUR MALES ISM CROATS
NEPALESE SISTERCARRIE
DRIVERED INTERSECTION
SALINAS ROADSIDEINNS

261

ACRE KLEE PJS ASPECTS
LOOM HANDGRIP MALLRAT
POPPSYCHOLOGY UFOLOGY
SKYLAB AMONG SLAW NOL
OCEAN TEETER SYNE
DEFY ROCKFORMATION
ALOES NEHI BBS HOSTS
MILDEW ATEAR POWWOW
EEK LATINSCHOLAR SIRE
WAITON GAIETY UNCA
BLING SITS BLAT TIGHT
REST GENRES VALETS
AIDE TAKINGTHERAP HOP
SCOLDS ASTRO SIMILE
SAMOA ARN APSE DEFER
PRECIOUSMETAL TTOP
SADE CRENNA UTICA
EGO ZHOU CLUED TIPTOE
PONTOON SOULSEARCHING
TROLLEY PITTANCE ORCA
SARCASM ALE UTES REED

262

AHME FAUST OHARE AKIN
TEEM ACTOR VEGAS LENO
ORKOFTHECOVENANT LIAM
NEO ATOP TORRID DELHI
CONBRIO COUSIN CEYLON
ENGAGE SAUCE TAI OLE
BORKUPTHEWRONGTREE
AHAB UNO RETINA
WARLORDS MEDICO CHOU
ESTEVEZ WALESA ASTERN
ISH AMUSEMENTPORK LBS
GLUMLY EDICTS ILIKEIT
HERA DEGEIS GLOMONTO
SALAMI ERE RASP
DORKHORSECANDIDATE
INA EON AWAIT SHARKS
PAMPAS TODATE SPANIEL
ITHAD GOWEST STEN FLA
NEON MAKETHESPORKSFLY
TAME EVENT ROARS GLEE
OREL TENSE SPREE TERR

263

RAWBAR CEDER WELSHMAN
OLEARY CRIME ALEHOUSE
T(O)LLED ROAST SEVENTHS
CELINEDION ALIC(I)AKEYS
ARID ARIA TNT
TOMBS PFA ELIS HEMI(N)
ERIE SPRINGSTEEN RISE
AINTHAY RIGA AMARILLO
R(O)UTES PIEAT HERBCAEN
ALTERS RILE NORDIC
TEEM EONS MARGO LAWN
INMATE MOUSE MACHU
HARDNOSE BASTE COPTE(R)
E(V)ILWAYS ELHI AUNTIES
ROME NATALIECOLE OOZE
EWERS SNOB ANC INNES
PPS ONUS BOON
CAROLEKING NORAHJONES
OPERATES INANE BUTANE
COATT(R)EE NORM(A) ORI(E)NT
OPPOSITE GREEK YESSES

264

CASE ERSE AFIRE MEDAL
AGOG LEON GATED IMAGO
NOFOOLING GULAG NEWER
ENATE GAR ILLBEDARNED
RESIDENT SEI STORY
SIR AGA STOOGE OTT
OLYMPIA ALL BRO TRUER
MOO UNBELIEVABLE ETRE
ABUTS SPONGER TRYONE
NODE DEEPEST SPOONFED
URPINES STANZAS
CONTENTS GASLESS RING
ACTING GINNERS EDGAR
RASA OHMYGOODNESS HBO
ELAND YAM NOG LOCATES
DAY OBSESS DEP ROB
EMITS ESS ABERDEEN
IMAGINETHAT DYE TORSO
DEIGN ROUTE HOLYSMOKE
LANAI ISLET ALTE EDEN
ENURE COLDS LASS NERD

265

VATS ORCA IOAM GODIVA
OPAH NEHI GNUS OUTRAN
CINEMAMARQUEES NISEIS
EGGSALAD TAEL IED NNE
KIP GINA ETRADE
SELDOM PAPARAZZI EPIC
AXER BERMS DEAL VALE
RANUP DEM SDAK HOPER
ALABAMAMASCOT BLATANT
HTS YESI BATE RAMESES
MARNE ALC HITME
CAPABLE ARLO AGEE MUY
SMALLER FROMAMARRIAGE
PUPAE STOP LID STOLA
ALAI AGER PULED IRIS
NEWS PAPALBULL INSIST
TEAPOT EARL STO
VAR CEL OCTI UNCLESAM
EGESTA BAHAMAMAHOGANY
RUEFUL RHFA RAKE OLOR
AESOPS BURN FRED NANA

266

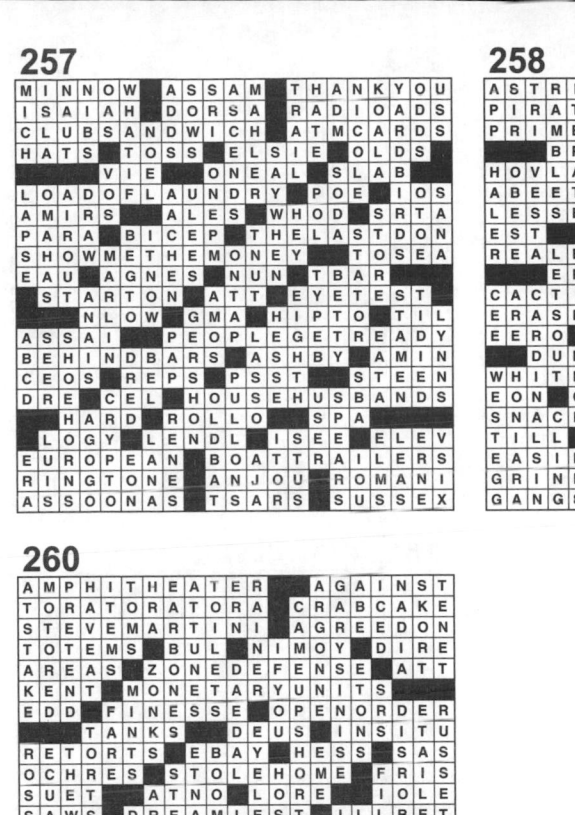

SILO ABOMB SAMBA JEEP
ENOS MEDIA ORATE OREO
CHESSPAINS FLOURCHILD
TOWIT RUNINTO ARNESS
STEERS MOLES ACTED
OPP WAROFTHEWORDS
AUTODIAL ROADIE EURO
WHINECLUB PALEST BON
LUNE ESCAPE TREADING
SHOOT CRAVAT INTAKES
FRASIEREPISODES
SOSUEME SENORA RHEIN
CAISSONS SPECKS IRMA
ATE SITCOM SHRINKRAP
REVS RECALL SOLOISTS
FREUDIANSLEEP CAB
RINSE ANNAL SLAVIC
NOLESS KIDSRUS ELITE
CROCKTALES MOTHERLOAD
ABBA ELOPE ALEUT ELLE
ASSN PANTS NESTS NAYS

267

SCION NANCE EMAJ GIFT
CANOE ONEON LOLA IDEA
RICHARDGERE THIN NEED
ARA VEERY ROADSIGN
MONTREAL BERIA NETS
HARRISONFORD TRIPE
ESSEN TWA SESE FIG
ANNETTEBENING SORTING
REC EARPS LEA SPREES
NECKLACE FENN OUST
RICHARDDREYFUSS
DOUG KEIR MORETHAN
SAPPHO STE IMACS OLE
UNEATEN DUSTINHOFFMAN
NIN YOUR ESL EREWE
GESTE PAULGIAMATTI
LEIA TIBIA USATODAY
STRAINED GASPS ORI
SHAH MAIN WILLEMDAFOE
NOME PLED ONAIR ATOLL
LIES SSRS KARMA WORLD

268

COBBLEDSTREET SYSTEMS
AMERICANEAGLE PALETTE
POTATOPANCAKE ONESAGE
POSIT PEEL FINESSED
DEFY TRIEDALITE
MESSROOM STRESS IRISH
ODE BOGUS ETAT SEANCE
NIE ALASKA ERECTS CHA
STING ICC DARTMOOR
TONY SIERRAMADRE AHOT
ERGS INQUISITIVE TELL
RIAS SOUNDASLEEP ERIE
MAHARANI SHA DRESS
ALE ELENAS ASSURE NOS
SWALES OSAS THRUM CUL
HEDID EXERTS ENTIRETY
BIGLEAGUES SATE
TAMENESS TVAD ADALE
ARMREST AFTERAFASHION
PICASSO THERAZORSEDGE
SELLSON PARESEXPENSES

269

PICCOLO GAPED PARAGON
ECUADOR IRATE ASARULE
THETENDERTRAP ASSAYER
EAGERLY AWRAP SOD
ABS DRAY BARR MEGA
BRIDGE HOTTEA DANES
LADYINCEMENT ADO EDDA
EDENS AVOW STIR ADIN
AHOLEINTHEHEAD OBJ
SAYS DIN REX UTRILLO
CLOTHO VEERY ISTLES
ABUSERS IVY NUN ESSE
REN NOTASASTRANGER
ERGS URSA HOPI CATER
UTAH SAP THEDETECTIVE
PATON PIGEON NEEDED
HOOT RANG SKID ESS
ROE TIBER STINGER
ALABAMA ANCHORSAWEIGH
PIRATES GOREN EMENDER
TOTTERS ETUDE TESTATE

270

BREWS ADES NOTAT CARD
RIGHT LOWE APISH AVER
INGER ERIE NARCO MONA
ASORE CANYOUHEARMENOW
RESEED GAD SPOOL
SPERO ELKO HOSTS
MIST BECAUSEIMWORTHIT
ORCH ADAMN ALERT ELY
DIRECTS UTERO AIRDATE
ENABLE ACID OCCUR
MAGEE LIKEAROCK BISON
EASEL MORT REVERE
SAFFRON MASSA MINERAL
ARE ADDIN INGOD RILL
FINGERLICKINGOOD SOBS
ELSOL RAHS AGLOW
RELIT ADS ENACTS
ITGIVESYOUWINGS SNARE
MULL NODES COAT ITSIN
ABEL ALONE ERLE TEENS
CANA SAGOS DEEM EDDIE

271

FESTA GNAT FIGS UTUBE
OUTON AIDA ISLE NOVEL
PRINCEIGOR SAINTSAENS
PARSES GRR CONDENSATE
ISR DALEYS DONAT
SIEGFRIED WARANDPEACE
HADRIAN BEMA ELAM
IFS CIS INFEAR OPA
MARNI GOTTERDAMMERUNG
ORB SAMBAR TOONE
AMIDSUMMERNIGHTSDREAM
SERIO STREET LIE
DAMONANDPYTHIAS WEILL
REA STEELE ODD MAP
ARIA ILET ATLEAST
WILLIAMTELL RIGOLETTO
ESTEE DRONES HAR
AMENCORNER ASS SEVERN
PONCHIELLI LATRAVIATA
OTTOI SEAT PREY ERRED
DESNA TYNE HYPE RETRO

272

ALLAH STAG EMIT TRUCE
TIARA HIRE MANS RERUN
RAZORBACKTOBACKJUDGES
AMENDERS FURS AIDED
HAI ARTY PADS
SCARFACETOFACEMUSIC
AWAIT RHEA UNCS MANE
HAIRSPRAY PRET APSES
ADD LOB PLANTS LISZT
BUSSTOP TEARAT APR
POPEYETOEYECATCHERS
ARS ARLENE ACADEME
EDENS ALPERT ERR VIA
NIXIE NEED IRSAUDITS
UNIS POND DRNO POSSE
FATHEADTOHEADOFFICE
SEES ALTO LIN
ZESTA ASTI DADAISTS
COWHANDTOHANDOVERFIST
ALEUT NINE GYRO MALAY
WASTE AXED SEAR STORE

273

CARDGAME CIRCA CLERKS
LEEREDAT ONEAT HOMILY
OSCULATE PREROGATIVES
NOAM GRR SESAMESTREET
EPPS IONA DEFILE
DONALD ESL LATER
WHALE LEECH MADELINE
REBINDS EELER RIALTOS
ALLEYOOP PALES ARTIST
PLED SALESSLIPS NHL
SOSO TRADESECRET ELIS
ERR STEAMSHIPS SADE
DRAMAS ONTAP GIAMATTI
ROMANCE SETON ARAMEAN
ALANKING DENIM WEDGE
GENTS SAL TRIADS
BISECT ONTO OMEN
FIREFIGHTERS ITE HALO
ASHWEDNESDAY BUSFARES
STEELE AGAIN ANNERICE
TOASTS TORTE RETREATS

274

SLAP TRUMP SAABS SHAW
PATE AUBER ASSES AERO
ATEAMPHOTO BSIDETRACK
DISCOERA SPREAD EATS
ENTERS TAPPET YANNI
SUP WED EBRO NBA
CNOTEPAPER DDAYTRADER
OAHU UPS MERGE VENA
PHAETONS ICAL PIXEL
SUR INC PRATE SAL
EMAILCHUTE FSTOPWATCH
MED NINES PIA ORE
LAGER TANS FANTASIA
OLLA SIRES COQ ICED
GMANFRIDAY HHOURGLASS
SAD LINY SAE EAR
SLATE COURTS PAVERS
ETON WOODED CASTANET
IBOOKVALUE JBARTENDER
RANK EVENT OSTIA NOVA
EYES GESTS BASER ANEW

275

EVER GRAD FAR POND
LIRE RICE ARES UVEAL
MARQUETTEPLACE TAURUS
URGES ALTARS RENO
SEEINGS GRE PACECARDS
ACMES HADNT HAUL
GLOM PAULO REFORM MOM
EAR FURMANTATION PALE
STY ALIAS ANNAL HERDS
BUNSEN DUCAT PERSIA
SPONGES MANES PORCHES
COATED CASTS AHIMSA
ACRID SAUTE ALINE LDS
RUDE HARVARDBEATS LEA
ESS PEWTER EARLS ELLS
RARE DRAFT GNATS
BROWNBRED EDT HEADWAY
IOWA SARAPE TORSO
BLENDS TULANEHIGHWAYS
ENDOR SITS SOSO EVIL
SAGA DOT PUTT DENY

276

ELCAR DROP SWIM SPIEL
NOONE RUBE HANA HOMEY
DESAC UNIS AVER ACORN
WASHINGTONWIZARDOFID
TANKS INE VAR FEE
ATLARGE LACES IDOS
HOUSTONROCKETSCIENCE
ENLIST URL THO OHNO
MILA OBDURATE FRIDA
OMNI OBI SPEEDOS
MILWAUKEEBUCKPASSER
POWELLS ADO IAMS
SPITS DUSTPANS ERIC
FUSS IDI ALE CAMETO
PHOENIXSUNWORSHIPPER
NATE ARISE WARTORN
EMT SET WAN LAITY
NEWJERSEYNETEARNINGS
ADIOS ONEI ALUM MEATS
CELEB DORA LIRE ESTER
TALLY ASSN LEAD STENO

277

GAZASTRIP PLATO IPANA
ICESHEETS ROBOT LOSER
DALLASSTAROFBETHLEHEM
ENL TEO OSAY OTTERS
WABE SWAT OBOES
ARIANA ONEI SNARL CTS
WASHINGTONCAPITALGAIN
ESSO REBA BROTH ONME
SPOONFULS SHINY ABABA
OREL MOOT SEEPED
BUFFALOSABRERATTLER
PARLEY TRES AMEN
ENSUE THEIR SPINALTAP
STUN TREES MOPS OHNO
CALGARYFLAMERESISTANT
IMA LUSTY ODER GESTES
EDITS ELIS GOTA
FLAXEN BLOC ANO SAS
LOSANGELESKINGOFCLUBS
ELECT MARIA CAMERAMAN
ELATE TIMEI CREDITORS

278

TRAPP THEMELESS AGING
OUTRE HALFPENNY RODEO
ONAIR EMBASSIES CLEAR
LENOS LIE DET ADARE
ROBOT NOM RECD
SEMINAR BOLAS MAILMAN
LEOTARD STEREO RATEDA
ARTISTS AIRGAUGE GRIM
NITE APT TURFTOE OGEE
GEOS BRET DEALER VETS
AMES TRES
CHAR TYPEAB EARS ILEA
BADE WEEVILS PIP MEAS
STOL ARSENALS GETPAST
THROWN TETRIS HAIRDYE
VANGOGH SLEPT TREESAP
USER YDS LASTS
ARSON ROO MAH AARON
ROUND OTHERWISE CREPE
NONCE IONIANSEA KINER
EDGED CROSSWORD SOUND

279

CRAB BARONS BACKBEND
ATTA AMINOR CASHIERED
VEALS1OPINI ASSERTIVE
SIDLE RENU ONETWOS
OLD RESCUER VERAS
PASTEUP EDT APB YOGI
ABA SHADYRE2ATION ORE
COBB SLOE DECLAIMER
TUBAS PENTECOST INFER
STANCH STELA SALSODA
TARA TENSILE TETR
EMINENT LARAM TRADER
LO1AW REABSORBS STILE
PRESUMING VEND ESCE
ATA POLITI1EADERS 2AS
SAVE ALG NUT EATHERE
OREOS MISSAID WEE
CASSATT GMAN VALUE
POTENTATE DE2YSHERIFF
ADINTERIM IRENEE TROT
METEORIC RESECT HESS

280

OCEANIA OLAF POETIZED
SALMONS PEPE ONEONONE
HALFTHEPEOPLEDONTVOTE
ANEMIA ADIEUS NIE KES
PROB XACTO ESME
REPO MMLI SCAUP UPEND
HALFDONOTREADTHEPAPER
USEFINESSE SOLON AERI
MEDLEYS ODA SEEST RAP
BIGO WURST ABEAD
NEAR LETUSHOPE CASA
DIMEA MORNS KURT
MEO PUNKS COB ATATIME
ALPO IDLES VACCINATOR
THEYAREINTHESAMEGROUP
TINED ENNEA EMES IRRS
DRAM KEELS ASOK
SAO YAD TRITER NEWAGE
FROMAQUOTEDYGOREVIDAL
PIROGUES RULE NOISILY
DESPOILS STER ANNEALS

PUZZLE #279:

1 = CALL

2 = PUT

PUZZLE #281: @ = NaCl

281

HAMSTERS BYTE COP PST
ARBOREAL SOIL AGO RHO
SEABORNE AURA SLICERS
POKES REMOTE ELIS
IRANI STOPS SARA@AKE
BENICE SDI DHOW NEWER
MAENAD ONCEA ALI
MA@ES I@ASSBYITSELF
CLOSURES ENATE CRIMEA
HAM BLAHS ELISA AMASS
RYE ETATS TEENS NSC
ISTLE SAROD REDUG CEE
STEALS ROMEO MEMORIES
MORMONTABER@E STOUP
POE ERROL ESSAYS
CIRCE NESS ULM RESTED
O@EARDAY EDIES BEETS
MANS ENESCO ENOLA
MINARET POST APERTURE
ARI ORR ARIA CHI@OSET
SEN DEY RENT ESSENCES

282

SEALUP GRITS SUPINE
ONLINE MANIAC RAPIDER
ANEMIA IMPALA UNICORN
KARATSINPUREGOLD ALOE
DEEN ETA IDEALS
OBIES SUDS DEADLYSINS
NANA CIA OURS NOVEL
DISNEYDWARFS SAX ARA
EDU ALE GIFT TIC INDY
CHRIS MACS AEGEAN
KIEFERSUTHERLANDDRAMA
FLEECE AVGS DEMON
TCBY ASH ASEA BOO ORI
EAR LPS WORLDWONDERS
APACE OPEN AAH OBIE
ROMANHILLS GWYN BRASS
STELLA AAA ADAM
BUSH BLACKBIRDSINAPIE
RHUBARB INATIE DANANG
AURALEE DOTELL INCITE
THERAW BERYL TAYLOR

283

LEVI CLAMS ALIBI CLAN
EVEN HASAT PEDAL HOME
DESKJOCKEY PEARLDIVER
ARTWORKS LEAK AMEND
ECUS LIAR MAITE
PABLOS WASTE ENMESHED
AXELS HASHSLINGER OLE
TOA ERODE MIEN BRAN
ENNS INERT OPAL BASIS
CORNER REVEL SERENE
GEOLOGY RIVAL STANDER
EQUALS FATAL STEREO
OUNCE JOKE STEAL SCAM
DATE HARE ILIAC TOO
ETE PAPERHANGER ORONO
SERRATES AMIRS SOARED
ATEST ZONE CALI
ANTIC FARE POLISHED
HEADHUNTER PRIVATEEYE
ERIE MIKED INNER HARE
MOLD PLOTS NATTY STEP

284

INSPIRATION LAIDASIDE
DELIVERANCE ANNOTATOR
THESEVENTHVOYAGEOFSIN
AREAS ONES NET MEANS
GUT NLER SPRUCES
SPIED CHA RAM AIDA
MORTONS THEPHANTOMMEN
ATEASE HEE EEL POINT
BERRY BONEDRY RERINSE
ERIC JUSTSO VERA
LIGHTATTHEENDOFTHETUN
ANTS SORTIE VINO
STJAMES ESTREET LENDL
IHOPE ELI TAD LINGUA
NEVERADULLMOM CANTEEN
GEES MAR EIN HONKS
WYNONNA TYNE PGA
MOOCH PET PUPS SCORN
UPTHECREEKWITHOUTAPAD
METALHEAD ALTERNATIVE
SCORPIONS FLINTSTONES

285

NEBULAS PULSES ARMADA
CLIPART ATONCE REISER
ALLTIME CANOLA TARTAR
RIGHTOFFTHEBATHER ADE
EEE UFOS TRU IRAS
BRIG TDS IMEANTIT
ITSME SMARTYPANTHERS
MANAGES OHARE NOWI
PRORATE IOWANS ASSES
ATWITHERSEND TAUR TAI
LEIA EMIT BUCS DARN
ASE TREE ONIONHERRING
STRAY NAPOLI ETHANES
SLAB RISEN SOONEST
NETHEREARNINGS NODTO
INHERING ERE WISE
ACES JEU PINT CBS
GAP JOINTHERATHERRACE
ASIMOV DIALER AVIATOR
RETINA ALIBIS LEFTOUT
ASSAIL SERENE ENTENTE

286

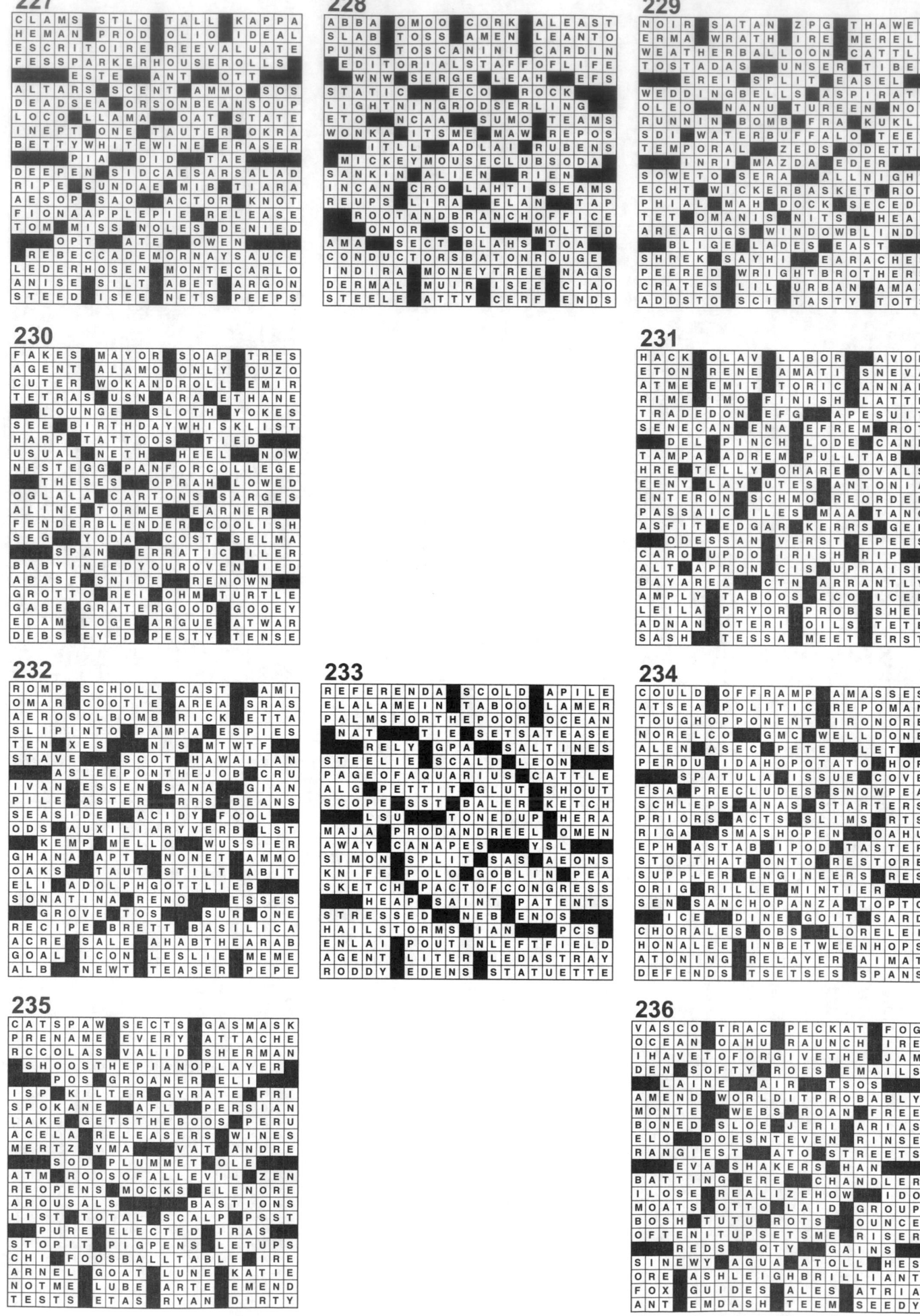

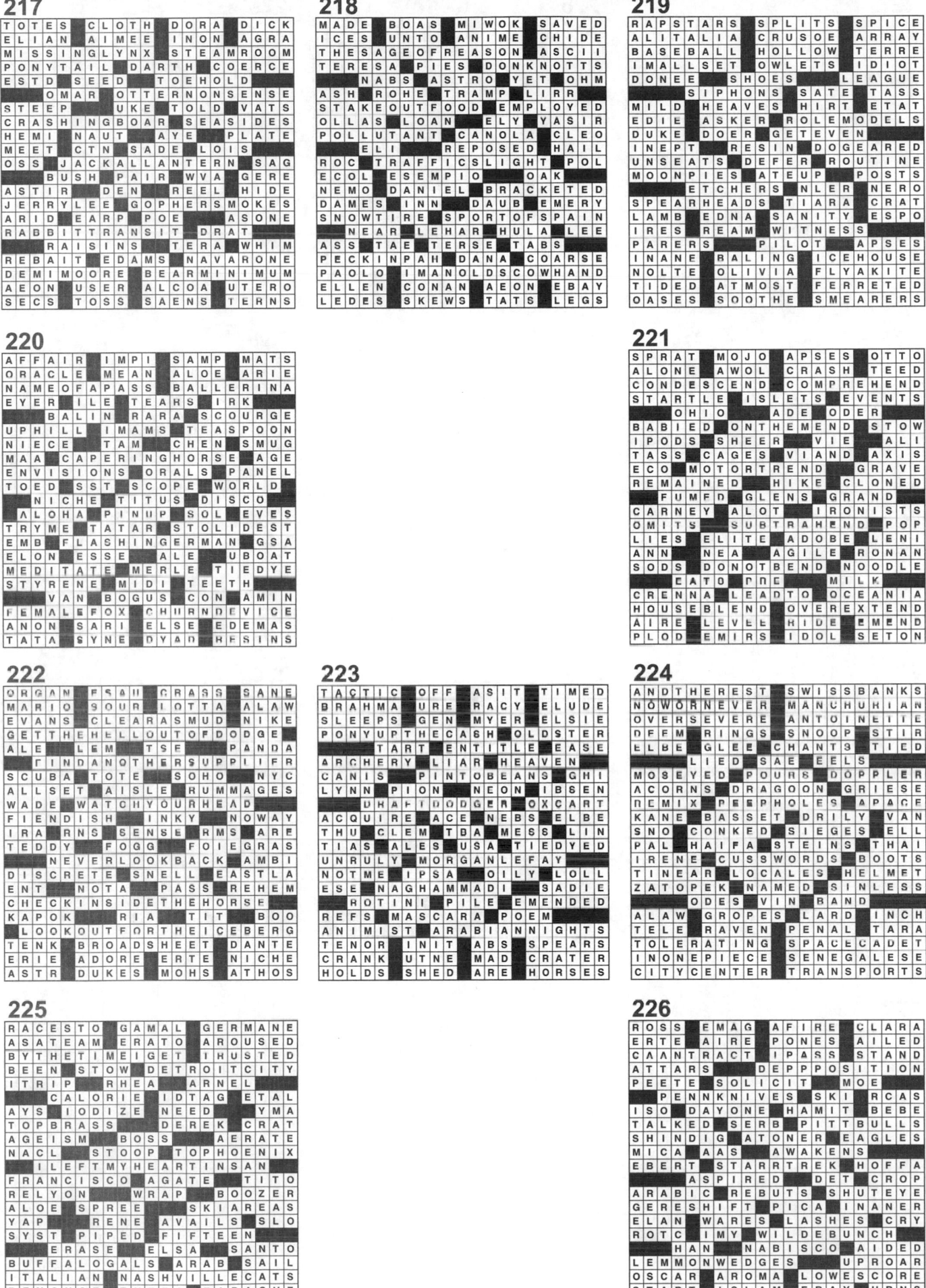

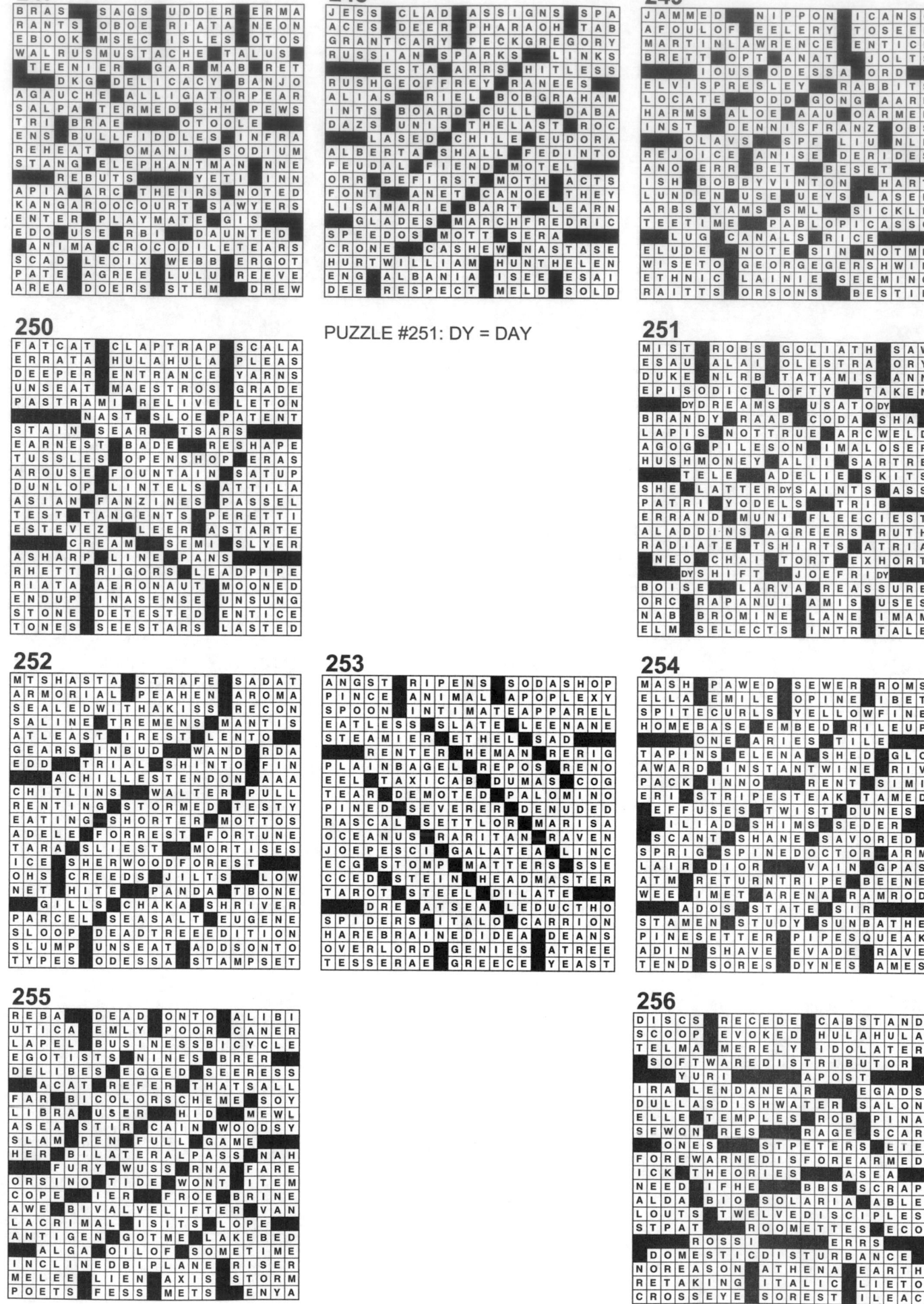

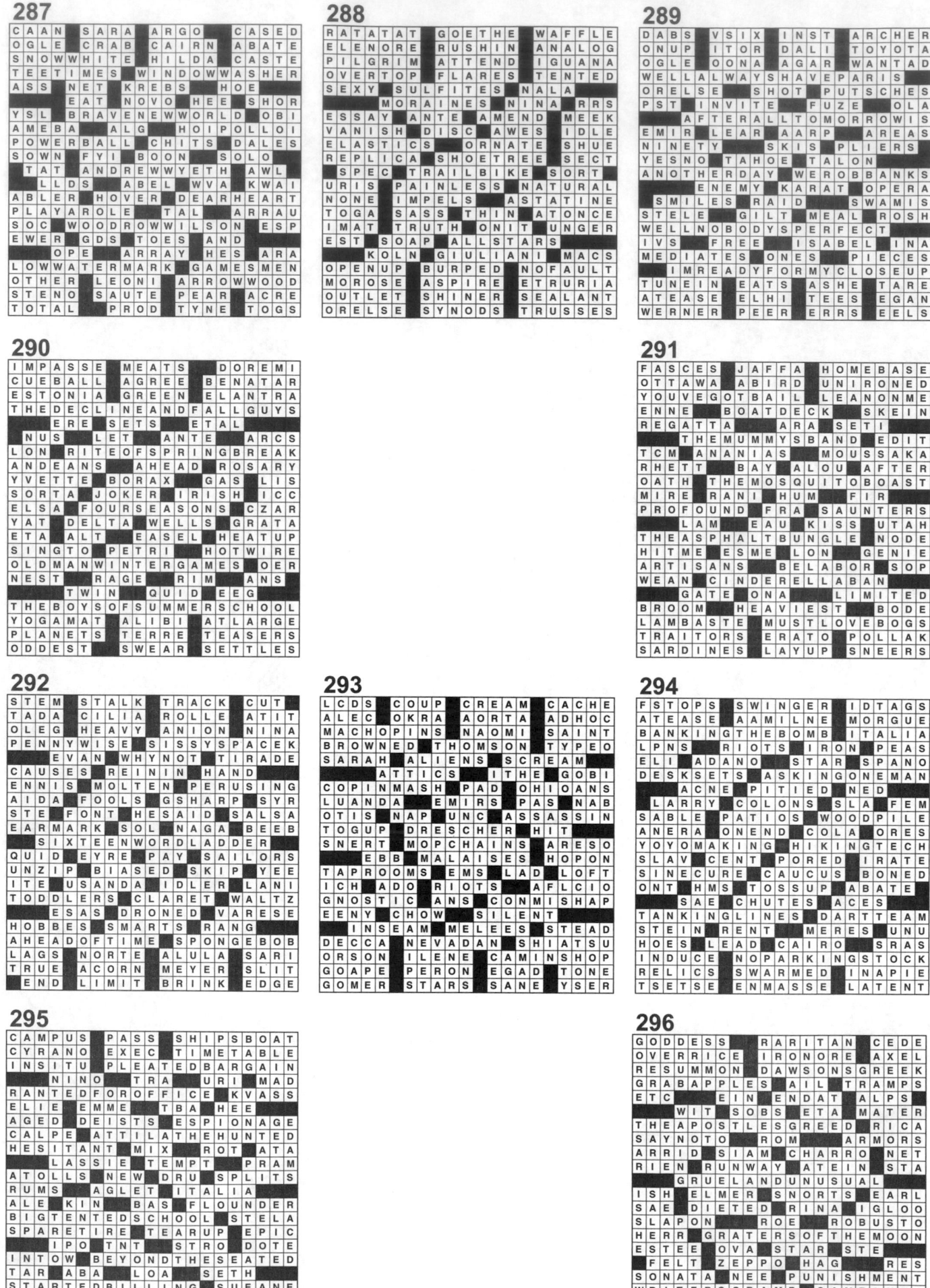

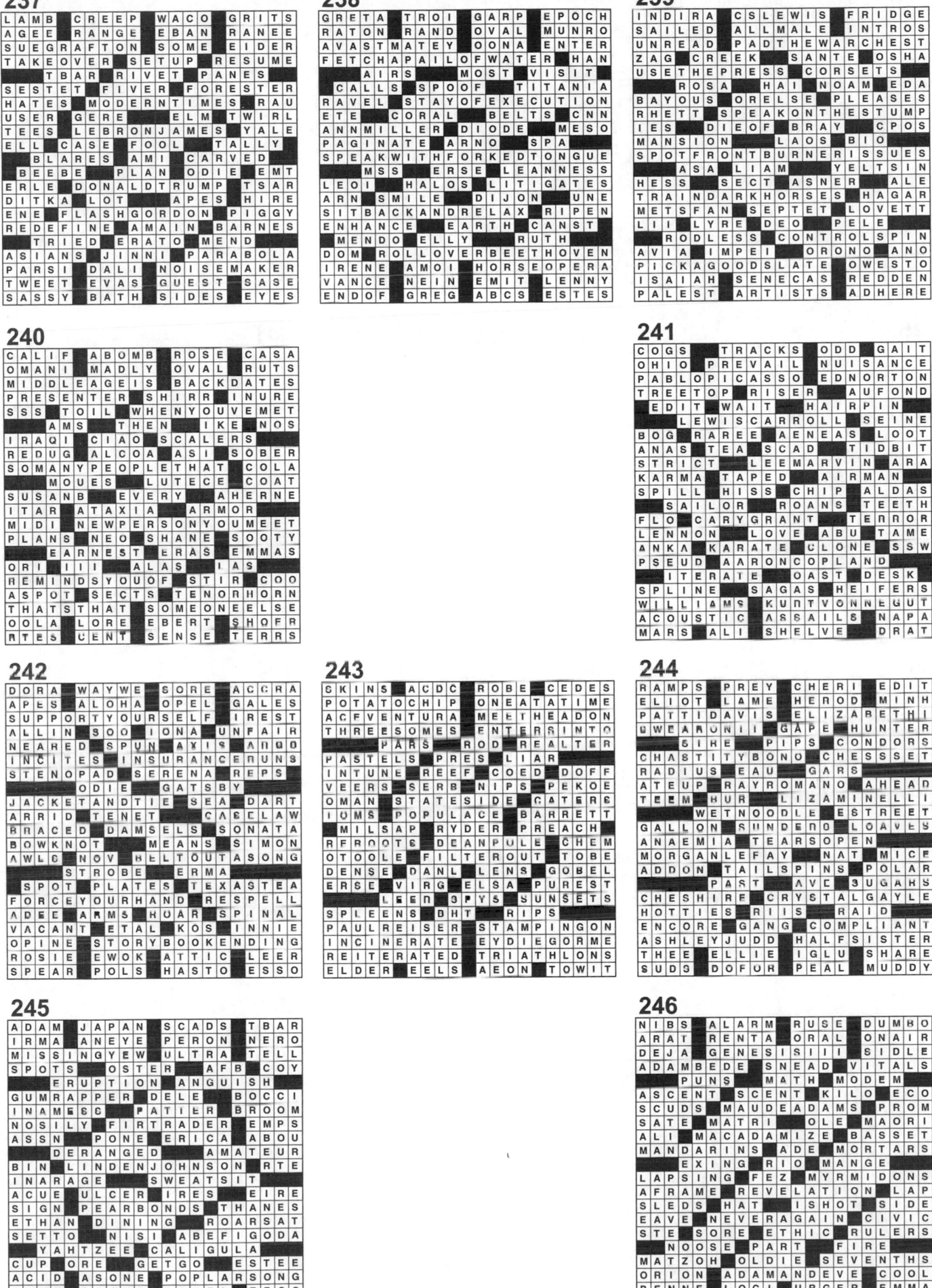

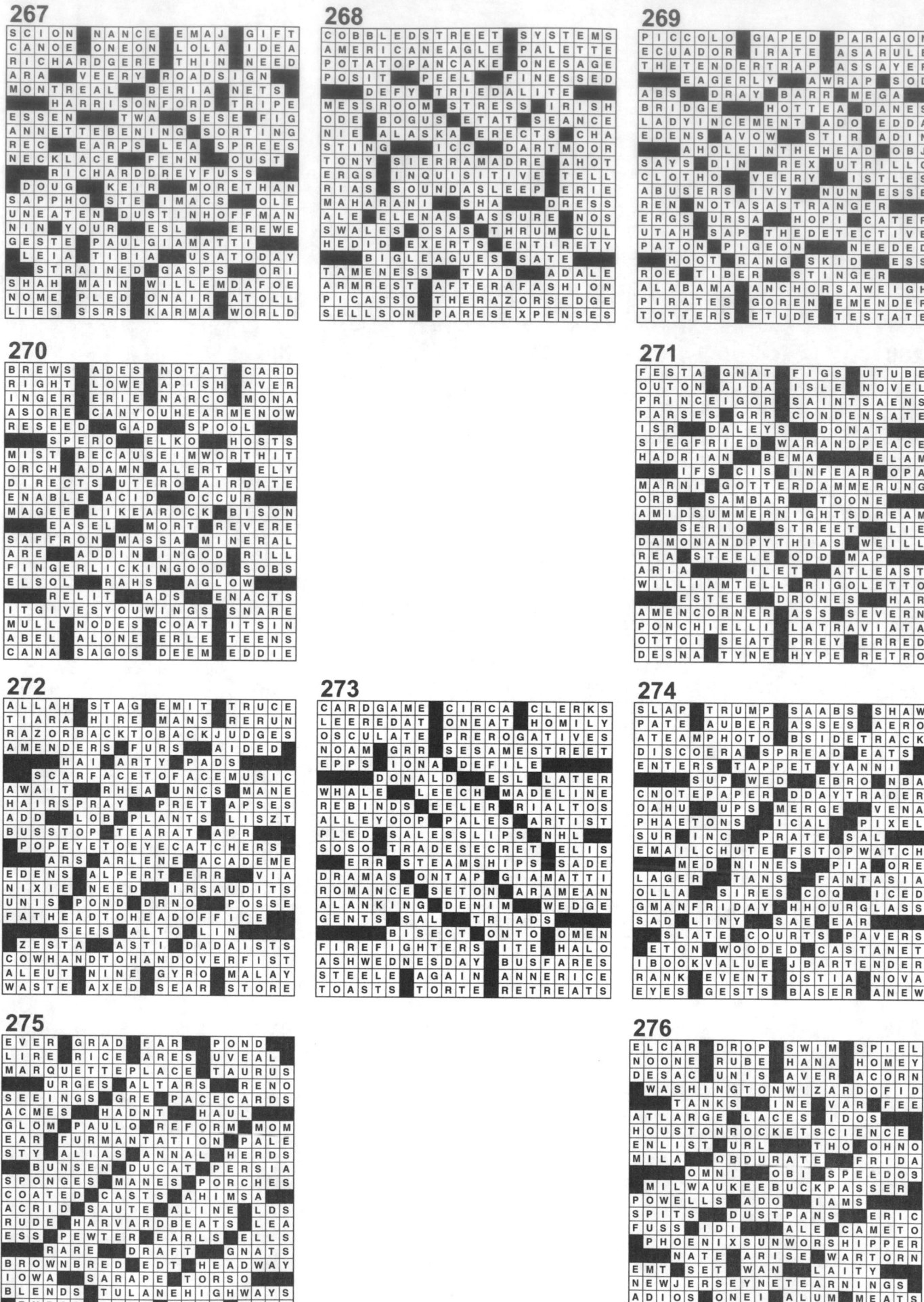

ASTA WAWA DEATH IDOL
CHAPS AJAX ELSIE LIMA
COPPERRAGE TOWERROVER
TREADON ESCAPE DIVERT
REOS HIE CELESTE
ADDERS STAIN KARL TAR
FERN ASTER CORSET
AKITA HANGERRON TACIT
REV GAINS QUAKES NITE
ERASED PUNKY TAGGER
STRAITS ELATE SUNLAMP
TORINO SLATY RUDDER
ADEN RIALTO BOISE RAH
YODEL CLEARROUT SPARE
DEMEAN AZTEC ASTI
CGS GIRD CANOE RASHER
RATTANS TAN PANT
OLEATE FENDER ENDORSE
WORKERRANT CONGERREEL
ERNE ABUSE HAIG EASEL
DEAN LINER ONLY LTDS

287

```
CAAN SARA ARGO CASED
OGLE CRAB CAIRN ABATE
SNOWWHITE HILDA CASTE
TEETIMES WINDOWWASHER
ASS NET KREBS HOE
EAT NOVO HEE SHOR
YSL BRAVENEWWORLD OBI
AMEBA ALG HOIPOLLOI
POWERBALL CHITS DALES
SOWN FYI BOON SOLO
TAT ANDREWWYETH AWL
LLDS ABEL WVA KWAI
ABLER HOVER DEARHEART
PLAYAROLE TAL ARRAU
SOC WOODROWWILSON ESP
EWER GDS TOES AND
OPE ARRAY HES ARA
LOWWATERMARK GAMESMEN
OTHER LEONI ARROWWOOD
STENO SAUTE PEAR ACRE
TOTAL PROD TYNE TOGS
```

288

```
RATATAT GOETHE WAFFLE
ELENORE RUSHIN ANALOG
PILGRIM ATTEND IGUANA
OVERTOP FLARES TENTED
SEXY SULFITES NALA
MORAINES NINA RRS
ESSAY ANTE AMEND MEEK
VANISH DISC AWES IDLE
ELASTICS ORNATE SHUE
REPLICA SHOETREE SECT
SPEC TRAILBIKE SORT
URIS PAINLESS NATURAL
NONE IMPELS ASTATINE
TOGA SASS THIN ATONCE
IMAT TRUTH ONIT UNGER
EST SOAP ALLSTARS
KOLN GIULIANI MACS
OPENUP BURPED NOFAULT
MOROSE ASPIRE ETRURIA
OUTLET SHINER SEALANT
ORELSE SYNODS TRUSSES
```

289

```
DABS VSIX INST ARCHER
ONUP ITOR DALI TOYOTA
OGLE OONA AGAR WANTAD
WELLALWAYSHAVEPARIS
ORELSE SHOT PUTSCHES
PST INVITE FUZE OLA
AFTERALLTOMORROWIS
EMIR LEAR AARP AREAS
NINETY SKIS PLIERS
YESNO TAHOE TALON
ANOTHERDAY WEROBBANKS
ENEMY KARAT OPERA
SMILES RAID SWAMIS
STELE GILT MEAL ROSH
WELLNOBODYSPERFECT
IVS FREE ISABEL INA
MEDIATES ONES PIECES
IMREADYFORMYCLOSEUP
TUNEIN EATS ASHE TARE
ATEASE ELHI TEES EGAN
WERNER PEER ERRS EELS
```

290

```
IMPASSE MEATS DOREMI
CUEBALL AGREE BENATAR
ESTONIA GREEN ELANTRA
THEDECLINEANDFALLGUYS
ERE SETS ETAL
NUS LET ANTE ARCS
LON RITEOFSPRINGBREAK
ANDEANS AHEAD ROSARY
YVETTE BORAX GAS LIS
SORTA JOKER IRISH ICC
ELSA FOURSEASONS CZAR
YAT DELTA WELLS GRATA
ETA ALT EASEL HEATUP
SINGTO PETRI HOTWIRE
OLDMANWINTERGAMES OER
NEST RAGE RIM ANS
TWIN QUID EEG
THEBOYSOFSUMMERSCHOOL
YOGAMAT ALIBI ATLARGE
PLANETS TERRE TEASERS
ODDEST SWEAR SETTLES
```

291

```
FASCES JAFFA HOMEBASE
OTTAWA ABIRD UNIRONED
YOUVEGOTBAIL LEANONME
ENNE BOATDECK SKEIN
REGATTA ARA SETI
THEMUMMYSBAND EDIT
TCM ANANIAS MOUSSAKA
RHETT BAY ALOU AFTER
OATH THEMOSQUITOBOAST
MIRE RANI HUM FIR
PROFOUND FRA SAUNTERS
LAM EAU KISS UTAH
THEASPHALTBUNGLE NODE
HITME ESME LON GENIE
ARTISANS BELABOR SOP
WEAN CINDERELLABAN
GATE ONA LIMITED
BROOM HEAVIEST BODE
LAMBASTE MUSTLOVEBOGS
TRAITORS ERATO POLLAK
SARDINES LAYUP SNEERS
```

292

```
STEM STALK TRACK CUT
TADA CILIA ROLLE ATIT
OLEG HEAVY ANION NINA
PENNYWISE SISSYSPACEK
EVAN WHYNOT TIRADE
CAUSES REININ HAND
ENNIS MOLTEN PERUSING
AIDA FOOLS GSHARP SYR
STE FONT HESAID SALSA
EARMARK SOL NAGA BEEB
SIXTEENWORDLADDER
QUID EYRE PAY SAILORS
UNZIP BIASED SKIP YEE
ITE USANDA IDLER LANI
TODDLERS CLARET WALTZ
ESAS DRONED VARESE
HOBBES SMARTS RANG
AHEADOFTIME SPONGEBOB
LAGS NORTE ALULA SARI
TRUE ACORN MEYER SLIT
END LIMIT BRINK EDGE
```

293

```
LCDS COUP CREAM CACHE
ALEC OKRA AORTA ADHOC
MACHOPINS NAOMI SAINT
BROWNED THOMSON TYPEO
SARAH ALIENS SCREAM
ATTICS ITHE GOBI
COPINMASH PAD OHIOANS
LUANDA EMIRS PAS NAB
OTIS NAP UNC ASSASSIN
TOGUP DRESCHER HIT
SNERT MOPCHAINS ARESO
EBB MALAISES HOPON
TAPROOMS EMS LAD LOFT
ICH ADO RIOTS AFLCIO
GNOSTIC ANS CONMISHAP
EENY CHOW SILENT
INSEAM MELEES STEAD
DECCA NEVADAN SHIATSU
ORSON ILENE CAMINSHOP
GOAPE PERON EGAD TONE
GOMER STARS SANE YSER
```

294

```
FSTOPS SWINGER IDTAGS
ATEASE AAMILNE MORGUE
BANKINGTHEBOMB ITALIA
LPNS RIOTS IRON PEAS
ELI ADANO STAR SPANO
DESKSETS ASKINGONEMAN
ACNE PITIED NED
LARRY COLONS SLA FEM
SABLE PATIOS WOODPILE
ANERA ONEND COLA ORES
YOYOMAKING HIKINGTECH
SLAV CENT PORED IRATE
SINECURE CAUCUS BONED
ONT HMS TOSSUP ABATE
SAE CHUTES ACES
TANKINGLINES DARTTEAM
STEIN RENT MERES UNU
HOES LEAD CAIRO SRAS
INDUCE NOPARKINGSTOCK
RELICS SWARMED INAPIE
TSETSE ENMASSE LATENT
```

295

```
CAMPUS PASS SHIPSBOAT
CYRANO EXEC TIMETABLE
INSITU PLEATEDBARGAIN
NINO TRA URI MAD
RANTEDFOROFFICE KVASS
ELIE EMME TBA HEE
AGED DEISTS ESPIONAGE
CALPE ATTILATHEHUNTED
HESITANT MIX ROT ATA
LASSIE TEMPT PRAM
ATOLLS NEW DRU SPLITS
RUMS AGLET ITALIA
ALE KIN BAS FLOUNDER
BIGTENTEDSCHOOL STELA
SPARETIRE TEARUP EPIC
IPO TNT STRO DOTE
INTOW BEYONDTHESEATED
TAR ABA LOA SETH
STARTEDBILLING SUEANE
MADECLEAR AREA ADAGES
ELEPHANTS NYET SEDATE
```

296

```
GODDESS RARITAN CEDE
OVERRICE IRONORE AXEL
RESUMMON DAWSONSGREEK
GRABAPPLES AIL TRAMPS
ETC EIN ENDAT ALPS
WIT SOBS ETA MATER
THEAPOSTLESGREED RICA
SAYNOTO ROM ARMORS
ARRID SIAM CHARRO NET
RIEN RUNWAY ATEIN STA
GRUELANDUNUSUAL
ISH ELMER SNORTS EARL
SAE DIETED RINA IGLOO
SLAPON ROE ROBUSTO
HERR GRATERSOFTHEMOON
ESTEE OVA STAR STE
FELT ZEPPO HAG RES
SONATA NEE PUNISHMENT
WRITERSGRAMP CAMEINTO
ACNE KNEECAP ONEINTEN
BEGS SADDENS TERNARY
```

297

C	H	A	T		R	O	P	E		S	T	O	I	C		N	A	V	A	L
B	O	T	H		A	C	I	S		T	O	N	T	O		E	R	I	C	A
E	P	E	E		T	H	E	G	R	A	P	E	S	O	F	W	R	A	T	H
R	I	N	G	T	O	S	S		E	B	R	O		S	I	M	I	L	A	R
			R	I	N		A	B	A	L	O	N	E		S	O	B			
A	T	S	E	A		A	F	A	R	E	W	E	L	L	T	O	A	R	M	S
F	R	I	A	R		B	E	A	U				M	O	E	N		E	Y	E
T	A	N	T	A	R	A			P	L	A	C	A	R	D		T	A	N	A
R	I	G	G		U	S	O	C		A	L	O	N	E		O	H	M	A	N
A	T	L	A	S	S	H	R	U	G	G	E	D		N	A	P	E			
	S	E	T	A	T		U	R	N		P	O	D		C	A	C	A	O	
			S	K	Y	E		S	O	P	H	I	E	S	C	H	O	I	C	E
G	L	O	B	E		C	R	E	M	E		L	E	T	T		L	O	T	S
L	I	L	Y		C	L	O	S	E	S	T			A	S	T	O	L	A	T
U	M	A		T	H	A	T				O	L	I	N		B	R	I	N	E
G	O	N	E	W	I	T	H	T	H	E	W	I	N	D		A	P	S	E	S
			C	O	S		S	H	U	S	H	E	S		F	L	U			
S	T	R	O	B	E	S		E	S	T	E		P	O	O	L	R	O	O	M
T	H	E	C	A	L	L	O	F	T	H	E	W	I	L	D		P	R	E	Y
R	O	S	A	S		I	S	T	L	E		A	R	G	O		L	A	I	R
O	U	T	R	E		P	O	S	E	R		Y	E	A	R		E	L	L	A

298

I	L	S	A		G	R	U	B		P	E	R	M	S		H	I	N	G	E
N	E	E	R		O	H	N	O		E	T	A	I	L		E	N	O	L	A
S	T	A	G	E	D	O	O	R	J	O	H	N	N	Y		A	C	T	O	R
H	I	T	U	P	O	N		K	A	R	A	T	E		S	T	U	M	P	S
A	N	T	E	A	T	E	R		M	I	N	S		B	A	R	R	Y		
P	O	L	S				A	R	E	A			D	A	N	A		C	A	D
E	N	E		P	R	I	C	E	S		T	H	E	S	E	S		U	T	E
			D	R	I	N	K	L	I	K	E	A	F	I	S	H		P	E	C
A	S	S	A	U	L	T	S			I	N	T	E	N	T		M	O	L	L
C	H	U	N	N	E	L		G	E	N	D	E	R	S		M	A	F	I	A
R	I	G	G	E	D		M	O	L	D	E	R	S		F	O	R	T	E	S
O	P	A	L	S		P	E	T	A	R	D	S		W	O	R	K	E	R	S
B	A	R	E		D	A	M	O	N	E			D	E	C	R	E	A	S	E
A	H	A		F	O	R	B	I	D	D	E	N	F	R	U	I	T			
T	O	N		O	N	S	E	T	S		N	O	L	E	S	S		N	U	S
S	Y	D		O	N	O	R			J	A	V	A				S	A	T	E
		S	A	T	I	N		B	A	U	M		T	A	C	I	T	U	R	N
A	S	P	I	R	E		B	A	R	R	E	L		D	O	N	A	T	E	S
S	L	I	M	E		C	O	N	D	O	L	E	E	Z	Z	A	R	I	C	E
P	A	C	E	S		U	N	D	E	R		I	S	E	E		E	L	H	I
S	W	E	E	T		T	O	W	N	S		A	S	S	N		D	I	T	S

299

L	I	P	S		C	L	A	R	A		S	T	D		M	C	C	A	B	E
I	D	E	E		R	O	B	O	T		P	R	O		T	H	E	B	E	S
S	E	S	Q	U	I	P	E	D	A	L	I	A	N		S	A	L	S	A	S
A	M	O	U	N	T	E	D		N	A	N	C	E			P	I	Q	U	E
			E	L	I	Z		J	E	N	N	I	E		M	E	N	U		
P	Y	K	N	I	C		D	U	N	C	E			R	E	L	E	A	S	E
E	D	I	C	T		W	I	D	D	E	R	S	H	I	N	S		T	W	A
I	S	L	E		U	R	S	A				M	A	M	E		C	U	E	R
				O	N	Y	C	H	O	P	H	A	G	Y		R	A	L	E	
N	O	S	T	R	I	L	S		S	O	A	R	S		T	O	D	A	T	E
A	N	N	U	I	T	Y		T	R	I	T	T		V	I	S	I	T	E	D
G	L	O	B	E	S		A	R	I	S	E		D	E	N	I	Z	E	N	S
	E	L	A	L		A	B	E	C	E	D	A	R	I	A	N				
H	A	L	L		E	L	E	V				S	U	N	S		B	A	S	E
I	V	Y		G	A	L	L	I	M	A	U	F	R	Y		S	U	R	L	Y
D	E	G	A	U	S	S			A	N	N	O	Y		G	A	L	E	R	E
		O	M	I	T		D	A	N	D	E	R		S	A	N	G			
M	A	S	O	N			U	L	T	R	A		E	P	I	T	A	P	H	S
E	S	T	E	E	M		V	A	L	E	T	U	D	I	N	A	R	I	A	N
T	I	E	B	A	R		E	M	E		E	N	T	R	E		I	P	S	A
H	A	R	A	S	S		T	O	S		N	E	V	E	R		A	S	A	P

300

M	O	T	H	E	R		M	A	N	I	L	A		A	G	R	A	F	F	E
A	R	I	A	N	E		U	R	A	C	I	L		M	E	A	L	I	E	R
S	I	E	R	R	A		S	O	C	I	A	L		A	L	G	E	B	R	A
C	O	L	P	O	R	T	E	U	R		M	U	L	L	I	G	R	U	B	S
A	L	I	E	N		R	U	S	E	S		V	O	I	D			L	E	E
R	E	N	D		F	A	M	E		E	L	I	T	E		O	M	A	R	S
A	S	E		S	I	C	S		S	T	O	A	T		F	L	U			
			B	O	D	Y		N	A	T	O			S	L	A	M	M	E	D
H	O	H	O	H	O		L	O	G	O	M	A	C	H	Y		P	A	R	E
A	N	E	M	O		B	A	T	S		S	C	O	R	N		S	I	R	S
S	E	R	B		H	O	P	I				A	M	E	N		I	L	I	A
S	I	M	I		O	W	E	N	S		A	C	I	D		A	M	E	N	D
A	D	I	N		P	I	L	G	A	R	L	I	C		S	M	U	D	G	E
N	A	T	A	L	I	E			L	I	M	A		M	A	T	S			
			T	E	N		O	M	E	G	A		D	E	U	S		L	B	J
P	A	D	E	R		A	L	A	M	O		L	E	N	D		F	A	R	E
E	I	O			I	M	I	T		R	O	O	F	S		S	A	P	O	R
P	R	O	C	A	C	I	O	U	S		S	C	I	A	P	O	D	O	U	S
I	L	L	U	S	E	D		R	A	S	C	A	L		E	M	E	R	G	E
T	O	I	L	E	R	S		E	S	T	A	T	E		S	M	I	T	H	Y
A	G	E	L	A	S	T		S	H	A	R	E	D		T	E	N	E	T	S